MIDDLE EAST CONTEMPORARY SURVEY

Volume XIII: 1989

MIDDLE EAST CONTEMPORARY SURVEY
Published for
The Moshe Dayan Center
for Middle Eastern and African Studies
The Shiloah Institute
Tel Aviv University

HAIM SHAKED, Founding Editor

Other volumes in this series:

Volume I, 1976–77
Volume II, 1977–78
Volume III, 1978–79
Volume IV, 1979–80
Volume V, 1980–81
Volume VI, 1981–82
Volume VII, 1982–83
Volume VIII, 1983–84
Volume IX, 1984–85
Volume X, 1986
Volume XI, 1987
Volume XII, 1988

MIDDLE EAST CONTEMPORARY SURVEY

Volume XIII

1989

AMI AYALON
Editor

Barbara Newson, Executive Editor

**The Moshe Dayan Center
for Middle Eastern and African Studies
The Shiloah Institute
Tel Aviv University**

Westview Press
BOULDER, SAN FRANCISCO, & OXFORD

Middle East Contemporary Survey

Copyright © 1991 by Tel Aviv University

Published in 1991 in the United States of America by Westview Press, Inc., 5500 Central Avenue, Boulder, Colorado 80301, and in the United Kingdom by Westview Press, 36 Lonsdale Road, Summertown, Oxford OX2 7EW

Typeset in Israel, Graph-Chen Ltd., Jerusalem

Library of Congress Catalog Card Number: 78-648245
    ISBN: 0-8133-1246-9
    ISSN: 0163-5476

Printed and bound in the United States of America

The paper used in this publication meets the requirements of the American National Standard for Permanence of Paper for Printed Library Materials Z39.48-1984.

10   9   8   7   6   5   4   3   2   1

About the Series and Editor

Established in 1977, the *Middle East Contemporary Survey* (*MECS*) is acknowledged as the standard reference work on events and trends in the region. Designed to be a continuing, up-to-date reference for scholars, researchers and analysts, policymakers, students and journalists, it examines in detail the rapidly changing Middle Eastern scene in all its complexity.

In each volume, the material is arranged in two parts. The first contains a series of essays on broad regional issues and on the overall relations of the region with other parts of the world. Subjects explored in detail include Arab-Israeli and inter-Arab relations, Islamic affairs, Palestinian issues, economic developments, and the relations between major world powers and the Middle East. The second part consists of country-by-country surveys of all the Arab states, as well as Iran, Israel, and Turkey. The North African states of Tunisia, Algeria, and Morocco are not covered separately. The emphasis in the second part is on elucidating the inner dynamics of each country's policy and society.

Ami Ayalon is Senior Lecturer in the Department of Middle Eastern and African History and Senior Research Fellow at the Moshe Dayan Center at Tel Aviv University.

Preface

The present volume of *Middle East Contemporary Survey* is the thirteenth in a series which provides a continuing up-to-date reference work recording the rapidly changing events in an exceptionally complex part of the world. Every effort has again been made to use the widest range of source material and maintain the highest possible academic standards.

Most of the essays in this volume have been researched and written by the members of the Shiloah Institute of the Moshe Dayan Center for Middle Eastern and African Studies at Tel Aviv University. Other contributions have been made by academics and experts from other institutions in Israel and abroad.

This volume covers the year 1989, the closing year of an ever-eventful decade in the Middle East. In several countries of the region major developments modified the rules of the domestic game. In Iraq, a war-weary country emerging half victorious from a long battle was forced to face the painful socio-economic aftermath, which drove its tough leader to take bold steps on an unpredictable course. Across the Gulf, Iran, licking its own wounds of war, also had to contend with the loss of Khomeyni, with the resultant resetting of its political scene. Elsewhere — in Jordan, Sudan, Lebanon — new forces and leaders came to the fore, introducing changes with far-reaching implications. In the Arab-Israeli arena, as the Intifada went on unabated, the peace process was gathering new momentum, giving birth to new ideas and generating feverish diplomatic activity. The inter-Arab system was realigned as new sub-regional groupings emerged and Egypt returned to the Arab League. Finally, the dramatic changes on the global scene toward the end of 1989 had significant repercussions in the Middle East, both direct and indirect.

The period surveyed in this volume, unless otherwise indicated, is from January to December 1989. In order to avoid excessive repetition while achieving a comprehensive survey of the affairs of each country individually, extensive cross-references have been used. Finally, in this volume, the order of chapters in the second section of country-by-country surveys has been rearranged and set to follow the alphabetical order of state names more strictly.

Ami Ayalon

Acknowledgments

While *MECS*, like all collective works, has an editor responsible for its merits and shortcomings, it is — perhaps more than most such publications — a team project. We are grateful to a large number of contributors who have made this volume possible. First and foremost, we recognize the work of the staff of the Moshe Dayan Center and its Shiloah Institute for Middle Eastern and African Studies at Tel Aviv University, whose individual contributions are acknowledged separately.

In the process of preparing this volume we were given much help by Avraham Altman. Barbara Newson's role as executive editor has been indispensable. The exacting work of indexing has been carried out by Ronald Watson. Ruth Beit-Or prepared the maps for publication, and David Levinson proofread large parts of the volume.

At the Dayan Center, Edna Liftman and Amira Margalith, assistants to the Head of the Center, were responsible for the complicated coordination of the production of the volume and fulfilled a variety of other executive tasks with accuracy, skill, and unflagging care. Others at the Center who must be singled out for special thanks are Lydia Gareh, whose skillful and devoted work has been an indispensable pillar of the production of *MECS*, Margaret Mahlab, Ilana Greenberg, Margalit Hochman, and the Moshe Dayan Documentation System team, headed by Yigal Sheffi. Finally, we would like to express our sincere thanks to Frederick A. Praeger, Barbara Ellington, Carolyn Richards, and the staff of Westview Press for their help in the production and distribution of this volume of *MECS*.

Haim Shaked gave form and purpose to the series as founding editor and has guided its publication for over a decade. The contribution made by the late Max Holmes and by Colin Legum to the launching of this project and to setting its standards remains invaluable and much appreciated.

A. A.

Table of Contents

PART ONE: CURRENT ISSUES

THE MIDDLE EAST IN PERSPECTIVE

THE MIDDLE EAST AND WORLD AFFAIRS

ARAB-ISRAELI RELATIONS

INTRAREGIONAL AND ISLAMIC AFFAIRS

PALESTINIAN ISSUES

PART TWO: COUNTRY-BY-COUNTRY SURVEY

List of Maps

Transliteration

The **Arabic** language has been transliterated as follows:

b	for	‍ب		q	for	ق
d	for	د ، ض		r	for	ر
dh	for	ذ		s	for	س ، ص
f	for	ف		sh	for	ش
gh	for	غ		t	for	ت ، ط
h	for	ح ، هـ		th	for	ث
j	for	ج		w (or u)	for	و
k	for	ك		y (or i)	for	ي
kh	for	خ		z	for	ز ، ظ
l	for	ل		’	for	١ ، ء
m	for	م		‘	for	ع
n	for	ن				

In addition, the following should be noted:

Long vowels are not marked for distinction from short ones. Thus ناظر = *nazir*, but also نظیر = *nazir*.

The *hamza* is used only in the middle of a word.

The *shadda* is rendered by doubling the consonant containing it.

The *ta marbuta* is not shown, except in construct phrases. Thus *madina, madinat Nasr.*

The definite article is always shown as "al-", regardless of the kind of letter following it.

Exceptions to the above are names of Lebanese and North African personalities who have adopted a French spelling for their names.

In transcribing **Persian**, frequent allowance is made for pronunciation; thus Khomeyni (not Khumayni). Names appearing in both Arabic and Persian texts are transcribed according to the language of the relevant text. Thus Hizballah (Arabic) or Hizbollah (Persian).

Recommended Method for Citation from *MECS*

In the interest of accuracy, consistency, and simplicity, the editors of *MECS* recommend the following method of citation. Based on the classification of *MECS* as a periodical, published annually, the method conforms to the *Chicago Manual of Style*.

In a footnote: Asher Susser, "Jordan," *Middle East Contemporary Survey*, vol. X (1986), p. 445.

In a bibliography: Susser, Asher. "Jordan," *Middle East Contemporary Survey*. Vol. X (1986), pp. 425–64.

The accepted abbreviation of the periodical's title is *MECS*. The year is that covered by the volume as indicated on the volume binding and title page, not the year of publication. No mention need be made of editors or publishers, who have changed several times since the establishment of *MECS*. Some styles may require mention of place of publication, usually in parentheses following the title of the periodical. For Volumes I through VII, the place of publication was New York; for Volumes VIII and IX, Tel Aviv; since Volume X, Boulder, Colorado.

List of Initials and Acronyms

ACC	Arab Cooperation Council
Agridev	Agriculture Development Research Corporation (Israel)
AI	Amnesty International
Aipac	America-Israel Public Affairs Committee
AOI	Arab Organization of Industry
Aramco	Arabian-American Oil Company
Awacs	airborne warning and control system (radar)
b/d	barrels per day
BDF	Bahraini Defense Forces
Benelux	Belgium, the Netherlands, Luxembourg
bn.	billion
BNL	Banca Nazionale del Lavoro (Italy)
BP	British Petroleum
BPC	Basic People's Congress (Libya)
Brig. Gen.	Brigadier General
CBJ	Central Bank of Jordan
CC	Central Council (PLO)
CFP	Compagnie Française des Petroles
CIA	Central Intelligence Agency (US)
Col.	Colonel
CPEs	centrally planned economies (comprise East Europe and the USSR, plus China)
CPI	consumer price index
CRM	Citizens' Rights Movement (Israel)
CSCE	Conference on Security and Cooperation in Europe
CSPF	Civil Service Pension Fund (Saudi Arabia)
DFLP	Democratic Front for the Liberation of Palestine
DGPI	Directorate General of Press and Information (Turkey)
Disk	*Devrimci Işçi Sendikaları Konfederasyonu* (Confederation of Revolutionary Trade Unions)
DLP	Democratic Left Party (*Demokratik Sol Partisi*; Turkey)
DUP	Democratic Unionist Party (Sudan)
EC	Executive Committee (PLO)
EEC	European Economic Community
Exxon	Standard Oil (formerly Esso)
FAO	Food and Agriculture Organization (of the UN)
FM	Field Marshal
FRC	Fath Revolutionary Council
GAP	*Güneydoğu Anadolu Projesi* (Southeast Anatolia Development Project)
GCC	Gulf Cooperation Council
GDP	gross domestic product
Gen.	General
GNP	gross national product
Gosi	General Organization for Social Insurance (Saudi Arabia)
GPC	General People's Congress (Libya)
GPCom	General People's Committee (Libya)
ha.	hectare

Hamas	*Harakat al-muqawama al-Islamiyya* (Islamic Resistance Movement)
HE	His Excellency
ICO	Islamic Conference Organization
ICP	Iraqi Communist Party
ID	Iraqi dinar(s)
ID (cards)	Identity (cards)
IDF	Israel Defense Forces
IESCO	Islamic Educational, Scientific, and Cultural Organization (of the ICO)
IMF	International Monetary Fund
IPSA	Iraqi Pipeline through Saudi Arabia
IR	Iranian riyal(s)
ISE	Istanbul Stock Exchange
JD	Jordanian dinar(s)
KD	Kuwaiti dinar(s)
KDP	Kurdish Democratic Party
LCP	Lebanese Communist Party
LF	Lebanese Forces
LPG	liquefied petroleum gas
Lt. Gen.	Lieutenant General
m.	million
Maj.	Major
Maj. Gen.	Major General
ME	Middle East(ern)
Mossad	*Mossad Merkazi le-Modi'in ule-Tafkidim Meyuhadim* (Central Institute for Intelligence and Security; Israel)
MP	Motherland Party (*Anavatan Partisi*; Turkey)
MTI	Islamic Tendency Movement (French: Mouvement de la Tendance Islamique)
MWL	Muslim World League
Nato	North Atlantic Treaty Organization
NCO	non-commissioned officer
NDP	National Democratic Party (Egypt)
NGL	natural gas liquid
NIF	National Islamic Front (Sudan)
NIS	New Israeli shekel(s)
NLP	Nationalist Labor Party (*Milliyetçi Çalışma Partisi*; Turkey)
NPUG	National Progressive Unionist Grouping (Egypt)
NRP	National Religious Party (Israel)
OAU	Organization of African Unity
OC	officer commanding
OECD	Organization for Economic Cooperation and Development
Opec	Organization of Petroleum Exporting Countries
p.a.	*per annum* (yearly)
PCP	Palestine Communist Party
PDRY	People's Democratic Republic of Yemen
Petromin	General Petroleum and Mining Organization (Saudi Arabia)
PFLP	Popular Front for the Liberation of Palestine
PFLP-GC	Popular Front for the Liberation of Palestine-General Command
PIF	Public Investment Fund (Saudi Arabia)
PKK	*Parti-ye Karkaran-e Kurdistan* (Kurdish Workers' Party; Turkey)
PLF	Palestine Liberation Front

PLO	Palestine Liberation Organization
PNC	Palestine National Council
PNSF	Palestine National Salvation Front
Polisario	Front for the Liberation of Al-Saqiyya al-Hamra and Rio de Oro
£E	Egyptian pound
£Sy	Syrian pound
PRC	People's Republic of China
PSP	Progressive Socialist Party (Lebanon)
PUK	Patriotic Union of Kurdistan
R.	radio
RC	Regional Command (Iraq)
RCC	Revolutionary Command Council (Iraq)
RCCNS	Revolution Command Council for National Salvation (Sudan)
RCom	Revolutionary Committee(s) (Libya)
Sabic	Saudi Basic Industries Corporation
SADR	Saharan Arab Democratic Republic
Sam	surface-to-air missile
Sama	Saudi Arabian Monetary Agency
SAVAK	State Intelligence and Security Organization (Iran)
SDPP	Social Democratic and Populist Party (*Sosyaldemokrat ve Halkçı Parti*; Turkey)
SIS	State Institute of Statistics (Turkey)
SLA	South Lebanese Army
SLP	Socialist Labor party (Egypt)
SNP	Sudan National Party
SPLA	Sudanese People's Liberation Army
SPLM	Sudanese People's Liberation Movement
SR	Saudi riyal(s)
Swapo	South-West African People's Organization
SYD	South Yemeni Dinar(s)
Texaco	Texas Oil Company
TKP/ML	Turkish Communist Party/Marxist-Leninist
TL	Turkish lira(s)
TPP	True Path Party (*Doğru Yol Partisi*; Turkey)
TRT	*Türkiye Radio Televizyon Kurumu* (Turkish broadcasting authority)
Türkis	*Türkiye İşçi Sendikaları Konfederasyonu* (Turkish Industrialists' and Businessmen's Association)
UAE	United Arab Emirates
UAEDh	United Arab Emirates dirham(s)
UK	United Kingdom
UN	United Nations
UNC	United National Command
Unesco	United Nations Educational, Scientific, and Cultural Organization
Unifil	UN Interim Force in Lebanon
UP	Umma Party (Sudan)
Upoc	Unified Political Organization Committee (PDRY and YAR)
US	United States
USSR	Union of Soviet Socialist Republics
w/e	week ending
WHO	World Health Organization
WICS	World Islamic Call Society
WP	Welfare Party (*Refah Partisi*; Turkey)

WTI	West Texas Intermediate
YAR	Yemeni Arab Republic
YCIOMR	Yemeni Company for Investment in Oil and Mineral Resources
Yepco	Yemen Exploration and Production Company
Yök	*Yüsek Öğretim Kurumu* (Council of Higher Education; Turkey)
YR	Yemeni riyal
YSP	Yemeni Socialist Party

List of Sources

Newspapers, Periodicals, Irregular and Single Publications

Name *(Place, Frequency of Publication)*	Abbreviation	Comments
Abrar (Tehran, daily)		
Africa Confidential (London, biweekly)	*AC*	
Africa Economic Digest (London, weekly)	*AED*	Published by *MEED* (see below)
Africa Report (New York, monthly)		
Al-Ahali (Cairo, weekly)		Organ of the National Progressive Unionist Grouping
Al-Ahram (Cairo, daily)		
Al-Ahram International (London, daily)		
Al-Ahram al-Iqtisadi (Cairo, weekly)		
Al-Ahrar (Cairo, weekly)		Organ of the Liberal Party
Al-Akhbar (Cairo, daily)		
Akhbar al-'Alam al-Islami (Mecca, weekly)		Published by the Muslim World League
Akhbar al-Khalij (Bahrain, daily)		
Akhbar al-Usbu' (Amman, weekly)		
Akhbar al-Yawm (Cairo, weekly)		
Akhir Sa'a (Cairo, weekly)		
Al-'Alam (London, weekly)		
'Al-Hamishmar (Tel Aviv, daily)		Organ of the United Workers' Party (Mapam)
Alif Ba (Baghdad, weekly)		
Alwan (Khartoum, daily)		
Amal (Beirut, weekly)		Official publication of the Shi'ite Amal movement in Beirut
Al-'Amal (Cairo, monthly)		
American-Arab Affairs (Washington, quarterly)		
Amnesty International Report (London, annually)		

Al-Anba
(Kuwait, daily)

ANKA Review
(Ankara, weekly)
Published by the Ankara News Agency

Arab Oil and Gas   *AOG*
(Paris and Beirut, fortnightly)
Published by the Arab Petroleum Research Center

Arab Studies Quarterly
(Belmont, MA, quarterly)
Published by the Association of Arab-American University Graduates

Arab Times   *AT*
(Kuwait, daily)

Al-Ard al-Muhtalla
(Nicosia, monthly)

Aziya i Afrika Segodnya
(Moscow, monthly)

Al-Ba'th
(Damascus, daily)
Organ of the Syrian Ba'th Party

Al-Bayadir al-Siyasi
(East Jerusalem, biweekly)

Al-Bayan
(Dubai, daily)

Beirut al-Masa
(Beirut, weekly)

Betzelem — Annual Report
(Jerusalem, annually)
Published by the Israeli Information Center for Human Rights in the Occupied Territories

Al-Bilad
(Jidda, daily)

Boston Globe
(Boston, daily)

British Army Review
(London, three per year)
Published by the Ministry of Defence, Army Training Directorate

Business Week
(New York, weekly)

Chicago Tribune
(Chicago, daily)

Christian Science Monitor   *CSM*
(Boston, daily)

Country Profile
(London, annually)
Published by Economist Publications

Country Reports   *CR*
(London, quarterly)
Published by Economist Publications
Formerly *Quarterly Economic Review*

Current History
(Philadelphia, monthly)

Daily Telegraph   *DT*
(London, daily)

Davar
(Tel Aviv, daily)
Organ of the Israeli Trade Union Federation (Histadrut)

Al-Da'wa
(Riyadh, monthly)

Al-Da'wa al-Islamiyya
(Tripoli, Libya, bimonthly)

Department of State Bulletin   *DSB*
(Washington, DC, weekly)

Al-Diyar
(Beirut, daily)

Al-Dunya
(Beirut, weekly)
Supplement of the Lebanese paper, *al-Haqiqa*

Al-Dustur
  (Amman, daily)
Al-Dustur
  (London, weekly)
The Economist
  (London, weekly)
Ettela'at
  (Tehran, daily)
L'Express
  (Paris, weekly)
Al-Fajr
  (East Jerusalem, daily)
Al-Fajr   English- and Hebrew-language
  (East Jerusalem, weekly)   editions of the daily *al-Fajr*
Al-Fajr al-Jadid
  (Tripoli, daily)
Le Figaro
  (Paris, daily)
Al-Fikr al-Dimuqrati
  (Nicosia, monthly)
Al-Fikr al-Islami
  (Beirut, monthly)
Filastin al-Muslima
  (Manchester, monthly)
Filastin al-Thawra   Organ of the PLO
  (Nicosia, weekly)
The Financial Times   *FT*
  (London, daily)
Foreign Report   *FR*   Published by Economist
  (London, weekly)   Publications
Fourteenth October   Organ of the Yemeni Socialist Party
  (Aden, daily)   (YSP)
Al-Fursan
  (Paris, weekly)
Al-Ghadd
  (Los Angeles, monthly)
Al-Ghuraba
  (Leeds, monthly)
Globes
  (Tel Aviv, daily)
The Guardian
  (London, daily)
Guardian Weekly
  (Manchester, weekly)
Gulf News
  (Dubai, daily)
The Gulf States
  (West Sussex, biweekly)
Gulf States Newsletter
  (Crawley, West Sussex,
  biweekly)
Ha'aretz
  (Tel Aviv, daily)
Haber Bülteni   The title ("News bulletin") of the *ad*
  (Ankara, irregular)   *hoc* press releases of the State Institute
                                                 of Statistics

Al-Hadaf		Organ of the PFLP
(Damascus, weekly)		
Hadashot		
(Tel Aviv, daily)		
Ha'ir		
(Tel Aviv, weekly)		
Al-Haqiqa		
(Beirut, daily)		
Hatzofeh		Organ of the NRP
(Tel Aviv, daily)		
Al-Hawadith		
(London, weekly)		
Al-Hayat		
(London, daily)		
Al-Hilal International		Organ of the "Islamic movement"
(London, biweekly)		
Al-Hurriyya		Organ of the DFLP
(Nicosia, weekly)		
Al-Idha'a wa'l Tilifizyun		
(Cairo, weekly)		
Ila Filastin		
(Culver City, CA, monthly)		
The Independent		
(London, daily)		
Al-Inqadh al-Watani		
(Khartoum, daily)		
International Financial Statistics	*IFS*	Published by the IMF
(Washington, DC, monthly)		
International Herald Tribune	*IHT*	
(Paris and Zurich, daily)		
International Journal of Middle East Studies	*IJMES*	
(Cambridge, England, quarterly)		
Iran Focus		
(Bonn, monthly)		
Al-'Iraq		
(Baghdad, daily)		
Israel and Palestine Political Report		
(Paris, monthly)		
Al-I'tisam		
(Cairo, monthly)		
Al-Ittihad		
(Abu Dhabi, daily)		
Izvestiia		Organ of the Government of the USSR
(Moscow, daily)		
Al-Jamahiriyya		
(Tripoli, Libya, weekly)		
Jane's Defence Weekly		
(London, weekly)		
Al-Jarida al-Rasmiyya		
(Damascus, monthly)		
Al-Jazira		
(Riyadh, daily)		
The Jerusalem Post	*JP*	
(Jerusalem, daily)		

The Jerusalem Post, International Edition (Jerusalem, weekly)		
Jeune Afrique (Paris, weekly)	*JA*	Reflects views of Tunisian expatriates
Jewish Exponent (Philadelphia, weekly)		
Jordan Times (Amman, daily)	*JT*	
Journal of Palestine Studies (Washington, DC, quarterly)	*JPS*	Published by the Institute of Palestine Studies and Kuwait University
Al-Jumhuriyya (Baghdad, daily)		
Al-Jumhuriyya (Cairo, daily)		
Jumhuriyye Islami (Tehran, daily)	*JI*	Organ of the Islamic Republican Party
Al-Jundi (Dubai, monthly)		
Kayhan (London, weekly)		
Kayhan (Tehran, daily)		
Kayhan al-'Arabi (Tehran, daily)		
Kayhan-e farhangi (Tehran, monthly)		Monthly supplement to *Kayhan*
Kayhan Hava'i (Tehran, weekly)		
Al-Khalij (Abu Dhabi, daily)		
Al-Kifah al-'Arabi (Beirut, weekly)		
Krasnaia Zvezda (Moscow, daily)		
Le Liberal (Casablanca, monthly)		
Libération (Paris, daily)		
Al-Liwa al-Islami (Cairo, weekly)		Islamic publication of the ruling National Democratic Party
Los Angeles Times (Los Angeles, daily)	*LAT*	
Ma'ariv (Tel Aviv, daily)		
Al-Madina (Jidda, daily)		
Magyar Hirlap (Budapest, daily)		
Al-Majalla (London, weekly)		
Manchester Guardian Weekly (Manchester, weekly)		
Al-Masa (Cairo, daily)		
Al-Masira (Beirut, weekly)		

May		Organ of the National Democratic
(Cairo, weekly)		Party
Al-Mawqif al-'Arabi		
(Cairo, monthly)		
Al-Mawqif al-'Arabi		
(Nicosia, weekly)		
Memo		
(Limassol, biweekly)		
The Middle East	*ME*	
(London, monthly)		
Middle East Economic Digest	*MEED*	
(London, weekly)		
Middle East Economic Survey	*MEES*	Published by the Middle East
(Nicosia, weekly)		Research and Publishing Center,
		Beirut
Middle East Executive Report	*MEER*	
(Washington, DC, monthly)		
Middle Eastern Studies	*MES*	
(London, quarterly)		
Middle East Insight		
(Washington, DC, bimonthly)		
Middle East International	*MEI*	
(London, monthly)		
Middle East Journal	*MEJ*	Published by the Middle East Institute,
(Washington, quarterly)		Washington
Middle East Review		
(New Brunswick, NJ, quarterly)		
Mideast Markets	*MM*	Published by *FT* Business
(London, biweekly)		Information
Milliyet		
(Istanbul, daily)		
Minneapolis Star and Tribune		
(Minneapolis, daily)		
Monday Morning		
(Beirut, weekly)		
Le Monde		
(Paris, daily)		
El-Moudjahid		French-language journal of the *Front*
(Algiers, daily)		*de Libération Nationale* (FLN)
Al-Muharrir		
(Paris, weekly)		
Al-Mukhtar al-Islami		
(Cairo, monthly)		
Al-Musawwar		
(Cairo, weekly)		
Al-Mustaqbal		
(Paris, weekly)		
Al-Nadwa		
(Mecca, daily)		
Al-Nahar		
(Beirut, daily)		
Al-Nahar		
(Jerusalem, daily)		
Al-Nahar al-'Arabi wal-Duwali	*NAD*	Weekly international edition of
(Paris and Zurich, weekly)		*al-Nahar*
Al-Nahda		
(Kuwait, weekly)		

Al-Nashra
  (Athens, biweekly)
Al-Nasr
  (Nicosia, frequency unknown)
Near East Report
  (Washington, weekly)
New African
  (London, monthly)
Newspot   Turkish digest, published by the
  (Ankara, weekly)   Directorate-General of Press and
                                                              Information

The New York Times   NYT
  (New York, daily)
New York Times Magazine   NYT
  (New York, weekly)   *Magazine*
Nidal al-Sha'b
  (Beirut, weekly)
Le Nouvel Observateur
  (Paris, weekly)
Al-Nur   Islamic publication of the Liberal
  (Cairo, weekly)   Party
The Observer
  (London, weekly)
October
  (Cairo, weekly)
Oil and Gas Journal
  (Tulsa, weekly)
Oil Daily
  (New York, daily)
Oil Market Report
  (Paris, biweekly)
Oman Daily Observer
  (Muscat, daily)
Orbis   Published by Foreign Policy Research
  (Philadelphia, quarterly)   Institute
L'Orient le Jour
  (Beirut, daily)
El Pais
  (Madrid, daily)
Petroleum Economist   PE
  (London, monthly)
Petroleum Intelligence Weekly   PIW
  (New York, weekly)
Philadelphia Inquirer
  (Philadelphia, daily)
Pogled   "Review" of the Bulgarian Journalists'
  (Sofia, weekly)   Union
Le Point
  (Paris, weekly)
Pravda   Organ of the Central Committee of the
  (Moscow, daily)   CPSU
Pravda Bratislava
  (Bratislava, daily)
Die Presse
  (Vienna, daily)
Problems of Communism
  (Washington, DC, bimonthly)

Al-Qabas
  (Kuwait, daily)
Al-Qabas International
  (London, daily)
Al-Qadisiyya
  (Baghdad, daily)
Al-Quds
  (East Jerusalem, daily)
Al-Quds al-'Arabi
  (London, daily)
Al-Quwat al-Musallaha
  (Khartoum, weekly)
Al-Rabita
  (Mecca, monthly)
Al-Ra'y
  (Amman, daily)
Al-Ra'y
  (Beirut, weekly)
Al-Raya   Organ of the National Islamic Front
  (Khartoum, daily)
Al-Ra'y al-Akhar
  (London, monthly)
Al-Ra'y al-'Amm   Conservative
  (Kuwait, daily)
La Repubblica
  (Rome, daily)
Resalat
  (Tehran, daily)
Resmi Gazete
  (Ankara, daily)
Al-Riyad
  (Riyadh, daily)
Ruz al-Yusuf
  (Cairo, weekly)
Al-Sabah
  (Tunis, daily)
Sabah al-Khayr
  (Cairo, weekly)
Al-Safir
  (Beirut, daily)
San Francisco Chronicle
  (San Francisco, daily)
Sawt al-Rafidayn
  (London, biweekly)
Sawt al-Sha'b
  (Amman, daily)
Al-Sayyad
  (Beirut, weekly)
Sekira Hodshit
  (Tel Aviv, monthly)
Al-Sha'b
  (Algiers, daily)
Al-Sha'b   Organ of the Socialist Labor Party
  (Cairo, weekly)
Al-Sha'b
  (East Jerusalem, daily)

Al-Sharq
(Beirut, daily)
Al-Sharq al-Awsat
(London, Jidda, and Riyadh, daily)
Al-Sharq al-Jadid
(London, monthly)
Al-Shira'
(Beirut, weekly)
Shu'un Filastiniyya   Published by the PLO
(Nicosia, monthly)   Research Center
Al-Siyasa   Organ of the Umma Party
(Khartoum, daily)
Al-Siyasa
(Kuwait, daily)
Al-Siyasa al-Duwaliya
(Cairo, quarterly)
Al-Siyasi
(Cairo, weekly)
Sovetskaya Kultura
(Moscow, three per week)
Der Spiegel
(Hamburg, weekly)
Al-Sudani
(Khartoum, daily)
Sunday Correspondent
(London, weekly)
Sunday Times   ST
(London, weekly)
Suraqiyya
(London, weekly)
Syrie et Monde Arabe   Published by the Office Arabe de
(Damascus, monthly)   Presse et de Documentation
Al-Tadamun
(London, weekly)
Die Tageszeitung
(Berlin, daily)
Ta'ir al-Shimal
(Oslo, monthly)
Al-Tali'a
(Jerusalem, weekly)
Al-Tayyar al-Jadid
(London, weekly)
Tehran Times   TT
(Tehran, weekly)
Tehran Times International   TT
(Tehran, weekly)   *International*
Al-Thawra   Organ of the Iraqi Ba'th Party
(Baghdad, daily)
Al-Thawra
(Damascus, daily)
Al-Thawra International
(Baghdad, daily)
Al-Thawra al-Islamiyya   Organ of the Islamic Revolutionary
(London and Washington, monthly)   Movement in the Arabian Peninsula
Al-Thawri   Organ of the Central Committee of the
(Aden, weekly)   YSP

Time
(New York, weekly)

The Times
(London, daily)

Tishrin
(Damascus, daily)

Turkey Briefing
(London, bimonthly)

Turkey Confidential
(London, 10 per year)

Turkish Press Review
(Ankara, daily)   A daily telex service, sent by the DGPI
                                       in Ankara to Turkish embassies abroad

Al-Ufuq
(Nicosia, weekly)

'Ukaz
(Jidda, daily)

'Uman
(Muscat, twice a week)

Al-Usbu' al-'Arabi
(Beirut, weekly)

Vanity Fair
(New York, monthly)

Al-Wafd   Organ of the New Wafd Party
(Cairo, daily)

The Wall Street Journal   *WSJ*
(New York, daily)

Washington Files   Releases by the USIS
(Washington, irregular)

Washington Jewish Week
(Washington, DC, weekly)

The Washington Post   *WP*
(Washington, DC, daily)

The Washington Times   *WT*
(Washington, DC, daily)

Al-Watan
(Kuwait, daily)

Al-Watan al-'Arabi
(Paris, weekly)

Weekly Petroleum Status Report   US Energy Information
(Washington, DC, weekly)   Administration

Wochenpresse
(Vienna, weekly)

The World Today   Published by the Royal Institute of
(London, monthly)   International Affairs

World Water
(London, monthly)

Al-Yamama
(Riyadh, weekly)

Al-Yaqza
(Kuwait, weekly)

Al-Yawm
(Amman, daily)

Al-Yawm
(Dammam, daily)

Al-Yawm al-Sabi'   Affiliated to the PLO
(Paris, weekly)

Yedi'ot Aharonot
(Tel Aviv, daily)
Al-Zahf al-Akhdar   Ideological weekly of the
(Tripoli, Libya, weekly)   Revolutionary Committees

News Agencies

Full Name	*Abbreviation*
Agence France Presse (Paris)	AFP
Algérie Presse Service (Algiers)	APS
Associated Press (New York)	AP
Gulf News Agency (Manama)	GNA
Iraqi News Agency (Baghdad)	INA
Islamic Revolution News Agency (Tehran)	IRNA
Jamahiriyya Arab News Agency (Tripoli)	JANA
Jordanian News Agency (PETRA; Amman)	JNA
Kuwaiti News Agency (Kuwait)	KUNA
Maghreb Arabe Presse (Rabat)	MAP
Middle East News Agency (Cairo)	MENA
Novinska Agencija Tanjug (Belgrade)	TANJUG
Opec News Agency (Vienna)	OPEC NA
Qatari News Agency (Doha)	QNA
Reuters (London)	
Saudi Press Agency (Riyadh)	SPA
Sudanese News Agency (Khartoum)	SUNA
Syrian Arab News Agency (Damascus)	SANA
Telegrafnoe Agentstvo Sovetskovo Soiuza (Moscow)	TASS
United Press International (New York)	UPI
Wakalat al-Anba al-Filastiniyya (Palestinian News Agency; Damascus)	WAFA

Radio and Television Stations, and Monitoring Services

(Radio stations known by the location of their principal transmitter are not listed — their names being self-explanatory.)

Name	*Abbreviation*	*Notes*
American Broadcasting Company	ABC	Headquarters in New York City
British Broadcasting Corporation	BBC	
British Broadcasting Corporation, Summary of World Broadcasting: The ME and Africa	SWB	Monitoring reports published in English translation
Cable News Network Inc.	CNN	Atlanta, GA
Columbia Broadcasting System	CBS	New York
Daily Report: Middle East and Africa	DR	Monitoring reports published in English translation by the US Foreign Broadcasting Information Service
Daily Report: Soviet Union	DR:SU	
Federal News Service		A Washington-based wire service that transcribes major Washington and international news events
Independent Television	ITV	London
Israel Defense Forces Radio	R.IDF	

Joint Publication Research Services:	JPRS	English-language translation from
Near East and North Africa		foreign press. Occasionally includes
Soviet Union		monitoring reports as well
Sub-Saharan Africa		
West Europe		
National Broadcasting Company	NBC TV	New York
Television		
Nippon Hoso Kyokai	NHK TV	Tokyo
(Japan Broadcasting Corporation)		
Public Broadcasting Service	PBS	New York
Al-Quds — Palestine Arab Radio	R. al-Quds	PFLP-GC radio,
		broadcasting from Syria
Radiodiffusion Télévision Marocaine	RTM TV	Rabat; government Station
R. Flag of Freedom		Radio station of the Paris-based
		organization, Flag of Freedom
R. Iran Toilers		Radio station of the Iranian
		opposition group with leftist
		tendencies, broadcasting from Iraq
R. Peace and Progress		Official USSR station transmitting
		from Moscow to the ME
R. SPLA		Voice of the Sudanese People's
		Liberation Army
United States Information Agency	USIA	Washington, DC
United States Information Service	USIS	Washington, DC
Voice of the Arabs	VoA	Cairo
Voice of Free Lebanon		Military station of the Lebanese
		Phalanges
Voice of Israel	VoI	Israeli national radio
Voice of Lebanon	VoL	Radio station operated by the
		Lebanese Phalanges
Voice of the Mountain		Radio station of the Progressive
		Socialist party, operating from the
		Shuf mountains
Voice of National Resistance		Radio station connected with *al-Amal*,
		Lebanon
Voice of the Oppressed		A Hizballah mouthpiece, Lebanon
Voice of Palestine (Algiers)	VoP (Algiers)	PLO daily program over R. Algiers
Voice of Palestine (Baghdad)	VoP (Baghdad)	PLO main radio station
Voice of Palestine (Clandestine)	VoP (Clandestine)	PLO clandestine station transmitting from Sidon
Voice of Palestine (San'a)	VoP (San'a)	PLO daily program over R. San'a
Voice of the People		Communist Party clandestine radio
		station, based in Lebanon
Wireless File	WF	Published by the USIA Library,
		Washington
Worldnet		USIS global television satellite
		network

Note: Radio and news agency material not otherwise attributed is available in Hebrew translation at the Moshe Dayan Center archives.

Notes on Contributors

AMI AYALON, PhD (Princeton University, 1980). Senior Research Fellow at the Moshe Dayan Center. Senior Lecturer, Department of Middle Eastern and African History, Tel Aviv University. Author of *Language and Change in the Arab Middle East* (1987) and numerous articles on modern Middle Eastern political and cultural history. Editor of *Regime and Opposition in Egypt under Sadat* (1983, in Hebrew).

GAD BARZILAI, LLB, MA, PhD (Hebrew University, Jerusalem, 1987). Lecturer, Department of Political Science, Tel Aviv University. Fields of specialization: Politics and governments in democratic regimes; Israeli politics; law, social order, and politics. Published articles on Israeli politics, national security crises and democracies, voting behavior, military force and politics. Author of *Wars and Social Order: The Israeli Society* (in Hebrew, forthcoming).

OFRA BENGIO, MA (Tel Aviv University, 1986). Research Fellow at the Moshe Dayan Center. Fields of specialization: Contemporary Middle Eastern history, modern and contemporary politics of Iraq and the Arabic language. Author of *The Kurdish Revolt in Iraq* (1989, in Hebrew) and articles.

MORDECHAI GAZIT, MA (Hebrew University). Senior Research Fellow at the Moshe Dayan Center and the Leonard Davis Institute for International Relations, Hebrew University. Formerly Director-General, Office of the Prime Minister of Israel (1973–75); Director-General, Israel Ministry for Foreign Affairs (1972–73); Ambassador to France (1975–79); Minister, Embassy of Israel, Washington, DC (1960–65); Fellow, Center for International Affairs, Harvard University (1980–81).

GIDEON GERA, PhD (Tel Aviv University, 1978). Senior Research Fellow at the Moshe Dayan Center. Fields of specialization: current politics of the Arab world; the Iraqi-Iranian War. Author of *Libya under Qadhdhafi* (1983, in Hebrew).

GAD G. GILBAR, PhD (University of London, 1974). Associate Professor in the Department of Middle Eastern History, University of Haifa. Fields of specialization: economic and social history of the Middle East. Recent books: *The Economic Development of the Middle East in Modern Times* (in Hebrew, 1990); editor of *Ottoman Palestine 1800–1914: Studies in Economic and Social History* (1990).

JACOB GOLDBERG, PhD (Harvard University, 1978). Senior Research Fellow at the Moshe Dayan Center. Chairman of the Editorial Board of the Moshe Dayan Center Occasional Papers Series. Fields of specialization: the modern and contemporary history of the Arab world with particular reference to Saudi Arabia. Publications: *The Foreign Policy of Saudi Arabia: The Formative Years, 1902–1918*; coeditor of *The Soviet-American Competition in the Middle East*.

JOHN P. HANNAH, PhD candidate (Stanford University). Deputy Director of Research and Fellow at the Washington Institute for Near East Policy. Field of specialization: Soviet foreign policy and East-West relations. Published articles on Soviet and US foreign policies in the Middle East. Author of *At Arms Length: Soviet-Syrian Relations in the Gorbachev Era* (1989).

WILLIAM W. HARRIS, PhD (University of Durham, 1979). Lecturer in Geography, University of Otago, New Zealand. Fields of specialization: Middle East politics and political geography. Frequent visits and periods of residence in Lebanon from 1983 to the present. Published papers on Lebanese political developments, especially on Syrian interventions. Author of *Taking Root: Israeli Settlement in the West Bank, the Golan, and Gaza-Sinai 1967–1980.*

JOSEPH KOSTINER, PhD (London School of Economics and Political Science, University of London, 1982). Research Fellow at the Moshe Dayan Center; Lecturer in the Department of Middle Eastern and African History at Tel Aviv University. Fields of specialization: history and current affairs of the Arabian Peninsula states. Published several papers on this subject. Author of *The Struggle for South Yemen* (1984) and *South Yemen's Revolutionary Strategy* (1990).

MEIR LITVAK, BA (Tel Aviv University, 1983). PhD candidate at the Center for Middle Eastern Studies, Harvard University, Junior Research Fellow at the Moshe Dayan Center, and Instructor in the Department of Middle Eastern and African History, Tel Aviv University. Fields of specialization: Modern Shi'i history and Palestinian politics.

BRUCE MADDY-WEITZMAN, PhD (Tel Aviv University, 1988). Research Fellow at the Moshe Dayan Center. Visiting Assistant Professor at Emory University and Visiting Fellow at the Carter Center, 1990–91. Fields of specialization: contemporary Middle Eastern history; inter-Arab relations; and the Arab-Israeli conflict. Published articles on Arab politics and the Iraqi-Iranian conflict. Forthcoming book on the Crystallization of the Arab state system.

ANDREW MANGO, PhD (School of Oriental and African Studies, University of London). Associate Research Fellow at the Modern Turkish Studies Programme, SOAS; member of editorial board of Turkish edition of *Encyclopaedia Britannica.* Formerly Head of French and South European Services, British Broadcasting Corporation. Author of *Turkey* (1968), *Discovering Turkey* (1971), etc.

DAVID MENASHRI, PhD (Tel Aviv University, 1982). Senior Research Fellow at the Moshe Dayan Center and Senior Lecturer in the Department of Middle Eastern and African History, Tel Aviv University. Field of specialization: the history and politics of Iran. Author of *Iran: A Decade of War and Revolution* (1990), *Iran in Revolution* (1988, in Hebrew), and *Education and the Making of Modern Iran* (forthcoming, 1991). Editor of *The Iranian Revolution and the Muslim World* (1990), and published papers on Iranian politics.

DAVID J. PERVIN (BA, Hampshire College, 1985; MA, the Johns Hopkins School of Advanced International Studies, 1989) is a student in the PhD program of the Department of Political Science, University of California, Los Angeles.

UZI RABI, BA (Tel Aviv University, 1986). Researcher at the Moshe Dayan Center and Instructor in the Department for Middle Eastern and African History and in the Preparatory Program, Tel Aviv University. Field of specialization: Persian Gulf states.

DAVID RACHOVICH, PhD (Tel Aviv University, 1990). Instructor in the Department of Middle Eastern History, University of Haifa. Field of specialization: Industrialization in the Middle East and Middle Eastern oil.

YEHUDIT RONEN, BA (Tel Aviv University, 1977). Junior Research Fellow at the Moshe Dayan Center. Fields of specialization: Sudan and Libya. Published articles and book reviews on the modern political history of Arab countries.

REINHARD SCHULZE, Dr. (University of Bonn, 1981), habil. (University of Bonn, 1987). Professor, Department of Islamic and Oriental Studies, University of Bochum and University Lecturer in the Department of Oriental Studies, University of Bonn. Fields of specialization: Social history of the Middle East (1500–1900); cultural sociology of the Islamic Middle East (18th–20th century); Islamic theology and mysticism. Author of *Die Rebellion der ägyptischen Fallahin 1919* (1981) and *Islamischer Internationalismus im 20. Jahrhundert* (1990).

HAIM SHAKED, PhD (School of Oriental and African Studies, University of London, 1969). Professor, Department of Middle Eastern and African History, Tel Aviv University. Head of the Shiloah (now Moshe Dayan) Center (1973–80); Dean of the Faculty of Humanities, Tel Aviv University (1975–80). Fields of specialization: modern and contemporary history of the Middle East. Author of *The Life of the Sudanese Mahdi* and coeditor of *From June to October: The Middle East between 1967–73* and *The Middle East and the United States: Perceptions and Policies*. Editor in chief of *Mideast File*. Chairman, Editorial Board of the Moshe Dayan Center Monograph Series.

STEVEN L. SPIEGEL, PhD (Harvard, 1966), is Professor of Political Science at the University of California, Los Angeles. He is the Author of *The Other Arab-Israeli Conflict: The War for Washington*, and coeditor of *Soviet-American Competition in the Middle East*, as well as of many articles on American foreign policy and Middle East politics.

ASHER SUSSER, PhD (Tel Aviv University, 1986). Senior Research Fellow at the Moshe Dayan Center and Head of the Center. Fields of specialization: history and politics of Jordan and the Palestinians. Author of *Between Jordan and Palestine: A Political Biography of Wasfi al-Tall* (1983, in Hebrew); *The PLO after the War in Lebanon* (1985, in Hebrew); monographs and papers on Jordanian and Palestinian history and politics.

JOSHUA TEITELBAUM, MA (Tel Aviv University, 1988). Junior Research Fellow at the Moshe Dayan Center and Instructor in the Overseas Students Program, Tel Aviv University. Fields of specialization: Palestinian history and politics, modern Islamic movements, and the history of the Arabian Peninsula. Researching PhD dissertation on "State and Society in the Hashimite Kingdom of the Hijaz, 1916–1925."

EYAL ZISSER, MA (Tel Aviv University, 1988). Researcher at the Moshe Dayan Center and Instructor in the Department of Middle Eastern and African History, Tel Aviv University. Fields of specialization: the political history of Lebanon, the Arab-Israeli conflict, and Palestinian armed operations. Title of MA thesis: "The Arab-Israeli Struggle over the Jordan Waters and the Inter-Arab System."

PART ONE: CURRENT ISSUES

THE MIDDLE EAST
IN PERSPECTIVE

The Middle East in 1989: A Year of Transition

HAIM SHAKED

Viewed from the dramatic pinnacle of the fall of 1990 — as this introductory chapter goes to the typesetters — 1989 could best be characterized as a year of transition, a bridge year.

The year under review is devoid of dramatic events such as those which highlighted the preceding one: the disengagement of Jordan from the West Bank (July 1988); the termination of the eight-year-long Iraq-Iran War (August 1988), and the opening of the US-PLO dialogue (December 1988). As Itamar Rabinovich put it in the previous volume of *MECS*, 1988 saw "a shift of accent" in that the termination of the Iraq-Iran War and the attention-riveting Intifada "shifted the focus from the Gulf area to the Arab-Israeli part of the region." In this regard, 1989 was a direct continuation of 1988, much more so than of 1987, with most international and regional attention focusing on the western part of the Middle East. With the Soviet pullout from Afghanistan and the cessation of the Iran-Iraq War, the eastern reaches of the ME were off the top of the regional and international agenda, at least for a short while. If the turn of the 1970s into the 1980s witnessed a very dramatic rise in the turbulence of the Gulf subregion — with the downfall of the Shah of Iran, the Soviet invasion of Afghanistan, and the outbreak of the Iraq-Iran War — the turn of the 1980s into the 1990s seemed, from the perspective of the main events of 1988 and 1989, to be highlighted by the return of the Arab-Palestinian-Israeli conflict to the center of the ME stage.

The inability of the Israeli authorities to quell the Intifada, and its success in persistently maintaining a high local, regional, and international profile, dominated Palestinian-Israeli relations, and therefore, the whole context of the Arab-Israeli conflict. Its impact was also felt in the relations of the US with several major actors in this conflict, primarily Israel, Egypt, and the PLO. As pointed out in *MECS* 1988, the Intifada "broke the pattern of Israeli-Palestinian relations as these had crystallized and existed for 20 years. Since June 1967, Israel had been able to control the West Bank and Gaza with relative ease...The dominant element in this configuration was the readiness of the bulk of the Palestinian population to comply with Israel's rule. This changed with and through the Intifada, as a sizable portion of the population willingly defied the Israeli authorities and participated in acts of semi-violent opposition."

In its second year in 1989, it became clear that the Intifada was neither a temporary convulsion of pain, nor a passing spasm of violence. As Meir Litvak points out in his chapter on the subject, in 1989 the "dual authority in the territories," that of the continuing presence of the Israeli Government and troops, and that of the Intifada activists, became an established, institutionalized fact. The Israeli Government, and in particular the minister of defense (under whose jurisdiction the territories have been since Israel occupied them in the war of 1967), opted for containment, rather

5

than forceful suppression of, or disengagement and withdrawal from the territories. The Palestinian activists, for their part, realizing that an escalation of their violence might trigger forceful Israeli suppression, and that de-escalation of their activities could wind the Intifada down into insignificance, shifted their focus "from the violent confrontations with the Israel Defense Forces" which was the characteristic pattern of 1988 "to the political arena." As time passed, the Intifada's full implications became more visible:

(a) A sociopolitical shift had been triggered among the inhabitants of the West Bank and Gaza, accelerating a generational change with the emergence of a new, younger leadership. These leaders were getting better organized under a clandestine United National Command (UNC). In 1989, the UNC eclipsed the older dignitaries — mayors, journalists, trade union, and civil organization activists.

(b) While all Intifada activists confronted a common enemy, Israel, it was clear that the leadership as well as the rank and file were split in more than one way — the primary cleavage being between the PLO-oriented Palestinians and a much fiercer, less compromising, militant Islamic group — the Islamic Resistance Movement, better known by its acronym Hamas. The growing appeal of the latter further complicated yet another, newer fissure characteristic of the Palestinian body politic — "the inside" (of the territories) versus "the outside" (the PLO leadership based in Tunis). These tensions resulted, among others, in significant numbers of "account settling" assassinations of Palestinians by Palestinians. The outside world, however, viewed their combined activities as an indication of the vitality of a Palestinian struggle for independence, which seemed to be gaining in legitimacy and at least tacit recognition. It was only natural that as the rather esoteric Arabic term Intifada was quickly becoming a household term internationally — mainly through the media, primarily the television screen — it deeply hurt Israel's moral image.

(c) As the Intifada was turning more and more into an established facet of Israeli-Palestinian relations, it continued to nourish the internal Israeli debate about the future of the territories beyond the "green line" — Israel's cease-fire lines with Egypt (in Gaza) and Jordan (in the West Bank) as demarcated in the wake of the war of 1948–49. In one sense, the Intifada reerected these lines creating a clear-cut differentiation between "Israel proper," and "the territories." Simultaneously, however, the Intifada also threatened to demolish the "green line," in that in 1989 there were more and more indications of the spread of the Intifada's defiant spirit into the Israeli-Arab sector. Thus, while in terms of the incidence of violent acts, the Intifada appeared to be stabilizing in 1989 at an overall low level of intensity, its political implications, far from diminishing in importance, grew in 1989 and continued to exert enormous pressures on the Israeli Government in particular, and on the Israeli-Palestinian Arab peace process in general.

Two elections held in November 1988 had a direct impact on this situation. In the US, a Republican Administration headed by George Bush was elected for a four-year term. As a former US ambassador and director of the CIA, and as Ronald Reagan's vice president for the preceding eight years, Bush was no stranger to the running of American foreign policy and to ME affairs. It was, therefore, expected that his Administration would "hit the ground running," and that its direction would not entail a radical departure from American ME policies in the later Reagan years. The outgoing Reagan Administration's surprise opening of the dialogue with the PLO in

Tunis, just as it was handing over the keys of the White House to its successor, provided an opportunity for the incoming Bush Administration to push, once settled in power in early 1989, for a resuscitation of the Israeli-Arab peace process.

The elections in Israel resulted in the formation, once again, of a "National Unity Government" in December 1988, composed mainly of Likud and Labor ministers. Unlike its predecessor (set up in 1984), the new government, headed by Likud leader Yitzhak Shamir, was not bound by the rotation-of-prime-minister principle. The government was thus poised to address the peace process as a strongheaded, but split body.

As fully analyzed in Mordechai Gazit's chapter devoted to the peace process in 1989, there were four main actors in this complicated game: Israel, Egypt, the PLO, and the US, with the last three forming a triangle of sorts. Among the highlights of relevant developments in the year under review was the Israeli peace initiative. It had been in the making since January 1989, but was officially launched only in May 1989 — an indication of the tortuous Israeli political debate in which it was begotten. It was born out of a sense of expediency: the combination of cumulative pressures generated by the Intifada, the US dialogue with the PLO, and the prodding by American friends of Israel anxious for Israel to deflect the damaging impact of the Intifada on American public opinion.

The Israeli peace plan started rolling in January 1989, with Prime Minister Shamir, Defense Minister Rabin, and the Knesset floating general ideas for a peace plan. It took five months of incubation before the Israeli Government officially adopted the plan in May 1989, based on a four-point plan presented by the prime minister to the US Government during his visit to Washington the month before. The plan was greeted by the US as new and not just a "warmed over" Camp David formula. The US, trying to steer a very difficult course between its own convictions and views, the PLO's expectations and demands, Egypt's ideas and objectives, and Israel's anxieties and apprehensions, found itself in increasingly stormy waters. Paradoxically, the process, which was intended to rekindle the peace process with the obvious objective of reducing tensions and enhancing a gradual reconciliation of profound differences between the antagonists, rapidly turned into a radicalizing force. The second half of 1989 thus witnessed the opposite of what had been intended. Egypt floated a list of 10 questions to Israel, which soon became known as President Mubarak's "Ten-Point Plan." In Israel, the Likud and Labor partners in government were being torn apart, while within the Likud a number of senior cabinet ministers were putting the screws on their own prime minister lest he demonstrate any softness under pressure. The US, actively working with Egypt, and at the same time with the PLO, was frantically seeking a formula that would incorporate conflicting demands and attitudes crystallizing in Jerusalem, Cairo, and Tunis. In this parallelogram of forces, the US was gradually shifting its position toward the Egyptian-PLO axis, and away from Israel. The unavoidable result was growing Israeli-American tension, amidst a flurry of Egyptian and American diplomatic activities culminating, early in November 1989, with US Secretary of State James Baker offering a five-point plan for an Israeli-Palestinian dialogue. As 1989 was nearing its end, it was clear that the intense action aimed at moving the peace process forward was not producing much progress, a factor which was gradually eroding the stability of the Israeli Government itself.

While these major moves were being played out on the center stage of the region, other trends, noticeable well before 1989, were becoming increasingly visible. In inter-Arab affairs, as Bruce Maddy-Weitzman points out in his chapter, Egypt was gradually regaining its seniority, which had significantly diminished as a result of its peace overture toward, and agreement with Israel in 1977–79. Back then, when Arab leaders threatened to isolate Egypt, President Anwar Sadat had reacted forcefully by stating that those Arab states could not possibly isolate Egypt from the Arab world. Rather, they would isolate themselves from Egypt. A decade later, the incremental readmission of Egypt into the Arab fold, begun in 1984 when Jordan renewed its diplomatic relations with Egypt, was crowned by two events: President Mubarak's participation in the Arab summit conference held in Casablanca in May 1989, and the restoration in late December of diplomatic relations with Syria, a major leader and instigator of the anti-Egyptian stance in the Arab world throughout most of the decade. Even the extremist Libya partially normalized its relations with Egypt toward the end of the year. It was now a matter of time before the headquarters of the Arab League, lodged in Tunis since Egypt's suspension from the organization in 1979, would return to Cairo (in 1990), thus fully restoring Egypt's seniority in the Arab world. Egypt's centrality in brokering the American-Israeli-Palestinian minuet-like peace process further accentuated Egypt's leading role as promoter of major Arab causes.

In most other respects, events and processes in 1989 were a direct continuation of 1988. The two foci of persistent internecine violence — Lebanon and southern Sudan — continued to bleed heavily, with no end to the hostilities in sight. While the Sudanese case was fairly isolated and its geographical remoteness kept it off the international agenda and out of public awareness, the carnage in Lebanon surfaced every so often on the world's television screens and front pages, only to recede soon until a further explosion. There was another difference between the Sudanese and Lebanese cases. The latter provided an arena for some of the ME's most ferocious wrestlers: Syria was aligned behind one (Muslim-Christian) Lebanese government, led by President Ilyas al-Hirawi and Prime Minister Salim al-Huss; Iraq — Syria's archenemy — was therefore, supportive of the "rebel," anti-Syrian Lebanese government, led by Christian Gen. Michel 'Awn. Iran continued its involvement with, and support of, military Shi'ites in Lebanon. Israel, for its part, maintained its active interest in the "security zone," which it had carved out in Southern Lebanon. Intense inter-Arab efforts, which led in October 1989 to the Ta'if agreement on a new Lebanese National Accord, did not translate into an acceptable solution in the field. A third conflict, that of the Western Sahara, was also not resolved in 1989, despite the good prospects for progress that were expected at the end of 1988-beginning of 1989.

In contradistinction to these foci of conflict, attempts at subregional cooperation continued in 1989. On the bilateral level, Egypt improved its relations with Sudan following the Sudanese military coup at the end of June 1989; and the People's Democratic Republic of Yemen sought closer ties with its northern neighbor, the Yemeni Arab Republic (YAR). On the multilateral level, in addition to the eight-year-old six-nation Gulf Cooperation Council (GCC), which continued its rather low-key function throughout the year, two new groupings were created in February: the Arab Maghrib Union (AMU), composed of five North African states (Mauritania, Morocco, Algeria, Tunisia, and Libya); and the Arab Cooperation Council (ACC), consisting of Egypt, Iraq, Jordan, and the YAR. The formation of the AMU made more sense in terms of geographical contiguity and took slightly longer to gestate. The formation of the ACC — initiated by Jordan in late 1988 — made less sense geographically and accentuated a notable exclusion, that of Syria. Indeed, the ACC was nothing but an institutionalization of the Iraqi-Jordanian-Egyptian axis, which had emerged during the eight-year war between Iraq and Iran.

With this major war over, the Gulf situation in 1989 was characterized by three traits: (a) an attempt to stabilize oil production and prices and satisfy Iraq's demands in this regard, through the November 1988 agreement by Opec members (the fourth since 1983); (b) efforts by the GCC to restore good relations with Iran; and (c) most significantly, Iraq's clear flexing of muscle in a renewed bid for leadership in the Gulf and, as it were, in the Arab world. Bruce Maddy-Weitzman's conclusion of his chapter on inter-Arab relations, and Ofra Bengio's chapter on Iraq, both written before the Kuwaiti crisis erupted in August 1990, bear ample witness to this important trend, perhaps encouraged by the continued American "tilt" toward Iraq. The relative decline in the importance of the Gulf as a ME subregion was thus transient, unreal, and misleading.

When the decade of the 1970s was coming to an end — 10 years before the year under review — a number of major events were indicative of some major facets of the unfolding 1980s: (1) the downfall of the Shah of Iran and Ayatollah Khomeyni's revolution were soon to turn into a terrible, protracted war between Iraq and Iran, triggered by Iraq's invasion of Iran in September 1980; (b) a little further to the east, the Soviet Union's intervention in Afghanistan, projecting strength and resolve, was about to develop into a long, bloody Russian involvement in a no-win situation; and (c) on the other side of the ME, the signature of the Israeli-Egyptian peace treaty of 1979 gave rise to hopes for accelerated progress toward a more comprehensive resolution of the Arab-Israeli conflict.

By the end of the 1980s, the picture was very different from what might have been expected. Khomeyni's death in June 1989 removed the charismatic spearhead of the Islamic militant wave unleashed 10 years before, albeit not its impact and disruptive potential. The Soviet Union's withdrawal from Afghanistan, the quick collapse of the USSR's iron grip on Eastern Europe, and the turmoil created by centrifugal forces and winds of reform within the USSR, signified the sharp decline of its ability to shape events in the ME. This was best illustrated by the USSR's public withdrawal of its blanket support of Syria in the latter's quest for strategic parity with Israel, and the simultaneous improvement of Soviet-Israeli relations resulting, *inter alia,* in an unequaled (and unexpected) mass exodus of Russian Jews to Israel. In the early 1980s, it appeared that American influence in the region — peaking with the Camp David Accords of 1978 — was facing a serious challenge with the collapse of its Iranian pillar, the imminent extension of the Soviet empire into Afghanistan, the inability of the US to make progress in the Israeli-Arab peace process, and the failure of American involvement in Lebanon during the early phases of the Israeli invasion in 1982. It was almost obvious that the decline in Soviet influence in the ME provided a major opportunity for the US to step in, to fortify and enlarge its influence in the region.

As the decade was coming to a close, it was clear that with all the changes in accent and focus, the basic problems of the ME had not been resolved. The ME remained a highly crucial, extremely volatile region, even as other regional conflicts — in Central

America, South-West Africa and Southeast Asia — were gradually being resolved and Europe was about to undergo a tremendous political renaissance. It was just a matter of time before the ME would, yet again, rivet world attention through a major crisis, arousing unprecedented anxieties because of the proliferation of lethal chemical and, potentially, biological and nuclear weapons in the hands of ruthless regimes. This dimension of horror, coupled with strong sentiments of Islamic bigotry and Arab nationalist xenophobia at the grass roots, did not augur well for the region. Toward the end of the 1980s, many experts on the ME were concerned that the next major round of violence might erupt over the growing scarcity of water resources. As it were, it would soon be demonstrated that oil and petrodollars still had enough "spark" in them to trigger a major crisis. As it turned out, unlike 1989, it was 1990 that was destined to become a watershed year, the momentous events of which demonstrated again that the ME had become a region where everything was possible.

THE MIDDLE EAST
AND WORLD AFFAIRS

The United States and the Middle East

STEVEN L. SPIEGEL and DAVID J. PERVIN

During 1989, American policy toward the Middle East was a mixture of change and continuity. There was a new administration in Washington, but the election of George Bush, Ronald Reagan's vice president, meant fewer changes than would have been likely had Michael Dukakis, the Democrat's candidate, been victorious. Many of Reagan's principal advisors on ME policy remained, but the ideological and emotional flavor of the Reagan era was replaced by the pragmatic and cautious approach of the Bush team.

The Reagan Administration left a twofold legacy to Bush's entourage. First, the active efforts of then secretary of state George Shultz to energize the peace process during 1988 resulted in much motion but little movement. Indeed, the limited movement which did occur was backward, as Jordan disengaged from the West Bank in July 1988, removing a traditional pillar of American diplomatic efforts for a settlement. The failure of Shultz's efforts, which included three visits to the region, reinforced the predilection for caution in the Bush Administration. Second, by recognizing and then beginning a dialogue with the PLO in the Administration's waning days, Reagan and Shultz removed a potentially contentious issue from the new Administration's agenda.

The high level of activity that characterized the final year of the Reagan Administration was thus replaced by a more circumspect approach. In part this was due to the decreased urgency of the various issues: the Intifada seemed to lose steam, or at least it was no longer of central concern to the media in the US, and the cease-fire between Iraq and Iran continued to hold, though not without tension. There was increased anxiety about the proliferation of missiles and unconventional munitions — chemical, biological, and potentially nuclear — but there was little the US could or would do directly to stem the flow. The momentous and historic events in Eastern Europe and the Soviet Union took central place in American foreign policy, leaving the ME on the back burner.

The cautious approach of the Bush Administration also reflected its analysis of the low likelihood of positive developments in the region and the conviction that there was little the US could do in the absence of action by the regional parties themselves. Although widely interpreted as a signal to Iran, Bush's statement, in his inaugural speech, that "goodwill begets goodwill" summed up his Administration's general approach to foreign policy. As to the ME, one unidentified administration official put it bluntly: "We don't have to rush....[I]f the parties don't want to move, it's their mess

The authors would like to thank Gitty Cannon, Miranda Ke, Thomas Neusom, and Kathleen Urbanik for their assistance in the preparation of this chapter.

and they can sleep in it. "[1] This approach was played out with respect to the Arab-Israeli peace process, as well as with Lebanon and the Arab radical states.

THE UNITED STATES AND THE PEACE PROCESS

Although not a completely unknown quantity, the policy the incoming Bush Administration would follow was a matter of concern and conjecture in the ME. The pragmatic approach implied that the relationship with Israel would be based less on sympathy or ideological affinity and more on its perceived political and strategic importance. Gone was the romantic vision that had characterized the Reagan years. The image of the Arabs, in particular the Palestinians, had improved as a result of the Intifada. But while the Reagan Administration appeared to have had a complete change of heart toward the PLO, paralleling a similar change in attitude toward the Soviet Union, the incoming Bush team placed greater importance on whether the PLO could deliver. Consistent with their outlook, Bush's advisers believed that the PLO would have to address Israel directly with promises of peace and examples of moderation if there was to be any hope of progress.

The new approach was a source of concern to Arabs and Israelis alike. Some Arabs were fearful that the appointment of officials with pro-Israel reputations, many of whom were Jewish, would lead to a definite tilt toward Jerusalem. Israelis were worried that the absence of high-ranking close friends like Reagan and Shultz would lead to a more "even-handed" approach, to Israel's detriment.[2]

There was ample evidence to support the fears and hopes of local parties on both sides of the ME divide. None of the new principal policymakers was known for his affinity to either the Arabs or Israelis. All had first emerged during the Ford Administration, when Arab strength on the energy question raised concerns in Washington that an unchecked Arab-Israeli dispute could adversely affect American strategic and economic interests in the ME. Thus, in 1976 George Bush had been director of the Central Intelligence Agency (CIA); Richard Cheney, now secretary of defense, had been the White House chief of staff; Brent Scowcroft was Ford's national security adviser and now became Bush's; and James Baker, now secretary of state, had managed president Ford's election campaign. Only two high-ranking individuals in the Bush Administration were often cited for their presumed Mideast partisanship. John Sunnunu, Bush's chief of staff, was the highest ranking Arab-American in US history. In the late 1980s, while Sunnunu was governor of New Hampshire, he had been the only state chief executive to refuse to sign a document criticizing the UN resolution equating Zionism and racism. Vice President Dan Quayle, widely seen as unprepared for his post and not regarded as a major player with policy input, made a special effort in the early months of the Administration to court Washington's pro-Israeli community.

On the second and third levels, however, there was an unprecedented number of officials — Jewish and gentile — who were generally seen as supportive of Israel. Many held posts previously occupied by Arabists or individuals skeptical of close relations with Israel. Several, if not most, of these officials tended to agree with the Israeli Labor Party's view of Israel's security or were skeptical and suspicious of the Likud formula. (For these parties' positions, see chapter on Israel.)

The president and his secretary of state set the tone for the Administration as a whole. Both of them had first become successful in Houston, Texas, where the oil industry has been particularly influential. Bush had had much experience and involvement in Arab-Israeli affairs, and there was contradictory evidence which might provide solace for either side. Bush was the vice president in an exceptionally pro-Israeli administration and had been a hero to the Israelis in arranging the secret exodus of Ethiopian Jews in the late 1980s. On the other hand, he was known to have been highly critical of the Israelis in two ME crises early in the Reagan Administration: the bombing of the Iraqi nuclear reactor in 1981 and the invasion of Lebanon in June 1982. His experiences at the CIA would also lead to the prediction that he would be more persuaded than his predecessor of the dangers of such issues as settlements in the West Bank and the Gaza Strip. By the end of 1989, his Secretary of State Baker had never been to Israel.

Given this background, it is not surprising that in its first year the Bush Administration's approach to the peace process was one of seeking to balance the preferences of various actors — Israel, the Palestinians, Arab countries, and domestic constituencies. If it was commonly observed that the Intifada had returned the Arab-Israeli conflict to its original communal nature, and if Jordan's disengagement from the West Bank had strengthened this conviction, then with the opening of the dialogue with the PLO the US was carefully balanced between the regional foes. The Bush approach was based on a belief that the actors in the region would have to make the first move, that the US would be a mediator, facilitator, and moderator, but it would not be an initiator. The US would seek the common ground between the two parties, but would also make it clear that whoever refused to play would bear the blame for any breakdown in the process. What ensued was a process in which each side sought to keep the ball in the other's court, akin to the game of hot potato.

The tone was set by the new president during a news conference on 27 January, when he said that the purpose of the dialogue with the PLO was "to try to facilitate peace in the Middle East....You crawl before you walk."[3] As Secretary of State Baker put it on 19 February, "I think that if you had to balance risks here, the risk would be greater in taking precipitous action than in waiting awhile, analyzing the situation, working on the ground carefully — tilling the ground...."[4] The emphasis was on procedure, in large part in the belief that progress on procedures would lead to progress on substance, both through building trust and because procedure and substance are deeply intertwined.

It should be clear that the emphasis on procedure still meant that the US had policy aims. The overarching goal, of course, was a mutually acceptable settlement. In his confirmation hearings, Secretary Baker outlined the themes that would characterize American policy throughout the year, and which were to be repeated on many occasions: the "message" to the PLO was that terrorism was unacceptable, that there was a need for "realism that makes practical progress on the ground possible," and that while "the Palestinians must participate in the determination of their own future," the US was opposed to an independent state because it would "not be a source of stability or contribute to a just and enduring peace." Toward Israel, Baker made clear that while American support was firm, "the legitimate rights of the Palestinians" had to be addressed, and any negotiations would have to be "based on UN Resolutions 242 and 338, which include the exchange of territory for peace."[5] Baker's testimony was in many ways a continuation of the Reagan Administration's policies, as outlined by Shultz in his final major statement on the ME, made before the Washington Institute for Near East Policy in September 1988. The basic message was that the US would not condone unilateral measures by either side, and that each had to talk to the other, not through the US, but directly.

The difficult task of balancing the demands of Israel and the Palestinians quickly became apparent. In the final days of the Reagan Administration, Yasir 'Arafat, chairman of the PLO, was accused by Israel of making threats against the lives of moderate Palestinians in the occupied territories who might want to negotiate with Israel.[6] Tensions increased after two member organizations of the PLO, the Popular Front for the Liberation of Palestine (PFLP) and the Palestine Liberation Front (PLF), attempted to raid Israel from Southern Lebanon early in 1989, and, in response, Israel called on the US to stop its talks with the PLO.[7] The American answer was, depending on one's point of view, calculated neither to please nor alienate either side, or was confused. On the one hand, the State Department condemned terrorism and said the PLO would be held responsible for its actions. Yet it refused to directly associate 'Arafat with the attacks, claiming that it was not clear whether he had control over the activities of the various constituent members of the PLO. On the other hand, Vice President Quayle expressed suspicion of the PLO and 'Arafat and warned that the Administration "needed to see real evidence of concrete actions by the PLO — actions for peace and against terrorism."[8]

While the issue of terrorism would continue to plague American relations with the PLO and Israel, the Bush Administration continuously sought to keep the peace process on-line. The first opportunity for the new team to convey its policy directly to regional actors came at the funeral of Japanese Emperor Hirohito in late February. After meetings in Japan with Jordan's King Husayn, Egypt's President Husni Mubarak, and Israel's President Chaim Herzog, Secretary Baker explained that the cautious US approach was based on the concern "that if we act too precipitously we might preempt promising possibilities that could surface if we adopted a more reasoned and measured approach." The policy was based on the belief that there was "a certain dynamic now in the region," a dynamic that had led to a "reexamination on the part of a number of the major players." In turn, that reexamination might lead to "direct negotiations that will ultimately lead to peace." The trick was to "somehow...find a way to get to these direct negotiations." An international conference might be an appropriate forum, but Baker argued that "there ought to be an extensive amount of practical groundwork accomplished before we rush off to have a big, high visibility conference under the television lights."[9]

Although Baker saw the dialogue with the PLO as part of the new dynamic, in the beginning of March the old scourge of terrorism quickly raised its head again. The Democratic Front for the Liberation of Palestine — a group that, like the PFLP and the PLF, opposed 'Arafat's concessions — attempted to raid Israel from Lebanon. In reaction to this incident, however, the US was more critical of the PLO. The State Department warned that "attacks against Israeli civilian or military targets inside or outside Israel are contrary to the peaceful objectives of the dialogue" and that the "PLO cannot escape responsibility for the actions of its constituent elements."[10] While reluctant to conclude that the dialogue should be aborted, Washington also sought to make clear to the PLO that its behavior merely reinforced opposition to the dialogue in the US and would increase Israeli pressure for a halt, and raised "questions about the PLO's ability to carry out its commitments."[11]

The unwillingness of the US to categorically hold 'Arafat accountable for the actions of his Palestinian opponents within the PLO was consistent with the Bush Administration's policy of keeping all doors open while seeking paths for progress. The criticism of the PLO may also have been an attempt to smooth the ground in preparation for the visit to Washington of Israeli Foreign Minister Moshe Arens, scheduled to commence on 13 March. Prior to his visit, there were reports that the US would propose steps to be taken by both sides in order to reduce tensions. Israel would be asked to release some of the Palestinians from the occupied territories who had been arrested, end or limit the use of administrative detentions against Palestinians, and reopen schools. The PLO, in turn, would be expected to halt violent demonstrations, cease the distribution of inflammatory leaflets in the territories, and block raids from Southern Lebanon.

The purpose of these proposals, administration officials made clear, was to "improve the situation on the ground so that hopefully the whole atmosphere and climate will improve to the point that we can then begin to talk about how...we get the parties together." Again, the US would not propose solutions and its goals would be limited to helping the parties "lay the proper foundations and proper frame as they go along"[12] the path of the peace process.

After meeting with Arens on 13 March, Baker said that they had "reviewed the current situation in the West Bank and Gaza and considered various reinforcing and reciprocal steps that might be taken to defuse the tensions there." While he also "reaffirmed our desire...to work closely with Israel in the search for peace," the differences between the American and Israeli positions were not far below the surface. According to one "senior administration official," Baker told Arens that "we need some general commitments from Israel and the Palestinians to a final settlement, so that the Arabs don't think we are simply trying to reduce tensions or buy off the Palestinian uprising as an end in itself....one without the other simply will not work."[13]

Although the statements made by Baker and Arens after their meeting showed little sign of tension,[14] differences reached the surface immediately. Baker, in testimony to a Senate appropriations subcommittee, stated that the US could not rule out direct negotiations between Israel and the PLO if other Palestinian interlocutors, i.e., from the occupied territories, could not be found.[15] While still in Washington, Arens said he was "disappointed" at Baker's comments, and claimed that neither the apparent change in the American position nor requests for specific actions by Israel had been raised in their joint discussions.[16] Yet, Arens was further disconcerted when he was told by members of the Senate Committee on Foreign Relations of a "movement of American public opinion to a more negative posture regarding Israel" and the need for Israel "to seize the initiative...to go the extra mile."[17] Baker's refusal, a week later, to dismiss the possibility of direct negotiations between Israel and the PLO, and his admission of "differences" in the respective positions of the US and Israel, were further evidence of a change in nuance, if not in policy, by the US.[18]

Israeli Prime Minister Yitzhak Shamir embarked on an effort to lower the heat prior to his visit to Washington, scheduled for early April. In a reversal of his earlier position,[19] he suggested that if the violence in the occupied territories ceased, elections could be held for negotiators to discuss interim measures and ultimately the final status of the territories. The Israeli leader also advocated the raising of funds to build new housing for Palestinian refugees in the territories.[20] This seemingly innovative proposal, which was similar to the Camp David Accords that Shamir had rejected in 1978, would become the centerpiece of all subsequent discussions regarding the peace process during 1989.

Prior to the Israeli prime minister's visit, Egyptian President Mubarak held discussions in Washington on 3 April. He expressed his support for the American policy of trying to improve the atmosphere in order to move the peace process forward. The similarity of the American and Egyptian positions was made clear by President Bush. After meeting Mubarak he said that the two countries "share a sense of urgency to move toward a comprehensive settlement through direct negotiations," as well as "the goals of security for Israel, the end of the occupation, and the achievement of Palestinian political rights."[21] The contrast with the aftermath of the Arens visit, scarcely three weeks earlier, was stark.

Yet the Egyptian leader also expressed doubts as to the realism of Shamir's elections proposal, in particular the Israeli demand that the Intifada cease before the election could be held. He also warned that Egypt could not support the idea "unless we are sure that it's going to keep the momentum [going] or will help the peace process."[22] According to a "senior" administration official who briefed reporters on Mubarak's discussions with Bush, the Egyptian president told the US that elections "certainly would not be acceptable to the Palestinians under the supervision of the Israelis."[23] The problems that would plague the elections proposal were thus apparent from the beginning.

Shamir's visit to Washington took place immediately after Mubarak's, and the Administration sought to depict the Israeli proposals as favorably as possible. After meeting with Shamir on 5 April, Baker said that their discussions were "productive, useful, and friendly" and that Shamir's proposals were "encouraging...hopefully [they] will form the basis under [sic] which we can move the peace process forward."[24]

Shamir met with President Bush the next day, after which he made public his four-point peace initiative. First, he reaffirmed the Camp David Accords. Second, he asked that the US and Egypt "make clear to the Arab governments that they must abandon their hostility and belligerence toward Israel" and that they "must replace political warfare and economic boycott with negotiations and cooperation." Third, he called for "a multinational effort under the leadership of the United States and with substantial Israeli participation to finally resolve the Arab refugee problem perpetuated by the Arab governments....This process does not have to await a political solution or to substitute for it." The fourth element was the centerpiece, in that it called for "free democratic elections" in the occupied territories in order to "produce a delegation to negotiate an interim period of self-governing administration." The interim period would "provide a vital test of coexistence and cooperation," and would lead to "negotiations for a permanent agreement," at which time "all proposed options will be examined" as to the final status of the occupied territories.[25] (For full text and a detailed discussion of the Israeli proposals, see chapter on the ME peace process.)

Shamir's initiative was meant to be an indivisible whole, i.e., if there was no progress on one section, there could not be movement on the other elements. Yet the fourth part received the most attention and for all practical purposes came to be divorced from the first three. While pleased that it now had a proposal, the Bush

Administration believed that there were severe difficulties to be overcome if Shamir's proposals were to be brought to fruition. Indeed, Bush himself struck something of a discordant note in his statement following his meeting with Shamir when he stated that: "Peace, security, and political rights can be attained through direct negotiations. The status quo serves the interests of no one." Bush further affirmed that the US did "not support an independent Palestinian state nor Israeli sovereignty or permanent occupation of the West Bank and Gaza."[26]

The president expressed qualified support for Shamir's plan, saying that he "believes that elections in the territories can be designed to contribute to a political process of dialogue and negotiation." Yet he added that the Palestinians would be free to bring any proposal to the table, that the final status of the territories would have to be satisfactory to all sides, and that the interim stage should not be the "end of the road" but rather the beginning of a "broader political process that includes negotiating and concluding an agreement on final status" of the territories.[27] Sounding a similar note, Baker said that the proposed elections would be "an important political act that can launch a process leading to negotiations on both transitional and final status issues."[28] The similarity between Shamir's position and that of the Administration did not, however, disguise the nuanced American warning that the elections would be the first stage of a process, not an end in and of themselves.

Below the surface there were important differences between the US and Israel. These differences would be exacerbated by a misunderstanding between Bush and Shamir. In his private session with Shamir, Bush repeated his well-known opposition to new Israeli settlements in the West Bank and Gaza Strip, an opposition consistent with long-standing American policy. Shamir responded that "this would not be a problem." The president apparently believed that he had received a commitment that Israel would not build additional settlements. Shamir seems to have meant that since the settlements had not been an impediment to the peace process in the past, they would not be so in the future. The president was therefore infuriated when he was informed only a few days later that the Israeli Cabinet planned to establish new settlements. From the president's point of view Shamir had deceived him. Here was the beginning of a deterioration in the personal relations between the two leaders with important future policy implications.[29]

Thus, notwithstanding American acceptance of Shamir's proposals, suspicion of his ultimate objectives was ever present. Administration officials clearly recognized the difficulties inherent in even reaching the elections stage. In an interview on the ABC News Program "This Week With David Brinkley" on 9 April, Baker alluded to these problems and the need to conduct negotiations over the terms of the elections, which themselves were to lead to negotiations. The central questions concerning elections, Baker said, included "Who is eligible to vote? After these people are elected, what is going to be their responsibility?....How will that fit in with the negotiations on permanent status?"[30] These questions would bedevil the process throughout the remainder of the year.

The Administration's emphasis on the elections received a qualified vote of approval from the next visitor to Washington, Jordan's King Husayn. After meeting with Baker on 19 April, Husayn said that "the idea of elections might be worth looking at within the context of a whole process...to a final settlement. Otherwise the idea is out of context."[31] Yet any hopes that Jordan would reenter the peace process[32] were dashed by Husayn's contention that "peace can neither be negotiated nor achieved without PLO participation." Husayn added that the "forum for a negotiated comprehensive settlement is a peace conference under the auspices of the United Nations."[33] In his own statement, President Bush addressed many of the same themes, though with different emphases. There was a "need to diffuse tensions, to promote dialogue, to foster the process of negotiations that could lead to a comprehensive settlement....properly designed and mutually acceptable elections could, as an initial step, contribute to a political process leading to negotiations on the final status of the West Bank and Gaza." Bush reaffirmed the "principle of territory for peace" and said that "a properly structured international conference could serve, at the appropriate time, as a means to facilitate direct negotiations between the parties."[34]

Even if Husayn's Jordan would not play a direct role in the peace process, Jordan continued to be an important element in American policy. As the president put it after meeting with Husayn, "Jordan's security remains a fundamental concern to the United States" since "an important part of this effort [for peace] and of the stability of the Middle East as a whole will be the continued economic and military strength of Jordan."[35] Little did Bush know how soon that premise would be put to the test, as Husayn was forced to cut short his visit after riots erupted in various Jordanian towns. The dangers of instability, and the fear that the Intifada would adversely influence events in the region, were demonstrated in stark relief (see chapter on Jordan). For many American policymakers, Husayn's troubled position at home merely confirmed Jordan's inability to play an active role in the peace process, and certainly seemed to put to rest any hope that it could be a substitute or surrogate for the PLO.

In the wake of the visits of the three main ME leaders with close relations with the US, the peace process had taken two steps forward and one step back: Shamir had produced a proposal that could serve as the foundation of American diplomacy and it had not been rejected (nor, for that matter, unconditionally accepted) by either Egypt or Jordan. With trouble at home, Jordan was even more removed to the sidelines. Given Israel's absolute refusal to talk with the PLO, some alternative would have to be tried, and Cairo and the Palestinians in the occupied territories appeared to be appealing options. Washington policymakers would spend the rest of the year trying to define and refine the procedures and implications of the proposed elections.

Having laid the initial groundwork in the region, the Bush Administration sought to gain Soviet participation in the peace process. Banking on the apparent desire of Gorbachev to improve relations with the US, Baker used the opportunity of a meeting on 9 May with Soviet Foreign Minister Eduard Shevardnadze to explain to the Soviets the broad outlines of the Administration's Mideast policy. He then offered Moscow a place in the process. The Soviets could play a positive role, Baker said, by seeking to convince the PLO to agree to American efforts to initiate negotiations for elections. He added that for Moscow to be an equal partner, it must restore diplomatic relations with Israel. Baker also expressed American displeasure with the continued Soviet supply of high technology weapons to the ME, in particular the recent sale of long-range bombers to Libya.[36]

The Kremlin's influence on its regional clients was reduced by its declining role in the Third World and by the turmoil in Eastern Europe and the Soviet Union itself. Moscow could at best play a quiet role supporting American efforts — in itself preferable to its past policy of unconditionally backing the positions of obstructionist states and actors in the region. The weight of the peace process would continue to fall squarely on the shoulders of Washington, a weight that was almost dropped in a stunning speech by Baker before the America-Israel Public Affairs Committee (Aipac) on 22 May.

In and of itself, the speech, appropriately entitled "Principles and Pragmatism: American Policy Toward the Arab-Israeli Conflict," departed little from statements of former secretary of state Shultz and previous declarations by Bush Administration officials. But the bluntness of the first major policy statement on the ME by the secretary of state caused an immediate stir. The controversy was undoubtedly magnified because the audience was the principal pro-Israel lobby.

Baker opened the speech with warm support for Israel, and then enunciated the "principles" of American policy. First, negotiations must lead to a comprehensive peace based on UN Security Council Resolutions 242 and 338, and "these negotiations must involve territory for peace, security and recognition for Israel and all the states in the region, and Palestinian political rights." Second, Baker argued that negotiations must take place directly between the parties. While an international conference might be "useful," it could "not interfere with or in any way replace or be a substitute for direct talks between the parties." Third, he admitted that there would have to be a transitional period. Fourth, he claimed that while no outside party could impose a settlement, unilateral actions by either Israel (i.e., annexation) or the Palestinians (i.e., the declaration of an independent Palestinian state) would not be supported by the US. The goal, Baker said, was a "reasonable middle ground" based on "self-government for Palestinians on the West Bank and Gaza in a manner acceptable to Palestinians, Israel, and Jordan."

Baker proceeded to emphatically call on all sides to rid themselves of illusions; any settlement would necessarily fail to satisfy the maximal demands of either side. The Palestinians would have to accept Israel's existence and an "end to the illusion of control over all of Palestine"; the covenant should be amended and the Intifada turned from a "dialogue of violence" into a "dialogue of politics and diplomacy." The Arabs would have to "take concrete steps toward accommodation with Israel," including an end to the economic boycott, no more challenges to Israel's standing in international organizations, and a repudiation of the "odious line that Zionism is racism."

Because of the audience and the tone, the media paid most attention to Baker's direct message to Jerusalem. Israel, he said, would have to recognize that the successful outcome of the peace process "will, in all probability, involve territorial withdrawal." "Now is the time," he continued, for Israel "to lay aside, once and for all, the unrealistic vision of a greater Israel....Foreswear annexation. Stop settlement activity. Allow the schools to reopen. Reach out to the Palestinians as neighbors who deserve political rights."[37]

The regional response was predictable. The PLO called Baker's speech a "big step forward," and of particular importance given that it was made to Aipac. Israel, on the other hand, reacted with undisguised anger, even disgust. On a visit to London, Shamir said "we cannot accept what he said...about a greater Israel or the settlement problem....I don't think it was useful to raise those issues now. It was useless." A spokesman for the Israeli Foreign Ministry called it "an explosive statement.... because it is not realistic. It makes an impossible request."[38]

In the wake of the Aipac speech, the peace process stalled. The US continued to provide support for Israel in the UN, vetoing on 9 June a Security Council resolution condemning Israel's actions in the occupied territories.[39] Yet, relations with Israel grew tense. First it was disclosed that Robert Pelletreau, the US ambassador to Tunisia and the sole authorized intermediary with the PLO, had met with senior officials of that organization for the first time.[40] Second, since Shamir was under pressure from the Likud's far right (see chapter on Israel), several Bush aides and American Jewish leaders persuaded the president to write a letter demonstrating US support for the Shamir plan, which might be used by the prime minister as ammunition against his opponents. Baker complained that such a letter might undercut his positions as stated in the Aipac speech. Therefore the letter, which was sent on 30 June, merely reiterated the president's message of May. When it arrived, the letter could not be used to bolster Shamir's position.[41] At the Likud party convention, Shamir accepted four points that effectively muted any possibility that the Palestinians might accept the proposed elections. The prime minister agreed that: (1) Arab residents of East Jerusalem could neither vote in nor run for the elections; (2) there would be no elections until the Intifada ended; (3) Israel would not give up territory and no Palestinian state would ever be established; and (4) settlements would continue to be built.[42]

The conditions Shamir accepted were not contrary to his own position, but they left him little room to maneuver and hedge. His Likud opponents made it clear that this was precisely their intention. The Bush Administration tried to paper over its dismay at the latest developments by claiming that these were the positions of a party, albeit the senior partner in the government, and not the official position of Israel's Government. Yet in an implicit criticism, the State Department, in true understatement, observed that "partisan declarations, particularly if they appear to be more restrictive or to impose conditions, do not advance the prospects for peace."[43] Fearing the strength of Likud's hawks, the Administration nevertheless counseled the Labor Party, the Likud's partner, against withdrawing from the government.[44]

Thus, Washington officially responded cautiously to the conditions set down at the Likud Party convention. Unofficially, the response was much harsher. An unidentified "senior US official" traveling with Baker *en route* to Europe via Oman was reported to have said that "if you can't make progress with this election proposal, then we would have to look a bit more closely at the prospects for an international conference. There is a lot of support for that...."[45] When Baker himself was widely identified as the source,[46] the pressure on Jerusalem was intensified.

Another negative development in American-Israeli relations was Israel's abduction of Shaykh 'Abd al-Karim 'Ubayd, a leader of Hizballah, from Southern Lebanon on 27 July (for details see chapter on armed operations). Although not directly linked to the process surrounding the elections proposal, Israel's actions had adverse effects on relations with Washington. A Shi'ite group threatened that if 'Ubayd was not released it would kill US Marine Col. William Higgins, who had been kidnapped while serving as an observer with Unifil. In a statement interpreted as a rebuke to Israel, President Bush said that "I do not think kidnapping and violence helps [sic] the cause of peace."[47] After Higgins's corpse was revealed in a grisly video tape, Bush made an "urgent call to all, all parties who hold hostages in the Middle East to release them forthwith," which was also interpreted as a criticism of Israel. Bush seemed to be calling 'Ubayd a hostage.

The incident began as an Israeli abduction of a guerrilla leader who Israel believed had information about terrorist operations and who hopefully could be exchanged for three Israelis being held in Lebanon. It quickly turned into a confrontation between Jerusalem and Washington. The situation further deteriorated when the Shi'ite terrorists threatened to kill another American hostage if 'Ubayd was not immediately released. In the ensuing emotional atmosphere, the Senate Republican minority leader, Robert Dole of Kansas, severely chastised what he regarded as Israel's unacceptable actions.[48] Lost in the media extravaganza was the assessment by the American intelligence services that Higgins had actually been killed months before.

Tensions between the Administration and Israel's supporters escalated as well. In mid-July, Bush and the Congress confronted each other over the issue of US talks with high-level PLO officials. At first, the Congress threatened to demand that the president certify that any PLO interlocutor had not been involved in terrorism against Americans. According to this plan, if the Senate was not satisfied with how the negotiations were proceeding, it would cut off funding for the talks. The Administration's objection to this restriction had two bases: first, the Congress had no constitutional right to tie its hands; second, such a resolution would damage American diplomacy and the peace process. In the end, Congress adopted a watered-down measure calling on the president to stop any talks with known terrorists. If he proceeded, then he would have to inform the Congress about the dialogue.[49]

The Administration also met resistance from the Palestinians over the proposed elections. In early June, the US had asked the PLO to allow Palestinians in the West Bank and Gaza Strip to take part in elections.[50] The PLO had continued to condition its willingness to enter negotiations over the elections on its ability to choose the negotiators, including Palestinians outside the occupied territories.[51] In response to the stipulations of the Likud convention, 'Arafat stated that the PLO could no longer consider the election proposal, and expressed displeasure with US policy.[52] The hopes of the Administration received a further setback in early August when, during a trip to the region, John Kelly, the assistant secretary of state for Near Eastern and South Asian affairs, was told by a delegation of West Bank Palestinians that there was no substitute for PLO participation in any negotiations.[53] A meeting between Ambassador Pelletreau and PLO officials in Tunis on 14 August, in which the US again called on the PLO to accept the election proposal and allow local Palestinians to take the leading role, led nowhere, and was characterized as "disappointing" (see chapter on the ME peace process).[54]

Thus stymied by both sides, the Administration allowed the peace process to float, refusing to offer a plan of its own. Wary of the deep internal divisions that both parties faced, Washington was reluctant to place too much pressure on either Israel or the PLO. The tacit message was, "we will wait: the next move is up to you."

The next move, however, was not made by either Israel or the Palestinians, but by Egypt. Clearly concerned that a breakdown in the peace process would endanger its revived position in the Arab world, and even threaten relations with both Israel and the US, Mubarak's government became actively engaged. It offered a "ten-point" program for working out the terms of the elections. Although reports of the plan had appeared as early as July and August,[55] it became the centerpiece of discussion on the peace process only in mid-September. Here was the opportunity the Administration was seeking: since the proposal came from an Arab party at peace with Israel and having close ties with the PLO, neither could reject it as tainted. Since it was proposed by a regional actor, American prestige would not be directly affected by the success or failure of the plan. Since it was concerned with procedures, it was hoped that with agreement the process would resume. That Egypt offered to host Palestinian and Israeli negotiating delegations in Cairo[56] was a further bonus.

The Egyptian "Ten Points" were an effort to find a common ground. As both Egypt and the US made clear, they were intended to be initial ideas for negotiations, not final conditions. The Ten Points (for official text see chapter on the ME peace process) were, briefly, as follows:

(1) All Palestinians in the West Bank, the Gaza Strip, and East Jerusalem should be allowed to vote and run for office.

(2) Candidates should be free to campaign without interference from the Israeli authorities.

(3) Israel should allow international supervision of the election process.

(4) Construction or expansion of Jewish settlements would be frozen during this period.

(5) The Army would withdraw from the area of polling places on election day.

(6) Only Israelis who work or live in the occupied territories would be permitted to enter them on election day.

(7) Preparation for the elections should not take longer than two months; Egypt and the US could help form the Israeli-Palestinian committee doing that work.

(8) The Israeli Government should agree to negotiate the exchange of land for peace, while also protecting Israel's security.

(9) The US and Israel should publicly guarantee Israel's adherence to the plan.

(10) Israel should publicly agree in advance to accept the outcome of the elections.[57]

If calculated to have elements acceptable to both Israel and the Palestinians, the Ten Points also included aspects to which either would object. The US heartily welcomed Egypt's proposal as a useful framework from which to start, one that did not replace Israel's election proposal but that built upon it.[58] Shamir rejected it outright, in the main because of the call for the exchange of territory for peace.[59] While Mubarak claimed that the PLO agreed to the plan,[60] 'Arafat refused to accept it unequivocally unless Israel did so first[61] (for a discussion of the Israeli, Egyptian, and Palestinian positions, see chapter on the ME peace process).

Baker took advantage of meetings with Israeli Foreign Minister Arens and his Egyptian counterpart 'Ismat 'Abd al-Majid at the UN General Assembly annual meeting to place pressure upon Israel to accept the Egyptian proposals. Baker's displeasure with Israel's foot-dragging was clear in his statement that:

> We want to see progress toward peace. We feel that the Shamir proposal represents an excellent opportunity to get there, and we just hope that the Israeli Government will be as firmly committed to that proposal as it has been in the past and will decide to move forward to elections.[62]

Mubarak's meetings in Washington with Bush and Baker on 2 October provided another opportunity to bring Israel on board. Baker suggested that the US, Egypt, and Israel could participate in determining the participants in the Palestinian delegation, thereby giving Israel "a chop [stamp of approval] on the [Palestinian] representation."[63]

Shamir's government was not reassured, however, and the cabinet meeting of 6 October ended in a deadlock, effectively a rejection of the Ten Points. Washington sought to place this development in the best possible light, refusing to call the absence of Israeli acceptance a rejection of the Ten Points and hoping that the setback would be temporary.[64] Yet it was increasingly clear that the US would have to become a more active mediator if success were to result from ongoing efforts. For example, Shamir and Arens demanded a written proposal detailing Baker's position on the nature of any talks to set up elections.[65] Israeli Defense Minister Yitzhak Rabin called for a greater role for the US, saying that "the only peace that was achieved...was achieved with a lot of United States' activities and participation."[66]

Although reluctant to take an active position, the Administration concluded that it had no choice but to try and reassure Israel, and particularly Shamir. On 10 October the State Department announced that in the wake of phone consultations with the Israeli and Egyptian foreign ministers, Baker had submitted to the parties a five-point proposal for consideration.[67] The five points were as follows:

(1) The United States understands that Egypt and Israel have been working hard and that there is now agreement that the Israeli delegation will conduct a dialogue with Palestinians in Cairo.

(2) The United States understands that Egypt cannot substitute for the Palestinians in that dialogue and that Egypt will consult with the Palestinians on all aspects of that dialogue. Egypt will also consult with Israel and the United States.

(3) The United States understands that Israel will attend the dialogue after a satisfactory list of Palestinians has been worked out. Israel will also consult with the United States and Egypt on this matter.

(4) The United States understands that the Government of Israel will come to the dialogue on the basis of the Israeli Government 14 May [election and peace] initiative. The United States further understands that elections and negotiations will be in accordance with the Israeli initiative. The United States understands, therefore, that the Palestinians will be free to raise issues that relate to their opinion on how to make elections and negotiations succeed.

(5) In order to facilitate the process, the United States proposes that the foreign ministers of Israel, Egypt, and the United States meet in Washington within two weeks.[68]

Like Egypt's Ten Points, Baker's Five Points were meant to be an elaboration and facilitation of Shamir's election proposal; and like Egypt's points, Shamir found much unsatisfactory material in the secretary of state's proposal. In particular, Shamir wanted point one to read a "delegation from Judea and Samaria," both as a matter of principle and to limit the Palestinian representation to residents of the occupied territories, thereby excluding outside Palestinians. He also wanted point three to be changed to allow Israel a veto of proposed Palestinian delegates. He further sought the elimination of the word "negotiations" from point four[69] so that the dialogue in Cairo would be limited to the elections described in his original plan, with no opportunity for the Arab side to raise additional issues — e.g., final status of the territories.

The Bush team clearly was not pleased with Shamir's demands. Prior to Israel's efforts to amend Baker's proposals, one "administration official" was blunt: "If we put together something that is sensitive and he [Shamir] comes up with more excuses, then it will show everyone that he was not serious" about the peace process.[70] Reacting to the prime minister's expressed willingness for a showdown with Washington, the State Department called his statements "unhelpful...we're disappointed." Baker proceeded one step further, saying that "as long as there is even a faint hope [for peace] we think that we should remain engaged. When we become satisfied that is no longer the case, then we'll have no alternative but to disengage."[71] The secretary refused to consider changes in the five points.[72]

When subsequently informed that Israel had conditionally accepted the points, the State Department provided qualified praise, stating that "they [Israel] are engaged and they are working really hard to try to bridge these gaps" that continue to hold up the process.[73] Nevertheless, the Administration sought to maintain the pressure on Israel. In an act which was widely considered to be a deliberate diplomatic snub, it refused to invite Shamir to meet with the president during his coming visit to the US.[74]

Although Israel sought to convince the Administration to amend elements of Baker's Five Points, any changes were resisted.[75] On 5 November, the Israeli Cabinet officially accepted Baker's proposals, though with the addition of six demands which substantively altered and limited Egypt's Ten Points and sought to bind the US to virtually unconditional support for Israel's positions. The National Unity Government's demands included the following: (1) that only residents of the occupied territories would be eligible for negotiations, and among them only those acceptable to Israel; (2) discussions in Cairo would be limited to Israel's election proposal; (3) any continuation of the talks would be based on the results of the first meeting; (4) Israel would not talk with the PLO; (5) Egypt and the US would reaffirm their commitment to the Camp David Accords; and (6) "the United States will publicly support Israel's position and back whatever Israeli actions are necessary if the agreement is broken."[76] The Administration perhaps optimistically saw potential in Israel's acceptance, though the problems inherent in attaining Egyptian, not to mention Palestinian, approval were obvious.[77] While rejecting Israel's conditions, Baker nevertheless called Israel's decisions "a very positive step," though only a "first step." Any future progress, Baker said, "will depend on what we hear from the Egyptians."[78] The spotlight thus shifted toward Egypt, in effect a surrogate for the Palestinians. The PLO responded to Israel's conditions with a set of its own. These included a direct role in naming the Palestinian delegation to any talks and a "final say in all stages of the peace process." The PLO also sought to tie the talks to a process leading to a comprehensive settlement, with an international conference as the forum. It also demanded that Israel accept the American contention that peace would have to be based on the political rights of the Palestinians and trading land for peace.[79]

In the wake of the Israeli Cabinet's qualified acceptance of Baker's Five Points, the Administration extended an invitation to Shamir to visit the White House. In the absence of an Egyptian and Palestinian response to the American proposal, some of the heat on Israel had been dissipated. Yet the day before Shamir's meetings with officials in Washington, the State Department strongly criticized plans for a new settlement in the Gaza Strip. The US was "disappointed" at the proposed settlement, as "it is our long-standing position that settlement activity...does not help the peace process."[80]

Shamir, nevertheless, came away from his meetings on 15 November with Bush, Baker, and Secretary of Defense Richard Cheney confident that there was "no more tension" between the US and Israel, and that the problems had been "clarified." Administration officials called the visit a "success." Yet similar to the meeting in April, the differences were just below the surface, as Bush again raised the issue of settlements, which "had become...the litmus test of whether the Israeli leader was taking him and the United States seriously."[81] Their meeting was called "acrimonious."[82] In addition, the Administration conveyed to Shamir its concern over the slow pace of the peace process, Israeli tactics in response to the Intifada, and, in particular, reports that Israel had been assisting South Africa in developing missiles.[83]

Shamir was subsequently upset by a letter signed by 41 prominent Jewish leaders which said that "most American Jews do not reject" the principle of land for peace. The letter sought to make clear that the prime minister should not "mistake courtesy for consensus, or applause for endorsement of all the policies you pursue."[84] The controversial letter was intended to demonstrate to the prime minister that there were differences of opinion within the American Jewish community. There was particular concern on the part of many who disagreed with Shamir's policies that he would again interpret silence to be tantamount to acquiescence, as had frequently been the case in the past.

By the end of November, the peace process had reached a stalemate: Israel had officially accepted Baker's Five Points, though with provisos that effectively created high hurdles. The PLO had yet to respond officially to the Five Points. It had indicated willingness to accept Baker's plan, but only if its conditions were met. These conditions threatened to scuttle the peace process as well. The gaps were large; the challenges to American diplomacy were huge. Debate continued, now with the UN as the forum.

The Arab states attempted to use the UN to legitimate the PLO as the leader of a Palestinian state. This effort had two elements: first, to have the Food and Agriculture Organization (FAO) cooperate with the PLO in assistance to agricultural development in the occupied territories, as if it were a sovereign entity; second, to upgrade the PLO's status in the UN from "observer organization" to "observer state." Despite American warnings that it would cut off its contributions to that organization if these actions were implemented, the efforts in the FAO were successful. But this victory proved to be temporary. The Administration's position was strengthened by pressure from Congress, including proposed legislation to punish the UN for these pro-PLO moves. The result was that the Arabs were forced to back down from their effort to upgrade the PLO's status.[85]

In the midst of the storm over these UN developments, and perhaps as a result of the failure of the Arab efforts, there were reports that the PLO had accepted Baker's Five Points, though like Israel with conditions. Reflecting the ambiguity of the PLO's purported agreement to Baker's points, one American paper's headline on 4 December read "PLO Accepts Baker's Plan for Mideast Peace," while another's stated that the "PLO Refuses to Take Invisible Role at Talks: US Plan Appears to Reach an Impasse."[86] Yet hopes were raised on 6 December, when Egypt, apparently with the approval of the PLO, accepted in "principle" Baker's proposal, and agreed to have talks on the basis of the Five Points. The Egyptian agreement was conditional, although administration officials hoped that the last disputes would be reduced so that a meeting of the foreign ministers of the US, Israel, and Egypt could be held early in 1990.[87]

By the end of the year, then, the Administration had made only minimal progress in the peace process. Both Israel and Egypt, as surrogate for the PLO, had agreed to talk about the possibility of elections which would perhaps lead to limited Palestinian autonomy and eventual negotiations on the final status of the occupied territories. Neither side was addressing the other, nor talking about substance. Both wanted to avoid being blamed for problems or breakdowns. The Administration was trying to trap both sides so that as they sought to avoid embarrassment they would suddenly find themselves too far along the road to negotiations to turn back. It was hoped that a policy of "creative ambiguity....[i.e.,] structuring something verbally that will allow everybody to get to the table"[88] would work. Yet, all parties were worried that the result would only harm their interests and therefore they were deliberately ambiguous, and for the same reason: to allow an out. They were later to take it. In the end, the Administration became trapped in its own tactics rather than cornering the regional parties.

UNITED STATES' RELATIONS WITH
THE RADICAL STATES AND LEBANON

If American policy toward the Arab-Israeli peace process met with frustration, the picture in respect to the radical states in the region — Iran, Libya, and Syria — was not much better. Not much more could be said for the situation in Lebanon. The hostages there continued to plague American policymakers; indeed, on his final day in office Reagan regretted that he could not have done more for them.[89] The US was increasingly concerned with the spread of chemical weapons and long-range delivery systems, a concern that threatened to spill over into relations both with Nato allies — in particular Germany — as well as with the Soviet Union. As with the peace process, the Administration was intensely active, but barely able to significantly influence events on the ground.

Perhaps ironically, perhaps fittingly, the Reagan Administration departed with a burst of military activity, as on 4 January two Libyan jet fighters were shot down in a battle with carrier-based American jets.[90] In the context of American objections to the Libyan chemical plant at Rabta, there were hints from Washington that this incident might be the precursor to an attack on the plant. For example, William Burns, director of the Arms Control and Disarmament Agency, claimed that an attack on Rabta would be justified on the basis of "legitimate self-defense." He dismissed the question of whether the US would in fact launch such an attack as "pure speculation."[91] Although the US did not attack the plant, the issue of chemical weapons production strained relations with Germany, as the US accused German firms of supplying Libya with technology and assistance.[92] Meanwhile, the Soviet sale to Libya of long-range Sukhoi Su-24 bombers, their capabilities augmented by in-flight refueling capabilities, giving them the ability to reach Israel, led many in Washington to question Moscow's commitment to lowering tensions in the area.[93] (For further discussion of Libyan-US relations, see chapter on Libya.)

American relations with Syria continued to be distant, although throughout the year improvements were widely anticipated by most analysts of the region in the wake of Moscow's weakening support for the Asad regime. Syria's alleged sponsorship of international terrorism continued to inhibit the Administration from moving to a closer relationship. American officials were especially focused on Syria's sheltering of Ahmad Jibril's Popular Front for the Liberation of Palestine-General Command (PFLP-GC), reportedly responsible for the destruction of Pan Am 103 in December 1988. Indeed, as early as April the Administration had made clear to Damascus that movement on this issue would be indicative of whether or not Syria could play a positive role in the peace process.[94] By the end of the year the issue had not been resolved.[95] In July, for example, the American discussion with Syria was characterized as "frank, direct, comprehensive" by Ambassador to Syria Edward Djerejian. He stated that while "US policy is not to exclude Syria from the peace process," the US was not "pulling any punches" in what he called a "serious dialogue."[96] (See also chapter on Syria.)

The situation in Lebanon also showed little improvement during 1989, notwithstanding American efforts to use what little influence it had on events in that divided country. In the wake of severe fighting in Beirut, the US felt it necessary to withdraw some of its staff from the embassy in February, while at the same time calling on "all Lebanese to work together to restore the legitimate national institutions of Lebanon."[97] In July assistant secretary of state John Kelly outlined the US commitment to "do all it can to promote a political solution that will bring Lebanon's turmoil to an end." He called on "all parties to the conflict...[to] show restraint and flexibility" in order for Lebanon to be "a reunited and sovereign country — free of foreign forces and armed militias."[98]

Fighting continued to escalate, however, to the point that the US withdrew its ambassador and embassy staff from the country. The State Department was particularly concerned about threats from Michel 'Awn,[99] the Maronite general who had split from the government after former president Amin Jumayyil's term had expired in 1988. In November, it momentarily appeared that the crisis might be abating when the various Lebanese factions reached a *modus vivendi*, which came to be known as the Ta'if Accords, and René Mu'awwad was elected president. The US extended its congratulations to Mu'awwad and expressed the hope that "all parties" would "refrain from violence and intimidation and aid President Mu'awwad in reunifying Lebanon." At the same time, the Administration condemned 'Awn for his "confrontational tactics and threats of partition" which were "a disservice to the state and people he claims to defend."[100]

Mu'awwad was assassinated on 22 November. When Ilyas al-Hirawi was elected to the presidency, 'Awn refused to recognize Hirawi's authority or legitimacy. His forces and those of Syria, claiming to support Hirawi, were heading toward conflict at the end of November.[101] The US, fearing an uncontrollable escalation, sought an "honorable exit" for 'Awn and expressed its opposition to a military solution to the problems plaguing Lebanon.[102] According to one administration official, Washington had "urged the Syrians to hold back" and was "telling the Israelis not to take advantage of the situation."[103] In the event, a major showdown did not occur; instead, sporadic fighting and constant confrontation continued. (For a discussion of domestic developments in Lebanon, see chapter on that country.)

Relations with Iran also did not improve. Bush's call for "goodwill" in his inaugural address met a cold response in Tehran. The plight of the hostages and Iran's sponsorship of terrorism continued to impede possibilities for a breakthrough. Instead Ayatollah Ruhollah Khomeyni called for the assassination of Salman Rushdie, author of the book *The Satanic Verses* (see chapters on Iran and on Islamic affairs). Although the Administration could not devise a specific response to the threat, Bush called it "deeply offensive to the norms of civilized behavior" and threatened that "should any action be taken against American interests, the Government of Iran can expect to be held accountable."[104] The Administration similarly termed as "appalling" and "outrageous" Speaker of the Iranian Parliament Hujjat al-Islam Hashemi Rafsanjani's call for Palestinian terrorism against the West. It again warned that the US would hold Iran responsible for "attacks on American interests or citizens."[105]

Despite expectations that relations might improve after the death of Ayatollah Khomeyni on 3 June, administration spokesmen were cautious. As assistant secretary Kelly put it on 12 July, "it is too early to tell whether Iran will move in a more positive direction," which would entail an end of its support for international terrorism and the use of its influence to bring about the unconditional release of hostages held in Lebanon by pro-Iranian groups. "The burden of proof," Kelly said, "clearly is on Iran to show that it is prepared to behave responsibly. Actions are required, not words."[106] As a symbol of goodwill, the Administration announced on 17 July that it was offering compensation to the families of those who had died in the Iranian passenger plane destroyed by the USS *Vincennes* in 1988.[107]

Ironically, the first sign of possible improvement only appeared in the wake of Israel's abduction of Shaykh 'Ubayd and the murder of Col. Higgins. In response, Rafsanjani, who in the meantime had become president of Iran, offered to assist in the solution of the hostage crisis.[108] The two conditions for Iranian assistance were Israel's release of 'Ubayd and American release of Iranian funds that had been frozen in the wake of the 1979 revolution. The official American answer, enunciated by White House spokesman Marlin Fitzwater, was that "we are not willing to link the Iranian asset question to the hostage question. That fits within the definition of our policy of not trading arms or money or whatever for hostages, of not paying ransom for hostages." Yet the unofficial response, represented by an unidentified "senior administration official" was more open: "If it gets to the point of them helping us with the hostages, they are going to want some indication that we are ready to talk turkey [i.e., be serious] on assets."[109]

As the crisis over 'Ubayd wound down, no American hostages were released and relations with Iran remained strained. Yet on 6 November the US agreed to return over $500m. from an account providing for claims of Americans against the Tehran government.[110] While it was denied that the release of the money was tied to the hostage issue, Bush did express the hope that it would "get this underbrush cleaned out" and that the Iranians "will do what they can to influence those who hold these hostages."[111] By the end of the year, no hostages had been released (see also chapter on Iran).

CONCLUSION

Befitting the cautious and pragmatic nature of Bush, Baker, and their top advisers, the first year of the Bush Administration concluded with neither grand achievements nor dismal failures. The occasional crises were addressed in a low-key manner, neither resolved nor allowed to escalate. There were no breakthroughs or sustained high-level public involvement. The new team, instead, took a behind-the-scenes, or backseat, approach: it would neither direct nor drive.

The Administration was concerned about regional developments, but also involved with more pressing concerns elsewhere. Whether even-handed or balanced, the Administration's policy was a waiting game. It was not averse to placing pressure on the recalcitrant, but would do so only in a low-key manner. Publicity meant commitment to one side, with the potential of needlessly alienating the other. In the end, a wide variety of activities yielded meager results during 1989. The Administration could claim that it had sown the seeds for future success, but its efforts certainly had yet to bear fruit.

NOTES

For the place and frequency of publications cited here, and for the full name of the publication, news agency, radio station, or monitoring service where an abbreviation is used, please see "List of Sources." Only in the case of more than one publication bearing the same name is the place of publication noted here.

1. *NYT*, 16 March 1989.
2. KUNA in DR, 26 January; *Boston Globe*, 27 January; *NYT*, 1 January 1989.
3. *DSB*, April 1989, p. 4.
4. NBC's "Meet the Press" in *DSB*, April 1989, p. 22.
5. *DSB*, April 1989, p. 15.
6. *NYT, WP*, 19 January 1989.
7. *NYT*, 7 February 1989.
8. Ibid., 11 February 1989.
9. Ibid., *WP*, 24 February 1989.
10. *NYT*, 1 March 1989.
11. Ibid., 4 March; see also *NYT, WP*, 6 March 1989.
12. *NYT*, 12 March 1989.
13. Ibid., 14 March 1989.
14. *DSB*, May 1989, p. 63.
15. *WP*, 15, 16 March 1989.
16. Ibid., 16 March 1989.
17. *NYT*, 15 May 1989.
18. *WP*, 22 March 1989.
19. Jonathan Karp, "Israel's Shamir Against Palestinian Elections for Peace Talks," Reuters, 7 March 1989.
20. *NYT*, 31 March 1989.
21. *DSB*, June 1989, p. 40.
22. *WP*, 5 April 1989.
23. Ibid., 5 April 1989.
24. *NYT*, 6 April 1989.
25. *DSB*, June 1989, p. 43.
26. *DSB*, June 1989, p. 42.
27. Ibid.
28. *WT*, 14 April 1989.
29. Confidential interview with US official. See also *NYT Magazine*, 6 May 1990.
30. *DSB*, June 1989, p. 12.
31. *NYT*, 21 April 1989.
32. *Minneapolis Star and Tribune*, 13 April 1989.
33. Personal Papers of the President, Administration of George Bush, 19 April 1989, p. 577.
34. Ibid., p. 576.
35. Ibid.
36. *NYT*, 9 May; *WP*, 10 May 1989.

37. *DSB*, July 1989, pp. 24–27. For press reactions, see *NYT*, 23 May 1989.
38. *WP*, 24 May 1989.
39. *NYT*, 10 June 1989.
40. Ibid., 2 July; *Washington Jewish Week*, 6 July 1989.
41. Daniel Schoor, "Bush's Ill-Advised Letter to Shamir," *NYT*, 25 July 1989.
42. *NYT*, 6 July 1989.
43. Ibid., 7 July 1989.
44. Ibid., 12 July 1989.
45. Ibid., 9 July 1989.
46. *The Manchester Guardian Weekly*, 16 July; *Chicago Tribune*, 16 July 1989.
47. *NYT*, 29 July 1989.
48. Ibid., 1, 2 August 1989.
49. Ibid., 19, 21 July; *WT*, 18, 21 July 1989.
50. *NYT*, 9 June 1989.
51. Ibid., 25 June 1989.
52. Ibid., 10 July 1989.
53. Ibid., 4 August 1989.
54. Ibid., 15 August 1989.
55. Ibid.
56. Ibid., 17 September 1989.
57. Ibid., 14 September; *Minneapolis Star and Tribune*, 13 September 1989.
58. *NYT*, 29 September 1989.
59. *WP*, 22 September 1989.
60. *NYT*, 21 September 1989.
61. Ibid., 22 September 1989.
62. Ibid., 30 September 1989.
63. *LAT*, 3 October; see also *NYT*, *WP*, and *WT*, 3 October 1989.
64. *NYT*, 7 October 1989.
65. *WP*, 7 October 1989.
66. *NYT*, 8 October 1989.
67. Alan Elsner, "US Sends Five-Point Paper on Elections to Israel, Egypt," Reuters, 10 October 1989.
68. Reuters report, based on *JP*, 13 October 1989.
69. *LAT*, 29 October 1989.
70. *NYT*, 11 October 1989.
71. Ibid., 19 October 1989.
72. Alan Elsner, "Baker Advises Israel Against Seeking Changes to Five Points," Reuters, 25 October 1989.
73. *WT*, 25 October 1989.
74. Howard Goller, "Israel's Shamir Plans White House Visit Despite Snub Threat," Reuters, 26 October; *WT*, 8, 9 November; *WP*, 10 November 1989.
75. *WP*, 3 November 1989.
76. Ibid., 6 November 1989.
77. *NYT*, 6 November; *WSJ*, 13 November 1989.
78. *WP*, 9 November 1989.
79. *WT*, 7 November; Naguib Megally, "PLO Sets Terms for Accepting Baker Plan," UPI, 7 November 1989 — based on a report in *al-Ahram*, 6 November; also *NYT*, 7 November 1989.
80. Carol Giacomo, "US Faults Israel For New Settlement on Eve of Shamir Talks," Reuters, 14 November 1989.
81. *NYT Magazine*, 6 May 1990.
82. *LAT*, 16 November 1989.
83. *WP*, 16 November; also *NYT* and *WT*, 16 November 1989.
84. *NYT*, *WP*, 17 November 1989.
85. *NYT*, 26, 28, 30 November, 1, 2, 5, 6, 7 December 1989.
86. Respectively, *WT*, and *WP*, 4 December 1989.
87. *NYT*, *WT*, 7 December 1989.

88. *WT,* 7 December 1989.
89. *NYT,* 20 January 1989.
90. Ibid., 5 January 1989.
91. Ibid., 5 January 1989.
92. Ibid., 1,6, 7 January 1989.
93. Ibid., 5 April 1989.
94. Ibid., 2 April 1989.
95. Reuters, "US Faults Syria Inaction Against Terrorist Groups," 3 November; *WT,* 15 December 1989.
96. *NYT,* 16 July 1989.
97. Ibid., 18 February 1989.
98. Assistant secretary of state for Near Eastern and South Asian affairs, John Kelly, statement before the subcommittee on Europe and the Middle East of the House Foreign Affairs Committee, *DSB,* October 1989, p. 45.
99. *NYT,* 6 September 1989.
100. Ibid.
101. Ibid., 29 November 1989.
102. Ibid., 2 December 1989.
103. Alan Elsner, "US Launches Diplomatic Effort to Avert Lebanese Bloodshed," Reuters, 30 November 1989.
104. *NYT,* 22 February 1989.
105. Ibid., 6 May 1989.
106. Statement by assistant secretary of state John Kelly, 12 July, op. cit. (see Note 98).
107. *NYT,* 18 July 1989.
108. Ibid., 5 August 1989.
109. Ibid., 9 August 1989.
110. Ibid., 7 November 1989.
111. Ibid., 8 November 1989.

The Soviet Union and the Middle East

JOHN P. HANNAH

Soviet policy in the Middle East in 1989 followed the same broad pattern evident since 1987. The main features of this policy were: an effort to improve relations with the region's more moderate, pro-Western states, including Israel; an attempt to redefine ties with traditional friends in the Arab radical camp, with the aim of making them less costly and dangerous; and a continued interest in securing a role in diplomatic efforts to stabilize and resolve both the Arab-Israeli and Iran-Iraq conflicts.

The highlights of Soviet policy included Foreign Minister Eduard Shevardnadze's visit to the region in the immediate aftermath of the Red Army's withdrawal from Afghanistan; the decision to allow near complete freedom of emigration for Soviet Jews, resulting in a record exodus with even greater numbers forecast for the future; and a significant improvement in relations with Iran.

AN ASSESSMENT: CONSTRAINED CHANGE

These changes were consistent with Soviet leader Mikhail Gorbachev's "new thinking" in foreign policy, which sought to reduce the most confrontational aspects of Moscow's traditional behavior in the Third World. This desire to de-escalate regional conflicts was driven by three main factors:

1. The need to focus Soviet energies and resources on *perestroika* — Gorbachev's attempt to reinvigorate a society and economy that were in a systemic crisis.

2. The need to improve dramatically relations with the West, at least in part to enlist its support for *perestroika*.

3. The judgment that the old confrontational policies had reached a dead end. By the late 1970s, the Soviet Union found itself relegated to the ME's periphery, isolated with a small group of radical, and generally unruly clients in Syria, Libya, the PLO, and South Yemen.

While a trend of growing moderation in Soviet ME policy was discernible, its clarity was by no means absolute. Threads of continuity with the past were not eliminated entirely. The improvement in relations with Israel had been constant, but marred by fits and starts, as the Soviets continued to reject reestablishing full diplomatic relations. Likewise, Soviet actions to limit support for the policies of radical Arab states like Syria occurred in tandem with the continued delivery to these states of several potentially destabilizing weapons systems.

The existence of these ambiguous elements in Soviet policy was particularly noticeable when viewed in contrast to the thoroughgoing transformations that occurred in Soviet policy in Europe in 1989. After 45 years of treating the domination of Eastern Europe as the *sine qua non* of its national security, Moscow, within a few months, passively watched and even actively facilitated the collapse of its Communist empire.

Such startling changes were largely absent from Soviet policy in the ME. Here, incremental evolution was the watchword rather than revolutionary reversals. Unlike in Europe, where the moderation in policy occurred immediately and by leaps and bounds, in the ME the more apt analogy of change was two steps forward, one step back.

The cause of the slower rate of change in the ME did not seem to derive from any devious strategy on Gorbachev's part to pursue the Soviet Union's old zero-sum goals by other means. The important moderating impact on the region, which even the limited shifts in Soviet behavior had effected, made such arguments dubious. Instead, other explanations were more plausible:

1. Precisely because Gorbachev decided to address the tremendous problem of European security first, his attention could not be focused on monitoring the application of "new thinking" to less pressing issues like the ME. In this environment, where the region was not a high priority, the influence of standard operating procedures and of mid-level officials less committed to the "new thinking" were probably significant.

2. Even on major issues of ME policy that the leadership probably did address, such as resuming relations with Israel and large arms sales to Arab clients, a decision was made not to apply fully the logic of "new thinking," because doing so would strengthen Gorbachev's domestic opponents who claimed his policies were dangerously undermining Soviet security. At a time when his conservative critics accused him of "giving up" in Europe, the central theater of superpower rivalry for 40 years, Gorbachev may have felt he could not be seen as giving up everywhere else as well.

The Soviets took note of US criticism that a gap existed between the theoretical breakthroughs of "new thinking" and the continuation of old patterns of behavior in the Third World.[1] In a speech to the USSR's newly constituted Supreme Soviet in October 1989, Shevardnadze acknowledged the gap between Soviet theory and practice in some areas, and called for an "unending process of constant correlation between policy and reality." At the same time, however, he cautioned that transforming Soviet relations with traditional radical clients would be a long process that could not be accomplished overnight.[2] This suggested that the Soviet leadership had little inclination, at a time of growing domestic trouble and revolutionary change in Europe, to renege completely on past commitments to the Third World and incur the costs that would accompany a drastic deterioration in relations with old friends like Syria.

Shevardnadze's remarks accurately reflected the course of Soviet ME policy under Gorbachev. The strategic decision to "correlate policy and reality" through greater moderation seemed evident, but it remained constrained by the leadership's preoccupation with other concerns and its desire to avoid the domestic and international costs of a rapid reversal of policy. As a result, policy shifts were generally slow in coming and incremental in nature, at times frustrating US and Israeli policymakers who called for a clear-cut application of "new thinking" to the ME.

SOVIET RELATIONS WITH ISRAEL

Two events at the end of 1988 seemed to augur well for Soviet-Israeli relations in 1989, providing the countries with unique opportunities to cooperate and expand political contacts. The first came when Israel played a critical role in helping resolve the hijacking of a Soviet airliner; the second involved the 7 December earthquake in Soviet Armenia and Israel's immediate provision of emergency medical aid (for more on both incidents, see *MECS* 1988, chapter on the Soviet Union and the ME).

The goodwill generated by these events was in evidence in January 1989. During an international conference on chemical weapons in Paris, Shevardnadze, in his first meeting with Israel's new Foreign Minister Moshe Arens, agreed to upgrade Israel's consular delegation in Moscow and allow it to conduct political as well as consular business.[3] In addition, he agreed to allow it to move from its offices in the Dutch Embassy to a wing of the former Israeli Embassy building.[4]

Sharp differences remained between the two countries over the peace process. Shevardnadze reiterated the Soviet position that Israel should negotiate a settlement with the PLO at an international conference, advice which Arens politely rejected. Perhaps more important in the long run, however, was that Shevardnadze made clear Moscow's new understanding that these differences in viewpoint could not be overcome through threats against Israel, but only by developing an ongoing and constructive dialogue with Jerusalem.

This emphasis on the necessity of contacts with Israel received a dramatic demonstration in mid-February, when Shevardnadze, during a high-profile, 10-day trip to the ME, extended an official invitation to Arens to meet in Cairo. The move had tremendous symbolic significance: on the first tour of the region by a Soviet foreign minister in 15 years, he met and spoke with Israel's leadership as he would with the Soviet Union's Arab friends (Shevardnadze held discussions with PLO leader Yasir 'Arafat hours after his talks with Arens). While this meeting again underscored the widely divergent Israeli and Soviet views on the specifics of the peace process, it sent an important message to both Israel and the Arabs: the efforts of the Brezhnev era to use intimidation and ostracism to *force* a change in Israel's diplomatic position was being abandoned; instead, the Kremlin would increasingly focus on negotiations as the best means to *persuade* Israel to shift its policy.

Shevardnadze openly expressed his satisfaction with the talks.

> This meeting today is another stage in our dialogue. It has been a useful meeting. We had constructive discussions in a good atmosphere, allowing open, frank and honest talks....I cannot say we have come to a solution over all these aspects. That was not our expectation and it would be naive to expect that.[5]

This new realism was also evident in Shevardnadze's response to Arens's statement that the 20-year absence of Soviet-Israeli communications had been detrimental to the cause of peace: "Basically, I agree with the Israeli foreign minister....The worst thing is the absence of dialogue."[6]

The positive impact of the meeting was blunted, however, by statements Shevardnadze made days later during a major speech in Cairo. In an address otherwise remarkable for its moderation and concern for stability, Shevardnadze expressed a very tough attitude toward Israel, harshly criticizing its policy in the territories. Most ominously, he warned that "the question will arise of the use of sanctions against Israel as a country that is flouting the rights of civilians on a mass scale."[7] For Israel, such threats and clearly biased exaggerations could only raise questions about how much "new thinking" really existed in Soviet policy.

Concerns were also raised when Shevardnadze dealt with the issue of reestablishing relations with Israel. Until the speech, the Soviet position under Gorbachev seemed relatively clear: the USSR would restore relations the day an international conference convened. But in Cairo, Shevardnadze appeared to add a new condition, one even more disagreeable to Israel than accepting the conference — talking to the PLO. "We would like the Government of Israel to know that if it chooses the conference *and agrees to enter a dialogue with the PLO* it will permit our two countries to take yet another step forward along the path of restoring full diplomatic relations."[8] (Emphasis added.)

Israel could take comfort from much of the rest of Shevardnadze's speech which stressed the dangers of the arms race and the need to take into account Israel's security interests. Some speculation suggested that the more hard-line sections of the speech were meant less to signal new Soviet positions than to assuage Arab anger over Shevardnadze's cordial meeting with Arens. In any event, the sanctions threat did not reappear in later pronouncements by the Soviet leadership. The demand that Israel speak with the PLO, however, was repeated. But signs emerged later suggesting that Moscow might be willing to apply this condition flexibly so that relations could be restored without Israel having to speak directly to the PLO (see further below).

Despite Shevardnadze's negative statements, the flurry of Soviet-Israeli political contacts in the first two months of 1989 hinted that Moscow would move quickly to restore diplomatic relations. This was not the case. Following Shevardnadze's trip, a lull occurred in Soviet-Israeli political contacts. For their part, Israelis took offense at Moscow's predilection for setting preconditions for reestablishing relations. According to Arens, "I do not think they should pose any preconditions....We believe in the universality of diplomatic relations, which should not depend on agreement, positions, or policies."[9] The Soviets, in turn, seemed to believe that they had already taken several unilateral steps to improve relations, steps for which they had suffered criticism in the Arab world. It was felt that Israel's Likud leaders had pocketed these "concessions" and offered nothing in return, not even the hint of a more flexible position on the peace process.

A manifestation of Israel's rising frustration came in early May. Shevardnadze's special envoy to the ME, Gennady Terasov, was visiting key Arab states in an effort to gauge their reaction to Israel's proposal for Palestinian elections (see chapter on ME peace process). He invited Israeli officials to confer with him in Cyprus. But rather than jump at the opportunity to meet with a Soviet representative, as it had done consistently for two years, Israel refused Terasov's offer, insisting that he come to Jerusalem.[10] Weeks later, Arens reportedly informed the Soviets that the next time Shevardnadze toured the region, Arens would be glad to meet him in Israel, but not anywhere else.[11]

This hiatus in Soviet-Israeli relations at the level of "high politics" had little effect on the continuation of progress in other areas of Soviet-Israeli relations. The most well-publicized example of such progress was that of Soviet-Jewish emigration. The upward trends apparent throughout the Gorbachev era rose dramatically in 1989. From an average of less than a hundred emigrants a month in 1986, to around 650 in 1987, to 1,600 in 1988, the figure by the end of 1989 had reached a record of about 6,000 per month.[12] Moreover, projections for the next six years suggested that 750,000 Jews might eventually leave.[13]

While Gorbachev's incentive for liberalizing emigration policy was largely a function of his efforts to reform Soviet society and improve relations with the US, the new policy inevitably had an ameliorating impact on Soviet-Israeli relations as well. The eventual codification into law of the more lenient emigration procedures promised to have a further positive effect. More important for Moscow, it would also satisfy the US criterion for waiving the Jackson-Vanik Amendment, which withheld most-favored-nation trade status until unreasonable impediments to free emigration were removed. The new Soviet law was drafted in 1989, but was not taken up by the new parliament during the year.[14]

The darker side of the increase in emigration was that, by the end of 1989, it was driven not only by greater opportunities to leave, but by a fear of rising Russian anti-Semitism. Gorbachev's policy of *glasnost* provided an outlet not only for the voices of democracy, but also for those of neo-fascism and extreme nationalism. This "new Russian right" was represented most notoriously by the group *Pamyat* ("Memory"), but also had advocates among the Soviet intelligentsia and officialdom. A central tenet of its philosophy was to make the Jews the scapegoats for the crises of Russian society. Incidents of Jews being harassed, Jewish cemeteries and businesses being desecrated, openly anti-Semitic material appearing in the media, and rumors of impending pogroms all increased in 1989. (On the Jewish emigration issue, see further below).

Ironically, this rise in unofficial anti-Semitism was coupled with Kremlin efforts to expand opportunities for cultural and religious expression for all Soviet citizens, including Jews. Two events in the first half of 1989 dramatized the changes. The first was the opening in Moscow of the Mikhoels Center, the USSR's first officially sanctioned Jewish cultural center.[15] And while it did not immediately live up to the most optimistic expectations, it did provide a potential for Jewish cultural expression unique in Soviet history.[16] Another event was the establishment in Moscow of a yeshiva, the first academy of Jewish learning in the USSR for over 60 years. Staffed by Israeli and American rabbis, the yeshiva's students were to be trained as the USSR's next generation of rabbis and Bible scholars.[17]

The first few months of 1989 also saw a number of other developments in Soviet-Israeli relations at the cultural, social, and economic levels. A sampling included: Soviet and Israeli basketball teams competing against each other in Israel and the Soviet Union for the first time since 1967;[18] the first direct economic agreements between Soviet and Israeli firms;[19] the visit to the Soviet Union of 15 Israeli businessmen to discuss the possibility of establishing joint ventures;[20] the first docking of a Soviet ship at an Israeli port since 1967;[21] and the participation of a Soviet delegation, led by an official from the Ministry of Culture, in the international Jerusalem book fair.[22]

These increased contacts were accompanied by a continued improvement in Israel's image in the Soviet media. Despite the anti-Semitism that began appearing in the commentary of certain journals and newspapers, much of the "mainstream" press demonstrated a more balanced approach in covering Israel and Jewish affairs. In one remarkable article, two historians criticized the official anti-Zionism that has been a fixture of Soviet policy since Stalin, comparing it to Nazi Germany's anti-Semitism.[23]

The shifting coverage of Israel was aided by the fact that more Soviet correspondents were traveling to Israel to report on the country first hand. While Israel was still rarely treated in positive terms, the depiction was certainly less negative. Israel's response to the Intifada and its positions on the peace process still came in for substantial criticism, but this was portrayed less as a condemnation of Israel *per se,* than as a warning of the harm Israel was inflicting on itself by pursuing shortsighted policies. A more complex picture of Israeli society also appeared. On the wane was the caricature of a political monolith merely doing the bidding of US imperialism; instead, a more variegated image emerged, with the media stressing the existence of social forces opposing official policy, the implication being that opportunities existed for constructive changes in Israel's position, changes that an active Soviet-Israeli dialogue might help achieve.

This dialogue finally picked up again in the summer at a more official level. As in December 1988, it was events surrounding tragedies within the USSR that provided a new impetus. One was a train accident in the Ural mountains in June; an Israel Defense Forces medical team was successful in saving several lives.[24] Another involved Israel's humanitarian gesture, later that month, of flying in 65 Soviet Armenians severely injured in the December 1988 earthquake for special medical treatment. The story received page one coverage in *Izvestiia.*[25]

Around this time, Terasov finally met with an Israeli official, though not one from the Foreign Ministry. Instead, he met in Paris with Nimrod Novik, the chief foreign policy aide to Deputy Prime Minister and Finance Minister Shimon Peres. The meeting focused on the peace process, with Terasov trying to get an accurate reading of Israel's position on Palestinian elections. Commenting afterward, Terasov stressed that discussions with Israel had to remain a regular part of Soviet diplomatic activity in the region.[26]

Soviet-Israeli contacts at various levels increased after July, particularly on the economic plane. Several developments took place in rapid succession: a group of Soviet economists and agricultural experts visited Israel and signed a multimillion dollar agreement with the government for the export of Israeli agricultural products and know-how;[27] a joint-venture agreement was reached for the first time, between the Ukrainian Republic and an Israeli corporation to manufacture medical diagnostic equipment in Kiev;[28] Agridev (Agricultural Development Research Corporation), Israel's government-run agricultural research company, signed an accord with the Soviet Academy of Sciences to set up a joint agriculture company;[29] and an Israeli wheelchair company signed a joint venture contract with the Georgian Republic to build a wheelchair factory.[30]

Interspersed with these agreements, several other incidents occurred affecting Soviet-Israeli ties. One of the more interesting involved a major article in *Izvestiia* by the maverick but influential political commentator Alexander Bovin. Bovin criticized the equivocacy of the PLO and argued that the Soviet Union should restore relations with Israel unconditionally, dropping its insistence on an international peace conference.[31] Within a month, two replies to Bovin's article appeared (the second by the Soviet ambassador to Syria, Alexander Zotov), both highly critical of Israel and insisting that relations could not be resumed until its position on the peace process changed.[32]

At a minimum, the exchange suggested that among the Soviet elite, ties with Israel had become an issue of debate. One radio broadcast noted that this in itself was a positive development since "for many years, the question of the resumption of diplomatic relations between the Soviet Union and Israel was not on the agenda at all." It went on to reject the traditional Soviet argument that diplomatic relations should be a reward for good Israeli behavior. After all, "we have diplomatic relations with many countries whose official policies we disapprove of." At the same time, the broadcast questioned Bovin's proposal for an immediate restoration, explaining that it:

> would create more problems than it would solve. After all, 20 years of brainwashing and the nurturing of an enemy image by the media have left behind huge obstacles of ignorance and distrust...what we should do now is to expand our cultural relations and exchanges of know-how at an accelerated pace in order to create the background for the development of normal official relations in all aspects.[33]

As part of expanding cultural relations, the Soviet author, Chingiz Aytmatov, visited Israel in August and September.[34] The chairman of the Supreme Soviet's committee for culture and a confidant of Gorbachev, he was the highest ranking Soviet personality to visit Israel since 1967. Two months earlier, the liberal editor and parliamentarian, Vitaly Korotich, had done the same.[35] At the conclusion of their visits, both Korotich and Aytmatov praised Israeli society and called for the early resumption of relations.

Visits by Israeli officials to the USSR, however, were not yet so easy. In early September, Israel's Minister of Agriculture Avraham Katz-Oz was invited by the Republic of Estonia to attend a flower exhibition. At the last minute, the Soviet Foreign Ministry denied Katz-Oz his visa. Reportedly, Soviet officials privately told Israel that this had less to do with Soviet-Israeli relations than with the Kremlin's desire to remind Estonia that foreign policy issues were still the domain of the central authorities.[36] A few weeks later, Finance Minister Peres was asked to visit Moscow. The invitation was issued by the Soviet Peace Committee, a nonofficial institution, but it was clear that it had official blessing. Moscow wanted to expand economic cooperation with Israel, with deals being discussed in medicine, agriculture, civilian aircraft construction, irrigation, tourism, and energy.[37] But it was also clear that the Kremlin viewed the visit as an opportunity to improve political ties since Peres would almost certainly meet with Shevardnadze.[38]

Getting Peres to Moscow, however, proved difficult. The trip was postponed in October and again in December. One reason given was the need to better prepare the proposed economic agreements. Toward this end, the Soviets promised to send an official delegation to Israel in January 1990.[39] A second reason cited more frequently was the Kremlin's refusal to accede to Peres's demand that he be guaranteed an audience with Gorbachev.[40]

The first visit to the USSR since 1967 by an Israeli cabinet minister finally took place in November, when Katz-Oz arrived in Moscow for talks with senior Soviet officials (but neither Gorbachev nor Shevardnadze). While his discussions were narrowly focused (as desired by Moscow) on advancing agreements for agricultural cooperation, Katz-Oz emphasized the trip's political importance, claiming that his interlocutors had hinted privately that Soviet-Israeli relations might be restored within six months.[41]

If hosting Israeli officials remained a sensitive issue for the Soviets, meeting them at the UN was already routine. In September, Shevardnadze and Arens held discussions there on the peace process, with Shevardnadze mentioning Moscow's goal of convening an international conference that could be preceded by consultations among the five permanent members of the Security Council. But they also discussed Israel's elections proposal and Egyptian President Husni Mubarak's Ten-Point Plan to implement it (see chapter on ME peace process). Without endorsing them, Shevardnadze made it clear that they were under serious consideration in Moscow: "We do not exclude the possibility of implementing the idea of elections...there are rational elements in the proposals that were put forward by Prime Minister Shamir. There are also interesting elements in the proposals made by President Mubarak." Shevardnadze endorsed the concept of arranging a "direct dialogue between the Palestinians and the Israeli leadership," which had become the main goal of US diplomacy. But he also stressed the need to include the PLO in the process, since "there will not be a settlement if you allow the PLO to be ignored. The PLO is a real force...that needs to be reckoned with."[42] To highlight this, Shevardnadze offered to host an Israeli-PLO meeting in Moscow, a nonstarter for Israel.[43]

Soviet-Israeli relations were sidestepped for the most part, with Shevardnadze simply noting that "this is not the most important issue right now. I think that what is most important now is the fact that a [Soviet-Israeli] dialogue is under way...on a systematic basis. This is very important."[44]

Moscow's growing willingness to explore US ideas on the peace process, however, raised the possibility that its position on restoring relations with Israel might be in transition. If the Kremlin was ready to accept that an Israeli-Palestinian dialogue was a logical starting point for negotiations, and that the international conference would be held only at a later stage, it seemed reasonable to assume that the USSR might be ready to restore relations once Israel agreed to talk with the Palestinians. One hint that this shift might be occurring could be found in the way some officials began answering the question of when Moscow would reestablish ties. Rather than repeat the catechism of demanding Israel's acceptance of an international conference, they started using the vaguer formula that relations were linked to "progress toward peace in the region."[45]

The sticking point remained the USSR's insistence on PLO involvement in the process. But if the US and Egypt succeeded in getting the PLO to sanction a dialogue between Israel and Palestinians from the territories, should this not be good enough for the Soviets as well? If so, the Kremlin might resume relations with Israel without guarantees of an international conference or direct participation by the PLO in the first stages of the process. Rumors to this effect circulated after the Bush-Gorbachev summit in Malta in December.[46]

Three other developments in 1989 should finally be mentioned for their impact on Soviet-Israeli relations. One was a shift in Moscow's attitude toward Israel in the UN. In October, the USSR decided to abstain in the vote to reject Israel's credentials at the General Assembly. This was the first time ever that the USSR had failed to support the annual effort to delegitimize the Jewish State.[47]

A second event took place in December, with the Kremlin's decision to allow the first nationwide gathering of Soviet Jews since the fall of the czar. Over 700 participants and observers gathered in Moscow for a spirited debate about the future of Soviet Jewry. And while the meeting illustrated the more benevolent official attitude toward Jews, it also illustrated the mounting dangers of Russian anti-Semitism — members of *Pamyat* were permitted to picket the meeting and threaten its participants, unimpeded by the police.[48]

The third issue that emerged as a major development in Soviet-Israeli relations in late 1989 involved the skyrocketing emigration of Soviet Jews. In October, the US imposed a quota on the number of Soviet Jewish emigrants it would accept.[49] In practice, this meant that going to the US would no longer be a realistic alternative for the swelling number of Jewish emigrants. This left Israel as their destination of last resort. The combination of a more liberal Soviet emigration policy and tighter US immigration restrictions had immediate results: in December alone, more Soviet Jews settled in Israel than in all of 1988.[50] These numbers continued to grow in the first part of 1990. This coincided with the conclusion of negotiations between El Al and Aeroflot for direct flights, a step whose implementation promised to further increase the number of emigrants going to Israel.[51]

Arab reaction to the realization that Israel was about to receive a massive influx of new citizens was swift and furious. By January 1990 their diplomatic and media campaign against Soviet emigration had reached fever pitch,[52] fed by Prime Minister Shamir's untimely statement that "a big Israel was needed for a big immigration."[53] Moscow's reaction to the storm of Arab pressure was twofold. To assuage Arab concerns, it issued several harsh statements denouncing any intention to settle the emigrants in the territories. More important, the Kremlin decided, for the time being, not to implement the agreement to commence direct flights with Israel.[54] On the other hand, however, Soviet officials also made it clear to the Arabs that their concerns would do nothing to alter Moscow's more liberal emigration procedures. Indeed, some statements even suggested that the Arabs would be better served by putting their energies into making peace with Israel rather than worrying about emigration.[55]

The emigration issue promised to be a major one in Soviet-Israeli relations in 1990. The broad strategic objective of Soviet policy to pursue a more positive approach toward Israel was rather clearly manifest in 1989, but the process was slow and somewhat erratic, susceptible to Arab pressures, the internal preoccupations, and other external priorities of the Soviet leadership.

RELATIONS WITH ARAB MODERATES:
EGYPT AND JORDAN

In 1989 the Soviet Union continued to show an interest in improving relations with the US's two closest Arab friends, Egypt and Jordan. Its motivation for doing so depended on three factors:

1. A recognition of the influential role these states, especially Egypt, played in Arab politics; expanding ties with them could enhance the USSR's regional influence.

2. A recognition of the status quo policies of these states resulting from the emphasis of the "new thinking" on international stability. In contrast to the past, Moscow's interest under Gorbachev seemed to be in bolstering Egyptian and Jordanian moderation, rather than undermining it.

3. A hope that mutually beneficial economic ties could be established.

The high point of Soviet contacts with both Egypt and Jordan occurred during Shevardnadze's tour of the region. Jordan was his second stop and it marked the first visit ever by a Soviet foreign minister to the Hashemite kingdom. As with Shevardnadze's meeting with Arens in Cairo, the importance of the Jordan trip was more symbolic than substantive. It reflected Moscow's realization that, even after Jordan's disengagement from the West Bank (see *MECS* 1988, chapter on Jordan), it would be involved in any Arab-Israeli settlement. Furthermore, the Soviets appreciated King Husayn's position as one of the strongest advocates of an international conference. Finally, Shevardnadze hoped to use the visit to expand Soviet-Jordanian economic contacts, following up on a trade agreement the two sides had reached in late 1988.[56]

During his one-day stay in Amman, Shevardnadze met with King Husayn, Prime Minister Zayd al-Rifa'i, and Foreign Minister Marwan al-Qasim. The talks were described as warm, friendly, constructive, and businesslike, though they were necessarily brief and no substantive results emerged. Topics discussed included the Palestinian issue, the need for inter-Arab unity, the Iran-Iraq peace talks, Lebanon, the Soviet withdrawal from Afghanistan, and Soviet-Jordanian bilateral relations.[57]

From Jordan, Shevardnadze went to Cairo. His visit to Egypt, the first by a Soviet foreign minister in 15 years, had great significance. It marked the culmination of Soviet efforts under Gorbachev to normalize relations with Egypt. The *rapprochement* occurred almost entirely on Egypt's terms, its strong relations with the US and its separate peace with Israel remaining fully intact. After years of participating in the campaign to isolate Egypt because of Camp David, Moscow's efforts at reconciliation were indicative of the *de facto* acceptance and tacit support of the accords by the "new thinking." Finally, the structure of Shevardnadze's stay in Cairo — it was the venue for meetings not only with Egypt's leadership but also with 'Arafat and Arens, as well as the place of his major policy speech — reflected Moscow's approval of the fact that moderate Egypt had reassumed a leading role in the Arab world.

In his meeting with Mubarak, Shevardnadze praised Egypt "as a major country of the Arab world....On the Soviet side a positive assessment is made of Egypt's...constructive and carefully weighed approach to solving urgent international problems."[58] He spoke of the "identical views" the two countries held on ways to settle the Arab-Israeli problem.[59] This apparently referred not only to Egypt's support for convening an international conference, but also to its awareness that a settlement would require addressing Israeli concerns and moderating the PLO's positions. Shevardnadze also emphasized Moscow's pleasure with the development of Soviet-Egyptian bilateral ties, noting that "we can with full justification place the full normalization of Soviet-Egyptian relations...on a level with the greatest political achievements of the recent period, which have so greatly promoted radical changes in the nature of world politics."[60]

It was at the bilateral level that Soviet-Egyptian contacts were mostly focused in 1989. Meetings on expanding economic cooperation proliferated. In January, a protocol was signed in Cairo in which the USSR undertook to finance the 'Uyun Musa power plant on the Gulf of Suez,[61] in addition to several other major industrial projects. Moscow's ambassador to Egypt reported that the Soviets would finance these projects through long-term soft government loans. In addition, the ambassador confirmed that Soviet-Egyptian military cooperation at a low level had begun again, with Moscow exporting spare parts for Egypt's old Soviet weaponry.[62] Furthermore, Egypt agreed to allow the USSR to reopen a military attaché's office in Cairo.[63]

In the spring, Egypt played host to three senior Soviet officials. The first was Gennady Terasov, who was visiting the region to discuss Israel's proposal for Palestinian elections.[64] Terasov claimed there existed a unity of Soviet-Egyptian views on the need for an international conference and skepticism regarding Prime Minister Shamir's plan.[65] The second Soviet visitor was the chief of the Foreign Ministry's press office, Gennady Gerasimov. His purpose was supposedly to expand media connections between Egypt and the USSR, but he met with Mubarak's senior political aides and spoke at length about the peace process (see below).[66]

The last visitor to Cairo was Minister of Foreign Economic Relations Konstantin Katushev. He led a delegation for the first meeting of the Soviet-Egyptian committee for economic, trade, and scientific cooperation. At the visit's conclusion, it was confirmed that construction of the 'Uyun Musa power station would be financed by a $200m. Soviet loan, repayable over 12 years at an interest rate of 3.5% following a five-year grace period.[67] In addition, a long-term protocol was signed calling for a major expansion in bilateral trade.[68]

In addition to Egypt, both Gerasimov and Terasov also made stops in Jordan. On the peace process, Gerasimov blasted the Shamir plan. On Soviet-Jordanian bilateral relations, he noted that political ties were very good, but that room for improvement existed in the area of trade.[69] During Terasov's stay in Amman, he was received by King Husayn and Foreign Minister Qasim. He stressed the common stand that Jordan and the USSR held on the peace process and the necessity of an international conference.[70]

In the late summer, several developments occurred in Soviet-Jordanian relations. Most important, Deputy Prime Minister Tahir al-Masri traveled to Moscow and won Soviet agreement to reschedule that part of Jordan's military debt (c. $190m.) due in 1989 and 1990. Apparently, some of the debt would be rescheduled over 10 years with a six-year grace period while the rest would be settled through Soviet imports of Jordanian goods.[71] Several weeks later, Terasov showed up in Amman to discuss the deepening crisis in Lebanon that pitted the Iraqi-backed Lebanese Forces of Gen. Michel 'Awn against the Syrian-backed government (see chapter on Lebanon).[72] Terasov had already been to Syria, Lebanon, and Iraq in an effort to avoid a further deterioration in the situation and to achieve a political settlement. In Amman, he sought Jordan's intervention on several fronts: with both Syria and Iraq to calm the situation; and with the Arab League's tripartite committee on Lebanon (see chapter on inter-Arab relations) to convince it to resume the peacemaking efforts it had abandoned earlier in the summer. Qasim highly praised Moscow's efforts to resolve the crisis.[73]

The last half of 1989 saw little other substantive activity in Soviet-Jordanian relations. And what interaction there was seemed largely negative, as Jordan began to voice concern and criticism about the growing numbers of Soviet Jewish emigrants going to Israel — an issue that was sure to have a major impact on Moscow's future relations with Jordan.

Regular contacts with Egypt continued during the final part of the year. More economic accords were announced, such as Moscow's granting of a loan to finance an

Egyptian paper factory,[74] Soviet agreement to help in the construction of a phosphate project,[75] and further progress on preparation of a long-term trade agreement.[76] Shevardnadze met with Mubarak at the UN in September and reiterated Moscow's interest in Egypt's Ten-Point Plan. A month later, Terasov made another trip to Cairo to consult with Egypt about the peace process. He expressed Moscow's continued support for an international conference. But he also reiterated the USSR's willingness to consider seriously the ongoing US and Egyptian efforts to bring Israel and the Palestinians together for preliminary discussions.[77]

The steady progress made in Soviet-Egyptian relations during 1989 was crowned by the announcement that Mubarak would visit Moscow in 1990.[78] The trip would be sure to further improve political and economic ties between the two countries. It would also serve as another signal of Egypt's growing importance in the USSR's changing strategy toward the Arab-Israeli conflict. (On Moscow's relations with Jordan and Egypt, see also chapters on the two countries.)

RELATIONS WITH THE PLO

The Soviet Union ended 1988 on an interesting note: it successfully pressed the PLO to moderate its declaratory positions toward Israel and terrorism, and welcomed the US-PLO dialogue that resulted when 'Arafat did so. This was in contrast to Soviet behavior of as recently as 1985–86, when Moscow fiercely opposed 'Arafat's alliance with King Husayn, designed to get the PLO to meet US conditions for peace talks with Israel. The USSR's main concern then was not with achieving progress toward a settlement, but with the possibility that the US would be able to mediate a Palestinian-Israeli peace unilaterally.

However, the PLO's moves in 1988 to establish a relationship with Washington were welcomed in Moscow as a necessary step for achieving peace. This reflected a change in the Soviet view of the PLO. No longer was the organization simply an instrument for frustrating American peace efforts. Instead, the PLO and US-PLO relations were seen as essential elements of a solution, suggesting that Moscow now considered a stable settlement of the conflict as taking precedence over its desire to compete with the US.

Moscow's new attitude toward the PLO and a peace settlement, however, did not mean abandonment of its interest either in being part of the settlement process or in the PLO. The Soviets coupled their praise of the US-PLO dialogue with a call to convene the international conference.[79] Furthermore, the first two months of 1989 saw an intensification of Soviet diplomacy in the region, beginning with the Arens-Shevardnadze meeting in Paris in January and ensuing with Shevardnadze's regional tour in February. Finally, to strengthen their influence and position with the PLO, the Soviets moved in 1989 to institutionalize regular contacts with 'Arafat.

This increase in the frequency of bilateral meetings was a major development in Soviet-PLO relations during the year. In January, the head of the Foreign Ministry's Middle East desk, Vladimir Polyakov, traveled to Tunis to talk with 'Arafat and reached an agreement "on making Soviet-Palestinian consultations more regular and intensive."[80] A month later, immediately following his discussions with Arens in Cairo, Shevardnadze met with 'Arafat. Reports of the meeting were scant, perhaps because 'Arafat felt slighted by Shevardnadze's decision to meet with the enemy —

Israel — on an equal footing with the PLO. An agreement was noted on the need to convene an international conference, but no mention was made of the PLO as the Palestinians' sole legitimate representative or of an independent Palestinian state.[81] Shevardnadze also pressed 'Arafat on the need for a Syrian-PLO *rapprochement* to ensure a unified Arab position behind the PLO's peace offensive.[82]

The PLO undoubtedly welcomed parts of Shevardnadze's speech in Cairo, with its praise of PLO policy changes, the harsh rhetoric against Israel, the demand that Israel talk with the PLO, and the rhetorical query as to whether it could "really be supposed that any solution is possible other than one that would satisfy the Palestinians and give them the opportunity to exercise their own inalienable right to self-determination." On the other hand, the PLO was probably less pleased with Shevardnadze's support for Israel's security and his warning regarding the continued use of terrorism in the ME: "It is difficult to count on a dialogue achieving results without precise commitments from the sides that they will neither directly nor indirectly encourage terrorism and other subversive activities against one another in any forms."[83]

Another Soviet-PLO meeting took place in March when 'Arafat's aide and PLO Executive Committee member Mahmud 'Abbas met with Shevardnadze in Moscow. Shevardnadze again praised the PLO's constructive new position, while calling for the convening of a conference that would secure a just solution of the conflict, including the right of the Palestinians to self-determination. In another attempt to push a PLO-Syrian reconciliation, Shevardnadze noted the importance of a coordinated inter-Arab stand on the peace process.[84]

In April, Polyakov returned to Tunis to meet with 'Arafat. Support was expressed for the international conference, but the main focus of the meeting seemed to be on Israel's plan for Palestinian elections. Reports of the talks suggested that neither the PLO nor the USSR rejected elections in principle, but both saw the Shamir plan as a deception to end the Intifada and avoid achieving a comprehensive settlement.[85]

However, by June, when 'Abbas met in Moscow with Soviet Deputy Foreign Minister Alexander Bessmertnykh, this position had begun to shift, with the Soviets showing a greater receptiveness to peace-process ideas other than the international conference. 'Abbas and Bessmertnykh spoke of "the practical aspects of a settlement," and underscored "the necessity of launching multiple approaches in preparing and convening an international conference." They noted that "measures of an interim character" could prove useful on the way to a comprehensive settlement.[86] These formulations suggested that Moscow was communicating to the PLO that the international conference might have to be postponed till a later date, in favor of other approaches such as the elections proposal. This conclusion was reinforced later that month after US and Soviet experts met in Washington to discuss the ME, with Moscow dropping its insistence on an international conference and instead pressing the US for details on the Shamir plan.[87]

Terasov went to Tunis in July to brief the PLO on the US-Soviet talks. He was reported to have told 'Arafat that the US might be willing to back a more specific linkage between elections and an overall political settlement.[88] Then, days later, during his meeting in Paris with Israel's Nimrod Novik, Terasov supposedly suggested that the PLO was now ready to accept elections conditionally, provided there was a prior Israeli acceptance of the land-for-peace principle.[89]

In September, Shevardnadze met the head of the PLO's political department, Faruq Qaddumi, at the UN. Details of the talks were not provided, but the two sides were reported to have had a "thorough exchange of opinions on the situation in the ME," a possible signal of disagreement.[90] One cause was probably Qaddumi's support for the hard-line resolutions of the fifth Fath Congress held in August, which called for the intensification of armed struggle against Israel (see chapter on the PLO). The Soviets were clearly uncomfortable with such deviations from the PLO's more peaceful image, a fact evident in the lack of coverage the Soviet media afforded the event.

Two Soviet-PLO meetings occurred in rapid succession in October. The first took place in Moscow where 'Abbas met with Polyakov and Deputy Foreign Minister Yuri Vorontsov.[91] The sides reportedly briefed each other on "multiple-option approaches toward preparing and convening an international conference." In addition, they noted the need for all interested parties to display political flexibility and realism in seeking "compromise ways to untangle emerging problems on the basis of balance of interests," an indication that they were seriously considering Israel's elections idea.[92] Several days later Terasov met with 'Arafat in Tunis, where the focus of discussion was clearly on US Secretary of State James Baker's attempt to initiate a Palestinian-Israeli dialogue (see chapter on the ME peace process). Reports suggested that Terasov communicated a US proposal that exiled members of the Palestine National Council (PNC) be allowed to take part in the dialogue, an idea unacceptable to Israel and one for which the US refused to take credit.[93] Subsequently, Terasov was said to be disillusioned that the US had reneged on its proposal.[94]

This sense of frustration with US diplomacy may explain a decidedly counterproductive step that Shevardnadze undertook in November. In a message to 'Arafat, which Terasov carried to Tunis, Shevardnadze warned that Israel's peace efforts were insincere and aimed only at excluding the PLO from the negotiating process. In response, Shevardnadze supposedly proposed a return to the international conference formula.[95] Though worrisome at the time, the message did not represent a reversal of Moscow's growing pragmatism on the peace process: in early 1990, Shevardnadze again endorsed an Israeli-Palestinian dialogue following a meeting with Baker.[96] Instead, the warning seems in retrospect to have been a genuine expression of concern that the US and Israel were maneuvering to keep the PLO and, by extension, the USSR out of the peace process.

The incident reflected Moscow's multiple purposes in intensifying contacts with the PLO. On the one hand, it hoped to further encourage 'Arafat's commitment to a political settlement with Israel. As the year progressed, it was clear that the Soviets were counseling the PLO to work with the US and Egypt to make Israel's elections plan workable, rather than reject the plan outright or make unreasonable demands that would torpedo the process. On the other hand, the efforts to encourage PLO flexibility and moderation were undertaken not simply for the purpose of achieving any settlement, but rather one in which the PLO and the USSR would have a role.

In addition to its stepped-up contacts with the PLO on the peace process, two other developments in Soviet-PLO relations in 1989 must be mentioned, both of which reinforced the image of increasing Soviet pragmatism. The first was Moscow's willingness to cooperate with the US in international fora to block PLO efforts to achieve member-state status. In May, the Soviets voted to postpone discussion of the

PLO's application for membership in the World Health Organization,[97] while in November they refused to support the PLO's bid for statehood status at the UN.[98] Both incidents caused tension in Soviet-PLO relations and indicated Moscow's strong interest in avoiding a fight with the US. At the same time, Moscow's caution seemed motivated by a recognition of Israel's sensitivity on the issue and the danger that a PLO victory could retard rather than advance the search for a settlement.

A second development involved Moscow's evolving attitude toward terrorism. Under Gorbachev, Soviet condemnation of Palestinian acts of terrorism had become more consistent and Soviet advice to the PLO had been strongly in favor of political, rather than armed, methods of struggle. This message was clearly sent prior to the 1988 PNC, especially to Soviet friends in the Democratic Front for the Liberation of Palestine (DFLP) and the Popular Front for the Liberation of Palestine (PFLP).[99]

US officials criticized the Soviets in early 1989 for failing to keep up the pressure on the PLO to abide by its renunciation of terrorism. Specifically, the USSR was chastised for not officially condemning several attacks launched against Israel by the DFLP and PFLP from Syrian-controlled territory in Lebanon.[100] In late January, the DFLP's leader, Na'if Hawatima, paid a visit to Moscow and granted interviews with the Soviet press, with little sign that Soviet officials protested against DFLP terrorism. There was no evidence, however, that the USSR had supported or encouraged the attacks; indeed, commentaries had earlier appeared in the Soviet press mildly criticizing PFLP and DFLP deviation from the PNC decisions.[101]

In July 1989, Moscow issued an immediate and surprisingly harsh condemnation of a terrorist incident in Israel, in which a Palestinian caused the crash of a civilian bus (see chapters on Israel and armed operations). Calling it a "despicable terrorist act against innocent people," for which "there is no justification...whatever the motive," the Soviets insisted that "it is the duty of all sane people, regardless of their views on Middle East political developments, to denounce this heinous act."[102] This was in marked contrast to the reaction of elements within the PLO, such as the DFLP, that applauded the tragedy. Interestingly, Hawatima again showed up in Moscow following the incident, but details of his trip were not reported.[103]

For many Palestinians, Moscow's changing positions on the peace process, terrorism, and relations with Israel were a clear sign of declining support for the PLO. Certainly, they signaled an end of support for two decades of failed PLO radicalism. But if the Palestinians' true interest lay in a resolution of the conflict with Israel, the USSR's efforts to achieve a settlement, including trying to make the PLO an acceptable negotiating partner, did not represent an abandonment of Palestinian aspirations. On the contrary, Moscow's heightened involvement with the PLO reflected a Soviet attempt to get the movement to make the necessary concessions to achieve those aspirations.

SOVIET-SYRIAN RELATIONS

The Soviet Union's ties with Syria seemed to be in transition in 1989. On the one hand, political relations suffered substantial strain. Moscow's efforts to improve ties with Israel and the Arab moderates, to encourage 'Arafat's peace offensive, and to entertain US ideas on the peace process all ran contrary to the confrontationist priorities of the Asad regime. Furthermore, senior Soviet officials publicly suggested that Soviet aid to Syria would be reduced. On the other hand, actual Soviet military support for Syria remained high during the year, including the delivery of qualitatively new weapons systems.

Tension between Moscow and Damascus was clearly on display at the close of 1988. The USSR's important role in convincing 'Arafat to moderate the PLO's positions and win a dialogue with the US infuriated the Syrians. A typical response was a Radio Damascus broadcast that categorically rejected Gorbachev's insistence that a "balance of interests" formulation could be applied to the Arab-Israeli conflict.[104]

Events in the early months of 1989 did nothing to improve the strained atmosphere. In January, Moscow appointed Alexander Zotov as its ambassador to Syria. His nomination could not have pleased the Syrians, for Zotov had been a major advocate of moderation in Soviet Middle East policy and was widely credited as one of the architects of the *rapprochement* with Israel.[105] Nor was Syria pleased by the Soviet withdrawal from Afghanistan, which came immediately before Shevardnadze's arrival in Damascus in February on the first leg of his regional tour. While the rest of the Islamic world greeted it with great fanfare, for Syria the Red Army's retreat carried a disturbing import: if the USSR was ready to turn its back on a Communist regime installed by the blood of Soviet troops, what was to prevent it from doing the same with an unruly and costly client like Syria? When queried about the implications of the withdrawal, President Asad could only muster this ambivalent response: "I think they [the Soviets] thought it was a good thing...[but] an outside observer might see things in an opposite way."[106]

Upon arriving in Damascus, Shevardnadze made sure to affirm Syria's status as the USSR's leading partner in the ME. But in his meetings with Syria's leaders — Asad,[107] Vice President 'Abd al-Halim Khaddam, and Foreign Minister Faruq al-Shar'[108] — all the recent tensions were on display. Reports of the talks noted "an exchange of opinions" which took place, with Shevardnadze "setting out the Soviet view," standard euphemisms for an absence of agreement. Shevardnadze urged Asad to mend his fences not only with archrivals like the PLO and Iraq, but with apostate Egypt as well. He also pointed out the existence of "quite a few problems" in Soviet-Syrian economic ties, highlighting Moscow's growing unwillingness, in an era of economic scarcity at home, to continue paying the bill for Syria's military buildup.

On the peace process, Syria could agree in principle with Shevardnadze's call for convening an international conference. But whereas the Syrians emphasized Israel's intransigence and the futility of trying to engage it in a diplomatic process, Shevardnadze focused on the ripeness of the situation for making progress toward peace. In a manner unprecedented for a Soviet leader, he laid out a vision of genuine Arab-Israeli coexistence that blatantly contradicted Syrian statements about the inevitability of continued confrontation.[109]

While Shevardnadze acknowledged that his discussions had dealt with "the development of ties in various fields, including the military field,"[110] his speech in Damascus was focused on the growing dangers of the ME arms race, especially in the realm of nuclear and chemical weapons. This trend, he warned, posed a direct threat to the international stability that "new thinking" supported. At best, the Syrians could interpret this as confirmation of Moscow's continued refusal to help Syria achieve strategic parity with Israel. At worst, it suggested that the Soviets might cut back on the existing levels of supplies.

The clarity of this message was brought into question the following month, however, when Soviet Defense Minister Dimitri Yazov visited Syria.[111] On the one hand, Yazov echoed Shevardnadze's alarm about the dangerous levels of armaments in the region.[112] On the other hand, the outcome of his visit was a pledge to provide Syria finally with at least one squadron of Su-24 bombers, an aircraft that would significantly improve Syria's ability to strike strategic targets inside Israel.[113] This came on the heels of Moscow's delivery to Syria in 1987 and 1988 of between one and two squadrons of MiG-29s, the most sophisticated fighter aircraft in the Soviet arsenal.[114]

After the Yazov visit, the focus of Soviet-Syrian relations turned to Lebanon and Syria's involvement in the latest round of that country's civil war, fighting the Iraqi-backed Lebanese forces of Gen. 'Awn. Rather than support the brutal bombardments Syria launched against Christian East Beirut, or ignore them altogether, Moscow, throughout the summer of 1989, consistently lent its support to international and Arab efforts to achieve an arrangement — an immediate cease-fire leading to the eventual withdrawal of foreign forces — that Asad ultimately saw as antithetical to Syrian national interests.

Moscow's activism on the Lebanese crisis was impressive. In May, Shevardnadze and Secretary Baker issued a joint statement that noted the dangerous escalation of hostilities and called on all sides to adopt an immediate cease-fire.[115] Two months later, in a joint statement with French President François Mitterrand, widely viewed as the protector of Asad's foes in Lebanon's Christian community, Gorbachev expressed "profound concern at the continuing crisis situation" and called "for an immediate cease-fire and strict observance of it." All sides providing weapons to the combatants — namely, the USSR's feuding allies in Syria and Iraq — were urged to end their arms deliveries. Finally, the statement expressed full support for the Arab League's tripartite committee that was seeking to mediate the crisis, and whose efforts to that point Syria had subverted.[116] The Soviets also sent two diplomatic missions to the region in efforts to moderate the crisis. Just prior to the Soviet-French declaration, Deputy Foreign Minister Bessmertnykh went to Baghdad and Damascus to urge both sides to take steps to alleviate the deteriorating situation around Beirut.[117]

In mid-August, with Syria threatening to launch an all-out ground assault on 'Awn's forces, Moscow dispatched Terasov on a feverish round of shuttle diplomacy to Jordan, Syria, Lebanon (where he met with both 'Awn and Muslim leaders), and Iraq. In each country, Terasov urged the parties to support a renewed mediation effort by the Arab League, while floating some ideas of his own regarding the possible elements of a Lebanese peace plan.[118] Though no immediate results from the trip were apparent, the feared Syrian assault did not occur, and by mid-September the Arab League had reactivated its peacemaking role. Subsequently, reports suggested that Terasov was instrumental in winning Syria's agreement to withdraw its troops to the Biqa' Valley as part of a formal Lebanese peace accord.[119]

As the Lebanese crisis momentarily subsided, tensions in Soviet-Syrian bilateral relations reemerged as a major issue. At the center of the controversy were several statements made by Ambassador Zotov. The first came in September during a trip to Moscow. At an impromptu press conference, Zotov claimed that Syria's requests for military aid for the next five years "are being scrutinized critically and if there are any changes they will be in favor of reductions." A primary factor behind the reevaluation was the fact that "the Syrian Government's ability to pay is not unlimited," with most estimates placing Damascus's military debt to the USSR at between $9bn. and $20bn.[120]

If these comments were not worrisome enough for Syria, Zotov issued a similar message two months later, this time in Damascus during an interview with Western reporters. The Soviet Union, he said, was encouraging Syria to abandon its quest for strategic parity with Israel in favor of a posture of "reasonable defensive sufficiency," by which Syria would not pose an offensive threat to Israel but would be able to repulse any Israeli attack. In an obvious reference to his Syrian hosts, he explained that "the feeling in this region is that the more arms you have the more secure you are. [But] military force is not a...certificate of security....We really believe the balance of forces is an out-of-date approach." He again highlighted Syria's economic difficulties and its inability to pay for Soviet weaponry.[121]

A few days later, in response to Syrian protests, Zotov gave a press conference in which he claimed that his remarks had been distorted. He stressed the USSR's continued commitment to provide Syria with military support to protect it against Israeli aggression.[122] He did not, however, retract the key points made in his earlier interview.

While Zotov was signaling Moscow's desire to reduce the burden of aiding Syria, intense negotiations were under way on a new Soviet-Syrian arms contract. In September, the commander of Soviet rocket and artillery troops met with Syrian Defense Minister Mustafa Talas in Damascus.[123] The following month, the Syrian army's chief of staff visited Moscow.[124] In late November and early December, Talas played host to both the Soviet deputy defense minister for armaments[125] and the commander in chief of Soviet air defense forces.[126] Talas himself traveled to the USSR in mid-December.[127] But perhaps the most important trip of the series was that of Moscow's Minister of Foreign Economic Relations Konstantin Katushev, who spent several days in Syria discussing the repayment of Syria's military debt.[128]

No details of these meetings were released, but reports appeared claiming that a planned trip by Asad to Moscow, originally scheduled for late 1989, had been postponed because the Soviets had failed thus far to accommodate Syria's desire "that the visit usher in a qualitative shift in Soviet-Syrian relations." Allegedly, Asad wanted the trip to culminate in the signing of a major new arms contract, but difficulties in the negotiations, especially Moscow's demand that Syria settle at least some of its outstanding military debts, were holding up the talks.[129]

A concrete manifestation of the changing Soviet-Syrian relationship occurred when Syria agreed to reestablish relations with Egypt, something Asad had pledged never to do as long as Camp David remained in effect. Sources throughout the Arab world identified the shifts in relations with the Soviet bloc as the key factor forcing Asad's humiliating reversal: "With the shift in Kremlin policy toward the Arab-Israeli conflict and the transformation of the Soviet role in the era of *détente,* Damascus has no option other than to review its calculations and reevaluate its policies."[130] (See also chapters on Syria and Egypt.)

As 1989 closed, it was hard to avoid the conclusion that Soviet-Syrian relations were entering a process of long-term deterioration. How extensive that deterioration would be, remained to be seen. Certainly, the continued delivery to Syria of large amounts of sophisticated armaments, including the Su-24s, suggested that, for the moment, the Soviets wanted it to be limited. But even so, the strategic significance for the region was already substantial, especially as it influenced Syrian calculations about war and peace. At the end of the year, Israeli Foreign Minister Arens offered this sweeping assessment:

> Syria can no longer embark on military escapades against Israel and enjoy Soviet support....In the past...we were very troubled by the fact that Asad was sure that, in every military adventure against us, the Soviet Union would be at his side and give him its full support. I am prepared to state that today he has no such assurance.[131]

Israeli Defense Minister Yitzhak Rabin added that "there is no doubt that Damascus knows that the new Soviet policy is different from the old one and calls for a solution to the Middle East problem."[132] If changes in Soviet policy do in fact help instigate such a fundamental evolution in Syria's strategic outlook, they would have to be viewed, limits and all, as extremely important. (On Soviet-Syrian relations, see also chapter on Syria.)

POSITIONS ON THE PEACE PROCESS

Soviet policy toward the Arab-Israeli peace process in 1989 exhibited a growing realism. As Soviet priorities evolved from scoring points with the Arab world at the expense of the US to promoting a stable regional settlement, Moscow's understanding of what a successful peace process would require became more sophisticated.

The most important changes involved the Soviet view of the international conference. Bombastic references to an "authoritative" conference, which would seek to impose a settlement on Israel, disappeared from Soviet statements in 1989. Commentaries even appeared that explicitly attacked the traditional position, arguing that it had led Israel to conclude, justifiably, that the Soviet Union supported an imposed solution.[133] Throughout the year, Moscow's understanding of the conference's role moved closer to that of the US: the conference would serve as an umbrella providing cover for direct negotiations between the local parties. After agreements were reached, the conference would bestow on them an international blessing and guarantees.

As the year progressed, there also seemed to be a gradual acceptance of the US argument that if a conference was to have any chance of success, it would require the prior completion of a "preparatory," or, in the US parlance, confidence-building stage. According to the initial Soviet formulations, this could include direct discussions among the local parties and certain outside powers — namely, the permanent members of the UN Security Council — with the aim of narrowing disagreements and assuaging fears about the conference's nature, purpose, and outcome. But by late 1989, even the Soviet view of the preparatory stage was shifting. While the utility of Security Council discussions continued to be advocated, the focus of Moscow's talks with the US, the Palestinians and Israel was increasingly on the idea, developed by the US, of arranging a direct dialogue between Israel and the Palestinians.

In Shevardnadze's January meeting in Paris with Arens, a shift had already occurred in his rhetoric about the peace process. He spoke of the need to establish "measures that lead to confidence and mutual understanding, and taking practical steps to unblock the Arab-Israeli conflict." In advocating the international conference,

Shevardnadze "laid particular stress on the need to carry out preparatory work aimed at convening it as soon as possible."[134]

During his regional tour in February, Shevardnadze again emphasized the necessity of convening the international conference (within nine months, he proposed), but also stressed the preparatory work that had to be done to ensure its success. In Amman, he spoke of the conference as "the strategic goal," which "cannnot be reached without serious preparation." Following his meeting with Arens, Shevardnadze displayed remarkable candor in discussing the problems of a conference. Rather than identify Israel as the only obstacle, Shevardnadze acknowledged that:

> The international conference is not a simple matter. Even if Arens and I are agreed on this today, it still does not mean that this conference will be held, because we also must take into account the positions of the Arab countries, the UN Security Council members, and the European countries.[135]

In his speech in Cairo (see above), Shevardnadze focused on the conference, but spent much time reassuring Israel that it could achieve security and peace through this process. Acknowledging Israel's concerns about a coercive conference, he stated that "the issue of the form of the international conference...what it should deal with, how it should work, and who should take part in it gives rise to discussions. These are all legitimate questions...answers must be given to them that are acceptable to all."[136] Subsequently, when asked about Israel's fears of being isolated at a conference, Shevardnadze stressed that it was essential to exclude any attempts to isolate anyone at all, whether Israel or the Palestinians; one of the main purposes of the preparatory phase, he said, would be providing guarantees against isolation.

As to the preparatory phase itself, Shevardnadze indicated that Moscow was willing to be flexible. The proposal for an informal meeting of the UN Security Council was simply a suggestion, not a demand. "We are not imposing a preparatory committee. At present it is difficult to determine the form of the preparatory process...we are not imposing anything at all."[137] During his meetings with Arens and 'Arafat, Shevardnadze reportedly raised an alternative idea — direct negotiations between Israel and the PLO in Moscow.[138]

The Soviet Union's growing seriousness about a political solution was indicated by its response to Prime Minister Shamir's proposal for Palestinian elections. Before Gorbachev, Moscow's reaction would almost certainly have been an immediate and unequivocal rejection. Israel's plan not only ruled out the PLO and a Palestinian state, it came in response to American pressures, said nothing about an international conference, and seemed to ignore a role for the Soviet Union.

The initial Soviet reaction to these perceived negatives was to express great skepticism and criticism. Elections per se were viewed as acceptable, but as presented in the Shamir plan were denounced as an effort to exclude the PLO and deny the Palestinians their right to self-determination. Thus, Gennady Gerasimov, during his visit to Cairo in April (see above), dismissed the plan as "a sham to divert world public opinion from the ongoing Intifada in the occupied territories, and from reaching a real solution to the Middle East problem."[139] Yet, rather than simply rejecting the plan, Moscow called for its clarification: What purposes would elections serve? What would be their connection to a comprehensive settlement? What would be the role of the PLO? This more constructive attitude was reflected after the Shevardnadze-Baker meeting in Moscow in May. Baker noted that:

> We think that there may be a fair amount of common ground with respect
> to our approach to the Middle East....We talked about the importance of
> giving the idea of elections a chance; working with Israelis and Arabs to see if
> we can convert elections into a...broader process that will ultimately bring
> about political negotiations."[140]

Shevardnadze reportedly told Baker that the elections idea was "worthy of attention,
while many points remain unclear."[141]

The more flexible Soviet approach was evident the following month in the meeting
between PLO representative 'Abbas and Soviet Deputy Foreign Minister
Bessmertnykh (see above). The mention of "multioption approaches" and "phased
steps" in preparing a conference and comprehensive settlement indicated that the
Israeli proposal was being considered seriously. And in the mid-June discussions on
the ME between US and Soviet officials, the Americans were reported to be
encouraged by Moscow's failure to press actively for a conference and its interest in
finding out more about Israel's initiative.[142]

This interest in working with the US was reflected in Soviet support for Egypt's
Ten-Point Plan, which sought to clarify the Shamir plan and make it more acceptable
to the Palestinians.[143] In September, at the UN, Shevardnadze referred to the positive
elements in both Israel's proposal and the Egyptian ideas, while again floating his
offer to host direct PLO-Israeli talks in Moscow.

While Shevardnadze's letter to 'Arafat in November (see above) caused some
tension between the USSR and the US over the peace process, by the time of the
superpower summit in Malta, the Soviets again seemed ready to support an Israeli-
Palestinian dialogue as the first step in the peace process. Shevardnadze's outright
endorsement of the dialogue in January confirmed this conclusion.

Increasing Soviet flexibility toward the US-backed peace process reflected a desire
to see the Arab-Israeli conflict begin moving toward a settlement. It did not, however,
signal Moscow's abandonment of all its former positions. An international conference
was still supported as the forum in which a comprehensive solution would be achieved;
some form of PLO involvement in the process was viewed as critical to its success;
and satisfaction of the Palestinians' demand for self-determination — either in an
independent state or in confederation with Jordan and/or Israel — was seen as an
essential element of a stable settlement. But Soviet attitudes on each of these issues
was more flexible; Moscow seemed prepared to put off satisfaction of them in order to
see the peace process get under way.

MOSCOW AND THE GULF

The most outstanding feature of Soviet policy toward the Persian Gulf in 1989 was a
dramatic improvement in relations with Iran. This was made possible by the resolution
of two conflicts that had been major obstacles to bilateral ties: the Iran-Iraq War, in
which Iran resented Moscow's role as Iraq's primary arms supplier; and the Soviet
intervention in Afghanistan, which Islamic Iran had viewed as an attack on all
Muslims.

The Soviets had multiple interests in a *rapprochement* with Iran beyond the obvious desire to increase their influence in an important country situated on their border. First, they hoped to encourage Iran to conclude a formal peace treaty with Iraq. Without it, the Soviets feared there would inevitably be another outbreak of hostilities, the consequences of which — in terms of destruction, instability, and superpower relations — could not be foreseen. Second, Moscow hoped to get Iran's help in Afghanistan. The Soviets wanted Iran to use its influence with rebel Shi'ite groups for two purposes: to allow the Red Army to withdraw in an orderly fashion; and, afterward, to help the USSR arrange a political settlement that would prevent a humiliating defeat of the Najibullah regime at the hands of Mujahidin groups backed by the US, Saudi Arabia, and Pakistan. Finally, the effort to improve relations was motivated by Moscow's concern with growing nationalist and religious fervor in its Muslim republics in Central Asia. At a minimum, the Soviets wanted Iran, as the symbol of revolutionary Islam, to desist from any activities that would inflame the unrest. At best, they hoped to enlist Iran as a partner in dampening the heightening passions and ensuring stability.

A major breakthrough in Soviet-Iranian political relations occurred at the very beginning of the year. In a somewhat bizarre scenario, Iran's supreme leader, the Ayatollah Ruhollah Khomeyni, sent a personal envoy to Moscow with a lengthy letter for Gorbachev. The letter was filled with praise for the Soviet leader, noting his courage and wisdom in admitting the failures of communism and for allowing Soviet Muslims to practice their faith again. It went on to instruct Gorbachev that the USSR's problems could not be resolved through *perestroika,* but by studying the ways of Islam.[144]

Despite the letter's didactic tone, it represented an obvious shift in Iran's attitude toward the Soviet Union. Like the rest of the world, Khomeyni finally seemed to believe that the changes in policy instituted by Gorbachev were genuine. This realization, in addition to Iran's need for immediate help in reconstructing its war-ravaged economy, was sufficient reason to seek an improvement in relations with the USSR.

This was evident when Shevardnadze visited Iran in February as the last stop on his regional tour. He was granted an unprecedented private meeting with Khomeyni, in which he claimed that "conditions are ripe for relations between our two countries to enter a qualitatively new stage of cooperation in all fields." Khomeyni endorsed the improvement in Soviet-Iranian relations, noting that strong ties would enable them to confront "the devilish acts of the West."[145]

Shevardnadze's discussions with Iran's other leaders focused on Afghanistan, the stalled Iran-Iraq peace talks, and bilateral economic relations. The Iranians welcomed the Red Army's withdrawal from Afghanistan and agreed to work with Moscow to achieve a peaceful resolution of the conflict.[146] Shevardnadze urged Iran to achieve a peace treaty with Iraq; Iran replied by insisting that the Soviet Union put more pressure on Iraq to withdraw its troops from Iranian territory. Finally, the two sides signed protocols agreeing to expand political, economic, and cultural cooperation significantly; reports also surfaced that discussions had begun on Soviet arms sales to Iran.[147]

All this was a prelude, however, to the event that marked the high point of Soviet-Iranian relations in 1989: the official visit to Moscow of Hashemi Rafsanjani, the speaker of Iran's parliament, in late June, just weeks after Khomeyni's death.

Though he would not be elected Iran's president for another month, Rafsanjani came to the USSR as his country's dominant political figure. The visit, therefore, had great symbolic importance, signaling Iran's intention to continue the policy, launched by Khomeyni, of improving ties with Moscow.

By all accounts, the trip produced significant results. Rafsanjani held several meetings with Gorbachev, in which both leaders called for an expansion in bilateral relations. A "Declaration on the Principles of Relations Between the USSR and Iran" was issued, describing ties between the two countries as having "entered a new stage," based on "rigorous observance of their equality, mutual respect for national sovereignty and territorial integrity, nonaggression, [and] noninterference in each other's internal affairs." This statement was important not only for Iran, with its historical concerns about Russian imperialism, but for the Soviets as well, who were seeking assurances that Iran would not exploit mounting tensions in Soviet Central Asia. Finally, without providing any details, the declaration on principles also spoke of a Soviet willingness to "cooperate with the Iranian side with regard to strengthening its defense capability."[148]

The joint communiqué released at the end of the visit noted that the two sides had signed a long-term program for economic, scientific, and technical cooperation until the year 2000. In addition, a commercial agreement and an agreement to build a Soviet-Iranian railway were reached. Interestingly, the communiqué also spoke of an understanding to expand cultural and spiritual contacts; this was immediately manifested when Rafsanjani stopped in Baku on his way back to Tehran and participated in Friday prayer services with Soviet Muslims.[149]

The Soviets quickly tried to put the burgeoning goodwill generated by Rafsanjani's trip to use. In early August, at the height of the crisis in Lebanon involving Israel's abduction of a Shi'ite cleric and the murder of an American hostage (see chapters on Lebanon and armed operations), Shevardnadze flew to Iran to try and engage Rafsanjani in some crisis management. For what it was worth in helping to defuse the immediate crisis, Shevardnadze succeeded in eliciting a statement from Rafsanjani that expressed "deep regret about what has happened." Jointly, Shevardnadze and Rafsanjani "condemned any acts of a terrorist kind and called for the adoption of urgent measures to prevent a further exacerbation of the situation."[150]

The remainder of 1989 continued to see a large volume of Soviet-Iranian contacts. Bilaterally, more progress was made on economic issues, including final arrangements to resume Iranian natural gas exports to the USSR.[151] Regionally, Iran's position on a political settlement of the Afghan conflict seemed to shift in Moscow's favor: following his August meeting with Rafsanjani, Shevardnadze claimed that Iran had adopted a "wholly positive attitude" on Afghanistan. Reportedly, Iran was willing to back down from its demand that the Najibullah government be excluded from any future Afghan regime.[152] In return for this shift, it was rumored that Moscow was ready to take a position on the Iran-Iraq peace talks more favorable to Tehran, by calling for a return of Iraqi forces to the status quo ante borders.[153]

Though Moscow's view of its vital interests in the ME increasingly focused on the need to attain a stable, working relationship with Iran, the Soviets remained willing to direct criticism at Iranian policies that threatened regional stability. Articles appeared in the press attacking Iran's human rights abuses, as well as its support for radical Islamic fundamentalists in both Lebanon and Saudi Arabia. Late in 1989, as the fragile Lebanese peace accord brokered by the Arab League unraveled, Shevardnadze sent a sharply worded message to his Iranian counterpart, warning that "all countries for whom Lebanon's fate at this crucial juncture is important should try to maintain its territorial integrity and unity."[154]

In part, this readiness to criticize Iran occasionally may have reflected Soviet sensitivity to Arab concerns that it was tilting too much in favor of the Islamic Republic. Especially in the wake of Rafsanjani's visit, several Arab regimes expressed alarm. Iraq, predictably, led the way, with its official press condemning the USSR's *rapprochement* with Iran as an opportunistic act that drew into question Soviet policy toward the Arabs.[155] A senior Iraqi official noted that "Iraq has declared the Soviet Union's supplying of Iran with weapons as unacceptable and as an act which does not serve the peace process."[156]

The Soviet media responded to these attacks with several commentaries that sought to downplay the significance of the military aspects of the Soviet-Iranian relationship.[157] More important, a special diplomatic effort was made to assure key Arab states that no major arms deal had been concluded with Iran for offensive weapons that could disrupt the Gulf's military balance.[158]

For the most part, this effort at damage limitation appeared successful. As it had done for much of the Gulf War, Moscow was able in 1989 to maintain and improve its ties with several Arab states in the Gulf at the same time as it was achieving a significant improvement in relations with Iran.

Thus, despite Iraq's displeasure with the Soviet-Iranian *rapprochement,* its ties with the USSR remained as they had been for years — very businesslike, but also very extensive. Shevardnadze visited Iraq on his regional tour and held discussions with President Saddam Husayn on bilateral relations and the Iran-Iraq peace negotiations. On the latter issue, differences were apparent, with Shevardnadze emphasizing to Husayn "the need to intensify efforts with a view to finding mutually acceptable solutions...both sides [must] show goodwill, a well thought-out approach and political realism."[159] But these differences had no visible adverse impact on bilateral ties; the USSR remained the major supplier of Iraq's massive Army, while Iraq remained the Soviet Union's primary trading partner in the ME.[160]

The Soviets were also able to sustain a gradual improvement in relations with several of the smaller Arab Gulf states with whom they had only recently established diplomatic relations. Thus, for example, Oman's minister of petroleum went to Moscow in January,[161] an official Soviet trade delegation visited Qatar in February,[162] and the UAE signed its first economic, trade, and technical cooperation agreement with the USSR in July.[163] Soviet contacts with Kuwait, with which it had had relations for decades, also expanded significantly. Economic cooperation, especially in the area of oil production, increased.[164] In addition, the two countries exchanged senior military delegations.[165] Reports, which the Kuwaitis denied, suggested that a major arms deal had been signed.[166]

The Soviets were less successful in cultivating relations with the most influential Gulf Cooperation Council state, Saudi Arabia. In 1988, there had been a significant multiplication of economic and political contacts between the two countries, culminating in the visit to Moscow of the Saudi foreign minister (see *MECS* 1988, chapter on Saudi Arabia). Many observers had anticipated that once the Soviets removed the last major irritant in relations — their military presence in Afghanistan

— Saudi Arabia would finally assent to an exchange of ambassadors. But whether because of Moscow's continued support for the Najibullah regime, or because of its wooing of Iran, the Saudis balked at taking this step, much to Soviet chagrin. Yet despite this continued caution on Riyadh's part, it still seemed likely that Soviet-Saudi ties would be upgraded sooner rather than later, especially since this remained a priority of Soviet policy in the Gulf. (For a more detailed discussion of Soviet-Saudi relations, see chapter on Saudi Arabia.)

NOTES

For the place and frequency of publications cited here, and for the full name of the publication, news agency, radio station, or monitoring service where an abbreviation is used, please see "List of Sources." Only in the case of more than one publication bearing the same name is the place of publication noted here.

1. For an example of the US criticism, see US Secretary of State James Baker's speech to the Foreign Policy Association, "The Points of Mutual Advantage: *Perestroika* and American Foreign Policy," 16 October 1989, transcribed by Federal News Service.
2. *Pravda,* 24 October 1989.
3. Reuters, 8 January 1989.
4. VoI, 27 January — DR, 27 January 1989.
5. UPI, 22 February 1989.
6. MENA, 22 February — DR, 23 February 1989.
7. *Izvestiia,* 24 February — DR:SU, 24 February 1989.
8. Ibid.
9. Israeli TV, 22 February — DR, 24 February 1989.
10. *Hatzofeh,* 9 May — DR, 9 May 1989.
11. *Hatzofeh,* 2 June — DR, 2 June 1989.
12. Figures provided by the Union of Councils of Soviet Jews, Washington, DC.
13. *JP International Edition,* w/e 16 December 1989.
14. The draft law is described in Reuters, 8 June 1989.
15. *NYT,* 8 February 1989.
16. Edgar Bronfman, president of the World Jewish Congress, cited several problems with the center's poor performance not related to official Soviet policy: infighting among Jewish groups over the center's goals, a lack of adequate programming to attract people, and persistent fear of anti-Semitic repercussions. *Jewish Exponent,* 31 March 1989.
17. *NYT,* 19 February 1989.
18. Reuters, 9 March 1989.
19. *Yedi'ot Aharonot,* 20 January — DR, 25 January 1989.
20. *Yedi'ot Aharonot,* 22 January — DR, 25 January 1989.
21. R. IDF, 13 February — DR, 15 February 1989.
22. VoI, 11 March — DR, 17 March 1989.
23. *Sovetskaya Kultura,* 9 February 1989.
24. Jerusalem TV, 8 June — DR, 8 June 1989.
25. *NYT,* 29 June 1989.
26. *Izvestiia,* 27 July 1989.
27. *Hadashot,* 30 July — DR, 11 August 1989.
28. TASS, 10 August — DR:SU, 11 August 1989.
29. *JP International Edition,* w/e 26 August 1989.
30. *Yedi'ot Aharonot,* 7 September — DR, 11 September 1989.
31. *Izvestiia,* 27 August 1989.
32. *Izvestiia,* 23 September 1989.
33. R. Peace and Progress (in Hebrew), 11 September — DR:SU, 13 September 1989.
34. *JP International Edition,* w/e 23 September 1989.
35. R. IDF, 15 June — DR, 15 June 1989.

36. VoI, 7 September — DR, 8 September 1989.
37. R. Moscow, 10 October — DR:SU, 11 October 1989.
38. R. Moscow, 11 October — DR:SU, 11 October 1989.
39. *NYT,* 27 December 1989. On the actual visit see AP, 25 January 1990.
40. R. IDF, 23 October — DR, 23 October 1989.
41. VoI, 29 November — DR, 30 November 1989.
42. TASS, 28 September — DR:SU, 29 September 1989.
43. *JP International Edition,* w/e 7 October 1989.
44. TASS, 28 September — DR:SU, 29 September 1989.
45. One example came in a statement by Foreign Ministry press spokesman Gennady Gerasimov in *Davar,* 22 September — DR, 25 September 1989.
46. *JP,* 6 December 1989.
47. *NYT,* 14 October 1989.
48. Ibid., 20 December 1989.
49. Union of Councils for Soviet Jews, Washington, DC.
50. *Ha'aretz,* 2 January 1990.
51. Reuters, 7 December 1989.
52. *NYT,* 29 January 1990.
53. Ibid., 18 January 1990.
54. Ibid., 31 January 1990.
55. *Mideast Mirror,* 2 February 1990.
56. *JT,* 14 December 1988.
57. The visit is reported in DR, 21 February, and DR:SU, 21 February 1989.
58. *Pravda,* 21 February — DR:SU, 21 February 1989.
59. R. Moscow, 20 February — DR:SU, 21 February 1989.
60. TASS, 20 February — DR:SU, 21 February 1989.
61. MENA, 15 January — DR, 17 January 1989.
62. MENA, 18 April — DR, 19 April 1989.
63. Reuters, 6 July 1989.
64. MENA, 26 April — DR, 27 April 1989.
65. *Al-Musawwar,* 5 May — DR:SU, 11 May 1989.
66. MENA, 30 April — DR, 1 May 1989.
67. R. Cairo, 15 May — DR, 17 May 1989.
68. TASS, 15 May — DR:SU, 19 May 1989.
69. *JT,* 27–28 April — DR:SU, 2 May 1989.
70. *JT,* 3 May — DR, 3 May 1989.
71. *MEED,* 1 September 1989.
72. R. Amman, 27 August — DR, 28 August 1989.
73. R. Amman, 27 August — DR, 28 August 1989.
74. *MEED,* 29 September 1989.
75. *Al-Ahram,* 21 November — DR, 24 November 1989.
76. *Al-Ahram,* 12 December — DR, 19 December 1989.
77. Reuters, 30 October 1989.
78. *Al-Akhbar,* Cairo, 12 December — DR, 19 December 1989.
79. *Pravda,* 18 December 1988.
80. R. Moscow, 18 January — DR:SU, 19 January 1989.
81. MENA, 22 February — DR, 23 February; *Pravda,* 23 February; Moscow TV, 23 February — DR:SU, 24 February 1989.
82. *Al-Watan,* Kuwait, 16 February — DR, 22 February 1989.
83. *Izvestiia,* 24 February — DR:SU, 24 February 1989.
84. *Pravda,* 30 March 1989.
85. *Al-Madina,* 30 April — DR, 3 May 1989.
86. *Izvestiia,* 15 June 1989.
87. *JP International Edition,* w/e 24 June 1989.
88. Reuters, 26 July 1989.
89. Ibid., 26 July 1989.
90. *Izvestiia,* 28 September 1989.

91. Ibid., 25 October 1989.
92. Ibid., 25 October — DR:SU, 1 November 1989.
93. Reuters, 29 October 1989.
94. *Mideast Mirror,* 30 October 1989.
95. *JP International Edition,* w/e 25 November 1989.
96. Federal News Service, 10 February 1989.
97. *Al-Anba,* Kuwait, 16 May — DR, 18 May 1989.
98. *WP,* 1 December 1989.
99. Galia Golan, *Gorbachev's "New Thinking" on Terrorism* (New York: Praeger, 1990), p. 67.
100. *Minneapolis Star and Tribune,* 23 March 1989.
101. For example, *Izvestiia,* 6 January 1989.
102. R. Peace and Progress (in Hebrew), 7 July — DR:SU, 12 July 1989.
103. TASS, 21 July — DR:SU, 25 July 1989.
104. R. Damascus, 16 December — DR, 29 December 1988.
105. *Al-Qabas,* 27 January — DR, 3 February 1989.
106. R. Damascus, 27 March — DR, 28 March 1989.
107. *Pravda,* 19 February 1989.
108. The Khaddam and Shar' meetings are reported in ibid., 20 February — DR:SU, 21 February 1989.
109. TASS, 19 February — DR:SU, 21 February 1989.
110. Ibid.
111. TASS, 28 March — DR:SU, 28 March 1989.
112. Reuters, 27 March 1989.
113. UPI, 12 April, 26 October 1989.
114. Charles B. Perkins, *Arms to the Arabs* (Washington, DC: America-Israel Public Affairs Committee, 1989).
115. TASS, 11 May 1989.
116. *Pravda,* 6 July 1989.
117. See the TASS reports in DR:SU, 3, 5 July 1989.
118. *WT,* 28 August 1989.
119. *Al-Qabas,* 29 August — DR, 31 August 1989.
120. Reuters, 18 September 1989.
121. *WP,* 20 November 1989.
122. *Mideast Mirror,* 23 November 1989.
123. SANA, 7 September — DR, 8 September 1989.
124. *Krasnaia Zvezda,* 18 October — DR:SU, 18 October 1989.
125. R. Damascus, 28 November — DR, 29 November 1989.
126. Damascus TV, 3 December — DR, 4 December 1989.
127. *Krasnaia Zvezda,* 20 December — DR:SU, 22 December 1989.
128. TASS, 29 December — DR:SU, 2 January 1990.
129. *Al-Qabas,* 25 October — DR, 12 October 1989.
130. *Mideast Mirror,* 13 December 1989.
131. Ibid., 28 December 1989.
132. *NYT,* 29 December 1989.
133. R. Peace and Progress (in Hebrew), 12 May — DR:SU, 19 May 1989.
134. TASS, 8 January — DR:SU, 9 January 1989.
135. VoI, 22 February — DR, 22 February 1989.
136. *Izvestiia,* 24 February — DR:SU, 24 February 1989.
137. TASS, 23 February — DR:SU, 24 February 1989.
138. UPI, 23 February 1989.
139. See Note 66 above.
140. Baker's press conference, 11 May 1989, Federal News Service transcript.
141. *WP,* 11 May 1989.
142. *Jewish Exponent,* 23 June 1989.
143. For example, *Izvestiia,* 20 September — DR:SU, 26 September 1989.
144. R. Tehran, 8 January — DR, 9 January 1989.
145. *MEED,* 10 March 1989.

146. *Pravda*, 28 February — DR:SU, 28 February 1989.
147. *MEED*, 10 March 1989.
148. TASS, 22 June — DR:SU, 22 June 1989.
149. *Pravda*, 24 June — DR:SU, 26 June 1989.
150. TASS, 2 August — DR:SU, 2 August 1989.
151. For example, the visit to Iran of the USSR minister of foreign economic relations, reported in TASS, 4 November — DR:SU, 6 November 1989.
152. *MEED*, 18 August 1989.
153. Ibid., 11 August 1989.
154. IRNA, 24 November — DR, 27 November 1989.
155. *Al-'Iraq*, 1 July — DR, 10 July 1989.
156. *Sawt al-Sha'b*, 24 July — DR, 25 July 1989.
157. For example, R. Moscow, in Arabic, 29 July — DR:SU, 3 August 1989.
158. *Al-Qabas*, 26 July — DR:SU, 28 July 1989.
159. TASS, 25 February — DR:SU, 27 February 1989.
160. *MEED*, 16 December 1989.
161. *Al-Ittihad*, Abu Dhabi, 16 January — DR:SU, 19 January 1989.
162. GNA, 13 February — DR, 14 February 1989.
163. TASS, 12 July — DR:SU, 13 July 1989.
164. *MEED*, 27 January 1989.
165. TASS, 14 July — DR:SU, 17 July; KUNA, 26 July — DR:SU, 3 August 1989.
166. KUNA, 24 July — DR, 25 July 1989.

ARAB-ISRAELI RELATIONS

The Middle East Peace Process

MORDECHAI GAZIT

It was no foregone conclusion that the peace process would gather momentum in 1989. It had stalled in the previous year, but not for want of efforts by the traditional go-between, the US.

The continuation of the Intifada in the West Bank and Gaza, Jordan's disengagement from these territories, and the decisions which the PLO adopted in November 1988, concatenated to keep the issue in the forefront. The Israeli peace initiative was launched officially in May 1989, but it had been in the making since January. It provided the missing element vitally needed to rekindle the peace efforts. The Israeli proposal contained hardly any provisions tailored to attract the Palestinians. It was modeled almost entirely on the Camp David Accords, which the Palestinians had rejected. It reiterated the three Israeli objections: to the establishment of a Palestinian state in the West Bank, to negotiations with the PLO, and to any change in the status of the West Bank other than in accordance with the basic guidelines of the Government of Israel. The only element that could make it acceptable to the Palestinians was a commitment that in the negotiations for a permanent solution, set to begin not earlier than in the third year after the establishment of the autonomy regime, the Palestinians would be free to present for discussion any subject they might wish to raise. This commitment was fortified by a unilateral Israeli declaration of intent that these negotiations would aim to achieve a solution acceptable to the negotiating parties, i.e., to the Palestinians as well as to Israel.

The US, a participant in the peace process both as a peace broker and near-partner, stated its belief that the Israeli ideas were something new and not just a "warmed over" Camp David. This proved crucial. Without the Americans' vouching for the seriousness of the Israeli move, and without American readiness to reengage US diplomacy to advance agreement, it was doubtful whether there would have been a peace process in the year under review.

The US, however, also clearly articulated its positions, which occupied the middle ground. Among them, one of the most important was based on the assumption that a settlement was attainable only if Israel agreed to exchange land for peace. This position split the Cabinet evenly into two. However, the US also had bad tidings for the Palestinians. It told them that it would not support an independent Palestinian state and would not expect Israel, at least in the "current effort," to negotiate with the PLO.

Israel's stand not to negotiate with the PLO complicated the US role. Israel's decision, however, was one the cabinet continued to support almost unanimously. As against it, there was the PLO's insistence that it alone was entitled to represent the Palestinians. Notwithstanding these difficulties, the US and Egypt made great efforts to find diplomatic formulas which, so they hoped, each side could accept without fearing that in doing so it would give up its basic positions.

In this situation, it was hardly surprising that a plethora of documents (Mubarak's Ten Points, Egypt's Four Points, Baker's Five Points) were devised by Washington and Cairo in tenacious attempts to get the two parties finally into a dialogue. This objective was not yet achieved by the end of the year, but neither had it failed.

The Bush Administration chose a nondramatic and partly indirect approach as it toiled throughout the year. US Secretary of State James Baker preferred the telephone to the air shuttle, but devoted much attention to the peacemaking process. Cooperation between the US and Egypt was close and crucial. Israel acknowledged Egypt's role as an important country that could help achieve agreement with the Palestinians. This Israeli attitude, in the face of Egypt's declared sympathy for the Palestinians and the PLO, was certainly noteworthy.

ISRAEL

In the year under review, Israel remained a key factor in the peace process. However, diplomatic activities, whether initiated by Israel or by others, were all carried out in a climate of heightened domestic tension in Israel. The results of the 1988 parliamentary elections, like those of 1984, forced the two rival large political blocs, Likud and Labor (also referred to as the Alignment), into forming a National Unity Government, supposed to be guided by a document entitled *Basic Guidelines*. In fact, however, the differences between the two parties over the settlement of the Arab-Israeli conflict were much too fundamental to be papered over by a series of general principles drafted in 1984.

The year 1989 was particularly busy diplomatically and necessitated hard decisions, which were adopted only after much strain and delay. Three reasons combined to persuade the Israeli Government, early in the year, that it had to advance a peace proposal of its own as soon as possible. In the US, the outgoing Reagan Administration had just started a dialogue with the PLO and had bequeathed the Shultz plan to its successors. Rather than wait for the new American Administration to make the first move, which would present Prime Minister Yitzhak Shamir with the same difficult questions as the Shultz plan had, it seemed preferable for Israel to venture forth with its own peace proposal. Moreover, the Intifada had entered into its 13th month as 1989 unfolded, and its end was nowhere in sight. Israeli leaders were convinced that military means could reduce its intensity down to more "tolerable" proportions, but that only a political settlement could terminate it completely.

A third reason impelling the Israeli Government to formulate a peace plan was the existence among the Israeli public of a clear majority in favor of an Israeli peace initiative.

It was to be expected that Shamir's move would adhere as closely as possible to the Camp David framework. Yet it soon became known that he was, nevertheless, considering one not insignificant change. The Camp David Accords laid down that the process would start with negotiations between Egypt, Israel, Jordan, and, possibly Palestinians from the West Bank and Gaza or other Palestinians as mutually agreed. The objective of these negotiations was to agree on the powers and responsibilities of the self-governing authority. Elections would be held thereafter for the purpose of choosing Palestinian delegates to run the autonomy. With Egypt refusing since 1982 to go on with the autonomy talks and with Jordan disengaging from the West Bank in

July 1988, it was evident that Israel could find the negotiating partner only among the Palestinians. However, for this to happen, elections would have to be held in the territories to choose the Palestinian representatives for talks with Israel. In line with the Camp David Accords, Shamir held that the autonomy regime would eventually, probably after a five-year transition period, be replaced by a permanent status for the territories which, in its turn, would also have to be negotiated. But Shamir was careful to add his own interpretation of these accords: the permanent status need not involve Israeli renunciation of territory — other options could be found.[1] For example, a confederative arrangement based on links between Israel and "Arab elements" east and west of the Jordan River could be considered.[2] Shamir was hopeful that Egypt would play some kind of useful role in this plan. It had signed the Camp David agreements and was, so he insisted, still bound by them.

Shamir was also willing to heed a US-Soviet call on the parties to the dispute — he was obviously thinking of Jordan and Syria — to open direct negotiations. He continued to oppose an international conference, but would acquiesce in some kind of formal UN auspices, if it was assured that the negotiations themselves were direct.[3]

The Knesset, for its part, soon gave support to these general lines of thinking, when on 3 January 1989 it adopted a resolution stating readiness to talk to Palestinian representatives who recognized Israel and who renounced terror. It reiterated its opposition to talks with the PLO.[4]

Defense Minister Yitzhak Rabin, who was to play a central role in the Israeli moves throughout the year, outlined his own plan for elections and autonomy in the territories for the first time soon thereafter (19 January). After three to six months of calm, Israel would let the Palestinians hold elections for representatives to negotiations. The elections would be held under Israeli supervision, but Rabin did not completely exclude some kind of neutral involvement as long as it was not the UN. The Palestinians would receive expanded autonomy for a transition period, a self-governing council would administer the areas, the Jewish settlements would remain in place, and Israel would control security. After the transition period, Palestinians in the territories would choose between federation with Jordan or with Israel. All Palestinians in the territories, but none of those living in the diaspora, could be partners to a dialogue with Israel, along with Jordan. Over the Arabic language programs of Israeli Television, Rabin appealed directly to the Palestinians in the territories, saying: "I want you to know that we are ready to talk to you. You are the partners to negotiations."[5] In another interview, he stated explicitly that he was not proposing municipal elections, but an election to provide a "political representation." Moreover, a "Palestinian entity" in the West Bank and Gaza "with links to Israel" would come into being.[6] In line with Labor policy, Rabin declared his opposition to talks with the PLO, since that organization demanded an "independent Palestinian PLO state between Israel and Jordan...withdrawal to the 1967 boundaries and negotiations over the 'right of return.'"[7]

Shamir's immediate reaction was that the plan reflected Rabin's private views.[8] However, this was not altogether accurate since, as Vice Premier Shimon Peres was quick to point out, the Labor Party had announced a similar plan on the eve of the 1988 elections.[9]

Early in the year under review, one Israeli cabinet member dissented from the nearly unanimous view that Israel ought not negotiate with the PLO. Minister of

Science and Development Ezer Weizmann declared himself in favor of talks with the PLO. His assessment was that no agreement could be reached through the Palestinians in the territories: they had no authority, and only the PLO could make decisions.[10] Throughout 1989, Weizmann reiterated this opinion, but without affecting government policy. Nor did the participation of dovish Knesset members in meetings with PLO personalities outside Israel have any concrete impact on national policy. However, they did raise doubts among some sections of the Israeli public, whether the authentic Palestinians to whom Israel was anxious to talk could indeed be found in the territories without PLO consent. All Palestinian leaders in the territories with whom prominent Israelis continued to meet refused, as in the past, to consider themselves qualified to represent the Palestinian people. It made no difference whether Israel talked to Palestinians it thought "moderate" or to Palestinians it thought to be staunch PLO supporters; the reply was the same. When some Israelis believed that the most prominent among the PLO supporters, Faysal al-Husayni, would be less inhibited than other Palestinian personalities to negotiate, they were soon disabused. The Palestinians in the territories refused to act independently of the PLO and thus rejected the Rabin proposal.[11]

Almost five months were to elapse between the early Israeli peace proposal and its actual emergence after adoption by the Israeli Government on 14 May 1989. During this period Shamir was unperturbed by calls from his Labor Party minister to expedite the process. He urged his colleagues not to grow impatient; the problem was much too complicated for instant results.[12] Furthermore, Shamir continued to hope that he would turn many countries back from their increasing acceptance of the PLO. In February, he visited Paris where he tried to persuade President François Mitterrand of Israel's determination to find Palestinian interlocutors in the territories. He pointed out that his quest was made considerably more difficult by countries like France, which not only had relations with the PLO, but was upgrading them and might invite Yasir 'Arafat, the PLO chairman, to visit Paris.[13]

While Shamir was in Paris, his foreign minister, Moshe Arens, met in Cairo with Eduard Shevardnadze, the Soviet foreign minister. In vain did Arens argue the Israeli case against the PLO. Shevardnadze was certain that 'Arafat could not appoint Palestinians from the West Bank and Gaza to negotiate in his stead. It was equally sure that without the PLO and the USSR no peace process was possible.[14] When Arens told him that the Soviet Union could play a role in such a process only after restoring diplomatic relations with Israel, Shevardnadze countered this by restating the Soviet position that Israel would first have to accept an international conference and a dialogue with the PLO. In an important speech that Shevardnadze delivered in Cairo, he said that in "denying freedom of choice" to the Palestinians "Israel was weakening both its security as a state and the legitimacy of its own self-determination."

Moreover, Israel was "losing support among her staunchest friends" and was becoming isolated, and the question of "whether to impose sanctions against Israel" was being raised.[15] There were not many people in Israel who thought, before Shevardnadze's Cairo address, that the time had come to see whether Israel could already accept a more active Soviet role, along with the US, in the peace process. His harsh words reduced their numbers even further. (For Shevardnadze's peace proposals, see chapter on the Soviet Union and the ME.)

The US was, therefore, as in the past the only country with which Israel could hope to cooperate in efforts to achieve a settlement with the Arabs. However, there was a new Administration in Washington headed by people not well-known in Israel. The fact that the Administration had committed itself to the policy of carrying on the dialogue with the PLO, started by the Reagan Administration in December 1988, raised many questions in the minds of the Israeli leaders. In these circumstances it was natural that the first high-level contacts were between Arens and the Bush Administration and were essentially preparatory. Indeed, a mere three weeks later his visit was followed by Shamir's.

Arens met with US President George Bush and Secretary of State Baker (13 March). Both American leaders introduced a note of urgency. Bush stressed that the "US does not want to miss an opportunity for peace in the Middle East," and that it expected "progress" and "new ideas." Baker was equally insistent. He noted, however, that he and Arens had agreed to accord the highest priority to the need for progress. He emphasized that the aim was direct negotiations, a point that certainly pleased Arens. Altogether, Arens was quite satisfied with his talks. He told newsmen that the president and secretary had not asked Israel to make any changes in its foreign policy.[16] Arens was also much encouraged by a letter signed by 14 Republican senators in which they recognized that Israel "must make its decisions based on its own security needs and its own sovereignty. Anything less would undermine the hope for peace."[17] However, one incident marred this otherwise positive picture. A day after his meeting with Arens, Baker told a congressional panel that if it proved impossible to have meaningful direct negotiations without involving the PLO, "we would then have to see negotiations between Israelis and representatives of the PLO." This statement caused Arens to remark that Baker had not said "anything like that" to him. Arens felt that Baker's statement would encourage local Palestinians, whom Israel wanted to engage in a negotiation, to spurn any Israeli overtures and to turn to the PLO. Baker, however, stood his ground and in additional testimony before a congressional committee a day later, he said that the US ought not to rule out anything if it could help to achieve peace, otherwise "we could be faulted if we did not."[18]

Despite this apparently determined US stand, a *New York Times* editorial thought that the "Baker approach might represent mere temporizing by a timid disorganized Administration."[19] This seemed at the end of the year, nine months later, a somewhat hasty judgment when one considered the continuous efforts, albeit low profile, that the Administration made in the year under review.

Shamir met with Bush three days after Egyptian President Husni Mubarak's meeting with him (see below). Bush, in his departure remarks to the Egyptian president (3 April) said, *inter alia,* that Egypt and the US shared the goals of "security for Israel, the end of occupation, and the achievement of Palestinian political rights."[20] The Arabs assessed these last two phrases ("end of occupation" and "Palestinian political rights") as highly significant and soon elevated them to the status of policy principles which they hoped the US would prevail upon Israel to implement. Shamir presented to Bush and Baker a rather complete outline of a plan for advancing the peace process. In its official formulation the plan was entitled "The Four-Point Plan" (see Appendix II).[21] It contained four suggestions: (1) that Egypt and Israel renew their commitment to the Camp David Accords; (2) that the Arab countries replace belligerency toward and boycott of Israel with negotiation and peace; (3) that an international effort, led by the US, be made to solve the problem of the Arab refugees; and (4) that free elections be held in the West Bank and Gaza to choose Palestinian representatives for negotiations on an interim settlement in which a self-governing administration would be set up.

The linchpin was the plan's fourth point which provided for the elections in the territories. Bush endorsed this idea. He felt that "elections...can be designed to contribute to a political process of a dialogue and negotiation." The Israelis and Palestinians ought to "arrive at a mutually acceptable formula for elections." He promised American help toward that end.[22] This was a carefully drafted endorsement of a general concept and Bush was perfectly aware of the many differences that existed between the US and Israel. However, the US president was much encouraged by Shamir's assurance that "all options are open to negotiation."[23] To a large extent, this statement persuaded the US that Shamir's ideas were "something new and different from Camp David."[24] Shamir himself elaborated on it in an interview: "We are committed to negotiations in which the future of the territories...will be determined without preconditions and without our defining that solution at this point — except for one thing: it must be a solution that will be acceptable to *both sides*."[25] However, Shamir also totally rejected negotiations with the PLO, any steps that could lead to a Palestinian state, or to a change of the status of East Jerusalem. Even the very demand to exchange territory for peace was anathema to him.

Peres viewed this outcome with skepticism. He wondered whether Shamir had won a time-out to achieve a turning point. In order to gain acceptance for the election idea the US would, so he believed, mediate between Israel and the PLO although this was not to Israel's taste. Arens vehemently denied this.[26] The Americans also denied that this was their intention. A senior US official explained that the US had a dialogue with the PLO, but that "was separate from being a mediator." The purpose of the dialogue was "to determine whether or not the PLO commitment in a rhetorical sense to the principles of peace can, in fact, and will be translated by the PLO into behavior that will support a practical peace process."[27]

Over the rest of the year the question of whether the US was indeed violating what had become an Israeli taboo and was, in fact, mediating between the PLO and Israel became the subject of frequent controversy in Israel. The Americans throughout were careful to make it appear that their dialogue with the PLO was quite distinct from their efforts to advance the election idea. Egypt became the conduit to the PLO. Israel formally refused to be briefed on what transpired in the US-PLO dialogue or what the Egyptians told the Americans about their contacts with the PLO. Shamir, Arens, and many other Israelis, including a fair number of Labor Party members absolutely refused to have anything to do with the PLO since this could imply acceptance of that organization's major demand — an independent Palestinian state as well as the "right of return" to Israel of the Palestinians living in the diaspora. These demands they viewed as a threat to Israel's very existence.

On 14 May, the Israeli Government adopted by a 20–6 vote a resolution constituting Israel's peace plan. It encompassed the elements of the Four-Point Plan which Shamir had presented to the Americans in April, but it contained more details about the elections in the territories. The elections were to be held in an "atmosphere devoid of violence, threats, and terror," a hint to the Intifada. They were to enable the 1.7m. West Bank and Gaza Palestinians to elect representatives to conduct negotiations for a five-year transitional period. Thereafter, negotiations for a "permanent solution" would follow. The interlock between the two stages was to be assured by a timetable limiting the transitional period. During the second stage "all the proposed options for an agreed settlement" would be examined. The Israeli Government was too divided to commit itself to anything beyond the expression of readiness to examine all options. There was no explicit mention of withdrawal from the territories. Resolutions 242 and 338 were referred to in a carefully circumscribed phrase which said that the "peace process delineated by the initiative is based on 242 and 338 upon which the Camp David Accords are founded." Some points were left ambiguous, others were skipped over altogether. Thus, for example, the important issue of the residents of East Jerusalem and whether they would participate in the vote was not mentioned. (For full text, see Appendix I.)[28]

The Israeli plan was the outcome of an understanding between Shamir and Rabin. Rabin had no objection to the "land for peace" formula or to let the East Jerusalem Arabs participate in the elections.[29] However, in deference to Shamir's views and to the strong opposition Shamir was facing from his right wing in Likud, Rabin did not insist on the inclusion of these two crucial elements.

Two weeks earlier, Secretary Baker had sent a letter to Arens expressing support for the elections proposal, but also enumerating the requirements he deemed necessary to make it more acceptable to the Palestinians. He mentioned such matters as the participation of "Palestinians who do not currently reside in the West Bank and Gaza" and of the inhabitants of East Jerusalem. Concerning Israel's readiness also to entertain options for a solution, Baker specifically said that this could include "the demands for sovereignty."[30]

That Shamir was totally opposed to any concessions more than those provided for by the peace plan, soon became clear when he said to the Likud Knesset faction that in his opinion the Arabs of East Jerusalem would not be permitted to vote and that Israel "will not give even one inch of land to the Arabs, we will not give them anything." This was his way of rejecting the "land for peace" demand. Even so, Shamir could not assuage his right-wing opposition, in particular his three Likud government colleagues, one of whom was his deputy. The three ministers had voted against the plan and attacked it publicly. They requested that a special meeting of the Likud Central Committee be convened to discuss the plan (see chapter on Israel).

The task facing Israeli diplomacy now was to muster international support for the plan. Egypt and the US were the two obvious key countries. Egypt certainly had to play a role in persuading the Palestinians that the Israeli initiative was sincerely meant and deserved their trust. If Mubarak consented to meet with Shamir this would mean that Egypt reaffirmed the Camp David Accords and fulfilled the expectations spelled out in the first of the four points. The US was even more crucial to the plan's success. Its attitude toward the plan could determine that of other countries, including Egypt's.

Arens met with Baker (19 May) and found him quite receptive. It was true that the latter continued to believe that without additional Israeli concessions of the kind he had mentioned in his letter, progress would be highly unlikely, if not impossible. However, Arens persuaded him not to press Israel to provide additional details on the nature of the Palestinian election. He appealed to him to be sensitive to the Israeli political scene and not to expect more decisions when there was no Arab negotiating partner in sight. On the whole, Arens won broad US support for the Israeli plan. Moreover, Baker had not stated that the US would hold negotiations with the PLO concerning the initiative.[31] This suited Arens very well.

However, only three days after this promising meeting there came a somewhat rude awakening. Baker delivered a speech to the annual conference of the America-Israel Public Affairs Committee, the pro-Israeli lobby. The speech was on the whole as supportive of Israel as any of the speeches made by the US secretaries of state in recent years, but there was in it a particularly jarring phrase. In referring to the occupied territories, he called upon Israel "to lay aside, once and for all, the unrealistic vision of a greater Israel" and to "forswear annexation, stop settlement activity." He balanced this by calling on the Palestinians to renounce their illusion of controlling all of Palestine and to accept Israel as "a neighbor and partner in trade and human contact."[32] But to the Israelis this appeal to the Palestinians was too evenhanded to alleviate the pain caused by the appeal addressed to them. Shamir considered the reference to greater Israel "superfluous and not useful," but nevertheless thought that "90% of the speech was correct." What mattered most was that Baker had expressed full support for Israel's initiative and had asked the Arabs, the Palestinians, and the Soviets to contribute to its success.[33] More significant than these exchanges was the Administration's obvious readiness to reassume an active role in the peace process. The State Department's spokesperson declared its "wholehearted" support for Israel's election proposal, adding that Israel had given the US something to work with and that the US was "now asking the Arabs to give it something to work with." This statement came a few hours before Rabin met with Bush, who declared his support for the Israeli initiative.[34]

The US Congress went even further. In an unusual display of unanimity, 95 US senators signed a letter to Secretary Baker in which they stated their conviction that Israel's peace initiative was "both sincere and far-reaching." They urged the Administration to endorse it strongly.[35]

Yet many difficult problems remained. Likud leaders believed that American attempts to persuade the PLO to signal discreetly to the Palestinians in the territories to accept the Israeli initiative, were doomed to fail. They considered it naive to assume that the PLO would release its grip on the Palestinians in the territories merely to accommodate the US.[36] For the PLO, the stakes were much too high to do this.

The Egyptians, too, were discouraged by Shamir and Arens from mediating between Israel and the PLO. In June (11–12) Minister of State for Foreign Affairs Butrus Butrus-Ghali came to Israel to offer Egypt's good offices in contacts with the PLO. Shamir told him that Israel was not interested in negotiations with the PLO, but welcomed Egypt's aid in encouraging local Palestinians to take part in the elections.[37] The Egyptians, like the Americans, met with the local Palestinians throughout the year, but devoted their main attention to the PLO.

The American dialogue with the PLO did not fare well. The US was continuing to adhere to its policy of "nonsupport" for an independent Palestinian state, a serious disappointment to the PLO. (For details, see sections on the PLO in this chapter and the chapter on the US and the ME.) The relations between Egypt and the PLO were under no similar constraints. Egypt had, in the immediately preceding years, again become the PLO's main patron. The relations between Mubarak and PLO Chairman Yasir 'Arafat were frequent and close (see chapter on Egypt). It did not take long before the Americans began to use the Egyptian channel to try and wrest from the PLO what they could not get directly. Obviously, the US and Israel continued to hold quite different views on the PLO's role. Israel saw its election proposal as a means of finding authentic Palestinian leaders outside the PLO; the US, however, was looking for ways to involve the PLO with the election proposal. These different strategies were bound to create tensions between Israel and the US. Thus, when in the summer months Egypt made a diplomatic move, Shamir and the Likud, weighing how best to react, were more concerned over repercussions in Washington than in Cairo. The specter of a confrontation with the US was never altogether absent.[38]

The Egyptian move was in the form of a questionnaire containing 10 questions about Israel's peace initiative. If Israel responded satisfactorily to them Egypt would rate Israel's initiative as worthy of consideration. The 10 questions seemed tailor-made to fit Labor, but showed no concern for Likud's proscriptions. The three particularly objectionable issues were the participation of East Jerusalem residents in the elections, termination of all settlement activities, and the acceptance of the territory-for-peace formula.[39] (For details see section on Egypt in this chapter.)

For three months the Israeli Government was spared the need to take a definitive position on the Egyptian move simply because Egypt did not transmit the ten-point document officially. Yet on 8 August, the Labor Party Central Committee adopted 12 principles to guide it in negotiations. Except for a declaration of opposition to an independent Palestinian state, a restatement of the demand for "security borders," and a reference to "areas of Jewish settlement that would remain in Jewish hands," Labor, in fact, accepted all 10 Egyptian demands.[40] This laid the ground for a crisis that was soon to come. A month later (8 September) Rabin met Baker again. The two men reportedly decided to seek a more active role for Egypt by which they meant that the Egyptian Ten Points deserved receiving fullest Israeli attention, if not support. Rabin was given a document of Egyptian provenance but which was prompted by the US, saying that the PLO agreed to negotiations between Israel and a Palestinian delegation consisting of residents from the territories and of Palestinians recently expelled from there, the Palestinian delegation would negotiate on the basis of Egypt's Ten Points, Egypt would assist the two parties in the talks, and the PLO would not insist on a UN role in the first stage of the talks.[41] The snag was the emphasis on the PLO as the only authority entitled to make decisions concerning the Palestinian delegation. Rabin could not but assume that the Israeli Government, with Labor support assured, would reject the document. To try and convince Rabin that Egypt had done its best and that the time had come for Israel to weigh the pros and cons of the Egyptian proposal, Mubarak invited Rabin to Cairo.

Now that the Egyptian Ten Points had assumed great importance there remained two possibilities. Either Israel accepted them as a basis for the negotiations as Labor had in effect already done, or, as a minimum, let the Palestinians base their opening position on it. In both cases, Israel would be told that the Ten Points would not be considered an alternative to the Israeli election proposal. A senior American diplomat explained that the Ten Points merely represented "Egypt's acceptance of the elections concept and Egypt's view on how to get to the elections and make them work."[42]

When Rabin returned to Israel from Washington he pressed for an early decision. However the "Forum of Four" top ministers[43] failed to resolve any of the differences. Shamir and Arens maintained their opposition to Mubarak's Ten Points, now at last officially transmitted by Cairo (15 September), and to the proposed nature of the Palestinian delegation, specifically that it include Palestinians who had been expelled from the territories. Peres and Rabin explained that Israel was not requested to embrace the Ten Points but merely to agree to a preliminary meeting with a Palestinian delegation.[44] This was quite true except that Cairo kept making it clear that without the PLO the peace process would stall. Mubarak said so himself often squarely, sometimes obliquely (see section on Egypt in this chapter). The "Forum of Four" deferred its decision to a meeting of the 12-member Inner Cabinet which would convene after Rabin's return from Cairo. Under these circumstances, Rabin's meeting with Mubarak could do little to move the process forward. Rabin was authorized to tell Mubarak that if other points of disagreement were worked out satisfactorily, the Israeli Government would accept an Egyptian invitation to talks in Cairo. This was, of course, a heavily qualified acceptance.[45]

Rabin's visit to Cairo incurred Shamir's displeasure. He said that Rabin had "surprised" him by adopting unexpected positions in his talk with Mubarak. Shamir had expected Rabin to coordinate his moves more loyally with him and not make irreversible commitments; but Rabin had extolled the merits of the Egyptian Ten Points, and it seemed that he had agreed to let Mubarak choose the Palestinian delegation after consulting with whomsoever he wanted. This meant the PLO.

Rabin explained that he had not said or done anything that ought to have come as a surprise to Shamir. He had not strayed from any government decision. The latest among them (of 23 July) had barely saved the Israeli peace initiative from Likud's attempts to make it much stiffer. Labor had threatened to quit the government if the damage was not rectified. To settle the crisis, Shamir agreed to let the government adopt a decision reaffirming the 14 May peace initiative and stating that it remained valid "without additions or changes."[46] This reaffirmation, and in particular the phrase "without additions or changes," went some way toward offsetting the effects of the resolutions adopted by the Likud Central Committee three weeks earlier (5 July) at the instigation of the three Likud ministers who continued to fight the peace initiative (see above). At the Central Committee meeting, Shamir, in what seemed a reversal of stand, instead of opposing the move, identified himself with the demands of the three ministers in a long speech.[47] The Central Committee's endorsement of his speech was seen as a victory for Shamir's opponents and a setback for the peace initiative. Thus, when Rabin said that he had been faithful in Cairo to the cabinet decisions, he meant, of course, the decisions as agreed by Likud and Labor with whatever flexibility they afforded.

Shamir, for his part, was not altogether mistaken when he thought, in the aftermath of Rabin's Cairo visit, that his defense minister had gone beyond the agreed guidelines. Rabin was publicly and almost unreservedly expressing agreement to let Egypt initiate a meeting with a Palestinian delegation and to be the one to issue the invitations. He also agreed that the Palestinians could raise Mubarak's Ten Points at the meeting with the Israelis.[48] Shamir could not but be concerned that the only Labor leader whom he had trusted was close to abandoning him. The Israeli media contributed considerably to deepen his concern. It carried such headlines as "Shamir-Rabin rift grows wider, defense minister lauds Mubarak Plan";[49] and published such articles as the one by a pundit about "Rabin's Transmutation."

It seemed for a while that the National Unity Government could not survive the

Shamir-Rabin contretemps. Two events that occurred in the three weeks that followed had a direct impact on the Shamir government's chances of survival. Arens's meetings with Mubarak, Baker, and with Egypt's deputy prime minister and foreign minister, 'Ismat 'Abd al- Majid, in Washington, proved crucial in assuring the government's continued existence. Then, an Egyptian document conveyed to Israel on 4 October almost caused its breakup. Labor threatened to leave the government if Israel did not respond positively to what they described as an Egyptian invitation to talks with a Palestinian delegation in Cairo. Labor insisted that the Israeli answer to the document be voted upon in the Inner Cabinet. It prepared a resolution that expressed readiness to accept the Egyptian proposal, but also made it clear that the Israeli delegation would go to Cairo on the basis of the Israeli peace initiative; further, that Israel would immediately start talks on the composition of the Palestinian delegation.[50] Peres and Rabin concluded that the Egyptian document, even though it stated positions that fell short of what was acceptable to them, ought to be tested in talks since there was no other way to attempt to make progress. When the resolution was put to the vote it resulted in a 6-6 tie. This meant that it had not been adopted. Still, Labor did not carry out its threat to quit. Instead, it went along with a proposal by Arens to encourage the US to become again directly involved in the peace efforts. Arens recalled that Baker had indicated to him American readiness to do just that. Moreover, after the Bush-Mubarak encounter (2 October), Baker stated publicly that the US, Egypt, and Israel could meet "in some way to determine the Palestinian representation"; such a meeting "would give Israel a chop on the representation of people in the occupied territories [who] would represent Palestinians."[51]

To bolster his argument, Arens quoted from the report of his talk with Baker (21 September). According to the report, Baker asked Arens what he thought of a joint Israeli-Egyptian-American agreement on the Palestinian delegation. Arens replied that this was a matter for the Israeli cabinet to decide, whereupon Baker urged him to take it up there. In the tripartite meeting (Baker-'Abd al-Majid-Arens) a day later, Baker again proposed that each of the three countries come to the meeting with a list of names of Palestinians.[52] Arens was convinced that the offer Baker had made was more advantageous to Israel than the Egyptian proposal. However, the Labor ministers remained doubtful whether a US offer existed at all. Even if it did, they did not think that it made all the difference. Notwithstanding their doubts they went along with Aren's idea.

It soon emerged that Baker had meant what he had said. The deadlock in the Israeli cabinet over the Egyptian document was certainly an added reason that prompted him to act. Within two days (8 October), he transmitted a brief text, which soon became known as the Baker Plan or the Five-Point Plan. This document, except for two minor changes, remained essentially unaltered throughout. It stated:

> 1. The United States understands that because Egypt and Israel have been working hard on the peace process, there is agreement that an Israeli delegation could conduct a dialogue with a Palestinian delegation in Cairo.
> 2. The United States understands that Egypt cannot substitute itself for the Palestinians and Egypt will consult on all aspects of that dialogue. Egypt will also consult with Israel and the United States.
> 3. The United States understands that Israel will attend the dialogue only after a satisfactory list of Palestinians has been worked out.

4. The United States understands that the Government of Israel will come to the dialogue on the basis of the Israeli Government's 14 May initiative. The United States further understands that Palestinians will come to the dialogue prepared to discuss elections and the negotiating process in accordance with Israel's initiative. The US understands, therefore, that Palestinians would be free to raise issues that related to their opinions on how to make elections and the negotiating process succeed.

5. In order to facilitate this process, the United States proposes that the foreign ministers of Israel, Egypt, and the United States meet in Washington within two weeks.[53]

Most of Israel's requests for textual changes were rejected. In paragraph 1, Israel asked to make it plain that Palestinian delegates would be residents of the West Bank and Gaza; in paragraph 3, it suggested specifying that the US, Egypt, and Israel would prepare the list of delegates. In paragraph 4, it asked to delete altogether the word "negotiations," twice mentioned in the first version of the Five Points. As a compromise, Baker agreed to replace "negotiations" with "negotiating process."

The negotiations having reached a fairly advanced stage and the red lines having already been drawn some time earlier, the US did not have much leeway left as it made its diplomatic move. The PLO had apparently not completely rejected Mubarak's Ten Points and therefore the US wanted to reopen the discussion. Moreover, as the Egyptian ambassador in Israel quite rightly pointed out, Israel had not rejected the Ten Points. Its Inner Cabinet had rejected the later (4 October) Egyptian document. He predicted that if Baker's Five Points did not contradict Mubarak's Ten Points, "everything will be fine."[54]

Shamir and Arens insisted on receiving the strongest possible assurances that the PLO would not be included in the dialogue in any way and that the talks would not stray to topics besides the elections. The US had no difficulty with the first requirement. On numerous occasions, Administration officials had stated publicly that the US would not try "to get Israel to negotiate with the PLO." Naturally, this was a promise the US was free to make. Concerning the second Israeli requirement, the US could do no more than promise *to try* to convince the Palestinians to focus on the election proposal.[55]

At the end of October, Shamir and Arens accepted Baker's Five Points.[56] They could not ignore completely the possibility that Israel's relations with the US would come under a strain if they did not. Shamir had accepted an invitation to address, in the US, the annual meeting of the largest American Jewish organization.[57] The close relations between the US and Israel made it almost *de rigueur* for an Israeli prime minister to meet with an American president when visiting the US. However, Bush kept delaying his reply concerning the meeting thereby signaling his discomfort with Shamir's positions. Only when the "Forum of Four" (see above) accepted the Five Points (5 November) did Bush announce the time for the encounter (16 November). Israel's decision in favor of the Five Points was made easier by Baker's indication of readiness to provide Israel with side assurances concerning those issues that were left vague in the document.[58] Israel's reply was drafted in the form of an Inner Cabinet decision. The acceptance was, in accordance with Baker's request, couched in unambiguous language. However, Israel added certain "assumptions" which it expected to materialize in order to make sure that the negotiations would indeed be consistent with Israel's 14 May Peace Initiative. (For full text, see Appendix III.)

Since Baker's Five Points had already covered much of the same ground, it seemed, on the face of it, that two of the "assumptions" posed no difficulty anymore. Thus, Israel expected the dialogue to begin after agreement on the composition of the Palestinian delegation. Baker's third point had already taken care of that. It stated the American understanding that Israel would attend the dialogue only after a satisfactory list of Palestinians had been worked out. Regarding Israel's assumption that the dialogue would focus on the election process in the territories, it appeared that Baker's fourth point dealt with that.

Israel had to wait over a month before it could begin to discuss its requirements, because Egypt had not yet given its reply to Baker. This happened finally on 6 December (see section on Egypt in this chapter). The US conveyed to Israel Egypt's response in a generally phrased document stating that the US was satisfied that the Egyptian reply was in the affirmative. Peres was quite correct in observing that Israel had no problem with the indirect manner by which Israel was informed of Egypt's consent. The US in its role of honest broker could vouch for Egypt.[59] Shamir and Arens joined Peres and Rabin in the "Forum of Four" to conclude (8 December) that Egypt had indeed accepted the Five Points, but they remained wondering whether Egypt had not really acted as proxy for the PLO. Arens was not ready to ignore a statement by the Egyptian ambassador in Washington who admitted that Egypt had conveyed the PLO's reply to Baker.[60] To Shamir and Arens this constituted proof that Egypt was acting as a "mailman" for the PLO, a totally unacceptable development to them and perhaps to Peres and Rabin as well. True, Peres and Rabin thought that Israel should not go over the Egyptian reply with a fine-tooth comb, but for them, too, there were lines they would not cross.[61]

In practical terms, these questions did not terminate Israel's cooperation with the US effort. In mid-December, it sent a senior Israeli official to Washington to discuss the Israeli requirements for US assurances. His mission was only partly successful. On the question of the PLO, the US was prepared to assure Israel in writing that "it was not the aim of the US, in the current effort, to get Israel into a dialogue with the PLO." The qualification "in the current effort" was disappointing. On the question of strictly limiting the talks to issues connected with the elections in the territories, the US said that in the opening statement of the talks each side would be free to raise any issue. As to Israel having a say in choosing the Palestinian representatives, the US said that it could not go beyond what was stated in the Five Points (paragraph 3) namely, that the US understood that Israel would come to the talks only after a satisfactory list of Palestinians had been worked out.[62] However, in conveying its responses to Israel the US did not completely close the door to further contacts with Israel on the question of assurances.

As the year came to a close, no date for the tripartite foreign ministers' meeting (paragraph 4 of the Five Points) had yet been set and plainly much work remained to be done.

EGYPT

The year 1989 saw the complete restoration of Egypt's standing in the Arab world. The Arab League summit in Casablanca (23–26 May) formally readmitted Egypt to the Arab League. In the second part of the year, Egypt restored diplomatic relations with Syria and was moving toward normalization of its relations with Libya after Mubarak and Mu'ammar Qadhdhafi convened together, thereby completing the process that had started six years earlier in September 1983, when Jordan renewed its diplomatic relations with Egypt. However, one problem remained to be resolved: Egypt was the only Arab country at peace with Israel. This was still irksome even though Egypt had been welcomed back to the Arab fold, respected by all Arab countries, including the radical ones, and had become the PLO's main protagonist since 'Arafat's dramatic meeting with President Husni Mubarak in December 1983. In 1988 Egypt played a leading role in the events that resulted in the decisions the PLO adopted at the 19th PNC at the end of that year. Egypt could also take credit for persuading the US to open the dialogue with the PLO. (See further in chapter on Egypt.)

Egypt was much encouraged by the success of its policy toward the PLO. It was determined to continue to exert further efforts to bring about negotiations between the Palestinian organization and Israel.[63] Mubarak announced this at the beginning of the year. He asserted that 'Arafat was a most moderate and strong Palestinian leader who spoke for most of his compatriots and who had clearly renounced terrorism.[64] He seemed convinced that the Palestinians, by which he meant the PLO, had already made all the concessions needed to enable peace to be established. In fact, as in the past he vouched for the PLO by affirming that it had accepted to live in peace alongside Israel in a "Palestinian state that ought to be linked with Jordan in a confederation."[65]

The terms for a settlement with Israel were, as far as Egypt was concerned, nonnegotiable. Since the more radical factions in the PLO did not support 'Arafat unconditionally, Mubarak knew that he could count only on 'Arafat and his mainstream followers to support Egypt's diplomatic efforts. Egypt accepted it as a fact of life that 'Arafat could not stray from his organization's decisions because of the radical groups. This explained the innumerable Egyptian protestations throughout the year that Egypt was not acting as a substitute for the PLO, that the PLO alone would decide what to accept and what to reject, and that Egypt would not impose its views on the PLO.[66] Egypt's long history of support for the Palestinian cause was frequently recalled by Egyptian leaders. Mubarak proclaimed on one occasion: "The Palestine issue is Egypt's issue. Egypt has been involved in it right from the beginning and we will support this cause, which we consider one of our fundamental concerns."[67] It seemed also self-evident to Egypt that eventually Israel would have to accept the PLO since there "could be no solution without the PLO."[68] Israel's search for non-PLO Palestinians was futile. Usama al-Baz, first under secretary of the Foreign Ministry and director of the president's office for political affairs, who played a key role in Egypt's efforts in 1989, went so far as to say that the PLO would be represented or actually be present in a dialogue with Israel "from the first day" of the talks. The only way the PLO could accommodate Israel, he added, was by choosing delegates to the talks who supported peace, but the PLO would do the choosing.[69]

Even if such declarations were made in order to play down the influence that Egypt could or did exert by virtue of its prestige and presumed selflessness in acting as a go-between, the fact remained that Egypt wanted the PLO itself to make the decisions.

The immediate objective of Egypt's diplomacy in the year under review was to bring about a high-level dialogue between Palestinians and Israeli officials with Egypt as host.[70] On several occasions PLO leaders had expressed readiness to participate in a preliminary meeting with Israeli officials as a step leading toward the international conference — one of their most insistent demands.[71] The Egyptians believed that this objective could be melded with the Israeli proposal to hold elections in the territories. It was obvious that Israel would have to find Palestinian representatives to discuss the elections and their modalities. Thus, if the PLO accepted the election proposal in principle, work could start on the formation of a Palestinian delegation to the preliminary meeting. First, however, Egypt had to overcome the PLO's reluctance to accept the Israeli election plan as announced. The plan had to be made to fit "Arab requirements," which were quite different from those of Israel.

The Egyptian moves materialized *pari passu* with the emergence of the Israeli peace initiative (see section on Israel above). Before they began to assume shape, Mubarak's meetings with Bush and Baker in Washington early in April were bound to affect them greatly. Mubarak was encouraged by Bush's declaration of support for the principle of land for peace and for the political rights of the Palestinians.[72] Still, he would have liked Bush to have announced his support for Palestinian *national* rights rather than merely for *political* rights. Mubarak indicated this clearly when, in his White House statement, he referred advisedly to Palestinian national rights.[73] Al-Baz elaborated on it in an interview. He said that *political* rights, as distinct from *national* rights, implied a state that was not wholly independent, pointing out that the Americans themselves had said so. For his part, he interpreted the US position as acceptance of a Palestinian state [i.e., a state less than fully independent] linked to Jordan. Al-Baz actually described those links as confederal, although the US itself had never used this term to define the status of a self-governing Palestinian entity acceptable to them.[74] The Egyptians concluded that the gaps between the Arab and American positions were narrowing, a finding that strengthened their resolve to be actively involved in the peace efforts.

Egypt was prudent in reacting to Israel's election proposal. One of Mubarak's first comments was that the proposal ought to have been part of an agreement in principle to convene the international conference at some date, so that the PLO, if it went along with the Israeli offer, would have something to look forward to. Moreover, the Israeli idea was not specific enough concerning such questions as who would supervise the elections, under what law would they be held, and whether East Jerusalem was included.[75] These were the kind of questions the Egyptians would soon develop further.

A month after Israel announced its peace initiative (14 May), Egypt sent its Minister of State for Foreign Affairs Butrus Butrus-Ghali to Israel. Butrus-Ghali told the Israelis that their plan contained "several positive elements but also negative ones, about which Egypt had reservations." He told them that Egypt wanted to attempt to revise the plan so as to include "certain Palestinian demands." Thus revised, it could serve as a basis for negotiations. Egypt had no formal "mandate" from either the Palestinians or the Israelis to mediate, but was nevertheless prepared to act as mediator. Interviewed on Israeli television, Butrus-Ghali did not hide that he was including the PLO in referring to the Palestinian people. After all, Egypt had "close relations with the Palestinian people and the PLO."[76]

Soon after Butrus-Ghali's visit, Cairo completed its list of queries about the Israeli plan and enumerated them in a 10-point questionnaire. However, for reasons never explained, this document was not conveyed to Israel for nearly three months. At the end of June, Mubarak gave it to a visiting US congressman,[77] who, in turn, apprised Shamir and Arens of its existence. Two-and-a-half months later Arens complained that Egypt had still not transmitted the document to Israel, in spite of the fact that Egypt and Israel kept embassies in their respective capitals and that he, Arens, maintained contact with Foreign Minister 'Abd al- Majid.[78] The Egyptian ambassador in Israel admitted to not having transmitted the document. One Israeli correspondent reported from Cairo that the Egyptians admitted that a "bureaucratic blunder" had occurred.[79] The confusion surrounding this document was further compounded by the existence of several different versions. Finally, on 19 September the Egyptian Embassy in Israel provided the authoritative version (for full text see Appendix IV). It turned out that the text was no longer a questionnaire, but had taken the form of a set of conditions some of which were known to be unacceptable to Shamir and Arens. Israel was asked to commit itself in advance to the land-for-peace formula, to let the residents of East Jerusalem participate in the elections, and to desist from building new settlements in the territories. The Egyptian text was bound to disappoint the Palestinians too: the PLO was nowhere mentioned and there was no demand for Palestinian self-determination or for a Palestinian state. However, Egypt had a convincing explanation to offer the PLO. The ten-point document did not constitute an Egyptian plan. It was merely a way to find out what Israel really had in mind and whether it was prepared to meet certain conditions which would prevent using the elections to install an autonomy regime of unlimited duration on the West Bank and Gaza Strip. The Egyptians insisted that the elections lead toward a final settlement of the Palestinian question.[80]

Mubarak and 'Arafat met frequently throughout this period until, by the second week in September, it became known that 'Arafat accepted the Ten Points "in principle" (see section on the Palestinians and the PLO in this chapter). Acceptance in principle meant, in effect, that many conditions were attached to the reply, which seriously diminished its value.[81] It was then that the US urged Egypt to cut the Gordian knot by addressing an invitation to Israel to send a delegation to Cairo to meet with a Palestinian delegation. Egypt agreed to do this, but in order to secure Palestinian, i.e., PLO cooperation, the invitation referred explicitly and repeatedly to the PLO. It was shown to Rabin in Washington (8 September). It stated:

1. The PLO will accept negotiations between an Israeli delegation and a Palestinian delegation consisting of residents of the territories and from among those recently expelled from them.

2. The PLO will be ready to authorize the Palestinian delegation to consider the election plan on the basis of Egypt's Ten Points.

3. Egypt will assist the parties in their talks.

4. The PLO will not insist on a UN role in the first phase of the negotiations.[82]

Israel, which was banning any contacts with the PLO, ignored this invitation. This prompted Egypt to make a new and somewhat unusual move. Mubarak invited Rabin to Cairo. The visit took place on 18 September. The talks were, according to Mubarak, "extremely good"; he and Rabin had agreed on some points and there was "great understanding" between them.[83] Rabin had probably agreed, subject to the Government of Israel's approval, to the participation in the delegation of two to three Palestinians from among the deported residents of the West Bank and Gaza. Furthermore, Rabin, who had since 1981 been in favor of East Jerusalem Arabs taking part in the elections, explained this personal view to Mubarak mentioning the Likud's opposition. From what Rabin said, it appeared that Egypt would not insist on mentioning the PLO in the invitation. He also said that it was agreed that Egypt would announce the names of the Palestinians. Yet, he admitted that problems remained concerning the composition of the delegation, which had to be coordinated with "various elements," a possible hint to the PLO. Another problem was the "principles on which the meeting would be based." In simple terms, this meant that there was still no agreement on the opening stand with which the Palestinians would come to the meeting.[84]

Mubarak felt encouraged enough by Rabin's visit to believe that Israel was ready to accept a formal Egyptian invitation to send a delegation to Cairo. The invitation reached Israel on 4 October, but the Inner Cabinet rejected a Peres-Rabin proposal to accept it with some reservations. Shamir and Arens thought that many issues remained to be clarified. Rabin himself had mentioned several of them on his return from Cairo.

The next phase opened almost immediately after the Israeli rejection. Baker suggested (8 October) a meeting of himself, 'Abd al-Majid, and Arens if the two sides accepted certain conditions, which he listed in a five-point document (see section on Israel in this chapter). One of the points stated that the US understood that Egypt would not substitute itself for the Palestinians and Egypt would consult with them on all aspects of the envisioned dialogue. Whatever Baker meant when he referred to the Palestinians, so far as Egypt was concerned, the term "Palestinians" was synonymous with the PLO. To Israel, even to Labor, such synonymity was not acceptable. Notwithstanding the Israeli position, Egypt announced openly that it would coordinate its reply with the PLO. Mubarak declared in a joint news conference with 'Arafat that it was entirely up to the PLO to decide whether to accept Baker's Five Points. It is worth quoting Mubarak verbatim:

> It is not up to Egypt to decide on Baker's proposals, but to the PLO. When we form an opinion we do this in consultation with the PLO and President 'Arafat, who discusses it with his colleagues and then comes to us to reach an agreement so that we can explain it to the Americans. It is, therefore, up to the PLO to approve or disapprove of these proposals. The PLO will decide on this matter after consulting its ranks, and once they come up with a view or an opinion, we will adopt it in our talks with the United States and Israel.[85]

By the end of September, the PLO had accepted, albeit conditionally, Mubarak's Ten Points.[86] The absence of a direct reference to Mubarak's Points in Baker's document obliged the PLO to reconsider its decision. There was not much Mubarak could or would do to influence the PLO's decision. He pointed out to the PLO that Baker's Five Points had a limited objective in mind: to bring about a dialogue between the two sides. The PLO ought to answer merely one question, namely whether it would agree to come to a dialogue. Mubarak wanted them to reply affirmatively, but Egypt would not impose anything on them.[87]

Finally, on 6 December Egypt announced that it had sent its response to Baker.[88] The PLO described this response as "positive" and "flexible" and termed it "a Palestinian response."[89] This claim was not surprising in the light of Egypt's repeated protestations that it was not a surrogate for the PLO.

As to the substance of the reply, Mubarak summed it up tersely: "The PLO poses conditions, and Israel poses conditions. The principle [itself] of Baker's Five Points is accepted conditionally, by both sides."[90] Al-Baz explained that the PLO agreed to elections in the occupied territories, but only if they were part of an unbroken series of steps aimed at reaching a comprehensive settlement.[91]

It was obvious, therefore, that the Egyptian response, which was to all intents and purposes that of the PLO, was hedged even though presented as "positive." It remained to be seen what precisely Egyptian diplomacy had accomplished in the many months of toil and would continue to attempt to accomplish in the months ahead.

JORDAN

When King Husayn announced Jordan's decision to sever its administrative and legal links with the West Bank (31 July 1988) many observers in Israel and elsewhere doubted the seriousness of this step. They were wondering whether the king's move was not essentially tactical. In view of Israel's adamant refusal to deal with the PLO, they found it extremely difficult to envision a continuation of the peace process when its success depended so much on Jordan. Indeed, the whole effort in 1988, engineered by US Secretary of State George Shultz, was essentially riveted on Jordan. And yet the very assumption that made the peace process so heavily reliant on that country, prior to Husayn's disengagement, was questionable. US and Israeli diplomacy refused to accept at face value the frequently repeated Jordanian disclaimer that Jordan would be a surrogate for the Palestinians or for the PLO. Even in times of tension between Jordan and the PLO, Jordanian officials, led by the king, remained absolutely determined not to appropriate for themselves the PLO's role. Thus, for example, in February 1986 when Husayn suspended Jordan's political coordination with the PLO leadership (see *MECS* 1986, pp. 442–49) he was careful not to cut Jordan's ties with the PLO completely. A more recent case was provided in April 1988, during the Shultz mission. Four months before Jordan's disengagement it handed the US a document which contained the solemn affirmation that "Jordan will not represent the Palestinian people at the [international] conference nor will it negotiate the settlement of the Palestinian problem on behalf of the PLO."[92]

Clearly, without belittling the role that Jordan might have assumed in the peace process prior to its disengagement, some questions remained as to whether it would have acted in the manner in which the US and Israel cast it.

In the year under review, there were no longer such expectations. The US and Israel recognized Jordan's secondary role, without however completely relinquishing hope that it would one day make a significant contribution to a peace settlement.

Husayn appeared at peace with his decision. He never tired of stressing the advantages that had accrued from it. Jordan was no longer suspected by the Palestinians of wishing to regain the territories in order to rule over them, nor could it be said that Jordan envied the PLO its role as representative of the Palestinians. The relations were no longer beset by "impurities," as one Jordanian minister put it. On the contrary, Husayn and 'Arafat congratulated one another on their close working relationship and on the atmosphere of trust that existed between them.[93]

More important than the change in atmosphere was the dramatic effect that the disengagement decision had on the peace process by prompting the PLO, as Husayn said, "to abandon the confines of ideological puritanism and enter the realm of political realism."[94] Jordan's departure from the scene forced the US to adjust its policy to the new circumstances and to the new and difficult interlocutor who claimed the right to be the sole representative of the Palestinians — the PLO. The new Administration in Washington, headed by Bush, a man Husayn trusted implicitly, appeared well-suited to restart the peace process. With Reagan and Shultz no longer at the helm, Husayn was free to reveal that he had what he called "strong proof" that the Reagan Administration had been influenced by the "extremist Israeli right wing" and therefore attempted to influence Jordan to act as a surrogate for the Palestinians and accept a settlement based on the "Jordanian option." Husayn saw this as an effort to persuade him to deny the existence of the Palestinians as a people and to disregard their wish to achieve self-determination.[95]

Husayn did not believe that new initiatives or special diplomatic envoys were needed to advance the peace process.[96] In the 22 years since 1967 many attempts had been made, every possible avenue had been explored. The time had come to look for a shortcut. The obvious one was via the international peace conference and rapid implementation of UN Security Council Resolution 242. The conference would tackle all outstanding issues. There was the Palestinian question, of course, but there were also the other territories occupied by Israel and claimed by Lebanon and Syria. They ought not to be overlooked. It was inadvisable to try to settle one component of the conflict while neglecting the remaining ones.[97]

Husayn declared himself wholly in favor of an independent Palestinian state on "Palestinian national soil." The last three words were prudently added to indicate that the state would be restricted to the West Bank and would not aspire to territory lying east of the Jordan River.

On 7 January, the PLO office in Amman was recognized by Jordan as an embassy of the State of Palestine.[98] In his letter designating Mudar Badran head of the Jordanian Government after the elections in Jordan at the end of the year (8 November; see chapter on Jordan), Husayn instructed him to support the "legitimate struggle of the Palestinians to exercise their right to self-determination and the establishment of their independent state on their national soil."[99] The extent to which the king deemed it necessary to proclaim his support for an independent Palestinian state was clearly demonstrated when, in addressing a pro-Nato group in London in the summer of 1989, he devoted his whole speech to this issue. He insisted that "such a state must be an essential component of any peace settlement."[100] It was noteworthy that Husayn decided to argue in favor of the need for a Palestinian state before an audience among whom there were certain to be people inclined to doubt whether such a state would be a boon to the West.

The possibility that a confederal arrangement between Jordan and the Palestinian state would come about was frequently raised with Jordanian leaders. The usual reply was that after Israeli withdrawal from the West Bank and Gaza the Palestinians would express their opinion on relations with Jordan. If they decided in favor of a confederation Jordan would *then* consider and decide.[101]

Husayn himself seemed to be leaning toward a more forthcoming position. He told a journalist that Jordan stood ready to discuss with the PLO any ideas it had about the future. This statement did not make it altogether clear if the king was expressing readiness to discuss the confederation idea with the PLO even before the Israeli withdrawal, but neither did it seem to exclude this.[102]

Husayn's first reaction to Israel's election proposal was negative. Later, reassured by Bush, whom he met in the spring (20 April), that the US supported the idea as part of an effort aimed at a comprehensive settlement, he promised to be of assistance.[103] He told reporters that elections could be one element of a process leading to a comprehensive solution, but could not be an end in itself.[104] Like Mubarak (see section on Egypt in this chapter) he, too, thought that the Israeli Government had yet to spell out many details. Also, the elections should not be a means of creating a new Palestinian leadership distinct from the PLO.[105]

Cooperation between Husayn and Mubarak was close. Husayn supported Mubarak's Ten Points.[106] He agreed with the PLO and Mubarak himself that they were the bare minimum for starting a dialogue.

Jordan's internal difficulties in 1989 (see chapter on Jordan) strengthened Husayn's belief that a settlement of the Arab-Israeli conflict was desperately needed. It would reduce regional tensions, make it possible to devote more resources to the economy, and stimulate economic cooperation in the whole region. It was in this spirit that throughout the year Jordanian leaders, and in particular Crown Prince Hasan, continued to be enthusiastic champions of regional development from which, after peace, Israel would no longer be excluded.

SYRIA

Early in the year under review (13 February), a Syrian presidential spokesman published a brief statement containing President Hafiz al-Asad's terms for a settlement of the Arab-Israeli conflict:

1. Israel's withdrawal from the occupied Arab territories.
2. The Palestinian people's right to self-determination.
3. The Palestinian state.
4. The PLO's participation in the peace process.
5. The suitable formula for the attainment of such a peace lying in the convocation of an international conference under UN auspices and the participation of all the parties concerned.[107]

Faruq al-Shar', Syria's foreign minister, annotated this by pointing out that before Syria would agree to attend the international conference Israel would have to announce unequivocally its preparedness to withdraw from all of the occupied territories, including the Golan Heights.[108] The kind of conference Syria was ready to attend was apparently somewhat different from that agreed upon at Arab summit meetings. Syria wanted the conference to be an "effective and authoritative" forum.[109] This notwithstanding, the conference ought not to have unlimited power. Syria did not want to surrender its freedom of decision to the conference. A conference endowed with excessive authority would expect Syria to enter into bilateral treaty arrangements with Israel and to recognize Israel. This Syria was not ready to do.[110]

Throughout the year, Syria viewed the peace efforts from the sidelines. It adhered to the posture it had adopted in 1988 during the Shultz mission and followed US endeavors skeptically and critically. Asad viewed the US-PLO dialogue as a positive step,[111] but held that 'Arafat had seriously erred when he made the concessions to the US and Israel which made possible the opening of the PLO dialogue with the US. Asad was convinced that nothing good could come out of it. 'Arafat's policy, even if successful, ran counter to Syria's, which, as Asad readily admitted, was embedded in its pan-Arab ideology. Syrian Vice President 'Abd al-Halim Khaddam explained that Syria was part of *Bilad al-Sham* (a concept embracing territories lying outside Syria's present boundaries), therefore Palestinian decision making could be independent only to the extent that it concerned the Palestinians alone. If, however, it bore upon the interests of Syria and others, it had to be clearly circumscribed.[112] This explained why Syria was carefully watching 'Arafat's actions. At the end of the year, it concluded that they had not yet posed a real threat to Syria. Should Syria find that a real threat was imminent it would no longer remain indifferent.[113]

Syria apparently adopted a similar wait-and-see attitude toward Egyptian efforts in the peace process in 1989, with one essential difference. Asad was much more circumspect where Egypt was concerned, especially as Syria's relations with it were improving. When Syrian Foreign Minister Faruq al-Shar' met with Secretary Baker (29 September) he merely told him that Syria would not be a party to Egyptian-Israeli moves under way and that Syria did not approve of Egypt's ten-point proposal.[114]

Simultaneously with the utterance of strong statements, Asad also displayed a talent for realism. At the end of the year (27 December), Syria resumed diplomatic relations with Egypt. Asad's rationale behind this decision was wholly pragmatic. He explained that to continue the rift with Egypt would serve only Israel's interests. The Arabs could not do without the Egyptian people. Although he would never change his mind about the Camp David Accords, "as an Arab citizen and as someone in a position of responsibility [he would] not let the estrangement [with Egypt] last forever on account of one document." The existence of peace between Egypt and Israel and the Israeli Embassy in Cairo were appropriately overlooked as if they mattered little.[115]

There were many good reasons for Asad's remarkable decision; among them Syria's suffering economy, his concern about relations with the Soviet Union, and the eternal Lebanese crisis. They all combined to enjoin steps to ease Syria's isolation (for further discussion of Syria's motives, see chapters on Syria and Egypt). Some observers were left wondering whether this could also have some effect on Syria's attitude toward the peace process.

THE PALESTINIANS AND THE PLO

The year under review was a critical one for the Palestinians and the PLO. On the one hand, 1989 was a year of soaring hopes. At the 19th Palestine National Council (PNC) meeting in November 1988 (see *MECS* 1988, chapter on the PLO), the PLO made what it believed to be very difficult concessions. The Americans, by starting a dialogue with the PLO, acknowledged that the organization had met the conditions set by the

US 13 years earlier. The PLO was encouraged to believe that it was, finally, nearing its goal. 'Arafat said frequently that the Palestinians were now a mere stone's throw away from their independent state.[116] They were much buoyed up by the international support they had rallied to their cause. The Soviets remained steadfast, the European Economic Community (EEC) was almost as supportive. At the end of the year, the Intifada had been going on for over two years and remained a potent weapon. It was, in fact, the strongest arm in the PLO arsenal, which it was unwilling to give up before reaching its goal. Israel seemed to be unable to quell the uprising altogether. As long as the Intifada continued, even if somewhat curbed, it served the PLO's purpose to keep the diplomatic momentum going.

However, as against these promising features, others were discouraging. The PLO's main problem was, of course, Israel. Both major Israeli parties, Likud and Labor, were determined not to negotiate with the PLO and were completely against the establishment of a Palestinian state. The PLO considered Shamir and his Likud party as immutably opposed to it. As for the Labor Party, the PLO tended to despair of it and to refer to it disdainfully.[117] Yet the PLO was encouraged by its many contacts with Israelis, some of whom were members of the Labor Party and others who belonged to parties or movements at the left of the political spectrum. The PLO hoped that in time Israeli public opinion would change and accept the terms for the settlement the PNC had laid down in 1988. When this happened, the Israeli Government would have no option but to go along.

Relations with the US did not develop satisfactorily for the PLO. 'Arafat, like Mubarak and Husayn, believed that the Bush-Baker combination was more sympathetic to the Arab cause than Reagan and Shultz had been.[118] Statements made by Bush (3 April) and Baker (22 May) raised the hopes of 'Arafat and other Palestinians (see section on Israel above). It pleased them that Bush had said that the "end of [Israeli] occupation" and the achievement of Palestinian political rights were goals that he shared with Mubarak.[119] Baker, for his part, had called on Israel to "lay aside...the unrealistic vision of a greater Israel."[120] The PLO's assessment was that the Bush Administration would make greater efforts to advance the peace process than had the preceding Administration. Still, they were concerned about other elements of the US position. The US put a definite stress on direct negotiations; it advocated a clearly noncoercive role for third parties, including the US, and accorded the international conference a secondary role in the peacemaking process. Even if the US did not completely discard the international conference, it wanted the conference to be "properly structured" and did not think that it was an urgent item on the diplomatic agenda.

The worst part was that the US affirmed its reservation toward the creation of an independent Palestinian state. It supported "self-government in the West Bank and Gaza in a manner acceptable to Palestinians, Israel, and Jordan."[121]

A prominent Egyptian diplomat, Usama al-Baz, was quite correct in pointing out that the Americans had, nevertheless, agreed to a "state" even if they meant an entity distinguishable from an independent state (see section on Egypt in this chapter).[122] This position went back to the Reagan Administration. It was Shultz who had been the first to agree to a Palestinian entity on the West Bank and Gaza, or most of it, affiliated with Jordan. What Shultz had had in mind for the Palestinians was a political entity that was not a full-fledged independent state.[123]

Given the wide difference between the PLO and the US, the dialogue between them did not fare very well from the very beginning. After the first formal meeting (16 December 1988) there was an interval of over three months before the second formal meeting in March. This was far from auspicious and top PLO leaders were quick to comment on it. One of them, Salah Khalaf ("Abu Iyyad"), a Fath Central Committee member, reminded the US that if it was "serious" about the dialogue with the PLO it must not delay the meetings and agree to discuss "fundamental issues."[124] The PLO was disappointed that the US had spent much of the first meeting discussing the need to end terrorism. Yasir 'Abd Rabbuh, a PLO Executive Committee (EC) member and the head of the PLO delegation to the talks with the US, admitted openly that the talks, in both their formal and informal settings, were going nowhere. He suspected that the US was trying to find "Arab or Palestinian alternatives" to the PLO.[125] This suspicion was temporarily allayed when Baker told a congressional committee that Israel might eventually have no choice but to deal directly with the PLO.[126]

In preparation for the second formal meeting the PLO drafted a working paper which did not merely restate PLO positions, but attempted to elucidate US positions. It queried whether the US was still committed to convening the international conference and how it viewed the PLO's role in such a conference. More significantly, it expressed readiness to hold preparatory meetings with Israeli officials anywhere and anytime, adding, however, that such talks must be only a prelude to the conference. Only at the conference could real peace negotiations take place. 'Arafat added one more condition: the preparatory dialogue must be supervised by the UN or the five permanent members of the UN Security Council.[127]

Despite heavy doubts about US policy, the PLO EC included a few words of praise for the "seriousness that characterized" the dialogue in a statement that it released on the eve of the meeting.[128] The meeting (22 March), however, proved to be as disappointing as the first. The Americans, headed by US Ambassador in Tunis Robert Pelletreau stated the US position, i.e., the four points which would guide the US in a search for a settlement (Resolutions 242 and 338, land for peace, Israel's security, and Palestinian political rights). The PLO, headed by 'Abd Rabbuh, expounded its viewpoint (complete Israeli withdrawal, UN supervision of the territories and the elections, self-determination, and international conference). As in the working paper, the PLO hedged its readiness to enter into a dialogue with Israel by insisting that the Palestinian representatives would have to be selected solely by it. In effect, the gaps between the two sides remained as wide as ever.

The US side proposed settling the conflict in two stages. The first would comprehend confidence-building measures so as to end the violence, the second would deal with the final settlement. Only then would the PLO "along with other distinguished Palestinian figures" from the occupied territories participate in the negotiations. There was no mention of the international conference or of an independent Palestinian state. The PLO told the Americans that it would refuse to participate in any kind of elections as long as the Israeli occupation persisted. 'Abd Rabbuh, who revealed these details, concluded that the US still failed to engage in a "serious dialogue."[129] It was wasting time in the hope of exhausting the Palestinians. Therefore, there was no point in letting the talks drag on; they really ought to do no more than prepare the ground for the international conference.[130]

One newspaper reported that the meeting was quite stormy at times. The storm broke out when the US criticized the violence of the Intifada. The PLO representatives strongly resented this and strongly defended the Intifada methods. They objected to what appeared to them to be American attempts to use the dialogue for the purpose of curbing the Intifada.[131]

The PLO Central Council met early in April and appointed 'Arafat as "head of the Palestinian state." Disregarding the unsatisfactory character of the second meeting, it expressed "appreciation for the dialogue and [hope for] its continuation."[132] The statement was issued on the very day Mubarak met with Bush (3 April), a coincidence that perhaps influenced its tenor.

In the period that followed, PLO-US relations did not improve. Two more meetings were held (8 June and 14 August) without bringing the two sides any closer. Nevertheless, all factions inside the PLO were one in advocating the continuation of the dialogue. Even George Habash, the head of the Popular Front for the Liberation of Palestine, took care not to urge the suspension of the talks although, as he observed, the dialogue went around in circles and was used by the Americans to "distract the PLO from its national goals." Na'if Hawatima, leader of the Democratic Front for the Liberation of Palestine, was equally annoyed with the dialogue but he too stressed the importance of continuing it.[133]

The third round (8 June) was held after the Israeli peace initiative (14 May) was launched and after US support for its central feature, the elections in the territories, had become known. Another equally important event, an Arab summit meeting, had also taken place (23–26 May). It planned to offset the impact of the Israeli election proposal and gave the PLO the backing it sought. The summit resolutions contained an appeal to the US to "develop its stand toward the PLO and the Palestinian people's national rights and to frankly recognize their right to self-determination."[134] The summit again reaffirmed the Arab resolutions since Fez 1982 (see *MECS* 1981–82, chapter on inter-Arab relations) on how to settle the conflict, but it also expressed support for the PLO's stand and the elections, and set forth in detail the terms under which they could be held.[135] (For more details, see chapter on inter-Arab relations.)

'Arafat was much encouraged by this outcome and after a meeting with Mubarak, he said that contacts with the US would continue "so that we may advance with firm steps in the peace process, and *elections* in the occupied territories may become a part of the peace process."[136] This statement made it evident that the PLO would accord the election proposal a higher priority than before.

The PLO prepared one more memorandum for submission to the US before the third meeting. It again urged the US to clarify what it meant by the term "political rights" and why it avoided the term "national rights."[137] The PLO also demanded a "declaration of principles" on the Palestinian question from the US.

This meeting also disappointed the PLO. At its conclusion, a terse news report announced that there had been no tangible results. 'Abd Rabbuh admitted that the PLO had received no clear answer to its questions.[138]

In subsequent weeks, senior American diplomats were to make statements that caused the PLO much concern. In one of them, the Israeli election proposal was termed "a very significant one"; the Israeli rejection of the PLO was viewed with understanding ("The PLO has certainly not convinced the Israelis of their commitment to peace"); the independent Palestinian state was deemed economically nonviable and a source of instability, both with regard to Israel and to Jordan; and the term self-determination was carefully eschewed since "in the context of the Middle East it had come to mean an independent Palestinian state."[139] Another US diplomat asserted that "no one, including the US Government, is going to deliver a settlement"; a settlement must emerge from an engagement between the parties themselves; the UN was called an "imbalanced forum" for the discussion of ME-related issues; the US would not expect Israel just then to articulate support for land for peace; this issue should be addressed when the parties engaged themselves in a dialogue; and the US believed that the outcome should be a reasonable "middle ground" which fell short of the independent Palestinian state.[140]

In July, the newly appointed US assistant secretary of state for Middle Eastern and South Asian affairs, John Kelly, added fuel to the fire when he called on the Palestinians to work out "in a realistic manner" who their representatives were going to be...to make it possible for the Israelis to sit down with them." Moreover, he thought the Israeli proposal had "shifted the ground" very constructively and the US had been trying to assist that shift. US policy was being aimed at "trying to get negotiations between Palestinians in the territories and the Government of Israel, thus leading to elections." Kelly also said that he did not know whether the PLO was acting in good faith. The Palestinian Covenant was an "outrageous document" which the PLO ought to abolish. Finally, in the dialogue with the PLO there had been no tangible progress and he doubted whether the dialogue could go on indefinitely.[141]

Initially, 'Arafat reacted calmly to these American statements, although they came on top of the inconclusive third meeting. In an address to the Pakistani Parliament (25 June), he described the talks with the Americans as "important." But he expressed hope that the US would forward the peace process more energetically through efforts to convene the international conference, instead of "providing absolute support for the so-called [Israeli] election plan in the occupied territories."[142] Two weeks later, however, 'Arafat was more outspoken in his criticism. He said that he feared the Americans were using the dialogue to gain time for Shamir to strike at the Intifada. They were backing Israeli policies and "ignoring the Palestinian peace proposals," which had been endorsed by the "Arab summit as well as 130 countries." He was convinced that the US could resolve the issue if only it made up its mind to do so. This unusually sharp criticism was probably caused by the US refusal to reply to the PLO's questions, which had been posed many months earlier.

The PLO protested against Kelly's remarks in a note to the US. It took exception to several of them and in particular to his unsparing support for the Israeli election plan. 'Abd Rabbuh said that this would cause the dialogue to remain unfruitful. He again urged the US to make a policy declaration so as to "enshrine" its position on Israeli withdrawal and Palestinian self-determination.[143]

The PLO was also annoyed by the US warnings that if the Palestinians rejected the election proposals the dialogue might end. Salah Khalaf asked rhetorically whether the purpose of the dialogue was to force the PLO to accept the proposition that it did not exist and that there were no Palestinians outside the territories.[144] The PLO organ, *Filastin al-Thawra,* published a highly critical article which enumerated all PLO grievances against the US and warned "that the clash [with the US] was inevitable and there is no other way to bring about a drastic change in US thinking."

However, not everything in the US position displeased the PLO. They appreciated being told that the US was not trying to drive a wedge between the Palestinians inside the territories and the PLO even when they insisted that the delegates to the talks with Israel on the elections would have to be, most of them if not all, residents of the territories.[145]

The fourth meeting (14 August) proved to be the most difficult of all. The Fath General Congress (3–8 August) adopted hard-line positions (see chapter on the PLO), making the US wonder if the Palestinians were not backtracking. The US State Department's spokesperson said that the "derogatory rhetoric on Israel, its tone of confrontation and violence, and its preference for unrealistic principles and solutions instead of practical ideas for peace are unhelpful." In particular, the decision to "intensify and escalate armed action and all forms of struggle" contradicted 'Arafat's explicit renunciation of terrorism (December 1988).[146]

The concluding statements at the end of the fourth meeting revealed that neither side had budged from its positions. 'Abd Rabbuh declared that "Shamir's plan is useless for advancing the peace process."[147] Pelletreau insisted that "the next, but not the last, cornerstone on [the] road [of peace] be elections in the occupied territories."[148] One PLO EC member claimed that the US delegation had refused to give assurances that the PLO would play a role in the future phases of the peace process, or even in the final stages of the settlement. According to him, Pelletreau had affirmed that the US would not pressure Israel into dealing with the PLO.[149]

At first it seemed that 'Arafat himself would go along with his more extreme collaborators. He warned that "patience had its limits" and that he might convene the PNC to reconsider the "moderate Palestinian peace strategy, if no visible progress is achieved."[150] But after a visit to Cairo and a meeting with Mubarak he became noticeably calmer. In a joint press conference with Mubarak he only remarked that the last meeting "fell short of the desired goal, due to the US Government insistence on adopting the Shamir plan."[151] As in the past, all these disappointments notwithstanding, the PLO considered it unwise to terminate the dialogue with the US.[152]

At this time of tension between the PLO and the US, Egypt again assumed a more active role by means of Mubarak's ten-point initiative (see section on Egypt above). 'Arafat showed interest in the Ten Points almost immediately. During his visit to Cairo (30–31 August) he mentioned them almost casually as if they posed no problem to the PLO.[153] Ten days later a PLO EC member stated flatly that the PLO did not object to the Ten Points.[154] The PLO, was, of course, perfectly aware that two elements essential to the PLO were not among the Ten Points — the exclusive representative role of the organization and self-determination.

Nevertheless, the PLO accepted the Egyptian explanation that the Ten Points were nothing but questions Egypt had addressed to Israel in the expectation that Israel would answer them in order to clarify its election proposal.[155] Soon, the PLO was ready to go further in its acceptance of the Ten Points. It said that it agreed to make use of them in the dialogue with Israel, except that it would add to them its own demands, such as self-determination, independent statehood, and exclusivity of Palestinian representation.[156]

The focus, however, did not remain on the Ten Points very much longer. It shifted away from them to the highly controversial questions: who would appoint the Palestinian delegates, who would the delegates be, and who would announce their appointment once the list was established. The shift occurred sometime in September coinciding with the Rabin visit to Washington (8 September) and to Cairo (18 September; see sections on Israel and Egypt above). The PLO quickly insisted that it was the only party entitled to form and announce the delegation.[157] In line with this it said that Baker's five-point document, which made no mention of the PLO, was unacceptable.[158]

A PLO Central Council meeting was convened in Baghdad (16 October) to discuss the Five Points, but refrained in its resolutions from saying anything about them. Instead, it endorsed all earlier PNC and Arab summit decisions and declared again that only the PLO had the right "to select and announce a Palestinian delegation from inside and outside [the occupied territories] for talks with Israel."[159] Some PLO leaders interpreted the council's decision as a flat rejection of the Five Points, others disagreed. They said that the PLO had simply not responded "either negatively or positively."[160] It was again Mubarak who provided the solution. After meeting with 'Arafat (2 November), he announced that it would be the PLO who could approve or disapprove of the Five Points. However, once the PLO reached a decision, Egypt would adopt it in its contacts with the US and Israel.[161] This meant, in effect, that the PLO had agreed to act through Egypt, the implication being that the PLO's independence would be protected, but Egypt would act as proxy.

Following this understanding with Egypt, the PLO's next step was to convene a meeting of the EC, which decided to ask the Americans, through Egypt, to provide several clarifications to enable the PLO to accept the Five Points. These clarifications concerned the status of the PLO in the formation and naming of the Palestinian delegation; the topic of the talks, which the PLO would insist to be its own peace proposals; the agenda of the talks, which must not be restricted to the election issue; the international conference, which must follow the preliminary talks; the participants in the talks, which, in addition to the PLO-appointed Palestinians and to Israel, must include the UN secretary-general, the five permanent members of the Security Council, Egypt, and Sweden (a total of 10) and finally the principles for a settlement must be Security Council Resolutions 242 and 338 and territory for peace.[162]

On 22 November, the PLO received, through Egypt, American clarifications.[163] The US conceded as follows:

> 1. The Palestinian delegation will be appointed by the main political and influential element in the Palestine movement.
> 2. Israel will not have veto power over the composition of the Palestinian delegation, but will not be forced to sit with interlocutors against its will. This principle will also apply to the Palestinian side.
> 3. The Palestinian delegation will include both Palestinians from inside and outside the territories, provided that the majority of its members are from inside the territories and that they include two deportees.
> 4. The "primary focus" of the proposed dialogue will be the elections in the territories. However, the Palestinians will be allowed to raise any topic they deem relevant, including those in President Mubarak's ten-point plan. The US believes that the most suitable time to raise topics other than the elections is in the opening statements of the dialogue.
> 5. The US views positively the convening of an international conference in accordance with US Security Council Resolutions 242 and 338, provided that

the conference is properly structured, adequately prepared, and convened at the appropriate time.

6. The US is committed to the peace-for-territories formula in accordance with 242 and 338, but this topic should be dealt with only at the appropriate juncture in the negotiations.

7. The US stands by its policy statement of 16 September 1988, given by former secretary of state George Shultz. The statement included US opposition to the establishment of a Palestinian state, as well as to Israeli annexation of the territories, recognized the "legitimate political rights" of the Palestinians, and said that an international conference could be an appropriate vehicle for direct negotiations.[164]

The American reluctance to confer a publicly visible role on the PLO was the main cause for its disappointment.[165] This disappointment prompted the PLO to stray from its understanding with Mubarak and transmit its reply to the Five Points directly to the Americans instead of through Egypt, as agreed. One of its top officials in Tunis, Hakam Bal'awi, met with Pelletreau (1 December) and handed him a document containing the reply.

The US, however, refused to consider this document as constituting the formal reply they awaited from Egypt. The US State Department spokesperson issued a statement (4 December) which said that "the US [had] never sought...a PLO response to the Five Points and [was] looking forward to an official Egyptian reply."[166] This statement added to the already existing tension between the PLO and the US.

Finally, on 6 December, the Egyptians delivered their response to the US, only after further coordination with the PLO[167] (see section on Egypt above). Egypt and the US did not release the text of the reply. The PLO was less reticent. From various PLO sources it became known that the document that Bal'awi had handed to Pelletreau also contained a two-page memorandum, wherein the PLO reviewed critically the dialogue with the US. Only then came the operative part which stated as follows:

> Based on the PLO's position outlined in its first answer to the plan, it can agree to dealing with the Baker plan presented on 6 October 1989 [only] [Egypt persuaded the PLO to delete the word "only"] in accordance with the PLO Central Council decision to hold a Palestinian-Israeli dialogue as follows:
>
> 1. A delegation to be formed by the PLO from inside and outside the occupied territory and to be announced by it.
>
> 2. An open agenda for the dialogue.
>
> 3. An international presence during the dialogue.
>
> 4. The dialogue is a preliminary step to pave the way for the international peace conference.[168]

A PLO official gave a fuller version of these four items as follows:

> 1. The PLO is ready for a dialogue between a delegation of its members, representing the Palestinian people inside and outside the occupied territory, and an Israeli delegation.
>
> 2. The agenda of the dialogue should be open, without preconditions. Each delegation should be able to raise whatever issues it wants, including elections in the occupied Palestinian territory and the 10 Egyptian points, in accordance

with the US statement of 16 September 1988 based on Security Council Resolutions 242 and 338, the exchange of land for peace, the right of all peoples of the region to secure and recognized borders, and recognition of the Palestinian people's political rights.

3. The dialogue should be held under the supervision of the United Nations, Egypt, Sweden, and the five permanent members of the Security Council.

4. The dialogue should be a step paving the way for an international peace conference on the Middle East with the participation of the five permanent members of the Security Council.[169]

Since the preamble expressed agreement to deal with Baker's Five Points, the US, so it was hoped, would consider the reply as satisfactory. Furthermore, according to one report, the Egyptians had succeeded in persuading the PLO to forgo the two-page memorandum. The Egyptians also achieved the deletion of the word "only" from the preamble.[170]

Some PLO leaders proceeded to describe the reply as "positive" and even "very positive," although the expressed acceptance of Baker's Points had been qualified by four assumptions or conditions. It was left ambiguous as to how adamant the PLO would be concerning them. Hawatima said that the PLO had "clearly rejected the Baker plan."[171] Khalaf believed the reply was "very flexible" but that the PLO had not conceded.[172]

At the end of the year, it was not clear whether the PLO had indeed accepted the Baker plan in a manner that would let the dialogue take place. The EC met again (15–17 December) only to repeat, among other things, the PLO's conditions about its "absolute right to form and announce" the delegation. On the basis of such unequivocal and determined declarations it was not certain that the PLO would resign itself to the invisible and indirect role the US asked it to play. The PLO would have to abandon some of its incessantly declared and deeply entrenched positions before differences could be narrowed.

APPENDIX I: THE ISRAELI FOUR-POINT PLAN (April 1989)[173]

1. The Camp David Partners — Reconfirmation of the Commitment to Peace

Ten years ago, the peace treaty between Israel and Egypt was concluded on the basis of the Camp David Accords. When the accords were signed, it was expected that more Arab countries would shortly join the circle of peace. This expectation was not realized.

The strength of Israeli-Egyptian relations and the cooperation between the three partners to the accords have a decisive influence on the chances for Middle East peace, and the Israeli-Egyptian treaty is the cornerstone to the building of peace in the region.

Therefore, the prime minister has called on the three countries whose leaders affixed their signature to the Camp David Accords, the US, Egypt, and Israel, to renew, 10 years later, their commitment to the agreements and to peace.

2. The Arab Countries — From a State of War to a Process of Peace

The prime minister urged the US and Egypt to call on the other Arab countries to desist from hostility toward Israel and to replace belligerency and boycott with negotiation and cooperation. Of all the Arab countries, only Egypt has recognized Israel and its right to exist. Many of these states actively participated in wars against Israel by direct involvement or indirect assistance. To this day, the Arab countries are partners in an economic boycott against Israel, refuse to recognize it, and refuse to establish diplomatic relations with it.

The solution to the Arab-Israeli conflict and the building of confidence leading to a permanent settlement require a change in the attitude of the Arab countries toward Israel. Israel, therefore, calls on these states to put an end to this historic anomaly and to join direct bilateral negotiations aimed at normalization and peace.

3. A Solution to the Refugee Problem — An International Effort

The prime minister has called for an international effort, led by the US and with the significant participation of Israel, to solve the problem of the Arab refugees. The refugee problem has been perpetuated by the leaders of the Arab countries, while Israel with its meager resources is absorbing hundreds of thousands of Jewish refugees from Arab countries. Settling the refugees must not wait for a political process or come in its stead.

The matter must be viewed as a humanitarian problem and action must be taken to ease the human distress of the refugees and to ensure for their families appropriate living quarters and self respect.

Some 300,000 people live in refugee camps in Judea, Samaria, and the Gaza district. In the 1970s, Israel unilaterally undertook the rehabilitation of residents of refugee camps in Gaza and erected 10 neighborhoods in which 11,000 families reside. This operation was carried out in partnership with the residents despite PLO objections.

The time has now come to ensure appropriate infrastructure, living quarters, and services for the rest of the residents of the camps who, at the same time, are victims of the conflict, hostages to it, and an element which perpetuates its existence.

Goodwill and an international effort to allocate the necessary resources will ensure a satisfactory solution to this humanitarian effort and will help improve the political climate in the region.

4. Free Elections in Judea, Samaria, and Gaza on the Road to Negotiations

In order to bring about a process of political negotiations and in order to locate legitimate representatives of the Palestinian population, the prime minister proposes that free elections be held among the Arabs of Judea, Samaria, and Gaza — elections that will be free of the intimidation and terror of the PLO.

These elections will permit the development of an authentic representation that is not self-appointed from the outside. This representation will be comprised of people who will be chosen by the population in free elections and who will express, in advance, their willingness to take part in the following diplomatic process.

The aim of the elections is to bring about the establishment of a delegation that will participate in negotiations on an interim settlement, in which a self-governing administration will be set up. The interim period will serve as an essential test of cooperation and coexistence. It will be followed by negotiations on the final settlement, in which Israel will be prepared to discuss any option which will be presented.

APPENDIX II: THE ISRAELI PEACE INITIATIVE (14 May 1989)[174]

The Government's Resolution:

It is decided to approve the attached peace initiative of the Government of Israel.

A Peace Initiative by the Government of Israel

General

1.   This document presents the principles of a political initiative of the Government of Israel which deals with the continuation of the peace process; the termination of the state of war with the Arab states; a solution for the Arabs of Judea, Samaria, and Gaza district; peace with Jordan; and a resolution of the problem of the residents of the refugee camps in Judea, Samaria, and the Gaza district.

2.   The document includes:

(a) The principles upon which the initiative is based.

(b) Details of the processes for its implementation.

(c) Reference to the subject of the elections under consideration.

Further details relating to the elections as well as other subjects of the initiative will be dealt with separately.

Basic Premises

3.   The initiative is founded upon the assumption that there is a national consensus for it on the basis of the basic guidelines of the Government of Israel, including the following points:

(a) Israel yearns for peace and the continuation of the political process by means of direct negotiations based on the principles of the Camp David Accords.

(b) Israel opposes the establishment of an additional Palestinian state in the Gaza district and in the area between Israel and Jordan.

(c) Israel will not conduct negotiations with the PLO.

(d) There will be no change in the status of Judea, Samaria, and Gaza other than in accordance with the basic guidelines of the Government.

Subjects to be Dealt with in the Peace Process

4.   (a) Israel views as important that the peace process between Israel and Egypt, based on the Camp David Accords, will serve as a cornerstone for enlarging the circle of peace in the region, and calls for a common endeavor for the strengthening of the peace and its extension, through continued consultation.

(b) Israel calls for the establishment of peaceful relations between it and those Arab states which still maintain a state of war with it for the purpose of promoting a comprehensive settlement for the Arab-Israeli conflict, including recognition, direct negotiations, ending the boycott, diplomatic relations, cessation of hostile activity in international institutions or forums, and regional and bilateral cooperation.

(c) Israel calls for an international endeavor to resolve the problem of the residents of the Arab refugee camps in Judea, Samaria, and the Gaza district in order to improve their living conditions and to rehabilitate them. Israel is prepared to be a partner in this endeavor.

(d) In order to advance the political negotiation process leading to peace, Israel proposes free and democratic elections among the Palestinian Arab inhabitants of Judea, Samaria, and the Gaza district in an atmosphere devoid of violence, threats, and terror. In these elections a representation will be chosen to conduct negotiations for a transitional period of self-rule. This period will constitute a test for coexistence and cooperation. At a later stage, negotiations will be conducted for a permanent solution during which all the proposed options for an agreed settlement will be examined, and peace between Israel and Jordan will be achieved.

(e) All the above-mentioned steps should be dealt with simultaneously.

(f) The details of what has been mentioned in (d) above will be given below.

The Principles Constituting the Initiative
STAGES
5.   The initiative is based on two stages:
   (a) Stage A — A transitional period for an interim agreement.
   (b) Stage B — Permanent solution.
6.   The interlock between the Stages is a timetable on which the plan is built; the peace process delineated by the initiative is based on Resolutions 242 and 338 upon which the Camp David Accords are founded.

TIMETABLE
7.   The transitional period will continue for 5 years.
8.   As soon as possible, but not later than the third year after the transitional period, negotiations for achieving a permanent solution will begin.

PARTIES PARTICIPATING IN THE NEGOTIATIONS IN BOTH STAGES
9.   The parties participating in the negotiations for the First Stage (the interim agreement) shall include Israel and the elected representation of the Palestinian Arab inhabitants of Judea, Samaria, and the Gaza district. Jordan and Egypt will be invited to participate in these negotiations if they so desire.
10.   The parties participating in the negotiations for the Second Stage (Permanent Solution) shall include Israel and the elected representation of the Palestinian Arab inhabitants of Judea, Samaria, and the Gaza district, as well as Jordan; furthermore, Egypt may participate in these negotiations. In negotiations between Israel and Jordan, in which the elected representation of the Palestinian Arab inhabitants of Judea, Samaria, and the Gaza district will participate, the peace treaty between Israel and Jordan will be concluded.

SUBSTANCE OF TRANSITIONAL PERIOD
11.   During the transitional period the Palestinian inhabitants of Judea, Samaria, and the Gaza district will be accorded self-rule by means of which they will, themselves, conduct their affairs of daily life. Israel will continue to be responsible for security, foreign affairs, and all matters concerning Israeli citizens in Judea, Samaria, and the Gaza district. Topics involving the implementation of the plan for self-rule will be considered and decided within the framework of the negotiations for an interim agreement.

SUBSTANCE OF PERMANENT SOLUTION
12.   In the negotiations for a permanent solution every party shall be entitled to present for discussion all the subjects it may wish to raise.
13.   The aim of the negotiations should be:
(a) The achievement of a permanent solution acceptable to the negotiating parties.
(b) The arrangements for peace and borders between Israel and Jordan.

Details of the Process for the Implementation of the Initiative
14.   First and foremost, dialogue and basic agreement by Palestinian Arab inhabitants of Judea, Samaria, and the Gaza district, as well as Egypt and Jordan if they wish to take part, as above-mentioned, in the negotiations, on the principles constituting the initiative.
15.   (a) Immediately afterward will follow the stage of preparations and implementation of the election process in which a representation of the Palestinian Arab inhabitants of Judea, Samaria, and Gaza will be elected. This representation:
   (I) Shall be a partner to the conduct of negotiations for the transitional period (interim agreement).
   (II) Shall constitute the self-governing authority in the course of the transitional period.
   (III) Shall be the central Palestinian component, subject to agreement after three years, in the negotiations for the permanent solution.
   (b) In the period of the preparation and implementation there shall be a calming of the violence in Judea, Samaria, and the Gaza district.

16.   As to the substance of the elections, it is recommended that a proposal of regional elections be adopted, the details of which shall be determined in further discussions.

17.   Every Palestinian Arab residing in Judea, Samaria, and the Gaza district, who shall be elected by the inhabitants to represent them — after having submitted his candidacy in accordance with the detailed document which shall determine the subject of the elections — may be a legitimate participant in the conduct of negotiations with Israel.

18.   The elections shall be free, democratic, and secret.

19.   Immediately after the election of the Palestinian representation, negotiations shall be conducted with it on an interim agreement for a transitional period which shall continue for five years, as mentioned above. In these negotiations the parties shall determine all the subjects relating to the substance to the self-rule and the arrangements necessary for its implementation.

20.   As soon as possible, but not later than the third year after the establishment of the self-rule, negotiations for a permanent solution shall begin. During the whole period of these negotiations until the signing of the agreement for a permanent solution, the self-rule shall continue in effect as determined in the negotiations for an interim agreement.

APPENDIX III: TEXT OF ISRAEL'S ACCEPTANCE OF US SECRETARY OF STATE JAMES BAKER'S FIVE-POINT PLAN FOR AN ISRAELI-PALESTINIAN DIALOGUE (5 November 1989)[175]

1.   The minister of foreign affairs will inform the US secretary of state that Israel accepts the amended five-point document of 12 November 1989 as proposed by Secretary of State Baker.

2.   This, on the assumption that following this agreement, and in accordance with the secretary's letter that accompanied the five-point document, the US will, for its part, undertake that the entire process will be consistent with the peace initiative of the Government of Israel of 14 May 1989, including the following clauses:

(a) The dialogue will begin after the composition of a list of Palestinian Arabs, residents of Judea, Samaria, and Gaza, acceptable to Israel.

(b) Israel will not negotiate with the PLO.

(c) The substantive issue of the dialogue will be the election process in the territories, in a manner consistent with the outline included in the peace initiative of the Government of Israel.

(d) The US will publicly support the above Israeli position and will stand by Israel in the event that another party to the dialogue deviates from what has been agreed upon.

(e). The US and Egypt will declare their support for the principles of the Camp David Accords, which are the foundation of the Israeli peace initiative, including the stages of negotiations and their substance.

(f) The first meeting will take place in Cairo. The next step will be considered according to the results of the first meeting.

APPENDIX IV: THE EGYPTIAN TEN POINTS[176]

1.   The necessity of participation of all citizens of the West Bank and Gaza [including the residents of East Jerusalem] in the elections, both in the voting and in the right to stand as a candidate for any person who has not been convicted [denounced] by the court of committing a crime. This is meant to permit the participation of those under administrative detention.

2.   The freedom of political mobilization before and during the elections.

3.   Acceptance of international supervision of the election process.

4.   Prior commitment of the Government of Israel that it will accept the result of the elections.

5.   Commitment of the Government of Israel that the elections will be part of the efforts which will lead not only to a temporary stage, but also to a final solution, and that all efforts from beginning to end [should] depend on the bases of the solution [which are in] the American concept; Resolutions 242 and 338, Territory for Peace, Protection of the Security of Israel and the Countries of the region, Palestinian political rights.

6.   Withdrawal of the Israeli Army during the elections process at least one kilometer outside the perimeters of the polling stations.

7.   Prohibition of Israelis from entering the West Bank and Gaza on election day with permission to enter only to those who work in these regions and the residents of the settlements.

8.   The preparatory period for the elections should last no longer than two months and these preparations should be accomplished by means of a joint Israeli-Palestinian committee. (The US and Egypt may assist in forming the committee.)

9.   Guarantee of the US of all the above points by means of a prior announcement on the part of the Government of Israel.

10.   Prevention of settlement in the Occupied Territories.

NOTES

For the place and frequency of publications cited here, and for the full name of the publication, news agency, radio station, or monitoring service where an abbreviation is used, please see "List of Sources." Only in the case of more than one publication bearing the same name is the place of publication noted here.

1. *Ma'ariv*, 1 January 1989.
2. Interview with the director-general of the Prime Minister's Office, *Ha'aretz*, 6 January — DR, 11 January; Israel TV, 12 February — DR, 13 February 1989.
3. *IHT*, 14 January; *JP*, 19 January; British ITV, 25 January-- DR, 26 January 1989.
4. Israel TV, 3 January — DR, 4 January 1989.
5. Israel TV, 20 January — DR, 24 January 1989.
6. Israel TV, interview in Hebrew, 20 January — DR, 24 January 1989.
7. *JP*, 20 January 1989.
8. Israel TV, 20 January — DR, 24 January 1989.
9. Israel Educational TV, 22 January — DR, 22 January 1989.
10. Interview with VoI, 26 January — DR, 26 January 1989.
11. Such were, for example, the reactions of the Palestinian mayors, Elias Freij, Hilmi Hanun, Mustafa al-Natsha and of Dr. Sari Nusayba (VoI, 21 January — DR, 24 January; *JP*, 22 January — DR, 24 January.) See also detailed article by Daoud Kuttab, *JP*, 29 January 1989 and leaflet No. 34 of the Unified National Leadership of the Uprising which declared its total rejection of the so-called Rabin and Shamir plans, as well as autonomy (*JP*, 9 February 1989).
12. *JP*, 27 February 1989.
13. *Le Monde JP*, 22 February; *IHT*, 25 February 1989.
14. *JP*, 23 February; VoI, 23 February — DR, 23 February 1989.
15. Speech before a convention of Egypt's National Democratic Party. Full text UN Document, GA SC A/44/157 S/20498, 2 March; *Davar*, 24 March 1989.
16. WF, story: NE 1130313, 13 March 1989; *JP*, 14, 15 March 1989.
17. WF, story: NE 2090314, 14 March 1989.
18. *NYT*, 15, 17 March; *WP*, 18 March 1989.
19. *NYT* editorial, 15 March 1989.
20. USIS Official Text, 4 April 1989.
21. *JP*, 14 April 1989.
22. Ibid., 7 April 1989.
23. Ibid.
24. Baker on ABC's *This Week with Brinkley*, as reported by *JP*, 10 April 1989.
25. Israel TV, 7 April — DR, 10 April 1989.
26. Peres's interview, *Yedi'ot Aharonot*, 10 April — DR, 10 April 1989.
27. Dennis Ross, director of the policy planning staff for the US Department of State, interview on PBS MacNeill/Lehrer News show, 27 April, USIS WF, story: NX 5050428, 28 April 1989.
28. *JP*, 15 May — DR, 15 May 1989.
29. Rabin to VoI, 3 May — DR, 4 May; *JP*, 4 May 1989.
30. Letter is dated 27 April 1989. Complete text (Hebrew translation) was published by *Ha'ir* (a local Tel Aviv paper).
31. Arens to VoI, and to Israel TV, 19 May — DR, 22 May; *JP*, 19 May 1989.
32. USIS Official Text, 23 May 1989.
33. Shamir to Israeli TV, 26 May — DR, 30 May; *JP*, 28 May 1989.
34. *JP*, 25 May 1989.
35. Ibid., 11 June 1989. The letter was dated 6 June 1989.
36. Y. Ben-Aharon, director-general of the Prime Minister's Office, R. IDF, 13 July — DR, 14 July 1989.
37. *IHT*, 13 June 1989.
38. Ben-Aharon to *JP*, 28 July — DR, 9 August; Shamir, quoted by *Ha'aretz*, 18 October 1989.

39. *JP,* 5 July — DR, 5 July; for a later and authoritative version see *JP,* 12 September 1989.
40. *Ha'aretz,* 9 August; VoI, 8 August — DR, 9 August 1989.
41. *Yedi'ot Aharonot,* 22 September 1989.
42. US Assistant Secretary of State John Kelly's testimony before the Europe and ME Subcommittee of the House Foreign Affairs Committee, 19 September, USIS Official Text, 21 September 1989.
43. Shamir, Arens, Peres, and Rabin.
44. Rabin to VoI, 13 September — DR, 14 September; Peres to Israel TV, 13 September — DR, 14 September 1989.
45. See Note 42.
46. VoI, 23 July — DR, 24 July 1989.
47. VoI, 5 July — DR, 5 July 1989.
48. Rabin addressing the Labor Party Central Committee, 23 September (*Ha'aretz,* 24 September 1989).
49. *JP,* 22 September; Y. Ben Porath, *Yedi'ot Aharonot,* 22 September 1989.
50. Full text in *Ha'aretz,* 5 October 1989.
51. *JP,* 27 October 1989.
52. In *Ma'ariv,* 8 October; the exchange is reproduced verbatim.
53. Text as released by the US Department of State, 6 December 1989 (*JP,* 7 December 1989).
54. Muhammad Basyuni to *Hadashot,* 5 November — DR, 6 November 1989.
55. Thus, for example, statement by US Department of State spokesperson, 17 October (*JP,* 18 October 1989).
56. Arens, quoted by *JP,* 24 October — DR, 25 October; Shamir to Israel TV, 3 November — DR, 6 November 1989.
57. The General Assembly of the Council of Jewish Federations.
58. Shamir to *Ma'ariv,* 10 November — DR, 13 November; Peres to VoI, 6 November — DR, 6 November 1989.
59. Peres to VoI, 7 December — DR, 7 December 1989.
60. R. IDF, 9, 12 December — DR, 11, 13 December. Arens could just as easily have referred to 'Abd al-Majid's statement that Egypt would convey the PLO's reply to the US, MENA, 21 November — DR, 22 November 1989.
61. R. IDF, 7 December — DR, 7 December 1989.
62. *Yedi'ot Aharonot,* 5 January; *Ha'aretz,* 8 January 1990.
63. Mubarak to *al-Ra'y al-'Amm,* 21 January — DR, 25 January 1989.
64. Mubarak to *Der Spiegel,* 2 January — DR, 6 January; talking to Israeli correspondents, MENA, 22 March — DR, 23 March; to *Le Figaro,* 13 July — DR, 18 July 1989.
65. Mubarak to *al-Musawwar* (MENA), 15 February — DR, 16 February; his White House statement, MENA, 3 April — DR, 4 April 1989.
66. For example, interview of the Egyptian ambassador in Israel with *al-Fajr,* East Jerusalem, 1 September — DR, 8 September; Mubarak quoted by MENA, 29 November — DR, 30 November; Usama al-Baz quoted by MENA, 9 December — DR, 11 December 1989.
67. MENA, 2 November — DR, 3 November 1989.
68. Mubarak quoted by MENA, 22 March — DR, 23 March 1989.
69. To *al-Hawadith,* 14 April — DR, 26 April 1989.
70. *Al-Ittihad,* Abu Dhabi, 26 March — DR, 28 March 1989.
71. Salah Khalaf in a video-taped speech to an Israeli peace gathering, *JP,* 23 February — DR, 23 February 1989.
72. See Note 20.
73. MENA, 3 April — DR, 4 April 1989.
74. See Note 69.
75. To *al-Siyasa* (MENA), Kuwait, 20 April — DR, 20 April 1989.
76. *JP,* 13 June; interview with BBC (MENA), 14 June — DR, 15 June; Israel TV, 12 June — DR, 14 June 1989.
77. *Ha'aretz,* 25 September 1989. The US congressman was William Gray.
78. To R. IDF, 12 September — DR, 13 September 1989.
79. To *al-Fajr,* East Jerusalem, 7 September — DR, 8 September; *Yedi'ot Aharonot,* 15 September 1989.

80. 'Abd al-Majid to *al-Musawwar,* 1 September — DR, 5 September 1989.
81. Mubarak told a news conference on 18 September that Egypt would attempt to make further efforts to convince 'Arafat to take a more flexible stand; MENA, 18 September — DR, 19 September 1989.
82. See Note 41.
83. Mubarak's news conference, MENA, 18 September — DR, 19 September 1989.
84. Rabin's news conference, MENA, 18 September — DR, 19 September; airport statement, VoI, 18 September — DR, 19 September; news conference, VoI, 18 September — DR, 19 September 1989.
85. Mubarak, 'Arafat in news conference, MENA, 2 November — DR, 3 November 1989.
86. Mubarak to *WP,* MENA, 29 September — DR, 2 October 1989.
87. Mubarak to *al-Ra'y al-'Amm,* 2 December — DR, 7 December 1989.
88. MENA, 6 December — DR, 7 December 1989.
89. Ibid.
90. Mubarak, Husayn joint news conference, 9 December — DR, 11 December 1989.
91. Al-Baz, quoted by MENA, 9 December — DR, 11 December 1989.
92. *JT,* 9 April — DR, 11 April 1989.
93. See e.g., Husayn's interview with NHK TV, 20 February — DR, 23 February; R. Amman, 20 October — DR, 23 October; 'Arafat, R. Amman, 19 December — DR, 20 December 1989.
94. Husayn's address to European Atlantic Group, *JT,* 22 July — DR, 24 July 1989.
95. Address to Jordanian senators and news media representatives, Jordanian TV, 29 June — DR, 2 July 1989; see also his address to the Atlantic Group, Note 94.
96. Prime Minister Zayd al-Rifa'i to *al-Ra'y,* 6 February — DR, 7 February 1989.
97. Crown Prince Hasan, "Jordan's Approach to the Peace Process," The Washington Institute for Near East Policy, Washington DC, 12 September 1989.
98. Jordanian TV, 7 January — DR, 9 January 1989.
99. R. Amman, 4 December — DR, 5 December 1989.
100. As in Note 94.
101. Prime Minister Marwan al-Qasim to *al-Ittihad,* Abu Dhabi, 12 March — DR, 15 March 1989.
102. Husayn to *al-Dustur,* Amman, 21 October — DR, 25 October 1989.
103. *NYT,* 20 April 1989.
104. *JP,* 21 April 1989.
105. To *WT,* R. Amman, 29 June — DR, 30 June 1989.
106. Husayn's Oxford lecture, R. Amman, 20 October — DR, 23 October; to *al-Dustur,* Amman, 21 October — DR, 25 October; Qasim to *al-Qabas,* 10 October — DR, 17 October 1989; Prince Hasan, see Note 97.
107. Presidential spokesman Jubran Kuriyya to R. Monte Carlo, 13 February — DR, 14 February 1989.
108. Joint news conference with three visiting EEC foreign ministers, R. Damascus, 13 February — DR, 14 February 1989.
109. R. Damascus, 23 February — DR, 24 February 1989.
110. Syrian Vice President 'Abd al-Halim Khaddam to *al-Anba,* Kuwait, 30 June — DR, 13 July; *Ha'aretz,* 26 February 1989, reported that the EEC ministers visiting Israel told their Israeli interlocutors that Syria feared too powerful a conference since it objected to imposition.
111. Asad's *Time* interview, R. Damascus, 27 March — DR, 28 March 1989.
112. Interview with *al-Anba,* Kuwait, 30 June — DR, 13 July 1989.
113. Asad's interview with *al-Qabas,* 9 December — DR, 11 December 1989.
114. R. Damascus, 30 September — DR, 2 October; an unnamed senior Syrian official to *al-Watan,* 1 October — DR, 3 October 1989.
115. See Note 113.
116. To Fath conference, R. Tunis, 3 August — DR, 4 August; to R. Monte Carlo, 9 December — DR, 11 December 1989.
117. 'Arafat's interview, *al-Qabas,* 6 March — DR, 8 March 1989. He said that the Labor Party "had lost its principles and the fight against Likud."

118. 'Arafat to *al-Riyad*, 3 January — DR, 11 January; to Hungarian TV, 27 February — DR, 28 February 1989.
119. USIS Official Text, 4 April 1989.
120. WF, 23 May 1989.
121. Ibid.
122. See Note 69.
123. Shultz said: "I am a Californian, whereas if you ask George Bush, he might say I'm a Texan, but we're also US (Shultz interview, Israel TV, 6 April 1988, USIS Official Text).
124. Khalaf to *al-Musawwar*, 17 February — DR, 28 February 1989.
125. 'Abd Rabbuh to *al-Bayan*, Dubai, 13 March — DR, 15 March 1989.
126. See Note 18.
127. *Al-Qabas*, 16 March — DR, 20 March; 'Arafat's Cairo news conference, MENA, 23 February — DR, 24 February 1989.
128. VoP (San'a), 25 March — DR, 27 March; 'Arafat expressed personal satisfaction; INA, 23 March — DR, 24 March 1989.
129. 'Abd Rabbuh to *Pogled*, Sofia, 1 May — DR, 9 May; to *al-Anba*, Kuwait, 11 April — DR, 13 April 1989.
130. *Al-Ittihad*, Abu Dhabi, 28 March — DR, 31 March 1989.
131. VoP (Algiers), 3 April — DR, 4 April 1989.
132. Habash to *al-Bayan*, Dubai, 25 July — DR, 27 July; to *al-Anba*, Kuwait, 30 July — DR, 2 August 1989.
133. Hawatima to *al-Anba*, Kuwait, 6 July — DR, 10 July 1989.
134. VoP (San'a), 27 May — DR, 30 May 1989.
135. The summit resolution said that they could be held "following withdrawal from the occupied Palestinian territories under international supervision and within the framework of the comprehensive peace process."
136. R. Monte Carlo, 27 May — DR, 30 May 1989.
137. EC member, 'Abdallah Hurani to *al-Anba*, Kuwait, 4 June — DR, 6 June; 'Abd Rabbuh, MENA, 31 May — DR, 1 June; MENA, 8 June — DR, 9 June 1989.
138. R. Tunis, 8 June — DR, 8 June; 'Abd Rabbuh to *al-Thawra*, Baghdad, 11 June — DR, 16 June 1989.
139. Dennis Ross, Worldnet interview, 14 June, Washington Files, USIS, 16 June 1989.
140. Daniel Kurtzer's speech, USIS Official Text, 21 June 1989.
141. Kelly before Subcommittee on Europe and the Middle East of the Senate Foreign Affairs Committee, 12 July 1989.
142. Islamabad address, VoP (San'a), 25 June — DR, 26 June 1989.
143. 'Abd Rabbuh, AFP, 18 July — DR, 19 July; to *al-Anba*, 15 July — DR, 17 July; to R. Monte Carlo, 16 July — DR, 17 July 1989.
144. Khalaf to *al-Sharq al-Awsat*, 21 July — DR, 26 July 1989.
145. VoP (Baghdad), 29 July — DR, 1 August 1989.
146. 'Abd Rabbuh to *'Ukaz*, 7 July — DR, 13 July; *al-Madina*, 7 July — DR, 19 July 1989.
147. VoP (Baghdad), 9 August — DR, 10 August 1989.
148. VoP (San'a), 15 August — DR, 16 August 1989.
149. Hurani to *al-Anba*, Kuwait, 20 August — DR, 22 August 1989.
150. 'Arafat's Amman news conference, *JT*, 23 August — DR, 23 August 1989.
151. R. Cairo, 30 August — DR, 31 August 1989.
152. Khalaf to *al-Sharq*, 22 August — DR, 23 August 1989.
153. See Note 151.
154. Jamal al-Surani quoted by *al-Ittihad*, Abu Dhabi, 10 September — DR, 12 September 1989.
155. Faruq Qaddumi, head of the EC's Political Department, Cairo, MENA, 13 September — DR, 14 September; 'Arafat to *al-Akhbar*, Cairo, 22 September — DR, 25 September 1989.
156. Hurani to *al-Majalla*, 3 October — DR, 3 October 1989.
157. Mahmud 'Abbas ("Abu Ma'zin") member of EC, Cairo, MENA, 11 October — DR, 12 October 1989.
158. 'Abd Rabbuh, interview with GNA, 12 October — DR, 12 October; also interview with *al-Bayan*, Dubai, 12 October — DR, 16 October 1989.

159. VoP (Baghdad), Final Statement, 17 October — DR, 18 October 1989.
160. Bassam Abu Sharif, political adviser to 'Arafat, R. Abu Dhabi, 29 October — DR, 30 October 1989.
161. Joint Mubarak-'Arafat meeting with reporters, Cairo, MENA, 2 November — DR, 3 November 1989.
162. Hurani, interview with *al-Watan,* Kuwait, 21 November — DR, 21 November; *al-Ahram,* 6 November — DR, 8 November 1989.
163. 'Arafat to *al-Hawadith,* 24 November — DR, 24 November 1989.
164. The last part of the sentence in the third concession, starting from "provided that" is based on the *al-Watan* article, 22 November — DR, 27 November 1989.
165. EC member, Jamal al-Surani, R. Monte Carlo, 27 November — DR, 27 November 1989.
166. State Department Briefing, USIS, 5 December 1989.
167. See Note 88 and MENA, 4 December — DR, 5 December 1989.
168. *Al-Ra'y,* 3 December — DR, 4 December 1989.
169. Sa'id Kamal, PLO ambassador in Cairo to *al-Sharq al-Awsat,* 8 December — DR, 14 December 1989.
170. *Al-Anba,* Kuwait, 3 December — DR, 5 December 1989.
171. *Al-Anba,* Kuwait, 5 December — DR, 8 December 1989.
172. *Al-Anba,* Kuwait, 4 December — DR, 6 December 1989.
173. *JP,* 4 April 1989.
174. *JP,* 15 May 1989.
175. *JP,* 6 November 1989.
176. *JP,* 12 September 1989.

Armed Operations

EYAL ZISSER

During 1989, the Palestinian uprising in the West Bank and Gaza Strip, now in its second year, continued to power Arab armed operations against Israel.

The heavy and permanent military pressure the Israel Defense Forces (IDF) used to suppress the uprising led to a certain reduction in the number of such Arab attacks. Armed assaults on Israeli targets, however, continued. So did disturbances of order — especially stone-throwing — in the occupied territories as well as inside Israel; their number in 1989 was twice that of the previous year.

Disturbances of order and armed attacks by squads or individuals (some of them driven by religious sentiments) in the West Bank, the Gaza Strip, and inside Israel characterized the Intifada. An incident on 6 July, in which a Palestinian man diverted a public bus *en route* from Tel Aviv to Jerusalem into an abyss, causing the death of 16 passengers, and the murder of two IDF soldiers, abducted while trying to catch a ride home, exemplified these solo operations; many incidents were religiously inspired, the last two being carried out by acknowledged Hamas activists.

The uprising overshadowed other armed encounters between Arabs and Israelis. The armed operations along Israel's borders were generally small scale. The Egyptian-Israeli border was quiet for the most part, and the number of incidents declined even in South Lebanon. Tension there increased only after IDF troops seized the Shi'ite leader Shaykh 'Abd al-Karim 'Ubayd in July. Otherwise, no armed operations directed against Israeli or Jewish targets were recorded. The only exception was the Jordanian-Israeli border, hitherto quiet, where the number of incidents increased significantly in 1989.

Major operations are discussed below. Statistical data on armed operations are provided in the appendix.

THE WEST BANK, THE GAZA STRIP, AND ISRAEL PROPER

THE WEST BANK AND THE GAZA STRIP

(This section is concerned with armed operations mounted in the context of the uprising. It covers mainly Arab armed operations carried out by means of lethal weapons [shooting, hand-grenades or incendiary bomb throwing, knife assaults], but also makes reference to disturbances of order [stone-throwing, the erection of roadblocks and the like]. For other aspects of the uprising see chapters on Israel, and the West Bank and Gaza Strip.)

In 1989, the uprising continued to power intensive Arab armed operations against Israeli targets. Yet, in the course of the year the number of these attacks decreased somewhat. In 1989 1,160 armed incidents were recorded, compared with 1,539 in 1988 — a decline of c. 25%. The number of incendiary bombs thrown came down from

1,390 in 1988 to 782 in 1989. Similarly, 14 incidents of hand-grenades thrown were recorded in 1989, compared with 34 in 1988; and there were 70 cases of explosive charges being planted compared with 85 in 1988. On the other hand, other types of incidents increased: 210 cases of knife assaults in 1989, compared with only 49 in 1988; and there were 84 incidents involving gunfire, compared with only 10 in 1988 (for further details see appendix). In November, an IDF patrol in the Gaza Strip was ambushed and two Israeli soldiers killed. At the time it was thought that the incident would trigger an escalation in the uprising, but this did not happen.

By and large, during the period under review Palestinians continued to refrain from using firearms against Israeli targets, including both IDF soldiers and civilians. One reason for this seems to have been fear that if they did use firearms, Israel would retaliate severely and employ drastic measures to quell the uprising. There was also another logic: by adhering mainly to "cold" weapons, such as stones and knives, the Palestinians in revolt were engaging the IDF in a kind of battle in which it had only limited advantage over them, or none at all.

This overall decline in the number of armed operations was due, at least in part, to the massive Israeli effort to suppress the Intifada. The IDF launched large-scale operations designed to capture the organizers of the uprising and perpetrators of attacks. These operations included long curfews and house-to-house searches, such as that carried out in Nablus in November following the capture of the "Red Eagle" and the "Black Panther" squads (see below). Moreover, in 1988 the IDF had permitted soldiers to open fire on those throwing incendiary bombs, which led to a significant reduction in the number of such incidents. In 1989, the permission to open fire was expanded, to include the increasingly common phenomenon of masked youths: they would be shot if they did not respond to the standard IDF "suspect arrest procedure" — an oral command to the suspect to stop, which — if not heeded — is followed by shooting above his head.

While the mass demonstrations which had taken place mainly in refugee camps disappeared almost entirely as a result of IDF pressure, and while the number of armed operations in the West Bank and the Gaza Strip had declined, the total number of disturbances, including stone-throwing, tire-burning, and flag-waving almost doubled, increasing from 23,092 in 1988 to 45,504 in 1989 (for further details see appendix). The number of Palestinian casualties also increased in comparison with the previous year: in 1989, 299 residents of the territories were killed compared with 272 in 1988 — a 10% increase; 5,832 were wounded in 1989 — a 44% increase over the previous year, in which 4,150 were injured. On the Israeli side, the increase in the number of casualties was bigger: 10 Israeli soldiers and civilians were killed in 1989, as against eight in 1988 — a 43% increase; the number of wounded nearly tripled, from 444 to 1,319 (for further details see appendix).

The continuing disturbances, mainly in the form of stone-throwing along all roads in the territories, especially in the West Bank, exacerbated the retaliation measures adopted by the Jewish settlers there. In 1989, violent clashes between Jewish settlers and Palestinians occurred in almost all parts of the territories. A total of 11 Palestinians were reportedly killed by Israeli civilians in these clashes.[1]

In 1989, about 9,000 Palestinians were held in Israeli detention camps, in addition to about 4,000 Palestinians held in Israeli jails, most of them imprisoned before the Intifada erupted.[2]

In 1989, then, the uprising came to be characterized by large-scale disturbances throughout the territories alongside armed operations of individuals and squads. Beyond that, the major characteristics of the armed operations were as follows:

Organizationally
Masked Youths
In 1989, the role of masked youths became prominent. As mass demonstrations disappeared, organized squads or individuals acting on behalf of popular committees, or the Hamas, but sometimes on their own, became the leading elements of the uprising and armed activities. That they posed a serious threat was made clear by the IDF's decision to permit its troops to open fire on them if they failed to respond to the standard "suspect arrest procedure."

A good example of this type of activity was that of the "Red Eagle" and the "Black Panther" masked youth squads, which were captured in Nablus late in the year. On the morning of 8 November, an IDF unit surrounded a deserted house on the outskirts of Nablus, in which 10 members of a squad calling itself the "Red Eagle" were hiding. Six of them were eating their breakfast, while four were on guard outside. The IDF unit broke into the house, shooting dead the leader of the squad as he tried to draw his gun. The others were captured after a chase. This squad, affiliated with the Popular Front for the Liberation of Palestine (PFLP), was suspected of having used knives and axes to murder nine local residents who were in turn suspected of collaboration with the Israeli authorities or of "immoral" behavior.[3] Three weeks later, on 1 December, another squad was liquidated in a confrontation with Israeli troops dressed as Arabs, who had prior intelligence concerning the squad's exact location. Calling their group the "Black Panther," its members were suspected of murdering 16 collaborators and of attacking Israeli targets.[4]

The "Popular Army"
The period under review witnessed a rise in the activity of groups calling themselves the "Popular Army." These were organized units which operated especially in deserted areas and villages in which the IDF presence was limited. They demonstrated in broad daylight, wore uniforms, and carried arms, mostly axes and clubs. Such demonstrations occasionally occurred in large cities, e.g., in the Qasba, or old city, of Nablus, and had greater propaganda than military significance, but they did attest to the fact that there were areas, especially in the West Bank, where the limited Israeli presence left actual control in the hands of popular committees and representatives of the Palestinian organizations.

Hamas Activities
The Hamas continued to take an active part in the uprising and in armed operations against Israeli targets. This was a part, and a result, of the struggle between the Hamas and the PLO for the control of the population.

The Hamas organization was established in December 1987 at a meeting between Shaykh Ahmad Yasin, leader of the Muslim Brothers in the Gaza Strip and six other religious leaders from Gaza. At this meeting, held at Shaykh Yasin's house, he set out the principles of Hamas: adherence to Islam as a way of life, *jihad* — holy war — against Zionism, and the "restoration" of the land of Palestine to Islam. These principles justified taking part in the uprising in the territories, including the use of firearms. The Shaykh suggested organizing regional committees to coordinate activities. Shaykh Yasin then developed ties with the leaders of the Muslim Brothers in the West Bank and in Jordan. The armed operations carried out by the Hamas under his leadership included the murders of local Arab residents suspected of collaborating with Israel, in February and May, the murders of two IDF soldiers abducted while waiting to catch a ride home (see below), and an ambush on an Israeli patrol, resulting in the death of two IDF soldiers in November.[5]

In mid-1989, more than 200 Hamas members, including Shaykh Yasin and his assistants, were arrested in a large-scale operation. Yet even from jail Shaykh Yasin continued to coordinate Hamas's activities so that the organization continued to function despite the arrest of its major leaders.

Operationally
Murder of Collaborators
Another significant tendency in the uprising in 1989 was the diversion of part of the violence from Israeli targets to Arabs in the West Bank and Gaza Strip, who were suspected of collaborating with Israel. At the beginning of the uprising, a collaborator was someone who openly cooperated with the Israeli security authorities, but the definition came to include all those whom the local popular committees or squads considered to have any connection whatsoever with the Israeli authorities. This wider definition included for example local employees of the Israeli civil administration. Liquidating "collaborators," about which there seemed to have been a general consensus in the territories at the beginning of the Intifada, eventually became a guise for murders motivated by criminal causes, power struggles between rival political factions, or family feuds. The increasing number of such murders was inimical to the prestige of the uprising both inside and outside the territories. It prompted PLO chairman Yasir 'Arafat himself to condemn blind actions that had not won the approval of the PLO authorities or the local popular committees.[6] In 1989, 150 Arabs were murdered for alleged "collaboration."[7]

Abductions
Another conspicuous mark of the uprising in 1989 was abductions of soldiers and civilians. One such case was the abduction, in June, of Chris George, a pro-Palestinian American who headed a charity organization in the territories. He was abducted under circumstances that raised the suspicion that he had cooperated with his kidnappers. He was subsequently released by an IDF force on 25 June. Another was the case of an Israeli jeweler who was kidnapped in August apparently for the purpose of blackmail. He, too, was released a few days later by the IDF.[8] (For the abduction of two Israeli soldiers, see below.)

ISRAEL
An important tendency in 1989 was the spillover of the Intifada into Israel proper: 176 operations, primarily the throwing of incendiary bombs, were recorded in 1989 as against 69 in 1988. In incidents perpetrated by Arabs from the territories, four Israeli soldiers and 17 Israeli and foreign citizens were killed. A common method of attack was by knife; six Israeli civilians died as a result of such assaults in 1989. The number

of disturbances of order and other such actions rose as well: 2,267 incidents of stone-throwing inside the Green Line as compared with only 1,468 in 1988, a 54% increase; 149 cases of Palestinian flags being waved as compared with 37 in 1988, in addition to 193 incidents of agitation as compared with 94 in 1988, 248 incidents of forest arson motivated by nationalistic sentiment as compared with a few dozen in 1988, and 80 incidents of roadblocks being raised — the same number as in 1988.[9]

Especially notable were the abduction and murder of two Israeli soldiers who were hitchhiking home. But the most lethal attack, with the largest number of casualties, was the attack on an Israeli civilian bus in July.

The Bus Incident

Perhaps more than any other incident in 1989, the bus attack symbolized the Intifada spilling into Israel. On 6 July, a civilian bus *en route* from Tel Aviv to Jerusalem, was attacked by one of the passengers, an Arab, about half an hour after its departure from Tel Aviv. As the bus was approaching the Neve Ilan junction, the assailant jumped at the driver, forcefully turned the steering wheel to the right and diverted the bus off the road into an abyss. The steepness of the abyss into which the bus fell imposed extreme difficulties on efforts to rescue the passengers and provide medical aid to those injured, who were trapped inside the bus or lay beside it. Sixteen passengers were killed and 25 were wounded. The attacker, who was only slightly injured, was arrested, and his interrogation revealed that he was a member of the Gaza-based Islamic Jihad.[10] He said he had wanted to avenge a friend of his who, he said, became paralyzed after being shot by Israeli soldiers, and a relative who had been beaten during interrogation by Israeli security forces. He also admitted having murdered an Israeli with whom he had worked at a Tel Aviv construction site.[11]

The incident caused intense anxiety in Israel. The official reaction was sharp. "It is a horrendous disaster," said Prime Minister Yitzhak Shamir, "it is a murderous act perpetrated by a man with a sick mind, brimming with hatred. This sets a new record of madness, stemming from hatred nurtured by incessant instigation. It is very difficult to prevent such actions, but everything must be done to strike at these murderers and those who dispatched them."[12]

In Israel, the incident brought into sharper focus the question of imposing the death penalty on members of Palestinian or other organizations who murder civilians. Among those who joined the ranks of the supporters of the death penalty for this crime was Minister of Police Haim Bar-Lev.[13] The fact that the incident had occurred on a main highway was a blow to the Israeli public's sense of security while moving on the roads and in public transportation; consequently, measures were taken to step up security in traffic centers, such as central bus stations, and new safety devices (special metal bars separating the driver from the passengers) were introduced into all buses. On 17 September, this increased alertness paid off when the security forces arrested a Palestinian man who tried to board a bus about to leave the Tel Aviv bus station for Jerusalem. A knife was found on his person and he admitted to his interrogators his intention to perpetrate an attack similar to the previous one, in order to mark the anniversary of the Sabra and Shatila massacres.[14]

The attack on the bus led to acts of vengeance by Jews against Arabs throughout Israel; 17 such incidents were reported, 11 of them in Jerusalem.[15] Many incidents involved Jews throwing stones at cars with license plates of the territories.

The bus incident was generally condemned by Western states, and even Moscow Radio did so. These condemnations, however, also stressed the need to find a peaceful solution to the wave of violence in the area.[16]

The tendency among the Palestinian organizations was to blame Israel for the incident. A PLO spokesman said that those killed were victims of the Israeli leaders, who had abandoned their responsibility for their own and for the Palestinian people.[17] The Voice of Palestine (VoP) from Baghdad even said that the attack had been a heroic suicidal act of a new type, executed by a young man crying out against the Israeli soldiers' oppression of his people. The assault, the VoP said, was part of a popular revolution which could not be prevented, let alone stopped.[18] At the same time, the Islamic Jihad assumed responsibility for the incident, saying that Mujahidin attacks would continue until the entire world recognized the Palestinian people's determination to live in its own land.[19]

The Abduction and Murder of Two IDF Soldiers
Two Israeli soldiers were abducted and murdered by two young Hamas members in two separate incidents in Israel proper. On 16 February, the murderers carried guns given them by a Hamas leader and stole a car. Disguised as orthodox Jews, they stopped at a military pick-up point at the Hodaya junction (east of Ashkelon) where a soldier waiting for a lift got into their car. Shortly after, they apparently shot the soldier dead and then buried the body, which was found some time later. On 3 May, the same two attackers picked up another soldier waiting for a ride in the Re'em junction (south of Gedera), likewise killed him and buried the body. The two Hamas members escaped to Egypt, but the head of their cell was arrested.[20] These two incidents shocked the Israeli public severely and deepened the feeling of insecurity on the roads. This, in turn, led to violence against Arabs, manifested mainly in stone-throwing mostly in the south of Israel, where the two soldiers had been abducted and murdered.

The Intifada in 1989 also influenced a growing number of Israeli Arabs to undertake activities against the state: 176 armed operations, primarily the throwing of incendiary bombs, were recorded as compared with 69 in 1988.

Forest Arson
The arson of forests, of which there had been a few cases in 1988, continued, but on a much larger scale: 248 such incidents were recorded in 1989, the peak of which was the destruction of over 7,000 acres of forest on Mt. Carmel, near Haifa, on 19 September. Three days were needed to overcome the blaze, which destroyed a scenic site in the area.

Organized Squads
Organized squads operating against Israel, some of them under orders from outside the country, became more active. One squad of 17 members operated in the Arab village of Jat. Called "The Popular Front of Jat," it was responsible for a series of armed assaults in the vicinity of the village, including attacks on public transportation, the most violent of which was an incident in which stones were thrown at a public bus and its driver injured. Another squad, of 10 members, operated in Nazareth. Among other operations, it threw incendiary bombs at public buildings in the city, including

those belonging to the Israeli Communist Party. These two squads were locally based, and apparently had no ties to Palestinian organizations in the territories or outside Israel. They managed to operate for long periods before they were discovered and arrested. The Jat squad, for example, operated for almost two years. At first, these squads limited themselves to waving Palestinian flags, but undoubtedly under the influence of the uprising in the territories, they expanded their activities to include violence, such as throwing stones and incendiary bombs, which characterized the Intifada beyond the Green Line.[21]

In addition to such locally organized, independent squads, PLO-controlled squads, too, were uncovered inside Israel proper. For example, a Fath squad was discovered in the village of Tayba in April. The squad had five members and its leader was recruited while he was abroad. It was uncovered before it became active.[22]

LEBANON

Armed operations against the IDF and the South Lebanese Army (SLA) in South Lebanon continued in 1989, although at a somewhat diminished intensity as compared with 1988: nine attempts of infiltration into Israel in 1989 as compared with 25 the previous year, 22 encounters between IDF and members of Palestinian and Lebanese organizations as compared with 23, and four cases of katyusha rockets being fired toward Israel as compared with 10 in 1988. In these incidents, two Israeli soldiers, 12 SLA soldiers, and 75 Palestinian and other activists were killed, as compared with 21 Israeli soldiers, 26 SLA soldiers, and about 250 Palestinian and other activists killed in 1989.[23] This decline was due to IDF activity, to SLA activity in the security zone, and the US warning to the PLO that it would regard any PLO attempts to attack Israel from the security zone as a violation of 'Arafat's pledge to the US to suspend armed operations against Israel from Lebanese territory: this pledge had been one of the reasons for the American decision to open a dialogue with the PLO (see chapters on the US and the ME and on the PLO). Another factor contributing to the decrease in the number of armed operations against Israel may have been the clashes between the Shi'ite organizations in South Lebanon.

Whatever the reason, armed operations against Israeli targets came to be undertaken mainly by hard-line organizations such as the PFLP, the Democratic Front for the Liberation of Palestine, and the Abu Nidal, Tal'at Ya'qub, and Abu Musa factions. Most of these hard-liners approved 'Arafat's November 1988 initiative, which involved the decision to suspend terrorism, including in Lebanon.

A typical example of the Palestinian hard-liners' armed operations was the infiltration into Israel of an Abu Nidal squad. On 3 October, its three members reached the Israeli-Lebanese border, near the Israeli village of Zar'it, after transiting the security zone at its narrowest point. At the border fence, the squad opened fire on an IDF patrol; the patrol returned fire and began combing the area for the squad which succeeded in fleeing under cover of darkness. It withdrew northward outside the security zone, but an hour and a half later it clashed with another IDF unit inside the zone. The IDF unit attacked the squad at short range, killing two of its members, while the third escaped.[24]

Other armed operations in South Lebanon were carried out by Lebanese organizations included in the National Lebanese Resistance Front. But these operations, although directed at IDF and SLA targets, were confined to Lebanese territory. Two such armed operations were carried out by the Lebanese Communist Party (LCP) on 9 and 11 September. In the first, an IDF force was ambushed in the Mount Dov area. In the second, an IDF patrol was ambushed about 1 km. north of the border.[25] The Lebanese organizations also assisted the Palestinian squads which tried to infiltrate into Israel and provided them with guides and shelter.

Despite these armed operations, the IDF continued to view the security zone and the SLA as precious assets. Thus, for example, on 4 October, a day after the above-mentioned clash with the Abu Nidal squad, OC Northern Command Gen. Yossi Peled said that whoever thought that it was impossible to infiltrate through the security zone had been mistaken, but that on the whole the system had proven itself: there was no need to reinforce the area with thousands of additional soldiers or to build a security fence north of the security zone.[26]

In 1989, the IDF carried out fewer large-scale operations against Lebanese targets than in the previous year. Israeli planes, however, continued attacking targets in Lebanon on the scale of 1988.

There was also IDF activity beyond the security zone against Palestinian organizations or Lebanese groups assisting them. On 26 December, for example, the IDF carried out an operation against an LCP base near the village of Nabi Safa, about 15 km. north of the security zone. In 1989, the LCP was one of the most prominent organizations acting against the IDF in the security zone. The Israeli force advanced in difficult terrain, reaching two buildings which served as departure points for Palestinian squads. The Israeli force stormed the two buildings and blew them up. At least four LCP members were killed and several others injured.[27]

THE ABDUCTION OF SHAYKH 'UBAYD

The 36-year-old shaykh, who was educated in Iran, became a dominant figure in the Hizballah and its commander in South Lebanon. 'Ubayd planned and approved armed operations against Israel and helped transfer arms and ammunition to Hizballah forces in the area. He masterminded attacks against IDF soldiers in the security zone, the firing of katyusha rockets, and the kidnapping of hostages.

'Ubayd was captured on 27 July by a helicopter-borne IDF unit that landed near his village, Jibshit, walked to his house where it overcame his bodyguards, broke into the house, captured the shaykh and two of his aides, and took them to the helicopter waiting in a nearby canyon.[28]

Israel's objective in this operation was to capture a hostage whom it could use in negotiations for the release of three Israeli soldiers held probably by the Hizballah or other Shi'ite forces in Lebanon. There is little doubt that Israel also hoped that these negotiations would lead to the release of Western hostages, thus helping it score a public relations victory. (About 19 Western hostages were being held by the Hizballah and other Shi'ite elements in Lebanon: eight American, three British, among them the clergyman Terry Waite, who was kidnapped on 20 January 1987 while on a goodwill mission to help release Western hostages, and two West German.)

Israel's seizing of 'Ubayd elicited an international reaction that was generally negative. The reaction became all the more negative after the Shi'ites threatened to harm the Western hostages in their hands,[29] and especially after they announced that they had hanged Col. William Higgins, an American. It quickly became clear, however, that Higgins had been executed some time before the seizing of the shaykh.[30] (See also chapter on the US and the ME.)

On 9 August, about two weeks after the seizing of 'Ubayd, a suicide attack by means of a car bomb carrying c. 250 kg. of explosives was launched on an Israeli military convoy in the security zone, but precautionary measures taken by the IDF foiled this assault and the two attackers were killed; five IDF and one SLA soldiers were wounded.[31] Hizballah assumed responsibility for the attack and reported that one of the attackers had been a Shi'ite clergyman close to 'Ubayd. It explained that the attack had been carried out as a gift for the Imam Khomeyni on the occasion of the 'Ashura feast.[32] Not long after the seizing of 'Ubayd, the tension dissipated (see chapter on Lebanon).

MARITIME ACTIVITY

The year 1989 proved once again the importance that Palestinian organizations, deterred by the massive efforts to prevent them from infiltrating Israel by land, accorded to seaborne operations against Israel. In April, an Israeli naval patrol spotted a Palestinian boat, opened fire on it and sank it together with the four Palestinians on board. On 30 October, an Israeli naval patrol boat spotted a Lebanese fishing vessel south of Tyre. When approached by the Israeli patrol boat, the Lebanese vessel exploded in what is believed to have been a suicide attempt to sink the Israeli boat. Three Israeli seamen were injured. The PFLP promptly claimed responsibility for the incident.[33]

Maritime activity also became more prominent when Israel attempted to prevent the Palestinians from moving men and ammunition to South Lebanon by sea. The Israeli Navy arrested vessels *en route* from Cyprus to Lebanon, one such being a yacht sailing from Cyprus to Sidon which the Navy detained on 3 November. The Navy took off three Palestinian members of Fath for questioning in Israel and then allowed the yacht to continue on its way.[34]

JORDAN

During the previous few years, the Jordanian border had been one of the quietest. But in 1989, there was a sudden and significant rise in the number of armed operations against Israeli targets along this border. Seven such incidents occurred, including infiltration into Israeli territory and the firing of katyusha rockets, causing the death of two Israeli soldiers and the injury of five others. Only two of these incidents were the work of members of Palestinian organizations. In one of them, on 17 March, a Palestine Liberation Front squad attacked an IDF patrol, killing its commander, and then escaped into Jordan where it was eventually captured.[35] In the second incident on 7 September, a PFLP squad fired katyusha rockets toward Israeli territory, but failed to cause any casualties. Some members of the squad were later apprehended by the Jordanian authorities.[36]

The other incidents along this border were the result of individual initiatives of Jordanian soldiers, some of whom had repeatedly deserted from their units. They fired at Israeli border patrols and on some occasions infiltrated into Israeli territory.

The main targets of these solo attacks were in the 'Arava (southern sector) and the northern Jordan Valley. Both sectors were relatively easily accessible: the 'Arava had no electronic border-fence and the guards there tended to be lax in fulfilling their duties; the northern part of the Jordan Valley was thought to have the advantage of proximity to Syria, which was believed to have been behind some of the operations.

The infiltration into Kibbutz Lotan, in the 'Arava, on 8 August exemplifies the infiltration of armed Jordanians into Israeli territory, which increased during the year. In the morning, a Jordanian soldier crossed the border into Israel near the kibbutz, north of Eilat. He then walked about 1 km. to the kibbutz orchards, where he encountered a civilian girl whom he shot and injured. He then encountered an IDF girl soldier whom he capured and held hostage for about two hours in a small warehouse nearby. Large IDF and police units as well as a special anti-terrorism force were brought to Lotan, commanded by Chief of General Staff Lt. Gen. Dan Shomron and by OC Southern Command Gen. Matan Vilna'i. The Israelis surrounded the warehouse, negotiated with the Jordanian soldier, then shot him dead. Abu Musa's organization assumed responsibility for the incident, a claim that appeared to be rather dubious. The same day, the Jordanians announced that one of their soldiers was missing from his unit, and it seemed likely that this had been the same soldier, who had acted on his own initiative out of religious or nationalistic reasons.[37]

Another incident of this type, similar to the 1989 incident, occurred in the Israeli-Jordanian border area in the first week of 1990. A Jordanian soldier, who had repeatedly deserted from his unit in the al-Hama area, crossed the border and took cover in a deserted house near the Israeli patrol road. Between 5 and 7 January 1990, he fired at IDF patrols three times. The IDF forces deployed in the area intercepted him and shot him dead. After the first attack on an IDF patrol the Jordanians hastened to announce that one of their soldiers had deserted from his unit and, at the same time, stepped up preventive measures all along the border with Israel.[38]

The deterioration along the Israel-Jordan border was interpreted in Israel as a symptom of the weakening of the Hashemite regime due to economic crises and political agitation (see chapter on Jordan). The Jordanians apparently continued to hold the view that it was in Jordan's vital interests to keep its border with Israel quiet. Indeed, they prevented several planned actions against Israel from being carried out, but they had insufficient control over their own soldiers, some of them of Palestinian origin, who acted out of Islamic motives or identification with the Intifada. According to some observers, some of the incidents were probably carried out with Syrian help as part of Damascus's efforts to deal a blow to the Israel-Jordan peaceful *modus vivendi*. The resurgence of religious activity in Jordan and Jordan's decision to give a free hand to certain Palestinian organizations have also been cited as reasons for the recurring incidents.[39]

Jordan tried to play down the infiltration incidents perpetrated by its soldiers into Israel; it gave these incidents minimal media coverage and sometimes ignored them completely. When two IDF soldiers were shot on 27 May by a Jordanian soldier east of kibbutz Hamadia (in the central sector of the Jordan Valley), the Jordanians declared that he had suffered from some "psychiatric problems."[40] In the same vein, after the 8 August incident in the 'Arava (see above), Jordan merely referred to a "missing soldier" who had defected from his unit, an explanation which they repeated after the January 1990 incident.

The recurring Jordanian statements concerning the mental instability of their soldiers who had crossed the border elicited an angry response in Israel. While wishing to keep the border area calm, Israel also warned Jordan that it was holding the latter responsible for security on the Jordanian side of the border; the prime minister, the minister of defense, and the chief of the general staff all spoke in this vein.[41]

EGYPT

The Israeli-Egyptian border in 1989 was Israel's quietest, with only four incidents being reported. On 15 March, two Palestinians — 15- and 17-year-olds — were captured about 14 km. southeast of Rafah. A third member of the squad escaped to Egypt, where he was arrested. The trio belonged to the Islamic Jihad and were promised a reward for any Israeli they killed or wounded while carrying out their mission to attack an Israeli border post, Israeli military patrols, and civilian cars along the border. The two captured members of the squad told their interrogators that the PLO was behind their operation.[42]

Another incident occurred on 5 December when an IDF patrol discovered signs of infiltration in the Mount Harif area. Troops combed the area for the infiltrating squad which was intercepted. In the ensuing battle, the squad's five members were killed; five Kalashnikov submachine guns and five hand-grenades were found in their possession. OC Southern Command Gen. Matan Vilna'i said that the squad, whose organizational affiliation was unknown, had planned to mount a spectacular attack against civilian targets in the Negev.[43]

Finally, on 15 December, fire was opened from the direction of the Egyptian border on an Israeli patrol, causing no casualties. Israeli sources which reported the incident declined to provide additional details concerning it, saying only that the IDF was investigating the matter. There was no Egyptian reaction.[44]

An incident of a different nature occurred in the bay of Eilat, on the border between the two states. On 3 June, an Egyptian patrol boat opened fire on an Israeli yacht which had been cruising near the Coral Island, killing an Israeli citizen who had been on board.[45] The Egyptians claimed that the Israeli yacht had penetrated into their territorial waters and disregarded orders to leave the area. Consequently, the Egyptians said, their soldiers fired overhead shots.[46] The incident, a result of the absence of clear regulations concerning cruising in the bay of Eilat, caused considerable distress in Israel, and the Israeli Government submitted an official protest to the Egyptian authorities.

The relative quiet along the Israeli-Egyptian border reflected the mutual resolve of Egypt and Israel to preserve the peace. This, despite the fact that Egypt permitted Palestinian organizations, especially those that looked to 'Arafat, to act in its territory and turned a blind eye to the activities of Palestinian deportees and refugees, some of them religiously inspired. The multifarious acts of smuggling along the border added to the burden of halting terrorist infiltration (see also chapter on Egypt).

THE INTERNATIONAL ARENA

The number of attempted and actual armed operations against Israeli and Jewish targets worldwide was especially low during 1989; one of the main reasons was the PLO's effort to hold on to its political achievements of 1988, the most significant of which was the dialogue with the US. The PLO also strove to preserve the international sympathy it had acquired thanks to the Intifada, and hence sought to dissociate itself from terrorist operations. Syria, and to some extent Libya, were also apprehensive about being accused of involvement in international terrorism. This apprehension increased after a Pan Am airliner exploded over Lockerbie, Scotland, on 21 December 1988.

In the absence of international terrorist operations carried out by Arab groups, attention in 1989 focused on the Lockerbie incident, in which 259 passengers and crew, among them two Israelis, were killed. Details became available thanks to the concentrated efforts of Western, mainly British and American, intelligence services. They discovered that the bomb that blew up the plane was constructed of a tape recorder connected to a barometric apparatus which activated the detonator. The device had been cached in a suitcase put aboard the plane in Frankfurt.[47] The operation was attributed to the Syrian-backed PFLP-GC, although the organization and its leader Ahmad Jibril repeatedly denied any connection with it.[48]

A few other terrorist operations were perpetrated during the year but were foiled. In one case, in May, six men were arrested in Larnaca, Cyprus, on suspicion of planning to attack Israeli or Lebanese Christian planes in Larnaca airport.[49] In another case, in July, a Lebanese student was arrested in West Germany on suspicion of planning to attack Israeli and American targets.[50] In August, a terrorist was killed when the bomb he had been preparing in his London hotel room exploded. London police said the bomb had been intended for use against Israeli and other targets.[51]

One other event in the international arena during 1989 was the murder in Brussels of a leader of the Belgian Jewish community. The assassins were not found, and the categorization of the murder as an armed operation against Jews was based on surmise only. On 4 October, Dr. Joseph Wybran, 48, who was one of Belgium's most prominent pro-Israel activists, was shot in the head at short range as he walked out of the Brussels University Hospital (where he headed a department) toward his car. The Belgian police investigation revealed that the bullet which killed him was of the same type that had been used in the murder of the driver of the Saudi ambassador to Belgium and of a member of the Belgian Islamic community earlier in the year. A Beirut-centered Lebanese organization calling itself "Soldiers for the Rights" assumed responsibility for the Wybran murder, but it was doubtful whether it had had a hand in the killing.[52]

APPENDIX: STATISTICAL DATA

The following statistical data are based on IDF sources.

TABLE 1: THE WEST BANK AND GAZA STRIP: TYPES OF INCIDENT

Date	Disturbances of order	Incendiary bombs	Knife assaults	Planting of charges	Gunfire	Hand-grenades
9 December 1988–12 January 1989	2,790	44	4	5	5	—
13 January–8 February 1989	2,372	67	2	6	1	1
9 February–8 March 1989	2,768	59	8	5	4	—
9 March–8 April 1989	3,508	60	6	2	2	2
9 April–8 May 1989	3,727	72	12	9	5	1
9 May–8 June 1989	3,395	86	17	7	9	1
9 June–9 July 1989	2,668	63	20	13	6	—
10 July–8 August 1989	2,933	39	26	10	12	1
9 August–10 September 1989	4,022	67	22	1	18	—
11 September–12 October 1989	4,571	66	27	3	6	4
13 October–9 November 1989	3,864	55	20	4	6	2
10 November–7 December 1989	3,793	50	22	1	8	—
8 December1989–9 January 1990	5,093	54	24	4	2	2
Total	**45,504**	**782**	**210**	**70**	**84**	**14**
Total: 1988	**23,092**	**739**	**46**	**80**	**10**	**34**

TABLE 2: THE WEST BANK AND THE GAZA STRIP: CASUALTIES

Date	Local Residents[a]		Israelis[b]	
	Killed	Wounded	Killed	Wounded
9 December 1989–12 January 1989	26	441	2	91
13 January–8 February 1989	27	417	—	59
9 February–8 March 1989	8	245	1	94
9 March–8 April 1989	23	523	—	138
9 April–8 May 1989	32	640	—	147
9 May–8 June 1989	38	568	1	140
9 June–9 July 1989	20	440	1	97
10 July–8 August 1989	21	431	1	77
9 August–10 September 1989	27	493	2	122
11 September–12 October 1989	26	446	—	139
13 October–8 November 1989	23	277	—	106
9 November–7 December 1989	13	426	2	29
8 December 1989–8 January 1990	15	485	—	80
Total	**299**	**5,832**	**10**	**1,319**
Total: 1988	**272**	**4,150**	**7**	**444**

a   Only local residents killed by IDF forces; excluded, e.g., 150 Arabs killed by other Arabs, and 11 Arabs killed by Jewish settlers.

b   Only civilians and soldiers killed and injured in the West Bank and the Gaza Strip.

NOTES

For the place and frequency of publications cited here, and for the full name of the publication, news agency, radio station, or monitoring service where an abbreviation is used, please see "List of Sources." Only in the case of more than one publication bearing the same name is the place of publication noted here.

1. *Betzelem — Annual Report 1989* (Jerusalem: The Israeli Information Center for Human Rights in the Occupied Territories), p. 21.
2. Ibid., p. 61.
3. *Ha'aretz,* 9 November 1989.
4. *Davar,* 3 December 1989.
5. *Ma'ariv,* 17 November 1989.
6. *Yedi'ot Aharonot,* 1 February 1990.
7. Statement by IDF spokesman to author, 9 January 1990.
8. *Ha'aretz,* 25 June, 27 August 1989.
9. Ibid., 21 January 1990.
10. *Ma'ariv,* 7 July, 11 September 1989.
11. *Ha'aretz,* 15 September 1989.
12. R. IDF, 6 July — DR, 7 July 1989.
13. *Ma'ariv,* 7 July 1989.
14. *Ha'aretz,* 18 August 1989.
15. Ibid., 9 July 1989.
16. *Ma'ariv,* 9 July 1989.
17. R. Monte Carlo, 7 July — DR, 8 July 1989.
18. VoP (Baghdad), 12 July — DR 13 July 1989.
19. R. al-Quds, 9 July — DR, 10 July 1989.
20. *Ha'aretz,* 10 November 1989.
21. *Ma'ariv,* 9 November 1989.
22. Ibid., 13 April 1989.
23. Statement by IDF spokesman to author, 9 January 1990.
24. *Ha'aretz,* 5 October; VoL, 4 October — DR, 6 October 1989.
25. *Ma'ariv,* 12 September; VoL, 11 September — DR, 12 September 1989.
26. *Ha'aretz,* 5 October 1989.
27. *Ma'ariv,* 27 December 1989.
28. VoI, 28 July — DR, 31 July 1989.
29. R. Beirut, 28 July — DR, 28 July 1989.
30. *JP,* 1 August; VoL, 29 July — DR, 31 July 1989.
31. *JP,* 11 August 1989.
32. VoL, 9 August — DR, 9 August 1989.
33. *Ma'ariv,* 31 October; R. Beirut, 31 October — DR, 31 October 1989.
34. *Ma'ariv,* 5 November 1989.
35. *Ha'aretz,* VoL, 19 March — DR, 19 March 1989.
36. R. Monte Carlo, 7 September; VoL, 10 September — DR, 11 September 1989.
37. *Ha'aretz,* 9 August 1989.
38. *Ma'ariv,* 8 January; Jordanian TV, 7 January — DR, 8 January 1990.
39. *Ha'aretz,* 8 August, 27 September 1989.
40. R. Amman, 27 May — DR, 30 May 1989.
41. *Ha'aretz,* 9 August 1989.
42. *Ma'ariv,* 16 March 1989.
43. Ibid., 6 December 1989.
44. R. IDF, 17 December — DR, 19 December 1989.
45. VoI, 3 June — DR, 5 June 1989.
46. MENA, 3 June — DR, 5 June 1989.
47. *Ma'ariv,* 5 January 1990.
48. R. al-Quds, 14 January — DR, 17 January; BBC TV, 30 November — DR, 4 December 1989.

49.   *Ma'ariv*, 30 May 1989.
50.   Ibid., 7 July 1989.
51.   *Ha'aretz*, 4 August 1989.
52.   *Ma'ariv*, 5 October 1989.

INTRAREGIONAL AND
ISLAMIC AFFAIRS

Inter-Arab Relations

BRUCE MADDY-WEITZMAN

Throughout the 1980s, the inter-Arab system came to be characterized by a number of central features: (1) a division into two blocs with regard to the main issues facing the Arab world, primarily the Iran-Iraq War, the Arab-Israeli conflict, Egypt's place in the system, the Lebanese crisis, and global orientation; (2) Egypt's steady, incremental successes in breaking down the isolation imposed on it in the late 1970s following its peace agreement with Israel; and (3) growing apprehension over the long-term consequences of both "local" issues such as inter-Arab fragmentation, demographic pressures, economic slow-down following the decline in oil-derived revenues, Islamic fundamentalism, and international developments, most notably the thaw in East-West relations and the movement toward economic integration in Western Europe. For most Arab leaders, the mitigation of inter-Arab tensions was a necessary prerequisite to any affective response to these multiple challenges. Consequently, efforts to promote dialogue among the various parties at odds with one another, referred to as "purifying the Arab atmosphere," were intensified.

Many of these trends jelled during 1989, resulting in a significant change in both the structure and patterns of inter-Arab affairs. The final phase of Egypt's return to the Arab fold, on its terms, had begun in 1987; in 1989, it was formally crowned by Husni Mubarak's presence at the Arab summit conference held in Casablanca in May, and the restoration, in late December, of diplomatic relations with Syria. Thus, the Egyptian-Syrian fault, one of the two most trenchant in Arab affairs during the 1980s, had been repaired, at least formally. Earlier, Lebanon (i.e., both competing governments) had restored full ties with Egypt. Only Libya held back, but even here bilateral ties were partially normalized. Given all this, the return of Arab League headquarters to Cairo from Tunis, its home since Egypt's suspension from the League in 1979, seemed to be a only a matter of time.

Another noteworthy development in 1989 was the creation of two new regional groupings, which took their place alongside the eight-year-old six-nation Gulf Cooperation Council (GCC): the Arab Maghrib Union (*Ittihad al-Maghrib al-'Arabi*; AMU), composed of five Arab states in North Africa, and the Arab Cooperation Council (*Majlis al-ta'awun al-'Arabi*: ACC), consisting of Egypt, Iraq, Jordan, and the Yemeni Arab Republic (YAR). The AMU's creation was the outgrowth of intra-Maghrib dynamics. The ACC's emergence was more sudden and less "logical" in geographic terms, and thus caused a number of ripples in the Arab world. Apart from its economic rationale, the ACC marked the formal institutionalization of the Egyptian-Iraqi-Jordanian alliance which had grown up during the Iran-Iraq War. In structural terms, the decade of the 1980s thus marked the formal division of the Arab world into more compact subunits, grouped around common political and economic

119

120

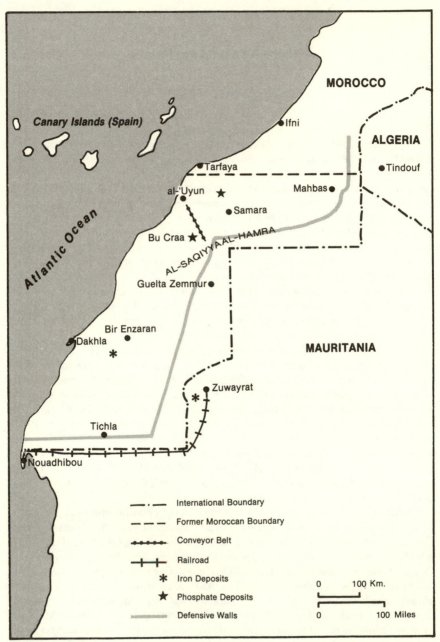

MOROCCO

Canary Islands (Spain)

●Ifni

ALGERIA

●Tindouf

Atlantic Ocean

●Tarfaya

al-'Uyun● ★

Mahbas●

●Samara

Bu Craa ★

AL-SAQIYYA AL-HAMRA

Guelta Zemmur●

Bir Enzaran●

MAURITANIA

Dakhla

✱

●Zuwayrat

✱

Tichla●

Nouadhibou

—·—·— International Boundary

— — — Former Moroccan Boundary

●●●●●● Conveyor Belt

┼┼┼┼ Railroad

✱ Iron Deposits

★ Phosphate Deposits

━━━ Defensive Walls

0   100 Km.

0   100 Miles

Western Sahara

interests: 15 of the 22 Arab League members were now also members of one of the three groupings.

The most important exception, of course, was Syria. Its absence from the ACC was clearly conspicuous but understandable, for the ACC was the least "organic" of the three bodies. No inter-Arab fissure had been more acrimonious during the 1980s than that between Syria and Iraq, largely, though not solely, thanks to Syria's support for Iran against Iraq. The cessation of hostilities in the Gulf brought no respite, for Iraq was more bent on extracting a measure of revenge than on amity.

The primary arena for Iraq's efforts to settle scores with Syria was Lebanon. Baghdad's active support for the anti-Syrian forces of Gen. Michel 'Awn greatly complicated Syria's efforts to impose order and helped to "Arabize" the crisis. Most of the Casablanca summit was devoted to Lebanon, and the level and intensity of Arab League-sanctioned mediation efforts in the Lebanese crisis were unprecedented. By the end of the year, however, the situation remained deadlocked.

In broader terms, Syria's regional posture was relatively weaker, due to a number of factors. In addition to the Lebanese imbroglio, Egypt's triumphant return to the Arab League and Damascus's exclusion from the ACC, one could point to Syria's continued failure to undermine Yasir 'Arafat's leadership of the PLO; Syria's unrealized hopes that the Palestinian Intifada would fundamentally alter Arab positions regarding the conflict with Israel; Syria's ongoing economic crisis; and, finally, the far less unqualified support which it received from its patron, the Soviet Union. Taken *in toto*, Syria's ability to shape events seemed more limited, although not completely exhausted, a situation which may well have engendered considerable soul-searching in Damascus, and undoubtedly underpinned its changed behavior *vis-à-vis* Egypt. Whether Syria would alter its long-held positions on the major issues facing the Arab world remained to be seen (see also chapter on Syria).

Subregional issues continued to command attention. The death of Iran's Ayatollah Ruhollah Khomeyni on 3 June further reinforced the more relaxed atmosphere which had taken hold among the GCC states after the cessation of hostilities the previous year. All of them were interested in restoring a sense of normalcy in their relations with Tehran, while seeking to maintain ties with Iraq — in essence, their traditional balancing act between two more powerful neighbors. In the Nile Valley, Sudanese-Egyptian relations first deteriorated, then improved dramatically following the overthrow of al-Sadiq al-Mahdi's government in July by the military. However, owing to its seemingly perpetual natural and man-made disasters, Sudan continued to rival Lebanon as the Arab world's reigning disaster area. On the other hand, by virtue of both the intractability of its problems and its relative isolation from the vortex of inter-Arab affairs, Sudan provided far less fertile ground than Lebanon for the acting out of inter-Arab (in this case Egyptian-Libyan) rivalries. In the south of the Arabian Peninsula, the People's Democratic Republic of Yemen (PDRY) continued to seek to move away from its previous isolation as a radical Marxist state by strengthening its ties with the GCC states and by maintaining a dialogue with the YAR regarding the unity ideal to which they both professed allegiance. The YAR-PDRY dialogue culminated in the very first summit meeting between their two heads of state, on 29 November in San'a. In addition, the PDRY probed the possibility of joining either the ACC or GCC, but without results. (For details on south Arabian affairs, see chapters on the PDRY and YAR.) Finally, Maghrib affairs were characterized by (a) a new era of good feeling in Moroccan-Algerian relations which had evolved during 1988 and catalyzed the creation of the AMU; (b) Algeria's overwhelming concern with the process of domestic political reform; and (c) generally more tempered behavior by Libya. However, the potential for renewed tension remained, as the prospects for resolving the Western Sahara conflict, which had looked so bright during the latter part of 1988 and early 1989, were not borne out.

Numerous important developments on the bilateral level are not treated in this chapter, or are done so only partially. For details, see relevant country chapters.

THE ARAB COOPERATION COUNCIL

The gestation period preceding the founding of the ACC was relatively short. The idea was first broached in 1988, spearheaded by Jordan's King Husayn.[1] A spate of inter-Arab consultations in the beginning of 1989 — visits by Iraq's President Saddam Husayn to San'a, by the YAR Prime Minister 'Abd al-'Aziz 'Abd al-Ghani to Amman and Baghdad, and by King Husayn to Cairo and Baghdad — quickly laid the groundwork. By the end of January, the Arab media were reporting on an imminent four-way summit conference among the heads of state of Egypt, Iraq, Jordan, and the YAR, which would establish an institutional framework to advance economic development and cooperation among them.[2] Ever mindful of maintaining proper relations with Syria, King Husayn sought to include Damascus in the grouping as well, or at least to appear to be doing so. Husayn argued that an inter-Arab economic grouping should not be influenced by political and ideological differences, citing the development of economic ties between Jordan and Syria between 1980–85, in spite of their serious political disputes, as a desirable model.[3] He was joined in his efforts to mediate between Syria and Iraq by YAR President 'Ali 'Abdallah Salih. These failed to bear fruit, owing to Iraq's firm opposition. Consequently, Husayn welcomed Syrian Prime Minister Mahmud al-Zu'bi to Amman on 9 February in order to ease Syrian displeasure with the upcoming four-way gathering and reassure Syrian leaders that Jordan did not view it as directed against Syria. Similarly, efforts to assuage Saudi apprehensions were made in separate visits to Riyadh by Husayn and Egypt's Foreign Minister 'Ismat 'Abd al-Majid.

Mubarak, Husayn, and Salih all led high-level delegations to Baghdad for the festive founding session of the ACC, hosted by Saddam Husayn, on 15–16 February. Upon conclusion, the four leaders issued a 17-clause document establishing the ACC. Article II defined the organization's aims as follows:

(1) "achieving the highest levels of coordination, cooperation, integration, and solidarity";

(2) working for gradual economic integration by coordinating development plans in a wide range of areas;

(3) "encouraging investment, joint projects, and economic cooperation"... between the various sectors of their respective economies;

(4) establishing a common market as a step toward an all-Arab common market and economic unity;

(5) "strengthening the ties and bonds among the citizens of the member states in all fields..."; and

(6) "bolstering and developing joint Arab action in order to strengthen Arab ties."
Institutionally, the ACC was to consist of the following:

(1) a supreme council, made up of the heads of the member states, which would meet annually in one of the member states on a rotational basis, with the host leader acting as chairman for that year; extraordinary sessions could be called for either by the council chairman or by two states;

(2) a ministerial council, consisting of the heads of government of the member states or their representatives, which was to meet once every six months, apart from extraordinary sessions; and

(3) a general secretariat based in Amman, headed by a secretary-general appointed to the post for two years, with a maximum of two renewals permitted.

With regard to decision-making, the members pledged to "strive to achieve unanimity and accord." However, if this proved unachievable, decisions were to be adopted by a majority vote, with the decisions binding on all. This was a departure from Arab League practice by which decisions were binding only on those who voted for them; it did not come as a surprise, given the four countries' repeated calls during the 1980s to change the League charter so as not to let a minority of countries (principally Syria) paralyze collective Arab decision-making. Only two areas required a unanimous vote: decisions pertaining to membership applications by other states (limiting the effectiveness of the declaration that ACC membership was "open to every Arab state wishing to join"); and amendments to the foundation agreement.

Both the Arab media and Arab leaders devoted considerable attention to debating and analyzing the motivating forces underlying the ACC. To what extent was it an economic organization? What were the political ramifications of the new grouping? The preamble to the agreement shed some light on these matters, as well as on the members' overall view of Arab and international affairs.

On the ideological level, the preamble laid forth what had emerged during the 1980s as a dominant theme in Arab nationalist thought: as "the positive and negative aspects" of previous experiments in forging Arab unity had shown, what was needed was buiding the "firm practical bases" for "the Arab nation's sublime objective of unity" from the ground up, and in all fields. Such action, the preamble noted, was legitimized by the Arab League charter, "which permits member states seeking closer cooperation and stronger ties to conclude any agreements fulfilling [the] aims...of solidarity and joint action" (Article IX of the League charter). Moreover, it was in harmony "with present world trends toward creating economic communities which ensure for their member states better conditions to safeguard their interests and achieve development and economic progress" (a reference to the upcoming European Economic Community [EEC] economic integration in 1992). However, the existing threats to "Arab national security" were not only economic in nature, but also involved "security, political...and cultural" elements as well. Thus, the preamble stated that:

> the maintenance of security, peace, and stability in the entire region calls for strengthening Arab awareness of the wholesomeness of pan-Arab security and its requirements and conditions, and also for entrenching this awareness through practical cooperation, coordination, and solidarity.

As for the four founding members, they were in "similar circumstances" in various fields, they adhered to the principles stated in the preamble and had already been promoting practical cooperation amongst themselves in recent years (a reference to the joint higher committees which had been established between Egypt and Iraq, Egypt and Jordan, Egypt and the YAR, Iraq and Jordan, and Iraq and the YAR. The ACC's creation was thus presented as a natural outgrowth of a decade-long trend. (For the complete text of the foundation agreement, see Appendix II.)

Subsequent statements on the ACC's *raison d'être* by high officials of the member states tended to vary in nuance, depending on their countries' priorities. Mubarak told an inteviewer that there was no purpose to the ACC other than promoting economic integration and growth. No steps in the political realm would take place on issues of all-Arab concern, he pledged, without going through established all-Arab channels, nor had military cordination been discussed at all.[4] The ACC, Mubarak declared at the post-summit press conference, was "not aimed at terrorizing anyone" (a statement designed to reassure those uneasy about Iraq's vastly enhanced military capabilities), but rather was intended to serve the whole Arab nation.[5] Mubarak's political adviser, Usama al-Baz, elaborated on the strategic elements of the grouping: a basic ACC principle, he told an interviewer, was that its member states would stand ready to combat any danger, threat, or attack to the Arab nation, and particularly the GCC states, from whatever source.[6] Baz's statement was consistent with Egypt's overall foreign policy outlook as it had evolved during the 1980s in the face of the Iranian threat in the Gulf (see *MECS* 1987, pp. 135–36).

The Iraqis were more explicit than the Egyptians in linking political aspects to the economic motivations underpinning the ACC. Without a "joint political agreement," stated Foreign Minister Tariq 'Aziz, a common understanding on economic issues and successful bilateral relations which had evolved over the previous decade could not have been achieved. While shunning the term "alliance" (*tahaluf*), he reiterated the four countries' like-mindedness on strategic issues: the Palestinian problem, relations with Iran, the Lebanese crisis, and the importance of Arab solidarity in the face of threats to "pan-Arab security." True, the ACC was open to others who might wish to join, but only on the condition that their political stands were not hostile — a clear reference to Syria which, he pointedly noted, did not even have diplomatic relations with Iraq and Egypt.[7]

As for the status of the Arab League, all the participants took pains to insist that the ACC's creation would strengthen the League, and not serve as a substitute for it. The League, declared Saddam Husayn, "was meant to be something more than what it is now." The ACC, as a "supportive body," would assist the League in "fulfilling its mission" and "reaffirming the principles on which it was founded."[8] Two concrete ways in which the ACC was envisioned as a model for the League were (a) carrying out the much-discussed, but long-delayed amending of the League charter in order to enable binding decisions to be taken by majority vote; and (b) holding regularly scheduled Arab summit conferences.[9] The GCC and AMU were viewed in a similar vein. As for cooperation between the different bodies, declared 'Aziz, it would be focused on the economic sphere; otherwise, the League would be left without any role at all.[10]

Official Arab reaction to the ACC's creation was uniformly favorable; even Syria avoided making negative comments. Behind the scenes, however, there was less enthusiasm. The Saudis and Syrians had both reportedly tried to pressure the YAR into not joining; the Saudis may even have exerted pressure in another way, by cultivating Yemeni tribal shaykhs in the disputed YAR-Saudi border region.[11] Concern with Iraq's future orientation was even more acute, and thus both Saudi Arabia and Kuwait sought clarifications. Saddam Husayn attempted to soothe their concerns. Kuwait, he declared, was "a fraternal Arab state that has made contributions to Iraq's combat capabilities." Thus, he pledged, the final border demarcation between them, a problem which they had inherited, would be solved amicably.[12] With the Saudis, he went further. Relations between Iraq and Saudi Arabia, Saddam Husayn stated, were based on both "human fraternity" and "practical reasons" and thus the two sides held continuous consultations on all matters.[13] To drive the point home, Saddam hosted King Fahd's three-day visit in late March, during which Fahd was awarded the highest civilian decoration in Iraq, the al-Rafidayn civilian medal of the first order, in appreciation for what was described as Saudi Arabia's unstinting generosity toward Iraq during the war with Iran. This was said to encompass monetary aid vital for Iraqi arms purchases, the use of a Saudi oil pipeline and Saudi territory to build another one in order to break the economic siege imposed by Iran and Syria, the placing of the Saudi port of al-Qadima at Iraq's disposal without cost, and continuous political backing. Another of Fahd's deeds, stated the decree, was a pledge to rebuild Iraq's nuclear plant destroyed in 1981 by Israel. (It was not clear whether this statement was a declaration of gratitude or a reminder of a pledge yet unfulfilled.)[14]

Never had the Iraqis been so full of praise for Saudi Arabia's behavior during the Gulf War. (For previous, less enthusiastic statements regarding the behavior of usually unnamed Arab states, see *MECS*, 1982–83, p. 195, and 1984–85, p. 119). But this was not all. Fahd's visit ended on 27 March with an agreement pledging the nonuse of force in their bilateral relations, the resolution of any disputes by peaceful means and noninterference in each other's internal affairs.[15] Such pledges were, as Fahd subsequently noted, already contained in previous agreements between Arab countries (the Arab League charter and joint defense pact of 1950 contained identical commitments).[16] Nonetheless, for Riyadh it was obviously important at this stage, in light of Iraq's vastly strengthened military posture, to have them reiterated. For Baghdad, the agreement was a further demonstration of its self-proclaimed benign intentions toward its GCC neighbors as well as an effort to further boost its regional standing both within the majority Arab coalition and *vis-à-vis* Iran and Syria.

Throughout 1989, ACC meetings took place at a dizzying place — they included two of the Supreme Council, three of the ministerial council, and no less than 13 four-way meetings of various cabinet ministers — as the member states strove to give teeth to their founding agreement. The two supreme council gatherings were held in Alexandria, on 15–16 June, and in San'a, on 24–26 September. In addition, the four heads of state met together in Casablanca on the eve of the Arab summit conference to coordinate positions.

The Alexandria meeting of the Supreme Council approved a number of recommendations drawn up by ministerial council meetings which had been held in Baghdad, on 10–12 April, and in Alexandria, on 14 June. These included the easing of movement and work of ACC nationals within each others' territories; enhancing cooperation in the legal and judicial fields and between their respective foreign ministries; choosing a secretary-general, Dr. Hilmi Mahmud Nimr — an Egyptian professor of economics, former president of Cairo University and former People's

Assembly member; and procedural matters concerning the working of the secretariat. They also set up a civil aviation council to study recommendations in the field of air transport. In foreign policy, they reaffirmed the principles of nonuse of force in their relations with other Arab countries (as Iraq had done with Saudi Arabia).[17] At the close of the summit, the new secretary-general issued a political statement reaffirming the four countries' support for (a) Iraq's position in the stalemated negotiations with Iran (see chapters on Iraq and Iran); (b) the "fraternal Palestinian people...their blessed Intifada...the [November 1988] resolutions of the Palestine National Council [PNC]...[and] the Palestinian peace unitiative"; and (c) the work of the tripartite Arab committee on Lebanon (established by the Casablanca Arab summit conference; see below), emphasizing "the need for the withdrawal of non-Lebanese (i.e., Syrian, as well as Iranian and Israeli) forces from Lebanon."[18]

The San'a meeting of the Supreme Council in September approved no less than 16 agreements which had been tendered to it by the ministerial council meetings of the previous week (16–17 September in Baghdad). They covered nearly every conceivable area, from economic, trade, and agriculture to education, transport, and drug-trafficking. The council also agreed on the secretariat's organizational structure and two-year budget.[19] The accompanying political statement by the secretary-general expressed support for international efforts to "eliminate the weapons of total destruction, whether...nuclear or chemical" (a reference designed to deflect Western concern with the proliferation of chemical weapons in the Arab world, especially Iraq's employment of them against Iran, but also to link it to Israel's apparent nuclear capability).[20]

Both Mubarak and Saddam Husayn cautioned against exaggerated expectations growing out of the ACC's establishment, at least in the short run. "The wheel has started to turn," stated Mubarak.

> We might think that it is turning slowly, but...we are taking calm and prudent steps so that no setback will occur.....It is easy to take quick steps which cannot be implemented.....The methods of the fifties, or the sixties, or even the seventies are not suitable for us.

The strategy being adopted, said Saddam Husayn, was "a call for reason...it does not mean abandoning the masses' romanticism, but adapting this romanticism to the facts and the resources."[21]

Indeed, these meetings and agreements, numerous as they were, established a skeletal structure only. The inherent difficulties in promoting meaningful integration among the four ACC countries were daunting. Unlike the GCC, this was not a club of oil-rich regimes with similar forms of government and social structure, and with clearly identifiable common interests. Nor did it have cementing factors akin to those of the AMU — fueled, as it was, by a Moroccan-Algerian *détente*, a keenly felt need to prepare for Europe's imminent economic integration, and a shared urge for a common Maghrib identity. Rather, the ACC was characterized by a lack of geographical contiguity (apart from Iraq and Jordan), diversity in regimes and social structures, and only a limited number of existing economic links. In trade, for example, only Jordan could count other ACC members (Iraq and, to a far lesser extent, Egypt) among its main trading partners.[22] Neither did the ACC have much practical economic value for Jordan in the face of its acute economic crisis which was highlighted by a wave of riots in April 1989 (see chapter on Jordan). Iraq did tender $20m. and pledge another $25m., but it was the GCC states, led by Saudi Arabia, which provided almost $400m. in emergency aid to prop up King Husayn following the April riots.[23] Most of all, wrote an authoritative Western source, "the potential for flourishing economic interdependence is retarded by the shortage of productive investment in the member countries, exacerbated by the size of their combined debt," estimated to be in excess of $80bn.,[24] a figure which did not include the massive loans made by GCC countries to Iraq during the Gulf War (and which Iraq may not have intended to repay). Obvious complementarity among the ACC states seemed to exist in only one, albeit important sphere: Egypt's manpower surplus, which had proved so vital to the maintenance of Iraq's civilian economy during the Gulf War. But this had predated the ACC, and moreover had ceased to be a factor following the termination of hostilities. With the cease-fire and partial demobilization of Iraqi troops, the number of Egyptians working in Iraq declined significantly, spurred on in late 1989 by widespread reports of violence against Egyptians by demobilized Iraqis seeking civilian employment. (For details, see chapters on Egypt and Iraq.)

Still, there was no shortage of ideas on how to strengthen intra-ACC links. Some were already under way, as the outcome of activities of various bilateral joint higher committees, such as improving the transportation networks among Egypt, Jordan, and Iraq, or linking the electricity grids of Egypt and Jordan; both of these, suggested Mubarak, could be expanded to include other neighboring states as well.[25] Egyptian-Iraqi cooperation in military industries was under way as well, and promised to continue for some time.[26] The YAR was hopeful that its ACC partners would make available expertise, capital, and materials to stimulate both large-scale village electrification and exploitation of newly discovered oil fields.[27] Secretary-General Nimr declared that one of the ACC's tasks was to restore investor confidence within the private sector in order to achieve greater balance between the public and private sectors. Regarding the massive food imports of the member states (Egypt alone imported some 60% of its needs), he suggested joint purchasing in order to obtain better prices, while working to expand agricultural production massively, particularly in Iraq.[28] One Egyptian official also suggested that the ACC framework might enable the members to cope better with their foreign debt problem by bargaining as a group with their creditors.[29] Another, an economist from Mubarak's ruling National Democratic Party, expressed the hope that ACC actions would lead to a drop in imports from nonmember countries (i.e., the industrialized nations).[30] However, even if the various ACC plans were implemented, it was estimated that the volume of mutual trade during the coming decade would be no more than 15% of the total foreign trade of any one of the members.[31]

The fact that progress toward the ACC's goals was bound, at best, to be incremental served as a reminder that the ACC had grown out of a convergence of *political* interests at the beginning of the 1980s. One could thus expect the "group of four" to seek to coordinate their political stands as much as possible. Indeed, this was soon manifested in the run-up to the Casablanca summit, as the ACC (and like-minded GCC as well) insisted that Egypt be invited to attend. At the same time, the ACC's essentially political nature meant that it was potentially vulnerable to possible future shocks (e.g., changes of regime or orientation, changes in the regional balance of power, etc.). More specifically, Iraq's growing power and aspirations to regional leadership, the potential for instability in Jordan, and differences between Iraq and Egypt over the situation of Egyptian workers in Iraq, the Lebanese crisis, relations with Syria, and policies regarding Arab-Israeli affairs, all carried the potential to cripple the ACC. Still, for the time being, the leaders of these states did see genuine value in promoting greater economic cooperation and development as a way to help stabilize the region, assist in coping with internal challenges, and respond to changes in the global economic and political environments, all under the heading of a more sober and mature ideology of Arab nationalism.

THE CASABLANCA SUMMIT, 23–26 MAY 1989

THE ROAD TO THE SUMMIT

The idea of holding an Arab summit was in the air at the beginning of 1989, for a number of reasons. During 1988, Lebanon had again become a significant arena of inter-Arab rivalries. Iraq's military backing for the anti-Syrian Lebanese Army under Gen. Michel 'Awn had contributed to Damascus's failure to stage-manage the election of a new Lebanese president, plunging Lebanon into its worst ever constitutional crisis. Consequently, the Iraqis trumpeted the idea of a special Arab summit to put Syria on trial. Others, particularly Jordan, sympathized with Baghdad but were more reluctant to hold a summit with an anti-Syrian tenor. They preferred instead a conference with a broader agenda and a less contentious mode, in which Syria could be cajoled into helping solve the Lebanese crisis, rescinding its last-ditch opposition to Egypt's return to the Arab League, and not placing obstacles in the way of the PLO. Indications from Syria that it was amenable to normalizing relations with Egypt, in order to shore up its weakened regional position, provided encouragement (see *MECS* 1988, p. 157). A further, if less striking indication of Syria's increasing flexibility was its renewal of diplomatic relations with Morocco on 9 January 1989 (for the background to the severing of ties in 1986, see *MECS* 1986, pp. 101–102).

Collective Arab involvement in efforts to solve the Lebanese crisis was formally legitimized on 12 January by an emergency meeting of the Arab League Council in Tunis, at the level of foreign ministers (called to discuss both US-Libyan tensions and Lebanon — for the former, see chapters on the US and the ME, and Libya). The council decided to create a six-nation committee of foreign ministers, chaired by Kuwait's Shaykh al-Ahmad al-Jabir al-Sabah, to mediate among the various parties in Lebanon "in order to achieve national concord."[32]

The council's session was officially left open, so as to allow it to reconvene readily as events unfolded. In fact, the efforts of Shaykh Sabah notwithstanding, the situation in Beirut rapidly deteriorated during March, as rival ports were mutually blockaded; Syrian troops blockaded east Beirut and fierce fighting took place between 'Awn's forces, on the one hand, and Syrian and Syrian-backed militias on the other (for details, see chapter on Lebanon). On 28 March, the Arab League Council, during its semiannual ordinary meeting in Tunis, appealed to "the combatant sides" for an immediate cease-fire and called on them to facilitate the work of the six-member committee.[33] The following day, the council, resuming its January session, endorsed the efforts of Shaykh Sabah's committee (which had submitted a 20-page report on its activities). The meeting was not tension-free, however. Iraqi Foreign Minister Tariq 'Aziz sharply criticized Syria, declaring that Iraq rejected any form of "custodianship" in inter-Arab relations and the notion that an Arab state should enjoy special status or privileges in any other state. In reply to 'Aziz (and to UN Secretary-General Javier Pérez de Cuellar's concurrent call for the withdrawal of non-Lebanese forces from Lebanon), Syrian Foreign Minister Faruq al-Shar' took pains both to reiterate the legality of Syria's presence in Lebanon and to emphasize that it was the Lebanese "nationalist forces," and not Syrian troops, who were engaged in the fighting.[34]

The fighting continued unabated, and the news that Iraq had supplied the anti-Syrian Christian forces with a number of ground-to-ground *FROG* missiles, capable of reaching Damascus, raised the diplomatic temperature even higher.[35] The bloodletting resulted in another emergency council session on 26–27 April in Tunis. Once again, 'Aziz and Shar' clashed sharply, as Syria sought to avoid any mention in the council's calls for an immediate cease-fire of its troop presence in Lebanon. On this point, Damascus partially got its way, as the council's statement referred only to "the parties involved in the fighting." (Ideally, Syria would have preferred that the statement refer only to "the Lebanese sides.") It also derived satisfaction from the council's call to implement UN Security Council Resolution 425 (an American-sponsored resolution passed in March 1978), which called for an immediate Israeli withdrawal (something which Syria insisted must precede the withdrawal of its own forces).[36] At the same time, the League moved to further institutionalize collective Arab involvement in the search for a solution by declaring its intention to establish a 321-man observer force, commanded by a Kuwaiti officer. Its function would be to monitor a three-month cease-fire, which would include the lifting of all blockades and the opening of all crossing points, to be followed by a round-table conference of Lebanese leaders who would choose a new president, agree on political reforms, and arrange for the withdrawal of foreign troops. Arab League assistant secretary-general Lakhdar Ibrahimi (an Algerian national) and Kuwaiti Ambassador to Syria Ahmad 'Abd al-'Aziz al-Jasim were charged with making contacts with all the parties to pave the way for the force to take up its positions.

As events in Lebanon unfolded, the majority of Arab states (the ACC and GCC groupings, and Morocco) moved to take advantage of Syria's difficulties there and its overall weaker regional posture by accelerating efforts to hold an all-Arab summit conference. In addition to further prodding Syria into loosening its grip in Lebanon, the intended summit would consecrate Egypt's return to the Arab League. It would also provide collective Arab backing to the PLO's diplomatic initiative of November-December 1988.

Originally, there had been some talk of holding, in March, the long-delayed "ordinary" Riyadh Arab summit conference, designated as such by the Fez summit of September 1982. The likelihood of this summit ever meeting soon faded, as the Saudis continued to prefer to have inter-Arab disputes thrashed out on someone else's turf. By the end of March, efforts to mobilize support for a special summit had moved into higher gear. A tripartite meeting of Mubarak, King Husayn, and 'Arafat in Isma'iliyya on 25 March concluded with both of Mubarak's guests endorsing the idea. Husayn went even further, declaring that the ACC states were in agreement that either they would attend a summit together, or would not attend one at all.[37] Their visit was followed immediately by that of King Fahd, arriving from Baghdad (see above). Before departing on 31 March, he, too, strongly endorsed a summit that would seal Egypt's presence in the Arab fold, something which, he stated, was "indispensable for joint concrete Arab work...in achieving the rights of the Arab nation." Fahd also informed Mubarak that the GCC states would not attend a summit if Egypt was not invited as well.[38] At the same time, the Saudis were concerned that too much pressure on Damascus with regard to Lebanon would have the opposite effect and poison the atmosphere of a summit.

Syria, for its part, now sought to ease its isolation regarding Lebanon by signaling readiness to be flexible regarding Egypt's return to the summit fold. For a time, Damascus still insisted on certain procedures: the summit should first be convened without Egypt, where the issue could be debated. Until then, Asad told American journalists, discussion of the matter was premature.[39] Syria's declared decision not to boycott a summit which would discuss Egypt's return was met with general satisfaction in Arab capitals. Some unnamed parties were even willing to accommodate Syria by having the first session of a summit, perhaps an unofficial one, formally invite Egypt to join them, the rationale being that since Egypt had been suspended by a summit decision, its return could only be secured by one as well.[40] But the Egyptians, who had never accepted the legality of the suspension (see *MECS* 1978–79, p. 230) would have none of this, or even of the idea that it would be invited by a preparatory foreign ministers' session. "The way for Egypt to attend the next Arab summit," declared the editor in chief of a pro-government Egyptian daily, "is a clear and unequivocal invitation, which...should suit Egypt's status and dignity." Otherwise Mubarak, who like all Egyptians cares for his homeland's dignity, would not attend.[41]

In late April, envoys of Morocco's King Hasan fanned out across the Arab world to firm up preparations for the summit, which Hasan would host in Casablanca the following month. As the summit date drew closer, the Syrians felt compelled to drop their procedural preferences. On 13 May, Syria announced officially that it no longer objected to Egypt's attendance.[42] Accordingly, on 16 May, Hasan telephoned Mubarak to formally invite Egypt to attend both the summit and a preparatory foreign ministers' meeting. The invitation was unconditional, as the Egyptians had insisted.[43]

With Syria having withdrawn its objections to Egypt's return, only Libya remained a question mark. Like Syria, Tripoli had also given sporadic indications during 1988 that it was not averse to improving relations with Egypt (see *MECS* 1988, pp. 160–61). Nonetheless, the Libyans publicly expressed their disapproval of Egyptian participation, unless Cairo could be impelled (with financial inducements, if necessary) to abandon its peace agreement with Israel; in fact, in Libya's view, existing circumstances in the Arab world were not ripe for a summit at all.[44] Moreover, at a meeting in Rabat on 13 May, Libyan leader Mu'ammar al-Qadhdhafi pressed Hasan to postpone the summit or cancel it altogether; he also accused Hasan of violating the AMU founding agreement by not consulting with the other members before issuing invitations to what he called a "suspect conference," for which there was no justification.[45] Qadhdhafi's other AMU partners, Algeria and Tunisia, as well as Syria, encouraged Qadhdhafi to attend; on the eve of the summit, Asad, Algerian President Chedli Benjedid, and Tunisian President Zayn al-'Abidin Ben 'Ali flew to Tripoli to press Qadhdhafi further and coordinate stands.[46] It was only on 22 May, the day before the summit's scheduled opening, that Qadhdhafi agreed to attend, although, he declared, he felt as if he was "walking on thorns." Should others take any steps "toward betrayal, surrender, and negligence," then he would immediately withdraw.[47]

The summit's preparatory meeting of Arab foreign ministers on 21–22 May was noteworthy mainly for the participation of Egyptian Foreign Minister 'Ismat 'Abd al-Majid. His welcoming by Morocco's 'Abd al-Latif al-Filali was met with applause by the other delegations.[48] Moreover, Egypt's presence was immediately felt, as its delegation took the lead in attempting to reconcile separate Palestinian and Syrian working papers on Arab-Israeli/Palestinian issues (see below). No Libyan or Lebanese representatives were present.

Nor was there any meaningful discussion on the Lebanese crisis. Meeting on the sidelines, the six-member committee prepared a detailed report on its activities for the summit. Submittted to the summit by Kuwaiti Foreign Minister Sabah, it claimed to have achieved the end to the shelling of civilian targets, while admitting that it was still unable to fully implement the Arab League resolution of 28 April. It also expressed disappointment with the unwillingness of other Arab states to contribute contingents to the proposed Arab observer force. The responsibility for Lebanon's future, the report concluded, was now in the hands of the summit.[49]

THE SUMMIT: THE INTER-ARAB WEB

The summit opened on 23 May. It was the ninth Arab summit of the last 13 to be held in a Maghrib state, and the sixth hosted by Morocco (Algiers had been the venue of two summits, and Tunis of one). In addition to Mubarak, 17 other heads of state were present, an extraordinarily high number; the PLO delegation was, as always, headed by Chairman 'Arafat; Kuwait was represented by its crown prince, and Mauritania by its foreign minister. Conspicuous by its absence was Lebanon: the summit's opening was held up for a few hours, as Syria successfully resisted King Hasan's proposal that the summit extend invitations to the two rival claimants to legitimate Lebanese authority, Gen. 'Awn and Prime Minister Salim al-Huss.[50] It was symptomatic of Lebanon's plight that it would not be represented at a summit whose discussions would revolve around it.

The summit's opening session consisted of two speeches, the first a welcoming address by Hasan, the other by Mubarak. Not only had Egypt been readmitted to the summit conference on its terms, it was being accorded pride of place. Mubarak barely mentioned Egypt's enforced absence from the Arab League in his address, nor did he engage in settling accounts. Rather, it was noteworthy in that he laid out in some detail his suggested directions for the Arab world in light of the widespread political and economic changes taking place in the international system as the 21st century approached — the moving away from the East-West nuclear balance of terror, the growing willingness to seek the resolution of regional conflicts by peaceful means, the upcoming EEC economic integration in 1992, and the development of "the Asian economic giant." The Arab world, he declared, must adapt itself accordingly, "in order not to miss the train." The path to be followed must be based on:

> a new conception of inter-Arab solidarity....We should benefit from the lessons of the past and its numerous experiences, for which we paid and are still paying heavily with the lives of our sons and our resources, at a time when other nations are vying with each other to entrench [themselves] in the world of today and tomorrow.

This concept, Mubarak continued, should be based on eight pillars. The most significant of them were:

(1) "an agreed Arab formula for peace," based on the "Arab peace plan" promulgated by the 1982 Fez summit (see *MECS* 1981–82, pp. 254–55), but wider and more comprehensive, so as to establish an "integrated framework" between the Arab countries and all of the neighboring states;

(2) a strict commitment to "the principle of noninterference in each other's internal affairs." It is not feasible, Mubarak declared, "that we should be enthusiastic in proposing this principle in the sphere of international relations" while failing to honor it;

(3) acknowledging "the law of life [which] calls for diversity and variation in views and methods," so that Arab countries may differ without fighting one another or drifting apart; and

(4) "laying down...practical policies which will lead to more economic, cultural, and political cooperation [and] creating the basic frameworks for joint development." This should include revising previous economic agreements, such as the Arab common market agreement of 1964 and the relevant resolutions of the 1980 Amman summit (for the latter, see *MECS* 1980–81, p. 234), as well as "a common vision" of the relationship with emerging international economic groupings. It also necessitated defining the relationship between the various Arab regional groupings and the Arab League, on the one hand, and those not affiliated with any of the groupings, on the other.[51]

Self-appointed mediators had invested considerable efforts at the previous two summits (Amman, 1987, and Algiers, 1988) to bring antagonists together in the hope of "purifying the Arab atmosphere." This trend continued at Casablanca, spearheaded by King Husayn, Fahd, Benjedid, Hasan, Salih, and the Kuwaiti crown prince. Their most notable failure was in the Iraqi-Syrian sphere: unlike in the previous two summits, Saddam Husayn and Asad held no face-to-face meetings, not even in the presence of others, thus providing further evidence that the rivalry between their two countries remained the most intractable of all inter-Arab disputes. By contrast, Asad did meet with 'Arafat on more than one occasion. The Asad-'Arafat meetings raised expectations for a Syrian-PLO breakthrough. These were not realized, although a measure of dialogue was maintained in subsequent months. At the summit itself, Syria attempted to water down the final statement's endorsement of the PLO, but without much success (see below). In any case, Damascus's differences with the PLO were not a top priority for Asad, and thus PLO-Syrian differences at Casablanca were played out in somewhat lowered tones.

Most noteworthy were Mubarak's meetings with Asad and Qadhdhafi, adding further proof that the latter two had chosen not to swim against the pro-Egyptian tide any longer. Mubarak's talks with Qadhdhafi took place "in an atmosphere of frankness and amity."[52] Most satisfying to Mubarak was that Qadhdhafi's rejection of Egypt's peace with Israel was no longer as big an obstacle to Egyptian-Libyan reconciliation as it had been hitherto. The two leaders agreed on the resumption of direct air links between their countries, the reopening of their common land border to traffic, and the cessation of propaganda campaigns against one another. Qadhdhafi also apparently agreed in principle to pay compensation to the tens of thousands of Egyptian workers summarily expelled from Libya in 1985 (see *MECS* 1984–85, pp. 560–61).[53]

Developments in the following months bore witness to the fact that the Mubarak-Qadhdhafi talks in Casablanca marked a breakthrough toward normalization. The highlight came on 16 October, with a Mubarak-Qadhdhafi summit in Marsa Matruh, an Egyptian town some 250 km. east of the border with Libya, followed by further talks the following day at a Libyan air force base in Tubruq. In December, Mubarak made another visit, to the Libyan town of Sirte. The result of their October meetings was an agreement to open diplomatic-interest sections in each other's capitals, as well as a host of cooperation agreements and easing of regulations regarding border crossings (for details, see chapters on Egypt and Libya). The only practical residue remaining from Qadhdhafi's opposition to the Egyptian-Israeli peace was his unwillingness to restore full diplomatic relations with Egypt, so that the Libyan flag would not have to fly alongside Israel's in the skies of Cairo. One practical manifestation was Qadhdhafi's refusal to meet with Mubarak there.

Mubarak's meeting with Asad was less dramatic. They had met previously at the Islamic Conference Organization's summit in Kuwait in January 1987 (for their tense exchanges, see *MECS* 1987, pp. 119–20); since then, the two leaders had reiterated on a number of occasions their mutual personal respect, dating back to their contacts during their air force careers. Neither did it lead to any immediate breakthrough in their bilateral relations — that would come only later, toward the end of the year. What was noteworthy about the meeting was Mubarak's treatment of the Lebanese crisis. On the one hand, he refused to confer special status or legitimacy on Syria's presence in Lebanon, explaining that his call during his opening speech for the withdrawal of "all" foreign forces as a part of a settlement was addressed to Syria as well as Israel and Iran. At the same time, Mubarak indicated that any solution must take Syria's position into account.[54] This pragmatic, noncontentious approach would guide Egypt throughout the summit's heated discussions on the Lebanese issue (see below). Asad, for his part, apparently sought Mubarak's assistance in staunching the flow of Iraqi arms to 'Awn (for further developments in Egyptian-Syrian relations after the summit, see chapter on Egypt).

THE PALESTINIAN QUESTION AT THE SUMMIT

The PLO's inter-Arab standing on the eve of the summit was unprecedentedly favorable, thanks to the Intifada-linked events of the previous year: the Algiers summit, King Husayn's disengagement from the West Bank, the PNC's declaration of independence and accompanying political program, and the initiation of PLO-US dialogue (for details on the inter-Arab aspects of these developments, see *MECS* 1988, pp. 144–52). Syria, the PLO's chief antagonist, was now both weakened regionally and preoccupied with Lebanon. The PLO thus came to Casablanca in a comfortable, if not commanding position, reasonably certain of an endorsement of the PNC's actions and of its opposition to Israel's newly promulgated plan for elections in the West Bank and Gaza Strip (see chapter on the ME peace process). One symbolic indication of the PLO's enhanced status was that its place at the conference table was labeled, for the first time, as the "State of Palestine."

The PLO's working paper, submitted to the preparatory foreign ministers' meeting, embodied 'Arafat's desire for a blanket endorsement of the PNC decisions and the PLO's political program. It began with a call for a reaffirmation of previous Arab summit resolutions regarding the need for: (1) "an Israeli withdrawal from all

Palestinian and Arab territories occupied in 1967"; (2) the establishment of an independent Palestinian state "on [Palestinian] soil" after a temporary period of supervision by the UN; (3) settling the Palestinian refugee problem in accordance with UN General Assembly Resolution 194 of 11 December 1948 (previous Arab summits, while insisting on the Palestinians' "right of return" or compensation, had never referred to this UN resolution specifically, owing to some of its less favorable language);[55] and (4) convening an international peace conference with the participation of the Security Council's five permanent members and all the parties to the conflict, "including the State of Palestine with an independent delegation" (previous summit resolutions merely called for PLO participation "on an equal footing," thus leaving open the possibility of subsuming PLO participation in either a joint Arab delegation or a Jordanian-PLO one). A further departure from the language of previous summit resolutions was the statement, taken from the 19th PNC's declaration, that the conference would be convened "on the basis of UN Security Council Resolutions 242 and 338," for the purpose of realizing "the inalienable national rights of the Palestinian people" and agreeing on "security guarantees for all countries of the region, including the State of Palestine." This last phrasing was also a departure from the Fez resolutions: while the Fez wording was that the Security Council would guarantee the peace, here the guarantees would be agreed on by the participants at the international conference (i.e., the belligerents would have a say in their formulation as well).

The working paper then called on the Arab states to:

(1) endorse the resolutions of the PNC's 19th session, and "the Palestinian initiative based on the Arab peace plan [the 1982 Fez resolutions] and international legitimacy [UN General Assembly Resolution 181 of 29 November 1947, advocating the partition of mandatory Palestine into a Jewish and an Arab state]";

(2) establish a committee of Arab leaders, headed by Morocco's King Hasan, to act in the international arena on the Palestinians' behalf;

(3) "support the Palestinian stand rejecting the Israeli Government's plan of holding elections under occupation," which, it stated, was intended to undermine the Intifada and bypass the PLO and Palestinian national rights;

(4) set up a commission composed of the five frontline states — Egypt, the "State of Palestine," Jordan, Syria, and Lebanon — to coordinate positions in advance of an international conference (by including Syria in preconference consultations, the PLO hoped to temper its opposition);

(5) fulfill the largely unmet financial pledges made at Algiers ($128m. immediately and $43m. monthly),[56] and channel aid to the territories solely through the PLO (the previous summit in Algiers had avoided such a commitment);

(6) call on the international community to prevent Israel from committing further "crimes" in the occupied territories, including the imposition of sanctions; and

(7) call on the US to recognize the Palestinian people's right of self-determination.[57]

Syria's working paper, by comparison, placed much greater emphasis on the pan-Arab aspects of the Arab-Israeli conflict, calling for the reiteration of previous resolutions pledging the mobilization of all Arab resources for confronting "the Israel enemy," in order to achieve the strategic balance which was a prerequisite for the liberation of Arab territories (Syria avoided explicit reference to the territories taken in 1967). Similarly, it rejected any settlement which was not comprehensive, and called for assistance not only to the Palestinians in the territories but also to those struggling against Israel in the Golan Heights and in Southern Lebanon. The working paper also pointedly downplayed the PLO's role: it did not employ the standard characterization of the PLO as "the sole legitimate representative" of the Palestinians, avoided the phrase "State of Palestine," made no mention of the PLO's "equal" or "independent" status at the proposed international conference, and refrained from praising the PLO's political program adopted at the 19th PNC. In this regard, it made no mention of UN Security Council Resolutions 242 and 338, nor did it explicitly mention UN General Assembly Resolution 194 when advocating the Palestinians' "right of return."[58]

It was the newly readmitted Egyptians who took the lead in preparing a formula to reconcile the two working papers. Egypt's efforts in this regard led to a number of disagreements between Syria's Shar' and Egypt's 'Abd al-Majid, centering on Syria's unwillingness to recognize the PNC's declaration of independence and political program, the explicit mention of UN Security Council Resolution 242 and the implicit endorsement of the 1947 UN partition resolution.[59] Shar' was at pains to tell an Arab interviewer that Syria was not opposed to the principle of a Palestinian state, but it rejected using the UN General Assembly partition resolution as a basis for its establishment (as the PNC had done), because the resolution entailed granting Israel recognition without getting anything in return.[60] Nor was the Egyptian document that was sent to the summit completely to Syria's liking, and it expressed reservations on a number of points. As it happened, however, Asad chose to avoid any further disagreements with Egypt and the draft was adopted by the summit *in toto*.

In essence, it was everything that the PLO wanted. To be sure, a number of additions designed to placate Syria were inserted: a call for Israeli withdrawal from all Arab territories taken in 1967, a pledge to mobilize Arab resources in all fields "to achieve comprehensive strategic parity," and a promise to extend material and moral support "for the Arab people's struggle in the occupied Golan Heights and in southern Lebanon." However, none of them infringed on the summit's confirmation of PLO primacy in all matters related to the Palestinian issues. Thus, the summit's final statement and accompanying resolution ratified every important point contained in the PLO's working paper, from endorsing the 19th PNC decisions, through according to the "State of Palestine" equal and independent status at the proposed international peace conference, reaffirming the Algiers summit aid pledges and agreeing to channel funds to the territories solely through the PLO, establishing a committee chaired by King Hasan to mobilize international support, and opposing Israel's election plan (thereby disappointing the US Administration, which had lobbied for more favorable language). One textual modification of some interest concerned UN Security Council Resolutions 242 and 338 as the basis for an international conference: whereas the PLO's working paper had coupled this proviso with a stipulation on realizing Palestinian "inalienable national rights," the final version of the summit resolution added the phrase "all the other related UN resolutions," thus leaving open, at least theoretically, the possibility that the demand for Israeli withdrawal would not be confined to the territories taken in 1967. As it happened, this was the language used by the 19th PNC. It appears that the drafters of the PLO's working paper had sought to move slightly beyond the PNC's formulation, but returned to it without difficulty as a small sop to Syrian sensibilities. In any event, this was the first Arab summit to have explicitly mentioned the UN Security Council resolutions as a basis for a peace settlement.

One more immediately operative area in which Egypt and the PLO did not succeed in budging Syria was the matter of consultations among the frontline states. Whereas they had hoped for a unanimous resolution proclaiming upcoming coordination, they had to settle for a summit call "to intensify coordination."[61] The less-binding language indicated Syria's unwillingness to follow their lead and perhaps have its hands tied with regard to the peace process.

Overall, however, the PLO's inter-Arab standing was further strengthened by the Casablanca resolutions. Syrian opposition had been of the rearguard variety[62] and Jordan had been completely passive, while Libya was alone in expressing reservations to the final product. Arab leaders, declared King Hasan, had "blessed the Palestinian plan and steps, thus adding legitimacy to their [i.e., the PLO's] legitimacy."[63] Henceforth, declared the head of the Democratic Front for the Liberation of Palestine, Na'if Hawatima, the Casablanca resolutions should serve as the common denominator between the PLO and the Arab states.[64]

THE LEBANESE CRISIS AT THE SUMMIT

As expected, it was the crisis in Lebanon that occupied the bulk of the summit's discussions (on 24–25 May). Syria strongly resisted the attempts of the other participants to include the withdrawal, or even redeployment of its troops, in a formula for reconstituting the Lebanese Government's authority. So charged was the atmosphere, and so difficult was it to reach a consensual resolution that 25 May, the summit's last scheduled day, was taken up by marathon meetings on both the foreign ministerial and summit level. Consequently, the summit's concluding, public session was postponed till the next day.

True to form, the Iraqis took the lead in castigating the Syrian presence in Lebanon. Baghdad's working paper on the Lebanese issue called for the establishment of a multinational Arab security (*quwwat al-amn al-'arabi*) under the flag of the Arab League, to replace Syrian forces, beginning in greater Beirut. This would allow the various Lebanese factions to reach a national reconciliation and restore the functioning of state institutions. The summit, the Iraqis suggested, should remain "open" so as to enable it to monitor the implementation of the plan.[65] As they had done at earlier foreign ministers' meetings, Iraq's 'Aziz and Syria's Shar' jousted sharply, even abusively, over the question of the legitimacy of Syria's presence in Lebanon and more generally, over their respective regional policies. So did Saddam Husayn and Asad; concurrently, Saddam Husayn rejected all offers by other Arab leaders to mediate between them.[66]

More problematic for Asad were the positions of the other participants: no one, not even his long-time ally Qadhdhafi, was willing to give Syria *carte blanche* in Lebanon. Qadhdhafi's declaration that Syrian forces must be removed from Lebanon surprised the participants: Saddam Husayn hastened to meet with Qadhdhafi afterward in order to try and win his support for Iraq's proposals.[67] The most substantive efforts to bend Syria's policies to the collective Arab will, however, came from the other important players: Egypt, Jordan, and Kuwait, backed by Saudi Arabia, Algeria, Morocco, and the YAR. At the same time, all were convinced of the futility of a head-on confrontation with Syria, and thus tried to include a measure of conciliation in their proposals. In a speech to one of the summit's closed sessions, King Husayn thus phrased his call for the deployment of an all-Arab force:

> It is high time for the Arabs to assume the burden and responsibility of dealing with the situation being undertaken by sisterly Syria and its forces, which entered Lebanon in the first place to stop bloodshed and achieve Lebanese reconciliation. This helps concentrate efforts on evacuating the occupying Israeli forces and the alien Iranian forces from the Lebanese territories.... With the attainment of this objective, Syria will have performed its full duty toward Lebanon and toward itself and its nation, considering it is the closest sister of Lebanon.[68]

The centerpiece of the Egyptian-led effort to find an acceptable formula was the call for the permanent withdrawal of all military and militia forces from greater Beirut during the month of June. Upon completion of the withdrawal, the Lebanese Parliament would convene to choose Lebanon's new president, who would then begin the process of reasserting the central government's authority over the entire country and ridding it of non-Lebanese forces. The Egyptians and Kuwaitis were willing to accommodate Syria by avoiding specific reference to the Syrian presence. Nonetheless, the call for the withdrawal from Beirut was too much for Damascus to swallow. The summit had two choices, declared Shar'. It should either recognize the legitimacy of the Syrian presence in Lebanon (and in greater Beirut) until Lebanese governmental institutions were reconstituted, or treat the Syrian role in Lebanon as it did Israel's, and act accordingly by synchronizing their troop withdrawals. (In essence, Shar' was throwing down the gauntlet.)[69] To demonstrate their determination further, the Syrians reinforced their military presence with additional troops and equipment, raising fears in the Lebanese Christian camp of imminent renewal of hostilities.[70]

With a deadlock looming, Arab foreign ministers called on Egypt and Kuwait to prepare a compromise formula for the summit's approval. They did so, and it was then adopted by the summit, except for one important point: missing from the summit's final statement and accompanying resolution on Lebanon was the Egyptian-Kuwaiti stipulation of the withdrawal of all military forces from greater Beirut. On this, Damascus had won out.[71] No less satisfying to Syria was the absence of any reference in the final product to the need to insure the withdrawal of Syrian (or even Iranian troops) from Lebanon. The only indirect reference to Syrian withdrawal in the final communiqué was the summit's expression of support for the yet-to-be established national reconciliation government's efforts to exercise its "full sovereignty" over Lebanese territory. Also missing from the final statement was any reference to the idea of creating an observer force to monitor the cease-fire.

Less satisfying to Syria was the fact that, operatively, the summit resolution further Arabized the Lebanese crisis. In the spirit of "the general Arab responsibility" for Lebanon and "the commitment of all Arab countries" to seek a solution, the summit established a three-member committee of heads of state — Saudi Arabia's Fahd, Algeria's Benjedid, and Morocco's Hasan — charging it with "full comprehensive authority" to achieve a resolution to the crisis.[72] Its task appeared to be similar to that of the six-member Arab League committee which had preceded it — to hold contacts "with all concerned parties" in order to enable the Lebanese parliament to convene to discuss a document of political reforms, followed by the choosing of a new president, who would then form a government of national reconciliation. All of this was designed to take place within six months; the summit conference was prepared to convene any time after that to examine the situation.

The results seemed meager, given the effort invested. Aware of this, Hasan sought in his postsummit press conference to stress the positive: the will of the summit, he declared, was one of "reconciliation and conciliation." But patience was needed, since the process was only beginning. Moreover, he stated with both frankness and optimism:

> we must understand that we have not yet found the way. When we find it we shall request a firm commitment and as I know the two men — be it President Asad or President Saddam — ....they cannot have committed themselves to the reconciliation of the Lebanese without having thought maturely about the nefarious consequences which continued violence would bring.[73]

Asad had cause to be sanguine about the resolution on Lebanon. By contrast (and regardless of the summit's backing for Iraq's position against Iran in their deadlocked negotiations), Saddam Husayn was unsatisfied with the Lebanese resolution, and undoubtedly with his ACC partners as well. He expressed his displeasure by leaving for home before the summit's concluding session at which the final statement and resolutions were made public. (Others who left early included Qadhdhafi, who did not want to be associated with the "shameful" summit resolutions either on the Palestinian or Lebanese questions,[74] Tunisian President Ben 'Ali, and Omani Sultan Qabus.) Iraq, Saddam Husayn declared from Baghdad, had reservations about the Lebanese resolution, but avoided making them official in order to provide "even a preliminary opportunity" to the committee of three leaders to achieve something.[75] As for relations with Syria, the Iraqis made sure to emphasize that nothing had changed. Efforts to achieve an Iraqi-Syrian reconciliation, Saddam Husayn declared, were out of the question until Asad reformed his "deviant and vicious actions and policies." As for the summit, it had given Asad "a last chance to save face and withdraw from Lebanon without an uproar."[76]

As was usually the case at Arab summit conferences, the balance sheet was mixed. Overall, Egypt and the PLO had achieved substantial gains; Syria had managed to withstand Arab pressure on Lebanon and buy time, albeit at the price of acquiescing to Egypt's return and to the resolutions on the Palestinian question, and despite its antagonizing other Arab leaders through its unwillingness to concede on Lebanese-related matters. Iraq showed itself unable to lead a coalition against Syria, but also served notice of its determination to continue trying to isolate Asad's regime as much as possible.

LEBANON AND THE COMMITTEE OF THREE

The Casablanca summit had prescribed the establishment of two committees: one, designed to lobby in the international community on behalf of the Palestinians, was not even formed during the remainder of 1989; the other, formed to deal with the Lebanese crisis, was peripatetic. Its guiding principle provided a clue to its efforts:

> Our committee is not a follow-up or a mediation committee [and therefore with limited authority], but a higher committee entrusted with the task of reviving the Lebanese State with all of its constitutional and security institutions in

order to preserve Lebanon's unity, independence, sovereignty, territorial integrity, and Arabism.[77]

Indeed, the committee's actions over the following months were unprecedented both in kind and degree during the 15 years since the outbreak of the Lebanese civil war. Also unprecedented was the constitutional crisis facing the Lebanese State, however fragmented. With the escalation of the fighting, the continued Syrian-'Awn standoff, and Iraq's stepped-up arms shipments to 'Awn, the urgency and intensity of the committee's work rose accordingly.

This state of affairs was reflected in the number of meetings and discussions held during the following months. Two tripartite summit meetings among Hasan, Benjedid, and Fahd were held in June, one in Rabat on 4 June, another in Oran, Algeria on the 27th. In between came a meeting in Jidda on 7 June of the three foreign ministers — Saudi Arabia's Sa'ud al-Faysal, Morocco's 'Abd al-Latif al-Filali, and Algeria's Boualem Bessaih — and Arab League assistant secretary-general Ibrahimi. Following this meeting, they went to Damascus (8 June) and Baghdad (10 June). These officials repeated their consultations with the Syrian and Iraqi leaderships twice more, on 2–3 and 9–10 July. They also held a series of meetings with various Lebanese politicians and spiritual leaders.

If Syria hoped for a respite from Arab pressure after Casablanca, it was mistaken. Instead, the tripartite committee continued to seek Syrian concessions regarding both the immediate security situation in greater Beirut and the long-term relationship between Syria and a reconstituted Lebanese State. As at Casablanca, the Syrians put all of their efforts into avoiding just that. Information regarding Syrian actions varied. During the initial stage of contacts, Syria reportedly sought to dissuade the committee from conditioning a meeting of Lebanese parliamentarians, who would discuss a reconciliation accord, on attaining a cease-fire in Beirut, lifting the sieges of all ports, and opening crossing points. Success in these efforts would both remove the onus from Syria for the continuation of the crisis and hopefully induce 'Awn and the Christian community to be more flexible. Foreign Minister Shar' was said to have pressed the point during his visits to Rabat and Algiers in mid-June. He found some sympathy in Algeria,[78] the committee member traditionally closest to Syria in its foreign-policy orientation. However, because the Moroccans and Saudis held sway, the Oran summit called for an easing of the situation in Beirut before the Lebanese reconciliation meeting could take place.[79] On the other hand, according to the committee's detailed report submitted to Arab leaders in mid-August, following a temporary cessation of its work (see below), Asad had expressed "Syria's readiness to help in achieving a cease-fire and reopening the crossing points without any condition." As for lifting the naval blockade, it was conditional on establishing a "security mechanism," whose task would be to prevent arms from reaching the eastern sector.[80]

Many of these arms were being sent by the Iraqis, rankling the Syrians no end. Indeed, reports of an increased flow of weapon deliveries from Baghdad multiplied during June and July. Particularly disturbing to Syria were declarations in the Iraqi media that Baghdad had supplied 'Awn with *Frog* surface-to-surface missiles capable of hitting Damascus.[81] The committee took up this complaint with Saddam Husayn and was satisfied with his response: at their first meeting, on 10 June, Saddam pledged to "immediately stop the dispatch of military hardware" once an agreement on a cease-fire and a lifting of the sieges had been reached." On the eve of their second meeting, on 3 July, Iraq issued a statement in which it pledged to stop supplying arms altogether. The fragility of Saddam's pledge was such that the three foreign ministers deemed it necessary to call on Saddam, in writing, to "fully adhere" to his commitments. Saddam's response was totally favorable, a fact the committee noted with appreciation.

Two months of intensive diplomacy resulted in the formulation of a comprehensive, multistage plan for political reform. However, the actual situation remained deadlocked. Thus, on 31 July, Fahd, Hasan, and Benjedid issued a joint communiqué declaring that their mission was at "a dead end." Two weeks later, they submitted a detailed report on their activities to Arab leaders. In what was an unprecedented move for inter-Arab mediators, the committee openly blamed Syria for the impasse. Their act was the more unusual since Saudi Arabia had, almost instinctively, always avoided public criticism of Damascus, while Algeria, as Syria's ally, had nearly always sympathized with Syrian policies.[82] On the immediate security level, the two states continued to differ with Syria on the terms for lifting the blockade. Still more important was the twofold political problem: the question of extending Lebanese sovereignty to all parts of the country, and the nature of future relations between Syria and Lebanon. The committee proposed a Lebanese-Syrian agreement establishing the principles of their bilateral relations, including a formula for the extension of Lebanese sovereignty over areas controlled by Syria and a Syrian troop withdrawal to the Biqa' Valley. It also proposed a second agreement, which would define the locations, size, and duration of the Syrian presence there. Both agreements were to be concluded under the committee's auspices. Syria, for its part, insisted that the questions of the Lebanese security forces extending their authority to all parts of Lebanon and of the Syrian troops withdrawing to the Biqa' could only be discussed *after* the establishment of a national reconciliation government. Moreover, Syria sought to exclude the committee from overall responsibility for the implementation of any agreement. As for overall Syrian-Lebanese relations, Damascus preferred to define them in much more intimate terms than the committee found desirable. Concluding its statement, the committee declared that the Syrian conception would "obstruct the possibility of an integrated, coherent implementation of the other parts of the proposed reconciliation document."[83]

The Syrian reaction was immediate and sharp, although Damascus sought to avoid exacerbating its differences with the committee any further. In a detailed letter to the committee's three foreign ministers, Faruq al-Shar' insisted that Syria remained unwavering in its support for the Casablanca resolutions and the tripartite committee's efforts. At the same time, he decried the absence of "an objective and fair evaluation" of the parties involved. The committee's treatment of the sea blockade issue was, in Shar''s view, particularly grievous. The committee had retreated from its intention, expressed during its meetings in Damascus in early June, to set up the mechanism for inspecting ships bound for east Beirut. Furthermore, Iraq's commitments to the committee regarding arms shipments were "refuted by facts and documents." More generally, Shar' emphatically rejected the committee's insinuations that Syria was not concerned with Lebanon's sovereignty or the need for the Lebanese authorities to reestablish their authority over the whole of the country. He noted that the Casablanca summit resolution did not refer even remotely to Syria in the context of Lebanon reasserting control over its territory, a point for which Syria had fought hard at the summit. The Casablanca resolutions, Shar' claimed, were also identical to the Syrian positions in another respect: that it was the yet-to-be-constituted Lebanese national reconciliation government which was entitled to exercise full sovereignty over Lebanese soil. Moreover, Shar''s letter reiterated Syria's long-standing position that its presence in Lebanon was "legitimate within the context of Lebanese sovereignty, and not in breach of it." In summing up, Shar' declared that the divergent perspectives on the sovereignty of Syria and the committee stemmed from the committee's "assuming the responsibilities of the government produced by the national reconciliation even before reconciliation is realized and a reconciliation government is in place."[84]

The suspension of the committee's work in July further raised the inter-Arab temperature. Jordan's support for the Arab consensus at Casablanca had rankled Syria. Morever, Amman's denials of having assisted in the transfer of Iraqi arms to 'Awn were not convincing in Damascus. In the wake of the diplomatic deadlock, Jordan reiterated, both publicly and privately, its hopes that Syria would cooperate with the tripartite committee; Syria, for its part, expressed its unhappiness with Jordan more actively.[85] Apparently, one way Syria did so was to permit Palestinian guerrilla groups under its supervision to launch cross-border raids against Israel via Jordanian territory, a Syrian tactic which dated back to the mid-1960s (see chapter on armed operations). Syria also signaled its displeasure with the Saudis, with a hint of threat, via a number of anti-Saudi articles in pro-Syrian publications in Beirut.[86] To further bolster its position, Syria stepped up high-level consultations with Iran, its decade-long ally against Iraq and (to a lesser extent) in Lebanon. One outcome of the contacts between Syria and Iran was their cosponsoring of a newly formed front of Lebanese and anti-PLO Palestinian organizations, which called for 'Awn's overthrow. According to Saddam Husayn, the Iranians were offering troops, equipment, and financial support to Syria if it would act to liquidate 'Awn.[87] (For more on Syrian-Iranian relations, see chapter on Syria.)

Iraq, for its part, immediately pounced on the tripartite committee's reprimand of Syria. It claimed justification for its own outspoken anti-Syrian stand at Casablanca, implicitly criticized those who preferred a policy of cajolement, and called for the convening of an emergency Arab summit to "assume its historic responsibilities" toward the Lebanese crisis. The summit's actions, declared Tariq 'Aziz, should be based on "collective Arab confrontation" with the Syrian regime.[88] The lack of Arab response did not deter Baghdad, as it repeatedly attacked Syria's "anti-Arab alliance" and "collusion" with Iran.[89] The visibility of Baghdad-based Syrian opposition groups was sharpened as well (for the increased activities of each other's opposition groups, see chapters on Syria and Iraq).

The tripartite committee may have desired a cooling-off period before resuming its efforts. But the intensification of the fighting dictated otherwise. On 15 August, the committee issued a "humanitarian appeal" for an "immediate and overall cease-fire."[90] Two weeks later, the diplomatic wheels began to turn again. Asad, Hasan, and Benjedid were all present in Tripoli, Libya for the 20th anniversary celebration of Qadhdhafi's ascent to power, and used the occasion to attempt to break the logjam. Reports of their three-way meeting differed. One journal stated that Asad responded favorably to Hasan's latest suggestions, while another source reported that each of them accused the others of deviating from commitments made at Casablanca.[91] Regardless of what transpired, what was most significant about the meeting was that it occurred, an indication that both Syria and the committee were interested in avoiding further friction. Additional talks were held during the same week between Shar' and the committee's foreign ministers on the sidelines of the summit of nonaligned nations in Belgrade.

The ground now seemed ready for the formal resumption of the committee's activities. On 6 September, Fahd, Hasan, and Benjedid met in Jidda. One week later, their foreign ministers did the same, and on 16 September they issued a seven-point plan, beginning with an insistence on an immediate cease-fire as a prerequisite for solving the crisis. The Syrians had cause to be satisfied: a centerpiece of the agreement was the formation of a "security committee," headed by the tripartite committee's representative Lakhdar Ibrahimi, which was charged with both supervising the cease-fire and, more important, with preventing seaborne arms supplies from reaching any of the parties. To insure balance, all sides were called on to halt arms supplies to the various factions. The sea blockade was to be lifted and Beirut airport reopened as soon as the committee began operating. Once all of these measures had been taken, members of the Lebanese parliament were to convene, on 30 September, to prepare a document of national concord.[92] Overall, it was clear that the committee had decided that its previous strategy of directly pressuring Syria had not borne fruit and that it should thus give greater weight to Syrian demands.

Indeed, three weeks of discussions among members of the Lebanese Chamber of Deputies in Ta'if (30 September-22 October) produced a "document of national accord" in line with Syrian conceptions (for details see chapter on Lebanon). Although a number of Christian deputies sympathetic to Gen. 'Awn sought a precise timetable for the complete withdrawal of Syrian troops, the accord spoke only of a two-year period during which Syria would assist the future government of national reconciliation in extending its authority over all of Lebanon. At the end of that period, Syrian troops were to be redeployed in the Biqa' region and at other points to be mutually agreed on; as would their numbers and the nature of their relationship to the Lebanese authorities. According to the text of the accord, the tripartite committee would assist Syria and Lebanon in reaching such an agreement if they so wished. On the other hand, an accompanying committee statement declared that an Arab summit meeting would be responsible for concluding and implementing the agreement, indicating the committee's desire to maintain collective leverage on future developments. In addition, the accord also included a paragraph defining the "special relationship" between Lebanon and Syria. Of particular importance to Damascus was the clause stating that:

> Lebanon should not allow itself to become a pathway or a base for any force, state, or organization seeking to undermine its security or that of Syria's.

In return, Syria was obligated not to "permit any act that poses a threat to Lebanon's security, independence, and sovereignty."

The tripartite committee's declaration which accompanied the accord further underscored its shift toward accommodating Syria. The committee expressed its "full appreciation" for Syria's "fruitful cooperation" which had made the accord possible, and particularly "sister Syria's...reiteration of its readiness to make a serious contribution to putting the national reconciliation document into effect." This may have also included a Syrian oral commitment to withdraw its forces from the Beirut area within six months after the formation of the new government.[93] To be sure, the committee's emphasis on its continued responsibility for and commitment to Lebanon's welfare, "backed by the Arab summit," marked a degree of collective Arab involvement greater than Syria deemed desirable. But on the whole, the document of national accord fitted Syria's requirements.[94]

Yet, for Syria, successfully deflecting collective Arab hostility to its Lebanese policies did not ensure a political settlement attuned to its needs. Opposition to the Ta'if agreement was widespread among the various Lebanese factions; most vocal in his rejection was 'Awn, Syria's number-one opponent, and Ibrahimi's efforts on behalf of the tripartite committee to obtain his cooperation came to naught. René Mu'awwad's election as president on 5 November briefly provided Syria with some hope that 'Awn's own legitimacy would be placed in doubt. However, Mu'awwad's assassination 17 days later dashed that expectation, and his hastily chosen replacement, Ilyas al-Hirawi, was a virtual unknown. In December, the tripartite committee engaged in another round of efforts, first with a foreign ministers' meeting in Riyadh on 3 December, followed a week later by consultations with Syria, Iraq, France, and the Vatican. The statement issued after the Riyadh meeting described 'Awn's rejection of the Ta'if agreement as the "main obstacle" to its implementation,[95] thus completing the shift which had begun in August. What had not been altered, however, was the continuing deadlock on the ground (for further discussion, see chapter on Lebanon).

While Syria remained stymied, and even embarrassed, in its efforts to forge a satisfactory solution to the 15-year-old Lebanese imbroglio, its position remained preeminent there and, in inter-Arab terms, Syria had weathered the storms of 1989. At this point, it chose to renew diplomatic relations with Egypt, an act designed to further ease its regional isolation, deflect attention from its lack of success in toppling 'Awn, and perhaps prepare for the eventuality of a renewed Arab-Israeli peace process. Coming at a time of tension between Egypt and Iraq over the treatment of Egyptian workers there (see chapters on Egypt and Iraq), Damascus may have even hoped to begin driving a wedge between Cairo and Baghdad.

MAGHRIB AFFAIRS

The creation of the AMU in February 1989 marked an important milestone in the modern history of the Maghrib. For the first time in the post-colonial era, the five Maghrib states — Morocco, Algeria, Tunisia, Libya, and Mauritania — had established an all-inclusive regional grouping to coordinate their political and economic relations with one another. In doing so, they sought to give a tangible expression to a long-expressed but previously ill-defined desire for institutionalizing a common Maghrib identity. However, the new grouping generated few visible results during the remainder of the year, indicating the continued gap between lofty aspirations and their realization. To be sure, the overall improved state of bilateral relations among the member states, most importantly between Algeria and Morocco, indicated that a new, less contentious era was emerging. Nonetheless, clouds remained on the horizon, generated mainly by the lack of further progress toward resolving the conflict in the Western Sahara.

THE ARAB MAGHRIB UNION

Most of the ground work for the AMU's establihment had been laid during 1988 (see *MECS* 1988, pp. 161–64). The progress registered had been made possible by a number of factors, the most important of which was Algeria's decision to partially delink its relations with Morocco from its longstanding support of the Polisario movement in the Western Saharan conflict. The Algerians were assisted in this by Morocco's readiness to cooperate with a mediation effort sponsored by UN Secretary-General Pérez de Cuellar, designed to conduct a referendum among the Saharans to determine the area's ultimate status. Algeria, King Hasan told an interviewer, was no longer a party to the conflict[96] (he had, in fact, made a similar statement to the BBC 18 months earlier, but its reiteration was nonetheless significant). Less central, but nonetheless important, was Libya's willingness to take part in the process of "building the Greater Maghrib edifice" (*bina'sarh al-maghrib al-'arabi*) on the terms laid down by the others.

Two events in January 1989 helped jell the all-Maghrib *rapprochement*. The first was the Moroccan-Libyan abolition of visa requirements for each other's nationals.[97] More significant was King Hasan's aboveboard meeting in Marrakesh on 4 January with three senior Polisario officials, an act he had long resisted. The meeting was immensely pleasing to Algeria, which had steadfastly insisted over the years that it was not a party to the conflict and that it could be resolved only by negotiations between Morocco and Polisario. Whether or not the holding of direct talks was an Algerian condition for sealing Algerian-Moroccan and all-Maghrib ties could not be determined. But surely Hasan was well aware of its significance for Algeria on the eve of the establishment of the AMU and thus agreed to receive the Polisario delegation. (For its significance in the Western Saharan context, see below.)

Final preparations for the AMU's establishment were made in late January and early February. On 23–24 January, the "Higher Maghrib Commission" (a body which included the Moroccan and Algerian foreign ministers, the Tunisian prime minister, and senior officials from Libya and Mauritania) met in Tunis to review the work of various all-Maghrib subcommittees and to discuss the upcoming all-Maghrib summit. Two weeks later, Algerian President Benjedid led to Rabat a high-level ministerial delegation designed to boost bilateral cooperation in fields such as transport, commerce, and energy. A "joint higher committee" was established for this purpose at the conclusion of the visit. Of particular significance were discussions on a proposed Algerian gas pipeline across Moroccan territory, which would link up with West Germany and France, via Spain. According to Algeria's energy minister, the project would both create hundreds of jobs in Morocco and supply thousands of Moroccan homes with gas.[98] No less important was their unannounced decision to resolve their long-standing border problems (Morocco had never ratified a 1972 treaty delineating the frontier) and to develop their common border areas, both agriculturally and industrially.[99]

The founding of the AMU was proclaimed at a festive gathering of the five Maghrib heads of state in Marrakesh on 16–17 February. Three documents were issued: a final communiqué of intent; the 20-article Marrakesh Treaty, laying out the AMU's institutional framework and guiding principles; and a resolution delegating the newly established bodies to draw up an action program and implementation timetable, based on the work of the higher commission and sectoral committees.

The final communiqué was a statement of lofty principles. It included references to both the ties of "religion, language, and history" binding the peoples of the Maghrib, and the "unity of aspirations and expectations"; to the "dire need" to achieve "effective cooperation" and "continuous integration in all spheres"; to the myriad political, economic, cultural, and social challenges facing their countries, particularly in view of the "rationally planned...and firm and unhurried steps" toward regional integration elsewhere; and to a belief that "a unified Arab Maghrib constitutes a fundamental phase on the path toward Arab unity" (this last stipulation was included to satisfy Qadhdhafi).

The Marrakesh Treaty spelled out in more detail the AMU's guiding principles. Article 2 spoke of "consolidating friendly ties between member countries and their peoples," which would be achieved by progressively ensuring the freedom of movement of persons, goods, services, and capital among the member states. Article 3 envisaged a political community which both preserved the independence of all members and promoted cooperation in all fields — diplomatic, economic, cultural, and educational. Article 14 stipulated that aggression against one of the members would be considered aggression against all of them. Even more important was Article 15: the member states pledged not to tolerate any activity within their territories which would harm the security, territorial integrity, or political system of any of the members. This was especially significant for Tunisia, which in 1980 had been exposed to Libyan-sponsored subversion (see *MECS* 1979–80, pp. 208–209). With regard to the Western Saharan conflict, this clause precluded Polisario attacks on Morocco proper (which had occurred during earlier phases of the conflict, but not for many years); however, this clause did not indicate an endorsement by either Algeria or Mauritania of Moroccan claims to the Western Sahara. Article 15 also implied the final determination of the Moroccan-Algerian border. Finally, the members pledged in Article 15 not to adhere to military or political alliances which threatened each other's independence or territorial integrity.

Institutionally, the AMU's supreme body would be the presidential council, made up of the members' heads of states. It would meet every six months, apart from extraordinary sessions, with the chairmanship being rotated accordingly. Its decisions were to be taken unanimously. A foreign ministers' council would prepare the sessions of the presidential council as well as oversee the work of specialized ministerial committees; the members' prime ministers were encouraged to convene whenever necessary. The treaty also stipulated the creation of a compact secretariat general, whose location would rotate along with the chairmanship of the presidential council. A consultative council made up of six representatives of each state, and a judicial organ, composed of two judges from each state to be nominated for six-year terms, were also to be established. Finally, any Arab or African state which desired to join the AMU could do so, as long as the members agreed. Leaving the AMU membership was a result of Qadhdhafi's demand that Niger, Mali, Chad, and Sudan be included in the pact.[100] (For the texts of the final communiqué and Marrakesh Treaty, see Appendix III.)

The third document was more technical, in that it sought to set up a timetable of implementation. Among possible issues to be discussed were the cancellation of entry visas and the establishment of a common Maghrib identity card for travel within the AMU. Encouragement of the movement of people, goods and services, and capital were seen as vital steps toward the establishment of a common market.[101]

Inevitably, Maghrib leaders varied in their public analyses of the AMU's underlying significance. Qadhdhafi, for example, adhered to his traditional "unionist" position. All Arab regional groupings, he insisted, "should be included in the framework of the Arab union from the [Atlantic] Ocean to the [Persian/Arab] Gulf." To reinforce his unionist thrust, he was keen to promote another regional grouping parallel to the AMU and ACC — "a Swahili union, which would protect the southern part of the Arab homeland littoral to the Arabian Sea and the Indian Ocean." To that end he dispatched Col. Abu Bakr Yunis to Somalia, Djibouti, the two Yemens, and Oman.[102] At the same time, he was especially concerned about the "negative effect" the new groupings had on those not belonging to any of them — most importantly, Sudan, but also Syria, Lebanon, and the PDRY. In fact, he considered Egypt's "abandonment" of Sudan in favor of the ACC framework was the cause of renewed instability in that country. Apart from the regional dimension of his policies, Qadhdhafi's comments contained a populist and revolutionary dimension missing from those of the others. For example, he stressed the need for women in the AMU to "move from the harem section to the section of human beings."[103]

Hasan, by way of contrast, stressed the AMU members' will to move rapidly, "but in an orderly manner." He also had special words of praise for Algeria: its economic and political liberalization, he said, served as a vital step which would strengthen the collective. As for the conflict in the Western Sahara, he insisted that it was never a subject for discussion in the plenary, even on a constitutional basis. Everyone agreed, Hasan declared, that this "grain of sand" (or, varyingly, "banana peel" or "historic fly") could disappear quickly.[104] Algerian Foreign Minister Boualem Bessaih, for his part, did not mention the Saharan conflict in a postsummit commentary. Rather, like Hasan, he called for a prompt collective Arab response to world economic trends:

> economic integration and...political unity are long-term, if not very long-term tasks and there is therefore a high price to be paid for any delay....[105]

Algerian-Moroccan relations, the keystone to the AMU's long-term viability, developed satisfactorily in subsequent months, although the renewal of Polisario-Moroccan fighting late in the year was a source of tension. Libyan-Tunisian relations, which in the past had been problematic as well, and Algerian-Libyan relations, also developed adequately (for details, see chapter on Libya). On 3 March, the anniversary of Hasan's ascension to the throne, he made public what had been agreed the previous month with Benjedid: his decision to have parliament ratify the 1972 Moroccan-Algerian frontiers (thus renouncing, in effect, long-standing Moroccan nationalist claims to the Tindouf area of Algeria).[106]

The month of March also witnessed a number of high-level contacts designed to revive previously unimplemented agreements in the areas of commerce, finance, culture, and imformation; the finishing touches were put on the border demarcation agreement during April,[107] and on 14 May the treaty took effect upon the exchange of the instruments of ratification. On 29–30 May, the foreign ministers of the two countries chaired meetings of a "joint higher committee." The meetings concluded with the signing of a number of agreements on bilateral matters; it was also decided that the committee would meet every six months, and that a follow-up committee would meet every three months.[108]

As for the AMU, a number of concrete steps were taken to activate the February proclamations. A consultative council (*majlis al-shura*), composed of 10 parliamentarians from each state, was proclaimed on 10 June at a meeting in Algiers; it first working meetings were held in October in Rabat. The AMU follow-up committee, which had been stipulated by Article 9 of the founding treaty, met on two occasions at the level of secretary of state for foreign affairs in charge of AMU affairs — in late July in Rabat and in mid-October in Algiers. The committee passed on its recommendations to the AMU's council of foreign ministers, which met on 29–30 October in Rabat. The council's main operative action was the adoption of the follow-up committee's recommendation to establish four specialized commissions dealing with: food security, economy and finance, basic infrastructure, and human resources.[109]

Politically, the AMU, led by Hasan, attempted to mediate during April in the sharp dispute between Mauritania, a fellow member, and Senegal, with whom the others had good ties. The results were inconclusive, yet as a first collective effort, it was noteworthy in and of itself.

Despite both the fanfare and the practical steps taken to put meat on the bare bones of the founding charter, the AMU remained more of an aspiration than anything else. Their collective problems were formidable, among them an exploding population (expected to increase by one third over the next decade, from 65m. to 100m. people),[110] large differences in levels of per capita income, a stagnant agricultural sector, the challenge of the EEC's impending unification in 1992, and the large foreign debts, particularly of Morocco and Algeria. These problems could be addressed effectively only over the long term, if at all.

In the meantime, the AMU failed to convene another summit during 1989, although one finally took place in mid-January 1990 in Tunis. The lack of a summit further highlighted the slow place at which Maghrib integration was progressing. Moreover, summit-level diplomacy was not without controversy. It had been expected that another AMU summit would take place on 1 September in Tripoli, on the sidelines of the 20th anniversary celebrations of the Libyan Revolution. However, Mauritania's president was absent; more importantly, Hasan irritated Qadhdhafi by remaining on his yacht, anchored in Tripoli harbor, and thus not attending the festivities. In return for the perceived snub, Qadhdhafi absented himself from a shipboard meeting of Hasan, Algeria's Benjedid, Tunisia's Ben 'Ali, and a senior Mauritanian official, delegating Maj. Khuwaylid al-Humaydi to arrive only at its end. Bruised feelings were subsequently soothed by Qadhdhafi's call on Hasan on 2 September, following which Hasan briefly left the ship to appear at a military parade (in which a symbolic contingent of Moroccan troops took part).[111] Given the often stormy history of Qadhdhafi's relations with Hasan and others, the personal dimension would undoubtedly play a role in future Maghrib developments.

THE WESTERN SAHARA CONFLICT

The prospects for the resolution of the conflict had never seemed so bright as at the beginning of 1989. Both Polisario and Morocco had given their assent in principle during the previous months to a UN-sponsored plan for a cease-fire and referendum to determine the territory's future (see *MECS* 1988, pp. 164–67). To be sure, a number of the particulars had yet to be worked out, most notably the determination of voter eligibility and the status of Moroccan troops and administration during the interim, prereferendum period. The overall atmosphere, enhanced by Polisario's declaration at the end of 1988 of a unilateral cease-fire, was nonetheless favorable.

A further breakthrough came on 4–5 January, when Hasan held two days of talks with three senior Polisario officials in Marrakesh. He had already indicated his intent to do so the previous month. Nonetheless, his assent to Polisario's and Algeria's long-held insistence on direct, aboveboard negotiations between Polisario and Morocco seemed to bode well for the future. According to a Gulf newspaper, Hasan promised his interlocutors that the Sahrawis in the Polisario-run refugee camps in Tindouf would be allowed to participate fully in any referendum.[112] Elsewhere, it was reported that Polisario and Moroccan officials had held a number of other secret meetings in Arab and European cities, that Polisario was no longer insisting on complete Moroccan withdrawal prior to the referendum, and that it was considering accepting an offer of meaningful autonomy for the territory in lieu of full independence.[113] Indeed, optimism reigned, at least for a short period following the Marrakesh meeting: Polisario praised Hasan for adopting a "constructive and courageous position," and one official spoke of a "climate of calm and trust" which hopefully would result in an agreement on the details of the UN plan.[114] The incipient peace process seemed to receive a further boost from a fact-finding tour of the region, in mid-January, of the UN secretary-general's special representative, Hector Gros Espiell.

However, matters developed no further. Having made the requisite gesture to Algeria and the UN of holding direct talks with Polisario, Morocco now chose to direct its energies elsewhere — toward consolidating its *rapprochement* with Algeria and matters connected to the founding of the AMU. Time, the Moroccans had apparently concluded, was on their side, not Polisario's. Thus, Moroccan officials downplayed the significance of the first set of Polisario-Morocco meetings,[115] and a second round, which Polisario had understood to be scheduled to take place on the sidelines of the Marrakesh summit, or shortly afterward, was not held.

The achievement of all-Maghrib *rapprochement* without Polisario, embodied by the AMU, highlighted Polisario's weakened position. However, Polisario's secretary-general and president of its government-in-exile (the Saharan Arab Democratic Republic — SADR), Muhammad 'Abd al-'Aziz, cast developments in a favorable light:

> Contrary to speculations, we Saharans do not believe that this union has harmed us. On the contrary, we believe it has stimulated the convening of the second Saharan-Moroccan meeting....[Moreover, the AMU treaty] has opened the doors to the SADR's membership and thus to the solution of the Western Sahara conflict without winners or losers....Building the greater Maghrib signifies the rallying of all its members' energies and it will eventually diminish their obsession with individual borders and place the emphasis on those of the whole, within a framework of mutual trust.[116]

Disappointed with Morocco's refusal to hold a second round of talks, Polisario proclaimed at the beginning of March the end of its two-month-old unilateral cease-fire;[117] but with its capabilities to inflict damage having been progressively constrained over the years by the extension of Moroccan fortifications, it mounted important armed operations only in the latter months of 1989.

The diplomatic stalemate compelled UN Secretary-General Pérez de Cuellar to undertake personally a round of diplomacy. He held a week of meetings in early June with Moroccan, Polisario, Algerian, and Malian officials (Mali's president also being the incumbent president of the Organization of African Unity [OAU], in what was officially a joint UN-OAU initiative). On 30 June, he established a "technical commission" at UN headquarters, under his chairmanship, "to study ways and means of implementing the settlement proposals" (accepted in principle the previous August). The commission prepared a draft timetable for the implementation of the proposals, which was conveyed to both parties on 12 July by Gros Espiell. Morocco's response was transmitted on 6 October, and Polisario's one week later.[118]

Pérez de Cuellar's public estimate of the chances for progress was positive. Other, unnamed sources in the UN and the region spoke of the difficulties of funding the project. However, the problems were apparently more substantive, as Morocco preferred to hold the referendum under existing conditions.[119] Hasan's explanation was forceful; he declared in a nationwide television address:

> We told the secretary-general that if we have to leave, then we will all leave; we will cut the telephone wires...dismantle all means of communications...fill in all the wells...take all vehicles with us, and...arm the population....Since the others are armed with tanks, we would not leave unless we left the tanks. Because of the abilities and numbers, I am convinced that our people would crush the others, but I did not want to reach this kind of breaking ranks.[120]

The lack of progress was frustrating for Polisario. Not only were the Moroccans biding their time, but Polisario's Algerian patrons were apparently encouraging it to be more flexible (although Polisario officials firmly denied the existence of any pressure).[121] One result was Polisario's decision to release 200 Moroccan prisoners of war as a goodwill gesture (which fell flat, as the Moroccans refused their repatriation). Another was a widespread shake-up in the Polisario leadership carried out at its seventh organizational conference at the end of April. The reasons for purging or demoting a number of Polisario's founding members, were numerous: differences stemming from varying tribal and national origins and personal conflicts were apparently determining factors. Most reports also stated that the changes marked a triumph of a more pragmatic group favoring a continuation of a strategy of negotiations, as advocated by Algeria, over a more hard-line group,[122] but this appears to have been unfounded. Indeed, Polisario's representative in France (and the brother of its number-two official) hastened to declare that Polisario was insisting on complete independence and would not settle for anything less.[123] Moreover, it would demonstrate in the coming months that, militarily, it had not been totally emasculated.

That all was not well with Polisario was evidenced by a number of defections of Polisario functionaries to Morocco.[124] Moroccan officials were active in encouraging their "return," as part of an effort to split Polisario ranks by playing up differences between Polisario members of Moroccan or Moroccan-controlled Saharan origin, and those who originated elsewhere.[125] The most prominent among them was Omar

Hadrami, who was one of its founding members and who up until the seventh conference had held a number of key military and political positions. Rabat trumpeted his "return" as indicating that Polisario was crumbling from within. Hadrami himself, having been given a high-profile position in the Ministry of Interior, spoke repeatedly of the internal divisions which, he declared, had wracked Polisario and the population of the Tindouf camps as a whole over the last year.[126] Although Polisario dismissed Hadrami's act as being motivated solely by personal gain, the Moroccans had undoubtedly scored a propaganda coup.

On the largely stagnant diplomatic front, Hasan apparently assented to Benjedid's and Qadhdhafi's request, made during the Libyan anniversary celebrations, that he hold the long-delayed second round of meetings with Polisario.[127] However, by mid-October, they had not yet taken place. To demonstrate that it was still a factor to be reckoned with, Polisario launched a series of attacks against Moroccan positions during October and November, mostly in the central sector between Amlaga and Guelta Zemmour. The fighting was at times fierce, with heavy casualties on both sides. Following the first attack, Hasan announced the cancellation of what he said were impending talks, an act which surely did not sit well with Algeria. The attacks also raised the level of tension between Morocco and Mauritania, since the Polisario forces had apparently been based in Mauritania.

The lack of progress and renewed tension was noted with concern at the UN. To Polisario's satisfaction, the General Assembly called in November for a renewal of the Moroccan-Polisario dialogue in order to pave the way for a diplomatic solution. Polisario could also take comfort in the fact that SADR was now recognized by 73 countries, and that its full-member status in the OAU was reinforced by the choice of its foreign minister as reporter of the OAU's foreign affairs council.[128]

However, on the ground, Polisario remained heavily constrained. Hasan, for his part, while taking care to maintain cooperation with the UN mediation effort, seemed emboldened. Toward the end of the year, he engineered a two-year postponement of parliamentary elections, until such time as the Saharan referendum would have been held. The area could then be included in the elections for parliament, while "the international community would recognize, for good, our borders." The two-year deadline, he hastened to add, was not a threat. "However, if after the two years the referendum has not taken place, then it will be time to deduce from that procrastination or delay the proper conclusions...."[129]

THE GULF STATES*

On the eve of the 1990s the GCC, grouping Saudi Arabia and the five Gulf states reviewed below, seemed to have reasons for optimism. The August 1988 cease-fire in the Gulf War brought immediate relief to the GCC states by ending eight years of constant threats to their individual and collective interests. Throughout the 1980s, the six monarchies had coped with the threat of the Iranian revolution that sent tremors through their peoples and societies. They could hope that the post-Khomeyni era would not be worse than the recent past. On a different level, the decade that had started with a collapse of oil prices unfolded with their stabilization, bringing expectations of an overall economic upturn.

*   This section was written by Uzi Rabi.

On the other hand, while the GCC could take pride in having emerged from this stormy period relatively unscathed, it could not turn a blind eye to the unwelcome lessons regarding its limited political influence and internal cohesiveness. Other problems, typical of a postwar period, stemmed from the greater expectations of such groups in society as were seeking more active participation in politics. These expectations could not be fulfilled in the short term because of the absence of adequate opportunities, and institutions that encourage internal instability. All these served as painful reminders that the GCC's path to security and prosperity was still fraught with danger. The question was: what direction should the GCC take to remain an effective entity in the 1990s?

THE POSTWAR CHALLENGE OF SURVIVAL: WALKING A TIGHTROPE BETWEEN TWO GIANTS

The Iraqi-Iranian conflict had receded for the time being, but the slow process of implementing the cease-fire agreement caused uneasiness about the agreement's fragility. The mutual rivalry and animosity of the two belligerents had not disappeared, none of the root causes of the conflict had been eliminated, and neither Iraq nor Iran had abandoned its claim to regional hegemony. The six GCC states evidently feared that the combination of political skill and good fortune, which had kept them from being swept into the war, might not save them if Iran and Iraq had recourse to arms once again. It was essential to the six GCC states that they find a way out of "no-war no-peace" and achieve a firm and lasting peace in the region. Council Secretary-General 'Abdallah Ya'qub Bishara stressed that the GCC was not sitting back, but "working hard to overcome the differences in negotiations between the parties in the Gulf War."[130] The Gulf War topped the GCC's political agenda during the 1980s; it seemed that a similar priority would be given to regional peace in the 1990s.

It was crucial that the GCC be seen to play a part in the restoration of regional peace; after all, its member states' security had been a prime reason for the GCC's establishment. The GCC wanted its concerns to be taken into account in any future peace settlement. The importance of this was emphasized when during Oman's incumbency as president of the council in 1990, it was entrusted with heading the council's mediation initiative.[131] The GCC seemed to have calculated that an impartial approach could help moderate Iran's antagonism and enhance the chances for regional peace. The communiqué issued at the end of the Supreme Council's summit in Muscat in late December, which urged the UN to "exert further efforts to arrive at a just peace that takes into consideration the legitimate rights of all parties," reflected a significant change in the GCC's attitude toward Iran (see Appendix V). The communiqué's obvious evenhanded approach to both belligerents was a shift from the tilt in Iraq's favor in most previous communiqués.

However, regardless of its generally pro-Iraqi policy, the GCC's first task was to gain Tehran's confidence by displaying its readiness to reintegrate Iran into the Gulf region. This task was given a triple expression. First, stress was placed on common denominators, which would facilitate the GCC-Iranian dialogue. GCC officials emphasized that "relations with Iran derive from a geographical, historical, and cultural reality....Adding to that are common interests, the most important of which is to ensure stability in the region."[132] Considerable efforts were also made to persuade Iran to act more rationally and more pragmatically in order to end its isolation in the

Arab world and internationally.[133] The fact that Iran was at a crossroads in the post-Khomeyni era encouraged hopes that such an appeal would not fall on deaf ears.

Second, the GCC moved to assuage some of Tehran's harsh feelings about the pro-Iraqi stance of some of its member states in the past. The GCC focused on allaying the Saudi-Iranian animosity, which reached an extreme in April 1988 with the severance of diplomatic ties. At the same time, the council made clear that "if Iran wishes to develop its relations with the GCC states, it must consider the need to improve its relations with Saudi Arabia."[134] Oman, as mediator, met with representatives of both sides; Iranian Foreign Minister 'Ali Akbar Velayati and Saudi Foreign Minister Sa'ud al-Faysal visited Muscat in February and March, respectively. Muscat was also reported to have hosted a secret meeting between both foreign ministers in June (for more details on Saudi-Iranian relations, see chapters on Islamic affairs and Saudi Arabia).[135]

Third, on the bilateral level, most members moved to improve their ties with Tehran: air links were renewed or expanded, and the level of diplomatic representation was upgraded. The broadening of ties, as well as the GCC's readiness and ability to assist Iran in its reconstruction efforts also made it worthwhile for Tehran to consider *rapprochement*. GCC officials had consistently reiterated that Tehran should abide by existing norms of international behavior, such as noninterference in the internal affairs of other countries and the cessation of attacks in the media.

On the whole, Tehran was receptive to the GCC's advances. "Iran covets no other country, including its neighbors in the south, and wishes to see tension removed from the region," asserted Foreign Minister 'Ali Akbar Velayati, adding that Tehran placed emphasis on promoting good neighborly relations with countries of the region.[136] Still, the atmosphere on both sides was not conducive to joint meetings. Tehran persisted in trying to drive a wedge between the GCC and Iraq, by suggesting, for example, that it establish an economic framework alongside the GCC.[137] The GCC, meanwhile, aware of the impact such proposals might have in Baghdad, chose not to aggravate any Iraqi suspicions.

The GCC, however, had little success in convincing Iraq of its good intentions. The GCC's evenhanded approach to Iraq and Iran, which replaced its previous clear-cut pro-Iraqi policy, gave Baghdad the ominous feeling that it was being gradually deserted by its Gulf allies. Claiming that it was impossible to have normal relations with some Gulf states while maintaining a state of war with others, Iraq warned the GCC not to develop exclusive relations with Tehran.[138] Much more alarming to the GCC were Iraq's efforts to promote itself as the region's dominant force. An outstanding example of Iraqi ambitions was its attempt to revive the long-standing conflict over demarcation of the Iraqi-Kuwaiti border hoping in that way to put on the alert Kuwait, which had supported Iraq throughout the war and had hoped that the issue was a thing of the past. Throughout the 1980s, the Iraqi-GCC interest in containing Iran's revolutionary zeal led to an improvement in Baghdad's relations with the GCC. The alignment with Iraq during the war had won the the GCC credit, allowing it to gain influence in Baghdad. Against this backdrop, the growing Iraqi threat to the GCC plus the diminishing menace from Tehran could justly be regarded as one of the postwar era's greater paradoxes.

In the final analysis, it was clear that the GCC states had to continue their struggle for survival as independent entities in the postwar era. Outnumbered demographically and militarily weak, the six had to pursue a carefully charted course between the Gulf's two giants, as other ways of coping with them were merely theoretical.

THE COMING DECADE: LESSONS TO BE LEARNED

The GCC states had successfully weathered the Iranian Revolution, the protracted Gulf War, and the overt or covert attempts to undermine them. Yet, the Gulf War — perhaps the most compelling reason for the GCC's establishment — had also shown the GCC's regional capacities to be limited. One of the more compelling, but least pleasing, conclusions drawn from the war concerned the limited effectiveness of the GCC's defenses. Neither now nor in the foreseeable future, could the GCC match Iraq or Iran militarily, despite the impressive GCC military build-up which was prompted by the war. All the GCC had was a brigade-sized, multinational six-state force, headquartered at Hafr al-Batin in Saudi Arabia. The lesson of this was that the GCC's dependence on extraregional elements for its security would prevail. Its defense doctrine of "self-reliance" was thus found invalid even before being put to the test. Hence, in 1989, defense matters occupied less time in the council's discussions. Individually, however, each Gulf state went ahead with its own program of military consolidation.

The Iraq-Iran War also exposed the GCC's limited political influence in the region. After the war broke out, the GCC made consistent efforts to halt or at least contain it. The GCC succeeded in securing limited Arab and Islamic support and in mobilizing the international community to take firm action to stop the war. Yet, the GCC was unable to get either of the belligerents to alter its policies. Evidently, it was ill-equipped to deal with the regional crisis by direct political means. Both in the case of external threats, such as the Gulf War, and also of disputes between member states, the GCC found it difficult to serve as a channel of influence. This weakness was best exemplified in the case of the Qatari-Bahraini dispute which erupted into a military conflict in 1986 (for an account of the dispute, see *MECS* 1986, pp. 294–96). So unsuccessful was the council in resolving the crisis that at a certain stage it considered referring the issue to the International Court of Justice at The Hague. The GCC also had limited success in patching up social and economic differences among the six members which came to the surface in the 1980s. As long as the Gulf War persisted, a degree of unity among the member states was unquestioned. What was to bolster it after the guns fell silent? Would not the six monarchies find it more difficult to cooperate after Iranian revolutionary zeal seemed to have receded? Entering the 1990s, the GCC had to attain a greater degree of cohesiveness, which presupposed common economic priorities and a common approach to internal and external security; it also had to seek ways of increasing its political influence. In other words, the GCC had to redefine its role if it wanted to become a significant entity in the region and beyond. The first indication that the GCC wished to play a more active role internationally appeared in a special declaration attached to the communiqué issued at the end of the Supreme Council's summit. Worded in general terms, such as "the new world climate which makes it incumbent on everyone to strengthen the basis of cooperation, which should replace confrontation and struggle," the Muscat Declaration (Appendix II) reflected the GCC's awareness of the changing international climate, particularly the East-West *détente* and its impact on Eastern Europe and Third World countries, and of the diminished antagonism in inter-Arab relations. Postsummit reports referred to the establishment of a three-member committee, headed by Oman's minister of state for foreign affairs, which was to monitor regional and international developments in both the political and economic spheres.[139]

SOCIOECONOMIC AFFAIRS AND OTHER ISSUES ON THE GCC AGENDA

On the eve of the new decade, the GCC's economic fortunes seemed brighter. It was generally assumed that the oil market would swing back to the seller, a most encouraging prospect for the GCC. Some of its member states, which had recently announced massive increases in their proven reserves — had staked claims to being Opec's senior members. The GCC seemed to be on its way to regaining its preeminence in the oil market by the end of the century. Not only was it anticipated that the world would become increasingly dependent on Gulf oil, but that the power of the Gulf states would be enhanced, as they moved downstream, through building domestic refineries and acquiring marketing outlets in the oil-consuming countries.[140]

No significant progress was made with regard to the GCC's socioeconomic integration. Implementation of the GCC's Unified Economic Agreement was held up because the signatories were reluctant to compromise their national interests. The results of the 10th summit (see below) were meager concerning matters crucial to the GCC's future, such as joint passports, a common currency, and common tariff rates. It did not seem that the 1990 deadline for the establishment of a Gulf common market would be met.

Absence of a common external tariff also blocked the conclusion of a free trade pact with the EEC. The issue was another clear indication that that the GCC's incomplete internal cohesion could hamper its activity on the foreign front. The GCC dreaded the prospect of the EEC — by far its largest trading partner — becoming a unified trading bloc in 1992, because it might erect barriers to protect its own petrochemical and aluminum products from the competition of GCC imports, thus striking at the GCC's main exports to the EEC.[141] An economic agreement stipulating the gradual liberalization of EEC-GCC trade, concluded in June 1988, was to take effect in January 1990. In December 1989, the GCC summit authorized the Ministerial Council to begin talks with the EEC aimed at concluding a full-fledged trade pact. Agreement, however, seemed distant because of deep-seated differences between the sides. It remained to be seen whether the GCC could overcome the particularist policies of its member states and cope with the economic challenges of the coming decade.

The GCC Supreme Council held its 10th annual meeting in Muscat in late December. Apart from the routine declarations about the need for regional coordination, the council discussed peace talks between Iran and Iraq and trade talks with the European Community. Consensus politics, most notably the Lebanese crisis and the Palestinian issue, which continued to figure on the summit's agenda, demarcated the limits of the GCC's capabilities. It was Saudi Arabia — the GCC's most influential member — that played a leading role in the Lebanese attempted appeasement in November in Ta'if (see chapter on Lebanon). The initiative gained due recognition by the GCC, but this was not reflected in a resolution. The council did nothing more than support the efforts to resolve the crisis on a "basis of legitimacy and national unity" and urged the Lebanese to practice self-restraint. The discussion of the Palestinian issue was perfunctory; realizing that it could do little to advance the

US-PLO talks, and even less regarding the Intifada, the council confined itself to denouncing Israel's activity in the West Bank and Gaza Strip.

CONCLUSION

The creation of two more regional economic and political groupings, the restoration of Egypt's membership in the Arab League, the deepening crisis in Lebanon, the reinforcing of the PLO's inter-Arab standing, and Iraq's growing bid for regional preeminence all made 1989 a momentous year for the inter-Arab system. Also of major importance was the restoration of diplomatic relations between Syria and Egypt, following a series of high-level exchange visits capped by Syrian Vice President 'Abd al-Halim Khaddam's journey to Cairo on 23 December.

For Egypt and the Arab system as a whole, Syria's decision marked the closing of a circle. Having been isolated and boycotted at the end of the 1970s for making peace with Israel, Egypt could now feel vindicated, justifiably, in its decade-long policy of working to restore its standing as a full and leading member of the system while not abandoning the Egyptian-Israeli peace treaty. The Casablanca summit drove home the scope of its success. In fact, a comparison of the Casablanca summit's resolutions on the Arab-Israeli conflict with the language of the Baghdad summit of 1978 may indicate the extent to which support for a political resolution of the conflict had gained currency.

In addition to the matter of Egypt's role in the system, the wheel seemed to have come full circle in other areas as well. Iraq had been engaging in a bid for regional preeminence, if not predominance, at the beginning of the decade: at the end of the decade, although perhaps partly chastened by its brutal eight-year war with Iran, it was now renewing its efforts in that same direction, and from a vastly strengthened position. In contrast to the end of the 1970s, Egypt and Iraq were now formal partners (in the ACC), not competitors. Nonetheless, to characterize the new situation as an irreversible departure from previous patterns was premature, given the geopolitical constants which historically have generated rivalry between them. The extent to which these factors would reassert themselves, and when, remained an open question. The challenge of the Iranian Revolution, which dominated Arab concerns for much of the decade, had now receded, as had Iran's unprecedented involvement, as a non-Arab state, in what was essentially an Arab system. On the other hand, the GCC states were already showing signs of renewed interest in relations with Iran in order to maintain regional equilibrium in the face of Iraq's growing power. This too was a familiar pattern.

One inter-Arab nexus which was neither transformed nor had journeyed full circle during the 1980s was the Iraqi-Syrian relationship. If anything, the relationship was in worse shape than it had been at the beginning of the decade, as it continued to be the most trenchant of all inter-Arab rivalries. What had changed for the worse, as far as Syria was concerned, was that Iraq had moved from being the "odd man out" in inter-Arab politics to a position of considerable importance. It now had both allies (if, at times, less than enthusiastic ones) and the capacity to meddle in Lebanon — Syria's traditional preserve. Furthermore, its vastly strengthened military capabilities and intentions now also had to be taken into account in any evolution of the Arab-Israeli balance of power (although Syria undoubtedly hoped that this could one day be turned to its advantage). For its part, Syria had led the "minority" or "opposition" camp in the Arab world throughout the 1980s on every important issue facing the Arab system: the Gulf War, the Arab-Israeli conflict and Palestinian question, relations with Egypt, the Lebanese crisis, and global orientation. Initially, this camp had been partially institutionalized through the Steadfastness Front. By the middle of the decade, however, the front was moribund, as its five members (Syria, Libya, Algeria, the PDRY, and the PLO) increasingly diverged over the various issues facing them. At the end of the decade, changes in all of these spheres seemed to be compelling Syria to reassess its policies, at least on the tactical level. Libya, for its part, had been Syria's staunchest Arab ally during the decade, while simultaneously promoting Qadhdhafi's particular brand of activism. By itself, Libya had never been a central actor in the Arab system, more so at the end of the decade. Even in North Africa, it was now compelled to take a back seat to Algeria and Morocco.

As for the Gulf states, and particularly Saudi Arabia, the fall in oil prices and production during the mid-1980s significantly reduced their ability to shape events, thus emphasizing anew their inherent vulnerabilities. Riyadh continued to stake its claim for the role of the premier inter-Arab mediator, but with considerably less leverage than previously.

Most analysts of inter-Arab relations characterized the early 1980s as a period of fragmentation and collective weakness, in which the system lacked a single center of gravity.[142] In this sense, inter-Arab relations appeared substantially different at the end of the decade from what they had been at the beginning, marked now by the existence of regional groupings, the restoration of dialogue and "normalcy" among nearly all Arab states, and more or less universal acceptance of the notion that meaningful Arab solidarity could be promoted only gradually, and from the ground up. At the same time, these changes did not cancel out the permanent mix of elements of intense competition and cooperation which have made the Arab system unique in the annals of international politics over the last 45 years.

APPENDIX I: FINAL STATEMENT OF THE ARAB SUMMIT CONFERENCE, CASABLANCA, 23–26 May 1989[143]

Upon the initiative of His Majesty King Hasan II, king of Morocco, and upon the invitation of his majesty, an emergency Arab summit was held in Casablanca from 23–26 May 1989.

At its opening session the conference welcomed the delegation of the Arab Republic of Egypt chaired by President Muhammad Husni Mubarak, president of the Arab Republic of Egypt, and Egypt's resumption of its full membership in the Arab League and in all the organizations, institutions, and councils belonging to the League. The conference expressed its conviction that the presence of the Arab Republic of Egypt in its natural place among its Arab sister-countries will contribute to boosting inter-Arab action, and strengthening the march of solidarity and unity of Arab ranks for the good of the Arab nation, its dignity, and its prosperity.

The conference expressed appreciation for the guiding address made by His Majesty King Hasan II at the opening session in which he affirmed the noble pan-Arab significance of the convening of the conference and in which he traced the scope for future inter-Arab action and for strengthening and expanding its institutions. The conference also welcomed the address made by His Excellency President Muhammad Husni Mubarak and decided to consider the two addresses as documents of the conference.

As a result of the contacts held between their majesties, their excellencies, and their highnesses, the Arab kings and presidents, and in response to an invitation by His Majesty King Hasan II of Morocco, the chairman of the conference, the leaders have been able to eliminate disputes that spoiled relations between some Arab states, a matter that had conferred on the work of the conference a climate of reconciliation, concord, brotherhood, and solidarity.

In a spirit of pan-Arab responsibility and out of its sense of the delicate nature of the stage traversed by the Arab nation, the conference discussed the most important issues and challenges facing the Arab nation. The conference greeted the blessed Intifada of the Palestinian people, expressed its appreciation and cherishment of its steadfast heroes, and prayed for God's blessings on the souls of its noble martyrs who, with their sacred blood, have irrigated the blessed land of Palestine. The conference decided to continue extending all types of support and backing for it so that the Palestinian people, under the leadership of the PLO, its sole and legitimate representative, may be able to continue its resistance and step up its valiant Intifada against Israeli occupation.

The conference condemned the crimes and practices of the Israeli occupation against the Arab people in the occupied Palestinian and Arab territories. The conference called on the UN Security Council to shoulder its responsibilities toward these crimes and practices including the possibility of imposing sanctions against Israel. The conference hailed the struggle of the Syrian citizens in the occupied Syrian Golan and the struggle of the Lebanese national resistance in South Lebanon against Israeli occupation.

The conference affirmed the foundations on which was based the peace plan laid down by the 12th Arab summit conference in Fes and which were affirmed by the Arab emergency summit in Algiers. These foundations aim at liberating the Palestinian and Arab territories, which have been occupied since 1967, from Israeli occupation and enabling the Palestinian people to exercise its inalienable national rights including its right to return, to self-determination, and to establish its independent national state with Jerusalem as capital and under the leadership of the PLO, its sole and legitimate representative and concentrating Arab sources in the various fields to establish a comprehensive strategic balance so as to face the hostile Zionist plans and protect Arab rights.

The conference welcomed the resolutions of the 19th Palestine National Council session and affirmed its support for the Palestinian initiative based on the Arab peace plan and international legitimacy and lauded the positive international response. The conference blessed the establishment of an independent Palestinian state and expressed its determination to make available to it all the elements of support and backing and expressed its consideration for the friendly states which officially recognized it. The conference also called on the remaining nations to fully recognize the Palestinian State and enable it to exercise its sovereignty on its national territory.

The conference supported the convening of an international peace conference on the Middle East with the participation of the five permanent members of the UN Security Council and all the parties in the conflict including the PLO, the sole and legitimate representative of the Palestinian people, with the aim of reaching a comprehensive and just solution to the Arab-Israeli conflict on the basis of UN Security Council Resolutions 242 and 338 as well as all the related UN resolutions and the national inalienable rights of the Palestinian people and agree on security guarantees of all the states of the region including the State of Palestine as well as solving the problem of the Palestinian refugees in accordance with UN General Assembly Resolution 194 and considering all the related UN resolutions as still providing the conditions for international legitimacy which guarantee the right of the Palestinian people to establish its independent state.

The conference decided to set up a higher committee chaired by His Majesty King Hasan II to start moves and undertake relevant international contacts on behalf of the Arab League in order to invigorate the [Middle East] peace process and take part in preparation for an international conference.

The conference backed the Palestinian position concerning elections affirming that they should take place after the Israeli withdrawal from the occupied Palestinian territories, under international supervision, and in the context of an overall peace process, as the Israeli plan is aimed at the Intifada and at transcending the PLO and the inalienable rights of the Palestinian people as a nation.

The conference underlined the need for an end to the Israeli occupation of the Arab and Palestinian occupied lands, and the putting of the occupied Palestinian territories under the control of the United Nations for a temporary period in order to enable the Palestinian people to exercise its right to self-determination.

The conference expressed its great concern over what is going on in Lebanon, a founding member of the Arab League that has always participated in the strengthening of inter-Arab action and defending Arab causes and taken part by its civilized radiance and its intellectual and cultural action in enriching the Arab and international culture.

The conference debated with great interest the tragic situation being experienced by Lebanon and its reverberations and effects on Lebanese unity and national security of the Arab nation and stressed the need for continuing inter-Arab action to achieve a settlement that brings back to Lebanon its stability and security and preserves its Arab character, its sovereignty, and its territorial integrity.

The conference urged all Lebanese parties to immediately respect the cease-fire, in a full and lasting manner, in accordance with the Arab League resolution issued on 27 April. The conference lauded the good efforts made by the Arab six-man committee and urged all the Lebanese parties to cooperate to attain an overall national reconciliation and realize a national concord that paves the way for a final solution to the Lebanese crisis in all its aspects.

The conference also expressed its commitment to safeguard the unity and Arab character of Lebanon and to protect its security, independence, and sovereignty, and to reject any attempt to divide it. The conference reiterated its commitment to offer support to reconstruct Lebanon and help it rebuild its national economy. The conference reaffirmed the Arab resolutions related to pan-Arab solidarity with Lebanon to help it get out of its ordeal, end its long suffering, and normalize its situation, as well as achieve national concord between its sons and support the Lebanese legitimacy based on concord.

The conference decided to set up a committee composed of His Majesty King Hasan II, the sovereign of the Moroccan Kingdom; His Excellency King Fahd Ibn 'Abd al-'Aziz Al Sa'ud, custodian of the two holy mosques and sovereign of the Kingdom of Saudi Arabia; and His Excellency President Chedli Bendjedid, president of the Democratic and Popular Republic of Algeria; and gave it comprehensive and full prerogatives to achieve the aims decided by the conference in order to solve the Lebanese crisis. This committee will be in charge of carrying out consultations, contacts, and procedures in order to provide an atmosphere suitable for inviting the members of the Lebanese Chamber of Deputies to discuss the political reforms document and hold the elections for the presidency of the republic and to set up a government of national concord on the understanding that this will be completed during a period not longer than six months. The conference announced its readiness to convene after this period in order to look into all that has been implemented and the subsequent developments, if necessary.

The conference also decided to support the Lebanese efforts internationally in their endeavor to end the Israeli occupation of

Lebanese territories and to support the establishment of the full sovereignty of the Lebanese state on all the Lebanese soil to protect its security and stability with its own power.

The conference affirmed its rejection of the Israeli occupation of the Lebanese territory and condemned the continuous Israeli aggressions against the land of Lebanon, its sovereignty, and its people, and it urged the UN Security Council to act for the fulfillment of its Resolutions 425, 508, and 509 that provide for an immediate, full, and unconditional withdrawal of the Israeli forces of occupation from the Lebanese territories.

The conference reviewed the developments in the Iraq-Iran situation since its last session in Algiers and expressed its deep satisfaction with the conclusion of the fighting and with the beginning of negotiations under the auspices of the UN secretary-general in order to achieve an overall, just, and lasting settlement of this conflict.

From its belief that the cease-fire must be a starting point for the establishment of an overall, just, and lasting peace between Iraq and Iran and for establishing security and peace in the region, the conference expressed its hope of seeing a quick move from the cease-fire stage to a stage of establishing peace and entrenching security and stability. The conference called for exerting international and regional efforts to invigorate and intensify direct negotiations under the auspices of the UN secretary-general in order to establish peace on the basis of the implementation of UN Security Council Resolution No. 598 for 1989 as a peace plan, in a way that guarantees the rights of Iraq and its sovereignty on its territory and in its waters, noninterference in its internal affairs, and the guarantee of the security of the Arab Gulf and the freedom of navigation in its international waters and through the Strait of Hormuz for ships in accordance with the convention on the law of the sea concluded in the United Nations. The conference stressed the need to face up to all attempts aimed at obstructing or delaying the implementation of the UN Security Council Resolution 598 at the expense of Arab national rights and pan-Arab rights.

The conference affirmed its full solidarity with Iraq in preserving the integrity and safety of its land and its historic rights in its sovereignty over Shatt al-'Arab, and it came out in support of a call to charge the United Nations with cleaning Shatt al-'Arab and making it good and safe for navigation.

The conference noted with concern the continuing tragedy of the prisoners of war and that there has been no start in releasing and exchanging them despite the conclusion of military operations since 20 August 1988 in contradiction to the provisions of UN Security Council Resolution 598 of 1987, and the third Geneva convention for 1949 concerning prisoners of war. The conference called on the United Nations and all the international organizations and bodies to adopt whatever measures they can for the release of the prisoners of war and their repatriation without delay, to put an end to their ordeal and that of their families.

The conference praised the efforts by the UN secretary-general and declared its support for his efforts aimed at ensuring a just, comprehensive, and lasting settlement for the conflict, which will lead to peace and security in the Arab Gulf region.

The conference accorded all its interest and care to the question of the clearing of the inter-Arab atmosphere and reiterated its faith in the need for solidarity among the Arab states and for setting disputes aside. The conference stressed that inter-Arab action is the only way to face up to the dangers and challenges surrounding the Arab nation. In this respect, the conference welcomed the establishment of the Arab Cooperation Council and the Arab Maghrib Union, in addition to the Gulf Cooperation Council, the regional groups that came to realize the dreams of past generations and to help future generations in the struggle for growth and prosperity, armed with their options and their determination.

The conference affirmed the adherence of member states to the Arab League as an overall institutional framework for inter-Arab action in which these states have acted and will continue to act in the spirit of the league's charter, its objectives, and basic elements. The conference expressed its belief that the pan-Arab umbrella institution and these groups will complement one another, and that any group should be an incentive for contacts and ties and for strengthening joint action. In order to be in harmony with the developments witnessed by the Arab homeland, the conference saw the need for promoting the administrative and structural organization of the League and for reviewing the project of amending its charter so that such an amendment may come as a prelude to new horizons and an entrenchment of the comprehensiveness of the role of the League in joint Arab action and in pushing this action forward.

The conference stressed the need for the Arab information media to be committed to the ethical and pan-Arab norms and to shun vituperations and provoking disputes, in implementation of the Arab information charter of honor.

The conference stressed its condemnation of the US aggression against the Great Socialist People's Libyan Arab Jamahiriyya and its support for it in the face of the continuous threats against its security. It also expressed its support and backing for Libya's sovereignty over the Gulf of Sirte in accordance with international conventions.

The conference expressed its satisfaction with the victory of the people of Namibia and the beginning of its national independence process. The conference underlined its full solidarity with the peoples of southern Africa and its condemnation of the policy of apartheid and the alliance between the Zionist entity and the racist Pretoria regime.

The conference reiterated its denunciation of terrorism in all its types, forms, and sources, and affirmed the need for adopting legitimate means passed by international treaties and for adhering to the principles of rights, justice, and international legitimacy in defending national interests and attaining noble aims.

On the occasion of the summit conference, His Majesty King Hasan II, chairman of the conference, received letters from His Grace Pope John Paul II, President George Bush, President Mikhail Gorbachev, President François Mitterrand, Spanish Prime Minister Felipe González, and from Javier Pérez de Cuellar, the UN secretary-general, in which they express their best wishes that the work of the conference be crowned with success in resolving the problems faced by the Arab world.

The conference recorded with satisfaction the growing international concord and expressed its hope that this positive development will help in the spread of security and peace and the realization of welfare and prosperity in the various parts of the world.

The conference expressed its great appreciation for the initiative of His Majesty King Hasan II of Morocco to convene this conference and for his majesty's efforts to provide for its chances of success. The conference lauded the wisdom and farsightedness with which his majesty managed the conference work, which led to the success of this conference and to its historic resolutions that will strengthen inter-Arab solidarity, boost joint Arab action, and contribute to the realization of progress and invulnerability.

The conference offered its thanks and appreciation to the fraternal Moroccan people for their warm welcome and generosity toward the delegations.

APPENDIX II: FOUNDATION AGREEMENT OF THE ARAB COOPERATION COUNCIL[144]
Issued in Baghdad, 17 February 1989

In the name of God, the merciful, the compassionate.

Whereas the Arab nation, with its ancient and rich cultural heritage and its big role in building the edifice of human civilization, cherishes a strong and legitimate aspiration for cooperation, solidarity, and joint action in all fields prompted by a profound yearning for unity and a desire to assert its national characteristics and distinguished cultural identity which have been firmly entrenched through the ages, safeguard its security, serve its legitimate interests, take firm steps toward progress and advancement, and consolidate its constructive and positive world role in serving the causes of peace, security, progress, and fruitful, equal cooperation among world nations;

Whereas the Arab nation had, in modern history, witnessed several experiments of joint action, cooperation, and solidarity, achieved certain forms of unity, and learned useful lessons from the positive and negative aspects of those experiments;

And, whereas the foremost of these lessons is cooperation in building the foundations for strengthening all forms of spiritual, cultural, and practical ties among the citizens of the Arab states, a cooperation which occupies a central place in any continuous, persistent, and serious endeavor for joint action and creates the firm practical, bases for advancement to higher levels and wider horizons toward achieving the Arab nation's sublime objective of unity as circumstances and practical possibilities permit;

Whereas this constructive, realistic trend is harmonious with present world trends toward creating economic communities which ensure for their member states better conditions to safeguard their interests and achieve development and economic progress;

Believing that cooperation among the Arab states in these fields is of special importance due to the threats to which Arab national security has been, and still is, exposed, threats which are of a security, political, economic, and cultural nature;

Proceeding from the reality that the maintenance of security, peace, and stability in the entire region calls for strengthening Arab awareness of the wholesomeness of pan-Arab security and its requirements and conditions, and also for entrenching this awareness through practical cooperation, coordination, and solidarity;

Considering the similar circumstances of the Hashemite Kingdom of Jordan, the Republic of Iraq, the Arab Republic of Egypt, and the Yemeni Arab Republic in the various fields, and out of these states' faith in the aforementioned principles and values and in expression of their profound desire to find a practical and realistic means to strengthen the formulas of cooperation and to further develop and promote this cooperation, which has continued between them for several years and bore important fruits, as circumstances and capabilities permitted, at every stage until it reached the highest levels of solidarity and joint action;

Guided by the Arab League Charter which permits member states seeking closer cooperation and stronger ties to conclude any agreements fulfilling these aims; and in accordance with what was agreed upon at the historic meeting which was held in Baghdad among His Majesty King Husayn Ibn Talal, king of the Hashemite Kingdom of Jordan; His Excellency Saddam Husayn, president of the Republic of Iraq; His Excellency Muhammad Husni Mubarak, president of the Arab Republic of Egypt; and His Excellency 'Ali 'Abdallah Salih, president of the Yemeni Arab Republic on 9-10 Rajab 1409 Hijra, corresponding to 15-16 February 1989, it has been decided, with God's blessing, to establish the Arab Cooperation Council according to the following:

Article I
The ACC shall be comprised of the Hashemite Kingdom of Jordan, the Republic of Iraq, the Arab Republic of Egypt, and the YAR in accordance with the provisions of this agreement. The ACC shall be considered one of the organizations of the Arab nation, adhering to the Arab League charter, the Treaty of Joint Defense and Economic Cooperation, and the institutions and organizations stemming from the Arab League, and establishing ties of cooperation with regional Arab and international communities.

Article II
The ACC aims at:

(1) Achieving the highest levels of coordination, cooperation, integration, and solidarity among the member states and promoting them gradually according to circumstances, capabilities, and experiences.

(2) Achieving economic integration gradually by coordinating policies on the level of the various productive sectors, coordinating the member states' development plans taking into consideration the different levels of growth and the economic conditions and circumstances experienced by the member states in moving from one stage to another, and achieving that integration and coordination in the following fields in particular:

(a) Economy and finance;

(b) Industry and agriculture;

(c) Transport, communications, and telecommunications;

(d) Education, culture, information, scientific research, and technology;

(e) Social, health, and tourist affairs;

(f) Regulation of labor, movement, and residence.

(3) Encouraging investment, joint projects, and economic cooperation between public, private, cooperative, and mixed sectors.

(4) Endeavoring to achieve a common market among the member states in order to arrive at the Arab Common Market and Arab economic unity.

(5) Strengthening the ties and bonds among the citizens of the member states in all fields.

(6) Bolstering and developing joint Arab action in order to strengthen Arab ties.

Article III

The ACC shall work toward the achievement of its objectives through plans and practical measures, including whatever legislation it might consider issuing, adjusting, or standardizing in the various fields.

Article IV

(1) Membership in the ACC shall be open to every Arab state wishing to join it.

(2) Membership in the ACC shall be with the approval of all member states.

Article V

The ACC shall consist of the following organizations:

(1) The Supreme Council.

(2) The Ministerial Council.

(3) The General Secretariat.

Article VI

The Supreme Council, which is the highest ACC authority, shall consist of the heads of the member states.

Article VII

The Supreme Council shall exercise the following powers:

(1) Drawing up the ACC's higher policies.

(2) Making the necessary decisions on recommedations submitted by the Ministerial Council.

(3) Empowering the Ministerial Council with any matter falling within its jurisdictions and functions.

(4) Approving the procedures governing its work and their amendments.

(5) Appointing the ACC's secretary-general.

(6) Approving new memberships.

(7) Amending the ACC's foundation agreement.

(8) Following progress in the implementation of the approved coordination, cooperation, and integration measures.

(9) Creating other organizations and standing committees as necessary.

Article VIII

(1) The Supreme Council shall hold an ordinary session once a year in one of the member states on a rotational basis. The Supreme Council shall be chaired by the head of the host state for one full-year term.

(2) Extraordinary sessions may be held at the invitation of the Supreme Council chairman or by a proposal from one of the member states, seconded by at least another member state. The extraordinary sessions shall be held in the state whose head chairs the Supreme Council.

(3) Special sessions may be held with the approval of the heads of the member states in any capital or city in the member states. The convening of such sessions does not change the rules pertaining to the chairmanship of the Supreme Council.

(4) The convening of the Supreme Council sessions shall be deemed correct by the attendance of the majority of the member states.

Article IX

The Ministerial Council shall consist of the heads of government of the member states or their representatives.

Article X

The Ministerial Council shall exercise the following powers:

(1) Studying affairs and issues related to matters concerning the ACC.

(2) Submitting to the Supreme Council plans, proposals, and recommendations concerning the achievement of the ACC's objectives.

(3) Taking the necessary practical measures to implement the Supreme Council's decisions.

(4) Examining any issue on cooperation, and whenever necessary referring it to *ad hoc* specialized committees to study it and present the appropriate proposals on it.

(5) Drafting the rules governing the ACC's work procedures and referring them to the Supreme Council for approval and also proposing any amendments to them when necessary.

(6) Approving and amending the General Secretariat's administrative and financial systems.

(7) Examining the secretary-general's reports concerning the ACC's work.

(8) Discussing and approving the General Secretariat's budget and final accounts as well as discussing the secretariat's administrative and financial status.

(9) Forming *ad hoc* committees as necessitated by the ACC's work.

(10) Drafting the Supreme Council's agenda.

Article XI

(1) The Ministerial Council shall hold an ordinary session once every six months in the member state chairing the Supreme Council. The Ministerial Council shall be chaired by the head of government of that state, or his representative.

(2) Extraordinary sessions may be held at the request of the Ministerial Council's chairman or by a proposal from one of the member states, seconded by at least another member state. Extraordinary sessions shall be held in the member state holding the chairmanship.

(3) The convening of the Ministerial Council sessions shall be deemed correct by the attendance of the majority of member states.

Article XII

When adopting decisions in all ACC organizations, the member states shall strive to achieve unanimity and accord among themselves. When this is not possible, decisions shall be adopted on the basis of a majority vote by the member states. The decisions shall be binding on all. Decisions pertaining to membership and amendment of the ACC foundation agreement shall be made by a unanimous vote.

Article XIII

(1) The ACC shall have a General Secretariat based in Amman, headed by a secretary-general and consisting of the necessary number of employees.

(2) The Supreme Council shall appoint the secretary-general from the citizens of the member states on the basis of personal qualifications and faith in the ACC's objectives. The appointment, which will be for two years, shall be renewable twice at the most.

(3) The General Secretariat employees shall be appointed from the citizens of the member states on the basis of their personal qualifications and faith in the ACC's objectives.

(4) The secretary-general and the senior employees of the General Secretariat shall enjoy the necessary immunities, privileges, and facilities to enable them to carry out their duties in the headquarters state as well as the member states.

Article XIV

(1) The secretary-general is the chief executive of the ACC's General Secretariat. He is directly responsible to the Ministerial Council for all the General Secretariat's functions and good conduct.

(2) The secretary-general shall assume the following tasks:

(a) Following up implementation of the decisions adopted by the Supreme Council and the Ministerial Council;

(b) Preparing the necessary reports on the ACC's work for submission to the Ministerial Council and the Supreme Council;

(c) Drafting the agenda of the Ministerial Council;

(d) Preparing the ACC's draft budget and final accounts;

(e) Proposing administrative and financial systems for the General Secretariat and submitting them to the Ministerial Council;

(f) Appointing and terminating the services of General Secretariat employees;

(g) Performing any tasks assigned to him by the Supreme Council and the Ministerial Council.

Article XV

The headquarters agreement shall be concluded between the host state and the secretary-general, acting on behalf of the ACC, after the agreement has been approved by the Ministerial Council.

Article XVI

The General Secretariat shall have an annual budget to which the member states shall contribute equally.

Article XVII

(1) This agreement shall go into force and become valid as of the date of its ratification by the signatory states in accordance with existing constitutional procedures and the deposition of the instruments of ratification with the Foreign Ministry of the Hashemite Kingdom of Jordan in its capacity as the headquarters state of the General Secretariat.

(2) This agreement shall be binding on the states which join the ACC in accordance with the provisions of Article IV from the date of depositing their membership documents with the ACC General Secretariat.

(3) This agreement may be amended in accordance with a unanimous decision by the Supreme Council. The amendment shall be valid from the date of its ratification by the member states in accordance with existing constitutional procedures and the deposition of the instruments of ratification with the ACC General Secretariat.

(4) The headquarters state of the General Secretariat shall deposit a copy of this agreement with the Arab League and shall register this agreement with the General Secretariat of the United Nations.

Signed in Baghdad on 10 Rajab 1409 Hijra, corresponding to 16 February 1989.

Col. 'Ali 'Abdallah Salih, president of the Yemeni Arab Republic;

Muhammad Husni Mubarak, president of the Arab Republic of Egypt;

Saddam Husayn, president of the Republic of Iraq; and

Husayn Ibn Talal, king of the Hashemite Kingdom of Jordan.

APPENDIX III: FINAL STATEMENT AND FOUNDING AGREEMENT OF THE ARAB MAGHRIB UNION[145]
Issued in Marrakesh, 17 February 1989

In the name of God, the merciful, the compassionate, the creation of the Arab Maghrib Union is declared. HM King Hasan II, monarch of the Kingdom of Morocco; HE Zayn al-'Abidin Ben 'Ali, president of the Tunisian Republic; HE Chedli Benjedid, president of the Democratic and Popular Republic of Algeria; Col. Mu'ammar al-Qadhdhafi, leader of the great 1 September Revolution and the Great Socialist Libyan Arab People's Jamahiriyya; and HE Col. Maaouya Ould Sid Ahmed Taya, chairman of the Military Committee for National Salvation and head of state of the Islamic Republic of Mauritania.

From the premise of the unity of religion, language, and history that binds our peoples, and the unity of aspirations and expectations, inspired by the glories of our forefathers who have contributed to the radiation of the Islamic Arab civilization and the enriching of a cultural and ideological renaissance which served as the best support for the common struggle for freedom and dignity;

In an embodiment of our common desire that we expressed at the Zeralda summit, which constituted a new starting point for the search for the best means leading to the edification of the Arab Maghrib;

Out of our awareness that the realization of our people's hopes through the aspirations of such a unity requires an additional mobilization of efforts and the establishment of effective cooperation between our countries as well as continuous integration in all spheres;

In view of the transformations and the ties and integrations under way at the international level as well as the challenges facing our peoples and our countries in the political, economic, cultural, and social fields in general, we are required to achieve more intersolidarity and support, and exert more effort in order to attain the sought-after goal;

In view of our awareness of the dire need that our countries cooperate in all fields as well as the need to fully coordinate our policies, our stances, and our economic and social choices;

Given the fact that our grouping will make our region a place for peace and security, a matter which will allow it to contribute further to strengthening the bonds of international cooperation and peace;

In announcing our firm will to provide the bases of justice and dignity for our peoples as well as consecrating individual and collective rights in our countries inspired by our civilized noble descent and our spiritual values; and in following the path taken by the rest of the projects for regional groupings throughout the world which were rationally planned and were achieved through firm and unhurried steps;

With respect to the human, natural, and strategic possibilities which the countries of the Arab Maghrib are endowed with, which qualify them to face up to these challenges, and to handle expected developments in future decades;

Out of our faith that a unified Arab Maghrib constitutes a fundamental phase on the path toward Arab unity;

Out of our belief that the establishment of the Union of the Arab Maghrib will consolidate the struggle of the Palestinian Arab people for the liberation and the recovery of the entirety of their firm national rights;

Out of our conviction that a developed Maghrib entity will enable our states to consolidate joint action with the rest of the brotherly African states for the development and prosperity of our African continent;

With respect to the fact that the Union of the Arab Maghrib is the ideal framework for the realization of the will of our peoples to strengthen bonds with all the friendly peoples, and to support the international organizations and groupings to which our states belong;

Due to the fact that the edification of international cooperation and the support of international peace compel the establishment of regional unions to serve as a framework for reinforcing and consolidating their edifice;

In response to the aspirations of our peoples, out of awareness of the sensitivity of the current period, and out of our consciousness of the historical responsibility laid on our shoulders;

While we stress our attachment to our spiritual values and our historical authenticity, our openness toward others, and our attachment to the principles of international morality;

We announce, with God's help and on behalf of our peoples, the creation of the Union of the Arab Maghrib, as an integrated group, based on a single will, cooperating with its regional counterparts, and as a compact bloc to contribute to enriching international dialogue, determined to support the principles of good, and mobilizing its peoples with the possibilities it is endowed with in order to consolidate the independence of the countries of the Union of Arab Maghrib, to preserve their gains, and to work with the international community in order to set up a world system where justice, dignity, freedom, and human rights prevail, and whose relations are characterized by sincere cooperation and mutual respect.

In accomplishment of these objectives, we concluded an agreement which specifies the principles and aims of this union and establishes bodies and institutions for it.

APPENDIX IV: TREATY INSTITUTING THE ARAB MAGHRIB UNION, 17 FEBRUARY 1989[146]

ANNEX I
In the name of God, the Clement, the Merciful
His Majesty Hasan II, king of the Kingdom of Morocco; His Excellency Zayn al-'Abidin Ben 'Ali, president of the Republic of Tunisia;

His Excellency Chedli Benjedid, president of the People's Democratic Republic of Algeria;

The leader of the Great First of September Revolution, Col. Mu'ammar Qadhdhafi, the Great Arab People's Socialist Libyan Jamahiriyya, and His Excellency Col. Maaouya Ould Sid Ahmed Taya, chairman of the Military Committee for National Salvation and Head of State of the Islamic Republic of Mauritania;

Having faith in the strong ties based on common history, religion, and language that unite the people of the Arab Maghrib,

In response to the deep and firm aspirations of these peoples and their leaders to establish a union that would reinforce the existing relations and provide them with the appropriate ways and means to gradually proceed toward achieving a more comprehensive integration among themselves,

Conscious that this integration will have effects that will enable the Arab Maghrib Union to acquire a specific weight allowing it to make an effective contribution to world balance and to the consolidation of peaceful relations within the international community and to the establishment of security and stability in the world,

Aware that the institution of the Arab Maghrib Union requires tangible achievements and the setting up of common rules embodying the effective solidarity among its components and ensuring their economic and social development,

Expressing their sincere determination to make the Arab Maghrib Union a means for the construction of total Arab unity and a starting point for a wider union comprising other Arab and African countries,

Have agreed on the following:

Article One

By virtue of this treaty, a union, to be called the "Arab Maghrib Union," is hereby instituted.

Article Two

The union aims at:

— Strengthening the ties of brotherhood which link the member states and their peoples to one another;

— Achieving progress and prosperity of their societies and defending their rights;

— Contributing to the preservation of peace based on justice and equity;

— Pursuing a common policy in different domains; and,

— Working gradually toward achieving free movement of persons and transfer of services, goods, and capital among them.

Article Three

The common policy referred to in the previous article aims at reaching the following goals;

In the international field: to achieve concord among the member states and establish between them a close diplomatic cooperation based on dialogue;

In the field of defense: to preserve the independence of each of the member states;

In the economic field: to achieve industrial, agricultural, commercial, and social development of member states and take the necessary measures for this purpose particularly by setting up joint ventures and working out general and specific programmes in this respect;

In the cultural field: to establish a cooperation aimed at promoting education on its various levels, at safeguarding the spiritual and moral values emanating from the tolerant teachings of Islam, and at preserving the Arab national identity, and to take the necessary measures to attain these goals, particularly by exchanging teachers and students and creating joint university and cultural institutions as well as joint institutions specialized in research.

Article Four

The union shall have a Presidential Council composed of the heads of state of the member states and constituting the supreme authority of the union.

The chairmanship of the council shall be for a period of six months in rotation among the heads of state of the member states.

Article Five

The Presidential Council of the union shall hold its ordinary sessions every six months; it may hold extraordinary sessions whenever deemed necessary.

Article Six

Only the Presidential Council shall have the authority to take decisions, and its decisions shall be taken unanimously.

Article Seven

The prime ministers of the member states, or their homologues, may meet whenever deemed necessary.

Article Eight

The union shall have a Council of Foreign Ministers which shall prepare the sessions of the Presidential Council and look into the points submitted by the follow-up committee and the specialized ministerial committees.

Article Nine

Each state shall appoint a member of its Ministerial Council, or General Popular Committee, to be in charge of Union Affairs; these appointees shall form a Committee for the Follow-up of the Affairs of the Union and shall submit the results of their proceedings to the Council of Foreign Ministers.

Article Ten

The union shall have specialized ministerial committees set up by the Presidential Council which shall determine their tasks.

Article Eleven

The union shall have a General Secretariat composed of one representative for each member state; the General Secretariat shall exercise its functions in the country presiding over the session of the Presidential Council under the supervision of the chairman of the session whose country shall cover the expenses involved.

Article Twelve

The union shall have a Consultative Council comprising ten members for each state, to be chosen by the legislative bodies of the member states or according to the internal system of each state;

The Consultative Council shall hold an ordinary session every year as well as extraordinary sessions at the request of the Presidential Council;

The Consultative Council shall advise on all draft decisions handed over to it by the Presidential Council, as it may submit to the Presidential Council any recommendations it might consider likely to strengthen the action of the union and achieve its goals;

The Consultative Council shall elaborate its rules of procedure and submit them to the Presidential Council for approval.

Article Thirteen

The union shall have a judicial organ, composed of two judges for each state to be appointed by the state concerned for a six-year period, and renewed by half every three years. The judicial organ shall elect a chairman from its members for a one-year period;

The judicial organ shall specialize in examining conflicts related to the interpretation and implementation of the treaty and the agreements concluded within the framework of the union and submitted by the Presidential Council or any of the states party to the conflict or as provided for by the statutes of the judicial organ, the verdicts of which shall be binding and final;

Likewise, the judicial organ shall give advisory opinions on legal questions laid before it by the Presidential Council;

The judicial organ shall elaborate its statutes and submit them to the Presidential Council for ratification. The statutes shall constitute an integral part of the treaty;

The Presidential Council shall determine the seat of the judicial organ and its budget.

Article Fourteen

Any aggression directed against one of the member states shall be considered as an aggression against the other member states.

Article Fifteen

Member states pledge not to permit on their territory any activity or organization liable to threaten the security, the territorial integrity, or the political system of any of them.

They also pledge to abstain from joining any alliance or military or political bloc directed against the political independence or territorial integrity of the other member states.

Article Sixteen

Member states are free to conclude any agreements between them or with other states or groups provided these agreements do not run counter to the provisions of this treaty.

Article Seventeen

Other states belonging to the Arab nation or the African community may join this treaty if member states give their approval.

Article Eighteen

Provisions of this treaty may be amended upon the proposal of one of the member states, and such amendment becomes effective after its ratification by all member states.

Article Nineteen

This treaty goes into effect after its ratification by the member states according to procedures in force in each member state.

Member states are committed to take the necessary measures to this end within a maximum period of six months from the date of signature of this treaty.

Done in the city of Marrakesh on the blessed day of Friday the tenth of Rajab 1409 of the Hijra [1398 of the Death of the Prophet], corresponding to 17 February [Nuar] 1989.

For the Kingdom of Morocco,
  Hasan II
For the People's Democratic Republic of Algeria,
  Chedli Benjedid
For the Republic of Tunisia,
  Zayn al-'Abidin Ben 'Ali
For the Great Arab People's Socialist Libyan Jamahiriyya,
  Mu'ammar Qadhdhafi
The President of the Islamic Republic of Mauritania,
  Maaouya Ould Sid Ahmed Taya.

APPENDIX V: FINAL STATEMENT OF THE TENTH GULF COOPERATION COUNCIL SUMMIT HELD IN MUSCAT[147]
Issued in Muscat on 21 December 1989

In the name of God, the merciful, the compassionate: the Sultanate of Oman, Muscat, 19–22 Jumada al-Ula, 1410 Hijra, corresponding to 18–21 December 1989.

In response to the invitation of His Majesty Sultan Qabus Ibn Sa'id, sultan of Oman, and with the help and care of God, the 10th session of the GCC Supreme Council was held in the city of Muscat from 19–22 Jumada al-Ula, 1410 Hijra, corresponding to 18–21 December 1989, in the presence of His Highness Shaykh 'Isa Ibn Salman Al Khalifa, emir of the State of Bahrain; King Fahd Ibn 'Abd al-'Aziz, custodian of the two holy mosques and king of the Kingdom of Saudi Arabia; His Majesty Qabus Ibn Sa'id, sultan of Oman; His Highness Shaykh Khalifa Ibn Hamad Al Thani, emir of the State of Qatar, and His Highness Shaykh Jabir al-Ahmad al-Jabir Al Sabah, emir of Kuwait.

The Supreme Council studied all aspects related to the development of the council's march and the means of bolstering it according to the aims cited in the basic law, the security situation in the region in the light of the stages of contacts on the implementation of Security Council Resolution 598, the situation in the occupied Arab territories and the dimensions of the Palestinian Intifada, the situation in Lebanon and the tripartite committee's efforts and Ta'if agreement, world developments, the current changes in Europe, and the international situation after the Malta summit.

The Council's March

From its follow-up of the march of cooperation and the requirements of collective action; recalling the principles and aims cited in the council's basic law; in confirmation of what was contained in the 1987 Riyadh declaration and the 1988 Manama declaration, particularly about intensifying joint ventures; taking cognizance of the Ministerial Council's recommendations on the stages of implementing the economic agreement; and in confirmation of the Supreme Council's determination to continue to adopt all suitable steps to implement the remainder of the economic agreement and to establish a unified Gulf market, the council decides the following:

— To approve the rules of exclusion from the exemption of custom duties according to Article 24;
— To approve what was cited in the Ministerial Council's recommendation on the unified customs tariff;
— To approve what was cited in the Ministerial Council's recommendation on the mechanism of joint work.

The council reaffirms its determination to implement the rest of the economic agreement for the sake of establishing a unified Gulf market.

Security Cooperation

Believing in the importance of military and security cooperation among the member states to maintain their security and stability, and desiring to achieve further coordination and integration in this field, the council endorsed the recommendations of the defense ministers on building self-reliance according to the common vision and on the basis of the defense policy document.

The Peace Talks Between Iraq and Iran

The council discussed the developments of negotiations between the two countries in light of Security Council Resolution 598 of 1987. The council expresses appreciation for the efforts of UN Secretary-General Javier Pérez de Cuellar to surmount all obstacles to these negotiations. The council underlines its support for these efforts, which aim at bringing about a just, lasting, and comprehensive settlement of the conflict with a view to establishing peace and security in the region. The council expresses conviction in the success of these efforts in light of the positive signs coming from both sides — signs that clearly indicated both countries' desire to establish peace and embark on a new stage of normal relations between them on the basis of mutual respect.

The council calls upon the Security Council, especially its permanent member states, to support these efforts by all available means, including direct negotiations under the supervision of the UN secretary-general, and to release the prisoners of war and return them to their homelands without delay to end their suffering and the agony of their families. This should help both sides achieve balanced benefits and interests that help implement Security Council Resolution 598.

The council also appeals to the international community to exert further efforts to arrive at a just peace that takes into consideration the legitimate rights of all parties.

The Current Arab Situation

The council reviewed the current Arab situation while recalling the resolutions of the extraordinary Arab summit in Casablanca on the Intifada and its support for it and the struggle of the Palestinian people and their right to self-determination and the establishment of their independent state on their land. The council pays tribute to the heroic Intifada and appreciates the sacrifices of the Palestinian people in the occupied territories. It underlines the council's support and backing for the valiant Intifada toward achieving its aims. The council appeals to the international community to support the Intifada, expose Israel's methods of oppression and terrorism, oppose Israel's measures against the Palestinian people in the occupied territories, and stop the acts of tyranny represented by deportations and demolishing houses, which contradict the principles of human rights and conflict with the most fundamental international norms and conventions.

The council also supports the call for convening an international conference within the framework of the United Nations and with the participation of all parties, including the PLO, with a view to reaching a lasting and comprehensive solution to the Palestine question.

The Situation in Lebanon

The Supreme Council, having been briefed by the custodian of the two holy mosques on the Ta'if accord and the efforts and contacts of the higher Arab tripartite committee, reiterates its appreciation of the prominent role played by the committee to reach the Ta'if accord, and renews its support for the higher tripartite committee's work, expressing its appreciation of the efforts exerted by the custodian of the two holy mosques, His Majesty King Hasan II, and His Excellency President Chedli Benjedid, stressing its readiness to contribute to boosting the committee's contacts and efforts. It reaffirms its support for Lebanese President Ilyas al-Hirawi and the Government of National Reconciliation and the principles cited in the Ta'if accord so that Lebanon's unity and territorial integrity can be achieved and so that its national soil can be preserved. The council appeals to the international community to continue to support the Ta'if accord and back the higher Arab tripartite committee's efforts and the Lebanese legitimacy strongly and clearly and to respect what is dictated by the recognition of legitimacy in dealing with the Lebanese state.

The council appeals to all Lebanese parties to practice self-restraint and deal with matters at this critical stage with wisdom and patience in conformity with the Ta'if accord and within the framework of legitimacy as a basis for solving outstanding problems and removing the present obstacles for the sake of guaranteeing the unity of Lebanon — land and people — and entrenching its freedom, sovereignty, and independence.

The International Changes

The council is closely following the world developments and events and calls for adopting steps that end tension and remove the causes of division in the world. It hopes that these developments will lead to an international understanding to find just solutions to the regional conflicts, particularly the Middle East issue.

The council also hopes that the world will witness closer economic cooperation that is based on reciprocal interests and that supports the economic development programs in the developing countries.

Negotiations With the European Group

The Supreme Council expressed its satisfaction over the completion of measures to ratify the cooperation agreement between the council's member states and the EEC which will come into effect on 1 January 1990.

On this occasion, the Supreme Council recalled the resolution adopted by it during the Bahrain summit to authorize the Ministerial Council to enter into official trade negotiations with the EEC, and expressed the hope that the two sides can reach a balanced trade agreement which contributes toward improving and freeing trade exchange between them and which corresponds to the development needs of the council's member states.

While welcoming the convening of the first joint Ministerial Council in Muscat in March 1990, the Supreme Council hopes that relations between the two parties will, under that agreement, witness positive improvement which corresponds to the importance of the relations and the mutual interests of both parties.

The council expresses its appreciation for French President François Mitterrand's initiative of resuming Arab-European dialogue, and hopes that the meetings of the Arab and European foreign ministers will yield positive results in the interest of the two sides.

The GCC leaders expressed great appreciation and deep gratitude for His Majesty Sultan Qabus Ibn Sa'id for the hospitality he accorded them as well as for the excellent arrangements to provide an appropriate atmosphere to achieve success.

The GCC leaders commend his majesty the sultan's initiative to honor the citizens of the GCC states who rendered prominent services to their societies and states. They also underlined the role of this initiative in deepening cohesion and links among the GCC citizens.

The council looks forward to convening its 11th session in the State of Qatar next December at the invitation of His Highness Shaykh Khalifa Ibn Hamad Al Thani, emir of the State of Qatar.

APPENDIX VI: THE MUSCAT DECLARATION[148]
Issued in Muscat on 21 December 1989

The political, social, and economic changes that have been taking place on the international scene since the convening of the ninth GCC summit in Bahrain and all their ramifications have compelled the countries of the world to develop their international policies and to follow a new line based on wider horizons and greater exchanges while each state, big or small, continues to preserve its national identity.

This new world climate makes it incumbent on everyone to strengthen the basis of cooperation instead of confrontation and struggle, from which mankind has reaped only ruin and destruction.

The GCC states have undertaken many good and constructive deeds within the Arab and Islamic families, as well as on the international level in general and presented a good example for joint brotherly work within the framework of national sovereignty. Their majesties and highnesses the GCC leaders have been eager for their 10th summit to contribute to supporting and encouraging the spirit of peace and understanding prevailing in the world today. In order to reaffirm the ties of brotherhood, faith, and common destiny among the GCC states, entrench the concept of genuine cooperation, whose foundation is steadily rising on all levels, and promote the joint interests of their peoples in establishing distinguished relations, their majesties and highnesses the GCC leaders declare the following:

(1) Affirming the principle of neighborliness as a basic and legitimate pillar to which the GCC states will adhere in their international dealing in conformity with the principles of Islamic religion and international conventions;

(2) Affirming mutual respect for national sovereignty as a basic principle that must be firmly established;

(3) Adopting dialogue and negotiations as an effective means to solve disputes among nations in line with the principles of peaceful coexistence defined by the United Nations and international law;

(4) Supporting joint Arab action within the framework of the Arab League, given that it is the Arab house under whose ceiling the Arabs meet to achieve stability and prosperity for their nation, and extending a hand of friendship and cooperation to all nations that care for truth, justice, and peace;

(5) Considering the principle of peaceful coexistence among nations to be the cornerstone for the achievement of world peace and security and exploiting the prevailing *détente* in the international atmosphere within the principle of peaceful coexistence among nations to enable man to devote all of his potential to tackling his problems, especially poverty, ignorance, illness, and environmental pollution;

(6) Boosting efforts aimed at consolidating peace between Iraq and Iran, continuing support for the persistent efforts to resolve the Lebanese crisis on a basis of legitimacy and national unity, and stressing the Palestinian people's legitimate rights to self-determination and the establishment of their independent state under the PLO;

(7) Commending the existing policy of accord between the two superpowers, urging the enhancement of this policy to achieve further accomplishments in the international arena, and paying tribute to the growing accord among the European states to remove the causes for confrontation and disagreement in Europe, thus contributing toward entrenching world peace and security.

NOTES

For the place and frequency of publications cited here, and for the full name of the publication, news agency, radio station, or monitoring service where an abbreviation is used, please see "List of Sources." Only in the case of more than one publication bearing the same name is the place of publication noted here.

1. According to Mubarak, the four states had discussed the matter for over a year prior to the ACC's establishment. (Interview in *al-Ittihad,* Abu Dhabi, 21 February 1989.)
2. *Al-Ittihad,* Abu Dhabi, 23 January; *al-Sharq al-Awsat, al-Muharrir,* 28 January 1989.
3. *Al-Hayat,* Beirut, 7 February 1989.
4. Mubarak interview in *al-Ittihad,* Abu Dhabi, 21 February 1989.
5. INA, 16 February — DR, 23 February 1989.
6. *Al-Dustur,* Amman, 17 February 1989. One prominent Egyptian intellectual declared that the ACC would help prevent Israel from trying to solve the Palestinian problem militarily (either in Southern Lebanon or Jordan). In the event of peace, the ACC would provide strategic depth for an initially demilitarized Palestinian state in the West Bank and Gaza Strip. (Sa'd al-Din Ibrahim, in *al-Jumhuriyya,* Cairo, 4 February 1989.)
7. *Al-Ra'y,* 15 February; *al-Musawwar,* 14 July — DR, 19 July 1989.
8. INA, 16 February — DR, 23 February 1989.
9. Interview with 'Ali 'Abdallah Salih, *al-Ra'y al-'Amm,* 23 February; interview with Saddam Husayn, *al-Sharq al-Awsat,* 8 March — DR, 14 March 1989.
10. QNA, 22 February 1989.
11. *Al-Muharrir,* 21 January, 25 February 1989.
12. Interview with Saddam Husayn, *al-Sharq al-Awsat,* 8 March — DR, 14 March 1989.
13. Ibid.
14. INA, 25 March — DR, 28 March 1989.
15. For the text of the agreement, INA, 27 March — DR, 27 March 1989. The two leaders also concluded a second agreement on unspecified "security coordination."
16. *AT,* 3 May — DR, 5 May 1989.
17. For the text of the resolutions, R. Cairo, 16 June — DR, 19 June 1989.
18. For the text of the statements, MENA, 16 June — DR, 19 June 1989.
19. For the text of the resolutions, Amman TV, 26 September — DR, 27 September 1989.
20. For the text of the statement, INA, 26 September — DR, 27 September 1989.
21. MENA, 17 June — DR, 19 June 1989.
22. *Country Profile: Jordan, 1989–90.*
23. *CR:* Jordan, No. 4, 1989.
24. *CR:* Jordan, No. 2, 1989.
25. Interview in *al-Ahram,* 12 July — DR, 17 July 1989.
26. Interview with Iraqi Minister of Industry and Military Industrialization Husayn Kamil Hasan, in *al-Akhbar,* 7 May 1989; Shlomo Gazit and Ze'ev Eytan, *The Middle East Military Balance, 1988–89* (Tel Aviv: Jaffee Center for Strategic Studies, 1989), p. 22.

27. MENA, 30 January 1989.
28. *Akhir Sa'a*, 21 June 1989.
29. Muhammad Wahby, "The Arab Cooperation Council and the Arab Political Order," *American-Arab Affairs*, No. 28, Spring 1989.
30. *Al-Ra'y al-'Amm*, 15 February 1989.
31. *Al-Yawm al-Sabi'*, 20 February 1989.
32. The other members of the committee were the foreign ministers of Tunisia, Jordan, the United Arab Emirates (UAE), Sudan, and Algeria, and the Arab League's secretary-general; R. Tunis, 12 January — DR, 13 January 1989.
33. R. Beirut, 28 March — DR, 29 March 1989.
34. R. Monte Carlo, INA, 29 March — DR, 30 March 1989.
35. *IHT*, 28 April 1989. In an interview with a team from *Time*, Asad characterized Iraq's involvement in Lebanon as "something new...serving neither Iraq nor Lebanon." For text of the interview, R. Damascus, 27 March — DR, 28 March 1989.
36. R. Monte Carlo, 27 April — DR, 28 April; *Le Monde*, 29 April; *al-Usbu' al-'Arabi*, 8 May 1989.
37. MENA, 25 March — DR, 27 March 1989.
38. *FT*, 1 April; *al-Jumhuriyya*, Cairo, 21 April 1989.
39. R. Damascus, 27 March — DR, 28 March 1989.
40. *Al-Sharq al-Awsat*, 27 April; *October*, 7 May 1989.
41. *Al-Akhbar*, 12 May 1989.
42. AFP, 13 May — DR, 15 May 1989.
43. R. Cairo, 16 May — DR, 17 May 1989.
44. *Al-Siyasa*, Kuwait, 16 May; *al-Zahf al-Akhdar*, 15 May 1989.
45. Qadhdhafi's speech to the General People's Congress (GPC), Tripoli TV, 22 May — DR, 23 May 1989.
46. *Al-Tadamun*, 22 May; R. Damascus, 22 May — DR, 23 May 1989.
47. Qadhdhafi's speech to the GPC, Tripoli TV, 22 May — DR, 23 May 1989.
48. R. Rabat, 21 May — DR, 22 May 1989.
49. Ibid. For the text of the committee's report, see *al-Musawwar*, 2 June 1989.
50. *Ha'aretz*, 23 May. Three ways of ensuring Lebanese attendance had previously been discussed: (1) inviting both 'Awn and Huss; (2) having them delegate representatives; and (3) forming a delegation not affiliated with either of the two competing governments, KUNA, 16 May 1989.
51. Rabat TV, 23 May — SWB, 25 May 1989.
52. Mubarak's address to the People's Assembly, R. Cairo, 30 May — DR, 1 June 1989.
53. For an Egyptian weekly's account of the meeting, *al-Musawwar*, 2 June 1989; Dan Avidan, in *Davar*, 20 October 1989.
54. *Al-Musawwar*, 2 June 1989.
55. The resolution had confirmed the "right to return" of all refugees (i.e., both Jews and Arabs) displaced by the 1948 war and the right of compensation for those choosing not to return, on the condition that the returnees intended to "live at peace with their neighbors." The question of the timing of their return remained unsettled: according to the resolution, it was to be implemented at the "earliest practicable date." Ironically, all of the Arab states voted against the resolution at that time.
56. On a number of occasions, the PLO's Salah Khalaf (Abu Iyad), bitterly compared the lack of Arab financial aid to the PLO with Arab (Saudi and Gulf states') generosity toward the Afghan rebels (*al-Anba*, 6 December 1988; MENA, 9 February 1989). At Casablanca, 'Arafat castigated Arab leaders for failing to meet their commitments: of the initial $128m. pledged, he declared, none had been paid; regarding the $43m. monthly payments, only Saudi Arabia, Iraq, the UAE, and Libya had made (unspecified) contributions. (VoP [Baghdad] 25 May — DR, 30 May 1989.) Statements on other occasions by Palestinian officials placed Kuwait on the list of contributors as well.
57. VoP (Algiers), 24 May — DR, 25 May 1989.
58. *Al-Usbu' al-'Arabi*, 5 June 1989.
59. R. Monte Carlo, 22 May — DR, 23 May; *al-Musawwar*, 2 June 1989.
60. *Al-Sharq al-Awsat*, 24 May 1989.

61. Interview with PLO Executive Committee member Mahmud 'Abbas, MENA, 25 July —
     SWB, 27 July 1989.
62. To its domestic audience, the Syrians presented a different picture, indicating the tenuous
     nature of their commitment to the Arab consensus behind the PLO. The Casablanca
     summit's final communiqué, broadcast over R. Damascus on 27 May 1989, was distorted
     considerably. References to the PLO were not accompanied by the description, "the sole
     legitimate representative of the Palestinian people"; the portions dealing with the 19th
     PNC meeting, the creation of a Palestinian state, and the issue of elections in the West
     Bank and Gaza Strip were omitted; as was any mention of UN Resolutions 242 and 338 as
     being part of the basis for an international peace conference.
63. Rabat TV, 30 May — SWB, 1 June 1989.
64. Al-Anba, 11 June 1989.
65. Al-Musawwar, 2 June 1989.
66. AFP, 25 May — DR, 26 May; IHT, 26 May; al-Sharq al-Awsat, 26 May 1989.
67. Al-Jumhuriyya, Cairo, 28 May 1989.
68. R. Amman, 25 May — DR, 25 May 1989.
69. MENA, 25 May — DR, 26 May 1989.
70. Ma'ariv, 26 May 1989.
71. Al-Musawwar, 2 June 1989. This may have been achieved by Asad's oral assurances that he
     would be flexible on the matter of troop redeployments. For example, one Egyptian
     weekly mentioned a "gentleman's agreement" with Syria by which its troops would be
     pulled back within three months; Akhir Sa'a, 31 May 1989.
72. Asad had preferred that the six-nation committee upgrade its representation to the summit
     level and continue its work, presumably because it would be less prone than the tripartite
     committee to pressure Syria. (Asad's interview with al-Qabas International, 9 December
     1989.)
73. Rabat TV, 30 May — SWB, 1 June 1989.
74. Qadhdhafi's speech to the 1990 Baghdad Arab summit conference; Tripoli TV, 30 May —
     SWB, 1 June 1990.
75. R. Baghdad, 27 May — DR, 30 May 1989.
76. Al-Thawra, Baghdad, 7 June 1989.
77. Text of report by the Higher Arab Tripartite Committee on Lebanon, submitted on 14
     August to Arab heads of state; al-Quds al-'Arabi, 18 August — DR, 23 August 1989.
78. Al-Qabas International, 1–2 July 1989.
79. SPA, 27 June — DR, 28 June 1989.
80. Communiqué issued by the tripartite committee, Algiers TV, 31 July — DR, 1 August;
     al-Quds al-'Arabi, 18 August — DR, 23 August 1989.
81. For expressions of Syrian concern to the tripartite committee, al-Muharrir, 17 June 1989.
82. Moroccan Foreign Minister Filali denied reports that his country had taken the lead in
     advocating an anti-Syrian stand in the committee; al-Safir, reported by KUNA, 4 December
     1989.
83. Algiers TV, 31 July — DR, 1 August; al-Quds al-'Arabi, 18 August — DR, 23 August 1989.
84. Text of Shar''s letter published in al-Safir, broadcast on R. Damascus, 7 August — DR, 8
     August 1989.
85. R. Monte Carlo, 31 August — DR, 1 September; MEI, 8 September 1989.
86. Oded Zarai, in Ha'aretz, 28 August 1989.
87. Al-Thawra, Baghdad, 7 September 1989.
88. Statement by Tariq 'Aziz to INA, 2 August — DR, 3 August 1989.
89. Letter to Arab League Secretary-General Klibi, INA, 18 August — DR, 21 August; INA,
     13 September — DR, 14 September 1989.
90. SPA, 15 August — DR, 16 August 1989.
91. Suraqiyya, al-Masira, 11 September 1989.
92. R. Riyadh, 16 September — DR, 18 September 1989.
93. AFP, 5 October — DR, 18 September 1989.
94. For the text of the national accord, al-Sharq al-Awsat, 24 October; for the tripartite
     committee's accompanying declaration, VoL, 24 October — DR, 25 October 1989.
95. SPA, 4 December — DR, 5 December 1989.

96. *Le Nouvel Observateur,* 12-18 January 1989.
97. R. Rabat, 1 January — DR, 3 January 1989.
98. APS, 8 February — DR, 9 February 1989. A jointly owned company was to be established for the purpose of studying the idea in detail; for text of the statement issued at the visit's conclusion, *al-Sha'b,* Algiers, 9 February 1989.
99. *Al-Sayyad,* 28 April 1989.
100. 'Umar 'Izz al-Rijal, "al-Qimma al-Thaniya Lil-Maghrib al-'Arabi," *al-Siyasa al-Duwaliyya,* April 1989, pp. 163–66.
101. Ibid.
102. Rabat TV, 16 February — DR, 17 February 1989.
103. Qadhdhafi's speech to the General People's Congress, Tripoli TV, 2 March — DR, 3 March 1989.
104. Hasan's postsummit press conference, Rabat TV, 17 February — DR, 23 February 1989.
105. Bessaih's article in *el-Moudjahid,* 19 February 1989.
106. *Al-'Alam,* Rabat, 4 March 1989. An earlier, if less explicit Moroccan acceptance of the territorial status quo had been contained in the 16 May 1988 Algerian-Moroccan joint communiqué announcing the resumption of diplomatic relations; 22 March 1989.
107. *Al-Sayyad,* 28 April 1989.
108. R. Rabat, 30 May — DR, 2 June 1989.
109. R. Rabat, 31 October — DR, 1 November 1989.
110. *Syrie et Monde Arabe,* May 1989, citing an economic study published in Marrakesh on the occasion of the AMU's founding summit.
111. Paris International Service, 2 September — DR, 5 September; *al-Hayat,* Beirut, 4 September 1989.
112. *Al-Ittihad,* Abu Dhabi, 20 January 1989.
113. *Al-Watan al-'Arabi,* 27 January 1989.
114. Paris International Service, 5 January — DR, 6 January; *Le Monde,* 12 January 1989.
115. Moroccan Foreign Minister Filali took pains to characterize the meetings as "contacts," not "negotiations," while Morocco's minister for Saharan affairs declared that Polisario could be a legitimate interlocutor only *after* it had triumphed in a referendum. (*Al-Hayat,* Beirut, 11 January, reported by MAP, 12 January — DR, 13 January; *al-Sayyad,* 6 January 1989.)
116. *El-Pais,* 26 February — DR, 21 April 1989.
117. Originally proclaimed at the end of December 1988, the cease-fire had been provisionly extended as a goodwill gesture on the eve of the February AMU summit. It was declared to have formally lapsed on 28 February; *al-Sha'b,* Algiers, 13 May 1989.
118. "The Situation Concerning Western Sahara: Report of the Secretary-General," United Nations Security Council, S/21360, 18 June 1990.
119. *Suraqiyya,* 26 June 1989.
120. RTM TV, 22 November — DR, 24 November 1989.
121. *Al-Muharrir,* 25 February; *The Economist,* 17 June 1989.
122. *Al-Dustur,* London, 8, 15 May; *al-Muharrir,* 13 May 1989.
123. *Al-Muharrir,* 20 May 1989.
124. According to the account of one prominent defector, Polisario was already rent by internal divisions during 1988. (Interview with Omar Hadrami, *JA,* 23 October 1989.)
125. As part of this policy, Hasan's references to Polisario had become more conciliatory, in a paternalistic way; ibid., 18 September 1989.
126. *JA,* 23 October 1989; *Le Liberal,* May 1990.
127. *MEI,* 20 October 1989.
128. Ibid., 8 September 1989.
129. RTM TV, 22 November — DR, 24 November 1989.
130. *Die Presse,* 8 January — DR, 19 January 1989.
131. *ME,* February 1990.
132. KUNA, 3 January — DR, 9 January 1990.
133. See, e.g., *al-Sharq al-Awsat,* 15 May 1989.
134. *Al-Majalla,* 26 December 1989.
135. *Beirut al-Masa,* 3 July 1989.

136. R. Tehran, 20 November — DR, 21 November 1989.
137. *Al-Dustur,* London, 3 January 1989.
138. *Al-Jumhuriyya,* Baghdad, 17 September 1989.
139. *Al-Siyasa,* Kuwait, 24 December 1989.
140. *The Gulf States,* 30 October 1989.
141. *The Gulf States,* 21 August 1989.
142. E.g., Bruce Maddy-Weitzman, "The Fragmentation of Inter-Arab Politics," *Orbis,* Vol. 25, No. 2, Summer 1981, pp. 389–407; Itamar Rabinovich, "The Politics of Fragmentation and Anticipation: Inter-Arab Relations In the Early 1980s," *Occasional Papers,* No. 87 (The Moshe Dayan Center for Middle Eastern and African Studies, Tel Aviv University), October 1984; Gabriel Ben-Dor, "The Politics of Fragmentation: The Middle East in 1984," *MECS* 1983–84 (The Dayan Center for Middle Eastern and African Studies, Tel Aviv University, 1986).
143. Rabat TV, 26 May — DR, 30 May 1989.
144. INA, 16 February — DR, 17 February 1989.
145. JANA, 17 February — DR, 21 February 1989.
146. *American-Arab Affairs,* No. 31, Winter 1989–90.
147. GNA, 21 December — DR, 22 December 1989.
148. Ibid., 21 December — DR, 22 December 1989.

The Forgotten Honor of Islam

REINHARD SCHULZE

On 26 September 1988, when Viking Press in London published Salman Rushdie's novel *The Satanic Verses,* the Islamic world was showing a growing readiness to settle the cultural and political conflicts between divergent Islamic tendencies. The cease-fire on 18 July 1988 in the Iraq-Iran War also effected a "verbal truce" between Iran and Saudi Arabia, the contestants for cultural hegemony in Islam. Both regimes demonstrated that they were interested in establishing an Islamic coexistence in order to freeze the Sunni-Shi'i conflict, to reduce the pilgrimage problem to a lower level, and to defuse the Lebanon question. Although the Saudi-Iranian quarrels continued, officials on both sides tried to ease the tension that had characterized the hot phase of the Gulf War. From 11 November 1988 on, Saudi media discontinued the propaganda war following an announcement by King Fahd,[1] and Iran made it understood that it would follow the Saudi example.

Only Saudi Arabia's Commission of the Great 'Ulama (*hay'at kibar al-'ulama*) perpetuated the pilgrimage conflict by issuing a remarkable *fatwa* in November 1988, stating that anybody committing acts of violence against public institutions, infrastructure, or public-supply services should be executed as a rebel, according to the *hadd al-haraba,*[2] after being tried in court according to the accepted procedure. This *fatwa* was a very late reaction to the pilgrimage issue, which had preoccupied the Saudi security forces since the bloodshed in Mecca on 31 July 1987. In August 1988, prominent Muslim scholars, such as al-Azhar rector Jadd al-Haqq 'Ali Jadd al-Haqq, had legitimated the Saudi claim that only the royal regime should be responsible for the security of the pilgrimage and that "the rulers of Mecca and Medina have the right and the duty to guarantee security."[3]

The cease-fire between Iran and Iraq freed the Saudi regime to concentrate on the Afghanistan issue. The Ta'if talks in December 1988 between a Soviet delegation headed by Ambassador in Kabul Yuli Vorontsov and a delegation of Afghan Mujahidin led by Burhan al-Din Rabbani[4] released Saudi Arabia from the pressure which the Gulf War had exerted on its politics. The Saudi regime could now play its cards in the effort to determine the structure of the Afghan political leadership after the Soviet troops' final withdrawal. Iran and the Shi'a question were thrust into the background. Even 'Abd al-'Aziz Ibn 'Abdallah Ibn Baz, the archmodel of Wahhabi scholarship, proposed a state-sponsored alms (*zakat*) tax to finance the final Afghan Jihad.[5] The demonstrations in Iranian cities on 27 December 1988, on the occasion of the ninth anniversary of the Soviet intervention in Afghanistan, were reported positively by the Saudi media.[6] Accordingly, Saudi Arabia unofficially welcomed the talks between the new leader of the Pakistan-based alliance of seven Mujahidin factions, Sibghat Allah Mujaddidi, and Iranian Foreign Minister 'Ali Akbar Velayati on 16 January 1989.[7] They agreed that the reconciliation of Sunni and Shi'i Afghan factions should result in a unified leadership and a broad-based Mujahidin government. The Saudi media optimistically awaited 15 February 1989, the day when all Soviet troops would evacuate Afghanistan, and foresaw an Islamic government seizing power in Kabul directly after the withdrawal.[8]

A day before the final withdrawal, however, the leader of the Islamic revolution in Iran, Ayatollah Ruhollah Khomeyni, promulgated his famous *fatwa* concerning Rushdie. This very short statement suddenly made Islam an international political issue once again.

THE RUSHDIE AFFAIR

In September 1988, two Muslim members of the Indian Parliament, Sayyid Shihab al-Din and Khurshid 'Alam Khan, started a successful campaign to prohibit publication of Salman Rushdie's book, dealing with the cultural and social situation of Muslims in Great Britain, which had just been published in London. The book, they claimed, contained a blatant defamation of Islam, of the Prophet, and of his wives. On 5 October 1988, the Indian government banned the novel, on the basis of Article 11 of the Indian tariff law, on the ground that it offended Islam. Pakistan, South Africa, Saudi Arabia, and several African countries followed suit during October. News about the book spread through the Arab states only very slowly. Nevertheless, in November 1988, al-Azhar rector Jadd al-Haqq published an urgent warning against a book called *The Satanic Verses* without mentioning the author's name. He said he had received small parts of the book from the Egyptian Foreign Ministry which had asked for his opinion on those passages containing the hero's vision of early Islamic history in Mecca.[9] In general, however, Muslim circles in the Arab world did not pay much attention to the book or its author. In November 1988, a certain Murtada Bozorgzadeh published a critique of the book in the literary supplement of *Kayhan Hawa'i*, stating that "some critics think that the book *The Satanic Verses* implicitly insults Iran, or is some sort of reaction of the West or Westerners toward Iran's Islamic Revolution."[10] Thus, instead of directly attacking Iran, the "Westerners" preferred to hit, to offend, and to insult Islam's "holy values."

The Rushdie affair blossomed in the Islamic diaspora in England and India. In London, the secretary-general of the Union of Islamic Organizations in Great Britain, Sayyid Pasha, protested against Rushdie in October 1988 and called on Prime Minister Margaret Thatcher to ban his book, which she refused to do, on 11 November 1988. The Saudi-backed Islamic Center in London organized a meeting of Islamic ambassadors (also attended by the Iranian chargé d'affaires) in the Regent's Park mosque on 29 November 1988, in order to examine the possibilities of involving the law against the book. On 11 December 1988, the affair reached the large Pakistani and Indian Muslim community in Bradford. After Attorney-General Sir Patrick Mayhew declared on 22 December 1988 that the book did not represent a major offense, the Bradford Muslim community began to demonstrate in public.

Whereas Islamic countries seemed to restrict their reaction to banning Rushdie's book, in Bradford the reaction was more radical. On 14 January 1989, several thousand Muslims took part in a public burning of the book; six days later, the Bradford Muslim community demanded for the first time that Rushdie be condemned to death for apostasy. Thus, a novel whose subject was the cultural reality of Muslim diaspora communities helped these communities express themselves. The language has now become that of Islam, a single word summing up a complex cultural identity perceived as having been offended for the last 30 years.

In India and Pakistan, the novel caused similar unrest, which reached a climax in the Islamabad riots of 12 February. Thousands of Pakistanis attacked the American Cultural Center leaving five people shot dead by the police and several others wounded. Among the wounded was the president of the *jam'iyat-i 'ulama'i Islam*, Mawlana Fadl al-Rahman.[11] The next day, one demonstrator was killed in Srinagar,[12] and Pakistani students also attacked Prime Minister Benazir Bhutto as a "witch" during an anti-Rushdie rally.

Significantly, from January 1989 on, not the book, but the author was the focus of criticism. Until then, Islamic governments had only banned the book without demanding action against its author. South Africa had barred entry to Rushdie, the only action taken against him. To most of the states that had hitherto taken action, the book was blasphemous, but did not constitute a criminal offense.

"THE MOST IMPORTANT *FATWA* OF THE 20TH CENTURY"
On 14 February, Ayatollah Khomeyni issued his *fatwa* declaring that the book's author was an apostate and its publisher a blasphemer. The Islamic community, Khomeyni said, should not only ban the book, but also punish the author and the publisher:

> In the name of God:
> "To him we belong, and to him we will return [in days to come]" [Sura 2/156]. I inform the pious Muslims of the whole world that the author of the book *The Satanic Verses* which was compiled, printed, and published against Islam, the Prophet, and the Qur'an, and the publishers who are acquainted with its contents are condemned to death.
> I call on every zealous Muslim to execute them immediately wherever they find them so that no one else will dare insult the holy values of the Muslims. Anyone killed on this path is, so God wills, a martyr. Meanwhile, if anyone has access to the author of the book *The Satanic Verses* but without the power to execute him, he should hand him over to the people that he may be punished for his offenses. Peace be upon you, the mercy of God and his blessings.
> [signed] Ruhallah Musavi [Khomeyni].
> [dated] 25 Bahman 1367 [= 13 February 1989].[13]

The ideological context of this *fatwa* was clearer than its traditional-legal validity. In many places, the *fatwa* was criticized on the grounds that Khomeyni did not have the legal authority to issue such a death warrant; this could only be done by an ordinary court empowered by Islamic law to carry out the *hadd*-penalties.[14] Critics also said that even if Khomeyni did have the legal authority in his role as Iran's supreme judge, he was not allowed to speak for the whole *umma* (nation of Islam), as this would constitute interference into the domestic affairs of other countries that delegitimated their legal system. Thus, by international law and even by the accepted standards of the Islamic law of *haraba*,[15] Khomeyni's sentence of death should be regarded as invalid, critics said.

Khomeyni, however, did not resort to an official *hukm* (binding judgment) as

Sunni courts would have done, but to the more moralistic instrument of a *fatwa*. Such a legal opinion, in principle, has no judicial force. On the contrary, it offers only a judgment which advises Muslims in general or courts in particular of the rules of a sentence or social behavior. In theory, a *fatwa* is not linked to any executive power;[16] other scholars might issue different opinions in the same case, and it would be up to the person who sought a *fatwa* to follow one or the other ruling.

Political *fatawa* (plural of *fatwa*), however, are different. In most cases, they are not sought. A mufti makes an ideological statement the form of a *fatwa*; or, he appeals to an unnamed public to execute his ruling, or to follow his order. As a result, a new legal structure transcending the borders of state law emerges; a moral statement embodied in a legal opinion becomes a judicial ruling without the force of the state's executive power. The *umma* itself becomes the new executive power, with the result that such a *fatwa* delegates state power to an anonymous public. Such *fatawa* were not unknown in the Muslim world. On 26 June 1983, for example, the Sunni mufti of Jerusalem, Sa'd al-Din al-'Alami, issued a similar *fatwa* condemning Syrian President Hafiz al-Asad to death and demanding of every Muslim that he execute Asad wherever he might be found.[17]

It may be assumed that Khomeyni deliberately used the form of a *fatwa* (though his statement was sometimes called a *hukm*) in order to mobilize his Islamic clientele by stressing his claim to being not only the leader of the Iranian Islamic Revolution, but also of the whole Islamic *umma*.[18] This could be interpreted as an attempt to counter the growing readiness of Shi'ite scholars to give state power a constitutional basis and to reduce the influence of informal Islamic groups that had exercised executive power. In fact, the *fatwa* was issued at a moment when the so-called Iranian liberals, led by 'Ali Akbar Hashemi Rafsanjani, pleaded for an Iranian form of open-door policy (see chapter on Iran).

A NEW LINE OF DIVISION

The reception of Khomeyni's *fatwa* coincided in general with its two aspects. On the one hand, scholars who held an etatist view of Islamic politics attacked Khomeyni on the ground that he did not have the authority to speak for the whole Islamic *umma* and to act as a grand inquisitor vested with judicial power. On the other hand, according to the new Shi'ite concept of *velayate faqih* (rule of the jurisconsult)[19] Khomeyni's judgment, even if clothed in a *fatwa*, had legal force because Khomeyni acted as the "agent of the Hidden Imam," whose will he personified. In addition, as the former Iranian president 'Ali Khameneh'i put it, "he is the leader of the Muslim communities and nation; to him, who is not only the leader of the Iranian nation, all Muslims of the world are bound by their hearts. As leader of the Islamic *umma*, he has to defend their rights."[20]

Etatist-oriental Islamic politicians countered this claim by stressing the responsibility of each Islamic state for its Muslim community. Therefore, only Islamic courts could deal with the Rushdie affair, and, as the secretary-general of the Supreme Council of Islamic Affairs of al-Azhar, Jamal al-Din Mahmud, stated, Rushdie as a Muslim had a vested interest in having a just trial.[21] The president of the *fatwa* commission of al-Azhar, 'Abdallah al-Mashar, said that Rushdie had to be killed, as he had insulted the Prophet, but he must be heard by a court and should have the opportunity to repent.[22] This legalistic approach was shared by 'Abd al-'Aziz Ibn Baz, who demanded that Rushdie be tried *in absentia* by a court consisting of scholars from Egypt, Pakistan, India, Morocco, and Jordan.[23] Ibn Baz, of course, would not hesitate to condemn Rushdie to death if he were a member of such a court. In January 1985, he had together with the secretary-general of the Muslim World League (MWL), 'Abdallah 'Umar Nasif, applauded both a Sudanese court's sentence of death on the mystic Mahmud Muhammad Taha for apostasy, as well as Taha's execution on 18 January 1985.[24]

Khomeyni's *fatwa* antagonized the legal-minded Sunni scholarly establishment. The informal Islamic groups, however, welcomed the clear delegation of executive power manifested by the *fatwa* and hurried to express their readiness to carry out Khomeyni's ruling. Here, the Sunni-Shi'ite cleavage was of no importance and it seemed that these informal political groups used the *fatwa* to demonstrate their identity, denying any legitimacy to existing Islamic regimes. A *fatwa* like Khomeyni's thus tended to strengthen Islamic community-building processes: by identifying with the executive power which Khomeyni's *fatwa* demanded, these informal political groups were able to provide their *jama'a* (community) with a political and legal identity, which helped to further the dissociation from state power and to question the legal legitimacy of the state to which the community originally adhered.

Little wonder that the *fatwa* was well received particularly in Muslim areas rent by conflict and where Muslims were a minority. In Lebanon, the Islamic Jihad Organization for the Liberation of Palestine (*munazzamat al-jihad al-islami li-tahrir filastin*) called for Rushdie's execution,[25] as did the Hizballah. Sa'id Sha'ban of Tripoli, an Iranian client, secularized the affair by claiming that Rushdie was a Zionist spy, who should be killed immediately.[26] Even Ahmad Jibril, the leader of the Baghdad-based Popular Front for the Liberation of Palestine-General Command, declared his readiness to carry out Khomeyni's execution order.[27] In Egypt, 'Umar 'Abd al-Rahman, head of *al-Jama'a al-islamiya*, likewise sided with Khomeyni and insisted on the *fatwa*'s legitimacy.[28] In April he organized rallies in Fayyum during which the *jama'a* claimed power to execute the *fatwa* among others. 'Abd al-Rahman and other Islamic militants were soon arrested (see chapter on Egypt). The female Turkish preacher Gülcin Tavsan called on all Muslim women to wage a holy war against the West and to start it by killing Rushdie.[29] The mufti of the Turkish town of Osmaniye also welcomed Khomeyni's *fatwa*.

THE ISLAMIC "DIASPORA" REACTS

Numerous Muslim scholars from India and Pakistan quickly expressed their conviction that the Islamic *umma* had to obey the *fatwa*.[30] Here, the non-Arab Muslim identity found a new forum: not only had Rushdie been born in Bombay in 1947 — a fact that Indian Muslims liked to highlight — but he had also discredited and defamed the Islamic culture in Great Britain, a country whose c. 1.5m. Indian and Pakistani Muslims formed the largest non-Christian community. It was, thus, largely a sense of shame which prompted their response. The reactions to the Rushdie affair in India and Pakistan were far more violent than elsewhere. In Bombay, with 15% of its population Muslim, c. 20 people were killed in riots on 24 and 25 February.[31] The common view was that Rushdie had deserted to the West in order to dishonor Islam. The reactions in the Indian subcontinent were connected to its cultural ambiguity, which was the theme of Rushdie's novel. Thus, the Rushdie affair was only one aspect of a growing dissociation of Indian and Pakistani Muslims from the hitherto accepted British culture. For many of them, the West had shown itself as a bulwark of impudence, be it with regard to women or to Islam.

Among European Muslim communities, the Rushdie affair boiled down to this: the more the Muslim communities defended the *fatwa,* the more they were socially isolated from the majority. Here, too, shame played an important role. Collectively, Muslim communities in Bradford, Paris, Hamburg, or Berlin were able to identify the offender of their culture and the impudence they experienced daily. Now he had a name: Salman Rushdie, the devil.[32] In general, however, the support for Khomeyni's *fatwa* was weak among European Muslim communities outside Great Britain. Even the most radical Turkish preacher in Cologne, Celalettin Kaplan, the head of the so-called Islamic Cultural Centers, pointed out: "We do not accept the call for murder."[33]

ARABISM AS AN EXAMPLE OF ISLAMIC SOBRIETY

Obviously, Arab Muslim communities reacted far less. Here the more legalistic and etatist tendencies of Sunni Islam were of minor importance: the Rushdie affair touched the honor of Islam, but not the honor of the Arabs. Suddenly, Arabism became an issue again. As the Libyan leader Mu'ammar al-Qadhdhafi stressed, Rushdie himself was not important; on the contrary, the "Christian-Jewish countries were behind this book....It was published by the Christian-Jewish group together with a warning against the Arabs and Islam."[34] Qadhdhafi linked the Rushdie affair to radical Islamic politics: "Extremist religious movements...want religion to prevail over pan-Arabism, because they are jealous of the Arabs who are the imams of the Muslims." Nevertheless, the "death threats against Rushdie were praiseworthy," Qadhdhafi added in another context.[35] No wonder that most Islamic heads of state or officials said nothing about the Rushdie affair. For them, it only strengthened the position of non-Arab governments and the power of informal Islamic political groups. Until the beginning of March 1989, only Pakistan and Iraqi Foreign Minister Nizar Hamdun had commented upon the *fatwa*: Pakistan supported Khomeyni, though indirectly; the Iraqi foreign minister, on the other hand, denied that Khomeyni had any legal power. Most governments restricted their reaction to banning the book, and Jordan, for example, declared that it had already banned the book on 15 November 1988. Nevertheless, in March 1989, Jordanian Minister of Religious Affairs 'Abd al-'Aziz al-Hayyat added that "Khomeyni was wrong to call for the killing of the author Salman Rushdie."[36]

The crucial point was how to deal with Rushdie and not with the book. It was the accepted wisdom that the book contained a defamation of Islam, of the Prophet Muhammad and his wives, and of all Islamic values. Iran's policy of attacking Rushdie had an adverse impact on inter-Islamic open dialogue. Saudi Arabia had the difficult task of continuing the *rapprochement* with Iran in order to restore its own Islamic supremacy, even over non-Arab Islamic countries, while avoiding being identified with Iran's politics by the West. At the same time, the Saudi regime had to dampen the reactions of Saudi 'ulama who had declared Rushdie an apostate on 21 February 1989.[37]

From 19–24 February, the Islamic Fiqh Academy of the MWL held its 11th session in Mecca.[38] The 22 participants had to discuss nine different topics, one of which concerned the apostasy of Rashad Khalifa, an Egyptian living in Tucson, Arizona, who had developed a far-reaching reinterpretation of Islamic law claiming that the *sunna* was no longer a source of Islamic law.[39] For the MWL Khalifa was closer to the pure type of an apostate than Rushdie, for Khalifa argued as a Muslim, whereas Rushdie openly declared his unbelief. Khalifa's heresies had occupied Saudi scholars since 1979; on 1 May 1979, the Saudi Great Scholars' Organization had issued a *fatwa* stating that Khalifa should be treated as an apostate. Now the members of the academy were discussing them once again as he had just declared that the two last verses of *surat al-tawba* (Qur'an IX, 128–29) were inserted into the Qur'an. In the League's eyes, this obvious heresy had far wider implications than Rushdie's book. The academy used the Khalifa issue to pronounce a general sentence against Rushdie, stating that he was an apostate; but the Rushdie case remained in the shadow of the Khalifa affair (for Khalifa's death, in January 1990, see below).

The MWL restricted itself to very short statements. League Secretary-General Nasif declared that the book was too "trifling to be refuted scientifically"; a columnist in the League's weekly, 'Amir 'Ubayd, added that "Salman Rushdie's work does not, by any measure, fall within the orbit of creative work and hence cannot be defended or protected."[40] In an earlier comment, the League demanded Rushdie's execution "as an apostate by whatever Muslim who gets hold of him."[41] This first reaction of the MWL seemed to have been influenced by Khomeyni's *fatwa*; but within a few days, the League dissociated itself from its own statement, perhaps because the Saudi Government controlled the Islamic reactions by censoring critics in the Saudi press.

Before disposing of the Rushdie matter, the MWL stressed that there was no need for a scientific reaction as some scholars, particularly from Egypt and Europe, had proposed. The United Arab Emirates' (UAE) paper *al-Ittihad* said the sole solution was that Rushdie should be declared an apostate because he was a Muslim. Any attempt to refute Rushdie's book would mean accepting Rushdie as an interlocutor, which was contrary to Islam.[42]

The official Saudi position was now clear. Saudi Foreign Minister Sa'ud al-Faysal said:

> The kingdom refuses to be dragged into this marginal and imaginary battle. Even though the kingdom appreciates the grief felt by Muslims as a result of the book's publication, the kingdom does not consider it the most dangerous provocation facing Muslims. All efforts to raise the problem make Islam out to be an easy prey for anyone who wants to damage or attack Islam.[43]

This was not only a clear statement against Iran, but more so against Rushdie himself who had suspected Saudi Arabia of being responsible for the unrest among Muslims in Great Britain and of financing the campaign against him.[44]

THE 18TH CONFERENCE OF ISLAMIC FOREIGN MINISTERS

Sa'ud al-Faysal's statement was an attempt to end the discussions on Salman Rushdie, which had also affected the proceedings of the 18th conference of Islamic foreign ministers that had convened in Riyadh from 13-16 March. The Islamic Conference Organization (ICO) had just entered a new era; in January, Niger's Prime Minister Hamid Algadib took up the post of its secretary-general (on his election at the 17th conference in Amman, see *MECS* 1988, p. 183),[45] and the organization could look back with some satisfaction to its success in helping achieve a cease-fire in the Gulf War. With the Soviet Union's withdrawal from Afghanistan, another critical issue in Islamic politics had been resolved, enabling the ICO to present itself again as a stronghold of moderate Islamic interests. Even the quarrel over the pilgrimage was now seen to be negotiable. Although Sadiq Khalkhali, the president of the foreign political committee of the Islamic Assembly in Iran, still insisted on Iran's demand to send 150,000 pilgrims to Mecca during the Hajj, Iran welcomed Pakistan's mediation.[46] In January 1989, Mehdi Karrubi, the "representative of the Imam" (who on 15 August 1989 was elected speaker of the Majlis), optimistically stated that a solution of the pilgrimage problem was in sight.[47]

For Iran, the Rushdie affair offered an opportunity to reenter the ICO with drums beating and flags flying. In 1987, Iran had boycotted the Islamic summit conference in Kuwait, and in 1988 it sent a foreign ministry official — rather than the foreign minister — to the Amman session of the Islamic foreign ministers' conference (see *MECS* 1987, p. 154; 1988, p. 181). With the Gulf War over, however, Iran urgently needed to reconstruct its Islamic foreign policy, which hitherto had been dominated by the politically shaped Sunni-Shi'i antagonism. No wonder that the Iranian Government took advantage of the Rushdie affair; once again, Iran could portray itself as the custodian of Islam and of Islamic values, fighting all forms of apolitical deviations, e.g., the so-called "American Islam." The 18th foreign ministers' conference should become the forum for the reconstituted Iranian Islamic identity which had suffered much after the end of the Gulf War. Amir 'Ali Mas'udi in a *Kayhan* editorial pointed out that, for the first time, the ICO conference was of importance. Hamid al-Ghadib was said to have encouraged Iran to improve its relations with the ICO, and Iran reacted by considering its possible participation in the Riyadh conference. Nevertheless, Mas'udi continued, the ICO's "ultra-conservative" tendency still offered the opportunity of turning the Rushdie affair into an intergovernmental and ICO problem. If Iran participated, the danger would arise that this would "lessen its value and dignity."[48] The Rushdie affair thus became a new avenue for Iran's reentry. The Organization of Islamic Propagation (*munazzame-y i'lam-i islami*), the Iranian counter to the Saudi MWL and the Libyan World Islamic Call Society, had to take a clear stand against Rushdie. Its secretary-general, 'Ali Jannati, had just paid a visit to the UAE and to Qatar in order to win their support. To underline the international aspect of the affair, Iran did not send its foreign minister, 'Ali Akbar Velayati, but Jannati's deputy, Muhammad 'Ali Taskhiri at the head of a small delegation to Riyadh.

In Riyadh, Taskhiri sought Pakistan's support to give the Rushdie affair high priority.[49] The issue was urgent: a draft agenda finalized on 11 March (two days before the conference convened) did not mention Rushdie. In addition, more and more Islamic countries tried to counter the Iranian threat by declaring that the Rushdie affair should not be "politicized." Nevertheless, Rushdie became a subject of the "cultural issues" at the beginning of the conference. The pressure on the ICO, and especially on Egypt and Saudi Arabia which had both tried to cool the affair, grew steadily. Kuwait and Qatar urged an immediate discussion of Rushdie.[50] In Saudi Arabia, the Rushdie affair disappeared from the pages of the daily newspapers on 13 March, the day the conference began. The Saudi Arabian Government was concerned lest Rushdie overshadow the Palestine and Afghanistan questions, the conference's two major issues, which were the Saudi focal points of concern. The Rushdie affair, however, was too hot to be thrust into the background. Saudi Arabia had to agree that it be referred to the political committee.[51] Sa'ud al-Faysal stated: "I cannot yet take a general position on the question of blasphemy against Islam as the conference has not yet made any final decision on it."[52]

On 16 March, the foreign ministers agreed on a "final statement" in which the Rushdie affair was dealt with as a political matter:

> The conference issued a declaration of joint Islamic action to combat the blasphemous campaign against Islam. It stressed its determination to coordinate the efforts of the Islamic states which rely on the Shari'a to combat blasphemy against Islam. The conference declared that blasphemy cannot be justified on the basis of freedom of expression and opinion. The conference strongly condemned the book *The Satanic Verses*, whose author is regarded as an apostate. It appeals to all members of society to impose a ban on the book and to take the necessary legislation to ensure the protection of the religious beliefs of others. The conference announced that the Islamic states will make effective and coordinated efforts to ensure respect for Islam and its noble values.[53]

DEAD HEAT AT THE CONFERENCE

The ICO had thus officially declared that Rushdie was to be regarded as an apostate. In Iranian propaganda, this statement came close to the "Imam's line," as all five Islamic schools of jurisprudence exacted the death penalty for apostasy.[54] In addition, Iran with great satisfaction pointed out that the conference's political committee had refused to discuss the Iraqi proposal concerning the exchange of prisoners of war. For the first time, an Iranian position had won over an Iraqi one.[55] Iranian newspapers soon reported worldwide support for Khomeyni's *fatwa*: in Egypt, the 'alim Fu'ad 'Abd al-Rahman al-Minyawi regarded it as the only way to combat Rushdie's "crime"; in Ankara, the preacher Molla Sadr al-Din Yüksel also openly stated his unqualified support for the *fatwa*.[56]

It was rumored that Iran had to make important concessions to get Saudi Arabia's agreement to a statement against Rushdie. Some sources reported that Iran would forgo the compensation that Saudi Arabia had intended to pay to the families of Iranian pilgrims killed in the July 1987 Mecca riots and that Iran was ready to accept the quota of 45,000 pilgrims set by Saudi Arabia following the resolution of the 17th Islamic foreign ministers' conference in Amman. Finally, Iran would also accept the Saudi condition not to stage any political demonstrations during the coming pilgrimage.[57] Clearly, this was a false report: Iran would never have accepted such preconditions. But Iran did have to pay a price. The more Iran concentrated on the Rushdie issue, the more Saudi Arabia was able to deal with the Afghanistan problem, which was another area of Iranian-Saudi political competition. The MWL commented contentedly that every effort to exploit the Rushdie affair in order to sow discord among the Islamic states had failed.[58]

AN ISLAMIC AFGHANISTAN?

On 9 March, Saudi Arabia recognized the new provisional Afghan Mujahidin government. Sibghat Allah Mujaddidi, the leader of the Afghanistan National Liberation Front (*jebh-i nejat-i melli-y Afghanistan*), a prominent figure of the Naqshbandi Sufi order and a graduate of al-Azhar, was elected acting president following long discussions in the Shura (Consultative Council) of Rawalpindi from 10–18 February. The new government was mainly one of the Peshawar-based Mujahidin parties, the so-called Seven-Party Alliance. The Iran-supported Shi'i Eight-Party Alliance had no influence in the new government. At the Riyadh conference, Saudi Arabia had introduced the Mujahidin government as the only legitimate representative of an Islamic Afghanistan and urged the ICO member states to recognize it by offering it the vacant Afghan seat at the conference. The conference approved the Saudi demand: 35 for, five against (Syria, Libya, North Yemen, South Yemen, and Iraq) and two abstentions (Iran and the Palestinian delegation).[59] The Iranian officials did not protest against the lack of representation for the Iran-supported Mujahidin. The Iranian press tried to delegitimate the new government by saying that the Afghan Foreign Minister Qulb al-Din Hikmatyar (*hezb-e islami*/ Hikmatyar) tended to submit to Soviet peace conditions.[60] This however, was only a secondary theater of war. At the same time, Iran was doing everything to improve its relations with the Soviet Union, also in order to counter the strong Saudi influence in the region.

POLITICS OF ISLAMIC APPEASEMENT

After the ICO foreign ministers' conference, Iran and Saudi Arabia began improving their bilateral relations. Taskhiri, the head of the Iranian delegation to Riyadh, stated that the presence of an Iranian delegation was a "positive step" toward a restoration of diplomatic relations between the two countries. Sa'ud al-Faysal answered that he was glad to hear this statement, which "is good proof of Islamic solidarity."[61] The diplomatic relations had been cut by Saudi Arabia on 27 April 1988, following explosions at a petrochemical plant in the Eastern Region. Optimistically, Iranian sources said that within three weeks Iran and Saudi Arabia would resume their diplomatic relations.[62] After Jannati's tour in March of every country on the Arabian Peninsula (except Saudi Arabia), Oman mediated between Iran and Saudi Arabia.[63] On 23 April, Mehdi Karrubi, as head of the Martyrs' Organization established after the bloodshed in Mecca in 1987, declared that Iran would send pilgrims to Mecca "when Saudi Arabia announces that it will host them in the following days."[64]

Both Iran and Saudi Arabia also tried to play down the murder of 'Abdallah Ibn Muhammad al-Ahdal in Brussels on 29 March. Ahdal, born in 1952 in Hudayda, had been director of the MWL's Islamic Cultural Center in Brussels since 1983. He was killed in front of the center together with his secretary, Salim al-Bahri from Tunisia. Two days later, a Lebanese group calling itself "Soldiers of the Right" (*jund al-haqq*) claimed responsibility for the murder. Ahdal, it was reported, had received several threats for two weeks after openly attacking the Khomeyni *fatwa* concerning Rushdie.[65] (The same organization had also claimed responsibility for assassinating Hasan 'Ali al-Amiri, a Saudi diplomat, in Bangkok at the end of 1988.)[66] The group did not associate the murder with the Rushdie affair; on the contrary, it accused Ahdal and Bahri of working for the Israeli Mossad and of being enemies of God and of Islam. 'Abdallah 'Umar Nasif, the MWL secretary-general, "reiterated that the uproar which was raised over Salman Rushdie's blasphemous book and the assassination of al-Ahdal and his aide may be a mere coincidence...[Ahdal] was the target of harassment and provocations long before Rushdie's book became a hot issue."[67]

Even the assassination of Lebanon's mufti Hasan Khalid, a member of the MWL constituent council since 1975,[68] in Beirut on 15 May 1989 was not connected with Iranian activities.[69]

BOMBING AT MECCA

Iran also tended to play down the Saudi-Iranian conflict. Two months before the pilgrimage started, Iranian Prime Minister Mir Husayn Musavi maintained that Iran refused to link the pilgrimage with its policy toward Saudi Arabia, but would continue to demand the admission of 150,000 Iranian pilgrims; this demand, however, should not weaken the new Iranian-Saudi bonds.[70] Yet, "the existing limit on the number of pilgrims set by Saudi Arabia [was still] the main obstacle."[71] On 5 May, Iranian First Deputy Foreign Minister 'Ali Muhammad Besharati, speaking at a Friday prayer service, said: "We have achieved some success in planning for the participation of Iranian pilgrims in the Hajj ceremony." But Mehdi Karrubi, acting as the imam's representative for Hajj affairs, pointed out that Iran's three conditions were still valid: "We will take part if there is a demonstration, if there is politics, and if our quota...is preserved."[72] Iranian Minister of Culture and Islamic Guidance al-Sayyid Muhammad al-Khatimi deplored that Riyadh had let time pass without trying to negotiate the pilgrimage problem.[73]

Saudi Defense Minister Sultan 'Abdallah Ibn 'Abd al-'Aziz took up this issue, stating that his government was still interested in improving its relations with Iran; he, too, separated the bilateral relations from the pilgrimage question.[74] Iran, in turn, welcomed the Saudi readiness to launch an Islamic *détente,* but criticized its quota-fixing policy, arguing that since the Amman foreign ministers' conference in 1988, the "general" (i.e., demographic) situation had changed profoundly, necessitating a new quota.[75]

From June onward the atmosphere of Iranian-Saudi relations carried a sense of latent aggression. As long as the pilgrimage was imminent there was no room in public for bilateral negotiations on other issues.

Meanwhile, Saudi Arabia, taking advantage of this political deadlock, intensified its activities to convene an emergency Arab summit conference, which met in Casablanca from 23–26 May. Some of the conference's major issues were the readmission of Egypt to the Arab League, the Lebanese war, and the Syrian-PLO conflict. On 31 March, King Fahd had said that he would support Egypt's return to the League.[76] On 3 April, Egypt returned to the Arab Mining Company, and on 13 May the Organization of Arab Petroleum Exporting Countries readmitted Egypt.[77] Syria then gave up its opposition to Egypt's readmission to the League. Thus, the official approval of Egypt's reentry into the Arab fold in Casablanca was little more than a formality[78] (see chapters on inter-Arab relations and Egypt).

Whereas Saudi Arabia was doing everything to shape a new Arab alliance (a touchstone was the problem of the Lebanese war, which was to be settled by a committee consisting of King Fahd, Morocco's King Hasan, and Algeria's President Chedli Benjedid; see chapter on inter-Arab relations), Iran's Islamic propaganda was costing it dearly. Iranian-Turkish relations were close to rupture after Iran's intervention in the Turkish debate on whether Muslim women should be allowed to wear the Islamic veil (*hijab*). When the Turkish Constitutional Court on 7 March invalidated a law allowing the veil to be worn in universities, Iran seemingly believed that the question could give it leverage to extend its influence in Turkey.[79] Tension between the two countries began to mount, and it took a visit by Iranian Deputy Foreign Minister 'Ali Muhammad Besharati to Ankara, on 2 June to cool things down. Besharati declared that Iran did not want to interfere with Turkish domestic affairs, although "defending the rights of the Muslims cannot be considered an intervention into another's concern."[80] Iran's commercial interests had won over its Islamic propaganda.

In June, Iran prepared to renew its boycott of the pilgrimage.[81] Ahmad Khomeyni poured oil on the flames: in an interview with an Iranian daily he admitted that Iran had smuggled explosives into Saudi Arabia during the 1986 Hajj. Khomeyni defended this act (which at the time had been criticized by 'Ali Montazeri, a criticism that had been the formal reason for removing Montazeri as the imam's successor).[82] In the following weeks, the Saudi press capitalized on the interview to maintain that the participation of Iranian pilgrims in the Hajj would pose real security problems.[83]

Having been elected as "leader of the Islamic revolution" immediately after Khomeyni's death, on 3 June, Sayyid 'Ali Khameneh'i quickly published a "message to pilgrims visiting Mecca and to Muslims throughout the world,"[84] in which he summed up Iranian criticism of "rulers of the Hijaz and the Wahhabis" and of the "American Islam" that governed Saudi Arabia. Khameneh'i gave no sign of compromise; on the contrary, he ignored every Iranian attempt at reconciliation. Chief Justice 'Abdul Karim Musavi Ardebili added in a Friday prayer that the Iranians "should throw the corpse of this *taghut* ["usurpatory government," a pejorative for Al Sa'ud] out of the house of God just as we discarded the Iranian *taghut*."[85]

In the middle of June, Saudi Minister of Hajj and Religious Endowments 'Abd al-Wahhab Ahmad 'Abd al-Wasi' published the annual pilgrimage regulations.[86] Once again, political activity was prohibited, as were the display of books and banners, the use of loudspeakers, demonstrations, and marches; every pilgrim was attached to a communal or national organization, which was responsible for its members' activities. These regulations, the minister said, should serve to "unite the pilgrims," by abolishing any distinctions of color, language, clothing, and culture.[87] Meanwhile, the Saudi press intensified its anti-Iranian campaign: "The behavior of the madmen and terrorists [rulers of Iran] can only be described as madness and foolishness," *al-Riyadh* wrote.[88]

On 10 July, large demonstrations and rallies were organized in Tehran in commemoration of the second anniversary of the Mecca bloodshed. On the evening of the same day, two bombs exploded next to the Haram (Great Mosque) in Mecca leaving one man dead and 16 others injured.[89] Next morning, Khameneh'i's office, in order to avoid any accusations, issued a statement that "the crime committed by the Saudi rulers in exploding two bombs in the holy city of Mecca is in line with the policy of global ignorance to violate the sanctity of Islamic shrines....The stupid action by the Saudi Government is indicative of the weakness and despondency of the US agents and American-style Islam."⁹⁰ The Iranian Foreign Ministry was less offensive. Velayati declared that the incident was "in line with the armed police attack on the pilgrims...two years ago."⁹¹ Rafsanjani blamed US agents for the explosions, which, he said, were an attempt to discredit Iran: "Maybe the Saudis themselves did it to free themselves of the pressure from true Muslims of the world, for depriving Iran from participating in the Hajj."⁹²

As previously, the Saudi Government was silent concerning the perpetrators of the explosions.⁹³ Riyadh soon started to search for them among Pakistani and Shiʻi pilgrims. In Beirut, a little-known group calling itself the "Generation of Arab Anger" claimed responsibility.⁹⁴ Although some Arab papers linked the bombing to Iran, and Iraq officially blamed Iran for the explosions,⁹⁵ King Fahd and Crown Prince ʻAbdallah did everything to keep Iran out of the affair. In their message on the occasion of the Hajj, they even stated, though cryptically, that "It is good news, to witness this year some Islamic and international *détentes,* not only in the political arena but also in other areas related to international relations."⁹⁶ During July, Saudi security forces arrested 29 suspects, most of them Kuwaitis.

In Iran, after the presidential election of 28 July (see chapter on Iran), officials entertained a more sober view of relations with Saudi Arabia. Encouraged by a statement at the Jidda meeting of the Gulf Cooperation Council (GCC) foreign ministers on 29 August that the Gulf countries would welcome an improvement of their relations with Iran, Sayyid Rajaʻi Khurasani, chairman of the Majlis Foreign Affairs Committee, said "that ties with Saudi Arabia should be expanded and that the GCC should take specific steps for improving relations."⁹⁷ Two weeks later, he even called for "resuming diplomatic relations with Saudi Arabia." Iran seemed to be coming out of its international isolation; West European countries, including West Germany and France, sought to settle bilateral problems with Iran.

But following the trial and execution of 16 Shiʻi Kuwaitis in Mecca on 21 September, Khurasani declared that there was no room for Iranian reconciliation with Saudi Arabia.⁹⁸ The Saudi-Iranian rift deepened again. Saudi television showed the leader of the arrested Shiʻi group, Mansur Hasan ʻAbdallah al-Muhmayyid, a 32-year-old teacher, who confessed that he had been trained to carry out the explosions by an Iranian, Muhammad Baqir al-Mahri, in June 1989⁹⁹ in Kuwait, where Muhayyid and another Kuwaiti, ʻAli ʻAbdallah Husayn Kazim, had assembled an informal group. Though most of its members were Iranian, they all had Kuwaiti passports and were students or teachers at Kuwait University. The group called itself a "party following the imam's line" (*al-hizb al-saʼir ʻala khatt al-imam*). Saudi Arabia now discarded its reserve concerning possible Iranian participation in the Mecca bombing; it blamed Iran and Shiʻism for the "terroristic acts" committed in Mecca.¹⁰⁰ Iran, in turn, renewed its fierce attacks against "Wahhabism" and the "*taghut* of Mecca." The new Speaker of the Majlis Karrubi stated that it had become clear that there were "two trends in Islam": the "Muhammadan Islam and the American Islam."¹⁰¹

The old pre-Rushdie conflict was renewed and even sharpened; Tehran and Riyadh continued to contest for hegemony with each standing at the head of divergent Islamic trends, polarizing Islamic culture. (For further discussion of Saudi-Iranian relations, see chapters on these two countries.)

ISLAMIC INTERNATIONAL ACTIVITIES

The activities of the international Islamic organizations were overshadowed by the deep-rooted dispute between Iran and Saudi Arabia. Both regimes did their utmost to absorb the Rushdie affair and the pilgrimage question into their struggle for hegemony, leaving hardly any room for independent activities by these organizations. Only the Libyan World Islamic Call Society (WICS) stood apart and continued its propaganda activities, especially in Africa and the Caribbean. On 31 August, Libya and Chad signed a peace agreement in Algiers, which was published the next day, on the occasion of the 20th anniversary of the Libyan Revolution. Both sides agreed to try to settle the Aouzou conflict within a year, otherwise the matter would come before the International Court of Justice at the Hague (see chapter on Libya).[102] The agreement helped reduce the stigma impressed on the WICS by the war in Chad and by the organization's often surprising changes in its Islamic orientation.[103]

While the Iranian Organization of Islamic Propagation was preoccupied with the Rushdie affair, the pilgrimage, and the Turkish *hijab* issues (see above), the MWL escaped the direct influence of these problems by following the general Saudi quietist political line that characterized Saudi pragmatism. After 1985, the MWL underwent a remarkable decline in its political influence. The League's bureaucratic apparatus, and especially the number of its emissaries and foreign bureaus had to be reduced. At the 29th meeting of the League's Constituent Council, on 12–16 November 1988, the secretariat general reported that it was extending financial aid to 50 organizations "all over the world" and that 409 officials "of different categories" were serving the League in Mecca. In addition to 329 officials, nurses, and doctors working in the 17 MWL clinics, c. 1,000 emissaries were in various Islamic communities. In September, the MWL had reported that 818 emissaries were under contract.[104] The obvious lack of MWL activities had led to the foundation of a new coordinating body in Cairo in 1988, the World Islamic Council for Propagation and Relief (*al-majlis al-islami al-'alami lil da'wa wal ighatha*); see *MECS* 1988, p. 180). The MWL's publications described this new council "as an offshoot of the Muslim World League,"[105] which was pure fiction, though one of its founding members, Kamil Isma'il al-Sharif, had been elected secretary-general.[106] The MWL was only one of 17 founding organizations, and together with al-Azhar, the Baghdad-based Organization of the Islamic Popular Conference (*munazzamat al-mu'tamar al-Islami al-sha'bi*), the Kuwaiti International Islamic Welfare Association (*al-hay'a al-khayriyya al-islamiya al-'alamiyya*) and the ICO, it was one of the more prominent members of the council.[107] The council, headed by the Azhar rector Jadd al-Haqq, had three committees: the Kuwaiti International Islamic Welfare Association, led by Farid Yasin Qurashi (who had originally held the office of general supervisor of the World Islamic Relief Organization, an offshoot of the MWL); the Iraqi Organization of the Islamic Popular Conference, led by Bishar 'Awwad al-'Ubaydi; and a Saudi one, headed by 'Abdallah 'Umar Nasif (MWL). The founding committee met twice in 1989, on 22 June in Cairo and on 4 August in Amman. From 20–22 September, the council held its second conference in Cairo under the chairmanship of Jadd al-Haqq.[108]

In spite of all endeavors, it was unclear how the new council would be able to coordinate international Islamic politics. Looking at the organizations and personalities in the council, it was clear that the council was a reincarnation of the former Conference of Islamic Organizations (1968–71) and the Supreme Coordination Committee of World Islamic Organizations, founded in April 1974 (both had been established by the MWL to coordinate the Islamic policy, among others, of the Azhar and its dependencies — the Academy of Islamic Research and the Supreme Council of Islamic Affairs — the Pakistani Islamic World Congress, the Indonesian International Islamic Organization, and the Jerusalem-Amman-based General Islamic Congress).[109] In the new council, the role of the Azhar had been upgraded, but the second most important Saudi Arabian international Islamic body, the Riyadh-based World Association of Muslim Youth (*al-nadi al-'alami lil shabab al-islami*), with a strong Wahhabi orientation, was not mentioned among the member organizations initially. In July 1989, its secretary-general, Mani' Hammad al-Jahni, took part in a council meeting in Cairo, in the course of which the council welcomed the establishment of the Arab Cooperation Council (ACC).[110] The International Islamic Council also tried to incorporate the ICO and 12 *waqf*-ministries, representing an etatist tendency, which, up to the 1980s, the MWL had tried to prevent.

In 1989, the council concentrated on missionary policy in Africa, in which the leader of the Sudanese Islamic Call Organization, 'Abd al-Rahman Siwar al-Dhahab, played an important role.[111] The still unsettled conflict between Mauritania and Senegal was also a major item on the council's agenda. From 11–15 February, the MWL's Supreme World Council of Mosques held its 13th session in Mecca.[112] Under its new deputy secretary-general (Nasif nominally acted as secretary-general) 'Abdallah Ibn 'Aqil Sulayman al-'Aqil,[113] the council tried to restructure its policies, especially concerning African and European Muslim communities; until then, the council had centered its activities in Malaysia, Sudan, and Egypt.

THE WORLD ISLAMIC CALL SOCIETY ON THE SIDELINES

In March, the WICS presented itself as the initiator of many rallies and demonstrations against Rushdie's book which took place in European cities.[114] As stated above, the society focused mainly on the "Christian and Jewish conspiracy" behind Rushdie. Posing as the true defender of Islam, this Libyan society did not explicitly call Rushdie an apostate who should be tried or put to death, nor did it publicly comment on Khomeyni's *fatwa*. Instead, the society reemphasized its view of Islam as a religion of freedom and revolution, and of Arabism as Islam's highest cultural expression.[115] Once again, the WICS purveyed Qadhdhafi's interpretation of Islam, that there is no need of a special body of legal scholars to judge cases of apostasy, heresy, or even "ordinary" crimes.

Meanwhile, the WICS did everything to strengthen its ties to African Muslim communities, especially in southern and eastern Africa. From 19–22 March, the WICS helped organize the fourth meeting of the Union of Islamic Councils of Eastern, Central, and Southern Africa at Harare, Zimbabwe. Its chairman, Musa Menk, declared that the WICS had also played an important role in organizing a special seminar on women in Islamic propagation (*da'wa*).[116] From Khartoum, the WICS received a letter of thanks from the leader of the Organization of Islamic Call, 'Abd al-Rahman Siwar al-Dhahab, who had just been nominated as representative of the Cairo-based World Islamic Council of Propagation and Relief, stating that he was "not surprised at the assistance" the WICS had offered the Khartoum group. In Sudan, the WICS obviously competed with the MWL to enlarge its influence in

Africa, which had never been a prominent sphere of MWL propagation politics.[117] Simultaneously, the WICS continued its efforts in West Africa. From 24–27 May, it held its fourth da'wa conference for West Africa in Nouakchott, Mauritania.[118] A total of 150 WICS emissaries from 14 West African states were said to have attended this conference.

From 12–15 June, a delegation of the Madagascar Association of Islam visited WICS headquarters and signed an agreement of cooperation.[119] The first project under this agreement was to be the 'Umar al-Mukhtar school in Antsiranana (in the north of the island), which would become the basis of Islamic propagation on the island. It was also agreed to build a new Islamic school in Mahajanga, the center of the Madagascan Muslim community. In addition, both sides prepared an Islamic radio program and agreed to train emissaries at the International Islamic Call Academy in Tripoli.

COMPETITION ABROAD: PORT OF SPAIN, TRINIDAD
In 1989, Port of Spain, Trinidad, with its c. 6% Muslim population, was the stage of Saudi Arabian-Libyan propagation competition. From 20–22 March, the MWL organized an Islamic congress of the Muslims of the Caribbean, with MWL secretary-general Nasif and Saudi officials attending. The MWL had started working in the Caribbean region in 1977, helping the Indian community build up an Islamic Coordination Council of South America and the Caribbean. It was led by Muhammad Shafiq al-Rahman of Trinidad, president of the Association of the People of Sunna and Community (jam'iyat ahl al-sunna wal-jama'a),[120] who had been appointed a member of the MWL constituent council in 1976. Some 50 representatives of Muslim organizations from 21 Caribbean and South American countries attended. As in other such conferences whose participants came from countries where Muslims were a minority, the agenda included the question of strengthening Islamic cults, improving the state of mosques, and the situation of women (although as usual no women took part in the conference.) The conference also approved the decision of the MWL's Legal Academy concerning Rushdie.[121]

Three months later, from 8–10 June, the WICS held its fifth Islamic Caribbean conference in Port of Spain.[122] (The conference had been held every two years since 1981.) The ally of the WICS in Trinidad, the Muslim Community Organization (munazzamat jama'at al-muslimin), convened 500 participants from Caribbean countries. Whereas the MWL had proposed founding a consultative council for the Caribbean countries, the WICS went further, and decided to establish an Islamic consultative commission with the task of preparing a regional Islamic union. The WICS also focused on the position of Muslim women in societies where Muslims were a minority, but in contrast to the MWL, the WICS allowed a woman to speak on women's affairs. The conference's 16-point final statement declared that the Islamic organizations should try to work up economic development programs in order to achieve self-sufficiency in the regional economy. The Muslims' Community Organization also stated that it had won 9,000 proselytes in Trinidad during the preceding 10 months.

As for cooperation with the ICO-linked Islamic Educational, Scientific, and Cultural Organization (IESCO), the WICS followed its schedule as set after the 16 August 1988 general agreement between the two organizations. Both sides stressed educational and cultural affairs,[123] but it was unclear how successful Libya was in imposing its own brand of Islam on the ICO cultural organization's policy.

In October 1989, speaking at an international Islamic conference convened at Benghazi with c. 250 participants from 48 countries, Qadhdhafi once again appealed to the Muslim world to build up "one world Islamic leadership; the one party should be the Party of God (Hizballah)."[124] This leadership, Qadhdhafi said, "will not be a king or amir; it will be nothing less than one book, the Qur'an."

MUSLIM BROTHERHOOD ACTIVITIES

In North Africa, independent Islamic political organizations blossomed during 1989. In March, a new organization to propagate Islam, the Islamic Call League (*rabitat al-da'wa al-islamiyya*) was founded by a scholar from Bi'r Murad Rayis (Algeria), Ahmad Sahnun.[125] In a declaration on 1 March, Sahnun stated that the League's aims were to implement the "Islamic system," to unify all propagation activities in Algeria, to standardize the heterogenous Algerian *fatwa* practice, to call for a "collective *ijtihad* in a code of civil procedure," to control morality, and to fight Westernization, secularism, and the Christian mission. On 10 March, a new Islamic Salvation Front led by the Islamic activist 'Abbas Madani was proclaimed and it soon tried to open offices in two mosques. The Algerian minister for religious affairs immediately rejected this request, saying that mosques had to distance themselves from politics.[126] After applying for approval by the Interior Ministry on 22 August, the Islamic Salvation Front was legalized as the country's fourth party on 14 September.[127]

In Tunisia, too, the former Islamic Tendency Movement (French: MTI) acquired a more legitimate status. On 29 January, it changed its name to the Islamic Renaissance Movement (*harakat al-nahda al-islamiyya*). Its secretary-general, 'Abd al-Fattah Moro, who had just been pardoned along with the Brothers' General Guide Rashid al-Ghannushi and other Islamic militants, was allowed to join the newly established Supreme Islamic Council, following the "peace agreement" between the state and the MTI on 7 November 1987.[128] Consequently, Ghannushi became very optimistic about the chances of the legalization of his movement.[129] However, the growing social unrest in Tunisia resulted in the arrest of Moro and two other members of the movement on 8 October.[130]

The informal Islamic political groups, both isolationist and integrationist, had far more success in North Africa than in the West Bank, the Gaza Strip, or Syria. The head of the Jordanian Muslim Brotherhood, 'Abd al-Rahman Khalifa, admitted in an interview that Islamic forces among the Palestinians were not as successful as expected.[131] Khalifa refrained from making a clear statement on Iranian policy toward Israel and the Palestinian question. His stance on the Iran issue typified the Brothers' tilt toward nonalignment: on the one hand, the Brothers had to criticize the clear pro-Shi'i tendencies in Iranian politics; on the other hand, they felt called upon to form the moral executive power that Khomeyni and other Iranian politicians had been demanding. This dilemma paralyzed the Brothers in the region. Although the success of the Jordanian Muslim Brotherhood in the 1989 elections (see chapter on Jordan) showed that the Brothers were able to collect protest votes, which gave them a high degree of political legitimacy, their field of social and cultural action became increasingly narrow. In Egypt, the Brothers were caught up in parliamentary maneuvering; in the West Bank, they became a political force by helping to organize the Hamas, on which Khalifa commented: "We are satisfied with it" (see chapter on the West Bank and Gaza Strip).

In contrast to Khalifa, the controller-general of the Syrian Muslim Brotherhood, 'Adnan Sa'd al-Din, did not deny the Brothers' weakness, especially in Syria.[132] Moreover, he reproached the Hamas for its lack of maturity. The PLO, he argued, was indispensable especially with regard to safeguarding the interests of non-Muslim minorities and to foreign policy. He therefore sought coexistence between Hamas and the PLO. Sa'd al-Din also pleaded for a Syrian and Islamic *perestroika* which would leave room for democracy and party pluralism. In this contest, he welcomed an attempt to build up a national coalition in opposition to the Syrian regime, modeled on the democratic movements in Eastern Europe.

ISLAMIC POLITICS AND SOVIET MUSLIMS

The dramatic changes in the Soviet Union and other socialist countries with Muslim minorities (Poland, Bulgaria, Yugoslavia, and Romania) also affected the strategies of the international Islamic organizations and of the governments sponsoring them. In January and February, the MWL revived a long discussion concerning the Muslim communities in the Soviet Union.[133] The MWL, which had maintained contact especially with the Tashkent muftis since 1968, found it difficult to judge the cultural, social, and political situation of the Muslim communities in the Soviet Union, both because these communities were regarded as representing an "example of atheist policy toward Islam" and because Islam in the Soviet Union was dissimilar to the MWL's view of Islam. The MWL stated repeatedly that the "cultural standard" of Soviet Muslims was not "very high." The Soviet Union became a field of Islamic missionary activity after the beginning of *perestroika*. Thus, in 1987, the MWL tried to strengthen its ties with the Ufa mufti, Tal'at Taj al-Din, who became a league spokesman.[134] Taj al-Din had visited the League in Mecca in 1962 and in 1976, and he had praised its activities and the results of *perestroika*.[135] The Soviet Union's large Muslim population, however, had yet to be absorbed into the hegemony conflicts governing Islamic political culture.

The MWL's newly initiated campaign was aimed at explaining the change of its policy toward institutionalized Islam in the Soviet Union. In February, the League moved to distance itself from the official Islamic establishment, especially that in Tashkent where the mufti Shams al-Din Babakhanov had been in office since the death of his father Diya al-Din, in 1982. In 1980, the latter had openly declared that there were no conflicts between the state and the Tashkent muftis;[136] Shams al-Din continued his father's policy. Both, however, were the best known representatives of Soviet Islam; the senior Babakhanov had even been appointed to the League's Mosque Council in 1979. Now the League declared that these official "Communist scholars" had no real influence on the Muslim communities. Their open pro-Communist tendencies encouraged the "informal Islamic groups," an MWL pejorative for mystical brotherhoods. The MWL now sought to establish direct links to *salafi* and neo-*salafi* groups in Uzbekistan in order to establish a new *da'wa* orientation.

In March, the MWL reported with greatest satisfaction that Shams al-Din Babakhanov had been deposed the previous month, because of "immoral behavior."

On 14 March, the 36-year-old rector of the Tashkent Islamic Institute, Mama Yusupov Muhammad Siddiq, was unanimously elected as the new mufti at the fourth Central Asian Muslim Congress.[137] The Libyan WICS was gratified because Yusupov was a graduate of its Islamic Call Faculty and in his inaugural speech had mentioned the need to cooperate with the WICS in providing the Tashkent Muslims with representative Islamic literature.[138]

In August, 'Abdallah 'Umar Nasif traveled to the Soviet Union where he visited the mufti of Ufa. It became clear once again that the MWL was trying to counter Libyan and Iranian influence in the Soviet Union by deepening its cooperation with Ufa. Thus, within a few months the Muslim communities were absorbed into the Islamic hegemony conflicts. Iran chose the mufti of Baku Shukrallah Bashazadeh as a bridgehead, which became important at the end of 1989 during the anti-Soviet uprising connected with the conflict between Armenia and Azerbaijan. The MWL aimed at the Ufa mufti with its long salafi tradition; and Libya strove for a footing in Tashkent. Only the Makhachkala mufti al-Hajj Mahmud Kiki was beyond the reach of the big Islamic organizations.

On a bilateral level, only Iran made direct advances to the Soviet Union. In an open letter in February, Khomeyni urged President Mikhail Gorbachev to "study Islam honestly," as Islam offered the only safeguard for Gorbachev's *perestroika* policy.[139] The bilateral *détente* reached a dead end during the Azerbaijan crisis in January 1990.

The fate of Bulgarian Muslims became an issue in the MWL's external policy, especially from March 1989 to March 1990. The League also exploited Bulgaria's ethnic problems to improve its relations with Turkey that were disrupted after the so-called "imam scandal" of 1984–85. After June 1989, as c. 60,000 Bulgarian Muslims fled to Turkey in order to escape Bulgaria's assimilation policy (see chapter on Turkey), the MWL posed as a guardian of Turkish Muslim interests. During the anti-Bulgarian campaign, the MWL tried to portray the Ottoman Empire as a cornerstone of Islamic identity.[140] On the Turkish side, the ministers Mesut Yılmaz, Abdalkadir Akso, and Halil Tugun appointed Salih Özcan, the former member of parliament of the National Salvation Party and member of the MWL Constituent Council since 1963, to coordinate the policy toward Bulgaria.[141] In August 1989, Nasif again went on a fact-finding mission to Turkey, declaring that Bulgaria's assimilation policy was nothing less than revenge for the 500 years of Ottoman domination.[142]

THE DEATH OF AN APOSTATE

On 31 January 1990, Reshad Khalifa, the League's most hated apostate, was killed in a mosque in Tucson, Arizona.[143] Throughout 1989, the MWL and the Azhar had warned of this "apostate," who had just declared that he was the new prophet and that the Islamic dogma of the seal of the prophethood was no longer valid. One of his closest followers, Ahmad Subhi, had published a book called *The History of the Prophets* in which he tried to clarify Khalifa's teaching. The Azhar had already pronounced a sentence on Khalifa and called upon him to repent; but (as the former secretary-general of the Azhar's Academy of Islamic Research, 'Abd al-Jalil Shalabi, stated) Khalifa refused.[144]

The MWL considered Khalifa as standing in the Baha'i tradition, whereas Rushdie was influenced by the Indian-Pakistani Ahmadiya.[145] To the MWL, the Baha'i movement was far more dangerous than the Ahmadiya, which might help explain why the League did not publish very much on Rushdie. Khalifa was the archetype of the League's foes, so that it was probably not a coincidence that he had to die, whereas Rushdie was able to survive the troublesome year of 1989.

NOTES

For the place and frequency of publications cited here, and for the full name of the publication, news agency, radio station, or monitoring service where an abbreviation is used, please see "List of Sources." Only in the case of more than one publication bearing the same name is the place of publication noted here.

1. *Al-Hilal International,* 31 December 1989.
2. *Akhbar al-'Alam al-Islami,* 15 February 1989; *al-Rabita,* 286 (December 1988-January 1989), p. 64. This term, uncommon in traditional Islamic law, denotes God's punishment for rebellion and/or highway robbery.
3. *Akhbar al-'Alam al-Islami,* 15 August 1988.
4. Born in 1942, Robbani was a university lecturer. See Jan-Heeren Grevemeyer, *Afghanistan. Sozialer Wandel und Staat im 20. Jahrhundert* (Berlin: Express Edition, 1987), pp. 132, 134.
5. *Akhbar al-'Alam al-Islami,* 26 December 1988.
6. E.g., ibid., 9 January 1989.
7. Ibid., 23 January 1989.
8. E.g., ibid., 30 January 1989.
9. Ibid., 28 November; *NYT,* 16 February 1989.
10. *Kayhan-e farhangi,* November-December 1988, p. 35.
11. *Kayhan al-'Arabi,* 13 February 1989. The main agitator against Rushdie's book in Pakistan, Senator Kauthar Nyazi, was also wounded.
12. *JP,* 14 February 1989.
13. *KH,* 22 February; *TT, Kayhan al-'Arabi, NYT,* 15 February 1989.
14. See N.J. Coulson, *A History of Islamic Law* (Edinburgh, 1964), pp. 131 ff. *Hadd* (pl. *hudud*) offenses are those offenses for which God himself has defined the punishments. Ibid., p. 124.
15. See Note 2 above.
16. For details see Reinhard Schulze, "Ifta' in Saudi Arabia, the Case of 'Abdal'aziz b. 'Abdallah b. Baz," a paper presented at the international conference "The Making of a *Fatwa,"* Granada, 10–13 January 1990.
17. Reinhard Schulze, *Islamischer Internationalismus im 20. Jahrhundert. Untersuchungen zur Geschichte der Islamischen Weltliga* (Leiden: Brill, 1990), p. 362, n. 171.
18. See the preamble of the Iranian constitution (1979); Sylvia Tellenbach, *Untersuchungen zur Verfassung der Islamischen Republik Iran vom 15. November 1979* (Berlin: Klaus Schwarz Verlag, 1985), p. 328.
19. Gregory Rose, "Velayat-e Faqih and the Recovery of Islamic Identity in the Thought of Ayatollah Khomeini," in Nikki R. Keddie (ed.), *Religion and Politics in Iran, Shi'ism from Quietism to Revolution* (New Haven: Yale University Press, 1983), pp. 166–88.
20. *KH,* 22 February 1989, Khomeyni was often referred to as "the epitome and embodiment of all Muslim teachings and divine religious standards...by himself an entire nation." See Generalkonsulat der Islamischen Republik Iran, (ed.) *The Islamic Republic of Iran, From Resolution 598 to Reconstruction,* Hamburg, file number 180-10/4818, 8 February 1990, p. 11.
21. *Al-Akhbar,* Cairo, 20 February 1989.
22. *Al-Liwa al-Islami,* 2 March 1989.
23. *NYT,* 23 February, *Kayhan,* London, 2 March 1989.
24. For details, see Schulze, op. cit., pp. 377 ff.
25. Tehran TV (in Persian), 23 February — DR, 24 February 1989.

26. *Kayhan al-'Arabi*, 18 February 1989.
27. *JP*, 5 March 1989.
28. *Al-Wafd*, 27 February 1989. The preacher and Cairo University lecturer 'Abd al-Rashid Saqqar made a similar statement. The Egyptian Muslim Brotherhood declared that, if necessary, Rushdie should be tried *in absentia*; the death penalty should be executed when the conditions were ripe. See *al-'Alam*, London, 15 April. An official statement of the World Organization of the Muslim Brothers said: "Concerning what the book *The Satanic Verses* contains, it can only be explained as unbelief, and as Salman Rushdie is said to be a Muslim, the judgment of the law is that he is an apostate by virtue of having written this [book]." Quoted in *al-Ghuraba*, April 1989.
29. *Die Tageszeitung*, 25 February 1989.
30. E.g., *Kayhan al-'Arabi*, 21 January 1989.
31. *Le Monde*, 25, 26 February 1989.
32. E.g., *al-'Alam*, London, 4 March 1989.
33. *Die Tageszeitung*, 25 February 1989.
34. *JP*, 7 March 1989.
35. *FT*, 7 March 1989.
36. Ibid.
37. IRNA, 24 February — DR, 24 February 1989.
38. *Akhbar al-'Alam al-Islami*, 20 February 1989.
39. Schulze, op. cit., p. 377.
40. *Akhbar al-'Alam al-Islami*, 6 March 1989.
41. Ibid., 27 February 1989.
42. *Al-'Alam*, London, 4 March. In this context, the MWL argued against Azhar rector Jadd al-Haqq, who later officially announced that the Azhar would publish a "scientific refutation" of *The Satanic Verses*; see *al-Da'wa*, 6 April. In April, an Indian scholar, Majid 'Ali Khan, declared that with the aid of the Center for Islamic Studies at New Delhi, he would soon publish a refutation called "The Holy Verses," see *TT*, 8 April and *al-Da'wa al-Islamiyya*, 24 May. In April, the Libyan WICS and the IESCO of the ICO organized a symposium on Rushdie in Rabat; the final statement called for a scientific refutation of Rushdie's book; see ibid., 7 June 1989.
43. *Al-Yawm al-Sabi'*, 27 March 1989.
44. *WP*, 21 February; *Le Monde*, 25 February 1989.
45. *Al-Fikr al-Islami*, 2 February; *al-'Alam*, London, 27 January 1989.
46. *Kayhan al-'Arabi*, 8 February 1989.
47. Ibid., 8 January 1989.
48. *Kayhan*, London, 11 March — DR, 22 March 1989.
49. *JP*, 13 March 1989.
50. IRNA, 13 March; KUNA, 14 March — DR, 15 March 1989.
51. SPA, 15 March — DR, 15 March 1989.
52. Ibid.
53. SPA, 16 March — DR, 20 March 1989.
54. IRNA, 18 March — DR, 20 March; *Kayhan al-'Arabi*, 18 March 1989.
55. *Kayhan al-'Arabi*, 18 March 1989.
56. Ibid.
57. R. Flag of Freedom, in Persian, 18 March — DR, 20 March 1989.
58. *Akhbar al-'Alam al-Isalmi*, 27 March 1989.
59. Ibid., 27 March 1989.
60. *Kayhan al-'Arabi*, 18 March 1989.
61. *Al-Yawm al-Sabi'*, 13 March 1989.
62. Ibid.
63. Ibid., *al-Hilal International*, 1–15 March 1989.
64. *Al-'Alam*, London, 23 April 1989.
65. *JP*, 30 March 1989.
66. R. Monte Carlo, 31 March 1989.
67. *Akhbar al-'Alam al-Islami*, 10 April 1989.
68. Schulze, op. cit., p. 228.

69. *Akhbar al-'Alam al-Islami,* 22 May 1989.
70. *Kayhan al-'Arabi,* 29 April 1989.
71. IRNA, 30 April — DR, 1 May 1989.
72. IRNA, 5 May — DR, 5 May 1989.
73. *Kayhan al-'Arabi,* 6 May 1989.
74. *Al-Majalla,* 24-30 May 1989.
75. IRNA, 27 May — DR, 30 May 1989.
76. DR, 31 March 1989.
77. *NYT,* 14 April 1989.
78. *Akhbar al-'Alam al-Islami,* 19 June 1989.
79. *Al-Yawm al-Sabi',* 10 April 1989.
80. *Kayhan al-'Arabi,* 3 June 1989.
81. IRNA, 13 June — DR, 14 June 1989.
82. *Ettela'at,* 16 May 1989.
83. SPA, 18 May — DR, 18 May 1989; *al-Yawm,* Dammam, 18 May; *al-Majalla,* 7–13 June 1989 (Letters of Khomeyni).
84. R. Tehran, 6 June — DR, 7 July 1989.
85. R. Tehran, 7 July — DR, 10 July 1989.
86. *Akhbar al-'Alam al-Islami,* 3 July 1989.
87. *Al-Hawadith,* 7 July 1989.
88. Quoted in *IHT,* 8–9 July 1989.
89. SPA, 10, 11 July — DR, 11 July 1989.
90. R. Tehran, 11 July — DR, 12 July 1989.
91. Ibid.
92. *IHT,* 12 July 1989.
93. AFP, 12 July — DR, 13 July 1989.
94. *JP,* 13 July 1989.
95. *Al-Siyasa,* Kuwait, 13–14 July 1989.
96. SPA, 14 July — DR, 17 July 1989.
97. DR, 5 September 1989.
98. Ibid., 29 September 1989.
99. *Al-Majalla,* 3 October; *al-Rabita,* 296 (October 1989), pp. 8–13.
100. *Al-Majalla,* 3 October; interview with Saudi Interior Minister, Na'if Ibn 'Abd al-'Aziz, in *al-Madina,* 30 September 1989.
101. Quoted in *al-'Alam,* London, 30 September 1989.
102. *Akhbar al-'Alam al-Islami,* 11 September 1989, p. 15.
103. Hanspeter Mattes, *Die innere and aussere islamische Mission Libyens* (Mainz: Grünewald, 1986), pp. 114–69.
104. *Akhbar al-'Alam al-Islami,* 11 September 1989.

MWL Emissaries 1973–90

	1973	1985	1987	1990
Africa		360	336	331
Asia	49	473	501	409
Europe, US		167	99	76

105. Ibid., 19 February 1990, p. 2.
106. Born 1926 in al-'Arish, al-Sharif studied Arabic literature at the University of Cairo, and in 1953 was elected secretary-general of the General Islamic Congress of Jerusalem/Muslim Brotherhood. From 1956–76 he served as Jordanian embassador and from 1976–82 as Jordanian minister of religious endowments.
107. Founded at the Islamic Propagation Congress, Cairo 4-9 March 1988, see *Akhbar al-'Alam al-Islami,* 7 March 1989, pp. 1, 14, and 14 March 1989, pp. 8–10. A total of 38 Islamic organizations are now members of this body.
108. *Al-Rabita,* 298 (December 1989), pp. 11–13.
109. Schulze, op. cit., p. 265–77.
110. *Akhbar al-'Alam al-Islami,* 31 July 1989. The ACC was established on 16 February 1989 at a summit meeting in Baghdad (see chapter on inter-Arab relations).

111. Ibid., 31 July 1989.
112. Ibid., 6, 20 February 1989.
113. 'Aqil was born in 1933/34 in Hurma and studied Islamic law at al-Azhar. Having lived for 25 years in Kuwait, he was a founding member of the Mosque Council and a member of the Riyadh-based World Association of Muslim Youth. He was appointed deputy general secretary in March 1988. Ibid., 7 March 1989.
114. E.g., Cologne, 21 March; al-Da'wa al-Islamiyya, 29 March 1989.
115. Ibid., 1 March 1989.
116. Ibid., 12 April 1989.
117. Ibid., 16 April 1989.
118. Ibid., 7 June 1989.
119. Ibid., 21 June 1989.
120. Schulze, op. cit., pp. 278, 288.
121. Akhbar al-'Alam al-Islami, 27 March, 10 April 1989.
122. Al-Da'wa al-Islamiyya, 21 June 1989.
123. Ibid., 29 March 1989.
124. Al-'Alam, London, 7 October 1989.
125. Al-Hilal International, 1–15 June 1989.
126. DR, 13, 18 March, 3 April 1989.
127. Akhbar al-'Alam al-Islami, 25 September 1989.
128. Ibid., 13 February 1989.
129. Interview in al-Hilal International, 1–15 June 1989.
130. DR, 10 October 1989.
131. Text in al-Watan al-'Arabi, 9 June — JPRS, 28 August 1989. Khalifa was born in Salt in 1919, studied agriculture and graduated in 1934. He studied at the Law Institute in Jerusalem, from which he graduated as a lawyer in 1944, then practiced law in Jordan until 1946, first as a judge, then as a lawyer. Khalifa soon became assistant to the Muslim Brothers' general deputy 'Abd al-Latif Abu Qura. In 1953, he was appointed controller-general of the Muslim Brothers' Jordanian branch.
132. Interview in al-Yawm al-Sabi', 10 April 1989.
133. Akhbar al-'Alam al-Islami, 16-30 January 1989.
134. Schulze, op. cit., pp. 269 ff.
135. See al-Rabita, 274 (1987), p. 22.
136. Akhbar al-'Alam al-Islami, 31 July 1989.
137. Ibid., 27 March 1989.
138. Al-Da'wa al-Islamiyya, 12 April 1989.
139. Die Tageszeitung, 27 February; NYT, 27 February 1989.
140. Akhbar al-'Alam al-Islami, 27 March 1989.
141. Ibid., 24 July 1989.
142. Ibid., 21 August 1989.
143. Ibid., 5 February 1990.
144. Ibid., 27 March 1989.
145. Ibid., 23 January, 12 June 1989.

PALESTINIAN ISSUES

The Palestine Liberation Organization

JOSHUA TEITELBAUM

In 1989 the PLO's main concern was to assure its role in the peace process as it unfolded once the US accepted the elections component of the Israeli peace initiative (for details see chapter on the Middle East peace process). While opposed to a focus on elections, the PLO made the decision to play the game in order to assure its position in future negotiations. Its greatest fear was that the elections would be used to create an alternative Palestinian leadership and thus undermine the PLO's status as "the sole legitimate representative of the Palestinian people." The leadership's immediate goal of a Palestinian state in the West Bank and Gaza Strip made it a sophisticated diplomatic player, willing to cooperate and make concessions, as long as that goal seemed attainable. The PLO responded to US Secretary of State James Baker's five points much in the same way as did Israel, with certain conditions or assumptions. While in principle agreeing to hold talks with Israel prior to an international conference, the PLO demanded that the dialogue have some international component, and that the organization be the one to form and announce the Palestinian delegation. By the end of the year it was still unclear if such a qualified acceptance of the Baker plan had really put the PLO on board.

The PLO continued its "yes-no" policy of making both conciliatory statements and hard-line pronouncements. No PLO official ever repeated the recognition of Israel, the unconditional acceptance of UN Resolutions 242 and 338, and the renunciation of terrorism stated by PLO Chairman Yasir 'Arafat in Geneva in December 1988 (see *MECS* 1988, pp. 256–57). Notwithstanding 'Arafat's statement while in Paris in May that the Palestinian National Charter was obsolete or null and void (*caduc*), and Fath Central Committee member Salah Khalaf's conciliatory videotaped address to an Israeli gathering in Jerusalem, in February, other senior PLO officials continued to maintain on occasion that the final goal was an Arab democratic state in all of Palestine. Such statements continued to indicate that the organization was still resisting a full commitment to a two-state solution.

Another major concern of the PLO during the year was gaining international recognition for "the state of Palestine." It was successful with many friendly states, but efforts to gain recognition in several international bodies were stymied by US opposition.

At the Fifth General Congress of Fath, in August, 'Arafat agreed to several personnel changes demanded by the rank and file, but it was clear that he emerged on top. The documents issued at the end of the congress reflected the hard line of the organization; yet, it seemed a price 'Arafat was willing to pay in order to insure organizational harmony.

Having effectively been removed from the Beirut area in 1988, in 1989 'Arafat's Fath strengthened its position in Southern Lebanon; the move was facilitated by the exploitation of the fighting between Amal and Hizballah, on the one hand, and the contending governments of Lebanon, on the other.

Fath's major opposition in the PLO, the Democratic Front for the Liberation of Palestine (DFLP), and the Popular Front for the Liberation of Palestine (PFLP), disagreed with 'Arafat's diplomacy, considering it based on concessions that would not advance the Palestinian cause. But the leaders of these organizations were not prepared to risk another split in the PLO, and so contented themselves with verbal attacks and demands for reforms within it. 'Arafat's continuing domination of the Palestinian arena, and the fact that the Palestinian component of US and Egyptian diplomatic efforts during the year were fully focused on convincing 'Arafat to discuss peace with the Israelis, made the views of the DFLP and the PFLP on the peace process relevant only for their internal PLO ramifications; these views are thus discussed below in the section on interorganizational developments.

THE PLO AND EFFORT TOWARD A MIDDLE EAST SETTLEMENT

The PLO's longtime policy of seeking to prevent the emergence of an alternative leadership in the West Bank and Gaza was tested during the year, as discussions got under way between Israel, Egypt, and the US on the subject of elections in the territories. While there was no doubt that the Intifada had succeeded in increasing the relative political weight within the PLO of the residents of the territories, the PLO leadership was successful in maintaining its primacy and control over the local leadership. This was accomplished by a combination of factors, first and foremost the PLO's all-powerful legitimacy as the embodiment of Palestinian nationalism. Leaders in the territories were wary of challenging that hard-won PLO status — it served their cause. For its part, the Fath-led PLO kept a flexible policy, jealously guarding its right to represent the Palestinians in negotiations, yet also allowing local Palestinians to maintain a high profile and meet with Israelis and visiting diplomats on certain occasions deemed useful to the PLO, whether in order to influence Israeli public opinion or to show that the West Bankers were firmly behind the organization. When local leaders bucked the PLO line, or did not operate in consultation with the organization, they were quickly called to order.

The PLO brooked no interference with its status as the "sole, legitimate representative of the Palestinian people." In January, Israeli Defense Minister Yitzhak Rabin floated a peace proposal which suggested a period of quiet elections in the territories and then a transition period to be followed by a decision by the residents to federate with either Jordan or Israel.[1] The PLO was quick to reject the proposal, terming it "absolutely worthless."[2] Several days later, following his release from administrative detention, Faysal al-Husayni, widely recognized as the most prominent supporter of al-Fath in the territories, expressed support for Rabin's proposed elections, provided they were carried out under UN or another form of international supervision.[3] Following apparent pressure from the PLO, Husayni later brought his position into line with that of the organization, which accepted elections only after an Israeli withdrawal.[4] Husayni's standing in the territories allowed him to make statements that were often more conciliatory and less ambiguous than those of PLO leaders outside. While PLO leaders rarely seriously addressed Israeli concerns that a

Palestinian state would be a staging ground for further attacks on Israel, Husayni was clear. "The solution we reach through negotiations will be a final one," he told a Tel Aviv audience, "after which we will have no further claims on one centimeter of your land. We're talking about a real peace with final borders." In Lausanne, in March, Husayni reportedly stressed that the right of return would be to the Palestinian state alone, and would not endanger Israeli security.[5] Similarly, West Bank journalist Ziyad Abu Ziyad addressed Israeli concerns about the "right of return": "We know that Israel was established as a Jewish state, and we know that the return of all the Palestinian people who left Palestine in 1948...will make Israel lose its Jewish character." Palestinians would, therefore, not ask Israel to lose its Jewish character, but that since UN resolutions spoke of a return or compensation, the issue would be subject to negotiation.[6]

The immediate goal of the PLO since the 19th session of the Palestine National Council (PNC) in November 1988 was to force Israel to an international conference (thereby avoiding the problem of direct negotiations), engineer a withdrawal from the territories, and establish a Palestinian state. The organization believed that several paths needed to be followed in order to work toward this goal. First, the Palestinian issue had to be kept on the international agenda, and this could be accomplished only if the uprising continued. A delegitimation of Israel was also deemed necessary, and this process was pursued by pointing up Israel's hard hand in confronting the Intifada. In the view of the organization, Israel could be forced to the international negotiating table only by the US, and it was in this direction that the PLO was particularly active (see below).

While guarding its exclusive representative status, the PLO demonstrated flexibility where it could. Such was the case with the issue of talks between local Palestinian leaders and Israeli officials. A "PLO official" told the London *Sunday Times* that in talks with the US in March, the organization had expressed a willingness to permit West Bank and Gaza Strip leaders to engage in official talks with Israeli government representatives. The "technical details don't matter as much as getting into a political process that leads to peace," stressed the official.[7]

The PLO's political and diplomatic dilemma remained, principally, as it had in previous years. The PLO believed that time was working in its favor. A Palestinian state in the West Bank and Gaza seemed realizable, and a democratic, Arab-dominated state in all of Palestine an inevitable outcome of the march of history. Yet for these to come true, the organization believed that it was essential for it to remain a part of the political process as the sole spokesman for the Palestinians. Allowing local activists to to meet with Israelis portrayed the organization as both flexible and responsive to its supporters in the territories. As long as the local Palestinian leaders more or less toed the line, they did not threaten the PLO's exclusive representative status.

Following the second formal meeting in March with the US delegation in Tunis, the PLO was decidely upbeat regarding the possibilities of the peace process. This was surprising, because the meeting had been preceded by acrimonious statements by both parties concerning incursions by the PLO to Israel from Southern Lebanon (see below). Apparently, the PLO had exhibited flexibility during the talks, and the US had not hammered too heavily on the incursion issue. According to a working paper prepared before the talks, the PLO was ready to hold "meetings, dialogue, and talks" (i.e., not negotiations) with Israeli officials, but they would have to be preparatory to an international conference, where the "real" negotiations would take place. 'Arafat, however, added on another occasion that even the preparatory talks would have to have an international component.[8] PLO-Israeli talks, were, in fact, a major US policy goal (see chapters on the ME peace process and the US and the ME),[9] a point borne out in excerpts from the protocol of the meeting published in the Paris weekly *al-Yawm al-Sabi'*.[10] 'Arafat himself was quite optimistic after the talks.[11]

The PLO's flexibility on the issue of preparatory talks did not go unrewarded for long. In early April, during a visit of Egyptian President Husni Mubarak to Washington, US President George Bush stated that "a properly structured international conference could play a useful role" in advancing the peace process. He added that "Egypt and the US share the goals of security for Israel, end of the occupation, and achievement of Palestinian political rights."[12] Bush's statement was warmly received by PLO leaders, and 'Arafat stressed that he was particularly gratified that the US had agreed to continue the talks, despite PLO armed operations and Israeli calls to put a halt to the dialogue.[13] An Executive Committee (EC) statement issued after the March meeting with the PLO voiced "appreciation for the seriousness that characterized it." At the same time, the statement firmly rejected the Rabin plan (see above) as aimed at splitting "the ranks of our people," and at outflanking "the PLO as the sole, legitimate representative of our people by trying to create substitutes for it."[14]

In early April, prior to Israeli Prime Minister Yitzhak Shamir's visit to Washington, his office made public a peace plan which he intended to discuss with Bush. The plan sought an internationalization of the Palestinian refugee question; elections in the territories for a delegation to negotiate a self-governing administration during an interim settlement; to be followed by negotiation on a final settlement (for details, see chapter on the ME peace process). The PLO's first reaction was vociferous rejection of the plan, which was termed a "travesty" and "dead the moment it was born."[15] But once it became clear that the plan — primarily the election component — was going to be accepted by the US as the basis for further discussion on a ME peace, the PLO had to play along, not assuming too strong a rejectionist posture. Nabil Sha'th, a top adviser to 'Arafat, said that he saw some "encouraging signs" in the plan.[16] West Bank journalist Daoud Kuttab seemed to have a sense of PLO tactics when he noted that since the plan had achieved some international backing, "it is very difficult for the Palestinians to say no to this idea....That is why we have to try to finesse this plan."[17]

The PLO initially chose to skirt the plan by accepting elections in principle, yet insisting on a prior Israeli withdrawal of some nature.[18] But the mainstream PLO leadership seemed intent on creating the impression that while the plan in its entirety was a nonstarter, it contained elements which were worth talking about. Fath Central Committee member Salah Khalaf said in May that as part of an internationally guaranteed peace process, elections could be held prior to an Israeli withdrawal.[19] The PLO was also being responsive to the demands of certain public figures in the territories, such as Sa'id Kan'an, who advocated a moderate response to the Shamir proposal in order not to jeopardize the dialogue with the US and keep the onus on Israel. They argued that a positive response to a partial Israeli withdrawal from major towns and elections under international supervision could bring American guarantees for PLO involvement at a later stage of the peace process.[20] Specific proposals of this type alarmed the PLO, since they threatened to leave the organization out of the process until the very end, but they were implicitly encouraged by 'Arafat in order to keep options open and give the impression that the PLO was ready to consider a compromise.[21] Shortly before 'Arafat's visit to France in May, for a meeting with President François Mitterrand, "PLO leaders" were quoted in the French press as saying that elections could take place after a partial — even symbolic — withdrawal of Israeli troops.[22] Writing in *Le Monde* the day after 'Arafat left Paris, and later in the US press, Bassam Abu Sharif, an adviser to 'Arafat, probably reflected the PLO leader's thoughts and tactics when he advanced a proposal for elections in the territories as part of the peace process. Couched in a positive tone — "The PLO is in favor of holding elections in the occupied territories of the West Bank and Gaza as soon as possible" — the document was reminiscent, both in content and in purpose, of a similar one drafted by Abu Sharif in 1988 (see *MECS* 1988, pp. 239–40). He stated that Israeli troops would not have to complete their withdrawal before elections as long as there was an internationally guaranteed timetable for a full withdrawal. The proposal was remarkable in that it did not include an explicit role for the PLO, but rather proposed elections for West Bank and Gaza Strip representatives in a "legislative body of the Palestinian people," presumably the PNC. This body would then appoint representatives to negotiate with Israel at a "well-constructed international peace conference" [the language employed by Bush] based on UN Resolutions 242 and 338 and the Palestinian right to self-determination.[23]

Something of an official convergence of opinion between those in the territories and PLO leaders outside was achieved toward the end of April, when similar and coordinated statements were issued by a group of 80 West Bank and Gaza Strip Palestinians and the EC in Tunis. The statements rejected the Shamir plan as a "propaganda maneuver" aimed at dividing the Palestinians and insisted that negotiations be held with the PLO, the representative of all the Palestinians, and not just a part of the Palestinian people. While "elections as proposed by Shamir" were rejected, the notion of elections in principle was not.[24]

The PLO's diplomacy for the rest of the year, following the adoption of the Shamir plan by the Israeli Government in mid-May, the subsequent Egyptian 10 points, and Baker's five points (see chapter on the ME peace process) remained essentially unchanged. The organization never officially issued a total rejection, being careful not to commit itself and often asking for further "clarifications." It was a kind of "yes, but..." — "no, but..." diplomacy. The PLO's main goal was to keep the process moving without being perceived as an obstacle to progress, while all the time guarding its right to represent the Palestinians. The US acceptance of the elections component of the Israeli initiative put the ball squarely in the PLO's court, forcing the organization to deal seriously with the question of elections. Around April-May, US Ambassador to Tunisia Robert Pelletreau began upgrading his contacts with the PLO to include additional top PLO officials and advisers, including Salah Khalaf, EC member Mahmud Darwish, and Bassam Abu Sharif.[25] The US move, apparently designed as a concession to the PLO in order to keep it involved in the peace process, was all the more significant since at the very moment when the level of these contacts became public (late June), Salah Khalaf was being indicted in a Venice court for gunrunning to the Red Brigades terrorist organization in 1979.[26]

While in public insisting that elections could be considered only as part of a process that would lead to an independent Palestinian state,[27] it was clear that the PLO was ready to negotiate without such an advance promise. The US believed, because it was told so either by Egypt or by the PLO, that the organization had agreed to the Egyptian Ten-Point Plan passed to Israel unofficially in July.[28] One Egyptian source even maintained that 'Arafat had had a hand in formulating the plan[29] (for details see chapter on ME peace process). The plan, which was acceptable to a large part of Israel's Labor Party, provided only for a limited withdrawal of Israeli troops "during the elections process." Since the 10 points made no reference to the PLO, it was illustrative of the organization's flexibility that it was willing to give them the nod.

The PLO's determination not to be shut out of the election process by Israel was evident in the flexibility shown by a series of conditions passed on to Israel by Soviet Deputy Foreign Minister Gennady Tarasov in July. The organization agreed to elections if (1) residents of East Jerusalem were allowed to take part; (2) candidates were assured freedom of speech and immunity from prosecution; (3) the IDF withdrew from population centers to predetermined areas on election day; (4) teams of Egyptians and Americans would serve as observers; (5) before elections, Israel would agree in principle to giving up territory. No mention was made of an international conference, a precondition of total withdrawal, or of prior agreement to the establishment of a Palestinian state.[30] Yet, again, in an official meeting with the US in Tunis on 14 August, the PLO told the US that any negotiations would have to result in a Palestinian state.

Such somewhat incompatible statements from various PLO spokesmen, both privately and publicly, were part and parcel of what the organization called its policy of "yes-no" (la'am). With respect to the political maneuvers of 1989, the PLO congratulated itself:

> The PLO has done very well using the diplomacy of yes-no toward Shamir's initiative. It has accepted the principle of elections and worked effortlessly towards international acceptance of the logical conditions of any elections. These conditions are so logical that the US saw eye-to-eye with some of them and was unable to reject the others.[31]

More of the same was evident in mid-September when Abu Sharif announced to the French radio that he was willing to go to Israel within 24 hours to negotiate with Labor Party leaders who had voiced support for Mubarak's 10 points. Abu Sharif's statement was termed "unauthorized" by an official PLO spokesman, a tactic that was reminiscent of that of the "Abu Sharif document."[32] The aim of both moves was to test the water and keep the parties interested in talks with the PLO.

Throughout the ensuing months until the end of the year, the goal of the PLO was to try to change the discussion of the Shamir plan from an emphasis on West Bank and Gaza Strip elections as being solely for a delegation to discuss an interim and final settlement with Israel, into preliminary talks with a PLO-appointed delegation on elections as well as other Palestinian concerns. In this it was partially successful, as was shown by the appearance of the Baker proposal.

With the advent of the five-point Baker proposal in mid-October, the PLO began to move closer to the concept of US-engineered talks with the Israelis in Cairo. The Baker proposal was more attractive to the organization than Mubarak's 10 points and certainly the original Shamir initiative, because Baker's proposal subordinated the elections issue in importance to the Israeli-Palestinian dialogue itself, and allowed the Palestinians to raise the issue of further negotiations as well. The PLO was thus free to understand the Baker proposal as providing for a preliminary dialogue which would go beyond elections. Yet, many obstacles still remained, such as the formation of the Palestinian delegation and who would announce it. As discussions developed with the US both directly and indirectly on the basis of the Baker points, the organization was prepared to be flexible, as long as its role was assured.

In order to extract maximum concessions from the US, the PLO continued its "yes-no" diplomacy. Baker's proposal was first met with a tide of rejections.[33] On 17 October, the Central Council (CC) issued an ambiguous statement which called, on the one hand, to "firmly confront the US policy" and "reject all alternative plans, projects or, proposals,"yet on the other hand offered five points of its own. The PLO's five points ignored the election issue totally, viewing any dialogue with Israel as preparatory to an international conference, and insisted that the international character of the dialogue be consecrated by the UN secretary-general and the five permanent members of the Security Council. The PLO would have the sole right to select and announce the Palestinian delegation.[34] While these points contained aspects with which the US (and certainly Israel) could not agree, the CC statement was not a clear rejection of the Baker proposal.

No one was more perceptive of this than the DFLP secretary-general, Na'if Hawatima, who expressed his dissatisfaction with the final statement. Convinced that the CC had rejected the Baker plan, Hawatima argued that the statement failed to reflect that stand, and was in fact a manipulation of the wording.[35] Yet, while PLO officials were saying that the proposal had been rejected, other officials in Cairo reported that in a meeting with Mubarak on 23 October 'Arafat had not rejected Baker's proposal and had requested further "clarifications."[36]

The PLO EC met in Cairo in early November to discuss the Baker proposals. It was the first meeting of that body in Cairo in 12 years, signifying the marked improvement in PLO-Egyptian relations (see chapter on Egypt). Faruq Qaddumi, head of the PLO's Political Department and a Fath representative, absented himself from the gathering, an apparent indication of his dissatisfaction with the direction in which the 'Arafat leadership was heading. Mustafa al-Zibri (Abu 'Ali Mustafa), the PFLP representative, was also absent, in protest against holding the meeting in Egypt.[37] The PLO added to the confusion by not issuing a final statement after the session, but it was clear that the organization was interested in the Baker proposals. It was reported that 'Arafat had secretly convinced the EC to accept the Baker proposals, but was waiting for several assurances or clarifications from the US.[38]

What ensued was what the PLO termed a "war of letters" with the Bush Administration over the composition of the Palestinian delegation, the PLO's visibility as the party forming it, the international component of the dialogue, and the issue of territory-for-peace. PLO leaders alternately "rejected"[39] and "accepted"[40] the Baker proposals, but the PLO was determined not be shut out of the process if it could maintain some of its minimum conditions. The Baker proposals were the item on the negotiating table — and the PLO was fully aware that without the US it could get nowhere.

The clarifications the US passed on to the PLO in November through Egypt (for text, see chapter on the ME peace process) fell short of PLO demands. They defined no explicit role for the organization, indicated that the international conference would come "at the appropriate time," and clarified that the Palestinian delegation would be comprised mostly of Palestinians from inside the territories, plus two deportees. In early December, the PLO passed on its "final and definitive reply" to the US. Using essentially the same method as had the Israeli Government when it accepted the Baker proposals in November, the PLO accepted the Baker points for a dialogue based on the October CC statement and on four assumptions, which more or less repeated the CC language:

> (1) a delegation [to the dialogue] will be formed by the PLO from inside and outside the occupied territory and will be announced by it;
> (2) the dialogue will have an open agenda;
> (3) there will be an international presence;
> (4) the dialogue is a preliminary step to pave the way for the international peace conference.[41]

The PLO's assumptions were at odd's with Israel's: for example, Israel insisted that it would not negotiate with the PLO, while the PLO insisted that it would form and announce the Palestinian delegation. But the US decided to view the "assumptions" of both parties as just that, and not "conditions" for accepting the Baker points. By so doing, it sought to gloss over differences and bring about the dialogue. The Bush Administration most probably hoped that once begun the dialogue would have a dynamism of its own which would help to overcome the differences.

The nature of the PLO reply to Baker was such that the Fath mainstream could present it as "very positive,"[42] while the DFLP could deny that the organization had agreed to the Baker plan.[43] PFLP leader George Habash continued to attack the PLO stand on the issue as a "policy of free concessions."[44]

With the PLO reply as problematic as Israel's, Washington began to focus discussions on the composition of a Palestinian delegation, in consultation with the PLO via Egypt. Apparently, the PLO agreed to accept the US demand for a delegation that would have a majority from the territories, and that the "outside" Palestinians would be two deportees.[45] They would be allowed to return to the West Bank or Gaza Strip, and thus for the Israelis they would constitute "inside" Palestinians, while the PLO could contend that they were from outside the territories. The PLO bridled at what it saw as the invisible role it was being forced to play. After all, it had received hard-won worldwide recognition and was now being forced to give it up. For this reason, by the end of the year, it was far from clear if the PLO really intended to play ball. Time and again, the organization insisted vehemently that it would publicly announce the delegation as its own.[46] An official EC statement reiterated this in mid-December.[47] Despite this official insistence, the PLO's overwhelming desire to be a part of the process left an opening, suggesting that even on this the organization could be flexible. Nabil Sha'th stated that the way in which the PLO would announce the delegation as its own could "be discussed and clarified."[48] It remained to be seen whether the DFLP and certain elements in Fath (Qaddumi, and even Khalaf) would go along with the charade.

By and large, the idea of direct Israeli-Palestinian talks in Cairo concentrating mainly on elections was not well received by the PLO; the organization put little stock in anything that was essentially based on the Israeli government initiative. Yet the

Fath mainstream chose to go along with the plan. While it was unclear how far the PLO would eventually go, the constant desire to guard the exclusivity of its representative status and to maintain the support of many of the West Bank and Gaza Strip residents was surely a powerful determinant that pushed the organization in a conciliatory direction.

The PLO mainstream's flexibility was goal-oriented. It saw a state on the horizon, and the policy of flexibility served this objective.[49] At the end of the year, the question remained: If the process developed toward the exclusion of a Palestinian state, would the PLO abandon its pragmatic policy and return to its more radical policy?

THE DIALOGUE WITH THE UNITED STATES: THE VIEW FROM TUNIS

For the PLO, opening a dialogue with the US was primarily of symbolic importance, evidence of its growing acceptance in the international community. The organization had little hope that in the short term it could change Washington's basic support of Israel, but it saw the US as the only country that could move Israel toward accepting a Palestinian state. The PLO weekly *Filastin al-Thawra* wrote that all real decisions in the ME took place in Washington, and Israel just did its bidding. In 1956, all then president Dwight Eisenhower had to do was order then premier David Ben-Gurion out of Sinai, wrote the magazine, and Ben-Gurion complied. "The moment Washington announces that the Palestinians have the right to self-determination and to establish an independent state, everything will end up in our favor, and Israel will have no choice but to comply with the American decision."[50]

This being the PLO's perception, it saw the greatest value of the dialogue in its very existence rather than in anything that it could actually accomplish by it. The dialogue made it easier for the PLO to present its case in the US, where it believed the public took a view of Israel opposite to that of the Administration.[51] While during the year the PLO began more and more to realize the need to address Israeli public opinion, it also continued to believe that the US held most of the cards. It was correct in believing that the uprising, Israel's response, and coverage in the media had made Americans more attentive to the Palestinian case, and that maximum effort had to be made to develop and expand this direction in the US. Nevertheless, there were indications that many Palestinians were far from satisfied with the PLO's performance in this regard. In October, Columbia University Professor and PNC member, Edward Said, led a blistering attack on the Palestinian leadership for bungling the public relations efforts in the US. Palestinians in the US felt "utterly disgusted," said Said, "by the neglect, corruption and incompetence in the Palestinian performance in this country." By early 1990, there were indications that the organization had responded and was overhauling its US operations.[52]

Skeptical about the PLO's renunciation of terrorism, the US used the beginning of the dialogue to determine how serious the PLO was on this issue. The problem was further complicated by several incursion attempts into northern Israel by PLO constituent organizations during the first quarter of the year (for the PLO's view of the armed struggle, see below; for details of the operations, see chapter on armed operations). Several reports citing PLO sources at the beginning of the year indicated that the US had demanded that the PLO disband the Force 17 operations unit and remove some terrorist leaders from the leadership, such as the EC member from the Palestine Liberation Front (PLF), Muhammad 'Abbas (Abu al-'Abbas), who was responsible for the *Achille Lauro* operation[53] (see *MECS* 1984–85, pp. 91–93). Both PLO and US officials issued denials of the reports.[54] In any case, the initial focus of the talks was the issue of terrorism. US State Department spokesman Charles Redman stressed this, but soon Baker made it clear that while PLO armed operations "gave us trouble," "we are not prepared to say at this time that this constitutes an action which would cause us to break off the dialogue."[55]

The PLO was furious that the US was so concerned about the terrorism issue, and demanded that it address such problems as recognition of the PLO, self-determination, and Israel's "daily state terrorism" in the territories. The US stand "smacks of hypocrisy," said EC member Yasir 'Abd Rabbuh.[56] PLO operations in February and March drew some — albeit muted — US criticism, to which the organization replied that the US would have to define terrorism, since the armed struggle was not terrorism.[57] But it was precisely such a definition as this which the US fought to avoid. Deputy Assistant Secretary of State for Near Eastern Affairs Ned Walker testified before a House subcommittee:

> I would like to avoid giving an exact prescription for when we would stop or not stop the talks; I don't think it would be useful to give the PLO guidelines, that this operation is permitted and another is forbidden. There are certain circumstances under which we would certainly halt the talks.

Walker, of course, declined to define these circumstances,[58] but the US refusal to suspend the talks during the year in response to attacks by the DFLP, the PLF, and the PFLP suggested that only an overt terrorist attack by 'Arafat's Fath would cause the US to do so. The US, which saw PLO participation in the peace process as essential, was not about to halt talks with it after Washington had spent so much effort in getting the organization to say the words that would allow the talks to begin.

When the dialogue moved on to discuss more substantive issues as the year unfolded, the PLO grew more appreciative of the "seriousness" of the discussions and was gratified by certain positive statements by US officials and talks held with top leaders (see above). But the organization was still quite disappointed that the talks were focused on elections in the territories rather than the more important issues of Palestinian statehood. The PLO insisted that the US assume a neutral role. Its emphasis on the Shamir plan showed that the dialogue did not represent a change in the US policy that was inimical to the Palestinians, but just a change in tactics. It was thus a dialogue of the deaf, and the US was guilty of bad faith. Khalid al-Hasan said that the dialogue could not really be called so. "It is made up of public relations meetings, ice-breaking, and the exchange of platitudes."[59]

THE DRIVE FOR INTERNATIONAL RECOGNITION: STRATEGY AND TACTICS ON THE ROAD FROM GENEVA TO *CADUC*

Underlying 'Arafat's great legitimacy as a Palestinian leader had been one major achievement: more than any other individual, 'Arafat was responsible for developing the Palestinian issue into one of international concern following the second defeat of 1967. His achievements were those of the Palestinians, and were the embodiment of Palestinian pride. His speech at the UN in 1974, the agreement of 150 countries to move the UN General Assembly session to Geneva in December 1988 to hear 'Arafat (when 'Arafat had been denied a visa to the US; see *MECS* 1988, pp. 254–55), the opening of the dialogue with the US — even having his likeness made for Madame Tussaud's Waxworks Museum in London[60] — all were milestones in this process. In his strategy, focused on achieving a Palestinian state, furthering the international legitimacy of his cause was paramount. With the declaration of the state of Palestine in November 1988, the PLO concentrated on attaining the symbolic trappings of statehood, such as recognition and membership in international organizations.

Part and parcel of this approach was to project an image of the PLO as a moderate, responsible party. This necessitated diplomatic pronouncements, some of which reflected real change in the PLO, such as the readiness to engage Israel in a dialogue (as long as it was preparatory to an international conference). But the long-term, strategic goals of the PLO — a Palestinian Arab state in all of Palestine — still remained. This was evident in many statements throughout the year, and could not be viewed solely as an attempt to appease radical elements under the PLO umbrella.

THE "STATE OF PALESTINE" AND INTERNATIONAL RECOGNITION

In early April, the CC proclaimed 'Arafat President. His official title then became "President of the State of Palestine, Chairman of the EC, and Commander in Chief of the Palestine Revolution Forces." 'Arafat's main rival in Fath, Faruq Qaddumi, was named foreign minister.[61] The move came just before 'Arafat's visit to Paris, and was designed to officially grant him the status of head of state. By mid-April 1990, 84 states had recognized the "State of Palestine" (see Appendix I).

In the PLO's drive to gain international recognition for the "State of Palestine," the European arena was the scene of some of the most important diplomatic gains of 1989. Foremost among them was 'Arafat's visit to France in early May. The French let it be known that the "price" for the visit would be "new and unequivocal statements" on the recognition of Israel and the renunciation of terrorism. The PLO chairman did make a dramatic statement, that the Palestinian national covenant was *caduc* (null and void, or obsolete; for the broader significance of the statement, see below). 'Arafat met with Mitterrand and other top French officials. Paris was very careful with its protocol, receiving 'Arafat not as the PLO had wished, as "President of the State of Palestine," but rather as "President of the PLO." Many of the trappings of the visit were, however, those of a head of state.[62]

During a visit to Spain, in late January, where he was received by President Felipe González and King Juan Carlos I, 'Arafat held his first official talks ever with representatives of the European Community, meeting with a committee made up of the foreign ministers of France, Greece, and Spain.[63] In other European-related developments, meetings took place at various levels between PLO officials and those of Great Britain, The Netherlands, Greece, West Germany, and the Scandinavian states.[64]

The second main arena in which the PLO was active was that of international organizations. In January, the PLO was granted the right to address the UN Security Council as "Palestine," on the same basis as any member state. Previously, the organization had to be sponsored by a member state.[65] In late November, the PLO formally asked the UN to change its status to that of the "State of Palestine," a nonmember state such as Switzerland and the Vatican; hitherto the organization's status was that of "observer." The US threatened to cut off funds to the UN if the PLO's status was changed. Following pressure by the US and the USSR, the Arab countries sponsoring the change agreed to withdraw it.[66]

The PLO devoted much attention during the year to gaining admission to a host of other UN and non-UN international organizations, the most important of which were the World Health Organization (WHO) and the United Nations Educational, Scientific, and Cultural Organization (Unesco).[67] Had they been successful, both attempts would have been major diplomatic victories, but a serious threat by the US to cut off funding to the WHO, and the belief by several friends of the PLO that it would be unsuccessful at Unesco led to failures in both forums.[68]

REALITY AND RHETORIC: SHORT-TERM IMPERATIVES
AND LONG-TERM DESIRES

In 1988, the PLO had come closer than ever to accepting a two-state solution to the conflict, yet statements by various leaders seemed to belie a true acceptance, as they implicitly and explicitly referred to a West Bank and Gaza Strip state as only one step in the drive for what the PLO saw as full Palestinian self-determination (see *MECS* 1988, chapter on the PLO). While in 1989 the PLO often seemed more sincere in its statements concerning the final, permanent nature of a settlement involving two states, the Fath mainstream still seemed to have remained committed to the phased strategy for a Palestinian Arab state in all of Palestine as approved by the organization in 1974. Apparently, this commitment was more than a mere tactical position taken in order to appease more radical colleagues, although that need sometimes played a role. The continuing appearance of contradictory statements was part of the "yes-no" policy noted above, and also reflected the Fath leadership's dialectical sense of the time factor. Pressure from residents of the territories for immediate political gains worked to moderate the leadership, yet the belief that victory over Israel would eventually be achieved made them reluctant to renounce the aim of liberating all of Palestine. In the view of the PLO, the long-term goal of an Arab state in all of Palestine would be guaranteed by exercising the right of former residents of the area "occupied by Israel in 1948" to return ("the right of return"); the inherent, internal contractions in Israeli society; and the higher birth rate of Israeli Arabs. This belief seemed to have remained unshaken, even though Fath, and particularly 'Arafat, had made a tactical decision to exhibit the maximum degree of flexibility and goodwill needed to attain the immediate goal of a Palestinian state in the West Bank and Gaza Strip.

Soon after 'Arafat had made his Geneva news conference statement in mid-December 1988, following which the US opened a dialogue with the PLO (see *MECS* 1988, pp. 256–57), PLO leaders exhibited clear evidence of backtracking both on the news conference statement and the content of 'Arafat's Geneva speech made a day earlier. In Geneva, 'Arafat had accepted UN Resolutions 242 and 338 and had recognized Israel (conditional upon the existence of the state of Palestine). These statements had been urged by the US precisely because previous PNC statements had grouped UN Resolutions 242 and 338 with other UN resolutions and/or "self-determination," effectively emptying 242 and 338 of their content (see analysis in *MECS* 1988, pp. 251–54). During 1989, 'Arafat often referred to his Geneva news conference statement and speech, but ignored their content. Other PLO leaders acted in the same manner, never publicly repeating the Geneva news conference language during the year. Instead, they tried to put a moderate face on the resolutions of the November 19th PNC, as if the Geneva statement had never been made. 'Arafat insisted that the PNC approval of Resolution 242 "was conditional on three basic constants: a Palestinian state, self-determination, and repatriation....The Palestinian approval included all UN resolutions, not just one resolution."[69] On another occasion 'Arafat stated: "Our constants consist of the PNC resolutions. These resolutions emphasize the Palestinian people's national and political rights, foremost being their right to repatriation, self-determination, and the establishment of an independent state on Palestinian soil with Jerusalem as its capital."[70] Such statements were incompatible with what had been said in Geneva, and the constant trilateral refrain, demanding an independent state, *in addition* to self-determination and the right of return, indicated a continuing adherence to the phased strategy.

PNC speaker 'Abd al-Hamid al-Sa'ih and other leaders likewise chose to disregard the Geneva statement, referring, again, only to the PNC resolutions: "Anyone who says that the decisions we took in Algiers contain recognition of Resolutions 181 [the partition resolution of 1947], 242, and 338 is not right...." For Sa'ih and others, the declaration of Palestinian independence was not based on Resolution 181, namely, the creation of a Palestinian *and* a Jewish state, since this was an historical injustice. Rather, the creation of the state of Palestine was based on "our natural and historical right to the territory of our homeland, Palestine."[71] Such statements after Geneva seemed to imply that despite a professed desire for a two-state solution, many Palestinian leaders continued to see the very existence of a Jewish state as illegitimate.

PLO claims that it was reconciled to a two-state solution were further undermined by other statements which seemed to suggest that — by definition — there could be no peace with Israel. 'Arafat said: "Israel cannot possibly be a peaceful neighbor for the simple reason that according to the Zionist creed the land of Israel extends from the Nile to the Euphrates. The Israeli flag has two blue lines, one representing the Nile and the other the Euphrates...."[72] An editorial in *Filastin al-Thawra* read:

> [Israel is a] parasitical body in the Middle East which has no ability to survive, despite 40 years of injections from overseas. The land upon which this entity stands has a different meaning and history. Shamir knows this...and therefore when he loses his rule over part of the land, he knows that the other part will slip through his fingers, despite all the promises...from Europe and America to guarantee that this deformed creature will feel secure....But no one will be able to do anything, once, after all the assurances, this entity will drown and disappear.[73]

'Arafat sometimes stated that he was offering the Israelis "the peace of Salah al-Din [Saladin]," or that the PLO's readiness for peace was based on the al-Hudaybiyya treaty made between the Prophet and the people of Mecca.[74] The peace of Salah al-Din and the treaty of al-Hudaybiyya are well known to Muslim and non-Muslim Arabs. Following his glorious victory over the Crusaders at Hittin in July of 1187, Salah al-Din captured Jerusalem later that year. Realizing that he could not capture all of the Holy Land, Salah al-Din signed a cease-fire with Richard the Lion-Heart in September 1192. About 100 years later Palestine was rid of the Crusaders. This was the sense in which 'Arafat used this historical analogy — eventually the Arabs would be rid of the Israelis. The treaty of al-Hudaybiyya was signed in 628. The Prophet, seeing that he was unable to conquer Mecca, concluded a treaty with the tribe of Quraysh at al-Hudaybiyya for 10 years, during which the Muslims would be allowed to make the pilgrimage to Mecca each year and stay for 10 days. For the next two years, during the pilgrimage, the Muslims converted many to their cause. In January 630, the murder of a Muslim by a Meccan was seized upon as a pretext for breaking the treaty, and the Prophet proceeded to capture the city. For Muslims, Muhammad's behavior at al-Hudaybiyya is considered the essence of *hilm*, a combination of restraint, moderation, and cleverness. The Prophet was diplomatic, accepting a (temporary) peace for the sake of a later victory.[75]

By comparing his actions with those of two of the most illustrious figures in Islamic history, who had settled for lesser, immediate gains only in order to win a final victory, 'Arafat was striking the perfect chord for his Arab audience. He made these statements when he was trying to show Arabs that the PLO was operating from a position of strength, not weakness, and was making a tactical conciliation for the sake of a greater victory later on. In such statements, 'Arafat played the role of Salah al-Din and Muhammad, while Israel was cast as the infidel people of Mecca or the Crusaders. The fate of the latter two was well-known.

PLO officials made several peace overtures and particularly conciliatory statements during the year. Fath Central Committee member Hani al-Hasan told an audience in London in December that the PLO "has no objection to mutually agreed border modifications [in the pre-1967 Green Line], insofar as they may be necessary for genuine security concerns and needs." In an attempt to allay fears that the PLO was still bent on a strategy of destroying Israel in stages, he said: "We know that once we sign the settlement with Israel, it constitutes mutual recognition, and *we will therefore be renouncing our right to any further struggle.*"[76]

Nabil Sha'th told audiences in the US that the PLO had a permanent and complete commitment to a two-state solution. The organization had abandoned its claim to 78% of historic Palestine, he maintained. With respect to the right of return, Sha'th stated that the return of Palestinians to the area inside the Green Line would pose no demographic threat to Israel. It would, rather, be part of the peace process whereby Jews could live in the State of Palestine and more Palestinians would come to·live in Israel. He envisaged a "Benelux arrangement" for a future relationship between the state of Palestine, Israel, Jordan, Egypt, and Lebanon. He told the Israelis that they had nothing to fear from the right of return, and "we have no tricks up our sleeves."[77]

Other statements by Sha'th, to Arab audiences, conveyed quite a different message. In these statements his idea of a "Benelux arrangement" was a "democratic, secular Palestinian state....One state on all of the Palestinian land,...organized in a confederation with all the surrounding Arab states. If we attain independence on part of our land, we will not give up our dream to establish one democratic state on all of the Palestinian land."[78] When questioned about the contradictory statements made by himself and other officials, Sha'th replied disingenuously: "If we continue to regurgitate fear and if we continue just to look at our differences, just to spot our semantics, just to spot our little linguistic flops, we are never going to build peace."[79]

The most dramatic conciliatory appearance of the year was that of Salah Khalaf, who sent a videotaped address to an international symposium on peace in the ME held in Jerusalem in February. Khalaf addressed the Israelis directly, and his tone was particularly forthcoming. He called for direct PLO-Israeli meetings prior to an international conference, which in turn would serve only as a witness to security arrangements worked out bilaterally. He said that the Palestinians sought normalization, and that "we do not seek to have a Berlin Wall or any other wall separating us; we want there to be openness."[80] Coming from a man who had headed the Black September terrorist group, these were truly remarkable words.

But other statements made by PLO officials during the year seemed to cast some doubt on the kind of "openness" Khalaf had in mind. The organization's leaders still envisaged an Arab state in all of Palestine. They believed that, with time on their side, such a development was inevitable, and could even be accomplished by peaceful means. Faruq Qaddumi admitted that, since the ideal solution — a "democratic state" in all of Palestine — could not be achieved soon, a phased strategy was desirable:

> That is why we follow a policy of stages in our political struggle, the objective being to provide freedom, justice, equality for all. To convince the world, including the Jews and Israelis of that fact, we must go through the stages....Building the Palestinian state on a liberated part of Palestinian territory does not conflict with our convictions. In fact, just the opposite is the case: it is the proper way to achieve the ideal solution. Standing on firm ground — a state whose existence and international legitimacy are recognized, as working via peaceful and legal means will lead us to the desired solution.[81]

A characteristic illustration of the PLO's "yes-no" diplomacy was 'Arafat's statement while in Paris that the Palestinian National Charter, which calls for the destruction of Israel, was "caduc."[82] What followed was a diplomatic game of dictionary hide-and-seek; in the world of "yes-no" diplomacy, a better word could not have been chosen. Of archaic usage, the word carries with it a host of meanings, from "lapsed," "obsolete," "antiquated," "null and void," to "decrepit," "broken down," "decayed," and "frail." Asked by reporters to choose the English equivalent, he told them to go and "look it up in the *Larousse*."[83] When Radio Monte Carlo broadcaster Antoine Nawfal translated "caduc" as "null and void," 'Arafat said: "Who am I to criticize your translation. Let us say that it [the charter] has become a thing of the past, superseded, superseded, superseded. Many verses in the holy Qur'an were superseded by other verses. Does this mean that the previous verses have been canceled? No."[84] In addition to 'Arafat, both Salah Khalaf and the PLO representative in Tunis and participant in the dialogue with the US, Hakam Bal'awi, denied that the charter had been canceled or declared null and void in Paris. Khalaf was right when he insisted that only the PNC could cancel the charter.[85]

A French listener could easily have understood 'Arafat to have said that the charter was null and void. By eventually saying that he had meant superseded, 'Arafat was implying that the covenant had only been set aside, but remained on the books. By refusing to clear up discrepancies, 'Arafat succeeded in focusing media attention on himself and the Palestinian cause, and this was, after all, the aim of the exercise.

ISRAELI ARABS IN THE EYES OF THE PLO: SECURING SELF-DETERMINATION FOR ALL OF THE PALESTINIAN PEOPLE

Throughout the year, the PLO's view about the status of Israeli Arabs in a future settlement remained unclear (see also *MECS* 1988, p. 254). Since the organization regarded an independent West Bank and Gaza Strip state as distinct from self-determination (see *MECS* 1988, pp. 251–54, and above), and since it demanded self-determination for all Palestinians, including Israeli Arabs, the PLO seemed to be implying that its independent state would have further demands which would include the Arabs living in Israel. 'Arafat said as much when he told Israeli reporters that the future of the Arabs in Israel would be negotiated at an international conference.[86]

During the Fath Congress in August (see below), a cable was read by Nabil Sha'th in the name of "1948-occupied Palestine's" youth; it drew great applause. The cable stressed that "Palestine's people under occupation since 1948 will remain rooted in their homeland...until the time for the great freedom comes."[87]

The uprising heightened nationalist pride among Israeli Arabs. One of its implications was the making of 1989 a record year for security offenses committed by them. By early December, the security forces had broken up 20 sabotage cells, compared with 15 in 1988 and two in 1987. The number of incidents of sabotage also increased dramatically (see chapter on armed operations).[88] Although not relating specifically to these developments, 'Arafat used the occasion of Land Day (30 March) to salute "our masses in the Triangle, the Negev, and Galilee [who] declare their joining of the Palestinian struggle march through their celebration of Land Day...." On Land Day, continued 'Arafat, "martyrs fell to water with their noble blood the tree of Palestine's liberty."[89]

George Habash went farther to extend publicly 'Arafat's thinking to its logical conclusion. "We have to prepare the way to transform the struggles of our popular masses in the areas [captured in] 1948 from the level of support to the level of participation...in order to expand the framework of the uprising until it encompasses all of Palestine."[90]

In the political ideology of the PLO, the establishment of a Palestinian Arab state in part of historic Palestine would accelerate the process of disintegration of the Israeli entity. This process was already under way, the organization maintained, because Israel was an unnatural creature. Israeli society was being undermined by the Intifada, and the "Arab Jews" [Jews originating in Arab countries], who formed a majority in Israel, were experiencing an awakening and were rejecting European culture, "indicating that the Jews themselves will eventually agree to — or even demand — the establishment of a democratic state in Israel."[91] The growth of the Israeli Arab population, the increase in its Palestinian identity, and the "right of return" would eventually complete the task, the organization believed. It was for this reason that the PLO began toward the end of the year to mobilize world opinion against the renewed flow of Soviet Jews to Israel, since this worked against what the organization saw as the natural process of disintegration of that country.[92]

INTERORGANIZATIONAL DEVELOPMENTS

There were increasing signs in 1989 that the main opposition to 'Arafat in the PLO, headed by George Habash's PFLP and supported by the secretary-general of the DFLP, Na'if Hawatima, was becoming more impatient with the political moves and the concessions of the 'Arafat mainstream. Both had rejected 'Arafat's Geneva press conference statement in 1988 (see *MECS* 1988, p. 257). While there was no indication of an approaching split in the PLO, these leaders continued to call forcefully for the implementation of the organizational reforms agreed upon at the 18th session of the PNC in 1987 (see *MECS* 1987, pp. 212–14), and argued with Fath about the formation of a provisional government.

DFLP attacks on 'Arafat were carried out mostly by Na'if Hawatima, since Yasir 'Abd Rabbuh, assistant secretary-general of the DFLP and its representative on the EC, had moved even closer to 'Arafat's thinking on the Palestinian issue and had drifted away from his boss. 'Abd Rabbuh seemed no longer to constitute a force in opposition to 'Arafat.[93]

Hawatima rejected 'Arafat's whole approach to the political process, including preliminary direct negotiations even under certain international auspices. The DFLP was particularly up in arms with the PLO leadership's acceptance of massive US involvement in the Palestinian issue, and had opposed the Amman Accord of February 1985 for just this reason. While critical of 'Arafat throughout the year, Hawatima delivered his hardest punch to the PLO leadership in a speech at the al-Yarmuk refugee camp in Damascus in February. He rejected 'Arafat's suggestion that a common market could be established among Israel, Palestine, and Jordan,[94] and criticized him for aligning himself with an Arab regional alignment, the Arab Cooperation Council.[95] When 'Arafat, in an interview with an Italian newspaper,[96] offered to go to Jerusalem, the DFLP denounced the idea, stressing that it had not been approved by the PLO.[97]

Fath hit back hard at Hawatima for his statements. Mahmud 'Abbas, a Fath Central Committee member and a member of the PLO CC, took the unprecedented step of publishing an open letter to Hawatima in the Arabic press. "May God fight those who stir up sedition," he wrote. He accused Hawatima of "extreme egotism" and of stressing differences instead of augmenting unity, when the PLO leadership was acting within the Palestinian consensus.[98] The Paris-based weekly, *al-Yawm al-Sabi'*, edited by one of the Hasan brothers, Bilal, stressed that Hawatima's attacks were uncalled for, since the PLO had no illusions about its talks with the US and realized that negotiations with the US were with "an enemy who protects Israel." Since the DFLP had often evinced the greatest enthusiasm for phased solutions, Hasan added that it was surprising that the organization opposed the current policies of the Palestinian leadership. Furthermore, he wrote, the DFLP could no longer define its policies toward the PLO leadership as "left" versus "right" since the Palestine Communist Party had joined the PLO (see *MECS* 1987, p. 210).[99]

A truce between the feuding parties seems to have been reached in early April, when several meetings were held between the Fath and DFLP leaderships; another meeting was held in July. Both final statements stressed obvious common denominators. The July statement noted "satisfaction with what has been achieved in the...organizational" sphere, although there was no indication during the year that anything had been done in this regard.[100]

As could be expected, PFLP leader George Habash was more vociferous in his condemnation of 'Arafat than was Hawatima. The Intifada was becoming stronger, the "Zionist entity" was becoming more and more isolated, and the Palestinian cause was gaining support, he argued. Therefore, time was on the side of the Palestinians, and hence there was no justification for 'Arafat's "festival of concessions."[101] Habash rejected many of the statements by 'Arafat and Salah Khalaf, claiming that they represented their own individual positions and did not commit the PLO or any of the organizations in it to anything. After 'Arafat's "*caduc*" statement, which drew intense fire from Habash, the latter noted: "Brother Yasir 'Arafat can establish a new organization if he wants....But the PLO, as understood by our Palestinian people and by our masses, is the Charter."[102] He opposed direct negotiations of any kind and the possibility of an economic federation. Such ideas, stressed Habash, caused confusion in the ranks of the masses within the territories and without.[103]

Habash threatened both 'Arafat and Egyptian President Husni Mubarak. Mubarak's fate, he warned, "will be like that of Sadat at the hands of Egyptian progressive forces."[104] When the EC met in Cairo in early November, the PFLP representative, Mustafa al-Zibri, denied receiving an invitation, but stressed that he would not go anyway since "there are attempts to place the PLO under the Egyptian trusteeship for political reasons in agreement with the US Administration's wishes and orientations."[105]

The political program issued following the Fath Congress (see below) came in for blistering criticism by the PFLP as equivocating and totally lacking in self-criticism. Fath, wrote the PFLP organ *al-Hadaf*, evaded specific answers to specific questions, such as its stand on the liberation of all of Palestine. Moreover, continued the magazine, Fath's use of the term "armed action" (*al-'amal al-musallah*) instead of "armed struggle" (*al-kifah al-musallah*) was certainly not solely a semantic matter.[106]

Again, it was Mahmud 'Abbas who took the lead in the Fath counterattack. Habash lacked a sense of responsibility and reflected haste in his political judgment, 'Abbas stated. "Such statements harm our people and their struggle."[107] A meeting held in July between the Fath and the PFLP leadership failed to yield any significant amelioration of differences.[108]

Fath also had its differences with the two fronts over the formation of a provisional government for the State of Palestine, a step which had been mandated by the 19th PNC (see *MECS* 1988, p. 250). Points of disagreement centered around the timing of the government's formation, who would be a member, and what its relationship would be with the PLO. Several meetings on the subject were held in the early part of the year, but it was decided that the subject "needed more study."

In essence, the Fath leadership opposed the process of setting up a government because the status quo was preferable. Since according to the PNC decision, the EC, controlled by Fath, was to perform the functions of the provisional government until it was constituted, to go about forming the government at the present was superfluous, and would simply bring about internal dissent. The trouble was just not worth it, and Fath argued that the formation of the government should be postponed until specific political advantages could be gained by declaring the government, such as just prior to the international conference. The bitter memory of the puppet "Government of All Palestine" formed after the 1948 war continued to deter some of the leadership. Moreover, it was reported that the leadership had been informed by friends in Western Europe that declaring the government at the present stage would hamper its cause.[109]

The PFLP supported Fath's position against the formation of the provisional government, mostly because it feared that the latter would use it to eliminate the PFLP's influence in the PLO. According to the PFLP, while the government should not be established now, when it did come about it should be a part of the PLO, representative of the various factions, and certainly not include the "traditional personalities," such as Gaza attorney Fa'iz Abu Rahma, Bethlehem Mayor Ilias Freij, and *al-Fajr* editor Hana Siniora.[110]

While sharing many of the same fears of the PFLP, the DFLP supported the immediate constitution of a provisional government.[111] In Na'if Hawatima's estimation, Fath was in reality planning to establish the provisional government and use it to carry out a kind of a coup. Hawatima believed that Fath wanted to bypass the structure of the PLO and form a government comprised of its well-known supporters in the territories, such as those mentioned by the PFLP. Although Fath was particularly silent about this, there were reports which confirmed Hawatima's fears.[112] For this reason, the DFLP believed that the government had to be established immediately. To assure this, Hawatima demanded that representatives of the territories be appointed by the United National Command (UNC) of the Intifada, where the DFLP had more influence.[113]

With 'Arafat and Khalaf continually making statements and following policies opposed by the DFLP and the PFLP, those organizations lost no opportunity to remind the leadership of the resolutions of the 1987 PNC which called for organizational reforms. These reforms had been passed at the PNC in order to limit the type of "deviationist policies" followed by the PLO leadership, such as the 1984 Amman Accord and the *rapprochement* with Egypt, yet they had never been implemented by the Fath-dominated PLO. After each PNC, which established a vague consensus, 'Arafat would proceed to do as he pleased.

Suspicious of the direction in which the leadership was now heading, Habash and Hawatima intensified their efforts to reform the PLO. They railed against the "individualistic" policies of the leadership which deviated from the Palestinian consensus, and demanded "deep democratic reforms" in the PLO in order to bring about "collective decision-making." Hawatima, in particular, held up the UNC as the paragon of the kind of democracy that should prevail in the PLO.[114] The PLO, said Hawatima, had to be purged, and its "many corrupt and bourgeois bureaucratic institutions...should respond to the calls of the Palestinian people...." Both organizations also raised questions of financial irregularity. For example, Hawatima pointed out that matters concerning the occupied territories should not be confined to the one [Fath-dominated] Department of Occupied Territories Affairs. They should, rather, be distributed fairly among the PLO's constituent organizations on a "front-determined basis" (*'ala asas jabhawi*). Such statements were aimed at bolstering the strength of the DFLP and PFLP and getting rid of the "independents," who were almost all loyal to Fath.[115] The PFLP and the DFLP also protested against Fath's domination of the PLO's diplomatic missions abroad.[116]

Fath was silent in the face of calls for organizational reform, although there were indications that it was planning to allow some organizational diversity in the personnel manning diplomatic missions. The notable exception was the criticism of PLO institutions by Salah Khalaf, which appeared in a DFLP publication; but since Khalaf was quiet on the issue everywhere else, this was most probably lip service paid to his hosts.[117]

Although strongly felt, the differences between the organizations were not sharp enough to cause a split in the PLO. The PFLP was not about to go back to the situation previous to the 18th PNC, when it was outside the only legitimate Palestinian framework. Moreover, all sides realized that such differences were not worth hurting the Intifada, which was the Palestinians' main political asset. Finally, the growing *rapprochement* in the Arab world was anything but conducive to such a development.

THE FIFTH GENERAL CONGRESS OF FATH

Fath's Fifth General Congress convened in Tunis from 3–9 August, with more than 1,100 members present. The previous congress had been held in Damascus in May 1980 (see *MECS* 1979–80, pp. 236–38, 259–62). The Fath leadership believed that the time had come to hold a new congress in order to tie up several loose ends. The Lebanon war, the Fath rebellion, and the uprising had all occurred since the previous congress. With the Intifada well under way and Fath riding high, a hiatus had been reached and Fath could afford the discussion and dissent that the congress was sure to generate. There were also several personnel issues to settle. Since the last congress two members of the Central Committee had joined the rebels (Nimr Salih and Samih Kuwayk) and three had been assassinated (Khalil al-Wazir, Majid Abu Sharrar, and Sa'd Sayil); their positions had to be filled. Moreover, many of the younger leaders were clamoring for positions that would reflect their contribution to the movement.

The congress was held in secret and details were few. While the Western media were taken up with the program and statement issued at the end of the congress, the Arab press concentrated mostly on personnel changes.

Radical elements in the organization, including those associated with Fath's military apparatus, al-'Asifa, were critical of 'Arafat's political moves during the congress. 'Arafat and his supporters decided that it was time for consensus-building within the movement, now that the Intifada was going ahead and the US was fully committed to a PLO role in the peace process. The leadership could, therefore, afford to have the concluding political program contain language that constituted a political common denominator and that was more reflective of the hard line of the rank and file. The pragmatic leadership also held these positions, but in the past had toned them down for the sake of achieving a dialogue with the US. Moreover, there may have been an assessment that the time was ripe for attracting young Palestinians to the movement — from among those living outside Israel and the territories — who may have been drawn to the more radical organizations in the past few years.

For all these reasons, the initial "Political Program" (*al-barnamaj al-siyasi*) issued on 8 August (see Appendix II for text) was a document harsh in tone that seemed a far cry from the vague resolutions of the 19th PNC, and certainly the conciliatory language of 'Arafat's December 1988 Geneva speech and press conference. The program recalled the "Zionist invasion" which came "to implant a Zionist entity designed to carry out the imperialist schemes." "The crime was consummated," the document continued, "by the partition of Palestine and the establishment of the Zionist entity state in 1948."

The congress called for an intensification of "armed action and all forms of struggle to liquidate (*tasfiyya*) the Israeli-Zionist occupation of our occupied Palestinian land." Since the congress had affirmed that the establishment of Israel was illegitimate and a crime, there could be little doubt that the "Israeli-Zionist occupation" did not refer solely to the West Bank and Gaza Strip. Concerned about the increase in "Zionist immigration" and its consequences for the "effect of the demographic factor on our conflict with the Zionist enemy," the congress decided to set up a committee "to oppose the Zionist immigration to our homeland and to assume all cultural, information, and political tasks to prevent the arrival of Jewish immigrants in our occupied homeland."

The political program did not mention UN Resolutions 242 and 338 at all. The congress seemed satisfied, rather, with simply extending a blanket endorsement of the PNC resolutions; the more moderate Geneva speech and press conference statement received no mention. The congress also rejected the Shamir plan by name and any elections plan that did not entail a prior Israeli withdrawal.

The Fath leadership may have miscalculated the response of the US to the political program. State Department spokeswoman Margaret Tutwiler issued a statement stressing that Fath's "derogatory rhetoric on Israel, its tone of confrontation and violence, and its preference for unrealistic principles and solutions instead of practical ideas for peace are unhelpful."[118] In response to the US criticism, Fath beat a semantic retreat. It took the unusual step of issuing an additional "Concluding Political Statement" (al-bayan al-siyasi al-khitami; see text in Appendix III) two days after the congress was over and the day following the US criticism. The statement toned down Fath's rhetoric; it omitted the establishment of the committee to curtail Jewish immigration; it endorsed 'Arafat's Geneva speech (but not the press conference statement), and denounced terrorism.

Most interest in the Arab world centered on the various personnel and organizational changes instituted by the congress. It appeared that there was a division between the supporters of Qaddumi, who pursued a hard line, and those of the pragmatist 'Arafat. In the organizational sphere, 'Arafat and his supporters acceded to demands to expand the 15-member Central Committee to 21 members (18 were elected at the congress and three were to be chosen later by the committee) and the 80-member Revolutionary Council to 108 in order to pave the way for greater participation. As long as 'Arafat kept a majority of supporters in these bodies, their expansion was purely procedural (similar steps were taken at the 1980 General Congress; see MECS 1979–80, p. 237). The congress also mandated the formation of a Political Bureau (maktab siyasi) which would be chosen from among the members of the Central Committee, where 'Arafat had the upper hand. The congress also mandated the eventual formation of a General Council of the Movement (al-majlis al-'amm lil-haraka), apparently to introduce more al-'Asifa activists into leadership positions. In order to have his Fath title conform to his status as president of Palestine, 'Arafat was elected to a new position, "general commander" (al-qa'id al-'amm) of the movement, and as chairman of the Central Committee, as opposed to his previous title, "commander of the revolutionary forces."

With respect to the personnel changes determined by the congress, it seems that 'Arafat was stymied in his efforts to have some of his supporters elected to positions. For example, he failed to have senior Fath operations officer Brig. Gen. ('amid) Muhammad 'Afana (Abu al-Mu'tasim) elected to the Central Committee, and was forced to take in Brig. Gen. Muhammad Jihad; his adviser Nabil Sha'th was also not elected.[119] One of 'Arafat's main opponents, PLO representative in Saudi Arabia Rafiq al-Natsha (Abu Shakir), was defeated in his attempt to have the congress reelect him to the Central Committee. He had been quite critical of 'Arafat in the past.[120] The new Central Committee was comprised as follows (the asterisk indicates newly elected members):

1. Yasir 'Arafat (Abu 'Ammar) — chairman.
2. Faruq al-Qaddumi (Abu al-Lutf) — secretary.
3. Salah Khalaf (Abu Iyad) — unified security.
4. Khalid al-Hasan (Abu al-Sa'id) — information.
5. Intisar al-Wazir* (Umm Jihad) — social affairs.
6. Sakhr Habash* (Abu Nizar) — ideological mobilization.
7. Hayil 'Abd al-Hamid (Abu al-Hawl) — head, western sector.
8. Muhammad Ghunaym (Abu Mahir) — organization.
9. Hani al-Hasan — foreign affairs.
10. Subhi Abu Karsh* (Abu Mundhir) — member, western sector committee.
11. Hakam Bal'awi* — second deputy secretary and deputy to the official in charge of unified security.
12. Al-Tayyib 'Abd al-Rahim* — political commissioning (*al-tafwid al-siyasi*).
13. Mahmud 'Abbas (Abu Mazin) — international and Arab relations, first deputy secretary.
14. Ahmad Quray'* (Abu 'Ala) — finance.
15. Col. Nasr Yusuf* — member, al-'Asifa forces command.
16. Brig. Gen. Muhammad Jihad* — member, Intifada committee, and al-'Asifa forces command.
17. Salim al-Za'nun (Abu al-Adib) — popular organizations.
18. 'Abbas Zaki* — secretary to the Intifada Committee.[121]

Fifty members of the Revolutionary Council were elected by the congress (of particular note was Akram Haniyya, deported editor of the East Jerusalem paper, *al-Sha'b*); 25 were to be appointed later from among the military personnel, 12 would be chosen from "qualified cadres," and 21 were members of the Central Committee. Among those appointed at a later stage were PLO spokesman Ahmad 'Abd al-Rahman, PLO representative in Moscow, Nabil 'Amr, and Nabil Sha'th.[122]

By the end of the year, there were no indications that the Political Bureau or the General Council of the Movement had been constituted. This was typical of 'Arafat, who had also ignored the decisions of the 1987 PNC which had called for the formation of similar bodies in the PLO (see *MECS* 1987, p. 210).

FATH AND THE ARMED STRUGGLE

More than any other PLO constituent organization, Fath realized the importance of the uprising to the standing of the Palestinian issue and the PLO. It believed strongly that all PLO efforts should be concentrated in that arena, and therefore gave orders to stop Fath infiltrations from Lebanon. If carried out, Fath believed they would hurt the PLO's diplomatic offensive *vis-à-vis* the US. But the several attempted terrorist infiltrations from Lebanon in the first quarter of the year by other PLO organizations (see chapter on armed operations) were not condemned by Fath; in fact, Fath defended the operations because they believed them to be legitimate armed attacks against the enemy.[123] Salah Khalaf stated Fath's case clearly: "We understand the abandoning of terrorism as relating to the stopping of operations outside of our occupied lands in which innocent civilians are killed. Any Palestinian who declares the abandoning of terrorism means these types of operation only, and not the armed struggle. We reject the identification the US makes between the armed struggle and terrorism."[124] On another occasion he elaborated: "We in Fath and the PLO never gave up the *fida'i* operations. However, we should choose the proper time for these operations to serve the PLO's political proposals. We do not call for fighting for the sake of fighting. We call for operations that have weight and meaning. At present, we believe that the continuation and support of the Intifada is better...."[125] In any case, the US had made a tactical decision not to belabor the terrorism issue if Fath itself was not involved, largely because 'Arafat was not capable of ordering them to stop. This arrangement suited the Fath leadership well.

Fath had suspended armed operations from Lebanon only; Israeli security sources cited several instances during the year when Fath was involved in armed attacks and organized cells in order to carry out operations from within Israel and the territories. In late July these sources identified 71 such operations, all carried out since 'Arafat had "renounced" terrorism in December 1988; 11 of these operations took place in Israel proper, and the rest in the territories. The sources also showed the foreign press a series of letters from Fath officials overseas to a cell based in the Gaza Strip, in which the officials asked the cell to claim credit for their operations as the "Revolutionary Eagles" in order "not to cause the organization responsibility in this period, because there is negotiation with the US on the political level."[126] Although Israel certainly had a motive to show Fath involvement, Fath itself was anxious to prove to the other constituent organizations that it still supported the armed struggle, just as the latter had carried out the attacks from Lebanon to prove to 'Arafat that he could not control them.

Fath's desire to show its fellow PLO constituent organizations that it was still committed to the armed struggle, but in the context of the uprising, seemed to be behind Fath's announced creation of a "Palestinian Popular Army" in the territories at the beginning of the year (see chapter on the West Bank and the Gaza Strip). Originally, this body was announced as an arm of Force 17, a Fath military operations unit close to 'Arafat. Protests by other factions, that Fath was trying to appropriate the uprising, led to retractions by Fath which stressed that the army was under the control of the UNC.[127]

THE PALESTINIANS IN LEBANON

After the fighting had ended in 1988 between Amal and 'Arafat's Fath, leading to the signing of an agreement between the feuding parties (which was in essence designed to make common cause against Hizballah), most of the Fath armed cadres were evacuated to the Sidon and Tyre areas, their Beirut strongholds being totally wiped out[128] (see *MECS* 1988, p. 257, and chapter on Lebanon). This move, along with the traditional Syrian-supported opposition to 'Arafat, was responsible for the series of assassinations and assassination attempts that plagued Fath in Southern Lebanon during the year, mostly in October. Fath was opposed by the rebels of Abu Musa, al-Sa'iqa, Sabri al-Banna's (Abu Nidal) Fath-Revolutionary Council (FRC), and Ahmad Jibril's Popular Front for the Liberation of Palestine-General Command (PFLP-GC). Fath officials in November stated that 10 of their leaders had been assassinated during the year. Several FRC members were also assassinated.[129]

In May, two senior Fath officials were shot: 'Isam al-Salim ('Isam al-Lawh),

'Arafat's personal representative in Lebanon, was critically wounded; Bassam Hawrani, a deputy battalion commander in Fath, was killed. An attempt was also made on the life of the senior Fath official in Lebanon, Zayd Wahba. A pro-Syrian magazine attributed the fighting to struggles within Fath-'Arafat over control of Fath in Lebanon. In fact, there had been some dissatisfaction and protests in the ranks during the year over low salaries; it was reported in August that 'Arafat had given Fath fighters a raise in pay.[130]

An unusual incident in mid-December illustrated that 'Arafat may not have always been in control of local Fath commanders in Lebanon. On 14 December, an estimated force of 100 Fath fighters loyal to 'Arafat attacked a post held by Syria's military intelligence in al-Rumayla, seven km. north of Sidon, killing six Syrians and also three members of Mustafa Sa'd's militia. The PLO denied responsibility, but later admitted that the attack had been carried out by members of Fath without the knowledge of the Sidon Fath command. Those responsible would be punished, said Khalaf.[131] The incident did nothing to further PLO-Syrian relations, which remained cool during the year.

The agreement between the Palestinians and Amal at the end of 1988 did not change the basic animosity between the warring parties; Amal continued to try to assert its control over the south, and Fath wanted to expand its positions beyond the close vicinity of Tyre and Sidon. When Amal began to turn its efforts against Hizballah in January and again at the end of the year in the al-Tuffah region southeast of Sidon (see chapter on Lebanon), Fath used the opportunity to consolidate its position in the region at Amal's expense. During the January fighting, the PLO disingenuously offered to mediate between the sides. During the end-of-the-year fighting, Fath took the initiative and was poised to interpose itself between the warring factions; the move was a good cover for expanding Fath positions. There were also reports, denied by the PLO, that the pro-'Arafat Fath forces had stepped up coordination with Hizballah. The atmosphere between Amal and Fath thus remained tense during the year, but there were no major outbreaks of fighting.[132]

The practical cessation of hostilities with Amal during the year permitted Fath to further strengthen its logistical position in the south. According to several reports, Fath moved in large numbers of fighters and was training them. The organization was reportedly also able to smuggle in sophisticated surface-to-surface and surface-to-air missiles through the ports of al-Jiya and Sidon.[133]

The crisis between the rival Lebanese governments during the year gave the PLO other opportunities to try to strengthen its position in Lebanon. 'Arafat met with Gen. Michel 'Awn during the year. The PLO in effect recognized his government, standing with it against the mutual Syrian enemy; logistical support may have even been extended to 'Awn.[134] In April, the PLO again tried to exploit the tense Lebanese situation, offering to send 4,000–5,000 armed men to monitor a cease-fire between the warring governments.[135]

DEVELOPMENTS IN THE PALESTINE LIBERATION FRONT AND FATH-REVOLUTIONARY COUNCIL (ABU NIDAL)

The PLF continued its attempts during the year to restore unity between its two factions (for previous developments in the PLF, see *MECS* 1988, p. 259). Unity agreements were announced in April and November, but by the end of the year it remained to be seen if they would be carried out.[136]

The FRC underwent a bloody split in 1989. While details were scarce, it appears that three high officials in the organization, 'Atif Abu Bakr, 'Abd al-Rahman 'Isa, and Mustafa Murad (Haj Abu Mustafa), the organization's second-in-command, developed personal and political differences with Sabri al-Banna. They advocated a policy of reintegration into the PLO and the halting of operations overseas.[137]

In early September in Beirut, the FRC announced the "execution" of 15 Palestinians on charges of "espionage."[138] A month later, 'Isa and Abu Bakr announced the formation of an "emergency command" in order to "rehabilitate the organization." The two also declared their loyalty to the PLO (it will be recalled that the FRC attempted prior to the 1987 PNC to enter the PLO; see *MECS* 1987, p. 208), and accused Banna of killing 156 FRC members in Libya in October, including Mustafa Murad. They said that the dead were buried in the foundations of Banna's office; Banna killed 20 of them himself, they claimed.[139] The announcement came from Tunis, so that the participation of Fath in the exercise cannot be ruled out, particularly given the fighting between the organizations in Lebanon.

There were reports during the year that Libya, as part of its efforts at *rapprochement* with Egypt and the rest of the Arab world (see chapter on Libya), had limited the activities of Banna, and may have even put him under house arrest; it was also reported that Banna was seriously ill. In the early part of the year, the FRC held a congress in Iran; this, together with the growing alienation from Libya, may have indicated that al-Banna was planning to set up shop in Tehran. According to Israeli sources, the first operation carried out by the FRC on behalf of Iran was the killing of the Belgian Jewish leader, Joseph Wybran, in early October, apparently in retaliation for Israel's apprehending of Hizballah leader 'Abd al-Karim 'Ubayd[140] (for both, see chapter on armed operations).

The *rapprochement* in the Arab world also had its effect on the moribund Palestine National Salvation Front (PNSF), which continued to limp along during the year. Syria, apparently, was interested in having the PNSF rejoin the PLO. Moreover, Libya urged the PNSF to open up to some of the factions in the PLO, such as the DFLP and PFLP, and to adopt more moderate stands. The PNSF leaders, on the other hand, were interested in restoring Libyan aid, which had been suspended at the beginning of 1988.[141]

APPENDIX I: COUNTRIES RECOGNIZING THE "STATE OF PALESTINE"[142]

1. Afghanistan	22. Djibouti	43. Maldives	64. Senegal
2. Albania	23. Egypt	44. Mali	65. Seychelles
3. Algeria	24. Ethiopia	45. Malta	66. Sierra Leone
4. Angola	25. Gabon (Embassy)	46. Mauritania	67. Somalia
5. Bahrain	26. Gambia	47. Mauritius	68. Soviet Union
6. Bangladesh	27. GDR	48. Mongolia	69. Sri Lanka
7. Benin	28. Ghana	49. Morocco	70. Sudan
8. Botswana	29. Guinea	50. Mozambique	71. Tanzania
9. Brunei	30. Guinea Bissau	51. Namibia	72. Togo
10. Burkina Faso	31. Hungary	52. Nepal	73. Tunisia
11. Bulgaria	32. India	53. Nicaragua	74. Turkey
12. Burundi	33. Indonesia	54. Niger	75. United Arab Emirates
13. Cambodia	34. Iraq	55. Nigeria	76. Uganda
14. Cameroon	35. Jordan	56. Oman	77. Vanuatu
15. Cape Verde	36. North Korea	57. Pakistan	78. Vietnam
16. Chad	37. Kuwait	58. Philippines	79. North Yemen
17. China	38. Laos	59. Qatar	80. South Yemen
18. The Comoros	39. Lebanon ('Awn)	60. Romania	81. Yugoslavia
19. Congo	40. Libya	61. Rwanda	82. Zaire
20. Cuba	41. Madagascar	62. São Tomé e Príncipe	83. Zambia
21. Cyprus	42. Malaysia	63. Saudi Arabia	84. Zimbabwe

APPENDIX II: POLITICAL PROGRAM OF THE FIFTH GENERAL CONGRESS OF FATH, TUNIS, 8 AUGUST 1989[143]

Palestine is a part of the Arab homeland. The Palestinian people are an indivisible part of the Arab nation. The Palestinian people have been living in their homeland, Palestine, from time immemorial. They have enriched human civilization in all spheres. They have always been a people defending their holy land. They held out in the face of the invasions of the Europeans [al-Faranja] and Tartars and have forged epics, along with their nation, in the battles of Hittin and 'Ayn Jalut. Since the dawn of Islam and up to the present, the Palestinian people have been the heart of the Arab and Islamic nation protecting the first Qibla and the third holiest shrine and safeguarding the sanctuary represented by the destination of Prophet Muhammad's nocturnal journey and the cradle of Christ; may God's peace and blessings be upon them.

The Zionist conquest came at the beginning of this century to uproot the Palestinian people, end their civilization, and implant a Zionist entity designed to carry out the imperialist schemes that seek to control the Arab homeland's resources and make this homeland a part of the colonialist's spheres of influence.

The Palestinian people have held out in the face of this Zionist-colonialist barbarism. The convoys of martyrs continued. Over the past 30 years, the Palestinian people have offered hundreds of thousands of martyrs, wounded, and prisoners. The crime was consummated by the partition of Palestine and the establishment of the Zionist entity state in 1948.

Most of the Palestinian people were scattered outside their homeland and forced to live in exile in the diaspora. However, these people have continued to believe in their civilizing and militant role, and thus they were builders of civilization wherever they live.

Under hard and extremely difficult circumstances, the Palestinian National Liberation Movement-Fath launched the armed revolution on 1 January 1965. Then, the Palestinian people poured into the river of the revolution. The challenges, massacres, and victories resulted in heroic epics that captured the attention of the world.

In the Karama epic in 1968, the 1970–71 massacres in Jordan, and the epic of steadfastness in Southern Lebanon and Beirut in 1982, the great Palestinian people have shown a unique ability to resist to safeguard their identity and their independent Palestinian national decision-making. This has led to large-scale international support by world states and various political organizations.

Then came the conspiracies hatched by the Syrian regime and carried out by its agent tools, including the dissension conspiracy, the double siege of Tripoli, and the war of siege and elimination against the sons of our people in the camps. The conspiracy sought to contain the Palestinian revolution and to end its effective role within the equation of the conflict.

However, the steadfastness of our people in the camps of steadfastness and the valor demonstrated by the combatants of the Fath Movement have foiled the schemes hatched by the conspirators. Our movement, Fath, has faced up to the challenge and managed to safeguard our national unity and the independent Palestinian national decision-making. This was demonstrated through its ability to hold consecutive Palestine National Council [PNC] sessions, thus deepening national unity, bolstering its cohesion, and paving the groundwork for the launching of the blessed Palestinian Intifada which was launched on 8 November 1987 and which has continued to escalate for more than 20 months. The Intifada has driven a deep crack in the barbarous Zionist entity, strongly attracted the world's attention to the justice of our cause, and imposed a new political reality that has had a great impact on all Palestinian, Arab, and international levels.

Thus, the Intifada has added and continues to add shining chapters to the record of the struggle of the Palestinian people and the Arab nation. The PLO has crowned the Intifada with a great political achievement that matches the greatness and sacrifices of our people. The 19th PNC session — the Abu Jihad [Khalil al-Wazir] session — issued resolutions that were received with satisfaction by the world states. At this session, we presented to our people the document of independence and the proclamation of the State of Palestine, which has been recognized by over 100 states.

Now, after these huge challenges and great achievements, we convene the fifth general congress of our Fath Movement with more resolve and determination to continue the struggle with all possible means — political and military — to liberate our homeland and establish our state, the independent State of Palestine with holy Jerusalem as its capital.

It has now become clear to all that the Palestinian people are a fact that cannot be ignored and that no peace, stability, or security in the Middle East can be achieved without recognizing this people's right to self-determination and national independence. Therefore, while paying tribute to our movement's achievements since its establishment on 1 January 1965, culminating in the proclamation of Palestinian independence and the establishment of the independent state of Palestine at the 19th emergency PNC session, the fifth general congress of Fath Movement specifies our future objectives as follows:

First: On the Palestinian Level:

1. The Palestine question is the core of the Arab-Zionist conflict.

2. Firm adherence to Palestinian Arab national inalienable rights in their homeland Palestine, including their right to repatriation, self-determination without foreign interference, and the establishment of their independent state with holy Jerusalem as its capital.

3. Asserting the unity of our Palestinian Arab people inside and outside Palestine and rallying around the PLO, the leader of their struggle and their sole, legitimate representative.

4. The fifth Fath general congress affirms the historic importance of the resolutions of the 19th PNC session, particularly the document of independence. The congress supports the establishment of the independent State of Palestine and extends thanks to the Arab and friendly states that have recognized it. The congress authorizes the movement's Central Committee to work on all levels to implement the resolutions of establishing the Palestinian people's national inalienable rights, headed by the right to repatriation, self-determination, and the establishment of the State of Palestine on Palestinian soil with holy Jerusalem as its capital.

5. Continuing to intensify and escalate armed action [al-'amal al-musalleh] and all forms of struggle to liquidate [tasfiyya] the Israeli-Zionist occupation of our occupied Palestinian land and guaranteeing our people's right to freedom and independence.

6. Bolstering national Palestinian unity on the various political and military levels, reiterating the PLO's leading role, and escalating the popular Intifada aimed at ending the Zionist Israeli occupation.

7. Reiterating that the PLO is the sole, legitimate representative of our Arab Palestinian people wherever they are; the leader of their national resistance; their spokesman in Arab and international forums; and that it will resist all attempts to encroach on it, bypass it, surround it, or create alternatives or partners in representing the Palestinian people.

8. Rejecting and resisting the autonomy plan and the other liquidation plans aimed at entrenching the colonialist Zionist occupation.

9. The Fath fifth congress rejects the Shamir plan on elections and affirms that any election in our occupied territory must take place in a free and democratic atmosphere under international supervision after the withdrawal of the Israeli forces, and that elections must be a link in an integrated plan for the final solution.

10. Taking into consideration the important achievements in the Palestinian arena as a result of our people's continuous struggle and their blessed Intifada as well as the new situations and facts created by the Intifada in the Arab and international arenas, the Fath general congress stresses the PLO's right to participate — independently and on an equal footing with the other parties — in all the international conferences and efforts on the Palestine question and the Arab-Zionist conflict.

11. Providing all forms of support to reinforce the steadfastness of our masses in Lebanon's camps to stand in the face of the Israeli aggression and all its schemes aimed at scattering and displacing them and to consolidate the right of the sons of these camps to defend their presence, security, and natural right to join the people's militant march under the PLO.

12. Continuing the dialogue with the Israeli democratic forces that reject occupation; understand our people's inalienable rights, including their right to repatriation, self-determination, and establishment of the independent state of Palestine; and recognize the PLO as the sole, legitimate representative of the Palestinian people.

13. In light of the significant effect of the demographic factor on our conflict with the Zionist enemy, and in light of the huge efforts exerted by the Zionist movement to encourage Zionist immigration to Palestinian territory, the congress has decided to set up an ad hoc committee within the Revolutionary Council to oppose the Zionist immigration to our homeland and to assume all cultural, information, and political tasks to prevent the arrival of Jewish immigrants in our occupied homeland.

Second: On the Arab Level:

1. The fifth general congress of the Fath Movement salutes the solidarity of the Arab masses with our Palestinian revolution and the blessed Intifada of our people and calls on them to embody this solidarity within in practical ways on the pan-Arab level.

2. The congress appreciates the resolutions of the Arab summits on the issue of the Intifada and those that support it, particularly the Algiers and Casablanca summits. The Fath congress calls on the Arab countries to abide by and implement all the resolutions and honor their financial commitments.

3. Promoting relations with all national and democratic parties, movements, and forces in the Arab homeland and working toward providing popular backing and support for the Intifada and the PLO. The congress also recommends the formation of support committees for the Intifada on the pan-Arab level.

4. Respecting the right of the Palestinian revolution to perform its militant tasks through any Arab land and mobilizing the Palestinian masses in a manner that serves our people's struggle for freedom, independence, and repatriation.

5. Our relationship with any Arab regime will be defined in light of its stand toward the Palestinian people's struggle, its noninterference in the internal affairs of the revolution, its respect of our national independent Palestinian decision-making, and its adherence to the resolutions of the Arab summits on the Palestine question.

6. Calling on the Arab countries, especially those on the confrontation lines, to unify their forces and mobilize their masses in order to confront the Israeli aggression.

7. Working toward protecting and looking after our people and their affairs wherever they live; adhering to their rights of residence, travel, work, education, good health, and security in accordance with the Arab League resolutions and world declaration of human rights; and guaranteeing the freedom of political activity as an embodiment of the fraternal Arab bonds and pan-Arab affiliation.

8. The fifth general congress of the Fath Movement expresses its pride in, and appreciation of, the fraternal Lebanese people and affirms the importance of the militant and brotherly relations between the Lebanese and Palestinian peoples in order to continue the confrontation of the Zionist invasion for the sake of liberating the Lebanese and Palestinian territory from the Zionist Israeli occupation. The congress affirms that the Palestinian revolution shall remain a support for the Lebanese people in their struggle to achieve their national unity, preserve their independence and territorial sovereignty, and remove the Israeli occupation from their territory.

9. Stressing the special and distinguished relations linking the fraternal Palestinian and Jordanian peoples, and working toward developing them in harmony with the national interests of the two fraternal peoples. Any future relationship with Jordan must be based on a confederation between the states of Jordan and Palestine.

Third: On the International Level:

1. Adhering to an effective international conference with full powers for peace in the Middle East, which must be convened on the basis of international legitimacy under UN supervision and patronage, and with the participation of five permanent members of the Security Council and the concerned parties, including the PLO on an equal footing and with equal rights as the other sides.

2. The fifth general congress of the Fath Movement stresses its adherence to the UN principles, charter, and resolutions which emphasized the Palestinian people's national inalienable rights and the right of all oppressed peoples under occupation to use all forms of struggle for their liberation and national independence. The congress also emphasizes its strong condemnation of all terrorist Israeli practices, which violate the principles of international law, the Geneva conventions and their appendices of 1949, the world declaration on human rights, and the UN Charter and resolutions.

3. The congress calls on the United States to recognize the Palestinian people's right to self-determination and the establishment of their independent state; to abandon the policy of bias in favor of Israel; and to end its unlimited assistance to it as this would consecrate the Zionist Israeli occupation of our Palestinian territory and increase its violation of our Palestinian people's rights.

The congress calls on the United States to agree to holding an international conference for peace in the Middle East as soon as possible in accordance with the resolutions approved at the United Nations. The congress also calls on the United States to cancel all laws and legislation passed by the US Congress against the PLO so that its dialogue with us will lead to positive results.

4. The congress commends the positions of support adopted by the Islamic Conference Organization, the OAU, and the Nonaligned Movement member states for the struggle of our Palestinian people under the leadership of the PLO. The congress also greets the friendly countries which hastened to recognize the State of Palestine and to establish diplomatic relations with it.

5. The congress also praises the friendly relations between the PLO and the socialist countries and emphasizes the constructive stand taken by these states, headed by the USSR and the PRC, in support of our people's just struggle and our inalienable national rights to repatriation, self-determination, and the establishment of our independent state on our national soil under the leadership of the PLO, the sole, legitimate representative of our Palestinian people.

6. The prominent change in the public opinion of West Europe, Japan, Canada, and Australia in favor of our Palestinian people's inalienable national rights and their just and legitimate struggle, which has developed as a result of the blessed Intifada and the impact of the PLO's political and diplomatic activity, has created favorable circumstances for these states to step up their support for the cause of Palestine. This was embodied in the invitation extended to brother Yasir 'Arafat, president of the State of Palestine, to visit France; in the Warsaw Pact statement in Bucharest; in the EEC states' declaration in Madrid; and in the upgrading of relations with the PLO in these states. The fifth general congress of the Fath Movement highly values these steps and calls on these states to promote these positive stands to the level of recognizing the State of Palestine.

7. The congress voices its support and backing of liberation movements in Africa, Asia, and Latin America, particularly the Namibian people's struggle under the leadership of Swapo [South-West African People's Organization] and the South African people's struggle against the racist regime in Pretoria.

APPENDIX III: FINAL POLITICAL STATEMENT OF THE FIFTH GENERAL CONGRESS OF FATH, TUNIS, 11 AUGUST 1989[144]

In the name of God, the merciful, the compassionate. At a stage that is one of the most delicate stages of our Palestinian people's national struggle for liberation, and at the climax of confrontation between the masses of our Palestinian people and the Israeli occupation forces — which used all its tools and powers in an attempt to liquidate our national cause, strike the PLO, the sole and legitimate representative of the Palestinian people, and confiscate their inalienable rights — and in light of the popular Intifada, which has entrenched its position in the conscience of the world and the calculations of international powers as a battle for national independence that is led by all our people along with the legendary steadfastness of our masses in the Palestinian camps in defense of their national cause and existence — under all these circumstances, the fifth congress of the Fath Movement was held in Tunis from 2–9 August under the patronage of Tunisian President Zayn al-'Abidin Ben 'Ali and with the warm fraternal embrace of the fraternal Tunisian Government and people.

The meetings of the fifth congress of the Fath Movement were permeated by a democratic atmosphere, a national and organizational responsibility, and responsible and comprehensive discussion of all the problems and issues of the Palestinian people related to their national cause.

The committees of the fifth congress have studied and analyzed these problems and searched for the best solutions to them. In light of this, the congress has adopted important resolutions on all the issues and developments, foremost of which are the blessed popular Intifada, the means to bolster and escalate it, and political and organizational issues.

From the position of pride and glory, the congress discussed in detail the valiant popular Intifada of our great people, its steadfast heroes and wounded, and its righteous martyrs, affirming that the Intifada has built the wall of steadfastness and determination, constituted a turning point in the course of conflict with the Israeli occupation, and secured the possibility for the Palestinian people to achieve what they could not achieve since the 1947 partition resolution — namely, the establishment of their independent state and the protection of its national fate from loss. The congress has made all the necessary decisions in order to provide all the means required to escalate and guarantee the continuation of the Intifada.

The congress, inspired by the principles of the Fath Movement and its history of struggle, has proceeded from the principle that the change will eventually be decided by the organized popular movement, which has a clear program, especially as through their blessed Intifada; our Palestinian people have entrenched their existence in the homeland in confronting the most serious Zionist conspiracy to liquidate their presence. Based on this, the congress has unanimously adopted a political program that has clearly defined the political stand of our movement on the national, pan-Arab, and international levels.

On the national level, the congress has debated at length the methods necessary to consolidate Palestinian national unity. It stressed the unity of our Palestinian people inside and outside Palestine, in exile, the diaspora, and the steadfast camps. The congress has greeted their firm rallying around the PLO, the leader of their struggle and their sole and legitimate representative, and their adherence to their inalienable national rights to self-determination, repatriation, and the exercise of their sovereignty in their independent Palestinian state with Jerusalem as its capital.

The fifth general congress of the Fath Movement also underlined the historical importance of the resolutions of the Palestine National Council [PNC] at its 19th session, particularly the document concerning the declaration of independence. It has also authorized the Fath Central Committee to work on all levels to implement these resolutions based on achieving the Palestinian people's inalienable national rights, foremost of which is their right to self-determination, repatriation, and the establishment of the independent Palestinian state on Palestinian territory.

The congress voiced its commitment to the Palestinian peace initiative approved by the PNC at its 19th session in Algiers and which was declared by brother President Abu 'Ammar [Yasir 'Arafat] before a UN meeting in Geneva. The congress meanwhile rejects all autonomy plans, substitute homeland, and other liquidatory schemes to consolidate the occupation, such as Shamir's plan. The congress regards elections as normal if carried out within the framework of an integrated and cohesive program for a comprehensive and final solution. The elections should take place in a free and democratic atmosphere, under international supervision, and after the withdrawal of the Israeli forces.

While the congress pledged adherence to the principles of international legitimacy, which grant our people the right to exercise all forms of struggle, including armed struggle, to confront the hateful Israeli occupation of the Palestinian homeland, it denounced all forms of terrorism, particularly state terrorism. The congress stressed the need to continue to work tirelessly for a just and lasting peace based on our people's inalienable national rights within the framework of an international conference to be attended by the UN Security Council permanent member states as well as all the concerned parties, including the PLO, on an equal footing with the other parties.

The congress underlined the need to continue the dialogue with the Israeli democratic forces within the framework of the constants endorsed by our PNC sessions.

The congress hailed our steadfast people in our camps in Lebanon, stressing their effective role in safeguarding the independent national Palestinian decision-making. The congress decided to secure all forms of support to preserve them and foil the plans to disperse them.

On the pan-Arab level, the congress emphasized the need for constant work to achieve Arab solidarity as part of the overall efforts and pan-Arab resources to support the Palestine question and Intifada and attain all the major pan-Arab goals. This requires the intensification of relations with the Arab masses, the ones who have the real interest in achieving victory and the Palestinian people's national objectives.

The congress voiced its solidarity with Lebanon and stressed the need to exert all possible efforts to save it from its ordeal and to safeguard its sovereignty, Arabism, and territorial integrity.

The congress reviewed the developments that led to the cessation of the Iraq-Iran War, emphasizing the need to establish a lasting peace between the two countries. The congress praised the efforts and sacrifices that the Iraqi people and Army made to defend the Arab nation's eastern gate.

On the international level, the congress expressed appreciation for the relations of fraternity and friendship with the Islamic, African, and nonaligned states, and with the socialist states, the USSR and PRC in particular.

The congress praised with high appreciation the positive and outstanding change in the stands of the West European states, Japan, Canada, and Australia in favor of the Palestinian people's inalienable national rights manifested in the invitation extended to brother Abu 'Ammar to visit France and in the EEC statement in Madrid. The congress praised the Warsaw Pact statement that embodied the member states' commitment to the Palestinian goals and aspirations.

The congress debated at length the issue of the Palestinian-US dialogue which began several months ago and expressed surprise at the very slow progress of this dialogue and at the absence of political comprehensiveness and practical rules of this dialogue, which prompted the congress to demand that the US Administration recognize clearly the Palestinian people's right to exercise their right to self-determination and establish their independent state, with Jerusalem its capital, and adopt an advanced practical stand to preserve Palestinian human rights, noting that a US human rights committee highlighted the magnitude of the Israeli occupation authorities' violation of the Palestinian people's rights.

The congress decided to request the US Administration to abandon its biased policy in favor of Israel and adopt a neutral stand enabling it to play its role. The congress pointed out that partiality cannot serve the peace process in the required practical way and that had it not been for US political, economic, financial, and military support, the continued Israeli occupation and fierce violation of Palestinian human rights, as well as the Israeli authorities' confrontation of our heroic people's Intifada and the child stone-throwers with bullets and daily killing — all this would not have been possible.

Regarding organizational issues, the organizational issue took a lengthy part of the congress's work. This is because consolidating the internal situation of any revolutionary movement, such as the Fath Movement, and the confrontation of some negative phenomena that have accumulated throughout the past 10 years of our movement's life on the domestic and foreign levels is considered a vital and basic matter on the road of preparing to develop the best means to wage political and military confrontation. In this regard, the congress has adopted several resolutions and introduced wide amendments to its bylaws. In an atmosphere saturated with appreciation, the congress has elected brother Abu 'Ammar as commander in chief of the Fath Movement. The congress has decided to increase the number of members of the Fath Central Committee and Revolutionary Council to secure a wider participation of the leadership. The Central Committee will choose a political bureau from among its members. In this respect, the congress has decided to charge the Central Committee and the Revolutionary Council with choosing a number of our struggling leaders inside the occupied territories to posts in their command organizations.

Based on the view that it is important that the cadres should participate in all political and organizational developments, it has been decided to establish the movement's general council as a new framework embracing cadres who represent the various active frameworks to adopt the necessary decisions when necessary.

The fifth general congress of the Fath Movement addresses greetings of appreciation and gratitude to fraternal Tunisia — president, government, and people — for its principled stands and for hosting the Palestinian leadership's presence on its soil. The congress expresses profound appreciation for the efforts Tunisian President Zayn al-'Abidin Ben 'Ali is exerting in the service of the Palestine question and for his decision to host the fifth congress of our movement in Tunisia and among its generous people.

The congress recalls with reverence and admiration all the hero martyrs, the latest of whom was the prince and symbol of martyrs Abu Jihad [Khalil al-Wazir], who sacrificed their lives.

The congress pledged to the heroes of the great and blessed Intifada; the steadfast heroes in the lofty Palestinian camps, villages, and cities; the captives and prisoners in the detention camps; the masses of the Arab and Islamic nations; and the free and honest men in the world that the flag of struggle will continue to flutter regardless of challenges, that the march will continue to advance toward its goals, and that we will not hesitate to offer sacrifices until our people regain all their national rights and the flag of Palestine flutters over holy Jerusalem, the capital of our independent state, Palestine, the place and the land of Prophet Muhammad's midnight journey and Jesus Christ's cradle; may God's peace and blessings be upon them.

In the name of God, the merciful, the compassionate. Verily we have granted thee a manifest victory: that God may forgive thee thy faults of the past and those to follow; fulfill his favor to thee; and guide thee on the straight way; and that God may help thee with powerful help. [Koranic verse] Revolution until victory!

NOTES

For the place and frequency of publications cited here, and for the full name of the publication, news agency, radio station, or monitoring service where an abbreviation is used, please see "List of Sources." Only in the case of more than one publication bearing the same name is the place of publication noted here.

1. *Davar*, 22 January 1989.
2. 'Arafat to VoP (Baghdad), 23 January 1989.
3. *IHT, FT*, 30 January 1989.
4. *JP*, 31 January; VoP (Baghdad), 30 January — DR, 31 January 1989.
5. *Davar*, 27 March 1989.
6. Zayyad to VoI, 16 February — DR, 17 February 1989.
7. *ST*, 26 March 1989.
8. *Al-Qabas*, 16 March; 'Arafat, MENA, 23 February — DR, 24 February 1989.
9. See also Dore Gold, "The Bush Administration and the PLO: Where to?," Memorandum No. 27, Jaffee Center for Strategic Studies, Tel Aviv University, June 1989.
10. *Al-Yawm al-Sabi'*, 30 April; *Ha'aretz*, 23 April 1989.
11. *JP*, 24 March 1989.
12. *IHT*, 5 April 1989.
13. Interview with 'Arafat quoted on VoP (Algiers), 22 April — DR, 22 April; Salah Khalaf to R. Monte Carlo, 6 April; Yasir 'Abd Rabbuh to VoP (Algiers), 5 April — DR, 7 April

1989. Similar remarks were made by US Secretary of State James Baker in a speech in May (see chapter on the US and the ME).

14. VoP (San'a), 25 March — DR, 27 March 1989.
15. VoP (San'a) 10 April — DR, 11 April; VoP (Baghdad), 8 April—SWB, 10 April 1989.
16. *JP*, 14 April 1989.
17. Kuttab to *FT*, 16 May 1989.
18. VoP (Baghdad), 21 April — DR, 24 April; Khalaf to R. Monte Carlo, 25 April — DR, 26 April 1989.
19. Khalaf to *al-Sayyad*, 5 May; a similar response was said to have been conveyed to the US by the PLO, *al-Ra'y al-'Amm*, 10 May 1989.
20. *WP, JP*, 14 April 1989.
21. See *MEI*, 28 April 1989.
22. *Ha'aretz*, 30 April 1989.
23. *Le Monde*, 4 May; *IHT*, 24 May 1989. The formulation concerning the UN resolutions and self-determination was based on the 1988 PNC resolutions, but was a retreat from the formulation on these resolutions announced by 'Arafat at his Geneva press conference and later approved by the EC (see below).
24. VoP (Baghdad), 27 April — DR, 28 April; *JP, Ha'aretz*, 27 April; VoP (San'a), 28 April — DR, 1 May; *Ha'aretz*, 28 April 1989.
25. Previously, the dialogue had been limited to EC members Yasir 'Abd Rabbuh, and 'Abdallah Hurani, and other, lower-ranking officials.
26. On upgrading the dialogue, *Ha'aretz*, 29 June; *JP, FT, NYT*, 30 June; on Khalaf's indictment, see *JP*, 30 June, *NYT*, 2 July 1989. 'Arafat was also under investigation, but was absolved of any involvement.
27. Khalid al-Hasan to *NYT*, 28 July; 'Arafat to *al-Ahram*, quoted in *Ha'aretz*, 28 July 1989.
28. This was told by the head of the State Department Policy Planning Staff, Dennis Ross, to Israeli Minister for the Environment Ronni Milo; see *Ha'aretz*, 28 July 1989.
29. *Al-Watan*, Kuwait, cited in *Ha'aretz*, 2 October 1989.
30. *NYT*, 27, 28 July 1989.
31. VoP (Algiers), 31 July — DR, 4 August 1989.
32. *JP*, 12 September; WAFA statement cited on R. Monte Carlo, 12 September — DR, 13 September 1989.
33. VoP (Baghdad), 14 October; 'Abd Rabbuh to AFP, cited in *Ha'aretz*, 26 October; Faruq Qaddumi quoted by GNA, 17 October — DR, 18 October; Khalid al-Hasan to *al-Anba*, 31 October 1989.
34. CC statement, VoP (Baghdad), 17 October 1989.
35. Hawatima to *al-Watan*, Kuwait, 18 October 1989.
36. *Ha'aretz*, 26 October 1989.
37. R. al-Quds, 4 November — DR, 6 November 1989.
38. *JP, Ha'aretz*, 7 November 1989.
39. 'Abd Rabbuh, quoted by KUNA, 17 November — DR, 17 November 1989.
40. Khalid al-Hasan to R. Monte Carlo, 19 November — DR, 20 November 1989.
41. *Al-Ra'y*, 3 December 1989.
42. Khalaf to R. Monte Carlo, 5 December — DR, 5 December 1989.
43. R. Monte Carlo, 8 December — DR, 8 December 1989.
44. Habash to R. al-Quds, 13 December — DR, 13 December 1989.
45. *Yedi'ot Aharonot*, 10 December 1989.
46. 'Arafat to R. Monte Carlo, 9 December — DR, 10 December; Khalaf, KUNA, 15 December — DR, 15 December; EC member 'Abdallah Hurani to *JT*, 23 December 1989.
47. EC statement, VoP (Baghdad), 19 December — DR, 20 December 1989.
48. Sha'th to *al-Majalla*, 12 December 1989.
49. *Filastin al-Thawra*, quoted on VoP (Baghdad), 29 July — DR, 1 August 1989.
50. *Filastin al-Thawra*, 7 May 1989.
51. Ibid., 19 February 1989.
52. *San Francisco Chronicle*, 2 February 1990.
53. *JP*, 23 January; MENA, 24 January — DR, 24 January 1989.
54. *Davar, Ma'ariv*, 24 January; AFP, 25 January — DR, 26 January 1989.

55. Redman in *Ma'ariv*, 24 January; Baker in *IHT*, 13 February 1989.
56. VoP (San'a), 25 January — DR, 27 January; 'Abd Rabbuh, quoted by AFP, 28 February — DR, 1 March 1989.
57. Khalaf, quoted by *JP*, 16 March 1989.
58. Walker's testimony (English translated from the Hebrew), *Ha'aretz*, 2 March 1989.
59. *Filastin al-Thawra*, quoted on VoP (Baghdad), 29 July — DR, 1 August; VoP (Algiers), 21 August — DR, 21 August; Khalid al-Hasan to *al-Anba*, 31 October 1989.
60. *Ha'aretz*, 18 May 1989.
61. VoP (Baghdad), 1 April, MENA, 2 April — DR, 3 April 1989.
62. *Ha'aretz*, 2 May 1989.
63. *Ma'ariv*, 27 January; *NYT*, 28 January 1989.
64. *Ha'aretz*, 10 January; *Ma'ariv*, 30 January; *FT,* 14, 31 July 1989.
65. *JP*, 13 January 1989.
66. *NYT*, 1, 7, 28 December; *JP*, 7, 28 December 1989.
67. Also included were the International Federation of Dentistry and the World Tourism Organization. The PLO attempted to gain admission to 10 sport federations and the International Olympic Committee, and the Swiss Government decided not to act on a PLO request to become a signatory of the Geneva Conventions. The State of Palestine was accepted as a full member state in the Nonaligned Movement, and the UN Food and Agriculture Organization voted to assist agricultural development in the territories "in close cooperation with the PLO" (*Ha'aretz*, 15, 17 May; *JP*, 30 August, 14 September; *al-Anba*, 23 January; R. Baghdad, 18 May; *NYT*, 20, 30 November 1989).
68. *NYT*, 13 May; *Ha'aretz*, 12 October 1989. The PLO's case in the WHO was further undermined by its use of its emblem — a map of Israel, the West Bank, and Gaza — in its application. Applying as the "State of Palestine," the implication was that its territory included that of a current member state (see *WP*, in WF, 1 May 1989).
69. 'Arafat, quoted by GNA, 6 January — DR, 6 January 1989.
70. 'Arafat to *al-Yawm al-Sabi'*, broadcast on VoP (Baghdad), 4 January — DR, 6 January 1989. See also 'Arafat's message to the UN Palestine Commission, VoP (San'a), 29 November — DR, 30 November 1989; and Abu Sharif's proposal, in which he called for an international peace conference "convened on the basis of UN Resolutions 242 and 338 and the Palestinians' right to self-determination" (*IHT*, 24 May 1989).
71. Al-Sa'ih to *al-Sharq al-Awsat*, 13 January; and to *al-Tadamun*, 23 January 1989.
72. *'Uman*, 26 January — DR, 17 February 1989.
73. *Filastin al-Thawra*, 26 March 1989.
74. *Al-Anba*, 3 January; GNA, 25 January — DR, 27 January 1989.
75. On Salah al-Din, see Amin Maalouf, *The Crusades through Arab Eyes* (New York: Schocken Books, 1984); on the treaty of al-Hudaybiyya, see Bernard Lewis, *The Arabs in History* (New York: Harper & Row, 1969), pp. 45–46; W. Montgomery Watt, *Muhammad at Medina* (Oxford: Oxford University Press, 1956), pp. 46–52; Hava Lazarus-Yafeh, *Chapters in the History of Islam* (Tel Aviv: Reshafim, 1967), pp. 71–72 (Hebrew).
76. *JP*, 12 December 1989; emphasis added. The full Arabic translation of the speech appears in *al-Siyasa*, Kuwait, 11 February 1990.
77. *Davar*, 14 March; *JP*, 17 March; *Ha'aretz*, 1 June 1989.
78. Sha'th to *al-Siyasa*, Kuwait, 29 January; see also his interview with *al-Ittihad*, Abu Dhabi, 6 February, quoted in GNA, 6 February 1989.
79. Sha'th to *NYT*, 2 May 1989.
80. *JP*, 23 February 1989.
81. Qaddumi to *al-Tadamun*, 23 January; for similar views on this issue, see Khalid al-Hasan's interview with *al-Madina*, 2 January, and *al-Musawwar*, 20 January 1989.
82. R. Monte Carlo, 2 May — DR, 3 May 1989.
83. AFP, 3 May — DR, 4 May 1989.
84. 'Arafat to R. Monte Carlo, 3 May — SWB, 5 May 1989.
85. Bal'awi, quoted by KUNA, 6 May — DR, 8 May; Khalaf to *al-Tadamun*, 29 May 1989. See also the explanation to readers in *Filastin al-Thawra*, 3 September 1989.
86. *Ha'aretz*, 24 February 1989.
87. *Al-Bayan*, Dubai, 6 August 1989.

88. *JP, Yedi'ot Aharonot*, 27 September; *JP*, 5 December; *Davar*, 28 March 1989.
89. VoP (San'a), 30 March — DR, 31 March 1989.
90. Habash to *al-Fikr al-Dimuqrati*, Summer 1989; see also Hawatima's comments along the same lines in the same issue.
91. Khalid al-Hasan to *al-Musawwar*, 20 January 1989.
92. *JP*, 19 December 1989. These new PLO moves were not the first against the immigration of Jews. In January 1973, Fath's Black September organization attempted an attack on a transit depot for Soviet Jewish immigrants at Schoenau Castle near Vienna, with the purpose of stemming the tide of Jewish immigration.
93. For reports on the internal dissent in the DFLP, see *al-Muharrir*, 11 February; *JP*, 24 February; *Le Point*, 24 March 1989.
94. 'Arafat had made this suggestion in the February issue of *Vanity Fair* (see *Israel and Palestine Political Report*, May 1979).
95. See text of Hawatima's remarks in *al-Hurriyya*, 5 March; see also R. Damascus, 24 February — DR, 27 February; R. Monte Carlo, 24 February — SWB, 28 February 1989.
96. *La Repubblica*, 12–13 March — DR, 14 March 1989. 'Arafat said: "I am prepared to take al-Sadat's road. I am prepared to go to Jerusalem. But I am not al-Sadat. I act with the full agreement of all Arab leaders."
97. *JP*, 16 March 1989.
98. *Al-Anba*, 2 March 1989.
99. *Al-Yawm al-Sabi'*, 29 March 1989.
100. VoP (Baghdad), 5 April — DR, 6 April; VoP (San'a), 6 July — DR, 7 July 1989.
101. *Al-Hadaf*, 22 January, 26 March 1989.
102. Habash to R. Monte Carlo, 3 May — DR, 4 May 1989.
103. *Al-Hadaf*, 5 March 1989.
104. *The Times*, 10 October; see also Voice of the People, 9 October — DR, 10 October 1989.
105. Al-Zibri to R. al-Quds, 4 November — DR, 6 November 1989.
106. *Al-Hadaf*, 20 August 1989.
107. 'Abbas, quoted by VoP (San'a), 13 October — DR, 16 October 1989.
108. *Al-Bayan*, Dubai, 25 July 1989.
109. Khalaf to *Akhbar al-Khalij*, 5 January; and to *al-Fikr al-Dimuqrati*, Summer 1989; *FT*, 1 February; INA, 15 January — DR, 17 January; Qaddumi to *al-Sharq al-Awsat*, 28 February; 'Arafat to *al-Majalla*, 5 April 1989.
110. *Al-Hadaf*, 5 February; *al-Fiqr al-Dimuqrati*, Summer 1989.
111. Yasir 'Abd Rabbuh supported Fath's position on the formation of the provisional government, and thus was again at odds with his superior Hawatima; see 'Abd Rabbuh to *al-Hayat*, London, 19 January 1989.
112. See, for example, the list of 'Arafat's government, published in *al-Nahar*, East Jerusalem, quoted in *Ha'aretz*, 22 January 1989. The list includes, among others, Mahmud 'Abbas; EC member and deported mayor of Halhul, Muhammad Milhim; Yasir 'Abd-Rabbuh; Khalid al-Hasan; Palestinian-American academic Edward Said; Hana Siniora; Faysal al-Husayni and Bethlehem mayor Elias Freij.
113. Hawatima to *al-Bayan*, Dubai, 17 January; *al-Anba*, 19 January; *al-Hurriyya*, 5 March 1989.
114. In the UNC, decision-making power was distributed on an equal basis among the PLO constituent organizations. In the PLO, Fath, by virtue of its greater strength, had three representatives on the EC; since almost all of the "independents" supported 'Arafat, Fath could dominate the institution.
115. For DFLP views on organizational reform, see Hawatima to *al-Anba*, 30 April, 11 July; and to *al-Fiqr al-Dimuqrati*, Summer 1989; see also *al-Hurriyya*, 21 May; *al-Fiqr al-Dimuqrati*, Winter 1989. For PFLP views, see *al-Hadaf*, 22 January, 5 November; Habash to *al-Anba*, 3 April, 21 October; and to *al-Fiqr al-Dimuqrati*, Summer 1989.
116. Al-Zibri to *al-Qabas*, 27 November; *al-Ittihad*, Abu Dhabi, 28 October 1989.
117. *Al-Ittihad*, Abu Dhabi, 28 October; Khalaf to *al-Fikr al-Dimuqrati*, Summer 1989.
118. *NYT*, 11 August 1989.
119. See *al-Siyasa*, Kuwait, 17–18 August; *al-Hawadith*, 18 August 1989.

120. *Al-Siyasa*, Kuwait, 17–18 August; see also Natsha's critical comments on Fath's announced formation of a "popular army" in the territories (*al-Watan*, Kuwait, 8 January 1989).
121. VoP (Baghdad), 9 August — DR, 10 August; *al-Anba*, 18 November; KUNA, 19 November 1989. The members of the Central Committee are listed by the number of votes cast for each, in descending order; the Western Sector is the body responsible for much of Fath's covert armed operations, and was previously headed by Khalil al-Wazir. By the end of the year, it remained unclear whether or not the three additional members of the Central Committee had been appointed. The official PLO magazine, *Filastin al-Thawra* (3 September 1989), reported that al-Natsha, 'Afana and "Hamdan" (not further identified; according to *al-Siyasa*, Kuwait, 20 September 1989, this is Mutlaq Hamdan) had been appointed, but authoritative reports continued to indicate that no appointments had been made; see, for example, *al-Yawm al-Sabi'*, 27 November 1989. In March 1990 it was reported that Nabil Sha'th had become a member of the Central Committee (see *Ha'aretz*, 27 March 1990).
122. *Filastin al-Thawra*, 3 September; *al-Ra'y*, 25 September 1989.
123. VoP (Baghdad), 9 February — DR, 10 February 1989. In typical "yes-no" fashion, 'Arafat told visiting US Congressman Wayne Owens (Democrat-Utah), that the raid carried out by the PFLP on 5 February had "upset" him, was "not his doing," and "contrary to his explicit instructions and did great harm to his cause"; *JP*, 16 February 1989.
124. *Al-Hayat*, London, 3 March 1989.
125. Khalaf to *al-Thawra*, Baghdad, 22 April 1989.
126. *Ha'aretz*, 26 July; *NYT*, 24 October 1989.
127. *Al-Ittihad*, Abu Dhabi, 7 January; UNC Call No. 32, VoP (Baghdad), 7 January — DR, 9 January; VoP (Baghdad), 21 January — DR, 24 January; *Ha'aretz*, 31 March 1989.
128. According to Israeli sources, in early November 1989 there were about 400 Fath-'Arafat men under arms in Sidon, and about 1,000 in Tyre (*Ha'aretz*, 5 November 1989). Other sources quoted higher figures, such as 2,500 (AFP, 1 January — DR, 3 January 1989) and 3,000 (*NYT*, 11 June 1989) in Sidon alone.
129. *NYT*, 11 June; *FT*, 16 November 1989.
130. *Al-Diyar*, 31 January; *al-Muharrir*, 1 April; AFP, 2 May — DR, 3 May; *JP*, 3 May; *al-Shira'*, 15 May; *al-Dunya*, 8 June 1989.
131. *NYT*, 15 December; VoP (San'a), 15 December — DR, 18 December; Khalaf to *al-Anba*, 19 December 1989.
132. VoL, 8 January — DR, 9 January; VoL, 9 February — DR, 10 February; VoL, 24 December — DR, 26 December; VoP (Algiers), 25 December — DR, 26 December; *NYT*, 31 December 1989.
133. CBS Evening News, WF, 25 January; VoL, 31 January — DR, 31 January; *Ha'aretz*, 1, 2 June 1989.
134. *Al-Sabah*, 2 February; Zayd Wahba to *al-Shira'*, 13 March; Khalaf to *al-Hayat*, London, 1–2 April 1989.
135. MENA, 20 April — DR, 21 April; 'Arafat to *al-Yawm al-Sabi'*, 1 May 1989.
136. INA, 30 April — DR, 2 May; MENA, 15 November — DR, 16 November 1989.
137. *Al-Bayadir al-Siyasi*, 6 May; *al-Nashra*, Nicosia, 24 July 1989.
138. *NYT*, 5 September 1989.
139. *Al-Nahar*, Beirut, 31 October; AFP, 2 November; *Ha'aretz*, 20 November 1989. For further details on the claims made by the dissidents against al-Banna, see *NYT*, 12 November, and *al-Yawm al-Sabi'*, 20 November 1989.
140. *NYT*, *Ha'aretz*, 28 November; *WT*, cited in WF, 29 November; *Akhbar al-Usbu'*, 30 November; *JP*, 11 December; *al-Bayadir al-Siyasi*, 16 December; R. Monte Carlo, 3 December — DR, 4 December 1989.
141. *Al-Anba*, 6 June; *al-Ittihad*, Abu Dhabi, 9 July 1989.
142. List provided by the Foreign and Commonwealth Office, London.
143. Based on the English translation, VoP (Baghdad), 9 August — DR, 10 August; Arabic text in *Shu'un Filastiniyya*, August; pp. 148–51, and *Filastin al-Thawra*, 13 August 1989.
144. Based on the English translation, VoP (San'a), 12 August — DR, 14 August; Arabic text in *Shu'un Filistiniyya*, August; *Filastin al-Thawra*, 3 September 1989.

The West Bank and the Gaza Strip

MEIR LITVAK

THE INTIFADA IN ITS SECOND YEAR: INSTITUTIONALIZATION AND INTERNAL FRICTION

The second year of the Intifada, the uprising against Israeli occupation, was characterized by several intertwined developments. Internally, it was characterized by the deepening institutionalization of the Intifada on the organizational and mass levels in the attempt to build an alternative governmental structure. The success of this effort, however, was mixed. The loose and decentralized makeup of the Intifada's leadership structure had initially been a source of strength against Israeli countermeasures. In 1989, however, it led to a certain loss of control over the strike forces, manifested primarily by growing intrafactional strife and unbridled killings of alleged collaborators with Israel. These internal differences undermined the effectiveness of the Intifada. In addition, the pro-PLO circles in the territories had to face a growing challenge from the fundamentalist Islamic forces both on the ideological and organizational levels.

During 1989, the focus of the Intifada moved from violent confrontations with the Israel Defense Forces (IDF) to the political arena. This shift somewhat weakened the leadership in the territories, "the Inside," vis-à-vis "the Outside," i.e., the PLO leadership in Tunis. Neither the leadership nor the rank-and-file activists developed new approaches and methods to confront the Israeli security forces.

Israeli policy toward the Intifada remained basically unchanged from 1988. In addition to employing stricter measures to quell the violence, the IDF assumed the initiative in its campaign against the organizational backbone of the Intifada. Israeli efforts notwithstanding, the situation of a dual authority in the territories — that of the Israeli Government and of the Intifada activists — remained unchanged. Despite indications of fatigue among the populace, its general support and commitment to the Intifada remained high.

THE LEADERSHIP

While the United National Command (UNC), the Intifada's clandestine leadership, appeared to have retained its role of guiding the Intifada inside the territories (on its emergence and structure see *MECS* 1988, pp. 278–83), its position was somewhat undermined by the reemergence of public figures as a central political factor. According to Israeli sources, the top echelon of the UNC comprised c. 40 persons who were engaged in providing general guidelines to the Intifada. The second echelon, comprising some 500 persons, dealt with organizational matters.

Both echelons remained a loose and decentralized coalition of the four leading PLO organizations in the territories. Behind the operating nuclei stood reserve teams, which enabled the UNC to withstand the frequent arrests of its members. The arrests, however, led to the appointment of lower echelon and less experienced activists, particularly the team writing the UNC's calls. This development led both to radicalization of the UNC and to several tactical errors which caused popular confusion toward the latter part of the year (see below).[1]

An additional important leadership group was composed of intellectuals, primarily university professors and journalists, who served as an informal public brain trust of the Intifada and maintained close relations with the diplomatic community of East Jerusalem. Some members of this group were mentioned as candidates for the Palestinian negotiating team from the territories. The popular backing of these figures, however, was weak. An indictment against four UNC activists in May 1989 mentioned two members of this group, Prof. Sari Nusayba of Bir Zayt University and Radwan Abu 'Ayyash, chairman of the Palestinian Journalists' Association, as taking part in composing several UNC calls and in the distribution of funds. The two, who denied the allegations, were not arrested.[2]

During 1988 public figures (*shakhsiyat*) — e.g., former mayors, journalists, trade-union and civil organization activists — who had comprised the public pro-PLO leadership in the territories, were totally eclipsed by the UNC. However, during 1989 their importance grew, particularly as greater attention was given to the peace process. Occasionally, nuances of opinion and even disagreements between Fath supporters within this group and the UNC came into the open (see below). It should be noted that the affiliation of various figures with either group was fluid, and some of them could belong to both. Unlike members of the UNC, some activists of the latter two groups enjoyed a certain immunity from detention due to "extralegal considerations," according to the IDF judge advocate, implying Israeli fear of international support on their behalf.[3]

The most important public figure was Faysal al-Husayni, head of the Institute of Arab Studies in Jerusalem, and reportedly the leading Fath activist in the West Bank. Husayni's status was based on prolonged public and military activity for the PLO including several prison terms, as well as respectable lineage (his father was 'Abd al-Qadir al-Husayni, leading military commander of the Jerusalem area in the 1948 war). His formal link to the UNC, however, was not clear.

The emerging leadership of the Intifada reflected an important political and possibly social change in the territories. The new leaders were young, many of them had higher education, and their position was based on their political activity rather than economic or family status. Significantly, some of them were of refugee origin which had formerly meant the lowest rung of the social ladder. The new leadership reflected the leading role of the youth in the Intifada and a certain rebellion against their elders. This change was widely acknowledged in the territories. When a group of public figures met Brig. Gen. Yesha'ayahu (Shayke) Erez, head of the civil administration in the West Bank, they advised him to meet members of "the Intifada generation," and not the aging leadership, since "the young generation does not heed the veteran leadership."[4]

THE UNITED NATIONAL COMMAND AND THE PLO

The *modus vivendi* between the UNC and the PLO leadership, which had been achieved in early 1988 (see *MECS* 1988, p. 281), was maintained in 1989, despite certain tensions between the two, particularly regarding the peace process. Paradoxically, one of the major achievements of the Intifada, generating the peace process, enhanced the PLO and diminished the importance of the UNC. The UNC was partly responsible for this development by rejecting any independent role for the inhabitants of the territories in the peace process and by stressing the PLO's status as the sole representative of the Palestinians (see below).

While insisting on the complete unity between the Inside and the Outside, Faysal al-Husayni described the link between the two leaderships as dialectic. Decisions on the tactical and operational spheres were the responsibility of the UNC, he explained, while decisions on the strategic level were taken by the national leadership as a whole. "We see the trees in the jungle," Husayni stated on another occasion, "but not the whole jungle."[5]

The worsening economic conditions in the territories (see below) enhanced the Inside's dependence on the funds channeled from the Outside. For instance, in Calls nos. 43 and 44, the UNC prodded the PLO to step up its financial support for the territories. (On the role and structure of the calls, see *MECS* 1988, pp. 283–84.) According to Arab press reports, the UNC appealed to the PLO to refrain from armed operations outside the territories, and devote all its resources to the aid of the Intifada, but apparently to no avail.[6] Complying with the request would have meant subordination of all other PLO priorities to the interests of the Inside, an option which the PLO could not have accepted without harming its own position.

The UNC, and particularly its leftist components, requested PLO approval to handle the distribution of PLO funds in the territories, claiming better acquaintance with local conditions. Handling the distribution would have given the UNC, rather than the PLO outside, effective control over large sectors of Palestinian society. Certain amounts were, indeed, given to the UNC for distribution, but it appeared that in addition to these amounts, the PLO and in fact Fath, channeled funds directly to other organizations and individuals in order to maintain its direct influence.[7]

The weakening of the UNC and the reemergence of the public figures served Fath, which had to share power with the other organizations in the UNC to a far greater extent than in the PLO's institutions, and which had always feared the emergence of an independent leadership in the territories. The Popular Front for the Liberation of Palestine (PFLP) and the Democratic Front for the Liberation of Palestine (DFLP), on the other hand, hoped to enhance their own influence through the UNC. Both organizations, inside and outside the territories, called for the establishment of "democratic relations" rather than the "bureaucratic" approach which had characterized the relations of the PLO with the masses in the territories, and advocated greater power to the UNC. Na'if Hawatima, for instance, demanded that only the UNC should appoint the territories' representatives in a Palestinian provisional government should it be set up.[8]

Both the PLO and the UNC were well aware of the newly acquired importance of the Inside which, consequently, had to be acknowledged in the decision-making process of the PLO. According to one survey in Gaza, "the creation of a national voice from *inside* [original italics] the occupied territories was regarded as a significant personal and political achievement by all of the refugees interviewed."[9] While describing the UNC as the "struggling arm of the PLO," deported UNC activists stressed the advantages it enjoyed over the Outside, as it was free of the interference by Arab states to which the PLO was often subjected.[10] Depicting the Intifada as a turning point in Palestinian history, the fifth Fath Congress announced the appointment of unidentified representatives from the territories to Fath's Revolutionary Council and Executive Committee (see chapter on the PLO).[11]

Interestingly, whereas in 1988 the signature affixed to the UNC calls placed the PLO before the UNC, the pattern was broken in 1989. In Calls nos. 31, 34, 38, 39, and 45, the UNC came first,[12] while in Calls nos. 43, 46, and the "Deportees' Call" (a special unnumbered call denouncing the deportation of activists) the PLO was completely omitted and the signature was "the UNC, the State of Palestine."[13] Significantly, this sequence was transmitted by the PLO radio itself, implying the organization's acquiescence. The changes may have reflected the UNC's desire to demonstrate greater importance or perhaps even independence.

The UNC managed to maintain a considerable degree of public unity during 1988 as long as the goals of the Intifada were the mobilization of society against the authorities, and thanks to Palestinian successes in the international arena. Although the various organizations probably never ceased to vie among themselves for greater influence, these conflicts did not come out in the open. However, with the institutionalization of the Intifada the first visible cracks began to appear.

Late in December 1988, leaflets in Gaza proclaimed the establishment of the Palestinian Popular Army, which was to be subordinated to Fath's Force 17. The new army, it was added, would not replace but complement the popular committees and strike forces. Fath spokesmen issued a similar statement on 1 January 1989. The declaration aroused great resentment across the Palestinian spectrum. Both the PFLP and the DFLP, which participated in the UNC, resented Fath's intention to "attribute the strike forces' achievements" to itself, and to subordinate the new army to its own authority. Even figures in Fath opposed Force 17's attempt to augment its own power, and subsequently, set up rival units, e.g., "the Abu Jihad Battalions" loyal to Intisar al-Wazir.[14]

Call no. 32 sought to remedy the situation. While praising the birth of the Popular Army, it stressed that it was "the army of the PLO, the army of the Intifada, which is composed in essence of the strike forces, includes all parties, and comes under the orders and instructions of the UNC." In other words, it was to be a joint force of all factions. According to Israeli sources, however, it was financed primarily by Fath.[15]

Leaflets distributed by local branches of the UNC during the following months called upon the populace to enlist in the new army which they claimed was composed of eight battalions. Marches under its banner were occasionally conducted in various localities. The Popular Army even issued official membership cards, signaling the institutionalization of the Intifada. On 5 June, the IDF announced the arrest and indictment of dozens of Popular Army leaders in the Gaza Strip.[16] The UNC itself, however, refrained from mentioning the new organization in its following calls, referring only to the strike forces, probably in order to calm the controversy. The Popular Army was successful in boosting morale and in enhancing the feeling of Palestinian statehood though it never became more than local groupings. It failed to become a significant factor because of its divisive nature but also, according to

Palestinian sources, because it might have lent the Intifada an image of a struggle between two armies rather than the image, which the UNC sought to portray, of an unarmed population facing an occupying army.[17]

POPULAR MOBILIZATION

With the Intifada entering its second year, the UNC faced the challenge of maintaining the momentum of the struggle. The shift away from mass demonstrations required that the UNC prevent a decline in the total mobilization of the populace lest the uprising be confined to a small nucleus of activists. The UNC was also worried about world attention turning away from the Intifada. Consequently, both the UNC and PLO repeatedly urged the escalation of the violence, which was regarded as the only way to induce Israel to accept Palestinian demands. Calls nos. 37 and 44, for instance, urged the population to "set the ground afire under the feet of the occupation troops," while Calls nos. 34 and 37 exhorted the use of knives, axes, petrol bombs, slingshots, and the throwing of heavy rocks from rooftops against IDF troops. Call no. 40 extended the struggle to the pre-1967 Israeli territory, encouraging the masses to "burn the Zionist fields and factories and inflict losses to the enemy's economy in response to the settlers' efforts to destroy our national economy."[18]

Growing frustration over the diplomatic stalemate and mounting Palestinian casualties were regarded by various Israeli observers as the main reason for the escalation of violence during the middle months of the year.[19] Palestinian frustration was manifested by renewed calls from radical factions and rank-and-file activists to use firearms against Israeli troops. In February, 'Arafat himself announced that he was considering the use of firearms in response to the Israeli "iron-hand policy."[20] On several occasions, leaflets issued by the Unified National Front, representing the organization that seceded from the PLO, criticized the UNC and the PLO for abandoning the strategy of armed struggle and for making concessions to Israel.[21]

Responding to the pressure from below, Call no. 40 distributed in leaflets urged the killing of an Israeli soldier or settler in return for every Palestinian casualty. Leading Fath supporters, however, including Husayni and Nusayba, met in Jerusalem and telephoned PLO officials outside the territories to argue against the passage. Fearing negative international reaction to the call, an official PLO spokesman denied the call had ever been made. However, whereas the transmission by the PLO radio omitted the disputed passage, *al-Hurriyya,* the DFLP organ, published the original version. Palestinian sources attributed the lapse on behalf of the UNC to the rise of more radical and less experienced activists following arrests of more experienced members. The UNC, however, did not oppose armed operations from outside the territories, and in Call no. 38 demanded of the Arab states that they open their borders to Palestinian fighters.[22]

Indeed, the number of violent incidents had been rising since January 1989 with the months of April, May, and July recording the highest numbers of Palestinian deaths — 34, 35, and 31, respectively. The number of daily incidents amounted throughout 1989 to c. 100 in the West Bank and 20 in the Gaza Strip, 85% of which, according to IDF statistics, involved stone throwing. A substantial rise in arson of cars (140 by October) and houses (22) was recorded in the Jewish neighborhoods of Jerusalem. It is noteworthy, however, that according to the IDF's own estimate, at least a third of all violent incidents were not reported and, therefore, not included in these statistics.[23] (For further details, see chapter on armed operations.)

Significantly, out of 1,571 violent acts committed by the strike forces and recorded by November 1989, at least 970 (c. 56%) were directed against Arabs. During 1988, the ratio between attacks on Jews and Arabs was inverse. Only since November was a visible decline in violence recorded. According to an Israeli watch group, 293 Palestinians were killed in clashes with Israeli troops during the year until 8 December.[24]

CIVIL ORGANIZATION

Parallel to the violent confrontations, the UNC continued its efforts to mobilize Palestinian society for building an alternative governmental structure in the territories. Its aim was to disengage the population from the Israeli authorities and to prepare the infrastructure for an independent state. The leftist organizations sought to turn this mobilization into a vehicle for a comprehensive social transformation. In the long run, these processes could prove to be as significant as the political gains of the Intifada. The popular committees (on their emergence and structure, see *MECS* 1988, pp. 284–87) were the main vehicle in these efforts. The UNC as well as various PLO spokesmen repeatedly called for the establishment of more popular committees and the expansion of their activity to all spheres of life.[25]

The popular committees continued to maintain their loose and decentralized structure throughout 1989. In addition to the local committees, however, there were attempts to set up supreme sectorial councils (*al-majalis al-quta'iyya al-'ulya*) for workers, women, youth, students, and health care which served as the UNC's operational arms. These councils were designed to supervise, coordinate, and improve the working of the various committees. The wording of Call no. 39 implied that the councils were supposed to unite members of the various political organizations. The relatively few references to the councils in other UNC calls, however, may suggest that they were not very successful in their efforts.[26]

Israeli officials estimated the hard core of the committees and strike force activists at 10,000–20,000 persons. The widespread arrests by the IDF, amounting to more than 40,000 by the first 18 months of the Intifada, failed to reduce their activities, indicating a broad base of support and willingness to replenish depleted ranks. In fact, the prisons and detention camps proved to be effective recruiting and indoctrination centers for the popular committees.[27] The composition of the popular committees, their prestige, and local power served as yet additional evidence of a significant social change, reflected primarily in the rising power of the younger generation.

The cutbacks in the deployment of the IDF in the territories and the closure of the Civil Administration offices in various localities, following attacks by strike forces, enabled many localities to function as independent zones. Daily life in these places and public services such as education, health care, and agriculture, were run by the popular committees. In certain regions popular courts were set up to deal with moral offenses, clan disputes, civil-law cases, and security matters. In the more conservative Hebron, for instance, representatives of the major clans signed a charter allowing the killing of thieves and robbers based on traditional tribal law in order to combat the increase in crime following the mass resignation of policemen. Whereas most popular committees in the rural areas were organized on a village basis, regional committees comprising several villages were set up in the Nablus area in order to provide mutual aid, e.g., collecting and marketing crops of villages under curfew.[28]

The popular committees also put a great emphasis on the symbolic aspects of independence. The local UNC in Nablus stated that the popular committees would no longer require contributions from the population, but would issue bonds to be repaid on the day of independence. It is unknown how widespread this practice became. Strike forces conducted marches of masked and uniformed youth carrying wooden weapons and Palestinian flags. Likewise, the UNC declared a Palestinian daylight-saving time in the territories distinct from the time used in Israel.[29] Overall, Israel never managed to reverse the emergence of the popular committees as a rival authority in the territories.

THE UNITED NATIONAL COMMAND, THE PLO, AND THE FUNDAMENTALIST CHALLENGE

The most serious challenge to the UNC and the PLO in the territories came from the fundamentalist Islamic wing of the Palestinian national movement, primarily the Islamic Resistance Movement (*Harakat al-muqawama al-Islamiyya;* Hamas) and the Islamic Jihad (*al-Jihad al-Islami*). Whereas all other organizations in the territories regarded the PLO as the sole legitimate representative of the Palestinians, the Islamic organizations were equivocal on that point. Consequently, they refused to subordinate themselves to the UNC and were engaged in a bitter struggle for influence and power in the territories.

Hamas originated from the Muslim Brotherhood movement, which had been active in the Gaza Strip since the 1950s. The Muslim Brotherhood had traditionally followed an evolutionist approach, calling for reformist action through education and infusion of Islamic practices into all aspects of life. The movement spread its influence through the network of mosques and various charitable and social organizations, under the roof organization of "the Islamic community" (*al-mujamma' al-Islami*; see *MECS* 1986, p. 221). The Brotherhood's approach set it in sharp contrast to the PLO organizations, which advocated the centrality of the armed struggle against Israel.[30] Nevertheless, during the 1980s the Brotherhood emerged as a powerful political factor in the Gaza Strip, challenging the influence of the PLO.

In 1987, the Brotherhood changed its approach, adopting a more nationalist and activist line including the principle of armed struggle, due to the growing threat to its position from the Islamic Jihad. Unlike the Brotherhood, the Islamic Jihad stressed the centrality of the Palestinian problem for Islam. Since Israel was the spearhead of imperialism against Islam, it argued, Jihad against it was the prerequisite for remedying the ills of the Muslim world.[31] Fearing the loss of its constituency following several much publicized terrorist activities by the Islamic Jihad and under pressure from younger activists, the Brotherhood embarked upon its new course under the name of Hamas.

Hamas was organized in three wings. Its spiritual leader, Shaykh Ahmad Yasin, who had been released in the 1986 prisoner exchange deal, also headed the political wing. The military wing called "the Palestinian holy warriors" (*al-mujahidun al-Filastiniyyun*) was engaged in operations against the IDF. The security wing named "glory" (*majd*) was responsible for intelligence gathering and the elimination of collaborators and other elements which corrupted Palestinian society, such as prostitutes and drug dealers. Hamas received financial support from fundamentalist organizations in Jordan and Great Britain. Whereas the Islamic Jihad remained a small terrorist organization, Hamas, combining political and military activity, spread its influence throughout the Gaza Strip.[32]

The fundamentalist challenge to the PLO was augmented because Hamas did not pose only as a religious alternative to the PLO, but also as a nationalist one. Departing from the pan-Islamic tradition of the Muslim Brotherhood, Hamas stressed its Palestinian nature and the importance of the Palestinian national struggle in its Islamic ideology. Whereas all other political organizations in the territories regarded themselves as extensions of the PLO and derived their legitimacy from it, Hamas's power base was in the territories. Consequently, Hamas saw itself as independent of and equal to the PLO, perhaps even an alternative to the PLO leadership, which had failed to realize Palestinian national goals. On one occasion, Shaykh Ahmad Yasin welcomed the idea of elections in the territories as the only way to elect representatives for the Palestinian people, implying that the PLO was not the natural sole legitimate representative.[33]

The PLO's attitude to Islam and its political strategy were the two major grievances Hamas raised against the organization in its covenant, published in August 1988. Adopting an ostensibly conciliatory tone, the covenant described Hamas's attitude toward the PLO as that of a son to his father, as a brother and relative. "Our fatherland is one," it stated, "our fate is one,...and our enemy is common." However, the covenant added, the PLO adopted the idea of the secular state which totally contradicted the religious thought. Hence "with all our appreciation to the PLO and without belittling its role," Hamas could not exchange the Islamic nature of Palestine for the idea of the secular state. Hamas would support all Palestinian movements as long as they did not profess loyalty to "the Communist East and the crusading West." The day the PLO adopts Islam as its way of life, the covenant concluded, we shall be its soldiers.[34]

Whereas the PLO regarded the conflict with Israel as a national struggle, Hamas perceived it as a religious war between Muslims and Jews, and as a continuation of the ideological struggle between the "crusading West" and the world of Islam. Palestine, the covenant states, was an Islamic *waqf* (endowment) and any concession on its part was tantamount to giving up part of religion. Consequently, the covenant totally rejected all "so-called peaceful solutions and international conferences." "There is no solution to the Palestinian problem except holy war (Jihad)," it concluded.[35] Hamas adhered to these principles throughout 1988–89 in numerous proclamations and statements.

The Islamic covenant adopted a sharp anti-Jewish tone echoing the notorious Protocols of the Elders of Zion and anti-Jewish utterances in the Qur'an and Muslim tradition. The Jews were accused of controlling world media as well as international and espionage organizations. They were described as the force behind all major revolutions and wars in the world. Other publications depicted the Jews as "bloodsuckers" and "brothers of apes."[36]

A greater degree of agreement existed between the Islamic Jihad and the PLO, particularly Fath, as both sides tended to postpone the debate over the nature of the Palestinian state until after victory was achieved. Significantly, both fundamentalist organizations refused to join the UNC due to their disagreements with the PLO and their insistence on maintaining their independence. In addition, Hamas expressed its distrust of the susceptibility of other organizations to Israeli penetrations. Hamas, however, pledged to honor all UNC calls for rebellious actions and strikes and to refrain from setting conflicting strike days.[37]

The attitude of the mainstream PLO and the UNC toward Hamas was ambivalent too. They resented Hamas's challenge to their authority, but could not ignore its wide constituency and effectiveness in the struggle against Israel. Moreover, although Fath professed a nonreligious ideology, it always maintained a favorable attitude toward Islam, regarding it as a crucial component of the Palestinian national heritage. Therefore, it could never come out openly and forcefully against the ideology of the two organizations.

Consequently, only rarely did the PLO organizations openly dispute with Hamas over the nature of the conflict and the desired final goal of the Palestinian national movement. On one such occasion, a leaflet issued by the "Steering Committee of the Palestinian Popular Army" presented a religious ruling (Fatwa) asserting that the two-state solution was permissable under Islamic law. Aware of the limited appeal of the Marxist-Leninist ideology *vis-à-vis* Hamas, the Palestinian left, except for the communists, shied away from confrontation with Hamas.[38] The fundamentalist extremism, on the other hand, helped to portray the PLO in the Western media as a moderate and reasonable alternative.

Throughout 1989, the PLO adopted several interrelated courses of action toward the fundamentalist challenge. On the one hand, both 'Arafat and Abu Iyad sought to belittle the significance of the separate stand of the Islamic organizations, claiming that the latter were part of the Palestinian national movement and were represented in the Palestine National Council (PNC).[39] The UNC appealed to Hamas in Calls nos. 32, and 43 to coordinate its activities "on the basis of a militant program to escalate the uprising."[40] Following meetings outside the territories, the two parties apparently agreed on coordination primarily regarding strike days and acts of civil disobedience. Faysal al-Husayni even spoke of extending the coordination into total union between Hamas and the UNC. The agreement, however, did not last long, with each side holding the other responsible for its failure.[41]

The failure, apparently, stemmed from the same reasons that prompted Hamas to maintain its independence of the UNC. In a statement issued on 3 February, Fath expressed particular anger over Hamas's support of elections which had previously been rejected by the UNC and accused it of undermining Palestinian unity. Fath was probably most incensed over Yasin's implied challenge to the PLO's exclusive representativeness.[42] Hamas, in its turn, continuously criticized the PLO for "kneeling to the Jews" by making unilateral concessions which strengthened "the spirit of the criminal enemy."[43] On 3 August, Hamas issued "a document to history," addressed to the fifth Fath Congress, in which it praised Fath for its pioneering role in declaring the armed struggle as the only course to liberation, but implicitly warned Fath of losing its legitimacy by pursuing the political strategy. Recognizing "the false Jewish entity," it stated, was not in the authority of any organization, and was tantamount to betrayal of God and of the faith. Whoever believed that Israel would reciprocate for any concession, it warned, was either ignorant or a fool. In conclusion, Hamas urged Fath to return to its original course and pledged its cooperation until final victory was achieved.[44]

The Islamic Jihad followed similar lines in its own calls. In June, it declared that the "filthy peace" for which the PLO had expressed its desire in the 19th PNC in Algiers was "null and void." Their common opposition to Fath's political course drew the Islamic organizations and the PFLP-GC toward each other, as indicated by the latter's transmission of the former's calls on its radio.[45]

Throughout 1989, Hamas enhanced its position in the territories, taking advantage of the stalemate in the violent confrontation against Israel and in the peace process. Beginning in June, growing compliance to Hamas's calls for strikes were visible in the West Bank, where it had hitherto been weaker. The conservative town of Hebron emerged as its stronghold in the West Bank. PLO supporters attributed this development partly to Israeli encouragement designed to undermine the PLO. The Islamic Jihad, on the other hand, assumed the lead in terrorist activity against both Jews and Arabs in the territories.[46]

Whereas the authorities had tolerated and encouraged the activities of the *Mujamma'* until 1987, they viewed the increased violent activity of the Islamic organizations as a serious danger. On 18 June, three small fundamentalist groups in Gaza were banned, and on 28 September Hamas itself was outlawed. Over 200 of its leading activists, including Shaykh Yasin and the other seven senior leaders in both the Gaza Strip and the West Bank, were arrested. Large quantities of weapons were impounded; Yasin was brought before a military court in November on charges of murder and kidnapping.[47] Though inflicting a blow to its infrastructure, the arrests did not check Hamas's growing influence.

Alarmed by this growing influence, both the PLO and its supporters felt obliged to confront it openly. The PLO was also worried by reports of Iranian financial support for Hamas. Abu Iyad berated Hamas for presenting itself as an alternative to the PLO, and in essence, serving Israeli interests. He warned that by allowing Iranian influence into the Palestinian arena, Hamas would destroy the Palestinian people. In an address to Israeli peace activists, Abu Iyad warned that unless Israel negotiated with the PLO, it would have to face the fundamentalists in the future. UNC activists chided Hamas for the Muslim Brotherhood's inaction against Israel since 1948, which did not match its high words on Jihad. Simultaneously, however, they tried to belittle Hamas's influence, claiming it enjoyed the support of only a minority.[48] Some Israeli observers, on the other hand, argued that a major reason for the UNC's opposition to elections in the territories was fear lest Hamas be the major beneficiary, a feeling clearly shared by Shaykh Yasin.[49]

The growing tension between Hamas and the UNC led to conflicting calls for strike days, which imposed a heavier burden on the population, and to violent clashes, particularly with supporters of the leftist organizations. Whereas the UNC was determined to preserve Muslim-Christian unity, the fundamentalists published leaflets denouncing the Christians and on some occasions assaulted Christian shops and houses. The factional clashes were particularly serious in the detention camps, leading Hamas to warn in its Call no. 47 that its "long arm would sever all hands extended against any one of our people."[50]

THE INTIFADA AND THE PEACE PROCESS

The peace process, accelerated by the Intifada, in turn influenced the situation in the territories in three ways. First, the significant degree of Palestinian unity, which had been maintained in public since the early days of the Intifada, was shaken due to differing attitudes toward various aspects of the process. Second, in an expression of the disagreements public figures, many of them Fath supporters, reemerged as an important political factor parallel to the UNC. Third, by stressing the PLO's exclusive role in any political process, the UNC and other PLO supporters relegated the initiative they had previously gained thanks to the Intifada to the PLO leadership. Unlike in 1988, Palestinians in the territories now reacted to developments rather than initiated them.

In spite of the UNC's voluntary subordination to the PLO, certain differences regarding the peace process emerged between the two, particularly toward the latter part of the year. Three rough trends of political opinions could be discerned during 1989: public figures supporting Fath, the radical camp composed of the leftist and Islamic organizations, and the UNC, which maintained a balance and wavered between these two extremes.

Israeli Defense Minister Yitzhak Rabin's plan of mid-January, to hold elections for representatives from the territories who would negotiate an interim settlement with Israel (see chapter on the ME peace process), elicited a generally negative reaction from the PLO and the entire Palestinian spectrum in the territories. In essence, the plan was rejected precisely for its very rationale, namely the election of a local leadership as an alternative to the PLO. Both al-Fajr, reflecting Fath's views, and the pro-Jordanian al-Nahar, as well as public figures chided Rabin for reiterating old formulas, which had been rejected in the past while ignoring the political developments brought about by the Intifada.[51] Official Israeli sources claimed, however, that the majority of c. 400 Palestinian public figures representing a cross section of political opinion had expressed "great interest" in the Rabin plan and particularly the election proposal during numerous meetings with Israeli officials.[52] Such alleged opinions were never stated in public.

Calls nos. 33 and 34 of the UNC sharply condemned the "stillborn" plans of the "criminal" Shamir or Rabin, and declared that the masses would send it "to the waste dump of history" as they had done to similar plans in the past. There is no alternative, Call no. 34 concluded, "to an independent Palestinian state with holy Jerusalem as its capital, and to the right of return and self-determination."[53] The UNC adhered to these principles throughout 1989 in all its following calls.

Most interesting, however, was the changing position of Faysal al-Husayni, which epitomized the political dynamics in the territories. Prior to his release from administrative detention on 29 January, Husayni was visited by Shmu'el Goren, the coordinator of activities in the territories, and reportedly expressed cautious support for elections under certain conditions. Upon his release, Husayni reiterated his conditional support for elections provided they were democratic, free from any Israeli interference and under proper international supervision. Cessation of violence, he added, depended on Israeli compliance with Palestinian demands.[54]

Husayni's statements, which were interpreted both in the territories and by the Israeli media as a conditional approval of the Rabin plan, caused an uproar in the territories. The PLO spokesman in Tunis, Ahmad 'Abd al-Rahman, asserted that elections could be held only after an Israeli withdrawal and under UN supervision. In a clear message to Husayni he added, "this is not only the PLO position, it is a Palestinian position." A group of prominent PLO supporters boycotted a meeting held at Husayni's house on the night of his release. In a meeting held on the same night in Jerusalem, they strongly criticized Husayni's statements, though without issuing any public condemnation, both in order to avoid an open friction and apparently in deference to Husayni's status.[55]

In view of the criticism, Husayni hastened to accommodate his position to the PLO's line, denying there had been any discrepancy between his own position and the organization's. In a series of statements, he argued that free and democratic elections were totally incompatible with the occupation, and could be held only after an Israeli withdrawal. Elections, he added, would in effect be a referendum on the PLO's platform. The elected representatives could serve only as a bridge, which would lead Israel to direct negotiations with the PLO.[56]

Shortly after his release, Husayni embarked upon what was termed by Palestinian sources as a "peace offensive" aimed at Israeli public opinion. The UNC had recognized the need to influence Israeli public opinion to accept Palestinian demands in the early stages of the Intifada, and appeals to the Israeli public appeared in several UNC calls during 1988. Opposition within the UNC (see below) presumably prevented the translation of this awareness into a concerted effort of direct contacts with Israelis. Only an activist of Husayni's stature could initiate such a move, but even he, as he said, required the PLO's prior approval.

During February, Husayni held several much publicized meetings with various Israeli circles, the most important being with senior members of the Israeli Labor Party. For that purpose he formed a delegation comprised, in addition to himself, of Prof. Sari Nusayba, the journalist Ziyad Abu Ziyad and three younger academics affiliated with Fath, as well as Sam'an Khuri of the DFLP, and Ghasan al-Khatib of the Palestine Communist Party (PCP). Representatives of the PFLP and the Islamic fundamentalists were not included. The delegation's composition was probably designed to project the large consensus behind the initiative and the PLO's approval.[57] Interestingly, in his meetings with Israelis, Husayni went much farther than the PLO and his own statements to the Arab media in presenting Palestinian moderation and in elaborating on the nature of future peace. Apparently, he was more aware than the PLO leadership of the need to gain Israeli public support.[58]

The publicity given to the meetings aroused opposition primarily from the PFLP, but also among Fath supporters in the territories. The opponents argued that meetings with Israeli politicians and government officials served only Israeli propaganda which tried to present a local alternative to the PLO, as well as create the false impression of diplomatic progress. Both points, they added, would only help Israel break its international isolation, but would not benefit the Palestinians.[59] In response, Husayni argued that the meetings were designed to "expand the [Israeli] belief that the only possible solution is through negotiations with the PLO." Zuhayr 'Abd al-Hadi, a deported UNC activist, explained that the meetings were aimed at "deepening the internal conflict in the Israeli political arena," and Sari Nusayba pointed to these conflicts as the "tangible evidence of the need to continue these meetings." The path various Israeli public figures had taken toward meeting with PLO officials, Nusayba added, began by meetings with Palestinians in the territories. Our aim, he concluded, was to persuade the Israeli public of the PLO's desire for peace and that dialogue with Palestinians in the territories did not differ from dialogue with PLO officials.[60] Thus, while both Palestinians and certain Israeli officials, Rabin included, supported the dialogue, each side maintained a completely opposite view of its purpose.

Call no. 35 sought to establish a compromise formula, but in fact led to a deeper disagreement on the issue when two conflicting versions appeared. The "official" version stipulated that all meetings should be held under the guidelines of opposition to the occupation, agreement to negotiate with the PLO in an international conference, and recognition of the Palestinian "right of self-determination." Significantly, the guidelines did not mention the right of return. The version disseminated by the PFLP, on the other hand, omitted all reference to the meetings. In its own leaflets, however, the PFLP strongly denounced the very idea and those Fath supporters, who had taken part in such meetings.[61]

PFLP activists in Nablus went farther and threatened with death prominent Fath supporters, who had met with Civil Administration officials, should they continue their meetings. Meetings between senior supporters of both camps were hurriedly convened in order to prevent an escalation of the factional rivalry. In mid-March, prior to Prime Minister Shamir's visit to Washington, the National Institutions (a euphemism for PLO-controlled institutions in the territories) published a leaflet calling for an immediate end to all meetings between Palestinians and Israelis. The suspension, it stated, was designed to foil Shamir's claim that there was an alternative leadership to the PLO.[62]

The concerted Israeli effort to continue the meetings with Palestinian residents in search for an alternative to the PLO was probably one reason which motivated the latter to depict them in late July as indirect negotiations between itself and Israel, thereby implying an unofficial Israeli recognition of the PLO. When Shamir confirmed he had met several Palestinian public figures but denied the PLO's claim, the latter named four persons who had allegedly taken part in them. Of the four, only Jamil al-Tarifi, deposed deputy mayor of al-Bira and a senior Fath supporter, publicly acknowledged the meeting. Aware of the UNC position on such meetings, Tarifi stated that he had merely presented to Shamir the well-known Palestinian positions on the conflict and informed the PLO of his meeting.[63]

Both the PLO's and Tarifi's statements proved somewhat of an embarrassment to the UNC, which had previously demanded an end to all meetings with Israeli officials in Calls nos. 37 and 39. Even worse was the announcement by PLO spokesman Ahmad 'Abd al-Rahman that the meetings had been conducted with the PLO's approval. Bashir al-Barghuti, editor of the East Jerusalem Communist weekly *al-Tali'a,* likened the UNC's situation in that regard to that of the wife who is always the last to know. Various public figures claimed that conflicting messages on the issue arrived from opposing factions in Fath. Slogans scrawled on walls in Ramallah and signed by the PFLP threatened Tarifi with death, and he had to leave for Jordan for several weeks. Adopting a harsher line than Fath, Calls nos. 43 and 44 warned those who contributed to any meetings with official and unofficial Israeli parties that did not accept Palestinian demands.[64] Significantly, Husayni himself did not adhere to this order.

Prime Minister Shamir's peace plan, announced in early April (see chapter on the ME peace process), was rejected outright almost unanimously by Palestinians in the territories regardless of their organizational affiliation. The elections it proposed were denounced as a deception aimed at buying time and relieving pressure on Israel, and as an attempt to foil the peace efforts. Like the Rabin plan, Shamir's was criticized for seeking to create a "farcical alternative leadership" to the PLO, of ignoring the key issue of Palestinian self-determination, and of seeking to separate the Palestinians inside from those outside, who were referred to only as refugees.[65]

Various Fath supporters, however, were willing to consider elections if they were approved by the PLO and were part of a process that would lead to an independent Palestinian state.[66] On 9 April, Sa'id Kan'an, head of al-Najah University Friends' Association in Nablus, joined Faysal al-Husayni in Cairo to present to the PLO and Egypt a counterproposal on behalf of various PLO supporters in the territories. Its main points were to hold elections under international supervision but without complete Israeli withdrawal, in which representatives of the PNC would be elected. The PLO would then choose several of those elected for the negotiating team. While it was clear that such proposals would be unacceptable to Israel, a major consideration, according to the pro-Fath weekly, *al-Bayadir al-Siyasi*, was to maintain the initiative on the Palestinian side and demonstrate flexibility to the US.[67]

The initiative reflected the growing importance of the Inside but also its limitations. Palestinians from the Inside could now initiate plans which the Outside had to take into consideration. Moreover, elected representatives from the Inside, rather than ones appointed from above, would grant greater weight to the Inside within the PLO. Significantly, however, the Outside approval was still the crucial element and, apparently, it was not given. On 26 April, the PLO Executive Committee officially rejected the Shamir plan, reiterating the previous conditions set by the PLO.[68]

A day after the PLO announced its decision, 80 leading public figures from the West Bank and the Gaza Strip issued a joint statement rejecting the Shamir plan for the reasons stated above. The declaration ruled out any elections "prior to the withdrawal of the Israeli Army." Negotiations must begin with the representatives of the Palestinian people as a whole, and not with the representatives of any fragment, it concluded.[69] Although seeking to present the widest consensus, the statement was not signed by PFLP supporters and by members of the fundamentalist organizations, nor did the moderate mayor of Bethlehem, Elias Freij, at the other end of the Palestinian spectrum endorse it.

Palestinian sources explained that the joint statement sought to prevent confusion over more moderate initiatives by individuals, e.g., Sa'id Kan'an's. In order to remove all doubt, Call no. 39 flatly rejected "all attempts to agree with the Shamir plan." Significantly, although probably coordinated with the PLO, both the joint declaration and Call no. 39 were phrased in a harsher tone than the PLO's own statement, which had tempered its rejection of the Shamir plan with positive preconditions for elections. Moreover, unlike the PLO's statement, which was also aimed at the US, Call no. 39 sharply denounced the US for seeking "to monopolize the solution" and for its support of Israel while praising the USSR.[70] Both points, as well as a condemnation of the Arab regimes for their inaction, reflected the growing importance of the leftist organizations within the UNC. The same principles were reiterated in Calls nos. 40, 41, and 42.[71]

Despite the efforts to present a unified Palestinian position, political differences in the territories were in fact intensified as the election proposal became the main issue of the peace process. American efforts to advance the proposal in the territories met with mixed reaction, partly because of the UNC's determination to exclude other parties from any role in the process. Consequently, a discussion on the elections held on 14 May at the American Consulate in East Jerusalem with Dennis Ross, head of the planning section of the US State Department, was boycotted by 11 out of 15 public figures invited. The four who attended were second rank figures.[72] In a letter to Ross, five of those who boycotted the meeting, headed by Nusayba, Ghasan al-Khatib of the PCP and Zuhayra Kamal of the DFLP explained their absence by the large number of those invited, including supporters of Hamas and pro-Jordanians, which would have prevented them from adequately presenting their views. Rather, they proposed a separate meeting in which Palestinians would choose the participants. Ross obliged and the meeting with six representatives of the main PLO factions took place on 15 May. While reiterating their rejection of the Shamir plan, Nusayba expressed both in the meeting and in public several ideas regarding the elections which in fact differed from those of the UNC calls.[73]

With the PLO's change of attitude, under American pressure, toward elections, a similar change took place in the territories. The debate now revolved more around the conditions of elections than whether or not they should be held. A poll conducted by *al-Bayadir al-Siyasi* among 104 leading public figures established that 83% supported elections under various conditions. Only 14% were willing to accept Israeli withdrawal from population centers as a sufficient condition, while 86% demanded total Israeli withdrawal. According to other sources, however, many Fath supporters accepted partial Israeli withdrawal as sufficient, while PFLP and DFLP supporters insisted on total Israeli withdrawal prior to any peace move. Interestingly, while still publicly opposed to the Shamir plan, various figures expressed satisfaction when the Israeli Cabinet officially approved the plan on 29 July.[74]

The Ten-Point Plan presented by Egyptian President Husni Mubarak in early September (see chapter on the ME peace process) again revealed sharp differences between the UNC and the PLO. Whereas the PLO delayed its official response fearing to alienate Egypt, reactions in the territories were swifter, reflecting again the basic pattern of opinions mentioned above. Several prominent Fath supporters as well as the two dailies, *al-Fajr* and *al-Quds,* welcomed the plan as a basis and a beginning for the process, which needed various changes to satisfy principal Palestinian demands, rather than as a comprehensive plan.[75] But supporters of the PFLP, the DFLP, the PCP, and even some of Fath rejected the 10 points as insufficient. Leaflets signed by the PFLP denounced the plan as "treacherous" and "conspiratory," accusing Mubarak of seeking to "undermine Palestinian national unity and weaken the power of the Intifada."[76] Reflecting the greater weight of the left in its composition, the UNC adopted the latter line. Call no. 46 criticized the 10 points as unbalanced and unacceptable "as long as they do not specify the final objective in accordance with the Palestinian people's right to return, self-determination, and the establishment of its independent state."[77]

Reactions in the territories concerning the Five-Point Plan, proposed by US Secretary of State, James Baker in October (see chapter on the US and the ME), followed the pattern outlined above. Again, the UNC adopted the radical line in opposing the Baker plan and denouncing American policy in the region, while the PLO took an ambiguous line.[78] The growing power of the left and Hamas exacerbated the internal debate among supporters of Fath itself, who were pulling in two opposing directions. Leaflets signed by Fath and distributed in the Ramallah area dismissed the peace process as a temporary and tactical cover for Palestinian revolutionary activity against Israel. The confrontation with the IDF, it added, was not aimed at attaining a political settlement, but was rather a phase of the armed struggle.[79] Faysal al-Husayni, on the other hand, in an interview to the Palestinian weekly *al-Yawm al-Sabi'*, called on the PLO to come out with a more concrete plan, which would regain the political initiative and play more effectively on international and Israeli public opinion. While stressing the need not to abandon any of the fundamental Palestinian demands, Husayni added that the plan must allay the Israeli fears about security (exaggerated in his opinion) after the Palestinian state had been established.[80]

Only a figure of Husayni's stature could "advise" the PLO in such a public manner. Another prominent Fath supporter, As'ad al-Siftawi, came out in July with a peace plan which greatly resembled President Mubarak's Ten-Point Plan and which went further than the official PLO line. However, unlike Husayni, he presented his plan to Fath's fifth Congress to get its approval rather than come out with it in public.

In order to break the political deadlock and recover the Palestinian initiative as well as overcome the centrifugal forces of Palestinian organization in the territories, Sari Nusayba during a trip to the US in October called for setting up a provisional Palestinian government. His main point was not the (rather ceremonial) council of ministers which would be drawn from the PLO Executive Committee, but the establishment of a complete bureaucratic apparatus in the territories, which would manage the daily life of the population. This government would be structured as a "pyramid-like integration of local institutions with the PLO leadership abroad" and would fill the vacuum created by the Jordanian disengagement. Such a step, he explained, would give meaning to the Palestinian declaration of independence and provide coherence and direction to the myriad of Palestinian institutions and committees which manage various aspects of Palestinian life. In addition, an institutional linkage between the ordinary citizen and the PLO would be established. Israeli attempts to abolish this government would be thwarted by its sheer size and Israel would be forced to give up control of the administration to the new government.[81]

The three proposals — by Husayni, Siftawi, and Nusayba — reflected the new relations between the residents and the PLO, as the former felt sufficiently confident to make proposals to the PLO. However, whereas both Husayni and Siftawi gave the PLO the leading role, Nusayba's plan sought to establish a new mode of relationships between the Inside and Outside. While the PLO would hold overall responsibility, the Inside would hold effective power over the population's life. All three, however, still subordinated themselves to the PLO, and felt that they had to obtain its approval for their proposals — but that was not forthcoming.

ISRAELI POLICY

Israeli policy toward the Intifada was guided during 1989 by the realization, phrased by the Chief of Staff, Lt. Gen. Dan Shomron, that the Intifada could not be eradicated militarily since in its essence it was an expression of national struggle. Rather, the Intifada was perceived by the IDF as a long war of attrition, in which the IDF's role was to reduce the level of violence to a tolerable minimum, which would enable the government to work for a political solution on the best possible terms. The motivation to continue the Intifada, Shomron hoped, would decline when the Palestinian inhabitants realized that violence would not lead them to any gains.[82] This attitude led to a certain tension between the IDF high command and some members of the Cabinet, including Prime Minister Shamir, who still believed that the Intifada could be put down by force.[83]

On the operational level, policy was made by the "territories forum," a weekly meeting of 30 senior civil and military officials headed by Defense Minister Rabin. Initially, the forum misunderstood the essence of the Intifada and was guided by false optimism as to its approaching end. As the months passed by, however, it was guided by a growing frustration over the failure of the measures applied to quell the violence.[84] As part of its new approach, which regarded the fight against the Intifada as equivalent to regular war, new commanders from elite units were appointed in sensitive areas. Special units serving long periods in policing duties were set up, as it was believed that such troops were less inclined to resort to shooting.[85]

In order to quell the violence, particularly stone throwing, the IDF during 1989 continued to apply the same combination of measures it had applied the year before (see *MECS* 1988, pp. 292–95), although it was fully aware of their limited effectiveness. These measures included curfews on rioting localities; stiffer sentences for petrol bomb and stone throwers, heavy fines on their parents, and sometimes the demolition of their houses (a total of 236 houses were demolished during the period December 1987-September 1989). The High Court of Justice, however, ordered the IDF to enable residents to appeal to the court before any demolition took place. Observation posts were set up in sensitive areas, and trees along roads where stone throwing was rife were felled (23,440 as claimed by Arab sources; less than 2,000 according to the IDF). The universities remained closed throughout the year, but schools began to be opened gradually in July 1989.[86]

In an attempt to reduce casualties among rioters, which only stimulated more violence, the IDF in October 1988 began to use plastic bullets which were deemed less fatal. In January 1989, the IDF amended its regulations on opening fire with plastic bullets: not only officers but NCOs were now authorized to fire them at stone throwers from a certain distance even in situations not involving mortal danger, but not at children and women. Justifying the change, Rabin argued that the rioting youth, who were well acquainted with the previous regulations, behaved more audaciously when officers were not present.[87] The state attorney-general pronounced the new regulations legal.[88]

Unofficial military sources expressed concern that the amended regulations would lead to heavier casualties and consequently to an escalation of the violence. Experience showed that plastic bullets, though less harmful than ordinary ones, could be fatal at certain shooting angles and distances, particularly when children were hit. At least 77 persons were reported killed by these bullets within 10 months of their use.[89] Some observers further argued that the regulations were now too confusing, exposing soldiers to impossible situations, which were bound either to lead to greater casualties or undermine the soldiers' effectiveness. Lt. Gen. Shomron, indeed, admitted that the IDF regulations left many "gray areas" in which the soldiers had to use their own judgment.[90] In order to combat the growing power of the "strike forces," troops were allowed in July to shoot at masked youths if the latter refused to stop when ordered.[91] This gave the troops greater latitude in resorting to shooting.

If the measures against rioters were mostly reactive in nature, they nonetheless allowed the authorities to assume the initiative in their struggle against the "strike forces" and popular committees. Thanks to close coordination with the General Security Service, scores of activists were arrested in nightly raids by troops. Among the detainees were more than 320 senior activists, some of whom were described by military sources as "department heads of the Intifada's general staff."[92] In one such raid on 13 April, in the village of Nahalin, a serious clash between the troops and the population took place and five residents were killed, while none of the wanted suspects were apprehended. A military investigative committee charged the troops with losing control and excessive shooting. The commanding officer was relieved of his post. The Israeli press strongly criticized the entire operation.[93]

Unlike suspects of violent activities, leaders of the popular committees were mostly held in administrative detention, whose term was extended in June to a year. By July, 1,954 persons were being held in administrative detention.[94] As mentioned above, the most senior political activists were not arrested out of extralegal considerations. Overall more than 18,000 persons were brought before military courts during the year, of whom 10,000 were convicted. Only 400 were acquitted (others were either awaiting trial or released without charges being brought against them). The exact number of those detained could not be ascertained. The military-court system was unprepared for such numbers of detainees, which led to procedural irregularities, particularly long pre-trial detention and pressures on detainees to confess. Too often convictions were based only on the accuseds' confession. Civil rights activists also charged that rules of evidence were often compromised in view of the pressure on the courts. Following public pressure, a court of appeals was established in April.[95]

Despite criticism in the US and Europe, the authorities deported two groups of senior committee activists, 15 on 1 January and an additional eight on 29 June. Some observers charged that the policy of deportations was more the product of inertia than any long-term political rationale. Such deportations, they added, eliminated the local leadership which could eventually form a future partner for negotiations and which could challenge the outside PLO leadership.[96]

The authorities retained the economic and administrative measures employed during 1988. The purpose of this policy was to demonstrate to the population both its dependence on Israel and the heavy cost of the Intifada in order to drive a wedge between the population and the UNC (see below for the struggle over taxation).[97] On 15 and 16 May all workers from the Gaza Strip were temporarily barred from entering Israel, and those already there were ordered to return home. The population should know, a military source stated, "that we, and not some leaflet, decide when and how life is to be disrupted." The measure was also aimed at showing that general strikes would be retaliated. Critics charged, however, that the sudden and indiscriminate order reflected Israeli confusion and could push the population to greater radicalism by creating a feeling that they had nothing to lose.[98]

In an attempt to improve control over the entry of Gazans into Israel and as a test of power vis-à-vis the UNC, the authorities introduced new computerized ID cards as of June, which barred security offenders from entering Israel. Though the struggle over the computerized cards was regarded as a success for the authorities and a defeat for the UNC, as it determined who would control the population's passage to Israel (see below), it was not extended to the West Bank, mainly due to the difficulties of controlling the numerous entry points to Israel. Security offenders and suspected political activists from the West Bank had already been issued special ID cards in March, which restricted their passage to Israel.[99]

Parallel to the military efforts, Rabin himself and Civil Administration officials conducted meetings with hundreds of Palestinian public figures throughout the year in an effort to advance the Israeli peace plans. In addition, several senior political activists, e.g., Faysal al-Husayni and Haydar 'Abd al-Shafi, head of the Red Crescent Association in Gaza and a veteran PFLP supporter, were allowed to go abroad where it was clear that they would conduct talks with PLO officials.[100]

Although the number of troops deployed in the territories declined compared to the most volatile months of 1988, confronting the Intifada exacted a heavy price from the IDF's manpower and budget, which exceeded NIS400m. Defense Minister Rabin and senior IDF officers charged that acts of vigilantism by Israeli settlers against Palestinians added to the burden on the IDF rather than helped it.[101] (For other aspects of the Intifada's impact on Israeli society and politics, see chapter on Israel.) All in all, the various measures the IDF employed failed to reduce substantially the level of violence, even though the IDF did regain the initiative in its struggle against the "strike forces." The Intifada's organizational structure was not broken. Although the Civil Administration resumed its activities in various towns and villages in the West Bank from which it had been forced out during 1988, the *de facto* dual authority in the territories remained an established fact as the Intifada ended its second year.

ORGANIZATIONAL FRICTIONS AND POPULAR FATIGUE

THE LOSS OF CENTRALIZED CONTROL

The Intifada's decentralized organization, which proved to be a great advantage in 1988 (see *MECS* 1988, p. 281) showed clear signs of strain in 1989, particularly during its latter half. It was manifested by the UNC's growing loss of control over the "strike forces" and by factional infighting. Israeli observers attributed the loss of control to the arrests by the authorities of experienced activists at all levels. Their replacements were less sophisticated politically, were more radical, and prone to spontaneous violence. Channels of communication between the leadership, both inside and outside the territories, and the rank-and-file activists were severed, making effective control more difficult. The proliferation of "strike forces" professing loyalty to rival factions in Fath and other organizations was another obstacle to coordination.[102]

Eliminating alleged collaborators with Israel was one of the main rolls of the "strike forces" since the beginning of the Intifada. Although social pressure, threats, and harassments were the main measures employed at first, 22 persons were killed during 1988 for collaboration.[103] In 1989, the campaign against collaborators assumed greater intensity. Popular committees set up interrogation centers where suspects were questioned and even tortured in order to obtain confessions and pledges to sever all ties with the authorities. Suspected informants were tried by clandestine "popular courts" and if found guilty, permission had to be obtained from top commanders in the territories and senior PLO officials outside before the killing took place.[104]

The growing power of the "strike forces" as well as numerous arrests of activists, which convinced the "strike forces" that their ranks had been penetrated by the authorities, combined to accelerate the killings of alleged collaborators. Call no. 38 by the UNC presented a landmark by setting 26 April as the day "of settling accounts" with the collaborators and urging the "strike forces" to use "all means" to punish "all those who deviate from the national line." Indeed, eight alleged collaborators were attacked on that day, and four of them were killed. The PLO radio reiterated similar calls throughout the period. The PLO's official organ, *Filastin al-Thawra*, expressed satisfaction that the "positive phenomenon" of eliminating collaborators received wide popular support.[105]

The following months witnessed a substantial increase in the number of murders, including quite a few cases of people who had little or no connection with the Israeli authorities. On at least three occasions, people murdered by one popular committee were declared martyrs by a rival one. Many of the victims were brutally tortured and their bodies mutilated. In Gaza, at least 13 women, whose husbands were suspected of collaboration or of disobeying the UNC's orders, were raped during April alone.[106] Official Israeli sources claimed that only about half of the victims were in fact informers. Many of the murders, they argued, stemmed from factional rivalries and in order to intimidate and impose the control of the "strike forces" over the population, while others were committed due to personal or family feuds. By 8 December, the Intifada's second anniversary, over 131 persons were murdered as alleged collaborators.[107]

The definition of collaborators deserving death became a source of disagreement among the various organizations. Fath supported the killing only of intelligence and police informants, and of land dealers who sold land to Jews. The leftist factions, on the other hand, advocated the elimination of all those who maintained any tie whatever with the authorities, including Civil Administration employees, village headmen, and even moderate pro-Jordanian figures, who harm Palestinian society and national effort. The Islamic fundamentalists added to the list criminal elements and those who corrupt Muslim society.[108]

The killing of people not clearly identified as collaborators raised the fear among Palestinians that the sense of common purpose forged during the Intifada would be destroyed. There was much concern that the fate of the Intifada would be like that of the 1936 Palestinian revolt, which deteriorated into an internal civil war.[109] Call no. 40, therefore, warned against accusing people of collaboration just "because they are political rivals with different points of view."[110] Aware of public reservations concerning wanton murders, popular committee members in various localities publicly read lists authorized by the UNC of the people murdered and the reasons for their killings. Confessions of alleged collaborators were publicized in order to demonstrate the harm they had done.[111] Collaborators, who had been provided by the Israeli authorities with weapons for self-defense, began to operate in groups against "strike force" committees.[112]

The UNC was caught in a dilemma in view of the alarming rate of murders, fearing total loss of control over the rank-and-file activists on the one hand and of public and international support on the other. Calls nos. 41, 44, 45, and 46 urged the continued persecution of collaborators, but warned the masses "not to liquidate any agent without a central decision by the higher command. Nor should any suspected agent be executed short of a national consensus on that decision or before he is warned beforehand or given a chance to repent."[113]

The principle of eliminating collaborators, however, was not disputed in public. Shaykh Zuhayr al-Diba'i, a prominent preacher from Nablus, asserted that while the people "looked with pride at the killing of agents," they resented the excessive violence and the mutilation of bodies. Both Faysal al-Husayni and Sari Nusayba argued for the right of every nation under occupation to fight collaboration. However, following three brutal murders in Gaza, the National Institutions there issued a statement condemning these particular cases and all "acts of revenge" as "counter to all laws and mores" and as adversely affecting the Palestinian situation.[114]

The UNC calls did little to stop the killings, leading to rifts among the various organizations. A Fath leaflet in Nablus in late November condemned the killings of "those who had erred in their ways," totally omitting the derogatory term of collaborators. Stressing that interrogations must be carried out under the orders of the "security apparatus" of the Intifada, Fath warned that the "military police and the UNC" would deal with groups violating the order. The leaflet also banned the arbitrary collection of "Intifada taxes" from shopkeepers or confiscating Israeli goods from shops. Both acts had been widely practiced by the "strike forces," often serving as a euphemism for extortion. Subsequent Fath leaflets stated that only PLO chief Yasir 'Arafat could authorize the killing of collaborators. In contrast, leaflets disseminated by the radical factions called upon the people to eliminate collaborators wherever they were found.[115]

The "Red Eagle," loosely affiliated with the PFLP, and the "Black Panther," comprised of c. 40 members and associated with Fath, were the two most notorious cases of "strike force" gangs which did not submit to UNC authority. Rather than confront the IDF, most of their actions were aimed at imposing their authority in the old section of Nablus (the Casbah) by eliminating alleged collaborators, levying taxes, and conducting marches carrying weapons. Nablus residents described both gangs as "out of control" for defying the UNC and PLO's calls to halt their unbridled killings. On 28 November, following the arrest of three of its members, the "Black Panther" imposed a curfew on parts of the Casbah, confiscated telephones to prevent contacts between residents, interrogated residents and even killed one.[116] The "Red Eagle" was apprehended on 9 November; the four leaders of the "Black Panther" were killed by IDF troops on 1 December, and five other members were arrested (see chapter on armed operations). Riots broke out in Nablus after both incidents. Members of both groups were hailed as popular heroes, and other youths joined their reorganized ranks.[117]

The dispute over the participation of schoolchildren in strikes was another expression of the organizational splits and loosening discipline. After almost 18 months of closure, in late July the Civil Administration allowed the gradual reopening of schools. The decision was greeted with enthusiasm in the territories, as a victory over Israel's "stultification policy," which was forced to bow to international pressure. In addition, there was fear among the populace that the prolonged closure would inflict long-term damage on a generation of children, particularly in view of the inadequacy of the attempts to set up an alternative school system (see below).[118]

Seeking to respond to these feelings, the UNC called for orderly studies, but, adopting a radical line, it instructed the students to participate in general strikes. The UNC's call was challenged from two quarters. It apparently misjudged the public mood as large numbers of students went to school during three strike days, 30 July, 9 and 16 August. Clashes erupted in several locations between PFLP supporters, who tried to block students from going to school, and supporters of Hamas and Fath, who sought to maintain orderly schooling in defiance of the UNC instructions.[119]

While urging the population to abide by the strikes, the UNC was forced to condemn the "irresponsible acts" of "reckless elements" disrupting schooling and drawing the students to the streets during ordinary school days. It urged the "strike forces" to confront these elements, and instructed the students to take part in the struggle only after school hours. Hamas took an even more moderate line, calling for leaving the schools out of the national struggle. Brawls between rival factions broke out on that issue too.[120]

The failure of the UNC's campaign against the computerized ID cards issued by the authorities further deepened the cracks in Palestinian unity and the lack of central control. During the weeks before 18 August, the day the new order came into effect, the popular committees confiscated hundreds of the new ID cards from local residents both in order to foil Israel's policy and to use the cards as an instrument of their own control over the population. The UNC declared a two-week-long solidarity strike of West Bank workers and an indefinite boycott of work in the Gaza Strip.[121]

Both calls proved to be too demanding in ignoring the economic plight of workers and their dependence on jobs in Israel. Whereas only several hundred workers in the Gaza Strip defied the call, in the West Bank only few heeded it, despite threats and active efforts of "strike forces" to prevent their going to their jobs. Moreover, a black market in the new ID cards developed due to the confiscations. The problem was aggravated as West Bank workers began taking the jobs vacated by the Gazans, despite the UNC's exhortations to the contrary.[122]

Realizing the failure of the strike and the growing economic plight in the Gaza Strip, the UNC wished, according to Palestinian sources, to revoke it. This was fiercely opposed, however, by the popular committees, particularly those affiliated with the PFLP. Call no. 45 reflected the UNC's difficulties: it praised the Gazan workers, but did not provide any specific instructions, thereby arousing some public resentment and confusion. Leaflets and slogans written on walls in Gaza eventually permitted workers to resume work in Israel in order to foil the authorities' attempt "to drive a wedge between the leadership and the people."[123]

The UNC could not publicly admit the failure of its efforts, nor could it risk open defiance by the popular committees. Calls nos. 46 and 47, therefore, exhorted the population in Gaza to continue its steadfastness, but could do little to stem the growing number of workers who disobeyed the calls. While Call no. 48 omitted any reference to Gaza, Call no. 49 urged the boycott of jobs in the Israeli settlements in the territories and stipulated specific strike days for both the West Bank and the Gaza Strip, thereby implicitly recognizing the failure of the campaign. Under popular pressure, the "strike forces" were obliged to return confiscated ID cards to the workers. By October the flow of workers from the Gaza Strip to Israel had returned to its pre-August days.[124]

The UNC's misjudgment on the two issues discussed above was attributed by Israeli observers both to the effect of arrests on its membership (see above) and to the growing influence of the radical organizations, particularly the PFLP. Additional factors seemed to have been resentment of former prisoners, who advocated a more radical line, against the intellectuals in the leadership, who enjoyed the media limelight, and who stressed the Intifada's political aspect; as well as Fath's fear of loss of support to Hamas, which prompted it to adopt a harder line.[125]

Parallel to the loss of central control, and partially contributing to it, was the growing factional rivalry particularly during the second half of the year. The main cause seemed to have been disagreements over the peace process and the continuous vying for influence, which were exacerbated by the growing difficulties in the confrontation against the IDF. In May, there were reports that several leading UNC activists, who had been arrested earlier, had been turned in to the authorities by factional rivals. During June, cars belonging to prominent Fath supporters in Ramallah, Jerusalem, and Bethlehem were set on fire.[126]

In early July, leaflets signed by the Palestine Popular Army-Fath circulating in the Nablus area sharply attacked 12 pro-Fath figures for embezzling funds (see below) and of living a life of luxury. Similar leaflets had been distributed in May, but at that time the National Institutions issued a statement rejecting the allegations as an Israeli fabrication.[127] In July, Palestinian sources expressed the concern that the leaflets may have been issued by radical factions as part of the ongoing interfactional struggle.[128]

Interfactional brawls became an alarming phenomenon, and at least some of the murders of alleged collaborators were in fact due to factional strife.[129] Reflecting the UNC's concern, Calls nos. 35 and 40 accused the Israeli authorities of sowing discord in Palestinian ranks, and called for the solution of "narrow-minded factional problems (*sic*)" in a "positive and patriotic manner."[130] In view of the growing discords, Calls nos. 44 and 45 urged the standardizing of slogans, demanding that they be signed only by the UNC. In addition, Call no. 45 urged the prisoners "to close ranks" and abide by the decisions of the prisoners' committees, which should represent all factions.[131] In November, a conciliation committee, headed by Faysal al-Husayni and other prominent public figures from other factions, was formed in order to solve the emerging factional disputes. The committee, however, remedied the symptom, but not the problem itself.[132]

THE FAILURE OF THE COMPREHENSIVE CIVIL DISOBEDIENCE CAMPAIGN

The attempt to transform the Intifada into a comprehensive civil disobedience campaign was unsuccessful primarily due to the continued economic dependence of the territories on Israel, and the worsening economic conditions in the territories. The frequent strikes and violent activity as well as economic sanctions imposed by Israel on rioting localities (see *MECS* 1988, p. 293) combined to bring about a severe recession in the territories. The strikes and curfews severely reduced the commuting of workers to Israel, thereby reducing a major source of income. In Gaza, where c. 50% of the work force was employed in Israel, this was felt acutely. Residents complained that the amounts levied by tax collectors were prohibitive and accused the authorities of a deliberate policy of impoverishing the population. Exports from the territories to Israel declined by c. 33% during 1988–89.[133]

The devaluation of the Jordanian dinar by almost 50% (see *MECS* 1988, chapters on Jordan and economic developments) was even more painful, since almost all business transactions, savings, and wages not earned in Israel were calculated in dinars. The decline in the dinar's rate in the territories was accelerated by the increased demand for Israeli currency in cash following the gradual closure of all Israeli banks in the territories during 1988 and by the need to pay the fines and taxes imposed on the population. As part of its own disengagement from the West Bank and in order to protect its own ailing economy, Jordan imposed additional restrictions on imports from the territories. Palestinians also complained that other Arab states restricted agricultural imports from the territories, ostensibly in order to prevent disguised Israeli exports.[134] Calls nos. 33, 35, 39, and 48 berated the Arab states for not fulfilling their pledges of financial aid to the Palestinians.[135]

Statistics on economic activity in the territories since the beginning of the Intifada were both fragmented and unreliable. According to the Ramallah Chamber of Commerce, the standard of living in the territories declined by c. 50% during 1988–89 as annual per capita income dropped from $1,500 to $700.[136] The growing economic hardship increased the dependence of the population on work in Israel. Consequently, the number of Palestinian workers in Israel gradually grew during the latter part of 1989 amounting to c. 105,000 daily, close to the pre-Intifada figures.[137]

The PLO had pledged to sustain financially the organizational activity of the Intifada and the population in general, particularly following Jordan's disengagement from the West Bank. Muhammad Milhim, director of the PLO's Occupied Homeland Affairs Department, claimed that $1m. daily were provided to individuals and institutions in the territories. Israeli sources, however, estimated the amount remitted as considerably smaller. Even Milhim, though, admitted that the funds channeled were insufficient to cover the growing population's needs. Moreover, some Palestinian sources criticized the large share allocated to the support of individuals rather than to investments.[138] Occasional reports on embezzlements by PLO officials in Amman and by various activists in the territories became a source of certain resentment in the territories.[139]

On the other hand, various sectors which had previously suffered from Israeli competition benefited from the boycott of Israeli products (see below). According to Palestinian sources, the number of egg-laying chickens in the West Bank had tripled since 1987, to 35,000, while the number of milch cows grew to an estimated 14,000 in 1989 from 10,500 in 1987. Some 1,100 small- and medium-sized manufacturing businesses mainly in cheap textiles, shoes, soft drinks, and cigarettes, were also given a boost. The main problems of these industries, however, were their inability to absorb large numbers of workers and their narrow range of products. The independent export of citrus from Gaza to Europe, which had been regarded as a symbol of independence and as a great financial hope, ended in a loss of $300,000 to the growers. The frequent general strikes also undermined the profitability of local businesses. Palestinian economists admitted that many of the newly established household industries were inefficient and were more important for morale than for long-term economic growth. The territories, they admitted, were still very far from shedding their economic dependence on Israel.[140]

The attainment of self-sufficiency particularly in food production was regarded by the UNC as essential both for reducing Palestinian vulnerability to Israeli pressures and for laying the infrastructure for the future Palestinian state. The population was encouraged to grow its own food and reclaim lands which had been neglected into disuse. Likewise, the repeated exhortations to boycott "Zionist goods," which could be produced locally, were largely, but never fully, obeyed. Call no. 50, for instance, denounced the attempts to market Israeli products under false labels. The "strike forces," therefore, occasionally destroyed Israeli goods secretly sold by local merchants.[141]

Simultaneously, the UNC sought to ease the burden on the lower classes, fearing that economic hardships were the greatest threat to the continuance of the Intifada.

Calls nos. 32, 33, and 39 instructed employers not to deduct the days of strikes from the workers' wages. Rather, they were urged to absorb more workers and raise wages by 40% to compensate for inflation and the dinar's devaluation. Landlords were told to lower rents by 25%. Calls nos. 42 and 43 urged merchants to take the plight of the peasants into consideration, and not to raise prices.[142] While Call no. 42 urged money changers to stop speculation on the dinar, the "strike forces" compelled money changers to artificially appreciate its value. In February, the money changers went on strike in protest against the intimidation.[143]

Having realized the limits of the population's endurance, the UNC did not call upon the workers to abandon their jobs in Israel. Moreover, even the campaign which started in 1988 to bring about the total resignation of the Civil Administration employees failed (see *MECS* 1988, p. 288). The repeated exhortations and threats throughout 1989 aimed at the remaining employees indicated that compliance was limited. Likewise, none of the rural councils and appointed mayors in the West Bank resigned during 1989.[144]

Both the UNC and Civil Administration regarded the withholding of taxes as a crucial element on the road to comprehensive civil disobedience. While the UNC repeatedly exhorted the population not to pay taxes, the Civil Administration conducted concerted collection campaigns and made various government services and permits conditional upon payment of taxes. On the whole, however, the Administration's revenue declined by a third in 1989, also because of the decline of economic activity in the territories.[145]

A collective tax revolt declared in July by the residents of Bayt Sahur, a town near Bethlehem, was quickly recognized as a new phase in the confrontation and as a crucial test of will for both sides with implications for the territories as a whole. In response to the strike, the IDF imposed a virtual siege on the town during September. Tax collectors accompanied by soldiers confiscated equipment and property belonging to the tax-delinquents worth c. NIS3m. Forty merchants were detained and heavily fined. Call no. 47 praised the residents of Bayt Sahur and urged the rest of the population to follow their example. The local "strike forces" threatened those who paid taxes with severe punishments. Faysal al-Husayni appealed to the foreign consuls serving in Jerusalem to intervene but to litle effect. The patriarchs of the three main churches in Jerusalem, who came to express solidarity with the residents, were not allowed to enter the town.[146]

By late October, the collection campaign was completed with both sides claiming victory. Some IDF officers admitted, however, that while the authorities collected the due debts, the entire affair ended in a political and a morale-boosting victory for the population. The residents' determination and morale were not broken, they added, while the extensive coverage of the affair in the world media further tarnished Israel's image. Some observers expressed the fear that the severe measures employed by the government would further radicalize the population into resorting to firearms. The severity of the measures, however, did seem to deter other localities from following the example of Bayt Sahur.[147]

The UNC's attempt to build an alternative educational system proved only partially successful. The Israeli authorities' prolonged closure of West Bank schools following student riots threatened the loss of the entire school year for more than 320,000 elementary and high-school students. Call no. 33, therefore, urged the establishment of national education bodies in every locality to encourage popular education as well as develop and "Palestinize" the curriculum.[148] Although networks of classes were organized by education committees, they did not provide a suitable alternative to the government school system as indicated by the enthusiasm with which the opening of schools was greeted (see above). The universities offered semiclandestine courses to which the Israeli authorities turned a blind eye. An attempt to launch an international campaign to exert pressure on the authorities to reopen the universities failed due to internal disagreements.[149]

The IDF measures and the growing economic pressures led to a certain weariness of the population, and to a decline in the number of those participating in acts of protest. Such weariness was strongly manifested when popular committees in Nablus, ordinarily the radical center of the Intifada, called upon the population to disregard the UNC's announcement of a five-day strike starting from 5 October. Residents complained that the town had suffered too much from curfews and strikes in the previous month, and the UNC had not taken the population's plight into consideration. In response, Call no. 47 exempted the people of Nablus from the strikes it had stipulated. Merchants committees in Ramallah, for instance, met to discuss the merchants' growing laxity in complying with the UNC orders.[150] The most alarming sign from the UNC point of view were the reports of increased emigration from the territories, estimated at 15,000 a year. Call no. 36 sharply attacked those "foreign agencies" encouraging Palestinian emigration and prodded the population to adhere to the homeland.[151]

On the whole, despite the signs of fatigue and laxity, the Palestinian community still manifested a considerable degree of social solidarity and willingness to sacrifice. Even if somewhat eroded, the overall commitment of the population to the Intifada and its political goals remained high.

NOTES

For the place and frequency of publications cited here, and for the full name of the publication, news agency, radio station, or monitoring service where an abbreviation is used, please see "List of Sources." Only in the case of more than one publication bearing the same name is the place of publication noted here.

1. *Ma'ariv,* 5 April; *Davar,* 20 October 1989; Ze'ev Schieff and Ehud Ya'ari, *Intifada* (Tel Aviv: Schocken, 1990) pp. 202–203.
2. *Ma'ariv,* 27 January, 5 April; *Ha'aretz,* 12 February, 5 May, 3 October; *JP,* 12 May 1989.
3. *Ma'ariv,* 5 April, 19 October; *Davar,* 20 October 1989.
4. Wahid 'Abd al-Majid, "Al-Shumuliyya al-Ijtima'iyya lil-Intifada," *Shu'un Filastiniyya,* April 1989; *al-Ittihad,* Abu Dhabi, 9 May; *'Al Hamishmar,* 10 March 1989.
5. *Filastin al-Thawra,* 23 April; *al-Watan,* 18 February 1989.
6. *Al-Hurriyya,* 30 July, 20 August; GNA, 18 February — DR, 21 February 1989.
7. *Ma'ariv,* 13 January; *al-Watan,* 8 March; *Yedi'ot Aharanot,* 14 May; *al-Hurriyya,* 8 October 1989.
8. *Al-Hadaf,* 16 April; *al-Hurriyya,* 5 March, 8 October 1989.
9. Sara Roy, "Changing Political Attitudes among Gaza Refugees," *Journal of Palestine Studies,* Autumn 1989, p. 74; see also interview with Mahmud al-Mi'ari, a Bir Zayt University professor, in *al-Ittihad,* Abu Dhabi, 9 May 1989.
10. See UNC activist 'Ata Abu Kirsh in *Shu'un Filastiniyya,* October 1989, p. 105.
11. *Ma'ariv,* 25 May; *al-Ittihad,* Abu Dhabi, 21 June 1989.

12. *Al-Hurriyya*, 1 January, 16 April, 7 May; VoP (Baghdad) 12 February, 30 April — DR, 13 February, 30 April; *al-Ard al-Muhtalla*, No. 57, September 1989.

13. *Al-Hurriyya*, 7 May, 2, 30 July, 1, 8 October 1989.

14. *Ma'ariv*, 2 January; *JP*, 29 January; *Ha'aretz*, 31 March 1989.

15. *Al-Hurriyya*, 15 January 1989.

16. *Ha'aretz*, 3, 6 February, 6 June; *Ma'ariv*, 17 March; *al-Nadwa*, 3 April; *al-Dustur*, Amman, 11 May 1989.

17. *Ha'aretz*, 31 March 1989.

18. VoP (Baghdad) 12 February, 17 August — DR 13 February, 18 August; VoP (San'a), 31 March — DR, 3 April; *al-Hurriyya*, 28 May 1989.

19. *Davar*, 19 May; *Ha'aretz*, 23 May, 28 November 1989.

20. *Shu'un Filastiniyya*, October 1989; *Filastin al-Thawra*, 5 March; *al-Nasr*, Nicosia, 10 March; *Ma'ariv*, 18 April 1989.

21. *Ha'aretz*, 8 January, *'Al Hamishmar*, 23 April, 3 May; R. al-Quds, 3 July 1989.

22. *Ha'aretz*, 21 May; *Ma'ariv*, 22 May; *JP*, 23 May; VoP (San'a), 23 May — DR, 24 May; *al-Hurriyya*, 16 April, 28 May; *IHT*, 16 June 1989.

23. *JP*, 15 June; *Ha'aretz*, 2 January, 2, 12 May, 8 October, 24, 28 November 1989.

24. *Ha'aretz*, 12 May, 21 August, 4 September, 6 December; *Ma'ariv*, 8 December 1989. The IDF and Palestinian sources provide lower and higher figures, 250 and more than 350, respectively.

25. E.g., 'Arafat's "uprising messages" on VoP (Algiers), 9 March — DR, 21 March and on VoP (San'a), 14 August — DR, 15 August; *al-Hurriyya*, 26 February 1989.

26. "Call no. 39," VoP (Baghdad), 30 April — DR, 30 April; *al-Hurriyya*, 27 August 1989.

27. *Ha'aretz*, 14 April, 5 July, 5, 19 December 1989.

28. See "Call no. 32," VoP (Baghdad), 7 January — DR, 7 January; *Hadashot*, 5, 16 January; *Yedi'ot Aharonot*, 26 March, 19 May; *Ha'aretz*, 6 March, 21 May, 16 June; *JP*, 16 June 1989.

29. Israeli TV, 23 April — DR, 24 April; *Ha'aretz*, 3 February, 12 December; *Filastin al-Thawra*, 7 May; *JP*, 23 February, 16 June 1989.

30. For the history of the Islamic movement in the territories, see Ziyad Abu'Amr, *Al-Haraka al-Islamiyya fi al-Diffa al-Gharbiyya wa-Quta' Ghaza* (Acre: Dar al-Aswar, 1989).

31. *JP*, 12 July; *al-Khalij; al-Anba*, Kuwait, 9 December 1989.

32. Shaykh Yasin to Israeli TV, 23 September — DR, 27 September; *Ha'aretz*, 26 November 1989.

33. *Al-Mustaqbal*, 11 February 1989.

34. Re'uven Paz, *The Islamic Covenant and its Meaning* (Tel Aviv: Dayan Center, Data and Analysis Series, September 1988; in Hebrew), pp. 46–47.

35. Paz, op. cit., pp. 33, 34, 35.

36. Paz, op. cit., pp. 41–42. See also Hamas Calls nos. 34, 37, 40, 42 cited in *Ha'aretz*, 16 January, 29 May; *Filastin al-Muslima*, March, May 1989.

37. *Ila Filastin*, No. 41, April 1989.

38. *Ha'aretz*, 26 March; *JP*, 2 February, 5, 24 March 1989.

39. *Al-'Alam*, London, 22 July; Abu Iyad to *al-Ra'y*, 8 December 1989.

40. VoP (Baghdad), 7 January — DR, 9 January; *al-Hurriyya*, 30 July 1989.

41. Call no. 35 in *al-Hurriyya*, 5 March; *Beirut al-Masa*, 6 March; Husayni to *al-Sharq al-Awsat*, 12 March; *al-'Alam*, London, 22 July, 18 December; *Ila Filastin*, No. 41, April; *Shu'un Filastiniyya*, October 1989, pp. 107–108.

42. R. Monte Carlo, 3 February; *al-Mustaqbal*, 11 February; *al-Nahar*, Jerusalem, 30 April 1989.

43. Hamas Call no. 37 of 3 March in *Filastin al-Muslima*, March; Yasin to *Filastin al-Muslima*, May 1989.

44. *Filastin al-Muslima*, September 1989.

45. *Al-Mukhtar al-Islami*, June 1989.

46. *Ha'aretz*, 23 May, 18 September, 27 November; *JP*, 28, 30 November; *Ma'ariv*, 20 October 1989.

47. *NYT*, 19 June; *Ha'aretz*, 29 September; *JP*, 12 November; *Ma'ariv*, 22, 23 May, 2, 17 November 1989.

48. *Ha'aretz,* 22 September, 27 November; *JP,* 6 December; *Filastin al-Muslima,* November; *al-Ra'y,* 8 December; *Shu'un Filastiniyya,* October 1989, pp. 106–107.
49. *JP,* 24 November, 8 December; *Ma'ariv,* 8 December; *Filastin al-Muslima,* July 1989.
50. *Al-'Alam,* London, 22 July; *al-Qabas,* 30 July; *Ha'aretz,* 22 September, 30 October, 22 December; *Filastin al-Muslima,* September 1989.
51. *Al-Nahar,* East Jerusalem, 21 January; *al-Fajr, Ha'aretz,* 21 January; *al-Sha'b,* East Jerusalem, 21 February 1989.
52. *'Al Hamishmar,* 7 March, 6 April; *JP,* 7 April 1989.
53. VoP (San'a), 22 January — DR, 24 January; VoP (Baghdad), 12 February — DR, 13 February; *Ma'ariv,* 27, 30 January 1989.
54. *Ma'ariv,* 27 January; *FT,* 28 January 1989.
55. *Ha'aretz,* 31 January; *JP,* 3 February 1989.
56. *Al-Quds,* 30 January; *JP, Ha'aretz,* 31 January, 3 February 1989.
57. *Ma'ariv,* 16, 17, 20, 24 February; *JP,* 16 February 1989.
58. Compare his statements in *Ha'aretz,* 31 July with those in *al-Bayadir al-Siyasi,* 4 March; *al-Sharq al-Awsat,* 11 March; *Filastin al-Thawra,* 23 April; *al-Wafd,* 24 April; *Akhir Sa'a,* 17 May 1989.
59. *Ha'aretz,* 23 February; Israeli TV, 19 February — DR, 24 February; *al-Fajr* (English ed.), 27 February; *al-Tali'a,* 16 March 1989.
60. *Al-Fajr,* 19, 22 February; *al-Fajr* (English ed.), 20 February; *al-Ghadd,* April 1989.
61. *Al-Hurriyya,* 5 March; *Ha'aretz,* 2 March; *'Al Hamishmar,* 26 March 1989.
62. *Al-Ittihad,* Abu Dhabi, 22 March; *JP,* 24 March; *Ha'aretz,* 26 March 1989.
63. *Ma'ariv,* 24 July; "Iltiqa'at fi al-Ittijahayn," *Shu'un Filastiniyya,* August 1989, pp. 141–43.
64. VoP (Baghdad), 20 July; *al-Tali'a, Ha'aretz,* 27 July; *al-Fajr* (English ed.), 31 July; *JP,* 11 August; *al-Hurriyya,* 30 July, 20 August 1989.
65. *Al-Fajr,* 8 April; *FT,* 8 April; *JP,* 9 April; *Ha'aretz,* 12 April; *al-Fajr* (English ed.), 17 April; *al-Hurriyya,* 30 April 1989.
66. *JP,* 7, 9 April; VoI (in English), 9 April — DR, 10 April; *al-Bayadir al-Siyasi,* 22 April 1989.
67. *NYT,* 15 April; *Ha'aretz,* 17 April; *al-Bayadir al-Siyasi,* 22 April 1989.
68. MENA, 26 April — DR, 27 April 1989.
69. *Al-Fajr* (English ed.), 1 May 1989.
70. *IHT, Ha'aretz,* 27 April; *al-Hurriyya,* 7 May 1989.
71. *Al-Hurriyya,* 28 May, 3 July; *al-Nashra,* Athens, 27 July 1989.
72. *Ha'aretz,* 15 May; *Ma'ariv,* 19 May 1989.
73. *JP,* 16 May; VoI (in English), 15 May — DR, 16 May; R. IDF, 16 May — DR, 16 May; *al-Fajr* (English ed.), 19 February 1989.
74. *Al-Bayadir al-Siyasi,* 1 July; *JP,* 12 July; *Ha'aretz,* 30 July 1989.
75. *Ha'aretz,* 8, 20 September; *al-Watan,* Kuwait, 12 September; MENA, 19 September, 11 October — DR, 17 October; *al-Hayat,* London, 22 September 1989.
76. *Ha'aretz,* 27 September; *al-Tali'a,* 28 September; *al-Hurriyya,* 8 October 1989.
77. *Al-Hurriyya,* 1 October 1989.
78. *Al-Fajr* (English ed.), 20 November; *al-Fajr,* 11 December; *al-Hurriyya,* 19 November 1989.
79. Israeli TV, 1 November — DR, 2 November 1989.
80. *Al-Yawm al-Sabi',* 18 September 1989.
81. *Al-Fajr,* 20 November; *JP,* 24 November, 8 December 1989.
82. *JP,* 11 January; *Ha'aretz,* 7 April; *Hatzofeh,* 9 May 1989.
83. *'Al Hamishmar,* 24 January; *NYT,* 31 January, 9 February 1989.
84. *Ha'aretz,* 10 January, 7 April; *NYT,* 31 January 1989.
85. *Ma'ariv,* 30 August; *Ha'aretz,* 2 October; *Davar,* 8 December 1989.
86. *Ha'aretz,* 18 January, 29 March, 28 August; *JP,* 4 January, 31 July; *Ma'ariv,* 21 May 1989.
87. *JP,* 12 January; *Ha'aretz,* 18, 22 January; *Ma'ariv,* 25 January; *Hadashot,* 27 January 1989.
88. *Ma'ariv,* 24 January; *JP,* 23 January, 2 February 1989.
89. *Ha'aretz,* 22 January; *Yedi'ot Aharonot,* 6 October; *Ma'ariv,* 31 May 1989.
90. *Ha'aretz,* 25 January; *JP,* 2 March 1989.

91. *'Al Hamishmar*, 15 August; *Ha'aretz*, 14 September 1989.
92. *Yedi'ot Aharonot*, 19 May; *Ha'aretz, Hadashot*, 2 October 1989.
93. *Ma'ariv*, 14 April; VoI, 4 May — DR, 5 May; *Ha'aretz*, 7 May 1989.
94. *Ha'aretz*, 5, 21 July; *Ma'ariv*, 13 August 1989.
95. *Ha'aretz*, 1, 15 December; *JP*, 18 January, 7 April. See also the US State Department Report on Human Rights published in February 1990, cited in *JP*, 21 February 1990.
96. *JP*, 30 June; *Ha'aretz*, 2 January, 8 September 1989.
97. *Davar*, 26 February 1989.
98. *JP*, 16, 17, 18 May; *Ha'aretz*, 28 May 1989.
99. *Ha'aretz*, 14 March, 21 October; *Yedi'ot Aharonot*, 12 September 1989.
100. *'Al Hamishmar*, 7 March, 6 April; *JP*, 7 April; *Ha'aretz*, 20 June 1989.
101. *Ha'aretz*, 17 January, 10 February; *JP*, 24 May; *Ma'ariv*, 15 February, 31 May 1989.
102. *Ha'aretz*, 29 August; *'Al Hamishmar*, 4 December; al-Diba'i to *al-Watan*, 2 September 1989.
103. AP estimate, cited in *Ha'aretz*, 6 December 1989.
104. *Ha'aretz*, 2 August; *JP*, 19 April; *Ma'ariv*, 2 May; *IHT*, 24 August 1989.
105. *Al-Hurriyya*, 16 April; *Ma'ariv*, 27 April; *Yedi'ot Aharonot*, 28 April; *Filastin al-Thawra*, 2 May 1989.
106. *JP*, 16 May, 20 August; *IHT*, 25 August; *Ha'aretz*, 23 April, 1 May, 21 August, 1 December 1989. See Taysir Nasrallah, a deported Fath activist, who admitted in *Shu'un Filastiniyya*, October 1989, p. 110, that several mistakes had been made.
107. *JP*, 20 August; *Ha'aretz*, 21 August; *Ma'ariv*, 8 December; AP estimate, cited in *Ha'aretz*, 6 December 1989.
108. *Ha'aretz*, 5 May; *IHT*, 24 August 1989.
109. UNC activist to *al-Hurriyya*, 3 September 1989. For the internal strife in the 1936 rebellion, see Yehoshua Porath, *The Palestinian Arab National Movement, 1929–1939, from Riots to Rebellion* (London: Frank Cass, 1977) pp. 249ff.
110. *Al-Hurriyya*, 28 May; *Ha'aretz*, 21 August 1989.
111. *Hadashot*, 6 August; *Ma'ariv*, 3 October 1989.
112. *Ma'ariv*, 4 September; *JP*, 26 September; *Ha'aretz*, 13 August, 4 October 1989.
113. *Al-Nashra*, Athens, 24 July; VoP (Baghdad), 17 August — DR, 17 August; *al-Ard al-Muhtalla*, No. 57, September; *al-Hurriyya*, 1 October 1989.
114. *Al-Watan*, 2 September; *Ha'aretz, al-Fajr*, 26 September; *Ma'ariv*, 29 September 1989.
115. *'Al Hamishmar*, 4 December; *Ma'ariv*, 14 July, 30 November; *JP*, 29 December 1989.
116. *JP*, 10, 29 November, 3 December; *Ha'aretz*, 3 November 1989.
117. *Ma'ariv*, 3 September; *JP*, 10 November, 3 December; *Ha'aretz*, 15, 19 December; *'Al Hamishmar*, 4 December 1989.
118. *Ha'aretz*, 23, 24 July; *al-Fajr*, 23 July; Call no. 43 in *al-Hurriyya*, 30 July 1989.
119. VoI (in Arabic), 31 July — DR, 31 July; *Ha'aretz*, 31 July, 10 August; *JP*, 11 August; R. IDF, 16 August — DR, 17 August 1989.
120. See Call no. 45 in *al-Ard al-Muhtalla*, No. 57, September; Call no. 46 in *al-Hurriyya*, 1 October; Hamas Calls nos. 45, 46, 47 in *Ha'aretz*, 23 July; *Filastin al-Muslima*, 14 September 1989.
121. *Ha'aretz*, 30 July, 13, 14, 18 August 1989.
122. *Ha'aretz*, 20, 21, 23, 24 August; *Ma'ariv*, 25 August; *Davar*, 17 September; *FT*, 10 November 1989.
123. *Al-Ard al-Muhtalla*, No. 57, September, p. 151; *JP*, 1 September 1989.
124. *Al-Hurriyya*, 1, 12 October, 19 November; *Yedi'ot Aharonot*, 27 September; R. IDF, 27 September — DR, 28 September; *Ha'aretz*, 5 December 1989.
125. *JP*, 12 July; *'Al Hamishmar*, 31 August, 4 December; *Ha'aretz*, 29 August 1989.
126. Israeli TV, 5 May — DR, 8 May; *JP*, 12 July 1989.
127. Israeli TV, 10 May — DR, 11 May; *al-Fajr*, 11 May 1989.
128. VoI, 17 July — DR, 18 May; AFP, 19 May; *Ma'ariv*, 20 July 1989.
129. *IHT*, 16 June; *Ma'ariv*, 31 July; *Ha'aretz*, 21 August, 9 November, 3 December; *JP*, 24 November 1989.
130. *Al-Hurriyya*, 5 March, 28 May 1989.

131. VoP (Baghdad), 17 August — DR, 17 August; *al-Ard al-Muhtalla,* No. 57, September 1989, pp. 153-54.
132. *Ha'aretz,* 9, 12 November; *JP,* 24 November 1989.
133. *JP,* 10, 13, 17 February; *Ha'aretz,* 17 February 1989.
134. *Ha'aretz,* 17 February; *JP,* 17 April, 18 October; *al-Majalla,* 8 January 1989.
135. *Al-Hurriyya,* 29 January, 5 March, 7 May, 19 November 1989.
136. VoI, 7 February — DR, 10 February 1989.
137. *Hatzofeh,* 7 June; *JP,* 27 November 1989.
138. *Al-Watan,* 8 March; *Ma'ariv,* 13 January, 8 December; *Yedi'ot Aharanot,* 14 May 1989.
139. *Al-Muharrir,* 1 April, 27 May; *Yedi'ot Aharonot,* 17 May 1989.
140. *JP,* 1, 17 February, 17 April; *IHT,* 7 September; *Ma'ariv,* 8 December; *al-Fajr* (English ed.), 1 February 1989.
141. See, e.g., Calls nos. 34, 38, 40, 41, 42, and 45 in *al-Hurriyya,* 19 February, 16 April, 9 July; *al-Nashra,* Athens, 24 July; *al-Ard al-Muhtalla,* No. 57, September, p. 154; VoP (Baghdad), 26 December — DR, 27 December; *Ha'aretz,* 27 January 1989.
142. *Al-Hurriyya,* 19 January, 19 February, 7 May, 9, 30 July; VoP (San'a), 22 January — DR, 24 January 1989.
143. *Al-Hurriyya,* 9 July; *Hadashot,* 12 February; *Ma'ariv,* 20 February; *Ha'aretz,* 24 February, 9 July 1989.
144. *Ma'ariv,* 23 February; Brig. Gen. Shay Erez, "The Intidafa: an Interim Report," *Sekira Hodshit* (Hebrew), January 1990, p. 30.
145. *Ma'ariv,* 18 August; *Ha'aretz,* 20 October 1989.
146. *Ha'aretz,* 4 July; 12 October, 11 November; *al-Hurriyya,* 12 October; R. al-Quds, 4 July, 20 August; *JP,* 4, 29 October 1989.
147. *JP,* 1 November; *Ha'aretz,* 11 November; *'Al Hamishmar,* 4 December 1989.
148. *NYT,* 8 May; Call no. 33 in VoP (San'a), 22 January — DR, 24 January 1989.
149. *Ha'aretz,* 19 April, 1 December 1989.
150. *Ha'aretz,* 5 October, 7 August; *al-Hurriyya,* 12 October 1989.
151. *Ha'aretz,* 30 August; *JP,* 18 October; *al-Hurriyya,* 19 March 1989.

MIDDLE EAST
ECONOMIC ISSUES

Middle East Oil Developments 1989

DAVID RACHOVICH and GAD GILBAR

INTRODUCTION

The fourth agreement since 1983 among members of the Organization of Petroleum Exporting Countries (Opec) on production ceilings and quota distribution, signed in Vienna in November 1988, came into force on 1 January 1989. (For the agreement, see *MECS* 1988, pp. 321-22). None of the earlier agreements, of March 1983, October 1984, and December 1986, had survived long. In Opec circles it was generally estimated that the November 1988 agreement would open a new chapter in the relationships among the members and that it would permit the existence of a stable price structure on the international market. Such estimates were based on the following developments:

1. Iraq was integrated into the new agreement and received a quota of the same size as Iran's. This was of great importance in view of the termination of the Gulf War, the reconstruction of Iraq's oil installations, and the expansion of its production and export capacity.

2. The different components of the production quotas were defined by agreement. In particular, the dispute between members over the mode of inclusion of the condensates (natural gas liquids; NGLs) in the production quotas was settled.

3. A new Monitoring Committee at the level of oil ministers was established, to ensure that the new quota agreement was honored and to monitor developments on the international oil market.

4. Several Opec members received a mandate from the organization to enter into discussions with "independent" oil states (namely, nonmembers of Opec) to persuade them to join in the effort to stabilize oil prices on the world market, i.e., to induce them to cut back on their own production. As is known, from 1979 to 1985 there was a fall in the share of Opec oil in the total world production and an increase in the elasticity of demand for oil. Clearly, therefore, any attempt to bring about a rise in the price level had to be made by coordination and cooperation with the large "independent" producers, or at least with some of them.

In signing the November 1988 agreement Opec members underlined the importance of cooperation with the "independents." They made it clear that without such cooperation stabilizing the reference price of $18 per barrel could not be assured. The organization thus let it be known that the burden of price stabilization could not be placed on its shoulders alone and that achieving this goal required that all the large oil producers and exporters without exception make their contribution.

Developments on the world oil market and the Opec members' production policy during 1989 showed that this cooperation was in fact of limited importance. Of incomparably greater impact on developments were the oil policy of the large producers on the Arabian Peninsula (Saudi Arabia, Kuwait, and the United Arab Emirates [UAE]), on the one hand, and a number of unforeseen events on the other — production breakdowns, mishaps, and disasters among several of the "independent" producers.

PRICE, SUPPLY, AND DEMAND

The year 1989 began with a tendency toward a rise in oil prices. The spot price of Dubai Fateh rose from $13.45 a barrel on 3 January to $14.35 on 24 January. The spot price of Brent rose during those weeks from $16.40 to $17.73 per barrel (see Table 1). This increase stemmed from the widely held evaluation on the world market that Opec members intended to uphold the quota agreement they had signed in November 1988. Of special significance were reports that Saudi Arabia had cut back its production by about half at the beginning of January (to 3.6m. barrels per day [b/d] in the week ended 8 January from 7.4m. b/d the previous week).[1] What had taken shape in January became a clearly marked trend in March and April. The spot price of Dubai Fateh reached $16.75 a barrel on 25 April and of Brent, $20.30. Compared with the price level at the end of November 1988, the rise in the first four months of 1989 was quite steep: an addition of $6.90 a barrel of Dubai Fateh (cf. *MECS* 1988, p. 328, Table 1) and of $5.90 a barrel of West Texas Intermediate (WTI).[2] The Opec Monitoring Committee convened on 29 March. It noted with evident satisfaction that the price of the seven types of crude oil included in the "Opec basket" was higher than the reference price of $18 a barrel fixed by the organization.[3]

Three major factors are pertinent to the rise in oil prices in the first months of 1989: first, an increase in world demand for oil.[4] Second, disruptions in oil supply from non-Opec sources, which applied in particular to the North Sea wells — the result of the effects of the explosion on the Piper Alpha rig (July 1988), the interruption of production at the beginning of 1989 at the Fulmar oil field, and the accident on the Cormorant Alpha rig.[5] The running aground of the Exxon tanker *Valdez* on 24 March and the consequent ecological disaster[6] also contributed to the disruption of the regular supply from non-Opec sources. Third, Opec itself cut back on production. The total production of the organization fell from c. 23m. b/d in December 1988 to c. 19.6m. b/d in February-March 1989.[7]

The rising trend was halted at the end of April; in May-September there was actually a decline in the prices of most grades of oil (see Table 1). The price of the "Opec basket" fell to $16.78 a barrel in July-September. The factors leading to this change were the excess production by several Opec members over their allotted quotas (see Tables 2, 3, and 4).[8] To this should be added the resumption of production and supply from North Sea fields, which had been inoperative for many months.[9]

At the beginning of October there was again a tendency toward a rise in prices, prompted mainly by an increase in world demand as a result of the severe cold spell that descended on Europe and North America at the end of 1989.[10] This tendency was marked in December, at the end of which the price of Dubai Fateh rose to $17.80 a barrel, that of Brent to $21,[11] and that of WTI to $22.[12] These were the highest prices recorded in 1989. The effect of excess production by several Opec members, which likewise persisted throughout the last two months of 1989, was thus fully offset by the increased demand (see Tables 2 and 3).[13] As they had in the opening months of the year (January-April), so in the closing months (October-December) the Opec members benefited from the average price of the "Opec basket" being higher than the reference price that the organization had set for itself (see Table 4).

A summary of developments in the sphere of oil prices throughout 1989 shows clearly that this was the best year for the producers since the grave crisis of 1986. The average "Opec basket" price of about $11 a barrel in 1986 rose to $14.28 in 1988 and to $17.31 in 1989. In other words, the average price rose in 1989 by 21.2% compared with the previous year. True, this average price of $17.31 a barrel fell short of the organization's reference price ($18), but such a small difference between the latter and the yearly average price of the "basket" had not existed in years. The Middle Eastern producers also profited from the widening gap in 1989 between the prices of light oil, which constituted the bulk of their exports, and of heavy oil. This difference in prices almost doubled (from $1.5 to about $3 a barrel).[14]

One development worth emphasizing in particular is that together with the rise in price levels in 1989 there was also a rise in the quantity that Opec produced (in average terms) as the year progressed (see below). This development could be accounted for by the rise in world demand for oil, on the one hand, and the fall in supply from several of the large non-Opec producers, on the other. Consumption by the non-Communist world rose in 1989 by about 2% (total consumption 51.9m. b/d), consumption by the OECD states rose by 1% (total consumption 37.4m. b/d), and that of the developing countries by 4.5% (14.5m. b/d).[15] The US and Japan among the developed states and South Korea and Taiwan among the others were especially prominent as economies with a rise in oil consumption rates.[16] At the same time, there was a fall in absolute terms in the supply of oil from the North Sea, the US, and the USSR. British North Sea oil production fell in 1989 on average by about 500,000 b/d as a result of a series of accidents on the production facilities.[17] US production also dropped by a similar amount.[18] In the USSR, the fall in production was apparently less: in the first nine months of the year it declined by an average of about 320,000 b/d.[19] The fall in production within the boundaries of the USSR together with the fall in coal and nuclear energy production there caused a drop in exports of Soviet crude oil of about 300,000 b/d.[20] As a result of these three developments, the demand for ME oil rose both in the US and in the countries of Eastern Europe.

It should be stressed that this increase in the amount produced by Opec and the parallel rise in prices was a function of the maturing of medium- and long-range processes (increase in oil consumption) together with casual factors (the accidents in the North Sea, coal miners' strikes in the USSR, and the like).

OPEC PRODUCERS

5–7 JUNE VIENNA CONFERENCE[21]

The 85th Opec conference on 5–7 June in Vienna took place during a Saudi-Kuwaiti dispute over the organization's production ceiling and the allocation of production quotas to the members for the second half of 1989, and hence over the target prices. In contrast to its position in previous years, Saudi Arabia at this conference supported an increase in the oil price above $18 a barrel, with a concomitant, relatively moderate, increase in the organization's production ceiling from 18.5m. b/d to 19.5m. b/d. As for the distribution of the new production total, Saudi Arabia proposed that it should be on a pro rata basis among Opec members (namely, the size of the addition would be proportionate to each member's share in total Opec production). As against this Saudi position, which basically sought to stabilize the price, Kuwait called for adopting a policy of increase in production. Kuwait's proposal was that instead of striving for prices above $18 a barrel, the organization's production ceiling should be raised to at least 20m. b/d. Moreover, Kuwait demanded for itself and for the UAE a relatively larger share of this extra production than each of them had been apportioned in the past. This dispute between the large producers of the Arabian Peninsula was settled by a compromise: the conference adopted the Saudi approach (maximum production of 19.5m. b/d), but at the same time agreed (by a "gentlemen's agreement") that Kuwait alone could exceed its official quota by 250,000 b/d. This was the first time that members of the organization had approved such an accord.

A change occurred in Saudi oil policy during 1989. In previous years Saudi Arabia, like Kuwait, had supported the maintenance of relatively low oil prices (between $15 and $18 a barrel). This price level was intended to foster a rise in oil consumption, to restrain non-Opec producers from exploring for new oil fields, and to reduce investments in the development of alternative energy sources. In 1989 this policy changed. Both King Fahd and Oil Minister Hisham Nazir now held that the price should be raised to $20 a barrel and even higher.[22] The assumption of the Saudi rulers was that it would be possible to sustain and even somewhat increase the total production at the high price level they proposed. In mid-1989 it seemed possible to increase Opec members' total revenue from oil exports in this way rather than by increasing production alone. The change in the Saudi position appears to have stemmed from domestic pressures that became more severe in 1989 owing to the continuous deficits in the current account, in the balance of payments, and in the regular budget (see chapter on Saudi Arabia). To this one may add the heavy pressures by Iraq and Iran for higher revenue from their own oil sectors. The Saudi position appealed to them, and the Saudis, for their part, did not find it difficult to respond to these pressures.

On the other hand, the Saudi posture on the mode of distribution of production quotas did not change. The Saudis insisted on the preservation of the status quo. Saudi sensitivity in this area arose from the serious erosion that had occurred in their share of Opec oil. In 1982, the Saudi quota took up 40% of total Opec production. From then on this share fell consistently. In 1989, it was only 24.45% (see Table 3). In June 1989, the Saudis held firmly to their position not to allow further attrition of their production quota, and so insisted that there be no change in the mode of quota fixing. The "gentlemen's agreement" that permitted Kuwait to increase its oil production remained, in the Saudi view, within the boundaries of the quota allocation. It did not require a change in the principles underlying the quota allocation structure.

Unlike Saudi Arabia, Kuwait adhered to its long-standing policy of exploiting any circumstances on the world market to increase its production. In June 1989, the exploitation was limited to keeping the price at $18 a barrel. The rise in the production ceiling was intended to get a fair deal for Opec members who, in the opinion of the Kuwaiti rulers, had been "deprived" in the allocation of production quotas in the past, primarily Kuwait itself and the UAE. In effect, Kuwait's desire was that about 50% of the extra production it proposed be added to its own quota and to that of the UAE, so each would reach 1.35m. b/d. The Kuwaiti rulers had no qualms about applying strong pressure and made it clear to the Saudis and others that their demand for a rise in their quota was unshakable. In preparation for the June conference they increased oil production from their fields to 1.7m. b/d (or possibly 1.9m. b/d), far higher than their approved quota at the time (just over 1.0m. b/d). Kuwait could afford to be heavy-handed in its pressures on its Opec colleagues because it was less exposed than they to the consequences of a steep fall in crude oil prices on the world market resulting from surplus supply. This was so because most of the oil produced in its territory was exported as refined products and not as crude. The prices of refined products on the world market reacted only partly to falls in crude oil prices; stated otherwise, the rate of fall in their prices was smaller. In addition, Kuwait had sizable revenues from its investments abroad, including the downstream industries in industrialized Western countries. This was the setting in which the Opec members were in fact forced to accept the compromise of allowing Kuwait two different quotas: one formal, at 1.1m. b/d, the other informal, at 1.35m. b/d (that is, an addition of over 300,000 b/d to the quota of January-July 1989). Kuwait, for its part, undertook not to exceed the new (informal) quota for three months, until discussions were renewed at the next meeting in September. But already in June, Kuwaiti Oil Minister 'Ali Khalifa Al Sabah warned Opec members that, if at the September meeting Kuwait's annual quota was not confirmed to its satisfaction, it would be unable to act in accordance with the organization's decisions.[23]

THE 23–27 SEPTEMBER GENERAL OPEC MONITORING MEETING
As mentioned, the Opec production ceiling for July-September 1989 was set at 19.5m. b/d. But, in fact, average production of the organization's members in July-August was higher by about 2.4m. b/d. The amount that Opec produced in those months, about 21.9m. b/d, was fully absorbed by the market, with relatively mild fluctuations in price. As in the past, the major deviations from the quotas fixed in June were on the part of Kuwait and the UAE. In July-August, Kuwait produced an average of 1.7m. b/d and possibly more, that is, at least 350,000 b/d above the amount to which Kuwait itself agreed in the "gentlemen's agreement" in June. The UAE went even further. It produced an average of 1.9m. b/d in those months, that is, an excess of 200,000 b/d over the quota approved in June (see Tables 2 and 3).

This was the background for a meeting on 23–27 September of the Opec oil ministers in Geneva, in the framework of an expanded conference of the monitoring committee. The demand of Kuwait and the UAE for a sizable increase in their production quotas was the most pressing issue on the agenda. This matter was, of course, linked to the fixing of Opec's production ceiling. In late September 1989, the Opec ministers had two proposals before them: (1) to retain the 19.5m. b/d ceiling decided upon in June and ignore excess production of Kuwait and the UAE; (2) to raise the ceiling to 20m.-21m. b/d.[24]

Contention at this meeting centered on the allocation of quotas among the organization's members. As at the June conference, the division focused on the Saudi Arabian approach, to which Iraq attached itself, as against the Kuwaiti approach.[25] Saudi Arabia was at that time amenable to the proposal to raise the ceiling, owing to encouraging forecasts in the summer of 1989 of increasing demand for Opec oil. Yet Saudi Arabia — and Iraq — insisted that the increase in production be divided among the members in proportion to the quotas existing in September, that is, adherence to the application of the pro rata principle. As expected, Kuwait rejected this proposal out of hand. The Kuwaiti oil minister announced that his country opposed any change in the level of the ceiling as long as the method of quota distribution remained unchanged. He did not conceal Kuwait's goals in this respect: a recognition by the organization of preferred status to Kuwait, namely, formal ratification of a higher proportional quota in light of its surplus production capacity. The UAE, too, demanded preferred status and a change in its share of production. A third position expressed at the September meeting was that of Algeria, Libya, and several other members, which opposed the raising of the production ceiling as long as the attainment of the $18 a barrel reference price was not assured.[26] It will be recalled that in the weeks preceding this meeting the price of the "Opec basket" was less than $17 a barrel.

In this situation Iran presented a proposal of its own: to raise the ceiling to 21.5m. b/d and to allocate the lion's share of the addition to the Persian Gulf states, thus satisfying the demands of Kuwait and the UAE. This proposal was turned down owing to opposition by Libya and the UAE, which aspired to higher quotas than those specified in the Iranian proposal.[27] In the course of the ministers' meeting a revised Iranian proposal was presented: a rise in the share of Kuwait (6.3%, instead of 5.6%) and of the UAE (6.3%, instead of 5.3%) of total production; maintenance of the share of Saudi Arabia, Iran, Iraq, Libya, Gabon, and Ecuador; and a reduction in the share of the other members of the organization. Underlying the Iranian proposal was the evaluation that most of the producers outside the Persian Gulf region were more interested in a rise in oil prices than an increase in the volume of their production. As a price rise was dependent on production discipline in the organization itself, and this discipline required that the Gulf producers with their considerable excessive production capacity be satisfied, it was assumed that members outside the Gulf would affirm this proposal.

In the event, the revised Iranian proposal was not accepted. At the concluding session of the monitoring committee the Saudis obtained a majority for a resolution more in keeping with their original position. First, it was decided to raise the production ceiling for the last quarter of 1989 to 20.5m. b/d. Second, and highly important for Saudi Arabia, it was decided that the increment be distributed in proportion to the existing quotas (pro rata).[28] Needless to say, the Kuwaiti and UAE representatives derived no satisfaction from this resolution. 'Ali Khalifa Al Sabah hastened to announce that Kuwaiti production would be determined by the government and that "we have given no pledges. Legally speaking we have reserved our position and given no commitment as to what we produce."[29] Nor was there any doubt that the UAE, too, would continue to exceed its approved quota (about 1.1m. b/d) for October–December. Another member that disliked the decision of the monitoring committee was Algeria, which, as stated, feared that raising the ceiling would harm crude oil prices on the market. It refused to ratify the agreement.[30]

THE 25–28 NOVEMBER VIENNA CONFERENCE[31]
The last conference of 1989, which took place in Vienna on 25–28 November, also centered on the rising demand for Opec oil. It also focused on large-scale deviations by Kuwait and, even more, by the UAE, whose excesses in the closing months of 1989 broke their previous records. The purpose of the conference was primarily to find a

way of restoring Kuwait and the UAE to the organization's disciplined production framework. These efforts were only partially successful. A proposal was placed before the committee to raise the production ceiling again and to depart from the pro rata method of allocating the production increments. Naturally, the deviation applied first and foremost to Kuwait and the UAE. It was decided to grant 30% to the former and 35% to the latter over the quotas approved for them in the past. All other producers, large or small, would, according to this proposal, receive an addition of only 7% above their quotas. Saudi Arabia gave its consent to this proposal, as did Kuwait. For both of them it was a compromise. The Saudis agreed to a deviation from the pro rata principle when it became clear to them that breaches were being made by Kuwait and the UAE in practice and that they would persist and even go farther if Saudi Arabia did not at least go part way toward meeting these two neighboring producers. Kuwait did not accept all the provisions (in fact it produced 1.7m. b/d while the proposal affirmed only 1.5m. b/d), but it preferred to ensure the smooth functioning of the organization in view of expected developments among producers inside and outside Opec.

The arrangement was spoiled by the UAE, which did not approve this proposal, because the increment projected for it was far from satisfying its requirements. It should be recalled that in the weeks preceding the conference the UAE raised its volume of production to about 2.3m. b/d. The quota approved for it in September was about only 1.1m. b/d. The addition proposed for it at the November conference would have raised that quota to 1.5m. b/d. This was inadequate for the UAE.

The November conference, therefore, ended with a decision to raise the organization's production ceiling in the first half of 1990 to 22.1m. b/d; to permit an enlargement of Kuwait's quota by 30% (from 1.15m. b/d to 1.5m. b/d) and of the other members' quotas by 7.3%. There was no change in the quota of the UAE, which rejected an addition of 35%. (Indonesia's quota similarly remained unchanged, because it provisionally waived the addition on its own initiative as it had no capacity for enlarging its production.) Concomitantly, the UAE announced its intention to produce at least 2.0m. b/d in the first half of 1990, that is, at least 900,000 b/d in excess of the quota. Thus, at the conclusion of the November conference, the Opec members were aware that together they would produce at least 23.0m. b/d in the first months of 1990, and that the pro rata principle had been infringed without production discipline being fully restored to the organization's ranks. An important member, the UAE, declared from the outset that it would act contrary to the organization's decisions, the dimensions of its breach of the official quota already being in excess of 100% in November (2.3m. b/d as compared with a 1.1m. b/d quota).

The November conference also adopted separate resolutions concerning prices. It decided that the reference price of $18 a barrel for the "Opec basket" would become the "minimum reference price" as of January 1990. This change attested to the wish of Opec members to attain a higher level of oil prices. Of great importance was the fact that producers with an excess production capacity, such as Saudi Arabia and Iraq, shared this desire.

The organization's oil policy and the disputes that persisted among its members during 1989 accurately reflected the fact that most Opec countries were still below the "comfort level" at the end of the 1980s (that is, below the level of revenue required by an oil exporter for the purpose of financing overall government expenditure).[32] In their efforts to increase their total revenue from oil exports, two groups formed, each suggesting a different way. The first group, led by Algeria and Libya, held that the increase in revenue would follow from a rise in prices. The second, whose foremost representatives in 1989 were Kuwait and the UAE, believed that an enlargement of the quantities produced would achieve that result. Alongside this difference in approach, there was evident antagonism within the group pressing for quantitative enlargement, which divided the large producers of the Arabian Peninsula — Saudi Arabia on the one hand, and Kuwait and the UAE on the other — regarding the shares of production. This was a new dispute within a group of producers among whom understanding, cooperation, and coordination of positions had prevailed in the past (occasionally these three producers had been termed the "mini-Opec"). They were members of the Gulf Cooperation Council and had many political interests in common. Kuwait and the UAE were determined to impose an increase in the production quotas on the organization, even if this should cause a fall in prices of the "Opec basket" in the short run. These two producers were motivated to adopt such a policy primarily as a result of the marked increase in the proven reserves in their territories. Kuwait also emphasized its need for additional revenue to pursue its intention of continuing to invest in downstream industries in the US and Europe.[33] The Kuwaiti and UAE rulers adduced further arguments to explain and justify their oil policy. One important factor was not mentioned, at least not publicly: these two producers' fear of Iraq's extensive production potential, and to a lesser extent Iran's. Kuwait and the UAE wished to establish for themselves a "high" starting point at a time when the struggle for the production quotas with Iraq and Iran was growing more fierce. Finally, it is worth emphasizing that Kuwait and the UAE, which cast off Opec discipline, were the only two states (together with Qatar) that in recent years had not suffered large deficits in their current accounts.[34] This fact certainly did not favor them in the course of their bargaining with the other Opec members.

Unlike its two neighbors, Saudi Arabia had suffered in recent years from heavy deficits in the regular budget, deficits in current accounts, and consequently from a steep fall in its financial reserves. In 1989, for the first time since 1954, the Saudi Arabian Government sought loans on the private market to cover its budget deficit. The Public Investment Fund borrowed $660m. from 11 financial institutions.[35] Against this background it was possible to understand Riyadh's resolute position that the increment in volume of production be distributed proportionally, a method that would ensure it the largest relative and absolute share and the largest increase in revenue.

The evaluation that Iraq was likely to be the organization's biggest troublemaker once it had rehabilitated its oil-producing capacity was disproved, at least in the period under review. During 1989, Iraq succeeded in reestablishing and considerably enlarging its export capacity, as a result of renewal of oil exports from the Persian Gulf and in consequence of completion of the IPSA-2 pipeline to the Red Sea. Nevertheless, Iraq did not exceed its approved production quota, nor did it demand any increase in it. In the dispute among Saudi Arabia, Kuwait, and the UAE, Iraq supported Saudi adherence to the pro rata principle in quota distribution. This Iraqi policy in Opec had apparently to be viewed in the context of its bitter rivalry with Iran: Iraq avoided giving Iran any pretext for making its own claims to extra quotas.[36] Another possible factor behind this policy was the Iraqi concern to bring about a raising of the price level on the international market.

NON-OPEC PRODUCERS

In 1989 an important change was observed in relations between Opec and the other oil producers. Its beginnings went back to as early as March 1986, when Opec, having adopted the "market shares" strategy, invited five "independent" oil producers — Mexico, Oman, Egypt, Malaysia, and Angola — to the Opec conference for an exchange of views in an effort to create a common basis for future cooperation. Less than a year later, in January 1987, an important European producer, Norway, made a gesture of support for Opec in announcing that production from its wells in the North Sea would be cut by 7.5% of the planned level.[37] At the beginning of 1988 additional coordination between the Opec and non-Opec producers was achieved. China and Brunei, together with the five "independent" producers mentioned above, formulated their own proposal: they were willing to cut 5% off their oil exports on condition that the Opec members did likewise. This signified a reduction in exports of c. 185,000 b/d by the seven non-Opec producers if Opec itself cut 850,000 b/d. In the event, Opec did not accept the seven's proposal, principally on account of serious differences between Iran and Iraq.[38]

In November 1988, the Opec members' position regarding cooperation with other producers changed. Large oil supplies, a fall in prices at the end of the year, and the end of the Iran-Iraq War all contributed to this change. At its November 1988 conference, the organization called for opening negotiations with the "independent" exporters, with the aim of reaching an understanding that would approve a cutback in production and attainment of stability on the market.

On 25–26 January 1989, representatives of the two groups of producers met in London.[39] This time, too, the discussions were with seven "independent" producers — with one change: Brunei dropped out and Colombia joined in. The overall production of the group of seven amounted to 7.5m. b/d at the beginning of 1989. An important innovation at the London talks was the presence of observers from the USSR, Canada (Alberta), the US (Texas and Alaska), Norway, and North Yemen. The London meeting ended with an understanding among all participants — Opec and non-Opec — that coordinated action was required to achieve a price of $18 a barrel on the world market. The non-Opec representatives also agreed to present their governments with recommendations for realizing cooperation with Opec. Opec for its part pressured the "independent" producers to agree on a common policy.[40] This pressure and the common interest yielded results. On 21 February, the independents announced their commitment in principle to a 5% cut in their oil exports in the months April-June 1989.[41] In March, the USSR joined the common effort to stabilize market prices; it announced a 5% reduction in its oil exports for the first half of 1989.[42] This was the first time in Opec's history that the USSR declared openly for cooperation with the organization. The non-Opec producers' reduction was c. 300,000 b/d from the amount they planned to export in the second quarter of 1989. True, this move was somewhat influenced by the total demand on the world market, but the fact that understanding and cooperation had been achieved between the two groups of producers raised the level of expectation for an oil price rise on the world market.[43]

The non-Opec producers met again on 16 May in London and on 5-6 October in Kuala Lumpur. At these two meetings, each of which preceded an Opec conference, no decisions were taken regarding the continued cutbacks in supply of oil to the world market. Market conditions, namely, the increasing demand for oil and the fact that Opec itself had decided on raising its own production ceiling during the second half of 1989, freed the "independent" producers from the obligation of making decisions on steps to restrain production.[44]

DEVELOPMENTS IN THE US PETROLEUM MARKET AND THEIR IMPACT ON MIDDLE EASTERN OIL

The fall in total US oil production, a development observed for years, accelerated in 1989. A special contribution to this was the decline in oil production in Alaska, after it had reached a peak of 2.0m. b/d in 1988.[45] Concomitant with this fall was a rise in demand for oil in the US. The result of these two developments was, of course, an increase in imports of crude oil and refined products. This import again assumed very large proportions in absolute and relative terms (see Table 7). It was the second time in US history (the first being in 1977) that total oil imports (including refined products) exceeded total domestic production.[46]

The American Petroleum Institute, in presenting the main data of domestic production and imports for 1989, stated that the trends of these developments were "very disturbing",[47] since total US crude production in 1989 was on average 7.6m. b/d, a fall in 6.8% (533,000 b/d) from the total production in 1988. In parallel, total oil imports (crude and refined products) rose to 7.9m. b/d — an increase of 8.2% compared with total imports in 1988, and an increase of about 60% compared with imports in 1985, when they had amounted to only 5.0m. b/d.

In this situation of a fall in total production, the number of new drillings declined, chiefly on account of the oil prices prevalent on the market in recent years.[48] The pollution of the sea caused by Exxon's tanker *Valdez* (see above) did not add to the chances of improving the US oil balance. It was also difficult to foresee the grant of approval for oil explorations in Alaska's Arctic National Wildlife Refuge, as long as the US public, especially in the large environmentalist camp, was not convinced that there was no danger of serious harm being caused to this unique region.[49]

Since in the year under review the increase in energy consumption, including oil, was continuing, there was no alternative to enlarging total imports of oil and refined products. The amount supplied by the Opec producers in this import steadily increased (see Table 8), and it was the ME oil producers that supplied most of the additional import of crude oil in 1989. These producers increased their exports to the US by 461,000 b/d, which was 90% of the added imports in the first half of 1989 (see Table 8). *In toto,* the ME exporters supplied 1.71m. b/d, which at the time was 31% of the total US imports of oil and refined products. In the equivalent period of 1988 the share of the ME producers in US imports was only 25%. This rise in the relative share of the ME producers in US oil imports was the result of a steep fall in the export of British oil to the US (from 332,000 to 138,000 b/d) owing to accidents on the North Sea oil installations.[50] The total exports of Canada and Venezuela also declined (by 60,000 b/d and 30,000 b/d respectively).

In the first half of 1989, most of the addition of ME exports to the US was from Saudi Arabia and Iraq. The former increased its exports to the US by 291,000 b/d (total exports to the US amounting to 1.12m. b/d), the latter by 167,000 b/d (total exports to the US amounting to 402,000 b/d). Kuwait, which exported negligible quantities to the US in the first five months of 1989, renewed its contract sales in June, when it supplied no less than 300,000 b/d.[51]

The increase in US oil imports impeded efforts to reduce its trade deficit.[52] In addition to the economic aspect, oil imports on such a relatively large scale also had political and strategic implications. In the last months of 1989, concern was voiced in Washington over the growing dependency on imported oil. In October, President George Bush stated decisively: "We are becoming increasingly dependent on foreign oil. This is not acceptable to any president who is responsible for the security of this country."[53] From past experience, fears focused chiefly on the interruption or reduction in oil supplies by the ME exporters. It should indeed be noted that the US in 1989 was not as vulnerable to the consequences of a possible reduction in ME oil supplies as it had been in late 1973 and early 1974, by virtue of the Strategic Petroleum Reserve, whose volume amounted to 600m. barrels.[54] The Arab exporters, Saudi Arabia at their head, acted to dispel fears created by the enlargement of the share of Arab oil in total imports. They stressed that, as suppliers, they needed the US market just as the US market as a customer needed Arab oil.[55] Indeed, as long as there was no clear case of overdemand ("sellers' market") for oil on the world market, the ability to exploit US dependency on imported oil for political gain was extremely circumscribed.

SUMMARY

Was 1989 a turning point in the history of oil production? Did it mark the end of the years of recession and the start of a new cycle of boom years in prices and revenue of the oil states?

It seems that the feeling of being at the threshold of a new era prevailed among circles close to Opec in the closing months of 1989. Prices that had stood at $22–$23 a barrel with an overall Opec production of 24.0m. b/d at the beginning of January 1990 reinforced this prediction. Early in 1990, a plethora of prognoses was published stating that there would be a considerable real rise in oil prices (up to 40%) in the first half of the 1990s. Indeed, there were sound reasons for stating that there was an absolute rise in the demand for oil and that in coming years it would be primarily the Opec members, in the first place those of the Persian Gulf, who would supply the increase in quantities required. This development in itself would not necessarily entail a sharp rise in prices.

Developments in 1989 brought home the power of the producers in the Arabian Peninsula apart from Saudi Arabia itself. Kuwait and the UAE had sizable and large proven reserves and an excess production capacity. Against this background, the conflicting interests in production policy of the Persian Gulf producers were even more marked. While Kuwait and the UAE strove to maintain a low price level on the world market, Iraq, Iran, and other producers sought to restrain the increase in production so as to achieve a high price level. Tension among these producers rose around this issue.

Finally, 1989 was a landmark in the process of increasing US dependency on imported oil generally and on that imported from Arab suppliers in particular. It seemed that US policy regarding the ME in the late 1980s and early 1990s should be scrutinized against the background of this development, among other factors.

TABLE 1: 1989 CRUDE OIL PRICES (Dollars per barrel)*

Date	Brent	Dubai Fateh	Date	Brent	Dubai Fateh
3 January	16.40	13.45	4 July	18.60	15.90
10 January	16.15	13.55	11 July	17.40	15.60
17 January	17.30	14.55	18 July	18.00	15.20
24 January	17.73	14.35	25 July	17.50	14.90
31 January	16.30	13.93	1 August	17.20	14.70
7 February	16.15	14.50	8 August	17.10	14.50
14 February	16.65	13.85	15 August	17.10	15.00
21 February	16.80	14.45	22 August	17.20	15.40
28 February	17.10	14.30	29 August	17.10	15.20
7 March	18.00	14.90	5 September	17.50	15.60
14 March	18.00	15.60	12 September	17.90	15.80
20 March	18.70	15.75	19 September	17.90	15.50
27 March	19.45	16.50	26 September	17.50	15.50
4 April	19.90	16.50	3 October	18.80	16.10
11 April	19.15	16.70	10 October	18.38	15.80
18 April	19.60	16.45	17 October	19.65	16.33
25 April	20.30	16.75	24 October	18.80	15.80
2 May	18.50	15.25	31 October	18.70	16.05
9 May	18.10	15.30	7 November	18.95	16.35
16 May	18.90	15.30	14 November	18.40	15.90
23 May	17.70	14.90	21 November	18.60	16.05
30 May	18.00	15.50	28 November	18.20	15.80
6 June	18.40	15.95	5 December	19.00	16.35
13 June	16.50	14.50	12 December	19.50	16.95
20 June	16.60	14.40	19 December	19.55	17.05
27 June	18.10	15.60	2 January 1990	20.60	17.80

*   A middle spot price.

SOURCE: Figures are from *MEED,* 1989–90, various issues.

FIGURE 1: SPOT PRICE OF BRENT BLEND CRUDE, 1989

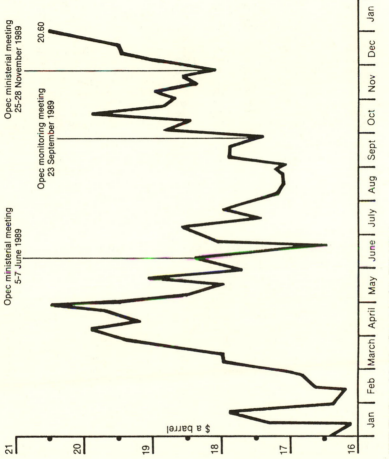

Opec ministerial meeting
25-28 November 1989

20.60

Opec monitoring meeting
23 September 1989

Opec ministerial meeting
5-7 June 1989

$ a barrel

Jan | Feb | March | April | May | June | July | Aug | Sept | Oct | Nov | Dec | Jan

21 —
20 —
19 —
18 —
17 —
16 —

NOTE: The diagram is based on figures taken from Table 1 above.
SOURCE: See Table 1.

TABLE 2: OPEC COUNTRIES' OIL PRODUCTION* IN 1989
(Volumes in thousands b/d)

Country	Jan.	Feb.	March	April	May	June	July	Aug.	Sept.	Oct.	Nov.	Dec.
Algeria	700	700	700	700	700	700	700	700	700	700	700	800
Ecuador	300	300	300	300	300	300	300	300	300	300	300	300
Gabon	200	200	200	200	200	200	200	200	200	200	200	200
Indonesia	1,200	1,200	1,200	1,200	1,200	1,200	1,200	1,200	1,200	1,300	1,300	1,300
Iran	2,800	2,900	2,800	2,900	2,500	2,800	2,600	3,000	2,800	2,900	2,700	2,900
Iraq	2,600	2,600	2,600	2,700	2,800	2,800	2,800	2,900	2,800	3,000	3,000	3,000
Kuwait	1,100	1,000	1,000	1,400	1,600	1,600	1,700	1,700	1,700	1,700	1,800	1,900
Libya	1,000	1,000	1,000	1,100	1,000	1,000	1,100	1,100	1,100	1,100	1,200	1,200
Nigeria	1,400	1,400	1,400	1,400	1,700	1,600	1,800	1,800	1,800	1,700	1,800	1,800
Qatar	400	400	300	300	400	400	400	400	400	400	400	400
Saudi Arabia	4,800	4,500	4,500	4,800	5,000	4,800	4,800	4,900	5,000	5,400	5,400	5,600
UAE	1,700	1,600	1,600	1,500	1,600	1,700	1,800	2,000	2,200	2,300	2,300	2,300
Venezuela	1,600	1,600	1,600	1,600	1,700	1,700	1,700	1,700 ·	1,700	1,800	1,800	1,800
Partitioned Zone**	400	300	300	300	400	400	400	400	400	400	400	400
Total	**20,200**	**19,700**	**19,500**	**20,500**	**21,100**	**21,200**	**21,500**	**22,300**	**22,300**	**23,200**	**23,300**	**23,900**

* Excluding NGLs.
** Output divided equally between Kuwait and Saudi Arabia.

SOURCE: *AOG*, 1989, various issues.

TABLE 3: OPEC QUOTAS (million barrels per day)

	January-June 1989	July-September 1989	October-December 1989	January-June 1990
Algeria	0.695	0.733	0.770	0.827
Ecuador	0.230	0.242	0.255	0.273
Gabon	0.166	0.175	0.184	0.197
Indonesia	1.240	1.307	1.374	1.374
Iran	2.640	2.783	2.925	3.140
Iraq	2.640	2.783	2.925	3.140
Kuwait*	1.037	1.093	1.149	1.500
Libya	1.037	1.093	1.149	1.233
Nigeria	1.355	1.428	1.501	1.611
Qatar	0.312	0.329	0.346	0.371
Saudi Arabia*	4.524	4.769	5.014	5.380
UAE	0.988	1.041	1.095	1.095
Venezuela	1.636	1.724	1.813	1.945
Opec Ceiling	18.500	19.500	20.500	22.086

* Including half the Partitioned (Neutral) Zone.

SOURCES: *ME*, January 1990, and *PE*, January 1990.

TABLE 4: OPEC ACTUAL BASKET PRICE, 1988–89 (Dollars per barrel)

First Quarter 1989	Second Quarter 1989	Third Quarter 1989	Fourth Quarter 1989	average 1989	average 1988	Change Volume	%
16.43	18.00	16.78	18.03	17.31	14.28	3.03	+21.2

SOURCE: Figures based on *MEES*, 8 January 1990.

TABLE 5: OIL SUPPLY AND DEMAND (million barrels per day)

1989	First Quarter	Second Quarter	Third Quarter	Fourth Quarter	Year
World Oil Demand					
(excluding CPEs)	52.8	49.8	50.8	54.1	51.9
Non-Opec Supply	28.6	28.5	28.8	29.3	28.8
Additional Requirements	24.2	21.3	22.0	24.8	23.1
Implied Call on Opec Crude	22.3	19.4	20.1	22.9	21.2
Opec Production					
Crude	19.9	21.1	22.1	23.7	21.7
NGL	1.9	1.9	1.9	1.9	1.9
Total	21.8	23.0	24.0	25.6	23.6
Supply/Demand Balance	-2.4	+1.7	+2.0	+0.8	+0.5

SOURCE: Figures are from the January issue of the International Energy Agency, *Oil Market Report*, as quoted in *MEES*, 15 January 1990.

TABLE 6: OPEC BASKET PRICE
(Dollars per barrel)

	Reference Price	Average Spot Price in 1989
Saudi Arab Light	17.52	16.21
Dubai Fateh	17.42	15.64
Algerian Saharan Blend	18.87	18.53
Nigerian Bonny Light	18.92	18.50
Indonesian Minas	17.56	17.63
Venezuelan Tia Juana Light	17.62	16.93
Mexican Isthmus	18.07	17.72
	18.00*	17.31

*   The reference price of $18 per barrel is calculated on the basis of the 1987 official price for each crude.

SOURCE: Figures based on *MEES*, 8 January 1990.

TABLE 7: US OIL BALANCE, FIRST-HALF 1988–89
(Volumes in thousands b/d)

	First-half 1988	First-half 1989[a]	% Change 1988–89
Supply			
Crude Production	8,280	7,767	-6.2
NGL	1,614	1,647	+2.0
Other[b]	833	905	+8.6
Total Production	10,727	10,319	-3.8
Crude Imports[c]	4,952	5,482	+10.7
Product Imports	2,223	2,337	+5.1
Total Imports	7,175	7,819	+9.0
Total Supply	17,902	18,138	+1.3
Demand			
Motor Gasoline	7,266	7,264	—
Distillate	3,194	3,118	-2.4
Heavy Fuel Oil	1,361	1,446	+6.2
Other[d]	5,274	5,378	+2.0
Total Domestic Demand	17,095	17,206	+0.6
Exports	835	834	-0.1
Total Demand	17,930	18,040	+0.6
Stock Change	-28	+98	—

a) Provisional estimate.
b) Unaccounted-for crude oil, refinery input of other hydrocarbons, and processing gain.
c) Excluding purchases for the Strategic Petroleum Reserve.
d) Jet fuel, LPG, and other hydrocarbons.

SOURCE: American Petroleum Institute, as represented in *PE,* September 1989.

TABLE 8: US CRUDE OIL IMPORT IN THE FIRST HALF OF 1989
(Volumes in thousands b/d)

	First half 1989	First half 1988	Change Volume	Change %	% Share First half 1989	% Share First half 1988
Total Crude Imports	5,518	5,003	515	10.3		
Imports from Opec	3,169	2,566	603	23.5	57.4	51.3
— ME Opec*	1,709	1,248	461	36.9	31.0	25.0
— Other Opec	1,460	1,318	142	10.8	26.4	26.3
Imports from Non-Opec	2,348	2,437	(89)	(3.7)	42.6	48.7

*   Of the ME Opec only Algeria, Iraq, Kuwait, Saudi Arabia, and the UAE exported oil to the US.

SOURCE: *MEES,* 4 September 1989.

TABLE 9: MIDDLE EAST OPEC: OIL EXPORT
REVENUES, 1986–89 (million dollars)

	1986	1987	1988	1989
Saudi Arabia	20,131	17,593	17,733	23,200
Iran	5,907	9,824	7,655	12,000
Iraq	6,633	11,611	11,666	15,400
Kuwait	4,928	4,557	4,483	8,700
UAE	6,074	7,939	6,601	10,300
Qatar	1,571	1,849	1,486	2,200
Divided Zone	1,700	—	—	2,200
Total ME Opec	**46,944**	**53,373**	**49,624**	**74,000**

SOURCES: *MEED*, 20 January 1989, and *Memo*, 23 March 1990.

TABLE 10: ESTIMATED OIL PRODUCTION: THE MIDDLE EAST
AND NORTH AFRICA, 1989 (thousand tonnes)

	1988	1989	% Change	*% Share in Total World Production* 1988	1989
Saudi Arabia*	251,890	255,000	+1.2	8.3	8.2
Iran	112,420	145,000	+29.0	3.7	4.7
Iraq	128,085	138,000	+7.7	4.2	4.4
Kuwait*	71,495	91,000	+27.3	2.4	2.9
Abu Dhabi	55,175	71,000	+28.7	1.8	2.3
Libya	48,820	53,000	+8.6	1.6	1.7
Algeria	46,665	52,000	+11.1	1.5	1.7
Egypt	44,234	45,000	+1.7	1.5	1.4
Oman	29,510	28,500	-3.4		
Qatar	16,040	20,000	+24.7		
Dubai	17,100	17,700	+3.5		
Syria	13,500	16,000	+18.5		
North Yemen	8,000	10,000	+25.0		
Tunisia	4,909	4,800	-2.2		
Turkey	2,584	2,600	+0.6		
Bahrain	2,150	2,150	—		
Sharja	3,135	2,000	-36.2		
South Yemen	650	850	+30.8		
Ra's al-Khayma	500	400	-20.0		
Total	**856,862**	**955,000**	**+11.4**	**28.3**	**30.7**
World Total	**3,030,276**	**3,109,415**	**+2.6**	**100.0**	**100.0**

*   Including the Partitioned (Neutral) Zone.

SOURCE: Figures are from *PE*, January 1990.

NOTES

For the place and frequency of publications cited here, and for the full name of the publication, news agency, radio station, or monitoring service where an abbreviation is used, please see "List of Sources." Only in the case of more than one publication bearing the same name is the place of publication noted here.

1. *IHT,* 10 January; *MEED,* 8 December 1989.
2. *AOG,* 1 May 1989.
3. *MEED,* 12 May 1989.
4. *AOG,* 1 April; *MEED,* 12 May, 8 December 1989.
5. *Oil and Gas Journal,* 25 December 1989.
6. *FT,* 28 March 1989.
7. *AOG,* 1 April 1989; see also Table 2.
8. *MEED,* 8 December 1989.
9. *IHT,* 29, 30 July; *PE,* September 1989, January 1990.
10. *MEED,* 27 October, 22 December; *PE,* November 1989; *MEED,* 12 January 1990.
11. *MEED,* 12 January 1990.
12. For the price of WTI see *MEED,* 8, 29 December 1989.
13. *PE,* January 1990.
14. *MEES,* 8 January 1990.
15. *IHT, FT,* 10 January; *MEES,* 15 January 1990.
16. *FT,* 8 May; *MEES,* 18 December 1989; *PE,* January; *The Economist,* 13 January 1990.
17. *FT,* 8 January 1990.
18. For US Petroleum Balance Sheet see Energy Information Administration, *Weekly Petroleum Status Report,* 4 January 1990.
19. *PE,* December 1989.
20. *Globes,* 5 December 1989; *PE,* January 1990.
21. For full details on the conference, see *MEES,* 12 June 1989.
22. E. g., *IHT,* 4 May; *NYT,* 31 May 1989.
23. R. Kuwait, 8 June — DR, 9 June 1989.
24. *IHT,* 25 September 1989.
25. *WSJ,* 25 September 1989.
26. Ibid.
27. *FT,* 28 September 1989.
28. OPECNA, 27 September — DR, 28 September 1989.
29. *JP,* 28 September 1989.
30. *WSJ,* 28 September 1989.
31. For the full details of the meeting, see *MEES,* 4 December 1989.
32. *MEED,* 8 December 1989.
33. See, for example, these arguments in *AOG,* 16 June; *PE,* July 1989.
34. *MEED,* 8 December 1989.
35. *AOG,* 16 July; *MEED,* 29 December 1989.
36. *CR:* Iraq, No. 4, 1989.
37. *PE,* May 1989.
38. Ibid.
39. *WSJ,* 26, 27 January; *MEES,* 30 January 1989.
40. *MEES,* 6 February 1989.
41. *MEES,* 27 February, 6 March 1989.
42. *MEES,* 13 March; *PE,* April 1989.
43. *MEED,* 12 May 1989.
44. *AOG,* 1 June, 16 October 1989.
45. *PE,* September 1989.
46. Ibid.
47. Annual Report of the American Petroleum Institute, quoted in *Ha'aretz,* 18 January; *MEED,* 2 February 1990.
48. *Business Week,* 13 March, 25 September; *PE,* March, September 1989.

49. *PE,* May, June 1989.
50. *MEES,* 4 September 1989.
51. Ibid.
52. *AOG,* 16 November 1989.
53. *PE,* October 1989.
54. *AOG,* 16 November 1989.
55. *MEES,* 20 February, 6, 27 November 1989.

PART TWO:
COUNTRY-BY-COUNTRY SURVEY

Middle East Countries
Basic Data

Country	Capital	Most Important Natural Resources	Area 1,000 sq. km.	Population in millions (mid-1988)	GNP per capita ($US 1988)
Bahrain	Manama	Crude Oil	1	0.473	6,340
Egypt	Cairo	Cotton, Crude Oil, Fruits, Vegetables, Iron	1,001	50.2	660
Iran	Tehran	Crude Oil, Natural Gas	1,648	48.6	NA
Iraq	Baghdad	Crude Oil, Dates, Cement	438	17.6	NA
Israel	Jerusalem	Fruits, Vegetables, Potash	21	4.4	8,650
Jordan	Amman	Phosphates, Vegetables, Fruits	89	3.9	1,500
Kuwait	Kuwait	Crude Oil	18	2.0	13,400
Lebanon	Beirut	Fruits, Citrus Fruits, Vegetables, Forests	10	NA	NA
Libya	Tripoli	Crude Oil, Vegetables, Fruits	1,760	4.2	5,420
Oman	Muscat	Crude Oil	212	1.4	5,000
Qatar	Doha	Crude Oil	11	0.411	9,930
Saudi Arabia	Riyadh	Crude Oil	2,150	14.0	6,200
Sudan	Khartoum	Cotton, Gum, Cereals	2,506	23.8	480
Syria	Damascus	Cotton, Crude Oil, Vegetables, Fruits, Livestock, Phosphates	185	11.6	1,680
Turkey	Ankara	Cotton, Wool, Tobacco, Chrome, Copper	779	53.8	1,280
United Arab Emirates	Abu Dhabi	Crude Oil	84	1.5	15,770
Yemen (North)	San'a	Coffee, Cotton, Sorghum, Fish	195	8.5	640
Yemen (South)	Aden	Cotton, Fruits, Vegetables, Tobacco, Fish	333	2.4	430

SOURCE: *World Development Report 1990* (New York: Oxford University Press for the World Bank, 1990).
NA = not available.

Currencies

| Country | Currency Unit | Approximate Equivalent in Other Currencies* | | | | |
		US Dollar	Pound Sterling	Deutsche Mark	Swiss Franc	French Franc
Bahrain	Bahraini Dinar (BD) = 1,000 Fils	2.64	1.55	4.91	4.33	16.63
Egypt	Egyptian Pound (£E) = 1,000 Milliemes	0.40	0.23	0.74	0.65	2.51
Iran	Iranian Riyal (IR) = 100 Dinars	0.014	0.008	0.026	0.023	0.088
Iraq	Iraqi Dinar (ID) = 1,000 Fils	3.21	1.88	5.97	5.27	20.23
Israel	New Israeli Shekel (NIS) = 100 Agorot	0.55	0.32	1.02	0.90	3.46
Jordan	Jordanian Dinar (JD) = 1,000 Fils	1.88	1.10	3.49	3.14	11.83
Kuwait	Kuwaiti Dinar (KD) = 1,000 Fils	3.45	2.02	6.41	5.65	21.72
Lebanon	Lebanese Pound (£L) = 100 Piastres	0.0019	0.0011	0.0035	0.0031	0.012
Libya	Libyan Dinar (LD) = 1,000 Dirhams	3.40	1.99	6.32	5.58	18.91
Oman	Omani Riyal (OR) = 1,000 Baiza	2.58	1.51	4.81	4.24	14.37
Qatar	Qatari Riyal (QR) = 100 Dirhams	0.27	0.16	0.51	0.45	1.52
Saudi Arabia	Saudi Riyal (SR) = 100 Halalas	0.27	0.16	0.50	0.44	1.69
Sudan	Sudanese Pound (£S) = 1,000 Milliemes	0.22	0.13	0.41	0.36	1.39
Syria	Syrian Pound (£SY) = 100 Piastres	0.047	0.028	0.088	0.078	0.30
Turkey	Turkish Lira (TL) = 100 Kurus	0.0005	0.00028	0.0009	0.0008	0.0030
United Arab Emirates	UAE Dirham (UAEDh) = 100 Fils	0.27	0.16	0.51	0.45	1.73
Yemen (North)	Yemeni Riyal (YR) = 100 Fils	0.10	0.060	0.19	0.17	0.64
Yemen (South)	South Yemeni Dinar (SYD) = 1,000 Fils	2.90	1.70	5.41	4.77	18.33
$US rate $1		—	0.59	1.8607	1.6421	6.30

* As quoted by the *Financial Times* in London on 24 April 1989.

Bahrain
(Al-Bahrayn)

UZI RABI

Relaxation in the Gulf, which allayed Bahrain's chronic anxiety, had a positive effect on the country at most levels. Regionally, relations with Iran were, on the whole, on the path to reconciliation, and attempts were made to take a more moderate approach in the dispute with Qatar over the island of Fasht al-Dibal. Internationally, Bahrain established diplomatic links with the People's Republic of China (PRC), its first ties with a Communist state. Assuming that the positive mood would continue, Bahrain embarked on optimistic medium- and long-term plans to make its economy flourish once again. Nonetheless, Bahrain maintained a swift pace of armament and continued treating its Shi'i community roughly.

INTERNAL AFFAIRS

THE ARMED FORCES

Bahrain was keen to maintain a level of military preparedness, especially in the event that its negotiations with Qatar failed. Accordingly, defense expenditures continued to rise; arms deals were concluded with Western allies, the US in particular. Following a visit by Foreign Minister Shaykh Muhammad Ibn Mubarak Al Khalifa to Washington in August, it was announced that the *Stinger* missiles, which initially were leased from the US for an 18-month period (see *MECS* 1987, p. 367), could remain in Bahrain's possession.[1] Bahrain also procured 80 M-113 armored vehicles and reportedly concluded the purchase of seven US multiple-rocket-launcher systems, apparently to protect itself from assault by landing aircraft.[2] Britain was another potential source of armaments. A bilateral military cooperation agreement was concluded during the May visit to Britain of Staff Maj. Gen. Shaykh Khalifa Ibn Ahmad Al Khalifa, Bahrain's minister of defense and deputy commander in chief of the Bahraini Defense Forces (BDF). Khalifa was said to have been interested in acquiring lightweight *Hawk*-200 fighters as well as portable surface-to-air *Javelin* missiles.[3]

The BDF of 3,350 volunteers was reorganized. A legislative decree announced the formation of a military defense council, which was to help review mobilization, administration, and financial planning; its makeup was to be decided by the heir apparent and BDF commander in chief, Shaykh Hamad Ibn 'Isa Al Khalifa. The decree emphasized the right of the Bahraini ruler, in his capacity as supreme commander of the force, to seek military assistance from friendly countries and to offer BDF services to Arab League members. The BDF duties were summarized as "defense of the homeland, protection and preservation of its security, independence, sovereignty, and territorial integrity."[4]

ATTITUDE TOWARD THE SHI'I COMMUNITY

Bahraini anxiety in the post-Khomeyni era affected the government's relations with the island's Shi'i community. The government's handling of the Shi'i religious gatherings after Ayatollah Khomeyni's death increased tension in June and it rose higher in August following the annual 'Ashura processions, commemorating the martyrdom of Imam Husayn. Before June, many Shi'i leaders were detained in larger than usual security clampdowns. Further evidence of government anxiety was the withdrawal of press cards from two journalists employed by foreign wire services, who reported on local reactions to Khomeyni's death.[5] Opposition sources reported that a Bahraini political activist, Muhammad Mansur, was found dead in Manama. Mansur, an employee of Gulf Air, had been detained in Manama International Airport, while on his way back from Damascus. Thirty young Bahrainis were reportedly arrested and tortured following a large-scale clampdown by the Bahraini security forces in February. No information was available on their whereabouts.[6]

ROYAL FAMILY POLITICS

According to opposition sources, the Bahraini ruler, Shaykh 'Isa Ibn Salman Al Khalifa, and his brother Prime Minister Shaykh Khalifa Ibn Salam Al Khalifa were so much in disagreement that whenever Shaykh 'Isa left the island, he put his son and heir apparent, Shaykh Hamad, in charge rather than his brother, as was customary.[7] A report that due to ill health, Shaykh 'Isa had decided to relinquish the throne in favor of Shaykh Hamad attested to his growing influence.[8]

ECONOMIC AND SOCIAL AFFAIRS

Bahraini expectations of an economic upturn in the wake of regional calm were realized as improved investor confidence contributed to a surge in domestic business activity. The construction sector stood to benefit considerably from impending major projects, such as the second causeway, linking Muharraq and Manama;[9] the banking sector on the whole showed improvement, reporting stable liquidity and higher profits. Yet another indication of the optimistic mood was the reintroduction of the biannual budgetary system during 1989–90. However, being a minor oil producer whose sources were dwindling, Bahrain benefited very little from the firming oil prices. Therefore, special emphasis was laid on diversifying the Bahraini economy in four main areas: finance, industry, tourism, and trade.

Bahrain strove to restore its once dominant position as a regional financial center. The opening of a stock exchange in mid-June — a significant move in and of itself — was regarded a first step to becoming a regional stock-trading center.[10] In another move, aimed at increasing Bahrain's involvement in the international business community, preparations were made to set up a major arbitration center for disputes arising between Gulf and European business partners.[11] More ambitious were the efforts made to consolidate the island's industrial base, gradually shifting the emphasis from consumption to production. Numerous Bahraini-based plants thus faced expansion. Aluminum Bahrain (Alba), for instance, undertook a huge expansion plan to more than double production.[12] Other plants, mostly small and medium-sized, such as the Bahrain Aluminum Extrusion Company (Balexco), were to be sold off to the private sector.[13] As part of its search for financial resources that would make these plans possible, Bahrain set out to attract extraregional investors in joint ventures by offering a wide range of incentives.[14]

The considerable attention given to tourism — predominantly regional — seemed to reflect a greater Bahraini understanding of that sector's potential revenue and the advantages accruing from receiving tourists via the King Fahd causeway, linking Bahrain and Saudi Arabia. Tourist attractions were to be built and entry procedures simplified.[15] With the prospects of an increased number of passengers, Manama international airport also underwent major expansion and renovation, with emphasis on entertainment and recreation areas.[16] Plans to turn Bahrain into a reexport center were also under discussion; preliminary studies were carried out for digging a new port, since Salman port was unable to handle the expected expansion of transit trade.[17]

The problem of unemployment became more acute because ever-growing numbers of nationals were about to enter the labor market. Efforts to create jobs through the industrial diversification program were insufficient, because Bahrain's revenue base was still too narrow. Hence, the obstacles on the road to Bahrainization still remained deeply entrenched. According to official Bahraini figures, the number of expatriates had not only not decreased since 1987, despite declining economic activity, but had increased by 5.6% yearly.[18] These difficulties had probably pushed the Bahraini Government into implementing a five-year accelerated Bahrainization program to replace a third of the foreign labor force employed in the private sector with Bahraini nationals.[19]

A second Arabic-language daily, *al-Ayyam,* was issued for the first time on 7 March as part of the effort to enable the Bahraini citizen to "express his conscience and embody his freedom of expression."[20]

FOREIGN AFFAIRS

BAHRAIN AND THE GULF

"We all act so that peace shall triumph and bring relief, stability, and prosperity instead of war and destruction."[21] These words, of Shaykh 'Isa, summed up Bahrain's regional policy in 1989: the use of every available means to preserve and strengthen the calm which followed the August 1988 cease-fire. The small island-state was well aware that its much needed economic growth was more likely to occur in times of peace. The January incident, when a Bahraini vessel hit a mine and exploded, killing its captain and wounding five crewmen, revived wartime memories and pushed Bahrain to exert every possible effort to bring about a new round of talks aimed at overcoming the obstacles to regional peace.[22] In its capacity as chairman of the Gulf Cooperation Council (GCC), Bahrain held discussions with both belligerents in order that the UN Resolution 598 "be fully implemented."[23] In this context, the Bahraini foreign minister visited Paris to confer with his Iranian counterpart, Dr. 'Ali Akbar Velayati.[24]

As part of the same endeavor, Bahrain made efforts to step up relations with both belligerents. The thaw in Bahraini-Iranian relations was maintained, although rather hesitantly; Bahraini officials were not known to have visited Iran and prominent

Iranians did not come to Bahrain. Contacts were maintained through Iran's chargé d'affaires in Bahrain, Husayn Naraqiyan, who conveyed several messages from President 'Ali Khameneh'i and from Foreign Minister Velayati to 'Isa and other Bahraini officials. The restraint in Bahraini-Iranian ties was not surprising considering their stormy relations throughout the 1980s. Since the summer of 1979, revolutionary Iran had given the Bahraini regime a cause for concern by its propaganda and threatening actions, as evinced by the Iranian-sponsored coup attempts in 1981 and 1987 (for details on the attempted coups, see *MECS* 1981–82, pp. 490–92, and 1988 pp. 429–30). The Bahraini prime minister on several occasions touched on the issue: "It is important that good intentions be shown clearly...time alone can reveal good intentions and with the lapse of time, relations [with Iran] will gradually improve."[25]

Bahraini-Iraqi relations were strengthened markedly; senior officials of both countries exchanged visits. In May, Shaykh 'Isa paid his first visit to Baghdad since the outbreak of the Gulf War, discussing bilateral as well as regional issues with President Saddam Husayn.[26] A comprehensive bilateral cooperation agreement in the economic and cultural fields was agreed upon in September, while in December a noninterference and nonaggression pact was concluded.[27] Iraq's chairing the Arab Cooperation Council (ACC; for details on the grouping, see chapter on inter-Arab relations) and Bahrain the GCC must have added another dimension to their relations in 1989.

Bahrain took a moderate approach in other regional disputes. Explaining the fragility of bilateral relations in the Gulf, Bahraini Minister of Information Tariq 'Abd al-Rahman al-Mu'ayyad said that "the Gulf region inherited many historical problems, which we hope will be settled peacefully, since there is no other way."[28] Accordingly, Bahrain hailed the Saudi-Iraqi efforts to settle their border demarcation disputes. But it soon became evident that the modest Bahraini tone was meant for Qatari ears. The efforts made to resolve their dispute over the island of Fasht al-Dibal had not been crowned with success, and it could well lead to another war in the near future. "We, inside the Gulf houses," asserted Shaykh Khalifa, "should solve our outstanding problems, or at least...forget that we have any problems until suitable conditions prevail and we are ready to face and settle them."[29] (For a full account of the Qatari-Bahraini dispute, see *MECS* 1986, pp. 294–96.)

BAHRAIN AND INTER-ARAB AFFAIRS

As chairman of the GCC, Bahrain often expressed its views on the Arab world's main problems, such as the Lebanese crisis and the Palestinian issue. Bahrain supported the efforts of the six-member Arab committee entrusted with tackling the Lebanese crisis, by appealing to "all parties inside and outside Lebanon" to support these efforts.[30] Shaykh 'Isa held that the crisis could be solved only by the Lebanese people and that the Arabs should only help do so.[31] Bahrain reiterated its support for the Palestinian uprising in the West Bank and the Gaza Strip. Declarations to that effect were made during 'Arafat's visit to the island in March. Addressing the UN on several occasions, Bahrain urged the international community to protect the Palestinians from what it called, Israeli persecution.[32]

The new Arab blocs — the ACC and the Arab Maghrib Union — were welcomed by Bahrain (for details on these groupings, see chapter on inter-Arab relations). Emphasizing that these groupings were not separatist organizations, Shaykh 'Isa said they were an embodiment of the Arab peoples' aspiration for unity.[33] Most states within the groupings considered moderate were on good terms with Bahrain, particularly Egypt. Bahrain supported wholeheartedly the reinstatement of Egypt in the Arab League as a full-fledged member, claiming that "Egypt's absence from Arab summits is abnormal."[34] In May, Shaykh 'Isa led a delegation to Egypt for a three-day visit and held discussions with Egyptian President Husni Mubarak and other senior officials. Economic issues were known to be the leading topics of the discussions; Bahrain was interested in expanding all forms of bilateral investment and trade as well as promoting economic cooperation between the GCC states and Egypt, hoping to become the focal point of such activity.[35] Security policy — fighting terrorism and drug trafficking — was coordinated during the November visit to Bahrain of Egyptian Interior Minister Gen. Zaki Badr.

Relations with the Maghrib states were strengthened as well. A Moroccan military delegation visited Bahrain in May and discussed cooperation with the Bahraini heir apparent, who paid a reciprocal visit in June. Bahraini-Tunisian bilateral cooperation was discussed during meetings held by a joint commission in October in Manama.[36] A Libyan envoy visited Bahrain in October with a message to 'Isa from Libya's Mu'ammar al-Qadhdhafi. Bahrain recognized the new regime in Sudan (see chapter on Sudan), hosting several Sudanese officials. During a visit in December by Chairman of the Sudanese Revolutionary Council Lt. Gen. 'Umar Hasan al-Bashir, it was announced that a Sudanese embassy was to be opened soon in Bahrain.[37]

RELATIONS WITH THE WEST
Forged during the heat of the Gulf War, Bahrain-US relations were especially amicable. The military aspect of relations came to the fore again in 1989 as the US continued to be the main supplier of Bahraini arms (see above). Among important official exchanges between the two countries was the visit of Gen. Norman Shwarzkopf, the commander of the US Central Command (Centcom), who came twice — in January and in November — and held talks with senior military officials. It was scarcely surprising, therefore, that Bahrain — in contrast with other GCC states — avoided a confrontation with the US on the Israeli-Arab conflict. It chose rather to define US policy in the Middle East as "positive and effective," and Bahrain's prime minister asserted while in Washington that relations between both countries had probably "never been better."[38]

Bahraini-British relations were typified by a stream of exchange visits throughout the year. Secretary of State for Home Affairs Douglas Hurd led a delegation in March for a two-day visit, during which security matters, such as the exchange of expertise in the police field, were discussed.[39] A bilateral military cooperation agreement was concluded during the May visit to Britain of Shaykh Khalifa Ibn Ahmad Al Khalifa, Bahrain's minister of defense and commander in chief of the BDF.[40]

RELATIONS WITH OTHER STATES
Seeking to "foster the bonds of friendship and cooperation," Bahrain established diplomatic ties with the PRC in April,[41] the fifth GCC state to do so. The PRC was the first Communist country to be represented in Bahrain; ties with the USSR were yet to be established, although such a step was likely since the USSR had withdrawn from

Afghanistan. For the first time, Bahrain established ties with an East European country, Yugoslavia. Relations were also slated with Panama and Columbia.

NOTES

For the place and frequency of publications cited here, and for the full name of the publication, news agency, radio station, or monitoring service where an abbreviation is used, please see "List of Sources." Only in the case of more than one publication bearing the same name is the place of publication noted here.

1. *Al-Sharq al-Awsat,* 5 August 1989.
2. *The Gulf States,* 12 June; *CR:* Bahrain, No. 3, 1989.
3. *The Gulf States,* ibid.
4. *CR:* Bahrain, No. 3, 1989.
5. Ibid.
6. *Al-Nashra,* Athens, 17 April; *al-Muharrir,* 29 April 1989.
7. *Suraqiyya,* 8 December 1989.
8. *Al-Sharq al-Jadid,* July 1989.
9. *CR:* Bahrain, No. 3, 1989.
10. *MEED,* 27 October 1989.
11. *The Gulf States,* 9 January 1989.
12. *MEED,* 27 October 1989.
13. *CR:* Bahrain, No. 1, 1989.
14. *ME,* February 1989.
15. *AT,* 16 May 1989.
16. *ME,* February 1990.
17. *Al-Qabas,* 20 October 1989.
18. *CR:* Bahrain, No. 2, 1989.
19. *The Gulf States,* 21 August 1989.
20. GNA, 7 March — DR, 16 March 1989.
21. *Al-Ra'y al-'Amm,* 5 March 1989.
22. GNA, 17 January — DR, 18 January 1989.
23. *Al-Bayan,* Dubai, 23 February 1989.
24. GNA, 7 March — DR, 8 March 1989.
25. *AT,* 16 May, 20 November 1989.
26. GNA, 14 May — DR, 15 May; *al-Bayan,* Dubai, 15 May 1989.
27. GNA, 2 September, 12 December — DR, 7 September, 12 December 1989.
28. *Al-Sharq al-Awsat,* 19 November 1989.
29. *AT,* 16 May 1989.
30. GNA, 7 March — DR, 8 March 1989.
31. MENA, 17 May — DR, 18 May 1989.
32. *Al-Bayan,* Dubai, 22 April 1989.
33. GNA, 8 April — DR, 11 April 1989.
34. GNA, 16 May — DR, 18 May 1989.
35. *Al-Bayan,* Dubai, 16 May; *The Gulf States,* 29 May 1989.
36. GNA, 7 September — DR, 12 September 1989.
37. R. Omdurman, 13 December — DR, 18 December 1989.
38. Prime minister's lecture in Washington — *American-Arab Affairs,* No. 30, Fall 1989, pp. 18-21.
39. GNA, 27, 28 March — DR, 29 March 1989.
40. GNA, 30 May — DR, 5 June 1989.
41. *Al-Bayan,* Dubai, 17, 19 April; *JP,* 10 April 1989.

Egypt
(Jumhuriyyat Misr al-'Arabiyya)

AMI AYALON

Closing a decade which after a turbulent start had been relatively calm for Egypt, 1989 was yet another peaceful year, one of continuity rather than change. The regime was stable and confident, notwithstanding economic troubles and domestic political opposition. Freedom of expression was palpably expanding, making Egypt a conspicuous model of political pluralism among the Arab states. A visitor to Cairo in 1989 could readily detect many recent improvements in infrastructure and services as well as a vivid momentum of construction, achievements that were a source of much satisfaction. And the state's remarkable foreign policy accomplishments further boosted the national moral. "Our ship," President Husni Mubarak stated assuredly, "is sailing safely ahead despite the storms."[1]

The ship may have been forging ahead — where to was a question with more than one answer — but the water was surely troubled by powerful undercurrents. Underlying this difficult reality was, as ever, economic plight, the result of an adverse population-resources ratio, "the mother of all problems" in Mubarak's words.[2] It exposed the government to repeated assaults by the legal opposition and led to periodic outbursts of protest in various quarters, not least by Muslim fundamentalists, imposing upon the security forces a constant state of alert. The harsh present was further overcast by the long shadow of future troubles, the seemingly inescapable outcome of ongoing demographic trends, which was already undermining the government's socioeconomic efforts.

As against this, the foreign scene was much more gratifying to Egypt. Cairo continued to improve its international standing, scoring impressive gains especially in the regional arena. The cycle of its ostracism in the Arab world was eventually closed in 1989, as Egypt was officially readmitted into the Arab League. Having subsequently renewed diplomatic relations with Syria and Lebanon and improved its ties with Libya, Egypt, now without adversaries among the Arab states, resumed the standing of a senior actor on the regional stage. It was the chief speaker for the Arab side in the political process that was designed to settle the Arab-Israeli conflict, was prominently outspoken on the Lebanese crisis, and was a founding member of a new subregional international framework, the Arab Cooperation Council (ACC). From Cairo's point of view, therefore, 1989 "rightly deserved to be called the year of clearing the Arab atmosphere," in the words of one enthusiastic journalist.[3]

This was also the year in which Taba, a tiny piece of land hitherto held by Israel, was returned to Egyptian sovereignty. Its return removed another stumbling block from Egyptian-Israeli peace, a vital pillar in Cairo's foreign strategy that remained stable after a decade of relations, despite many visible difficulties. Finally, Egypt's

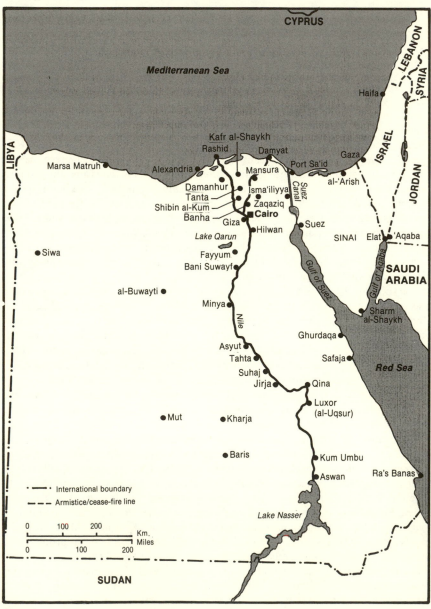

Egypt

international prestige was given a boost in Africa, where Mubarak was elected to head the Organization of African Unity (OAU) for 1989–90.

DOMESTIC AFFAIRS

ECONOMIC PRESSURES AND SOCIOPOLITICAL TENSIONS

Awareness of the dangers inherent in rapid population growth was clearly increasing among the country's political and intellectual leadership. The Egyptian population — 54m. on 16 March, 55m. on 17 December — was growing at a staggering rate of 1.33m. annually,[4] undermining the government's achievements in economic and infrastructural development and threatening to completely offset all such efforts in years to come. In 1989, this demographic menace was the subject of extensive public debate in newspapers and journals and in the Consultative Council.[5] President Mubarak, profoundly concerned, missed no opportunity to discuss it publicly and express his alarm. The problem, he repeatedly warned, was truly "horrifying," for people were procreating "without any consideration or calculation." 'What will happen," he admonished his audience, "when there are 70m. of us, keeping in mind that resources do not increase at the same rate as population?...What about houses, food, education, medical treatment, and many other needs for [these]...millions? Where will we get these things?"[6]

> In Luxor [Mubarak told an audience] I once met a police sergeant who said: 'I need a house, Mr. President.' I asked him: 'how many [children] do you have?' He said 13. My God! What he needs is an apartment block. If each of you needs a whole apartment block to yourself, how can we build a million of them? Not even in a thousand years will we be able to build them...Yes, we all trust in God, but the Prophet said: 'Do your duty and trust [in God,]' He did not say: 'Fool around.'[7]

The problem was particularly intricate as it stemmed from traditional cultural concepts and social conventions that were deeply rooted in large segments of Egyptian society. Changing these attitudes called for a comprehensive educational campaign in which many forces would act in concert. This was hard to attain. Securing a legal opinion (*fatwa*) from Shaykh al-Azhar to the effect that birth control was compatible with the Shari'a, and enlisting mosque preachers to propagate the need for family planning,[8] could not have more than a marginal effect, for most mosques (still a major channel of communicating a message in Egypt) were not controlled by the state religious establishment; rather, they were often guided by spiritual leaders who strongly objected to family planning. Similarly, it was one thing to allocate resources for the purpose (£E20m. for 1989),[9] or broadcast the slogan of "a small family is a happy family" in the media and street posters; it was quite another to bring women to the birth control distribution stations, or make them agree to be examined by male gynecologists. Mubarak often voiced his frustration in the face of such difficulties.[10] Asked why the government was not taking more effective measures, such as refusing to extend health, educational, and supply assistance to families with more than two or three children, he admitted that the government's ability to remedy the situation through such means was very limited: "We cannot implement these programs," he said in dismay, "unless the people realize the future danger that population growth poses."[11]

While the demographic forecast portended a grim material future for Egypt, the socioeconomic circumstances of the present were bleak enough in themselves. Chronically short of the hard currency required to finance the imports of foodstuffs (over 50% of all food consumption) and other goods, and sunk deep in debts, Egypt in 1989 suffered from yet another acute foreign currency crisis. According to Mubarak, the country's foreign exchange earnings in 1988–89 amounted to a mere $6.1bn., while imports reached $10.6bn., including $1.1bn. in wheat and $2.2bn. in consumer goods.[12] The long-term remedy was in increased production and exports. But meanwhile, the country badly needed the forbearance of its creditors, to whom it owed a total of about $50bn., serviced at $4bn.–$5bn. annually. Egypt was the largest debtor in Africa and, apart from Iraq, in the Middle East.[13]

The road to improving the conditions of debt repayment passed through the International Monetary Fund (IMF). An Egyptian-IMF agreement was a prerequisite for rescheduling some $10bn. of the country's debts to its chief foreign creditors, grouped in the Paris Club, and for obtaining another major loan from the World Bank. Since the collapse of the May 1987 agreement with the IMF a few months later (see *MECS* 1987, p.333; 1988, p. 391) Egypt had sought to reach a revised agreement. Egypt's failure to meet performance targets in reforming its economy as agreed upon in 1987 prompted the fund to take a more rigid stance and ask for firmer Egyptian commitments. The IMF demanded that Egypt should considerably reduce its budget deficit, take steps toward unifying its multitiered exchange rate system, raise the prices of domestically consumed energy and adapt them to world prices, markedly increase interest rates to encourage savings and, perhaps most significant, gradually reduce subsidies for basic commodities in preparation for abolishing them later on. The Egyptian Government acknowledged, in principal, the need to rationalize its economic structure and began to introduce some effective measures: it cut some of the budget deficit; marginally raised interest rates on savings; raised energy prices; set taxes on certain commodities, such as cigarettes; and effectively increased the price of bread (see below).[14] All these measures still left a gap between the government and the fund concerning both the scope of the desired changes and the timetable for their implementation: the IMF demanded more drastic measures, to be introduced mostly within 18 months, while Egypt insisted on a lenient and gradual approach, believing it needed three-to-five years for some changes, seven-to-ten for others.[15] Of all the points of disagreement, the issue of subsidies for basic staples was the most sensitive and intricate. "The fund considers it from a purely economic point of view," the editor of *al-Ahram* complained, "while we look at it as a political and social, not merely economic matter."[16] In a country as poor as Egypt, cutting sharply on subsidies was a risky matter, as recent precedents had shown, and the government had no intention of taking the risk to meet IMF demands. Negotiations between Egyptian economic leaders and IMF representatives continued throughout the year in Cairo and Washington, and there were reports of the gap between their positions being narrowed down.[17] By the end of 1989, however, Egypt's revised agreement with the IMF was still to be signed.

The country's financial hardship, of course, was no mere abstract figure in state budget books and balance-of-payments tables. It was felt in the market daily and acutely, especially by the poorer. The prices of staples, notably wheat, rice, sugar, cooking oil, fruits, and vegetables, rose sharply during the period under review; in some cases they doubled, or more. A steep increase in the price of bread was especially grave, because of its symbolic connotations. Its doubling in 1989, affected through the introduction of an "improved loaf" and phasing out of the standard loaf, elicited repeated protests that were occasionally violent. In the middle of March, a bread shortage crisis occurred, resulting from a temporary want of wheat. It produced long and angry queues at bakeries and an extensive black market. Shopkeepers engaged in manipulatory stockpiling of wheat, while bus and taxi drivers were reported to be purchasing bread in Cairo and selling it in the countryside for double the price.[18] Small-scale outbursts of indignant consumers took place here and there, prompting the police to interfere and enforce order at bread distribution centers.[19] The crisis came to an end in late April, as sufficient quantities of wheat arrived from abroad. But the government, sensitive and concerned, announced it was moving to "take strict measures to achieve discipline in the markets," through tightening its control over commodities and prices; transgressors, the government warned, would be swiftly punished.[20]

Imposing stricter control was one way of handling the burdensome supply situation. Another was trying to educate the public to more economic consumption. Alongside rapid population growth, Mubarak stated in his May Day speech, overconsumption was the country's gravest problem. The people had "unfavorable habits and modes of conduct" that were both "unacceptable and unreasonable": they threw foodstuffs in the garbage or fed them to livestock, and consumed many products wastefully, at a rate far exceeding the world average. Just as in previous years they were advised to economize by quitting smoking or by eating vegetables instead of meat, they were now called upon not to eat cucumbers and tomatoes out of the summer season. "Stop behaving like aristocrats!" Mubarak scolded his audience. "Since when have we eaten cucumbers in the winter? Don't you live in this country?"[21]

A serious breach of the fragile sociopolitical calm occurred in August in Hilwan, where a labor strike at the large iron and steel plants led to a violent confrontation between workers and the security forces. Following the suspension from the company's board of two elected labor representatives who sought a better deal in the annual decision on production bonuses, about 1,500–1,800 workers went on strike on 1 August to show solidarity with their colleagues. The next morning the police staged a dawn raid on the plant, using armored cars and tear gas. They killed one person, wounded several others, and arrested about 600 workers, thus putting a speedy end to the strike.[22] In the aftermath, the government agreed to a sizable increase in bonuses as a conciliatory measure. But at the same time, it also took steps that were strikingly reminiscent of its tactics during the January 1977 food riots (see MECS 1976–77, pp. 290–92) and in subsequent incidents of a similar nature. Interior Minister Zaki Badr was quick to discover "a conspiracy" behind the incident by "extremist communist and religious elements," and vowed to expose them. Three weeks later, the police "uncovered" an "illegitimate underground communist organization" and arrested its 52 alleged members, among them three journalists, three lawyers, students, and workers. They were accused of "trying to promote communism" during the Hilwan strike.[23]

Most of the detainees were released shortly afterward, as tempers cooled down. But the official reaction clearly indicated the government's alertness to expressions of popular discontent, however mild, and its mindfulness of their dangerous potential.

Perhaps, as one observer suggested, the authorities had never got over the trauma of the January 1977 events.[24] Whether or not that was so, given the country's material reality they surely had good reasons for being nervous.

THE REGIME'S ENCOUNTER WITH ITS ISLAMIC AND LEFTIST OPPONENTS

The exposure of numerous clandestine groups, extensive arrests, and recurrent clashes between the police and the regime's opponents were clear marks of the tension that dominated the Egyptian domestic political game in 1989. As in the previous two years, the tension surfaced mainly in limited-scale encounters which, as such, did not seriously threaten the state's basic stability. They indicated, however, that defiance of the government was anything but abating.

The opposition's leftist-Nasserite wing was relatively calm in 1989. The trial of members of the terrorist "Egyptian Revolution" group (see *MECS* 1987, pp. 336–37; 1988, pp. 393–94) continued intermittently throughout the year and beyond, attracting limited popular attention. Expressions of solidarity with the defendants and their cause were likewise fewer than before. Only the appearance of senior politicians, such as Foreign Minister 'Abd al-Majid and Interior Minister Badr, as witnesses in court drew some public interest.[25] In April, a "communist cell," linked to the illegal Egyptian Communist Party, was exposed in Mansura and Alexandria, and its members were arrested for possessing tracts "designed to stir up social agitation and revolution."[26] Another "communist conspiracy" was unveiled in September, following the events in Hilwan (see above); and a third group of 13 alleged communists was uncovered in al-Mahalla al-Kubra the next month.[27] "The communists are uniting with the Nasserites, they all work together," Interior Minister Badr stated, shedding light on the reasons for his high sensitivity to the problem; "it is a unified plan until they reach their prey."[28]

The regime's confrontation with the Islamic opposition, always more intensive than its encounter with the left, was considerably more violent in 1989 than in the previous year. At the background to the heated atmosphere were the 'Ayn Shams incidents of late 1988, especially the clashes in December in which a police officer was killed (see *MECS* 1988, pp. 394–95). It seemed as if they caused the police to lose much of the patience it had displayed hitherto. During the period under review, Muslim fundamentalists were repeatedly harrassed all over the country and thousands of them were arrested. As in the past, it was mostly in the fundamentalist strongholds of Upper Egypt — Asyut, Minya, Qina, Sawhaj, Bani Suwayf, Aswan — that these encounters took place.[29] One particularly violent clash between demonstrating radicals and the police took place in Asyut on 12 December; 40 people, including 10 policemen, were reportedly injured, and 300 were detained.[30] Incidents were also reported in Cairo, Alexandria, and the Delta.[31]

Another major center of radical action was Fayyum, an oasis town about 100 km. southwest of Cairo. In 1989, it became a stage of intense quarrels between Muslim militants and the authorities. Fayyum's Shuhada mosque was the theater of the blind theologian and preacher 'Umar 'Abd al-Rahman, a 51-year-old charismatic fundamentalist leader, the mufti of al-Jihad organization and the spiritual mentor of president Sadat's assassins in 1981. Having been tried twice following Sadat's assassination and acquitted for lack of evidence, 'Abd al-Rahman had been arrested several times thereafter. In 1989, he won prominence again. Under his inspiration Fayyum was restive during the early months of the year, and small-scale incidents took place there in February and March.[32] On 7 April, following Friday noon prayers at al-Shuhada mosque, a group of slogan-chanting al-Jihad affiliates clashed with the police. Four people, among them a police officer, were injured; 37 people, including 'Abd al-Rahman, were arrested. 'Abd al-Rahman and 54 other members of his group were accused of opposing the authorities and "exploiting religion to propagate ideas with the intention of creating sedition."[33]

The radical leader's arrest generated a wave of angry protests throughout the country, to which the police reacted by a massive crackdown, arresting another 1,500–2,000 people over the next two weeks.[34] During the following weeks more demonstrations of solidarity with the imprisoned preacher took place, leading to more arrests. On 10 August, a court in Cairo released 'Abd al-Rahman pending further hearings. But on the next day Interior Minister Badr issued a warrant to rearrest him "in accordance with the emergency regulations."[35]

The danger posed by the Islamic radicals, however limited their concrete power for the time being, was in their representing the most credible ideological and political alternative to the government's message, as the latter was facing growing difficulties in responding to the people's basic needs. The Islamic movement's militant wing may not have been its most dangerous component in the long run: the more moderate Muslim Brothers may have formed a greater peril, due to the consolidation of their position in the official political system — not least in the People's Assembly — and the popular attractiveness of their more temperate style. But the militant challenge — some 45 radical groups were counted in Egypt in 1989, according to one report[36] — was more immediate and required a prompt response. One kind of response, which the authorities had used ever since Sadat's assassination, was engaging the radicals in an ideological-theological dialogue (*hiwar*) with prominent 'Ulama (cf. *MECS* 1981–82, p. 450). The government, said Minister of Religious Endowments (*Awqaf*) Muhammad 'Ali Mahjub, was seeking "to arrange mass meetings with youth to explain correct Islamic concepts."[37] Men arrested for affiliation with such groups were sometimes taken upon their release directly to a meeting with leading 'Ulama for an educational talk.[38] Badr, the chief architect of the battle against Islamic radicalism, favored tougher measures. "It is a grave error to deal with these people through dialogue," he warned, since they were "a stock [of people] who cannot be redirected [to the correct path]...I see them as mad dogs, with all due respect to dogs." Badr preferred to employ "violence against violence and weapons against weapons":

> I say in a crystal-clear way that killing, mutilation, and the use of live ammunition is the method against those who use terrorism as their means. There is no other way. To hit at the very heart [of terrorism] is the only solution.[39]

Badr's method was to order wholesale arrests of suspects after every incident, major or minor, and even without any outburst of open violence. Most suspects would be released after days or weeks of detention in harsh conditions which, according to numerous accounts in the opposition press and Amnesty International reports,[40] were frequently accompanied by torture. Those who remained in custody were prosecuted, in trials that lasted many months or years. In April, the trial of 18 youngsters involved in the December 1988 'Ayn Shams incidents began in a Cairo court, where they were indicted.[41] In September, the Supreme State Security Court issued a sentence against 33 defendants of the group calling itself the "Rescued from Fire" (al-Najun min al-nar), arrested two years earlier (see MECS 1987, p. 336): five members were sentenced to life imprisonment, 21 to periods of 1–10 years in prison, and seven were acquitted.[42]

Another facet of the radical Islamic challenge, one with roots outside the country, was the appearance of pro-Iranian Shi'ite organizations in Egypt. Such groups had been exposed several times in the past (see MECS 1987, p. 336; 1988, p. 395). On 2 August, the police in Mansura and Tanta arrested 41 suspected members of a clandestine Shi'ite group that aimed to prepare the ground for the forcible establishment of an "Islamic republic" in Egypt. Another 16 members of the group managed to escape, among them four Saudis and an Iranian. The suspects, mainly university professors, physicians, and students, were allegedly trained in Iran, Syria, and Cyprus in preparation for attacking civilian targets in Egypt.[43] This spillover of Iranian militancy into Egypt was not directly associated with the indigenous phenomenon of Islamic radicalism, although the group's Egyptian members may have been induced to join it by the same grievances that gave birth to Egyptian fundamentalism. Be that as it may, from the regime's point of view this surely exacerbated the already intricate problem of Islamic opposition.

Interviewed early in the year, Badr estimated that the radical Islamic movement was "on its deathbed or, as we say, like the bird dancing in the throes of agony."[44] Judged by the vigor of the radicals' confrontations with the authorities, and the large number of arrested members in later months, this movement "on its deathbed" surely displayed an impressive degree of vitality. Badr himself almost became a victim of this aggressive vitality in December when, in what seemed to be an attempt on his life, a car bomb exploded near his motorcade in Cairo as he was driving over a bridge.[45] While the blast failed to cause any injuries or damage, the passionate reactions in the press indicated that its message was well received. "The radical religious movement will continue to exist and use its terrorism," one journalist suggested soberly, "if it pauses it is only a temporary pause, until it regains its vigor."[46]

THE REMOVAL OF ABU GHAZALA

On 15 April, in a surprise motion, Mubarak removed the second most powerful man in Egypt, FM 'Abd al-Halim Abu Ghazala, from his post as deputy prime minister and minister of defense and war production. Abu Ghazala was appointed to the vaguely defined post of presidential assistant, and was presented with the "Collar of the Republic," the country's second highest decoration. He was replaced as defense minister by Gen. Yusuf Sabri Abu Talib, hitherto governor of Cairo. The shift was sudden and swift. Asked how long he had been thinking of the change, Mubarak answered that it was a simple matter; "the thing began on Wednesday and was finished on Wednesday."[47]

If sudden and swift, the move was nonetheless of profound political significance. It was no doubt the most important change in personnel ever to have taken place under Mubarak. The 59-year-old Abu Ghazala had served as minister of defense since March 1981 (i.e., still under president Sadat) and as deputy prime minister since August 1982 (Mubarak's first year in office). Under Mubarak he had always been regarded as unquestionably the strongest man in the state after the president, and had often been mentioned as a natural candidate for the vice presidency (a post which Mubarak, however, had chosen to leave vacant). What accounted for Abu Ghazala's unique standing — beside the mutual trust between him and the president, his longtime comrade-in-arms — was his effective control of the Army, the regime's main support, which was completely restructured and reequipped during his tenure. As one who had made indefatigable efforts to improve service conditions for the troops, Abu Ghazala was very popular among the armed forces, and was often said to have "established something of a personal fief in the military."[48] Thus, unlike any other cabinet minister, he had what seemed to be his own powerful and independent constituency. Fully appreciative of this advantage, Abu Ghazala had reportedly resisted two previous attempts by Mubarak to lure him from the defense ministry by offering him the vice presidency and the prime ministry.[49]

Speculations about tacit tensions between the top two leaders had appeared from time to time, but such rumored tensions had never come to the surface, nor had they had concrete political implications. Thus the announcement about Abu Ghazala's dismissal was unexpected and surprising. The authorities themselves declined to elaborate on the move; Prime Minister 'Atif Sidqi laconically remarked that "President Mubarak needs by his side a figure to help him in tremendous tasks," hence he appointed Abu Ghazala as his aide.[50] The absence of a satisfactory official explanation prompted, again, extensive speculations concerning the reasons for the change and its significance. Most observers, rejecting Sidqi's implied suggestion that the shift was meant to enhance Abu Ghazala's standing, generally agreed that it rather weakened his position, since he was assigned an essentially ceremonial job (an assessment vindicated in later months). Some commentators sought to trace the background for what could be Mubarak's recent discontent with Abu Ghazala's professional and ethical standards. As possible reasons for Mubarak's displeasure with his defense minister, which led to the latter's removal, they mentioned "substantial corruption" in the Defense Ministry,[51] Abu Ghazala's personal corruption,[52] his involvement in the 1988 scandal of smuggling high-technology military materials from the US (see *MECS* 1988, p. 413),[53] his role in an alleged plan to build a chemical-weapons factory in Egypt,[54] his reported consent to give the US a military base west of Cairo for storing strategic weapons,[55] and his insistence that the Army press ahead with an expensive modernization program rather than contribute its share to the state's austerity budget.[56]

There were also other explanations, tracing the decision not to Abu Ghazala's performance but to Mubarak's desire to "boldly assert his own exclusive authority." It was suggested that, in view of the difficult decisions lying ahead for him, especially in the economic field, Mubarak felt it was necessary that he thus pronounce his firm control "over civilian and military life." Having a clear alternative leader such as Abu Ghazala on the scene in such hard times was undesirable. A new and loyal defense minister, on the other hand, was unlikely to harbor larger political ambitions, at least for the time being. More specifically, it was suggested that Mubarak had decided to cut military spending substantially so as to decrease the country's budget deficit, a policy that was easier to implement with Abu Ghazala out of the way.[57]

While it was true, as one journalist had remarked, that "in the Byzantine world of Egyptian presidential politics the real reasons are unlikely to be known for some time, if at all,"[58] it seemed reasonable that at least some of the above reasons had motivated Mubarak to make the move. The president himself denied the speculations about his displeasure with Abu Ghazala; "these rumors are just for fun," he said.[59] His own explanation was rather predictable if not quite illogical:

> I felt we needed to make this change so that there will be new thinking and new blood in one of our most important institutions, the armed forces. Abu Ghazala had spent eight years in this position, during which he had given a great deal. I think that after such a long period, it would be wise to seek a new talent that can offer new things in order to continue and renew the performance in what concerns the firm strategic objectives of our armed forces.[60]

Whatever the reason for Abu Ghazala's dismissal, the move certainly strengthened Mubarak's authority. Having convincingly demonstrated the broad scope of presidential power, Mubarak further consolidated his centralistic grip on the government by unseating his obvious successor. In the words of Tahsin Bashir, a seasoned Egyptian diplomat, Mubarak was "making public that he is the king and master."[61] After Abu Ghazala's deposition there was no "number two" in Egypt. This, of course, clouded the question of who would lead Egypt if and when Mubarak is gone.

The new defense minister, 60-year-old Gen. Abu Talib, had been an artillery officer trained both in the US and the Soviet Union. Aside from his military assignments during 35 years of service, he had served as governor of Northern Sinai, minister of state for popular development and, since 1983, governor of Cairo. A hard-working and incorruptible public servant with a pleasant personality, he was credited with many improvements introduced in the capital during his tenure. Asked why he had elected Abu Talib to the post, Mubarak praised him as "one of the most efficient military cadres," an experienced officer with a superb "organized mentality," who commanded "a great deal of respect within the ranks of the armed forces."[62]

THE MULTIPARTY "SAFETY VALVE"

"I believe that parties are necessary in Egypt," Mubarak told a foreign interviewer, "responsible parties contribute to reform and act as the people's watchdogs. I am for freedom of opinion. It is our safety valve."[63] In Mubarak's Egypt, freedom of opinion was primarily freedom of speech rather than of political action. There was hardly any restriction on free expression; opposition groups and individuals could assail the government verbally on any subject and with any wording. And since, on the other hand, there were various limitations on the formation and activities of legal parties, opposition forces took full advantage of the available freedom of speech to conduct a perpetual campaign of harsh indictment against the regime. The "safety valve," then, essentially meant a channel for vocal protest. As such, it was undoubtedly a vital device in a system as pressed as that of Egypt. This was clearly reflected in the way the multiparty game evolved in 1989.

The scene during the period under review was basically that of recent years. There were six officially licensed parties: the ruling National Democratic Party (NDP); the Wafd; the National Progressive Unionist Grouping (NPUG; locally known as *al-tajammu'*); the People's (*umma*) Party; the Socialist Labor Party (SLP, or *'amal*), and the Liberal (*ahrar*) Party. The last two groups were bound in a loose "coalition" with the Muslim Brothers. Several other groups organized and sought official status, among them a Nasserite party headed by Farid 'Abd al-Karim as well as a "Greens" party, formed to fight for environmental issues, under Dr. Baha al-Din Bakri.[64] The licensing of parties being a long and protracted process, none of the new groups was approved in 1989. In general, the government was reluctant to admit new parties into the system: "We will not have a carnival of parties," Mubarak stated, "we do not want to have to accept duplicate parties."[65]

There were no significant changes in the structure or functioning of the parties in 1989. The one exception was the SLP, which experienced a severe crisis. During the party's congress in March, a split occurred in its ranks, as a group of members broke off in protest against party leader Ibrahim Shukri's "continuous readiness to succumb to pressures by the Muslim Brothers" (the SLP's coalition partners). Calling itself "the socialist front," the group accused Shukri of straying away from the party's original course and changing its character. When the congress moved to adopt the motto "comprehensive reform by Islamic standards," the group, headed by People's Assembly member Ahmad Mujahid, announced it was leaving the party and henceforth professed to represent the "real SLP."[66] In later weeks, efforts were made to bridge the gap, through mediation between Shukri and Mujahid, and otherwise; they were unsuccessful, and the party remained split.[67]

While the opposition continued to attack the regime on domestic and foreign issues, the question of political freedom was a major bone of contention in 1989. Two main developments accounted for this. On 29 April, the Supreme Administrative Court ruled that the results of the 1987 People's Assembly elections had been forged by the Interior Ministry through tampering with the ratio of workers and peasants (according to the Egyptian constitution, at least one half of all assembly members must be workers and peasants). The court was acting upon a government appeal of a decision by a lower court, which in April 1987 had concluded that the elections had been rigged (for the opposition's complaints following the elections see *MECS* 1987, p. 329); the Supreme Court now turned down the appeal. According to the court's verdict, 78 representatives had entered the assembly illegally due to this falsification. Rectifying the situation by replacing them would mean a loss by the NDP of as many as 23 assembly seats to the Wafd and the Coalition.[68] It was up to the People's Assembly to decide whether to uphold the ruling, something which the assembly, with its heavy NDP majority, did not hasten to do. After some delay, the assembly on 26 June rejected the court's decision, affirming, somewhat cynically, that it was "the only authority empowered to authenticate or invalidate the membership of any of the people's deputies."[69]

Opposition reaction was wrathful. The legal ruling, they argued, did not merely confirm what they had been claiming all along — that "the will of the nation [was] being violated, forged, and encroached upon"; it also disgraced those who were responsible for the rigging, above all Zaki Badr. The ruling, said an editorial in *al-Wafd*, "fell like a sword on the heads of those who wronged. It decisively and unequivocally proves that these elections were neither clean nor honest, and that those who committed the rigging have no honor." Worse still, "the thieves who robbed people of their will and encroached upon their dignity are still in their positions." Wafd leader Siraj al-Din was bitter: "Had we lived in a democratic country, as they claim, the government would have resigned immediately after the ruling, or at least it would have relieved Interior Minister Zaki Badr, who had killed the nation's will, of his post."[70] As the assembly refused to carry out the decision, the opposition again approached the court in July, asking it to force the assembly to comply. The court repeatedly postponed discussion of the matter; in December it announced that the case would be taken up in June 1990.[71]

The other issue which pitted the government and its critics sharply against each other was the Consultative Council (Shura) elections in June. The 1989 elections to the council — the legislature's upper house, essentially a deliberative body — were not a matter of scheduled routine. Rather they were a result of exceptional political and legal developments, quite reminiscent of the circumstances that had led to the 1987 People's Assembly elections (see *MECS* 1987, pp. 324–25). In the middle of April, the Supreme Constitutional Court, acting on the opposition's appeal (see *MECS* 1986, p. 275), ruled that certain clauses in the 1980 Consultative Council electoral law were unconstitutional, hence the council elected under that law, and indeed every council elected under it since 1980, was legally invalid. The court's decision disqualified elections conducted by party lists, in which individual candidates could not be contestants. Anticipating the ruling, President Mubarak had already instructed the People's Assembly in January to prepare an amended version of the law; by the time the court issued its verdict, the new law was ready. On 22 April, following the announcement of the court's decision, Mubarak dissolved the Consultative Council, and set 8 June as election day under the amended law.[72]

The new law increased the council's membership from 210 to 258, of whom two thirds (172) would be elected and the rest nominated by the president. The elections would be held in 86 constituencies, instead of the previous 26, each electing two members including at least one worker or peasant. The contest would be open to both parties and individuals. This last stipulation also meant the annulment of another rule, the "8% hurdle," which required parties to poll at least 8% of the votes nationwide in order to be represented in the council. According to the amended version, entering the council depended upon attaining a simple majority in the constituencies.[73]

As the elections were announced, the Wafd and the NPUG made public their intention to boycott them for lack of trust in the government's ability, or will, to run a free contest and for "want of any guarantees for a proper election process."[74] The other opposition parties decided to compete: leaders of the SLP and Liberal Party said they were "eager to integrate with the masses and take part in any general elections."[75]

The elections took place on 8 June in a quiet atmosphere, although small-scale clashes between NDP and opposition affiliates took place here and there[76] — a normal phenomenon in Egyptian elections of recent years. According to the official figures, 69.7% of the 14.6m. registered voters cast their votes to elect 172 representatives. Of 162 members elected in the first round (i.e., by absolute majority), 161 were NDP candidates, including 19 who were unopposed in their constituencies; one was an independent candidate. In the second round on 15 June, all of the other 10 elected members were from the NDP.[77]

As a matter of routine, the opposition — the parties which boycotted the elections and those which participated in them alike — received the results with a blend of bitterness and contempt. Their leaders described the elections as "a farce," "a big tragedy," and "a calamity that destroys the democratic experiment." Again they spoke of rigging, violence, and blackmail by the police and the NDP, and derided the official statement on the results as "a mere joke."[78] "We are neither surprised, nor amazed by the government's rigging of the Consultative Council elections in such a blatant way, since we have expected this," read an editorial in *al-Wafd*; the regime "keeps proceeding on the wrong course, which has made democracy a deluding 'shop-window,' exploiting it for its own purposes without regard for the nation's good....These rulers turn the country into a shambles."[79]

On 20 June, Mubarak announced the names of his 86 appointees (one third of the council's membership). Among them were ex-ministers, veteran politicians, prominent intellectuals, and Coptic leaders. Mubarak also nominated two opposition party leaders, Mustafa Kamil Murad of the Liberal Party and Ahmad al-Sabbahi of the People's Party, both of whom accepted the appointment.[80] In its first session on 24 June, the council elected Dr. Mustafa Kamal Hilmi — formerly deputy prime minister and minister of education — as its chairman.[81]

The unpleasant climate continued to dominate the government-opposition dialogue until the end of the year. Mubarak, who often reiterated his commitment to democracy, also criticized the opposition, referring to "People...[who] resort to shouting and high-sounding speeches instead of working and contributing, or to deliberately falsifying the will of the masses and their desires by fabricating priorities that have no foundation or echo in the political street."[82] His critics answered in kind in their newspapers and, on one occasion, they managed to unite around a joint statement. On 13 November, a much dramatized press conference took place in Cairo, attended by Wafd leader Fu'ad Siraj al-Din, SLP leader Ibrahim Shukri, NPUG leader Khalid Muhyi al-Din, Liberal Party leader Mustafa Kamil Murad, Muslim Brothers' parliamentary representative Ma'mun al-Hudaybi, and a representative of the banned Communist Party, Mahmud Amin al-'Alim. The participants made strongly worded anti-government speeches and issued a communiqué which they all signed, expressing their concern about the government's poor performance and especially its attitude toward the opposition. The communiqué was a disappointing document: it called for a new constitution, new general elections, repeal of the state of emergency, and a firmer government commitment to the rule of law and to the protection of individual and political liberties[83] — demands that were hardly new or inspired. Nor could the joint appearance of six leaders on one platform disguise their profound differences. "I expected them to make an important announcement or issue a new plan," said Musa Sabri, a veteran journalist, "but I have discovered that I have been quite naive."[84]

FOREIGN AFFAIRS

EGYPT AND THE ARAB WORLD

Ten Years After Baghdad: Closing the Cycle of Ostracism

Ten years after having been boycotted by the Arab consensus and ousted from inter-Arab bodies, Egypt in 1989 recovered its place as a full member of the regional system. The cycle of ostracism was closed. An Arab decision to renew diplomatic relations with Cairo on an individual state basis had already been made in 1987, and all Arab states but three — Syria, Libya, and Lebanon — had done so thereafter. In

1989 came the time of Egypt's formal and unconditional return to the regional organization, the Arab League. Mubarak had reason to be satisfied, as the blend of patience and resolve he had displayed toward the Arabs since his access to power now appeared to be paying off. His address to the Arab summit in Casablanca, where Egypt was readmitted to the League, clearly reflected, in substance and style, the restoration of Egypt's position as a senior member of the organization. Following the summit, Lebanon and Syria resumed full diplomatic relations with Cairo, and relations with Libya improved markedly. During the second half of the year, Egypt was again playing a key role in the regional game, adopting an active and firm stance concerning the central issues of the day, notably the Palestinian and Lebanese problems. Perhaps one mark of Egypt's normalized inter-Arab position was the crisis that occurred late in the year in the relations with Iraq, over the conditions of Egyptian workers there: if, during the years of Arab boycott, Cairo sought to grasp the hand of whoever offered friendship in the region and courted the often-reluctant Baghdad, now, back as a full member, it could afford a crisis with an Arab ally (see further below).

Already before Egypt's return to the Arab League, its previously severed ties with various Arab organizations were resumed (this process had begun in 1988 — see *MECS* 1988, p. 398). These included the Arab Organization of Agricultural Development,[85] the Arab Labor Organization,[86] the Arab Mining Company,[87] the International Association of Arab Labor Unions,[88] the Arab Health Council,[89] the Organization of Arab Petroleum Exporting Countries,[90] and the General Association of Arab Writers.[91] Likewise, it was admitted as a new member of the Arab World Institute in Paris.[92] In February, Egypt joined Iraq, Jordan, and North Yemen in founding the ACC, essentially, though not exclusively, a framework for economic collaboration. Egypt's role as a founding member of the ACC — whose creation, alongside other developments, may have marked a change in the rules of inter-Arab politics (see chapter on inter-Arab relations) — was yet another indication of its normalized regional position. The council elected an Egyptian as its first secretary, Dr. Hilmi Nimr, a professor of management at Cairo University and member of the People's Assembly.[93] Mubarak traveled to Baghdad to the ACC inauguration session, then to San'a, in September, to attend the council's summit. In June, he played host to the other three ACC heads of state, in a council summit in Alexandria.

During the early months of the year, it was becoming clear that Egypt's return to the Arab League would take place shortly. Arab diplomats worked to remove the obstacles still delaying the convening of the conference that would formally readmit Egypt, namely, the opposition of its only two Arab foes, Syria and Libya. Syria, which already in late 1988 had signaled, if half-heartedly, its readiness to withdraw its objection (see *MECS* 1988, p. 405), continued to let it be known that its opposition was abating, and on 13 May a presidential spokesman in Damascus officially announced Syria's consent to Egypt's readmission.[94] Libyan leader Mu'ammar Qadhdhafi was still adamant; but left totally isolated in his dissent, he grudgingly put up with Egypt's participation. (On Cairo's relations with Syria and Libya see further below.) The question of procedure now remained to be settled: how should Egypt be invited to rejoin the League? A proposition, that the Arab heads of state would meet for a preliminary discussion, then invite Mubarak to attend, was quickly rejected by Egypt as "compromising its dignity and that of its people."[95] Cairo was particularly sensitive to the apparent lingering Arab misgivings: "Why this reservation?" a vexed newspaper editor asked, "why this style of inviting Egypt? Why does Egypt not get a frank and direct invitation?...the invitation should suit Egypt's status and dignity and its president's efforts."[96] At this stage, Cairo's membership of the ACC began to yield it dividends, as the leaders of Jordan, Iraq, and North Yemen threatened to boycott the summit if Egypt was not invited.[97]

On 16 May, King Hasan II of Morocco, host of the summit, called Mubarak and officially invited him to attend. On 21 May, Arab foreign ministers, including Egypt's 'Abd al-Majid, met in Casablanca and decided to readmit Egypt into the League. Syria's Foreign Minister Faruq al-Shar' even made a statement, congratulating Egypt on its return; Libya, on the other hand, absented itself from the occasion (although Qadhdhafi did appear at the summit itself).[98] Two days later, as the summit began, Mubarak delivered a forceful speech, asserting himself as a senior Arab leader who undertook to define the regional system's priorities. Mubarak chose to overlook the years of ostracism, except for remarking briefly that during that period "the Arab world was not absent from Egypt and Egypt was not absent from the Arab world." Instead, he focused on challenges of the future. He spoke of "pillars" on which Arab solidarity should rest, foremost among them, rather significantly, the need "to arrive at an agreed-upon Arab formula for peace...in a world that now places the realization of peace at the head of its aims."[99] During the conference, Mubarak met with both Asad and Qadhdhafi for cordial talks.[100] By and large the summit, from which only Lebanon was absent, was a rather rare display of Arab amity. The climate was one of moment and excitement. The Egyptians felt the joy of eventual triumph (in the words of one Egyptian journalist, "the return of the soul to the body, the triumph of reason and maturity");[101] and their fellow Arabs gave ample expression to their great relief with the termination, finally, of Egypt's anomalous ouster (see further in chapter on inter-Arab relations).

For Egypt, its readmission to the League despite its refusal to relinquish the peace with Israel meant full vindication of its regional strategy. The credit for this went almost exclusively to Mubarak; the name of the late president Sadat, the first architect of that peace, was conspicuously missing from the voluminous public discussion of the event. "Through patience, perseverance, and commitment to higher Arab interests, Egypt under President Mubarak managed to again hold together the strands of the Arab fabric that had become worn and tattered," ran a typical article in al-Musawwar.[102] Egypt's peace with Israel was not an error by a former president which the Arabs were now prepared to forgive. Rather, it was an inseparable part of Egypt's international policy, which the Arabs — their fabric "worn and tattered" — agreed to recognize. The Arabs needed Egypt, which, "due to many cultural and social factors, in addition to geographic considerations," was bound to remain "the conscience of the Arab nation and the minaret of its thought," as well as "the reservoir of expertise, ability, and skill" of the Arab world.[103]

A conference of Arab interior ministers, held in Cairo in early December, was already something of a routine event for Egypt, now a full member of the regional system. Yet its position could scarcely be that of the powerful leader it had been in the past. The system itself had changed profoundly from what it had been a decade or more earlier. Power and influence had been redistributed. The consolidation of Arab statehood, especially significant in the smaller states, the proliferation of high-quality communications and media where the voice of Cairo was once paramount, the discovery of the limits of revolutionary-ideological action — all processes begun in the 1970s and accelerated in the 1980s — seemed to have molded a system in which no single state or leader was likely to attain dominance. The Arab League, no longer "a step on the sure path to Arab unity," was now more of a concert of equals seeking stronger solidarity. Egypt itself had also changed. The limits of its economic potential, whether in irrigable land, industry, or oil, had become all too apparent, as had the fact that its sizable population, once an asset, had become a liability. Likewise, it had ceased to be the unmatched military giant of the Arab world, following the tremendous expansion of the Iraqi and Syrian armies. Egypt, therefore, was not returning to the League as its natural leader but rather as a natural member, one that still had much to offer to the other members but also one with heavy problems.

It was perhaps symbolic of this shift in status that the League did not hasten to return its headquarters to Cairo after the latter's readmission. Moved to Tunis in 1979, the headquarters remained there until the end of the period under review. Returning the offices to Egypt was no obvious matter; rather, as Mubarak said, it was "a sensitive issue."[104] Six months after Casablanca, League Secretary-General Chedli Klibi on a visit to Cairo stated that "this issue is contingent upon an Arab decision, and when such a decision has been made it will be implemented."[105] The decision was made only in March 1990.

The Bilateral Dimension of Readmission: Broadening the Cycle of Allies

If recovering its place in the Arab League was highly gratifying to Egypt, an equally important aspect of its return to the fold was the ongoing improvement in bilateral relations with Arab states. The resumption of diplomatic relations with Syria and Lebanon and the reconciliation with Libya — all long overdue, from Cairo's perspective — were prominent events that generated much joy and pride. There were other reasons for content in this arena. During the period under review, Egypt played host to no fewer than nine Arab heads of state, among them leaders whose visit was the first since the 1970s: Saudi King Fahd, who, after repeated delays (see *MECS* 1988, p. 404), came to Cairo in March and was given a particularly enthusiastic reception; the emir of Bahrain, Shaykh 'Isa Ibn Salman Al Khalifa, who arrived in May; the emir of Kuwait, Shaykh Jabir al-Ahmad Al Sabah, who came to Cairo in August; the president of North Yemen, 'Ali 'Abdallah Salih, who visited Egypt in October; and the emir of Qatar, Shaykh Khalifa Ibn Hamad Al Thani, who arrived on 1 January 1990. King Husayn of Jordan made frequent visits, in January, June, and August; Oman's Sultan Qabus, an old friend, came in May; as did the UAE heir apparent, Shaykh Khalifa Ibn Zayid Al Nuhayyan. (Two other heads of state to visit Egypt were Libya's Qadhdhafi and Sudanese leader 'Umar al-Bashir — see below.) Similarly, Mubarak traveled extensively to the Arab countries: he went to Iraq in February and October; to Jordan in April, November, and December; to Sudan in July and December; to Tunisia, Algeria, and Yemen in September; and to Libya in October and November. Relations with these states were now warm and friendly, comprising cooperation in various fields and close coordination of policies on regional and international issues. One joint project of infrastructural development launched in 1989 had perhaps a symbolic value for the new spirit in Cairo's regional relations: the "King Fahd bridge" over the Gulf of 'Aqaba, designed to link Egypt and Saudi Arabia. Decided upon during the king's visit to Cairo, the bridge would form a part of a land route stretching from Sharm al-Shaykh in Sinai, through the island of Tiran, to mainland Saudi Arabia.[106] Generally, then, an air of optimistic communion dominated Egypt's relations with the Arab states, compensating somewhat for years of banishment.

Undoubtedly the most important of these developments was the renewal of ties with Damascus, the formal part of which took place just a couple of days before the decade ended. The rivalry with Syria, an important actor on the Arab stage in many respects, had been a particularly painful reality for Egypt. It had been painful, both due to their close alliance in earlier periods, not least during the 1967 and 1973 wars against Israel, and because Egypt had basically shared the nationalist-Arab values propounded by Syria, albeit in a different fashion. Beyond the bitter disagreements over strategies, the two countries had recognized that in the final account they were seeking the same pan-Arab goals. There had also been a personal angle: the longtime friendship between Husni Mubarak and Hafiz al-Asad, two air force commanders who had shared important chapters in their careers as pilots. During the decade since 1979, however, strategic disagreements had almost completely overshadowed the sense of common destiny. Damascus refused to renew the dialogue with Cairo even after most Arab states had done so, and this largely compromised Egypt's satisfaction with its improved inter-Arab position. During the decade's last year this estrangement gave way to a thaw, which paved the way to the restoration of diplomatic relations.

What caused the change? Above all it was Syria's growing sense of isolation in both the inter-Arab and international arenas. The resumption of relations between Cairo and the majority of Arab states following the Amman summit of 1987 left Syria among the handful of Arab countries which declined to do the same. The reconstruction of Arab bridges to Egypt, far more than just a series of bilateral events, was a collective development which marked a change of spirit in the inter-Arab system. This change of spirit had been prompted by the desire to close ranks so as to form a unified Arab front against Iran, in the Gulf War (see *MECS* 1987, chapter on inter-Arab relations); and Syria, Iran's chief Arab ally, had found itself outside this emerging unified camp. The climate of Arab solidarity evidenced during the last months of the Gulf War in 1987-88 had remained after the termination of hostilities, with Syria (and Libya) out of the consensus. Such self-imposed isolation, at first entailing mostly diplomatic inconvenience, came to be more problematic as Iraq, Syria's neighbor and traditional adversary, ceased to be engaged in active confrontation on its eastern front. With a formidable, highly experienced army at its disposal, Iraq now began to appear as a potential threat to Syria. An indirect Iraqi-Syrian encounter began to develop in Lebanon (see chapter on Lebanon), an arena where Syria's activities had long been a subject of vocal Arab criticism. Syria's isolation in the regional system was coupled with a cooling in its relations with the Soviet Union, its main strategic support, which was engrossed in domestic *glasnost* and international *détente*. Moscow began to pressure Damascus for greater moderation, clarifying that it no longer shared Syria's "military option" concept (see chapter on the Soviet Union and the ME). Damascus, therefore, must have felt an urgent need to bail itself out of a growingly inconvenient corner. Warming up its relations with Egypt was a sure recipe for that. (For further discussion of the change in Syria's policy, see chapters on Syria and inter-Arab relations.) As for Egypt, it had always aspired to reconciliation with Syria, both before and after the Amman summit, but without sacrificing its other interests. Cairo could only welcome Asad's readiness for a renewed dialogue.

An improvement in Egyptian-Syrian relations was already noticed in late 1988 (see *MECS* 1988, p. 405). Their open exchanges lost their former acrimony, and Asad began to signal that he might drop his objection to Egypt's return to the Arab League. In a meeting with a delegation of Egyptian lawyers in January, for example, Asad praised Mubarak as "the brother, the friend, the comrade-in-arms, and the genuine Arab" and hailed Cairo's "Arab positions."[107] He also informed the kings of Jordan and Saudi Arabia, who were instrumental in mediating between Damascus and Cairo, that he "wished to remove all outstanding problems with Egypt and to open a direct dialogue" with it.[108] Mubarak willingly reciprocated by often mentioning the historical bonds of the two countries, which "were partners in the October [1973] war and experienced unity," and his old friendship with the Syrian leader.[109] As the Arab summit approached, Syria's opposition to Egypt's presence was abating and on 13 May an official Syrian spokesman announced that Damascus no longer objected to Egypt's return. Mubarak, the spokesman said, was "not to be equated with former Egyptian president Anwar al-Sadat, who signed the Camp David Accords"; Syria was "not blind to the positive aspects of President Husni Mubarak's policies."[110] The summit itself offered an opportunity for a friendly meeting between Asad and Mubarak. The general feeling was that from now on relations could only improve.

There was, however, one important issue on which a sharp disagreement between the two states still remained — the Syrian presence in Lebanon. Cairo was highly critical of the Syrian attitude, for Mubarak believed that terminating the Lebanese tragedy was predicated upon a total evacuation of the non-Lebanese forces from there. In his speech in Casablanca, Mubarak mentioned the need for "withdrawal of all the foreign forces" from Lebanon, without a direct reference to Syria. But on later occasions he was more explicit: "I do not like Syria to take a stand at variance with the general Arab public opinion," he said, "there is consensus on the need to effect political reform in keeping with Lebanon's interests. All foreign forces must evacuate Lebanese territory."[111] Egyptian criticism of the Syrian presence in Lebanon continued throughout the year, cautiously worded yet unequivocal. As they were about to renew their diplomatic relations, one leading Egyptian journalist remarked that their new dialogue "should not contravene the responsible Egyptian stand on the Lebanese issue."[112]

The later months of 1989 witnessed a further thaw in Egyptian-Syrian ties. In August-September, Egypt participated in the Damascus international fair for the first time since 1976.[113] In late October, Syrian Vice President 'Abd al-Halim Khaddam came to Cairo, carrying a "cordial" message from Asad to Mubarak.[114] Thereafter, the pace of exchanging words of praise was accelerated, as was the pace of diplomatic contacts. In mid-December, Egyptian Information Minister Safwat al-Sharif went to Damascus, followed a few days later by Prime Minister Sidqi; Khaddam traveled to Cairo, again; and the foreign ministers of the two states met in Paris. Early that month, Egyptian and Syrian airlines renewed commercial flights between Cairo and Damascus, and toward the end of the month they resumed their routine schedule. Eventually, on 27 December, the two states announced the formal restoration of their diplomatic relations. The renewal, one observer noted, summing up the Egyptian view, meant that "Egypt has consolidated its Arab relations while maintaining the dignity of the homeland. This affirms the sincerity of the Egyptian approach toward pan-Arab issues."[115]

Unlike the relations between Cairo and Damascus, Egyptian-Libyan relations at the beginning of the period under review were characterized by mutual suspicion and mistrust. Yet, although Libya was an immediate neighbor, Qadhdhafi's enmity seems to have been somewhat less annoying to Egypt than Asad's. This was so perhaps because Libya had always been a rather marginal member of the regional system, and because Mubarak's mistrust of Qadhdhafi was also shared by many other leaders, Arab and non-Arab. Nonetheless, Cairo was unhappy with its tense exchanges with Tripoli. And if it did not aspire for warm friendship — something, Egypt felt, would be unrealsitic to expect from the unpredictable Qadhdhafi — it at least sought a peaceful atmosphere. "All we want from them is good neighborly relations," Mubarak said; "No problems, no border violations or operations. I do not ask for more than this."[116] But Qadhdhafi, who declared that "the main benchmark for Libya's relations with any country" was "that country's stand toward imperialism and Zionism,"[117] continued to hold grudges against Egypt for its ties with Israel and the US and to assail Egypt periodically.

During the early months of 1989, relative calm marked Cairo's relations with Tripoli, a situation which Mubarak contentedly defined as "good."[118] On the eve of the Casablanca summit, however, Qadhdhafi was the main opponent of the invitation to Egypt. Eventually, Egypt was invited despite his opposition, and was readmitted to the League notwithstanding Libya's absence from the discussion (see above). Qadhdhafi, who now chose not to remain in total isolation, showed up at the summit, embraced Mubarak and met with him for two rounds of "very realistic, serious, and frank talks."[119] The meeting, the Egyptians assessed, was "a step toward full reconciliation," although they reckoned that "it will require patience to surmount the years of estrangement."[120]

Following the summit, there was a flurry of diplomatic contacts between the two states. An emissary of Qadhdhafi, his cousin Ahmad Qadhdhaf al-Dam, came to Cairo in late May for an eight-day visit, and an Egyptian Foreign Ministry delegation went to Tripoli.[121] The Egyptian-Libyan border, closed since 1977, was reopened,[122] and on 4 June the Egyptian-Libyan airspace was reopened for commercial flights.[123] The cordial climate and friendly exchanges continued in later months. Qadhdhafi invited Mubarak to the 20th anniversary celebrations of his revolution, and Mubarak sent Deputy Prime Minister and Agriculture Minister Yusuf Wali to represent him there. Six weeks later, a double Egyptian-Libyan summit took place. On 16 October, Qadhdhafi went to Marsa Matruh, a Mediterranean resort town about 250 km. from the Libyan border, where he was greeted by Mubarak who conferred with him for several hours. The next day, Mubarak went to Tubruq, across the Libyan border, to continue his talks with his Libyan counterpart. The two visits, much dramatized in the local and international media, were held in an atmosphere of demonstrated amity. "I am not a guest in this place, but I am among my family, relatives, and brothers," Qadhdhafi stated in Marsa Matruh. Mubarak, typically less emotional, hailed his session with the Libyan leader as "characterized by reason and logic."[124] The two leaders discussed and agreed to cooperate in such areas as electricity, telecommunications, roads and railways, agricultural projects, and oil exploration.[125] The momentum of reconciliation persisted until the end of the year. In November, a

Libyan industrial delegation arrived in Cairo, and signed a protocol of industrial and technical cooperation.[126] In December, Mubarak again went to Libya and met with Qadhdhafi in Sirte, where they discussed cooperation in agriculture, industry, energy, transport, communications, and information.[127] In this, and in other frequent meetings between Egyptian and Libyan officials, progress was also made on an issue that had been a source of much aggravation — Libyan compensation to thousands of Egyptian workers who had been expelled from Libya in 1985 (see *MECS* 1984–85, pp. 560–61; 1987, p. 309). Tripoli agreed to pay, and the two sides decided to form a joint committee to complete the procedure for disbursing the money.[128]

This amicable spirit notwithstanding, the two sides did not hurry to renew their diplomatic relations. Both Cairo and Tripoli felt that the time for such a move had not yet come. The fact that the two leaders met in towns other than their respective capitals was a clear sign that obstacles still lay on the road to a more harmonious rapport. Qadhdhafi would not go to an Arab city where the Israeli flag was flying, and would not put up with Cairo's peace strategy, although he was prepared to put the issue aside for the time being. On the Egyptian side, too, much skepticism remained — a result of the frustrating experience in the vicissitudinous relations with the Libyan leader. These limitations meant that more time was needed to overcome the problems of the past and disagreements of the present. By the end of the period under review, much remained to be done in Egyptian-Libyan reconciliation.

Like Syria, but unlike Libya, Lebanon decided to renew its diplomatic relations with Egypt following the Casablanca summit. Immersed in a bitter domestic war, Lebanon had hitherto been too insecure to take such a step, especially as long as Syria was categorically opposed to Egypt's return to the Arab League. On 29 June, five weeks after the summit, the Lebanese Government moved to restore relations with Egypt. According to the new Lebanese ambassador in Cairo, the two rival "governments" in Lebanon were in favor of the change, and "rather than fighting each other [over it] we saw the reverse — they competed with each other in winning Egypt's friendship."[129] The resumption of relations, the ambassador stated, was "not merely a measure rectifying the situation"; it was also going to benefit Lebanon, which would "use Egypt's prudent policy and good ties with all Arab and international parties" to resolve its problems.[130] Egypt, which already before the resumption of relations had given ample expression to its view, that the Lebanese problem was the most acute crisis facing the Arab world, continued to voice this view repeatedly thereafter. Cairo welcomed the "national accord" for Lebanon reached in Ta'if in October (see chapter on Lebanon), and supported the elected presidents René Mu'awwad and Ilyas al-Hirawi.[131]

The Crisis in Egyptian-Iraqi Relations
If Egypt's relations with the Arab states and the Arab League were back to normal in 1989, this resumed normalcy was also seen in a development of a different nature: a crisis with an Arab ally over a purely bilateral issue. The Egyptian-Iraqi tension was yet another clear indication of Cairo's recovered freedom of maneuver in the regional arena. Had such a crisis occurred two years earlier, Egypt — with most of its Arab alliances not yet reinstitutionalized — might have chosen to overlook the problem and keep silent about it. In late 1989, however, Cairo could afford to allow its relations with one of its closer allies to cool down somewhat, and perhaps even benefit from it.

During the first 10 months of the year, Egyptian-Iraqi relations were warm and cooperation in various fields persisted. In January, the second session of their joint higher committee for economic, scientific, and technical cooperation was held in Cairo (the committee was founded in May 1988 and met for its first session in Baghdad — see *MECS* 1988, p. 401). Iraq's First Deputy Prime Minister Taha Yasin Ramadan headed the Iraqi delegation to the talks, which offered an opportunity for mutual expressions of friendship and support.[132] In February, Mubarak went to Baghdad to attend the ACC inaugural session, where optimism and amity were again voiced. During the following months, the routine of friendly dialogue and close cooperation continued, Mubarak and Saddam Husayn frequently exchanging words of praise and high-level Egyptian and Iraqi officials exchanging frequent visits. Iraq was one of the most active and firm supporters of Egypt's participation in the Casablanca summit and readmission to the Arab League. In October, Mubarak again traveled to Baghdad to attend the Faw reconstruction celebrations (see chapter on Iraq).[133]

The crisis that broke out in early November revolved around a reported Iraqi maltreatment of Egyptian workers in Iraq, which prompted a massive flight of Egyptians back home. That something of this kind should happen could perhaps have been anticipated long before. During Iraq's eight-year war with Iran, Egyptian workers formed a sizable segment of Iraq's labor force as Iraqi men were mobilized in the Army. The Egyptians, whose number in Iraq was estimated at 2m., did mostly menial jobs or worked in agriculture. As the war ended in summer 1988, hundreds of thousands of demobilized Iraqi troops found Egyptians in their jobs. This Iraqi problem was coupled with another, a severe financial crisis resulting from Iraq's heavy war debts and the need to reconstruct its infrastructure. To tackle the double problem, Baghdad decided in July to discourage the presence of foreign workers by sharply cutting down the remittances they were allowed to send back home and to delay payments to foreign workers. The ruling went into effect in October.[134] By mid-November, the value of all delayed remittances to Egyptians was estimated at $350m.[135] Consequently, Egyptians — whose number had already dwindled to 1m., or less[136] — forced out of their jobs and unable to make do with the allowable remittances, began to rush back home at an accelerated pace.

These developments were painful enough, both for the returning individuals and for the Egyptian economy which badly needed the remitted hard currency. What turned the problem into an acute crisis were rumors that began to spread among the Egyptians in Iraq in late October, of angry unemployed Iraqis attacking Egyptians and even murdering them. Such rumors turned the Egyptian exodus from Iraq into a panicked escape. As tens of thousands of Egyptians fled Iraq by air and land, means of transportation became inadaquate. On 15 November Iraqi Airways added 10 daily flights between Baghdad and Cairo, but even that was insufficient. Thousands of terrified Egyptians crowded the Baghdad airport, and a black market in flight tickets to Cairo reportedly developed. Egyptian officials and the foreign press estimated that, if continued at the same pace, the Egyptian exodus from Iraq would reach 100,000–150,000 people by the end of the year.[137]

The reports and rumors brought to Cairo by the escaping Egyptians were soon amplified in the Egyptian media. Unable to get reliable information on what was really happening, the press relied on these partial reports and often inflated rumors.

Trying to investigate the matter, it produced more ambiguity. There were reports of large numbers of Egyptian corpses flown in from Baghdad — 1,052 bodies during the first 10 months of the year, as against 980 for the whole of 1988 — many of which had marks of violence on them, or bullet holes.[138] There were also reports about cruel treatment of Egyptians by the Iraqi police,[139] and about mass attacks on groups of Egyptians in the streets of Baghdad, which resulted in many casualties.[140]

The Egyptian reaction was one of shock and puzzlement as much as rage. Cairo was puzzled, due both to the former background of cordial relations with Baghdad — officials and commentators indeed recalled the exemplary Iraqi attitude toward Egyptian workers in previous years — and because there was no accurate knowledge about the true nature of events. There was a general feeling that the Iraqi Government, its difficulties acknowledged, had mishandled the operation of replacing Egyptian workers by Iraqi citizens and allowed the situation to get out of control. This, many Egyptians felt, was unacceptable: Egyptians should "raise their voice against the wave of racist persecution of Egyptian workers in Iraq....We do not accept an Iraqi government that does not control the situation and allows Iraqi citizens to chase Egyptian workers in the streets and to beat, insult, and sometimes kill them."[141] Several papers referred to the possibility that Iraq's "repressive measures" against Egyptians resulted from its dismay with the improvement in Egyptian-Syrian relations,[142] thereby implying that the attacks were inspired from above. Egyptian writers who were invited to participate in an Iraqi festival turned down the invitation in protest.[143] As a precaution, Iraqi institutions in Egypt, such as the embassy, the Iraqi Airlines office, and the Iraqi bookstore in Cairo, were placed under heavy police guard.

As the crisis developed, Egyptian and Iraqi officials held intensive contacts with the aim of defusing the tension. Mubarak and Saddam Husayn conferred by telephone and ordered an inquiry into the reports of Iraqi mistreatment. Another session of the joint higher committee, scheduled to meet in Cairo on 18 November, was set to focus its discussions on the crisis. One day before arriving in Cairo for the committee's meeting, Taha Yasin Ramadan, in an interview with the Middle East News Agency (MENA), offered the Iraqi version of the crisis. The decision to cut down and delay remittances, he said, was "related to certain economic conditions." The "brothers in Egypt" should appreciate that it was not an easy decision to make. It was only natural, he went on to say, that some of the Egyptian workers would consequently leave Iraq; but Iraq was "not withholding its hospitality even to hundreds of thousands of unemployed workers. Iraq is their home for as long as they want to stay." Ramadan rejected the news about Iraqi assaults on Egyptians as mere "attempts to harm Egyptian-Iraqi relations" and predicted that they would fail, due to the "deep love, friendship, and fraternity between the presidents, governments, and peoples of the two countries."[144] In the committee's meeting, Iraq agreed to pay $50m. of the amount due to Egyptian workers by the end of the year — a partial solution to the problem, which Prime Minister Sidqi termed "not complete, but positive." Sidqi also added that "the plight of Egyptians in Iraq is temporary and...the problem of remittances, which is considered the heart of the issue, has been solved."[145] Subsequently, voices calling for putting aside the differences began to be heard in Egypt. "It is not in anyone's interest to exacerbate differences," said the editor in chief of *October,* "the feeling of responsibility makes the two countries duty-bound to do other essential tasks."[146]

The plight of Egyptian workers in Iraq may have been temporary, and it was certainly in the government's interest to bring it to an end. Yet the crisis that erupted around it focused attention on other latent points of dispute between the two states. The improvement in Cairo's relations with Damascus was clearly much to Baghdad's disliking, and hence a potential source of Egyptian-Iraqi tension. There was also disagreement over Lebanon: while Egypt supported the Syrian-backed Ta'if agreement, Iraq supported the adversary, Gen. Michel 'Awn, who pledged to end Syria's role in the country (see chapters on Lebanon and inter-Arab relations). In addition, the termination of the Gulf War rekindled the Gulf states' apprehension about Saddam Husayn's long-term regional intentions; and Cairo, to whom the alliances with these states was important, had to be cautious not to alienate them by too close an alliance with Iraq. Weighed within the new context of options available to Egypt in the regional arena — more diverse than those it had had until recently — the scene of Cairo's interests concerning Baghdad seemed to be more complex and problematic.

Cairo and the Change of Regime in Sudan

Ever since the change of government in Khartoum in 1985, Egyptian-Sudanese relations had followed a love-hate pattern. Underlying these relations was a basic community of interests and a clear recognition by both sides that their destiny was bound together by many strings. Such awareness had accounted for their full diplomatic relations, even in years when Egypt was boycotted by most other Arab states, for their extensive cooperation in various fields, and for the mutual support in international matters. At the same time, there had also been quite a bit of friction, for a variety of reasons. Al-Sadiq al-Mahdi's government had never put up with Cairo's extending political asylum to the deposed and much hated president Ja'far Numayri, and repeatedly demanded his extradition — an issue that marred the climate of their rapport considerably. Cairo, for its part, had been sensitive to, and suspicious of, what it regarded as Sudan's overly friendly ties with Libya, Egypt's longtime adversary. In addition, and not least important, there seemed to have been a lack of mutual personal sympathy, perhaps a lack of mutual trust, between Mubarak and Mahdi. The result of this state of affairs was a somewhat nervous mixture of amicable exchanges and often sharp mutual criticism. During the first half of 1989, it was the latter that dominated relations between Cairo and Khartoum.

The chief cause of Egyptian-Sudanese friction during the early months of the year was disagreement on the form and scope of support that Egypt was extending the Sudanese Government in its struggle against the southern rebels. Sudan had a joint defense pact with Egypt since 1976. Mahdi's declared intentions to annul it (see *MECS* 1987, p. 344) had never taken effect and Khartoum insisted that the pact committed Egypt to a more direct and massive military support, since the war in the south was "not a domestic civil war but rather an external flagrant aggression against Sudan."[147] Mahdi was strongly critical of Egypt's "insufficient assistance" to his government in crushing the revolt. At the same time, however, he also requested Mubarak's help in mediating between the government and the southern rebels. Cairo willingly assisted in mediating, as it believed that negotiations were the preferable, and perhaps the only possible way, of settling the problem. Mubarak accused Mahdi's government of being uncooperative in the mediation efforts,[148] and the Egyptian press angrily rejected

Mahdi's complaints. Mahdi, one paper suggested, was one of "the only two international leaders left with their old principles without trying to change them" (the other being Israeli Prime Minister Shamir). He "had not found any person or state whom he could blame [for his domestic failures] but Egypt, having forgotten that for 30 years, Egypt has not been interfering and does not wish to interfere in Sudan's domestic affairs."[149] Such an attitude, said another paper, "puzzles us and fills our hearts with sorrow. It is, however, comforting to know that the great majority of Sudanese do not share Mahdi's strange position toward Egypt."[150] Egyptian officials were quoted as saying that they wanted to see Mahdi's government replaced by another.[151] Mahdi, for his part, announced at the end of March — as he had done several times before — that he was abolishing the defense treaty with Egypt.[152] Typically, a month later Sudanese Foreign Minister Sayyid Ahmad al-Husayni came to Cairo, praised Egypt for its cooperative attitude and stated that "the joint security of the two states is a fact, whether governed by agreements or not."[153] Then again, in early June, Mahdi notified the Egyptian prime minister in writing of his "intention to abrogate the joint defense pact."[154]

On 19 June, there was an attempted coup in Khartoum, which was foiled by the Army (see chapter on Sudan). In a statement before the Sudanese Constituent Assembly, Mahdi announced that the coup was designed to bring Numayri back to power, and accused Egypt of conspiring with him against Sudan.[155] The accusation was quickly and vehemently rejected by Egypt. Mubarak voiced his "extreme astonishment" about Mahdi's "imagining" that Egypt would act in such a manner,[156] and the press expressed its resentment of Mahdi's being "still determined to bring Egypt's name forcibly into his domestic problems."[157]

In interviews following the 30 June change of regime in Khartoum, Mubarak broadly elaborated on his grievances with the now deposed Mahdi. "When Mahdi assumed power, he filled the world with anti-Egyptian clamor," said Mubarak, "whenever anything happened in Sudan, Mahdi would involve the name of Egypt [in it], as if Egypt was the reason for Sudan's deterioration....[It was] as if he was telling the Sudanese people to hate Egypt." Efforts to come to terms with Mahdi always failed because he kept changing his mind; trying to get to terms with him was "absolutely futile." Frankly, Mubarak admitted, "I was happy when it [the coup against Mahdi] happened though I do not like military coups. I was happy because Sudan was almost lost."[158]

Egypt, then, had reasons for rejoicing over the change of regime in Khartoum. This gave ground to extensive speculations about its probable involvement in the coup that brought Mahdi down. One fact that was quoted as evidence for a possible Egyptian involvement was that the Egyptian news agency was the first to report the coup, about 30 minutes before the coup communiqué itself was broadcast. Cairo, however, categorically dismissed these allegations. Mubarak ascribed the quick reporting of the news by MENA to "journalistic skill" and insisted that Egypt had "absolutely no part" in the coup. "I heard about the coup the day it occurred, just like you," he told a journalist. "We had nothing whatsoever to do with the coup, but we expected it because circumstances pointed in that direction."[159] But Cairo did not hide its satisfaction with the change, brought about by people who had "the political awareness needed to confront the serious challenge facing sisterly Sudan...after the country was exhausted by irresponsible adventures and maneuvers during the rule of al-Sadiq al-Mahdi."[160] Cairo immediately recognized the new government in Khartoum and warmly wished it success.[161]

From the very beginning, it was obvious that the new regime in Khartoum was more interested than the old one in as full as possible cooperation with Cairo, and that the latter was all too eager to respond. Four days after the coup, a delegation on behalf of the Sudanese Revolutionary Command Council came to Cairo to confer with Mubarak — the first official visit to any foreign country by such a delegation.[162] Two weeks after seizing power in Khartoum, the leader of the Sudanese revolution himself, Lt. Gen. 'Umar al-Bashir, arrived in Egypt on a visit "aimed at rectifying the situation which some former Sudanese leaders had attempted to undo." Bashir asked Mubarak to continue mediating in Sudan's southern problem.[163] Several days later, Mubarak, *en route* to the OAU conference in Addis Ababa, stopped over in Khartoum for further discussions of the same issue.[164] On the sideline of the conference, Mubarak met with the leader of the southern Sudanese People's Liberation Army, John Garang, and presented him with a proposed "peace plan," which Garang accepted.[165] Egypt's efforts to mediate between Bashir and Garang continued in later months, and both commended Mubarak for his contribution.[166]

There were also intensive Egyptian-Sudanese contacts concerning other areas of cooperation, and visits of high-level officials were exchanged frequently: Bashir himself came to Cairo again, in late November, amidst a series of visits by Sudanese ministers; Egypt sent a delegation to Khartoum, headed by Deputy Prime Minister and Agriculture Minister Yusuf Wali and including Deputy Prime Minister and Foreign Minister 'Ismat 'Abd al-Majid, to "confirm...the entire Egyptian people's support" for Sudan;[167] and Mubarak himself went to the Sudanese capital, once more, in late December, to attend celebrations of the 34th anniversary of Sudan's independence.[168] In distinct contrast with Mahdi, Bashir announced that the Egyptian-Sudanese defense pact was in effect: "the agreement was never abrogated," he said, "although it was signed by Numayri, it reflects the wishes, expectations, and interests of the Sudanese people."[169] In September, a Sudanese economic delegation came to Cairo and signed a trade protocol of $322m. for 1989–90.[170] By the end of the period under review, the road of friendly relations and cooperation between Cairo and Khartoum seemed to be wide open, clear of any obstacles and stumbling blocks.

Egypt and the PLO

As Cairo assumed the role of chief spokesman for the Palestinian cause in the intensively evolving Arab-Israeli peace process, Egypt's relations with the PLO in 1989 were closer and warmer than ever. Having scored diplomatic successes in the Arab arena and in his dealings with Israel, Mubarak, deeply committed to the all-Arab cause, sought to employ his own experience and his country's international weight in helping to settle the Palestinian problem. Since Israel would not talk to the PLO, Egypt willingly became Israel's partner for negotiating the proposed elections in the West Bank and Gaza Strip, and for identifying Palestinians with whom Israel would deal. Cairo likewise offered to be host to the preliminary Israeli-Palestinian negotiations that were to precede the proposed elections (for details on these moves, see chapter on the ME peace process).

Far more than a mere mediator, however, Cairo was an active initiator in the process. Mubarak's ten-point plan, which he devised in the summer, was presented to

Israel and the US before it received the PLO's blessing. And when the PLO later expressed reluctance to accept US Secretary of State James Baker's plan, Cairo, finding the plan beneficial, pressed the PLO to adopt a more flexible stance. "We do not pressure anyone," Mubarak said, "but we must help to push the process forward."[171] In the PLO's case, showing more flexibility meant being prepared to play a less visible role in the process in order to avoid giving Israel a reason, or a pretext, to torpedo it. For Cairo this was essentially a tactical line: Egypt was consistently opposed to raising any doubts about the PLO being "the Palestinian people's sole legitimate representative."[172] The PLO, while unhappy with the idea of becoming invisible, was eager to benefit from the Egyptian commitment and was grateful to Cairo for its "fraternal and committed stand."[173] PLO chairman Yasir 'Arafat frequently applauded "Egypt's constructive, positive, and visible role in promoting the cause of the Palestinians and the Arab nation."[174] 'Arafat also showed his appreciation of Egypt by enthusiastically supporting its readmission into the Arab League; once this was achieved, he stated that "the presence of Egypt, with its cultural, historical, and human achievements, and of brother President Husni Mubarak, with his stature, position, wisdom, and courage, in the Arab League will give great impetus to our Arab nation's march on all levels."[175]

The situation whereby Egypt was playing the role of chief actor at center stage and the PLO a semi-invisible one behind the scenes necessitated close coordination between them. 'Arafat came to Cairo no less than 17 times in 1989 — feeling "at home in Cairo, which is his country and where he has many friends and brothers"[176] — and senior PLO officials and delegations followed suit on numerous occasions. In October, the PLO representative in Cairo, Sa'id Kamal, was accredited as the first Palestinian ambassador to Egypt.[177] Whatever was initiated in the peace process, 'Arafat said, was so "only after consultations at various levels, involving several echelons of the PLO and Egyptian leaderships. There has been complete coordination with Egypt."[178] (See further in chapter on the PLO.)

EGYPT AND ISRAEL: SHARED INTERESTS AND MUTUAL MISTRUST

The period under review was one of heightened diplomatic exchanges between Egypt and Israel, as Cairo sought to use its improved international position to push the Arab-Israeli peace process forward. It was also a period of intensive and often angry verbal exchanges over a variety of bilateral issues. Egyptian-Israeli relations thus frequently topped the public agenda in both countries in 1989.

Tension and bad spirit marked the atmosphere of Egyptian-Israeli relations as the year began, due to a controversy over the implementation of the Taba arbitration ruling of September 1988 (see *MECS* 1988, p. 411). Israel, having lost the case, did not rush to evacuate the Taba area and tried to use its effective presence there to gain concessions from the Egyptians on two main issues: compensation for the Israeli-built tourist facilities in Taba (in particular a big hotel, for which Israel demanded $70m.) and entry arrangements for Israelis once the area went back to Egyptian control (Israel demanded free access without passports). Certain Israeli politicians, notably Industry Minister Ariel Sharon, even insisted that Israel should not implement the ruling until Egypt abided by its commitment to "full normalization of relations with Israel."[179] Such demands caused much anger in Cairo, which accused Israel of "a systematic attempt at blackmail."[180] By bargaining to attain the highest possible price for the hotel in Taba, a Radio Cairo commentator warned, Israel was "submitting the entire peace process to the danger of a setback or collapse, for a mere few pennies."[181] Cairo offered to pay $20m. for the hotel, and insisted that Israelis — like all non-Egyptian nationals — would need their passports when visiting Taba. The negotiation of these issues took place in a nervous atmosphere, and a US mediator was called upon to intervene to keep the dialogue going. At the peak of tension, toward the end of January, the Egyptians demanded an immediate and unconditional Israeli withdrawal from Taba and threatened to take control of the area unilaterally.[182]

Neither side, however, was interested in letting the issue cause permanent damage to their relations, and the talks continued. On 26 February, an agreement was finally reached, providing for an Israeli evacuation by 15 March. Egypt agreed to pay Israel $40m. for the tourist facilities in Taba, and it was agreed that Israelis wishing to visit the area would need passports but no entry visas.[183] The hoisting of the Egyptian flag over Taba on 15 March was celebrated with much ceremony and excitement all over Egypt. Four days later, Mubarak arrived in Taba to join the celebrations and pronounced Egypt's lesson from the Taba affair: that "peace will never be the impossible goal."[184] Other Egyptians, however, drew a different lesson: "Israel took a tough position regarding Taba, and the result was that Egypt lost faith in it," said the editor-in-chief of *al-Akhbar*; Israel's lesson should be that "it will eventually have to withdraw from Gaza and the West Bank, no matter how long it takes. Hence it better leave of its free will, rather than be forced to withdraw."[185]

Once settled, the Taba question was soon supplanted as the main item on the Egyptian-Israeli agenda by the new momentum in the peace process. In 1989, the process revolved around the search for Israel's future Palestinian interlocutors. Such Palestinians were to be identified through elections in the West Bank and Gaza Strip, as Israel proposed, or otherwise (for a detailed discussion of these issues see chapter on the ME peace process). By and large, Israel — its government a delicate coalition of political rivals — was extremely cautious and hesitant, to the extent of giving the impression that it was reluctant to go along with its own proposed plan. This Israeli position caused dismay in Egypt, to which the Egyptian media gave explicit expression. In this there was scarcely any difference between the establishment press and that of the opposition: both voiced profound lack of faith in Israel's declared intentions and strongly criticized its "perpetuation of the policy of foiling any effort or initiative to establish peace."[186] The Israeli proposal of elections in the West Bank and Gaza was denounced as no more than "a gimmick that seeks to evade talking to the PLO." Prime Minister Shamir, it was argued, continued "to stumble in his attempts to invent new methods for evasion and procrastination in a bid to gain time to stop the wheel of peace"; he thus resembled "a drowning man who clings to a straw that may save him from his inevitable fate." Shamir "would be mistaken if he believes that he can escape from the ring of international pressure," one editorial warned.[187] When the leading Likud Party, in July, decided to add far-reaching qualifications to the elections idea (see chapters on Israel and the ME peace process), the move was seen in Egypt as yet additional "flagrant evidence of the animosity to peace harbored by Shamir and a handful of extremists in Israel" and of their "persistent effort to pour fuel on the fire to perpetuate the occupation." At the same time that Shamir announced the elections plan, Israel "intensified its oppression, expulsions, destruction of houses, and killing of the innocent" in the occupied territories, one paper claimed.[188]

Such Egyptian reactions to specific Israeli moves accompanied daily expressions of solidarity with the Palestinians in revolt in the territories and of harsh indictment of Israeli "bestial practices against the Palestinians."[189] The Intifada, which lent special urgency to the peace process, also caused the response of the Egyptian media to be markedly emotional and sharp. Mubarak, ever cool and patient, tried to display more understanding for the Israeli misgivings: "We must understand that there are different opinions in Israel. We, therefore, must not expect miracles from [Israeli Prime Minister] Shamir because public opinion must get involved so that a consensus can emerge," he said at a press conference.[190] Such statements by Mubarak, while calling for forbearance, also betrayed his frustration with Egypt's Israeli partner to the dialogue.

Yet, if the palpably pressing Palestinian problem and developments in the peace process gave ground for bitter verbal assaults, they also prompted intensive diplomatic contacts and exchanges of high-level visits. This highlighted the basic fact that Egyptian-Israeli peace, if tense, was still a vital reality, which both Cairo and Jerusalem were eager to preserve. Israeli Foreign Minister Moshe Arens came to Cairo in February, where he conferred with Mubarak as well as with Soviet Foreign Minister Eduard Shevardnadze (see below). Arens was followed by Minister of Science and Research Ezer Weizmann, who came to Egypt in March to participate in a modest ceremony marking the 10th anniversary of Egyptian-Israeli peace; Interior Minister Arye Der'i, and cabinet secretary Elyakim Rubinstein, who came in July; and Defense Minister Yitzhak Rabin, who came to Cairo in September. Egypt, for its part, sent Minister of State for Foreign Affairs Butrus Butrus-Ghali to Jerusalem in June. Mubarak met again with Arens and with Israeli Deputy Prime Minister and Finance Minister Shimon Peres during the UN General Assembly's annual meeting in New York in September (see further in chapter on the ME peace process).

Mubarak thus met with three Israeli leaders — Arens, Rabin, and Peres — out of four who served as an informal higher political forum, popularly known in Israel as "the Forum of Four." But he consistently refused to meet the fourth, Prime Minister Shamir. Shamir's requests for a summit were repeatedly turned down by Mubarak, who claimed that holding such a meeting would be futile unless the attainment of significant progress in it could be guaranteed in advance. "What is the point of seeing and embracing him?" Mubarak asked an Israeli interviewer, "do you want to score success and leave me to tell public opinion that Mr. Shamir and I came up with nothing?"

> I want to tell you something: a fruitless meeting with Mr. Shamir, I can predict, will psychologically complicate things between the Egyptian and Israeli people...I announced that I was ready to go to Israel and meet Mr. Shamir if this would help push forward the peace process...Shamir reacted as follows: No, to the international conference and no, to land-for-peace barter...God! you close all doors and invite me? I will, of course, say no, I am not going...You locked the door too firmly, and you still say come in?[191]

Asked by an Egyptian journalist whether he believed that there was "no hope of reaching a just settlement with Shamir" as prime minister in Israel, Mubarak replied: "Regrettably, this is what I see."[192]

Such frustration as was reflected in Mubarak's statements dictated the strident tone of the Egyptian-Israeli dialogue on all issues, not just those related to the peace process. Israeli leaders, especially Shamir, and the people of Israel as a whole, were attacked in harsh language for their "intransigent" attitudes and "corrupt values." Thus, an article in *al-Musawwar* criticizing the Israeli Government's policy, was entitled "Shamir, Hitler number two, must go away before his loathsome crimes finish his own people off."[193] Similarly, a cartoon on the front cover of *Ruz al-Yusuf* portrayed Shamir in Nazi garb, decorated with both a swastika and the Star of David, raising his right arm in a Nazi salute and holding a club in his left.[194] In the same vein, the deputy chairman of the Egyptian lawyers' association drew his readers' attention to "the full scope of the Zionist menace threatening our Arab nation, its future, present and past...The Zionist enemy disdains the monotheistic religions, and has murdered prophets in the past. Today it is slaughtering the innocent and deriding our faith."[195] Egypt strongly condemned the Israeli kidnapping of the Shi'i Lebanese leader, Shaykh 'Ubayd, in July (see chapter on armed operations), a "piratical" act which showed that "Israel was still preferring to resort to the methods of organized crime"; and labeled Israel responsible for the subsequent execution of the US hostage, Col. Higgins[196] (see chapter on Lebanon). Israeli leaders and the media declined to respond in kind. They did, however, repeatedly charge Egypt with failing to honor its commitments according to the peace treaty, which had an inevitable negative impact on Israel's faith in the Arabs in general and hence on its readiness to consider concessions in the peace process. "Had there been normal relations [between Egypt and Israel] in all aspects of life, it would have had positive implications for Egypt and us and would have reflected on our relations with the other Arab countries," Shamir said.[197]

The often tense atmosphere also found its expression in ways other than verbal. There were a number of border incidents, both on land and sea. Early in June, an Egyptian guard boat opened fire on an Israeli boat sailing close to the Egyptian coast near Taba, killing one man. The Egyptian authorities expressed their regret over the incident, which prompted the two sides to negotiate and agree upon more specific and precise rules of navigation in that area.[198] In October, an Israeli oil tanker was held in the southern Suez Gulf for allegedly polluting the gulf waters. The ship was detained for about three weeks, and the captain was taken off it, arrested, and brought to court. It took the intervention of high officials on both sides, including the two foreign ministers and eventually Mubarak himself, to release the ship and the crew.[199] In early December, Israeli troops killed five armed men who crossed the Egyptian border.[200] Later that month, shots were fired at an Israeli army patrol from across the Egyptian border.[201] A spate of reports in the Egyptian press, toward the end of the year, about an Israeli intention to peddle counterfeit dollars in the Egyptian markets,[202] was at the background to the arrest of several Israeli tourists, who were charged with trying to import false currency into Egypt. This was viewed by Israel as a "deliberate Egyptian campaign" to "victimize Israeli tourists."[203] All these incidents, and the indignant reactions they generated, further exacerbated the already unpleasant climate.

Yet peace itself was never in jeopardy in 1989. Israeli tourists, 80,000–100,000 during the period under review, continued to form the fourth largest group of foreign visitors to Egypt.[204] In November, an agreement for agricultural cooperation between the two countries was signed in Cairo.[205] In the same month, a group of Egyptian researchers went to Israel to participate in a seminar on tropical and contagious diseases.[206] And in December, an Egyptian trade delegation arrived in Israel.[207] Another development that helped to clear the air somewhat was an Egyptian tribunal's ruling in January, after a delay of over three years, on compensation to be paid to the Israeli victims of the Ra's Burqa' tragedy of October 1985 (see *MECS* 1984–85, pp. 371–72.) The tribunal ordered the payment of sums that were considerably higher than the accepted standards in similar cases in Egypt, and this was received with satisfaction in Jerusalem. It was "a gesture of goodwill" on the part of the Egyptian Government, the Egyptian ambassador to Israel stated, adding that his country sought "to settle all our problems [with Israel] quickly, so we can embark on effecting comprehensive peace in the region."[208] This, however, was a rather small step in what seemed to be a very long and arduous road.

EGYPT AND THE SUPERPOWERS

Relations with the United States: Solid Alliance and Latent Grievances

Egypt's relations with the US in 1989 continued to evolve along the same lines as in recent years and in a similar climate, revolving basically around two main axes, the international and the bilateral. The US continued to regard Egypt as its most stable Arab ally and a mainstay in the ME political process, which therefore deserved to be supported substantially. Egypt, highly appreciative of the American friendship, was also keenly aware of the direct correlation between US aid and its own moves in the ME arena. Thus, if Egypt's regional strategy was shaped by a variety of constraints, the need to appear before the US as a peace-seeking country in a turbulent region was surely among them. Beyond closely coordinating its peace policy with Washington, therefore, Cairo in 1989 made a special contribution to the preservation of the political momentum by formulating its own diplomatic plan (for a discussion of the Egyptian proposal and other aspects of its involvement in the peace process, see chapter on the ME peace process). Egyptian and US officials frequently referred to their "common views" regarding the direction and objectives of the ME political process; during the period under review, they often spoke in similar terms of the need to start an official Israeli-Palestinian dialogue. "Egypt and the US share the goals of security for Israel, the end of occupation, and achievement of Palestinian political rights...[as well as] a sense of urgency to move toward a comprehensive settlement through direct negotiations," President George Bush stated following a meeting with Mubarak at the White House. The Egyptian president confirmed that he and his host found themselves "in agreement on most issues at stake."[209]

Yet, if Cairo and Washington held common views on the ME, the limits of their partnership were nonetheless clearly felt in Egypt. Egyptians were inclined to weigh their friendship with the US against the background of the US-Israeli alliance, and the imbalance was all too evident: America's commitment to Israel was more profound, its readiness to back Israeli policies far more consistent. There was also a vast disparity in per capita disbursement of US aid, with Israel receiving some $700 per capita in grants compared with $50 for Egypt, mostly on a loan basis; and while Israel fully controlled the use of these funds, there were many restrictions on Egypt's access to the money.[210] Many Egyptians felt that Washington's policy toward their country was dictated primarily by Israeli interests. The Egyptian media gave expression to this feeling from time to time, criticizing the US — at times rather acidly — for its overly pro-Israeli slant. Commenting on the change of administrations in Washington early in the year, Mubarak himself implied as much: "I do not expect miracles from the new US president," he admitted, "and I do not expect a tilt toward the Arab position."[211] An editorial in a leading daily was more explicit and blatant when, following an American veto of a UN Security Council resolution condemning Israel, it charged that "US insistence on regularly employing the veto right to prevent...any resolution expressing the international community's indignation with Israel's inhuman practices [means that]...Washington supports these brutal practices"; this, the paper stated, amounted to a "clear contradiction to its role as a partner and a mediator."[212]

Many Egyptians likewise felt that their country was not getting the share of US appreciation it deserved for its contribution to the region's stability. Blinded by its alliance with Israel, the US was unable to see its real interests in the ME, said Ibrahim Nafi', editor-in-chief of *al- Ahram*. This alliance rested primarily on the role the US had assigned to Israel in the past, that of an advanced post against the Soviet Union. "Israel's former role in the post-cold-war era made sense, but it does not any longer," Nafi' suggested. Instead, Egypt, which had "paved the way for fair peace and stability" in the region, had come to play a role far more vital to Washington. "The Egyptian role and its realistic achievements along the path of peace match the importance the world is giving to the thaw in US-USSR relations." Still, the US failed to assist Egypt with sufficient funds, while Israel was getting "unconditional aid and assistance" as a "moral obligation." Was there "no American moral obligation toward the constructive Egyptian role?"[213]

Egypt was in dire need of US financial support. The second largest recipient of US foreign aid after Israel, it was designed in 1989 to receive an estimated $2.6bn. in economic and military aid, an increase of c. 10% over the previous year.[214] A sizable portion of this sum, however, was eaten up by the repayment of debts to the US. By mid-1988 Cairo's outstanding debts to Washington had reached c. $11.7bn. (including c. $5.8 in military debt). Servicing these debts in 1989 was estimated at c. $950m.[215] Egypt found it increasingly difficult to meet repayment deadlines and risked being cut off from all US aid (by US law, countries falling behind more than 12 months in repaying their military debts may not get any more government money). Egypt's growing needs and financial crisis made it pressure Washington for more aid and for canceling its military debt to the US, in whole or at least in part. These questions of aid and debts had been sensitive points in Egyptian-US relations for several years (cf. *MECS* 1987, pp. 337–38; 1988, pp. 412–13). The Administration, with its own financial and political constraints, was not prepared to increase the level of aid by a significant margin. Moreover, Washington (like the IMF, though somewhat less rigidly) demanded that Egypt show its will and ability to improve its economic structure as a prerequisite for getting US financial assistance: "We shall transfer funds once you lay down a strategy for economic growth," said US Ambassador in Cairo Frank Wisner.[216] In February, the Administration announced it was freezing $230m., a two-year accumulation of cash aid, until Egypt undertook to introduce economic changes stipulated by the IMF.[217] Nor was Washington prepared to wipe out Egypt's military debt. Instead, it proposed that Egypt refinance the debt at reduced interest rates through deals with US commercial banks.[218]

Economic issues were prominent, alongside diplomatic regional matters, on Mubarak's agenda during his two visits to Washington, in April and October.

Reminding his hosts of Egypt's being a vital ME asset to the US and a main driving force in pushing the peace process forward, Mubarak tried to convince them that his government deserved special consideration in financial matters, so as to sustain its political stability. Mubarak agreed that the Egyptian economy needed restructuring; indeed, he explained in Washington, Egypt had already "put together a comprehensive program for economic reform" and had made "great strides" to "consolidate the foundations of a strong economy."[219] But he wanted to dissuade the Administration from making aid contingent upon a speedy enforcement of such a plan. He hoped to convince his hosts that such economic reform had to be implemented gradually to avoid sociopolitical unrest. Moreover, he wanted them to help persuade the IMF of that. During his visit in April, Mubarak stated that the Egyptians were "offended" by the US freezing of $230m.; this, he said, "will never push us in any direction."[220] Instead, Washington should show more flexibility out of appreciation for Egypt's international role and understanding of its domestic difficulties.[221]

Mubarak's visits, important and gainful in other respects, produced results unsatisfactory to Egypt in financial matters. The Administration's reluctance to grant Cairo's demands and its resorting to economic criteria — not merely political ones — in deciding the scope of aid and debt repayment generated anger and frustration in Egypt. "Neither the quality nor the quantity of this aid is sufficient for the material and moral burden that Egypt has been shouldering for the sake of peace," one journalist argued:

> Although Egypt appreciates this US aid, it believes that the US attitude toward Egypt is based solely on figures. This attitude does not represent a comprehensive political vision for the future. If the US wants to adopt a sound view on the issue, it must deal with it from the political angle...rather than [the] mathematical one.[222]

Such disagreement cast a constant shadow on what the same journalist described as the "special relationship between a superpower such as the US...and Egypt, the oldest state in history."[223] There were other matters that spoiled the atmosphere. Early in March, US newspapers reported that Egypt was producing chemical weapons in a plant west of its capital. Cairo was upset and vehemently denied the reports, ascribing them to an attempt by "some American circles" to create an artificial crisis in US-Egyptian relations. Mubarak, "outraged" and "really shocked," dismissed these "false allegations" in his April meeting with Bush, who accepted his clarifications.[224] Another unpleasant affair was the exposure of two Egyptians who allegedly spied for the US. They, and their alleged CIA contact, were prosecuted in July in a quick trial (the latter was tried in absentia) and sentenced to long prison terms. In the trial, the defense claimed that the authorities fabricated the case in order to pressure Washington to release an Egyptian citizen detained since 1988 for trying to smuggle sophisticated chemicals to Egypt (see MECS 1988, p. 413) — thereby recalling yet another irritating recent affair.[225]

Beyond such problems and temporary tensions, however, there remained the solid alliance between the two states. If Washington sought to "educate" Egypt to rationalize its economy, it did not intend to exert unbearable pressure on Cairo. The aid money frozen in February was released in August,[226] following the Egyptian Government's adoption of certain economic measures in the summer (see above). And when it became clear that Cairo was unable to meet a July deadline for repaying an installment on its debt — and hence would become subject to losing all aid — the Administration, through some creative bookkeeping, circumvented the legal requirement and postponed the deadline to November.[227] Such measures, it could be argued, were barely more than palliatives for a potentially dangerous ailment of a long-term nature. Yet they were surely indicative of Egypt's importance to the US. By the end of the year, however, a more convenient arrangement for debt repayment was still to be worked out.

Egypt and the US continued their cooperation in the military sphere. During a visit by the commander in chief of the Egyptian Air Force to Washington in April, the two states agreed on the delivery of an unspecified number of F-16 fighters and EC-2 early-warning aircraft to Egypt by 1992.[228] In May, a cooperation document was signed on manufacturing parts of the F-16 by Egypt.[229] And in November, another round of joint military maneuvers, of the biannual series codenamed "Bright Star," took place in Egypt.[230]

Egypt and the Soviet Union: Expanding Bilateral Cooperation

The most conspicuous event in Egyptian-Soviet relations in 1989 was Soviet Foreign Minister Eduard Shevardnadze's visit to Cairo in late February, the first by such a senior Soviet official in 17 years. Shevardnadze came to Egypt as part of an extensive tour in several Arab states designed to boost Moscow's hitherto secondary role in the region's political process (see chapter on the Soviet Union and the ME). His visit was a focal event of a busy diplomatic week, during which Israeli Foreign Minister Arens and PLO Chairman 'Arafat came to the Egyptian capital to confer with Shevardnadze. Cairo was proud to serve as the venue for this activity; not only did this prove that Egypt was "the heart of the Arab world, the most efficient and influential" state, it also highlighted the fact that in Soviet-Egyptian quarrels of the past, the latter's cause was right. Egypt's peace strategy, observed one commentator, "was not a political error" and proved to be an effective line, while "those on whose steadfastness the USSR had betted achieved nothing." This showed that "whoever loses Egypt wins little in the region."[231]

Statements by Egyptian and Soviet officials during Shevardnadze's visit and thereafter reflected their proximity of views on regional and international issues. Moscow welcomed the establishment of the ACC, of which Egypt was a founding member, in February and Egypt's return to the Arab League in May (see above).[232] As for the peace process, the two states agreed upon the vital need to include the PLO in it. The Soviets, however, still favored the option of an international conference in which they would play a major role as the best avenue to a comprehensive solution. This option was not a central item on the ME diplomatic agenda in 1989; rather, it was the idea of elections in the West Bank and Gaza Strip that served as the focus of the international political activity. Egypt was a main actor in the game that revolved around this last idea. The Soviets, on the other hand, were less enthusiastic about the plan, having been accorded no role in it; on several occasions they dismissed it as "a sham to divert world public opinion from the ongoing Intifada in the occupied territories and from reaching a real solution to the ME problem."[233] (On the Soviet position, see further in chapter on the Soviet Union and the ME.) Consequently, broad ME issues did not figure prominently in Egyptian-Soviet contacts during the period under review.

As against this, bilateral ties were intensified in 1989. In January, a delegation of Soviet economic officials arrived in Cairo to sign with their Egyptian counterparts a new trade protocol for 1989, totaling £E620m. This marked a 20% increase over the level of Egyptian-Soviet trade in 1988. Moscow agreed to help finance the construction of a 640-MW power station (i.e., equivalent to half the production capacity of the huge station in Aswan) at 'Uyun Musa in Sinai, through a £E120m. "soft loan"; offered Egypt £E100m. to assist in the expansion of the Hilwan iron and steel works; and undertook to help in various other projects.[234] In May, Soviet Foreign Economic Relations Minister Konstantin Katushev arrived in Cairo at the head of another economic group to attend the first session of the joint Egyptian-Soviet committee on economic and trade cooperation, established in 1988 (see *MECS* 1988, p. 414). Seeking to lay a basis for a closer long-term relationship, the committee discussed a new five-year agreement to replace the 1987 three-year trade protocol. The agreement, covering the years 1990–95, envisaged an increase of some 60% in the trade between the two states, to c. £E1bn. annually. It was designed to be finalized during the committee's second round of talks to be held in Moscow in early 1990.[235] Such farsighted planning for an expanded cooperation seemed to confirm the Soviets' assessment that their relations with Cairo were undergoing "a process of stabilization and improvement." An Egyptian official concurred: "We are resuming the practice of long-term trade agreements typical of the Nasser period."[236]

EGYPT IN AFRICA

The election of Mubarak, at the OAU summit in July, as head of the organization for 1989–90 made Africa a central arena for Egyptian diplomatic activity during the period under review. Mubarak's candidacy for the post was proposed and promoted by Arab states and, being the only candidate, he was elected unanimously. Mubarak was the third Arab head of the OAU in its 25-year history, after Egypt's Abdel Nasser and Algeria's Boumedienne (both of them headed the organization in the 1960s).

Mubarak pledged to meet two major challenges in his new role: promoting solidarity and mitigating tensions in the continent, and coordinating African efforts to negotiate a collective solution to the continent's debt problem. There were several regions of dispute in Africa on which his attention and efforts were primarily focused: South Africa, Namibia, the Libyan-Chadian border dispute, and the Mauritania-Senegal conflict. In August, Mubarak traveled to Harare, to chair a conference on South African apartheid and Namibia's future.[237] In the following month, he visited both Mauritania and Senegal, where he presented a six-point peace plan that would start a process of reconciliation with Egyptian mediation.[238] The debt problem was equally important: Africa's total foreign debt amounted to c. $240bn., and Mubarak believed that a far greater cooperation between the continent and the industrialized countries was needed to ease Africa's unbearable debt burden. In August, a major seminar on international debt was held in Cairo, which Mubarak saw as "a starting point in discovering new ideas for reaching a mutual agreement between North and South regarding the debt problem."[239] He also raised the debt issue during the Non-Aligned Movement conference in Belgrade in September[240] as well as in his address to the UN General Assembly in the same month. The problem, he stated, had "become not one of development and growth but one of existence in the real sense of the word"; hence it was imperative that Africa and the advanced industrial countries engage in "a fruitful dialogue...on the basic economic issues."[241]

This was also a year of intensive contacts with African states on the bilateral level. Exchanges of senior officials took place at an accelerated pace throughout the year. Among those visiting Cairo were several heads of state: the presidents of Somalia, Uganda, Nigeria, and Tanzania arrived in January; the Ugandan president came again in July; and in September Cairo played host to the president of Guinea-Bissau.

NOTES

For the place and frequency of publications cited here, and for the full name of the publication, news agency, radio station, or monitoring service where an abbreviation is used, please see "List of Sources." Only in the case of more than one publication bearing the same name is the place of publication noted here.

1. Mubarak's interview in *al-Musawwar,* 17 February 1989.
2. Mubarak's May Day address, R. Cairo, 1 May — DR, 3 May 1989.
3. *Al-Ahram,* 29 December 1989.
4. *Al-Ahram,* 20 December; also *October,* 1 January; *al-Ahram al-Iqtisadi,* 13 February 1989.
5. *Al-Ahram al-Iqtisadi,* ibid.
6. Mubarak's May Day address, R. Cairo, 1 May — DR, 3 May 1989.
7. Mubarak's speech at National Democratic Party congress, *al-Ahram,* 23 July 1989.
8. *Al-Akhbar,* Cairo, 15 November 1988; Mubarak's speech on Preachers' Day, R. Cairo, MENA, 5 March — DR, 7 March; *NYT,* 8 July; Shaykh al-Azhar's interview in *al-Idha'a wal-Tilifizyun,* 23 September 1989.
9. *Al-Nur,* 18 January 1989.
10. See Alan Cowel's lively descriptions and discussion of this issue in *NYT,* 8 July 1989.
11. Mubarak's interview in *al-Anba,* Kuwait, 6 May; similarly *al- Jumhuriyya,* Cairo, 4 May 1989.
12. Text of Mubarak's speech in *al-Ahram,* 12 November 1989. The figure for earnings quoted by Mubarak, if correct, marked a steep decline from Egypt's foreign currency revenues of $11.3bn. in fiscal year 1987–88; *CR:* Egypt, No. 4, 1989, pp. 9–10.
13. *FT,* 23 June, 3 August; *IHT,* 3 July; *NYT,* 12 November 1989.
14. Minister of State for International Cooperation Maurice Makramallah's statements to *al-Musawwar,* 13 January, and to R. Cairo, 20 June — DR, 21 June; *al-Musawwar,* 14 April, 27 October; *Ruz al-Yusuf,* 19 June; *IHT,* 3 July; *FT,* 3 August 1989.
15. Makramallah to *al-Musawwar,* 13 January 1989.
16. *Al-Ahram,* 31 March 1989.
17. *FT,* 31 July, 3 August, 21 September; *ME,* November 1989.
18. *Akhbar al-Yawm,* 11 March; *al-Ahali,* 15, 22 March; *al-Akhbar,* Cairo, 23 March; *Ruz al-Yusuf,* 27 March; *FT,* 31 March 1989.
19. *Al-Wafd,* 3 February; *al-Ahrar,* 13 March; *al-Ahali,* 15, 22, 29 March; *Ruz al-Yusuf,* 27 March; *al-Sha'b,* Cairo, 28 March 1989.
20. *Al-Ahram,* 4 May 1989.
21. Mubarak's May Day address, R. Cairo, 1 May — DR, 3 May 1989.
22. AFP, R. Cairo, MENA, 2 August — DR, 3 August; *Akhir Sa'a,* 9 August; *al-Musawwar,* 11 August; *NYT,* 30 August; *ME,* November 1989.
23. *Al-Wafd,* 4 August; MENA, 11, 24 August — DR, 17, 25 August; *NYT,* 30 August 1989.
24. *ME,* November 1989.
25. R. Cairo, MENA, 11, 25 October — DR, 17, 26 October 1989.
26. MENA, 14 April; *al-Ahram,* 4 May 1989.
27. *Al-Wafd,* 19 October 1989.
28. Badr's interview in *al-Watan al-'Arabi,* 3 February 1989.
29. See eg., *al-Wafd,* 19, 21 January (Minya), 26 April (Qina), 12 August (Sawhaj), 25 September (Bani Suwayf), 18 November (Asyut); AFP, 14 April — DR, 17 April (Asyut); R. Cairo, MENA, 14 June, 12 December — DR, 15 June, 14 December (Sawhaj); *al-Nur,* 6

September (Sawhaj), 13 September (Qina), 12 November (Bani Suwayf); *al-Sha'b*, Cairo, 3 October (Sawhaj, Qina, Aswan); *al-Haqiqa*, 9 December 1989 (Qina).

30. Zaki Badr quoted by MENA, 14 December — DR, 18 December; *al-Ahram*, 14 December; *al-Haqiqa*, 16 December 1989.
31. E.g., *al-Wafd*, 14 January (Cairo, Alexandria), 22 August (Manzila), 30 October, (Gharbiyya); *al-Akhbar*, Cairo, 10 August (Mahmudiyya, in the Delta); R. Cairo, MENA, 30 August — DR, 5 September (Alexandria); *al-Sha'b*, Cairo, 5 September, *al-Nur*, 6 September; *al-Ahrar*, 30 October 1989 (Gharbiyya).
32. *Al-Wafd*, 13 February, 18 March; *al-Ahram*, 18 March; *al-Jumhuriyya*, Cairo, 20 March 1989.
33. *Al-Wafd*, 8, 10 April; AFP, 8 April — DR, 10 April; *al-Jumhuriyya*, Cairo, 10 April; *Ruz al-Yusuf*, 24 April; MENA, 10 August — DR, 11 August 1989.
34. AFP, 17 April — DR, 18 April; *NYT*, 27 April; *FT*, 11 May 1989. According to Interior Minister Badr, 1,500 were arrested; MENA, 24 April — DR, 25 April 1989. *Al-Wafd*, 2 May 1989, reported 2,100 detainees.
35. MENA, 10 August, R. Monte Carlo, 12 August — DR, 11, 15 August; *NYT*, 11 August; *al-Wafd*, 12 August 1989.
36. *Al-Ahrar*, 5 May 1989.
37. *Al-Jumhuriyya*, Cairo, 3 March 1989.
38. E.g., ibid.
39. Badr's interview in *al-Watan al-'Arabi*, 3 February 1989.
40. *CR:* Egypt, No. 4, 1989.
41. *Al-Akhbar*, Cairo, 23 April 1989.
42. R. Cairo, MENA, 2 September — DR, 5 September 1989.
43. *Al-Wafd*, 19, 22 August; *NYT*, 22 August 1989.
44. Badr's interview in *al-Watan al-'Arabi*, 3 February 1989.
45. MENA, 16 December — DR, 18 December 1989.
46. 'Abd al-Sattar al-Tawila in *Ruz al-Yusuf*, 25 December 1989.
47. MENA, 15 April — DR, 17 April; *NYT*, 16 April; *al-Musawwar*, 21 April 1989.
48. *FT*, 18 April 1989.
49. *NYT*, 16 April 1989.
50. Ibid.
51. *JP*, 18 April 1989.
52. Mubarak's interview in *AT*, 20–21 April; *al-Mawqif al-'Arabi*, 8 May 1989.
53. *FT*, 18 April; *IHT*, 19 April; Mubarak's interviews in *al-Musawwar*, 21 April and *al-Anba*, Kuwait, 6 May 1989.
54. Mubarak's interviews, ibid.
55. Ibid.
56. *FT, JP*, 18 April; Mubarak's interview in *al-Anba*, Kuwait, 6 May 1989.
57. *FT*, 17, 18 April; *JP*, 18 April 1989.
58. Tony Walker in *FT*, 18 April 1989.
59. Mubarak's interviews in *al-Siyasa*, Kuwait, 19 April, *AT*, 20–21 April, and *al-Anba*, Kuwait, 6 May 1989. Mubarak, however, did not deny the allegations about the relation between Abu Ghazala and corruption in the Army: "corruption exists in all parts of the world," he replied on an interviewer's question, "it will continue to exist as long as there are human beings"; *AT*, ibid.
60. Mubarak's interview in *al-Musawwar*, 21 April 1989.
61. Quoted in *FT*, 18 April 1989.
62. Mubarak's interview in *al-Musawwar*, 21 April 1989.
63. Mubarak's interview in *al-Majalla*, 12–18 July 1989.
64. See *FT*, 14 March 1989.
65. Mubarak's interview, *al-Majalla*, 12-18 July 1989.
66. *Al-Akhbar*, Cairo, 13, 14, 15 March; *al-Sha'b*, Cairo, 14, 21 March; *Ruz al-Yusuf*, 20 March 1989.
67. *Al-Ahali*, 22 March; *Ruz al-Yusuf*, 17 April, 1 May; *al-Ahram International*, 29 April; see also Ibrahim Shukri's interview in *al-Sharq al-Awsat*, 22 April 1989.
68. *Al-Wafd*, 30 April, 2 May 1989.

69. R. Cairo, 26 June — DR, 27 June 1989.
70. *Al-Wafd*, 2, 8 May 1989.
71. *Al-Wafd*, 5 July, 22 November; *al-Akhbar*, Cairo, 4 October, 12 December 1989.
72. *Al-Ahram*, 11 January; R. Cairo, 17 January; *JP, al-Ittihad*, Abu Dhabi, 23 April 1989.
73. *Al-Ahram*, 11 January; R. Cairo, 28 February 1989.
74. *Al-Wafd*, 11 June 1989.
75. *Al-Ahram*, 1 May 1989.
76. E.g., *al-Ahram*, 9 June 1989.
77. R. Cairo, 9 June — DR, 12 June; *AFP, al-Haqiqa*, 10 June 1989.
78. *Al-Haqiqa*, 10 June; *al-Wafd*, 11 June; *al-Nur, al-Ahali*, 14 June 1989.
79. *Al-Wafd*, 11 June 1989.
80. MENA, 20 June — DR, 21 June 1989.
81. R. Cairo, 24 June — DR, 27 June 1989.
82. Mubarak's speech, R. Cairo, 22 July — DR, 25 July 1989.
83. *Al-Wafd*, 14, 15 November; *al-Masa*, Cairo, *al-Akhbar*, Cairo, 14 November; *al-Ahali*, 15 November; *al-Ahrar, al-Ahram al-Iqtisadi*, 20 November; *al-Sha'b*, Cairo, 21 November 1989.
84. Musa Sabri in *al-Akhbar*, Cairo, 15 November 1989.
85. KUNA, 18 January 1989.
86. MENA, 6 March — DR, 8 March 1989.
87. MENA, 3 April — DR, 4 April 1989.
88. MENA, 22 April 1989.
89. R. Cairo, 9 May — DR, 10 May 1989.
90. MENA, AFP, 13 May — DR, 15 May; *NYT*, 14 May 1989.
91. MENA, 17 May 1989.
92. *Le Monde*, 16 February 1989.
93. Nimr's interviews in *al-Musawwar*, 23 June; *October*, 25 June 1989.
94. *AFP*, 13 May — DR, 15 May 1989.
95. *Al-Ahram*, 13 May 1989.
96. *Al-Akhbar*, Cairo, 12 May 1989.
97. Ibid.; *al-Ahram*, 12 May 1989.
98. R. Monte Carlo, 22 May — DR, 22 May 1989.
99. Mubarak's address, R. Rabat, 23 May — DR, 24 May 1989.
100. MENA, 23 May — DR, 24 May 1989.
101. Makram Muhammad Ahmad in *al-Musawwar*, 19 May 1989.
102. Ibid.
103. Ibid.
104. Mubarak's interview in *al-Ra'y al-'Amm*, 7 June 1989.
105. MENA, 29 November — DR, 30 November 1989.
106. For details see *al-Akhbar*, Cairo, 4 April; *Akhir Sa'a*, 12 July 1989.
107. *Al-Ra'y al-'Amm*, 5 January 1989.
108. *Al-Wafd*, 18 January 1989.
109. Mubarak's interview in *al-Anba*, Kuwait, 6 May 1989.
110. AFP, 13 May — DR, 15 May 1989.
111. Mubarak's interview in *al-Ra'y al-'Amm*, 7 June 1989.
112. Makram Muhammad Ahmad in *al-Musawwar*, 22 December 1989.
113. *Al-Thawra*, Damascus, 6 September; *al-Ahram*, 7 September 1989.
114. *JP*, 24 October 1989.
115. *Al-Musawwar*, 22 December 1989.
116. Mubarak's interview in *al-Anba*, Kuwait, 6 May 1989.
117. Quoted in *al-Ahali*, 21 June 1989.
118. Mubarak's interview in *al-Anba*, Kuwait, 6 May 1989.
119. Mubarak's interview in R. Monte Carlo, 24 May — DR, 25 May 1989.
120. *Al-Sharq al-Awsat*, 25 May 1989.
121. R. Cairo, MENA, 31 May, 2, 4, 7 June — DR, 1, 5, 8 June 1989.
122. *JP*, quoting Reuters, 1 June 1989.
123. MENA, 4, 5 June — DR, 5, 6 June 1989.

124. R. Tripoli, MENA, 16 October — DR, 16 October 1989.
125. *FT,* 26 October 1989.
126. MENA, 16 November — DR, 17 November 1989.
127. MENA, 12 December — DR, 13 December 1989.
128. *Al-Masa,* Cairo, 3 November; *al-Wafd,* 7 November; MENA, 17 December — DR, 20 December 1989.
129. Lebanese Ambassador 'Abd al-Rahman al-Sulh's interview in *Akhir Sa'a,* 5 July 1989.
130. MENA, 29 June — DR, 29 June 1989.
131. *Al-Jumhuriyya,* Cairo, 25 October; MENA, 6, 25 November — DR, 9, 28 November 1989.
132. R. Cairo, MENA, INA, 7, 8 January — DR, 9 January; *Akhir Sa'a,* 11 January 1989.
133. MENA, 16 October — DR, 17 October 1989.
134. MENA, 3 November — DR, 7 November; *al-Jumhuriyya,* Cairo, 9 November; Taha Yasin Ramadan's interview with MENA, 16 November — DR, 17 November 1989. According to *al-Jumhuriyya,* Cairo, the transferable remittances were reduced from 40 Iraqi dinars ($120) monthly to ID10–30 ($30–90), depending on the sector in which the worker was employed and on his social security coverage.
135. *Al-Sharq al-Awsat,* 14 November 1989.
136. *NYT, IHT,* 15 November; *FT,* 17 November 1989. Other sources quoted smaller numbers, of 560,000–650,000 Egyptians still employed in Iraq by November; *al-Jumhuriyya,* Cairo, 9 November; *al-Akhbar,* Cairo, 25 November; *October,* 26 November 1989.
137. *Al-Wafd,* 12 November; *FT,* 17 November. For descriptions of these events see *al-Wafd,* 6 November; *al-Ahram,* 7 November; MENA, 13 November — DR, 14 November; *al-Sharq al-Awsat,* 14 November; *NYT,* 15 November; *al-Akhbar,* Cairo, 16 November 1989.
138. *NYT,* 15 November; *FT,* 17 November; *JP,* 20 November; *al-Musawwar,* 24 November 1989.
139. *Al-Wafd,* 6 November 1989.
140. *Al-Akhbar,* Cairo, *al-Wafd,* 22 November 1989.
141. *Al-Wafd,* 6 November; similarly *al-Jumhuriyya,* Cairo, 9 November; *al-Musawwar,* 24 November 1989.
142. *Al-Wafd,* 9 November; *al-Musawwar,* 24 November 1989.
143. *Al-Jumhuriyya,* Cairo, 16 November; *al-Wafd,* 26 November 1989.
144. MENA, 16 November — DR, 17 November 1989.
145. R. Cairo, MENA, 19 November — DR, 20, 21 November 1989.
146. Salah Muntasir in *October,* 26 November 1989.
147. Mahdi's interview in *al-Ahali,* 5 April 1989.
148. *Al-Ahram,* 28 February 1989.
149. *Al-Jumhuriyya,* Cairo, 5 March 1989.
150. *Akhbar al-Yawm,* 11 March 1989.
151. *NYT,* 5 March 1989.
152. R. Monte Carlo, 2 April — DR, 3 April; *al-Ahali,* 5 April 1989.
153. MENA, 3 May — DR, 4 May 1989.
154. R. Cairo, 9 June — DR, 12 June 1989.
155. MENA, 19, 20 June — DR, 20 June 1989.
156. *Al-Musawwar,* 28 June 1989.
157. *Al-Akhbar,* Cairo, 20 June; similarly *al-Ahram,* 20 June; *al-Jumhuriyya,* Cairo, 20, 22 June 1989.
158. Mubarak's interview in *al-Ahram,* 11 July; *al-Majalla,* 12–18 July 1989.
159. Mubarak's interview in *al-Majalla,* 12–18 July 1989.
160. *Al-Ahram,* 7 July 1989.
161. R. Cairo, 1 July — DR, 3 July 1989.
162. MENA, 4 July — DR, 5 July 1989.
163. *Al-Akhbar,* Cairo, 14 July; *al-Wafd,* 15 July 1989.
164. *FT,* 24 July 1989.
165. *Al-Wafd,* 5 August 1989.
166. SUNA, 21 October — DR, 23 October; MENA, 25 December — DR, 28 December 1989.
167. SUNA, 30 October — DR, 31 October 1989.
168. MENA, 31 December 1989 — DR, 4 January 1990.

169. Quoted by *al-Madina,* 1 August; also *al-Majalla,* 23–29 August 1989.
170. R. Omdurman, 15 September — DR, 18 September; *al-Wafd,* 24 September 1989.
171. Quoted by *IHT,* 21 November; also *FT,* 28 November 1989.
172. Mubarak's address to the UN General Assembly, R. Cairo, 29 September — DR, 2 October 1989.
173. 'Arafat's speech, MENA, 2 November — DR, 3 November 1989.
174. 'Arafat's interview in *al-Musawwar,* 10 November 1989.
175. R. Cairo, 12 June — DR, 13 June 1989.
176. Mubarak at a news conference, R. Cairo, 12 June — DR, 13 June 1989.
177. *Al-Wafd,* 10 October; MENA, 26 October — DR, 27 October 1989.
178. 'Arafat's interview in *al-Musawwar,* 10 November 1989.
179. *Ha'aretz,* 17 January; *Ma'ariv,* 19 January 1989.
180. *Al-Ahram al-Iqtisadi,* 23 January 1989.
181. R. Cairo, 3 February 1989.
182. *Ha'aretz,* 22, 26 January 1989.
183. For details, see *Ha'aretz,* 23 February; MENA, 25, 26 February — DR, 27 February 1989.
184. Mubarak's speech in Taba, R. Cairo, 19 March — DR, 20 March 1989.
185. *Al-Akhbar,* Cairo, 9 March 1989.
186. Ibid., 9 October 1989.
187. Ibid., 12 January, 10 April 1989.
188. *Al-Jumhuriyya,* Cairo, 8, 9 July; likewise *al-Ahram,* 10 July 1989.
189. *Al-Akhbar,* Cairo, 22 June 1989.
190. MENA, 18 September — DR, 19 September 1989.
191. Mubarak's interview on Israeli TV, 20 September — DR, 22 September; similarly, Mubarak's interview in *Yedi'ot Aharonot,* 24 March 1989.
192. Mubarak's interview in *al-Musawwar,* 21 April 1989.
193. *Al-Musawwar,* 14 April 1989.
194. *Ruz al-Yusuf,* 17 July 1989.
195. *Al-Ahrar,* 1 May 1989.
196. *Al-Akhbar,* Cairo, 1, 2 August; MENA, 2 August — DR, 3 August 1989.
197. Shamir's interview, Jerusalem TV, 16 March — DR, 17 March 1989.
198. *Ma'ariv,* 4, 6, 12 June; *Ha'aretz,* 6, 11 June, 10 October; *al-Ahram,* 7 June; VoI, 10 June — DR, 12 June; *al-Sha'b,* Cairo, 26 September 1989.
199. *JP,* 29 October, 2, 10 November; *Ma'ariv,* 3 November; *Ha'aretz,* 5 November 1989.
200. *IHT,* 6 December; *JP,* 8 December 1989.
201. R. IDF, 17 December — DR, 19 December 1989.
202. E.g., *Ruz al-Yusuf,* 11 September; *al-Ahrar,* 20 November 1989.
203. *JP,* 21 December 1989.
204. Ibid.
205. *Ma'ariv,* 19 November 1989.
206. *Ha'aretz,* 22 November 1989.
207. *JP,* 25 December 1989.
208. *Ma'ariv,* 30 January 1989.
209. *NYT,* 4 April 1989.
210. *Country Profile, Egypt,* 1989-90, p. 8.
211. Mubarak's interview in *al-Musawwar,* 17 February 1989.
212. *Al-Akhbar,* Cairo, 12 June; similarly *al-Akhbar, al-Jumhuriyya,* Cairo, 6 August 1989.
213. *Al-Ahram,* 29 September 1989.
214. *Country Profile, Egypt,* 1989-90, p. 53.
215. Ibid.
216. Wisner's interview in *al-Jumhuriyya,* Cairo, 30 March; similarly *IHT,* 3 July 1989.
217. GNA, 14 March; *NYT,* 4 April 1989.
218. *CR:* Egypt, No. 2, 1989.
219. Mubarak's address to US businessmen, MENA, 3 April — DR, 4 April 1989.
220. Mubarak's interview on NBC TV, 6 April, quoted in WF, 6 April 1989.
221. *Al-Musawwar,* 7 April 1989.
222. Ibrahim Nafi' in *al-Ahram,* 29 September 1989.

223. Ibid.
224. *Al-Musawwar,* 24 March, 7 April; *al-Jumhuriyya,* Cairo, 30 March; VoA, *al-Anba,* Kuwait, 4 April, 6 April 1989.
225. *Ruz al-Yusuf,* 24 July; *al-Sha'b,* Cairo, 25 July; *al-Ahali,* 26 July 1989.
226. MENA, 27 July; *CR:* Egypt, No. 3, 1989.
227. *IHT,* 3 July; *ME,* November; *CR:* Egypt, No. 3, 1989.
228. *Al-Ahram,* 9 April 1989.
229. MENA, 29, 31 May — DR, 1 June 1989.
230. MENA, 8, 18 November — DR, 15, 21 November 1989.
231. 'Abd al-Sattar al-Tawila in *Ruz al-Yusuf,* 27 February 1989.
232. Shevardnadze, quoted by MENA, 23 February — DR, 24 February; Gennady Gerasimov, quoted by MENA, 9 June — DR, 15 June 1989.
233. Gerasimov, quoted by MENA, 30 April — DR, 1 May 1989.
234. MENA, 9, 15 January, 18 April — DR, 10, 17 January, 19 April; *FT,* 1 June 1989.
235. MENA, 18 April, 14, 15 May — DR, 19 April, 15 May; *FT,* 1 June; *al-Ahram,* 11 December 1989.
236. *FT,* ibid.
237. *Ha'aretz,* 21 August 1989.
238. MENA, 6, 7 September — DR, 8 September; *al-Musawwar,* 8 September; *al-Ahram,* 8, 10 September 1989.
239. Mubarak's address to the seminar, MENA, 28 August — DR, 29 August 1989.
240. Mubarak's interview with MENA, 31 August — DR, 1 September 1989.
241. Mubarak's speech at the UN General Assembly, R. Cairo, 29 September — DR, 2 October 1989.

Iran

(Jumhuri-ye Islami-ye Iran)

DAVID MENASHRI

The year 1989 was a year of change of the guard in the Islamic Republic. The leader, Ayatollah Ruhollah Khomeyni, died on 3 June and was replaced swiftly by Hujjat al-Islam (thereafter commonly referred to as Ayatollah) Muhammad 'Ali Khameneh'i. The heads of the three branches of government changed positions — Hujjat al-Islam 'Ali Akbar Hashemi Rafsanjani, formerly Majlis speaker, was elected the fourth president and formed a new government; Hujjat al-Islam Mehdi Karubi replaced Rafsanjani as the speaker; and Ayatollah Muhammad Yazdi replaced Ayatollah 'Abdul Karim Musavi Ardebili as the president of the Supreme Court. The post of prime minister was abolished by the new constitution.[1] The Council for Ascertaining the Interests of the State (*Shura-ye tashkhis-e maslahat-e mamlekati*) was reformed and by-elections for the Majlis were held. No less significantly, a new constitution was drafted by a constitutional-amendment body and approved by a plebiscite. All this was done swiftly but with impressive efficiency in the traumatic atmosphere following Khomeyni's death.

In the nature of things, most of this chapter will be devoted to the reinstitutionalization of the revolutionary organizations and their manning. The rest of the chapter will contain an analysis of the initial policy of the new leaders. But first the death of Khomeyni must be discussed.

Khomeyni's death was undoubtedly the year's major event. The long-expected — and occasionally prematurely announced — death finally came. Popular response to it proved that mass support for Khomeyni had not declined much since his return to Iran a decade earlier. His disciples in power successfully overcame the crisis of his death, realizing that only unity and coordination could guarantee their continued rule. Hence, the country's various powerful elements almost immediately pledged allegiance to the new leader and, later, to the new president. Yet, beneath the surface the struggle for power continued on different levels, with each of the leaders and groups laboring to improve their positions in the post-Khomeyni hierarchy of power and to advance their worldviews. The power struggle thus remained a major theme of Iranian politics. It appears as a crimson threat throughout this chapter.

This transitional period had elements of continuity. First, the clerics loyal to the imam's ideology remained in exclusive power. The succession of Khameneh'i and the *de facto* policy (see below) might not have conformed to Khomeyni's vision of Islamic rule, but one of Khomeyni's major aims was preserved: clerics still governed the country. Second, all prominent officials of the revolutionary establishment declared their loyalty to Khomeyni's ideology. Third, the opposition continued to be sterile, weak, and divided, unable to use the death of Khomeyni to challenge the regime. But

334

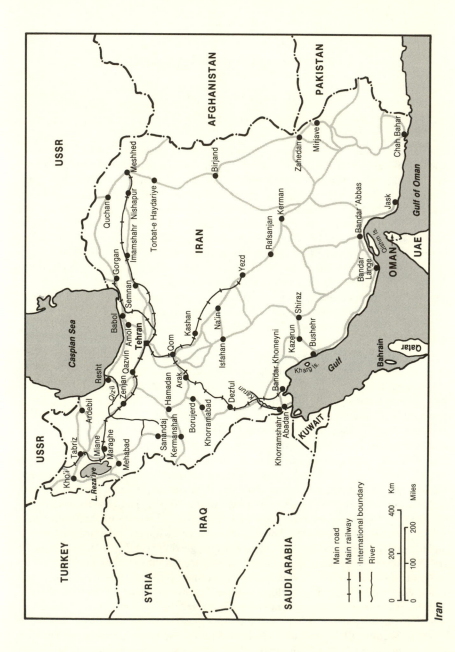

Iran

there were also elements of change in the transition period. First and foremost, in Khomeyni's absence, his disciples now had to settle their disagreements themselves and give their own answers to the new problems. Second, and related to the first, there was no leader who enjoyed the authority and power that Khomeyni had commanded.

As far as the internal struggle for power was concerned, Khameneh'i and Rafsanjani emerged as the twin pillars of the new political order. "It is obvious now that Khameneh'i and Rafsanjani have joined camps," an Iranian observer said. Their doctrinal views on critical issues facing the country (such as the role of private business, foreign loans, land reform, and relations with the outside world) "are not clearly defined, but their records suggest a relatively flexible approach" (for such similarities see, for example, *MECS* 1988, pp. 479–81). The two, as some observers pointed out, "are in some respects complementary individuals." While Khameneh'i was "a somewhat scholarly figure," Rafsanjani was a more worldly type "better equipped to communicate with the masses."[2] They maintained close relations with each other throughout the period under review, at least for tactical reasons.

In such a transitional period, all officials expressed loyalty to Khomeyni's philosophy. This meant that the voices heard from Tehran — even by those considered pragmatists — became more radical. Yet, given the views that Khameneh'i and Rafsanjani had expressed in the past, the problems facing the country, and the growing expectations for rapid change, it was not unlikely that they would eventually adopt a more pragmatic approach. The *Tehran Times* expressed such a hope when it declared that with this team in power, in "very high probability the country will soon be on its way to adopt such a politico-economic strategy as to suit the second decade of the Islamic revolution."[3] Yet, the struggle for power was by no means over. Although those known to be more radical lost their posts in government, strong tendencies for radicalism existed among many revolutionaries. As was the case throughout the regime's first decade in power, a period of radicalism had followed each period of relative pragmatism and vice versa (see *MECS* 1988, pp. 493–96). Thus, the radicalism of the spring of 1989 gave way to a growing pragmatism (in action, though not necessarily in words) later in the year. Was this another cycle prior to a new wave of radicalism? Was it the beginning of a new, uninterrupted, long-lasting pragmatism? It was too early to say.

THE DEATH OF AYATOLLAH KHOMEYNI

Khomeyni's death, though long anticipated, was a dramatic event ending an important chapter in the Islamic revolution's history and probably in that of modern Iran as well. Almost as soon as he came to power, it became clear that the ayatollah was sick and that his days were numbered. Rumors about his health continued throughout his rule. Many observers doubted whether the regime would last until his death; even fewer believed that its leader would survive throughout the whole decade.

The immediate popular reaction to the death of the ayatollah was emotional. The Iranian nation was plunged into mourning and similar sentiments were shared by many believers in other Muslim communities. Tehran television's live broadcast of the funeral showed the Iranian people's love and affection for Khomeyni. The mourners wished to come close to the dead imam, to touch the body of their leader. The initial attempt to take the body to the cemetery was thwarted by mourners surging forward and pushing the body to the ground from the wooden stretcher. His shroud was grabbed from the open coffin and torn to pieces. The crowd swarmed over the cemetery; they did not want to depart from their beloved leader. The burial was delayed for some six hours. The body was returned to the hospital and brought back by helicopter in a metal coffin. The outpouring of popular emotion at the imam's death surprised even Iran's leaders whose plans for the funeral were upset by the crowd's religious frenzy. The outpouring of emotion was overwhelming, as it had been a decade before when Khomeyni returned victorious from Paris. For days people continued to cry uncontrollably, wailing and beating their chests and heads in traditional expressions of grief. They shouted: "We wished we were dead, so as not to see our beloved imam dead."

Khomeyni's religious position, his charismatic personality, his political shrewdness, and the personal attachment to him of wide segments of society all had made him the revolutionary movement's undisputed leader. His success in leading it to power and his initial success in tightening the clerical grip on power added to his authority. To the *mostaz'efin* (disinherited) Khomeyni was the symbol of the revolution and a source of their hopes; within the establishment his word was law and even his opponents had given up hope of toppling the regime as long as the ayatollah was alive. Even the long war with Iraq and its end in unfavorable conditions, the economic difficulties (partly the result of the war and the revolutionary situation), and the fact that the initial expectations leading to the revolution had not been met a decade later neither affected his position as the father of the revolution, nor did they significantly tarnish the popular support for his leadership and ideology. For most Iranians, Khomeyni and the revolution were one. He was not merely the leader of the revolution, he was its symbol; his ideology — no matter how distinct it was from the Shi'i thought of the last centuries and how much his disciples had deviated from it during their decade in power — was viewed as representing Islam, the true Islam.

It was still too soon to sum up the impact Khomeyni and Khomeynism had on Iran and the region. It was possible, however, to indicate some basic trends and examine their impact on the country.

BALANCE OF SUCCESSES AND FAILURES: A PRELIMINARY APPRAISAL

After their seizure of power, the new rulers of revolutionary Iran set themselves two major goals: the consolidation of their rule, and the implementation of their doctrine. Taking a broad view of Khomeyni's 10 years in power, it seems that while he succeeded in achieving the first aim, he failed in the second. Below is an appraisal of his major successes and failures as they appeared soon after his death.

Khomeyni's most significant achievement seems to have been the appropriation of all state powers from the monarchy and concentration of all authority, spiritual and temporal, in the hands of the *vali faqih* (the jurisconsult). This was the primary sense in which the revolution was "Islamic." Khomeyni formulated the vision of the *velayat-e faqih* (the rule of the jurisconsult) and it became a reality under his leadership. His vision of the unification of "religion" and "state" remained a reality throughout his rule.

Khomeyni had been a revolutionary theologian who developed an Islamic-revolutionary theory, headed a revolutionary movement, and led it to success. He changed basic concepts in Islamic (Shi'i) theology, created new ideas and symbols and gave new meanings to the old ones. Above all, he developed a new model of revolutionary-activist-political Islam and led it to victory, which will undoubtedly have an important impact on Islamic thought for generations to come. Although Iranians may deviate from his line, as his disciples had already done under his own rule (*MECS* 1988, pp. 469–76), and other Muslim communities may not follow his example (as they, generally speaking, had hitherto proven reluctant to do), the ideology will certainly influence Islamic radical movements in Iran and elsewhere (cf. below).

Khomeyni rejected the distinction that Muslim rulers made between religion and politics. For him, as he often said, "Islam is political, or else nothing." He preached the political engagement of clerics, telling them this was an important religious duty. He encouraged them to become more activist and revolutionary and to confront — and, if need be, to sacrifice their lives — in the struggle against despotic regimes at home and imperialist exploitation from abroad.

Another important element in his legacy, related to the above, was his view of the politicization of the people. He made clear that popular participation in politics was essential and, moreover, clearly part of Islam. Active political participation also meant permanent struggle against injustice, whether of rulers or imperialists, and struggle also meant sacrifice of one's life in a just cause. Active popular participation was not only a means of overthrowing the old regime, or tightening the clerical grip on power. It was also the believers' everlasting duty. Thus Khomeyni and his rule had contributed significantly to the politicization of the Iranian people and proved to them the potential power of the masses. The awareness of the strength of popular will — first demonstrated in the movement against the tobacco concession (1891–92), later in the constitutional revolution (1905–11), and in the movement led by Muhammad Mosaddeq (1951–53) — became clearer than ever.

In its first stage, Khomeyni's movement was a success. It toppled a powerful regime, the monarchy which had a tradition of 25 centuries behind it, and was supported by some half a million soldiers as well as the strongest superpower, the US. It made a mockery of the US (among others, in the hostage crisis and in Lebanon), and was also successful, at least in the initial stages of the war, in preventing the Iraqi invaders from achieving any significant victories. The relative stability the young republic experienced under his leadership must also be considered a success. Compared with the frequent changes of government in the first two years of the republic, this stability was an additional mark of Khomeyni's ability to stabilize Islamic rule. This achievement becomes even more impressive when the revolutionary situation and the war conditions are kept in mind. Similarly, he succeeded in holding the core of the revolution together throughout the decade of revolution and war (an achievement which, as has been clearly manifested, was not lost in the initial months after his death).

Khomeyni offered revolutionary movements, mainly in Muslim countries, and particularly the Shi'is, an example of a revolutionary movement capable of seizing power without much bloodshed by devotion to religion, loyalty to the religious leadership, and belief in the path of Allah. He made the entire world more aware of Islam (mainly Shi'i Islam), and presented it (mainly to the Muslims themselves) as a political power to be reckoned with, thus giving Muslims all over the world a sense of pride, self-confidence, and power. For Shi'is, and other Muslims, the revolution represented a success after a long series of failures throughout Shi'ite history. The revolution reverberated far beyond the boundaries of its home country and the immediate region. It aroused enthusiasm throughout the Muslim world and became a force to be reckoned with by local as well as foreign governments.

In discussing the Iranian revolution as a model, one has to consider two distinct aspects: that of toppling a strong regime, both Westernizing and supported by the West; and its successes and failures in solving the problems which led to the revolution. As far as the first is concerned, while different ideologies were part of the revolution, their main driving force was unquestionably Islam and the clerics were the masters of the day. Even if the Iranian Revolution comes to grief, fundamentalists will undoubtedly continue seeing its advent to power as a source of inspiration. One way or another, it proved the power of Islam and the capacity of a popular movement led by the 'Ulama' and motivated by Islam to overthrow a hated regime and to make a mockery of the superpowers. In fact, much of the enthusiasm of fundamentalist movements centered on the revolution's advent to power, rather than its subsequent fate.[4] Moreover, even losing credibility at home did not mean that the "oppressed elsewhere could not continue to hope for global salvation through Khomeynism," just as Stalinism continued to be viewed by many devoted communists in Europe as the hope of the masses long after it lost credibility in the Soviet Union.[5] (For the failure of its achievements to become a model, see below.)

Alongside these significant achievements there were major failures, some of them in the Islamic regime's most basic concepts and aims.

For the new rules of Iran, an "Islamic revolution" was not only a slogan or a title of their revolutionary movement, and the seizure of power was not the aim: they were the means for adapting all spheres of life to genuinely Islamic norms as interpreted by Ayatollah Khomeyni. No less important, by implementing their ideology the revolutionary leaders wished to solve the problems of Iran and the Iranians. On this score, the record of the revolution was far less impressive. If one accepts that the roots of the revolution were much deeper than what Western observers called "religious," the question remains to what degree such broader aims were achieved fully or partially? Clearly there was no greater freedom in Khomeyni's Iran than under the shah, and the social and economic pressures on the *mostaz'efin* were not eased. The regime offered many explanations, such as the war, the animosity of the superpowers, the drop in oil income, etc. But were these not, at least in part, the result of the revolution? How long could such explanations and excuses continue to convince the people? For many Muslims, the new Iranian regime came to be identified with poverty, fanaticism, and lack of freedom. The events in Iran aroused not only curiosity abroad, but also a "fear of Islam."[6] Thus, while encouraging interest in Shi'ism, the Islamic revolution did not change the basic attitudes, mostly distorted, toward it in the West and among Sunnis. By and large, both tended to identify Shi'ism with disorder, executions, lack of freedom, martyrdom, fanaticism, terrorism, and hostage-taking.

Although Islamization was introduced in many fields, significant material achievements were absent. In many regards — the economic situation of the *mostaz'efin,* the health services, housing, education, etc. — conditions even deteriorated after the revolution. Similarly, Iran did not become more democratic. Under the shah, opposition to the regime was a crime; it was now regarded as a sin. Except for Lebanon, the "export" of the revolution similarly failed to achieve meaningful results, and the policy of "Neither East nor West" caused economic problems — as did Iran's almost total isolation, which was clearly illustrated by the absence of world leaders from Khomeyni's funeral. If successful in holding power, Khomeyni thus proved unsuccessful in solving the problems which had brought him there. If the "Islamic revolution" was the means, not an aim, then in the balance it was not impressive. Under Khomeyni Iran found excuses in the shah's policy, the revolutionary process or the war, and there was a leader whose appeals for postponing expectations of material gains found attentive ears. His successors, however, would be called upon to present results rather than excuses or explanations.

The war with Iraq was not Khomeyni's initiative, but he was undoubtedly responsible for the cease-fire not being accepted earlier, on much better terms for Iran. Thus, the destruction caused by the war was due, in part at least, to his stubbornness. By accepting the cease-fire, for the first time, he himself admitted a failure (see *MECS* 1988, pp. 476–79).

But Khomeyni's most significant success also turned out to be his most devastating failure, i.e., the concentration of all power in the hands of the *vali faqih*. More than being an Islamic revolution, Khomeyni's revolution was a revolution *in* Islam. He brought with him to power clerics of a lower — third or fourth — level. None of the *ayatollah 'uzam* (grand ayatollahs; see below) supported Khomeyni's doctrine regarding the *velayat-e faqih*. In the latters' view clerics should, by and large, limit themselves to consulting the government and supervising it rather than running the state. This view had its bearing on the succession question. The very fact that a Hujjat al-Islam ('Ali Khameneh'i) was selected to replace Khomeyni as the *vali faqih* (see below) was the greatest tragedy of Khomeynism and evidence that his doctrine reached a deadlock, at least temporarily. Finally, no less a failure was the fact that already under Khomeyni's rule his disciples blatantly deviated from his doctrine (see *MECS* 1988, pp. 469–76).

Although touched by the popular identification with the imam, Western observers varied in their assessment of his contribution to his country and the region. Pointing to his failure to solve the country's problems, they could not ignore, however, his initial success in toppling the shah's regime and the challenge he posed to the West. "He came to symbolize everything the West found incomprehensible and baffling about the East," one American magazine commented: "His intense, ascetic spirituality and air of other-wordly detachment; his medieval, theocratic mind-set...the mystical certitude that he spoke in the name of God, his country, and Muslims everywhere," it continued. Although pointing to the devastating outcome of his rule, the magazine went on to compare his role to that of other 20th century great revolutionaries: Lenin, Gandhi, and Mao.[7] "Perhaps only Lenin and Hitler in this century," a British newspaper suggested, "have mounted a comparable challenge to the world hegemony of post-Enlightenment Western liberalism." Yet, Khomeyni's challenge was "less formidable than theirs in that Iran is not...a military power comparable to Germany or the Soviet Union"; but "it is in one sense more radical, because it purports to come from right outside the Western tradition."[8] Many other commentators pointed to the failures of Khomeyni's movement. For most Iranians, however, such an analysis was irrelevant: Khomeyni was their unchallenged leader.

Whether such failures will change popular attitudes toward the imam is yet to be seen. It is possible, for some time at least, that the achievements will be credited to him (and/or Islam), while the failure will be blamed on others (imperialists, his successors). The popular reaction that followed his death, however, pointed to the continued mass support for the imam and his ideology.

POSSIBLE DOMESTIC IMPLICATIONS

Khomeyni's funeral testified to the depth of popular support his revolution commanded. The mass participation and the authentic emotional response was a proof that revolutionary zeal was still intense. Despite failures and setbacks, a deep sense of identification remained, not only with the man but also, it seemed, with his doctrine and revolution, although it was not clear how long this identification would continue. This sense also gave his followers a starting point from which to continue the revolution. Khomeyni, who throughout his rule tried to incite revolutionary fervor and to identify for his followers major issues around which all could unite (e.g., the American hostages, the war, Salman Rushdie), now encouraged revolutionary zeal and provided a focus for public attention in his death. Khomeyni had the power not only to incite tempers, but also, if he considered it necessary, to calm his people. When disagreements threatened the unity of the revolutionaries' ranks, he was able to restore order. He was above all groups and his word above all law; what he decreed was always accepted.

Khomeyni's image and the admiration for him may remain a valuable asset for his successors. It seemed, however, that in the long run, the love for the imam, even if the popular attitude toward him remained unchanged, would not suffice. His disciples would depend on themselves and would be judged by their own achievements. More importantly, Khomeyni's position in Iran was unique: he and his policies were beyond argument. His followers may not be accorded the same treatment.

The love and affection for Khomeyni and identification with him was not of necessity a guarantee that they would continue for long. Neither did they assure the implementation of the revolution's basic philosophy or its goals. In this connection, the funeral of another famous Middle Eastern leader — Egyptian president Jamal Abdel Nasser — is instructive. Nasser died in 1970 after suffering a series of political setbacks (the war in Yemen, the 1967 war with Israel) and Nasserism was already in decline. His funeral, like Khomeyni's, reaffirmed the man's popular appeal. The Nasser mystique still lingers on in Egypt. But very soon after his death, the country went through a tumultuous period of critical rethinking and less emotional, more rational analysis of Nasser's policies, culminating in his successor Anwar al-Sadat deviating from Nasser's philosophy of the revolution. In Iran, too, the death of the leader followed a series of political setbacks, most significant of which was the cease-fire with Iraq. One question still loomed ahead in 1989: when and whether the new Islamic Republic, built on ancient Persian ground, would go through a similar period of soul-searching.[9]

It was only natural that Khomeyni's successor would declare alliance to his path and that the contenders for power would compete with each other over who was more faithful to the imam's philosophy. Thus, greater radicalism became the order of the day. This trend became evident a few days after the funeral. On 6 June, for example, Khameneh'i was quoted as stressing to visiting world dignitaries that he intended to follow in Khomeyni's footsteps, vowing "to follow the ideals" of Khomeyni.[10] Rafsanjani tried to upstage the "radicals" even before Khomeyni's death by calling for random attacks on American and European targets in the name of the Palestinian cause. However, in a press conference on 8 June, as typical of him while speaking to the world media, he tried to sound more conciliatory and left room for optimism for those wishing to see Iran follow a more pragmatic policy; but at the same time he also labored to sound faithful to the line of the imam.[11] Those usually referred to as more radical did not lag behind. In practice, however, the gap between the two camps remained as wide as ever.[12]

REINSTITUTIONALIZATION OF THE
REVOLUTIONARY ORGANS

MONTAZERI'S DISMISSAL

The question of the succession to Khomeyni was a critical issue facing the young republic since its first days. For one thing, in a movement so closely identified with the person of its leader any successor would have difficulty stepping into the imam's shoes, let alone commanding the same loyalty of the people and the revolutionary leaders. Moreover, the position of the *vali faqih* — in Khomeyni's revolutionary thought, as well as in the original (1979) Islamic constitution — was tailored to fit Khomeyni. The combination of charismatic personality, Islamic scholarship, and political leadership could be found in Khomeyni, but hardly in any other prominent cleric. Matters were further complicated when shortly prior to Khomeyni's death his heir apparent, Ayatollah Husayn 'Ali Montazeri, was dismissed.

While Montazeri did not have full religious qualifications for the position of the *vali faqih* (see *MECS* 1981–82, pp. 539–40), he was undisputably a prominent ayatollah. His disqualification posed a significant challenge both ideologically (i.e., the adherence to the Khomeyni doctrine of the *vali faqih* when no qualified candidate was available) and politically (i.e., the need to fill the highest position in the Islamic regime).

Although Montazeri's nomination as the heir apparent in 1985 (see *MECS* 1984–85, pp. 433–35) was not entirely in line with Khomeyni's *velayat-e faqih* doctrine and although he did not seem sufficiently qualified to succeed to the leadership, Montazeri was the best available candidate whom the men in power could find among prominent clerics loyal to Khomeyni's dogma. The imam's followers labored long to groom Montazeri to the succession, initially by referring to him as an *ayatollah 'uzma* (see *MECS* 1979–80, p. 455) and later by officially selecting him as the successor. Although the imam did not clearly support this nomination, neither did he oppose it. He made it known that under the circumstances Montazeri was the most suitable candidate. However, it became clear preceding the celebrations of the republic's 10th anniversary that Montazeri, who publicly criticized the regime's politics, could no longer be considered sufficiently loyal to the philosophy of the revolution, let alone to the policies carried out by Khomeyni's disciples in the name of Islam.

On 26 March, following an emergency meeting of the Council of Experts, which was empowered, under certain circumstances, to choose the next *vali faqih,* Khomeyni asked Montazeri to resign. Montazeri replied in writing (27 March) declaring himself unqualified for the position of the next leader. He said he had "strongly disagreed" with his nomination in the first place and added: "if mistakes and weaknesses [on my side]...have occurred, God willing these will be rectified through Your Eminence's leadership."[13] Khomeyni confirmed the "resignation" (28 March).

Khomeyni's letter in reply to Montazeri revealed some of the reasons for his dismissal. First, Khomeyni wrote, the task of a leader is a "heavy and august responsibility which requires more strength" than you have which was why "from the start both you and I were against your choice [as the heir apparent]." But, Khomeyni added, since the Council of Experts decided to name you "I did not wish to interfere." Khomeyni continued: "Everyone knows that you have been the product of my life and that I am very fond of you," but he then criticized Montazeri harshly for associating with improper elements, even with people whom Khomeyni viewed as enemies of the regime. He "advised" Montazeri that "in order that former mistakes" may not be repeated, "[you should] cleanse your household of unsuitable individuals" and prevent the opponents of the [Islamic] system from entering your house. Khomeyni reminded Montazeri that he had given him similar advice two years before with regard to Mehdi Hashemi,[14] thus implicitly accusing him of failing to take that advice. (Hashemi was the brother of Montazeri's son-in-law, Hadi. He was executed in 1987 following the scandal around the Iran-Contra affair; see *MECS* 1987, p. 400.)

It must be stressed that although Khomeyni had made it known that under the circumstances Montazeri was the favorite candidate as successor, he had never shown any marked enthusiasm for Montazeri; he even refused to declare openly whether he advocated a single successor or preferred a leadership council. Montazeri lacked the religious authority, the political qualifications, and the personal charisma for leadership. Since this was by no means new to Khomeyni, why did he, nevertheless, move against Montazeri at that point? There were two main reasons:

(1) Khomeyni had no confidence that Montazeri would be able to exercise the authority of the *vali faqih* as envisaged in his doctrine. The concentration of all powers in the hands of the clerics was perhaps the revolution's most significant achievement. Khomeyni feared that Montazeri's appointment would ultimately wipe out this achievement either by leading to the reseparation of "religion" and "state" or by moving Iran into directions incompatible with his own revolutionary philosophy.

(2) Montazeri was blamed for associating himself with "opportunistic elements." These "elements," *Kayhan* wrote,[15] created the climate which led Montazeri "to raise new issues [i.e., criticism] in letters addressed to officials." (Some examples of Montazeri's harsh criticism of the executive in the summer of 1988 were publicized by former president Abul-Hasan Bani Sadr in Paris.) Montazeri's more recent statements on the revolution's shortcomings (for examples, see *MECS* 1988, p. 488) were much more than the imam was willing to tolerate. In the past Montazeri had criticized the functioning of the executive, but what he said on the eve of the republic's 10th anniversary was much harsher than anything that he or other revolutionary leaders had ever said. Thus, for example, he went as far as justifying young people who criticize the revolutionary regime. Among the problems existing under the Islamic rule he mentioned: extremism, selfishness, factional inclinations, and injustice. *Ettela'at* claimed that what Montazeri was now saying was not criticism, but rather statements that echoed the propaganda of antistate and antirevolutionary groups.[16]

In a letter to Montazeri,[17] Ahmad Khomeyni (the imam's son) provided a long list of accusations (documented by exchanges of letters between the imam and Montazeri, as well as extracts from Hadi Hashemi's confessions) to prove that Montazeri's appointment could harm the revolution. The main argument centered around Montazeri's relations with the Hashemi brothers: Ahmad Khomeyni accused him of ignoring the imam's warnings, going back three years before his dismissal, not to allow those "misguided people" to infiltrate his house and "create catastrophe." Montazeri remained under their influence. "Was it not because of your affection for Mehdi Hashemi that you created so many problems for Islam and the revolution," he asked? "What hand was at work that separated you so far from the imam...that you [said that you] consider the intelligence [officers] and the officials of the Islamic regime to be worse than the Shah's SAVAK?" In conclusion, Ahmad Khomeyni appealed directly to the people:

> ...See how well-documented and clearly I have revealed the inauspicious plan of this dirty band and showed that the issue of Mr. Montazeri was never the result of a few slight criticisms about the affairs of the country....It was not because of his foul-mouthing and thoughts in regards to officials of the regime or purges of one faction within the regime, against another. It has been the result of calculated conspiracy against the person of the imam and the high officials of the regime. A conspiracy...which was going to be implemented by a pious jurist though not necessarily with him fully aware of their plan.

As many sources in Tehran claimed, Khomeyni's decision proved once again that he was loyal first and foremost to Islam and the revolution. For the sake of Islam, *Resalat* wrote,[18] the imam even sacrificed his best friend. An editorial in *Ettela'at* said that Khomeyni's acceptance of Montazeri's "resignation" was his "second glass of poison" (the first being his acceptance of the cease-fire).[19] To Khomeyni, personal sentiments were insignificant. When he realized that Montazeri's appointment could endanger the revolution's future, he supported Montazeri's resignation.

Montazeri's disqualification was also influenced by the growing radicalism in Tehran (see *MECS* 1988, pp. 493–95). Although Montazeri could hardly be regarded a "pragmatist" — his views on domestic issues were relatively liberal, but he was radical, for example, regarding the doctrine of exporting the revolution — the timing of his dismissal, its background, and the charges against him all worked against the pragmatists. Thus, strange as it may seem, while the execution of Mehdi Hashemi was considered a blow to the radicals (see *MECS* 1987, p. 400) Montazeri's disqualification, in the short run at least, was accompanied by the growing power of the more radical elements within the Islamic administration. Most important among them were:
(1) The alliance between Ahmad Khomeyni and 'Ali Akbar Mohtashami became stronger. Ahmad Khomeyni, who had been closer to Rafsanjani, now cooperated with his greatest rival and the leader of the radicals, and with other leading radicals.
(2) The appointment of Hujjat al-Islam 'Abdollah Nuri, as the imam's representative in the Revolutionary Guards with the power to approve all appointments and dismissals, gave the radicals additional significant support. (Nuri was a leading radical who maintained close ties with Ahmad Khomeyni, but also with Rafsanjani.)
(3) The resignation of Muhammad Javad Larijani (deputy foreign minister in charge of relations with Europe and America), another leading pragmatist and architect of the policy of improving ties with the West, also strengthened the radicals. His resignation was announced a few days before Montazeri's without any explanation.
(4) The replacement of Muhammad Ja'far Shirazi Mahalati (ambassador to the UN),

another pragmatist, for health reasons, although it seems that his pragmatic positions were the real reason.

The atmosphere in Iran thus became much more radical. The pragmatists and their policies were attacked constantly. As always under such circumstances, the pragmatists kept a low profile. The best evidence for the new atmosphere was probably the fact that even Rafsanjani made much more radical statements in his public appearances (e.g., on the Rushdie affair, on "exporting" the revolution).

The growing radicalization of the atmosphere notwithstanding, the most serious and immediate challenge following Montazeri's dismissal was the question of the succession. Whether one successor "emerged" or a council of leadership was formed, it was unlikely that Khomeyni's doctrine of *velayat-e faqih* would survive, at least not as the imam had envisioned. The problems were not insignificant before Montazeri's dismissal; now they became even more pressing.

In Khomeyni's doctrine, the spiritual leadership (*marja'iyyat*) and the "temporal" rule were one; this was also stipulated in the 1979 constitution (see *MECS* 1979–80, pp. 443–45). Khomeyni's problem was that none of the prominent clerics (with the rank of *ayatollah 'uzma*) supported his revolutionary doctrine. Some of his most ardent opponents had died ('Abdollah Shirazi in 1984, Kazem Shari'atmadari in 1986). The others, in addition to Khomeyni and Montazeri, were Seyyed Muhammad Reza Musavi Golpaygani (in Qom), Seyyed Shihab al-Din Mar'ashi-Najafi (in Qom), Hasan Tabataba'i Qomi (in Meshhed), and 'Abdul Qasem Kho'i (who lived in Iraq).

The revolutionary doctrine and the Islamic constitution allowed two options, neither of which was free of problems: first, all could rally around a single leader. This solution was undoubtedly better than any form of collective leadership. But because none of the prominent candidates fully supported Khomeyni's doctrine, the appointment of a more junior cleric could have led to a retreat from its most basic principle.

Second, a council of leadership consisting of three or five prominent clerics could be formed. Doing so also involved several problems: (a) if not even one *ayatollah 'uzma* was loyal to Khomeyni's doctrine, how could three or five such prominent clerics be found to form a council, as required by the constitution and Khomeyni's doctrine; (b) all candidates of *ayatollah 'uzma* rank were old and would soon have to be replaced; (c) a council would be incompatible with the traditional Iranian tendency to personify complex ideas through one charismatic figure; (d) since the council was supposed to concentrate within itself all powers, spiritual as well political, it seemed unlikely that a collective leadership could effectively govern the country since it was bound to be riven by conflict.

Faced with such a challenge and in order to prevent a power vacuum from being formed in the case of the imam's death, the leaders set out to amend the constitution to allow a candidate lacking the *marja'iyyat* qualifications to assume the leadership. Before the constitution was amended, however, Khomeyni died. Only by adapting the constitution to the new realities could it legitimize the selection of Khameneh'i (see below).

THE AMENDMENT OF THE CONSTITUTION

Pressing Need for Constitutional Amendment

In Iran, as in other regimes in the Middle East where constitutions exist, constitutions have not always been adhered to. Rather, governments have often adopted policies that ignored the wording and spirit of the constitution. Khomeyni, too, did so, even while declaring his wish to remain loyal to the Islamic constitution, which reflected his own views. The appointment of Khameneh'i was a blatant deviation from the constitution, certainly not the first one. Rafsanjani openly admitted that, during the course of the revolution, "with the imam's permission" the regime had "ignored parts of the constitution." He added that this was "not anything new."[20]

The changes during the first decade of the revolution, the new facts created by Montazeri's disqualification, and the approach of the presidential elections, made the need to adapt the constitution to the new realities more urgent. The two most presssing problems were to change the procedure for choosing Khomeyni's successor as *vali faqih,* and the authority of the next president. In this way amending the constitution was linked to the power struggle, with each group having its own proposals for changes. The changes approved reflected not only the power of the contending groups, but also influenced it.

While the need for amendment had long been felt, Khomeyni and his disciples took the initiative only after Montazeri's dismissal and with the approach of the presidential elections. In mid-April, some half of the Majlis deputies and members of the Supreme Judicial Council appealed to Khomeyni to appoint a group to review the constitution and prepare the changes "so that it can be put to a referendum by Your Eminence after having been approved [by you]."[21] Both radicals and pragmatists signed the appeal, Rafsanjani being among the signatories.[22] One obvious shortcoming of the 1979 constitution was that it did not contain an amendment procedure. The signatories, therefore, suggested the above procedure since Khomeyni, as the *vali faqih,* was "above the constitution...and the legitimacy of others results from his authority" (these are the words of Rafsanjani).[23] Khomeyni accepted the proposal.

On 24 April, Khomeyni wrote to President Khameneh'i ordering the formation of a council to propose constitutional amendments. He specified that the council would discuss formulating regulations regarding the succession, centralizing the executive and the judiciary, restructuring the management of the radio and television in such a way that the three branches of government would supervise them, increasing the number of Majlis members, defining the authority of the 13-member council formed in 1988 to ascertain the interests of the state, formulating regulations regarding amendment of the constitution, and changing the name of the Majlis from National Consultative Majlis to the Islamic Consultative Majlis. The council was given a two-month deadline,[24] but it was extended and on 11 July the council presented its proposals. They were presented to Khamench'i on 16 July and he approved them on 19 July. On 28 July, the new constitution was approved in a referendum. (For the composition of the council and the constitutional amendments, see below.)

What were the reasons for such an initiative? First, as mentioned above, the need for amendment had long been felt. Before the original constitution was approved in December 1979, Khomeyni promised to change some of its articles mainly to meet the demands of ethnic minorities for autonomy. Since then, the ethnic question had become less pressing, but the need to amend the constitution was raised repeatedly by those charged with administering the state's affairs (see below). Finally, in 1989, all the state functionaries came to the conclusion that amendments could no longer be delayed. The problem was that the constitution was drafted by clerics and liberal intellectuals without experience in government and this under the pressure of the initial days of the revolution. Experience was lacking, in Iran and elsewhere, in implementing the kind of ideology they wished to advance, and the members of the Council of Experts then empowered to prepare the draft constitution had significantly different views on the subject. Referring to these shortcomings of the constitution, Rafsanjani said in a Friday sermon in April 1989 that any constitution, anywhere, requires amendments or supplements every few years.[25] *Abrar,* a paper that often supported radical policies, stated that while "many laws seem to be perfect...before implementation," sometimes the "circumstances call for major changes."[26] When appointing the constitutional committee, Khomeyni declared that the shortcomings were the result of the tense atmosphere prevailing in 1979 and that "because of the lack of precise knowledge of administrative problems, these weaknesses were not properly attended to."[27] In their letter to the imam, the Majlis members made it clear that despite its "strong points" and "lofty ideals," the constitution was not "devoid of flaws and shortcomings." They added that since "some of its conclusions and principles" were "fundamentally incorrect" managing the country's affairs "will face serious problems, if changes are not made. This is apparent to all who have been involved in affairs over the past 10 years."[28]

Second, strange as it may seem, the need to reconsider — and consequently change — the procedure governing the succession was not confronted. Although it was clear that no cleric of the rank of *ayatollah 'uzma* supported Khomeyni's philosophy, Khomeyni's disciples thought they could guarantee Montazeri's succession and thereby the perpetuation of the revolution. They groomed Montazeri for the succession, but his dismissal and the absence of an appropriate prominent candidate underlined the urgent need to change the constitution's relevant articles.

Third, no less pressing was the lack of sufficient clarity regarding the division of power among the three branches of the government, and even more importantly, within each of them, e.g., between the president and the prime minister, and between the different courts (regular state courts, revolutionary courts, military courts, and the courts of economic crimes). In the past, amendments were demanded, mainly by the presidents: all had done so, from Bani Sadr, after his election in 1980, to Khameneh'i mainly on the eve of the 1985 elections (see *MECS* 1984–85, p. 430). Now Rafsanjani made his candidacy for president conditional on amending the constitutional articles regarding the executive. Late in April 1989, Khameneh'i said that in wishing to get away from the shah's "excessive centralization" those formulating the Islamic constitution in 1979 had gone to the other, no less undesirable extreme of "excessive dispersion."[29] The issue came to the fore once again as the fifth presidential elections approached, against the background of the growing struggle for power and the pressing problems facing the executive.

Two things made the issue urgent: the danger that a political vacuum might be created in the event of Khomeyni's sudden death, and the approaching presidential election. Of the two, the first was more crucial. While the presidential election could be delayed without affecting the functioning of the regime, the issue of the succession could not be avoided, because without a new leader the regime could face critical problems. Hence Khomeyni's decree of 24 April, which declared that "any delay in this regard might bring about bitter results for the country and the revolution."[30] As with many other problems, Khomeyni wished to use his authority to settle this one too during his lifetime, being aware that if left unresolved it could endanger clerical rule. No less anxious for his decision were his disciples who wanted Khomeyni's blessing for their intended changes.

The Constitution Amendment Body

The Council for the Study and Codification of the Amendment to the Constitution (*Shura-ye hey'at-e barresi va-tadvin-e motammem-e qanun-e assasi*) was composed of 25 members, 20 appointed by Khomeyni and five Majlis members selected by that body. The council's first meeting on 26 April elected a presidium consisting of Ayatollah 'Ali Meshkini (who was also president of the Council of Experts) as president; Rafsanjani and Khameneh'i, deputy presidents; and Hasan Habibi and Muhammad Yazdi, secretaries.[31] The composition of the body showed that Khomeyni wished to maintain a balance between radicals and pragmatists, religious scholars and "politicians," and the different branches of government.

Based on institutional affiliation, the new council had five groups of five members each: the Council of the Guardians; the Majlis; the Executive and Judiciary (which together had five members: the president, the prime minister, the minister of justice, the president of the supreme court, and the attorney general); the Council of Experts; and five from the two factions of the Combatant Clerics (three from the radical wing and two from the more pragmatic one; see *MECS* 1988, p. 491).[32] By setting up the council in this manner, Khomeyni intended having the amendments approved by representatives of all branches of government, including all prominent state functionaries. (For some reason, the radical Minister of Interior Mohtashami was not included.)

Although it seems that Khomeyni wished to keep a balance between the radicals and the pragmatists, it was difficult to divide the members into clear-cut categories in terms of affiliation to either of the camps. This difficulty notwithstanding, given the members' statements during the last decade one could note that the president of the council (Meshkini) was radical, but his two deputies Rafsanjani and Khameneh'i were pragmatists. The chairman of the most important committee — the one discussing the leadership — was Ardebili, then viewed as a radical, but previously regarded more of a pragmatist. Another important committee — regarding centralization of the executive — was headed by Khameneh'i. The chairmen of the other two — regarding centralization of the judiciary, and radio and television — were, respectively, Meshkini and Rafsanjani. Khomeyni's decree that decisions were to be approved by a majority of at least 14 votes was additional proof of his intention to have the decisions widely accepted.

Balance was apparently also sought between "religion" and "state." The appointment of religious experts was calculated to keep the new constitution within the bounds of Khomeyni's Islam; the appointment of experienced officials from all branches of government was calculated to remove past political deficiencies. By naming these two types of member to the council, Khomeyni apparently hoped that the proposed constitution would be both "Islamic" and "practical."

As in the first Council of Experts that drafted the 1979 constitution, no grand ayatollah was appointed. (Montazeri, who was chairman of the Council of Experts, was not considered then a grand ayatollah.) Though many of the 1989 members were presented as scholars, and some were ayatollahs, most of them were Hujjat al-Islams and were better known for their political credentials rather than their Islamic scholarship.

On 8 July the council approved the final draft of the new constitution. In a referendum on 28 July it was approved by a vote of 16,052,459 against 398,867 (32,445 votes were declared spoilt).[33]

The Qualifications of the "Leader"

The most crucial question facing the council was the qualifications of the leader. With the dismissal of Montazeri, there was no candidate for this position of the rank of *ayatollah 'uzma* loyal to Khomeyni's doctrine. Khomeyni's disciple had to retreat from the imam's ideal and allow a less prominent cleric to succeed Khomeyni. When the council was formed there was more than a measure of support for a collective leadership. Typical were the arguments put forward by former interior minister 'Ali Akbar Nateq Nuri and *Jumhuri-ye Islami,* suggesting that Khomeyni was such a unique leader that no one person could succeed him and that the theory of the *vali faqih* was tailored for Khomeyni. Therefore, the argument went, the hitherto mandatory requirement of "supreme religious authority" (i.e., *marja'iyyat*) could be waived in favor of a lower-ranking *mujtahid* (jurisprudent) who met the other qualifications stipulated in the 1979 constitution (i.e., just, virtuous, aware of the needs of the time, and courageous).[34] But the disadvantages of a collective leadership were enormous (see above). Pointing them out, *Ettela'at* suggested that such a collective leadership "is either practically impossible or otherwise falls short of accomplishing the ultimate goals."[35]

Such a solution, however, seemed to have significant potential advantages at this stage. During the trauma following his death a collective leadership, representing different trends, could add an element of cohesion: they could overcome the immediate challenge of Khomeyni's death, face the opposition together, and postpone the internal struggle for power. A collective leadership could also help solve the immediate problem of the lack of an appropriate grand ayatollah to fill the position of the *marja'.*

The council's discussions were held amidst public debate on these issues. The press mentioned names of possible candidates. *Ettela'at* considered Rafsanjani as having "the necessary qualifications for heading the leadership council,"[36] as did the *Tehran Times,* which named him and Khameneh'i as having the "qualifications needed for the post."[37]

Before the council reached final agreement, the imam died. The Council of Experts then convened and chose Khameneh'i. The Council for the Study and Codification of the Amendment to the Constitution gave its blessing to the *fait accompli.*

Under the new constitution, the leader need not be *marja'.* This allows any *mujtahid* to assume the leadership (Articles 5 and 107). It was sufficient that he have "scholastic qualifications for issuing religious decrees" (i.e., any *mujtahid*). Similarly, the formalities governing the "emergence" of a new *marja'* were dropped. According to the new constitution "the task of designating a leader shall rest with the Council of Experts elected by the people"(Article 107). The stipulation (Article 5) that the leader should, among others, be "recognized and accepted as the leader by the majority of the people" (a condition needed for *marja'iyyat*) was also dropped. At the same time, the new constitution stressed that preference should be given to those who, in addition to expertise in religious jurisprudence, were versed in "political and social issues" (Article 107). (In the old constitution the need for "political and social insight" has been mentioned [Article 109]; in the new constitution it was repeated there as well as in Article 107). In other words, the level of religious scholarship was lowered and political experience was given greater weight, which was a significant retreat from the philosophy of the revolution.

In line with this approach, Article 110 specifying "the duties and responsibilities of leadership" envisioned greater responsibilities for the leader than did the original constitution. Among them was to "delineate the general policies" of the state and "supervise the execution of the policies," a responsibility not explicitly stated in the first constitution.[38] In other respects, however, the leader's authority was more restricted. He had to consult with the Council for Ascertaining the Interests of the State, as stipulated in the same article, when resolving "the problems that afflict the system and which cannot be solved by conventional methods."

It is also important to note (Articles 5, 110, and elsewhere) that all references to "Council of Leadership" were dropped. Such a possibility does not exist under the new constitution.

The Executive

The need to better define the authority of the president was coupled with the calculations of the competing groups seeking to guarantee their power. On this question, the pragmatists had a clear answer: they wanted more power for the president and the abolition of the post of the premier, which "will end the present bifurcate nature of the executive body."[39] Their candidate for such a powerful presidency was Rafsanjani. The radicals were less clear. They wanted to limit the presidency to a purely ceremonial institution. Less than that they would be ready to compromise for a clear definition of the functions of the president and the prime minister, giving the latter sufficient power to neutralize the president. Thus, for example, *Abrar* suggested that the aim should not be the elimination of either post; by making the prime minister an aide to the president, not only will the question of centralization be solved, but the power of the executive will also be increased.[40]

The constitutional amendments regarding the presidency were in line with Rafsanjani's aspirations. The constitution eliminated the post of the prime minister and transferred the executive authority to the presidency, except in "matters directly entrusted to the leadership by virtue of this constitution" (Article 60). The presidency, as the first constitution also stated, was "the next highest official position...after the position of leader" (Article 113). The president was also the head of the Supreme Council for National Security, a body which can concentrate much power in itself under certain circumstances. The president may appoint, with Majlis approval, one or more vice presidents. Although elected directly by the people, the president is answerable to the Majlis (Article 88), two thirds of whose members can vote non-confidence in him (Article 89). The way was paved not only for the election of Rafsanjani (see below), but also for the concentration in his hands of power much greater than other presidents had had.

Many observers pointed out that the problem of the bifurcate nature of the executive was not resolved in the new constitution. The council did not choose "between the 'presidential' and the 'parliamentary' systems," but "probably a combination of the two, something which in the long run will create problems for the system."[41]

Other Amendments

Among the other amendments, the following seemed noteworthy:

* The constitution defined the functions of the Council for Ascertaining the Interests of the State, which Khomeyni had established in 1988 (see *MECS* 1988, pp. 472–73). It was to help the leader resolve disagreements (Article 110). It would convene upon the request of the leader whenever the Council of Guardians judged a proposed law to be contrary to the principles of the Shari'a law or the constitution. It would also convene to discuss issues presented to them by the leader. Council's regulations shall be formulated by its members subject to the approval of the leader (Article 112). The council will also select the *faqih* of the Council of Guardians who is to be a member of a council of leadership (whose other members are the president and the head of the Judiciary Council) which is to function in case of the death, dismissal, or resignation of the leader until a new leader is selected (Article 111). While the Council for Ascertaining the Interests of the State gained prominence, the Council of Guardians, which enjoyed absolute power to approve legislation under the new constitution, lost much of its power.

* The name of the Majlis was changed to "The Islamic Consultative Majlis" (*Majlis-e Shura-ye Islami*) from The National Consultative Majlis (*Majlis-e Shura-ye Melli*) as in the first constitution (Article 69).

* Although the old constitution stipulated that every 10 years the size of the Majlis would increase at the ratio of one member for every 150,000 growth in population (Article 64), the new constitution contained no such clause. (If there had been such a clause, about 100 new members would have been added to the Majlis.) Instead, the constitution laid down that the size of the Majlis may (though not necessarily) increase by no more than 20 additional members for each 10-year period, depending on human, political, and geographical factors.

Two new articles were added: Article 176 that concerns the formation of "Supreme Council for National Security" presided over by the president, and (Article 177) that defines the process of amending the constitution.

KHAMENEH'I SELECTED AS NEW LEADER

On 4 June, the day after Khomeyni's death, the Council of Experts chose Khameneh'i as his successor. The council first discussed the possibility of forming a leadership council, but rejected it. Other candidates were considered — Montazeri was reportedly one of them — and then Khameneh'i was chosen: c. 60 out of the 74 members present reportedly voted for him.

This decision had several noteworthy aspects. First of all, a technical one, namely that it was essential to solve the succession question immediately by naming the successor. Aware of the sensitive nature of the issue, the regime had established the Council of Experts (1982) which selected Montazeri (1985) in order to avoid a power vacuum upon the imam's death. Since Montazeri was dismissed in March 1989 (see above), it was essential to convene the council and name a successor promptly. Failure to do so might have led to rifts even before the ayatollah was buried. As former deputy foreign minister Muhamamd Javad Larijani put it, such swift action was "a sign of the strength of the revolution."[42]

It might have been preferable to choose the successor when Khomeyni was still alive and could approve the choice, but Khomeyni had refused to interfere in the issue. He went to the extent of refusing to declare whether he supported a single, even unidentified, successor or a collective leadership. Even when Montazeri was chosen Khomeyni did not express his view, though he accepted the decision. Even when he referred to the issue in his will (first written in 1983, then amended in 1987) he mentioned the two possibilities together ("the leader or the council of leadership"). Furthermore, the selection of Khameneh'i when Khomeyni was still alive, but in hospital, might have caused rifts. Under the trauma of the death, the decision was more easily accepted.

The very fact that the Council of Experts had to decide was in itself proof that Khameneh'i was not acceptable to many. According to Shi'i tradition, to Khomeyni's doctrine, and the Iranian constitution of 1979 — which was based on both the former — if a leading religious authority is widely accepted (as was the case with Khomeyni 10 years before) there is no need to elect him. The Council of Experts must decide only in cases when it is not clear who is the most acceptable candidate. In the case of Khameneh'i, he even lacked the basic qualifications demanded by the constitution. After he was chosen, the press dubbed Khameneh'i an "ayatollah" even though he lacked the scholarly credentials and certainly could not even claim to be as prominent as an *ayatollah 'uzma*. In the long run, amending the constitution was meant to overcome these difficulties.

Ideologically, the choice of Khameneh'i was a fatal blow to the most basic principle in Khomeyni's revolutionary doctrine. Even the presentation of Ayatollah Muhammad 'Ali Araki as the *marja'*[43] could not solve the problem. The separation of the position of the *vali* and the *marja'iyya* was a crucial step toward the separation of "religion" and "state." Although clerics were still at the top of both hierarchies the separation distanced Iran from the revolutionary dogma.

In their attempts to justify the choice of Khameneh'i, the revolutionary leaders only made it clearer how far they had deviated from Khomeyni's doctrine. They now claimed that such a separation was Khomeyni's initial ideal. Rafsanjani said that Khomeyni had expressed this "in private discussions with us" just before his death and that this was "the last thing that he told me."[44] Quoting from the imam's letter to Meshkini dated 29 April 1989, he added: "Since the very beginning I [Khomeyni]...insisted that the condition of *marja'iyya* was not necessary [for the leadership]. The just *mujtahid* who is confirmed by the honorable [council of] experts...will be sufficient [to fulfill such a task]." Rafsanjani even lowered the qualifications needed, claiming that "the term *mujtahid* is interchangeable with the term *faqih*. Hence, since a *faqih* (i.e., Khameneh'i) had been chosen by the experts (who were themselves elected by the people), "there is a pledge of allegiance (*bay'a*)" between the people and the new leader.[45] Ayatollah Ebrahim Amini, a member of the Council of Experts' secretariat, said that such separation was due to the constraints of the time. In future, if a candidate combining religious scholarship with political capabilities appeared, the two spheres would be recombined.[46]

The revolutionary leaders also labored to convince the people that, following

Montazeri's disqualification, the imam had wanted Khameneh'i to succeed him. Rafsanjani said that in a meeting with the heads of the three branches of government (Rafsanjani, Khameneh'i, and Ardebili) at which Prime Minister Musavi and Ahmad Khomeyni were also present, they pointed out to Khomeyni that the old constitution's provisions regarding the selection of the successor might lead to a political vacuum. Khomeyni, Rafsanjani claimed, then said that this was unlikely "since we have the appropriate people for the position. When we asked whom, he pointed to Khameneh'i."[47] Ayatollah 'Abdul Qasem Khaz'ali, a member of the Council of Guardians, added that, when close to death, Khomeyni stated three times that he considered Khameneh'i the most appropriate successor.[48]

Eager to prove that Khameneh'i was the perfect choice, the leaders often raised arguments clearly at odds with Khomeyni's philosophy. While Khomeyni wanted the leader to be a prominent cleric, his students tended to claim that political and administrative experience were no less important than scholarship for leadership. "Familiarity with national issues," Rafsanjani said, was "far more important than all the other conditions such as...[religious] knowledge, [and even] justness." Khameneh'i. he added, had the experience of eight years as president, but "if we select a leader from a seminary, by the time he becomes familiar with national issues," Iran will have "suffered irreparable harm."[49] Meshkini added, similarly, that senior religious leaders could not qualify for the leadership of the state automatically because "they do not have enough knowledge of the current conditions in the world and the political, social, and cultural [sic!] issues facing Muslims."[50] A Radio Tehran commentary also pointed to Khameneh'i's political experience and added that he had the qualifications for the post that Khomeyni had specified in his book Velayat-e Faqih.[51]

All this revealed another source of concern for those who sincerely supported Khomeyni's revolutionary dogma. The politicians in power (some of them lower-rank clerics) used their political authority to impose their own views as Khomeyni's. They based their arguments on what the imam had said (or supposedly said), disregarding Khomeyni's worldview as a unity. Different groups and individuals are likely to continue basing their arguments on what the imam presumably told them. Important in this context is that the interpretations of those in power are given the validity of the imam's views. One example will suffice. For reasons of their own, Khomeyni's disciples did not consider collective leadership appropriate for governing the state (see above). While they may have been right, politically, Khomeyni's disciples claimed that Khomeyni himself had disapproved of collective leadership. As "proof," it was pointed out that Khomeyni's letter to Meshkini did not mention such an option.[52] They admitted, nevertheless, that the meeting of the Council of Experts that chose Khameneh'i had first discussed the possibility of having a Council of Leadership. Hujjat al-Islam Muhammad 'Ali Dastgheib disclosed that when such a proposal was put to the vote, 44 of the council's 76 members approved.[53] Was it likely that the 44 would have done so had Khomeyni disapproved? The original constitution and many of his statements clearly allowed such a possibility. Moreover, his last will constantly mentioned such an option; whenever he mentioned the future leader in his will he added "or the Council of Leadership."

All this notwithstanding, once Khameneh'i was chosen, all prominent figures in the establishment declared their loyalty to him, and made clear that he was the most suitable candidate for the post and had the talent needed by a new leader.

Given the above background to his selection as leader, Khameneh'i may be faced with serious challenges. First, his religious authority may be called into question. Some of the grand ayatollahs may issue decrees taking issue with his views and policies. His religious scholarship will be inadequate for disputing with them. He will, thus, have to depend on the support of Araki or one or more of the clerics with the rank of *ayatollah 'uzma*. His political power, too, may be challenged. Contrary to Khomeyni's vision of the rule of *velayat-e faqih*, and to the practice during Khomeyni's leadership, the cleric-politicians in senior positions may wish to concentrate more power in their own hands.

In order to strengthen his rule, after being selected Khameneh'i tried to balance between the two major camps competing for power, and at the same time, to establish closer ties with the grand ayatollahs. In his public statements he clearly echoed Khomeyni. His message to the people vowed loyalty to the path of the imam and promised to fight "any move which is directed against the sacred system of the Islamic Republic." He reminded the people that it was their "revolutionary duty" to remain "vigilant...and be aware of the enemies' conspiracies." He called for the preservation of unity, in words almost similar to those that Khomeyni so often used. "The duality of theories, and even viewpoints, must not...lead to squabbles and conflicts, especially as shared principles are creating profound bonds among the nation,"[54] he said.

What were the implications for the radical-pragmatist struggle for power? The choice of Khameneh'i as a single successor was a blow to the ultraradicals that signified a "silent revolution"; the election of Rafsanjani as president was another step in the same direction.

RAFSANJANI ELECTED PRESIDENT

The 1989 election campaign was neither as turbulent and colorful as the first in 1980, nor did it proceed under the shadow of terror that had darkened the second and third in 1981. It was much more similar to the fourth in 1985: in both, the regime demonstrated a great degree of stability. In all, however, the victory of the successful candidate was not questioned.

The elections were held on 28 July, three weeks before the date first designated by the Ministry of the Interior, because, according to Mohtashami, "of the great importance that the late imam attached to the country's political stability." Candidates were given five days, as of 28 June, to submit applications to the Ministry of Interior.[55] Some 80 candidates applied, but the council approved (9 July) only two[56] — Rafsanjani and 'Abbas Sheybani. Explaining why the others had been disqualified, Muhammad Yazdi, a member of the Council of Guardians, said that most of them lacked the basic political and administrative qualifications for the post. Some aspirants were as young as 22 years of age, others described themselves as "ordinary workers," drivers, or university freshmen, another gave his academic qualification as a certificate from the shah's Literacy Corps. In short, Yazdi said, they had only "wasted the time" of the Ministry of Interior and the Council of Guardians.[57]

Given Rafsanjani's position and Sheybani's record,[58] it seems the latter did not have much chance of getting massive support, not to speak of challenging Rafsanjani. Sheybani's campaign was very limited, a fact he justified by the need to economize.

Rafsanjani's candidacy was first proposed by the radical Combatant Clerics of Tehran (*Ruhaniyyan-e mobarez-ye Tehran*) and later by the conservative Association of Combatant Clerics (*Jame'e-ye ruhaniyyat-e mobarez*), the president, and many others. Supporting him, the *Tehran Times* wrote that if elected he would not favor any political groupings.[59] Already before his own nomination as the leader, Khameneh'i said that Rafsanjani's candidacy revived his hope for "a much brighter future."[60]

When the constitution was amended to give the president almost exclusive control over the executive — although final approval by plebiscite was scheduled for election day — Rafsanjani agreed to run. That he would be elected was not doubted; the question was how massive the popular support would be. Rafsanjani did not set up campaign headquarters, saying that "a campaign in its conventional form will be counterproductive."[61] He added: "Everyone recognizes me and I do not want my pictures and electioneering posters to be displayed. Such a display is not in the interest of the system and should be avoided."[62] In his campaign, Rafsanjani tried to avoid raising unrealistic expectations among his supporters and giving credence to the assumption that he could find fast solutions to the country's social, economic, and political problems.

During his campaign and immediately following his election he raised the following issues:[63]

Economy: Giving the economy priority, Rafsanjani pledged "to cut the government's role in the flagging economy." This, he said, was the country's "main concern" and one of the topics "that heads the list of our programs." Most importantly, he argued that Iran should strive for economic independence.

Private Sector: On this highly controversial issue, Rafsanjani said it was essential that the private sector participate in economic life. Therefore, "conditions should be created for the people to put their capital to work." It was wrong, he added, "for everything to be done by the government."

Foreign Relations: On the idea of "Neither the East nor the West," he said that it did not mean "the severance of relations with the East and West. This policy means healthy relations by negating expansionism and by preserving independence."

Both candidates made their programs sound as loyal as possible to Khomeyni's ideas. Rafsanjani emphasized the need to expand and improve education, strengthen defense, improve the lot of the "disinherited," advance industry and production, improve housing services, block inflation, advance agriculture, and reconstruct areas damaged in the war. He promised to remain loyal to Khomeyni's revolutionary ideals and implement the pledges that Khomeyni had made 10 years earlier.[64] Commentators, however, said that people mainly expected that Rafsanjani's presidency "will usher in fundamental economic reforms."[65]

Sheybani emphasized the three areas in which he had personal experience: agriculture, education, and health. In international affairs, he vowed to continue the doctrine of "Neither the East nor the West," though he mentioned that Iran would have good relations with countries having good relations with it.[66]

As in previous campaigns, the election of the candidate supported by the administration being guaranteed, the top leadership campaigned primarily with a view of ensuring the highest possible voter turnout. A high turnout, they claimed, would prove to the enemies of Iran and Islam that the people were still aware and active and the system was stable despite Khomeyni's death. *Jumhuri-ye Islami* wrote[67] that the elections and the constitutional referendum was "the first trial indicating the people's presence in the scene" after Khomeyni's death. It added that each additional vote was "a bullet fired at the enemies of the revolution."[68] As in previous elections, the leadership spoke of balloting as a national and religious duty. Thus, for example, Khameneh'i, echoing statements by Khomeyni, called on the people to vote and, by doing so, "once again deliver a mighty blow" to the "windbags and opponents, and bring despair to the enemies." Voting, he said, "is a religious...and revolutionary duty," while not doing so would bring about irreparable harm.[69] Ayatollah Muhammad 'Ali Araki said that voting was every Iranian's religious duty.[70]

Opposition movements urged the people to boycott the elections, as they had ever since 1981. Explaining the decision, the *Fada'iyyan-e khalq* (the majority wing) said that the government had denied even candidates supporting the system the right of running for office. "What is being held," it said, "is not a true election but a sham, stage-managed by the government."[71] Similarly, the Tudeh Party said the referendum and presidential elections were "nothing other than a charade" and their results were clear to everyone before they started. Manuchehr Ganji, the secretary-general of the Paris-based Flag of Freedom Organization, also supported the boycott.[72] But their calls fell on deaf ears for the most part. According to the official count, 16,454,378 votes were cast in the presidential elections, and c. 68% of those qualified. Altogether 97.4% of the voters supported the new constitution and 94.5% voted for Rafsanjani.[73] (Voting percentages in the first four rounds were: 75%, 69%, 73%, and 57%, respectively.) The minister of the interior said that the "wide participation" was "a token of the devotion of the people to Imam Khomeyni and to the path of the Islamic revolution."[74] Yet, the leaders warned against "irrational expectations" and "miraculous effects from the changes," as *Jumhuri-ye Islami* put it, and warned that "it will be wrong" to assume that the new president and his government would achieve immediate success in meeting the country's grave problems.[75]

All leaders, including Musavi, Ahmad Khomeyni, and Mohtashami, welcomed Rafsanjani's election and expressed their belief that he would advance the imam's aims. Most commentators said that the election of Rafsanjani, who was so closely identified with the revolutionary movement, manifested the "people's trust in the high-ranking officials of the revolution and the concordance between the people and the officials in continuing the path of the imam."[76]

Khameneh'i urged Rafsanjani to work hard to solve the nation's problems. Given his own experience in the presidency and his long familiarity with Rafsanjani, he believed that Rafsanjani would fit the post well. But echoing Khomeyni's exhortations when confirming the presidents, he reminded Rafsanjani that "this confirmation" depends on his loyalty to the same path. He also rejected the idea that the country was entering a new era: "A new era, if it means turning against the main line drawn by our dear imam, will never come...America and other arrogant enemies...will [have to] take this dream to the grave." Rafsanjani stressed his long history of friendship and cooperation with Khameneh'i. In the past few years, it was mainly Khameneh'i who repeatedly stressed the ties between himself and Rafsanjani, always recalling their cooperation since the late 1950s. This time it was Rafsanjani who used this language. He made it clear that he had been and was still loyal to Khomeyni's path. His was not a new path or a new direction, only a new phase[77] (see above).

Several conclusions could be drawn about the elections. First, the results of the referendum and presidential elections were not surprising. The fact that the government could approve such important constitutional changes and guarantee

Rafsanjani's election without much opposition was telling evidence of domestic stability. Second, all major decisions since the death of the ayatollah were supported — willingly or not — by all main figures. Yet, beneath the surface there was much tension, mainly between Rafsanjani and Mohtashami who continued to express independent views. Third, Rafsanjani needed Khameneh'i's cooperation to be in a better position to select his government and pursue his policies. And finally, Khameneh'i seemed to take leadership very seriously. Judging by his public appearances and messages such as that to pilgrims leaving for the Hajj and his message at Rafsanjani's inauguration, he seemingly attempted to echo Khomeyni. This made it imperative for Rafsanjani to firmly establish his authority as president and most powerful leader as soon as possible. The challenge to his authority came both from Khameneh'i and from elements in the executive (such as Musavi, Mohtashami, and Reyshahri, see below).

THE NEW GOVERNMENT

The Composition of the New Government

Following his election, Rafsanjani used his success to consolidate his own power and advance Iran's interests as he viewed them. His immediate concern was to form a competent and loyal government. On 27 August he presented his candidates for the 22 ministerial portfolios to the Majlis. All his nominees were approved by the Majlis (for the formation of the government see below).

Concerning the composition of the new government, the following points seemed to be particularly significant:

Those known for their radical views were excluded from the Cabinet. Rafsanjani could either get rid of his opponents gradually or leave them out of his government altogether. He opted for the second, with the result that the two most radical ministers, Mohtashami and Muhammad Reyshahri, and former prime minister Musavi were excluded. That he took such a step attested both to Rafsanjani's self-confidence and determination and to his authority and power. This was also confirmed by the fact that Rafsanjani came under fire from radicals for dumping their leaders, and that the radicals had failed both to deter him and to have the Majlis reject his nominees. True, Mohtashami and Reyshahri were replaced by other radicals — 'Abdollah Nuri and 'Ali Fallahiyyan — but they seemed to have less political clout, were believed to be personally close to Rafsanjani, and their challenge seemed less than that of their predecessors. At this stage, Rafsanjani, seemed to have outmaneuvered the radicals.

The fact that all his 22 nominees were approved was also significant. In all previous governments, some of the ministers were always rejected by the Majlis; it was unprecedented in the Islamic regime's short history that all candidates presented — until then by the prime minister — should be approved.

Rafsanjani selected a cabinet of technocrats, many of them Western-educated, rather than of revolutionary ideologues, which indicated the general direction in which he wished to move: rehabilitation of the country, mainly of the economy (see below). As a *Tehran Times*[78] editorial had made clear before Rafsanjani made his nominees known — the main criteria for nomination should be competence and not allegiance to any faction: "Any of the ministers chosen," the paper said, "should be a man of action before being a political figure." The paper added that the selection of ministers should be based "on realism and not on airy thinking or impractical sloganeering." When the list became known, *Abrar* voiced the conviction that "the new cabinet is the one suitable for a period of growth and renovation and is highly qualified as regards to specialization in economic, social, and cultural aspects."[79]

The government was one of change. More than half of the ministers — 12 of the 22 — had not served in the outgoing government though some of them had served in previous governments; a third had studied in the West, eight had Ph.D. or M.D. degrees, nine were engineers, and only four were Hujjat al-Islam (one, Muhammad Khatami is both a Dr. and a Hujjat al-Islam). Of special interest was the appointment of technocrats to several important portfolios associated with the economy: Economics and Finance, Industry, Heavy Industry, Mines and Metals, and Commerce. New ministers were also chosen for the portfolios of Higher Education, Health, Justice, Labor and Social Affairs, Intelligence, and Defense and Armed Forces Logistics. Rafsanjani made it clear that he wished to have a government of experts, not of politicians. It was enough, he said, that he himself was political; the ministers should be "experts in their field and their professional and administrative knowledge" as is needed "in the period of reconstruction." Referring to criticism of the large number of Western-educated ministers, he said that he did not think it advisable to limit ministerial appointments only to people who had studied in Iran. He said: "Studying in American universities was not and is not a negative point."[80] It should be added that preference for technocrats goes back to the first days of the revolutionary regime — to the government of Mehdi Bazargan (in 1979). While there was some retreat from this policy when the clerics become firmly established (mainly since 1981–82), a reversal to preference for professionals became clear in 1988, as was evident among others, with the election of the Third Majlis in that year (see *MECS* 1988, pp. 490–91).

Another sign of Rafsanjani's strengthening grip on the leadership was the naming (2 August) of Justice Minister Dr. Hasan Habibi as his first vice-president.[81] Rafsanjani also nominated 'Ata'ollah Mohajerani (35) as vice president for legal and parliamentary affairs, and Hamid Mirzade as vice president for executive affairs. In September, Rafsanjani named 10 advisers, one of them being Musavi.

The radicals did not give up. As mentioned above, some radical ministers still served in the cabinet, others held senior positions in different government agencies. In addition, the Majlis speaker from mid-August was a radical (Hujjat al-Islam Mehdi Karubi) who had defeated a pragmatic candidate (Hujjat al-Islam 'Ali Akbar Nateq-Nuri).[82] Similarly, although Rafsanjani succeeded in excluding the radicals, radical Majlis deputies were highly critical of the exclusion of the hard-line politicians.[83]

Explaining his selection of ministers, Rafsanjani said that the decision was based on "my personal knowledge" though he had consulted Khameneh'i, the former president; Musavi, the former prime minister; and Ardebili, head of the judiciary. Experience, he said, was an important criterion; affiliation "to this or that faction" played no role. He was convinced, he said, that "in the eyes of God" he had succeeded in deciding "what was good for the country and the Islamic revolution, despite all pressures and propaganda."[84] Yet, it was clear to everyone, whether pragmatist or radical, that the trend of his policy was to weaken opponents of Rafsanjani (see below, section on the new team in action).

The Policy

In addition to signaling the degree of power already concentrated in Rafsanjani's hands, the composition of the government also suggested that he wished to work with a largely centrist team of technocrats with the explicit aim of reviving Iran's economy, and the implicit purpose of improving relations with the outside world. These aims were clarified additionally in his policy declarations before and after his government was approved.[85]

Tactical or Strategic Changes: Policy must be appropriate to the times. But in an attempt to justify deviation from the policies of Islamic Iran, he viewed his proposed changes as "tactics and not [relating] to principles," although in reality this process may go far beyond tactical changes.

Rehabilitation of the Country: The coming decade was called "the decade of reconstruction" and Rafsanjani stressed that the prime motive behind his acceptance of the presidency was this goal.

Private Sector: Although he did not go into much detail regarding the role of the private sector, he made it clear that his economic policy — as against that of the more radicals — would encourage investment by the private sector. He also said that the initial idea of preventing the private sector from investing in private schools was unrealistic. He encouraged investment in education "from the primary stages up to university." Similarly, he welcomed private participation in "the management of our industries and economic centers." He promised that factories confiscated in the early stages of the revolution would be sold to the people, with the factory workers being given priority.

Lowering Expectations: Although pledging to work hard to improve the lot of the poor, he made clear that popular expectations would be difficult to meet, and it would take a long time before the problems could be solved. Thus, for example, economic independence was an important aim, but "in such a country, which for hundreds of years has been crushed under the jackboot of the world's dastardly elements, [it] is no doubt difficult." Elsewhere, he added that the people's expectations "exceed the [present] possibilities."

Iraq: Rafsanjani always took a hard line when expressing publicly views regarding Iraq. "We are not sure that the war has ended," he said. Yet, it seems, not only that he did not wish to resume the fighting — he seemed willing to settle the conflict.

The Superpowers: Rafsanjani tried to avoid voicing extremist sentiments when referring to the US, though his tone was not conciliatory either. Iran opposed "illegitimate domination...and injustice" in relations between countries, but in principle accepted bilateral relations based on "international norms and without interference in other's internal affairs." In another place he said: "In our new course, we are prepared to establish friendly relations with all countries — except two or three — who have discarded the idea of relations based on plundering." But even with these countries Rafsanjani reportedly maintained at least indirect contact after his election.

Other Changes

Appointment of Members of the Council for Ascertaining the Interests of the State: In a letter to Rafsanjani (4 October), Khameneh'i appointed as members to the council the six clerics of the Council of Guardians (Ahmad Jonati, Muhammad Gilani, Abul-Qasem Khaz'ali, Aqa Emami Kashani, 'Ali Akbar Rezvani, Muhammad

Mo'men); the heads of the three branches of government (Rafsanjani, Karubi, and Yazdi); Hujjat al-Islam Mahdavi-Kani; Hajj Shaykh Yusef Sane'i; Seyyed Ahmad Khomeyni; Seyyed Muhammad Musavi Kho'iniha; Hajj Shaykh Muhammad 'Ali Muvahedi-Kermani; Hajj Shaykh Hasan Sane'i; Hajj Shaykh Muhammad Reza Tavassoli; Shaykh 'Abdollah Nuri; and Mir-Husayn Musavi. In addition, the minister with whose office a proposed law is concerned and the head of the relevant Majlis committee would join the council on an *ad hoc* basis.[86] The number of members in the council was increased from 13 to 20.

New President of Supreme Court: By a decree of the leader, Ayatollah Muhammad Yazdi was named president of the Supreme Court to succeed Ayatollah Ardebili. Muhammad Moqteda'i was appointed chief justice and Muhammad Reyshahri replaced Kho'iniha as prosecutor-general.

Majlis By-Elections: Elections were held in 15 December to fill nine vacancies. (Mohtashami was elected to the Majlis; he gained 225,570 votes out of the total of 661,487 votes in Tehran).

RAFSANJANI'S GOVERNMENT

Hasan Habibi	First Vice-President
(Engineer) Akbar Torkan*	Defense and Armed Forces Logistics
Hujjat al-Islam 'Ali Fallahiyyan*	Intelligence
Dr. Mohsen Nurbakhsh*	Economic Affairs and Finance
(Engineer) Gholamreza Aqazade	Oil
(Engineer) Bizhan Namdar-Zangane	Energy
(Engineer) Muhammad Reza Ne'matzade*	Industries
Dr. Muhammad Hadi Nezhad-Husayniyyan*	Heavy Industries
(Engineer) Husayn Mahluj-chi*	Mines and Metals
Dr. 'Isa Kalantari	Agriculture
Husayn Kamali*	Labor and Social Affairs
Dr. 'Ali Akbar Velayati	Foreign Affairs
Hujjat al-Islam 'Abdollah Nuri*	Interior
'Abdul Husayn Vahaji*	Commerce
(Engineer) Sarraj al-Din Kazeruni	Housing and Urban Development
Hujjat al-Islam Dr. Muhammad Khatami	Islamic Guidance
Dr. Muhammad 'Ali Najafi	Education and Training
Dr. Mustafa Mo'in*	Culture and Higher Education
Dr. Iraj Fazel*	Health, and Medical Education and Treatment
(Engineer) Seyyed Muhammad Gharazi	Post, Telegraphs, and Telephones
(Engineer) Muhammad Seyyed-Kiya	Roads and Transport
(Engineer) Gholamreza Foruzesh	Construction Jihad
Hujjat al-Islam Esma'il Shoshtari*	Justice

* Did not serve in the outgoing Cabinet.

SOURCE: R. Tehran, 19 August — SWB, 21 August; *Ettela'at,* 30 August 1989.

THE NEW TEAM IN ACTION

THE POWER STRUGGLE

The selection of Khameneh'i as leader and Rafsanjani as president made them the leading figures in the revolutionary institutions following Khomeyni's death. That the two of them became the twin pillars of post-Khomeyni Iran did not bode well for the more radical elements in the Administration. Although the victory in this round went to the more pragmatic elements, the struggle for power was not over. Rafsanjani's cabinet excluded the radicals, yet he had to give them prominent positions; he could not ignore them entirely. This may have been calculated to serve his own aims (not overantagonizing the radicals, keeping them around him, appeasing them, gaining more time to set out against them). The radicals made it clear that they had not given up their determination to struggle for their views.

The potential challenges facing the new team derived from the political arena and the socioeconomic problems. Politically, the potential challenge to the Rafsanjani-Khameneh'i team lay in a clash between the two leaders themselves, and in the opposition to the president's pragmatic policy. In 1989, the latter was more of a problem.

Ever since the formation of the new institutions, the radicals made it clear that they had not abandoned their goal of directing the revolution in terms of their interpretation of Khomeyni's legacy, which, they argued, was the true interpretation. For example, they criticized Ayatollah Yazdi, the president of the Supreme Court, for giving an audience (26 September) to the sister-in-law of Roger Cooper, a British citizen imprisoned since December 1985. The radicals seized upon the meeting to criticize a move taken by a leading pragmatist. Another example was their determination to use the 10th anniversary of the seizure of the American hostages to incite tempers once again against the US. They organized a petition signed by 146 Majlis members appealing to Rafsanjani for a "glorious commemoration" of the anniversary.[87] Earlier, Muhammad Ebrahim Asgharzade — one of the leaders of the students who occupied the American Embassy in 1979 — said in the Majlis (27 September) that Iran could have common interests with the West — or for that matter with Saudi Arabia — "only when we step down from our revolutionary positions." He blamed officials speaking on behalf of the Foreign Ministry for voicing arguments and theories which "prepares the religious ground for resumption of ties with the US."[88] This statement, and others, were signs that the pragmatist trend would be challenged by the radicals on both domestic policies and foreign relations.

But even more serious than such political challenges were the social and economic problems. These problems could not be easily solved, and they were likely to continue and press even harder on the government. With the growing social and economic repercussions, Rafsanjani and his policies may be accused of responsibility for these problems. That he did not have a prime minister whom he could dismiss in case of popular resentment might prove another disadvantage. Since Rafsanjani was viewed as the man responsible for shaping all policies, in the event of growing criticism it would make it difficult to put the blame on others.

While Rafsanjani concentrated in 1989 on rehabilitating the economy, Khameneh'i worked to strengthen his own authority. As long as the struggle was against the radicals, both were on the same side. Khameneh'i wished to maintain his leadership along the lines of Khomeyni's rule, as was evident in the "unity conference" held in mid-October, when Iranian participants and foreign guests joined to support his leadership.[89] In these cases, Rafsanjani and Khameneh'i appeared to support each other.

The rift with the radicals, however, grew so wide in December that Khameneh'i was forced to intervene and call for unity in general, and for support for Rafsanjani in particular. Those opposing Rafsanjani, but not only they, used the visit of former Romanian president Nikolae Ceauşescu as a pretext to voice criticism. Although it was directed at the Foreign Ministry, or the foreign minister, it was criticism of Rafsanjani as well.

Ceauşescu's visit was a disgrace for revolutionary Iran, coming so soon before the Romanian people rose up against the dictator. What added to the disaster was that Tehran claimed that the popular uprisings in Eastern Europe were modeled on the Islamic-Iranian example. Such a claim now put them in the position of those who had hosted "the Romanian Shah," a decidedly uncomplimentary description. Criticism was not long in coming. Some of it focused on the wisdom of inviting Ceauşescu, since his record was clear to all and the opposition of his people was no secret. Others questioned the timing of the visit. Most observers even criticized the Foreign Ministry, though it was clear that some of the criticism was meant to be directed at Rafsanjani. *Ettela'at* asked the Foreign Ministry to explain why it had arranged for Ceauşescu to visit "at [such] an inappropriate time when his ouster from power was not difficult to foresee." The ministry, the paper went on, should have had studied his political record "as a dictator who had imposed his relatives on the Romanians, and who on the international scene acted as a bridge of communications between Israel and the Arab countries." It expressed the hope that Ceauşescu would be "the last falling star to come to the Islamic Republic for his last meal."[90] *Jumhuri-ye Islami* claimed that it was not the first time that "irresponsible [policy] and lack of awareness on the part of our policymakers cause[d] problems incompatible with the reputation of a revolutionary country."[91] The *Tehran Times* took a similar line though it blamed the Iranian ambassador at Bucharest for the mistake.[92] *Kayhan* wrote that it was shameful to see how the foreign media (always trying "to fish in troubled waters") were showing pictures of Ceauşescu and Rafsanjani side by side in the last days of the dictator's rule. This, the paper said, was detrimental to the revolution's reputation.[93]

When the wave of criticism mounted, Khameneh'i interfered. He tried to prevent the criticism from dividing the revolutionary camp and diminishing public support for the revolution. He also tried to prevent the criticism from turning against Rafsanjani, and thus challenging the stability of the regime. He first made these points on 27 December. Although only hinting at the political intentions of those making the criticism, it was clear that he accused certain groups and individuals of orchestrating the criticism: such divisive voices "will [not] again" be allowed to make themselves heard. Although not mentioning the specific issue to which he was referring, it was clear that he meant the Ceauşescu visit. To make his point even clearer, he praised the Foreign Ministry for its valuable service and attacked those who were always "looking for excuses [to criticize our diplomats]."[94] Rafsanjani, Karubi, Yazdi as well as other leaders and institutions praised Khameneh'i and vowed to preserve unity. After Khameneh'i's statements, the criticism waned. The *Tehran Times* warned against using the issue "to settle sectarian goals."[95] But criticism did not altogether cease.

That Khameneh'i was forced to repeat his plea for unity (8 January 1990) and to openly support Rafsanjani made clear that behind-the-scene criticism continued and that some of it was aimed at Rafsanjani. Khameneh'i made it clear that he supported and trusted Rafsanjani. The government, he said, was headed by "an outstanding personality" who was "trusted by the imam and the nation." Khameneh'i not only supported Rafsanjani, but also described those whom he believed were behind the criticism as persons wishing to keep the Iranian nation poor and "conspire" in order "to oppose this government." Although he did not identify the critics, it would be safe to conclude that he meant those who opposed Rafsanjani's pragmatic policies, primarily concerning social and economic issues. Such people, Khameneh'i continued, could also be found among Majlis members: "There have always been a handful of individuals in the Majlis who ignored these duties and went astray, and perhaps they may still be there today."[96]

Another indication of internal division was Mohtashami's replies in December to a number of questions put to him by *Ettela'at* before the Majlis by-elections. The Majlis, he said, was "the real base for the protection of the lofty values of the Islamic revolution." This statement must be understood as conveying criticism of the government and making clear his intention of using the Majlis as the forum for promoting his own ideas. "Political pressure" had been exerted "to prevent deputies from making accurate assessments of various issues. On certain occasions, unfortunately, the Majlis succumbed to such pressure and deviated from its revolutionary policy." Asked what were the main problems facing the nation, he replied that "in order of importance, [they are] the political, cultural, social and, finally, economic problems." This ranking made clear the gap between him and Rafsanjani. Mohtashami went on to say that the enemies of the country were those who gave top priority to the economic problems. In his view, these problems stemmed from political and cultural ones and were their "natural concomitant."[97]

It was premature to reach any ultimate results of the domestic struggle for power. Rafsanjani seemed powerful and had Khameneh'i's support. Together, they had the winning cards, but the more radical camp still held on to its hope. As former foreign minister Ebrahim Yazdi put it: "There is no big fish capable of eating all the other fish," they are unable "to eliminate each other, so they are spending much of the time checking each other's aggressions."[98]

THE ECONOMY

The economy remained a major concern in 1989. The leaders were aware of the pressing economic hardships and their possible political consequences. (For the economic problems see in *MECS* 1987, pp. 401–404; 1988, pp. 475–76, 479–81). Parallel to their attempts to plan an economic program, they concentrated on lowering expectations, particularly on the eve of the presidential elections and following the formation of the new government (see above). But they were aware that the government had to achieve some success in this field, if it wished to avoid discontent.

To this end, in September the government approved the five-year economic plan. Morteza Alviri (head of the Majlis Plan and Budget Committee) said that the plan aimed to lead the country to "self-reliance" (*khod etteka'i*), though not yet to "self-supply" (*khod kafa'i*). The policy was to invest oil revenue in economic projects that would decrease Iranian dependence on foreigners.[99] On 8 October, Rafsanjani outlined the plan's basic points at a press conference:

* For increasing the scope of domestic industries (in order to decrease dependence on foreign countries), it was decided to allocate $9bn. in order to advance the industrial sector.

* Dependence on oil revenue would be decreased.

* Immediate steps would be taken to rehabilitate war-damaged areas. The sum of $1.5bn. would be added to the IR35bn. (c. $5bn., which had already been allocated for

this purpose for the next five years). This sum, it was now decided, should be used in the first two years of the plan.

* Although foreign loans were not approved, foreign resources would be used as "a kind of loan."

* The government would take steps to insure for government employees appropriate salaries, which would not be affected by inflation.

* Tourism would be developed in order to make people in the world familiar with the revolution's achievements and to earn revenue.[100]

As far as the rehabilitation policy was concerned, the amounts allocated under the plan were insufficient for the needs of the country. Estimates of these needs ranged from $150bn. to as much as $500bn. Iran would need to use its oil revenue to supply the basic needs of the growing population, including food imports; to allow greater room for the private sector and to take — in one way or another — foreign loans; and to improve relations with the outside world and unfreeze assets in the US. More than any other leader, Rafsanjani seemed to be aware of these needs. In October, the different ministries made their policies public, in order to prove that the government was fully aware of the problems, that it had the necessary plans to solve them, and was determined to implement them soon. Rafsanjani went as far as to state publicly that to improve the economic situation it would not be sufficient to repeat slogans and cling to sentiments and emotions. If necessary, he implied, the government should deviate from revolutionary conviction and radical dogma. Slogans and emotional attachments were important but rehabilitation also depended on "material, economic, and physical aspects." He made it clear that Iran could not "raise its head" if it lacked "material means." In other words, that a degree of pragmatism was essential.[101]

After Rafsanjani presented the economic plan's main guidelines the media discussed different aspects of it. The leadership acknowledged that a more pragmatic policy must be pursued. The main policy lines were:

* The government would vigorously fight any sign of "economic terrorism" and take steps to ensure fair prices. The people were assured that those committing economic crimes would be punished. This repeated what had appeared in the "economic plans" of all previous revolutionary governments.

* Subsidization of basic goods would continue in order to guarantee sufficient supplies at low prices, an important step to quell disquiet among the *mostaz'efin*.

* Government officials, and mainly Minister of Economy and Finance Mohsen Nurbakhsh, appealed to the people to trust the government's economic policy and to invest in economic projects. The government, he said, would encourage private investment.[102] Rafsanjani promised that the government would encourage and guarantee investments: "We have plans for our banks to guarantee credits for the private sector."[103]

* In another indication of pragmatism, Rafsanjani disclosed the government's intention of dealing with the problem of rapid population growth (the Iranian population has grown from c. 37m. on the eve of the revolution to some 52m. late in 1989. According to official estimations the annual rate of growth in 1989 was 3.9%. As sensitive an issue as it was, he made clear in a press conference (23 October) that the government was determined to inhibit population growth by explaining the importance of the issue to the people and asking their cooperation.[104]

* The need for professional manpower in achieving economic goals was stressed.

Minister of Culture and Higher Education Mustafa Mo'in made it clear that although it was preferable to have Iranians trained in Iran, the government should also send university students abroad for training.[105] Education was not only one of the main obstacles to economic development but also a major cause of popular resentment. A recent report from the Ministry of Education maintained that in the not-too-distant future, education would become a major national problem, which the public sector would be unable to solve. Quoting the report, *Ettela'at* said that qualitatively the educational system had deteriorated during the decade of revolution. In some regions (and mainly in Tehran) there were elementary schools operating in three, and even four shifts; and even so there were often as many as 60–70 children in each class.[106] Habibi claimed that the government could not guarantee equal educational opportunities for all as stated in the constitution.[107] He concluded that the public sector should be encouraged to invest in the educational system as well, another deviation from the initial revolutionary ideology that education, at all levels, should be in the hands of the government.

GUIDELINES OF FOREIGN RELATIONS

Relations with the West

Following Khomeyni's death, leaders used harsh terms to criticize the US. Especially radical were Ahmad Khomeyni, Nuri, and Karubi.[108] Khameneh'i left no room for compromise, continuing to echo the views of Ayatollah Khomeyni. Even Rafsanjani had to join the radicals in his statements. In a Friday sermon on 1 September he denied that Iran had to change its policy *vis-à-vis* the West in order to hasten the country's reconstruction. To do so, he declared, "Iran does not need the West at all (*aslan*)." But, unlike the radicals, Rafsanjani did not close the door completely. He stated that Iran would maintain relations with those who did not have imperialist intentions and would give up "their dreams" (to exploit Iran), a declaration that could be interpreted as a signal to the US, although the statement was a denunciation of the US.[109]

In any case, the US seemed clearly willing to give Rafsanjani credit for being willing to improve relations. As one observer suggested, the Americans "are treating Rafsanjani with the same type of respect that they give Mikhail Gorbachev, as a man "committed to reforms who deserves to be supported'."[110] In 1989 Rafsanjani did not discourage such an attitude, but was in no position to satisfy the US in any way.

With the approach of the 10th anniversary of the seizure of the American Embassy in Tehran, there were growing signs of anti-Western and anti-US radical sentiments. Asked whether Tehran would approve American firms' taking part in economic rehabilitation, Rafsanjani said that since they did not have a "good record," Iran "cannot count on them." He disclosed that Washington was sending him messages through neighboring countries, but he maintained that Iran could not trust US promises, unless the US gave practical expression to its intentions, such as unfreezing Iranian assets in the US.[111]

Beneath the surface, the two countries reportedly maintained contact, particularly on the issues of unfreezing the Iranian assets and of releasing American hostages, the two major themes around which American-Iranian relations have revolved for a decade. Iran did not have any difficulties in organizing a united domestic front against the US. In November, the anniversary of the occupation of the American Embassy provided the pretext; in December, criticism of the American invasion of Panama was another occasion for demonstrating the leadership's "unity." For the radicals, this was another reminder to the people of the imam's true "line"; for the pragmatists, it was another occasion to prove loyalty to the revolution's basic principles (see also chapter on the US and the ME).

The Soviet Union

Rafsanjani's visit to the USSR that began on 20 June was the highest-level visit of an Iranian official to that country, or to any other European country, since the revolution. Rafsanjani, then Majlis speaker, was greeted with much respect and was treated as a head of state. He conferred several times with Gorbachev, and in a special gesture of friendship he was allowed to visit Azerbaijan and meet Muslims there.

Even in this atmosphere of friendship, however, the Iranians made no secret of their criticism of the Soviet Union's past policies toward their country. Iranian leaders made clear that historically, relations between the two countries had "never been desirable." Heading the list of their charges were the colonialist ambitions of czarist Russia in Iran, support for Iraq in the war, and Soviet policy in Afghanistan.[112]

But there were also important reasons for a change in Iranian policy as well as for the visit. The cease-fire in the Gulf, the Soviet withdrawal from Afganistan, and the policy of *glasnost* in the Soviet Union impressed the Iranians. For example, Velayati said: "We believe that the changes and developments in the Soviet Union are not superficial or temporary."[113] Iranian leaders viewed the developments in the Soviet Union as constituting a revolutionary change and welcomed it. They believed, as Rafsanjani put it, that the Soviets finally "comprehended the reality of the [Islamic] revolution."[114]

The visit to the USSR was a continuation of a process which Khomeyni had started several months before.[115] The fact that Iran did not cancel the trip after Khomeyni's death meant above all that it was interested in improving ties with the USSR. By Rafsanjani's trip the Iranians also wished to show the world that their country enjoyed stability.[116] Iran also needed to complete the economic projects about which there had been long discussions with Moscow. The discussions revolved mainly around infrastructure — export of gas, dams, power stations, railways, and technology transfer. Protocols of good-neighborliness and for technical, scientific, cultural, and economic cooperation up to the year 2000 were signed. The ministers of economy of both countries also signed an agreement for the exchange of goods. A third agreement concerned the construction of a railway between Tedzhen in the Soviet Union and Meshhed.[117]

But developments in Azerbaijan pointed to the potential difficulties in bilateral relations. They presented Iran with serious dilemmas, both ideological and national. Ideologically, Iran felt obliged to support the Muslim struggle in Soviet Azerbaijan; after all, was not the "export of the revolution" an axiom of the revolutionary ideology? But pursuance of such a policy would confront Tehran with two serious problems: it could lead to tension with its strong neighbor; the success of the movement in Soviet Azerbaijan could present a serious challenge to Iran's control over Iranian Azerbaijan, which might lead to problems with Iran's other ethnic minorities. The policy ultimately adopted was additional proof of the prevailing pragmatism: it was in line with Iranian national interest at the expense of revolutionary dogma (see also chapter on the Soviet Union and the ME).

Neighboring Arab States

In Iran's relations with its Arab neighbors, there were fluctuations following Khomeyni's death, as there have been before. Wishing to improve relations, Rafsanjani, for example, expressed the hopes at a meeting with the new Iranian ambassador to the United Arab Emirates that ties with the Gulf states would improve (see similarly a declaration by Karubi on 19 September).[118] Tension reemerged in Iran's relations with Saudi Arabia and Kuwait, mainly after the execution of 16 Kuwaitis in Saudi Arabia accused of terrorist activities inspired by Tehran.[119]

On the occasion of the Islamic unity conference in early October, harsh accusations were made against some Arab countries, mainly Saudi Arabia, for obstructing Muslim solidarity. In a speech in the Majlis, Speaker Karubi criticized Saudi Arabia on this score,[120] as did other Iranian leaders, mainly Musavi. An even more radical tone was heard in statements against Iraq. Rafsanjani made it clear that if there was no progress toward peace, "we will be forced to use another way [to advance our aims]." Appealing to the Iraqi people, he said that if they rose against the regime they could "free themselves" from their rulers though he did not promise Iranian support.[121]

In July 1989, for the second successive year, Iran did not participate in the pilgrimage to Mecca. As in previous years, regardless of whether or not Iranian pilgrims participated, tension peaked in relations between the two countries on the occasion of the Hajj. In 1989, the Saudis wished to see a change in the Iranian reaction, which would indicate the beginning of a new phase in their relations following Khomeyni's death. But Tehran continued to use the same harsh words in criticizing Saudi Arabia, as if it wished to use the Hajj to prove to the Gulf states, to the outside world, as well as to its own people that even though the ayatollah was dead, the revolution continued along the same lines. The statements made in Tehran, particularly those of Khameneh'i, to the pilgrims, Iranians, and others clearly reflected an attempt to echo Khomeyni.

In his message to the pilgrims (6 July), Khameneh'i condemned the Saudis for having "blocked the path of God" for Iranian pilgrims. He blamed the rulers in Riyadh for being "the sinful idols of arrogance and colonialism...who are ignorant of God." Also in line with Khomeyni's statements, Khameneh'i called the Saudi clerics "court preachers" and their religion an "American Islam."[122] Other Iranian leaders followed suit, and went as far as calling for an end to Saudi rule over the holy shrines and questioning the Saudis' faithfulness to Islam. The president of the Supreme Court, 'Abdul Karim Musavi Ardebili, prayed to God that "the corpse of Mecca's *taghut* [illegitimate rulers]" would be removed from Saudi Arabia.[123] Majlis vice-speaker (and former representative of Khomeyni in the Hajj) Mehdi Karubi said the Saudi rulers were "disqualified to administer the holy sanctuaries."[124] Mohtashami called to put the "Al Sa'ud clan" on trial "for the numerous crimes it has perpetrated...against Islam."[125] These statements, indicating the difficulties in bilateral relations since Khomeyni's death, increased tension between Tehran and Riyadh. Iran was faced with an emotionally charged issue for which a drastic change in policy was impossible in the short run. (For further discussion of these relations, see chapter on Saudi Arabia.)

Late in 1989, tension between Iran and Syria increased as well around two major issues: their policies concerning Lebanon and the renewal of ties between Damascus and Cairo. While Iran and Syria took different positions on Lebanon and while Tehran was upset by Asad's decision to renew ties with Cairo, the Iranian media and the spokesman for the Foreign Ministry continued to praise the close relations between the two countries. Beneath the surface, however, difficulties became more and more visible.

Tehran tried to explain to its people that the Syrian inclination toward Egypt was acceptable since it was meant to create a united Arab front against Israel. The *Tehran Times* warned, however, that the Syrian move should not "divert the attention of Muslim nations from Islam's strategic objectives."[126] It was clear that the Syrian attempt at *rapprochement* with Egypt was met with much Iranian opposition and added another cause for tension in Iranian-Syrian relations. Given the Iranian hostility toward Egypt — and keeping in mind that Egypt was the only country which had signed a peace treaty with Israel — Tehran was not indifferent to Syrian diplomacy. Moreover, Tehran was concerned by Syrian attempts to improve its relations with the Arab world.

Another source for concern was the policy in Lebanon. According to Arab diplomatic sources, Syria had undertaken — in a secret article in the Ta'if agreement — to limit the Iranian presence in Lebanon by preventing Iranian soldiers and arms from transiting Syria en route to Lebanon. Syria, the same sources said, had similarly undertaken to prevent Iran from sending supplies to Lebanon by sea or by air. When in mid-January 1990 Tehran tried to test Syrian intentions, the Syrians blocked the supply of arms to Lebanon, apparently in Damascus airport. They also prevented the entry of c. 160 Revolutionary Guards into Lebanon via Syria. Iranian and Syrian policy was at loggerheads, but Tehran could not do much about it. (See also chapter on Syria. For Iran's relations with Iraq, see chapter on Iraq.)

NOTES

For the place and frequency of publications cited here, and for the full name of the publication, news agency, radio station, or monitoring service where an abbreviation is used, please see "List of Sources." Only in the case of more than one publication bearing the same name is the place of publication noted here.

1. The heads of the three branches of government maintained their positions for at least eight years. (See *MECS* 1983–84, p. 428; 1984–85, pp. 423–24, where this phenomenon, since the fall of 1981, is referred to as a sign of the regime's stability.)
2. *FT,* 7 June 1989.
3. *TT,* 17 June 1989.
4. See David Menashri (ed.) *The Iranian Revolution and the Muslim World* (Boulder: Westview Press, 1990), mainly the introduction and the article by Shahram Chubin.
5. Ibid., article by J.J.G. Jansen.
6. James Piscatori, *Islam in a World of Nation States* (Cambridge: Cambridge University Press, 1986), p. 2.
7. *Time,* 12 June 1989.
8. *FT,* 5 June 1989.
9. Such soul-searching was already witnessed at the time of the 10th anniversary of the Islamic Republic (see *MECS* 1988, pp. 486–89), but it was interrupted by Khomeyni's decree against Rushdie and the more radical atmosphere created in Iran since then.

10. IRNA (in English), 6 June — DR, 7 June 1989.
11. Tehran TV, 8 June — DR, 10 June 1989.
12. Khomeyni's last will has not been discussed here, because it contains no significant new material. In it, Khomeyni repeated his basic ideology and appealed for loyalty to the revolution. The Embassy of the Democratic and Popular Republic of Algeria, Interest Section of the Islamic Republic of Iran (Washington DC: 1989), has published *Imam Khomeini's Last Will and Testament* in Persian, English, and Arabic. Brief references to the will will be made below.
13. *Ettela'at*, 29 March; R. Tehran, 28 March — SWB, 30 March 1989.
14. R. Tehran, 28 March — SWB, 30 March; *Ettela'at*, 29 March 1989.
15. *Kayhan,* Tehran, 29 March 1989.
16. *Ettela'at*, 5 April 1989.
17. *Resalat,* 15, 16, 17 May — DR, 6 July 1989. The letter, dated 29 April 1989, was widely distributed in Iran in pamphlet form before its publication in the paper.
18. *Resalat,* 29 March 1989.
19. *Ettela'at* — DR, 4 April 1989.
20. R. Tehran, 8 June — SWB, 12 June 1989.
21. *Ettela'at*, 16 April; R. Tehran, 16 April — SWB, 18 April 1989.
22. *TT,* 18 April 1989.
23. R. Tehran, 21 April — SWB, 24 April 1989.
24. R. Tehran, 24 April — SWB, 26 April 1989.
25. *Ettela'at*, 22 April 1989.
26. *Abrar,* 19 April — SWB, 22 April 1989.
27. R. Tehran, 24 April — SWB, 26 April 1989.
28. R. Tehran, 16 April — DR, 18 April 1989.
29. R. Tehran, 28 April — SWB, 1 May 1989.
30. R. Tehran, 24 April — SWB, 26 April 1989.
31. *Ettela'at*, 27 April; R. Tehran, 26 April — SWB, 28 April 1989.
32. Such categorizations are somehow problematic. Thus, for example, Rafsanjani was a member of the Council of Experts and of the Majlis. But, generally speaking, it seems that such an intention guided the composition of the council.
33. *TT International,* 3 August — DR, 20 September 1989. The source lists all the articles amended, comparing the 1979 version with the 1989 amendment. For the relevant articles in the 1979 constitution, see also *MECS* 1979–80, pp. 433–34. For the result of the referendum, see SWB, 31 July 1989.
34. *Resalat,* 22 April — SWB, 26 April; *JI,* 3 May — SWB, 4 May; *Ettela'at*, 25 April 1989.
35. *Ettela'at*, 25 April 1989.
36. Ibid.
37. *TT,* 1 May 1989.
38. This does not mean that the authors of the constitution wished to give the new leader more power than Khomeyni had had, or that the authors of the first constitution wished to limit Khomeyni's authority. Khomeyni did not have to depend on the constitution, he was above it. By contrast, the very need to specify the new leader's additional powers testifies to his weakness, not to his strength.
39. *TT,* 23 April — SWB, 26 April 1989.
40. *Abrar,* 25 April — SWB, 28 April 1989.
41. *TT,* 27 June 1989.
42. IRNA (in English), 12 June — DR, 13 June 1989.
43. Araki (nearly 100 years old) was once Khomeyni's teacher. Following Khameneh'i's nomination, a group of prominent theologians declared him a *marja'-e taqlid*: IRNA (in English), 12 June — DR, 12 June 1989.
44. Such arguments based on what Khomeyni said privately had little legal weight, since the imam in his last will warned against attempts to attribute views to him. He wrote that no view attributed to him is acceptable "unless I have said it in my own voice [therefore available on tape] or has my signature, with the affirmation of the experts, or what I said on the television of the Islamic Republic" (see Khomeyni's will mentioned in Note 12, p. 62).
45. R. Tehran, 9 June — SWB, 12 June; *Kayhan,* Tehran, 11 June 1989.

46. IRNA, 16 June — SWB, 19 June 1989.
47. R. Tehran, 9 June — SWB, 12 June 1989.
48. *Resalat* — DR, 5 June 1989.
49. R. Tehran, 8 June — SWB, 12 June 1989.
50. *Ettela'at*, 17 June; IRNA (in English), 16 June — SWB, 19 June 1989.
51. R. Tehran, 13 June — SWB, 15 June 1989.
52. Such arguments were raised by Rafsanjani and Hujjat al-Islam Muhammad 'Ali Dastgheib who based their conclusion on Khomeyni's letter to Meshkini, which referred to the selection "of someone," in the singular. *Kayhan,* Tehran, 11 June, and R. Tehran, 9, 12 June — SWB, 14 June 1989.
53. R. Tehran, 12 June — SWB, 14 June 1989.
54. R. Tehran, 8 June — DR, 9 June 1989.
55. *Ettela'at*, 19 June; IRNA (in English), 19 June — SWB, 21 June 1989.
56. In the previous four elections, the Council of Guardians also used its constitutional prerogative to thin out the ranks of the candidates. No fewer than 124 applied in 1980, but only eight were approved; in 1981, 71 applied, but only four were approved; again in 1981, 45 applied but only four were approved; and in 1985, 45 candidates applied, but only three were approved. (For a similar argument while thinning out the ranks of candidates in previous election campaigns, see *MECS*, 1979–80, p. 447; 1980–81, pp. 539 and 544; and 1984–85, p. 425).
57. R. Tehran, 10 July — DR, 11 July 1989.
58. Sheybani (58) was a medical doctor trained in France. He was a member of the Council of the Revolution (1979) and following the resignation of Prime Minister Mehdi Bazargan (November 1979) he was minister of agriculture. He won a seat for Tehran in all three Majlis elections and was one of the candidates in the first presidential elections, when he received 2.8% of the votes, as compared with 91% for Abul-Hasan Bani Sadr, 4.4% for Raja'i, and 1.8% for Asghar-Owladi. He later served as the chancellor of Tehran University and headed Iran's Medical Association. Sheybani was often critical of the social and economic situation under the Islamic regime. In 1982, he published an open letter criticizing the high rents, inflation, shortages (including those of essential medicines), and the sorry state of public transport. The nation could not be expected to bear this state of affairs much longer, he said. He rejected the argument customarily put forward by the government that "revolutionary patience" was needed; time was running out, he said (see *MECS* 1981–82, p. 548).
59. *TT*, 11 April 1989.
60. *Ettela'at*, 8 May 1989.
61. R. Tehran, 17 July — SWB, 19 July 1989.
62. *JI*, 11 July — DR, 18 July 1989.
63. The following statements are from his campaign speech, Tehran TV, 20 July — DR, 21 July; interview with *Resalat* — DR, 7 August; his speech upon taking his presidential oath, R. Tehran, 3 August — DR, 4 August 1989, and in taking his oath before the Majlis on 17 August, R. Tehran, 17 August — DR, 19 August 1989.
64. Tehran TV, 20 July — SWB, 22 July 1989.
65. *TT*, 20 July 1989.
66. R. Tehran, 25 July — DR, 26 July 1989.
67. *JI*, 19 July 1989.
68. Ibid., 23 July 1989.
69. R. Tehran, 14 July — SWB, 17 July 1989.
70. IRNA (in English), 27 July — DR, 27 July 1989.
71. R. Iran Toilers, 19 July — SWB, 21 July 1989.
72. R. Iran Toilers, 27 July — SWB, 31 July 1989.
73. R. Tehran, 3 August — DR, 4 August, and SWB, 5 August 1989.
74. R. Tehran, 30 July — SWB, 1 August 1989.
75. *JI*, 30 July — DR, 11 August 1989.
76. R. Tehran, 31 July — DR, 8 August 1989.
77. R. Tehran, 3 August — DR, 3 August, and SWB, 5 August 1989.
78. *TT*, 9 August — SWB, 10 August 1989.

79.   *Abrar,* 20 August — DR, 21 August 1989.
80.   IRNA (in English), 27 August — SWB, 29 August; *Ettela'at,* 27, 28, 29, 30 August 1989. Some people, Rafsanjani said, suggested ministerial portfolios should be offered only to those who had studied in Iran.
81.   Habibi (52), French-trained in law and sociology, was minister of justice since 1984 (he has also served for a brief period as minister of higher education in 1979).
82.   Karubi (52) joined Khomeyni's movement in the early 1960s and was imprisoned several times under the shah. In 1987, he was Khomeyni's representative to the Hajj, when clashes led to hundreds of casualties. His brother Hujjat al-Islam Hasan Karubi was involved in the arms deals with the US and Israel; *Iran Focus,* 5 November 1989.
83.   Over half of the Majlis deputies urged Rafsanjani to retain Mohtashami as the minister of the interior. In a letter signed by 138 deputies — and read in an open session of the House on 19 August — they claimed that because of the "sensitivity of the arrogant world" towards this issue, "the presence of powerful personalities in the future cabinet is inevitable," IRNA (in English), 19 August — SWB, 21 August 1989.
84.   R. Tehran, 27 August — SWB, 29 August 1989.
85.   Rafsanjani presented the policy guidelines at the swearing-in ceremony in the Majlis on 17 August (R. Tehran, 17 August — SWB, 19 August); at a meeting with the Foreign Ministry's staff on 23 August (R. Tehran, 23 August — SWB, 25 August); when presenting his government to the Majlis (R. Tehran, 27 August — SWB, 29 August); and in a Friday prayer sermon on 1 September (R. Tehran, 1 September — SWB, 4 September 1989).
86.   Tehran TV, 4 October — DR, 5 October 1989.
87.   *Iran Focus,* November 1989, p. 2.
88.   *Iran Focus,* November 1989, p. 3.
89.   *Ettela'at,* 17 October 1989.
90.   *Ettela'at,* 23 December 1989.
91.   *JI,* 24 December 1989.
92.   *TT,* 24 December 1989.
93.   *Kayhan,* Tehran, 25 December 1989.
94.   *Ettela'at,* 28 December 1989.
95.   *TT,* 31 December 1989.
96.   Tehran TV, 8 January — DR, 9 January 1990.
97.   *Ettela'at,* 12 December — DR, 21 December 1989. See also his interview in *Kayhan,* Tehran, 11 December 1989.
98.   *NYT,* 10 October 1989.
99.   *Ettela'at,* 2 September 1989.
100. Ibid., 9 October 1989.
101. Ibid., 23 October 1989.
102. Ibid., 28 October 1989.
103. Ibid., 23 October; *Iran Focus,* November 1989, p. 3.
104. *Ettela'at,* 23 October 1989. See, similarly, words of Iraj Fazel, ibid., 17 October 1989.
105. Ibid., 22 October 1989.
106. Ibid., 24, 25 October 1989.
107. Ibid., 25 October 1989.
108. See their statements quoted in ibid., 9, 18, 20 September, respectively.
109. *Ettela'at,* 2 September 1989.
110. *Middle East Insider,* 16 September 1989.
111. *Ettela'at,* 23 October 1989.
112. For Rafsanjani's views, R. Tehran, 20, 30 June — SWB, 22 June, 3 July 1989.
113. Tehran TV, 28 June — SWB, 1 July 1989.
114. R. Tehran, 24 June — SWB, 26 June 1989.
115. This continuity was pointed out by Rafsanjani: R. Tehran, 20 June — SWB, 22 June 1989.
116. This could be inferred, for example, from the commentary of R. Tehran, 22 June — SWB, 24 June 1989.
117. R. Tehran, 24 June — SWB, 26 June 1989.
118. *Ettela'at,* 20 September 1989.
119. Ibid., 24 September 1989.

120. Ibid., 10 October 1989.
121. Ibid., 23 October 1989.
122. R. Tehran, 6 July — SWB, 10 July 1989.
123. R. Tehran, 7 July — SWB, 10 , 11 July 1989.
124. R. Tehran, 10 July — SWB, 12 July 1989.
125. R. Tehran, 14 July — SWB, 17 July 1989.
126. *TT*, 1 January 1990.

Iraq
(Al-Jumhuriyya al-'Iraqiyya)

OFRA BENGIO

The period of no-peace no-war that followed the cease-fire with Iran in August 1988 exposed the imbalances in the Iraqi polity and society. Iraq looked like a giant trying to balance himself on a tightrope and though quite successful, the inherent dangers in the situation could not be overlooked. If geographically Iraq emerged from the war intact, the outcome was less clear-cut on the national level. About 20% of the Iraqi population — the Kurds — proved they were "Kurds first," and it was now the task of the rulers in Baghdad to inculcate them with the Iraqi patriotism which they had always rejected, and to integrate them forcibly into the national body. The Hashemite family, which had ruled Iraq from 1921-58 and which the Ba'th had vilified as a symbol of anti-Iraqism, was now suddenly raised from the ashes to provide the depth lacking in Iraq's modern history and nationalism. This search for positive symbols of unity was complemented by energetic efforts to reconstruct both ancient Babylon and the modern cities and towns which had been damaged during the eight-year-long war.

But the manipulation of history did not hide the problems of the present and the growing pressures for change in the totalitarian system. The regime attempted to swim with the tide by declaring its commitment to democracy, but it did little more than make cosmetic changes. The disliked Ba'th Party was losing more and more ground, but no alternatives were allowed to emerge. Nor was a free press tolerated beyond providing a safety valve for public frustration.

This frustration was sharpened by the lack of progress in the peace talks with Iran, by the serious economic and social dislocations which both the war and the move toward privatization had caused, and finally by the heavy expenditures on the standing Army and the development of military industry. If Iraqis had expected that the end of the war would alleviate pressures and better their economic conditions, they were deeply disappointed. The military industrialization gained further impetus after the war, throwing into relief the imbalance between a developed arms industry and a fragile economy, between a strong Army and a weakened society.

Displaying Iraq's military might became an important device not only for quelling dissent at home but also for promoting Iraq's standing abroad. The conventional and nonconventional arms in its arsenal and the reputation it had gained by using them were manipulated by Iraq to deter Iran from renewing the fighting. In also signaling its peaceful intentions toward Iran, Iraq often threatened Israel, thus attempting to strike a renewed balance between its orientations on the Gulf and on the Fertile Crescent. Iraq's self-projection as a regional power encouraged it to stake a claim, however disguised, to a leading role in the Arab world. Though the general atmosphere in the Arab arena was no longer congenial to such a role, Baghdad came to be viewed

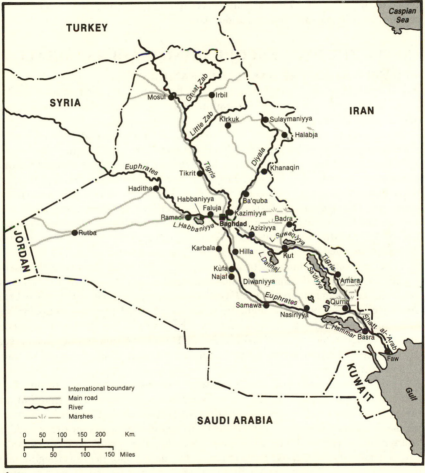

Iraq

by some, not merely by itself, as actually playing such a part. Iraq's preoccupation with its military buildup overshadowed all other issues in its foreign relations. The secret network which it had spread out in Western Europe and the US was aimed at securing sophisticated technologies, officially banned by the West for export, and at bypassing the problem of Iraqi debts, which weighed heavily on those relations.

Thus, the more precarious the internal social and economic situation became, the stronger was Baghdad's tendency to display its military strength and project to the world the image of an invincible country, commanding the awe of its neighbors and the respect of its partners in the world at large.

AFTER THE WAR: ENCOURAGING IRAQI NATIONALISM

REHABILITATING THE HASHEMITE FAMILY

No sooner had the war ended than the Iraqi leadership launched an all-out effort aimed at deepening the sense of Iraqi nationalism by arousing pride in ancient glories and the more recent past.

One of the most extraordinary developments of the period under review was the rehabilitation of the Hashemite family, which had been ousted from power in July 1958 and had been reviled ever since as traitorous and anti-Iraqi. President Saddam Husayn's visit on 4 July 1988 to the royal cemetery at al-A'zamiyya (together with King Husayn of Jordan) signaled the beginning of this effort. The government earmarked 1m. Iraqi dinars (ID) for the reconstruction of the cemetery in which King Faysal I and King Ghazi were buried, and to where the remains of King Faysal II, who had been killed during the July 1958 revolution, were moved.[1] The rehabilitation drive also included the publication of books and articles portraying the Hashemite family as patriots and builders of new Iraq, the construction of a special museum devoted to the family, the classification of 2m. documents belonging to the Hashemite era,[2] and the placing of a replica of Faysal I's statue where it had stood before being destroyed in July 1958. Throughout, it was emphasized that the campaign was undertaken on the initiative of Saddam Husayn and was not the result of outside pressures (such as by Jordan's Hashemite king, Husayn). A sign at the cemetery read: "The cemetery was reconstructed at the time of President Husayn to remind Iraqis who protected their past."[3]

On the national level, the rehabilitation of the past was designed to give Iraqi nationalism historical content and to emphasize elements of continuity, tradition, and unity, rather than the discontinuity and disunity that were broadly current among the people. The concern to cut loose from the image of the one-party state drove Saddam Husayn to weaken the Ba'th, or at least lower its public profile and to stress that national interests stood above party interests. On the sociopolitical level, legitimizing the Hashemite family implied a legitimization of the middle and upper class of the monarchy with a clear message of tolerance toward the emerging new middle class which Husayn was keen to encourage. Husayn, who no longer believed that peasants and workers could form the backbone of his regime, was looking for a new class which would both benefit from and acclaim his policies. The move could also be interpreted as a signal that Iraq was distancing itself still further from the revolutionary era and embarking on a period of stability and construction. It was also a gesture of gratitude to King Husayn of Jordan, who had stood by Iraq throughout the war. On the personal level, the gesture was meant to help portray Saddam Husayn as a national figure of historic magnitude, who could forgive and forget, who stood above any party and group and could thus forge the unity of the people, bringing them grandeur and glory. As one poet put it: "Saddam in this country is the country."[4]

The link that Husayn sought to create between himself and the Hashemite family was illustrated by his order to write a history book entitled *From Faysal I to Saddam Husayn*.[5] Furthermore, Husayn sought to create a firmer link to the history of Mesopotamia by posing as Nebuchadnezzar II[6] with all that figure's historic connotations. To lend more substance to this link he ordered the reconstruction of ancient Babylon while the war was still raging. It took three years and 1,000 workers to complete the project by September 1989, and the huge sums of money required while the economy was in deep crisis showed where Husayn's priorities lay. Indeed, focusing attention on the past became a way of diverting attention from the difficulties of the present.

THE RECONSTRUCTION DRIVE

The nationwide reconstruction program embarked upon at the beginning of the year had different motives and aims. To start with, it reflected Husayn's vision of his own role in history: having adopted a new honorific, "the leader of victory and peace," and seeking to pose as the builder of the Iraqi nation and state, he could not let the ruins lay untouched for long and cast a shadow on this image. It was also of utmost importance to efface the war from the Iraqis' memory. The involvement of different sectors of the Iraqi society in the reconstruction projects was meant to increase their patriotism, to provide them with employment, and to keep an eye on them. Externally, the projects were meant to demonstrate Iraq's peaceful intentions, win support from Arab countries, and attract international investment.

Basra, which had been hit most by the war, was first on the list for reconstruction. By Iraqi accounts, it was rebuilt in the record time of 120 days and nights — between February and June — with the participation of 20,000 architects and technicians, all under Husayn's direct supervision.[7] Military units from the 3rd and 7th Corps, as well as the Republican Guard and government ministries, contributed to the effort which cost %5bn.[8] and in which 15m. Iraqis reportedly participated.[9] The authorities offered various benefits to people willing to live in Basra, while obliging proprietors of houses to rebuild them at their own expense.

The reconstruction of Faw, which began immediately afterward (in mid-June) had symbolic, emotional, and psychological implications. According to Husayn, 52,858 Iraqis had died in Faw.[10] If the estimate (by foreign observers) of 160,000 dead was correct,[11] then the death toll in Faw was about one third of the Iraqi total. To emphasize the city's importance in Iraq's national life, its name was changed to "The City of Sacrifice and the Gate of the Great Victory"; 17 April, the day of its liberation, was declared a national holiday (along with 8 August, the end of the war). The government also called on all Iraqis to participate in the reconstruction endeavor either by volunteering a day's work or by contributing money; immediately, more than 2m. Iraqis reportedly volunteered and more than 3m. contributed money.[12]

Wishing to turn Faw into a pan-Arab symbol as well, Baghdad set up a special Iraqi-Arab committee for the reconstruction of the town and called on all Arabs to contribute money for the project, "so that every Arab can feel he has participated in one way or another in the reconstruction of Faw."[13] Upon completion of the rebuilding in mid-October, huge celebrations were held in the town with the participation of leaders from all over the Arab world. Probably facing pressures from other parts of the country, especially Mosul, which had been put in the shade, Husayn ordered that reconstruction projects begin there concurrently with that of Faw. At the same time, work went ahead on other sites, such as new Halabja in the north and the offshore terminals in the south.

MOVES TOWARD DEMOCRACY: MUCH ADO ABOUT NOTHING?

In November 1988, Saddam Husayn had already raised the idea of democratizing the Iraqi political system (see *MECS* 1988 p. 503), but only in early 1989 did the debate on it become public. There were domestic and foreign stimuli for this move. There was no doubt that the Soviet-style reforms had been a model for emulation. Iraqi papers had discussed the Soviet *perestroika* (economic liberalization) and, though more rarely, *glasnost* (political liberalization) too.[14] Domestically, the economic and social pressures were of utmost significance. The economic reforms that had been introduced two years earlier demanded a political complement. The Iraqis, like the Soviets, understood the dialectical relation between the two, though they may not have been willing to go as far.

The public debate revolved around three central issues: drafting a permanent constitution (the country had had several "provisional constitutions" since the July 1958 revolution), introducing a multiparty system, and granting freedom to the press. Although the three elements were interrelated and complementary, each had its own rationale and was meant to achieve a different goal (see below).

On 26 February, three committees were set up to discuss the political system's democratization. One, headed by 'Izzat Ibrahim al-Duri, deputy chairman of the Revolutionary Command Council (RCC) and assistant secretary general of the Ba'th Party Regional Command (RC), was to prepare the draft of a new constitution. Another, headed by RCC member and First Deputy Prime Minister Taha Yasin Ramadan, was to draft a law for the reorganization of party life. The assignment of the third, headed by Minister of Culture and Information Latif Nusayyif al-Jasim, was to draft a law on the freedom of the press. Meanwhile, the question of democracy and a multiparty system was thrown open for discussion. Taking the lead, Saddam Husayn rejected claims that the leadership had been forced to take the step as the result of a crisis. He asserted that he had raised the idea of the multiparty system in 1982 and though his colleagues were initially reluctant, they finally accepted it. Discussing the content and essence of democracy, Husayn warned repeatedly against copying blindly Western concepts and practice of democracy, because "we would be committing a historic mistake, which could bring about dictatorship instead of democracy." He explained that Iraq had been practising democracy for a long time but that it "had not succeeded in showing it"; therefore, the task was now to implement "better forms of democracy."[15] Elaborating further on the democratic model suitable for Iraq, the minister of culture and information said it should be "a centralized democracy" *dimuqratiyya markaziyya* (i.e., a communist-style democracy), not a liberal Western one. Furthermore, "democracy in its right form" he asserted, should not be confused with anarchy.[16] On the question of "democratic administration" and the role of the leader, *al-Thawra* maintained that the latter should keep his leading role in society, especially in a time of ordeals and challenges.[17]

If opposition parties had entertained any hopes of being included in the move toward democratization, they were soon disappointed. Concerning a multiparty system, *al-Thawra* explained that Iraq must have special rules governing it, among them that "negative parties" should not be licensed, that the Ba'th should retain its leading role, and that the formula of a National Front be finished with (the National Front was set up in 1973 and included pro-Iraqi Kurdish groups). Regarding the "positive parties," the following criteria should be applied to them:

(1) They should be patriotic (*wataniyya*) in breed and tendencies.

(2) Their concepts and deeds should be commensurate with the revolution's "pan-Arab and progressive line."

(3) "Qadisiyyat Saddam" — the war with Iran — would be the touchstone of their patriotism and loyalty. Accordingly, parties which had supported the enemy would not be licensed, even though they tried to appear under "new names." *Al-Thawra* mentioned specifically the Iraqi Communist Party (ICP) and al-Da'wa — an underground Shi'i movement.[18] For their part, different officials made it crystal clear that in the new democracy there would be no place for the ICP, al-Da'wa, or for Kurdish groups headed by Mas'ud Barazani and Jalal Talabani.[19]

By the end of the year, the promises for political reforms had hardly been fulfilled. None of the committees published their conclusions; no "new" opposition parties were allowed to organize; freedom of expression was suppressed; and many of the laws limiting personal freedoms remained in force.[20] An opposition paper ridiculed the idea from the outset: "Here the winds of democracy and the gases of freedom [i.e, an allusion to the chemical weapons used against the Kurds] are peeping at you once again....A new sun has arisen...Square-like with a green spot on it. This is the sun of democracy in the era of the Arabs' second Nebuchadnezzar."[21]

EXPERIMENTING WITH A FREE PRESS

For a brief period at the beginning of the year, an outstanding experiment in liberalizing the press took place. Hitherto, the press had been under the complete control of the authorities and hence only a propaganda tool. Behind this initiative were the grievances caused by both the war, and the transition to peace, and the need to allow them a legitimate outlet. Undoubtedly the Soviet *glasnost* was an important model for imitation. The timing might have been influenced by three unconnected events: the coup attempt by the military; the formation of the Arab Cooperation Council (ACC) in mid-February (see below), and the desire to project a democratic image to the other members, especially Egypt; and finally, the elections to the National Assembly scheduled for 1 April.

Giving the green light to the new experiment, Saddam Husayn told journalists on one occasion: "Write without reservation, hesitation, or fear that the state might not be satisfied with what you write." This pronouncement became the motto of the democratization campaign in the months to come,[22] and behind which the more daring journalists attempted to hide. Not leaving Husayn's statement hanging in the air, the RCC on 16 January issued a directive to Minister of Information Latif Nusayyif al-Jasim, to enable Iraqis to complain against misdeeds of officials and ministries, and to publish these complaints in the press.[23] Going a step further, Jasim later called on the journalists, on behalf of the leadership to listen to different views and to "criticize and analyze wrong social phenomena," but in "a balanced manner."[24]

A few journalists dared to take up the challenge, though very cautiously. One of them — who, however, chose to write under the pseudonym "Juhayna" — in a series of four articles in al-Thawra, attacked the Iraqi press for relying solely on the official Iraqi News Agency (INA) as a source of information; for lacking the courage to criticize and to investigate incidents; for being dull, unimaginative, and superficial; and, in short, for not being genuine journalists.[25] Another exceptional event was the press conference held by RCC member and Foreign Minister Tariq 'Aziz on 22 February on orders from Saddam Husayn. The conference was unique because, for the first time, an Iraqi official other than Saddam Husayn himself was allowed to hold a press conference for the local Iraqi press.[26] It was a rare case of Iraqi journalists criticizing the government or at least questioning some of its policies. One hundred journalists attended the press conference, and it was reported in all the Iraqi media, but only al-Thawra printed the questions and the names of the journalists asking them. As the conference was occasioned by the formation of the ACC, some journalists questioned the wisdom of this new alignment on different ideological, political, and social grounds (see below).[27] An even more outspoken deviation from the accepted code of Iraqi journalism was a satirical article in al-'Iraq, the pro-Iraqi Kurdish organ, which used allegory to attack the misdeeds of the Ba'th regime, the corruption of officials who had become millionaires, and the suffering caused to the people by corrupt economic policies. Even President Husayn did not escape unscathed, being referred to as "the leader whose justice is sharper than the sword." Aware that he might have gone too far, the writer Sabah al-Lami remarked that in spite of the danger to himself, he could not remain silent concerning these corrupt policies: "God will not be pleased with you if you choose to remain silent," he asserted.[28]

Another article in al-'Iraq by 'Abd al-'Aziz al-Rawi chided journalists and editors who did not dare to write freely as they had been asked to do and, moreover, attempted to hinder others from criticizing under the pretext that "the enemy might benefit from this." He concluded by saying that "democracy means democracy," and advised his colleagues to read Husayn's views on the issue.[29] Another paper, al-Qadisiyya, criticized some journalists and men of letters for becoming "men for all seasons," writing without target or aim and neglecting their duty of telling the truth to the new generation. Another journalist in the same paper complained of attempts to bribe him in order to silence his criticism, indicating that he had managed to escape pressures.[30] He called on his colleagues to break their silence, quoting the Talmudic question: "If not now, then when?"

This was too much for the authorities to swallow. Fearing that the trickle might become a flood, they quickly dammed it up. An article in al-Thawra attacked journalists for criticizing for the sake of criticism and for attacking the authorities as if they were Iraq's "worst enemies." The minister of information made an open attack on journalists who had lost their balance, who used pseudonyms and hid their identity, in a "surrealistic" manner, who interpreted democracy as anarchy, and "who rose as stars and fell as quickly."[31] With this, the experiment ended. The more daring journalists had already stopped writing, the others toed the line. The committee headed by the minister of information, which was set up in February to plan for freedom of the press, had not published its conclusions by the end of 1989. What did not change, however, was the publication in the press, of letters of complaint, but these were only on the social and economic problems of the individual himself.

NATIONAL ASSEMBLY ELECTIONS: THE SAME OLD GAME
The National Assembly (*al-majlis al-watani*) elections, held on 1 April, were described by the authorities as a major turning point in the democratization of the country's political system. In fact, they were not. A comparison with the assembly elections in June 1980 and October 1984 shows that no substantial change had taken place with regard to the assembly's powers and to the political forces entitled to be represented in it (see *MECS* 1979–80, pp. 506–507; 1984–85, pp. 464–65).

If the Iraqi opposition had interpreted Husayn's promises of November 1988 regarding the multiparty system as permission to nominate candidates to the assembly, they were greatly mistaken. Rather than opening up toward opposition groups, the authorities actually increased their precautions against such an eventuality. An amendment to the Assembly Law of 1980 in February 1989 added the following conditions for candidacy: the candidate's parents should not be of foreign origin (i.e., not Iranian?); the candidate should have contributed effectively to the war against Iran, and should share the belief that the war had crowned Iraq with glory "and had been the indispensable means of safeguarding Iraqi territory, waters, airspace, security, and shrines"; the candidate should not have deserted from the Army or failed to enlist during the war; and should not have plotted against the regime.[32] Taken together, these restrictions were meant to ensure that no opposition groups or individuals would find their way into the legislature.

Nor was the government any more inclined to allow the military and security services to vote than it had been in the 1984 elections, even though this was a violation of the law (see *MECS* 1984–85, p. 464). This ban was all the more striking since at the time of elections this element of the population numbered more than 1m. people, who had carried the main burden for the regime's survival and the war's outcome. That the regime disregarded such an important sector of society, who had expected to vote, indicated its concern about the possibility of their intervention in politics and its determination to prevent this by all possible means. On election day, all the military and security services were ordered to remain with their units.[33]

As if these restrictions were not sufficient, the government took additional steps which emptied the elections of any political content. Although the authorities had had a seven-month period to prepare the list of candidates (the elections had been postponed twice since August 1988), the list was published only a fortnight before the elections. Campaigning itself was very poor and the little that occurred focused on the candidates' personal qualifications — mainly their contribution to the war effort — rather than their political views (elections were held on a personal, rather than party basis). To grant all candidates equal opportunities, the government paid the campaign expenses, but stipulated that a candidate who failed to win 5% of the vote would have to repay the government.[34] In addition, there were various organizational problems on election day, such as erroneous voters' lists, lack of transportation, and difficulties for illiterates to participate.

Nevertheless, the outcome of the elections was instructive, shedding light on the changes in the Ba'th Party and its place in politics. Most striking was the relatively low number of successful Ba'thi candidates: c. 100 out of a total of 250, or about 40% of the assembly, compared with 90% in 1980 and 73% in 1984.[35] This steep fall in Ba'thi representation could hardly be accidental. True, in part, it reflected "natural" erosion in the party's standing. But perhaps to a greater extent, it seemed to have been the result of premeditated policy on the part of Husayn. One indication of this was the small number of Ba'thi candidates: 260 out of 910.[36] According to *al-Yawm al-Sabi'*, the Ba'th directed its cadres not to present their candidacy so as to allow other social sectors to present theirs.[37] Another was the meager representation of trade union leaders, which in the past used to be totally subordinated to the Ba'th. Husayn doubtless wanted to prove that the Ba'th no longer had a monopoly on power; election results proved this, and showed that Iraq was entering a new era of democracy and political pluralism. Yet the truth remained that while Ba'thi membership was cut by half, no alternative party or oppositionist was allowed to emerge. Those "independent" assemblymen were in one way or another dependent upon the government. Out of 250 assemblymen, more than 150 were government officials.[38] In contrast to the past, no ministers were included in the assembly, and the only one who presented his candidacy, Hashim Hasan 'Aqrawi, failed. Furthermore, the number of women representatives was cut by six, from 33 to 27, indicating their loss of status in society.

Another point worth noting was the high percentage of new faces: only 20 members of the former assembly remained in the new one.[39] One important figure who lost his post was former speaker Sa'dun Hammadi, who did not even present his candidacy, probably because of certain disagreements regarding the assembly's powers (see *MECS* 1988, p. 509). During the discussions on political reforms, Hammadi had been most critical of the Assembly Law and had demanded increasing the body's power.[40] The new Speaker, Sa'di Mahdi Salih, a member of the Ba'th Party RC since 1982, seemed readier to follow the government's line. Husayn appeared to have used the elections to get rid of persons more clearly identified with the Ba'th and to refurbish the assembly by introducing new faces, persons who had little parliamentary experience and thus less likely to make trouble.

Speaking on the eve of the elections, 'Izzat Ibrahim al-Duri, chairman of the higher committee supervising the elections, raised the possibility of dissolving the RCC, the country's highest legislative and executive body, and distributing its powers among the parliament, the council of ministers, and the president. But nothing had happened by the end of the year, and the assembly continued to be a rubber stamp of the government. It neither passed any important laws nor did it use its prerogative to dismiss ministers. (One of the laws it did pass permitted using corneas of persons condemned to death for surgical transplants.)[41] For all intents and purposes, the assembly became another vehicle for mobilizing support for the regime in general and for Husayn in particular. One of the first "projects" of the assemblymen was to contribute in person to the reconstruction of Faw and thus lead the campaign for mobilizing the people's support for the reconstruction effort.[42]

FUNCTIONING OF THE GOVERNMENT

THE FAMILY MUSICAL CHAIRS

Despite all the talk on democratization of the system, family rule remained unchanged. Yet 1989 witnessed the decline in the influence of one branch of Husayn's family and the ascendancy of two others. The former, the maternal branch, included Husayn's wife — Sajida Talfah — who was also his cousin, and her brother 'Adnan Khayrallah Talfah, the defense minister and deputy prime minister. The causes of the estrangement between the Talfahs and the president were not altogether clear, but persistent rumors maintained that it was due to Husayn's marriage to a certain Samira Shahbandar, or his taking her as a mistress. Incensed, Talfah sided with Sajida, as did Husayn's son, 'Uday, who in October 1988 had killed Husayn's personal bodyguard for having reportedly acted as an intermediary between Husayn and Samira[43] (for the killing, see *MECS* 1988, p. 507–508).

There was no way to verify this story, which seemed like one out of "the tales of a thousand and one nights." More important, however, was that it circulated widely in Baghdad, causing Husayn considerable embarrassment. His sensitiveness to the matter and his attempts to refute the rumors could be gauged by his allowing his wife a degree of access to the media, something he had never done before.

These intricate family relations may or may not have affected Talfah's standing, but beyond doubt, his power began to decline after the cease-fire with Iran (see *MECS* 1988, p. 505), indicating that political considerations may also have been at play. Talfah had been defense minister since 1977. That he remained in office so long was unusual, because Husayn used frequent reshuffling of ministers and officials, including his own relatives, to prevent them from gathering excessive influence and followers. As long as the war with Iran went on, Talfah was needed as a symbol of continuity and for his loyal link to the Army. Changes began to appear when the war ended. Indications of differences between him and Husayn appeared over the strategy to be followed after the Iraqi offensive on Faw, in April 1988; Talfah seemed to have sought to carry it into Iranian territory. After Iraq's military successes, Talfah might have envisaged a bigger role for himself or he might have been suspected of such by Husayn. Another suggested cause of the rift between the two was a failed military coup, which was unearthed in early January 1989 (see below). In any case, in early 1989 Talfah was put in the shade: his public appearances became very rare and his involvement in political affairs declined. So conspicuous was the decline that in early March a non-Iraqi journal reported his imminent removal from office.[44]

However, on 5 May Talfah was killed in a helicopter crash. According to the official version, the helicopter was caught in a windstorm while *en route* from Mosul to Baghdad, but against a background of rumors and speculations, this version was met with much skepticism. Speculations had it that Husayn himself or the Army had been behind the killing. The official version had serious loopholes: two other helicopters which had accompanied Talfah's had not been overcome by the storm. Also, the report of the committee investigating the causes of Talfah's death was very ambiguous.[45] One could not exclude the possibility that the Army, or one of the security services, was behind the killing, or that at least Husayn held them responsible for not preventing it. Less than two months after the event, Husayn dismissed Hamid Sha'ban, the air force commander, and Fadil Barrak, chief of intelligence, who wrote a

382

Figure 1: Saddam Husayn's Family Tree

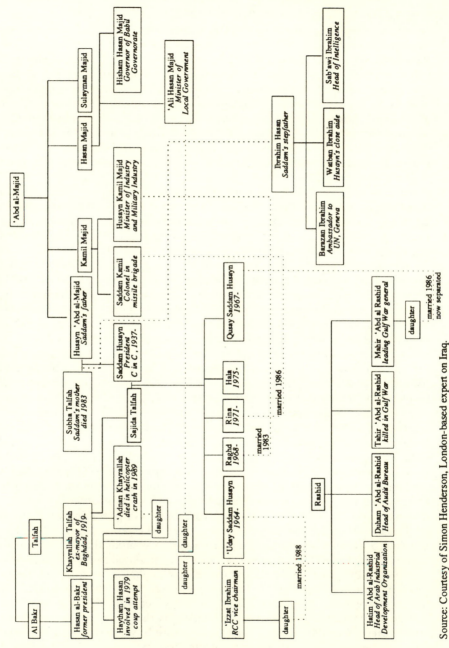

Source: Courtesy of Simon Henderson, London-based expert on Iraq.

long obituary on Talfah shortly before his own dismissal.[46] Husayn might have decided not to act immediately after the accident in order to keep up the facade of normalcy and to dispel rumors that the crash had not been an accident.

After his death Talfah was accorded the status of a national hero; among the honors bestowed on him was to have the Iraqi advanced-warning aircraft named "'Adnan 1'" after him.

The family's paternal branch fared better. The president's cousin and son-in-law, Husayn Kamil, continued to command the very important Ministry of Industry and Military Industrialization, whose achievements during the year brought him much prestige and influence. Husayn Kamil's brother, Saddam Kamil, who was also another son-in-law of the president, held another important post in the military industries. Another paternal cousin, 'Ali Hasan al-Majid, was appointed on 2 June minister of local government, replacing Dawud Salman. Majid had previously been secretary-general of the Ba'th Party's northern bureau. Other members of the family who also fared well in 1989 were Husayn's half-brothers: Barazan Husayn al-Tikriti, Sab'awi, and Watban, all of whom had been dismissed from their posts in October 1983 (see *MECS* 1983–84, pp. 468–69). Barazan, who had been chief of intelligence until then, was appointed ambassador to the Committee on Human Rights in Geneva in January 1989. In December 1989 Sab'awi was named chief of intelligence[47] while Watban became Husayn's close aide. The rehabilitation of these three half-brothers illustrates a technique widely used in 1989: advancing persons who had lost influence or fallen into disfavor. It might also have been connected with some obscure family relationship and the need to balance one branch against another, as rumors of rivalry between Husayn's cousins and his brothers might have suggested. In any case, the appointment of his half- brothers to key roles once again, gave the impression of *plus ça change plus c'est la même chose.*

RESHUFFLES

The reshuffles in government bodies in 1989 reflected three problems: socioeconomic, security, and the endemic Kurdish problem. Within five months from the beginning of the year, three Kurdish ministers and long-standing "allies" of the Ba'th lost their jobs. Babakr Mahmud Rasul (al-Pishdari), labor and social affairs minister since 1977 and member of the National Assembly in 1984, was replaced on 3 January by another Kurd, Umid Midhat Mubarak, a physician. The latter had been member of the National Assembly and adviser to the president. Another long-time Kurdish minister, 'Abdallah Isma'il Ahmad, a minister of state since 1974(!), was dismissed on 11 February, without a replacement being named. The third, Hashim Hasan 'Aqrawi, who had been state minister since 1977, was dismissed on 15 May for "poor health," and no replacement was announced. Poor health or not, 'Aqrawi was already in decline; his failure to be elected to the National Assembly was probably the final blow. The common element in these three cabinet changes was Husayn's desire to get rid of men who were no longer useful to the government or reliable go-betweens with the Kurdish population.

Acute agricultural problems (see below) were probably behind the dismissal of Minister of Agriculture and Irrigation Karim Hasan Rida (a Shi'ite) on 7 March. The decree blamed Rida for "complete failure in managing his ministry despite the chances he was given."[48] When he was appointed, Rida was considered a bright technocrat, but the difficult agricultural problems probably overwhelmed him. It was not unlikely that he was made a scapegoat to appease popular indignation over the lack of basic food commodities, such as eggs and meat. Customers, peasants, middlemen, and the minister of agriculture, accused each other but no one took responsibility for the acute situation.[49] 'Abdallah Badr Dannuk was then appointed an acting minister of agriculture and irrigation as part of the regular practice of testing a politician by giving him a problematic ministry. Dannuk failed the test and was dismissed on 7 October, without a replacement being named.

On the same day, Minister of Finance Hikmat 'Umar Mukhaylif was also dismissed for the slowness of the economic and financial reforms, as well as for inefficiency,[50] but in his case, too, the criticism seemed to reflect general frustration with the economic reforms. Mukhaylif was also said to have fallen out with President Husayn's protégé, Minister of Industry and Military Industialization Husayn Kamil, over the latter's spending policies.[51] Trade Minister Muhammad Mahdi Salih was appointed acting finance minister. The post of acting minister was often a step up the bureaucratic ladder; thus, 'Abd al-Salam Muhammad Sa'id, who since August 1988 had been acting minister of health, a problematic portfolio, was made minister on 16 July 1989.

The serious social dislocations which appeared after the cease-fire in different parts of the country were probably behind the dismissal of Dawud Salman as minister of local government, and the appointment of a strongman 'Ali Hasan al-Majid, in his stead. At the same time, six other senior officials in the ministry were dismissed. No doubt the mobilization of all the provinces for the rebuilding of Basra (see above) had been burdensome and there was a need for scapegoats.

This last group of changes was related to Talfah's death. 'Abd al-Jabbar Shanshal was appointed minister of defense on 7 May. Shanshal had been the chief of general staff and minister of state for military affairs. An apolitical figure and a close confidant of Husayn, Shanshal was to represent continuity, stability, and the noninterference of ambitious officers in political affairs. Talfah's other post, that of deputy prime minister, was given to Sa'dun Hammadi. A Shi'ite and veteran Ba'thi, Hammadi had until the new appointment held the powerless post of minister of state for foreign affairs. His appointment could be considered a form of "rehabilitation," because since 1983 he had not held an important position. In his new post he was in charge of economic affairs, in which he had much experience, having been minister of agriculture and oil. His "rehabilitation" might also have been connected with Husayn's intent to introduce political reforms which Hammadi was known to support staunchly. Talfah's other posts of member of the RCC and RC were not filled.

LOWERING THE PROFILE OF THE BA'TH

Michel 'Aflaq, the Syrian founder-leader of the Ba'th Party, died on 23 June at the age of 79. Since the Ba'th's advent to power in Iraq in July 1968, 'Aflaq had served in the symbolic post of secretary-general of the (pro-Iraqi) Ba'th Party National (i.e., all-Arab) Command, seated in Baghdad. Over the years he had witnessed the severe erosion of the Ba'thi doctrine whose chief ideologue he was, but he had continued, nevertheless, to openly support the Iraqi Ba'th Party against its (and his) enemy, the Syrian branch, headed by Hafiz al-Asad. 'Aflaq's death provided another opportunity to display the Iraqi Ba'th's purity and voice allegiance to the original Ba'th, in contrast to the Syrian version. President Husayn himself attended the funeral in Baghdad, and stressed in his eulogy the deep friendship and ideological affinity between himself and the late 'Alfaq (though there was known to have been friction between the two in the past.) To honor 'Aflaq's memory and in keeping with the new policy of erecting statues of various people, the government decided to erect a statue of 'Aflaq in front of the Ba'th building. There was, however, one discordant note: the Ba'th announcement of 'Aflaq's death was accompanied with the "revelation" that the Christian 'Aflaq had converted to Islam at an unspecified date. Neither he nor the party had wished to publicize the conversion "in order not to give it a political interpretation."[52] Made after 'Aflaq's death, the validity of the "revelation" will probably never be known. More important was the Ba'th's attempt to detach itself from anything concerned with 'Aflaq's Christian background in order to deflect charges of unbelief and heresy which Iran kept making against the Ba'thi regime.

In a way, 'Aflaq's death symbolized the end of Ba'thi ideology. Significantly, he had no successor as the party's secretary-general. In an era when leftist-communist doctrines were undergoing reappraisal, it was only natural that the Ba'th do the same. The process had begun in early 1987, when the regime started moving away from the socialist economy (see *MECS* 1987, pp. 425–27). Most leading members of the Ba'th opposed the attempt to introduce a multiparty system which might further curtail the party's power and their own as well. The formation of the ACC (see below) was an additional drift away from the ideal of Arab unity, because it sanctioned other forms of cooperation between such Arab countries as Egypt and Iraq which were ideologically distinct. Answering a question on the contradiction between the Ba'thi ideology and the formation of the ACC, Tariq 'Aziz defended Saddam Husayn, saying that as "a true Ba'thi" and a "100% Ba'thi," he would not have taken any decision that undermined the ideology.[53]

In fact, Saddam Husayn, who sought to appear as a national leader, preferred to keep his distance from the party and its activities: gone were the days when he was referred to by his party title. If, at the beginning of the year, he was still conferring the party's insignia on Ba'thi members of 25 years' standing, he later delegated the task to 'Izzat Ibrahim al-Duri. On one occasion he even chided Ba'thi members who presented themselves to him as Ba'this, emphasizing that he would much rather have them present themselves as Iraqis "for I am sitting here on this chair on behalf of the entire Iraqi people."[54] On another occasion, he criticized Ba'this for believing that they were entitled to special privileges and that the state owed them official positions.[55]

The results of the elections to the National Assembly (see above) did not enhance the prestige of the Ba'th, or the claim of its members to public posts. The speaker of the new assembly declared that the status of those party members who had not been elected would be reconsidered.[56] The erosion in the party's position was also reflected in the decision to "freeze" the Popular Army, the Ba'th Party's militia. The decision probably meant that the Popular Army had become redundant, and rather than mobilizing support for the regime it had encouraged dissatisfaction. Despite the erosion, the Ba'th remained, until a better one appeared, the regime's chief civilian mainstay and the body which in Husayn words "leads, organizes, and mobilizes the masses."[57]

MILITARY AFFAIRS

KEEPING THE MILITARY IN CHECK

Since the end of the Gulf War, President Husayn had been following a two-track policy in military affairs: lowering the Army's public profile as far as possible, but also embarking on an ambitious program for developing Iraq's arms industry. Lowering the Army's public profile was aimed at curbing any political ambitions it might have had after the long war, and at preventing it from interfering with the political solution of the conflict with Iran. Simultaneously, Husayn had to keep the Army in good humor and prove to it that its interests were high in Iraq's order of priorities. One way of doing this was to develop the arms industry,which was also construed as serving the regime's other goals as well.

Signs of friction between the military and Husayn appeared early in the year when Army Day celebrations scheduled for the 6 January were canceled without explanation. One month later — enough time for rumors to come out into the open — non-Iraqi papers carried the story of an attempt coup against Husayn at the end of December 1988 or beginning of January 1989. The sources differed on whether there had been a coup attempt, general unrest among the military, or a preemptive measure by Husayn which cost the lives of 7–200 persons, depending on the source. It was claimed that units from the 1st, 2nd, and 5th army corps and the Republican Guard (in charge of protecting the president) were involved.[58] Foreign Minister Tariq 'Aziz promptly denied these reports. Addressing the question a month later, President Husayn ridiculed these "fabrications," saying: "Anyone currently contemplating a coup must first consider whether the Army would back it and whether the people would tolerate it for days or even hours." Husayn blamed the Jews and Zionism, which were "very unhappy about the Arab victory," for fabricating stories about the coup attempt.[59] It was impossible to verify any version of events. But it was clear that Husayn and the military had disagreed and that Husayn was out to prove that his word was final in military affairs as well. Thus, he revealed in early January that "all the commanders in the Iraqi armed forces, without exception, were very dissatisfied when Iran accepted [in July 1988] Resolution 598," because they were pursuing the Iranian forces inside Iran and "wanted to take revenge." However, Husayn asserted, "we stopped the Iraqi armies and pushed them back to their positions."[60] In the same vein, articles written by military commanders and a two-day symposium on the victory at Faw attributed to Husayn both the strategic and the tactical planning of the various battles and, hence, the victory.[61] On other occasions, Husayn sought to settle accounts with commanders who either were too ambitious or failed their duty. He referred to them as people who had "lost their balance," or had sought to evade their duty, adding that he knew each one of them. Husayn promised not to forget certain "policies and acts that resulted in the needless shedding of blood in the eight years of fighting."[62] During a meeting with the military at the end of May, Husayn extolled Hamid Sha'ban, the commander of the Air Force, for not losing his composure.[63] However, less than two months later Sha'ban was dismissed and succeeded by Muzahim Sa'b Hasan. The reasons for the dismissal were unknown, but Sha'ban, who had held the post for many years, was one of the very ambitious, publicity-conscious army officers who boasted continually about the Air Force's great role.[64] Husayn might have also held the Air Force responsible for the accident which caused Talfah's death (see above).

Until the fall of the year, Husayn sought to put the military in the shade and to keep it at arm's length. While in the past he used to confer medals of valor in person, he now delegated this task to the chief of staff or other senior commanders, who then reverted to anonymity (except for Air Force commanders, most officers were not mentioned by name). Only civilian officials were invited to take part in the opening of the military fair in Baghdad. By the end of the year, however, Husayn seemed to have mended fences with the military. On the occasion of conferring medals of valor on some of the fighters, he said: "Although this meeting comes late, rights are never lost because of the passage of time."[65] Similarly, meetings with the military high command grew more frequent, including one with the RCC and the RC of the Ba'th Party. This exceptional meeting might have been an indication of Husayn's willingness to appear as sharing power with his colleagues.

DILEMMAS OF DEMOBILIZATION

One of the most serious problems confronting the regime at the end of the war was demobilization. The dilemmas were manifold. First, there were pressures for quick demobilization from soldiers and their relatives who had become weary of military service, but rapid demobilization might have caused serious social and economic problems. Second, keeping an army of 1m. men mobilized put a heavy burden on the Iraqi treasury, not to speak of the political pressure the Army might apply. Third, as long as there was no peace with Iran, the Army was needed for any eventuality, but such a large army was an obstacle to peace, because it posed a threat to Iran. The solution was a gradual process of demobilization.

At the end of June, the government dissolved the 1st Special Army Corps, one of eight remaining ones. The corps, which was set up in May 1986 and was stationed at Wasit in the central sector, had brought back to service retired army officers "as part of the president's strategy to involve former military experts in the country's defense."[66] Iraq presented the dissolution of the corps as a signal to Iran of Baghdad's peaceful intentions. But Baghdad's choosing to start with this corps seemed to indicate that it was the least effective and least organized one. Husayn's speech before this corps one month prior to its dissolution reflected pressures by soldiers in the corps to evade service or to be demobilized. Anyone who felt that his health or economic condition did not allow him to remain in service could ask to be pensioned off, Husayn said. He emphasized, however, that some soldiers in good health were affected by "unpatriotic" influences and did not contribute to the war effort. Over and over again Husayn repeated the theme of patriotism and betrayal, concluding that "the man's professionalism is the way to express one's patriotism."[67] In August, he declared that from October 1988-July 1989, Iraq demobilized 203,211 soldiers.[68] By the end of the year, it announced the dissolution of another 10 divisions (c. 120,000 persons). As to those remaining in service, the government employed them in reconstruction work all over the country.[69]

At the same time, the government had to look after the soldiers still in the Army and those who had been demobilized. Among the measures it took were: granting medals of valor to officers and soldiers; allowing men with three medals of valor to live in Baghdad (even if they were not originally from the capital); giving them a car on the anniversary of the liberation of Faw;[70] setting up "central markets" with subsidized prices for families of the military, security services, and dead soldiers;[71] accepting members of the armed forces and the security services into all colleges and universities regardless of their age and even though they were five points below the required minimum average;[72] and, finally, erecting 69 statues of heroes who had fallen in Basra.

AMBITIOUS ARMS INDUSTRY PROGRAMS

The vision of Iraqi grandeur and leadership had been a permanent feature of Husayn's policies, but the means to attain it had changed from time to time. At the end of the inconclusive war, Husayn chose to focus on military industrialization, a project with far-reaching implications for both the domestic and foreign fronts. Being the initiator of the move, Husayn was out to prove that he has remained the leader and the inspiration of Iraq's future development. To further emphasize the identity between himself and military industrialization, he chose to open the first international military fair in Baghdad on the day of his birthday, 28 April, under the title: "Defensive arms in the service of peace and prosperity." Husayn's personal involvement in the military industry could also be inferred from giving his name to the "Saddam's company for military construction."[73] On the regional level, he sought to propel Iraq to a formidable position as the first Arab country to have developed sophisticated arms, thus increasing its allies' respect and its rivals' awe. (Iraq was reported to have more guns, tanks, heavy mortars,and combat aircraft than any other Arab country.)[74] The immediate address of the new message was Iran, and to a lesser extent Israel. As peace talks with Iran were deadlocked, Iraq hoped to discourage Iran from initiating any military action, by demonstrating its own armed capacity. Iraqi officials stressed Iraq's peaceful intentions and that the arms industry was intended only as a deterrent and protector of national and pan-Arab security: "We have acquired these capabilities to safeguard the dignity of this nation and to preserve its image as a nation cherishing tolerance, generosity, magnanimity, and human interaction."[75]

The intensive industrialization effort won Iraq the title of "a Middle East superpower." In a short while, Iraq had succeeded in developing various conventional and nonconventional arms, including chemical and possibly biological weapons,[76] cluster bombs, the *Ababil* missile, and the *Asad Babil* (Lion of Babylon) tank (a copy of the Soviet T-72 M-I). The Iraqi industry also modified the MiG-23 for refueling in midair, and produced an airborne warning and control system (Awacs), a project that was completed in July. On 5 December, Iraq announced the launching of a rocket capable of putting satellites into space, thereby completing the first phase of its space program. At the same time, it announced the development of two different missiles of 2,000-km. range. There were also reports on the development of the *Condor* II missile, with a 1,000-km. range, following the abandonment of the joint project with Egypt and Argentina,[77] as well as reports about the development of nuclear arms: Iraq was believed capable of achieving production capacity within five to ten years.[78] (Iraq, however, totally denied these reports.) Thus, by the end of the year, Iraq could claim to be nearing the stage of self-sufficiency in weapon production. A non-Iraqi source reported that it had started exporting Kalashnikovs, mortars, and side arms in a bid to become "an arsenal for the Third World."[79]

Iraqi officials kept declaring that Iraq was not dependent on foreign assistance for development of its arms industry, but it became clear that, in fact, this was not so. Iraq had established a secret network for acquiring technological know-how, especially in Western countries whose governments turned a blind eye to the activities of the local companies.[80] West German companies were probably in the lead, with "dozens of them" providing technology, including nuclear, to the Sa'd armament complex near Mosul.[81] Other companies were from France, Italy, Great Britain, Austria, possibly Sweden, the United States, and Canada.[82] No less important was the cooperation on the governmental level of the Soviet Union, France, Argentina, Brazil, China, and Egypt.[83] The extent of interest in Iraqi armaments and the possibilities of investment was indicated by the participation of 150 companies from 28 countries in the Baghdad international military fair.

This ambitious enterprise had occasional setbacks as well. The mysterious explosion on 17 August in the military complex for the development of missiles or chemical weapons near Hilla was a case in point. News about this explosion began to leak out three weeks later. The London daily, *The Independent,* which first carried the report, claimed that 700 persons, including scores of Egyptians, had died in the explosion, that a third of the complex was destroyed, and that it took fire-fighting planes nearly a week to extinguish the conflagration.[84] *Le Monde* reported that as many as 1,500 might have died in the explosion.[85] No longer able to conceal the matter, Baghdad released its own version: an explosion took place at a petroleum by-product factory, causing the death of 19 Iraqis, but no Egyptians; the fire was extinguished in only a few hours.[86] There was no way to verify either of the versions, but the fact that the government's statement was released so late clearly detracted from its credibility.

More serious were the strains that this program created in the economy. According to Associated Press, allocations for this sector in the next few years could amount to $20bn.[87] *Mideast Markets* foresaw a possibility of domestic disquiet over the amount being spent on the missile program.[88] There were also indications of friction between different ministries concerning allocations from the state budget. Husayn Kamil, the strongman in the Ministry of Industry and Military Industrialization, boasted in an interview that his ministry had carried out various civilian projects in record time, while other ministries, including Housing and Reconstruction, had failed altogether. He called on the other ministries to emulate the example of the arms industry.[89]

SOCIAL AND ECONOMIC PROBLEMS

The economic strains grew worse after the war, because of the burden of the huge reconstruction and industrialization projects, and a foreign debt of $50bn.–$82bn.[90] Symptomatic of the difficulties were an annual inflation rate of 35%–40%[91] and increasing unemployment, which threatened to jeopardize internal stability and foreign relations. To cope with the problem, Baghdad unleashed a two-pronged propaganda campaign to quell discontent at home and to convince its foreign partners to continue doing business with it. The line adopted stressed the following that: (1) the economic difficulties were the natural outcome of the war, and that Iraqis should endure the hardships exactly as they had in wartime; (2) Iraq's problems were not structural; hence, Iraqis and foreigners alike were advised to distinguish between short-term liquidity difficulties and a long-term economic problem; (3) most importantly, Iraq's huge oil reserves, estimated at more than 100bn. barrels, held out the promise of a bright future for the economy.

Meanwhile, Iraq continued to develop new oil projects, including the beginning of oil production in east Baghdad, to mark Husayn's birthday at the end of April. In

September, the second stage of the Iraqi-Saudi pipeline was completed, boosting its capacity from 500,000 barrels per day (b/d) to 1,650,000 b/d. At the end of November, Iraq's Opec-allotted quota was increased from 2,926 m. b/d to 3,140m. b/d. However, for all the optimistic outlook, Iraq's major foreign creditors became impatient with its tactics of playing off different countries against others, and pressed for settlement of the debts. Some countries like Great Britain, France, Turkey, and Japan reached an agreement during the year for the rescheduling of debts (see also below). Others, like India or Brazil, did not. Iraq's payments of debts were made mainly with oil.

TENSIONS BETWEEN STATE EMPLOYEES AND THE PRIVATE SECTOR
One of the government's most difficult problems was to reconcile privatization with the pressing needs of the Iraqi individual. This commitment to privatization was a departure from the Ba'th's socialist ideology in the party's early years. All private-sector enterprises were granted complete tax exemption for 10 years.[92] State enterprises in the fields of agriculture, tourism, transport, and other nonmilitary industries were put up for sale to private individuals. For the first time the private sector was allowed to advertise in the media. The government even suggested establishing private banks that would compete with the state banks (al-Rafidayn and al-Rashid). Other incentives given to the private sector included the possibility of importing without foreign transfers, the easing of price controls on local products, and their lifting entirely on wages.[93]

The privatization policy had its genesis at the height of the war (see *MECS* 1987, pp. 430–34), but it was continued after it. It was stressed that the economy would become even freer and that this change did not contradict the socialist policy of the past. The new direction had a number of economic, social, and political roots. As the experience in the Communist bloc has shown, there was great disillusionment with the socialist economy. The need was felt to ease pressures on the state budget, to encourage foreign investment, and to improve the standard of living. Saddam Husayn also hoped to turn the emerging middle and upper class into a new bastion of support in the form of political parties that would compete with the Ba'th. Although he disbanded the public-sector trade union in 1987 (see *MECS* 1987, pp. 432–34), he allowed the formation, in May 1989, of the chamber of industry (separately from the chamber of commerce).[94] Even earlier, the monthly *al-Hadara,* and the weekly *al-Ittihad,* representing the views of these sectors, were allowed publication.[95]

The rapid growth and enrichment of the private sector antagonized many elements in Iraqi society. Wartime hardships were not only still being felt in many areas, but had even increased now that the war was over. Letters of complaint filled the newspapers, and journalists criticized undesirable economic and social phenomena, which they blamed mostly on the private sector.[96]

Rising prices were the most acute problem. An article in *al-Thawra* complained that prices had increased tenfold in a very short period, a rate which it claimed was unparalleled throughout the whole world.[97] The price rises affected basic foodstuffs and housing. House rents in Baghdad were greater than the monthly salaries of employees.[98] Basic foodstuffs and commodities disappeared from the market, a black market developed, and economic crime became common. Criticism was so outspoken that the government redoubled the efforts of the economic security administration (*mudiriyyat al-amn al-iqtisadi*), sent its personnel to all parts of the country, and encouraged citizens to complain through a special telephone line open around the clock.[99] But these measures had no effect: even the head of security had to admit that price rises and economic crime continued unabated.[100]

Husayn was unwilling to antagonize such wide sectors of society lest not only the new economic policy but also the regime's very survival be put in jeopardy. Accordingly, he adopted a series of measures meant to redress these social and economic imbalances, particularly as they affected state employees and members of the armed forces and the security services, either because he considered them the most vulnerable to the liberalization policy or because he sought to buy their goodwill, or both. He ordered the opening of "central markets" for state employees and members of the armed forces, where fruits and vegetables would be available at prices lower than in the free market. State employees and soldiers were also entitled to buy one electronic item every five years,[101] itself an indication of the severe shortage. Then he imposed a ban on the sale of more than one enterprise to one person or group, which he justified by the "need to distribute the national wealth in a manner that does not lead to the creation of monopoly."[102] In March the government decided to sell houses to members of the above-mentioned group at reduced prices, in addition to other benefits. In April, it imposed price controls on basic commodities, which had been lifted in 1988. However, these measures were probably ineffective because, in June, Husayn ordered an ID25 wage increase for government employees as well as for military and public security personnel. According to *al-Thawra,* this was a substantial increase, because monthly wages were ID54-ID78. The paper said that 10.6m. wage earners benefited from the increase.[103] In addition, the government also froze prices for one year.

Far from easing pressures, these measures only served to exacerbate the basic problems. The "central markets" created new problems of rationing, queuing, the disappearance of commodities, crowded markets, and favoritism to certain customers. Despite the price controls, newspapers continued to complain about skyrocketing prices. Nor was the salary increase any consolation to its recipients, who saw the growing gap between themselves and people in the private sector. They sought to solve their economic problems by engaging in private enterprise as well, undoubtedly exploiting their official positions to gain access to this additional source of income. This phenomenon seemed to have reached such endemic proportions in agriculture, where all activity became concentrated in private hands and quick enrichment became so common, that in March the government forbade leasing of agricultural land to state employees, including members of the armed forces.[104] *Al-Thawra* sharply criticized the "illogical" and "unnatural" enrichment of government employees by various legal and illegal methods and called on the government and the Ba'thi apparatus to weed out this phenomenon. Yet the rush to private enterprise continued unabated, forcing the government to devote a special session at the end of the year to discuss the problem. Husayn explained that he had proposed discussing whether to allow civil servants to work at part-time jobs, because the law banning it was no longer suitable. He warned, however, against opening the private sector to all state officials, stressing that it was not right to open the private sector to senior officials, because doing so would create an economy neither capitalist nor socialist.[105] Some officials disagreed, thus facing Husayn with a dilemma: either to clash with his colleagues and the bureaucracy or to approve of processes he himself had unleashed, but was no longer able to control.

TENSION BETWEEN IRAQIS AND EGYPTIANS

The socioeconomic crisis pitted Iraqis against Egyptians, whose number was estimated at 1m.–2m.[106] The Egyptians started arriving in Iraq in small numbers in 1973, but their number grew during the war, when they played a crucial role in saving the Iraqi economy from total collapse. However, with the war over, they became more of a liability than an asset. They became an easy target for frustrations and dissatisfactions felt by different Iraqi groups. The Egyptians occupied jobs which were now badly needed by soldiers demobilized from the Army and the Popular Army. The remittances Egyptians sent home weighed heavily on Iraqi finances. Not only Egyptian laborers came to be regarded with envy, but even more so Egyptian doctors, university professors, engineers, and technicians, who earned more than their Iraqi counterparts.[107] Egyptians also came to be blamed for corruption and immorality.

An inkling of Iraqi xenophobic feelings toward Egyptians was given by an Iraqi journalist who questioned the wisdom of allowing Egyptians free entry into the country, because, he claimed, they were largely responsible for the price rises, especially of foodstuffs, which affected the average Iraqi. At the formal declaration of the ACC (see below), Tariq 'Aziz angrily rejected the allegations and emphasized that on the contrary, the Egyptians had benefited the Iraqi economy. He justified the free-entry policy by the needs of Iraq's dynamic economy and its huge reconstruction programs.[108] However, despite such public statements defending the free-entry policy, government policy was quite ambiguous. On the one hand, the authorities neither wished to antagonize Egypt nor to turn the ACC agreement into a dead letter. But, on the other hand, they also had to contend with growing economic and social pressures for a quick reduction in the number of Egyptians. It was also possible that the government feared the undesirable effects the problem might have on domestic politics — there were rumors that friction was especially severe between Iraqi Shi'ites and the (Sunni) Egyptians, and that Egyptian displays of excessive religiosity were not to the government's liking. Accordingly, the government "encouraged" the exodus of Egyptians by placing ever-growing restrictions on their remittances home. Egyptian sources even claimed that the Iraqi authorities had turned a blind eye to misdeeds against Egyptians in order to hasten their departure. Nor did Iraqi officials hide the fact that this policy was prompted by the problems of unemployment and the huge Iraqi debts, which would take four or five years to ease.

At the beginning of the year, an Egyptian paper reported the growing unemployment faced by Egyptians remaining in Iraq, the maltreatment they sometimes experienced, and the hostility Iraqis harbored toward them.[109] Another paper in June reported the cumbersome Iraqi regulations governing the dispatch of remittances, which were sometimes delayed for as much as 18 months, thus prompting Egyptians to leave the country.[110] Egyptian workers were also required to work extra hours without pay and to contribute two months' salary for the reconstruction of Faw.[111] Meanwhile, tension continued to build up following the explosion in August (see above), which caused the death of an unverified number of Egyptian workers, and the authorities' decision at the beginning of October to further restrict remittances. Matters came to a head following reports in early October of physical assault and unexplained deaths of

Egyptians.[112] In less than two months, 200,000 panic-stricken Egyptians left.[113] The Egyptian media reacted with many stories of Egyptians being robbed, discriminated against, and intimidated in an organized fashion. Anti-Iraqi feeling became so widespread among the population in Egypt that Saddam Husayn felt it necessary to meet Egyptian workers, on 15 November, and explain the situation by postwar difficulties and by the growing number of traffic incidents, in which those Egyptians met their death.[114] However, his hope of containing the crisis was dashed two days later when, during a public demonstration by c. 5,000 Egyptians in Baghdad celebrating Egypt's victory over Algeria in a hotly contested world cup football match, an Iraqi-owned car ran over some Egyptians. In the violent clashes which ensued between Iraqis and Egyptians, one Egyptian died and 70 were injured (several Egyptians died, according to *Le Monde*).[115]

Those developments aroused the concern of the Iraqi authorities, not only because of their effect on relations with Egypt, but more so because of their domestic repercussions. A centralized and a totalitarian regime, such as the Ba'th, could not allow matters to get out of hand, or permit such spontaneous demonstrations or clashes to occur. Neither could the regime tolerate secrets concerning domestic developments being divulged by individual Egyptians and the Egyptian media. Accordingly, the government quickly arranged additional flights to Egypt and promised to pay $50m. in compensation by the end of the year to Egyptian workers who had returned and to whom Iraq owed a total of c. $350m. But such palliatives neither satisfied the returnees nor appeased Egyptian popular sentiments. In the midst of all this, RCC member Taha Yasin Ramadan affirmed that relations between Iraq and Egypt were "ideal" both on the popular and official levels.[116] (On the Iraqi-Egyptian crisis, see also chapter on Egypt.)

OTHER SOCIOECONOMIC PRESSURES

Economic distress, combined with a general sense of slackening the reins in the aftermath of the war, caused social problems about which one could learn from the drastic measures taken to meet them. One such area of pressures was road accidents. So severe must have the problem become that the government decided to confiscate cars breaking the speed limit on quick roads. In July alone it confiscated 40 such cars. Husayn justified this measure by the need to stop the "anarchy" on the road and to teach others a lesson, "as we are a people in the making, which needs to be disciplined."[117] Husayn explained the high number of accidents by the inexperience of "military personnel" who had bought cars at reduced prices during the war but did not know how to drive. He further attributed "violence" in society to the long years of war as "some of those who fought during this long period use their fists more readily than their tongues."[118]

Socioeconomic pressures were felt primarily in three main fields: health, education, and housing. As in the past, health services suffered most. These services, which could not cope with the double burden of the military and civilians, added insult to injury by collecting fees from civilians for services that had been free in the past. The government explained the measure by the need to grant incentives to personnel and to improve the health services. The pressures on public clinics prompted the flourishing of private sector clinics which, as in other areas, exploited the situation to accumulate quick riches. Hundreds of such clinics were closed down by the government for their poor services.[119]

The pressures on the education system, especially the universities, also increased after the war as more and more demobilized soldiers felt entitled to enter them. To meet the problem, the authorities imposed a number of restrictions, such as that an entrance application could be submitted only two years after graduating from high school, that only persons below 40 years of age could apply, and that applications could be sent only to one university at any one time.[120] No less acute was the problem of housing which according to *Alif Ba* was in a real state of crisis.[121] The problem was compounded by the continuous influx into Baghdad and by the great number of people married between August 1988 and August 1989, which reached 500,000 people,[122] compared with 228,658 in the two years between 1985–87.[123] Symptomatic of the severity of the problems and the government's inability to cope with them was that it no longer encouraged *publicly* a higher birthrate, indicating a break with a policy adopted in 1986.

THE CRISIS OF THE OPPOSITION

In a book published shortly before the end of the war, Muhammad Taqi al-Mudarrisi, the leader of the Shi'ite opposition group *Munazzamat al-'amal-al-Islami*, lamented the weakness and ineffectiveness of the Iraqi opposition. He attributed it to the lack of self-confidence; reliance on outside forces, such as Iran, to do the opposition's job; internal conflicts and lack of unity; its inability to reach out to the Iraqi masses; and, finally, the opposition's inability to adapt to the regime's new methods of crushing it.[124] This weakness increased after the war, reaching what even the opposition described as "stagnation."[125] Each of the opposition parties, the Communists, the Kurds, and the Islamic fundamentalist groupings, underwent a severe crisis in 1989. Its general causes were Iraq's conceived victory in the war, which made it easier for the Ba'th to crush the opposition and to tighten its control over the country; Iran's diminishing support of all opposition groups; and, finally, deep frustration of Iraqis over the opposition's ability to improve the situation. More specifically, the Kurdish groups had to face the destruction of their bases in the Kurdish region; the Islamic groupings had to deal with further disintegration and inaction; while the ICP had to adapt itself to the swift changes in the Communist bloc, which ended whatever commitment the Soviet Union had for the ICP, and put the party's legitimacy into question. Aware of the vulnerability of the ICP, which had come to lead a shadowy existence, the regime increased its propaganda attack on it. The move for democracy initiated by the Ba'th at the beginning of the year bewildered the opposition even further, because it was not included. In addition the move was likely to refurbish the regime's image and to strengthen its standing at home and abroad. In March, the opposition groups attempted unsuccessfully for the umpteenth time to form a united front, this time under Syrian auspices.

THE PLIGHT OF THE KURDS

The situation of the Kurds after the war resembled in many respects that after the collapse of the Kurdish rebellion in March 1975. In both cases, Iran, the major supporter of the Kurdish national movement, stopped giving aid for political reasons, thus dealing the movement a death blow. In both cases, there was also an exodus of

Kurdish refugees who feared the retaliation of the Ba'thi authorities (in the first case to Iran and in the second to Turkey). In both cases, the Iraqi Government seized the opportunity not only to crush the rebellion and to extend its control over the Kurdish area, but also to introduce changes in the infrastructure and the social fabric of the area that would make any new revolt impossible. However, for all the similarities, the change in Kurdistan this time was much more thorough, systematic, and drastic, making it appear at times irreversible. It seemed that the eruption of the Kurdish rebellion during the Iraqi-Iranian War, in spite of the earlier measures, convinced Baghdad to adopt a much more severe policy this time.

Immediately after the collapse of the Kurdish movement in the autumn of 1988 (see *MECS* 1988, pp. 521–25), the authorities began a large-scale relocation of Kurds residing reportedly at a distance of 30 km.–60 km. from the Syrian, Turkish, and Iranian borders.[126] Initially, Baghdad denied having taken such action; however, the picture began to emerge first from indirect reports in the Iraqi press, and then directly from Iraqi officials. At first, they said that both Kurds and Arabs living along the Iranian border had been moved in compensation for their suffering during the war, or as the information minister, put it, "they have spent many years not having life at all."[127] Then they said that the villagers were being relocated from remote areas closer to the center to enable the government to provide them with the services and facilities of modern life. In this vein, Husayn claimed that "if they remain in those distant mountains...we cannot reach or protect them under such difficult circumstances. They also cannot live a decent and stable life or improve their economic conditions. We want another standard of living for them. This is the whole truth".[128] Behind this humanitarian language lay the real motive, which, according to Tariq 'Aziz, was to establish a 30 km.-deep security belt empty of any population.[129] This policy had four aims: to cut the lifeline to Iran and Syria of the Kurdish guerrillas who had their headquarters near the borders; to prevent Kurdish villagers from giving logistical support to the guerrillas; to put the population of the border areas under close surveillance by moving them to more accessible areas; and, finally, to destroy Kurdish loyalties and social structure so as to make it more difficult to organize against the regime. Admitting the lack of loyalty of the Kurds in those areas, Husayn said: "We have decided that they should be moved to enable them to get rid of this dualism in personality. At night, they are blackmailed by the rebels, during the day, they say that they are with the government...therefore this area has remained in trouble."[130]

The 1989 transfer program was different from that of 1975 in three respects. First, it encompassed not only Kurdish villages, but towns; second, it involved razing all structures in areas included in the plan; and third, the population was probably transferred within the Kurdish area itself, not to the Shi'i south, as in 1975. The first phase of the plan called for laying down the infrastructure for cluster settlements (*tajammu'at sakaniyya*) or "modern towns," mainly in the governorate of Irbil, which was more accessible than other areas and in Sulaymaniyya; in Irbil, there were reportedly 20 such settlements.[131] This part of the plan seemed to have been completed by April, when Husayn made three visits to the area, probably in an attempt to convince the Kurds to move to the new settlements voluntarily. Simultaneously, the government announced various incentives, such as the decision in April to provide free housing,[132] a plot of agricultural land, and from ID1,500–ID3,000 for constructing new houses. Townspeople were given the higher sum but these sums were hardly an incentive or compensation, because the cost of building a house was estimated at ID5,000–ID10,000.[133]

The resettlement program began with the inauguration at the end of April of the "new Saddamiyyat Halabja" to replace the old Halabja, which Iraqi forces had attacked with chemical weapons a year earlier. Named after Husyan and inaugurated on his birthday, the new town was 32 km. from the border inside the Sulaymaniyya governorate[134] and under the watchful eye of a nearby military camp.[135] The government then proceeded to destroy other villages and towns and move their inhabitants deeper within Kurdistan. This action included Twasoran, Khalkan, Dukan, and Surdash, the latter having been the headquarters of Jalal Talabani, the leader of the Patriotic Union of Kurdistan (PUK).[136] The strongest resistance was put by the town of Qal'a Diza, whose inhabitants were warned to leave it by 18 June. Only 1,000 families, of the town's 70,000 inhabitants, did so. Earlier in April, the senior Kurdish religious leader, Muhammad Delgaii, came to Baghdad to get Husayn to change the plan, but he was jailed. The authorities then offered an indemnity of ID10,000 to the town's residents,[137] but even this sum did not convince them to move. In the face of continuing resistance, the authorities decided to evacuate them by force, including the reported use of tanks.[138]

There were contradictory reports as to the fate of these places, but most agreed that they were leveled to the ground. Other reports suggested that some places remained intact to enable the government to move on to the second stage of the plan, namely to Arabize the region by populating it with Iraqi Arabs, or even with Egyptians.[139] There were also contradictory reports as to the number of deportees. Tariq 'Aziz stated that "all of these residents were evicted 30 km. within Iraqi territory,"[140] including, he said, people from the Basra, Diyala, and Wasit areas in the south. But it seemed quite probable that non-Kurdish areas were not included. Ja'far 'Abd al-Karim al-Barzanji, the then governor of Sulaymaniyya, and a strong supporter of the regime, stated that 595,000 families [sic!] had been resettled by August.[141] Al-Jumhuriyya reported that 134,000 houses would be built in the new towns in the north by the end of the year.[142] The Economist claimed that 1,500,000 Kurds had been relocated.[143] Other non-Iraqi sources and the Kurdish opposition estimated the number of people included in the last wave of resettlements — small-scale ones had begun in 1987 — at 200,000–300,000 people.[144] There were also conflicting reports regarding the number of villages involved. The government announced in January its intention to contract the number of villages which had reached 12,500 in order to overcome the problem of the dispersal of villages over a large area, but it did not mention the Kurds.[145] According to the Kurdish opposition sources, 4,000 villages had been destroyed since 1975, a similar number being cited by The Economist, which probably used the same sources.[146] Other sources put the number in the hundreds. There was no way of verifying these figures, but even if the lower estimates were correct, the campaign had been ruthless. A reporter who visited the area said it had been turned into a desert.[147]

At the same time and in an attempt to belittle the importance of the Kurds in the state, Iraqi officials initiated what might be termed a "campaign of demographic disinformation." For example, only 36 Kurds were elected to the National Assembly (see above) which, the new Speaker said, represented their true proportion in the population, i.e., less than 15%.[148] Later, he lowered this percentage, stating that Kurds numbered 2m. in a population of 17m. or less than 12% and that they were the fourth largest Kurdish community in the world, i.e, after the USSR.[149]These assertions, which were later repeated, either indicated wishful thinking on the part of the government or future plans. In 1985, the lowest estimate of the Iraqi Kurdish population put it at 3m. and the highest at 4.3m. The number of Kurdish-speakers was estimated at 3.39m. or 22% of the total population.[150]

The regime accompanied the resettlement efforts with measures designed to spread its control over the north. The Iraqi Army, with two of its nine corps stationed in strategic areas, moved to what used to be "the Kurdish liberated zone" and in the newly depopulated zone. A non-Iraqi journalist who visited the area said army control was total.[151] Renewed efforts were also made to spread the Ba'th Party organization in the Kurdish area. Paradoxically, when party activity was significantly weakened in other parts of Iraq, it was reinvigorated in the Kurdish area. The man who carried out this policy was none other than the Shi'ite Hasan 'Ali (al-'Amiri), an RCC and RC member who assumed the office of the secretary-general of the Northern Bureau around April. At the same time, the regime apparently became disillusioned with the Kurds allied with it, because they proved unreliable or ineffective. Various pro-Iraqi Kurdish personalities and groupings were purged and, as mentioned above, two long-standing Kurdish ministers were deprived of their portfolios, leaving the Cabinet with only four Kurdish ministers, which may have indicated the government's intention to decrease Kurdish representation. Another reshuffle occurred in the pro-Iraqi Kurdish Democratic Party (KDP): its veteran secretary-general Hashim Hasan 'Aqrawi was replaced for "health reasons" by Muhammad Sa'id al-Atrushi. Additional changes followed elections to the Legislative Assembly.

The regime gave great publicity to the elections, on 9 September, to the Legislative Assembly of the Kurdish autonomous region. Husayn and other officials contended that the Kurds had "a right and a half," as they were entitled to vote in elections to the National Assembly in Baghdad and to the Kurdish Legislative Assembly.[152] Ostensibly the Legislative Assembly represented the autonomous will of the Kurds, but it was doubtful whether the elections to the sixth assembly were freer than to the previous five, and whether representatives of different shades of opinion were elected. It appeared that the scrutiny of the candidates became even stricter. Not even one member of the pro-Iraqi Kurdish groups — the KDP and the Kurdish Revolutionary Party — or of the Kurdish opposition was allowed to run for election. Many of the candidates, perhaps the majority, were Ba'this, which was a contradiction in terms: a Kurd who was supposed to represent the Kurdish nationality became an instrument for spreading a pan-Arab ideology. Candidates also had to have contributed to the war effort, or participated in the Popular Army or the auxiliary Kurdish forces which had been used against the Kurdish population and the guerrillas. Fifty new members were elected, two of them women. The Legislative Assembly's new Speaker was Baha al-Din Ahmad Faraj (succeeding 'Ahmad 'Abd al-Qadir al-Naqshbandi) and the new head of the Executive Council — the "Cabinet" of the autonomous region — was Ja'far 'Abd al-Karim Barzanji (succeeding Sirwan al-Jaff), a veteran Ba'thi.

The Kurdish opposition in exile called the elections a farce, and even Kurds inside Iraq dared criticize them and the autonomy in general. Reflecting this criticism, Saddam Husayn said at the swearing-in ceremony on 17 October: "Whoever wants to settle down and voice his own ideas on how to apply the autonomy better than we do, let him come forward." But he said he would not grant privileges "to the misled and the deviants," who had brought the Iranians to Halabja and "almost gave them al-Sulaymaniyya" (for the Kurdish-Iranian collaboration, see *MECS* 1988, p. 521). Probably reacting to criticism of the assembly's limited powers (on this, see *MECS* 1979–80, pp. 511–12), Husayn told members: "When you work better...you encourage us to consider how to improve your powers." However, he warned them to read their powers carefully and not to amend them unless they "accorded with Saddam Husayn's instructions."[153]

The Kuwaiti *al-Siyasa* described the Kurdish autonomy in Iraq as "the Hyde Park" of the Arab world;[154] Iraqi officials also stressed the superior status of the Kurds in Iraq as compared to other countries, especially Iran. The Speaker of the National Assembly said that there were 18 Kurdish papers and periodicals, and that both the radio and the television had special programs in Kurdish.[155] Still, the question remained whether these privileges counterbalanced the social and economic misery brought on by the regime's ruthless policies. One problem that was probably more acute in Kurdistan than elsewhere was unemployment. Referring to it, Saddam Husayn explained that "since some of our sons in the Kurdistan region...got used to living by their guns," it was extremely important to teach them to live by their work and bring stability to the area.[156] Another problem was political persecution. Both Amnesty International and the Arab Organization for Human Rights pointed to severe persecution of Kurds, including the torture and even execution of hundreds of children for political reasons.[157] Most antagonizing of all was the policy of mass deportation, which had caused economic and social dislocation all over Kurdistan.

The Kurdish movement became all but paralyzed after the government campaign in the north where guerrilla activities almost stopped. There was no organized resistance against relocation. Leaders and many rank-and-file members of the various groups, and their families, fled abroad and were dispersed in various countries: Turkey (with the 50,000–60,000 refugees), Iran, Syria, and European countries, especially West Germany, Great Britain, and France (which in the fall accepted 300 Kurdish refugees from Turkey). What changed the picture overnight was the use of chemical weapons against Kurdish civilians (see *MECS* 1988, pp. 521–23). Kurdish leaders admitted that fear of this weapon had reached the level of "mass psychosis."[158] It forced them to change their tactics. Instead of the traditional guerrilla operations inside Kurdistan which could turn their families into victims of chemical attacks, Kurdish leaders considered using hit-and-run operations by well-trained commandos against Iraqi military installations, oil installations, and other targets, as well as terrorist attacks on government officials, and members of the Army and security services in central and southern Iraq.[159] But the guerrillas' access to Kurdistan became more and more difficult. Turkey would not permit attacks from across its border. Iran, which would have welcomed the revival of Kurdish action, was reluctant to jeopardize the fragile cease-fire. Syria did not use the Kurds against Iraq, in spite of the latter's extensive support for Syria's enemies in Lebanon (see chapter on inter-Arab relations). But what weakened the Kurds most was the security belt.

Faced with these difficulties, the Kurdish opposition, which had belatedly awakened to the importance of political activities abroad, attempted to mobilize world public opinion to stop the mass deportations and Western military aid to Iraq. But beyond propaganda achievements, such as the first international conference on the Kurds held in October in France, political gains were nil. Ridiculing those Kurds "who have chosen to knock on the doors of Paris, Washington, and London," Husayn said that even if they continued to do so for a thousand years, the Kurds would never achieve their aims: "We are not afraid of five or six persons who speak to the press."[160] The Kurdish opposition did not present much of a challenge, either at home or abroad. In 1988, all the Kurdish groups including the KDP headed by Mas'ud Barazani and the PUK headed by Jalal Talabani, and four other smaller groups, formed the Iraqi Kurdish Front with the declared aim of fighting for self-determination. Seen from the perspective of 1989, they appeared farther than ever from achieving their goal, but neither was the government any closer to its declared aim of molding the entire population into an Iraqi nation. The government had gained physical control over the Kurds, but at the price of raising a wall of spiritual and emotional separation which probably also deepened the Kurds' national identity.

FOREIGN RELATIONS: THE REGIONAL ARENA

IRAQ AND IRAN: NO PEACE, NO WAR

The cease-fire between Iran and Iraq which came into force in August 1988, ushered in a new era of no-peace no-war between the parties. Their relationships were marked now by sterile and half-hearted attempts to negotiate for peace, coupled with mutual propaganda attacks and occasional cease-fire violations.

During the period under review, the UN secretary-general undertook three initiatives to bring the parties to the negotiating table, in January-February, April, and November. After three failed rounds of talks in 1988, the parties appeared keener in early 1989 on reaching an understanding. In a gesture of goodwill, Baghdad consented to the formation of a joint Iraqi-Iranian military committee (to which it was opposed earlier). It lifted the ban on civilian flights to and from Tehran through its airspace and released 255 wounded Iranian prisoners of war. Iran reciprocated by releasing 233 Iraqi prisoners. The immediate cause of this newfound flexibility was the parties' desire to secure the renewal of the UN peacekeeping force's mandate, which was due to expire in February. On 8 February, the Security Council renewed the mandate for another six months and Secretary-General Javier Pérez de Cuellar took the opportunity to hold talks with the foreign ministers of the two countries, who, after a one-hour face-to-face meeting, agreed to renew direct peace talks at the end of March. However, no sooner was the renewal secured than the parties reverted to their hostility. The joint military committee was never formed, mutual acrimonious attacks were renewed with greater vigor, and in mid-March there was a serious case of exchange of fire in the southern sector. A UN report, warning about the fragility of the cease-fire, said that, since August 1988, there had been 1,960 complaints concerning cease-fire violations, 25% of which were confirmed by UN observers.[161] After a long delay, the two foreign ministers held another round of talks between 20–24 April in Geneva with the UN secretary-general, but nothing came of them. Another mediation attempt was made in November by the secretary-general's representative during a 14-day shuttle between Baghdad and Tehran, but this failed as well.

That the negotiations failed was hardly surprising. The effects of the long years of war could not be effaced easily, however eager the parties were to achieve a peace agreement. In fact, they may not have been eager to pay the price for peace. The way the war ended, in addition to various internal and external developments in its aftermath, hardly encouraged making concessions to each other, so the parties once again found themselves locked in a no-peace situation. Iraq held three trump cards in its hands: the confidence of a victor, its control of Iranian territory (2,600 sq. km., according to Iran), and its mighty military industry. It used every opportunity to project itself as victor; as one commentary maintained: "The Iraqi negotiator goes to Geneva out of positions of victory and stabilized confidence and belief in peace."[162] Husayn emphasized that there was a difference "between a country that calls for peace while still capable of winning militarily and a country that cannot continue on the field of battle."[163] But Iran had its own trump cards as well: it held 70,000 Iraqi prisoners of war (against 30,000–50,000 Iranians in Iraqi hands), to which Iraq had become increasingly sensitive, possibly because of pressures from their families at home; Iran still held the keys to the opening of the Shatt al-'Arab to navigation; and it was emerging from its international isolation, as illustrated in the middle of the year by the Soviet decision to sell it weapons. Emphasizing that "Iraq cannot live without the Arvand River" (the Shatt al-'Arab), an Iranian commentary called on Iran to exploit the time factor in order to achieve military self-sufficiency and to strengthen its armed forces.[164] Clearly, the military buildup in both countries hardly encouraged the holding of serious peace talks.

But the fundamental problem underlying all others was the validity of the 1975 Algiers agreement which divided sovereignty over the Shatt al-'Arab between Iraq and Iran along the *Talweg* line (before that, Iraq had sovereignty over the whole Shatt). Iraq maintained that the agreement was no longer valid as Iran had abrogated it *de facto,* though not formally, even before Iraq had done so on the eve of the war. Hence, Iraq called for a new agreement that would take into consideration the war and its results. Iran, however, contended that the agreement was still in force as Iraq had abrogated it unilaterally, and that it should remain the starting point for the peace settlement. This divergence was the main stumbling block during the various phases of the talks. When Iraq suggested exchanging prisoners of war "on a humanitarian basis," without regard to the other outstanding issues, Iran insisted on linking the exchange with general political questions, and agreed to the exchange only if it was simultaneous with the withdrawal of Iraqi troops. Iraq, however, agreed to withdraw its troops on condition that Iran recognize "Iraq's historical rights" to the Shatt al-'Arab. Similarly, when Iraq demanded that the Shatt al-'Arab be dredged and opened to navigation as part of the cease-fire on the sea, Iran demanded that the troops be withdrawn before or together with the dredging. Then Iraq again demanded Iran's recognition of Baghdad's rights in the Shatt al-'Arab which Iran again denied, with the two of them moving round and round in the same circle. Indeed, a concession by either of the parties on the Shatt al-'Arab would have undermined the reason for the war and would have made it even more senseless in the eyes of their people. For Iraq to give up sovereignty to the Shatt-al-'Arab would have meant that even the minimal original war aims had not been achieved. For Iran to renege on this point, would have implied the same, but also acquiescence to the unilateral abrogation of treaties, which could have had implications for any future agreements.

When all was said and done, there seemed to be a certain asymmetry between the two: Iraq showed itself more anxious than Iran to achieve a settlement. In one of his speeches, Saddam Husayn declared: "You will find that we are not harboring grudges despite the depth of the tragedy the Iranian regime's behavior left in our hearts and in the society. You will also find that we care for peace as much as we care for the pupils of our eyes. We covet nothing in Iran...."[165] Iran usually belittled such declarations as a propaganda ploy. Even so, there seems to be a certain truth to them. First, Husayn wished to enter history as "the hero of peace," as he had come to be referred to. Second, though posing as the victor, Husayn was fully aware of the precariousness of the victory and that strategically speaking, Iran was the stronger of the two. Finally, Husayn might have calculated that the military advantages that had helped him tip the balance of war to his side, such as chemical weapons or long-range missiles, might not remain an Iraqi monopoly for long. He seemed to be playing a double game: flaunting Iraq's deterrent capabilities while also signaling his desire for peace.

Among the many steps that Iraq had taken to demonstrate its goodwill toward Iran and its commitment to peace, Husayn mentioned the withdrawal of Iraqi troops from deep within Iran on the eve of the cease-fire contrary to the advice of his military commanders, but in order to give Iran "a chance to reconsider its stands" (it was claimed that Iraq had pulled out of an area of 10,000 sq. km.).[166] Other gestures mentioned by Husayn were the demobilization of forces (see above) and the reconstruction of the cities hit by the war. With regard to the Shatt al-'Arab, although Iraqi officials kept declaring that it was "by all standards and definitions — an Iraqi river,"[167] the impression created was that they attempted to play down the issue and even suggested that the sovereignty problem could be discussed during peace negotiations.[168] In fact, Iraq had reduced even further its dependence on the Shatt al-'Arab as its only outlet to the sea by building oil pipelines to Saudi Arabia and deepening the small ports of Mina al-Bakr, Khor al-Zubayr, and Umm Qasr. Iraqi officials also mentioned the plan to divert the Shatt al-'Arab, although nothing seemed to have been done in this regard.

A very cautious evaluation at the end of 1989 would have it appear that the government was signaling to Iraqis to lower their expectations regarding the return of the Shatt to Iraqi sovereignty, while also preparing the ground for a compromise on this issue with Iran.

IRAQ, ISRAEL, AND THE PALESTINIANS

The emergence of Iraq as a regional power caused concern not only to Iran and some of Iraq's Arab neighbors, but to Israel as well. The latter's anxiety was due to three simultaneous developments signifying that after eight years of a degree of aloofness from the Arab-Israeli conflict, Iraq could once again play an active part in the dispute: Iraq's manufacture of missiles which could reach Israel, its growing involvement in Lebanon, and the deepening military cooperation with Jordan. The Israeli anxiety was counterbalanced to an extent by three other factors: the unresolved conflict with Iran was still a major Iraqi burden, the establishment of the ACC linked Baghdad even more closely with the Arab camp favoring peace negotiations with Israel, and, more directly, the green light Iraq had given to the PLO to proceed unhindered in the peace process.

The development of Iraq's military industry created a new area of friction between Iraq and Israel. When proclaiming achievements in this field, Iraq addressed itself to Israel rather than to Iran. Doing this enabled Iraq to divert the attention of the Iraqi Army and public from the conflict with Iran, and, at the same time, defuse tension with Iran by signaling that Israel, not Iran, was the main enemy. As the Iraqi Air

Force commander put it: "In our calculations, we attribute special importance to this entity [Israel], because it is the Arab nation's main enemy."[169] Iraq also sought to impress upon other Arab states that it, not Syria, had the key to the strategic balance with Israel. Last, but not least, Iraq also intended warning Israel not to repeat its attack on Iraqi military facilities such as the bombing of the Iraqi nuclear reactor in 1981, and reminding Israel that the score on that issue had not yet been settled. The recurring theme in the media and in officials' speeches was that Iraq of 1989 was completely different from that of 1981. "The special circumstances that prevented Iraq from reacting to the hostile Zionist action against the Tammuz atomic reactor for peaceful purposes in the year 1981 no longer exist," *al-Thawra* wrote. It warned that the Arabs had refrained from directing a legitimate preemptive attack against Israeli nuclear facilities for various geographical and demographic reasons. However, should "the Zionist entity attempt to harm Iraq's security, then it would expose its fragile fences to destruction."[170] The language at times became more threatening. For example: "Israel is aware that the Arab armies have in the last three years succeeded in purchasing long-range missiles capable of reaching the Zionist entity and destroying it in its strategic depth."[171] Such pronouncements usually followed revelations of the development of new weapons, such as the long-range missiles, and warnings voiced by Israeli personalities or media. Unlike the past, Iraq no longer refrained from responding to Israeli reactions to Iraq's arms development. Iraq interpreted these reactions as attempts to divert international attention from the Intifada and from Israel's own atomic, chemical, and biological weapons; to prevent progress in the Iraqi-Iranian peace talks; to denigrate Baghdad's reputation; and to inflame world public opinion against Iraq.[172]

Iraq maintained that the heart of Israel's strategy was to maintain its qualitative superiority over the Arabs. However, Iraq's technological achievements in the realm of military industry jeopardized this Israeli aim: "Israel sees that a strong and a culturally developed Arab country is rising now in the Arab East," which will play an important role in "any future confrontation with the Zionist enemy."[173] Thus, Iraq had destroyed "the myth of Israeli superiority" and created a balance of power between the Arab nation and its supporters.[174] In Iraq's view, the Intifada was also an important factor that changed the balance of power with Israel and put its very existence at risk. *Al-Thawra* predicted that the Zionist ideology and together with it Israel would cease to exist by the end of the 20th century as the country was already disintegrating socially, politically, and demographically.[175]

Iraq continued to support the Palestinians' "right of return," self-determination, and future independent state.[176] Iraqi officials declared Iraq's support for the Intifada, but only token support was given. In May, Husayn declared his decision to grant 100 scholarships to Palestinian students whose father or brothers had been martyred in the Intifada, emphasizing that Iraq did not distinguish between Palestinian martyrs and its own. In another symbolic gesture, Iraq initiated the establishment in December of the Popular Arab Front made up of various Arab countries to support the Intifada, but which remained powerless. More significant was Iraq's having given PLO chief Yasir 'Arafat a free hand in the peace process. Iraq appeared to be adopting policies similar to those of 'Arafat. Thus, when asked about Iraq's acceptance of Resolution 242 (which implied recognition of Israel and peace settlement with it), Tariq 'Aziz answered: "Our policy is to follow the PLO on this subject. After all, it is their business. In light of the fact that the PLO was prepared to accept 242, we supported it."[177] Even though Iraq itself did not formally accept Resolution 242, such a stance was a far cry from the initial Ba'thi ideological tenet which regarded the Palestinian question as an all-Arab one, the fate of which should be decided by all of them collectively.

Iraq, however, sought to increase its influence in this arena through another avenue, namely military cooperation with Jordan. This raised in Israel the specter of the revival of the "eastern front" of the late 1960s, which had included Syria as well. President Husayn offered to send military units to help King Husayn quell the unrest but the king refused (see below). In September, Iraqi corps commanders visited Jordan as King Husayn allowed two Iraqi reconnaissance flights along the Jordanian-Israeli border. The flights, which were probably aimed at obtaining information about the Israeli nuclear facility at Dimona, produced strong protests from Israel.[178]

Israel's concern over Iraq's growing military capabilities and its renewed interest in the "eastern front," prompted Israel to search for an opening to Iraq, possibly with the help of Iraq's ally, Egypt. While on a visit to Cairo in April, Reuven Merhav, director-general of the Israeli Foreign Ministry, declared Israel's wish to obtain Iraq's support to normalize relations, and even reach a peaceful settlement with it. The Iraqi response was prompt and unequivocal: the call was termed "a figment of the imagination and a scheme by the Zionist entity to conceal its aims against the sons of the Palestinian Arab people and the Arab nation." The Iraqi spokesman asserted that Iraq regarded Israel as "its enemy" and "the enemy of the Arab nation"; therefore, it was not seeking and would not seek "to normalize relations with those who usurped the land of Palestine."[179]

On 8 June, *Foreign Report* claimed that Iraq itself had approached Israel twice. In April, it had sent Jerusalem a message saying that it need not be concerned about Iraq's nuclear program, which would take 10 years to complete, and that Iraq had no intention of attacking Israel. Two months later, Baghdad asked Israel to allow freighters carrying arms and ammunition for the Maronite Christians in Lebanon to dock in the Israeli port of Haifa or the South Lebanese port of Naqura which was under Israeli control (the freighters could not dock in Beirut harbor because of Syrian bombardment). According to *Foreign Report,* Israel rejected the proposal for fear of antagonizing Syria. On the same day, an Iraqi spokesman rejected the report as "ridiculous," "empty lies," and "mere wishful thinking by Zionism," adding that "Zionism already knows Iraq's clear and frank attitude toward the Zionist entity" occupying Arab territory.[180] On 25 September, following a comment by Egyptian President Mubarak that President Husayn was not interested in maintaining a state of war with Israel, Israeli deputy foreign minister, Binyamin Netanyahu called on Mubarak to invite both the Israeli prime minister and the Iraqi president to peace talks in Cairo. Baghdad did not comment this time.[181] Another Israeli proposal in November for "reaching a strategic understanding"[182] with Iraq, with which Israel had no border disputes, likewise remained unanswered.

It appeared that while Baghdad regarded Iran as an enemy with which it needed to make peace, Israel was seen as a distant enemy with which there was no urgency or pressure to make direct peace, but which could be exploited to promote Iraq's leadership role, if the option of peace negotiations failed.

REVIVED LEADERSHIP AMBITIONS IN THE ARAB WORLD

More than 10 years had lapsed since Iraq had last made its bid for a leadership role in the Arab world (see *MECS* 1978–79, pp. 572–74). This initiative had been checked by the eight-year war with Iran, which made Iraq dependent on other Arab states, but with the war over, this ambition was revived, though on different grounds. Iraq now claimed that its victory over Iran — described by Baghdad as the first Arab victory in modern history — highlighted Iraq's role in safeguarding the entire Arab world from a catastrophe and, by implication, entitled Iraq to a leading role in the Arab world. Iraq repeatedly used this argument to pressure the weaker Arab countries into making concessions. Another, and more impressive argument, was its arms industry, which had made Iraq the most important Arab producer of weapons, thereby lending substance to its claim of holding the key to the strategic balance between the Arab world and its enemies in the region.

Given these claims, what were Iraq's expectations? Iraq expected to be accepted into the regional alliance of the Gulf Cooperation Council (GCC), set up in 1981, and to be recognized as the Gulf's new policeman; it hoped for all-Arab support in its unresolved conflict with Iran and its long-standing rivalry with Syria; and it hoped to deepen military cooperation with the Arab countries, thus turning them into the main clients of its military products, and simultaneously to attract Arab investments in the Iraqi economy.

Iraq's failed efforts to join the GCC were compensated by the formation in February of the Arab Cooperation Council (ACC) together with Egypt, Jordan, and North Yemen (for details, see chapter on inter-Arab relations). In joining the ACC, Iraq's motivations were manifold: to demonstrate its strategic depth *vis-à-vis* Iran; to use the ACC as a lever against Syria and members of the GCC, especially Saudi Arabia, and Kuwait; to demonstrate its adherence to the goal of Arab unity; to use the ACC to divert attention from difficulties at home; to strengthen its claim to a leading role in the Arab world; and, finally, by deepening economic cooperation with member states, to solve some of Iraq's financial and economic problems. Although the ACC's declared goal was economic, Iraq did not hide its intentions of diverting it along military and strategic lines, which Egypt tried to brake. The Arab countries of the Gulf realized the ACC's strategic implications and the additional leverage it gave Iraq in the Gulf. Thus, shortly after the formation of the ACC, Saudi Arabia's King Fahd visited Baghdad, where he signed "an agreement of noninterference in the internal affairs and the nonuse of force" between the two countries.[183] The timing and high level of the visit, the fact that of all four members of the ACC, Saudi Arabia felt it urgent to sign an agreement with Iraq, as well as the general context of Saudi-Iraqi relations seemed to indicate Saudi Arabia's wariness of Iraq's growing hegemonic ambitions and its need to contain them or to adapt itself to them. It was not known what Saudi Arabia paid for the agreement, but even before the signing, Iraq publicized the Saudi contribution to the reconstruction of Basra. In addition, during Fahd's visit Husayn reminded him of Saudi Arabia's earlier promise to finance the reconstruction of the atomic reactor which had been hit in 1981, implying either that Saudi Arabia had already started financing the project or that it was being pressured into doing so. (See also chapter on Saudi Arabia.)

Another member of the GCC, Bahrain, signed in December a similar agreement with Iraq. Coming after the visit of a high-ranking Iraqi military delegation to

Bahrain, the agreement aroused speculation that it was meant to provide naval facilities to Iraq.

For years Baghdad had been pressuring Kuwait to lease the islands of Warba and Bubiyan to improve its outlet to the Gulf. The leasing of the islands had acquired greater urgency because the talks with Iran were bogged down and the Shatt al-'Arab remained closed. Iraq attempted to use its border problem with Kuwait to pressure Kuwait into yielding on the issue, knowing well that Kuwait was eager to reach an agreement. (Since its establishment as a state in 1920 Iraq had been reluctant to recognize the Kuwaiti state and its borders.) During the talks, which began in February, Iraq called on Kuwait not to forget "the lessons of the war" and to keep Kuwait's interests in mind. Baghdad also described the border problem as "a thorn in the flesh" of Iraq.[184] However, neither the border agreement nor Iraq's threatening stance overcame Kuwaiti reluctance to lease the islands.

Alongside its benefits, the ACC also had certain shortcomings as far as Iraq was concerned. First, as Egypt was a partner in the alliance, Iraq could not claim the leading role. Nevertheless, it did attempt to attain the position of *primus inter pares* as indicated by the fact that Baghdad was the venue of the inaugural meeting, and that the council's chairmanship went to Husayn. Second, the ACC aroused criticism inside Iraq on ideological, political, and economic grounds. It was argued that the alliance was a far cry from the Ba'thi goal of Arab unity, that the four member states had nothing in common, that their economies were very weak, and that the other partners only, but not Iraq, would benefit from the free movement of citizens.[185] Nor did the formation of the ACC guarantee automatic support of the other members for Iraq's positions on different Arab issues. The most glaring example was their stand, notably Egypt's, on the Syrian-Lebanese problem at the Arab summit in May. So frustrated was Husayn with his inability to mobilize ACC support for Iraq's position on the issue, that he had left the summit before its end (see chapter on inter-Arab relations). Yet another annoying point was the clause in the ACC agreement, signed in April, which provided for "the noninterference in internal affairs and the nonuse of force or military intervention,"[186] thus indicating that suspicion still permeated relations among the members.

The Casablanca summit in May could be considered an important turning point in the relationship between Iraq and Egypt. Notwithstanding their membership in the ACC, relations became strained for various reasons. The two had become less dependent on each other than they had been during the war and prior to Egypt's readmission to the Arab League. Egypt's *rapprochement* with Syria during the second half of 1989 (see chapter on Egypt) angered Iraq and aroused its fears. Then came the reports on the harsh treatment of Egyptian workers in Iraq (see above), which itself might have been triggered by this *rapprochement*. Finally, there was the sharp conflict between their views on the Lebanese question (see chapter on inter-Arab relations). Thus, soon after the formation of the ACC, which marked the high point in the Iraqi-Egyptian friendship, their relations began to deteriorate. While cooperation continued in various fields, relations seemed to be losing the intimacy and special status of recent years.

As against this, Iraq's relations with Jordan continued to develop and expand to new areas. One area in which relations made progress was military cooperation. With the outbreak in April of disturbances in Jordan (see chapter on Jordan), President

Husayn rushed to Jordan to assure the king of Iraq's backing and to propose military support including the sending of Iraqi troops, and possibly the establishment of a missile base in Jordan.[187] No doubt Iraq attempted to exploit this crisis to achieve broader military cooperation, but Jordan, for its own reasons, was rather reserved: it did not agree to the entrance of troops although it was more forthcoming on other issues. It consented to the shipping of Iraqi arms via 'Aqaba to Michel 'Awn who was fighting Syria in Lebanon (see chapter on Lebanon), and to Iraqi reconnaissance flights along the Jordanian-Israeli border (see above). The king's consent to such moves, which were not devoid of risks for Jordan, was given either because it suited Jordan's interests at the moment or because he could not resist Iraqi pressures, or both. In any case, even the deepening of cooperation in this area could not paper over such problems in the economic field as the Iraqi debt to Jordan[188] and the decreased Iraqi imports and exports through 'Aqaba, which harmed the Jordanian economy.

Although Iraq did not help alleviate Jordan's economic problems, it hoped that it could solve its own with Arab aid, particularly by attracting investments from the Gulf. To this end, Iraq granted Arab investors the incentives it had granted to Iraqis, but it seemed that the response was cautious. Iraq also called on Arab countries to buy Iraqi arms at prices lower than demanded elsewhere.[189] It was not known whether Iraq succeeded in this enterprise, because it had to compete with Egypt in this field. But what was clear was that Baghdad was visited by many military delegations from Arab countries which showed increasing interest in developing arms and cooperating with Iraq to this end. Baghdad was also visited by many other Arab delegations, some of which included their countries' leaders, on different occasions, such as the Baghdad military fair and the celebrations at Faw. All this seemed to indicate the important role Iraq had begun to play in the Arab scene.

But Iraq's achievements were marred by its enmity with Syria, its chief foe in the Arab world. Iraq could neither forgive nor forget Syria's support for Iran during the war; hence Iraqi attempts to take revenge by supporting President Hafiz al-Asad's enemies in Lebanon. But Iraq's hopes were not fulfilled: it neither won unreserved Arab backing for its anti-Syrian effort, nor did it dislodge Syria from Lebanon. (See chapter on Syria and Lebanon. For further discussion of Iraq's relations with Arab states, see chapter on inter-Arab relations.)

FOREIGN RELATIONS: THE GLOBAL ARENA

THE SOVIET CHALLENGE

During the period under review, the Soviet Union posed two sets of challenges to Iraq. One was indirect: Moscow's accelerated policy of *perestroika* and *glasnost,* which had spillover effects on the whole Soviet bloc and was likely to affect Iraq as well. The other, more direct, was the Soviets' growing *rapprochement* with Iran, which peaked in the middle of the year. Linked to this was the emergence of Moscow as a major go-between in the attempts to advance peace talks between Baghdad and Tehran.

Moscow's policy of liberalization, its growing reconciliation with the West, and the breakup of the Soviet bloc system was likely to affect Baghdad in three ways: it could weaken the Soviet commitments to it as a Third World ally, it could further weaken the ICP, and it could pose as a model for emulation and, perhaps, popular demands. Judging from the discussions in the Iraqi press, *perestroika* did not go unnoticed in

Baghdad. Iraqi papers were agreed that Soviet policy would have far-reaching implications for the entire world, but refrained from discussing the implications for Iraq itself, preferring instead — rather subtly — to talk about the negative effect this policy had on its rival, Syria.[190] Baghdad also drew great satisfaction from the negative impact on the ICP, and missed no opportunity to demonstrate it. It emphasized that the Communist ideology had lost much of its attractiveness, both in the Communist world and elsewhere, that the Communist parties in the Arab and other countries proved an ineffective tool for the Soviet Union, and that these parties were shocked by the new Soviet policy which had cast them in deep crisis and isolated them further from their society.[191]

The domestic significance of *perestroika* for Iraq was discussed with much greater caution. On the one hand, *perestroika* was used to justify economic changes in Iraq itself, and its drifting away from the socialist economy. An article in *al-Thawra* put into relief the total failure of the Soviet socialist economy and the USSR's lagging behind the West in different spheres, most importantly that of technology. On the other hand, however, it would appear that Iraqi journalists used the discussion of *perestroika* as a very subtle means for criticizing the Iraqi system itself. Thus, it was pointed out that in the USSR freedom of speech had become an important pillar of this policy; that Western papers were allowed free access and that the Soviet people began to criticize the government freely, including President Mikhail Gorbachev himself. Thus, it was maintained that the Soviets had lost their fear and "gained back their tongues,"[192] because in the Soviet Union political and economic liberalization went hand in hand. By contrast, the journalists noted the problems which accompanied economic liberalization in the USSR including the quick enrichment of certain groups in society. Another implied message to the Iraqi authorities was what one journalist described as the Soviet realization of the inapplicability of Clauswitz's dictum that war was the continuation of politics by other means.[193]

At the same time as the Iraqi authorities had to contain the undesired influence of *perestroika* at home, they also had to contend with the damage done by Soviet *rapprochement* with Iran (see chapter on the Soviet Union and the ME). Although the war was over, the improved Soviet-Iranian relations were perceived by Baghdad as extracting Iran from its international isolation, paving the way to its rearmament, and encouraging it to stiffen its positions in the peace negotiations. Most alarming to Baghdad were the visit to Moscow at the end of June of Iranian Parliament Speaker Hashemi Rafsanjani and reports on an arms deal that was signed between the two countries during the visit. Iraq promptly reacted through an article in *al-'Iraq,* on 1 July, which took the opportunity to settle accounts on other issues as well. Ridiculing Gorbachev as "the international star," *al-'Iraq* maintained that he was destroying the Soviet Union and fragmenting the socialist countries "in the name of *perestroika* and *glasnost,* with all the chaos they have caused inside the Soviet Union, in the Warsaw Pact countries, and elsewhere." *Al-'Iraq* further ridiculed Gorbachev for attempting "to export his ideas and to picture *perestroika* and *glasnost* as new theories for the world." Talking more directly on relations with Iraq, the article sharply criticized Gorbachev for his "opportunistic" behavior and for his "disrespect" for the agreements and treaties that linked the USSR to others (i.e., the Iraqi-Soviet Friendship Treaty of 1972). Because of that treaty, *al-'Iraq* maintained, selling arms to Iran was no longer "a purely Soviet affair," but one that concerned Iraq as well. The Soviet Union was thus "playing the role of the fireman who starts the fire instead of the role it must play — the fireman who puts out the fire." Thus, Iran might use its agreement with the Soviets to argue against negotiations and to maintain its threat of resuming the war against Iraq. Finally, the article "recommended" Iraq as a better partner, because of its stable political system, its dynamic economy, and because, as a member of the ACC, "Iraq is four states in one."[194]

Having made its point, Iraq continued business as usual with the Soviets, and even strengthened relations. On 6 July, only five days after the attack in *al-'Iraq,* a Soviet delegation came to Baghdad to discuss military cooperation. Earlier in the year, when Moscow was still looking for an opening to Tehran, it sought to maintain a low profile on the issue, reflected also by its inconspicuous presence in the Baghdad fair. The Iraqi minister of industry and military industrialization even complained about the Soviets' unwillingness to help Iraq develop its arms, thus prompting Baghadad to do so by itself.[195] At the same time, however, he was reported to have held talks with Soviet officials on bolstering cooperation in the field of military industry. Similarly, Baghdad sought to purchase 48 Sukhoi Su-24 long-range fighter planes and seemed to have obtained Moscow's agreement. The July delegation was believed to have discussed the transfer of technology needed to develop Iraq's aircraft industry, possibly for the production of MiG-29s by Iraq.[196] Iraq remained the main client for Soviet arms, having purchased in the years 1981–88 *matériel* at the cost of $21.37bn., as compared with $370m. by Iran.[197]

Following the minicrisis of early July, Soviet delegations increased their visits to Iraq on an unprecedented level. Throughout the year more Soviet delegations came to Baghdad than Iraqi delegations visited Moscow. On these occasions, agreements were signed on cooperation in various fields, including oil, power stations, and gas pipelines. On the level of trade, the countries envisaged the increase of the trade volume from $1.8bn. to $2.5bn. in 1989.[198]

On the political level, the most important event was Soviet Foreign Minister Eduard Shevarnadze's visit to Baghdad at the end of February, the first such visit since the two countries established relations 45 years ago.[199] The visit — part of a tour to other countries including Egypt, Jordan, and Iran — was aimed at involving the Soviet Union in the peace process of both the Arab-Israeli conflict and Iraqi-Iranian conflict (see chapter on the Soviet Union and the ME). However, in neither did Moscow make great headway. Subsequent Soviet attempts to mediate between Iran and Iraq only aroused suspicions on each side of Soviet attempts to favor the other.

AMBIVALENT RELATIONS WITH THE UNITED STATES
Iraq's attitude toward the US oscillated between two extremes: a strong desire to develop relations in all fields, but also to lambaste it for its stand in the Arab-Israeli conflict, Iraq's development of nonconventional weapons, and human-rights violations.

Iraq had become increasingly aware of the need to attract Washington to its side, both in order to prevent an American tilt toward Iran and, no less important, to obtain US economic, financial, and technological support so badly needed in the postwar era. With regard to the possibility of a US-Iranian *rapprochement,* Baghdad had little or no leeway in trying to stop it, short of criticism in the Iraqi media as in

November, when the US came under strong attack for its "unbalanced" and "unfair" stance toward the Arabs. What occasioned this attack was the American decision to release some of the frozen Iranian funds (see chapter on Iran) in the US. On the other hand, Baghdad made great efforts to attract American business and know-how. To prepare the atmosphere, Baghdad agreed in March, after a year of negotiations, to pay $27.3m. in compensation to the families of 37 American sailors killed in the Iraqi attack on the frigate *Stark* in 1987 (see *MECS* 1987, p. 444). In early June, a delegation of representatives of 57 major American companies and establishments in the field of finance, agriculture, communications, manufacturing, oil, and automotive industries came to Baghdad. The delegation, which represented "the US-Iraq Business Forum" set up in 1985, had unprecedented access to the most senior government officials and was given unusual media coverage. The importance of the visit could be gauged by the fact that President Husayn himself held discussions with the delegation. The Iraqi side sought to convey the impression that an important breakthrough had been achieved through this visit. Writing in *al-Tadamun* after the visit, Fu'ad Matar, Husayn's biographer, predicted that 1990–91 "would be the year of Saddam Husayn in the United States." Matar described at length the great impression that Husayn had made on members of the delegation, who reportedly described him as "a man of steel," charismatic, creative, frank, decisive, and even a "handsome 'Dynasty' star" (a reference to a popular TV series). Matar believed that the change in Husayn's image in the US would lead Americans to wonder "why should Saddam Husayn not be the region's policeman given the real vacuum for such a policeman...."[200] No doubt, these expressions reflected Iraq's aspirations to assume such a role in the Gulf — which in the early 1970s had been reserved for Iran — and obtain Washington's recognition of it.

For all this optimism, relations had still to go a long way before reaching such a level. Even in the most promising field, trade, there were still major obstacles to overcome. Trade between Iraq and the US increased to $2.6bn. in 1988, from $1.2bn. a year earlier, and it was envisaged to increase further, to $3bn. in 1990.[201] The US had also become the major source of Iraqi food and raw material imports, including grain, cotton and wool, sugar, and even tobacco.[202] For its part, the US had become a major buyer of Iraqi oil; selling 500,000 b/d of oil to the US, Iraq was the sixth largest supplier of America's oil.[203] Nonetheless, these relations were still far from fulfilling Iraqi expectations. One reason for the slow pace of their development was Iraq's financial problems. Talking to the US-Iraq Business Forum in November in Washington, deputy assistant secretary of state Edward Gnehm explained that money was a major problem. Hence "we'll have to start small and stick with it over the long haul." Gnehm stated that "not only the US but every other major source of finance has been cautious with Iraq." He expressed his hope for a bright future, but "just a future that takes a little more time and a little more effort to reach than many had supposed."[204]

American caution increased further after what became known as the "Lavoro Affair," which exploded in September. The Atlanta branch of Italy's Banca Nazionale del Lavoro (BNL) apparently secretly approved some 2,500 letters of credit, totaling $3bn., to US and European exporters to finance sales to Iraq. The suspicion was that part of the credit, which had been guaranteed by the US Department of Agriculture's Commodity Credit Corporation and which was supposed to help American farmers to sell their grain to Iraq, went instead to finance a number of companies in the US, Great Britain, and West Germany that produced machinery and chemicals, thus helping Iraq to build poison-gas facilities and long-range missiles (see further below).[205] The uproar which this affair caused in the US came amid revelations that American companies were helping Iraq develop chemical and biological weapons and long-range missiles,[206] at a time when the US Administration was spearheading the campaign among Western countries to ban such aid.

The development of chemical weapons and long-range missiles became a major source of friction between the two countries. Baghdad was incensed by what it perceived as the American role in banning the export of high technology to Iraq and its calls of alarm after each new Iraqi military development. Iraq reacted by attacking "the pro-Israeli" American bias, its "obedience to the Zionist lobby," and its unwillingness to recognize Iraq's cultural progress.[207] The US relations with Israel remained a major source of tension between the two. In April, the Iraqi media lashed out at the US for declaring that the US and Israel had a common problem in confronting surface-to-surface missiles and that cooperation in the Strategic Defense Initiative was intended to solve that problem.[208] Washington was advised to reconsider its "cards" in the region and its attempt "to save the Zionist entity, its aggressive spearhead in the region." Iraq further warned that the Arabs, to whose rights and cause America turned a blind eye, "can upset its cards and affect its interests in the region."[209] The US also came under attack for what Baghdad described as its anti-Palestinian bias, which should rule America out as a mediator in the negotiations between Israel and the Palestinians, and for its backing of Syria's designs in Lebanon.

THE SCANDAL WITH ITALY

During the second half of 1989, Italy was in the center of an international financial scandal connected with Iraq, about which the latter remained silent. The affair was not limited to the sphere of finances, but had wide economic and military ramifications. It began with the granting of a $3bn. credit to Iraq by the Atlanta branch of the Italian BNL (see above). Following investigations which began in early August, it became clear that a great part of the sum was not authorized either by the main office at Rome or by the US authorities, which meant that those sums were guaranteed by Iraq alone. As BNL itself did not possess this huge sum, it used interbank lines which involved between 40 and 50 US, European, and Japanese banks. An Italian paper suggested that the BNL had been transformed "into a sort of clandestine, Baghdad-directed banking operation."[210] Another, and the most severe aspect of the issue, was that part of the credit went to finance Iraq's purchase of military equipment and technological know-how, instead of different civilian projects. The affair brought into the open a very complicated Iraqi network spread out in the West for the purchase of such technology. This network had to overcome an agreement signed in 1987 between different Western countries including Italy, France, West Germany, Great Britain, Spain, and the US, by which they pledged to halt the international spread of medium- and long-range missile technology.[211] To overcome this obstacle, Iraq sent Iraqi trainees to work at European-based companies. "In this way Iraq...[could] tap the West's most sophisticated industrial and military technologies without necessarily breaking the law."[212] Iraq used the BNL credit to finance deals with two types of companies: (a) existing Western concerns that supplied civilian or dual-purpose equipment; and (b) Iraqi-controlled companies that also received BNL financing for exports to Baghdad and had started to implement projects in Iraq by approaching other industrial companies. Interestingly, BNL credit also went to finance a Bulgarian armaments and trading company, which had signed an agreement on joint weapons production with Iraq.[213]

Both Italy and Iraq were pushed into a tight corner as a result of the revelations. In Italy, the affair shocked the financial and economic system. There were even suspicions that senior BNL officials were involved, both in Italy and the US. As for Iraq, though it did not mention the affair at home, there is no doubt that it accounted at least in part for the dismissal in October of the ministers of finance and agriculture (see above). There were also fears in Baghdad that the affair might damage relations with Western countries, or at least slow down the pace of procurement of military technologies. Of special concern were the relations with Italy. These relations had been strained for some years, following the embargo which Italy had put in 1986 on the delivery of 11 naval vessels at the cost of $5bn., ordered by Iraq in 1981. In retaliation, Iraq had suspended all payments estimated at $2.6bn. to other Italian companies.[214] In January 1989, following a visit to Italy by RCC Member Taha Yasin Ramadan, Rome agreed to lift the embargo, although delivery itself was delayed because Iraq refused to make the outstanding 50% payment, insisting on a credit instead.[215] By the time the BNL affair exploded, the problem of the ships had not yet been solved and there were growing fears in Italy that Iraq would link the two. Indeed, the Iraqi ambassador warned that it was "evident" that Italian companies would suffer the severest consequences if the BNL did not disburse the remaining $920m. of the $3bn. loan which had already been given. Moreover, Iraq threatened to withhold scheduled interest payments to the BNL unless the extra loans were disbursed. By the end of the year, however, the parties reached the conclusion that they had more to lose than to gain from the affair, and moved to resolve the dispute. Italy acceded to virtually all Iraqi demands, from credit terms (extended to 10 years) to additional supplies of military equipment.[216] The BNL controversy came to an end in January 1990, when Italy agreed to disburse the remaining loan, while Iraq promised to use at least two thirds of the amount that had yet to be disbursed to make purchases in Italy. Iraq also promised to use BNL branches for commercial operations and to deposit "substantial" amounts of liquid funds in it.

COOLING RELATIONS WITH FRANCE

Iraq's "special relationship" with France, which had started in 1975, cooled significantly during the period under review. The main cement for this friendship had been the huge French arms sales to Iraq, which were estimated at $17bn. for the war years alone.[217] Until 1986 Iraq was quite punctual in its payments, but after that year Baghdad stopped paying France or the French companies because of economic and financial difficulties, with the result that by 1989 Iraq's debt to them totaled $6bn.[218] In attempting to reschedule these debts, Iraq used the argument of their "special relationship" as well as promising to reward French companies with new deals. However, the negotiations that went on for one year from October 1988-September 1989 proved to be very tough. The French Government was placed on the horns of a dilemma: it was pressured by French companies to extend new lines of credit and to guarantee them, so as to enable the companies to make new deals with Iraq. But the government, reluctant to extend new credits when old ones had not yet been repaid, was at the same time afraid lest it jeopardize its already huge investments in Iraq. Paris was also furious that other countries, such as Great Britain, while less generous in granting credits, sometimes got better repayment conditions. Iraq seemed to have attempted to apply pressure on Paris by way of the French companies. A director of one company declared that "if the [French] government does not realize that Iraq is potentially the best market in the Arab world then I must say we are being misgoverned."[219]

While negotiations for debt rescheduling were going on, Iraq approached French companies for new deals. Thus, it held talks with Dassault for the purchase of 50 *Mirage*-2000 jets worth $3bn. It also approached another company for the purchase of missile technology. Both were eager to reach an agreement with Baghdad, but the French government stopped them by not extending credit. Nor was Paris more forthcoming on Baghdad's demand for rebuilding the nuclear reactor bombed by Israel in 1981.

Attempting to belittle problems between the two countries, Tariq 'Aziz in August defined these problems as technical only. At the same time, however, he blamed "some circles in France" for having taken advantage of the financial disputes "to undermine relations between Baghdad and Paris."[220] On 14 September the parties reached an agreement for the repayment of debts, some of them immediately and the balance in nine years.[221] However, in spite of the settlement of the financial dispute, relations did not reassume their cordial spirit. No new deals were known to have been struck.

On another level, Baghdad had been displeased that Paris was the venue of the January conference on the nonproliferation of chemical weapons, which French President François Mitterrand had convened after the Iraqi chemical attacks on the Kurds in 1988. Nor was Baghdad any more pleased with the Kurdish conference in November and the active part played by Mitterrand's wife, Danielle, in the issue. All that Baghdad did was to invite her to Iraq.

THE IRAQI-BRITISH COMPLEX

Of all the Western countries, Great Britain's relations with Iraq remained the most complex, not least due to the legacy of the British mandate in Iraq (officially terminated in 1932) and the deep-seated antagonism it had instilled in the heart of many Iraqis, which kept cropping up whenever relations became strained.

Besides this legacy, Great Britain adopted during the period under review certain positions which further antagonized Iraq. London took a tough line on Baghdad's demand to have its debts rescheduled and to have new credit lines made available for exports to Iraq. Although Britain remained a favored creditor — Iraq owed other countries much larger sums — Britain was unwilling to increase credit lines.[222] At the end of the year after several rounds of talks, Britain decided to reduce sharply its annual line of credit for exports to Iraq to £250m. for 1990 from £340m. in 1989.[223] A no less severe setback was the British decision in July to block the sale of 50 *Hawk* training jets to Iraq. Great Britain feared jeopardizing the shaky truce between Iraq and Iran, and chances for restoring diplomatic ties with Iran (see chapter on Iran). British officials also cited Iraq's human rights record and its use of chemical weapons against the Kurds as reasons to oppose the sale. Mas'ud Barazani, head of the KDP, had been in London to lobby against the sale, arguing that Iraq had a year earlier converted a Swiss trainer to drop chemical weapons on the Kurds.[224] What incensed Baghdad most was what the Iraqi foreign minister described as "tendentious attempts by the British Foreign Office and mass media to harm Iraq,"[225] referring to British criticism of the use of chemical weapons against the Kurds and the campaign of mass deportation. The Iraqi ambassador to Britain attacked the "suspect" British media campaign as aimed at blackening Iraq's reputation.[226]

It was doubtful whether the British media were more hostile to Iraq than the French or the American. But there was no doubt that Baghdad was intent on teaching the British a lesson and taking revenge for London's stance on Iraq. On 15 September, Iraq arrested Farzad Bazoft, a journalist of Iranian origin, employed by *The Observer* newspaper and who had been invited together with 200 foreign journalists to cover the elections to the Kurdish Legislative Assembly.[227] During the visit, Bazoft had investigated reports on the August explosion in the military complex (see above), probably with the assistance of a British nurse. He and the nurse were accused of spying for Israel. After a month of silence and failure to solve the problem through diplomatic channels, London protested to Baghdad about the arrest, the pair's being held incommunicado, and their confession having been secured by force. Baghdad was only too eager to fight back. In an unprecedented attack in the Iraqi media, Great Britain was ridiculed for living in the past because "the time of hegemony and custodianship and exercising pressure on other countries has gone once and for ever and that the wheel of history can never go back." Great Britain was advised to face the new reality: that Iraq was an independent state that rejected all pressures. An article in *al-Thawra* stated: "The sun set on the British Empire, it never rose over the ruling British political mentality."[228]

The great publicity Baghdad gave to the issue indicated that it had been designed for domestic purposes as well. As on other occasions in the past a case of spying was used to divert public attention from the social and economic crisis at home. The "coincidence" of a British journalist of Iranian origin spying for Israel only served to highlight the multifaceted conspiracy being hatched against Iraq. As for Great Britain, despite these public insults it continued to do business with Baghdad and to send delegations there. In March 1990, it was stunned by Bazoft's execution.

NOTES

For the place and frequency of publications cited here, and for the full name of the publication, news agency, radio station, or monitoring service where an abbreviation is used, please see "List of Sources." Only in the case of more than one publication bearing the same name is the place of publication noted here. In the present chapter, however, all references to *al-Thawra* and *al-Jumhuriyya* are to the Baghdad papers of these names.

1. *Al-Thawra,* 4 January; *Alif Ba,* 1 March 1989.
2. *Alif Ba,* 11 January 1989.
3. Ibid., 1 March 1989.
4. Ghazi Dar' al-Ta'i, *Al-Bahr al-Akhdar* (Baghdad: Dar al-shu'un al-thaqafiyya al-'amma, 1988), p. 7.
5. *Le Monde,* 26 July 1989.
6. *IHT,* 20 April; *FT,* 29 September 1989.
7. *Al-Thawra,* 14 June 1989.

8. *The Economist,* 24 June 1989.
9. *Al-Jumhuriyya,* 17 April 1989.
10. *Al-Thawra,* 27 March 1989.
11. *IHT,* 9 February 1989. Earlier estimates put them at c. 300,000.
12. *Alif Ba,* 28 June 1989.
13. *Al-Usbu' al-'Arabi,* 3 July 1989.
14. *Al-Thawra,* 25 February 1989.
15. *AT,* 15 February — DR, 17 February; *al-Sharq al-Awsat,* London, 8 March 1989.
16. *Al-Thawra,* 3 May 1989.
17. Ibid., 7 January 1989.
18. Ibid., 1, 5 April 1989.
19. R. Monte Carlo, 30 March — DR, 31 March; *al-Tadamun,* 28 August; *al-Siyasa,* Kuwait, 1 October — DR, 4 October 1989.
20. For these laws, see the report "On Human Rights in the Arab Homeland," *al-Nashra,* 18 May, 3 July 1989.
21. *Al-Tayyar al-Jadid,* January 1989.
22. *Al-Thawra,* 4 February 1989.
23. *Alif Ba,* 25 January 1989.
24. *Al-Thawra,* 4 February 1989.
25. Ibid., 1, 2, 6, 11 February 1989.
26. *Alif Ba,* 1 March 1989.
27. *Al-Thawra,* 23 February, cf. INA, 22 February — DR, 23 February; *al-Jumhuriyya,* 23 February; *Alif Ba,* 1 March 1989.
28. *Al-'Iraq,* 6(?) March 1989.
29. Ibid., 21 March 1989.
30. *Al-Qadisiyya,* 1, 12 February 1989.
31. *Al-Thawra,* 2 March, 3 May 1989.
32. Ibid., 8 February 1989; for the original law, ibid., 17 March 1980.
33. *Alif Ba,* 5 April 1989. The paper asserted, mistakenly, that the law did not give the military the right to vote.
34. *Al-Thawra,* 21 May 1989.
35. *Alif Ba,* 5 April 1989, cf. *MECS* 1979–80, p. 507; 1984–85, p. 464.
36. *Alif Ba,* 29 March 1989.
37. *Al-Yawm al-Sabi',* 10 April 1989.
38. *Alif Ba,* 5 April 1989.
39. Ibid., 5 April 1989.
40. *Al-Yawm al-Sabi',* 12 February 1990.
41. *Al-Jumhuriyya,* 16 May 1989.
42. *Al-Thawra,* 1 June 1989.
43. *ST,* 26 March; *MM,* 15 May 1989.
44. *The Observer,* as quoted by *JP,* 9 March; *MM,* 20 March; *ST,* 26 March 1989.
45. *Al-Thawra,* 11 June; *Alif Ba,* 14 June 1989.
46. *Al-Thawra,* 11 June 1989.
47. *CR:* Iraq, No. 4, 1989.
48. *Al-'Iraq,* 8 March 1989.
49. *Al-Jumhuriyya,* 19 May; *Alif Ba,* 23 August 1989.
50. *CR:* Iraq, No. 4, 1989.
51. Ibid.
52. *Al-Thawra,* 25 June; *Alif Ba,* 28 June 1989.
53. *Al-Thawra,* 23 February 1989.
54. *Al-Jumhuriyya,* 29 April 1989.
55. *Al-Thawra,* 5 May 1989.
56. *Alif Ba,* 5 April 1989.
57. *Al-Sharq al-Awsat,* 8 March 1989.
58. *Al-Tayyar al-Jadid,* January; *Philadelphia Inquirer,* as quoted by WF, 8 February; *NYT, IHT,* 9 February; *al-Nashra,* 13 February; *MM,* 20 February 1989.
59. *Al-Sharq al-Awsat,* 8 March 1989.

60. R. Baghdad, 11 January — DR, 12 January 1989.
61. E.g., *al-Thawra*, 6 January; *al-Jumhuriyya*, 8, 20 April; *Alif Ba*, 19 April 1989.
62. *Al-Thawra*, 22 June; INA, 23 September — DR, 23 September 1989.
63. *Al-Thawra*, 22 June 1989.
64. Ibid., 6 January; INA, 22 April — DR, 22 April 1989.
65. INA, 7 November — DR, 8 November 1989.
66. Chief of General Staff 'Abd al-Karim al-Khazraji, INA, 22 June — DR, 22 June 1989.
67. *Al-Thawra*, 22 June 1989.
68. Ibid., 6 August 1989.
69. *Le Monde*, 20 July 1989.
70. *Al-Jumhuriyya*, 10 April 1989.
71. *Al-Thawra*, 3 July 1989.
72. *Alif Ba*, 9 August 1989.
73. Mentioned in *al-Thawra*, 13 August 1989.
74. *Near East Report*, 15 January 1990.
75. Jasim to INA, 20 December — DR, 21 December 1989.
76. *NYT*, 18 January; *British Army Review*, No. 91, April; *MM*, 1 May; WF, 28 July 1989.
77. *MM*, 15 May 1989.
78. *Ma'ariv*, 15, 21 December; *Der Spiegel*, 18 December — DR, 20 December; *Le Monde*, 28 December 1989.
79. *Near East Report*, 15 January 1990.
80. *IHT*, 27 January; *FT*, 21 November; *NYT*, 1 December; *Der Spiegel*, 18 December — DR, 20 December 1989.
81. *Der Spiegel*, 18 December — DR, 20 December 1989.
82. *Le Monde*, 14 September, 9 December; *MM*, 18 September; *FT*, 21 November; *NYT*, 1 December 1989.
83. AP, 2 May 1989; *FT*, 21 November 1989; *Near East Report*, 15 January 1990.
84. *The Independent*, 6 September — DR, 18 October 1989.
85. *Le Monde*, 8 September 1989.
86. INA, 7 September — DR, 8 September 1989.
87. AP, 2 May 1989.
88. *MM*, 8 January 1990.
89. *Al-Jumhuriyya*, 2 May 1989.
90. *ME*, April, December; *CR:* Iraq, No. 2; *Middle East Executive Report*, No. 5, May; *MM*, 21 August 1989.
91. *CR:* Iraq, No. 4, 1989.
92. *Al-Siyasa*, Kuwait, 1 February; Saddam Husayn to *AT*, 15 February — DR, 17 February 1989.
93. Husayn to *al-Sharq al-Awsat*, 8 March 1989.
94. INA, 14 May — DR, 14 May; *al-Thawra*, 15 May 1989.
95. *Al-Siyasa*, Kuwait, 2 February 1989.
96. E.g., *al-Thawra*, 25 January, 3 July, 24 September; *al-Thawra International*, 15 May; *Alif Ba*, 17, 31 May 1989.
97. *Al-Thawra*, 15 March 1989.
98. *Alif Ba*, 4 October 1989.
99. *Al-Thawra*, 4, 6, 16 January; *al-Jumhuriyya*, 18 April; *Alif Ba*, 31 May 1989.
100. *Alif Ba*, 3 May 1989.
101. *Al-Thawra*, 2 March 1989.
102. INA, 4 March — DR, 6 March 1989.
103. *Al-Thawra*, 9 July 1989.
104. *Al-Jumhuriyya*, 9 March 1989.
105. INA, 12 December — DR, 13 December 1989. For the other officials' views, see *al-Thawra*, 10, 11 December 1989.
106. *Al-Wafd*, 3 February; *Le Monde*, 31 June, 16 November; *al-Akhbar*, 20 June; *MEI*, 1 December; *al-Masa*, Cairo, 1 December 1989.
107. *Le Monde*, 31 June 1989.
108. *Al-Thawra*, 23 February 1989.

109. *Al-Wafd,* 28 January, 2, 3, 4 February 1989.
110. *Al-Akhbar,* 20 June 1989.
111. *Le Monde,* 16 November 1989.
112. 1,052 bodies were returned to Egypt by November 1989, as against 980 for the whole of 1988; *NYT,* 15 November 1989.
113. Ibid., *Le Monde,* 16 November; *al-Wafd,* 25 November 1989, clamied that 1m. out of 2m. Egyptians had left the country since June.
114. R. Baghdad, 15 November — DR, 16 November 1989.
115. *Philadelphia Inquirer,* WF, 20 November; *Le Monde,* 20 November 1989.
116. MENA 16 November — DR, 17 November; INA, 20 November — DR, 21 November 1989.
117. *Al-Thawra,* 20 July 1989.
118. R. Baghdad, 15 November — DR, 16 November 1989.
119. *Al-Thawra,* 28 March, 4 August; *Alif Ba,* 17 May 1989.
120. *Al-Thawra,* 17 January 1989.
121. *Alif Ba,* 20 September 1989.
122. *Al-Tadamun,* 4 September 1989.
123. *Al-Thawra,* 30 January 1989.
124. Tawfiq al-Shaykh (ed.), *Al-'Iraq wal-Haraka al-Islamiyya* (London: Al-Safa lil-nashr wal-tawzi', 1988), pp. 32, 41–42, 77, 81–83, 98.
125. *Sawt al-Rafidayn,* November 1989.
126. *ME,* July 1989.
127. *Al-Tadamun,* 28 August 1989.
128. INA, 17 October — DR, 19 October 1989.
129. *Al-Musawwar,* 14 July 1989.
130. INA, 17 October — DR, 19 October 1989.
131. *Le Monde,* 22 July 1989.
132. *Al-Thawra,* 10 June 1989.
133. *Le Monde,* 21 September 1989.
134. *Al-Siyasa,* Kuwait, 12 August 1989.
135. *Le Monde,* 22 July 1989.
136. *FT,* 15 June; *Le Monde,* 21 September 1989.
137. Tariq 'Aziz to *al-Musawwar,* 14 July 1989.
138. *FT,* 15 June; *The Economist,* 24 June 1989.
139. *ME,* July 1989.
140. *Al-Musawwar,* 14 July 1989.
141. *Al-Siyasa,* Kuwait, 12 August 1989.
142. *Al-Jumhuriyya,* 11 July 1989.
143. *The Economist,* 24 June 1989.
144. *IHT,* 2 May; *FT,* 3 June; *Le Monde,* 17 June 1989.
145. *Al-Qadisiyya,* 26 January 1989.
146. *The Economist,* 24 June; *Le Monde* 22 July 1989.
147. *Le Monde,* 21 September 1989.
148. *Al-Dustur,* London, 29 May 1989.
149. *Al-Musawwar,* 15 September 1989.
150. Erhard Franz, *Kurden und Kurdentum* (Hamburg: Deutsches Orient-Institut, 1986), p. 12.
151. *Le Monde,* 21 September 1989.
152. *Al-Musawwar,* 15 September 1989.
153. INA, 17 October — DR, 19 October 1989.
154. *Al-Siyasa,* Kuwait, 7 September 1989.
155. *Al-Musawwar,* 15 September 1989.
156. *Al-Thawra,* 2 August 1989.
157. *FT,* 1 March; *Le Monde,* 2 March; *al-Nashra,* 8 May 1989.
158. *Le Monde,* 21 September 1989.
159. *ME,* February; *Le Monde,* 21 September 1989.
160. INA, 17 October — DR, 19 October 1989.
161. GNA, 2 April — DR, 3 April 1989.

162. INA, 20 April — DR, 21 April 1989.
163. R. Baghdad, 5 March — DR, 6 March 1989.
164. IRNA, 20 July — DR, 26 July 1989.
165. R. Baghdad, 11 January — DR, 12 January 1989.
166. INA, 11 January — DR, 12 January 1989.
167. Husayn to *al-Sharq al-Awsat,* 8 March — DR, 14 March 1989.
168. *Middle East Insight,* Vol. 5, No. 5, Spring 1989.
169. *Al-Thawra,* 6 January 1989.
170. *Al-Thawra,* 21 January 1989.
171. *Al-Jumhuriyya,* 14 March 1989.
172. Ibid., 3, 6 April; INA, 5 April — DR, 5 April 1989.
173. *Al-Jumhuriyya,* 8 April 1989.
174. *Al-Thawra,* 21 April — DR, 25 April 1989.
175. *Al-Thawra,* 20, 26 March 1989.
176. *Al-Jumhuriyya,* 15 May; *al-Thawra,* 10, 14, 30 June 1989.
177. *Le Figaro,* 13 January — DR, 19 January 1989.
178. *MM,* 18 September; *CR:* Iraq, No. 4, 1989.
179. INA, 18 April — DR, 19 April 1989.
180. INA, 8 June — DR, 9 June 1989.
181. *JP,* 26 September 1989.
182. Ibid., 23 November 1989.
183. *Al-Thawra,* 28 March 1989.
184. Ibid., 8 February 1989.
185. Ibid., 23 February 1989.
186. *Alif Ba,* 19 April 1989.
187. *Ma'ariv,* 3 April; *Yedi'ot Aharonot,* 17 July 1989.
188. According to *Sawt al-Sha'b,* Amman, 10 August 1989, the Iraqi debt was $450m. Iraq did not fulfill an agreement of 1988 to pay back the debt.
189. *Al-Jumhuriyya,* 2 May 1989.
190. *Al-Thawra,* 19 February 1989.
191. Ibid., 7, 19 February; *al-Jumhuriyya,* 11 October 1989.
192. *Al-Thawra,* 17 March 1989.
193. Ibid., 19 February, 17 March 1989.
194. *Al-'Iraq,* 1 July — DR, 10 July 1989.
195. *Al-Jumhuriyya,* 2 May 1989.
196. *JP,* 16 July 1989.
197. *MM,* 21 August 1989.
198. *Ha'aretz,* 13 June 1989.
199. INA, 23 February — DR, 24 February 1989.
200. *Al-Tadamun,* 10 July — DR, 26 July; INA, 9 November — DR, 13 November 1989.
201. Ibid.
202. *Middle East Executive Report,* September 1989.
203. *WSJ,* WF, 8 January 1989.
204. WF, 14 November 1989.
205. *FT,* 2 November; *NYT,* 1 December 1989.
206. *IHT,* 27, 30 January; *WP,* WF, 3 May 1989.
207. E.g., INA, 3 April, 10 December — DR, 3 April, 11 December 1989.
208. INA, 20 April — DR, 21 April 1989.
209. *Al-Thawra,* 2 April — DR, 25 April 1989.
210. *FT,* 9 September 1989.
211. *ME,* October 1989.
212. *FT,* 13 September 1989.
213. Ibid., 20 September 1989.
214. Ibid., 6 December; *CR:* Iraq, No. 2, 1989.
215. *CR:* Iraq, No. 2, 1989.
216. *FT,* 6 December 1989.
217. *IHT,* 12 June 1989.

218. *Le Monde,* 2 June 1989.
219. *IHT,* 20 March 1989.
220. KUNA, 29 August — DR, 29 August 1989.
221. *Le Monde,* 18 September 1989.
222. *FT,* 10 October 1989.
223. Ibid., 1 December 1989.
224. Ibid., 24, 28 July 1989.
225. *Al-Musawwar,* 14 July — DR, 19 July 1989.
226. INA, 14 June — DR, 15 June 1989.
227. *Le Monde,* 21 October 1989.
228. INA, 23 October — DR, 24 October; *al-Thawra,* 24 October — DR, 31 October 1989.

Israel

(Medinat Yisrael)

GAD BARZILAI

Ever since the November 1988 parliamentary (Knesset) elections and the formation of a National Unity Government in December of that year, the Israeli political system had to contend with a succession of major problems. Some of these were partly legacies from the past; others cropped up as the consequence of developments during the course of 1989 in Israel, in the Middle East generally, and in other parts of the world. The most significant sociopolitical events in Israel itself were those directly associated with the ongoing occupation of the West Bank and Gaza Strip. The Palestinian uprising in the territories, which had erupted in December 1987, continued to impair the smooth functioning of daily life within Israel proper. Continuous attempts to minimize that damage, by suppressing the Intifada and restoring normalcy and order to the territories, dominated the Israeli political agenda during 1989.

The year, however, also witnessed a number of other important events, all of which deserve analysis. This chapter, therefore, discusses the Israeli political setting in its different dimensions.

DOMESTIC POLITICAL AFFAIRS

DILEMMAS AND POLITICAL DEBATES REGARDING THE INTIFADA

The Israeli public, Jews and Arabs alike, enjoyed access to a considerable volume of reliable information, published by the local and foreign press. The spate of daily news released during 1989 about the bitter intercommunal conflict in the territories and its (mainly Palestinian) victims gave rise to renewed, and increasingly bitter, controversy about the future of those territories, an issue already debated in Israel for more than 20 years. Although still concerned by economic problems and the country's relations with its neighboring Arab states, Israelis began to show clear signs of regarding the solution to the territorial issue as the most vital matter on their national agenda.[1]

The Israeli political parties suggested their diverse solutions to the conflict. In reaction to the growing number of fatalities, many of them children, among the Palestinian civilian population, parties on the left, especially Mapam and the Citizens' Rights Movement (CRM, or Ratz), called ever more vociferously for immediate negotiations with the PLO, notwithstanding the great likelihood that they would pave the way for the establishment of a separate Palestinian state.[2] Their efforts to alter the public consensus, which was opposed to negotiating with the PLO, were intensified following the declarations by the organization's chairman, Yasir 'Arafat, and the decisions reached at the November 1988 conference of the Palestine National Council in Algeria (see *MECS* 1988, chapter on the PLO). The Israeli left interpreted those

Israel, the West Bank, and the Gaza Strip

declarations and decisions as expressing the PLO's acceptance of UN Resolutions 242 and 338, its recognition of Israel's right to exist, and as the long-awaited proof of the fundamental changes occurring in Palestinian thinking.[3]

The right-wing parties, at the other end of the political spectrum, saw the reality entirely differently and demanded the adoption of measures harsher even than those applied in 1988 to suppress the Palestinian uprising. Tzomet and Tehiya pressed strongly for an immediate annexation of the territories and for the expulsion of the Intifada's leaders. Moledet spokesmen went considerably further, asserting that nothing short of the "voluntary" exodus of all Palestinians from the territories would ultimately produce a viable solution.[4] Some religious groups, including members of the National Religious Party (NRP, or Mafdal), reflecting attitudes prevalent among certain of the Jewish settlers in the territories, also supported similar notions in favor of deporting thousands of Palestinians.[5]

Neither such right-wing views, nor those held by elements on the radical left, nor yet those propounded by such extrapolitical groups as Peace Now and Gush Emunim, were able to exert much influence on the state's policy. This, to the extent that it was definitively formulated, was determined almost entirely by the two largest parties, Likud and Labor, which together formed the overwhelming majority in the National Unity Government. On one issue, particularly, their views coincided: both were opposed to the creation of an independent Palestinian state in the territories.

The Labor Party remained faithful to its plan of maintaining Jordan as a major interlocutor in the attempt to resolve the conflict by means of some territorial compromise. In a departure from its pre-1988 approach, however, Labor accepted the idea that progress in resolving the conflict was going to require direct negotiation with Palestinians representative of the population of those territories. The Labor Party also accepted that such representation could include a limited number of Palestinians expelled by Israel for engaging in hostile activity on behalf of the PLO, and even on behalf of groups known to be more extreme in their anti-Israeli attitudes.[6]

In conformity with that approach, the Israel Defense Forces (IDF) coordinator in the territories, Shmuel Goren, with the knowledge and support of a prominent Labor Party leader, Defense Minister Yitzhak Rabin, met in January with Faysal al-Husayni, a local Palestinian leader affiliated with the PLO. The purpose of the meeting was to explore the chances of creating a local Palestinian leadership in the territories, not necessarily obeisant to orders issued by the PLO in Tunis. Rabin hoped that such local leadership would prove wise enough to reach some agreement with Israel that would assist in solving the problems of both the Palestinians and of the territories.[7]

It was Yitzhak Rabin, too, who contributed significantly to the design of the 14 May Israeli peace program, according to which elections would be held in the territories for Palestinian delegates with whom Israel could then conduct negotiations for solving the Palestinian problem (for details, see chapter on the ME peace process). On 8 August, the Labor Party central committee decided that it would see to the downfall of the National Unity Government if it did not take the steps necessary to ensure that the peace program was carried out.[8] Consonant with that decision, Labor Party leaders declared on 17 September their acceptance of the ten-point plan put forward by Egyptian President Husni Mubarak, who suggested holding a Palestinian-Israeli meeting in Cairo to push forward the plan for elections in the territories and to start negotiating a settlement between Israel and the Palestinians.[9] The Labor Party leaders made it clear that from their point of view the notion of holding such a meeting in Cairo was acceptable if it was understood that, while two Palestinian deportees, who no longer engaged in acts of terror, could be included in the Palestinian delegation, members of the PLO could not.[10] Subsequently, following the announcement of the "Baker plan" on 7 October, the Labor Party decided that it would be conditioning its continued participation in the National Unity Government on Israel giving its assent to the five points contained in that plan.[11] The party placed special emphasis on the need, as specified by the "Baker plan", for the foreign ministers of Egypt, the US, and Israel to meet, and on the benefits likely to accrue from a meeting between Israeli and Palestinian delegations in Cairo.[12] (For details on Mubarak's proposal and the Baker plan, see chapter on the ME peace process.)

The Likud, by contrast, had initially rejected out of hand any idea of negotiating with the Palestinians. As 1989 unfolded, though, some of its members began to change their minds. With the casualties of the prolonged Intifada mounting, and the US Administration applying pressure on Israel to demonstrate more flexibility in its diplomatic stance, certain Likud members, among them hard-liners, relented their opposition toward negotiating with expelled Palestinian activists on condition that they were not PLO members.[13] Still, most Likud ministers and senior members consistently rejected the notion of holding formal, public negotiations with the PLO. Prime Minister Yitzhak Shamir, Foreign Minister Moshe Arens, and other senior Likud leaders consistently made it a point to state that the PLO had always been, was, and would for ever be a terrorist organization and that it was entirely unacceptable as a partner for negotiations with Israel.[14]

Some Likud members, however, interpreted the Israeli Government's peace program as a sign of Shamir's "weakness." Three of them — Minister of Economic Planning Yitzhak Moda'i, Minister of Housing David Levy, and Minister of Trade and Industry Ariel Sharon — reacted by organizing a convention of the Likud Party central council on 4 July. The council decided that the Likud's representatives in the government would be obliged to stay loyal to two basic principles: first, that since East Jerusalem would for ever remain a part of a united Jerusalem, the Palestinian residents there would be barred from participating in the proposed elections in the territories; and second, that no PLO representatives, or any person who had taken part in acts of terrorism against Israel, could participate in any Palestinian delegation with which Israel would negotiate.[15] Pursuant to the Likud central council's decision, which did much to constrict Prime Minister Shamir's room for maneuver, Likud spokesmen issued several statements toward the end of 1989 expressing their opposition to any Palestinian deportees taking part in the proposed discussions. Any such possible participation, they considered, could be interpreted as granting legitimacy to the participation of representatives from the PLO and other terrorist organizations in talks over the future of the territories.[16]

In principle, both major parties essentially continued to cling to the ideologies they had advocated since the end of the Six-Day War (1967) and, to a considerable degree, to those which had shaped their respective policies ever since the establishment of the State (1948). Thus the Likud maintained its powerful devotion to the concept of Jewish-Israeli dominion over the "Eretz Yisrael" (the Land of Israel), often giving expression to its deep-seated wish eventually to annex the territories to Israel.[17] The Labor Party, on the other hand, remained loyal to the formula of territorial compromise.[18]

Where attitudes of the general public in Israel were concerned, the overall scene was one of puzzlement. Having grown used to its military forces scoring outright victories in conventional wars against Arab adversaries, Israelis became increasingly frustrated by the prolonged conflict in the territories, waged between regular army units and an undisciplined rabble of civilians, many of them children, who were employing "cold" weapons rather effectively. In a battle of this type, so it seemed, the IDF was losing its traditional edge.

As a result, the Israeli public's attitudes during 1989 were characterized by division. In contrast with the past, no single dominant approach to the conflict was apparent. On the one hand, an increase occurred in the percentage of those prepared to countenance the possible establishment of a Palestinian state alongside Israel; by mid-1989, about 14% of the public had come to support that idea, representing almost twice the proportion in favor on the eve of the Intifada. They were influenced by events of the Intifada and believed there was no alternative to bringing it to an end and solving the Palestinian problem by employing political moderation. About 37%, on the other hand, were of the view that Israel ought to go on administering the territories (30% favoring their annexation and 7% prepared to see a continuation of the status quo). However, 25% of the public were in favor of granting the Palestinians autonomous rule in the territories and 24% supported the notion of some form of territorial compromise.[19] In other words, 38% of the public were clearly in favor of the compromises involved in an Israeli withdrawal from the territories. Another 25%, those supporting autonomy, were ready to consider such a possibility since in principle they recognized the need for some kind of compromise. Comparing these figures with those for previous years indicates that, following the outbreak of the Intifada, moderation in Israeli public opinion began to increase. For example, in mid-1987, prior to the beginning of the Intifada, 56% of the public had favored continued Israeli rule over all of the territories.[20]

This incipient moderation in Israeli public opinion, however, was only partial in nature and stipulated certain conditions. A majority of the public, 52%, held the opinion that should peace-making efforts fail, Israel would have to expel the Palestinians forcibly from the territories and send them off to live in Arab countries.[21] In addition, it appeared that the effect of certain, especially lethal, acts of terror committed during 1989 was to cause a certain hardening in Israeli public opinion and prompt demands for using more force against the Palestinians. A prominent example was the reaction to the terrorist attack on the bus on the Tel Aviv-Jerusalem highway on 6 July; a Palestinian riding on that bus, who later admitted to being a member of the Muslim Jihad group, caused the vehicle to swerve off the road and topple into a ravine, resulting in the death of 16 people, with another 25 injured (for more details, see chapter on armed operations). The impact of this attack was to raise the degree of the Israeli public's support for utilizing force in the attempt to solve the Palestinian problem.[22]

Overall, then, the trends in Jewish public opinion in Israel were not clear-cut in either direction. It was apparent that any real decline in tension over security issues, in conjunction with moderate political leadership, contained the potential for bolstering moderate tendencies in the country. On the other hand, any increase in the number or severity of terrorist acts, combined with a militant political leadership, were capable of reinforcing conservative and hawkish forces within public opinion, too.

THE RULE OF LAW: NATIONAL SECURITY
AND DEMOCRATIC PRINCIPLES

Throughout the long history of the conflict, successive Israeli governments had continually tried to defend national security by methods which did not violate the country's democratic values, such as freedom of expression and organization, media pluralism, full suffrage, and free elections. Israel, despite having fought six wars (or seven, if one includes the Intifada) and having been engaged in thousands of additional, more limited military operations, had managed to preserve the precious democratic principles on which it was based. In 1989, despite the intensification of the intercommunal conflict in the territories, which tempted the country's leadership to sacrifice some basic democratic values on the altar of "Security considerations," Israel seems to have succeeded reasonably well in maintaining its citizens' human rights.

The challenges entailed therein were difficult because Israel had no written constitution. Its regime was founded on special, so-called "Basic Laws," intended to ensure its functioning as a democracy. But such laws failed to ensure certain rights, such as freedom of the press and of religion. Those had to be enacted by decisions of the Israeli Supreme Court, thus becoming part of an unwritten constitution.

Two significant events in the development of that unwritten constitution occurred in 1989, both entailing matters of censorship. On 10 January, the Supreme Court in Jerusalem ruled that the press possessed the right to comment and pass judgment on any lapse or malfunctioning that it might detect in the Israeli intelligence services, including direct criticism of the people it considered responsible.[23] This ruling, issued notwithstanding Israel's being effectively in a state of war, had limited the degree of secrecy in which information about national security affairs could henceforth be shrouded. The Supreme Court additionally ruled that democratic values, such as freedom of the press, were an essential ingredient of national security. Censorship could be justified, the court said, only if the publication of information could clearly be demonstrated to threaten national security.[24] In so ruling, the Supreme Court formulated its attitude to the relationship between freedom of expression and national security.

A similar ruling had previously been made by the Supreme Court as long ago as 1952.[25] Its 1989 pronouncement, however, was rather more definitive and focused specifically on the issue of publication by the media of information and criticism pertaining to vital security matters. Since the Israeli legal system is based on precedents, the Supreme Court's ruling was tantamount to a law.

Another significant event took place on 3 April, when the Knesset voted to abolish all censorship of theatrical productions for a trial period of two years. It had been possible until then to impose censorship on a play if there existed serious suspicion that it might be either offensive to "public sentiment" or injurious to "national security." Such censorship was resorted to only quite rarely, but it aroused severe disputes.[26] These two developments in 1989 served to enhance freedom of expression in Israel and to seriously narrow the degree of censorship imposed on matters previously perceived as impinging on national security.

These important democratic reforms in the rule of law, however, were confined to Israel proper. The situation in East Jerusalem (formally annexed by Israel), and the Golan Heights (subjected, since 1981, to Israeli law) and in those territories remaining merely "occupied," stayed as seriously problematic as ever. Indeed, one of the hardest challenges confronting the government throughout 1989 was how to succeed in subduing the turmoil in those territories without resort to measures which would seriously violate democratic principles, such as by always abiding by the due process of law. The growth in the number and gravity of acts of violence, perpetrated or spurred by nationalistic elements, which occurred in the territories during 1989, signified an intensification of the Intifada in that year in comparison with 1988.[27] The Israeli legal system made an attempt to provide a reasonable degree of freedom of action to the state's military and police authorities in dealing with the realities of this violent intercommunal conflict. At the same time, though, it tried to prevent these authorities from engaging in excesses and to compel them to limit their use of counterviolence to only the most threatening situations.[28] The intent was to help the authorities maintain law and order, but only by employing means rigorously incapable of condemnation as breaching democratic values. This aim proved to be difficult to realize.

The regulations governing the use of live ammunition in firing on demonstrators, saboteurs, or other perpetrators of violence, were reformulated again on 14 September jointly by the military authorities and the Ministry of Justice. They prohibited using live ammunition in all circumstances, other than those which entailed a palpable threat to the life of Israelis, those necessitating the apprehension of masked agitators (whether armed or not), or those which involved attempts to arrest any suspect trying to flee after having been ordered to halt. Notwithstanding these regulations, both the military and civilian legal systems found themselves forced to contend with the most severe violations. In a number of cases, Israeli officers and soldiers applied inordinately excessive zeal in their encounters with apparently innocent civilians.

A particularly prominent instance came to light in the trial of four soldiers from the combat force of the "Givati Brigade." The accused were charged with seriously assaulting a Palestinian, resident of Jibaliya in the Gaza Strip, to the extent of causing his death. Acquitted of manslaughter, they were nevertheless found guilty of grievous assault and of obeying an illegal command. The four were sentenced, in September, to a few months in jail, demoted in rank, and transferred from their unit. Later, in October, they were pardoned by the Commanding Officer, Southern Command, Gen. Matan Vilna'i,[29] by the authority which the law conferred on him. In justifying his decision, Vilna'i stressed that he had taken due consideration of the fact that the men had committed their crime while serving in circumstances in which their lives were daily in danger. But his writ of pardon nevertheless confirmed the gravity with which he viewed their act, which fully warranted their being demoted and dishonorably removed from a prestigious brigade.[30]

Another notable instance involved the case of Col. Yehuda Meir, who was charged with having given an order in January 1988 for 20 innocent Palestinian civilians, residents of the villages of Beita and Hawarra in the West Bank, to be physically assaulted. The Chief Military Prosecutor ruled that, in issuing his order, the officer had clearly contravened the law, but that his punishment would be confined to dismissing him from the Army and subjecting him to a disciplinary tribunal, rather than a military court. The prosecutor explained this ruling by citing the fact that the regulations governing use of force in the territories had been somewhat obscure at the time the colonel's act was committed. For their part, some of the Palestinian victims of the assault, in company with the Association for Civil Rights in Israel, petitioned the High Court of Justice, demanding that Col. Meir be tried by a military court authorized to hand down a sentence of severe punishment. It should be noted that, in accordance with international law, the High Court of Justice was prepared to hear petitions against the Israeli authorities submitted by residents of the territories, despite the fact that those were "occupied" territories. This practice enabled the court, subject to the various constraints imposed by the actual circumstances and by Israeli law, to exercise a certain degree of supervision, founded on democratic principles, over the manner in which the security forces behaved. In the case under review, the court ruled that since Col. Meir had apparently indeed committed a crime, he would have to stand trial before a military court and should be suspended from his army duties.[31]

The High Court of Justice found itself obliged to contend during 1989 with a most difficult state of affairs in the territories: a number of Palestians were deported; in several instances the homes of Palestinians were sealed closed or blown up by the Army; there were many occurrences of arrests being committed without prior notice to the detainee's relatives; and arrests were often conducted without a court order. The High Court was therefore compelled to establish norms facilitating some fundamental protection of human rights. During the course of the year, it issued a number of rulings, including those prescribing that neither the deportation of Palestinian agitators nor the blowing up of their homes would henceforth be tolerated except when the security forces considered these to be the only means of preventing hostile acts against the troops.[32] One of the court's most important contributions, in addition, was its addressing itself to the basic human right of any detainee to have his family and lawyer informed of his arrest and where he was being detained. A petition to this effect, presented to the High Court by relatives of an arrested Palestinian, was only retracted when the Israeli Army consented to the terms of the petition. The court made it clear to the authorities that they were duty-bound to adhere to the provisions of the Geneva Convention on this matter.[33] This was yet another example of how, despite all the hardships entailed in contending with the furor of the Intifada, the Israeli legal system strove to apply civilian controls over the security forces' freedom of action in an effort to preserve some of the basic human rights of the adversary.

But the military and political struggle over the future of the territories also had an impact on the rule of law within Israel proper. A greater use of emergency laws was resorted to, especially in East Jerusalem, which restricted individual rights. Two prominent examples were the imposition, for security reasons, of censorship of political articles appearing in the Arabic newspapers in East Jerusalem, and the invocation of emergency laws to facilitate placing suspected PLO members in "administrative detention," thus effectively denying them their liberty without any court being seriously able to intervene. An instance of this practice involved the order issued on 6 December against Faysal al-Husayni, a resident of East Jerusalem, limiting his freedom to travel from there to places in the occupied territories. The order was for a period of six months and stated that he would be arrested if he transgressed any of its provisions.[34] The Army explained the order by claiming it to be "necessary for the protection of the public's security."[35] It appeared, however, that the step was taken for the purely political reason of limiting the political liberty of a leader suspected of being a prominent PLO activist in the territories. Husayni, in point of fact, was a rather moderate Palestinian leader.

Within the boundaries of the pre-1967 "green line," by contrast, the legal system traditionally tended to a more liberal approach. Yet the period under review witnessed considerable controversy over the employment of a specific aspect of Israeli law. The issue revolved around an intended amendment to the Prevention of Terror Order, promulgated in August 1986, which made it illegal for Israeli citizens or residents to meet with representatives of the PLO; the maximum penalty for transgressing was three years in jail.[36] A notable case in which that amendment was enforced was that of Abie Nathan, an Israeli citizen known for his many efforts to bring peace closer, often through unconventional, spectacular, and sometimes risky means. In September, Nathan was sentenced to six months in jail for having met with the PLO's Yasir 'Arafat, plus a suspended sentence of another year, to be activated if he met PLO representatives again.[37] Reactions to this application of the order were extremely vigorous. While Israel's right-wing parties lauded the court for Nathan's conviction and punishment, those on the left of the spectrum claimed the order constituted a piece of antidemocratic legislation.[38]

In any event, the fact that it was enforced seemed to suggest that the Israeli legal system was becoming more and more politicized. There were probably two main reasons for this. First, in the absence of a constitution, Israeli legislators and courts tended to react to current events with increasing intervention in the country's political life, and not always in a manner founded strictly on democratic-liberal values. Thus, due to the intensification of the intercommunal conflict in the territories, which occasionally also expressed itself in violence by Israeli Arabs too, the regime was inclined to making political use of the law, thereby harming the country's democratic-liberal rule of law. Second, the legal system had become increasingly obliged to contend with politically motivated instances of noncompliance with the law. Illegal meetings with PLO members have already been referred to in this context. But breaches of the law were also committed by Jewish settlers in the territories, whose most common offense was opening fire randomly on Palestinians,[39] and by those members of the military forces who refused to serve in the territories because they opposed Israeli dominion there.[40] When attempts were made to enforce the law in these sorts of cases, the usual result was that pressures were brought to bear on the courts. When settlers were charged with offenses, the pressures tended to be applied by right-wing political groups; when soldiers were charged on counts of draft refusal, the pressures came from groups on the left.[41]

During 1989, in addition to the Israeli legal system becoming ever more politicized, the rule of law could be said to have become characterized by several opposing tendencies. Israeli citizens found themselves enjoying greater freedom of expression allowed in the media and on the stage. But, at the same time, they also saw an effective tightening of the practical controls over political behavior in matters concerning contacts with the PLO. Residents of East Jerusalem found themselves more frequently subjected to the application of emergency laws limiting their individual liberties. Residents of the occupied territories saw the Israeli legal system granting legitimacy to the use of force in suppressing the Intifada, on condition that such resort to force be limited to situations where civilians, not directly involved in any armed confrontation, were being confronted. Overall, in 1989 the Intifada succeeded in wreaking damage on the rule of law. This was because the effect of the continuing conflict was to push the Israeli legal system into markedly less liberal and less democratic dispositions.

PROBLEMS OF NONGOVERNABILITY

In addition to the aforementioned problems, it became quite clear during 1989 that Israel lacked an efficient and far-sighted government capable of successfully contending simultaneously with major economic, social, and security issues. This reality became most particularly apparent at the uppermost echelons of the national political elite. Not only did differences exist between the respective political-ideological positions held by the two major parties; their representatives within the government evidenced an irresistible proclivity to clash, with their dissonance rooted in disagreement over the disposition of state assets as well as in purely personal incompatibility. There were many examples of this sort of strife. The government, for instance, was characterized by a perpetual state of mutual suspicion between Prime Minister Yitzhak Shamir and his deputy, Finance Minister Shimon Peres. Shamir was inclined to believe that Peres, as finance minister, sought to allocate funds to the (Labor Party-linked) Histadrut, the general federation of labor, at the expense of financing the Jewish settlement activity in the annexed and occupied territories. Peres, for his part, was wont to complain that Shamir was deliberately hindering the Finance Ministry's programs.[42]

In addition, within the Likud itself, 1989 witnessed considerable disharmony between Yitzhak Shamir, on the one hand, and three of his senior ministers, Ariel Sharon, David Levy, and Yitzhak Moda'i, on the other (see above). Such disharmony, which progressed to outright antagonism, derived essentially from the personal grudges the three ministers harbored against Shamir's failure to consult with them sufficiently or to promote their political careers. Sharon and Levy were inordinately offended by Shamir's reluctance to let them influence his proposed plan for promoting ME peace. Moda'i, likewise, clearly resented having his opinions substantially and consistently ignored, and was unwilling to condone the fact that his faction within the Likud, the Liberals, had never been accorded any real positions of influence within the overall Likud framework. Since Shamir, throughout, demonstrated rigorously uncharismatic leadership, the three disgruntled ministers considered themselves very seriously as candidates for the mantle of the premiership.[43]

This cut and thrust effectively paralyzed the government and prevented it from producing solutions to several pressing issues. Not once during the entire course of 1989 did the government manage to decide on a single fundamental step toward solving any of the problems begging for urgent attention in Israel's public life. Governmental policy was simply characterized throughout by "no solution" and "nongovernability" politics. The prime example was the government's inability to advance in the peace process. It was incapable, for instance, of formulating any response to the American Administration's request for clear-cut answers to its query whether, and under what conditions, Israel might be ready for talks with some Palestinian delegation.[44] In these respects, therefore, the Israeli Government seemed to exhibit a preference for the status quo. Practically speaking, it opted for paralysis on vital foreign policy matters. It conducted itself similarly in regard to urgent social issues.

In Israel, social problems tended to be neglected. Ever since the Six-Day War, Israeli politics centered more and more solely on national security, with social issues pushed very much to one side. This situation was further aggravated by a growing political mood which appeared to posit that the country was essentially nongovernable.

Throughout the whole of 1989, the political parties making up the coalition engaged in almost continuous struggles for power. This had a fairly strong adverse effect on achieving progress on all matters generally considered as being less important than national security.

This very sorry state of affairs worsened in 1989. In November, for example, when details of the extent of poverty in Israel were published as part of the National Insurance Institute's annual report (see above), the political leadership failed to address itself seriously to the problem. Instead, accusations and counteraccusations were leveled, particularly between the coalition's two major parties.[45] The spokesmen for both parties, quick to blame the other for the poverty, used the issue as a convenient pretext for settling political scores. The Likud postulated that it was attributable to the policies of the Labor Party-controlled Histadrut and to the measures adopted by Minister of Finance Peres, Labor Party chairman. The latter, in turn, protested that the poverty was a clear indication of the grave extent to which the Likud had become a right-wing party bereft of all sensitivity to the weaker sectors of the population, and that it showed how incapable Prime Minister Shamir was of functioning effectively.[46]

Nongovernability, as a conspicuous rule in Israeli politics during 1989, also expressed itself in the debates over matters associated with the national budget. In lieu of serious discussions over the national priorities which ought to dictate allocation of budget resources, the debates quickly turned into interparty and interpersonal squabbles, such as those conducted between Deputy Prime Minister and Housing Minister David Levy and Finance Minister Peres. Thus, rather than dealing with fundamental issues — such as immigrant absorption, the reduction of unemployment, improving the situation in development towns, and alleviating the distress of chronically unprivileged sectors — the country's leadership all too often dealt with threats (made particularly by the ultra-Orthodox parties, and Labor) to leave the government and set up an alternative coalition.[47] One of the main features characterizing the Israeli political system during 1989, therefore, was the rival parties' tendency to focus primarily on advancing their own interests, while neglecting matters of national public policy.

LOCAL GOVERNMENT

Since their annual revenue deriving from municipal taxes is generally extremely low in comparison with their expenditures, local authorities in Israel are essentially dependent on central government subsidization. During the course of 1989, because of the widening gap between their tax revenue and expenditures, the finances of almost every single local authority became unprecedentedly bad. For its part, the government refused to cover their huge deficits which, during the 1988–1989 fiscal year, swelled by more than $100m.[48]

The economic slump especially hit the 30 development towns in Israel. Practically no new capital was invested in any of them, their revenue from municipal taxes dwindled almost to zero, and their percentage unemployment figures rose alarmingly. The root of their problem was a severe lack of workplaces for their respective populations. In many towns, unemployment rose to about 15%, so that about 30% of their residents found themselves below the poverty line.[49] Additional data indicated how very serious the situation in the development towns had become. Roughly 25% of their high-school pupils had no option but to abandon their studies, either because their parents were simply unable to afford to pay school fees or because the pupils themselves got such extremely bad grades.[50] All of these factors motivated many residents of development towns either to migrate to the country's central cities or to leave Israel altogether. For example, as many as 40% of the population of Ofakim, a development town in Israel's southern Negev region, expressed their desire to leave the city.[51] This phenomenon was not restricted solely to development towns but occurred also in a number of more established municipalities, relatively distant from the country's center and, therefore, deprived of allocations of central-government budgetary resources. For example, about 60% of the inhabitants of the large city of Beersheba (commonly called the "capital of the Negev") indicated their wish to leave their city within the near future.[52]

Notwithstanding the severity of the situation, the government failed to hold any serious discussions about methods of financing the local authorities. As a result, despite the protests voiced by the weakest of those authorities, there was still a gap between the allocations granted to councils located in or near the center of the country and those located on its northern and southern peripheries. The unprecedented reaction of the financially strapped authorities was to organize themselves to apply pressure on the Knesset to intervene far more actively in decision-making on financial matters relating to their municipalities.[53] This step looked like producing an eventual change in the way in which public policy decisions were taken, with greater consideration given to the needs of the development towns and local authorities in general. December 1989, in fact, saw the commencement of genuinely serious negotiations between the relevant government ministries (Finance and Interior) on the one hand and representatives of local authorities and development towns on the other.[54]

ELECTIONS

Municipal and local council elections, held in February, and elections to the Histadrut in November, served both as important power tests in the political system in 1989. The local elections, which took place on 28 February (with the second round, involving 13 municipalities, held on 15 March), had a distinctly political flavor, reminiscent of the 1988 Knesset elections. Likud leaders issued statements claiming that support for their party in those local elections would be tantamount to a demonstration of confidence in the Likud's foreign and security policies, and particularly in its refusal to compromise over the matter of continued Israeli dominion over the West Bank and Gaza.[55] The Labor Party, on the other hand, felt it to be quite wrong to confuse national with purely municipal issues, and it thus entirely refrained from attempts to suggest any connection between the local authority elections and the disputes about the territories.[56] As it turned out, the Likud's chosen tactics appeared the more successful of the two: the Likud won in the elections to all of the large local councils in the country, except for Haifa and Jerusalem. The Labor Party won the elections in just one large municipality, Haifa, and achieved that victory very narrowly and only after having to fight a second round, necessitated by a tie in the first. Teddy Kollek, the Labor Party's long-serving Jerusalem mayor, managed to win yet again, but on an independent ticket, which he had opted for despite his personal identification with the policies advocated by the Labor Party.[57]

The results of the local council elections underscored the gradual decline over the last several years in the Labor Party's capability to attract new voters. The elections showed the Likud to be still the country's most popular party and, therefore, did much to buoy up the Likud's confidence in anticipation of its political struggles with Labor, particularly in regard to the problem of the territories.[58]

While the results of the local council elections in Israel are naturally important to the local authorities themselves and also indicate the relative strength enjoyed by each major political party, the winners of the elections to the Histadrut gain control over a powerful, nationwide organization possessing vast assets which, together with the Employers' Association and the government, effectively dictates the nation's economic policies in its entirety. Although, historically, the Histadrut had always been dominated by the Labor Party, the leaders of the Likud, encouraged by their party's successes in the 1989 municipal elections, came to hope that control of this large labor organization might be within their grasp too.[59] That, however, was not to be.

The results of the Histadrut elections, held on 13 November, were very clear-cut. While the Labor Party lost a shade of its previous support, it scored an outright electoral victory, gaining 55% of the votes cast, as against the 27% for the Likud. Its candidate, Yisrael Kessar, was therefore reelected to the post of Histadrut general secretary, which remains one of the most influential executive positions within the Israeli economy.[60] The results of the elections indicated that, although with Labor leader Peres as finance minister, unemployment in Israel was actually growing, Labor Party representatives were still largely preferred as labor union leaders. This could be attributed to the social-democratic tradition with which the Labor Party was identified. By contrast, the Likud, a right-wing party, was still finding it difficult to assume control over centers of power of this sort.

REFORMATION OF THE ISRAELI POLITICAL SYSTEM

Ever since the State of Israel was established, elections, free and democratic in every respect, had been held whenever necessary. But that should not obscure the fact that certain fairly apparent distortions, nevertheless, existed within the Israeli political system, and needed to be dealt with via comprehensive reforms.

Israeli democracy was in considerable difficulties. The political system made it very hard to rule effectively or to govern the country in accordance with proper long-term planning. Another severe defect was rooted in the absence in Israel of any supra-legislative document containing a definition of its citizens' civil and human rights. These were anchored only in a ruling issued by the Israeli Supreme Court which, though it set down the principles of the country's democratic regime, did not give itself the authority to countermand laws passed by the Knesset. The judiciary system alone was, therefore, incapable of assuring the survival of the country's democratic processes. A prolonged state of emergency, for example, could, by the enactment of emergency legislation, seriously impair civil rights. The Supreme Court would be obliged to uphold such legislation, thereby damaging the foundations of the democratic system.

Given this situation, a number of proposals for the reform of the political system were raised during 1989. It was suggested, *inter alia,* that the country adopt a presidential system of government, that the electoral system be altered, and that a liberal constitution be drafted and approved.[61] But because both of the major parties,

Labor and Likud, clearly preferred to maintain very cordial relations with the religious parties, though never quite knowing when such cordiality might prove useful in some future process of coalition building, none of these proposals had any real chance of being realized in 1989. All of them were opposed by the religious parties on the grounds that any type of reform, such as that suggested in the electoral system, would diminish their political power and, without doubt, resoundingly reduce the degree to which the larger parties depended on them.[62]

The most important reform proposal raised in the Knesset during 1989 took the form of suggested legislation by the Ministry of Justice on human and civil rights, whose formulation was approved as the draft of a possible Basic Law in April. This proposal, if carried, would assure every person in Israel human and civil rights which could not be countermanded by any other authority whatsoever or in any conceivable circumstances, other than in a limited manner during states of emergency.[63] Most of these rights, like that of free speech and organization, were already recognized by virtue of the Supreme Court's ruling. But the proposed law would endow the Supreme Court with judicial supervision, enabling it even to abrogate legislation approved by the Knesset if such was deemed an infringement of human or civil rights.[64]

From that standpoint, 1989 may well yet be considered as having been a year of breakthrough in terms of democratic-constitutional matters, too. But, unless there was some change from the political state of affairs prevailing during 1989, the likelihood of the law being approved by the Knesset was very small. The religious parties were opposed to it, because they suspected it would prevent the passage of any religious laws and because they realized that it might define Israel as a secular state rather than as a state in which the Jewish religion had a special status.[65] If the major parties found themselves obliged to go on depending on the religious parties, the latter could be counted on to thwart the proposed law in the Knesset, so that the legal-political situation, which assured a future for additional legislation of a religious nature, was very likely to persist.

SOCIAL AFFAIRS: RELIGIOUS AND ETHNIC RIVALRIES

Israel's Jewish society is characterized by a solidly engrained communal gap between citizens of North African and Asian descent (known as "Sephardim") and those originally hailing from Eastern or Western Europe ("Ashkenazim"). The social tensions deriving from that gap explode from time to time, in varying degrees, depending on the circumstances. Toward the end of 1989, for example, it gradually became apparent that due to developments in Eastern Europe, the next five years were likely to witness an immigration into Israel of hundreds of thousands of mainly Russian "Ashkenazi" Jews. In the period October-December, about 60% more such immigrants reached Israel's shores than during the parallel months in 1988. Not only were these people "Ashkenazim," they were mostly also religiously nonobservant and a great many of them were highly educated. In these respects, too, they seemed to differ from Israel's "Sephardi" community which understandably developed some concern over this new phenomenon of potential competition. Moreover, since mass immigration has always been one of the principal cornerstones of Zionist doctrine, the newcomers from Eastern Europe were accorded economic and other benefits of various kinds, including assistance in the acquisition of housing. This aroused a measure of envy and bitterness in certain "Sephardi" quarters which felt themselves underprivileged and gave rise to incipient social tension.[66]

An additional factor behind the outbreak of social tensions was the publication in November 1989, of the National Insurance Institute's annual report, which indicated that about 400,000 Israeli citizens were living beneath the "poverty line" in 1988. The great majority of these were people of North African, mostly Moroccan, descent. The result was that a conference attended by about 200 political activists on behalf of the "Sephardi" community passed a resolution rebuking the government for widening the communal gap by investing funds in the absorption of new immigrants instead of solving the basic problems suffered by underprivileged ethnic communities long resident in Israel.[67] One of the initiators of the conference explained the resolution:

> It is unacceptable that the State of Israel has the money for a million immigrants and yet, for the past 40 years, has never been able to produce the funds required for solving the problems faced by the underprivileged communities. We should issue a call for people to take to the streets and, upon leaving this conference, each one of us should go out and incite his community against the government.[68]

The governmental authorities responded that the accusation was baseless. The chairman of the World Zionist Organization, Simcha Dinitz, dismissed as "demagogic" the suggestion that efforts invested in the absorption of immigrants were being undertaken at the expense of alleviating poverty. The truth, in his opinion, was quite to the contrary. The expected immigrants, he contended, would in part choose to settle in currently impoverished neighborhoods and in development towns, thereby entitling them to increased budget allocations. Moreover, the overall population increase was likely to stimulate economic activity throughout the entire country, if previous experience with the benefits resulting from mass immigration was any guide.[69]

At the time of this writing, it was impossible to assess with any certainty whether or not the apparent trend toward a deterioration of intercommunal relations would continue. What seemed clear, though, was that the Israeli political system had not yet succeeded in producing any permanent solutions to the long-standing problem of communal divisiveness within the country, with all of its conceivably negative implications for the absorption of new immigrants.

An additional social rift, typical of Israel, was that between its religious and secular Jews. The differences between the interests of these two sectors of the populace were highlighted during 1989 when the "Who Is A Jew" issue was again hauled onto the national agenda. As in the past, the debate revolved around the question of whether or not to amend the "Law of the Return," which prescribes the automatic conferral of citizenship on Jews immigrating to Israel. The law, enacted in 1950 and amended in 1970, defined a Jew either as a person born to a Jewish mother or as someone who had converted to Judaism and did not belong to any other faith.[70] The religious parties demanded an amendment which would recognize converts as Jews only if they were converted in accordance with strictly Orthodox procedures. Upon raising this matter again in 1989, the religious parties aroused an impassioned public debate and threatened to resign from the government *en bloc* if their demand for the amendment was not met. The other parties, mainly those of socialist and leftist bent, opposed them tenaciously, digging in their heels very firmly.[71]

The regime in Israel operates on the basis of coalition compromises. By virtue of the results of the 1988 general election, in which all of the religious parties (and especially the "haredi," ultra-Orthodox parties) did exceptionally well (see *MECS* 1988, chapter on Israel), the Likud, which emerged as the largest party, found itself unable to form a government unless ready to entertain far-reaching concessions on religious matters to the religious parties. It therefore promised, *inter alia*, to support the passing of amendments to the "Law of the Return" in accordance with Orthodox religious requirements. However, when pressed during 1989 to make good its promise, the Likud objected on the ground that it refused to permit actions pertaining to such divisive religious matters to jeopardize either the survival of its National Unity Government or the maintenance of cordial relations with American Jewry.[72]

The latter, regarding the proposed amendments as a derogation of the authority of the institutions within the Jewish Reform movement in the US (as well as contempt for all those who had converted to Judaism under its auspices), had strenuously resisted any tampering with the status quo.[73] The issue reflected the conflicting interests represented, on the one hand, by the Orthodox religious establishment in Israel, which has exclusive jurisdiction in matters of personal status, including the registration of marriages and divorces and, on the other, by the religious Reform movement in the US, which carries great weight among American Jewry. Their bitter dispute over the proposed amendment threatened to sour relations between Israel and the most powerful Jewish community in the diaspora, which had traditionally been of great help in getting successive American administrations to consider Israel's interests favorably when shaping its policies toward the ME.[74] Alarmed by the prospect, the Likud chose to notify the religious parties that their planned "amendments" stood no chance of acceptance by the Knesset within the near future.[75] The religious parties, nevertheless, decided not to pull out of the government. Any such step would merely have served to relegate them to the opposition benches, bereft both of influence and benefits, while the government, being so widely based, would have remained in office unscathed.[76] Accordingly, 1989 saw the status quo on matters of religion and state preserved unchanged, because, in spite of their growing importance, the religious parties were still unable to undermine the foundations of the National Unity Government.

ECONOMIC DEVELOPMENT

As long ago as July 1985, an economic stabilization program was launched with a view to curing two of Israel's foremost ills — the deficit in its balance of payments and the high rate of domestic price inflation. The intention, additionally, had been to bring about a change in the structure of the economy. In 1989, though, the government in practice retreated somewhat from those plans.

Whereas in 1985 the government had established a policy of refraining from supporting companies which had fallen on hard times, it reneged on that policy during 1989, arranging massive financial bailouts for economic enterprises such as the Koor Corporation, the various kibbutz collective settlements, and the moshav farms.[77] In parallel, 1989 saw a deficit of NIS4bn. in the state budget, a decline of about 4% (compared with 1988) in gross domestic investment in the economy, and only a slight increase over 1988, amounting to 1%, in gross domestic production. These developments, added to the rise in inflation (20.7% in 1989, compared with 16.4% in 1988) and the high level of unemployment (about 8.9% in 1989, compared with 6.4% in 1988), clearly indicated that the Israeli economy was in difficulties in 1989.[78] Nevertheless, in certain fields such as electronics, there were clear signs of an imminent increase in exports, even to such electronically developed countries as Japan.[79]

Overall, it became apparent during 1989 that the government was failing to realize its economic goals. The main aims, of reducing inflation and stimulating economic growth, were not achieved. Indeed, when the time came to draft the budget for 1990–91 and the finance minister proposed a decreased total budget of NIS55.2bn. (c. $28bn.), based on reductions in public housing expenditure and a freeze in outlays on security, almost all of the government's ministers objected, and even went so far as to demand additions to their respective ministries' allocations.[80]

In contrast with what occurs in democratic regimes headed by an elected president, the control over a given government ministry in Israel is often the outcome of political bargaining. A satellite party pledging its parliamentary support to the ruling party is rewarded by being given control over a ministry. This has negative implications for the process of efficient budget planning, as was most evident in 1989. The Finance Ministry, right up until the end of the year, found itself unable to put together a budget to which all members of the government agreed because the different cabinet ministers insisted on budget supplements for their respective ministries.[81] Any minister incapable of securing such a supplement ran the risk of being regarded by his party as having failed politically, both on a personal and party level. The disputes over the proposed budget, therefore, largely took the form of political wrangling.[82] The arguments surrounding the budget for the Housing Ministry, for example, were essentially based on a political altercation between Housing Minister Levy, a Likud politician with hawkish tendencies, and Finance Minister Peres, the chairman of the Labor Party.[83]

Security matters played their own role in aggravating the many difficulties in formulating an agreed national budget. As much as $400m. of the Defense Ministry's budget ($5.3bn.) went to cover the costs of dealing with the Intifada in 1989.[84] This prompted demands by the ministry for a supplement of between $50m. and $75m. over and beyond the appropriation suggested by the minister of finance for the 1990–91 national budget.[85] The argument these two ministries conducted over the issue in 1989 was very similar to that traditionally waged between them. The minister of defense always requests more funds for the purpose of developing the deterrent and defensive capacity of Israel's military forces. The minister of finance always tries to explain that budget cuts are necessary to ensure a balanced budget (or, at least, a budget deficit as low as possible) so as to weaken inflationary pressures. In 1989, as in the past, the Ministry of Defense issued stern warnings that if it did not receive the requested supplement, it would have to reduce its purchases of matériel, the number of training hours given to the military forces, and its long-term reequipment programs.[86]

A further issue that reared its head during the debates over the national budget was that of funding the Ministry of Immigration and Absorption. Indications of the likely arrival of between 100,000 and 200,000 new immigrants from the Soviet Union alone during the period from October 1989 to December 1992 (over and beyond those anticipated to come from other countries), stirred the ministry to demand a far larger than normal budgetary allocation.[87] The Finance Ministry found it difficult to resist that plea. It was becoming clear that the need to accommodate, feed, and retrain the many people arriving in the unexpectedly large waves of immigration from Eastern Europe, and the need to create places of employment for them, were going to necessitate the recruitment of financial means on a much greater scale than envisaged when the state budget was initially drawn up.[88] It was also becoming apparent that this influx of human resources was likely to exercise a decisive impact on the national economy as a whole. But no one was sure what the nature of that impact would be.[89]

FOREIGN RELATIONS

In addition to the perennial issues generated by the ongoing Arab-Palestinian-Israeli conflict, two principal matters occupied the attention of those responsible for determining Israel's foreign policy during 1989. One was the country's relations with the US, which were largely affected by the conflicting manner in which each side tended to regard the problem of the Palestinians and the Arab-Israeli conflict in general. The other was the development of relations with the states in Eastern Europe generally, and with the Soviet Union in particular, in the light of the very dramatic reforms and changes occurring there during the year.

ISRAEL AND THE UNITED STATES

Israel had long sought to convince the US Administration that it was prepared to talk peace with the Arabs, even to the Palestinians, provided that it would not lead to the creation of an independent Palestinian state.[90] In this context, the diplomatic relations between the two states were characterized by a fairly standard pattern: the more urgent the US's demand for a formal Israeli expression of preparedness to negotiate with a Palestinian delegation, and the more insistent Israel was on first receiving assurances that such a delegation would not contain PLO representatives, the tenser their diplomatic relations became.

A switch occurred during 1989 in the attitude held by the US Administration toward Israel. For the first time in a decade, some fairly basic differences of opinion were revealed in the manner in which the two states regarded the future of the occupied territories and the solution to the conflict in general. On the face of things, the primary cause of tension between Israel and the US was the different ways in which each approached the question of defining the identity of the PLO. The American position was that the PLO no longer constituted a terrorist organization, since it had declared its acceptance of the limitations implied by UN Resolutions 242 and 338. The Government of Israel, by contrast, and especially its Likud component, stood by its view that it was untrue that the PLO was not now a terrorist organization, maintaining that the PLO continued to employ unjustified violence for the purpose of realizing its aims and that it was an organization unworthy of being negotiated with by Israel.[91] Accordingly, while the US was busy advocating direct diplomatic negotiations among Israel, Egypt, the US, and the Palestinians, Israel was demanding explicit written guarantees that neither the PLO nor anyone identified with it would be permitted to participate in the negotiations, either directly or indirectly.[92] Eventually, therefore, the American Administration provided guarantees approximating the Israeli Government's formal demands. On 18 December the State Department issued a declaration clarifying that Israel would not be obliged to negotiate with the PLO and that the central, though not the sole, issue to be discussed at the intended meeting with Palestinians in Cairo would pertain to the proposed elections in the occupied territories.[93] Nevertheless, the Israeli Government was slow to budge in its formal position. The hesitancy exhibited by Prime Minister Shamir over whether, and under what conditions, Israel should enter into a dialogue with the Palestinians, contributed to the eventual fall of the National Unity Government in March 1990.

The US agreed to Shamir's program for elections and included it within the plan put forward by US Secretary of State James Baker, known as the Baker plan, of 7 October (for further particulars, see the chapter on the peace process). But, at the insistence of the Likud, Israel let it be known that the meeting in Cairo, proposed by the Baker plan, would have to be dedicated solely to the matter of the elections and that, in contradiction to what the plan suggested, Israel would refuse to discuss in Cairo any other issues related to the peace program.[94] Furthermore, Israel insisted that the Baker plan would have to contain a written guarantee stating that the Palestinians would not be represented by the PLO, and that Israel would be accorded a right of veto over the composition of the Palestinian delegation and the agenda for the Cairo discussions.[95]

Israel's apprehension about the possibility that an independent Palestinian state would eventually be formed, explains why, despite Israel's clear dependency on the US and their strategic-military alliance, some right-wing Israeli politicians leveled very hard-hitting accusations against the US. Thus, reacting to the hesitancy exhibited by President George Bush to meet with Prime Minister Shamir (almost certainly resorted to as a device for pressuring Israel into concessions), Minister of Housing Levy called the US president's behavior "a national insult to Israel."[96]

The Likud, almost unanimously, evinced a tough and uncompromising stand toward the proposals put forward by the US and known as the Baker plan. The Likud's fundamental assumption was that accepting the American suggestions in the form in which they were advanced would likely result in Israel's eventual destruction. In any event, they contradicted the Likud's desire to continue governing the occupied territories, which constituted part of "Eretz Israel," to which the Jewish People had historic rights. This attitude was often expressed by Likud leaders. One prominent statement was made by Shamir, who spoke of the Jewish People's need for, and rights to, a "large" Land of Israel.[97]

By and large, the Likud attempted to play down the significance of the political pressures exerted by the US. The prime minister was of the opinion that superpower pressure applied on Israel had never achieved anything and that the Government of Israel would, therefore, be entirely mistaken if it permitted differences in outlook with the US to warrant altering its policies in regard to issues of war or of peace. To Israel, he argued, its own security was a paramount interest, while to the US, a superpower involved in so many international affairs, it could only be a matter of secondary concern.[98] Foreign Minister Moshe Arens shared this view. Toward the end of November, when asked to comment on Washington's views regarding the composition of the Palestinian delegation and the agenda in Cairo, and regarding the notion that the US might apply sanctions if Israel persisted in opposing those views, he declared that Israel would not agree to "receiving orders" from the US and that it was capable of standing up to pressures exerted by the American Administration.[99]

In spite of all these differences of opinion, no cutback in American aid of c. $3bn. to Israel occurred during 1989, and relations between the two countries remained generally very favorable. The US went on giving Israel diplomatic assistance: on 10 June, for example, it exercised its veto in the UN Security Council, thereby blocking passage of a resolution condemning "Israel's activities in the territories."[100]

Notwithstanding the forthright manner in which the Government of Israel repeatedly declared its firm intention to frustrate any possibility of creating a Palestinian state, neither the prime minister nor any of his more hawkish ministers actually did anything rash enough to severely sour relations with the US. Accordingly, although Shamir was verbally bound by all of the Likud's formal positions, his practical policies (whether those he himself had designed or those to which he was merely a party) were actually rather more cautious. Even though he was wont to state that an Israeli government headed by the Likud would be obliged to continue the process of establishing Jewish settlements in the West Bank and Gaza, in actual fact the National Unity Government limited scope of such settlement activity during 1989.[101] Again, although Shamir declared that "the Likud's positions would not alter even if the Intifada were to continue for another 10 years,"[102] the Likud's stance was actually shaped with a view to inducing a political situation that would bring about an end to the Intifada, though naturally not at the price of a Palestinian state coming into being. The Likud's positions, therefore, caused tension in diplomatic relations between Israel and the US, but not a real crisis. The American Administration, for its part, clarified its view that despite the thaw in relations between the superpowers and the end of the cold war, Washington's commitment to Israel would not be allowed to diminish and that the cooperation between the two states, including the strategic-military, would proceed as before.[103]

In contrast with the positions of the Likud regarding the US, the Labor Party's were to respond positively to the Baker proposals in order to prevent a diplomatic crisis from erupting.[104] This difference also reflected a basic divergence in how the two parties regarded the nature of the desired relationship between Israel and the US. The Labor Party, not being ideologically commited to continued Israeli rule over the territories, has traditionally tended to be more considerate of the attitudes of the American Administration (for further discussion of Israeli-US relations, see chapters on the US and the ME, and the ME peace process).

ISRAEL, THE SOVIET UNION, AND EASTERN EUROPE

Although the need to obtain Washington's support for its positions occupied much of Israel's diplomatic attention, considerable efforts were also made to develop diplomatic relations with the countries in the Eastern bloc. This was prompted by three main motives: a desire to realize the Zionist goal of large Jewish immigration from those countries; the hope that, thereby, Israel might obtain both diplomatic support and more extensive political legitimacy; and the expectation that the development of diplomatic relations with Eastern bloc countries would open up possibilities for establishing commercial and economic ties with them.

One of the first signs of the upcoming renewal of relations with the Eastern bloc occurred in January with the visit to Israel of the Hungarian minister of agriculture. His stay in the country was partially devoted to talks about the possibility of establishing diplomatic relations between Israel and Hungary, and an agricultural cooperation agreement was signed.[105] These first steps toward understanding paved the way for a visit by Israeli Minister of Religions Zevulun Hammer to Budapest in February, where he met with Hungarian Prime Minister Miklos Nemeth.[106] An important development on the road to the establishment of diplomatic relations, and also a factor of considerable significance in facilitating the transfer of Eastern European Jews to Israel, was the signing of an air transport agreement between the two countries on 28 February; on 27 March Israel's national airline El Al inaugurated a new route, Budapest-Tel Aviv.[107] The likelihood of the political relations between Israel and Hungary being improved became even stronger when, on 27 March, for the very first time since 1948, the Hungarian parliament publicly commemorated the 600,000 Hungarian Jews who had perished in the Holocaust.[108] More progress yet was made on 4 July when an agreement was signed providing for a mutual reduction of import duties between the two countries. The signatures to this document, which was likely to facilitate much freer trade in both directions, were appended simultaneously in Jerusalem and Budapest.[109] Mutual economic relations were given a further impetus when Israeli Minister of Energy Moshe Shahal made an official visit to Hungary, pursuant to which a further economic cooperation treaty was signed. This series of compacts served to pave the way for a full resumption of diplomatic ties between the two countries, which finally occurred on 18 September.[110]

Opportunities for the possible forging of diplomatic links with yet another Eastern European country came on 29 January with the visit to Israel of the East German minister of religions, which emerged as more than a mere diplomatic mission. The minister made an official visit to Yad va'Shem, Israel's national shrine to the memory of victims of Nazi persecution. In so doing, he seemed to be offering a hint that East Germany was prepared to shoulder its part in the historical responsibility for the Nazi crimes against the Jews during World War II.[111]

Diplomatic relations with a further country, Poland, gradually developed during 1989. The two states signed an agricultural cooperation agreement on 2 March, and on 27 March a direct air route between Warsaw and Tel Aviv was inaugurated.[112] A more important diplomatic contact with Poland took place when Minister of Religions Hammer went on an official visit to Poland on 16 August and acted to secure the removal of a Carmelite convent which had been sited within the Auschwitz extermination camp.[113] These political developments led to the full resumption of diplomatic relations between the two countries in March 1990.

The initial foundation stone for the resumption of diplomatic relations between Israel and the Soviet Union was laid during 1989 when Israeli Foreign Minister Arens met with his Soviet counterpart, Eduard Shevardnadze. Following their talks, the Israeli consular mission to the Soviet Union was rehoused, for the first time since the Soviets severed diplomatic ties with Israel in 1967, in the Israeli Embassy building in Moscow, which had remained unoccupied for 23 years.[114] Thereafter, as had been the pattern in regard to other Eastern bloc countries, diplomatic relations between Israel and the Soviet Union were gradually strengthened through the signing of various cooperation agreements covering matters of culture and trade. A significant step forward was taken on 11 April when an accord was signed between the Association of Soviet Authors and the Hebrew Writers' Association in Israel.[115] Subsequently, an Israeli medical mission went to the Soviet Union on 10 June to assist in treating the victims of the gas explosion disaster in the Ural Mountains. In July and August, an official delegation of journalists from Tel Aviv met with their colleagues from the Soviet Union.[116] A further, very clear, expression of the change in Soviet attitudes toward Israel was voiced on 17 October when the UN General Assembly debated a resolution proposed by Arab states in favor of ejecting Israel from membership in that body: notwithstanding its opposition to Israeli rule over the occupied territories and to the Israeli manner of dealing with the Intifada, the Soviet Union refrained from supporting the resolution, thereby contributing to its rejection.[117]

Overall, therefore, 1989 was characterized by a historic change in the nature and scope of Israel's relations with the Eastern bloc. This appeared to be a significant change, which reflected a deliberate desire on the part of the countries comprising that bloc to expand their diplomatic ties with Israel.

ISRAEL AND THE AFRICAN STATES

The diplomatic relations between Israel and the African states improved in the course of 1989. On 16 January, the Central African Republic announced that it was resuming diplomatic ties with Israel.[118] On 4 February, Israel opened its embassy in Nairobi, Kenya and, on 24 August, Foreign Minister Arens paid an official visit to that country, the first Israeli minister to do so since 1973. During his stay in Kenya, Arens signed an agreement on economic and technical cooperation between the two states, which was followed by an air transport agreement.[119] An additional major achievement for Israeli foreign policy came when, on 3 November, diplomatic relations with Ethiopia were resumed after a break of 16 years.[120]

Israel attached considerable importance to strengthening its ties with African states, partially because such states could provide much-needed support for its positions at the UN, where Israel had always suffered significant numerical inferiority in comparison with the many countries in the Arab and Muslim world. That numerical inferiority was very relevant when resolutions were submitted for decision at sittings of the General Assembly and debates in the UN's various committees, although not in the Security Council, where the US often used its veto to defend Israeli interests. Israel's relations with African countries were also of appreciable economic value. Those countries required Israeli assistance in areas such as agriculture, building construction, and industrial development, as well as security. They were, therefore, capable of serving as a very useful source of export earnings.

ISRAEL, WESTERN EUROPE, AND JAPAN

In contrast with the diplomatic developments occurring in other areas of Israel's foreign policy, its diplomatic relations with the countries of Western Europe did not undergo any major changes during 1989. Western Europe, in general, maintained a posture in regard to the Palestinian question which was quite different from that held by the Israeli Government. Most of the European countries continued to believe that Israel ought to recognize the PLO and should engage in negotiations with it. This stance was made very clear to Prime Minister Shamir, for example, when he visited Italy on 23 November.[121]

Nevertheless, Western Europe's relations with Israel continued to be as amicable as before. This proved itself in the various commercial, industrial, and economic contacts maintained between them, as well in cultural exchanges. During 1989, for example, Israel's cultural and scientific relations with Spain were given a boost when, in

October, a cooperation agreement was entered into between the Hebrew University in Jerusalem and a number of Spanish universities.[122] On 19 November, France announced that it would renew its supplies of military equipment to Israel for the first time since 1968, when it had placed an embargo on shipments of equipment of that type.[123] The cordial diplomatic relations maintained with all the other Western European countries similarly continued undisturbed.

But Israel's interest in Western Europe went beyond the mere matter of diplomatic ties. Europe would be economically unified in 1992, and this unification threatened to have severe repercussions on the Israeli economy. Europe, with its 320m. consumers, bought about 30% of all Israeli exports and spent about $500m. in Israel each year.[124] Accordingly, a European-Jewish lobby was organized in November, designed to represent the Israeli Ministry of Trade and Industry, the Foreign Ministry, and the Finance Ministry on matters requiring discussion with the European Common Market.[125] The lobby undertook to fulfill a number of important functions, including that of coordinating resistance to the boycott which the Arab states and the PLO were trying to impose on countries prepared to engage in trade with Israel. In addition, Israel decided to set up an embassy to the institutions of the Common Market. By virtue of budgetary problems, however, the establishment of that embassy was subsequently deferred to 1990.[126]

The general trend of improvement in the relations between Israel and the European states was marred by its relations with Austria. In response to the appointment of Kurt Waldheim, suspected by Israel of having collaborated with the Nazis during World War II, as President of Austria, Israel recalled its ambassador from Vienna. In reaction, Austria announced on 18 September that it would lower the level of its own diplomatic representation in Israel for as long as Israel chose to persist in its opposition to Waldheim's presidency and failed to restore full diplomatic relations.[127]

An additional goal of Israel's foreign policy was to improve its relations with Japan, a country that was emerging as a superpower in political terms and not only in the area of economics. Trading contacts between Israel and Japan, inaugurated in 1985, continued to develop during 1989. In November, Foreign Minister Arens paid a visit to Japan, during which it became clear that the differences of opinion between the two countries over the Palestinian issue remained essentially unchanged. The Japanese Government's position was clearly in favor of direct negotiations between Israel and the PLO.[128] However, although Israel saw the matter entirely otherwise, extensive trading contacts between the two were expected to continue, mainly in areas associated with electronics and computers.[129]

By and large, in 1989 Israel generally succeeded in preserving its international status as a country which, though small, was important to the joint effort to maintain order throughout the world. In addition, the year witnessed breakthroughs in forging diplomatic links between Israel and certain countries which, for long periods, had refrained from conducting diplomatic relations with it. The year saw Israel extending the scope of international legitimacy accorded it, one of the reasons being that Israel, in spite of its difficulties and the many constraints imposed by military-security problems, remained a democracy. In a vastly changing world, which tended to attach ever-increasing significance to democracy as the favored form of regime, this was considered important, even by those Third-World countries with which Israel was developing relationships.

SUMMARY

The year 1989 was crowded with important events in Israeli politics. Overall, it was a year in which the political system was forced to contend with extremely difficult problems concerned with national security, economic and social matters, the rule of law and social order, and Israel's relations with the rest of the world. This, for such a small country, still developing as it shaped democratic rules and tried to preserve the democratic values it had already made its own, was a task of supreme proportions. Indeed, so manifold were the public issues with which Israel had to contend, the entire year passed without it chalking up a single genuinely major achievement. It turned out, in fact, to be a year of considerable hardship for the country and for its citizens — a pallid, even bitter, period endured in the shadow of dilemmas perceived by most Israelis as being hard existential dilemmas. It was a year in which Israelis became thoroughly aware of the real price that they had to pay for the privilege of their independence in a sovereign state. It was a year in which they were reminded, over and over again, how very difficult it was to be an Israeli.

And yet 1989 was a year during which the state preserved its basic fundamentals and prevented the many challenges it faced from becoming wholly uncontrollable. The problems associated with national security were not solved but, nevertheless, remained under the firm control of the government and the security forces; the economy still faced very severe difficulties, but showed considerable signs that some significant opportunities for growth might be around the corner; underprivileged social sectors were still clearly enduring hardship, but their problems were gradually being attended to and were certainly not of colossal proportions; the rule of law still ensured the preservation of democracy (within Israel proper) and the maintenance of social order. And, where the country's foreign relations were concerned, Israel was doing a great deal to bolster up the degree of the political legitimization being accorded it by the outside world, even though this might eventually intensify the pressure to agree to withdraw from the occupied territories.

As in the past, Israelis came to realize, during 1989, that their country was succeeding in its goal of maintaining a fairly open society in spite of having to contend with ongoing existential insecurity. That insecurity, one had to acknowledge, was to a very large degree determined by the essential characteristics of what was perhaps the world's most problematic region — the Middle East.

NOTES

For the place and frequency of publications cited here, and for the full name of the publication, news agency, radio station, or monitoring service where an abbreviation is used, please see "List of Sources." Only in the case of more than one publication bearing the same name is the place of publication noted here.

1. Public opinion polls conducted by Modi'in Ezrachi (a polling service) and Gad Barzilai (April 1989).
2. *Ma'ariv* 23 October 1989.
3. Ibid.
4. Protocols of the Knesset, 13 February 1989, pp.13–28.
5. Manifesto issued by the Mafdal in July 1989 regarding the Intifada.
6. Interview with Peres in *Der Spiegel,* 23 January; *JP,* 14 September 1989.

7. VoI, 29 January — DR, 31 January 1989.
8. *Ma'ariv*, 9 August 1989.
9. Interview with Peres, VoI, 17 September 1989.
10. Ibid.
11. *Ha'aretz*, 8 October 1989.
12. Ibid.
13. Declaration of Moshe Katzav, minister of transportation, VoI, 14 September — DR, 14 September 1989.
14. Interviews with Shamir, *Le Monde,* 1 February 1989.
15. *Ha'aretz*, 5 July 1989.
16. *Ma'ariv* 17 September; *Ha'aretz,* 23 October 1989.
17. Interview with Shamir in *Yedi'ot Aharonot,* 8 December 1989.
18. Israeli TV, 13 September; *Ma'ariv*, 14 September 1989.
19. See Note 1.
20. Modi'in Ezrachi polls for 1987.
21. *Ha'aretz,* 10 November 1989.
22. Ibid.
23. High Court 680/88 Shniser *et al* v. The Censorship and the minister of defense, *Collection of Judgments,* Vol. 42, No. 4, p. 617.
24. Ibid.
25. High Court 73/53 Kol Ha'Am v. Ministry of Interior, *Collection of Judgments,* Vol. 7, p. 871.
26. The formula adopted by the Supreme Court was that censorship is unjustified unless the danger for the public's safety or sentiment is clear and the damage is great.
27. Annual Report of the Israeli Information Center for Human Rights in the Occupied Territories for 1989; *Ma'ariv* 20 December 1989.
28. VoI, 8 February — DR, 8 February 1989. '
29. *Ma'ariv*, 2 October 1989.
30. Ibid.
31. *Ha'aretz,* Friday Bulletin, 6 April 1990: the annual report of the Israeli Information Center for Human Rights in the Occupied Territories (1989), p. 100.
32. High Court 358/88 The Civil Rights Organization v. The Commander of the Central Area, *Collection of Judgments,* Vol. 43, No. 2, p. 529. The decision was made in 1989.
33. *NYT*, 12 August; *Ma'ariv*, 6 December 1989.
34. *JP*, 7 December 1989.
35. Ibid.
36. Clause 4 (8) of the Prevention of Terror Ordinance.
37. *Ha'aretz,* 28 September 1989.
38. *Ma'ariv*, 22 October 1989.
39. *JP*, 13 December; Zeev Schiff in *Ha'aretz,* 21 November 1989.
40. *JP*, 13 September 1989.
41. Ibid., see also sources quoted in Note 39.
42. *Ma'ariv*, 10 September 1989.
43. Yuval Elitzur in *Ma'ariv*, 2 October 1989; *Ma'ariv*, 29 September 1989.
44. *Ha'aretz,* 12 October; *NYT,* 7 August 1989.
45. *Ma'ariv*, 1 December 1989.
46. Ibid.
47. *Ha'aretz,* 13 October; *Ma'ariv*, 25 December 1989.
48. *Ha'aretz,* 28 December 1989 (data based on information supplied by the Israeli Central Bureau of Statistics).
49. *Ma'ariv*, 27 November 1989 (data based on information supplied by the Israeli Central Bureau of Statistics).
50. *Ma'ariv*, 25 October 1989.
51. Ibid., 28 September 1989.
52. Ibid., 7 September 1989.
53. *Ha'aretz,* 22 November 1989.
54. *Ma'ariv*, 27 December 1989.

55. Shamir's declaration, *Ha'aretz*, 25 February 1989.
56. Labor Party spokesmen's declarations throughout the election campaign.
57. *Ha'aretz*, 1 March 1989.
58. For an analysis of the results, see ibid.
59. Shamir's statement, *Ma'ariv*, 28 September; statement by Yaakov Shamay, the Likud candidate for Histadrut general secretary, *Ha'aretz*, 11 October 1989.
60. The formal results were published in a special bulletin of the Histadrut, 4 December 1989.
61. Yoram Peri, *Reforms in the Political System in Israel* (Tel Aviv: The Israel-Diaspora Institute, 1989; in Hebrew); Gabriel Shtrasman in *Ma'ariv*, 16 November 1989.
62. For attitudes during the Knesset debate on the proposed Civil Rights Law and reactions of the religious parties, see *Ma'ariv* 16, 20 November, 21 December 1989; for debates in the Knesset Constitution and Law Committee, see *Ha'aretz*, 6 December 1989.
63. The draft of the suggested law was published by the Ministry of Justice in April 1989.
64. Ibid., clause 26 and appendices.
65. For such declarations and attitudes, see *Ma'ariv*, 16 November; *Ha'aretz*, 6 December 1989.
66. *Ha'aretz*, 6 December; *Ma'ariv*, 7 December 1989.
67. Ibid., and *JP*, 22 November 1989.
68. *Ha'aretz*, 6 December 1989.
69. *Ma'ariv*, 7 December 1989.
70. Law of Return, 1950.
71. *Ma'ariv*, 16 November 1989.
72. Ibid.
73. Ibid.
74. Ibid.
75. Ibid.
76. Gideon Alon in *Ha'aretz*, 11 October; *Ma'ariv* 22,23, 26, 31, October 1989.
77. Ibid., 22 October 1989.
78. Monthly bulletin of the Israeli Central Bureau of Statistics, February 1990.
79. *Ha'aretz*, 11 December 1989.
80. *Ma'ariv*, 19, 27 December 1989.
81. Ibid.
82. Ibid.
83. *JP*, 25 December 1989.
84. Ibid., 19 December 1989.
85. Ibid.
86. See Note 68.
87. Interview with Minister of Immigration and Absorption Rabbi Yitzhak Peretz in *Ha'aretz*, 3 November 1989.
88. Ibid.
89. Ibid.
90. *Ma'ariv*, 24 November, 11 December 1989.
91. *Ma'ariv*, 17 September 1989.
92. *JP*, 23 October 1989.
93. Israeli TV, 16 December 1989.
94. *JP*, 29 October 1989.
95. Ibid.
96. *Ma'ariv*, 1 November 1989.
97. Ibid., 27 November 1989.
98. Ibid., 10 November; R. IDF, 9 November 1989.
99. *JP*, 21 November 1989.
100. *Ha'aretz*, 11 June 1989.
101. *Ma'ariv*, 27 November 1989.
102. Ibid.
103. *Ha'aretz*, 30 November 1989.
104. Peres's response to Baker's proposal, VoI, 24 October 1989.
105. *Ha'aretz*, 4 January 1989.

106. Ibid., 19 February 1989.
107. *Ma'ariv*, 28 March 1989.
108. Ibid.
109. Ibid., 5 July 1989.
110. *Ha'aretz*, 19 September 1989.
111. *Ma'ariv*, 30 January 1989.
112. Ibid., 28 March 1989.
113. *Ha'aretz*, 17 August 1989.
114. Ibid., 9, 30 January 1989.
115. *Ma'ariv*, 12 April 1989.
116. Ibid., 11 June, 19 July 1989.
117. *Ha'aretz*, 18 October 1989.
118. Ibid., 17 January 1989.
119. *Ma'ariv*, 25 August 1989.
120. *Ha'aretz*, 4 November 1989.
121. *Ma'ariv*, 24 November 1989.
122. Ibid., 24 October 1989.
123. *Ha'aretz*, 20 November 1989.
124. *Ha'aretz*, 16 November 1989.
125. *Ma'ariv*, 30 November 1989.
126. *Ha'aretz*, 16 November 1989.
127. *Ma'ariv*, 20 September 1989.
128. Ibid., 10 November 1989.
129. Ibid.

Jordan

(Al-Mamlaka al-Urdunniyya al-Hashimiyya)

ASHER SUSSER

Three major events shaped the domestic scene in Jordan during 1989, all indicative of a steadily worsening economic and political crisis: an agreement with the International Monetary Fund (IMF) in mid-April on the rescheduling of Jordan's relatively massive foreign debt (more than $8bn.); the outbreak of widespread riots in southern Jordan a few days later, in the wake of new austerity measures imposed in accordance with IMF requirements; and the general elections in November, which resulted in an impressive showing of Muslim fundamentalist groups, whose candidates secured over a third of the seats in the new 80-member Chamber of Deputies.

King Husayn faced the most serious challenge to his regime since the civil war of 1970–71. Sharp reductions in Arab economic aid to Jordan, declining remittances from Jordanian workers in the Gulf states, and excessive borrowing were at the root of Jordan's economic woes. The internal crisis was exacerbated by demographic pressures, mounting unemployment, and an uneven distribution of wealth among different regions of the country and between the various strata of society. The rise of Islamic fundamentalism, apparent in Jordan since the late 1970s, gathered momentum against the background of widespread popular disaffection and steadily declining standards of living. Jordanians were compelled to tighten their belts after a decade of relative prosperity that had lasted until the mid-1980s.

Faced with domestic trials, Jordan sought regional political and economic support when it joined Egypt, Iraq, and North Yemen to form the Arab Cooperation Council (ACC) in February. Apart from expanding trade relations with the members of the ACC, Jordan presumably hoped to enjoy Iraqi economic aid at some time in the not too distant future. The ACC was also probably intended to allow Jordan, particularly in coordination with Egypt, to maintain a foothold in the Middle East peace process. Despite Husayn's disengagement from the West Bank in July 1988 (see *MECS* 1988, pp. 591–95), Jordan still had an interest in playing a central role in the ultimate determination of the political fate of the Palestinians. Any future settlement of the Palestinian issue was bound to have far-reaching ramifications for Jordan and its own large Palestinian population.

But Jordan's domestic stability was a fundamental precondition for an effective Jordanian role in any negotiations. The events of 1989 indicated a certain weakening of Husayn's previously firm grip on affairs in the country. There were rumors that the king had suffered a heart attack. In July he had a medical checkup in London, which, according to an official release "centered on the heart and the digestive system."[1] Unless Husayn had his own house in order, discussion of Jordan's role in the peace process could become increasingly irrelevant.

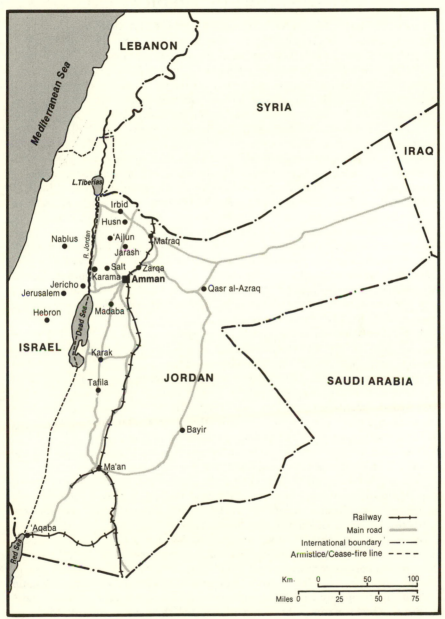

LEBANON

SYRIA

IRAQ

Mediterranean Sea

L.Tiberias

Irbid

Husn

Nablus

'Ajlun

R. Jordan

Mafraq

Jarash

Salt

Zarqa

Karama

Amman

Jericho

Qasr al-Azraq

Jerusalem

Hebron

Dead Sea

Madaba

ISRAEL

Karak

JORDAN

SAUDI ARABIA

Tafila

Bayir

Ma'an

Railway

Main road

'Aqaba

International boundary

Red Sea

Armistice/Cease-fire line

Km. 0   50   100

Miles 0   25   50   75

Jordan

JORDAN'S DOMESTIC PREDICAMENT

THE ECONOMIC CRISIS; NEGOTIATIONS WITH THE IMF

The impact of Jordan's economic crisis, already apparent since the mid-1980s, was particularly severe in 1989. Austerity measures taken in late 1988 (see *MECS* 1988, pp. 362–63) were unable to halt the further deterioration of the country's economy. Jordan was now being forced to pay dearly for the accumulation of an enormous external debt (some $8.3bn.),[2] after having borrowed heavily to offset declining remittances from Jordanian expatriate workers and reduced Arab aid. In early 1989, as foreign currency reserves continued to dwindle, pressure on the Jordanian dinar mounted.

In February, the government revoked the licenses of all the country's nonbank exchange firms and closed their offices. Money changers had been trading dinars at around 660 fils to the dollar, compared to the official rate of the Central Bank of Jordan (CBJ) of 570 fils (as opposed to 380 fils in October 1988), amidst speculation that Jordan intended to reschedule its debts and seek assistance from the IMF.[3] The CBJ fixed the rate of exchange at 540 fils to the dollar.

By early 1989, Jordan was indeed unable to service its external debt due to bunched repayment commitments.[4] King Husayn and Prime Minister Zayd al-Rifa'i were reluctant to approach the IMF because of the possible political ramifications. But Jordanian economists were convinced that the country had no choice. Jordan faced debt repayments of over $1bn. a year for the coming three or four years and its cash reserves were virtually nonexistent.[5]

In mid-April, the government concluded an agreement with the IMF. The initial recovery program was to last for five years, until 1993. It was aimed at steadily reducing the budget deficit from 24% of gross domestic product (GDP; excluding external grants) in 1988 to 10% at the end of the process. Real GDP growth was expected to revive, reaching 4% by 1993. Export earnings were to increase from a projected $1.1bn. in 1989 to $1.7bn. in 1993. Foreign reserves excluding gold were to be replenished to the level of $500m., to cover three months of imports. Inflation was to be brought down from the official estimate of 14% in 1989 to 7% in 1993. (Subsequent revelations that inflation was actually in excess of 25% suggested that the problem of inflation had been underestimated in the negotiations.)[6]

Once the IMF had ratified the accord in the summer of 1989, Jordan was able to start discussions with its creditors on the rescheduling of debt repayment. The agreement made Jordan eligible for a $125m. loan from the IMF as well as a restructuring loan of $150m. from the World Bank.[7]

During the talks with the IMF delegation, Rifa'i and other ministers made reassuring public statements to the effect that the government had already taken all the necessary corrective measures and would therefore not be required by the IMF to take any further action, relating to subsidies for basic foodstuffs or to the devaluation of the dinar.[8] People were therefore unprepared for the government decision to raise the prices of fuel and some other commodities, such as cigarettes and soft drinks, by 15–50%, as of 16 April. Fees for vehicle registration and licensing, television licensing, and telephone services were also raised considerably.[9] Though these measures to reduce the budget deficit did not affect subsidies of some JD60m. p.a. for basic foodstuffs (such as flour, sugar, rice, and meat), the price hikes sparked a wave of mass protest in many parts of the country (see below).

On 20 May, Muhammad Sa'id al-Nabulsi was reappointed governor of the CBJ. He had been governor from 1973 to 1985.[10] The appointment of Nabulsi heralded increased intervention by the CBJ to try and stabilize Jordan's currency and renew confidence in the dinar. Nabulsi, a tough and single-minded administrator, was said to have accepted the post on condition that the CBJ be restored to the role of principal agency of financial and monetary control. Restoration of confidence in the dinar was seen as the major precondition for any economic recovery.[11]

At the end of May the CBJ announced a set of measures designed to replenish the country's foreign currency reserves, and thus to provide the CBJ with the means to intervene and stabilize foreign currency trading. The measures included linking the dinar to a basket of currencies instead of solely to the dollar; requiring that all banks deposit 35% of their total foreign currency holdings at the CBJ; and rationalizing spending of foreign currency according to national priorities determined by the CBJ.[12] The CBJ abandoned the rigid exchange rate of 540 fils to the dollar set in February and resumed the daily setting of rates starting at 570 in late May.[13]

Despite an infusion of c. $300m. aid from Saudi Arabia, Kuwait, Oman, and Iraq, reported in June,[14] Jordan's shortage of foreign currency remained acute. CBJ efforts to stabilize the dinar did not initially bear fruit. In mid-June the dollar was being traded on the black market for 670 fils, compared to the official rate of 571.1–577.1.[15] Remittances from Jordanian workers in the Gulf declined as confidence in the Jordanian currency and economy continued to deteriorate.[16] In late July the dinar crashed on the black market to an all-time low of 960 fils to the dollar.[17] This prompted Nabulsi and even Husayn to accuse Israel of having plotted against the dinar. Israel, they said, had induced residents of the occupied territories to get rid of the dinar.[18]

The CBJ responded by launching a two-tier exchange system in an effort to curb the black market and to encourage expatriates to send their dollars home through the official banking system. The system set a lower official rate (570 fils to the dollar) for government imports and allowed for a higher free-market rate (which ranged between 850–870 to the dollar) for commercial banks to finance private sector imports.[19] Citizens were also deterred from purchasing dollars by repeated warnings in the local press about the circulation of counterfeit dollars on the black market.[20] However, the key to Jordan's solvency lay in external Arab support. It was only the rapid injection of aid from Saudi Arabia and major Arab banks that restored stability to Jordan's currency, by bolstering its reserves. Following a visit by King Husayn to Jidda in early August, Saudi Arabia extended a grant of $200m. to Jordan.[21] Further aid was received from Abu Dhabi, Qatar, and Dubai.[22] The CBJ was consequently able to intervene more aggressively in the currency market, supplying dollars and bolstering the dinar.

At the end of August Jordan's reserves were said to have risen to over $500m., compared to $20-30m. in May, partly as a result of the measures taken by the CBJ to rationalize the outlay of foreign currency, but mainly due to the influx of Arab aid. The dinar regained in value and was restabilized on the free market at 675/705 fils to the dollar.[23] The official rate was altered gradually by the CBJ and, by the end of the year, the official and free-market rates had converged.[24] In an effort to secure Jordan's reserves for a longer term, an agreement was negotiated with five Gulf states (Saudi Arabia, Kuwait, the United Arab Emirates, Qatar, and Oman) to deposit a total of $300m. with the Abu Dhabi-based Arab Monetary Fund, for use by Jordan.[25] In October, replenished reserves allowed the Cabinet to lift the ban imposed in late 1988 on the import of certain luxury items, as of 1 January 1990.[26] But, to be on the safe side, customs duties on these items were subsequently raised by 10–25%.[27]

The replenishing of Jordan's reserves would have been impossible without the agreement with the IMF and the subsequent rescheduling of Jordan's debts. In July, a rescheduling agreement was reached with the Paris Club of creditor governments, according to which debts due in 1989–90 were rescheduled over a period of 10–11 years, with a grace period of five to six years.[28] A similar agreement was concluded in November with the London Club of creditor commercial banks.[29] Jordan also secured long-term concessionary loans from the World Bank and the Governments of Japan and West Germany, totaling $317m., for balance-of-payments assistance. The US was to provide Jordan with $247m. of various forms of aid for the fiscal year beginning September 1989.[30]

Jordan's regional and international allies had come through with the aid to prevent the immediate collapse of the kingdom's economy. This had no bearing, however, on Jordan's structural deficiencies. King Husayn and other senior spokesmen repeatedly referred to the imbalance between population and resources. More than at any time in the past, the king drew attention to Jordan's demographic pressures and to the need for family planning and for a national policy to control the birth rate.[31] At 3.8% Jordan's rate of natural increase was one of the highest in the world. The population was growing at a pace that the Jordanian economy could not sustain. Unemployment was steadily increasing as the numbers of people joining the work force vastly outnumbered available jobs inside the country. Though the official rate of unemployment was around 10%,[32] 20% was much closer to the mark.[33]

Government efforts to alleviate unemployment centered on securing jobs for Jordanian professionals in other Arab states (some 10,000 positions were said to have been secured in Libya and North and South Yemen);[34] creating jobs in the bureaucracy; and taking measures to control the employment of foreigners in Jordan. There were some 70,000 legally employed foreigners and a similar number were illegally employed. Many of the foreigners were Egyptians who did menial jobs unattractive to Jordanians.[35] About 55% of the unemployed were high-school, community college, and university graduates.[36] Government efforts to direct students to vocational training instead of university education did not seem to have much effect.

According to Crown Prince Hasan, by the year 2000 Jordan would have a population of 4.5m. with a work force of 1.25m., compared with 650,000 at present.[37] If these figures were correct, it meant that no less than 60,000 jobs would have to be created annually until the end of the century.

As Husayn warned, unless people were made aware of the importance of family planning, on the one hand, and of the need to increase the productivity of the state's economy, on the other, the imbalance between resources and population would inevitably worsen.[38]

The overpopulation of Amman was becoming acute. Constant migration from rural areas to the capital, typical in other Middle Eastern countries, was also a central feature of Amman. The city's infrastructure was incapable of meeting the rising demand for services.[39] A concerted effort was made by the authorities to promote development in the underpopulated south of the country. The southern governorates of Karak, Tafila, and Ma'an, 50% of the kingdom's total area, were home to only 10% of the population. Hasan urged people who had left these governorates for Amman to return to the south to participate in the economic development of the region.[40] As one Jordanian observer noted, Jordan, like other ME states, had to stem the trend of "cities mushrooming at the expense of a stagnant rural sector." The alternative was "further rural disruption, urban difficulties and, most of all, a terrible dependence on food imports."[41]

The deterioration of Jordan's economy resulted in a rapid decline in the standard of living. Per capita income had dropped dramatically from its peak of $1,800 in 1984 to $750 in 1989.[42] During 1989, the cost-of-living index rose by 31%.[43] With salaries more or less stagnant and no unemployment insurance, poverty was on the rise. The government cushioned the fall somewhat by continuing to subsidize certain basic foodstuffs (bread, rice, sugar, beef, poultry, milk, barley, and corn).[44] Stern measures were also taken against merchants who hoarded staples for sale at prices higher than those fixed by the ministry of supply. Hoarded staples were seized by the police as over a hundred violators were detained. Some were fined, others were imprisoned.[45] The Ministry of Supply, through the Civil Service Consumer Corporation, provided basic foodstuffs and other commodities to civil servants. Similar supplies were made available to military and public security personnel through the Military Consumer Corporation.[46] Salaries of army personnel were increased to compensate for rising prices, but cutbacks in military expenditure had some serious ramifications for Jordan's armed forces. In March, the planned purchase of eight *Tornado* fighter bombers from Britain was postponed indefinitely. Husayn even conceded publicly that pilots had been grounded for economic reasons.[47] According to Western intelligence sources, the combat readiness and fighting capability of Jordan's armed forces had deteriorated following serious cutbacks in training and maintenance levels, constantly dwindling supplies, and shortage of spare parts.[48]

In an address to a conference dedicated to "safeguarding the future," Husayn pointed to the essential link between peace and development. It was impossible, he said, for many countries to achieve their demographic and developmental objectives as long as they had to maintain military machines to defend themselves against "the dangers of wars and the ambitions of expansionists."[49]

Jordan's budget for 1990, much like that of 1989, was one of austerity. The primary objective was deficit reduction. According to Prime Minister Zayd Ibn Shakir, Jordan had no choice but to learn to live within its means. It could not rely on foreign aid forever.[50] The draft budget, approved by the cabinet in November, totaled JD1,105m. (compared to JD1,035m.. for 1989). The deficit of JD199m., though higher than the 1989 deficit (JD122m.), was equivalent to only 16.5% of the projected GDP for 1990, down from 20.2% in 1989 and 24% in 1988,[51] when GDP had actually decreased by 3.5 %.[52] The coverage of total expenditure by local revenue was to rise from 59% to 63%. Self-sufficiency was still far off, and Jordan would remain in need of external aid for the foreseeable future.[53]

THE APRIL RIOTS

Jordan's economic crisis had no easy solution. Public distress was bound to have some political fallout. On 18 April, just two days after the government announced price rises following the talks with the IMF, riots erupted in the southern town of Ma'an. Sparked by taxi, bus, and truck drivers who were hit particularly hard by a fuel price hike not initially matched by an increase in fares, the riots soon developed into the worst disturbances that Jordan had witnessed since the 1970–71 civil war. Thousands demonstrated against the rising cost of living and the alleged corruption in the Rifa'i government, setting banks and warehouses on fire and attacking police cars.[54] The Ministry of Transport decision to increase fares of privately owned buses and taxis as of 19 April proved to be too little and too late, and had no effect on what was obviously widespread popular disaffection in the south. For four days violent demonstrations continued, spreading from Ma'an to Tafila, Karak, and other towns and villages in the area, where a variety of public utilities such as clinics and telephone networks were vandalized. In Ma'an at least five people were killed and 14 wounded as armed civilians confronted police and army units trying to enforce a curfew.[55] Curfew was also imposed on Tafila and Karak. On 20 April, the three towns were reported to be under the control of army units dispatched to quell the disturbances instead of the regular public security (police) forces.[56]

As order was gradually restored in the southern towns, the disturbances edged northward, to certain areas dangerously close to the capital. In clashes between civilians and troops of the bedouin desert force (*al-Badiya*) on 19 and 20 April, five people were reported killed in the village of Mazar, southwest of Amman.[57] On 20 April, riots also broke out in the town of Madaba, a mere 30 km. south of Amman. The next day, violent demonstrations rocked the city of Salt. In what was probably the most disturbing development in the crisis, some 3,000 demonstrators, chanting antigovernment slogans, filed out of the city's main mosque after midday prayers, smashed the facades of banks and shops, and set fire to government vehicles. Police and rock-throwing protesters fought for four hours, before a curfew was imposed on this main city.[58]

During the riots, Amman itself was generally quiet, apart from two peaceful demonstrations by about 100 students at the University of Jordan on 19 and 22 April.[59] All the same, security in the capital was strengthened. Heavily armed police patrolled the streets, and vehicles armed with heavy machine-guns were deployed in strategic locations.[60] By 22 April order had been restored throughout the country. By early May all curfews had been lifted and life returned to normal.[61] According to official accounts, eight people, including two security officers, were killed in the riots; 89 were injured, among them 47 men of the security forces.[62] According to press sources, 10 people were known to have been killed and over 100 injured.[63]

The entire crisis was managed by Crown Prince Hasan, acting as Regent, while King Husayn was in the US on an official visit. Husayn, who had left the country on 16 April, chose not to curtail his stay in the US. He, however, returned directly to Jordan from the US on 23 April, canceling a scheduled private visit to the UK. Calm had already been restored by the time the king landed in Amman, but his return may well have had a reassuring effect by giving rise to public expectations of high policy decisions to deal directly with popular grievances. The king's decision to remain in the US until the end of his scheduled engagements was presumably motivated by his unwillingness to admit the severity of the crisis back home or to take action that could be interpreted as lack of confidence in Hasan's capacity to deal with the turmoil. Available evidence suggests that Hasan handled the situation well. Security forces showed considerable restraint. Casualties were relatively light, considering the scope of the riots and the number of people involved. Hasan claimed that at least some of the casualties were caused by protesters who had used firearms in their possession.

The moderation shown by the security forces was no doubt also a result of the fact that the core of the disturbances was in the south. The south was traditionally ultraloyalist and many of the men in crack units of the security forces were themselves of southern bedouin origin. Even when the riots spread northward, they remained a purely East Bank affair. In Salt the police fired teargas, but frequently seemed to back off from more violent confrontation. "They are our children," a senior police officer said. "We cannot beat them too hard."[64]

Jordan's large Palestinian population, concentrated mainly in the Amman, Zarqa, and Irbid areas, did not take part in the disturbances, most importantly because they must have assumed that the regime would not have shown the same measure of restraint toward them. For the regime, massive Palestinian protest would certainly have been perceived as a mortal threat, rather than an expression of discontent with the economic situation. The memories of "Black September" still served as a potent deterrent to the Palestinians. The PLO had good reasons of its own to keep the Palestinians in Jordan in check. It was hardly in the PLO's interest to have international attention diverted from the Intifada in the West Bank and Gaza to Jordan. Moreover, appearing to have a hand in the destablization of Jordan could have wrecked the PLO's dialogue with the US. Therefore, while some of the more radical factions, such as the Popular Front for the Liberation of Palestine (PFLP) and the Democratic Front for the Liberation of Palestine (DFLP), did in fact seek to incite the Palestinians in Jordan to join in the fray, the PLO leadership made a deliberate effort to restrain them. Indeed, King Husayn subsequently made special note of the "pacifying nature" of the role played by the PLO leadership during the crisis.[65]

Generally the southern periphery of the kingdom had benefited less than the center and the north from Jordan's decade of prosperity, from the mid-1970s to the mid-1980s. The south was consequently relatively depressed economically. Less than 10% of the population lived in this arid region and for many years people had been migrating from the area to the more prosperous urban centers to the north. The regime was not unaware of the disparity between the south and other parts of the country. Only days before the announcement of the new austerity measures, Hasan called upon people of southern origin to return to their hometowns to participate in their development. At a development conference in 'Aqaba, several recommendations were made for the promotion of tourism, vocational training, agriculture, and transport in the southern regions.[66] It seems that the regime had displayed uncharacteristic insensitivity to the plight of the poor in introducing the new measures, with such minimal preparation of the public for the steps to come.

As the economic crisis was felt more acutely in the south, some of the new austerity measures were particularly painful there. The majority of the breadwinners in the south earned fixed salaries from the government or the army, that did not keep abreast with rising prices. Small farmers were hit by soaring fertilizer prices.[67] A sizable segment of the breadwinners in the Ma'an region were employed in transport and trucking which had experienced a boom of sorts during the Gulf War, due to the lucrative transit business on the supply line from ʻAqaba to Iraq. The end of the war drastically reduced the volume of transit traffic and the rising fuel prices and license fees were the last straw. The latest measures were introduced with little warning and the shock waves soon followed.

The public anger, however, was not directed toward the monarchy itself, but rather against the Rifaʻi government and against Rifaʻi personally. Ever since his first term as prime minister (1973–76) Rifaʻi had acquired a reputation for corruption (see *MECS* 1984–85, p. 510). His opulent life-style stood in stark contrast to the privations of the protesters,[68] and though Jordan's profound economic problems were clearly structural, the frustrated people of the south tended to simplistically put the blame on Rifaʻi's corruption and mismanagement. They called for Rifaʻi's ouster and even for his trial, together with others in government accused of embezzlement and mismanagement. At the same time, protesters in the southern towns, and in Salt, made the point of accompanying their demands, that heaped abuse on Rifaʻi, with expressions of loyalty to the king and the Hashemite family.[69]

The initial outburst of protest seemed to have been a spontaneous reaction to the price hikes. But, as the unrest spread, there were indications that Islamic fundamentalist groups were playing an important role in fanning the unrest. In an apparent allusion to Muslim radicals, Hasan referred to "some bearded gentlemen" who had been "very influential over the people in the street" in Maʻan.[70] In Salt, the demonstrations began at the town's central mosque and were said to have had an "overtly Islamic...profile."[71]

Even so, the demonstrators in the south were, for the most part, the king's loyal subjects. This was naturally cause for particular concern to the regime. Hasan consequently sought to strike a balance between controlled repression and conciliation. The first, albeit belated, government statement on the situation was issued on the morning of 21 April. It explained the need for the austerity measures that were needed to fulfill the IMF requirements and condemned the rioters for protesting in a manner "uncharacteristic of our [Jordanian] people." The Jordanians, according to the statement, "usually use the channels of dialogue to express their opinions" and these were "always open for all classes of society." Noting that the authorities had hitherto exercised great self-restraint in restoring order, the government warned the populace that it would not tolerate those who abused the current circumstances to meddle with the country's security and stability.[72] To lend this warning added credibility, the authorities began arresting political activists throughout the country, especially in Amman. Some 130 people were detained, including communists, pan-Arab nationalists (including the Karaki member of the Chamber of Deputies, Riyad al-Nuwayisa), Palestinian activists associated with the DFLP and PFLP, and some Muslim fundamentalists.[73]

Shortly before the outbreak of the riots, the Jordanian election law was finally amended to exclude the West Bank constituencies (see below). In early April it was reported unofficially that elections had been slated for November.[74] Following the riots, the issue of elections became more acute. Under Rifaʻi, the heavy hand of government had become increasingly repressive, as calls for the democratization of Jordan's political system continued. The so-called "channels of dialogue" were steadily stifled. In October 1988, a large group of generally left-wing activists criticized

Husayn for having failed to consult the public before his disengagement decision (see *MECS* 1988, pp. 591–95). Now, after important decisions were taken without any form of public involvement or consultation, popular resentment mounted amidst calls for greater press freedom and parliamentary elections.[75]

On 22 April, representatives of professional associations sent a petition to the Crown Prince, calling for the replacement of Rifaʻi's government by one that would enjoy the people's trust and would be accountable to a parliament elected in fair elections. If the situation remained unchanged, the petitioners warned, "the king's credibility...will be undermined."[76] In what was clearly a direct response to these expressions of profound political disaffection, Hasan told a press conference on the same day that it was essential to "enhance participation" of the populace in decision making and to entrench dialogue. Elections, he said, could be expected to take place during 1989.[77] Hasan also castigated government economic policy. He accused the government of "arbitrariness in economic decision making," contending that "successive budgets over the past 15 years could have identified different priorities."[78] It was not unusual in Jordanian politics for the government to serve as the monarchy's "lightning conductor" in times of crisis. It was, however, uncommon for the monarchy to criticize the government in public. The king, and particularly the crown prince, shared much of the responsibility for Jordan's economic policies. For many years Hasan had assumed a leading role in charting the course of Jordan's economic development. Though, for the most part, the protesters leveled their criticism at the government, there were those in the political elite — such as the outspoken fundamentalist member of parliament, Layth Shubaylat — who did not conceal their misgivings about King Husayn's handling of the country's affairs. Shubaylat accused him of complicity in the mistakes committed by a government "under his protection."[79] Hasan's criticism of the government was, therefore, correctly seen as an attempt to deflect popular anger from the monarchy, by distancing it from the day-to-day running of the government.[80]

At the same time, however, Hasan made it clear that riots would not deter the regime from implementing the economic reform program agreed upon with the IMF. The new austerity measures were essential for economic recovery, he stated, and the "wanton violence" had to stop. "Security [was] the basis of everything...it [could] not be compromised."[81] Government firmness was also displayed by the Ministry of Education, which instructed the schools to collect at least ten fils (one hundredth of a dinar) from every student to help cover damages caused during the riots. This symbolic contribution was intended to impress upon the students the need to safeguard public property, as a national duty.[82]

While the new prime minister (see below), Zayd Ibn Shakir, noted that his government would review its economic policies in order to avoid "confrontation in this phase of economic adaptation,"[83] Hasan emphasized that such a review would only be guided by "logical reconsideration" and "not by public opinion in the street or by slogans raised in demonstrations."[84]

OUSTER OF RIFAʻI; APPOINTMENT OF IBN SHAKIR

Husayn returned to Amman from the US on 23 April. He immediately met with cabinet officials, economists, and political figures to discuss measures to defuse the crisis. The most urgent question was the fate of the government. Husayn faced a dilemma. He had to choose between sacking his boyhood friend and long-standing confidant, thus exposing himself to charges from his closest associates that he had bowed to violent pressure, and maintaining Rifa'i at the helm, thus risking further unrest.[85] Although the government had reacted slowly to warnings of Jordanian economists and Rifa'i had become unpopular, Husayn had hitherto chosen to ignore the rumblings against his prime minister. The riots, however, had had a strong, disturbing effect. One day after Husayn's return to Jordan, on 24 April, Rifa'i resigned.[86] Husayn's decision was sharp and swift, so much so that Rifa'i was removed from office before the king had appointed a new prime minister, a move that was out of step with standard practice. Rifa'i's ouster, as could be expected, was well received in Jordan.[87]

Husayn hastened to explain to the people that the ouster of Rifa'i was in itself no solution to Jordan's problems. The government, he admitted, may have erred "here or there." Its failure to explain the recent economic measures was clearly a mistake. But, Husayn now conceded, Jordan's economic crisis was of such magnitude that these errors were only of marginal consequence. Husayn put most of the blame for the country's economic woes on the wealthy Arab states that had failed to honor their pledges of financial support to Jordan. In order to develop its economic infrastructure and to provide for the armed forces, he explained, Jordan had borrowed, trusting in the ultimate fulfillment of these Arab pledges. Jordan had thus accumulated an enormous foreign debt which, according to the king, was exactly equal to the shortfall in projected Arab aid.[88] While it was true that the failure of certain Arab states to meet their commitments was a root cause of Jordan's crisis, it was also true that the regime's failure to take the necessary steps earlier, and the excessive borrowing on international markets designed to evade drastic decisions, only made matters worse. For this miscalculation the regime had only itself to blame — an admission Husayn, of course, never made.

Husayn, in a long overdue revelation, said that Jordan was now in a "stage of economic adaptation." Those who refused to adapt, he warned, were destined to face decline and eventual collapse. Austerity measures were therefore essential. However, Husayn did suggest that the measures would be studied and revised to reduce the burden on the public. As for the popular protest, he noted, if expressions of discontent were understandable under the circumstances, the violent and self-destructive form they had taken was intolerable. Husayn appealed to the people to share in the responsibility of overcoming Jordan's present difficulties and to eventually attain economic self-reliance. To allow for greater public participation in the political process, he promised "quicker steps" toward the holding of parliamentary elections.[89]

On 27 April Husayn entrusted Sharif Zayd Ibn Shakir with the formation of a new cabinet. Ibn Shakir, who had been the commander in chief of the armed forces since 1976, was appointed chief of the royal court in December 1988. He was a distant cousin and contemporary of Husayn who had started his military career as Husayn's aide-de-camp in the mid-1950s. Ibn Shakir's long military career had enabled him to form especially close ties with the population of the south, heavily represented in the armed forces. As commander of the Third (Armored) Division in the 1970–71 civil war, Ibn Shakir played a key role in the routing of the fida'iyyun and the reestablishing of government control. He therefore seemed to be amply suited to head the government in the wake of the riots, and as Jordan entered a period of further potential domestic destabilization.

Only nine of the 26 ministers in the outgoing Rifa'i cabinet remained in the new government (see Table 1). It was noteworthy that the Palestinian Minister of Interior Raja'i al-Dajani, responsible for domestic security, was replaced by the East Banker Salim Masa'ida, a former senior official in the Ministry of Interior. Masa'ida, a critic of Rifa'i, had been minister of finance under premiers Sharif 'Abd al-Hamid Sharaf and Mudar Badran in the late 1970s and early 1980s. Former foreign minister Tahir al-Masri was appointed deputy prime minister and minister of state for economic affairs, a newly created post. The appointment of Masri, a Palestinian, to this new post was viewed as a gesture designed to increase the confidence of Jordan's (mainly Palestinian) expatriate work force in the economy. Most of the major economic portfolios were given to experienced senior technocrats who had never served in ministerial positions. Basil Jardana (minister of finance) was a former executive director of Jordan's Central Bank. Ziyad Radi 'Innab (minister of industry and trade) served for many years as director-general of the Industrial Development Bank. Ziyad Fariz (minister of planning) was also a former senior official at the Central Bank and under secretary at the ministry of planning. Jamal al-Budur (minister of labor) had been assistant to the Royal Scientific Society's director for administrative affairs since 1985. Ibrahim 'Izz al-Din (minister of state for cabinet affairs) was, since 1986, the director-general of the civil service. Ibrahim Ayyub, minister of supply in the Badran and 'Ubaydat cabinets from 1980–85, was recalled to that office. Southerners were also prominently represented in Ibn Shakir's new cabinet, holding five of the 24 portfolios: Nasuh al-Majali (of the powerful Karak family that had provided Jordan with numerous senior army officers and government officials for decades) was appointed minister of information and culture. Ziyad Radi 'Innab was also from Karak and Jamal al-Budur came from Tafila. Nasir al-Din al-Asad and 'Awad Khulayfat, both members of the Rifa'i cabinet who remained in office, were likewise southerners, from 'Aqaba and Wadi Musa respectively. The ratio of Palestinians in the new cabinet was reduced from just over a third in Rifa'i's last cabinet to just under a quarter. Dhuqan al-Hindawi, deputy premier and minister of education in Rifa'i's cabinet, replaced Ibn Shakir as chief of the royal court.[90]

In his directives to the new cabinet, Husayn described the situation as one of transition in which it was incumbent upon the government to direct the country's political and social readjustment to a new era of economic austerity. The government was instructed to prepare for what amounted to a controlled democratization of the political system, coupled with guarded concessions to Islamic fundamentalist demands. New general elections were to be held, the first since 1967. The "responsible freedom of expression" was also to be permitted and a special effort was to be made to expand the "channels of dialogue" with the younger generation to develop their national pride and "to acquaint them with the concerns and interests of their homeland." While "attempts to politicize religion," had to end, the "cultural role" of religion in the shaping of the "conscience of the nation" was to be enhanced. This role of religion was to affect both decision making and legislation. The government was also to "entrench the bases of social justice"; reexamine the system of taxation; and "uproot favoritism and corruption" wherever they existed.

On the other hand, the king instructed the government "to show no leniency toward any attitude or behavior" that could be detrimental to national unity. The professional associations (which were highly politicized, serving essentially as fronts for left-wing and pro-PLO groups) were to be encouraged to return to "their professionalism," the role for which they had been originally established, i.e., to abstain from political activity. Insuring domestic stability was obviously the main priority of the new government, and Husayn instructed the government "to place a premium on individual and public discipline" and to guarantee "public order as a societal requirement."[91]

CONTROLLED LIBERALIZATION OF THE POLITICAL SYSTEM

The April riots shook the regime's self-confidence and complacency. It prompted the king and his closest advisers to embark upon a process of guarded liberalization, in order to shore up the damaged legitimacy and credibility of the regime. The heavy hand of government, increasingly apparent under Rifaʻi (see *MECS* 1986, pp. 427–28, 437–38; 1988, pp. 603–4) was gradually lifted. As leaflets condemning corruption and demanding liberalization of the political system continued to be circulated by various groups (influential clans, professional unions, and others unidentified),[92] the regime made a concerted and highly publicized effort to bridge the gulf between ruler and ruled. The government worked to enhance direct communication with various sectors of the population, withdrew certain restrictions on the press, and began preparations for general elections.

In late April and early May, Husayn held meetings at the Royal Court in Amman with community leaders, representing the various regions of the country. Husayn called for national unity, in the face of Jordan's difficulties, assuring the local leaders of the regime's intention to hold elections and pave the way for the "full participation" of the citizenry in affairs of state through the exercise of "responsible freedom." The king also expressed the hope that the dialogue with the people would ultimately result in the formulation of a new political contract, the National Charter, that would govern the politics of the country.[93]

Husayn subsequently held similar meetings with youth, students, and labor union leaders, and toured Salt, Irbid, and other towns and villages in the north. In May, prime Minister Ibn Shakir received a delegation from Maʻan, the core of the April riots. The mayor of Maʻan paid homage to King Husayn, declaring the unswerving loyalty of the people of Maʻan to the Hashemite Crown. He did not, however, fail to use the opportunity to air the grievances of his town in the spheres of public services and unemployment. A month later, Ibn Shakir toured Maʻan, where he informed a public rally of his government's determination to improve public services and to create new jobs.[94] Ibn Shakir also met with the presidents of professional associations and the Writers' Union to discuss domestic issues.[95] The professional associations protested against what they described as the resentment of "certain centers of power," i.e., the domestic security establishment, toward the new, more liberal climate.[96]

In February, before the April riots, King Husayn had declared an amnesty for administrative detainees, to commemorate the formation of the ACC. All political prisoners were said to have been released.[97] In May, 68 people detained for involvement in the April riots were released.[98] In July, the king offered amnesty to 45 prisoners, including 19 political prisoners[99] and in early September a further 60 people, detained during the April riots, were released. According to Director-General of Public Security ʻAbd al-Hadi al-Majali, all those arrested in connection with the April riots had been released.[100]

Shortly after the April riots and the removal of Rifaʻi, government control over the press was relaxed, though not abandoned. In 1986 and again in 1988, measures had been taken by the government to effectively nationalize the Arabic dailies. A number of local journalists were blacklisted and prevented from writing (see *MECS* 1986, pp. 437–38; 1988, p. 604). Local journalists, who were deemed "biased" or "critical" in their contributions to foreign publications, either had their press credentials withdrawn, were banned from writing in the local press, or had their passports confiscated. Some suffered from all these measures combined.[101] In early 1989, the government's Social Insurance Institution purchased most of the remaining private shares in *al-Ra'y* (which also published the *Jordan Times*) and *al-Dustur,* thus completing the effective nationalization of the daily press.[102] Following the April riots, and in accordance with Husayn's directives to the new government, the prime minister announced his government's intention to "protect the freedom of the press and to advance the profession of journalism."[103] Banned journalists were allowed to return to their jobs, but the practical extent of press freedom remained unclear. Husayn's directives referred to the need to respect a diversity of opinion that would be "neither...indisciplined nor unduly regimented,"[104] and Ibn Shakir's support for freedom of the press was qualified by the reservation that it be governed by a "sense of responsibility," designed to "serve the country's interests and the people's unity."[105]

Issues related to the liberalization policy, such as the limits on free expression and the legalization of political parties (see below), began to be discussed, often critically, in the press.[106] The papers began to air public grievances on a wide range of issues, such as the rising cost of living, unemployment, and the level of public services. The government and the press were also more open and informative on the gravity of Jordan's economic difficulties. Addressing a special meeting of the Senate and representatives of the local media, at the end of June, Husayn admitted that the "real state of affairs" had previously been kept from the public. Husayn now acknowledged that the people ought to be fully informed, to enable them to "adapt, give, and offer what is needed so that the homeland is not endangered from near or far."[107]

Still, no change was made in the Press and Publication Law. The law empowered the government to suspend or close down any newspaper or punish journalists without recourse to the judiciary. The government still controlled editorial policy, and neither the government nor the king were directly attacked by the press. The freedom granted, therefore, did not signify a radical departure from Jordan's authoritarian tradition. It was the regime that granted this freedom and determined its parameters. Journalists remained cautious and uneasy as they groped to define the bounds of their newly acquired freedom. Some advocated immunity for journalists, arguing that the Press and Publication Law exposed the press to "impossible pressures." Others called for the revision or abolition of the law which held the press "in terror."[108] One (unnamed) editor was said to have "voiced the frustration of many in the profession about the lack of a clearly defined information policy." He complained that journalists were still receiving "mixed signals" from the authorities about what was allowed and what remained "taboo in [their] reporting."[109]

In early October, in preparation for the elections, Minister of Culture and Information Nasuh al-Majali banned the entry of certain foreign newspapers into Jordan.[110] The papers published in Jordan were apparently self-disciplined to the satisfaction of the government.

In early November, just before the elections, the Ministry of Culture and

Information published a new information strategy. One of its points referred to the government's intention to "modernize" the Press and Publication Law and other laws and regulations concerning the Jordan Press Association and control over radio, television, video films, and the cinema. Local journalists were to be given access to all information to enable them to "convey the information message to the public."[111] Until the end of the year, however, the Press and Publication Law remained unchanged.

Following the elections, a newly formed government under Mudar Badran (see below) made further conciliatory gestures toward the press. It reversed a government decision of August 1988, to take over the management of the three main dailies, *al-Ra'y, al-Dustur,* and *Sawt al-Sha'b* (see *MECS* 1988, p. 604), and the original boards of directors were reinstated. Reporters and editors who were dismissed from their jobs during the tenure of the government-appointed supervisory committees were returned to their former positions.[112] In mid-December, the Jordanian Writers' Association, dissolved by the government in 1987 (see *MECS* 1987, p. 492), was reconstituted. The alternative Writers' Union established with government sanction in 1987 was now dissolved.

The newly elected Amman deputy, Fakhri Qa'war, himself a journalist, thanked Premier Mudar Badran for the steps he had taken to facilitate freedom of the press. He, however, went on to suggest that the weekly meetings between the minister of information and newspaper editors be abolished. Badran denied that these meetings were intended for "imposing anything." They were necessary to keep editors abreast of events. Once they knew the situation, Badran added, the editors were "free to self-censor what they feel could be harmful to the country."[113]

THE GENERAL ELECTION CAMPAIGN

The Chamber of Deputies (*majlis al-nuwwab*), the elected lower house of parliament, was dissolved in July 1988, shortly before Husayn's disengagement from the West Bank (see *MECS* 1988, p. 591). In mid-April 1989, amendments to the election law of 1986 (see *MECS* 1986, pp. 425–27) were approved by royal decree. The amendments canceled the 60-seat representation for the West Bank and abolished the 11 East Bank seats that represented Palestinian refugee camps. The amendments thus accorded a stamp of finality to the disengagement from the West Bank while fully incorporating the refugee camps of the East Bank into their respective constituencies. This corresponded with the official view that Palestinians permanently residing on the East Bank, including refugees, were Jordanians in every sense. Refugee camps were now officially referred to as "populated centers,"[114] whose status did not differ in any respect from that of other residential areas. These changes halved the total number of seats to 71. A seat was added for the Amman area, making the new total 72.[115] In July, a further amendment was approved by royal decree, raising the total number of seats to 80.[116]

Even before the April riots, elections were expected to be held in November.[117] The outbreak of the riots was, therefore, not the reason why general elections were called for 8 November. The riots did, however, convince the regime of the need not to procrastinate on this issue. The holding of elections did seem to reflect the regime's genuine conviction that a measure of democratization was in its own best interest in this hour of severe domestic crisis.

Though political parties were not formally legalized, known political activists of banned political parties and organizations were allowed to run in the elections for the first time since 1956. Article 18e of the 1986 election law forbade the candidacy of anyone belonging to an illegal group, whose objectives or principles contradicted the Jordanian constitution. This article was firmly criticized by political activists[118] (cf. *MECS* 1986, p. 427), who argued that it gave the government sufficient leeway to prevent opposition candidates from running in the elections. Though the article remained unchanged, in practice the government chose to ignore it.[119] Another serious grievance against the law related to seat distribution. The large metropolitan area of Amman and Zarqa was severely underrepresented. In increasing the number of seats from 72 to 80, some consideration was given to this complaint, but the changes were too slight to be of significance (see Table 2). The seat distribution remained advantageous to rural areas and to the south in particular. It was disadvantageous to the densely populated urban centers which had large Palestinian communities. These urban areas were the more natural home ground for radical politics, whether Muslim fundamentalist or secular leftist.

Over 630 candidates vied for the 80 seats in the Chamber of Deputies. Twelve of them were women, running and voting for the first time in a general election since they were given the vote in 1974.[120] The candidates represented a wide spectrum of political opinion that included leading figures in the illegal Jordanian Communist Party, members of the newly formed Jordanian Popular Democratic Party (*Hizb al-sha'b al-dimuqrati al-Urdunni*, hitherto the clandestine Jordanian branch of the DFLP), candidates associated with the Jordanian wing of the PFLP, pro-Iraqi and pro-Syrian Ba'this, members of the Unionist Democratic Alliance (see *MECS* 1981–82, p. 674; and 1984–85, p. 503), traditional pro-establishment and establishment figures, including former cabinet ministers and other senior officials,[121] Islamic fundamentalists associated with the Muslim Brethren, 26 of whom formed the Islamic Movement Bloc (*Kutlat al-haraka al-Islamiyya*), and other independent representatives of the Islamic trend.

Candidates of all persuasions campaigned for the upholding of the constitution and the liberalization of the Jordanian political system (i.e., against the excesses of the security authorities, especially the confiscation of passports and travel restrictions); for the release of political prisoners; legalization of political parties; freedom of expression and of the press; and the abolition of martial law, in force since 1967. A widely discussed issue was corruption: candidates demanded punishment for those in positions of authority, who were suspected of having lined their pockets while in office, thereby contributing to Jordan's economic crisis. Some on the radical left or the Islamic right condemned the agreement with the IMF and even called for its abrogation.[122]

Officially, campaigning was to begin only 25 days before the election. In practice, it began earlier with candidates holding meetings and debates in their respective constituencies. Radio and television time was not available to candidates, who had to wage their campaigns by direct contact with prospective voters or by notices in the press. The public debate leading up to the elections was open and uninhibited by the government. In September, Maj. Gen. Fadil 'Ali Fahid was appointed director of Public Security (police), replacing Lt. Gen. 'Abd al-Hadi al-Majali.[123] Husayn subsequently directed Public Security to ensure the full respect for law and order, not only by the citizenry, but also by the security apparatus itself.[124] This seemed to indicate a generally more liberal approach to domestic security and regard for public criticism of security excesses.

Of the various groups competing for election, the best organized and most impressive during the campaign were the Muslim Brethren. They alone formed a recognized nationwide bloc. Generally, Islamic fundamentalist candidates drew the largest crowds to their rallies. They and their slogan, "Islam is the solution," were popular and it was clear, well before election day, that they would do well. Apart from the popularity of their message, they enjoyed a number of organizational advantages over their rivals. As opposed to other political groups, the Muslim Brethren had enjoyed relative political freedom over the years. As an "association" rather than a "party" they had never been banned. Some of their leftist rivals had only been released from prison or had emerged from hiding just before the elections. That the election campaign was brief (officially only 25 days) offered an obvious advantage to those who had previously been allowed free political activity, and broad public exposure, for a long time. Mosques, in theory out of bounds for electioneering, served as useful campaign grounds: preachers did endorse religious candidates in their sermons and urged their flock to vote for them.[125]

The program of the Islamic Movement Bloc noted that the Muslim Brethren had been established to liberate the Islamic world from foreign domination and to "apply the Islamic Shari'a." Islam was to be the sole source of legislation and the solution to all the nation's political, social, economic, and moral problems. All existing legislation ought to be revised to conform with the Shari'a. The program also called for the trial and punishment of those responsible for the mismanagement of Jordan's economy and those who had made personal gain by exploiting their positions.[126]

The Islamic Bloc upheld political freedoms, including the freedom of the press, the freedom of expression, and the freedom of religion, and demanded the abrogation of all laws that infringed upon these rights. Yet, in the same program, it also called for the formation of committees to "direct the [mass] media in accordance with the rules and morals of the Islamic Shari'a." These committees would monitor all that was published, approve what was useful, and ban what was harmful. Any book that slandered Islam or "misrepresented historical facts" would be banned,[127] the program noted.

An indication of Islamic fundamentalist self-assurance and intolerance was given during the election campaign, when two fundamentalists brought charges of apostasy against a woman candidate before an Islamic religious court in Amman. The candidate, Tujan Faysal, running against a fundamentalist for one of the Circassian seats in Amman, had published a forceful defense of women's rights and a strong condemnation of conservative religious perceptions of feminine physical and intellectual inferiority.[128] The plaintiffs demanded that she be declared an apostate, her candidacy be canceled, her marriage be dissolved, and immunity be given to anyone who chose to shed her blood.[129] Secular intellectuals appealed to the king to oppose this form of "psychological terrorism"[130] and articles in the daily press condemned religious extremism.[131] The case was subsequently dismissed by the court, on the grounds that the charges were beyond its jurisdiction.[132] Religious courts dealt, in the main, with matters of personal status.

The religious challenge to the essentially Westernizing secularist regime was clearly on the ascendancy. The Islamic factor had surpassed the long-standing Palestinian nationalist challenge as the potentially most powerful opposition force in Jordan, at least for the time being. In public statements by the king shortly before the elections, he repeatedly warned the electorate against the excesses of religious extremism and called for dialogue within the framework of "centrism, moderation, and rationality...in line with our faith, which rejects the exploitation of religion...as a means to achieve political objectives."[133]

The PLO and the Palestinians in Jordan adopted a line of calculated caution, seeking to avoid confrontation with the regime in the elections. The PLO issued an official statement on 1 November, urging candidates to refrain from involving the organization in their campaign propaganda and emphasizing the PLO's determination not to interfere in the domestic affairs of any Arab state.[134] That the PLO found it necessary to issue such a statement reflected the political sensitivity aroused by the question of identity and allegiance of Jordanian citizens of Palestinian origin.

During the campaign, candidates of Palestinian origin were often challenged to relate to the contention that their participation in parliamentary elections in Jordan lent support to an Israeli claim that Jordan was the homeland of the Palestinians. Palestinians who chose to run naturally refuted this contention, on the grounds that Jordanians and Palestinians were united by inseparable bonds.[135] Many others, however, were said to have decided not to run, precisely because of the "alternative homeland" factor. This factor, and the constituency distribution (see above), accounted for the low number of Palestinian candidates (8%) as compared to their relative weight in the population (about half). Even Palestinian voter registration was said to have been low, at least in part, due to the fear that participation in the election could "help to fix them into a permanent diaspora, in which they will forfeit the right to a homeland and to self-determination."[136]

On the other hand, while the PLO, as a body, formally advocated neutrality, some PLO factions, most notably the DFLP and the PFLP, rallied behind candidates and openly campaigned for them.[137]

THE SUCCESS OF THE ISLAMIC TREND
The elections were held on 8 November in a relaxed and free atmosphere. Government intervention was virtually nonexistent. Even so, voter participation was relatively low. Out of a total of just over 1,400,000 eligible voters, 1,019,852 registered. Of these, 877,000 collected their voter cards, but only some 63% of them actually voted,[138] i.e., a mere 54% of the registered electorate and some 40% of all eligible voters.

The elections, much to the consternation of the regime[139] resulted in sweeping gains for the Islamic trend. The Islamic Movement Bloc (Muslim Brethren) won 20 seats and other fundamentalist candidates won a further 13 seats, i.e., just over 40% of the seats in the new chamber. Evidence of Islamic fervor could also be found in the fact that not even one of the dozen women candidates was elected. Tujan Faysal was trounced in her district by a 6–1 margin by her religious rival.[140] The leftist secular opposition also did well, but was far less successful than the Islamic trend. Their 12–14[141] seats gave them a more significant parliamentary representation than they had ever enjoyed since the last relatively free elections held in November 1962. (For final seat distribution, see Table 3.)

Tribal and clan loyalties had weakened. The tribal consensus was fractured and the tribal vote was split between a number of candidates rather than uniformly supporting an agreed tribal representative. The authority of tribal elders had diminished and the multiplicity of tribal candidates led to the defeat of many of them. Particularly noteworthy was the total absence, among the newly elected representatives, of members of the large and traditionally influential Majali clan of Karak.[142]

However, the most notable result of the election was the success of the Islamic trend. Above all, the authenticity of the Islamic approach was readily acceptable to a large segment of the electorate. This was particularly true against the background of severe economic hardship at home and the declining appeal of alternative ideologies of the Marxist variety that were perceived to have failed in the Arab world and were even being discarded throughout Eastern Europe.[143] The Muslim Brethren fully exploited their organizational advantage and staged a well-orchestrated campaign. They united their forces in the Islamic Movement Bloc, while the secular Arab nationalists and leftists as well as the traditional supporters of the regime and tribal candidates could not legally indulge in party activity and failed to form nationwide blocs. In many instances candidates of similar persuasion ran against each other, inadvertently facilitating fundamentalist victories.

The relatively low participation in the election also aided the fundamentalists who were effective in mobilizing their supporters to vote. In some of the well-to-do upper-middle class residential areas of Amman and other cities, participation was particularly low, to the detriment of secular leftist or even pro-government candidates.[144]

While these factors did help the fundamentalist cause, it would be erroneous to conclude that the election results were less than a true reflection of public sentiment. There is no evidence to support the contention that those who did not vote were opponents of the Islamic trend.[145] The fundamentalist trend had very widespread popular support. Were it not for the underrepresentation, in the present system, of the urban areas of Amman and Zarqa, the Islamic trend may have even done better.

In the immediate aftermath of the elections, spokesmen for the regime and the local press voiced concern over the possible impact of the religious success at the polls.[146] Leaders of the Islamic movement responded with an effort to allay fears of fundamentalist extremism or coercion. They emphasized their demand for complete executive accountability on economic policies, past and present, as well as the need to punish those responsible for corruption. As a rule, they called for a generally more balanced and equal relationship between the executive and the legislature in the formulation of policy. On matters of religious legislation, they were united on the banning of alcohol and the legal institutionalizing of the Islamic dress code for women and for segregation between the sexes in public. The universal application of the Shari'a was, however, only a long-term objective.[147]

The Muslim Brethren sought no immediate confrontation with the regime that might have brought a premature end to the democratization process and thus upset their strategy for the gradual and evolutionary Islamization of the state. The regime, for its part, had no intention of precipitating a head-on collision with the fundamentalists. The process of democratization was required as a legitimizing instrument for the monarchy. But, at the same time, as one of the king's advisers put it: "great powers are accorded to the head of state. We are not going to have a monarchy like Sweden."[148]

THE REGIME AND PARLIAMENT AFTER THE ELECTIONS

Though impressive, the gains of the Islamic trend in the elections did not give its representatives a majority in the Chamber of Deputies. Moreover, the upper house (the Senate, *Majlis al-a'yan*), as a body appointed by royal decree, was a readily available counterweight to a potentially unruly lower house. A new 40-member[149] Senate was appointed as of 23 November.[150] It was, as always, overwhelmingly dominated by stalwarts of the regime, though it did include a few members with either religious or leftist inclinations. Noteworthy additions to the Senate were the first woman Senator Layla Sharaf (see *MECS* 1984–85, pp. 504–5) and Tariq 'Ala al-Din, hitherto Director of General Intelligence (*mukhabarat*). He was replaced in this last post by Mustafa 'Abd al-Karim al-Qaysi, in what was seen as a move designed to loosen the grip of domestic intelligence on the lives of politically active individuals.[151] 'Ala al-Din's removal may also have been prompted by royal displeasure with the failure of the *mukhabarat* to provide the king with a more realistic appraisal of political trends on the eve of the elections.

The first trial of strength between the regime and the Chamber of Deputies was over the election of the speaker of the house. Intense political activity preceded the elections, the outcome of which for the first time in many years was not a foregone conclusion. The leading loyalist candidate was Sulayman 'Arar, a former deputy premier and minister of interior. He was opposed by two fundamentalist candidates. The one was Yusuf al-Mubayyidin, an independent representative of the Islamic trend from Karak, endorsed by the Muslim Brethren. The other was Layth Shubaylat, a leading fundamentalist politician from Amman, very prominent in the previous chamber, but in competition with, and not supported by, the Muslim Brethren.

A few days before the vote, 14 leftist deputies formed a parliamentary bloc called the Democratic Alignment (*al-tajammu' al-dimukrati*).[152] With the loyalist and religious blocs commanding a more or less equal number of votes, the leftist bloc determined the outcome. The election of the speaker followed the inauguration of parliament by the king on 27 November. In the first round none of the three candidates secured the required absolute majority. Mubayyidin received 35 votes, 'Arar 31, and Shubaylat, supported by the Democratic Alignment, 14. In the second round, the Democratic Alignment supported 'Arar, who defeated Mubayyidin by 44 to 36 votes.

Opening parliament with his speech from the throne, King Husayn reaffirmed the regime's commitment to the democratic process and the eradication of corruption. He assured the people that the government would work toward the suspension of martial law, the legalization of political parties, and the formulation of a national charter to be approved by popular referendum.[153]

THE NEW CABINET OF MUDAR BADRAN

On 4 December, Husayn charged Mudar Badran, the chief of the Royal Court, with the formation of a new cabinet. Badran had been prime minister from mid-1976 to late 1979 and again from late 1980 to early 1984. The outgoing premier, Zayd Ibn Shakir, replaced Badran as chief of the Royal Court.[154]

In the past, the appointment of a new prime minister by the king was followed by the almost immediate formation of the new cabinet. This was not the case now. Badran entered into two days of intensive negotiations, particularly with deputies associated with the Muslim Brethren, on the composition of the cabinet. The Brethren demanded six portfolios, including education, information, and Islamic affairs.[155] Badran turned them down and included three other, nonaffiliated religious deputies. Altogether 10 deputies were included in the cabinet (see Table 1).

Immediately after the formation of his cabinet, Badran authorized a series of liberalizing measures that came in the wake of a review of martial law. Passports seized from the regime's political opponents were to be returned and other restrictions imposed on their travel and ability to obtain employment were also lifted.[156] The powers of the military courts were curtailed; various offenses were removed from their jurisdiction and transferred to regular civilian courts.[157]

Presenting his government's policy statement to the Chamber of Deputies on 19 December, Badran undertook to gradually suspend the rule of martial law until such time as it could be revoked altogether. He noted that his government viewed "the principle of consultation and democracy as the best formula to demonstrate...freedom, human dignity, and equality." Freedom and authority, however, were not contradictory. Indeed, Badran clarified, there could be "no freedom without order."[158]

The debate preceding the vote of confidence in Badran's government went on for three days — the longest and most intensive in Jordan's history. Some of the criticism leveled against the government was not only particularly harsh but was also reported extensively in the local press. Badran was attacked by fundamentalist deputies, Ya'qub Qirsh and Layth Shubaylat,[159] and by the leftist Fakhri Qa'war, who charged that as a former director of General Intelligence Badran was hardly the appropriate person to watch over the new process of democratization. Qirsh even questioned the justification for some of the king's constitutional prerogatives such as his right to postpone elections. Reforms were meaningless, he argued, unless the people really were the source of authority.[160] Ahmad 'Uwayd al-'Abadi, a former senior police officer, raised questions about the manner in which the prime minister had obtained his wealth, intimating that Badran himself was not above suspicion of corruption. 'Abadi also warned against an erosion of the efficiency of the domestic security apparatus and the dangers this portended for the country's stability.[161]

Most significant, however, was the speech of 'Abd al-Latif 'Arabiyat on behalf of 20 members of the Islamic Movement Bloc. He demanded, inter alia, that the government take concrete steps to implement the Shari'a and set a deadline, not later than six months hence, for the complete abolition of martial law.[162] Other deputies, particularly from the left, called for the abolition of the restrictive defense law (qanun al-difa'), promulgated by the British mandatory authorities and still in force.[163]

Replying to his critics, Badran rejected the aspersions cast on his own integrity. However, he had little choice but to make conciliatory gestures to the Islamic bloc, to ensure their support for his government. He stressed his government's determination to abolish martial law within four to six months and its commitment to review all legislation, including the defense law, which inhibited complete political freedom. Though stopping short of committing his government to the application of the Shari'a, Badran spoke at length of the respect Jordan had always shown for its Islamic heritage and of the important role of the Shari'a in Jordan's legislation.[164] This satisfied most of the religious delegates and, on 1 January 1990, Badran won the vote of confidence by the handsome margin of 65 to 9, with 6 abstentions. Most of the 15 deputies who did not vote for the government were leftists, while the great majority of fundamentalists voted for Badran[165] (see Table 3).

FOREIGN AFFAIRS

JORDAN, THE PALESTINIANS, AND THE MIDDLE EAST CONFLICT

Jordanian Perceptions of Israeli Policies

For about a decade, Jordan has been disturbed by the notion that Israel, under a right-wing government, may seek to solve the Palestinian question in Jordan (see *MECS* 1981–82, pp. 677–78). As some in the Israeli right continued to argue that "Jordan is Palestine," King Husayn believed that such ideas were "real threats" and posed a danger to the Hashemite Kingdom.[166] These Jordanian anxieties were reinforced by reports in the second half of 1989, on expected massive Soviet Jewish immigration to Israel. Crown Prince Hasan claimed that Israel sought "to evict the Palestinian people from their land and drive them across the river into Jordan and other Arab countries in a bid to make way for newcomers."[167] The Israelis, he said, were posing the "threat of transfer" of Palestinians to Jordan, coupled with the "ever-looming emigration" of Soviet Jews.[168] In December, the new Chamber of Deputies called for the cessation of Jewish emigration. The chamber warned that Soviet Jewish emigration was detrimental to the aspirations of the Palestinian people and was "bound to harm relations between the Socialist bloc and the Arab world."[169]

Israel's reported nuclear potential was another source of Jordanian anxiety. Foreign Minister Marwan al-Qasim stated that Jordan was situated in "the heart of an area" in which there were chemical and nuclear weapons.[170] Israel's possession of a nuclear capacity, he said, was the reason for the spread of chemical weapons in the ME.[171] According to Husayn, the availability of weapons of mass destruction in an area where conflict over scarce resources was a real danger, exposed the ME to potentially destructive conflict.[172] He, therefore, urged the superpowers to tackle the Arab-Israeli conflict and ensure the convening of an international conference for that purpose.

As far as the Jordanians were concerned, the PLO's acceptance of Resolutions 242 and 338, in November 1988, had finally paved the way for the convening of such a conference (see *MECS* 1988, p. 601). No new initiative was needed, aside from pressure on Israel by the US and the other permanent members of the Security Council. The conference would convene to negotiate an Israeli withdrawal in accordance with the relevant Security Council resolutions.[173] Jordan initially dismissed the Israeli idea of elections in the West Bank and Gaza (see chapters on the ME peace process and Israel), as a tactic designed to play for time, to drive a wedge between the Palestinians in the occupied territories and the PLO, and to evade the convening of an international conference.[174] However, once the Israeli plan had been officially communicated to the US in April, and then published, in May 1989, the Jordanian position mellowed somewhat. What prompted Jordan to adopt a more positive approach was the US acceptance of the Israeli initiative as the basis for a reinvigorated peace process, and its own realization that the international conference was not a feasible option in the near future.[175] Though not the optimal process, from the Jordanian perspective it was better than no process at all.

The Jordanians still rejected the elections in the occupied territories as an end in itself. But, as Husayn clarified during his visit to the US in April, they were prepared to accept elections as a part of an integrated process leading to a comprehensive settlement,[176] i.e., one that would not exclude Jordan. According to Marwan al-Qasim,

Jordan had urged the PLO not to reject the principle of elections as part of a "sound and healthy process,"[177] which would have to be crowned by an international conference. Only there could a comprehensive settlement be negotiated, with the PLO negotiating the Palestinaina settlement with Israel, and Jordan addressing the "Jordanian-Israeli dimension" of the conflict.[178] As Crown Prince Hasan put it, the resolution of the Palestinian-Israeli tier of the conflict ought not to be pursued in isolation from the second, Arab-Israeli, tier. "Decoupling those two tiers is not only inadvisable, it may be detrimental to the process as a whole."[179] The elections had to be linked to negotiations over the final outcome. They could then become "an important element as part of interlocking moves toward a comprehensive settlement."[180]

Jordan endorsed the ten-point plan put forward in the summer of 1989 by Egypt's President Mubarak (see chapter on the ME peace process), as it provided for precisely such an interlock between the elections and final status negotiations. Yet the Jordanians still found it necessary to reiterate that the "most appropriate vehicle" and the "only venue" for direct negotiations for a comprehensive settlement was an international conference to be attended by both Jordan and the PLO.[181]

As for the principles of the settlement, these, according to Husayn, remained: (1) the unequivocal commitment to the formula of land for peace; (2) acknowledgment of the right of the Palestinian people to self-determination; and (3) the security of all states in the region.[182] The Israeli Government, the king complained, was beset with "political paralysis" resulting from the split between the Likud and the Labor parties in the governing coalition (see chapter on Israel). Israel's resultant inability to reach a decision on the future of the occupied territories remained the only obstacle to just peace.[183]

Jordan, the PLO, and the Future of the West Bank
Husayn's decision to disengage from the West Bank paved the way for improved relations between Jordan and the PLO. Jordanian spokesmen repeatedly maintained that the previous atmosphere of doubt and suspicion that had shrouded Jordan-PLO relations had been replaced by one of mutual confidence and trust. One may safely assume that mutual trust was somewhat less than that proclaimed. But it was clearer now that Jordan supported the PLO as the sole legitimate representative of the Palestinian people, that it would not speak for the Palestinians, and that it had no territorial ambitions in Palestine.[184]

The improved relations were marked with symbolic gestures. On 7 January, the flag of Palestine was raised over the PLO office in Amman, which had become the embassy of the declared independent State of Palestine.[185] In early April, Husayn congratulated 'Arafat upon his election as President of Palestine. From then onward Jordanian spokesmen and media referred to 'Arafat by his new title.[186] 'Arafat and other senior PLO officials made frequent visits to Amman during the year for talks with Jordan's leaders. For the most part these consultations were related to coordination on the ME peace process.[187]

In August, the headquarters of the Palestine National Fund, closed since 1986 (see *MECS* 1986, p. 450), were reopened in Amman. Coming in the wake of Jordan's currency crisis (see above), the move was designed by the PLO to bolster confidence in the Jordanian economy. This was intended to be particularly helpful to the West Bank population, who had suffered heavily from the loss of value of Jordan's currency.[188]

The joint Jordanian-Palestinian committee for supporting the steadfastness of the occupied territories continued to meet. However, due to arrears of $450m. in payments from Arab states to the joint committee, it was unable to fulfill the task for which it had been initially established, i.e., to channel aid to the West Bank and Gaza.[189]

Jordan's improved relations with the PLO, its support for PLO involvement in the peace process, and its consequent support for the PLO-US dialogue[190] did not mean Jordan's acquiescence in its own exclusion from the peace process. On the contrary, the Jordanians appeared to be concerned that their disengagement might be misconstrued to mean the inclusion of the PLO instead of Jordan, rather than together with it. According to King Husayn, Jordan was not an idle spectator in the peace process. Jordan, he noted, had a longer border and cease-fire line with Israel than any Arab state and longer than those of the West Bank and Gaza put together. No solution could be reached "unless all of us are involved."[191] Crown Prince Hasan clarified that the fact that the PLO was now "in the driver's seat" did "not exempt [Jordan] of responsibility."[192] Whenever the possibility of direct Palestinian-Israeli negotiations was raised, the Jordanian media were quick to denounce the notion as an undesirable substitute for an international conference.[193] Jordan did not believe that "separate action by any...party" could lead to desirable results. Peace between Palestinians and Israelis could not be isolated from the other parties. That was why Jordan urged the "comprehensiveness of the solution."[194]

As for the future of the West Bank and Gaza, Husayn explained that Jordan had ceded sovereignty over the West Bank. He dismissed the notion that an independent Palestinian state in the West Bank and Gaza would pose a threat of any kind to Jordan. On the contrary, he contended, such a state was an essential component of any peace settlement.[195] Crown Prince Hasan was less categorical on this matter: Jordan, he observed, was in "a very sensitive position, and as long as treason is possible, there will always be danger."[196]

While the PLO continued to support the idea of confederation between a future Palestinian state and Jordan, the Jordanians remained reserved and would not commit themselves in advance to the confederative formula. Jordanian spokesmen reiterated that a Palestinian state had to be established before the question of confederation could be raised.[197]

Jordan, however, had not abandoned the historic perception that its relations with Palestine were of a special nature. A new government "information strategy" released in early November noted, *inter alia,* that "despite the decision to sever ties with the West Bank...the special relationship and the strong [bonds] between the two peoples on both banks of the River Jordan can never be disrupted."[198] As in the past, Husayn emphasized that Palestinians and Jordanians were actually "one people and family" and it was their common destiny to build together in the future.[199]

In the meantime, Jordan remained committed to the economic support and development of the West Bank and Gaza.[200] Jordan continued to finance the religious establishment in the West Bank and to support families of people killed in the Intifada. Pensions were also paid as of early 1989 to former Jordanian government officials who had been appointed after June 1967.[201] Jordan even continued to give assistance to organizations in the Gaza Strip that it had supported before the disengagement.[202] At the end of the year, following questions raised in Jordan by

Islamic groups and requests from the PLO, the government agreed to ease restrictions, imposed after the disengagement, on the movement of people and goods from the West Bank to Jordan.[203]

Deteriorating Situation Along the Border with Israel

During 1989, there was a marked deterioration of the security situation along Jordan's border with Israel. After many years of almost total tranquillity, a considerable number of incidents, involving armed infiltration into Israel and clashes, took place along the border, from the northern Jordan valley to the Wadi al-'Araba desert region south of the Dead Sea. Palestinian groups claimed responsibility for some of the incidents. Other cases involved individual Jordanian soldiers crossing into Israeli territory. Jordan denied responsibility for these actions and the Israeli authorities were of the opinion that the Jordanians were making a genuine effort to prevent such incidents and to keep the border area calm.[204]

A particularly serious incident took place in early September. Several katyusha rockets were fired from Jordan into Israeli territory in the northern Jordan Valley.[205] The PFLP claimed responsibility, and in early October the Jordanian authorities arrested several members of the PFLP in Jordan whom they accused of having been connected with the attack.[206] They were released in early December in a government gesture to the opposition.[207]

Jordan had no interest in provoking a confrontation with Israel. However, control over the border area seemed to have slackened. This was another indication of the regime's domestic weakness. It may also have reflected a certain Islamic fundamentalist infiltration into the rank and file of the Jordanian armed forces.

JORDAN AND THE ARAB WORLD

Jordan's severe economic crisis and its urgent need for economic aid was a central theme in the kingdom's relations with the Arab world in the period under survey. The Jordanians laid much of the blame for their economic plight at the doorstep of the wealthy Arab states (always excluding Saudi Arabia) that had not honored their pledges of support to Jordan (see above). They urged consistently that Arab aid to Jordan was vital for the kingdom's stability as a bastion protecting the Arab world from the expansionist menaces of Israel.[208]

On 16 February, Jordan, Egypt, Iraq, and North Yemen joined to form the ACC. From the outset, Jordan emphasized the economic potential of the ACC. The countries of the ACC had a total population of 80m., a total gross national product of more than $100bn., total annual exports of about $15bn., and imports of $30bn.[209] The council was to work toward the strengthening of economic ties between the four member states, boost trade and tourism, promote freer movement of goods and labor, set up joint ventures, and increase exports and investment.[210] The Jordanians hoped the formation of the ACC would expand the market for Jordanian goods; increase job opportunities for its skilled unemployed; and provide business opportunities for its private sector.[211] (For further discussion of the ACC, see chapter on inter-Arab relations.)

Whatever the future potential of the ACC might have been, in the short term the member states were unified mainly in debt. Each one of the four members owed staggering sums of money, primarily to foreign creditors.[212] It did not appear realistic to expect the ACC to be helpful in solving Jordan's economic problems, at least in the foreseeable future. For Jordan, however, the ACC had obvious political importance. It provided the kingdom with a focal position in an inter-Arab framework enhancing Jordan's status in the aftermath of its disengagement from the West Bank. It was a potentially important legitimizing instrument for Jordanian involvement in Palestinian affairs. Furthermore, it signified a cementing of ties with two major regional powers, Egypt and Iraq, in matters relating to the diplomatic and military dimensions of the Arab-Isaeli conflict.

Jordan's relations with Egypt were devoted to a large degree to coordination in matters pertaining to the ME peace proces. Because of Egypt's importance to, and centrality in, that process, Jordan was instrumental in having Egypt readmitted to the Arab fold at the Casablanca emergency Arab summit in May[213] (for details, see chapters on inter-Arab relations and Egypt). Jordan's support for Egypt's reinstatement in the councils of the Arab League was accompanied by another move designed to enhance Arab flexibility. Jordan returned to an argument it had made several years earlier (see *MECS* 1984–85, p. 518), in favor of majority decision making in Arab League forums[214] instead of the potentially paralyzing consensus, which gave veto power to radicals like Syria or Libya.

Unlike its ties with Egypt, the kingdom's relations with Iraq revolved more around the military dimension of the Arab-Israeli conflict and Jordan's efforts to bolster its military posture *vis-à-vis* Israel. Jordan and Iraq continued to maintain important transit trade links through the port of 'Aqaba. According to the Iraqi minister of transport, 'Aqaba remained the largest port for import-export for Iraq, even after the end of the Gulf War. Nearly 29,000 tons of goods were transported daily from 'Aqaba to Baghdad,[215] and 90% of the 'Aqaba port's facilities were used for transit trade to Iraq.[216] However, during 1989, the importance of transit trade was overshadowed by increasing indications of military cooperation between Jordan and Iraq. In August, Israeli sources revealed that Israel had conveyed a protest to Jordan, through the US, for having allowed Iraqi aircraft to fly reconnaissance missions along Jordan's border with Israel. The Iraqi and Jordanian air forces were said to have carried out joint exercises and senior Iraqi officers had visited Jordan's front with Israel.[217]

Though relations with Iraq were especially close, Jordan still maintained a stable and not overtly unfriendly relationship with Syria. This was true despite differences over Lebanon and even though Jordan had allowed Iraq to send military equipment via 'Aqaba to the anti-Syrian forces of Michel 'Awn in Lebanon[218] (see chapter on Lebanon). Jordan supported the replacement of Syrian forces with an Arab force and an overall settlement for the Lebanese question sponsored by the Arab League.[219] The *status quo* in Lebanon, the Jordanians feared, might pave the way for the partition of that country and the subsequent expulsion of Palestinians to Jordan.[220]

Neither Jordan nor Syria was interested in creating mutual tension. Various joint committees continued to function, including the one dealing with the al-Wahda dam project, that was to be jointly constructed across the Yarmuk River (see *MECS* 1987, pp. 507, 647–48). A tunnel built to divert the river's water before construction could begin was completed, but Jordan and Syria still had to raise the necessary funds ($350–400m.) for actual construction.[221]

Jordan's relations with Saudi Arabia remained as friendly as in the past despite the formation of the ACC, which was said to have aroused Saudi displeasure.[222] Riyadh remained as interested as ever in the stability of Jordan's monarchy. Saudi Arabia was the only Arab state to fully honor its pledge of economic support made to Jordan at the Baghdad summit of 1978. The last installment of this aid was paid in February 1989.[223] Saudi Arabia, however, continued to lead the Gulf states in propping up Jordan's faltering economy much to the relief and gratitude of the Jordanians.[224]

JORDAN AND THE GREAT POWERS
Relations with the United States
The new Administration of George Bush was received with optimism and high expectations in Jordan. Bush and Husayn were well acquainted and were said to have a good rapport. The fact that the president was thought to be well informed on ME affairs was seen as an Arab asset that would offset Jewish pressure groups and alter US ME priorities.[225] From the outset the Jordanian media urged the new Administration to pressure Israel to agree to an international conference.[226] In early April, during his talks in Washington with Egyptian President Husni Mubarak, President Bush called upon Israel to put an end to its occupation and to recognize the political rights of the Palestinians. He also noted that a properly structured international conference could play a useful role at the appropriate time. This US policy statement was very well received in Jordan. According to Foreign Minister Marwan al-Qasim it showed a "new spirit" in US policy on the ME.[227]

The Jordanians were therefore disappointed when Bush accepted the Israeli Government's proposal for elections in the West Bank and Gaza. In the Jordanian analysis these two US positions were incompatible and further proof of the lack of US credibility.[228] (For Jordanian grievances on US policy in the ME, see *MECS* 1988, p. 608.)

King Husayn paid an official visit to the US in mid-April. Following talks between Bush and Husayn on 19 April, the president restated the position he had outlined to Mubarak on the Arab-Israeli conflict. But more important for Husayn — with the riots in southern Jordan still raging (see above) — was the statement by Bush to the effect that "Jordan's security remains of fundamental concern to the US." Bush assured Husayn that the US would "do its utmost to help meet Jordan's economic and military requirements."[229]

On Arab-Israeli issues, the Jordanians remained critical of what was seen as a fundamental pro-Israeli bias in US policy. This was expressed in reference to the use of the US veto in the UN Security Council to block anti-Israeli resolutions, and to the massive economic aid given by the US to Israel.[230]

Relations with the Soviet Union
For the most part, Jordan's relations with the USSR were friendly and positive. On the ME peace process they shared a "common stand" on both the procedure of an international conference and on the substance of future negotiations.[231] Soviet-Jordanian consultations on the peace process were frequent. Soviet Foreign Minister Eduard Shevardnadze visited Jordan during his ME tour in February (see chapter on the Soviet Union and the ME) and Gennady Tarasov, assistant to the Soviet foreign minister, came to Jordan on a number of occasions during the year (April-May, August, November).

At the end of the year, the question of Jewish emigration from the Soviet Union to Israel introduced a sense of doubt and uncertainty in Jordan about Soviet ME policy. The Arabs were urged by the Jordanian media to exert pressure on the Soviet Union to change its emigration policy which could "open the doors to complications in the region, the nature of which could not be foreseen."[232]

Jordan and Western Europe
As in the past, Jordan's relations with Western Europe were concerned primarily with the ME peace process, as part of an effort to alter US policy, and with arms procurement. The EEC position on the ME was welcomed by Jordan. An EEC statement in June, endorsing the land-for-peace formula, calling for PLO involvement in the peace process, and condemning Israeli practices in the occupied territories, was praised in Jordan as a "highly positive development."[233]

In the sphere of arms procurement, Jordan suffered a setback, when it was compelled in March to indefinitely postpone a deal with the UK for eight *Tornado* aircraft (see *MECS* 1988, p. 610). Jordan's economic difficulties rendered the £500m. deal impractical.[234]

TABLE 1: JORDANIAN CABINETS — 1989

Portfolio	27 April	6 December
Prime Minister and Defense	Zayd Ibn Shakir	Mudar Badran
Deputy Prime Minister and Interior	Salim Masa'ida	Salim Masa'ida
Deputy Prime Minister and Minister of State for Economic Affairs	Tahir al-Masri(P)[1]	--------
Deputy Prime Minister and Foreign Affairs	Marwan al-Qasim*	Marwan al-Qasim
Supply	Ibrahim Ayyub	Nabil Abu al-Huda(P)
Awqaf and Islamic Affairs	'Abd al-'Aziz al-Khayyat(P)*	'Ali Faqir[2]
Health	Zuhayr Malhas*	Muhammad 'Addub al-Zabn[4]
Social Development	Zuhayr Malhas	'Abd al-Majid Shurayda[4]
Energy and Mineral Resources	Hisham al-Khatib(P)*	Thabit al-Tahir(P)
Education	'Abdallah Nusur[1]	Muhammad Hamdan(P)
Higher Education	Nasir al-Din al-Asad*	Muhammad Hamdan(P)
Municipal, Rural, and Environment Affairs	Yusuf Hamdan*	'Abd al-Karim al-Dughmi[3]
Public Works and Housing	Shafiq al-Zuwayda*[1]	'Abd al-Ra'uf al-Rawabida[4]
Youth	'Awad Khulayfat*	Ibrahim Ghababisha[3]
Tourism	Yanal Hikmat*	'Abd al-Karim al-Kabariti[4]
Agriculture	'Adnan Badran	Sulayman 'Arabiyat
Water and Irrigation	Muhammad Salih al-Kaylani(P)	Da'ud Khalaf(P)
Information	Nasuh al-Majali	Ibrahim 'Izz al-Din
Culture	Nasuh al-Majali	Khalid al-Karaki
Industry and Trade	Ziyad Radi 'Innab	Ziyad Fariz
Transport and Telecommunications	Hikmat al-Khammash(P)	Ibrahim Ayyub
Finance	Basil Jardana	Basil Jardana
Justice	Ratib al-Wazani	Yusuf Mubayyidin[2]
Planning	Ziyad Fariz	'Awni al-Masri(P)
Labor	Jamal al-Budur	Qasim 'Ubaydat[4]

| Minister of State for Cabinet Affairs | Ibrahim 'Izz al-Din | ------ | |
| Minister of State for Parliamentary Affairs | --------- | | 'Abd al-Baqi Jamu[2] |

*	Member of outgoing Rifa'i cabinet.
(P)	Palestinian origin.
1	Masri, Nusur, and Zuwayda resigned in August to run in the general elections. Masri was not replaced. 'Adnan Badran replaced Nusur and Basam al-Sakit was added to the cabinet to replace Badran as minister of agriculture.
2	Religious deputy but not member of Muslim Brethren.
3	Moderate leftist deputy not identified with any political party.
4	Loyalist deputy.

TABLE 2: POPULATION AND SEAT DISTRIBUTION PER GOVERNORATE

Governorate	Population[1]	and	Percentage	Seats	and	Percentage
Amman	1,249,000		41.6	21		26.25
Irbid	728,000		24.2	19		23.75
Zarqa	434,000		14.5	6		7.5
Balqa	207,000		6.9	8		10
Karak	128,000		4.3	9		11.25
Mafraq	105,000		3.5	3		3.75
Ma'an	105,000		3.5	5		6.25
Tafila	44,000		1.5	3		3.75
Total	**3,000,000**		**100**	**74***		**92.5***

Country Profile, Jordan, 1990–91, (London: The Economist Intelligence Unit, 1990), p. 2.

Six seats were reserved for bedouin tribal representation: two for each of the "bedouin of the north," "bedouin of the center" and "bedouin of the south." Bedouin who still abided by a tribal life-style accounted for 5–6% of the population, but had 7.5% of the seats in parliament.

TABLE 3: JORDANIAN CHAMBER OF DEPUTIES — 1989

Constituency	Deputies	Political Affiliation
Amman — First	'Ali Mustafa Muhammad al-Faqir	Islamic fundamentalist
	'Abd al-'Aziz Jabr Shabana(P)	Islamic Movement Bloc
	Majid Muhammad Khalifa	Islamic Movement Bloc
Amman — Second	'Abd al-Mun'im Abu Zant (P)	Islamic Movement Bloc[1]
	'Ali 'Id al-Hawamida	Islamic Movement Bloc
	Ya'qub Jum'a Qirsh (P)	Islamic fundamentalist (Dar al-Qur'an)
Amman — Third	Layth Farhan Shubaylat	Islamic fundamentalist (Dar al-Qur'an)[1]
	Faris Sulayman al-Nabulsi	Leftist (Independent)[2]
	Tahir al-Masri (P)	Loyalist
Circassian Seat	Mansur Sayf al-Din Murad	Leftist (Independent)[1]
Christian Seat	Fakhri Anis Qa'war(P)	Leftist (Independent)[1]
Amman — Fourth	Nayif Minwir al-Hadid	Loyalist
	Hamza 'Abbas Mansur(P)	Islamic Movement Bloc
Amman — Fifth	Humam 'Abd al-Rahim Sa'id(P)	Islamic Movement Bloc
	Muhammad 'Abd al-Qadir Abu Faris(P)	Islamic Movement Bloc
	'Ata Fadil al-Shahwan	Loyalist
	Ahmad Salih 'Uwayd al-'Abadi	Loyalist[1]
Circassian Seat	Da'ud Qujaq	Islamic Movement Bloc
Amman — Sixth	Ahmad Qutaysh al-Ayayida	Islamic Movement Bloc
	'Abd al-Hafiz Ahmad 'Alawi	Islamic Movement Bloc
Christian Seat	Sa'd Butrus Haddadin	Loyalist

Irbid	Ahmad al-Kufahi	Islamic Movement Bloc
	'Abd al-Rahim Muhammad 'Ukur	Islamic Movement Bloc
	Kamil Sari al-Umari	Islamic Movement Bloc
	Yusuf Mahmud Ahmad al-Khasawna	Islamic fundamentalist
	Muhammad Ibrahim al-'Alawina	Muslim Brethren
	Dhuqan Salim al-Hindawi	Loyalist[1]
	Husni Ahmad al-Shayyab	Leftist (Ba'th)[1]
	'Abd al-Ra'uf Salim al-Rawabida	Loyalist
Christian Seat	Dhib Sa'd Marji	Leftist (Jordanian wing of PFLP)[2]
Zarqa	Dhib Anis 'Abd al-Hafiz Shihada (P)	Islamic Movement Bloc
	Muhammad Ahmad Mahmud al-Hajj(P)	Islamic Movement Bloc
	Salama 'Attallah al-Ghuwayri	Loyalist
	Ziyad Muhammad Mahfuz Abu Mahfuz(P)	Islamic fundamentalist
Circassian/Chechen Seat	'Abd al-Baqi Jamu	Islamic fundamentalist
Christian Seat	Bassam Salama Haddadin	Leftist (Popular Democratic Party)[2]
Jarash	'Isa 'Abid al-Rimuni	Loyalist
	Husayn Muhammad Mujalli al-Rawashida	Leftist (Independent)[1]
'Ajlun	Ahmad Mahmud Salim 'Innab	Loyalist[2]
	'Abd al-Salam Nur al-Din Furayhat	Leftist (Independent)
Christian Seat	Jamal Riyad Haddad	Loyalist
Ramtha/Bani Kanana	Muhammad 'Ali Muhammad Dardur	Loyalist
	Qasim Muhammad 'Ubaydat	Loyalist
	Salim Muhammad Salim al-Zu'bi	Leftist (Independent)[1]
Al-Kura/Northern Jordan Valley	'Abd al-Majid 'Abdallah al-Shurayda	Loyalist
	Nadir Muhammad al-Dhuhayrat	Loyalist
Mafraq	'Abd al-Karim al-Dughmi	Leftist/Loyalist
	Muhammad Musallam Abu 'Alim	Loyalist
	Nawaf Faris al-Khawalida	Loyalist
Balqa	'Abdallah 'Abd al-Karim al-Nusur	Loyalist
	'Abd al-Latif 'Arabiyat	Islamic Movement Bloc
	Ibrahim Mas'ud Khuraysat	Islamic Movement Bloc
	'Awni 'Abd al-Rahman al-Bashir	Leftist
	Marwan al-Nimr al-Humud	Loyalist
	Sultan Majid Sultan al-'Adwan	Loyalist
Christian Seat	Fawzi Shakir Tu'ayma	Loyalist
Christian Seat	Samir Farhan Qa'war	Loyalist
Karak	Ahmad 'Ali Salim al-Kafawin	Islamic Movement Bloc
	Jamal Ahmad al-Sarayira	Islamic fundamentalist
	'Atif Muhammad Khalil al-Butush	Muslim Brethren
	Mahmud 'Abd al-Latif Huwaymil	Islamic fundamentalist
	Mutayr Ahmad al-Bustanji(P)	Islamic fundamentalist
	Yusuf Salim al-Mubayyidin	Islamic fundamentalist
	Muhammad Faris al-Tarawina	Leftist (Ba'th)[2]
Christian Seat	'Isa Sulayman Madanat	Communist Party[2]
Christian Seat	'Abdallah Ghanim al-Zurayqat	Loyalist
Tafila	'Abdallah al-'Akayila	Islamic Movement Bloc
	Ibrahim 'Abd al-Rahman al-Ghababisha	Leftist/Loyalist
	Fu'ad Mustafa al-Khalafat	Islamic Movement Bloc
Ma'an	Yusuf al-'Azm	Muslim Brethren
	Sulayman 'Arar	Loyalist
	Ziyad Kamal al-Shuwaykh	Loyalist
	Hisham al-Sharari	Loyalist
	'Abd al-Karim al-Kabariti	Loyalist

Bedouin-North	Muhammad al-Mu'ar'ar	Loyalist
	Sa'd al-Surur	Loyalist
Bedouin-Center	Jamal Haditha al-Khuraysha	Loyalist
	Muhammad 'Addub al-Zabn	Loyalist
Bedouin-South	Faysal Ibn Jazi	Loyalist
	Nayif Abu Taya	Loyalist

Cumulative Figures	
Loyalists	33–35
Islamic Movement Bloc	20
Other Islamic fundamentalists	13
Leftists	12–14
	80

SOURCES:

Based on Jordan TV, 10 November — DR, 13 November; *JT*, 11, 23–24 November; *al-Watan*, Kuwait, 12 November; *Sawt al-Sha'b*, 19 November, *al-Siyasa*, Kuwait, 9 December 1989; *al-Ra'y*, 2 January 1990.

NOTES

Loyalists — pro-establishment, generally former cabinet ministers, army officers, government officials, or traditional and tribal community leaders.

The Islamic Movement Bloc — all members of the Muslim Brethren who ran as part of a defined and published bloc. Some known Brethren ran separately and are listed accordingly.

Those listed as Islamic fundamentalists are not associated with the Brethren and no clearly defined organizational affiliation is known for them unless stated otherwise.

Leftist — supporters of the illegal political parties such as the Communist Party, the Ba'th (Iraqi and Syrian), other pan-Arab nationalists, and supporters of various PLO factions.

1   Voted against Badran in vote of confidence.
2   Abstained in vote of confidence.
(P)   Palestinian origin.

NOTES

For the place and frequency of publications cited here, and for the full name of the publication, news agency, radio station, or monitoring service where an abbreviation is used, please see "List of Sources." Only in the case of more than one publication bearing the same name is the place of publication noted here.

1.   Jordan TV, 12 July — DR, 12 July 1989.
2.   Public estimates by the Rifa'i cabinet had been lower — $6–6.5bn. *JT*, 20 May; *JP*, 24 May 1989.
3.   *JT*, 9–10 February; *FT*, 9 February 1989.
4.   *Country Profile, Jordan, 1990–91*, p. 11.
5.   *FT*, 21 February 1989.
6.   *Country Profile, Jordan, 1990–91*, pp. 11–12; *FT*, 11 April 1989.
7.   Ibid.
8.   *JT*, 28 March; *FT*, 3 April 1989.
9.   *Al-Ra'y*, 16 April; *JT*, 17 April 1989.
10.   *JT*, 21 May 1989.
11.   *MM*, 12 June 1989.
12.   R. Amman, 29 May — DR, 31 May; *JT*, 30 May 1989.
13.   *JT*, 31 May 1989.
14.   *JT*, 1–2 June; *FT*, 29 June 1989.
15.   *Al-Watan*, 17 June 1989.
16.   *JT*, 1 July 1989.

17. *FT,* 1 August; *JT,* 15 August 1989.
18. R. Amman, 28 July — DR, 31 July; Jordan TV, 30 July — DR, 2 August 1989.
19. *JT,* 29 July; *Sawt al-Sha'b,* 2 August 1989.
20. E.g., *Sawt al-Sha'b,* 30 July, 2 August 1989.
21. *JT,* 5 August 1989.
22. *Al-Ra'y,* 5 August; *JT,* 9 August 1989.
23. *JT,* 27 August 1989.
24. Jordan TV, 15 December — DR, 27 December 1989.
25. *JT,* 2 December 1989.
26. *Al-Ra'y,* 11 October 1989.
27. *JT,* 3 December 1989.
28. R. Monte Carlo, 20 July — DR, 21 July; *JT,* 25 July 1989.
29. *FT, JT,* 12 September; *JT,* 22 November 1989.
30. *JT,* 10, 17 October 1989.
31. Husayn at cabinet briefing, R. Amman, 10 May — DR, 10 May; similarly *JT,* 13 June; R. Amman, 2 October — DR, 12 October; Husayn's letter of appointment to Mudar Badran, R. Amman, 4 December — DR, 5 December 1989.
32. *JT,* 28 June 1989.
33. *JT,* 13 August 1989.
34. *JT,* 1 October 1989.
35. Ibid.
36. *JT,* 9 October 1989.
37. *JT,* 31 October 1989.
38. R. Amman, 2 October — DR, 12 October 1989.
39. *JT,* 16 May 1989.
40. *Al-Ra'y,* 6 April; *JT,* 8 April 1989.
41. Riyad al-Khouri in *JT,* 12 April 1989.
42. *JT,* 13 August 1989,
43. *JT,* 27 November 1989.
44. *JT,* 5 March 1989.
45. *Sawt al-Sha'b,* 11 July; *JT,* 31 July; *al-Dustur,* Amman, 6 August 1989.
46. *JT,* 5 February 1989.
47. R. Amman, 27 April — DR, 28 April; *ME,* June 1989.
48. *JP,* 15 June 1989.
49. R. Amman, 2 October — DR, 12 October 1989.
50. Jordan TV, 18 August — DR, 22 August 1989.
51. *JT,* 27 November 1989.
52. *JT,* 24 September 1989.
53. Dr. Fahd Fanik in *JT,* 3 December 1989.
54. AFP, 18, 19 April — DR, 19 April 1989.
55. R. Monte Carlo, AFP, 19 April — DR, 19 April; *IHT, NYT,* 20 April; Jordan TV, 21 April — DR, 24 April 1989.
56. AFP, 20 April — DR, 21 April 1989.
57. AFP, 20 April — DR, 21 April; *FT,* 21 April 1989.
58. AFP, 21 April — DR, 21 April; R. Monte Carlo, 21 April — DR, 24 April; *NYT, FT,* 22 April 1989.
59. AFP, 19 April — DR, 20 April; *JP,* 23 April 1989.
60. *FT,* 22 April 1989.
61. R. Monte Carlo, 24 April — DR, 25 April; MENA, 25 April — DR, 25 April; AFP, 1 May — DR, 1 May 1989.
62. *JT,* 23 April 1989.
63. *NYT,* 23 April; *FT,* 24 April 1989. In June another person died of injuries sustained in the riots in April (AFP, 24 June 1989).
64. *NYT,* 22 April 1989.
65. Husayn in interview to *al-Siyasa,* Kuwait, broadcast by R. Amman, 27 April — DR, 28 April 1989.
66. *JT,* 6–7, 8 April 1989.

67. *MEI*, 28 April 1989.
68. *IHT*, 25 April 1989.
69. R. Monte Carlo, 20, 21 April — DR, 20, 24 April 1989.
70. *IHT*, 20 April 1989.
71. *NYT*, 22 April 1989.
72. R. Amman, 21 April — DR, 21 April 1989.
73. *FT*, 23, 26 April; *MEI*, 28 April; *al-Bayadir al-Siyasi*, 29 April 1989.
74. *Al-Ittihad*, Abu Dhabi, 3 April 1989.
75. *FT*, 22 April 1989.
76. R. Monte Carlo, 22 April — DR, 24 April; *MEI*, 28 April 1989.
77. Jordan TV, 22 April — DR, 24 April; *JT*, 23 April 1989.
78. *NYT*, 23 April 1989.
79. *FT*, 22 April 1989.
80. *NYT*, 23 April 1989.
81. *JT*, 23 April 1989.
82. *Al-Dustur*, Amman, 11 May 1989.
83. R. Amman, 9 May — DR, 10 May 1989.
84. *Al-Sharq al-Awsat*, 4 May 1989.
85. *NYT*, 24 April 1989.
86. Jordan TV, 24 April — DR, 25 April 1989.
87. R. Monte Carlo, 25 April — DR, 26 April; *IHT*, 26 April 1989.
88. Husayn in speech to the nation, Jordan TV, 26 April — DR, 27 April; Husayn in interview to *al-Siyasa*, Kuwait, broadcast on R. Amman, 27 April — DR, 28 April 1989.
89. Ibid.
90. Jordan TV, 27 April — DR, 28 April; *al-Dustur*, Amman, 28 April; *JT*, 29 April; *MEI*, 12 May 1989.
91. Jordan TV, 27 April — DR, 28 April 1989.
92. *MEI*, 12 May; *AT*, 5 June — DR, 8 June 1989.
93. Husayn in meetings with delegations from the governorates of Tafila, Irbid, Karak, and Balqa and the city of Salt, *JT*, 1 May; R. Amman, 1, 4, 10 May — DR, 2, 5, 11 May 1989.
94. R. Amman, 15 May — DR, 16 May; *JT*, 10 June 1989.
95. R. Amman, 18 May — DR, 19 May; *MEI*, 26 May; *al-Ra'y*, 29 June 1989.
96. *MEI*, 26 May 1989.
97. *JT*, 19 February; *al-Sharq al-Awsat*, 20 February 1989.
98. *Sawt al-Sha'b*, 22 May 1989.
99. R. Monte Carlo, 11 July — DR, 12 July 1989.
100. *JT*, 3 September 1989. In May, Majali had made a similar statement after the releases made then (*Sawt al-Sha'b*, 22 May 1989). The September releases proved the May statement to be untrue. There was no way of knowing whether the statement in September was true.
101. *MEI*, 26 May 1989.
102. *Al-Sharq al-Awsat*, 2 March; *AFP*, 23 March 1989.
103. Jordan TV, 15 May — DR, 16 May 1989.
104. Jordan TV, 27 April — DR, 28 April 1989.
105. Jordan TV, 15 May, 18 August — DR, 16 May, 22 August 1989.
106. E.g., *al-Ra'y*, 18 May, 25 May; *Sawt al-Sha'b*, 23 May 1989.
107. Jordan TV, 29 June — DR, 3 July; *al-Ra'y*, 17 July 1989.
108. *JT*, 18–19 May, 19–20 October; *Sawt al-Sha'b*, 23 May 1989.
109. *JT*, 3 June 1989.
110. *Al-Dustur*, Amman, 5 October 1989.
111. *JT*, 7 November 1989.
112. *JT*, 12 December 1989.
113. *JT*, 16, 17, 18 December 1989.
114. See statements by Interior Ministers, Raja'i al-Dajani and Salim Masa'ida, R. Amman, 17 April — DR, 18 April; R. Monte Carlo, 6 July — DR, 7 July and *al-Dustur*, Amman, 20 July 1989.
115. R. Amman, 15, 17 April — DR, 17, 18 April; *al-Dustur*, Amman, 17 April 1989.
116. R. Amman, 5 July — DR, 10 July 1989.

117. See statements by Minister of Information, Hani al-Khasawna, in January and early April in *al Ra'y,* 7 January and *al-Watan al-'Arabi,* 7 April 1989; *al-Ittihad,* Abu Dhabi, 3 April 1989.
118. *JT,* 5 July 1989.
119. R. Monte Carlo, 4 October — DR, 6 October 1989.
120. *JT,* 8 November 1989.
121. In August, the Chief of the Royal Court Dhuqan al-Hindawi, the Mayor of Amman 'Abd al-Ra'uf al-Rawabida, and three cabinet ministers, Tahir al-Masri, 'Abdallah Nusur, and Shafiq Zuwayda, all resigned from their posts to run in the elections.
122. *Al-Hurriyya,* 19 August; *JT,* 2, 23 October; *MEI,* 20 October; *al-Ra'y,* 7 November; *JP,* 7 November 1989.
123. R. Amman, 13 September — DR, 14 September 1989.
124. *JT,* 23 September 1989.
125. *JT,* 12–13 October 1989.
126. *Al-Ra'y,* 25 October 1989.
127. Ibid.
128. *Al-Ra'y,* 21 September 1989.
129. *JT,* 30 October 1989.
130. JNA, 1 November — DR, 2 November 1989.
131. *Sawt al-Sha'b,* 31 October; *al-Ra'y,* 2 November 1989.
132. *JT,* 5 November 1989.
133. Jordan TV, 7 October, 4 November — DR, 10 October, 6 November 1989.
134. *JT,* 2–3 November 1989.
135. *Al-Yawm al-Sabi',* 25 September, 2 October; *JT,* 8 October 1989.
136. *FT,* 1 November 1989.
137. *JT,* 2–3 November 1989.
138. *JT,* 2–3, 9 November 1989.
139. *NYT,* 10 November 1989.
140. *JT,* 11 November 1989.
141. Political identities of some candidates were not clearly defined.
142. *JT,* 6, 12 November 1989.
143. *JT,* 13 November; *al-Dustur,* Amman, 19 November 1989.
144. *JT,* 11 November; *al-Ra'y, al-Watan,* 12 November; *al-Dustur,* Amman, 25 November 1989.
145. For conflicting arguments on this issue, see articles by Fahd Fanik in *al-Ra'y,* 12 Novermber, and Muna Shuqayr in *al-Dustur,* Amman, 26 November 1989.
146. *Al-Dustur,* Amman, 14 November 1989.
147. *Sawt al-Sha'b,* 14, 18, 22 November 1989.
148. *FT,* 14 November 1989.
149. According to the constitution, the number of senators was always half of the number of deputies. The Senate was therefore increased from 30 to 40.
150. *JT,* 23–24 November 1989.
151. JNA, 26 November — DR, 29 November; *MEI,* 1 December 1989.
152. *Sawt al-Sha'b,* 23 November; *JT,* 23–24 November 1989.
153. *JT,* 28 November 1989.
154. R. Amman, 4 December — DR, 5 December; *JT,* 7–8 December 1989.
155. R. Monte Carlo, 5 December — DR, 6 December 1989.
156. R. Amman, 10 December — DR, 11 December; *JT,* 12 December 1989.
157. Jordan TV, 26 December — DR, 27 December; *JT,* 27 December 1989.
158. R. Amman, 19 December — DR, 20 December 1989.
159. Even so, Qirsh eventually voted for the government.
160. *Sawt al-Sha'b,* 31 December 1989; *JT,* 1 January 1990.
161. Ibid.
162. *Al-Ra'y,* 31 December 1989; *JT,* 3 January 1990.
163. *Al-Ra'y,* 1 January 1990.
164. *Al-Ra'y,* 2 January 1990.
165. Ibid.

166. E.g., Jordan TV, 30 July — DR, 2 August; R. Amman, 10 November — DR, 14 November 1989.
167. *JT*, 19–20 October; similarly *al-Hawadith*, 27 October 1989.
168. *JT*, 17 October 1989.
169. *JT*, 25 December 1989.
170. *Le Figaro*, 11 January — DR, 18 January 1989.
171. *JT*, 11 January 1989.
172. Jordan TV, 30 July — DR, 2 August; London Press Association, 19 October — DR, 20 October 1989. Jordan was already said to be "struggling to meet its requirements of water supplies." (*JT*, 11 December 1989).
173. *Al-Ra'y*, 31 January; Rifa'i in *al-Ra'y*, 6 February 1989; Husayn quoted on R. Amman, 12 February — DR, 13 February 1989.
174. *Al-Ra'y*, 31 January 1989; Husayn to CNN, quoted on Jordan TV, 25 February — DR, 27 February 1989.
175. Zayd Ibn Shakir quoted in *Sawt al-Sha'b*, 15 June 1989.
176. Husayn quoted on Jordan TV, 20 April — DR, 21 April; *NYT*, 21 April 1989.
177. *Al-Dustur*, Amman, 10 July 1989.
178. Marwan al-Qasim in *al-Hawadith*, 28 April 1989.
179. Hasan in a speech at the Washington Institute for Near East Policy, 12 September 1989, *Proceedings of the Washington Institute* (October, 1989).
180. Hasan's speech, 12 September 1989, p. 6.
181. Ibid., pp. 6–7.
182. *JT*, 14 October 1989.
183. *JT*, 12–13 October 1989.
184. E.g., Minister of Information Hani al-Khasawna in *al-Ra'y*, 7 January; Foreign Minister Marwan al-Qasim in *al-Dustur*, Amman, 10 July 1989.
185. Jordan TV, 7 January — DR, 9 January 1989.
186. *JT*, 4 April 1989.
187. E.g., R. Amman, 3 May — DR, 4 May; *JT*, 24 September 1989.
188. *JT*, 16 August; R. Amman, 21 August — DR, 22 August; *MEI*, 25 August 1989.
189. *JT*, 19 June; *al-Ra'y*, 29 June 1989.
190. *JT*, 1 April, 14-15 September 1989.
191. Husayn on Macneil-Lehrer Newshour, 21 April — WF, 23 April 1989.
192. *Wochenpresse*, 12 May — DR, 18 May 1989.
193. *Al-Ra'y*, 15 March, 13 September, 16 October; *JT*, 27 March 1989.
194. Marwan al-Qasim on R. Monte Carlo, 2 March — DR, 3 March, and to *al-Qabas*, 10 October 1989.
195. *JT*, 17, 22 July 1989.
196. *Wochenpresse*, 12 May — DR, 18 May 1989.
197. E.g., Zayd al-Rifa'i to *al-Ra'y*, 6 February, Marwan al-Qasim to *al-Ittihad*, Abu Dhabi, 12 March and King Husayn to *al-Dustur*, Amman, 21 October 1989.
198. *JT*, 7 November 1989.
199. Jordan TV, 29 June, 30 July — DR, 3 July, 2 August 1989.
200. Hasan quoted in *JT*, 17, 25 October 1989.
201. *Al-Sha'b*, E. Jerusalem, 28 February; Premier Badran in a speech to the Chamber of Deputies, R. Amman, 19 December — DR, 20 December 1989.
202. *Ha'aretz*, 14 July 1989.
203. *JT*, *NYT*, 27 December 1989.
204. *NYT*, 9 August 1989.
205. *NYT*, 8 September 1989.
206. R. Monte Carlo, 5 October — DR, 6 October 1989.
207. *JT*, 3 December 1989.
208. Husayn on R. Amman, 1 May — DR, 2 May; Hasan to *al-Hawadith*, 27 October 1989.
209. *JT*, 16–17 February 1989.
210. *JT*, 15 February 1989.
211. *JT*, 19 February 1989.
212. *MM*, 20 March; *MEI*, 25 August 1989.

213. *JT*, 26 March 1989.
214. Husayn on Jordan TV, 7 March — DR, 8 March and in a speech to Arab summit, R. Amman, 25 May — DR, 26 May 1989.
215. *JT*, 8-9 June 1989.
216. *Al-Ra'y*, 5 August 1989.
217. *Ha'aretz, JP*, 21 August 1989.
218. R. Monte Carlo, 27 August — DR, 28 August; *al-Qabas,* 10 October; *al-Safir,* 12 October 1989.
219. Husayn's speech at Casablanca summit, R. Amman, 25 May — DR, 26 May 1989.
220. *MEI*, 8 September 1989.
221. *JT*, 6 June; JNA, 5 October — DR, 6 October 1989.
222. *MM*, 15 May 1989.
223. *JT*, 5 February 1989.
224. Zayd Ibn Shakir on Jordan TV, 18 August — DR, 22 August 1989.
225. Hani al-Khasawna in *al-Ra'y*, 7 January; Husayn to CNN, quoted on Jordan TV, 25 February — DR, 27 February; Rifa'i to *al-Sharq al-Awsat*, 3 March 1989.
226. E.g., *al-Ra'y*, 22 March, 5 April 1989.
227. *JT*, 6-7 April 1989.
228. *JT, al-Ra'y*, 8 April 1989.
229. *DSB*, July 1989.
230. *JT*, 14 May; *al-Dustur*, Amman, 10 June 1989.
231. *JT*, 3 May 1989.
232. *Al-Ra'y*, 18 October 1989.
233. *JT*, 12, 13 February, 29-30 June 1989.
234. *FT*, 22 March; R. Amman, 25 March — DR, 27 March 1989.

Kuwait

(Al-Kuwayt)

JOSEPH KOSTINER

In 1989, Kuwait was influenced by events and processes that had been evolving in the Gulf region since the end of the Iran-Iraq War. This influence was expressed in Kuwaiti inhabitants' optimism that they would be able to live in peace, develop their country, and regain political rights curtailed during the war. Kuwaitis also anticipated that years of recession would be followed by economic rehabilitation, since the postwar period coincided with the rehabilitation of Western economies and forecasts of higher oil prices. But, at the same time, this postwar period also posed problems to Kuwaiti leaders, some of which derived from insecurity in the Gulf, as a result of Iraq and Iran not signing a full peace treaty. Both Iraq and Iran kept reinforcing their military positions, while the Iranian Revolutionary Guards continued to export Iran's revolution, which affected Kuwait's security and alarmed its leaders. States in Kuwait's immediate proximity added to its anxiety. With the Gulf War over, Kuwait ceased being an ally of Iraq, but a small state, surrounded by major regional powers with conflicting interests, each trying to win Kuwait to its camp: Iran wanted to refurbish its image in the Arab world, Saudi Arabia was haunted by fears of Shi'i subversion, and Iraq made territorial demands on Kuwait.

There were also problems at home. Some of them stemmed from grand expectations, typical of a postwar period, both of the government and of different social groups, which could not be satisfied in the short run and forebode frustration and conflict. Some problems were sociopolitical in nature. The Shi'i minority was incited by Iranian propaganda and under economic pressure. The Sunni business elite and professional middle class sought to restore the National Assembly dissolved by the ruler, Jabir al-Ahmad Al Sabah, in 1986, and gain the right of political participation. Their ambitions were encouraged by democratization in Eastern Europe and in some Arab states such as South Yemen. The excess number of foreign workers, which confounded Kuwaiti demographic forecasts, cost concern to the government. It was feared that some of these problems, such as Shi'i unrest, could easily develop into Iranian-backed insurgency.

Kuwaiti leaders coped with these problems in a variety of ways. They gave first priority to security by strengthening the security forces and cracking down on potentially subversive Shi'i elements. Filled with a new spirit of optimism, they embarked on new development schemes and on programs to improve Kuwait's financial situation, thereby satisfying most Kuwaiti elements. The government simultaneously planned to reduce the number of foreign workers. It sought to maintain a balance both in regional relations and in its ties with the superpowers, in

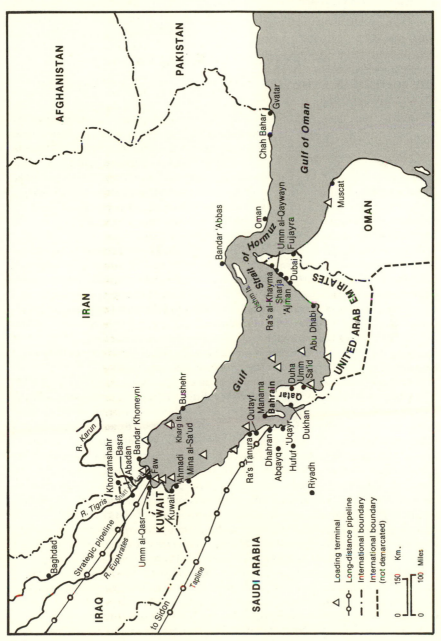

The Gulf

order to help establish regional stability. To achieve this aim, Kuwaiti leaders adopted a number of tactics, which transformed the country into a key state in inter-Arab affairs during 1989.

INTERNAL AFFAIRS

THE SOCIETY AND THE ECONOMY: PROBLEMS AND PROSPECTS

Sociopolitical Difficulties

The Kuwaiti regime evolved out of a tribal, but urban trade-oriented community, by means of a coalition between the ruling Al Sabah family and other leading professional or merchant families. The latter supported the Al Sabah rule in return for a stake in Kuwait's business affairs which facilitated their access to wealth, and for a public forum where they might voice grievances and express at least minimal criticism of the Al Sabah-dominated government. These families constituted the country's leading banking and trading elements, as well as its professional and intellectual elite. They also formed its select electorate of c. 65,000 Kuwaitis (out of a total population of 1,958m.), whose families lived in the kingdom before 1920.[1]

In recent years this elite sustained two major setbacks which increased its opposition to the regime. Kuwaiti commerce, which in the 1970s had been one of the country's most profitable sectors, was curtailed following the breakdown of the unofficial stock market (Suq al-Manakh) in 1981. This collapse impoverished many businessmen, and Kuwaiti banks were saddled with debts amounting to KD2.2bn. left by the investors. Kuwait subsequently lost its position as the Gulf's major business center to Abu Dhabi. Limitations caused by the Gulf War and the Arab states' boycott of Egypt following the Camp David Accords forced Kuwaiti businessmen to reduce or sever ties with Egypt and Iran, which further affected their activities.[2]

A second setback was the suspension of the 50-member National Assembly in 1986. It had been a forum of political debate for different factions — supporters of the regime, leftists, Arab nationalists, and Muslim fundamentalists, most of them members of elite families. Fearing the assembly's reaction to antigovernment and even subversive activities at the height of the Gulf War, the ruler, Jabir al-Ahmad Al Sabah dissolved the assembly.[3] However, former members, encouraged by its achievements, strove for its recall, redoubling their efforts after the cease-fire. The recall, they believed, would remove the last obstacle to the "restoration of parliamentary life." In February 1989, secret petitions to that effect were distributed, signed by 40,000 Kuwaiti males, identified as members of the electorate. Western observers believed that former members of the assembly, who represented the Kuwaiti elite, were behind this petition.[4] The government could not afford an open struggle with its "pro-democracy" elite groups, and had to deal with their grievances.

Kuwait also had difficulties in absorbing the foreign workers, which in 1989 were 70% of the population and 80% of the work force. The end of the Iraq-Iran War prompted the Kuwaiti authorities to examine the status and numbers of foreign workers. The problem was twofold: on the one hand, the government sought by the year 2000 "to balance" the composition of the Kuwaiti population, namely to increase the number of Kuwaiti nationals and particularly in the work force. Foreigners, who had been exposed to outside ideologies and suffered discrimination at the hands of the

Kuwaitis, were considered a disturbing factor, which could become a potential threat to Kuwait's security. On the other hand, the government had to consider Kuwait's dependence on foreign workers, who did work either too difficult or too menial for most Kuwaitis. Both the public administration and major Kuwaiti contractors and businessmen were, therefore, interested in employing foreign workers.[5] The government had to devise a policy to cope with this complex problem.

The Shi'is comprised c. 9% of the population and were another threat to stability. Most of them were in the lower strata of society; they were antagonistic toward the government, quite receptive to Iranian propaganda directed against Gulf rulers, and participated in opposition rallies and even in terrorist activities. When the Gulf War ended, Kuwaiti leaders feared that Kuwaiti Shi'is would remain a dissatisfied faction which could undermine stability if exploited by the Shi'i revolutionary underground organizations active in the region, such as al-Da'wa and Hizballah.[6]

The Problems of Ending Economic Recession

Due to the war and therefore to the fall in oil production, the official budget deficit for 1989 was estimated at KD800m. ($2.7bn.). The government's need to draw on its reserves to cover deficits ate into the Central Bank's foreign assets, which had fallen in December 1988 to a 15-year low of KD399.4m ($1.4bn.), the lowest since 1973. Financial problems were aggravated by the tremendous defense expenditure — $1.9bn. in 1988 for US arms and $300m. for Soviet arms — which, as Finance Minister Jasim Muhammad al-Khurafi said, were "continuously increasing."[7]

The economic problem was worsened by the government's readiness to increase the volume of economic activities, despite the deficits. Revenue increased, on improved tax collection and a higher oil production quota from 996,000 barrels per day (b/d) to 1,038 m. b/d as allocated at the Vienna meeting of the Organization of Petroleum Exporting Countries (Opec) in November 1988. This rise enabled the government to increase public expenditure by 9% and to raise interest rates on investments, in order to encourage large-scale investment in banks and trade.[8] This policy had two risks: the possible inability of the government to satisfy the growing expectations of different groups through government expenditure and business opportunities, and overspending, which would increase the deficit.

Hence, in 1989, the government faced problems carrying over from the years of war and recession, and from the plans and expectations of the postwar period. These problems, expressing themselves in subversion and social unrest, also gave ground to economic rehabilitation.

CONTAINING DOMESTIC PROBLEMS
Coping with Shi'i Subversion
In the Kuwaiti leaders' view, Shi'i subversion, possibly directed by Iran, was a dangerous security problem. They considered Shi'i dissatisfaction, when stirred up by Iran to the extent of terrorist activities in Kuwait, as a likely tactic in the postwar period, when subversion might replace conventional warfare to achieve regional revolution. The government asserted its determination to maintain a high level of security in several ways. Jabir al-Ahmad stressed that Kuwait "will not be an easy prey" and the security forces constituted "a protective shield" against "all those who

sought to tamper with the safety and security of this country."[9] Defense Minister Nawwaf Al Sabah stressed that as long as Iran and Iraq had not signed a peace agreement, Kuwait would maintain "maximum alert and vigilance." He stressed that Kuwait would develop its naval forces and set up a brigade of military reservists.[10] Great emphasis was put on security procedures in Kuwait's airport. It was also proposed that a coast guard, with speedboats, radar equipment, and frogmen be established under the authority of the minister of interior,[11] to prevent outside assistance to internal subversion and seaborne sabotage against Kuwaiti targets, which Kuwaiti Shi'is had carried out in the past with Iranian support.

Apart from such security measures, the government closely monitored the activities of the Shi'i community. In February 1989, it attempted to pacify Shi'i opposition groups by releasing two of the 17 terrorists imprisoned in Kuwait, as these groups had repeatedly demanded (see *MECS* 1988, pp. 437–38, 440–41).[12] But a month later it was announced that the government had decided to indict 33 people for plotting to overthrow the government, divulging state secrets, planning the assassination of leaders (observers thought that Foreign Minister Sabah al-Ahmad al-Jabir was the main target), belonging to outlawed groups, and spreading subversive literature.[13] Several of the accused escaped, but on 13 May, in the State Security Court, the trial of 20 defendants began in camera and of others in absentia; 22 of the accused were sentenced to prison terms of up to 15 years each, and 11 were found innocent of all charges.[14]

Among the 33 accused , 18 were Kuwaitis, nine were Iraqis, and two Iranians. The Kuwaiti Shi'is included a doctor from a state-run hospital, a former policeman, oil refinery workers, and communications ministry officials.[15] Either the seeds of opposition were deeply implanted within the local Shi'i community, or the authorities believed this to be so. The trial was a result of the authorities' suspicions, continuous surveillance of the Shi'i community, and its repression. At the same time, it was formally stated that the security authorities had arrested 47 Iranians who had attempted to enter the country via the sea,[16] which only increased the Kuwaiti leaders' nervousness.

In late summer, the Kuwaiti-Shi'i community was again stirred up against the government, as a result of the Saudi execution, on 20 September, of 16 Kuwaiti Shi'is, and the imposition of long-term prison sentences on four others for allegedly planting bombs during the pilgrimage to Mecca in July. The accused reportedly confessed that they were contacted in June and subsequently trained in the use of explosives by members of the Iranian Embassy in Kuwait, but were apprehended in Mecca before they could carry out their plan. The Kuwaiti Government was caught on the horns of a dilemma: it had to consider Kuwait's relations with both Iran and Saudi Arabia (see below), and to balance its anxiety over Iranian-backed Shi'i insurgency with its policy of not executing Shi'i terrorists. The government withheld its response for a while, but finally expressed its support for the Saudi handling of the matter;[17] it even arrested a radical Shi'i cleric, Salih Jawhur, possibly to preempt outspoken attacks on Kuwait and Saudi Arabia.

The public beheadings, rumors of torture inflicted by the Saudis on their Shi'i prisoners, and the Kuwaiti support for the Saudi action, inflamed the Kuwaiti Shi'is. They were described as "seething," their feelings "high and tense,"[18] but since they did not embark on any active antigovernment action, the authorities had no reason to adopt a more aggressive policy toward them. However, mutual suspicion and hostility increased.

Kuwaitis and Foreign Workers

The government's policy to replace as many foreign workers as possible with native Kuwaitis was given top priority. Foreigners had no valid reason to remain in Kuwait and would have to leave. The assistant under secretary for administrative development in the Civil Service Commission, Nasir al-Sani', noted in November that of 144,286 employees in ministries and government agencies, 64,203 were Kuwaitis. Their numbers in government offices were rising as a result of a developing educational system, which in 1988 produced 18,365 university graduates (11,212 from Kuwait University), the balance having studied abroad on scholarships.[19]

Under the terms of a new labor law for foreign workers initiated by the Ministry of Social Affairs and Labor and enacted on 22 March, private employers could import, or hire foreign employees already in Kuwait, only for a three-year period. Employees could not be moved from one employer to another during this period, or later, without ministry permission. If permission was not granted, the employee had to return to his country of origin. Private employers would not be able to recruit workers from abroad for positions which could be filled by Kuwaitis or citizens of Gulf states. The law strictly banned foreign employees from working for anyone other than their sponsor. Only workers who had resided in Kuwait for 10 consecutive years were exempted from the law.[20]

The policy stimulated much discussion in government circles and in public about the feasibility of removing foreign workers and the practicality of such a policy. Social Affairs and Labor Minister Nasir Muhammad al-Ahmad, addressing the Arab Labor Conference in Rabat in March, conceded that Kuwait had misgivings about inflicting hardships on foreign nationals and withholding visas from them, particularly Arabs, since Kuwait was a "state for all the Arabs."[21] Planning Minister 'Abd al-Rahman al-'Awdhi admitted that Kuwait's need for a large number of foreign workers would continue for the next 25 years, when their number would drop to 50% of all public employees.[22] Nevertheless, the government was determined to regulate the import and employment of foreign workers, and to encourage their replacement by Kuwaitis, in order to restore the demographic balance.

Kuwaiti businessmen, who employed foreigners, were skeptical about the government's policy in general and notably the above law. They complained that it would force them to dismiss workers and replace them by higher-paid Kuwaitis, or licensed foreign workers, to fill part-time jobs hitherto held by those without permits. The employers stressed that Kuwait's economy would suffer and social mobility slow down.[23]

The Parliamentary Movement: Challenge and Response

The government did not respond favorably to the petitions to recall the National Assembly. Information Minister Nasir Muhammad Al Sabah even hinted that the petitions might be "contrary to the law."[24] Moreover, during the ensuing weeks, the government did not lift the press censorship (see *MECS* 1988, pp. 436–37) which even prompted the Arab Human Rights Organization to call on Kuwait to change its policy.[25] The advocates of the assembly's recall, notably former assembly members, sought support mainly from different social groupings at informal gatherings, mostly in private houses (*diwaniyya*), as was customary in Kuwait.

Toward the end of 1989, *diwaniyya* gatherings focusing on these issues became more frequent and attracted growing numbers of participants; several thousand people held meetings in mosques in mid-December. Another petition with 20,000 signatories, calling for the assembly's recall, was submitted to the ruler.[26] In order to avoid censorship, journalists alluded to the fate of the deposed Romanian leader, Nikolae Ceauşescu, as a very discreet warning to oppressive rulers,[27] thus indicating that the Kuwaitis were inspired by the East European liberation movements. The government, however, did not give in. From its point of view, a new national assembly, based on the practice of its predecessor, could become a center of opposition activities, an intolerable situation for Kuwait. Addressing a news conference in Cairo, Prime Minister and Crown Prince Sa'd 'Abdallah Al Sabah did not rule out a measure of democratization though he excluded the restoration of the 1986 National Assembly. Although during 1989 the ruler did not reply to the petitioners officially, his policy echoed the crown prince's ideas. Hence, in early December, the police, using stun grenades, dispersed the *diwaniyya* of the assembly's former deputy chairman, Ahmad al-Shayran, and detained him and former assembly chairman, Ahmad Sa'dun, but both were released after several hours. The government also activated some of its leading supporters in the 1986 assembly to dampen the restoration movement, by pointing out dangers inherent in the 1986 assembly. Sa'dun, however, remained adamant: "The parliament is coming...it cannot be touched or amended,"[28] thereby setting the tone for the struggle for the assembly in 1990.

Economic Development

Kuwait's economic plan had two aims: to recover from recession by establishing profitable areas of commerce and business, and to encourage social integration by meeting the economic needs of different groups in society. Kuwait's rulers decided to achieve these aims by avoiding fundamental changes in Kuwait's economy (by developing for instance, indigenous, basic industries). Instead, they rather favored the policy of recovering oil and business profits, which had been Kuwait's main sources of revenue before the recession and which showed signs of improvement in 1988[29] (see above). The leaders' attitude also indicated their wish to promote rapid, and evident, economic growth, both to alleviate mounting social unrest and to improve Kuwait's image in the international business community, as an attractive financial center.[30]

Business development was a main focus. The Finance Minister Jasim al-Khurafi decided in December 1988 to raise the interest rates on investments made in Kuwaiti dinars in order to attract investors in Kuwaiti businesses and increase the Central Bank's currency holdings.[31] In December 1989, 1,350 of the main debtors of the Suq al-Manakh collapse (c. 54% of all debtors) who had hitherto been unable to engage in new investments and whose debts had been covered by a collateral, were allowed to write off up to KD250,000 of their debt to enable them to resume activities and enter new business enterprises.[32] In July, expatriates were permitted to invest in Kuwait through local representatives acting on their behalf, and non-Kuwaiti shopowners and craftsmen were permitted to conduct business without a Kuwaiti partner.[33] Consequently, non-oil revenues for 1989 were estimated at KD228.5m., up by KD176.5m. over the previous year.[34]

The relative improvement in oil prices enabled Oil Minister 'Ali Khalifa Al Sabah to reject the quota of 1,037 b/d allocated to Kuwait at the Opec meeting in June; he insisted that it was essential economically that Kuwait produce not less less than 1.35m. b/d. Observers believed, however, that Kuwait's production in fact exceeded 1.5m. b/d[35] (see also chapter on oil developments).

Moreover, Kuwait actively engaged in the refining and shipping of oil.[36] Khurafi announced in June that oil revenues were estimated at KD1,942bn. (c. $3.4bn.); during the first five months of 1989, the government's oil revenues increased by 56% in comparison with the previous year.[37]

Kuwait considered this upswing as a triple achievement. First, it indicated the end of recession and the economic slowdown. Although the budgets of "spending ministries," such as Public Works, Energy, and Water were cut by several percent, Prime Minister Sa'd 'Abdallah stressed that economic growth was compatible with world trends — with a new wave of "prosperity and growth," while "stagnation has now receded."[38] Second, it reflected the fact that the government had larger currency reserves (i.e., 4% greater at the end of the first quarter of the year),[39] but that the flourishing of a "financial sector," namely, the compensation of the private financial elite was also expected.[40] As in other Gulf states, the private sector was expected to invest in economic enterprises and, in return, enjoy an improved social status. Third, in an attempt to pacify the lower social strata, notably the Shi'is, Kuwaiti spokesmen made it clear that subsidies for education and food, as well as basic welfare measures, would not be cut, and that any budget would be planned in accordance with "the people's needs."[41]

The government also decided to exploit the financial upturn to plan several new major construction projects. They included the development, within a decade, of Kuwait's main ports, al-Shuyukh and Shu'ayba, and of the international port at the city of Kuwait and Kuwait's airport.[42] Another project was the establishment by 2020 of a new city, al-Sabiyya, on Bubiyan Island, about 45 km. south of the Iraqi border, for 250,000 inhabitants, in order to solve the housing problems expected to develop by then.[43]

ROYAL FAMILY DIVISIONS

By the end of 1989, Kuwait had not dampened social and political unrest. The Shi'is were restive, and although the native Kuwaitis were better off economically, the question of the recall of the National Assembly continued to agitate them. Outwardly, the country's leaders were of one mind and the government followed a clear-cut policy, but senior members of the royal family were reported to be in disagreement. The ruler reportedly favored using "a strong hand" to crack down on dissidents. Crown Prince Sa'd 'Abdallah was said to advocate a more conciliatory approach toward Shi'is and other social groups, as well as toward Iraq over border questions (see below), contrary to the view of Foreign Minister Sabah al-Ahmad. Observers speculated whether these disagreements might diminish Sa'd 'Abdallah's prospects of succeeding to the throne,[44] but no crisis over this issue was reported in 1989.

FOREIGN AFFAIRS

RELATIONS WITH GULF ZONE STATES

The Gulf region contained a prospective security threat for Kuwait: the main dangers to its existence originated there and had to be kept under constant observation and control, even in the aftermath of the Iran-Iraq War. Minister of Defense Nawwaf Al Sabah explained, in February 1989, that as long as the two protagonists did not sign a peace treaty the situation "prompts us to prepare for any emergency."[45] However, Kuwait's leaders believed that Iran and Iraq were war weary and wanted a relaxation of tension. They were, therefore, less concerned with the prospects of a renewal of full-scale warfare between the two hostile neighbors, which might draw Kuwait into the line of fire; Minister for Cabinet Affairs Rashid 'Abd al-'Aziz stressed that the interests of both parties lay in maintaining the cease-fire, while Crown Prince Sa'd 'Abdallah regarded "the continuation of the dialogue and the prominent role to be played by the big powers" as a basis for a favorable conclusion to the Iran-Iraq dispute.[46] Kuwaiti leaders were more concerned with routine and small-scale war efforts by both sides, which were a substitute for conventional warfare: terrorism and sabotage, fortification of military positions in Kuwait's immediate vicinity, and plans to use Kuwaiti territories as strategic outlets or deployment grounds in future battlefields, which would jeopardize Kuwait's territorial integrity.

As a small state, Kuwait's main strategy in tackling these problems was through bilateral negotiations, focusing on political and economic cooperation with its neighbors, and on political appeasement to avoid potential tension.

Relations with Iraq

Iraqi policy created problems for Kuwait's territorial integrity: Iraq did not recognize Kuwait's borders and had voiced its ambition to annex Kuwaiti territory. In 1961, Iraqi forces had threatened to invade Kuwait and retreated only after Arab League and British intervention. Kuwait feared that increased Iraqi confidence after the Gulf War might encourage its ambitious ruler, Saddam Husayn, to try to reannex Kuwaiti territories. More specifically, Iraq sought to control — by lease or through territorial exchange — the Kuwaiti islands of Bubiyan and Varba, at Iraq's entrance to the Gulf from the Shatt al-'Arab River, a location Baghdad considered vital for its strategic interests in the Gulf. Moreover, without a peace treaty with Iran, Iraq was unwilling to drop its demands for these islands, which if controlled by Iraq could deny Iran access to the northern parts of the Gulf. But Kuwait was unwilling to cede parts of its territory and was determined to avoid potential Iranian retaliation triggered by territorial concessions to Iraq.[47]

This territorial disagreement influenced Kuwaiti-Iraqi relations during 1989. Crown Prince Sa'd 'Abdallah's visit to Baghdad in early February was prompted by Baghdad's anger over the Kuwaiti decision to establish the city of Sabiyya on Bubiyan Island (and link it by a causeway to the Kuwaiti mainland) because it indicated Kuwait's determination to assert its sovereignty there. Kuwait, for its part, expected Iraq to reciprocate Kuwait's assistance to Iraq during the war, by dropping its territorial demands.[48] Sa'd 'Abdallah employed a moderate approach toward Iraq, but his negotiations with the Iraqi authorities produced no results. A visit by Defense Minister Nawwaf to Iraq in early May was equally fruitless.[49] Sa'd 'Abdallah's failure prompted the Kuwaitis to employ two other tactics to ease their relations with Iraq and avoid a crisis; they reemphasized that, despite territorial differences, they identified strategically with Iraq, that in time of need Kuwait would again collaborate with Iraq. In the words of Nawwaf, "the security and the fate of both countries are one and the same."[50] Kuwait and Iraq also engaged in technical cooperation projects: the visit by the Kuwaiti ruler to Iraq in September did not focus on territorial disagreements, but on a project to develop a water installation at Iraq's al-Gharaf River, 16% of which would be financed by Kuwait. Kuwait would also receive 500m. gallons of water per day from al-Haritha in Iraq. The planning of these projects started in October.[51] Jabir's visit and the inauguration of the new projects created a more relaxed atmosphere in Kuwait-Iraq relations toward the end of 1989.

Relations with Iran

Kuwait and Iran were definitely interested in improving their mutual relations. Kuwaiti leaders sought to neutralize Tehran's subversive designs on Kuwait by posing as friendly and cooperative. After Saudi Arabia severed diplomatic ties with Iran (see chapter on Saudi Arabia), Kuwait also hoped to develop a channel of communication with Tehran on behalf of the Gulf states. Iran, in turn, viewed improved relations with Kuwait as a springboard to regional cooperation, and to changing its image in other Arab states. These mutual interests encouraged both states to steadily develop what Western observers called "a modest *détente*," despite ensuing difficulties.

In March, Kuwait took a first step toward cooperation with Iran by responding to Iran's call to ban Salman Rushdie's *The Satanic Verses* and to lobby at the Islamic Conference against its distribution.[52] However, Iranian Revolutionary Guards blocked this first step by hijacking (probably without official backing) two Kuwaiti vessels, in March and May. In the first incident, a private yacht was highjacked but was released after a few hours. In the second incident, on 9 May, a coast-guard ship and its six-man crew were highjacked while on duty. The ship and crew were released after Minister of State for Foreign Affairs Sa'ud al-'Usaymi attended Khomeyni's funeral in Tehran in early June and after Jabir appealed directly to Iranian leaders on 19 June. Kuwait was thus prepared to make conciliatory moves toward Iran, and Tehran, which had been seeking ways to end the incident, was ready to respond.

The resolution of this incident and the interest of both sides in turning over a new leaf in their relations in the post-Khomeyni era, helped relax their strained relations. Kuwaiti Minister of Cabinet Affairs Rashid 'Abd al-'Aziz explained that "Kuwait has no dispute with Iran" and given Iran's interest in peace with Iraq, Kuwait regarded the situation as ripe for improving relations with Tehran.[53] However, these good intentions were again somewhat frustrated when Kuwait tried the Shi'i insurgents (see above) who, it seemed, were being supported by Iran. In September, the Iranian media criticized Kuwait for acquiescing in Saudi Arabia's execution of the Kuwaiti Shi'is and for detaining a leading Shi'i cleric (see above).[54] However, this time both parties were predisposed to allow their state interests to prevail; Kuwait understood that good relations with Iran could help prevent Shi'i insurgency in its territory and Tehran did not want its partisan insurgency operations to jeopardize its rehabilitation in the Arab world. The two sides decided to upgrade their diplomatic ties and on 29 September, a new Iranian ambassador arrived in Kuwait.[55]

Attitude Toward the Gulf Cooperation Council and Saudi Arabia

During the postwar period, Kuwait's interest diminished in the Gulf Cooperation Council (GCC) as an organization with military capabilities, able to provide for Kuwait's security (see *MECS* 1988, pp. 438–40). Kuwait still objected to signing a security treaty with other GCC states, preferring to rely mainly on diplomatic initiatives to fend off any serious danger and, if necessary, on its own counterinsurgency measures to safeguard its security. This attitude reflected Kuwait's new priorities: to focus on its immediate problems rather than on strategic regional cooperation. Indeed, Kuwaiti leaders regarded the GCC as a forum for coordinating the views of Gulf states in their foreign relations, and their economic policies, employment of foreigners, and oil production. Kuwaiti spokesmen also stressed the need to strengthen personal ties among GCC citizens, especially the youth.[56]

Kuwait's relations with Saudi Arabia exemplified Kuwait's attitude toward the GCC states in general: there was basic cooperation and mutual trust interrupted by minor instances of tension. Prior to Opec's meeting in June, there was a disagreement over quotas, generated by Kuwait's determination to demand a rise in its quota and thereby a higher Opec production ceiling, to which the Saudis objected. Refusing to abide by Opec's decision, Kuwait unilaterally raised its quota (see above),[57] which elicited no Saudi response. More tension was reported in late May at the Casablanca summit, which decided to appoint a three-member committee to mediate the crisis in Lebanon instead of a Kuwaiti-led six-member committee (see below). Jabir viewed this decision as a blow to Kuwait's diplomacy and raised it with the Saudis at a GCC meeting.[58]

The detention and execution of the Kuwaiti Shi'is in Saudi Arabia strained relations further. Kuwait apparently feared retaliation by Iran and its own Shi'is. Aware of Kuwait's fears and unwilling to spoil its relations with Kuwait, Riyadh reported continuously to GCC states about the case and sought Kuwaiti approval.[59] King Fahd's statement on 25 September after the execution, that Saudi-Kuwaiti relations "are deep-rooted...stronger than any plots or schemes"[60] was a way of putting pressure on the Kuwaiti leaders to reciprocate to the Saudi leaders' loyalty to Kuwait. After several days of official silence, Kuwaiti Ambassador to Riyadh 'Abd al-Rahman al-Bakr told the press that "Kuwait believes in the efficiency of the Saudi judiciary and believes in the execution of the sentences as if they were pronounced by Kuwait."[61] Several days later, a Kuwaiti spokesman noted that the three-member committee's initiatives about Lebanon (leading to the convention of the Lebanese Parliament in Ta'if) was "a constructive step" which would produce positive results[62] (see chapters on Saudi Arabia and inter-Arab relations), thereby supporting Saudi Arabia's Lebanese policy. Kuwait obviously decided to avoid a crisis in its relations with Saudi Arabia and adopted its policies to those of Riyadh.

KUWAITI ATTITUDES TOWARD OTHER ARAB STATES

Kuwait's policies toward the broader Arab world was determined by two main factors. Kuwait wished to maintain good relations with states, notably Egypt and Syria, that indirectly affected Kuwait's security by their defining the Arab Middle East's ideological climate and by their military might, which could tip the balance of power in the Gulf. Kuwait's policy, therefore, was to foster Arab solidarity, enabling it to cooperate with most of the Arab states under the common denominator of

Arabism. For Kuwait, the distant Arab states were its peripheral security belt, which could be utilized in different ways (see also *MECS* 1988, pp. 441–42).

Kuwait developed several tactics to foster Arab solidarity and cooperation. It did not object to Arab regional cooperation, even when it could lead to competition with another regional body, as was the case with the Arab Cooperation Council, comprising Egypt, Iraq, Jordan, and the Yemeni Arab Republic, which tacitly competed over economic development with Kuwait's organization, the GCC (see chapter on inter-Arab relations). In the words of Sa'd 'Abdallah, regional unions will "strengthen the Arab League, make it more effective, and enhance coordination and cooperation within it."[63] Kuwait underlined these words by avoiding clashes with any Arab state belonging to a different regional organization. Kuwait also mediated inter-Arab disputes, a role which encouraged Arab solidarity and rendered Kuwait significant to most Arab states, thereby strengthening its own security. Sa'd 'Abdallah explained further: "Kuwait considers such good offices a duty...we believe in cooperation, understanding, and negotiation as the means of resolving problems...[Kuwait] is happy to shoulder them individually or in cooperation with brothers and friends to end conflicts." He indicated that mediation was a continuous role, which has suited "the nature of Kuwait's people" over the years.[64]

Kuwait's Bilateral Relations with Arab Parties

After Egypt (see *MECS* 1987, pp. 374–75) reentered the Arab fold, Kuwait found in it a power which could help build up its own security by supplying arms and by acting as a counterpoise to Kuwait's immediate powerful neighbors. As Egypt was eager to develop its industry, Kuwait also found in Egypt a country ripe for investment and development. Although there was no formal agreement, cooperation flourished in these fields. In May, Kuwait received from Egypt the first 400 *Fahd* armored personnel carriers which it had ordered and in July 11 Kuwaiti technical officers graduated from an Egyptian officers' course. Kuwait's ambassador in Egypt stressed that there were over 400 technicians and officers-in-training in Egypt.[65] Both he and Kuwaiti Minister of Information Jabir Mubarak Al Sabah stressed that Egyptian military equipment was as good as any Western hardware and that political coordination between Egypt and Kuwait resulted in a common approach to many Arab and international issues.[66]

According to Egyptian Minister of Finance Yusri Mustafa the volume of Kuwaiti investments in Egypt reached £E496.445m. by June 1989, and "the last few months," he said, "have witnessed an increase of 286% in these investments." An additional Kuwaiti investment of c. £E500m. in 110 Egyptian projects was planned.[67] Kuwaiti investments in spheres such as military equipment, paper, tourism, petrochemical plants, and others, were granted favorable terms, which turned Egypt into a tempting area for Kuwaiti investors. Agreements signed in May and August protected investors from nationalization and expropriation, facilitated the flow of foreign capital into both countries, and eased trade and customs regulations.[68] More such cooperation was anticipated in 1990. Visits by Egyptian President Husni Mubarak to Kuwait in January and by Jabir to Cairo in August crowned Kuwaiti-Egyptian relations in 1989.

On 12 January, an Arab League conference of Arab foreign ministers appointed Kuwaiti Foreign Minister Sabah al-Ahmad to head a six-member committee, which was to achieve a "national accord" among Lebanese fighting factions. Kuwait's efforts were meant to win its prestige in the Arab world and to improve its bilateral relations with the Arab and Muslim parties involved in the Lebanese dispute, notably Syria, Iraq, and Iran (see chapters on Lebanon and inter-Arab relations). Sabah al-Ahmad tried to develop two main avenues of negotiations: to bring together representatives of the Lebanese factions to negotiate a regional, acceptable settlement (Sabah even invited them to Kuwait in March) and to obtain the support of Arab states, notably Syria, for these initiatives.[69] However, in May it became evident that Kuwaiti efforts had reached a dead end. Sabah later explained that the Lebanese factions had breached the cease-fire agreement Kuwait had achieved in April. Consequently, the fighting increased to Kuwait's evident dismay and Arab support for Kuwait's initiative was reported to be waning.[70] The six-member committee lost control of the situation which was deteriorating as a result of the dispute between Syria and Michel 'Awn's Maronite faction. To salvage their mission, Kuwaiti leaders proposed broadening the military authority of the six-member committee by establishing "Arab Observation Forces" composed of units from all Arab states to supervise the cease-fire, but this proposal was not accepted. Sabah al-Ahmad referred the issue back to the Arab League, which led to the formation of the three-member committee at the Casablanca summit.[71] The Kuwaiti press and leaders lamented that Lebanon had become "a prime example of the Arab situation,"[72] namely, inter-Arab fragmentation. Kuwait had to accept the formation of the three-member committee, led by Saudi Arabia, and eventually it officially supported the initial breakthrough achieved by the new committee, as was evident in the Ta'if meeting (see chapter on inter-Arab relations).

During Kuwait's involvement in Lebanon, it was in close contact with Syria. In early April, Jabir was reported to have asked Syrian President Hafiz al-Asad to support the work of the six-member committee in Lebanon in return for increased Kuwaiti financial support, which had diminished (see *MECS* 1988, p. 443). However, Kuwait was dissatisfied with Syria's partisan and aggressive role in Lebanon. A heated exchange of words was reported between Sabah and Syrian Foreign Minister Faruq al-Shar' at an Arab League council meeting in April.[73] The Kuwaiti press occasionally praised 'Awn as "a real representative of Lebanese aspirations,"[74] implying that the Syria-backed factions were less authentic representatives. Observers noted a strain in relations between Kuwait and Syria following the dissolution of the Kuwaiti-led six-member committee.[75]

Kuwait made relatively few comments on the evolution of the Israeli-Palestinian peace process, as its foreign policy was primarily focused on the Gulf region. Kuwait reiterated the need for direct negotiations between the parties under Egyptian and US auspices (see below), hopefully leading to the establishment of an independent Palestinian state.[76] In practice, Kuwait identified with the Palestinian struggle. It hosted PLO leader Yasir 'Arafat during several visits for discussions. Kuwait permitted the PLO (including a representative of the leftist Democratic Liberation Front) to strengthen its organizational hold on local Palestinians and to provide them with special PLO-issued identity cards.[77] Kuwait continued its support of the Intifada, by giving both immediate emergency funds for food and medicine and continuing its financial assistance, in accordance with the decisions of the Algiers summit of 1988. In June 1989, it was reported that Kuwait had already contributed $22m. and would continue its assistance.[78] The Kuwaiti media published several anti-Semitic articles on Israel, and justified every violent attack on Israeli Jews.[79]

Kuwait also tried to assist the People's Democratic Republic of Yemen (PDRY) in its reforms, particularly by mediating, though unsuccessfully, between the PDRY and the US for the reestablishment of diplomatic relations (see chapter on the PDRY).

RELATIONS WITH THE UNITED STATES AND WEST EUROPEAN STATES
The termination of the Gulf War led Kuwait to adopt a new policy of distancing itself from US military and strategic assistance. This change was partly motivated by the desire to maintain relations with all regional powers in the Gulf, and avoid their suspicion (notably by Iran and Iraq) of Kuwait's dependence on the US for its defense. Kuwait also wanted to diversify its foreign policy and arms purchases in a way that would give it access to the Soviet Union and many other Arab and European states. One major step in this direction was taken in January 1989, when Kuwait reregistered under its own flag, six of the 11 tankers which had been sailing under the US flag since July 1987.[80] Moreover, Kuwait did not conclude any security agreements with Washington during 1989.

Kuwait, however, was interested in reducing the US defensive military presence in the Gulf, not eliminating it entirely. It definitely appreciated the deterrent value of the American presence on its potential foes; it therefore left registered under the US flag, the remaining five Kuwaiti tankers which were still accompanied by US military escort. On 1 November, the commander in chief of the US Central Forces Command paid a visit and discussed strategic issues with his Kuwaiti counterparts.[81]

Kuwaiti leaders were optimistic that the Bush Administration would become more involved in ME affairs and promote regional tranquillity. They hoped that the personal bond Bush had established as vice president with Sa'd 'Abdallah and his experience in international affairs would make him supportive of Arab interests and that he would tend to resolve ME disputes.[82] Kuwaiti leaders, therefore, expected the US to intervene in regional politics as a "super mediator" to help resolve the Palestinian-Israeli dispute, on the basis of the Egyptian Ten-Point Program. Kuwait supported a step-by-step approach leading to the convening of an international conference.[83] Sabah al-Ahmad also justified Washington's interest in releasing the hostages in Lebanon.[84]

The Kuwaiti media were less sanguine. They criticized Washington's support of Israel during the Palestinian uprising, which they said kept Israel from withdrawing from the occupied territories.[85] American criticism of Libya, of the Fath conference's aggressive decisions in August (see chapters on Libya and the PLO), and Secretary of State James Baker's pressure on the Soviet authorities to discourage Syrian aggression against Israel (see chapter on Syria) were depicted by the Kuwaiti media as offenses against "the Arab people" while letting the real villain, Israel, escape unscathed.[86] Toward the end of 1989, with the stalemate in Palestinian-Israeli relations still unsolved, this type of criticism was also voiced by Kuwait's politicians. Ambassador to Washington Sa'ud Nasir Al Sabah said in October that Washington's (and Israel's) proposal to hold elections in the territories was prompted only by the uprising and focused on pressuring the PLO to make concessions; the US had no intention of putting similar pressure on Israel. He concluded that the Administration, and particularly Congress, jeopardized American relations with the Arab world.[87]

Kuwait enjoyed improved ties with Great Britain. Foreign Secretary Sir Geoffrey Howe visited Kuwait in January and explained that Kuwait would be permitted to reduce its stake in British Petroleum from 21.6% to 9.9% (as required by British law) in three years, to avoid immediate damages (see *MECS* 1988, p. 445).[88] In May, Secretary for Trade and Industry Lord Young came to Kuwait to discuss how to increase trade between the two states.[89] Kuwait was indeed willing to allow the dust of the BP affair to settle quickly, and in February, Nawwaf signed a contract with a representative of a British helicopter manufacturing company to purchase (an unspecified number of) helicopters and other accessories.[90]

Kuwait's relations with France were particularly cordial in 1989. During a visit by Interior Minister Pierre Joxe in early September, an agreement to "exchange expertise" in fighting terrorism and drug trafficking was signed, drawing on France's experience in these fields.[91] On 22 September, Jabir visited France in what was his first visit to Europe. In discussions with President François Mitterrand, Jabir reached an understanding to coordinate policy concerning Lebanon and the Arab-Israeli dispute.[92] There were rumors later that Kuwait was seeking to sign a major arms deal with France (including the purchase of the latest *Mirage* aircraft), but these were denied by Kuwaiti spokesmen.[93]

RELATIONS WITH THE SOVIET UNION
Kuwait's interest in improving relations with the Soviet Union was anchored in its wish to balance and diversify its foreign policy and arms purchases in order to avoid dependence on one source of arms and one defending power. Kuwaiti leaders appreciated Moscow's influence in the region, for instance, its "persistent and positive efforts to find a formula to end the Iran-Iraq War"[94] (see also *MECS* 1988, pp. 444–45). The Soviet new look as a peaceful superpower that no longer pursued revolutionary goals also appealed to Kuwait. In March, *al-Ra'y al-'Amm* stressed that "the loss of international balance is not in our interest...there is no need [for the Arabs] to refrain from close relations with the socialist bloc and the Soviet Union."[95] However, the government was interested in improving relations with Moscow solely as a counterbalance to Kuwait's relations with the US, and not as a new strategic axis. It therefore did not devise a clear policy for improving relations with the Soviet Union, which was left to limited and sporadic initiatives. Thus, Kuwaiti Chief of Staff 'Abd al-Rahman al-Sani' visited Moscow in January and Soviet Deputy Defense Minister Konstantin Kochetov visited Kuwait in July.[96] Rumors then spread that Kuwait intended to conclude a major arms deal with the Soviet Union, which the Ministry of Defense strongly denied.[97] In November, Soviet Minister for production of Oil and Gas Vladimir Chirskov visited Kuwait to discuss oil matters with his counterpart, 'Ali al-Khalifa, a visit which did not lead to any new agreements.[98] Hence, Kuwaiti relations with the Soviet Union were friendly and cooperative in 1989, but without any economic or strategic breakthroughs.

NOTES

For the place and frequency of publications cited here, and for the full name of the publication, news agency, radio station, or monitoring service where an abbreviation is used, please see "List of Sources." Only in the case of more than one publication bearing the same name is the place of publication noted. However, all references to *al-Siyasa* and *al-Anba* in this chapter are to the Kuwaiti publications bearing that name.

1. *FT,* 13 March 1990.
2. Ibid., *ME,* No. 185, March 1990.
3. See J.E. Peterson, *The Arab Gulf States, Steps Toward Political Participation,* The Washington Papers, No. 131 (New York: Praeger, 1988), pp. 27–61.
4. AFP, 28 February 1989.
5. *Al-Ra'y al-'Amm,* 15 August; Nasra M. Shah and Sulayman S. al-Qudsi, "The Changing Characteristics of Migrant Workers in Kuwait," *IJMES,* Vol. 21, No. 1 (February 1989), pp. 31–55.
6. J. Kostiner, "War, Terror, Revolution: The Iran-Iraq Conflict," in B. Rubin (ed.), *The Politics of Terrorism: Terror as a State and a Revolutionary Strategy* (Washington, D.C., Foreign Policy Institute, The Johns Hopkins University, 1989), pp. 95–128; *al-Nashra,* Athens, 20 March; *MM,* 29 May 1989.
7. *AT,* 2 March; *CR:* Kuwait, No. 2, 1989.
8. *ME,* No. 185, March 1990.
9. *AT,* 2 March 1989.
10. Ibid., 8 January; KUNA, 29 March — DR, 30 March 1989.
11. *AT,* 23 May; *al-Watan,* 11 June 1989.
12. USIS, 13 February 1989.
13. KUNA, 16 March — DR, 16 March; *al-Siyasa,* 16 March; *al-Hayat,* 6 May 1989.
14. *IHT,* 26 June; *al-Ra'y al-Akhir,* 10 July 1989.
15. *NYT,* 19 March; *MM,* 29 May 1989.
16. *Al-Anba,* 21 May; *al-Qabas,* 23 May 1989.
17. R. Riyadh, 27 September — DR, 28 September 1989.
18. *FT,* 21 September; *NYT,* 22 September 1989.
19. *AT,* 13 November 1989.
20. KUNA, 16 January — DR, 18 January; *AT,* 25 January, 22 March 1989.
21. *AT,* 8 March 1989.
22. Al-'Awdhi's interview, *al-Anba,* 14 May 1989.
23. *AT,* 22 March 1989.
24. AFP, 28 February 1989.
25. *Al-Wafd,* 24 April 1989.
26. *FT,* 28 November, 30 December 1989; *al-Ahali,* 3 January 1990.
27. *AT,* 26 December 1989.
28. Reuters, 11 December 1989; *al-Ahali,* 3 January 1990.
29. *ME,* No. 185, March 1990.
30. Cf. *IHT,* 3 May 1989.
31. *AT,* 4 July 1989; *CR:* Kuwait, No. 1, 1989.
32. *FT,* 13 March 1990.
33. *AT,* 22 January, 24 July 1989.
34. KUNA, 3 July — DR, 6 July 1989.
35. *CR:* Kuwait, No. 2, No. 4; *al-Ra'y al-'Amm,* 28 September 1989.
36. *Memo,* 18 August 1989.
37. KUNA, 3 July — DR, 5 July; *CR:* Kuwait, No. 4, 1989.
38. *CR:* Kuwait, No. 3, 1989; Sa'd 'Abdallah's interview, *AT,* 12 December 1989.
39. *AT,* 29 July 1989.
40. *CR:* Kuwait, No. 2, 1989.
41. Cf. al-Khurafi's interview, *al-Ra'y al-'Amm,* 30 July 1989.
42. *Al-Anba,* 4 February 1989.
43. *Al-Qabas,* 25 March 1989.

44. *FR*, 23 February; *MM*, 29 May 1989.
45. Nawwaf's interview, *'Ukaz*, 17 February 1989.
46. Sa'd 'Abdallah's interview, *al-Watan al-'Arabi*, 27 January; Rashid's interview, *al-Sharq al-Awsat*, 23 July 1989.
47. *FR*, 23 February; *al-'Alam*, London, 23 September 1989.
48. *Al-Anba*, 6 February; *CR:* Kuwait, No. 1, 1989.
49. R. Baghdad, 7 May — DR, 8 May 1989.
50. Ibid.
51. *Al-Siyasa*, 13, 24 September 1989.
52. KUNA, 19 February, 14 March — DR, 24 February, 15 March; *CR:* Kuwait, No. 3, 1989.
53. KUNA, 17 June — DR, 19 June; Rashid's interview, *al-Sharq al-Awsat*, 23 July 1989.
54. *CR:* Kuwait, No. 4; *Kayhan*, 25 September — DR, 20 October 1989.
55. KUNA, 29 September — DR, 29 September 1989.
56. Sa'd 'Abdallah's interview, *al-Siyasa*, 14 May 1989.
57. AFP, 8 June; R. Kuwait, 6 June — DR, 8 June; *Ha'aretz*, 6 June 1989.
58. *Al-Muharrir*, 17 June 1989.
59. *Al-Bayadir al-Siyasi*, 16 September 1989.
60. KUNA, 25 September — DR, 26 September 1989.
61. R. Riyadh, 27 September — DR, 28 September 1989.
62. KUNA, 1 October — DR, 3 October 1989.
63. Sa'd 'Abdallah's interview, *al-Hawadith*, 21 April 1989.
64. Ibid.
65. *AT*, 2 May; MENA, 9 July; *al-Ahali*, 16 August 1989.
66. Cf. *al-Anba*, 10 September 1989.
67. Mustafa's interview, *al-Ra'y al-'Amm*, 2 September 1989.
68. KUNA, 16 May, 29 August — DR, 19 May, 30 August 1989.
69. KUNA, 7 February — DR, 10 February; *al-Qabas*, 5 March 1989.
70. Cf. *al-Safir*, 20 May 1989.
71. KUNA, 24 April, 15 September — DR, 25 April, 19 September 1989.
72. *Al-Ra'y al-'Amm*, 25 May 1989.
73. *Al-Watan al-'Arabi*, 14 April 1989.
74. Cf. *AT*, 24 March, 26 April 1989.
75. *Al-Bayadir al-Siyasi*, 3 June 1989.
76. Cf. Sabah al-Ahmad's interview, *al-Usbu' al-'Arabi*, 18 September 1989.
77. *Al-Hadaf*, 29 October 1989.
78. *Al-Siyasa*, 9 June 1989.
79. Cf. *al-Qabas*, 29 March; *al-Watan*, Kuwait, 16 July 1989.
80. *Al-Anba*, 20 January 1989.
81. *Al-Ra'y al-'Amm*, 1 November 1989.
82. Sa'd 'Abdallah's interview, *al-Watan al-'Arabi*, 27 January; *al-Hawadith*, 25 April 1989.
83. Cf. Sabah al-Ahmad's interview, *al-Watan al-'Arabi*, 3 February 1989.
84. KUNA, 15 September — DR, 19 September 1989.
85. Cf. *al-Ra'y al-'Amm*, 11 May 1989.
86. Ibid.; and 1, 7 July, 14 August; KUNA, 5 January — DR, 5 January 1989.
87. KUNA, 1 October — DR, 4 October 1989.
88. KUNA, 1 January — DR, 4 January 1989.
89. *Al-Qabas*, 29 May 1989.
90. KUNA, 7 February — DR, 7 February 1989.
91. KUNA, 11 September — DR, 12 September 1989.
92. *Al-Anba*, 26 September 1989.
93. *Al-Hawadith*, 6 October; *al-Anba*, 22 October 1989.
94. Sa'd 'Abdallah's interview, *al-Qabas*, 28 February 1989.
95. *Al-Ra'y al-'Amm*, 11 March 1989.
96. *AT*, 8 January; KUNA, 18 July — DR, 19 July 1989.
97. *Al-Ittihad*, Abu Dhabi, 23 July; KUNA, 24 July — DR, 26 July 1989.
98. KUNA, 19 November — DR, 24 November 1989.

Lebanon
(Al-Jumhuriyya al-Lubnaniyya)

WILLIAM W. HARRIS

One feature dominated events in Lebanon during 1989: Gen. Michel 'Awn's challenge to the entrenched status quo of fragmentation and foreign occupation, and the political consequences. 'Awn, head of an interim military administration, who had been appointed by President Amin Jumayyil in September 1988 after the collapse of attempts to elect a successor to the latter, soon made it clear that he regarded his primary function as not to prepare presidential elections, but to force fundamental shifts territorially before elections or constitutional reform. 'Awn's approach involved consolidation of his geographical base in the East Beirut enclave, refusal to acknowledge inter-Lebanese differences in relations with West Beirut, and a military showdown to force the Syrian Army to expose itself as a principal participant in the Lebanese crisis. In March 1989, 'Awn embarked on an extraordinarily risky escapade without precedent in the 15 years of turmoil: a "war of liberation" against Syria, the overlord of West Beirut and 60% of Lebanon. His explicit aim was to create a sufficiently dangerous military emergency to impel international intervention in favor of a solution reuniting the country and pushing back the influence of the regional powers.

In his campaign 'Awn assured himself of a formidable array of opponents. First, the structure of authority within East Beirut came under great and continuous strain. Traditionalist leaders, including Christian parliamentary deputies and the Maronite patriarch, looked to a mildly reformed version of the sectarian National Pact of 1943 and compromise with Syrian strategic hegemony; 'Awn's open-ended confrontation terrified them. The politico-military complex consisting of the Lebanese Forces (LF) militia and the Phalangist (*Kata'ib*) party inevitably opposed 'Awn's aspiration for a single East Beirut power center under the "legitimate authority" — the military government in the Ba'abda presidential palace. The LF-Phalangist leadership had no sympathy for 'Awn's vision of a new united Lebanon, which they perceived as impractical and a threat to the East Beirut Christian "canton."

As regards West Beirut, the combination of notables and militia bosses assembled in Salim al-Huss's Administration, the rump civilian Cabinet of the Jumayyil period which viewed itself as the natural and only heir of "legitimate authority," rejected 'Awn's representation of the Lebanese problem as primarily stemming from the Syrian presence. Most of the non-Christian leadership ranked priorities in a different order: reforms, elections, Syrian withdrawal — the reverse of 'Awn's priorities. Syria was no more loved in West Beirut than in the Christian sector, but many saw no alternative to Syrian weight to budge Maronite supremacy. Damascus knew well how to manipulate non-Christian resentments in the service of its own hegemonic drive.

Lebanon: Geopolitical Divisions, 1989

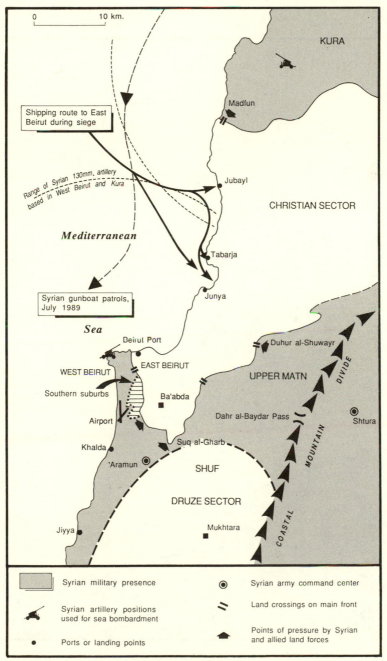

Syrian Siege of East Beirut, May–August 1989

502

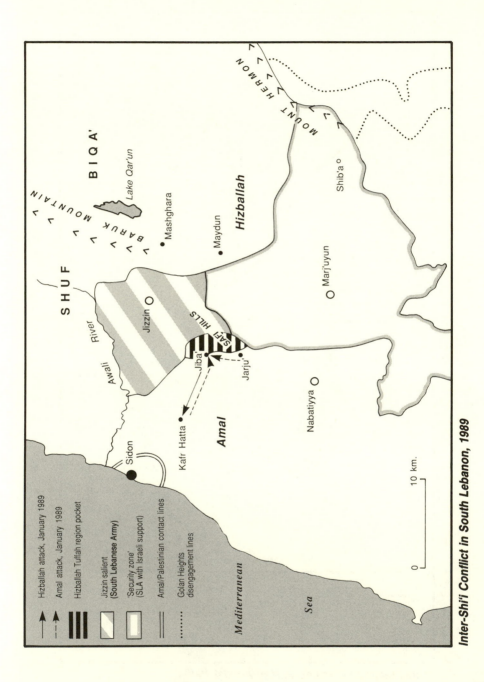

Inter-Shi'i Conflict in South Lebanon, 1989

Hizballah attack, January 1989

Amal attack, January 1989

Hizballah Tuffah region pocket

Jizzin salient
(South Lebanese Army)

'Security zone'
(SLA with Israeli support)

Amal/Palestinian contact lines

Golan Heights
disengagement lines

MOUNT HERMON

BIQA'

SHUF

BARUK MOUNTAIN

Lake Qar'un

Mashghara

Maydun

Hizballah

Shib'a

Marj'uyun

Jizzin

SAFI HILLS

Jiba

Jarju

River

Awali

Kafr Hatta

Amal

Nabatiyya

Sidon

Mediterranean

Sea

0   10 km.

On the international level, 'Awn's effort to mobilize intervention against Syria was doomed from the outset. The US, as the leading major power involved in the Middle East, demonstrated rigid hostility to any reappearance of "Lebanon" as a primary item on the international agenda. An undercurrent of vindictiveness tinged Washington's attitude toward Beirut, the scene of bitter humiliations. From the American perspective, pressure on the general Syrian alignment in Lebanon would be unproductive before substantive progress in the Arab-Israeli peace process was achieved, which would weaken Syrian strategic excuses. 'Awn certainly attracted a surge of Arab and international concern in mid-1989, but this merely determined the Americans to remove Lebanon from the "spotlight" without treating fundamentals considered intractable. The arrangement was embodied in the so-called Ta'if Accord of October 1989.

The simplicity — some would say simplemindedness — of the 'Awn adventure contrasted starkly with the enduring underlying intricacy of Lebanese politics and society. The year 1989 in Lebanon could not be understood without an appreciation of this interaction between the simplicity and the complexity. On the one hand, collision with reality frustrated and intensified 'Awn's impetus. At the same time, the trial of strength between 'Awn and Syrian President Hafiz al-Asad influenced every aspect of the Lebanese crisis. On the regional level, it was associated with an unparalleled Iraqi intrusion into Lebanese affairs. An Iraqi-Syrian contest taking precedence over Syrian-Palestinian-Israeli or Syrian-Iranian dimensions, however temporarily, was a novelty in the Lebanese war. Also, Syria had difficulties coping simultaneously with 'Awn and the continuing Amal-Hizballah competition in the Shi'i community. Hizballah and its Iranian patrons benefited from the Syrian-East Beirut confrontation, though not from its aftermath at Ta'if.

As for Beiruti politics, the 'Awn irruption reoriented relations between the power centers in both the eastern and western sectors. It pushed Christian and non-Christian traditionalists closer together, a process encouraged by Saudi Arabia and the US and consecrated at Ta'if. It thus deepened the suspicion and hostility between the traditionalist and "leftist" poles in West Beirut. The latter, vigorously sponsored by Druze boss Walid Junblat, feared any West Beirut drift toward either 'Awn or the Christian traditionalists. In East Beirut, a partial coalescence occurred, but with potentially deadly consequences — the LF militia, seeking spoils and security, found increased common ground with the traditionalists and openly parted company with 'Awn concerning the Ta'if Accord. The divergence between 'Awn and the LF became particularly dangerous in December, with the election of a president, Ilyas al-Hirawi, satisfactory to both the militia and the Syrians.

The dramatic developments in Beirut overshadowed events in South Lebanon, a somewhat detached arena of Shi'i, Palestinian, and Israeli interactions where continuation of the normal perennial disturbances brought only limited shifts in established local realities. This mainly applied to the sustained fundamentalist pressure on the secularist Amal movement, with two bouts of hostilities for control of the Tuffah area above Sidon at the beginning and end of the year. Such competition encouraged external exploitation, particularly manifested in the heightened connections of both sides with Palestinian factions in Sidon. Shi'i diversion and 'Arafat's involvement with the US, added to the commanding Israeli geostrategic position (see *MECS* 1988, chapter on Lebanon), meant that the Israeli-dominated "security zone" faced nothing beyond nuisance incursions. There was the usual rhythm of raids by Hizballah and radical Palestinian organizations, answered by Israeli air strikes and Israeli-South Lebanese Army (SLA) ground operations, but on a reduced level compared with 1988.

Lebanon's economic and social infrastructure, already in advanced decay, suffered further major damage as a result of the artillery exchanges on the main fronts between March and September. Parts of West Beirut, suburban areas of East Beirut near Ba'abda, Junya port, Shtura, and mountain villages in the Shuf and Matn were hit hard, with deliberate targeting of important national facilities such as the gas and oil storage tanks at Dura, in East Beirut. One preliminary assessment estimated damage between March and August at $800m.,[1] before the outburst connected with the mid-August Suq al-Gharb battle. This figure does not include such aspects as losses consequent on semiparalysis of business and closure of schools and universities for much of the year. The central bank managed to maintain minimal financing for the rival governments in East and West Beirut, covering notional salaries and sporadic functioning of essential services, despite virtually no tax or revenue collection, only by virtue of backing by long-standing gold and foreign exchange reserves,[2] profits of currency speculation, and rationing or shutdown of such basic facilities as electricity.

Lebanon's geographical fragments (see map No. 1, Lebanon: Geopolitical Divisions, 1989), however, sustained the ramshackle existence of previous years through the usual variety of *ad hoc* measures and sustenance: local "tax" extraction, remittances from the diaspora, support from interested foreign powers, smuggling using wide-ranging Lebanese commercial connections, and the multibillion dollar drug trade centered in the Biqa'. The East Beirut enclave, insulated from Syrian exactions and containing at least 60% of Lebanon's industrial capacity, especially light manufacturing that benefited from the exchange rate collapse, continued as the most dynamic area despite the constriction of the six-month Syrian siege. In the Shuf, the Druze entity, with less than one fifth of East Beirut's population and little internal productive capability, faced a perpetual economic and demographic crisis,[3] though leadership cohesion spared it some of East Beirut's uncertainty, which arose from the multipolar political structure. Tripoli escaped the year's fighting and much of its impact, but had to endure a demanding Syrian presence as well as a steady infiltration of Syrian 'Alawi settlers, which alarmed the Sunni population. Everywhere unemployment probably exceeded one third of the economically active population, with the salaried middle class almost destroyed as a socioeconomic category. For most technical and professional workers, unemployment or emigration had been the only alternatives since the mid-1980s.

This review divides treatment of 1989's political and military events into three parts: the new context given to the East-West Beirut struggle over Lebanon's orientation by 'Awn's "war of liberation" against the Syrian presence; the consequences of the 'Awn irruption as inaugurated by the Ta'if arrangement; and the partially autonomous developments in the South Lebanon Shi'i arena.

MICHEL 'AWN GOES TO WAR

PRELIMINARIES

The September 1988 establishment of the military government in East Beirut brought the secular nationalism of the Lebanese officer corps into the center of Lebanese politics. Formally, the Army had split into two segments with the Huss Cabinet's appointment of Sami Khatib as provisional army commander in West Beirut, the personnel being divided roughly equally between East Beirut and the rest of Lebanon. 'Awn's general staff at Yarza, however, remained the real center of gravity, with the only four fully operational brigades, out of the 12 technically existing, controlling 90% of the heavy equipment acquired from the US in 1983–84, including all the 155 mm. howitzers. Yarza also disposed of virtually all "command and control" and intelligence facilities, maintaining close links with many non-Christian officers in the brigades outside East Beirut.[4]

For 'Awn and his senior officers, the powerful army "rump" surviving in East Beirut was the final bastion of autonomous state legitimacy. Holding the East Beirut lines tended to be considered as preserving a free base for the later resurgence of central government authority — not as asserting a Christian canton. 'Awn and his circle viewed with scorn other remnants of regime machinery — the parliamentary deputies and the Huss cabinet — as potential tools of foreign powers and militias. In a nation beset by corruption and dishonor, the Army would express a supracommunal popular will for restored dignity, leading the struggle against internal and external enemies: "Only [the military] together with the living force of our people can shatter the cell bars and release our captive country from the prison of foreign interests."[5]

Considerations related to the Army's composition also necessitated a commitment by the army command to Lebanon beyond East Beirut. Apart from the intimate professional and personal links between Yarza and the largely non-Christian brigades, up to 20% of army manpower in East Beirut was Sunni or Shi'i. Also, a disproportionate part of Christian manpower came from peripheral rural areas outside East Beirut — the north Biqa', the 'Akkar, and South Lebanon. In early 1989, at least 50% of the soldiers in the East Beirut brigades had their homes in other parts of Lebanon.[6] Yarza exhibited a pan-Lebanese and to some degree a multicommunal flavor, with stress on the indivisibility of the whole Army.

'Awn's power center at Ba'abda and Yarza certainly embodied deep national frustrations cutting across sectarian identities, in this respect diverging from the normal Lebanese spectrum of semi-feudal *zu'ama* (bosses) and sectarian militias. As the months passed, however, it continued to lack organizational coherence and proper advisory support. Apart from the three-man military government, reduced from the intended six by an immediate Syrian and West Beirut prohibition on participation by non-Christian officers, 'Awn was surrounded by an "inner circle" of trusted East Beirut associates of mainly military background and dangerously limited political experience.[7]

Both the populist strength and the structural weakness reflected 'Awn's own past: humble origins in the mixed Maronite-Shi'i Harat Hurayk neighborhood leading into a long professional military career. 'Awn came to Ba'abda with little tolerance for the traditional political class or for militia usurpation of state functions, no fundamental commitment to the Maronite "establishment," and almost no familiarity with the intricacies of Middle Eastern and international diplomacy. What he did bring included a Gaullist-style leadership concept and a conviction of the need for prompt action to salvage Lebanon from the attrition attributed to foreign presences and militia depredations. With no clear program or proper grasp of the politically possible, this determination for a collision with complex geopolitical realities promised explosive results.

'Awn's prominent role in derailing the Syrian-US agreement for a new presidency in late 1988 guaranteed that the Syrians, previously indifferent toward the army commander, would confront the new regime installed in Ba'abda. In November 1988, the Syrians compelled the divided Huss cabinet to appoint a Sunni officer, Sami Khatib, the new interim army chief, as a preliminary step toward a Lebanese "nationalist army" under Syrian patronage. Initially, 'Awn's attention was concentrated on conditions within East Beirut, where coexistence with the LF militia constrained the military government's authority at its source. In the context of facing the Syrian presence 'Awn required a reduction of the militia to buttress his negotiating position, to lessen opportunities for Syrian splitting tactics, and to display nonsectarian credentials to West Beirut.

The interpenetrated distribution of the two largest Lebanese military apparatuses — 'Awn's brigades and the LF — in the compressed space of the eastern sector constantly threatened internal instability. The leaderships had been temporarily pushed together by the external pressures of late 1988, but a history of enmity, differing views of Lebanon, and an absence of real political coordination meant the arrangement was unlikely to last. The LF had attempted to penetrate and subvert the Army through links with sympathetic officers, while Yarza rejected any equalization with a militia and perceived the LF as a long-term menace to "legitimate authority." The LF political outlook centered on a Christian canton, whereas 'Awn had a romantic Lebanese nationalist orientation. He had his own federalist ideas,[8] but as an option for national coherence rather than as a necessity for sectarian security. More immediately, the LF's behavior as a state structure with taxes, ports, and military autonomy represented a daily challenge to the credibility of the military government.

Arab maneuverings in early 1989 at once increased mutual suspicions between Ba'abda and the LF and irritated the Syrians. Syrian failure with the presidential conjunction encouraged other Arabs to question Syrian aspirations to monopolize the Lebanese arena to an extent unparalleled since the 1970s. More worrying for Damascus, the emergence of 'Awn's military government coincided with the Gulf War cease-fire: Iraqi hands were freed for revenge on Syria for its alliance with Iran, and Saddam Husayn saw encouragement of 'Awn's defiance as a splendid opportunity for "baiting" Asad only 80 km. from the Syrian capital. Iraqi arms shipments, already reaching the LF, were accelerated with a new emphasis on 'Awn's brigades as well as continued supply for the militia. This had profound implications for inter-Lebanese balances. It significantly augmented the general military weight of East Beirut, thus forcing West Beirut elements, including Junblat's Druze "canton," into greater dependence on Syria. The rising stockpiles also had a destabilizing effect on LF-army relations, which was clearly not appreciated by the Iraqis. Ba'abda feared erosion of its authority in East Beirut, and the militia perceived an increased need to assert its position.

Arab diplomatic intervention, discussed by a meeting of Arab foreign ministers on

12 January, involved the establishment of a six-state committee[9] chaired by Kuwaiti Foreign Minister Sabah al-Ahmad Al Sabah to survey solutions to the Lebanese crisis (for details, see chapter on inter-Arab relations). Superficially impelled by the prospect of Lebanon's formal partition after the presidency fell vacant — supposedly a danger to the "Arab nation" — the move more likely came as a bid by Iraq and some conservative regimes to restrict Syria. Damascus, concerned about "Arabization" of Lebanese affairs in 'Awn's favor, warned that any committee must be "consultative not executive," and rejected discussion of Palestinian camp issues or of any external presence in Lebanon except Israel. The Iraqi-Syrian divide was stressed by the Iraqi foreign minister: "It is not permissible to leave one Arab state — Syria — to operate by itself in Lebanon."[10]

Both 'Awn and the Syrians scored points from the first major political round, when 'Awn, Huss, and Shi'i parliamentary Speaker Husayni were in Tunis at the beginning of February for discussions with the committee. 'Awn made a good impression, received a measure of recognition, and registered his insistence on giving priority to a Syrian pullback, thus "freeing the Lebanese decision."[11] He also met PLO leader Yasir 'Arafat, who caused anger in West Beirut by a statement about putting "the Palestinian gun" at 'Awn's disposal "as a representative of the legality."[12] It was to be 'Awn's only venture outside East Beirut for the year. The Syrians could not prevent the emergence of the notion of Arab military observers being stationed in Beirut, but, particularly with Husayni's help, scuttled anything highlighting the Syrian presence in Lebanon. The pattern of deadlock was set.

'Awn's diplomatic foray aroused LF suspicions, especially since it was combined with his failure to inform the LF leaders of the results of the Tunis discussions and with his stalling on including the LF in his government, apparently in deference to American appeals for avoidance of partitionist measures. 'Awn's expanding web of Arab contacts encouraged rumors about "bazaars" at LF expense.[13] In return, 'Awn felt he had done nothing against the LF outside East Beirut, while the LF continued to eat away at Ba'abda's political primacy inside, the latest challenge being an LF "National Development Council."

At this point, the army-LF contest intersected with 'Awn's policy concerning Syria. 'Awn had the possibility of using the suppression of the militia, historically hated in West Beirut and suspected by the Syrians as promoting a "balkanization" which might destabilize Syria itself, for an attempt at a general Lebanese realignment to his advantage. Damascus could obviously benefit from experimenting with the matter, if only to have the two East Beirut power centers in violent confrontation. Contacts allegedly occurred between army officers and representatives of Ghazi Kan'an, chief of Syrian military intelligence in Lebanon.[14] The contours of a "deal" were reasonably clear: if 'Awn threw the LF out of urban East Beirut and made his peace with Syria's strategic position, the Syrians might pull back in the Beirut region, allow reunification of the Army in a Greater Beirut security plan, and acquiesce in a national role for 'Awn.

On 14 February, after a succession of incidents between soldiers and militiamen and an army mobilization, 'Awn struck at the LF in the Matn and East Beirut suburbs.[15] After two days of street fighting causing the death of about 80 people, the Army held the upper hand in the main urban area, though without a conclusive military decision. 'Awn accused the LF of plotting a coup, termed them a "fascist mafia," and demanded that the ports be handed over, the end of taxes, abolition of the "National Development Council" and other parastate institutions, and a retreat of militiamen to barracks outside "administrative Beirut."[16] LF leader Samir Ja'ja' showed signs of shock[17] and took a concessionary line, but rejected any complete subordination of the militia. The Syrian reaction was interesting, with references to the LF wanting destruction of "Gen. 'Awn's forces which refuse to be an instrument for execution of the Zionist program in Lebanon."[18] (Previously the military government had itself been a "Zionist project.")[19] One West Beirut "government source" even hinted that 'Awn was "halfway to the presidency" following the East Beirut events.[20]

The late February settlement between 'Awn and the LF, however, did not at all coincide with Syrian preferences. 'Awn achieved the surrender of the militia's primary illicit port, the Beirut "fifth basin"; elimination of major LF taxes; evacuation of some urban militia barracks; and Ja'ja''s formal acknowledgment of Ba'abda's political supremacy. He thus consolidated his East Beirut base significantly, but without producing anything of value to Damascus. The militia remained a strong autonomous entity and retained its presence in Beirut. Far from fulfilling Syrian expectations, 'Awn seemed to have an improved *modus vivendi* with the LF. At the same time, 'Awn registered a worrying "public opinion" advance in Syrian-dominated territory: traditionalist Muslim politicians and northern Christians welcomed 'Awn's assault on the militia and the takeover of Beirut port, with Huss and West Beirut army commander Khatib moving for similar measures in West Beirut and more crossings between the two sectors.[21] All this implied political strengthening of 'Awn for no return, and Damascus swiftly reined in the more forward West Beirutis. By early March, the uniform "message" from Syria and West Beirut was that even a "partial opening" to 'Awn depended on prior submission of an acceptable political proposal regarding constitutional reform.[22]

'Awn came to feel thwarted and deceived on several levels. Within East Beirut, he exhibited anger toward the mediating religious and traditionalist personalities, perceiving them as treating the Army and militia as identical, and suspecting a "hidden wish" against a decisive resolution. He intimated that they had pressed him to "finish with this and this" and when he responded, they immediately shifted their positions.[23] Unsympathetic maneuverings in East Beirut increased the urgency of momentum elsewhere; it would be difficult to sustain reduction of one militia on the ports issue without a parallel retreat by West Beirut militias. Initial reactions by Huss and others encouraged 'Awn to believe he could "stampede" an extension of the military government's writ beyond East Beirut. On 24 February, even before reaching a settlement with the LF, he rushed into a fateful decision to close all "illegal ports" and to force shipping to use the army-controlled Beirut port,[24] though implementation was delayed. 'Awn considered that he had made a maximal beginning concerning the LF, which should be answered by gains for "legitimate authority" in West Beirut before further steps in the eastern sector. This was an unrealistic expectation.

Druze leader Walid Junblat played a central role in the following events. In early 1989, Junblat attempted his own *rapprochement* with East Beirut, but aimed at the Maronite religious institution rather than the Army or militia. The main issue was Junblat's proposal for a phased return of Christian refugees to the Shuf. The Druze region badly needed economic and demographic buttressing of its position in the

"Islamic and nationalist" arena; Druze leaders feared eventual Palestinian and Shi'i territorial inroads.[25] On 9 February, however, one of Junblat's most senior aides, Anwar Futayri, was murdered while on a tour connected with the refugee initiative. Junblat showed every sign of a conviction that East Beirut militia elements had organized the killing, aiming to prevent any change in the demographic status quo and perpetuate Druze vulnerability.[26]

Junblat was, thus, already in a nervous mood when 'Awn hit the LF and tried to trespass on West Beirut politics, with Huss apparently responsive to 'Awn on the ports matter. The Druze Progressive Socialist Party (PSP) ports at Khalda and Jiyya, the Shuf lifelines to the outer world that had been subject to Syrian squeezing since 1987, represented the main target, together with an Amal landing point at Awza'i. After some Junblati rumbles of warnings, 'Awn, drawn on by some Christians linked with Damascus, tentatively suggested a broad compact on cooling Suq al-Gharb, returning refugees, and opening the Damascus highway.[27] Junblat, furious about 'Awn's ports decision and with his long-standing suspicions of Huss and other traditionalists fully aroused, replied on 5 March by publicly abandoning his refugee proposal amid denunciations of the Army and Huss. For Junblat, Huss worked "to please some Beirut traders — ''Awn gives an order in Yarza and they execute it here' — the war is still at its beginning and we refuse a settlement on the basis of no victor and no vanquished."[28]

By this stage, such an approach well suited the Syrians, who were not merely angered by 'Awn's bid to accelerate events but also greatly disturbed by the trend in the meetings of the Arab committee, where insufficient attention was being given to "isolationists," with the Kuwaitis seeming to lean toward 'Awn.[29] The basic political impasse over the future of the Lebanese regime persisted undiminished while 'Awn made his February push; the maneuver to "extend legitimacy" had nothing underpinning it. At a gathering of Lebanese religious notables sponsored by the Arab committee in late February, Maronite Patriarch Nasrallah Sufayr repeated Maronite requirements that priority be given to presidential elections and resistance to reduction of presidential powers. The Syrians and allied West Beirut "nationalist parties" responded with hints of a boycott of the committee and by stressing the necessity for sweeping political reform before all else.[30] 'Awn took the Syrian and Junblati attitudes badly and on 6 March activated the Army's "marine operations room," thus inaugurating the blockade of West Beirut militia ports. Mutual escalatory measures ensued over the next week; Druze artillery fire commenced at Suq al-Gharb, Beirut port was shelled, 'Awn ordered the airport closed, and on 14 March came the first heavy, widespread bombardment.

CONFRONTATION WITH SYRIA

Partly through belief in the urgency of cracking the geopolitical mold of the Lebanese crisis, partly through misplaced hopes of an international impact, and partly through the immediate background of disappointments and misunderstandings regarding West Beirut and Syria, 'Awn plunged into his war for "sovereignty," immediately elevating it to a "war of liberation" (*harb al-tahrir*) from Syria. Because of the prevailing local and regional power balance, the hostilities became a six-month epic of static artillery duels, blockades, and limited frontal probing, in which c. 850 people died and c. 3,000 were wounded, and which primarily confirmed the rigidity of the territorial status quo. The developments could be divided into two phases, intersected by an emergency Arab summit in Morocco in May. From March to May, intermittent, but often intense, land bombardment on both sides was the main feature, with ʿAwn reaching deep into the Biqaʿ and the Shuf, while the Syrians and their allies targeted East Beirut ports and infrastructure. In May, a decrease in land shelling, which was pressed by the Arab committee, preceded and accompanied the Arab summit, with the Syrians shifting the emphasis to artillery interdiction of shipping approaches to East Beirut. From June to August, the Syrians steadily tightened their siege, looking to exhaust and split East Beirut by attrition, thereby politically emasculating ʿAwn. ʿAwn responded vigorously against the Syrian Army, leading in turn to an abortive Syrian experimental land probe at Suq al-Gharb in mid-August. Such escalation finally brought a forceful international diplomatic intervention, producing a September cease-fire and energizing the new Arab committee which was established by the May summit (see below). For Lebanon, however, the "war of liberation" proved only a long prologue to a second, more terrible upheaval — the ferocious time of reckoning between ʿAwn and the LF which was to tear East Beirut apart in February 1990.

After 14 March 1989, there was no going back for Michel ʿAwn. In the frustration of his bid to impose "legitimate authority" on "illicit ports" and to ease interaction between the two sectors of Beirut, ʿAwn saw only the hand of Damascus. Buttressed by the Iraqis, encouraged by Syria's unpopularity with other Arab states, and believing that the banner of an assault on "smuggling, terrorism, and piracy"[31] would bring Western support, ʿAwn swiftly declared war on the Syrian Army: "The question is no longer one of ports. We have passed this and defined the ceiling — Syrian withdrawal from Lebanon."[32] "Today we have one target," he announced, "we shall liberate our land; the depth of the difference, material and moral, is with Syria, not between Lebanese."[33]

On a visit by the author to the underground bunker at Baʿabda in the midst of the siege, ʿAwn explained his self-confidence in embarking on what most observers viewed as a reckless gamble: "As you know, the Syrians are much stronger in numbers, means, and resources, but we feel in our territory that we are stronger. Maybe that's a false impression but it's like that, the way everyone feels when he is at home, that he is the master."[34]

As no one had conceived of such a stand by a Lebanese party, ʿAwn at least had an opening advantage of surprise. Initial Syrian participation in bombarding East Beirut, far from having the deterrent effect obviously intended by Damascus, was welcomed as an opportunity for unprecedented large-scale targeting of Syrian military installations, from the Beirut region to the central Biqaʿ. ʿAwn built his whole military approach on forcing Syria to expose itself as a direct and aggressive participant in Lebanese hostilities, in this way to discredit its propaganda about playing a peacekeeping role. It was hoped that this would undermine Lebanese, Arab, and international props for Syrian territorial occupation. Thus ʿAwn kept up a barrage of invective against Syria and its president Hafiz al-Asad,[35] and insisted that any security committee to monitor a cease-fire be Lebanese-Syrian rather than Lebanese-Lebanese.

For a time, the Syrians were on the defensive, never before having faced anything quite like ʿAwn's attack. On the diplomatic level, French criticism and the unsympathetic attitude of the Arab committee on Lebanon, particularly its Kuwaiti chairman, considerably disturbed the Syrian regime.[36] The French, however, soon retreated; and the Arabs, despite Iraqi stirring, demonstrated timidity. Damascus, incensed by what it viewed as Ba'abda's impudence and infuriated by 'Awn's rejection of linkage between Syrian and Israeli withdrawals,[37] maintained an uncompromising line. On the military side, this comprised steady attrition by siege and shelling, accompanied by standard denials of Syrian involvement, and on the political side, coordination of West Beirut elements in order to demand Christian political concessions in advance of a cease-fire and to refuse any dealings with 'Awn. Asad avoided a personal response to 'Awn until early May, when he referred to "those raising the slogan of liberation from Syria" as "enemies of Lebanon" and "a small gang within a minority on a territory less than 10% of the area of Lebanon."[38]

Inside East Beirut the tough posture of Syria and its allies helped 'Awn to preserve the minimum necessary cohesion through some difficult months. However, given the unhappy relations between the Army and the LF, and traditionalist jealousies of 'Awn, dissent was sure to surface as the hostilities lengthened. Having itself always made a slogan out of "liberation," the LF had little option but to back 'Awn's position, yet it resented a campaign which promised to have consequences detrimental to the militia's cantonal base whatever the outcome. In early April, one LF source intimated to the West Beirut daily *al-Safir* that "if 'Awn wins, he wins alone; if he loses, all East Beirut loses."[39] Phalangist leader George Sa'ada, a close associate of Ja'ja', supported 'Awn publicly until September, but from the outset leaked subversive private comments. In mid-April, Patriarch Sufayr, urged on from West Beirut by such personalities as parliamentary Speaker Husayni, conducted contacts for a broad traditionalist "Christian meeting" of parliamentary deputies and party notables, certain to try to undercut 'Awn.

The "broad meeting" took place at the Bkirki Patriarchate on 19 April and condemned the destruction on both sides. Far from demanding Syrian withdrawals, it ignored the "occupation" issue, and even recognized a Syrian security role in policing a cease-fire. Deputy Edmond Rizq made a direct attack on 'Awn, speaking of the "exploitation of the people" in a "gamble for [personal] gains."[40] 'Awn denounced the deputies as not representing anything and was backed by large street demonstrations, their sustained vehemence reflecting genuine popular sentiment.[41] Syria and its allies then acted effectively to buttress 'Awn by taking the Bkirki communiqué as an invitation to tighten the screws on East Beirut. When in May, Arab mediation obtained Ba'abda's agreement to lift the blockade of "illegal ports" in exchange for a cease-fire supervised by Arab observers, Junblat and others demanded searches of all ships entering East Beirut ports for weaponry, and the Syrians refused to lift the maritime siege of the eastern sector without political capitulation. In these circumstances, 'Awn's traditionalist Christian opponents risked appearing as outright Syrian agents. Their lack of popular legitimacy brutally exposed, for the moment, they retired into obfuscation[42] or silence.

Through May, tortuous Arab diplomatic convolutions encompassed an emergency summit in Casablanca, but no resolution of the struggle in Beirut. At this stage, the main international aspects of the Lebanese contest were American insistence that treatment of the hostilities remain on the Arab level, with no referral to the UN; and Asad's manipulation of Egypt's need for his support of its reentry to the Arab League to thwart the Iraqi efforts to Arabize Lebanese affairs.[43] Before the summit began on

23 May, Syrian implacability finally disposed of the Kuwaiti-chaired Arab committee and its ideas for the introduction of an Arab force into Beirut. At the summit, Asad faced a strong Iraqi-Jordanian challenge in favor of a substantial Arab peacekeeping contingent and Syrian withdrawals.

The Syrian president, in a classic performance, neutralized the Egyptians, maneuvered with Saudi Arabia and the Gulf states, and reiterated Syrian absolutism in an epic three-hour harangue: "The relationship between Syria and Lebanon has a special historical, geographical, and human character without parallel in Lebanon's relationship with any other Arab state. Syrian forces will not leave Lebanon except by a Lebanese agreement in a national referendum or by a request from a unified central government." In bitter exchanges between the Syrian and Iraqi leaders, Saddam Husayn accused Asad of bringing the Iranians to Lebanon while Asad mocked the Arab-force notion: could those calling for it turn words into action?[44] In the end, the Arabs fell back before the Syrian trump card of presence on the ground, and the Iraqi president walked out of the summit in a rage a day before the final session (for further discussion, see chapter on inter-Arab relations).

For Lebanon, the summit created yet another committee, but this time under the auspices of the three heads of state, Morocco, Saudi Arabia, and Algeria. The section of the 28 May closing communiqué on mechanisms for quietening the Lebanese crisis reflected an international consensus for using the parliamentary deputies to approve suggestions for a new regime, and against any initial priority for foreign troop withdrawals. This consensus was in line with previous American-Syrian and Saudi-Syrian consultations,[45] and set an order of precedence gratifying to Damascus: political reform, presidential elections, establishment of a unity government, and measures to implement territorial sovereignty. Only as regards Israel were "withdrawals" explicitly demanded. It read ominously for 'Awn, though with the positive feature that it represented high-level Arab intervention, with the crystallization of a firm scheme only after "tripartite committee" contacts involving all parties.

Despite 'Awn's far-reaching ambitions and the now powerful determination of the Syrians and others to have him removed, subsequent events principally emphasized the strength of the elements tending to stalemate. First, Ba'abda acted on the basis of highly distorted perceptions of possibilities in the local and international environments, while the Syrians and their allies failed to appreciate the popular undercurrents generated by the 'Awn enterprise. In fact, Ba'abda headed for political isolation, but conditions in West Beirut put severe constraints on Syria's capacity to mobilize any effective Lebanese opposition. Second, local and regional geostrategic factors tended to block any advance by 'Awn or a military decision in favor of Damascus. These dimensions, which provided a setting that critically affected the consequences of the "siege," deserve close attention.

'Awn, West Beirut, and the Americans
'Awn's inner advisory circle, dominated by officers, maintained an image of the Lebanese and international contexts conditioned less by realistic analysis than by romantic nationalism, simplistic conspiracy theories concerning Syrian and Israeli roles, and inflated views of likely international responses.[46] 'Awn distrusted civilians, and a considerable East Beirut reservoir of experience in dealing with the outer world

went unused. Perspectives such as those of Elie Salem and Ghassan Tuwayni, senior Orthodox advisers to the Jumayyil presidency, were seen as too cautious and concessionary, and made little impact on the military government.[47]

In the local arena, Ba'abda misjudged the intricate relationship between the Syrians and the non-Christian communities. Certainly the Syrians were widely hated,[48] and 'Awn's promotion of the Army as the nucleus for a nonsectarian Lebanon aroused much enthusiasm, especially amongst the Shi'ites. Damascus, however, could always play on deep suspicions of Maronite "privilege" and of the Army's historical association with the "Maronite regime." Many non-Christians viewed the Syrian military presence as necessary to extract political concessions from East Beirut and to balance Maronite armed strength. The combination of Ba'abda's rejection of reform "in the shadow of occupation," substantial Iraqi arms supplies shifting the military equation against West Beirut, and 'Awn's efforts to internationalize the Lebanese crisis, could only drive the West Beirut leadership into deeper dependence on Damascus, and assist Syria and its friends to represent 'Awn as just another face of political Maronitism.

'Awn's failure to translate his personal preference for nonsectarian politics[49] into a distinctive, publicized reform package counted as a crucial lost opportunity for embarrassing the Syrians and attracting a receptive but wavering West Beirut audience. The repeated argument that an understanding could not be achieved while West Beirut was constrained by a foreign presence made no impact on the non-Christian parties. For all their continuing divisions, the West Beirut political bosses came together on one point, summarized by Junblat thus: "It is impossible to reach a common denominator with 'Awn: he wants to skip the internal conflict."[50] Ba'abda's weakness on this subject helped inflate other fears and accusations. Huss and Junblat seized on the military nature of 'Awn's structure, asserting that a book by a Col. Fu'ad 'Awn contained an army program for complete military domination of the state.[51] Amal leader Nabih Barri and Junblat expressed alarm about the "flood" of Iraqi weapons entering East Beirut, a matter inflamed by 'Awn's own remarks: "I am annoyed with the large amount of ammunition — my warehouses are not large enough to accommodate the ammunition."[52]

The Army's tendency to retaliate against Syrian and Druze shelling of East Beirut residential areas by bombarding Druze villages and parts of West Beirut was also counterproductive. The LF militia and, according to rumor, even the Syrians, contributed to the shelling of non-Christian areas; both had interests in maintaining the confrontation between 'Awn and West Beirut. Thus, despite common popular disgust concerning militias and Syria in the two parts of Beirut, sufficient suspicion endured to easily outweigh common feelings, principally to the benefit of Damascus.

Beyond preventing 'Awn from extending his base, however, none of this helped Syria to construct a solid West Beirut alignment as a credible spearhead for getting rid of 'Awn. Only the Druze and Syria's closest Lebanese and Palestinian clients, the latter all lightweight groups in conventional military terms, proved reliable in fighting East Beirut. The Syrian Army had no choice but to participate directly and on a large scale, even to sustain nonmobile warfare. Apart from the diversions of inter-Shi'i competition and squabbles between Junblat and the Huss government, Syria faced two main inconveniences in orienting West Beirut against 'Awn. First, the traditionalist Muslim "pole," chiefly represented in the Sunni "Higher Islamic Council," had no enthusiasm for the confrontation. Sunni Chief Mufti of the Republic

Hasan Khalid made cease-fire appeals to the Kuwaitis and other Arab states,[53] which could only have irritated Damascus. On 16 May, Khalid was assassinated by a huge car bomb. As usual, responsibility could not be determined, but on the eve of the Arab summit, many took it as a warning not to complicate the Syrian position. Second, Amal, Syria's main ally in West Beirut, had little interest in fighting 'Awn. Some in Amal and the associated Sixth Brigade of the Army still viewed Yarza as a component of the "legitimacy" — informal connections were maintained — and Amal was absorbed with watching Hizballah. Amal leader Barri made the pronouncements Damascus expected from him, but spent as much time as possible away from Beirut, and his fighters avoided any significant role in the battles.

As for the wider world, Ba'abda entirely underestimated diplomatic and political reluctance for new embroilments in the Lebanese drama. In particular, it quickly appeared that 'Awn had a most naive and unrealistic appreciation of the chances of moving the US against the Syrian deployment.[54] The Bush Administration indicated immediate dissatisfaction with 'Awn's bid to make Lebanon's geopolitical status quo a major international issue and worked consistently to contain any challenge to the existing ME order, and to keep the Lebanese matter under Arab cover. One American official even observed to the Senate Foreign Relations Committee that "if Syria withdraws I expect the situation would worsen rather than improve."[55] The American policy-making apparatus had established firm guidelines in 1988 (see *MECS* 1988, chapter on Lebanon) for treating the Lebanese crisis in coordination with the Syrians, and attempts by 'Awn's supporters to mobilize pressures in Congress and even from the French convinced Administration officials of the need to have 'Awn curbed.[56] With such a hardening in Washington's position, Ba'abda's gains in Paris, in the Vatican, and with some Arab actors could only serve as temporary advantages in the struggle for survival. Indeed, regarding the Arabs, the Americans consulted with Saudi Arabia after the Arab summit in May to have Arab intervention parallel American policy.[57]

Geostrategic Aspects

In mid-1989, East Beirut possessed a solid defensive base, but nothing to encourage Ba'abda's aggressive challenge to the Syrian presence surrounding the Christian sector, apart from Iraqi encouragement of 'Awn's impulsive nationalism and worries concerning long-term Syrian attrition of the enclave.[58]

The army brigades in East Beirut, with 15,000 troops, amounted to the Army's effective core. Iraqi supplies increased 'Awn's strike capacity by at least 30%, raising his tank strength to almost 200 and his heavy artillery pieces to a similar number.[59] For defense against a fundamental external threat to East Beirut, one could add the LF's 8,000 men to the Army's capacity, giving a total of 25,000–30,000 troops in East Beirut (counting some mobilization, for example of students as *ansar al-jaysh,* army auxiliaries), 300 tanks, and more than 300 heavy artillery pieces.

Regarding the Syrians and their allies and proxies, the maximum manpower that could be brought into play against 'Awn could not realistically be above 40,000. The Syrian Army would have to provide more than three quarters of such a total, given Shi'i noninterest, Druze fears about losses, the unreliability of northern Christians, the diversions of the south, and the irrepressible internal conflicts of West Beirut.

Assembling the equivalent of two divisions would mean stretching Syrian logistics to breaking point even in summer, stripping the Syrian alignment everywhere else in Lebanon, and bringing large armored reinforcements from Syria. Even this would still be much beneath the 3:1 military ratio theoretically required for a general assault on East Beirut, certainly without use of air power. Air-power considerations immediately came up against an Israeli "red line."

The balance dictated siege-style warfare. The chief Syrian option, given the need to maintain an appearance of an inter-Lebanese conflict and a fiction of Syrian noninvolvement, was prolonged bombardment to tire the East Beirut population and to interrupt supplies, undercutting 'Awn by prising the traditionalist and militia poles of the enclave's power structure away from Ba'abda. 'Awn only had the means for a defensive contest, yet he had launched an offensive project — his single chance to shake off the Syrian presence was by internationalization through escalation. This made Ba'abda's incompetence in relating to the US a most significant strategic deficiency.

Local physical and human geography reinforced the likelihood of stalemate, though with siege conditions giving an advantage to the Syrians. On both sides of the main lines, a surface dissected by growth-covered mountains combined with extensive expanses of reinforced concrete apartment buildings — an ideal urban fabric for defense — militated against easy offensive penetration. In the south, the Syrians and Druze had the benefits of height, with the Upper Matn and Shuf as natural highland artillery platforms overlooking the chief East Beirut urban area. East Beirut was forced to concentrate its main forces in a relatively limited southern pocket containing the sector's vital facilities and nerve centers, with the army brigades holding a semicircle comprising the Duwayr al-Shuwayr, Suq al-Gharb, and East-West Beirut fronts (see map No. 2, Syrian Siege of East Beirut, May-August 1989). The northern line, though topographically better sited, was not as well defended and the Syrians had the possibility of trying to seize ground here, while keeping East Beirut's main strength pinned southward. 'Awn, with numerical inferiority and facing greater Syrian firepower, had virtually no option for offensive action in the critical southern theater beyond commando raids.

For its part, East Beirut represented a geographical "hedgehog." Compact and well-settled, the enclave contained over 30% of Lebanon's population in 20% of the country's territory. Internal communication lines, with the coastal autostrada as the backbone, gave an advantage over opponents attempting to coordinate operations near Beirut and in the north on much longer external lines. This asset was only partially offset by the exposure of the coastal freeway to artillery interdiction. The southern pocket made up for altitudinal inferiority by being packed full of impressive geographical obstacles, encompassing an intricate topography and the East Beirut urban maze, a vast and anarchic highrise sprawl more than equivalent to its West Beirut counterpart.

Even a limited operation to reach Ba'abda via Suq al-Gharb was impossible without a large-scale commitment of Syrian regular forces.[60] In any case, 'Awn had the capability to ensure that such an exercise could not be kept limited, but turned into extended warfare on all axes. Subjugation of East Beirut promised military nightmares for Syria, with each ridge, suburb, and village a hostile fortress, and most roads narrow, winding, and circuitous, with successive ascents and descents, all inviting ambushes at every corner. An entire Syrian division might evaporate in East Beirut, with serious consequences for Syria's general strategic posture.

All this plus Iraqi activity turned Syria's attention seaward — in the context of Israeli aerial "red lines," East Beirut's most vulnerable direction. Coordinating between the Kura in the north and Ra's Beirut in the south, Syrian heavy artillery covered all the sea approaches to the enclave (see map No. 2, Syrian Siege of East Beirut, May-August 1989). For most of the six months of interdiction, Syria made no effort to conceal its direct operation of the siege as Iraqi shipments to 'Awn transformed the matter, from the Syrian perspective, into a regional confrontation with Iraq. Since only land-based artillery was deployed, however, the siege had limited effect. Despite scores of shells fired at individual ships, only about eight vessels were hit during the six months — for example, two out of 97 entering Junya port in June (see Table 1 below). By May-June, after more than two months of fighting, East Beirut faced a crippling fuel shortage but few problems regarding other commodities, whereas disruption of the land crossings meant considerable difficulties for West Beirut. Poor Syrian targeting and deficient radar left openings for such East Beirut countermeasures as night runs direct to the Jubayl coast, at a maximum range from Syrian guns, with the radar thereafter confused by a coast-hugging progress to Junya (see map No. 2, Syrian Siege of East Beirut, May-August 1989). Of course, the spectacular consequences of a direct hit on a fuel ship, for example, did have detrimental effects on morale.

Real strangulation began in early July, when Damascus decided to effect a gunboat blockade. Reports of the imminent arrival of a large Iraqi consignment including *Frog* 7 surface-to-surface missiles, which East Beirut could use against the Syrian capital, alarmed the Syrian leadership[61] and provided an excuse for action with implications beyond the Lebanese arena. Using Tripoli as a base, up to six gunboats at any one time cruised 10–15 km. offshore, shelling and arresting incoming vessels. Table 1, depicting shipping movements into Junya for the first seven months of 1989, indicates the impact. The April-July statistics show Junya taking over from Beirut port, close to the main urban front, and the July statistics demonstrate the dramatic effect of the gunboat patrols. By early August, the situation of the civilian population raised doubts in Ba'abda for the first time as to whether 'Awn could continue.[62]

TABLE 1: CARGO SHIPPING INTO JUNYA PORT
JANUARY-JULY 1989

	Number of Ships	Goods Emptied (tons)	Goods Loaded (tons)	Total Goods (tons)
January	1	294	22	316
February	1	318	30	348
March	1	811	345	1,156
April	41	7,304	3,472	10,776
May	93	15,017	5,488	20,505
June	97	21,725	5,580	27,305
July	16	5,715	1,463	7,178

SOURCE: *Al-Nahar*, 27 September 1989.

The decisive block on Syria, when added to local power balances and geography, was a residual Israeli geostrategic interest against Syrian hegemony in Beirut. Iraq, physically separated from Lebanon by Syria and with a lengthy, vulnerable sea route as its only access, could not in the end compete with Syria's immediate proximity to Lebanon. Israel, as Lebanon's other neighboring regional power, could compete, if it so wished.

Israeli officials and specialists were not impressed by 'Awn's "war of liberation."[63] First, bad experience had taught Israel to be distrustful of East Beirut's perambulations. Second, with no prior consultation, 'Awn was trying to change the regional strategic environment without realistic prospects for success, in the Israeli view, and in ways which might face Israel with difficult choices in relation to Syria. Third, 'Awn's connections with Iraq and 'Arafat stimulated Israeli concern. 'Awn had little room for maneuver in the matter: to acquire military necessities and to hold his position against Syria in the Arab world required an Arabist stance. 'Arafat had advised him: "Speak on an Arab path and we are all with you."[64] Thus, on the general Arab-Israeli issue, 'Awn answered "true" when asked by the Kuwaiti daily *al-Qabas*: "You mean you are with Syria and against Israel?"[65] — this in the midst of his struggle with the Syrians! It was only after three months of hostilities, with the "Arab path" not producing practical results, that 'Awn began to look in a tentative and erratic fashion toward Israel, the real "counterforce" to Syria in Lebanon. One exasperated senior Israeli official bluntly defined 'Awn's performance up to July as "obtuse."[66]

Israel, however, did not share the US Administration's animus against 'Awn or its indulgence of Syria. LF militia sources fed the Israelis' analysis which was unsympathetic to 'Awn, but the relevant personnel in Tel Aviv had learnt to look beyond particular Lebanese factions. 'Awn, for his part, compensated for his more tactless assertions about Syrian-Israeli collusion with enough overtures to avoid decisively alienating the Israelis.[67] Israel emphasized nonintervention except in relation to "vital interests," which the Israeli press hastened to limit to the South Lebanon border zone, but which officials deliberately left vague. A reasonable interpretation of "vital interests" thus still extended to preserving strategic cover for Israel's position in the south, cover including an East Beirut resistant to Syrian domination.

The main approach involved minimum-cost psychological devices to keep the Syrians unsure of Israeli intentions and possible reactions. For example, during one Syrian invasion "scare" in late May, Israeli aircraft carried out mock bombing raids over West Beirut and south of Suq al-Gharb.[68] In July, Israel ignored the Syrian gunboat activity for some weeks, presumably because of its own annoyance with Iraqi intervention, though when fighting subsequently intensified some "low profile" Israeli messages helped deter any Syrian thoughts of movement.[69]

INTERNATIONAL INTERVENTION

August proved to be the critical month of the hostilities. Both sides were pressed for time, 'Awn by East Beirut's maritime vulnerability and its potential impact on the enclave's political balance, and Syria by financial costs and rising international rumblings about the direct Syrian military involvement.[70] Radio Damascus set the tone on 18 July, with its most vigorous attack hitherto on 'Awn and Iraq: 'Awn was demanding an end to the siege "to keep up an inundation of weapons" from an Iraqi regime "submerged in treason...which has sent its servants to East Beirut to be side by side with Zionists to give specialist knowledge to 'Awn's band."[71] A few days later, LF chief Samir Ja'ja' finally agreed with 'Awn for a coordinated "belt" of artillery fire to help ships enter.[72] Having held back since May from a general response to the tightening siege, 'Awn now pursued escalation, including commando attacks, to force immediate internationalization. The Syrians stepped up shelling for attrition of civilian morale rather than for military effect, and brought armored reinforcements across Dahr al-Baydar. Residents fled many parts of metropolitan Beirut; by 10 August, up to 350,000 — perhaps 40% of the population — had evacuated West Beirut and the southern suburbs,[73] heading for Sidon and the south, while many East Beirutis left for the mountains.

On 14 August, the Syrian command experimented with an assault on Suq al-Gharb, the only bid to seize territory in the six months of hostilities. To avoid too much Syrian exposure, Druze (PSP) militiamen and Palestinians were given the frontline role, with Syrian stiffening.[74] In the difficult Suq al-Gharb terrain such an attempt to reconcile a military operation with political constraints could not succeed. The limited push inevitably collapsed, leaving Syria with a painful political embarrassment. 'Awn trumpeted a victory, which had an electric popular effect in East Beirut, and the international community reacted sharply. With urgent French pressure and a Soviet-American concord, the UN Security Council assembled on 15 August and called for an immediate cease-fire — the first such Security Council move since 'Awn had begun his war.

After five months 'Awn finally appeared to have an edge on the Syrians. Sporadic bombardments continued until mid-September, but international attention compelled Syria to retreat behind Lebanese political and military cover, with the West Beirut army command asserting direction of siege shelling. This halted gunboat operations and any plans for frontal assaults, as these were Syrian matters. For the moment, Damascus was greatly restricted by Israeli warnings, an unfavorable Arab committee report (see following section), arrival of French warships in the vicinity of Lebanon, and the late-August movements of Soviet and French envoys. On a visit to the border "security zone," Israeli Defense Minister Yitzhak Rabin pointedly remarked: "Growing international pressure and the strength of the Lebanese Army are enough to stop action by the Syrian Army — the restraints which Israel imposes by land, sea, and air are well known to the Syrians and there is no need to restate them daily."[75]

Appearances, however, were treacherous. 'Awn had not been able to extend himself one centimeter beyond the lines enclosing East Beirut, and the Syrians cooperated with West Beirut leaders in a powerful lobbying effort with the Arab committee. 'Awn could not balance this, especially as the US worked actively against him. The Americans had very briefly relaxed their opposition to a UN appeal not to support real international interference, but to quieten hostilities in preparation for steering the Arabs into an arrangement to remove both 'Awn and Lebanon from international visibility. Significantly, the UN cease-fire call did not mention Syria, and, to circumvent the details of cease-fire stabilization, the US planned to progress immediately to laying constitutional reform proposals before a conference of Lebanese deputies, as recommended by the Arab summit in May.

In the end, the events of March-September 1989 confirmed the resilience of a fragmented Lebanese territorial order which both mirrored local geographical and military realities and expressed major ME and international interests. Locally, the

East-West Beirut divide was set in the Lebanese mind and the tactics of 'Awn and Syria only further cemented this. Concerning foreign withdrawals, especially by Syria, Hizballah's spiritual mentor Muhammad Husayn Fadlallah was not far from the truth in remarking: "Too many balances would be upset by that."[76]

THE TA'IF ACCORD AND ITS AFTERMATH

SYRIA ADVANCES

On 31 July the foreign ministers of Morocco, Saudi Arabia, and Algeria, comprising the Arab tripartite committee on Lebanon, issued a report expressing sharp differences with Syria on two central issues: extension of Lebanese authority over all Lebanese territory, and the relationship between Lebanon and Syria.[77] On the first, the committee favored a "comprehensive security plan," including a timetable for the geographical expansion of Lebanese state authority and contraction of the Syrian presence. Syria demanded that the whole matter be left undetermined until after formation of a Lebanese national unity government. On the second, the committee indicated that the Syrian strategic alignment for facing Israel in the Biqa' should be defined in a rigorous fashion, and that other dimensions of Syrian-Lebanese relations be coordinated in a loose manner to respect Lebanese sovereignty; Syria still maintained the "strategic integration" concept of the 1985 Tripartite Agreement, covering "strategic, economic, social, and other aspects," which substantially eroded Lebanese sovereignty.[78] Radio Damascus bitterly condemned the report, voicing "astonishment" at its "political errors in ignoring the stand of the isolationist band,"[79] and the military events of August were in part a Syrian reply to an Arab step viewed as hostile.

Six weeks later, on 17 September, the Arab committee produced a draft "National Unity Charter" to be discussed by Lebanese parliamentary deputies meeting in Saudi Arabia.[80] This document, strenuously pressed by major Arab and international actors, was accepted almost unchanged by the Lebanese deputies on 22 October, after three weeks of sterile haggling at the resort city of Ta'if. The committee draft, as compared with the initial report, represented a major retreat in the face of Syrian strategic requirements, carefully combined with constitutional reform proposals which could be accepted by Christian parliamentarians, notables, and senior religious personalities. Criticism of Syria thus collapsed in favor of a deal with Syria: Damascus would curb West Beirut "radicals" and Iranian influence in exchange for acknowledgment of Syrian strategic primacy in Lebanon and the marginality of 'Awn. Syria's basic demand for adherence to the priorities set by the May Arab summit resolutions was more than satisfied, and the 31 July report now seemed merely a brief aberration.

Three features of the draft that appeared in the final Ta'if Accord buttressed Syrian influence in Lebanon. First, constitutional adjustment in advance of any Syrian pullback obviously exposed the adjusted structure to increased Syrian manipulation. Executive authority would shift from the Maronite presidency to a national unity cabinet based in West Beirut, an area from which the Syrians would withdraw within two years of the government's formation. 'Awn certainly did not object to change regarding the presidency — he had said he did not care if the president was a Muslim[81] — but he did object to implementation of such a change while Syrian forces remained in Beirut. Also, the new government would have the right to fill new and vacant parliamentary seats with appointees for an unspecified period before "elections," a disturbing conflation of the executive and the legislature, especially in the contingency of a continued Syrian presence. Second, the Syrians were given the formal role of "assisting the legitimacy to extend the authority of the Lebanese State," if this was "requested." In the context of a regime vulnerable to Syrian management such a provision implied impeccable cover for opportunist interventions. Third, regarding the two-year limit for an initial Syrian redeployment, the draft specified a new Syrian line at Hammana, well down the seaward side of the coastal mountains, preserving Syrian control of the main pass and topographic domination of Beirut. Beyond the vaguest wafflings about a "joint Lebanese-Syrian committee" to determine "redeployment," the document did not contain a commitment or timetable for any other Syrian movement. Far from resisting any of this, the Christian deputies at Ta'if even acquiesced to the addition of a provision allowing the government to make secret Lebanese-Syrian agreements, with no obligation for disclosure to the emasculated legislature, let alone to the people.[82]

Why was there such a shift in the Arab approach in so short a period? The main reason related to the American stand. State Department and CIA staff involved with the Lebanese crisis more than ever had no patience with 'Awn's complication of ME affairs. They viewed the first Arab report as taking an impractical position; persuading the Syrians to move without attention to the Israeli presence in the south was seen as a nonstarter, and the Americans had no interest in opening up either the Israeli or Syrian aspects of the Lebanese problem in isolation from the Arab-Israeli conflict. Further, the Israeli seizure of the Shi'ite cleric 'Abd al Karim 'Ubayd in early August (see below) brought the foreign hostage issue back into media prominence, and Washington was ever hopeful about possible Syrian "good offices" in obtaining hostage releases. After a short episode of criticism of Syrian shelling around the time of the Suq al-Gharb battle, the Americans, reflecting the annoyance of some with Syrian intransigence, settled back by late August into de-emphasizing any Syrian role in hostilities, and blocking new recourse to the Security Council.[83]

'Awn's success in embarrassing Damascus internationally at this time was thus inconvenient to the US Administration. French and Soviet activity, including visits by a senior Soviet official to Beirut and Damascus and a joint French-Soviet agreement[84] noting the need to "convince the Syrian leadership to withdraw its forces from Beirut and the mountain to the Biqa' according to a fixed timetable," helped spur American diplomatic activity with the Syrians and the Arab committee. One American diplomat boasted to a Lebanese deputy that "the US Administration has more influence on Syria than the Soviet Union has."[85] American officials apparently indicated to members of the Arab committee that Washington had no immediate interest in "withdrawals" and wanted the committee's initial report "passed over."[86]

'Awn reacted to information about American maneuvers with accusations that "the US puts pressure on friendly states [France] to stop them giving military assistance to the Lebanese" and "has sold Lebanon to Syria."[87] Noisy demonstrations outside the American Embassy in East Beirut accompanied such comment. The Americans, who had apparently been considering closure of their embassy for some weeks, presumably to aid flexibility in discussions with Damascus,[88] then used 'Awn's alleged references to the efficacy of Hizballah-style hostage-taking as a pretext to evacuate all American staff on 6 September.

At the same time, the Arab committee, in abeyance since professions of failure in August, was resuscitated. The Syrians adjusted swiftly and cleverly to the American impetus, which promised new possibilities for eliminating 'Awn. As the July Arab report had possibly gone against Syria because of Syria's Iranian connection and a meeting of Syria's Lebanese allies in Tehran, Asad personally contacted Gulf state leaders and others to "clarify" the limited nature of the connection. Syria also used the argument about the creation of a "security vacuum" if there were Syrian withdrawals without an "alternative security force,"[89] thus becoming more cooperative on a solidified cease-fire as the whole withdrawal issue receded. On the committee, Algeria and Saudi Arabia pulled Morocco with them in a return to a stress on security stabilization through internal Lebanese adjustments. By mid-September, France and the Soviet Union had both abandoned an independent line, and fallen into step with the main tendency of the Arab committee. Facing mounting international and Arab pressure and, within East Beirut, restiveness in the political and religious establishment stirred by the US, 'Awn had little choice but to let the East Beirut deputies go to Ta'if. He warned them against "any treason" concerning sovereignty, and extracted assurances that they would hold fast to "withdrawals," but he obviously had few illusions about their likely drift once out of Lebanon.

At Ta'if, the Saudis and Americans quickly got to work on the Christian deputies. Saudi Foreign Minister Sa'ud al-Faysal told them that Syrian acceptance of the Arab draft, including relatively moderate political reforms, hinged on the existing wording of the "extension of sovereignty" clause, which was reached after long negotiations with Damascus.[90] An American diplomat was on hand with the same message: the clause could not be changed. West Beirut deputies refused any linkage of Syrian withdrawals to reforms, while the more radical "Islamic and nationalist" parties gathered in Tehran to attack the emerging Ta'if compact as "consecrating sectarian privileges." Some said Syria allowed such a gathering to proceed to highlight its own "moderation." Toward the end of the conference, Sa'ud al-Faysal traveled to Damascus for consultations with Syrian leaders. The Syrians were prepared for a reduction in the size of the new Lebanese Parliament, at the expense of their Shi'i and Druze allies, but rejected any alteration in the highly favorable provisions for their own strategic interests. The Saudis concentrated on converting Phalangist chief George Sa'ada, deploying the draft's substantial "holding of the line" for Christian and non-Christian traditionalist prerogatives, unwritten "secret" assurances about eventual Syrian withdrawals, and perhaps even hints about the presidency for Sa'ada. Sa'ada finally decided that the draft document represented the best deal available to keep radicalism at bay. At the closing ceremonies 58 of the 62 deputies signed the accord, including all 31 Christians.

Despite impressive international endorsement, the Ta'if Accord did not face an easy passage in Beirut. Ta'if reconciled Syria to the traditional Christian and Muslim political class: Christians were not depressed below a 50% role in parliament or the new executive cabinet; the abolition of political sectarianism was delayed into a hazy future; and the chief individual beneficiary was the Sunni prime minister. The Druze and Shi'i communities received almost nothing; Druze aspirations for an upper house of parliament (a house for the communities) and decisive administrative decentralization were ignored, and a tacit Sunni-Maronite convergence curtailed Shi'i hopes for progression toward numerical democracy. In answer to Sunni West Beirut Premier Huss's welcome of the Ta'if result, Druze leader Walid Junblat accused Huss of "sabotaging the nationalist cause," caustically observing that Ta'if "carries the seed of new civil wars — the Maronite-Sunni alliance triumphs — tomorrow political Maronitism will remove 'Awn in one way or another."[91] Amal's Nabih Barri referred to the "Ta'if scandal."[92]

The most colorful condemnation came from Hizballah, next to 'Awn probably the main target of the Ta'if "axis." The "Voice of the Oppressed" radio station defined Ta'if as a "cargo cult" (a reference to a South Pacific messianic cult) occurrence: "the deputies will receive blessings from his [Saudi] majesty — a few hours later, Lebanese cargo planes will land in Beirut and Halat airports, discharging heavy loads of special Saudi garments, beads, rings, and other items." The accompanying comment was sarcastic, ending with a clear threat:

> This charter gives everyone the impression that the war in Lebanon broke out because of a disagreement over opening a window, parking a car, or avenging someone killed 200 years ago — it contains language that has nothing to do with the problem of someone whose rights have been usurped — the war did not break out so that the number of deputies would become 108, or so that the sons, brothers, and uncles of the deceased deputies would inherit the seats of their fathers, grandfathers, and friends — the people will ignore all those who filled their stomachs with the fattening Saudi meals — sooner or later these deputies will have to pay the bill for their treason.[93]

In East Beirut, Ta'if brought an immediate showdown between 'Awn and the traditionalist politicians. On one side, Patriarch Sufayr and the Phalanges joined the deputies in pressing acceptance of Ta'if and cooperation with West Beirut to elect a new president. They argued that the basic Christian position was sufficiently preserved, and that rejection would open a fresh round of fighting, with East Beirut standing alone. The Arab committee had hopes of making 'Awn out to be a "good nationalist," but such hopes proved fatuous, precisely because of 'Awn's nationalism. For 'Awn, Ta'if compromised "sovereignty," and beside this the matter of maintaining sectarian political status was unimportant. Large crowds began to congregate daily at Ba'abda, reaching tens of thousands in the last days of October, to hear 'Awn's pronouncements terming Ta'if "hell," "an unforgivable crime," and a "repair to a rotten regime."[94] It appeared that 'Awn's line on resisting "surrender" to Syria continued to carry much more weight with the East Beirut masses than traditionalist pragmatism, regardless of potential consequences. Most Christian deputies did not dare to return to Beirut, moving to Paris to await the call to a parliamentary session to elect the new president and ratify Ta'if. (For further discussion of the Ta'if Accord and its inter-Arab implications, see chapter on inter-Arab relations.)

BUBBLINGS IN THE CAULDRON

It quickly became evident that the Americans and Saudis intended to proceed without delay to assemble the Lebanese deputies for a presidential election, even if a neutral zone in Beirut could not be assured, and the session had to be held in Syrian-controlled territory. 'Awn reacted by abruptly dissolving parliament in early November, claiming power had devolved on his "transitional government" from President Amin Jumayyil, and declaring any further step by the "former deputies" to be void. Even in East Beirut, there was fierce controversy as to whether an interim authority could take such action, and outside East Beirut it was, of course, dismissed as having no effect. Parliamentary Speaker Husayni, with full American backing, immediately summoned the deputies to a 5 November electoral session at the Qulay'at airstrip, deep in the Syrian-dominated north. Three names had been discussed already between the Syrians and the Saudis;[95] with the shift of executive authority to the cabinet the Syrians were more relaxed on this subject. In the event, the deputies elected their northern colleague René Mu'awwad, more an American-Saudi candidate than a Syrian one.

Mu'awwad was a first-rank political figure from Zgharta, the center of the semiautonomous fiefdom of ex-president Sulayman Faranjiyya. Faranjiyya, though an old and trusted friend of the Syrian president, had been suspected by West Beirut leaders as having sympathies with 'Awn during the siege. Faranjiyya hated Ja'ja' and the LF militia because of their responsibility for the death of his son in 1978. Overall, Mu'awwad had the assets of a local power base, something of a buffer against Syria and the militias, a conciliatory approach, and international backing, though the latter could be expected to weaken. In his inaugural speech, Mu'awwad pledged himself to form a broad government, with the hint of a door left ajar for 'Awn.[96]

Mu'awwad lived only 16 days after his election. During that time, some very strange crosscurrents affected Lebanese politics. Syria displayed commitment to the emerging regime; within 48 hours Vice President 'Abd al-Halim Khaddam had invited himself on a tour of the north, blustering in his habitual fashion that "our help will not be small — Syria will give any assistance requested by the National Unity Government for extension of its authority to every part of Lebanon."[97] The Syrian leadership also emphasized its preference for a government led by Huss, and dragooned Junblat, Barri, and even Hizballah into superficial compliance with Ta'if.[98] Iraq had promised the Arab committee to suspend weapons shipments to East Beirut and not to oppose the Mu'awwad regime, but in reality encouraged 'Awn's defiance — 'Awn had no imminent need for extra weaponry. Israel did not reveal its position, waiting to see if Mu'awwad had any potential for limited autonomy from Syria.

Inside East Beirut, the LF militia gravitated toward its Phalangist associates and maneuvered for inclusion in the proposed National Unity Government, while 'Awn's hold on the population only increased as he appeared to drift into an unviable political stance. One crowd, for example, invaded the Maronite Patriarchate at Bkirki, and angrily confronted Patriarch Sufayr regarding his support for Ta'if. Sufayr was disgracefully manhandled in the encounter, and promptly left East Beirut for the north. As for the Phalanges, 'Awn threatened to occupy their headquarters, which brought LF militiamen into the streets in readiness for confrontation with the Army. Ja'ja' described Ta'if as positive and a West Beirut "source" indicated to al-Safir that he would be a government minister,[99] yet there were hidden obstacles to LF entry into a Mu'awwad Administration — perhaps a veto from Faranjiyya, perhaps a fear of East Beirut implications, perhaps a tug from Iraq? Thus, the LF could not yet cut away completely from 'Awn and take their revenge for his subordinating them. 'Awn himself did not slacken in his public rejections of the new order: "Do you believe in a Syrian withdrawal in the presence of a government and a parliament formed by Syria? Why was I absent from Ta'if? Why were the key Lebanese figures, who represent the

Lebanese people, ignored? There must be a fraud."[100] According to one well-informed source, however, quiet indirect contacts proceeded between Mu'awwad and 'Awn, on 'Awn's integration into the new structure and on promoting a Syrian pullback in the rural north.[101] The Syrians might have become suspicious of such contacts.

On 22 November, conditions were abruptly transformed, when Mu'awwad was killed in West Beirut by a car bomb, before even forming a government. Accusing fingers pointed in a number of directions. In Hizballah terminology, whether or not the fundamentalists were involved, Mu'awwad had "paid the bill."

The Syrians now tried to "crack" East Beirut psychologically with a series of quick political and military moves. With American cooperation, the deputies were promptly assembled in Shtura, the Syrian military nerve center, and Ilyas al-Hirawi, a Zahla deputy chiefly interesting for his connections with both Syria and the LF militia, was elected president without opposition. On 26 November, Hirawi announced a government headed by Huss and consisting primarily of parliamentarians. This time there was no pretense about broad consultations; some of the government members, for example Phalangist leader Sa'ada and Amal's Barri, only heard about their appointments on the radio. Two days later, the government dismissed 'Awn as army commander, replacing him with Emil Lahhud, who had left East Beirut some months before. Before the end of November, more than 7,000 Syrian troop reinforcements crossed Dahr al-Baydar amid talk of a military operation to capture Ba'abda and end 'Awn's "rebellion." Lahhud's command called on 'Awn's brigades to transfer allegiance immediately.

The Syrian bubble quickly burst. 'Awn declared his intention to fight, even with "kitchen knives," and the East Beirut brigades remained steadfast in their loyalties. Further, in a most extraordinary manifestation of mass popular feeling, many tens of thousands of East Beirutis formed a human wall around Ba'abda. By early December, the numbers perhaps exceeded 150,000, which apparently unnerved Syrian leaders.[102] Despite the widespread international approval for Ta'if, Syria also had foreign relations problems in taking any action. The Vatican, which exhibited more sympathy for 'Awn than for Ta'if, watched Damascus coldly, and the French hastened to inform Hirawi of their view that any "call for Syrian assistance" in a military operation contradicted "the spirit of Ta'if."[103] The US, according to some reports not against a "limited military move" after Hirawi's election,[104] soon feared a "massacre" and discouraged the idea.

Other factors were decisive in themselves. Given 'Awn's armed capacity and East Beirut's geography, as already discussed, the additional Syrian manpower was insufficient for a credible ground operation, even limited to the Ba'abda area. Conditions would have been different if supposed international backing for the new political framework had meant a weakening of "red lines" concerning aerial support for a land push. Syrian aircraft tested the matter in overflights of East Beirut, but the Israelis promptly indicated that their strategic imperatives stood regardless of Lebanese regime technicalities, and that Syrian air force deployment risked an Israeli response. In contrast to their view of Mu'awwad, Israeli officials had no doubt about Hirawi's status as a Syrian "stooge."[105] It is likely that in the last days of November, Syrian army commanders seriously considered a quick strike,[106] presumably including helicopters and air power, but Asad had to accept the deterring elements.

Hirawi's chief contribution to the drama, as the new figurehead of the "Ta'if regime," consisted of threats to parallel the Syrian military posture, slipping from being in Ba'abda "in 48 hours" to "not excluding a military act" as the Syrian impetus declined. Without the Syrians, the Hirawi-Huss government was militarily threadbare, as Lahhud's "army" could hardly muster three usable battalions.

Unlike Mu'awwad, Hirawi had no personal power base, being a Maronite from a largely Greek Catholic town, and the family business and lands in the Biqa' were vulnerable to Syrian interference. According to one well-informed Zahla source,[107] Hirawi only communicated seriously with the Syrians about the presidency in the month before the Ta'if conference, the path being smoothed by a nephew well connected with the Damascus apparatus. Links with the LF militia in East Beirut were long-standing; Hirawi had become a Zahla contact for LF founder Bashir Jumayyil in the early 1980s. As for political competence, Hirawi's posturing in the first week after the Shtura election demonstrated a notable noncomprehension of political and military realities. In any case, Premier Salim al-Huss was to be the leading government personality.

Toward the end of 1989, the most disturbing feature of the Lebanese central political arena was no longer the direct 'Awn-Syria confrontation, but the almost complete alienation of East Beirut's poles of authority from each other. First, a prominent group of Christian deputies now formed a vital component of the Hirawi-Huss government. Buoyed by international recognition, fearful of living under Syrian patronage on non-Christian territory, and anxious to return to East Beirut to enjoy the fruits of high status in the new system, these people sought any available lever to get 'Awn out of Ba'abda. With no military option except Syria, unacceptable in the Christian context, this meant diplomatic, economic, and publicity warfare to undermine 'Awn in East Beirut.

Second, asymmetry and estrangement between the Army — with its massive popular support — and the LF-Phalangist complex — with its large apparatus, but thoroughly marginal in public opinion terms — put East Beirut's whole structure at risk. On 29 November, while committing the LF to stand with the Army "to defend the eastern area until the end," Ja'ja' observed that "President Ilyas al-Hirawi is the son of the eastern area, which remains in his heart and mind. We are relying on President al-Hirawi in particular to protect the eastern area."[108] The LF felt more confident about a deal with Hirawi than with Mu'awwad, and thus now had even more reason to stall on questioning Ta'if, which in turn magnified 'Awn's anger and suspicion. The LF concept was that once Hirawi was planted in East Beirut he could be detached from Syria and, with his international acceptability, used as a cover for perpetuated LF domination of the enclave, i.e., an updated version of the 1976–82 Sarkis period.[109] Objectively, the notion could not work; the Maronite president was not the real pinnacle of the "Ta'if regime," and Asad had absorbed the lessons of past experience.[110] Syria, however, had good reason to encourage Hirawi to be receptive. 'Awn, for his part, through December and early January came gradually to the view that coexistence with the LF as an autonomous power center had finally become impossible.

ANOTHER LEBANON: SHI'I AFFAIRS AND THE SOUTH

HARB AL-SHAQIQAYN: THE WAR OF BROTHERS

For Lebanon's Shi'is, West Beirut's largest communal bloc and the majority population of South Lebanon and the Biqa', 1989 represented a second year of inconclusive struggle between the Amal movement and Hizballah for mastery of the community. As Syria dominated West Beirut and the Biqa', and as the south contained the primary Shi'i population concentration, the contest for "political decision" in the community necessarily meant a contest for preeminence in the south. Apart from the division between secularism and religious orthodoxy, there was also the central ideological issue of orientation toward the "Israeli enemy." Amal, despite theoretical commitment to liberation of the "security zone," had no interest in Arab-Israeli matters beyond South Lebanon, and sought order and quiet to stabilize its shaky local dominance. This dictated avoidance of provoking the Israelis as much as possible. Hizballah, on the other hand, viewed itself as being in total confrontation with Israel, and sought to use the south as a theater for maximum provocation of the "enemy." Amal's character as a loosely coordinated aggregation of political tendencies further contributed to tension by encouraging Hizballah infiltration as well as attracting competing foreign influences — Syrian, Palestinian, Iranian, and Israeli.

In March 1988, Amal launched a successful offensive against Hizballah in the Nabatiyya area, center of the Shi'i south. It was followed in May by a Hizballah onslaught on Amal in the southern suburbs of Beirut, where Syrian intervention enabled Amal to hold out. By the end of the year, Amal was increasing pressure on the main surviving fundamentalist bastion in South Lebanon east of the Baruk mountain — the high villages of the Tuffah region, inland from Sidon (see map No. 3, Inter-Shi'i Conflict in South Lebanon, 1989). Amal leaders argued that Hizballah had plans to expand southward to Jarju', in the direction of Nabatiyya,[111] and on 22 December 1988 secured their rear positions facing the Palestinians in Sidon by an agreement with 'Arafat's Fath. This arrangement relieved a long-standing constriction of Amal communications around Sidon. It was conveniently facilitated by 'Arafat's suspension of Fath military activities against Israel, which for the first time enabled the Amal and Fath approaches regarding the south to converge. In parallel, Palestinian factions rejecting 'Arafat's diplomatic maneuvers consulted closely with Hizballah about maintaining South Lebanon "resistance" bases, as indicated by a mid-December "Palestinian-Islamic" meeting in West Beirut's Carlton Hotel.[112]

In such an atmosphere, minor incidents in Beirut's southern suburbs sufficed to spark a renewal of heavy fighting on 31 December, extending to the Tuffah villages on 2 January. Amal advanced from Jarju' toward Jiba',[113] while each side accused the other of "Zionist" connections and reintroducing the Palestinian factor into local conflicts. On 8 January, Hizballah, compressed into a small pocket between Amal forces and the Israeli-backed SLA (see map No. 3, Inter-Shi'i Conflict in South Lebanon, 1989), but with some hundreds of fighters and a topographic advantage on the Safi hills, launched a sudden attack westward, taking five villages and reaching halfway toward Sidon. Amal had to respond promptly, as the thrust potentially impinged on sensitive alignments in the Sidon area. By the next day, using armored vehicles, Amal had returned to the fringes of Jiba'. Both sides then gathered reinforcements, Amal concentrating more than 1,000 troops and Hizballah bringing

500 from the Biqa'.[114] At this point, however, bad weather and Syrian-Iranian consultations intervened, and the hostilities degenerated into static exchanges with no further significant geographical shifts before a 25 January cease-fire. At least 140 had died in the month's clashes.

Four non-Lebanese actors had immediate interests in the Amal-Hizballah conflict. Syria, though technically Amal's patron, also found connections with the fundamentalists serviceable and perceived no particular benefit in victory for either side. In the south, the Syrians preferred the status quo, with a leading role for Amal, but with maintenance of the radical option in advance of wider ME "deals." As regards Beirut's southern suburbs, Syria wanted to avoid taking full security control, which would have meant confronting the fundamentalists, assuming full responsibility for the foreign hostages, and greatly disturbing the strategic relationship with Iran, which was still useful for leverage in the Arab world. Syria thus tolerated Amal-Hizballah altercations, as long as these did not have implications for the general situation in West Beirut. Matters were different in the Biqa', the location of the main military dispositions covering the Syrian border, where the Syrian Army moved swiftly to curb any obstreperous Hizballah behavior.[115]

The Iranian position was complicated by the clear emergence of two major tendencies in the Iranian leadership since the later phases of the Gulf War. The rising "pragmatic" group, promoted by House Speaker Rafsanjani and backed by President Khameneh'i, downgraded the idea of an "Islamic Republic" in Lebanon, made openings to Amal, and cooperated with Damascus to dampen inter-Shi'i rivalry. In contrast, potent radical forces championed by Interior Minister Mohtashemi continued a total alignment with Hizballah, and deeply suspected Syria's Byzantine maneuvers between Iran, the Arabs, and the US. As a result, despite a very favorable reception in Tehran in early January for the Amal-connected Shi'i religious leader Muhammed Mehdi Shams al-Din, Amal maintained the view that Iran sought monopoly influence amongst the Lebanese Shi'i, a view which inspired such hostile comment as "Iran must leave [Lebanon] as our people reject it."[116] At the same time, the Rafsanjani trend did not please some in Hizballah, who asserted that only they, not Tehran, could find a solution to the inter-Shi'i problem.[117] Overall, Iran, in a somewhat weakened regional position, aimed to preserve its Lebanese assets without the former expansionary impetus. This, at least temporarily, eased the interaction with Syria.

Various Palestinians, as noted, made their arrangements with the two sides, and some Lebanese believed that 'Arafat's Fath aspired to exploit the fighting to achieve a geographical extension outside Sidon, at first as a "separation force" between Amal and Hizballah.[118] Israel, as always, monitored events closely, but made no visible moves. Amal's new link with 'Arafat obviously annoyed Israeli officials, who were also concerned about possibilities for Palestinian expansion created by the conflict. On the other hand, the fighting in the Tuffah region diverted "resistance" energies from the Israeli-SLA "security zone" and the Jizzin salient.

Joint worry about unpredictable implications of escalation in the Amal-Hizballah hostilities brought strong pressures from Syria and the Iranian "pragmatic" camp for an agreement to perpetuate the existing Shi'i political and military balance. On 29 January, the Syrian and Iranian foreign ministers drew up a draft text and urged it on leaders of the two sides, who had been summoned to Damascus. Amal and Hizballah accepted the document, which called for a "joint operations room to coordinate activities against Israel," recognized "the right of the two sides to conduct operations independently," and confirmed Amal as "responsible for security in the south."[119] These clauses contained glaring contradictions, but a measure of exhaustion added to the Syrian-Iranian coalescence proved enough to enable the conflict to be formally suspended in early February.

Between March and December 'Awn's war and general concentration on primary West-East Beirut issues helped prolong the truce between the Shi'i parties. Syria was forceful on the undesirability of fratricide behind the West Beirut lines, though it had no chance of forming any real combination against 'Awn. In July, Amal and Hizballah issued a joint statement from Tehran against "the regime based on sectarian privileges and Michel 'Awn's gang, who are protected by Zionists and the criminal Iraqi regime."[120] During the same month, the two parties clashed repeatedly in the West Beirut streets, even as East and West Beirut bombed each other. The "joint operations room" of the Damascus agreement was forgotten, and further shifts in Iran toward "pragmatism" after Ayatollah Khomeyni's death on 3 June caused some to talk of a "crisis" in the "Islamic movement" in Lebanon.[121] Hizballah appeared on the defensive regarding the Ta'if arrangements and attempts to establish a new central regime.

A resumption of serious inter-Shi'i trouble coincided with the recession of the Syrian threat to 'Awn in early December. Unusually, the first major incident came in the south Biqa', with an Amal-Hizballah fight in Mashghara and Suhmur on 6 December, causing an Amal reverse and Syrian intervention. Two days later, heavy clashes occurred in the Beirut suburbs, and the two sides began organizing and assembling forces in the Tuffah region.[122] At dawn on 23 December, Hizballah struck out from the Safi hills in an almost exact repeat of its 8 January attack, bringing a similar Amal response, though with less ground recovered. The second Tuffah battle continued into 1990, with no decision like the first.

This time the conflict had a more active Palestinian adjunct, as Fath took the opportunity to reach out of Sidon. On 14 December, Palestinian fighters attacked a Syrian position north of the Awali River and, as the Tuffah hostilities continued, 'Arafat's men manipulated Palestinian contacts with the two sides to have a Palestinian buffer force inserted. Real fears now arose about possible Palestinian ambitions to create a "canton" east and north of Sidon.

PROJECTIONS OF ISRAELI POWER
The year 1989 saw no significant challenge to the border "security zone" policed by the 2,500-man SLA militia buttressed by Israeli troops, or to Israel's general geostrategic domination of South Lebanon. 'Awn preoccupied the Syrians; Fath, the largest organization in the Sidon Palestinian redoubt, withdrew from "armed struggle" to pursue its diplomatic option; and Hizballah faced competing priorities. Radical Lebanese and Palestinian groups continued to raid SLA positions and, less frequently, to bother the Israelis, but the level rarely rose above the routine. On the ground, Israel responded with only two modest raids, a penetration of the Hizballah's south Biqa' base area in the direction of Maydun, and a commando assault on the Lebanese Communist Party (LCP), also in the south Biqa'. Israel also made 15 air attacks, causing about 40 deaths,[123] less than half the 1988 toll. Twelve of these were on radical Palestinian organizations, including five on facilities occupied by Ahmad Jibril's

Popular Front for the Liberation of Palestine-General Command (PFLP-GC), an extremist splinter patronized by Syria. No raids were made on Fath.

Within the "security zone," Israel attempted to expand SLA recruitment from the Shi'ites and Druze, and fenced off some lands as "military areas," leading to vociferous local protest. In particular, the Israelis came into conflict with the Sunni village of Shib'a, on the Hermon slopes near the Golan border. Shib'a refused to participate in a "civil administration" plan and, in January, the Israelis expelled 65 villagers viewed as inconvenient. In April, territory used by 300 Shib'a farmers was fenced off.[124]

Israel's larger-scale influence in the Lebanese arena in 1989 concerned two matters: quiet fine-tuning to discourage any Syrian thoughts of attempting a strategic coup in Beirut, and interactions with Lebanese Shi'is and Iranians affecting the issue of foreign hostages. The first has been discussed, apart from some interesting air-raid details. The largest raid of the year targeted a PFLP-GC base close to primary Syrian military concentrations north of Zahla, coinciding with the initial artillery exchanges between East Beirut and the Syrians in March. Another attack, in December, came in the midst of the Syrian strategic alignment in the central Biqa' against the LCP. Such target selection appears to have been part of the "signals" system to put the Syrians off balance.[125] Israel also refrained from major air activity in September to avoid creating a diversion which might rescue Syria from its international difficulties following the Suq al-Gharb battle.[126]

As regards the foreign hostages held by Hizballah offshoots, Israel dramatically returned the issue to international prominence with the 28 July abduction of Shaykh 'Abd al-Karim 'Ubayd, reportedly an important Hizballah operative, from his South Lebanon home (for details, see chapter on armed operations). This came after the failure of "enormous efforts" by Israeli officials to achieve a deal for the release of two Israeli soldiers captured by Shi'i radicals, efforts presumably including contacts with Iran.[127] The radicals replied by displaying the body of hostage American Col. William Higgins and threatening to murder another hostage if 'Ubayd and others were not released. Hizballah ruled out any exchange with Israel in a bid to drive a wedge between Israel and the US, as Israel had not consulted Washington before seizing 'Ubayd. The Americans grumbled about the Israeli action, but indicated that more murders of hostages by the fundamentalists would bring a military strike, and dispatched a naval force (see also chapter on the US and the ME). Meanwhile, the Israelis claimed that interrogation of 'Ubayd had revealed his role in the Higgins kidnapping and his intimate knowledge of Hizballah activities.

All this worried the Syrians, who had no wish for additional external complications at the height of their confrontation with 'Awn. Also, the "pragmatists," who now had the upper hand in Iran, faced the possible wrecking of their opening to the West. The fundamentalist kidnappers decided not to take further steps, and the crisis subsided. Interstate contacts over the hostage issue, including Syria and Iran, returned to subterranean depths, but the Israelis had a new bargaining card, and for Syria and Iran the antics of the kidnappers were becoming an embarrassment.

NOTES

For the place and frequency of publications cited here, and for the full name of the publication, news agency, radio station, or monitoring service where an abbreviation is used, please see "List of Sources." Only in the case of more than one publication bearing the same name is the place of publication noted here.

1. VoA, Arabic service, 12 August 1989.
2. *FT*, 18 August 1989.
3. Author's interview with senior PSP source, January 1990.
4. In early 1989, the 10 army brigades were distributed as follows:

Brigade	Area	Principal Sect	Manpower
First	Biqa'	Shi'i	3,000
Second	Tripoli	Sunni/Christian	3,000
Sixth	West Beirut	Shi'i	4,500
Seventh (1/2)	Batrun	Christian	1,000
Eleventh	Hammana	Druze	1,100
Twelfth	Sidon	Sunni	2,500
Fifth, Eighth)			
Ninth, Tenth)	East Beirut	Christian,	c.15,000
Seventh (1/2))		20% Sunni, Shi'i	
Commando units)			

SOURCE: Author's interviews, fieldwork in Beirut.

5. 'Awn to *al-Nahar,* Beirut, 6 January 1989.
6. Author's fieldwork, interviews at Yarza.
7. 'Awn's inner circle comprised such people as Kalas (commander of the eighth brigade); Sassim (head of the military police); Shahin (commander of the commandos); Shihab (chief of the intelligence, *al-maktab al-thani*); Fawzi Abu Farhat, Fu'ad 'Awn, 'Izzat Haddad (officers), and Simon Khoury (a lawyer).
8. One Druze officer noted 'Awn's interest in a "Belgian solution"; *The Observer,* 20 August 1989.
9. The committee consisted of Kuwait, Tunisia, Sudan, Algeria, Jordan, and the United Arab Emirates. Syria did not even request inclusion, reportedly confident that its Lebanese allies would not or could not desert (Sarkis Na'um in *al-Nahar,* Beirut, 14 January 1989).
10. Ibid., 12 January 1989.
11. Ibid., 14 February 1989.
12. Ibid., 1 February 1989.
13. Ibid., 15 February 1989.
14. Author heard this from a source close to the Army, Beirut, January 1990.
15. *Al-Nahar,* Beirut, 18 February 1989. Na'um quotes 'Awn supporters as saying "you can't fry an omelet without breaking eggs."
16. *Le Monde,* 19–20 February; *al-Nahar,* Beirut, 17 February 1989.
17. *Al-Nahar,* Beirut, 18 February 1989. Ja'ja' even remarked that "the Lebanese Forces won't remain if the reason for their existence has gone."
18. *Tishrin,* 20 February 1989.
19. *Al-Thawra,* Damascus, 25 September 1988.
20. *Al-Nahar,* Beirut, 21 February 1989.
21. Huss on R. Lebanon, 23 February — DR, 24 February 1989. In the north, Robert Faranjiyya spoke of transferring Sila'ta to the "legitimate authority."
22. *Al-Nahar,* Beirut, 3 March 1989.
23. Ibid., 24 February 1989.
24. *Al-Safir,* 25 February 1989.
25. Author's interview with senior PSP official, January 1990.
26. *Al-Safir,* 6 March 1989. In a speech Junblat asserted that Futayri had been killed "to keep the Druze in the mountain on the same path as the Maronites," *al-Nahar,* Beirut, 8 March 1989.

27. *Al-Nahar,* Beirut, 7 March 1989.
28. *Al-Safir,* 6 March 1989.
29. Ibid., 13 March 1989.
30. Ibid., 9 March 1989.
31. 'Awn's "address to the nation," VoL, 17 March — DR, 21 March 1989.
32. *Al-Nahar,* Beirut, 18 March 1989.
33. Ibid., 15 March 1989.
34. Author's interview with 'Awn, May 1989.
35. In an 18 April interview with the VoL, 'Awn referred to Asad as follows: "What remains to be broken is the head of Asad. How long will this criminal continue his bombardment? Nevertheless, Lebanon will be his graveyard and that of his regime." DR, 18 April 1989.
36. *Al-Nahar,* Beirut, 25 March 1989. Asad toured the Maghrib and Foreign Minister Faruq al-Shar' was dispatched to Paris.
37. 'Awn is quoted as "refusing to link a possible Syrian withdrawal with a withdrawal of the Israeli Army from South Lebanon," VoL, 24 March — DR, 24 March 1989.
38. *Al-Safir,* 5 May 1989.
39. Ibid., 10 April 1989; Sa'ada is reported as observing: "'Awn's decision was spontaneous, and furthermore he is alone in it."
40. *Al-Safir,* 19 April 1989.
41. Ibid., 24 April 1989. Madani's column accepted this in quoting East Beirut deputies: "Political leaders and media in West Beirut have participated in inflaming public opinion in East Beirut against them [the deputies] by representing positions in the Bkirki communiqué in such a way as to make them appear as contradicting East Beirut popular feeling."
42. See, for example, interview with Patriarch Sufayr in *Libération,* 22–23 April — DR, 27 April 1989.
43. On contacts between Syria and Egypt regarding Lebanon prior to the Arab summit, see *al-Safir,* 29 May 1989.
44. Ibid., 26 May 1989.
45. The Murphy-Asad agreement of September 1988; *al-Safir,* 29 May 1989, Madani on the Fahd-Asad and Saudi-Syrian understandings regarding parallelism of reforms and elections, December 1988.
46. Author's impressions from Ba'abda, May 1989.
47. Observations to author by a former senior Jumayyil adviser, June 1989.
48. Senior PSP official remarked to the author: "No one likes the Syrians," January 1990.
49. 'Awn's interview with *al-Ra'y,* Amman, 31 August — DR, 10 April 1989:

    Q. Can we conclude that you are more Lebanese than Maronite?
    A. Yes, because I have a different view of authority. My concept of reform also differs from the current one and from that of the school of thought that has dominated Lebanon since 1920 or 1943.

50. Junblat's interview with Voice of the Mountain, 8 April — DR, 10 April 1989.
51. *Al-Nahar,* Beirut, 1 April 1989 (Huss). The book was entitled *The Army Remains the Solution.*
52. 'Awn's interview with *al-Qabas,* 3 July — DR, 7 July 1989.
53. *Al-Nahar,* 30 March — Mufti appeal to Kuwaiti Foreign Minister Al Sabah; *al-Safir,* 18 May — last act of Mufti telegram to King Hasan of Morocco appealing for Arab help for Lebanon.
54. *Al-Safir,* 4 April, refers to misleading reports sent to 'Awn from a Victor Musa, supposedly close to the Administration, about prospects for American backing regarding the exit of foreign forces. American reserve apparently came as a surprise to Ba'abda. See also David Ottaway in *IHT,* 2 May 1989, "US Policy in Lebanon: Once Burnt, Twice Shy."
55. Assistant secretary of state Lawrence Eagleburger, quoted by *al-Nahar,* Beirut, 16 March; ibid., 18 March 1989 for 'Awn's angry reply.
56. For example, on 1 June 1989 a House of Representatives' panel issued a resolution condemning Syria. Deputy assistant secretary of state Edward Walker tartly observed that "we would simply point out that Syrian withdrawal doesn't resolve all of Lebanon's problems"; WF, 1 June 1989.

57. Indicated in White House statement after Bush's meeting with Saudi Foreign Minister Sa'ud al-Faysal, 14 June; WF, 14 June 1989.
58. The author heard such concern in East Beirut. Also see I. Rabinovich, "Paralysis in Lebanon," *Current History,* Vol. 89, No. 544, 1989.
59. *The Economist,* 24 February-2 March 1990. Also, author's fieldwork in Beirut.
60. Ze'ev Schiff supports this view in *Ha'aretz,* 17-18 August 1989.
61. *Al-Nahar,* Beirut, 6 July 1989 — Syrian demands through Western and Arab channels for withdrawal of any missiles that might have arrived. 'Awn found the uncertainty of the affair useful for morale and propaganda purposes, though later investigation by Western intelligence agencies could not establish physical evidence for the presence of the missiles.
62. As indicated to the author by a source close to 'Awn.
63. Author's discussions with Israeli officials.
64. *Al-Safir,* 1 April 1989.
65. *Al-Qabas,* 3 July — DR, 7 July 1989.
66. Observation to author.
67. Indications to author in East Beirut and Israel.
68. Author observed this personally. *Al-Safir,* 25 May 1989, quotes Uri Lubrani (Israeli coordinator for Lebanese matters), as saying: "We expected a Syrian attack a few days ago, but nothing happened."
69. *Ha'aretz,* 17–18 August 1989.
70. *Al-Nahar,* Beirut, 8 August 1989.
71. Ibid., 19 July 1989.
72. Ibid., 28 July 1989.
73. Ibid., 17 August; *Ha'aretz,* 17–18 August 1989, reported the influx of 600 refugees per day from Beirut into the "security zone" in early- to mid-August.
74. *Al-Nahar,* Beirut, 17 August 1989, gives a preliminary survey from various viewpoints.
75. Ibid., 18 August 1989. Ze'ev Schiff analyzed the evolution of Israeli "red line" definitions in "weekly roundup," *Ha'aretz,* 17–18 August 1989. Intelligence assessments prepared for the 19 August Israeli cabinet meeting agreed that "Syria froze its attack in Lebanon due to international pressure, but Syria would renew its military activities if international pressure ceased," ibid., 24–25 August 1989.
76. Fadlallah's interview with *La Repubblica,* 28 August — DR, 31 August 1989.
77. *Al-Nahar,* Beirut, 1 August 1989.
78. Arab committee communiqué specifically noted the points of disagreement — DR, 1 August 1989.
79. *Al-Nahar,* Beirut, 9 August 1989.
80. Ibid., 18 September 1989.
81. 'Awn's interview with *al-Qabas,* 3 July — DR, 7 July 1989.
82. Text of the Ta'if Accord in *al-Safir,* 23 October 1989. An excellent critical commentary on the accord is to be found in *Muqarrarat al-Ta'if wa Huquq al-Insan* ("The Ta'if Decisions and Human Rights," Beirut: Institute for Human Rights in Lebanon, 1990).
83. *Al-Nahar,* Beirut, 21 August 1989.
84. *Al-Qabas,* 29 August — DR, 31 August 1989.
85. *Al-Nahar,* Beirut, 2 September 1989.
86. Ibid., 16 September 1989 (Emil Khoury column, quoting political sources close to Damascus).
87. Ibid., 2, 4 September 1989.
88. *IHT,* 9–10 September (Jim Hoagland referred to "reliable sources" on the matter of prior discussion about withdrawing embassy staff); *al-Nahar,* Beirut, 7 September 1989 (Na'um's analysis on reasons for embassy closure).
89. *Al-Nahar,* Beirut, 16 September 1989.
90. Ibid., 7 October 1989.
91. Ibid., 24 October 1989.
92. Ibid., 21 October 1989.
93. Voice of the Oppressed, 24 October — DR, 26 October 1989.
94. *Al-Nahar,* Beirut, 25 October (on demonstration numbers) and 26 October 1989.
95. Ibid., 27 October 1989.

96. Ibid., 6 November 1989. Perhaps significantly, the Syrian-influenced *al-Safir* did not report some of Mu'awwad's remarks (*al-Safir*, 6 November 1989).

97. *Al-Safir*, 8 November 1989.

98. Ibid., 13, 20 November 1989.

99. Ibid., 15 November 1989.

100. 'Awn's interview with *al-Anwar*, 18 November — DR, 21 November 1989.

101. Author's discussion with Abbot Bulos Na'aman, East Beirut, January 1990.

102. As heard by author, January 1990.

103. *Al-Safir*, 30 November 1989.

104. *Al-Nahar*, Beirut, 1 December 1989.

105. Author's discussion with senior Israeli source, February 1990.

106. Certainly this was the Israeli view, as heard by the author. Na'um gives an interesting analysis of factors deterring the Syrians in *al-Nahar*, Beirut, 25 December 1989.

107. Observations to author, January 1990.

108. Ja'ja' to Voice of Free Lebanon, 29 November — DR, 30 November 1989.

109. LF High Command member to author, East Beirut, January 1990.

110. *Al-Nahar*, Beirut, 23 February 1990.

111. *Al-Safir*, 5 January 1990.

112. Ibid., 11 January 1990.

113. *Al-Nahar*, Beirut, 4 January 1990, reporting 'Ayn Abu Suwar as not being under direct control of either side.

114. Ibid., 10 January 1990.

115. Syrian military intelligence watched closely for attempts "to spread dissension to the Biqa'" (*al-Nahar*, Beirut, 13 January 1990), and on 16 January Syrian troops acted against Hizballah in Suhmur, in the south Biqa'.

116. *Al-Nahar*, Beirut, 11 January 1990.

117. *Al-Safir*, 4 January 1990.

118. Senior PSP source to author, January 1990.

119. *Al-Nahar*, Beirut, 31 January 1989.

120. R. Tehran, 24 July — DR, 25 July 1989.

121. *Al-Nahar*'s interview with Muhammad Husayn Fadlallah, 4 December; *WP*, 28 July 1989, claimed that the $3m. monthly Iranian payment to Hizballah was being redistributed and shared with Amal and Syrian-backed factions.

122. *Al-Nahar*, Beirut, 25 December 1989.

123. Numbers derived from *al-Nahar*, Beirut, *al-Safir*, and *Ha'aretz* reports.

124. *Al-Safir*, 21, 24, 27 April 1989.

125. Senior Israeli source to author, February 1989.

126. Ze'ev Schiff in *Ha'aretz*, 14–15 September 1989.

127. Ze'ev Schiff in *Ha'aretz*, 2 August 1989.

Libya
(Al-Jamahiriyya al-ʿArabiyya al-Libiyya al-Shaʿbiyya al-Ishtirakiyya al-ʿUzma)

YEHUDIT RONEN

In 1989, the Libyan regime headed by Muʿammar al-Qadhdhafi celebrated its 20th anniversary in power. By all criteria, the event constituted a remarkable achievement — personal, political, and ideological — for the Libyan leader. Not only was the longevity of the regime highly impressive, but also its relatively stable hold on the country.

Aware that the anniversary celebrations would put his regime in the internal and, even more important, in the international limelight, Qadhdhafi in 1989 appeared more eager than ever that it should appear to be a consolidated and successful regime, and that he shed his bellicose image for one of a responsible, moderate, and peace-seeking leader.

Domestically, he continued to enhance the relaxed atmosphere which he had projected a year earlier. He adhered to the economic reforms which were designed to loosen government control over trade and to lift restrictions on travel to neighboring countries. These changes, though made without fanfare, helped the regime to placate the people and give them a greater sense of freedom. These changes were especially important given the continuing stagnation in the country's oil revenues, which were the major source of income.

Qadhdhafi's efforts, launched in early 1989 to divert international attention, which had been focused on the Jamahiriyya since the fall of 1988 because of its alleged establishment of a chemical-weapons industry, should be seen within this context. The worldwide preoccupation with this affair caused Tripoli much damage by counteracting its effort to present itself as nonmilitant and peace-loving. Qadhdhafi, quite experienced with such situations, seized upon the atmosphere of crisis to enhance his political prestige. Not only did he use the sense of threat to mobilize the people's support, but also to create favorable conditions at home for holding the annual conference of the country's ostensibly highest political authority — the General People's Congress (GPC). The conference, held in Benghazi in early March, served Qadhdhafi's political needs well by providing, first of all, additional proof that the "People's Power" political system was functioning and that the regime had firm foundations.

As had become customary, a series of changes in personnel and structure of the General People's Committee (GPCom), i.e., the Cabinet, was announced at its last session. These, however, did not signify any substantial change in domestic or foreign affairs.

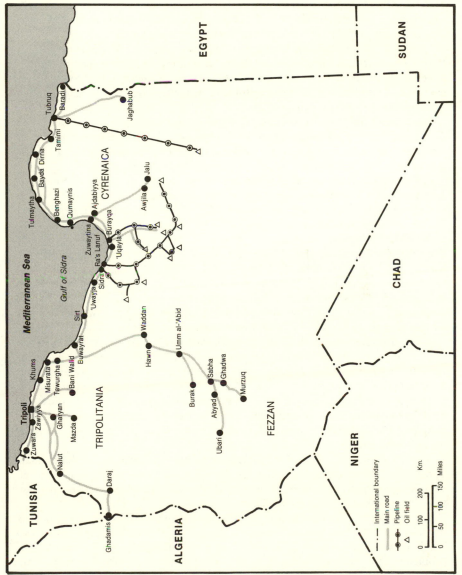

EGYPT

SUDAN

Tubruq
Baradi
Jaghabub

Tamimi

CYRENAICA

Bayda Dirna

Jalu

Tulmaytha

Benghazi
Qumaynis

Awjila

Ajdabiyya

Burayqa

Zuwaytina

Ra's Lanuf
'Uqayla

Sidra
Zuwara
'Uwayja

Sirt

Mediterranean Sea

Gulf of Sidra

CHAD

Buwayrat

Waddan

Umm al-'Abid

Khums

Hawn

Misurata

Tawurgha

Bani Walid

Burak

Sabha
Ghadwa

Tripoli

Gharyan

Murzuq

Zawiyya

Mazda

TRIPOLITANIA

Abyad

FEZZAN

Ubari

Nalut

NIGER

Daraj

TUNISIA

Ghadamis

ALGERIA

International boundary
Main road
Pipeline
Oil field

Km.
Miles

0 100 200
0 50 100 150

Libya

Despite the regime's strenuous efforts in the period under review to placate the people and assuage their grievances, Qadhdhafi faced increasing dissent by Islamic fundamentalists. While the precise scope of the dissent remained unknown, its very existence and especially its subversive activities were particularly alarming. Undoubtedly, this phenomenon was a great threat to the regime. It not only endangered Qadhdhafi's ideological revolution but also, much more seriously, challenged his political position, though not in the short term.

It remained unclear whether the two alleged attempts upon Qadhdhafi's life early in the spring and later in the summer were connected in any way to the fundamentalists. Whether they were or not, it should be added that the opposite end of the opposition spectrum, the secular expatriates, continue to be ineffective, thus leaving the stage almost entirely to the fundamentalists.

Qadhdhafi's own style of *perestroika* was also introduced into the Jamahiriyya's foreign affairs. During the whole of 1989, he sought a new accommodation with traditional enemies, both among neighboring countries and farther afield, in Black Africa and in the US.

The Arab world was accorded considerable attention as part of Libya's policies of appeasement. The most dramatic event was the reconciliation with Egypt, Tripoli's sworn enemy for about a decade and a half. In May, Egyptian President Husni Mubarak and Qadhdhafi met for talks in Casablanca, during the Arab summit conference. Additional rounds of talks between the two leaders took place in October and December. Yet, by the end of 1989, the two countries had not formally announced the resumption of diplomatic relations.

Links with Sudan remained unchanged notwithstanding the ousting, in June, of al-Sadiq al-Mahdi's government which had been close to Libya. Moreover, Tripoli succeeded immediately in establishing political rapport with the new leadership in Khartoum, seizing upon Sudan's economic and military dependence.

A new dynamism was introduced into relations with Syria, in part thanks to the latter's initiative. Tripoli enjoyed the new development, utilizing it to enhance its interests in the broader Arab scene. In Lebanon, Tripoli continued to support the Iraqi-backed Christian government of Michel 'Awn rather than the Syrian-backed Muslim government of Salim al-Huss. This, interestingly, seemed to have little effect on Libyan-Syrian reconciliation. Qadhdhafi repeatedly referred to the Lebanese quagmire during the year, providing him with a most convenient opportunity to wave his pan-Arab flag.

Nor did Qadhdhafi miss any opportunity to refer publicly to the Palestinian uprising in the Israeli-occupied territories. He was at pains to create the impression of being a staunch patron of the Palestinian cause. However, he was cautious enough not to be involved in the Intifada directly.

The African continent, too, attracted Qadhdhafi's attention. He made efforts to improve bilateral ties there, and scored noteworthy gains. One exception was the relations with Burundi, where a crisis broke out. Relations with Chad, highly problematic for years, were characterized by ups and downs in 1989. But the fact that the war between Tripoli and Ndjamena was not rekindled was in itself an important achievement.

Libya's persistent wish to establish a framework of unity in North Africa, i.e., in the Maghrib, was crowned with success. In mid-February, Libya joined Algeria, Tunisia, Morocco, and Mauritania, in forming the Arab Maghrib Union (AMU).

Qadhdhafi's desire to patch up his dispute with the US received further urgency in 1989. Tripoli hoped that the new Bush Administration would encourage, or at least welcome, an improvement in their strained relations. Washington, however, proved less enthusiastic than expected.

Political relations with the USSR and the Eastern Bloc were low-key. However, significant military deals were allegedly concluded and partially implemented between Moscow and Tripoli during 1989.

All in all, and despite the ongoing economic difficulties, the growing fundamentalist challenge, and the continuing standstill in relations with the US, Qadhdhafi had good reasons to feel more gratified in 1989 than in the earlier part of the decade. His ability to hold on to the country's reins for 20 years was the most solid proof of his extraordinary performance, which was blessed with favorable local political developments, and perhaps also, with a certain measure of good luck.

INTERNAL AFFAIRS

THE CHEMICAL-WEAPONS AFFAIR
At the end of 1988 and the beginning of 1989, Tripoli was preoccupied with refuting Washington's persistent charges that Libya was completing the construction of a chemical-weapons plant in Rabta, southwest of Tripoli. Libya clung to its explanation that the plant was confined solely to the production of pharmaceuticals. Whatever the plant's real objectives, there was no doubt that it had the potential of producing chemical weaponry. Taking these data together with Qadhdhafi's well-known bellicose behavior, it was not surprising that the issue drew a great deal of international attention for almost half a year. As expected, it also occupied a prominent position in the tightly controlled Libyan media, eclipsing almost all other domestic subjects.

While aiming his verbal aggression at Washington, which had brought the chemical-weapons affair to the fore, Qadhdhafi tried to exploit the matter to achieve political benefits at home. "Our battle is not actually the battle of the Rabta [plant] only, it is the battle of the nation's existence, its future, and its status in the world,"[1] was a typical statement released in Tripoli in early 1989, one of many that were designed mainly for Libyan domestic consumption. Strengthening the Jamahiriyya's image as a victim — a small Arab country fighting to fend off the threat of a superpower's onslaught — was meant to enhance Qadhdhafi's political prestige and heighten the Libyans' sense of national identity.

Nevertheless, the chemical-weapons controversy, its remaining the object of international concern, and, more important, the consequent mounting tension with the US, carried dangerous threats, particularly of an American military strike. (The trauma of the US air attack on Libya in 1986 was undoubtedly still fresh in Qadhdhafi's mind; see *MECS* 1986, pp. 512–13.) When all was said and done, Qadhdhafi was concerned with avoiding worsening the strain with the US. Thus, during January, trying to play down the matter, he restrained the "masses' fury" by limiting it to sit-in protests at the plant.[2] The protests, orchestrated by the authorities, were staged by "the masses" of the Basic People's Congresses (BPCs), that convened throughout the Jamahiriyya at the beginning of the year, in keeping with the annual routine. (For the BPCs' place in the "People's Power" system, see *MECS* 1976–77, pp. 526–27.) The BPCs' dealing with the chemical-plant affair, and especially with the real, or perceived,

American threat to Libya, rallied the people around Qadhdhafi and created conditions favorable to the imminent annual GPC meeting (see below).

During one of the GPC sessions, Qadhdhafi chose to clarify his stand on the subject of chemical weaponry. Underlining the importance and legitimacy of a state possessing such arms, either by production or by procurement, he said: "Whoever wants to manufacture a [chemical] weapon, let him do so....The Israelis have made chemical weapons and no one told them not to. But we have built a pharmaceutical plant...and a hue and cry was raised worldwide, and a world war nearly broke out over it." Therefore, Qadhdhafi went on, manufacturing chemical weapons "is not prohibited, because they are all manufacturing them....Any state, if an enemy enters its territory, is free to use all means of destruction against it."[3]

Qadhdhafi referred only to the case of a country defending itself, but ignored the use of chemical warfare while initiating a military offensive, as was, for example, the case of Libya's military intervention in Chad during the 1980s. When facing specially serious setbacks in its war in Chad in 1987, the Libyan Army was said to have attacked a Chadian raiding column with mustard gas (apparently supplied by Iran). Six Libyans and no Chadians died, because the wind was blowing the wrong way.[4] Qadhdhafi also ignored Iraq's continued use of chemical weapons in its war against Iran, a conflict definitely not perceived by Libya as an Iraqi defensive war.

Another possibility which Qadhdhafi chose to overlook was the use of chemical weapons as a bargaining counter for other weapons and for political influence over countries requesting the chemical matériel for their internal and external needs. Iran's supply of chemical weapons to Libya in 1987, in exchange for Soviet underwater mines,[5] illustrates such a possibility. Yet another example was Libya's allegedly supplying chemical weapons to Somalia in late 1988, which the two countries categorically denied.[6] Considering Qadhdhafi's effort at *rapprochement* with Somalia in 1988, one cannot entirely rule out the possibility that he had provided the weapons.

As implied by a foreign source based on a report by US aid agencies in southern Sudan, Libya also delivered chemical gas to the Khartoum government[7] for use in its war against Sudanese rebels in the south. (See chapter on Sudan.) The report did not give the date or quantities of gas delivered, and none of the parties allegedly involved referred to the allegation.

Later in the year, the controversy over the chemical-weapons plant disappeared from the international headlines, owing mainly to foreign factors, just as they had exposed the affair. Qadhdhafi was well served by this silence, which enabled him to devote additional efforts to project an image of a modernizing leader and to further improve his international standing.

RUNNING THE "PEOPLE'S POWER" SYSTEM
The General People's Congress Conferences
The GPC — formally the Jamahiriyya's highest political authority — was scheduled to convene once a year. In the course of 1989, however, it held four conferences.

The first, and most important, took place on 2–9 March in Benghazi, "the city of *al-Bayan al-Awal*," to coincide with the 12th anniversary of the "People's Power" system and the establishment of "history's first Jamahiriyya." (For details on Libya's becoming a Jamahiriyya and on the "People's Power" system, see *MECS* 1976–77, pp. 531–33, and subsequent volumes.) Unlike earlier occasions, Qadhdhafi attended most of the conference sessions, together with 'Abd al-Salam al-Jallud, who was known as the Libyan leader's right-hand man.[8] Their extraordinary joint appearance at the GPC sessions seemed to be a well calculated move aimed at refuting persistent claims about their rivalry. (On the alleged rivalry between them in 1986–87, see *MECS* 1987, pp. 549–50.)

Though the conference dealt with a wide spectrum of issues, its decisions did not herald any new development, neither domestically nor in foreign affairs. The long list of resolutions,[9] which only echoed Qadhdhafi's earlier ideas and policies, highlighted the GPC's major function as a rubber stamp and bestower of legitimacy to the regime's handling of the country's affairs. The conference ended with an announcement about changes in both the GPC secretariat and the GPCom (for the latter, see below). The changes in the GPC secretariat dealt only with personnel. A remarkable innovation, however, was the appointment of a woman, Salmin 'Ali al-'Uraybi, to a senior post in that body. The new composition of the GPC secretariat was announced as follows:

> Secretary-General of the GPC: Muftah al-Usta 'Umar
> Assistant Secretary of the GPC: Misbah Abu Khazzam
> Assistant Secretary of the GPC: Salmin 'Ali al-'Uraybi
> Secretary for Congresses' Affairs: 'Umar Muhammad Ishkal
> Secretary for People's Committees Affairs: Sulayman al-Shuhumi
> Secretary for Professional Congresses' Affairs: Bashir Huwayj

On 28 March, an extraordinary session of the GPC was held in Tubruq. Its aim was to formulate the decisions of the BPCs, convened throughout the country from 18-25 March regarding the ratification of the AMU, which was founded in February (see below). As expected, this forum stressed the importance of the union and detailed the Jamahiriyya's efforts to consolidate it.[10]

On 1 September, the 20th anniversary of Qadhdhafi's revolution, the GPC convened for another extraordinary session in Tripoli. Attended by visiting heads of state, the session was a highly prestigious event, designed mainly to magnify the regime's position at home and abroad. Finally on 7 October, the GPC held an "emergency" session in Tripoli. This time, the justification for convening it was Qadhdhafi's wish to mark, in a more dramatic manner, the 19th anniversary of the Italians' expulsion from Libya. Focusing the GPC's attention on the "crimes" colonialist Italy had committed against the Libyan people, Qadhdhafi stated dramatically that "we will never forgive Italy...".[11] In this case, too, the GPC forum has mainly a stage setting for the Libyan leader's political show.

All in all, the frequent meetings of the GPC served Qadhdhafi well. Not only did they strengthen the facade of the Jamahiriyya as being run by the people, they also "proved" that the "revolutionary" system was functioning properly — a significant achievement to which Qadhdhafi could point proudly on the revolution's 20th anniversary.

Changes in the General People's Committee

On 9 March, the GPC conference announced the new composition of the GPCom. The noteworthy changes were the appointment, for the first time, of a woman, Fatima

'Abd al-Mukhtar, to hold a portfolio — the Education Secretariat (equivalent of ministry) — and the appointment of an Egyptian citizen, Amin Hilmi 'Uthman Kamal — formerly Egypt's minister of industry under then-president Abdel Nasser[12] — as secretary of light industries. Both changes had mainly a symbolic nature, and were intended to highlight two of Qadhdhafi's principles: first, the need to elevate the status of women further in Libyan society and integrate them into public life and, second, the stress on the pan-Arabic character of the Jamahiriyya, which as Qadhdhafi had reiterated many times, considered itself the home of all Arabs. Presumably, the choice of an Egyptian citizen was not accidental and it was aimed at sending an additional signal to Cairo that Tripoli desired to normalize relations with it (see below).

Other important changes were the setting-up of seven new secretariats, most of which were the result of splitting up already existing portfolios. Of special significance was the creation of the new Secretariat for Revolutionary Guidance, hitherto part of the Secretariat of Information and Culture. The new ministry was responsible for administering the mosques and controlling the contents of the all-important *Khutba* Friday sermons. 'Ali al-Shahiri, known as a Qadhdhafi loyalist and a hard-line revolutionary, was "elected" head of the secretariat, although he lacked any status as a religious authority. Given the alarming growth of growing fundamentalism (see below), Qadhdhafi needed a tough, loyal, and most obedient person in this post.

The composition of the GPCom was as follows:

Portfolio:	Incumbent, 9 March 1988	Incumbent, 9 March 1989
Secretary of the GPCom	'Umar Mustafa al-Muntasir	unchanged
Health	Mustafa Muhammad al-Zaydi	unchanged
Strategic Industry	Fathi Hamad Ibn Shatwan	unchanged
Light Industries[a]		Amin Hilmi 'Uthman Kamal[b]
Treasury	Muhammad al-Madani al-Bukhari	unchanged
Economy	Farhat Sharnana	unchanged
Planning	Muhammad Lutfi Farhat	unchanged
Petroleum[a,c]		Fawzi al-Shakshuki[d]
Foreign Liaison and International Cooperation	Jadallah 'Azuz al-Talhi	unchanged
Communications and Transport	Mubarak al-Samih	unchanged
Higher Education[a,e]	Ahmad Ibrahim	unchanged
Education[a,e]		Fatima 'Abd al- Mukhtar[b]
Scientific Research[a,e]		Nuri al-Fayturi al-Madani[b]
Information and Culture	Rajab Muftah Abu Dabbus	unchanged
Maritime Resources	Muftah Muhammad Ku'ayba	unchanged
Vocational Training	Ma'tuq Muhammad Ma'tuq	unchanged
Mass Moblization and Revolotutionary Guidance[a]		'Ali al-Shahiri[b]
Justice		'Izz al-Din al-Hinshiri[b]
Agrarian Reform and Land Reclamation[a]		'Abd al-Majid al-Qa'ud[b,f]

NOTES:

a New portfolios.

b New secretaries (ministers).

c In earlier years, there was no separate portfolio for petroleum. In 1985, Shakshuki served as acting secretary of petroleum.

d Shakshuki was a member of the GPCom since 1982, holding intermittently the portfolios of Planning and Public Services. In 1989, the latter was abolished.

e In 1989, the post of Education and Scientific Research was divided into three separate portfolios: Higher Education, Education, and Scientific Research.

f A veteran political figure. Held top ministerial positions from the late 1970s to the mid 1980s.

GROWING ISLAMIC FUNDAMENTALIST DISSIDENCE

During 1989, the regime watched with alarm the growth in Islamic fundamentalism. The increase in the number of young women wearing headscarves in Tripoli's al-Fatih university and in the capital's streets, and the outspoken discussions in the mosques during the Friday prayer sessions were explicit symptoms of the phenomenon. Much clearer and more serious signs were the eruptions of fundamentalist-inspired turmoil on the university campus at the end of 1988 and on 8 January 1989, as reported by foreign sources. The January disturbances were so troubling that the security authorities had to intervene and arrest several people.[13] The tightly controlled media, however, did not mention the incident.

Qadhdhafi's strongly worded public reference to the growing impact of fundamentalism a day after the outbreak of the turmoil, added credibility to the foreign reports. "Any exploitation of religion [for political aims] will be nipped in the bud," Qadhdhafi stated, without specifying which religious groups he was warning. "The Qur'anic verses are clear and explicit. They forbid partisanship..., or sectarianism.... Anyone who calls for dogma, factionalism, or any religious ritual — any gathering of this sort would be an imitation of the Jews and the Christians. The Qur'an forbids this."[14]

On 20 January, Qadhdhafi's strict warning notwithstanding, clashes broke out between worshippers in Tripoli's mosques and members of the regime's Revolutionary Committees (RComs) — the bodies responsible both for safeguarding security and for boosting the "revolutionary" spirit throughout the country. Since 1987, it should be recalled, the RComs had taken an ever closer interest in the activities of the mosques (see *MECS* 1987, p. 550). The clashes reportedly resulted in injuries and arrests, and one mosque was thought to have been burned down.[15] The trigger for the riots and their scope remained unknown. Adhering to its policy, the official media remained silent on the event.

Later the same day — it was unclear whether there was any direct connection with the earlier clashes — unrest surfaced near Tripoli's main football stadium. Thousands of spectators, who had assembled for a World Cup match between Libya and Algeria, were incensed by an official announcement that the game would not be held. The Libyan football federation stated that in light of the planned union between Libya and Algeria, the two teams "are in fact one team" and, therefore, "no conventional competition" should be held between them. Furthermore, Libya made the gesture of awarding the game to Algeria.[16] This explanation regardless, one could not avoid the impression that by doing so, the authorities wished to prevent the outbreak of anticipated violence, given the prevailing tense atmosphere. However, the decision to cancel the match brought about the results that the move was designed to prevent. The crowd poured into the streets, chanting "God is most great" and "Qadhdhafi is the enemy of God." The Army, summoned to put down the riots, fired into the crowd, killing "at least three people."[17] According to another foreign source, the shots were fired into the air and "there were no serious incidents."[18] The local media, again, did not report the incident.

A clear indication of the perceived gravity of the situation was Qadhdhafi's warning that he would strike "mercilessly" against Islamic extremist groups, which was released on 30 January in *al-Zahf al-Akhdar,* the ideological publication of the RComs. The Libyan leader accused the extremists of "abusing religion for political ends," which he said was "tantamount to high treason." He also blamed the extremists for violent acts in eastern Libya, especially around the towns of Benghazi, Ajdabiyya, and al-Kufra.

The growing fundamendalist threat gave the Libyan leader no rest. On 8 March, he repeated in public his concern with the rising Islamic radicalism.

> Nowadays, there is hypocrisy, fear of religious men....The most dangerous thing is the continuation of the so-called tendency of moving towards politics....The religious tendencies coming to us are from Asia and from non-Arab countries. Non-Arab Muslims are spreading the Islamic calls of al-Da'wa, al-Jihad, al-Takfir wal-Hijra, al-Tabligh, the Muslim Brotherhood, and the Islamic Liberation Party [all names of fundamentalist groups active in various parts of the Middle East]....Naturally, the victim in this case is Arab nationalism, Arab unity, socialism, and progress....

These organizations, he went on, "want to obtain power in the name of religion" and they act in the interests of the Israelis and the Americans. On the same occasion Qadhdhafi attacked Salman Rushdie's book, *The Satanic Verses,* strongly denouncing its claim that "a large part of the Qur'an consists of satanic verses" (for details on the book and its international impact, see chapter on Islamic affairs). According to Qadhdhafi, "the Christian and Jewish Western countries were behind the book," exactly as they stood behind Islamic fundamentalism.[19]

Worried by the growing fundamentalism, which could pose a real threat to his leadership, Qadhdhafi ordered massive arrests of fundamentalists, mostly young people, during the spring.[20] Of the more than 4,000 taken into custody, 700 were kept incommunicado. On the night of 3–4 May, in another effort to frighten potential Islamic dissidents, 21 men were secretly executed. Another round of arrests followed several days later,[21] just before Qadhdhafi's trip to Casablanca (see below). The arrests, which should be regarded mainly as preventive measures, seemed to produce the desirable calm, at least temporarily.

Almost half a year elapsed before Qadhdhafi felt the need to put the fundamentalist issue on the public agenda once again. On 25 September, while attending the opening session of a two-day Islamic world seminar in Benghazi,[22] he delivered a speech in which he divided Islamic activities into two parts: "A fundamentalist part which wants to return to the basis of Islam and resurrect Islam once more..., [and] keep its morals and its customs"; and another, "which took a secret, violent, terrorist, and extremist trend...." Referring to the latter, he said it "does not hold dialogue, has no logic...[and] it hides in darkness, bombs, and kills...."[23] Two weeks later, Qadhdhafi revealed to the Libyan people the exposure "in the past months" of cells of the extremist groups in Ajdabiyya, Misurata, and Benghazi, which had carried out violent actions. Qadhdhafi used the occasion to elaborate a most bleak and frightening scenario of what would happen if the extremists seized power. Significantly, he referred to the fundamentalist threat as "more dangerous than cancer and Aids, even more than war with the Israelis or the Americans." Therefore, he added, "an end should be put to this....Anyone who embraces such religious hypocrisy must be outlawed....He is finished. You cannot possibly plead on his behalf....He must be crushed."[24]

Qadhdhafi seemed to be so troubled by the fundamentalist threat that he went out of his way to stress his commitment to Islam. He rejected the fundamentalists' reference to him as an infidel. "I have led the imams into prayer....I lead millions of people into prayer in Africa and I lead thousands into prayer in Libya," he stated indignantly. "How can someone come and say that we are nonbelievers? This is completely rejected by any standard, and would be resisted with every force and very firmly."[25]

Journalists who visited Tripoli in late October were told of two incidents in which fundamentalists had allegedly burst into mosques and killed eight worshippers. In one, an elderly man was beheaded in an apparent attempt at a ritual Islamic execution. On surrendering, the assassin said he regarded his victim as being a supporter of the "atheist Qadhdhafi."[26]

Most worrying to the regime was that young people were the main advocates of Islamic fundamentalism and that it apparently enjoyed support among the military. (Two years earlier, three soldiers, allegedly members of the Islamic Jihad organization, were executed by a firing squad in Benghazi; see *MECS* 1987, p. 550.) The Libyan people in general were affected by the general trend toward fundamentalism, which had developed in the ME, particularly since the outbreak of the Islamic revolution in Iran in 1979. Particularly important was the impact of the swelling tide of fundamentalism in neighboring Egypt and Algeria. Qadhdhafi's relative liberalization of travel abroad, announced in 1988, which had been enjoyed since then by more than half a million Libyan citizens,[27] apparently contributed to the growing fundamentalism. The return home of many exiled fundamentalists, especially members of the Muslim Brotherhood, who had fled the country in 1984, after their alleged attack on Qadhdhafi's headquarters and residence (see *MECS* 1983–84, pp. 585–86) may also have added to the trend. Furthermore, the return of large numbers of soldiers from the Chadian front in 1987 contributed to unemployment and dissatisfaction, which may in turn have propelled some of them toward fundamentalism.

One should also note that Qadhdhafi himself served as a spark for Islamic fundamentalism: since the end of the 1970s relations between the Libyan leader and the top religious establishment had been tense. Especially furious with him were the 'Ulama who rejected, among others, Qadhdhafi's postulate that they had no useful role within the Islamic Jamahiriyya since, as he repeated time and again, every Libyan and every Muslim could understand the Qur'an, without the need of their interpretations. He also emphasized the primacy of the Qur'an as the Muslims' sole authority and claimed that Sunna and Hadith (practices and sayings of the Prophet) were man-made and, therefore, open to error. (For more details on Qadhdhafi's concept of Islam, see *MECS* 1977–78, pp. 633–34.) Qadhdhafi had also caused urban religious circles economic difficulties while he was implementing his "revolutionary" concept of socialism during the late 1970s (see *MECS* 1977–78, pp. 631–34).

Thus, in 1989, the fundamentalist dissidence seemed to be a major threat to Qadhdhafi's hold on power. The fact that Islam has always provided an attractive prescription for coping with undesirable governments, which the extremists considered as illegitimate — and, more seriously, for their removal — undoubtedly rang a bell with Qadhdhafi.

ATTEMPTS UPON QADHDHAFI'S LIFE

The expatriate Libyan opposition continued to be ineffective, weakened as it was by additional fragmentation and personal rivalries. About 15 opposition groupings resided abroad during 1989,[28] but there was almost no connection, not to speak of collaboration, among them. In any case, the pale threat of the opposition abroad was largely eclipsed by the growing challenge of Islamic fundamentalist dissidence at home (see above).

It remained, however, unclear whether the Islamic extremists were connected in any way to the two alleged attempts upon Qadhdhafi's life during the year. The first took place on 16 March, when an unidentified Libyan attacked Qadhdhafi with a knife. The incident occurred while the Libyan leader hosted Syrian President Hafiz al-Asad (see below). As further reported, Asad's guards thwarted the assassination attempt and killed the man.[29] No Libyan or other element claimed responsibility for the attack and the Libyan media ignored the affair. According to a foreign report, the attacker was a fundamentalist.[30]

Another attempt at Qadhdhafi's life was thwarted on 20 June. A group of army men fired on Qadhdhafi's entourage, killing three of his guards.[31] Possibly referring to the same incident, another foreign source reported that when Qadhdhafi was in Misurata, more or less at the same time, an attacker suddenly dropped two hand grenades he had intended to throw at the colonel. An accomplice attempted to continue the attack but Qadhdhafi's bodyguard shot him.[32] Also with regard to this reported case, or cases, the Libyan media remained completely silent, in keeping with its longstanding policy of ignoring any subversive actions against the Libyan leader.

FOREIGN AFFAIRS

LIBYA IN THE ARAB WORLD

Egypt — A Breakthrough in Relations

Qadhdhafi's persistent efforts to achieve political *rapprochement* with Egypt, as had already been evident in 1988, gathered increasing momentum during the first months of 1989. Striving to achieve this goal, Tripoli resorted to the tactics of "stick and carrot." On the one hand, it exerted political pressure on Cairo: it opposed the candidacy of Egyptian President Husni Mubarak as chairman of the Organization of African Unity (OAU) — a post which was scheduled to be filled in the summer; it also opposed the readmission of Egypt to the Organization of Arab Petroleum Exporting Countries, being the only member to vote against Cairo during the meeting of the organization's Council of Ministers in Kuwait on 13 May.[33] On the other hand, Qadhdhafi simultaneously intensified his courting of the Egyptian regime. He offered Egypt significant financial aid, if Cairo only canceled the Camp David agreements.[34] ("Stable David" was the appellation which became the standard Libyan designation of Camp David.) Libya had been totally and persistently opposed to Egypt's peace agreement with Israel and had described it as the major stumbling block in Tripoli's relations with Cairo.

Since Tripoli was eager to defuse tension with Cairo, the Libyan authorities though they did not say so publicly, in fact continued to play down Egypt's commitment to the Camp David Accords. Tripoli continued its conciliation of Cairo, assisted by the mediation of other Arab countries, such as Morocco, Algeria and, at a later stage, even of Palestinian elements.[35] In late May, Tripoli's efforts peaked as Qadhdhafi and Mubarak met for talks in Casablanca, where both attended the Arab League summit. (On the summit, see chapter on inter-Arab relations.) The meeting with Mubarak was described by the Libyan leader as "positive and successful."[36] Whatever the content of their discussions, the importance of their meeting lay mainly in its very occurrence, symbolizing as it did a turn for the better in the relations of the two regimes. Thus, Qadhdhafi tacitly signaled his acquiescence to Egypt's return to the Arab League and, by implication, to Egypt's preeminent role in the Arab system. (See also chapter on Egypt.) The improvement of bilateral ties soon followed: on 29 May, the Salum overland crossing point was reopened to an immediate massive movement of travelers between the two countries.[37]

Seeking to speed up the pace of *rapprochement,* a special Libyan envoy arrived in Egypt in late May. The Libyan media did not dwell on the visit or its results, but a foreign source reported that Ahmad Qadhdhaf al-Damm, the Libyan leader's cousin and a top official in the secret security apparatus, discussed with his hosts the restoration of relations on the basis of "common interests." As further elaborated, he offered Cairo economic and technical "cooperation,"[38] presumably a less embarrassing term than "financial and economic help." Libya also offered to settle the dispute regarding compensation to the thousands of Egyptian workers expelled from Libya four years earlier[39] (see *MECS* 1984–85, pp. 560–61).

Following Qadhdhaf al-Damm's mission, the normalization process gathered speed immediately. On 4 June, the two countries resumed civilian flights. To mark the festive occasion, Jamal Muhammad Husni Mubarak, the Egyptian president's son, arrived in Tripoli on the first flight for a brief visit.[40] Libya, for its part, announced its support of Mubarak as the OAU chairman.[41] This move was accompanied by repeated Libyan calls, with Qadhdhafi's being foremost, to strengthen Arab support of "fraternal" Egypt. "What is required now is not to attack Egypt, but to help it and to ally ourselves with it," the Libyan leader stated.[42] Other clear signs of improvement were the reopening of the maritime line between Tripoli and Alexandria on 16 June;[43] the arrival of thousands of Libyans in Egypt,[44] including 200 experts in various fields;[45] and Libya's renunciation in July of $300m.,[46] which had been frozen in Egyptian banks since 1977 as a punitive act against Tripoli. The renunciation had only symbolic significance, since this money had been considered lost at any rate.

A sense of disappointment was felt by Tripoli on 1 September, when the Egyptian president, the newly elected OAU chairman, did not attend Libya's anniversary celebrations, although he had been officially invited. Egypt was represented — for the first time since the early 1970s — by an official delegation led by Yusuf Wali, deputy prime minister and minister of agriculture.[47] Qadhdhafi's indignation over Mubarak's absence was reflected in the relatively cool welcome senior Libyan officials gave to the Egyptians.[48]

Nevertheless, *rapprochement* gained momentum. On 16 October, Qadhdhafi arrived in the Egyptian city of Marsa Matruh for a meeting with the Egyptian president that lasted several hours. A day later, the two leaders met once again, this time in Tubruq, on Libyan territory. At the end of the meeting, a joint communiqué was issued, detailing an agreement for cooperation in various fields.[49] More significantly, however, there was no announcement of the restoration of diplomatic ties, which had been severed about a decade earlier. Clearly, both sides had their reasons for being reluctant on this point. Instead, they announced their agreement to open a "bureau" in each other's capital,[50] thus opting for a gradual warming in their formal relations rather than their unequivocal official revival. Reference to the issue made by both sides indicated that they regarded the opening of "bureaus" as tantamount to restoring diplomatic relations.[51] By the end of the year, Libya still had not reestablished full diplomatic relations with Egypt.

On 12 December, the Egyptian president paid his second visit to Libya, remaining in Sidra for several hours for talks with Qadhdhafi. The latter referred to the aim of the visit when he stated that "we are now laying the groundwork on which we will be able to stand firmly."[52] The two leaders agreed to cooperate in the areas of industry, agriculture, energy, transport, communication, and information.[53]

Sudan

A survey of the relations between the two countries should be divided into two parts: the first, covering the first half of the year when al-Sadiq al-Mahdi's government was still in office in Khartoum; the second, covering the second half of 1989, from 'Umar Hasan Ahmad al-Bashir's successful military *coup d'état* on 30 June (see chapter on Sudan). Throughout the year, however, Sudan was an important asset to Libya, especially against the background of Tripoli's still somewhat problematic relations with Egypt.

The first months of 1989 witnessed additional Libyan economic and military aid to Sudan. The arrival of Mahdi in Tripoli on 7-8 March, while facing growing discontent at home and successive defeats in the war in the south, suggested that the pace and volume of the aid were significantly smaller than Sudan's urgent needs at that time. (On events in Khartoum, see chapter on Sudan.) Though neither of the sides gave details of the visit's aims or results, one could assume that stepping up Libyan aid was at the top of the agenda.

Tripoli found it especially expedient at that stage to strengthen the impression of having close ties with Khartoum, while simultaneously trying to shift its conciliatory offensive toward Cairo into higher gear. The flow of visits of top Sudanese leaders to Tripoli in the first months of the year further played into Libya's hands (see chapter on Sudan).

At the end of June, a new military regime seized power in Khartoum, ousting Mahdi's government. Libya did not waste its time and started immediately to establish close ties with the new leadership. Especially urgent was the need to forestall an Egyptian attempt to enhance its political influence in Khartoum. Thus, on 1 July, only a day after the coup, a Libyan delegation arrived in Khartoum for a four-day visit. Two days later, a Sudanese delegation visited Tripoli. On the surface, the exchange of visits resulted in an understanding on mutual interests, probably accompanied by new Libyan promises for assistance. On 8 July, the Libyan foreign liaison secretary released a special statement affirming "the depth of the brotherly and fateful ties" between the two countries.[54]

Libyan political encouragement, and perhaps even immediate military and economic support, soon paid off. On 2–5 August, Bashir paid an official visit to Libya. The joint statement released at the end of the visit stressed the two countries' common interests and views on various Arab and African issues. Bashir seized the occasion to praise in public the Jamahiriyya's "gigantic" achievements.[55] According to a foreign source, it was during this visit that both countries reaffirmed the validity of their military agreement,[56] which had been signed in 1986 and which had become a source of controversy in Khartoum (see chapter on Sudan).

On 31 August, Bashir arrived in Tripoli once again and took part in the regime's anniversary celebrations. Undoubtedly, the tightening of ties with Khartoum played into Tripoli's hands and aided Libya's efforts to speed up simultaneous *rapprochement* with Egypt.

In late October, however, as his ties with Cairo reached a new high, Qadhdhafi could afford to be less agreeable toward the Khartoum leadership. Choosing an Egyptian publication in which to present his views, Qadhdhafi criticized the Bashir regime, calling on it to prepare a "national plan" to bring to an end the "vicious circle" in which "power was moving from the civilian regimes to the military and so on and so forth." The Libyan leader went on to warn the Sudanese regime, albeit implicitly, not to consider "any change in the country's Arab identity," as Sudan's southern rebels were persistently demanding. To accede to such a demand, Qadhdhafi added, would be "dangerous" and "unacceptable," since it might be a precedent for what could happen in other Arab states with non-Arab elements, such as Iraq, Algeria, and Morocco.[57] Thus, the Libyan leader virtually faced the Sudanese regime with a contradictory, if not impossible demand: to stabilize the country's political affairs, while vetoing any significant compromise for Sudan's African identity, which was one of the conditions set by the negroid southern Sudanese for a settlement with Khartoum. By eliminating the possibility of such a compromise, Qadhdhafi left Khartoum only with the military option, without saying so explicitly. Unfortunately for Khartoum, both options entailed many problems, a situation which strengthened Khartoum's political, economic, and military dependence upon Tripoli. Bashir's discreet visit to Libya on 18–19 November[58] (immediately following his talks with former US president Jimmy Carter, who tried to mediate between Khartoum and its rebellious south), clearly attested to such dependence.

Syria

In the course of 1989, a new measure of dynamism was introduced into Tripoli's relations with Damascus. It was not clear which of the two countries had contributed more to the new political concord; evidently, both had good reasons to do so. Damascus's concern over Tripoli's decision, made in October 1988, to support the Christian Iraqi-backed government of Gen. Michel 'Awn in Lebanon against the Syrian-backed Muslim government of Salim al-Huss, made Syria eager to reach a *rapprochement* with Libya. The dispatch of Syrian Vice President 'Abd al-Halim Khaddam to Tripoli in October and December 1988 clearly attested to this. Another factor was the setting-up of two new Arab groupings — the AMU and the Arab Cooperation Council (ACC) in mid-February — which aggravated Syria's relative political isolation in the Arab world and apparently pushed Damascus closer to Tripoli (see below and chapter on inter-Arab relations).

In mid-February, a military delegation headed by the commander in chief of the Libyan armed forces, Abu Bakir Yunis Jabir, paid a two-day official visit to Syria. Libya did not release details on the visit's goals. Possibly, Libyan political and military involvement in Lebanon and the manning of Libyan planes by Syrian pilots were discussed. (Later in the summer, the number of Syrian pilots serving in Libya's Air Force was estimated at 30.)[59] In addition to other assignments, they reportedly flew the Soviet-made Su-24 fighter bombers,[60] which arrived in Libya in the spring (see below).

On 16-18 March, Syrian President Asad paid an official visit to Libya, accompanied by a top-level entourage. His talks with Qadhdhafi dealt with the "general situation in the region" and with "methods to rally Arab resources to defend the Arab nation's interests."[61] Most likely, Lebanon was high on the agenda. On 21–22 May, the Syrian president visited Libya once again; he met with his Libyan host and the presidents of Algeria and Tunisia (see below). On 31 August, Asad arrived in Tripoli for the third time in 1989, to take part in Qadhdhafi's anniversary festivities.

As reported repeatedly later in the year, Qadhdhafi, who had succeeded in warming up his ties with Cairo, became actively involved in advancing the process of reconciliation between Syria and Egypt[62] (which ripened on 27 December, when they announced the restoration of their diplomatic ties).

Lebanon

During 1989, Tripoli reacted to the war in Lebanon with greater vigor than previously. Enjoying a relatively strengthened position in the Arab arena, Libya allowed itself to behave more freely in accordance with its interests in Lebanon. Tripoli's recognition of 'Awn's Iraqi-backed government rather than Huss's Syrian-backed Muslim government, attested to this new approach. Not only was it surprising that Qadhdhafi sided with the Christians, but his position also conflicted sharply with Syrian interests. Despite 'Awn's fierce "war of liberation" against Damascus and despite the latter's pressure imposed on Tripoli to withdraw its support, Qadhdhafi did not change his position throughout the year under review. "Our position stems from our understanding of the tragic situation in that fraternal country....In all our actions regarding the Lebanese problem..., our top priority is to spare Lebanon the threat of partition..." top Libyan officials stated on many occasions.[63]

Qadhdhafi presented a more detailed analysis of the Lebanese "quagmire" in one of his interviews — an illuminating exposé that merits extensive quotation. "The Jamahiriyya's role is a pan-Arab one. But the situation has become so complicated that we have refrained from getting involved....There is nowadays a settling of accounts between other parties on Lebanon's soil....The Iraqis want to settle their accounts with the Syrians. The Iranians want to settle their accounts with the Iraqis. We are not a party to the game of settling accounts...." Nevertheless, the Libyan leader continued, "the situation today is better than it was at the beginning of the war, because the alliances have become inter-Arab. 'Awn and his group are allied to Iraq and Saudi Arabia," he added, omitting Libya for some reason from this list. "This is better than being allied to Israel...." The problem in Lebanon, Qadhdhafi went on, is basically that of Christian Arab and Muslim Arab:

> The mistake is the existence of Christian Arabs. The error right from the beginning, regardless of whoever committed it, be it the Prophet Muhammad himself, was allowing Christians to remain. The basis of the call to Islam is that Arabs must be Muslims. Jihad, the confrontation of infidels and hypocrites, and beheadings were all meant for non-Muslim Arabs. The Arabs must fight

among themselves until they become Muslims. Religion has called since the time of the Prophet for turning the Arabs into Muslims so that no Jews or Christian Arabs would remain. The result is what we see today. As for Christians who are not Arabs and non-Arab infidels, there is no such thing as Jihad against them. The Qur'an says: 'And argue with them in ways that are best.' Islam calls for arguing with non-Arabs, such as Persians, Turks, Greeks, and others, in ways that are best. As for the Arab, he should not remain in his old faith. He should become a Muslim through the sword and through fighting, because if you had killed 10 at that time it would have been better than having constant fighting till now between Muslim and Christian. The result of this is clear in Lebanon. It might happen in Egypt, in Syria, or in Iraq, because there are non-Muslim Arabs in those countries.

Provoked during the interview by a remark that even in Lebanon there was a Sunni-Shi'i dispute within the same Islamic religion, Qadhdhafi answered:

The Shi'i-Sunni problem should not exist. I know what the present dispute is about, and it is not about religion. Jihad means that the Arabs should have one religion, namely Islam. From the first day of Islam the sword should not have stopped until all the Arabs became Muslims. Shi'a is not a religion but a political stand that supports 'Ali against Mu'awiyya. What has this to do with religion? Shi'a is a political party that supports 'Ali.[64]

On another occasion, the Libyan leader further noted that since the Jamahiriyya was not adjacent to Lebanon, it was free of various "sensitivities" and "national calculations," and, therefore, its policy on Lebanon was the "correct" one. Qadhdhafi also outlined the road to a solution: "We should promote an atmosphere that will enable the Lebanese Chamber of Deputies to meet to elect a president of the republic and enable us to work for a cease-fire." The Lebanese problem as a whole, Qadhdhafi suggested, was "incurable." Yet he proposed in the same breath how to solve it: "Only a Jamahiri system" will bring an end to the crisis there.[65]

Qadhdhafi's Attitude Toward the Intifada and the Palestinian State

Qadhdhafi's perception of the Arab-Israeli conflict remained as firm as ever: a total rejection of the right of the State of Israel to exist, and, therefore, the necessity to bring about its liquidation and to give Palestine back to the Palestinians. According to Qadhdhafi, the only legitimate and effective way to achieve the annihilation of the Israeli State was through armed struggle.

Considering Libya's consistent anti-Israeli policy, it could be expected that Qadhdhafi would warmly adopt the Intifada. Indeed, daily reports, accompanied by numerous pictures, appeared in the official Libyan media, virulently denouncing "the Zionist occupation forces," "the Zionist mob gangs," and using many other defamatory expressions that were normal for Tripoli within this context.[66] But as in the previous year, Qadhdhafi's verbal backing of the Intifada did not develop into more active support. Libya was cautious not to go beyond ideological and moral commitment. With regard to Libya's financial support, if there was any, no information about it was available.

Thus, Libya throughout the period surveyed continued to repeat calls for establishing a Palestinian state "in the land between the Jordan River and the

Mediterranean Sea," entirely rejecting any possibility of establishing a Palestinian state only in part of this area. "To take part of the land and say that in return for this part you will relinquish the rest of the land to the enemy and recognize him" was entirely unacceptable. But,

> when you seize a portion of your land and set up a state with the aim of liberating all of Palestine from the river to the sea, this is the kind of state we could recognize....To say that you were given this inch and that you have given up everything else — and this is what actually happened [a reference to the Palestinian state declared by the PLO in November 1988] — we do not recognize such a state.[67]

In a somewhat contradictory move late in the fall, Qadhdhafi expressed the opinion that "there is nothing that should prevent the Palestinians from sitting down with the Israelis for a dialogue and negotiations. It happens everywhere."[68] Given that such a dialogue, if opened, would negotiate a compromise settlement and, therefore, would not satisfy Qadhdhafi's maximal demands, this opinion appeared to be quite exceptional and rather odd.

LIBYA IN THE AFRICAN ARENA

Libya's efforts to mend fences in Black Africa continued during 1989. (For the momentum given to Tripoli's ties in the continent during the previous year, see *MECS* 1988, pp. 650–51.) On 28 March, while addressing the OAU Defense Committee meeting in Tripoli, Qadhdhafi seized the opportunity to convey his perception of the continent's major pitfalls and vulnerable points, all a result in his view of "White imperialism." Qadhdhafi stated: "Western imperialism and racism in Europe and the US, Brothers, is determined to violate Africa's independence and sanctity as well as drain its resources." The Europeans' contempt for blacks "reached such a level that they carried out experiments on them just as they do on mice and rabbits." They think that "every individual who lives on the African continent is a slave to the white Europeans." Qadhdhafi singled out two elements of which the African continent should rid itself immediately: "the racist regime" in South Africa and the "foreign colonialist European forces on African soil." It was "disgraceful" for African countries to exchange visits, negotiate, or recognize the "racist and dirty regime" in South Africa, which was "against the black race. We should only meet such a regime in a battle and nowhere else." Qadhdhafi thus exploited the broadest common denominator uniting the meeting's participants — their strong rejection of the South African Government — to gain their sympathy, while trying, at the same time, to consolidate the Jamahiriyya's position as an integral component of the all-African system, rather than merely of the nonblack North African (Maghrib) region. In the same vein, referring to the presence of foreign troops in Africa (and ignoring his own country's military intervention in Uganda and Chad in the past) Qadhdhafi employed equally harsh language: "We must eliminate Western military bases from the African continent immediately," he stated, apparently alluding primarily to Chad. African states "should totally refrain from carrying out military maneuvers with foreign sources," he said, presumably referring to Egypt, whose routine military exercises with the US was a major source of concern for Libya. These maneuvers, he charged, "are all preparations for the renewed invasion of this continent...."

In the same long speech, Qadhdhafi hailed the Jamahiriyya's contribution to the security and liberation of Africa. Having no massive forces stationed outside his country's borders, for the first time in a decade, the Libyan leader found the circumstances appropriate to declare that:

> We are proud that we have trained thousands of Africans on Libyan soil, using Libyan instructors who took part in the liberation of a number of African countries that had been colonized, and which are currently fighting in South Africa and South-West Africa....Soldiers of the following countries and organizations were trained and graduated in Libya: Zimbabwe, Guinea-Bissau, People's Republic of Benin, Guinea, Burundi, São Tomé and Príncipe, Djibouti, Uganda, Chad, Saharan Democratic Arab Republic, Swapo, Ghana, Sudan, Rwanda, Togo, Central Africa, Lesotho, Mozambique, Burkina Faso, Zambia, Madagascar, Pan-African Congress, African National Congress.

Summing up, the Libyan leader stated: "Libya is the guard of Africa....It will remain the gate which will not be crossed by the enemy unless over the dead bodies of its sons."[69]

The participation of about 15 African heads of state[70] in the Libyan regime's 20th anniversary celebrations on 1 September reflected not only the great efforts Libya had made to ensure such an impressive representation. It also attested to Qadhdhafi's improved political standing in Black Africa and, certainly, to the African countries' hope of benefiting politically and economically from relations with Tripoli.

Bilateral Ties

Libya's relations with Zaire, Liberia, Senegal, Nigeria, Niger, and Mali continued to be friendly, a trend that began at the end of 1988. The specially cordial ties with Burkina Faso and Ghana were also strengthened.

Libya's relations with Somalia were given a boost in 1988-89. At the end of 1988, high-level Somalian delegations visited Libya, headed by Somalian President Muhammad Siad Barre. Also at the end of 1988 there were deliveries of Libyan military supplies to Mogadishu, allegedly including nerve gas canisters.[71] (While Libya ignored the allegation, Somalia released an official denial.)[72] The political and military links between the two countries remained close during 1989, as clearly attested by another visit to Tripoli of Somalia's president, on 30 August-2 September, on the occasion of the anniversary festivities, and of top Somalian army commanders on several other occasions during the year.

Other noteworthy visits of Black African presidents in Tripoli during the year were those of Moussa Traoré, the president of Mali and chairman of the OAU, on 30-31 January and again during the anniversary celebrations. Qadhdhafi briefly visited Bamako in July, attending a minisummit to discuss his dispute with Chad (see below). On the same occasion (22 July) Qadhdhafi visited Niger, returning the visit to Tripoli on 21–22 March of 'Ali Seibou, chairman of the Supreme Military Council and president of Niger. The latter also attended the 1 September celebrations. On 16 July, the president of Burkina Faso, Capt. Blaise Compaoré, began a three-day visit in Tripoli. As expected, he returned to attend the 1 September celebrations.

Against the general background of Libya's improved political status on the continent, the sharp deterioration in relations with Burundi was an exception. On 5

April, Burundi announced its decision to expel all Libyan nationals and diplomats within 48 hours, because of their alleged "destabilization activities." The deportations involving 70 people[73] caused "astonishment" in Tripoli, which called the decision "unjustified," since the "Libyan citizens are present in Burundi for mutual economic, cultural, and political interests."[74] Though neither of the sides gave details of the causes of the crisis, a French source linked it with an abortive plot to kill President Buyoya during a military parade on 11 March.[75] Another possible reason for the crisis could have been the claim that Libya had granted asylum to former Burundian president, Jean Baptiste Bagaza, who had been deposed in 1987.[76] This possibility was, however, disputed by another foreign source.[77]

Relations with Chad, which improved dramatically in 1988, fluctuated throughout 1989 (for the 1988 reconciliation, see *MECS* 1988, pp. 648–50). In early spring, new tension crept into their relations. On 1 April, Idriss Deby, former Chadian chief of staff, attempted a coup against Hissène Habré, the Chadian president since 1982 and until 1988 Qadhdhafi's sworn enemy.[78] A claim that Deby had been seen in Tripoli[79] left room for suggestions that Libya was in some way connected to the coup attempt. Preoccupied at the time with promoting its image of moderation, Tripoli ignored this implicit accusation. Two months later, however, Libya moved to react. On 4 June, it responded to an official memorandum released that same day by Ndjamena, accusing Tripoli of aiding Chadian dissidents and preparing a military attack against Chad.[80] Tripoli expressed its "amazement" at the allegation, stressing it had "no expansionist greed" as regards Chad, and that it had "absolutely nothing to do" with that country's domestic conflicts. The more important part of the official Libyan statement declared that the Jamahiriyya "is within its own borders, [and] does not occupy any Chadian territories."[81] By saying that, Tripoli reiterated that the Aouzou Strip, paralleling the two countries' common border and the major bone of contention between them, was part of Libyan territory. Chad also claimed sovereignty over the Aouzou Strip, and was unwilling to reach any compromise over it (see all previous volumes of *MECS*). It was not surprising, therefore, that the meeting of the *ad hoc* OAU committee in Gabon on 17 June called to discuss the Libyan-Chadian dispute, was suspended within an hour. The reason for the meeting's failure was Libya's refusal to put the subject at the top of the agenda, as Chad had demanded.[82]

On 20–21 July, another attempt was made to bring the two sides to the negotiating table. A minisummit was held in Bamako under the auspices of the heads of state of Mali, Gabon, Algeria, and Nigeria with the participation of Qadhdhafi and Habré. But this time, too, the talks ended in a deadlock.[83] Nevertheless, maintaining the momentum of dialogue they helped Libya to portray itself as a peace-seeking force, an image especially important to the regime on the threshold of its 20th anniversary celebrations.

The anniversary festivities played an important role in Libya's readiness to iron out its difficulties with Chad, or at least to give such an impression. August witnessed unprecedented activities to this end: at the beginning of the month, an official Chadian delegation arrived in Tripoli and on 21–25 August, senior Libyan and Chadian top officials held talks in France under the aegis of Algeria and France and with the "secret mediation" of Kuwait.[84] Jallud was reportedly visiting Paris at the same time,[85] perhaps even taking an active role in the talks. On 31 August, the intensive contacts of the sides made tangible progress: they signed an "outline agreement" in Algiers, confirming their decision to settle their territorial dispute by political means within a year. Failing a political settlement, the issue would be submitted to the International Court of Justice at The Hague. The parties also agreed to cease all hostile media campaigns, release all prisoners of war (there were c. 2,000 Libyan prisoners in Chad),[86] and refrain from any interference in each others' internal affairs.[87]

The presence of a Chadian official delegation at the 1 September celebrations, the first since Habré's advent to power, was another sign of the conciliation. Renewed tension in the winter, however, clearly indicated that their mutual distrust was not removed. On 30 October, Chad reported the killing of 600 men of the Libyan Islamic Legion, which, Ndjamena claimed, had attacked it from its base in the Sudanese Darfur region. Accusing Libya of "military aggression," Ndjamena denounced Libya's violation of the Algiers agreement, which showed "that the Libyan leaders have not renounced their original sin of betraying their word and commitments."[88] Libya responded a day later in the form of a special statement which expressed its "astonishment" at the injection of its name into the internal Chadian dispute. Libya "has no link whatsoever with the conflict raging between Habré and his companions [the Chadian opposition led by Idriss Deby]. Moreover, there is no truth in the existence of any link between Libya and the so-called Islamic Legion, which is an imaginary thing that has no presence on earth." Libya also reaffirmed its adherence to the Algiers agreement.[89]

LIBYA AND THE MAGHRIB

Relations between the Maghrib countries and Libya continued to be dynamic during 1989. Libya's long-proclaimed goal of building the "Greater Arab Maghrib" was crowned with success. On 15–17 February, a summit conference attended by the heads of state of Algeria, Libya, Mauritania, Morocco, and Tunisia was held in Marrakesh. A document establishing the AMU was signed by all participants. (For the full text of the document, the intra-Maghrib activities which led to its signing, and the contacts which followed, see chapter on inter-Arab relations.) Qadhdhafi attributed major importance to the AMU, saying it was necessary for the Arabs to have a large grouping capable of dealing with a united Europe.[90] He further referred to the newly created AMU as an important step "along the path leading toward comprehensive Arab unity from the ocean to the Gulf."[91] Not belonging to the ACC comprising Iraq, Jordan, Egypt, and North Yemen that was established in mid-February, Qadhdhafi now must have felt a sense of relief upon emerging from isolation and belonging to an important Arab bloc.

Bilateral Ties

Relations with Algeria — the most important political and military power in the Maghrib — continued to be close in 1989. Senior officials exchanged visits between Tripoli and Algiers. Most important was the visit on 21–22 May by Algerian President Chedli Benjedid to Tripoli, where he met with his Libyan counterpart and the Tunisian and Syrian presidents. (For more details on this meeting, see chapter on inter-Arab relations.)

Wishing to encourage the stability of the Maghrib and to further cultivate bilateral ties with Tripoli, the Algerians provided Qadhdhafi with essential mediatorial services throughout the year: it contributed to the easing of tension in Libya's relations with Morocco, Chad, Egypt, and perhaps even with the US.

Given the high level of Libyan-Tunisian cooperation that has developed steadily since late 1986, and given the general cordial spirit that dominated intra-Maghrib relations in 1988–89, it was only natural that relations between Tripoli and Tunis continued to flourish in 1989. The frequent exchange visits by top political figures and the many economic cooperation agreements they signed attested to their good relations. Most conspicuous was the visit on 22 May of Tunisian President Zayn al-'Abidin Ben 'Ali, who participated in the meeting of the four Maghrib presidents (see above).

Libya's hitherto hostile relations with Morocco took a turn for the better in 1989 (for details see *MECS* 1986, p. 518, and 1987, pp. 115–17, 559). The increased dynamism in intra-Maghrib policies in 1988–89 and Algerian pressures, which had been exerted apparently on both Morocco and Libya, prompted the latter to improve its ties with Rabat. Syria's restoration of diplomatic relations with Morocco in early 1989 (broken off by Damascus in mid-1986 in protest against King Hasan's meeting with Israeli Prime Minister Shimon Peres), apparently was an additional catalyst for Qadhdhafi's willingness to reach a *rapprochement* with Morocco. Results of that process were noticed in early 1989, with Qadhdhafi's arrival in Morocco in mid-February (see above). On 13 May, Qadhdhafi paid an additional visit in Morocco, where he held talks with King Hasan II. The two sides issued brief and general communiqués stating that they had discussed bilateral relations, Maghrib issues, and the forthcoming Arab summit.[92] Qadhdhafi also requested King Hasan's help to end the Libyan-Egyptian dispute.[93]

On 24–26 May, Qadhdhafi arrived in Morocco once again, where he attended the Arab summit conference. The summit was the occasion for Qadhdhafi's reconciliation with Mubarak, seemingly with the assistance of King Hasan II.[94] On 9–12 July, Libya expressed its gratitude by sending a senior delegation to Morocco to participate in the celebrations of Youth Day, which coincided with the Moroccan king's 60th birthday.[95] Furthermore, it was reported early in October that Qadhdhafi asked the Polisario movement to close its office in Tripoli,[96] thereby removing a major source of dissension with Morocco. Later in the month, the Libyan leader stated that his country had ceased its military support of the Polisario, since it believed that the settlement of the conflict could be achieved only through negotiations.[97] This new approach, which contrasted sharply with Libya's hitherto militant support of the Polisario, was additional evidence for Qadhdhafi's wish to defuse tension in foreign relations, especially in Libya's immediate vicinity.

LIBYA AND THE SUPERPOWERS
The United States
Libya was at pains during the year to bring about a thaw in its frozen relations with the US. This new policy contrasted sharply with Libya's earlier bellicosity, which had brought bilateral relations to a low ebb. After the tension in their ties peaked at the turn of 1988–89, mainly over the chemical-weapons affair which culminated in a dogfight between aircrafts of the two sides in early January, Qadhdhafi tried to reduce the strain in links with Washington. (For more details on the renewed hostility and the

air battle, see *MECS* 1988, pp. 654–55 and above.) Not only had he tempered his anti-US rhetoric but much more significantly, on 7 January, he invited the incoming Bush Adminstration "to sit face to face" and discuss the dispute, which had dogged the two sides for years.[98] On 13 January, wishing to show further his goodwill, Qadhdhafi returned, through the good offices of the Vatican representative, the body of an American pilot killed during the US bombing of Libya in 1986.[99]

Whether influenced by the Libyan goodwill gesture or not, the Reagan Administration announced a week later that it was modifying its trade restrictions against Libya to allow American oil companies to resume operations there and to avoid a Libyan takeover of their assets.[100] It should be recalled that these assets, worth c. $2bn.,[101] were frozen in early 1986, after the US imposed severe economic sanctions on Tripoli (see *MECS* 1986, p. 511). Qadhdhafi had, indeed, stepped up pressure on the American companies and the US Administration by indicating that he would not renew the three-year "standstill agreement" under which the assets were frozen, when it expired in June 1989. Though trying to win political concessions, Libya was no less desirous of bringing to an end the boycott on oil exports to the US and of returning US personnel to run its oil industry. It also wanted the American companies to increase their commitment to exploration.[102]

Wishing to inject some dynamism into the stalled relations, Qadhdhafi, as well as other senior Libyan officials, repeatedly voiced the Jamahiriyya's wish to establish a direct dialogue with the new Administration.[103] The Bush government "is reasonable and mature; it understands international politics and cannot repeat the ignorance of Reagan...."[104]

Qadhdhafi did not limit his efforts to words alone. In June, he sent Muhammad Lutfi Farhat, a loyal aide and since 1987 the planning secretary, to Washington for talks with senior US officials.[105] Later in the summer, Tripoli further encouraged and, in fact, held meetings with high-ranking American officials.[106] From 27 June-3 July, an American delegation representing "the US good offices committee" visited Tripoli. Though not an official visit, it indicated some progress, since this was the first American delegation to arrive in Libya since 1986 when Washington forbade its citizens to travel to Libya. (This prohibition continued in force in 1989 as well.)

But no turn for the better followed. The freeze in bilateral relations was reinforced on 19 July, when President Bush announced his decision to maintain the three-year-old economic sanctions against Libya. He explained his move by Libya's continuing "to pose an unusual and extraordinary threat to the national security and foreign policy of the US."[107]

Qadhdhafi did not sit idly by and on 1 September, when delivering his anniversary speech, revealed the reasons which, in his view, prevented the thaw in his relations with Washington. The latter, he said, staged two conditions for opening a dialogue: recognition of Israel and the cessation of Libyan support of "the people of Panama," i.e., Gen. Manuel Noriega's regime. The Jamahiriyya, Qadhdhafi stated, rejected both conditions unequivocally.[108] The end of 1989 witnessed further "secret talks" between the two countries,[109] but apparently they did not produce any significant results.

The Soviet Union

Political and economic relations with Moscow proceeded in a relatively low-key manner. Not only was Moscow preoccupied with its own problems at home and in the Eastern Bloc, especially in the last quarter of 1989, but Libya, too, preferred in 1989, more than ever, to concentrate its foreign policy interests in its vicinity. (Nevertheless, with regard to the dramatic change of guard in Romania at the end of the year, Tripoli declared its support of the new Romanian leadership, after it had been accused of involvement with the Ceauşescu regime's efforts to survive.[110] In early April, American official sources disclosed that Libya had bought up to 15 Sukhoi-24 fighter bombers from the Soviet Union. Six of them were thought to be in Libya already.[111] In August, an Egyptian source reported the arrival in Libya of six MiG-29 fighter bombers. The same source also reported that 32 Libyan pilots had been sent to the Soviet Union for training.[112]

NOTES

For the place and frequency of publications cited here, and for the full name of the publication, news agency, radio station, or monitoring service where an abbreviation is used, please see "List of Sources." Only in the case of more than one publication bearing the same name is the place of publication noted here.

1. Tripoli TV, 17 January — DR, 18 January 1989.
2. *Al-Fajr al-Jadid*, January 1989, passim.
3. Tripoli TV, 6 March — DR, 7 March 1989.
4. *The Economist*, 7 January 1989.
5. *NYT*, 6 November, 24 December 1989.
6. *Al-Majalla*, 4–10 January, an interview with Foreign Minister al-Talhi. AFP, 10 February 1989, quoting the Somalian Government's statement.
7. *Africa Report*, March-April 1989.
8. *Al-Fajr al-Jadid*, first 10 days of March 1989.
9. Tripoli TV, 9 March — SWB, 14 March 1989.
10. Tripoli TV, 28 March — DR, 28 March 1989.
11. Tripoli TV, 7 October — DR, 13 October 1989.
12. *Al-Mustaqbal*, 18 March 1989.
13. *IHT*, 11 January 1989.
14. Qadhdhafi's speech to a BPC meeting in Tripoli, R. Tripoli, 9 January — DR, 11 January 1989.
15. *AC*, 3 February; *al-Sharq al-Jadid*, March 1989.
16. R. Tripoli, 20 January — DR, 23 January 1989.
17. *AC*, 3 February 1989.
18. TANJUG, 21 January — DR, 23 January 1989.
19. Tripoli TV, 8 March — SWB, 10 March (English version); *al-Fajr al-Jadid*, 9 March 1989 (Arabic version).
20. *Al-Ghuraba*, April; *al-Dustur*, London, 1 May; *AC*, 26 May 1989.
21. *AC*, 23 June 1989.
22. For more details on the seminar and the Tripoli-based and -sponsored World Islamic Call Society (*Jam'iyyat al-da'wa al-islamiya al-'alamiyya*), which organized it, see chapter on Islamic Affairs in *MECS* 1981–82, pp. 293–94.
23. JANA, 26 September — DR, 27 September 1989.
24. Tripoli TV, 7 October — DR, 13 October 1989.
25. Ibid.
26. *MEED*, 17 November 1989.
27. Ibid.

28. *Al-Dustur*, London, 10 April 1989.
29. *Al-Watan al-'Arabi*, 7 April 1989.
30. *Al-Nashra*, Athens, 13 November 1989.
31. *Al-Dustur*, London, 3 July 1989.
32. *AC*, 23 June 1989.
33. *Al-Wafd*, 9 May; AFP, 13 May — DR, 15 May 1989.
34. *Al-Sha'b*, Cairo, 23 May; *al-Wafd*, 15 June 1989, quoting Qadhdhafi.
35. See below, and *May*, 23 October 1989.
36. Qadhdhafi's interview with *al-Ittihad*, Abu Dhabi, 16 June 1989.
37. *Al-Ahram*, 4 June 1989.
38. *Al-Ittihad*, Abu Dhabi, 2 June 1989.
39. *MEED*, 23 June 1989.
40. JANA, 5 June — DR, 6 June 1989.
41. *Al-Wafd*, 5 June 1989.
42. Qadhdhafi's speech on the 19th anniversary of the evacuation of US bases in Libya, *al-Fajr al-Jadid*, 13 June; see also Qadhdhafi's interview with *al-Ittihad*, Abu Dhabi, 16 June 1989.
43. *Al-Fajr al-Jadid*, 18 June 1989.
44. *Akhbar al-Yawm*, 24 June; *al-Ahram*, 4, 27 June, 20 July 1989.
45. *Al-Dustur*, London, 19 June 1989.
46. *Al-Shira'*, 24 July 1989.
47. *Al-Sha'b*, Cairo, 5 September 1989.
48. *Al-Ahali*, 13 September 1989.
49. *Al-Ahram*, 18 October 1989.
50. MENA, 17 October — DR, 18 October 1989.
51. For the Libyan stand, see Qadhdhafi's interview with *al-Musawwar*, 27 October; for Egypt's, see an interview with a top official from the Egyptian Foreign Ministry, *al-Hayat*, London, 21–22 October 1989.
52. MENA, 12, 13 December — DR, 12, 13 December 1989.
53. MENA, 12 December — DR, 13 December 1989.
54. R. Tripoli, 8 July — DR, 10 July 1989.
55. JANA, 5 August — DR, 7 August 1989.
56. *Suraqiyya*, London, 14 August 1989.
57. *Al-Musawwar*, 27 October 1989.
58. *Al-Sharq al-Awsat*, 22 November 1989.
59. *Al-Watan al-'Arabi*, 7 July 1989.
60. *Al-Dustur*, London, 7 July 1989. In fall 1987 Libya allegedly "absorbed" 40 Syrian pilots into its Air Force, while reinforcing its Army in case the war in Chad was rekindled.
61. R. Damascus, 16 March — DR, 17 March 1989.
62. *Al-Bayadir al-Siyasi*, 28 October; *al-Majalla*, 31 October; *al-Wafd*, 7 November; *al-Dustur*, London, 13 November 1989.
63. *Al-Majalla*, 4-10 January; *al-Sharq al-Awsat*, 12 January 1989.
64. *Al-Mawqif al-'Arabi*, Nicosia, September 1989.
65. *Al-Hawadith*, 30 June 1989.
66. *Al-Fajr al-Jadid*, in the course of the whole year under survey.
67. E.g., *al-Mawqif al-'Arabi*, Nicosia, 1 September 1989.
68. Interview with *al-Musawwar*, 27 October 1989.
69. Tripoli TV, 29 March — DR, 30 March 1989.
70. For a detailed list of the guests, see JANA, 31 August, 1 September — DR, 1, 6 September 1989.
71. *Africa Report*, March-April 1989.
72. AFP, 10 February 1989.
73. AFP, 5 April 1989.
74. JANA, 5 April — DR, 6 April 1989.
75. *CR:* Libya, No. 3, 1989.
76. *JP*, quoting Reuters, 6 April 1989.
77. *Al-Usbu' al-'Arabi*, 7 August 1989.

78. *Al-Hayat,* London, 6 April; for details on the abortive coup, see an interview with Chadian Foreign Minister al-Shaykh Ibn 'Umar, R. Libreville, 9 August — DR, 12 August 1989.
79. AFP, 5 May 1989.
80. Ibid., 4 June — DR, 6 June 1989.
81. JANA, 4 June — DR, 5 June 1989.
82. R. Ndjamena, 18 June — DR, 18 June 1989.
83. *Le Monde,* 22 July 1989.
84. *Al-Qabas,* 2 September; *al-Bayadir al-Siyasi,* 18 November 1989.
85. *Al-Dustur,* London, 11 September 1989.
86. *IHT,* 1 September 1989.
87. R. Algiers, 31 August — DR, 31 August; see also *Le Monde,* 1, 2 September 1989.
88. R. Ndjamena, 2 November — DR, 4 November 1989.
89. JANA, 3 November — DR, 4 November 1989.
90. Qadhdhafi's interview with *al-Ittihad,* Abu Dhabi, 16 June 1989.
91. This idea was repeated many times, e.g., Qadhdhafi's interviews with the BBC, broadcast by R. Tripoli, 17 September — DR, 20 September, and with *al-Musawwar,* 27 October 1989.
92. Tripoli TV, 13 May — DR, 15 May 1989.
93. *Al-Sha'b,* Cairo, 23 May 1989.
94. *Al-Majalla,* 31 October 1989.
95. R. Rabat, 10 July — DR, 12 July 1989.
96. *Al-Majalla,* 3 October 1989.
97. Qadhdhafi's interview with *al-Musawwar,* 27 October 1989.
98. *Al-Fajr al-Jadid,* 8 January 1989, addressing 200 journalists at Tripoli's al-Kabir Hotel.
99. *Al-Fajr al-Jadid,* 14 January 1989.
100. *NYT,* 20 January 1989, for the White House statement.
101. *MEED,* 3 February 1989.
102. Ibid., 23 June 1989.
103. In an interview aired on the American ABC News TV, quoted by *JP,* 29 January. For similar statements released by other top Libyan figures, see *al-Sharq al-Awsat,* 12 January; *al-Yaqza,* 7–13 April; and *al-Hawadith,* 30 June 1989.
104. Qadhdhafi's speech marking the 19th anniversary of the evacuation of US military bases in Libya, *al-Fajr al-Jadid,* 13 June 1989.
105. *Al-Watan al-'Arabi,* 23 June 1989.
106. *Al-Ittihad,* Abu Dhabi, 16 June, 20 August; *al-Sharq al-Awsat,* 26 July; and *al-Watan al-'Arabi,* 18 August 1989.
107. USIS, 19 July 1989.
108. Tripoli TV, 1 September — DR, 5 September 1989.
109. *Sunday Correspondent,* 5 November — DR, 6 November 1989.
110. JANA, 26 December — DR, 26 December; R. Tripoli, 28 December — DR, 28 December 1989.
111. *NYT,* 5 April 1989. For an up-to-date survey on Libya's Air Force, see S. Gazit (ed.), *The Middle East Military Balance 1988–89 (The Jerusalem Post/*Westview Press, for the Jaffee Center for Strategic Studies, Tel Aviv University, Tel Aviv, 1989), pp. 223–25.
112. *Ruz al-Yusuf,* 21 August 1989.

Oman

('Uman)

UZI RABI

Omani efforts to balance its pro-Arab and pro-Western inclination with a friendly approach to Iran paid off. The ability to remain on good terms with all sides was given expression by Oman acting as a go-between for Iran and the Arabs, as well as other states. Accordingly, Arab and Western states viewed Oman as a country able to carry out discreet diplomacy which more often than not succeeded where others had failed. Oman was also seen as being able to influence the course of events. In line with its recent policy of increased involvement in Arab affairs, Oman strove to help define an Arab consensus on the most pressing regional issues, as was best demonstrated during Sultan Qabus's first visit to Arab and European capitals in May. In another development, diplomatic ties were reportedly set up with Libya, a radical Arab state, as well as with Ghana and Chad.

Oman became more integrated into the Gulf Cooperation Council (GCC) by settling some of its differences with fellow members. It was symbolic that Muscat had headed the 10th GCC summit and that Oman was the chairman of the GCC during its 20th anniversary year in 1990.

INTERNAL AFFAIRS

MEET-THE-PEOPLE TOUR — A REFLECTION OF THE SULTANATE'S PRIORITIES

In keeping with Omani tradition, Qabus, escorted by his Cabinet, embarked in February on his annual meet-the-people tour, listening to local grievances and experiences. These contacts kept Qabus informed of the public's mood and needs, and enabled him to define the sultanate's priorities. Qabus repeated his call about the need for greater discipline in the use of water, which is not abundant in Oman. The problem was crucial: it was estimated that the area under cultivation in Oman could be increased by c. 80% if water was consumed through a proper irrigation system.[1] The Ministry of Water Resources was set up as part of an effort to cope with water problems effectively.[2] Attempts were made to uproot certain traditional Omani customs, which Qabus held, had bad effects on daily life, such as the high dowry which prevented many couples from getting married.[3] More important was the announcement that the next five-year plan, due to commence in 1991, would focus on bringing the interior areas — hitherto rather neglected in terms of development — into the center of attention.[4] Apart from being yet another step toward integrating all the Omani territory, the announcement seemed to reflect a precautionary step to

559

preempt any disaffection in the interior stemming from the unequal distribution of material benefits.

Rapid development, however, brought new challenges to Oman, as was best reflected in the field of education. Expansion of educational facilities was considered the most prominent achievement of the Qabus era. Compared to three schools in 1970 — the year he came to power — Oman now had 719 educational institutions. "Qabus University," which was inaugurated in 1986, was to graduate its first students in 1989. However, the relatively large number of secondary-school graduates — c. 4,000 a year — plus austerity measures necessitated by stagnant oil revenues, created a difficulty in satisfying their occupational requirements. Furthermore, Omani nationals were reluctant to work in the private sector, preferring government employment which offered far better terms: wages were higher as well as the type of jobs offered.[5] Employment in the public sector was expected to become even more attractive following the announcement that, as of July, Oman's civil servants would enjoy a five-day working week.[6] But the government's ability to employ more nationals was hampered chiefly due to the employment of many still irreplaceable foreigners. "From now on, all that an Omani can do is to take over from one of the 23,000 foreigners in the civil service," lamented Civil Service Minister Ahmad Nabi Makki.[7] This complex problem was blocking the road to Omanization. Small wonder that in his speech on Oman's National Day in November, Qabus referred to the issue by saying:

> We [the Omani Government] wish to stress the importance of continuing such efforts to gradually replace expatriates with Omanis...as a national necessity....The percentage of expatriates in our country is still high, the majority of whom are in the private sector in the building and construction industries and other companies. Much of this work could be done by Omanis.... We call on every Omani to apply themselves to work seriously and participate...in the building of their country.[8]

However, speeches such as these did not seem to have much effect on the Omani people, and the government, not wishing to pursue the matter overenthusiastically, could only hope that economic realities would compel the Omanis to change their attitudes.

ECONOMIC AFFAIRS

Already producing close to capacity, the sultanate could not raise oil production in order to compensate for the decline in prices; it was thus compelled to continue preaching for restraint. Not a member of the Organization of Petroleum Exporting Countries (Opec), Oman had a hand in the agreement for a 5% production cut, reached during the non-Opec meeting in London in February.[9] Shuttling between non-Opec capitals in preparation for the meeting, the sultanate's minister of oil and mineral resources stopped over in Moscow, which agreed for the first time to take part in such a meeting.[10] Nonetheless, Oman continued seeking ways of increasing its oil production; exploration was continued in an effort to increase proven reserves and the al-Fahl refinery was undergoing improvements to enlarge its refining capacity.[11] Natural gas, in abundance and largely untapped, was seen as another potential source of revenue in light of the growing world demand for methanol, a by-product. Plans were under way to build the world's first floating methanol plant; it was to move from field to field and tap smaller accumulations of gas.[12]

Meanwhile, much emphasis was put on non-oil industries. Throughout 1989, the "Year of Agriculture"(for details, see *MECS* 1988, pp. 449–50), Oman's fish and date industry was vastly expanded in order to achieve self-sufficiency in food within seven to eight years.[13] Funds were expanded for improving Oman's infrastracture with the unveiling of plans for the increased development of the road network and telecommunications system. Since these projects required investments not available at home, Oman took a $500m. loan in Europe in March.[14] In another development, Oman's stock exchange started trading on 20 May, aiming to channel privately held funds into economic development.[15] Various relevant laws and regulations seemed also to mark the beginning of a new economic era.

THE ARMED FORCES — AN INCREASED COOPERATION WITH FRANCE

In spite of regional calm, defense continued to be high on Oman's list of priorities. Yet, in May, the sultanate announced its decision to "postpone for the present" its plan to buy eight *Tornado* fighter aircraft because of the need for "prudent financial management."[16] Concluded in 1985, the deal was to go through by 1992. Instead, Oman negotiated a cheaper air-defense package, which sufficed for the medium term. The purchase of *Hawk* fighters, which were to replace the old *Hawker Hunter,* as well as *Javelin* ground-to-air missiles, suggested that Oman — hitherto without a proper air defense of its own — might in the near future be released from its long-standing reliance on the Saudi air umbrella.

Defense needs also underlay the increasingly close ties with France, particularly following the comprehensive agreement concluded during Qabus's visit to that country (see below). The agreement provided a framework for acquiring French *matériel,* easier access to information, training, and after-sales services. Among the items reportedly on Oman's shopping list were antitank missiles, helicopters, and armored vehicles.[17] Oman's particularity with regard to arms purchases was well reflected in the realistic words of Omani Deputy Prime Minister for Security and Defense Affairs Fahr Ibn Tamur: "We [Oman] never faced any problem in acquiring the arms we need. The sources of our armament are varied, and we intend to maintain that line."[18] Pointing to other facets of military cooperation, an Omani official confirmed that French vessels were being serviced in Omani ports and that Omani officers were being trained in France.[19]

The Navy was kept up-to-date as well: Oman's fourth missile, the *Musandam,* was commissioned in October.[20] The skills of the armed forces were also cultivated through an integrated large-scale maneuver, the "Great Adventure," held in September on Omani soil.

FOREIGN AFFAIRS

OMAN AND THE GULF

With the calm in the Gulf, Oman continued to aspire for an end to the Iraqi-Iranian conflict. As Qabus put it: "...a truce is not the extent of our hopes. We would like to see the truce turn into true peace, based on solid foundations."[21] In line with this view, regional peace remained on the top of Oman's foreign policy agenda. Throughout the eight-year war, Oman had maintained better relations with Iran than most other GCC states. The ability to balance its pro-Arab and pro-Western stance with a friendly approach to Iran made Oman a fitting choice for mediation between Tehran and Arab capitals. Besides mediating between Baghdad and Tehran, Oman made concerted efforts to remove "certain complex issues" which still hampered the prospect of peace. Reconciling Saudi Arabia and Iran — both had severed their relations in April 1988 — was of prime importance. Meetings were held with representatives of both sides; Iranian Foreign Minister 'Ali Akbar Velayati and Saudi Arabian Foreign Minister Sa'ud al-Faysal visited Muscat in February and March, respectively, and conferred with Omani officials. Muscat was also reported to have been a neutral location for a clandestine meeting between both foreign ministers in June.[22] Another issue which attracted Omani attention was the minor crisis of the Kuwaiti warship captured by Iran in May 1988.

Omani-Iranian relations, chiefly economic, improved steadily. Iranian Minister of Heavy Industries Bahzad Nabavi led a delegation to Oman in March, where he attended the opening of the first Iranian heavy industries exhibition in Sib and signed a memorandum providing for the establishment of joint industrial and commercial companies. The economic bond again came to the fore in August, when an Omani delegation visited Tehran to inquire about the role the sultanate could play in Iran's reconstruction efforts.[23] *Rapprochement* efforts reached a peak in September with the appointment of Oman's first ambassador to Iran since the Islamic Revolution broke out. Iran appointed its ambassador to Oman in October 1988.

This, however, did not mean that Oman was going all the way to Iran. Careful not to appear as though Oman was tilting toward Iran, Minister of Information 'Abd al-'Aziz al-Rawwas clarified that relations with Iran would under no circumstance be at the expense of Iraq. Throughout the year, messages were exchanged between Qabus and Iraqi President Saddam Husayn. In October, Rawwas led a delegation to Iraq, and an Omani representative took part in the ceremonies marking the rebuilding of Faw.

Oman attempted to settle long-standing disputes with some GCC states. Relations with Kuwait improved following Qabus's first visit to the country in May. A "turning point needed for the development of both countries' bilateral relations,"[24] the visit was expected to end Omani-Kuwaiti differences over several aspects of GCC policy, most prominently the policy toward Iran. While Kuwait was the supporter of a harsher attitude, Oman advocated a more moderate approach. Now that the guns had fallen silent and the general mood in the region was that of appeasement, those differences were superfluous. Qabus's largely ceremonial visit was preceded by a four-day visit of Kuwaiti Interior Minister Shaykh Salim Al Sabah, to Muscat in March, aimed at boosting cooperation in the field of security.[25] The setting up of a joint naval force to police the Strait of Hormuz and the visit of an Omani vessel to Kuwait in August marked the beginning of such a cooperation.[26]

While in the United Arab Emirates (UAE), Qabus visited Ra's al-Khayma — one of the UAE's seven emirates — apparently bringing to a close a long-standing dispute over Omani-UAE border demarcation.[27] A border demarcation agreement was also reached with Saudi Arabia.[28] As though summing up his efforts for a fresher atmosphere within the GCC, Qabus asserted in his opening speech of the 10th GCC summit of heads of state in Muscat:

the importance of developing and revitalizing the mechanisms of cooperation...gives our joint action more vitality and flexibility. It also helps us achieve what we have always worked for...deepening contacts and coordination and bringing closer the efforts exerted to translate our goals of cooperation into a tangible reality that the Gulf citizens can feel.[29]

On the other side of the peninsula, the improvement of relations with the People's Democratic Republic of Yemen (PDRY) proceeded apace, although minor problems of border demarcation had not been solved. In May, the first agreement regulating civil aviation between Aden and Muscat was concluded.[30] Omani financial relief was given to the PDRY following the floods in March (for details, see chapter on the PDRY). Nonetheless, it was Omani fears for the stability of the regime in Aden which led Oman to support the two Yemens' steps toward unity, hoping that it would draw the PDRY into the more moderate Arab Cooperation Council (ACC) whose members were Egypt, Jordan, Iraq, and North Yemen (for further details on the ACC, see chapter on inter-Arab relations).

OMAN AND INTER-ARAB RELATIONS
Oman's inter-Arab and international relations were spotlighted during Qabus's tour, begun in mid-May, to Kuwait, Egypt, and Jordan, and thereafter his participation in the emergency Arab summit in Casablanca. Visits to Spain and France, the European leg of Qabus's tour, followed.

Cheered by the unprecedented combination of *détente* between the superpowers and the generally less contentious atmosphere in the Arab world, Qabus apparently believed that a successful conclusion to the Casablanca summit could become a cornerstone in resolving some of the Arab world's most critical problems. Accordingly, during his visits to Arab countries, largely in preparation for the Arab summit, Qabus spared no efforts to reach an understanding on the most pressing issues on the Arab agenda, i.e., Egypt's return to the Arab League, the Lebanese crisis, and the Palestinian issue.

Egypt's return to the Arab fold was a prime Omani foreign policy objective. The sultanate had been one of three Arab League members who refused to sever links with Egypt after the 1978 Baghdad summit. Following the restoration of diplomatic ties between Arab states after the 1987 Amman summit, Egypt still remained excluded from the Arab League. Oman made efforts to end this anomaly. This was deemed essential because Egypt's expulsion from the Arab League was followed by "many ordeals which befell the Arab nation."[31] Demonstrating his eagerness to tackle the problem, Qabus said publicly that he would not attend the summit unless "definite results that serve our Arab objectives" could be expected.[32] While in Jordan, he discussed the matter with King Husayn. Their constant efforts, added to those of others, bore fruits. By the time Qabus left Jordan on his way to Egypt, Mubarak had already been invited to the summit. Qabus, it seems, deserved the enthusiastic welcome he received in Egypt. (See also chapter on inter-Arab relations.)

Two of the most pressing regional issues — the Lebanese crisis and the Palestinian question — hitherto not known to have gained Omani attention, were at the top of Omani policy toward the Arab world. Interests extending beyond the Gulf region clearly indicated that Oman's self-centered, somewhat separatist policy was being replaced by stronger links to the larger Arab body.

The Lebanese Crisis

"A deep wound in the Arab body" as one Omani official termed it, the Lebanese crisis also figured prominently on the agenda of Qabus's tour. Qabus was highly in favor of Arab assistance to resolve the crisis, but let it be understood that the matter was basically up to the Lebanese themselves, stressing that only a government recognized by all parties concerned could decide "who was to leave Lebanon and who was to stay."[33] The issue had been dealt with especially in Kuwait, which headed the six-member committee appointed by the Arab League to tackle the crisis. Consultations were also held with Syria, another party with vested interests in Lebanon, during a visit by Omani Minister of State for Foreign Affairs Yusuf Ibn 'Alawi to Damascus.

The Palestinian Issue

Omani-PLO *rapprochement* (see *MECS* 1988, pp. 451–52) became more conspicuous in 1989. PLO Chairman Yasir 'Arafat paid his first visit to the sultanate in January, conferring with Qabus and other senior officials. Although no details of the discussions were released, it seemed obvious that Oman would be asked to take a more crucial part in the efforts to promote the PLO's new line of moderation, as well as to allow a PLO office to operate in Muscat. In spite of its Arab identity, Oman had not been an enthusiastic supporter of the Palestinians or the PLO. Its attitude toward Israel was less negative than that of most Arab states; at times, it had advocated recognition of Israel's right to exist along with recognition of Palestinian political aspirations. However, increased Omani involvement in inter-Arab affairs in recent years and the momentum the Palestinian issue has gained since the outbreak of the uprising called for a change in Omani policy. A PLO office was not yet reported to have been opened in Muscat, but Oman's favoring of the Palestinians became more strongly felt. The changed Omani attitude toward the Palestinian issue was best exemplified in the words of Rawwas that "... we [Oman] believe that dialogue in itself without power to support it cannot achieve the Arab nations' aspirations."[34] Israel gained its share of criticism; Oman complained to the UN Human Rights Committee that Israel had made a mockery of the international decisions regarding human rights in the occupied territories.[35]

QABUS'S EUROPEAN TOUR

Oman's much improved status in the Arab world was further highlighted by the decision to have Qabus present the issues dealt with in Casablanca in his forthcoming European tour.

The sultanate's rapid pace of modernization as well as its role in bringing Iran and Iraq closer raised its stock in the European Community, which was also interested in keeping the Gulf sea routes open and secure. The Omani reputation was to be exploited to promote the Palestinian cause in Europe; more specifically, to pressure the Europeans into taking a firmer stand in favor of the Palestinians. France and Spain, the tour's European leg, were targeted for this purpose since they held senior positions in the community. France, in particular, was considered more receptive than others, having accorded 'Arafat his first state visit. Given its special relations with the Lebanese belligerents, France was also urged to act for a swift settlement to the Lebanese crisis. The visits to France and Spain — the first by an Omani ruler — dealt with bilateral relations as well. Economic and agricultural issues were discussed with both, while an Omani-French military cooperation agreement (see above) made France one of Oman's most important extraregional allies.

OMAN AND THE SUPERPOWERS

Omani-US relations focused on the military sphere. Commander in Chief of the US Central Command Gen. Norman Schwarzkopf came to Oman twice, in March and November, to meet with leading military figures. Talks apparently focused on the US plan to improve facilities in key areas in the region and, as concerned Oman, to turn a disused stone quarry into an aviation-fuel storage complex, to serve both the Omani and US air forces. Meanwhile, the US undertook construction work at the air bases of Masira, Sib, and Thamarit, where US forces were permitted to land and receive service.[36]

Omani-USSR relations maintained their slow and careful momentum. In the first ministerial official visit since relations were established in 1985, Oman's minister of oil and natural resources stopped over in Moscow in January and concluded a series of economic agreements (see above). Discussions to that effect were also held in February, when a Soviet economic delegation arrived in Muscat.

NOTES

For the place and frequency of publications cited here, and for the full name of the publication, news agency, radio station, or monitoring service where an abbreviation is used, please see "List of Sources." Only in the case of more than one publication bearing the same name is the place of publication noted here.

1. *Al-Bayan*, Dubai, 3 April; *CR:* Oman, No. 3, 1989.
2. *CR:* Oman, No. 4, 1989.
3. *Al-Bayan*, Dubai, 4 March 1989.
4. Ibid., 19 February, 3 April 1989.
5. *ME*, June 1989.
6. *CR:* Oman, No. 3, 1989.
7. *ME*, ibid.
8. *Oman Daily Observer*, 19 November 1989.
9. *FT*, 2 March 1989.
10. *The Gulf States*, 20 February 1989.
11. *Al-Fursan*, 2 September 1989.
12. *FT*, 4 April; *CR:* Oman, Nos. 2 and 3, 1989.
13. *Al-Bayan*, Dubai, 15 February; *The Gulf States*, 26 June 1989.
14. *CR:* Oman, No. 2; *al-Fursan*, 15 July 1989.
15. *MEED*, 2 June; *CR:* Oman, No. 3, 1989.
16. *Al-Bayan*, Dubai, 4 May; *The Gulf States*, 15 May 1989.
17. *The Gulf States*, 12 June 1989.
18. *Al-Bayan*, Dubai, 23 April 1989.
19. Interview by 'Alawi with *al-Watan al-'Arabi*, 9 June 1989.
20. *Al-Jundi*, August; *The Gulf States*, 16 October 1989.
21. R. Muscat, 8 May — DR, 10 May 1989.
22. *Beirut al-Masa*, 3 July 1989.
23. *CR:* Oman, Nos. 2 and 4, 1989.
24. *Al-Bayan*, Dubai, 15 May 1989.
25. *CR:* Oman, No. 2, 1989.
26. *Al-Anba*, Kuwait, 22 August 1989.
27. *Ta'ir al-Shimal*, December 1989.
28. R. Muscat, 23 December — DR, 26 December 1989.

29.   R. Muscat, 18 December — DR, 19 December 1989.
30.   *Al-Bayan,* Dubai, 28 May 1989.
31.   Ibid., 17 May 1989.
32.   Ibid., 9 May 1989.
33.   MENA, 21 May 1989.
34.   R. Monte Carlo, 2 June — DR, 14 June 1989.
35.   *Al-Bayan,* Dubai, 6 February 1989.
36.   *MM,* 3 April; *CR:* Oman, No. 4, 1989.

Qatar

UZI RABI

Qatar's entry into the 1990s was not unclouded. Hopes for economic prosperity grew stronger as the first phase of the North Field offshore gas project neared completion. To facilitate its progress into a new economic era due to begin with the commissioning of the North Field offshore gas reservoir, Qatar revised its decision-making apparatus by reshuffling its Cabinet. The bright hopes, however, were overshadowed by the problem of Qatar's still undemarcated maritime borders; a sudden Iranian claim for a third of Qatar's North Field coupled with the still unresolved dispute with Bahrain (for details, see *MECS* 1986, pp. 294–96) was a painful reminder that Qatar's path to security and prosperity was still fraught with danger. Internationally, Qatari-US relations remained under a cloud following the *Stinger* missiles imbroglio (for details see *MECS* 1988, p. 459); in contrast, Qatar's relations with Moscow seemed to be developing nicely.

INTERNAL AFFAIRS

CABINET RESHUFFLE — ON THE MARCH TO A NEW ECONOMIC ERA

On 18 July, a royal decree announced a reshuffle in the Qatari cabinet, the most extensive since Qatar gained its independence in 1971. The members of the new cabinet were:[1]

Heir Apparent and Defense Minister	— Shaykh Hamad Ibn Khalifa Al Thani
Minister of Finance and Petroleum	— Shaykh 'Abd al-'Aziz Ibn Khalifa Al Thani
Minister of Economy and Trade	— Shaykh Hamad Ibn Jasim Ibn Hamad Al Thani
Minister of Interior	— Shaykh 'Abdallah Ibn Khalifa Al Thani
Minister of Information and Culture	— Shaykh Hamad Ibn Suhaym Al Thani
Minister of Justice	— Shaykh Ahmad Ibn Sayf Al Thani
Minister of Public Health	— Shaykh Khalid Ibn Muhammad Ibn 'Ali Al Thani
Minister of Municipal Affairs and Agriculture	— Shaykh Hamad Ibn Jasim Ibn Jabr Al Thani
Minister of Amiri Court Affairs	— Dr. 'Isa Ibn Ghanim al- Kuwari
Minister of Transportation and Communications	— 'Abdallah Ibn Salih al-Mani'
Minister of Foreign Affairs	— 'Abdallah Ibn Khalifa al-'Atiyya
Minister of Education	— 'Abd al-'Aziz 'Abdallah Turki
Minister of Electricity and Water	— Mubarak 'Ali al-Khatir
Minister of Industry and Public Works	— Ahmad Muhammad 'Ali al-Subay'i
Minister of Labor, Social Affairs, and Housing	— 'Abd al-Rahman Sa'id al-Dirham.

The cabinet was increased from 11 to 15 members, restoring several long-vacant posts and creating new ones. Only two ministers had been members of the outgoing government, the minister of defense and the minister of finance and oil; 11 ministers were replaced. Many were relatively young and some were promoted from the rank of under secretary.[2]

The fact that nine portfolios were given to members of the Thani ruling family indicated clearly that government in Qatar remained a family affair. The position of Shaykh Khalifa's sons was consolidated. The Ministry of Interior was given to his third son, 'Abdallah, while the fourth, Muhammad, was appointed under secretary in the Finance and Petroleum Ministry. The second son, 'Abd al-'Aziz, remained as finance and oil minister, but most notably, the political influence of Shaykh Hamad, the eldest son, was greatly enhanced. Apart from the confirmation given to his position as heir apparent, Hamad remained minister of defense and commander in chief of the Qatari armed forces. His more active involvement in government was evidenced by his appointment, in May, as chairman of the newly created Supreme Planning Council (see below).

Nonetheless, some of the key changes involved the promotion or introduction of outsiders. Particularly important was the elevation of the former information minister, Dr. 'Isa Ghanim al-Kuwari, to head the newly established Amiri Court Affairs Ministry, formalizing his position as Khalifa's chief adviser. Concurrently, Hamad's adviser, 'Abdallah Ibn Khalifa al-'Atiyya, was made foreign minister, a post that had been vacant since 1978. The promotion of both protégés to so high a level in the official hierarchy implied more harmonious relations between the ruler and the heir apparent, who were reported to have disagreed on regional policy, in particular the line to be followed in the dispute with Bahrain.[3]

The cabinet changes also had considerable economic significance. Industry, hitherto in one ministry together with agriculture, was now linked with public works, in a portfolio given to Ahmad Muhammad 'Ali al-Subay'i, chairman of the Qatar Steel Company and the head of the Aluminum Project Steering Committee. It was intended that the newly created Ministry of Industry and Public Works would also be responsible for plans to utilize Qatar's enormous offshore gas reserves. Shifted to the ministry was the Industrial Development Technical Center, responsible for industrial planning, which had hitherto reported directly to the royal court.[4] The economy and trade portfolio, unmanned since 1986, was given to Shaykh Hamad Ibn Jasim Ibn Hamad Al Thani. The new grip on economic affairs became apparent in May when Shaykh Hamad set up a Supreme Council for Planning. Independently staffed and budgeted, the council was responsible for drafting new development plans and monitoring their implementation, as well as for proposing legislation and reorganizing government activities.[5] These far-reaching administrative changes — uncharacteristic of Qatar — together with the relatively youthful new cabinet indicated that the country was gearing itself for a new economic era, due to begin with the commissioning of the North Field offshore gas reservoir.

THE DEVELOPMENT OF THE NORTH FIELD GAS PROJECT

Relying on oil for 90% of its export earnings, but having one of the lowest production levels of the Organization of Petroleum Exporting Countries, Qatar's economy in recent years had slowed down and its budget was in deficit. It was hardly surprising, therefore, that Qatar moved gingerly toward the development of the North Field gas project as the underpinning of its economy. The project was expected to provide

Qatar with the feedstock needed to fuel and expand its manufacturing industries, meet its hard-pressed domestic power requirements and, ultimately, leave a healthy and growing surplus for export. Various large-scale plans indicated that Qatar aimed at making the most of that unique opportunity. With 70% of the engineering work already completed, the first stage of the project was due to be commissioned in early 1991. It was to fulfill Qatar's domestic needs by supplying much-needed feedstock to meet the pressing demand for electricity that quadrupled over the last decade.[6] Gas was also needed for the expansion of domestic manufacturing industries, such as fertilizer production and the projected ferroalloy smelter; but most prominent was the planned Doha Aluminum Smelter, expected to be the largest in the Gulf. Expectations for expanded economic activity were so great that it was planned to set up a new industrial zone at Ra's Qirtas at the end of the decade, should the zone at Umm Sa'id no longer suffice.[7]

The large surplus was planned for export during the second and third phases of the project. Accordingly, a natural-gas pipeline to Dubai's Jabal 'Ali industrial zone was under consideration.[8] In the world market, it was expected that a large volume of exports would go to Japan, and officials of both countries held talks on the subject in Doha and Tokyo.[9] However, financing most of these projects remained a problem. Since these projects required investments not available at home, Qatar took two syndicated loans totaling $600m. on the international market.[10]

FOREIGN AFFAIRS

QATAR AND THE GULF STATES

Qatar expressed satisfaction with the continuing regional calm and the Iraqi-Iranian peace talks. Its newly appointed foreign minister, 'Abdallah Ibn Khalifa al-'Atiyya, gave assurance of Qatar's firm support for the efforts made to secure peace in the region, since "it is a vital necessity not only for us but for the whole world."[11] The thaw in Qatari-Iranian relations was best evinced by visits of the Iranian delegations to Qatar in January and February during which the strengthening of economic and cultural ties was discussed. Throughout the year messages were exchanged between both countries.

This *rapprochement,* however, came under challenge in June, when Iranian Oil Minister Gholam Reza Agazadeh laid claim to a third of Qatar's North Field. After having determined the exact quantity of gas in its territory, Iran would pump its share of the gas from the field to a nearby processing plant, he said.[12] Qatar remained silent, perhaps because of its surprise and consternation. In reaction, it chose to lay more emphasis on the "good neighborliness and Muslim brotherhood" in Qatari-Iranian relations. Qatar's development and exploration works were concentrated in Qatari territory, but there was no saying what might occur when both countries decided to exploit the part of the field adjacent to their marine boundaries. Added to its unresolved dispute with Bahrain, which was a constant threat to the integrity of the Gulf Cooperation Council (GCC), the Iranian claim was undoubtedly perceived by Qatar as a potential threat to the region. Both aggravated Qatari fears of becoming the catalyst of instability in the Gulf. Given its minuscule size, Qatar increased its reliance on the GCC, encouraging the six member states to stand together and strengthen their resistance against any outside intervention in Gulf affairs.

QATAR AND INTER-ARAB AFFAIRS

Traditionally passive in the inter-Arab arena, Qatar did not miss any opportunity to advocate Arab solidarity. It welcomed the end of the Gulf War and the generally less contentious Arab atmosphere. It also hailed the launching of the two new groupings, the Arab Cooperation Council and the Arab Maghrib Union (for details, see chapter on inter-Arab relations). As in previous years, the Lebanese crisis and the Palestinian issue figured prominently on Qatar's inter-Arab agenda. It affirmed its full support for efforts to help settle the Lebanese crisis and its readiness to participate in them; it called on the Lebanese belligerents to cooperate with the six-member Arab committee charged with tackling the problem, so that its efforts might succeed.[13] Qatari support for the Palestinian cause reached a high in January when it recognized the new declared Palestinian State and upgraded the PLO office in Doha to ambassadorial level. Qatar raised the Palestinian issue in various inter-Arab and international forums; in the UN, it called on international public opinion to help protect the Palestinians in the West Bank and Gaza Strip from what it called Israeli persecution.[14] Its foreign minister favored allowing the Palestinians to decide on their destiny without outside interference, since "we [Qatar] support everything which is acceptable to our Palestinian brothers."[15] The Qatari media were more outspoken; the weekly *Akhbar al-Usbu'* demanded that Arab assistance be given to the Palestinians under Israeli rule so as to enable the uprising to escalate to civil war.[16] Qatar's generous financial support for the Intifada made the country a favored site for visits by PLO officials: Chairman Yasir 'Arafat came in March and conferred with Shaykh Khalifa; Salah Khalaf (Abu Iyad) arrived twice at the beginning of the year. Apart from general policy coordination, these visits may have been used to resettle c. 150 Palestinian policemen who were reportedly expelled from Qatar in January.[17]

Qatar continued to cultivate ties with the more conservative Arab states. Besides support for Egypt's return to the Arab League, one issue was prominent in Qatari-Egyptian relations — Egyptian workers in Qatar. The interest in the uninterrupted flow of Egyptian teachers — highly appreciated by most GCC states — was well expressed during the visit of Qatari Minister of Culture Shaykh Ahmad Ibn Hamad Al Thani to Egypt in February.[18] Conclusion of a Qatari-Egyptian cultural cooperation agreement was discussed the following month when Thani's Egyptian counterpart, Dr. Ahmad Fathi Surur, paid a reciprocal visit.[19] The welfare of Egyptian workers in Qatar was dealt with during the visit to Egypt in May of Qatari Minister of Social Affairs 'Ali Ibn Ahmad al-'Ansari. Mutual coordination on security-related matters, probably drug-trafficking and terrorism, was also brought up during a visit to Qatar by Egyptian Interior Minister Zaki Badr in November.

As part of the Arab efforts to help Jordan overcome its economic crisis (see chapter on Jordan), Qatar agreed to provide economic aid to Amman during a visit by Jordanian Prime Minister Zayid Ibn Shakir to Qatar in August.[20] Relations with Libya, which was known to have a hand in the 1983 coup attempt in Qatar (see *MECS* 1983–84, pp. 457–58), seemed to be on the mend. Qatari Minister of Information and Culture Shaykh Hamad Ibn Suhaym Al Thani reportedly visited Libya in September; the following month, a Libyan envoy visited Qatar, bringing a message to Shaykh Khalifa from Mu'ammar Qadhdhafi. Solidarity with Libya was expressed after the January clash between US and Libyan aircraft[21] (for details on the incident, see chapter on Libya).

QATAR AND THE SUPERPOWERS

Qatari-USSR relations after the establishment of diplomatic ties in 1988 developed further particularly following the Soviet withdrawal from Afghanistan. The USSR Embassy in Qatar was formally opened in June and Soviet Ambassador Vladimir Vodiachin presented his credentials in October.[22] In another development, the first Soviet economic delegation to Qatar arrived in February to discuss expansion of bilateral ties; issues such as coordination in the field of extraction and marketing of gas as well as the holding of a joint exhibition were raised.[23] However, a joint economic cooperation agreement was not concluded.

Qatari-US relations, however, remained under a cloud following the *Stinger* missiles imbroglio (for details, see *MECS* 1988 chapter on Qatar, p. 572). No formal meetings or exchange visits of any kind were reported. The Qatari media continued to lash out at the US for its links with Israel. The daily *al-'Arab,* for instance, suggested that the US was unfit to serve as a go-between in the Israeli-Palestinian dispute because of its "double talk" on issues related to the Middle East.[24]

In line with its policy of having ties with the largest possible number of states, Qatar established diplomatic relations with the Socialist Federal Republic of Yugoslavia, Poland, Peru, and Cuba.

NOTES

For the place and frequency of publications cited here, and for the full name of the publication, news agency, radio station, or monitoring service where an abbreviation is used, please see "List of Sources." Only in the case of more than one publication bearing the same name is the place of publication noted here.

1. MENA, 18 July — DR, 18 July 1989.
2. *The Gulf States,* 6 August; *CR:* Qatar, No. 3; *MEED,* 20 October 1989.
3. *The Gulf States,* ibid.; *CR:* Qatar, ibid.
4. *The Gulf States,* 21 August 1989.
5. *Al-Bayan,* Dubai, 11 May; *CR:* Qatar, ibid.
6. *Al-Hawadith,* 24 February; *Memo,* 27 February 1989.
7. *The Gulf States,* 26 June 1989.
8. *Memo,* 5 July 1989.
9. Ibid., 16 March; *ME,* June 1989.
10. *Suraqiyya,* 3 June; *MEED,* 20 October 1989.
11. *Al-Usbu' al-'Arabi,* 23 October 1989.
12. *ME,* June; *CR:* Qatar, No. 2, 1989.
13. *Al-Bayan,* Dubai, 2 February 1989.
14. Ibid., 4 February 1989.
15. *Al-Usbu' al-'Arabi,* 23 October 1989.
16. QNA, 8 October 1989.
17. *Al-Nashra,* Athens, 6 March; *al-Muharrir,* 11 March 1989.
18. *Al-Bayan,* Dubai, 5 April 1989.
19. Ibid., 29 May 1989.
20. *Al-Bayan,* Dubai, 10 August 1989.
21. GNA, 5 January — DR, 6 January 1989.
22. TASS, 12 June, 23 October 1989.
23. GNA, 16 February — DR, 16 February; *Memo,* 16 March 1989.
24. GNA, 31 July — DR, 1 August 1989.

Saudi Arabia
(Al-Mamlaka al-'Arabiyya al-Sa'udiyya)

JACOB GOLDBERG

Nineteen eighty-nine was the first positive year for the Saudi economy in a seven-year recession. Gross domestic product (GDP) grew by over 3% for the second consecutive year and there were signs of renewed confidence within the business community. The royal family hoped that the shift represented a reversal of conditions in the oil market and signified the beginning of a new trend which would gather momentum in the 1990s. It was still premature to assess whether this optimism was predicated on realistic assumptions or on wishful thinking. What was certain, however, was the Saudi perception that a strong recovery in oil prices was the key, if not the prerequisite, for bringing an end to budgetary deficits, large-scale borrowings, and the drain on financial reserves.

Indeed, new emphases in Saudi oil policy revealed that it had become totally linked, if not subordinated, to revenue requirements. This was the underlying reason for the Saudi search for "downstream" joint ventures around the world: the need to carve out permanent markets for Saudi oil in order to secure guaranteed revenues. The critical dependence on oil revenues exposed an ominous reality about the kingdom. Despite 15 years of planned industrialization and modernization, three elaborate five-year plans, and hundreds of billions of dollars in investments aimed at diversifying the economy, the kingdom remained by and large a one-crop economy with non-oil income being largely derived from financial investments overseas. It was still the flow of hard-to-predict oil revenues which could make or break budgetary projections, and could determine the size of the deficit and the need to resort to borrowing.

This negative state of affairs accounted for the fourth five-year plan being reoriented toward the private sector and the privatization of state-owned companies. The underlying goal was to create new sources of capital inflow by such methods as offset investments in Saudi projects, private capital repatriation, and even foreign borrowing.

The cumulative impact of the seven-year recession also resulted in severe social strains, exacerbating the erosion of traditional values caused by a speedy pace of modernization. High unemployment, especially among university graduates, a growing drug problem, rising waves of crimes and executions, all pointed to heightening social malaise. These could threaten and rip apart the delicate social fabric of the society. In the long run it could potentially translate into a challenge to the political stability of the kingdom and the royal family.

In foreign affairs, the Saudis were facing at the end of 1989 a regional situation not as favorable to the kingdom's interests as they had expected. New developments in the Middle East forced the Saudis to try to influence the various new alignments and reshuffles in order to be certain that the kingdom was not outmaneuvered by any

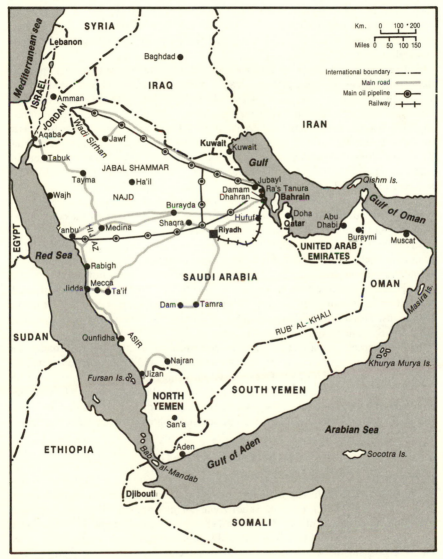

Saudi Arabia

realignment. The royal family had hoped that the end of the Iran-Iraq War and the death of Ayatollah Khomeyni would free Riyadh from an obsessive preoccupation with events threatening their "soft belly" in the Gulf region. But the unresolved dispute between Baghdad and Tehran raised serious questions about the latter's long-term intentions and continued to constrain Saudi strategic planning. The growing desire of Gulf Cooperation Council (GCC) members to pursue foreign policies independently of Riyadh also served as a major source of anxiety for the Saudi leadership.

But Saudi preoccupation with the Persian Gulf extended to another, perhaps more dangerous, threat — a new, powerful Iraq — which demonstrated that the end of the war entailed negative consequences as well. In fact, fear of Iraq became the most dominant single feature in Saudi regional policy. The royal family viewed Iraqi aspirations as centered on the Gulf area and the ME as a whole, but primarily focused on the Arabian Peninsula — the Gulf states and the Yemens, areas in the Saudi orbit. The establishment of the Arab Cooperation Council (ACC), with Iraq as its linchpin, was a case in point. But while the Saudi anxiety concerning the ACC considerably lessened by the end of the year, the fear of Iraq remained intact. This generated, surprisingly, a new Saudi interest in seeing a strong Iran as a counterbalance to Iraq's regional aspirations. Saudi overtures to Tehran, eventually foiled by the controversy over the Hajj quota, must be viewed also in this context.

In the Arab arena, Saudi Arabia could finally point to a success: the resumption of diplomatic relations between Syria and Egypt, though it was doubtful whether Riyadh could take credit for this development. The Saudi mediation in the Lebanese crisis ended in mixed results: success in convening the Lebanese Parliament in Ta'if, but failure in standing up to Syria, which exposed the limited Saudi leverage on Damascus. This also explains why all Saudi attempts to mediate between Syria and Iraq, and Syria and the PLO ended in failure.

In the international arena, the Saudis continued their attempts to broaden the range of their foreign relations. Arms deals with Britain and France demonstrated the desire "to diversify the sources of weaponry." Growing trade relations with the USSR and China reinforced the Saudi willingness to expand relations even with Communist countries. But all these could not obliterate the clear Saudi awareness that the US was still at the center of both Saudi foreign policy and military procurement plans.

DOMESTIC AFFAIRS

ECONOMIC AND FINANCIAL PROBLEMS

The most conspicuous factor in the 1989 budget was the projection of expenditures at 1988 levels — $37.65bn. (141bn. Saudi riyals). This signaled an end to successive reductions in government spending since 1983. The decision to check the decline in spending reflected Saudi realization that dwindling expenditures had reached a red line, the crossing of which might result in adverse political consequences. This assessment was substantiated by updated figures for 1987, showing that actual spending reached SR173bn. against a projected SR160bn. Hence, further expenditure cuts were deemed impossible.[1]

Revenues were projected at $31bn. (SR116bn.), up from $28.08bn. (SR105.3bn.) in 1988. No indication was given as to the expected breakdown of income between oil and non-oil revenues, most probably because of the uncertainties surrounding oil prices. It was reasonably expected that non-oil income would fall in 1989. For one thing, no new revenue-raising taxes or fees were introduced and subsidies were kept intact, largely because of the king's promise to protect living standards. For another, investment income appeared to have been traditionally overstated; in 1988 it was budgeted at SR15bn.–SR18bn., while in reality it could not have exceeded SR7bn.–SR8bn. Assuming non-oil revenue of SR25bn., the Saudis were hoping for SR91bn, in oil revenues. While this looked unrealistic at the beginning of the year, strong oil prices combined with rising quotas throughout 1989 seemed to have made it possible (see below).

Built into the budget was a SR25bn. deficit, compared to a projected SR38bn. and actual SR35.9bn. deficit in 1988. The royal family, for the second consecutive year, decided to resort to borrowing by means of bond issues to finance the deficit. In 1988, only part of the deficit — SR30bn. — was to be financed by borrowing, with the balance being drawn from the financial reserves of the kingdom. In 1989, however, the entire SR25bn. deficit was to be funded by borrowing.

The bond issues in 1988 were not a great success, to say the least, with the commercial banks taking up only 30%-50% of the SR30bn. bonds. This forced the government to dispose of all the unsold bonds by using the large sums of money deposited with two government agencies: the Civil Service Pension Fund (CSPF) and the General Organization for Social Insurance (Gosi).

There was a consensus among Saudi bankers that the bond issues failed to appeal to individual Saudis and that all efforts to create a secondary market had ended in failure. This was attributed partly to the absence of trading regulations. Consequently, the Saudi Arabian Monetary Agency (Sama) formed a committee of bankers to draw up trading guidelines and procedures.[2]

While in 1988 the government resorted only to CSPF and Gosi funds, in 1989 it placed bonds also with other quasi-official bodies such as Aramco, Petromin, and Sabic. But it soon became apparent that the government had to resort also, for the first time, to direct dollar-denominated loans. Breaking an official taboo against such borrowing, Finance Minister Muhammad Aba al-Khayl signed in early August an agreement with a syndicate of 11 banks for a $660m. loan to the government-owned Public Investment Fund (PIF). Technically, this did not constitute a government loan. But it was abundantly clear that the cash-rich PIF took on debt in order to cover purchases of government bonds. This technique gave the Saudi leaders access to reserves previously deemed untouchable. It was expected that the government would repeat the PIF pattern using Gosi and CSPF funds in order to avoid the impression of direct foreign loans. The need to resort to foreign borrowing was evidence of the failure to raise the necessary funds at home.[3]

The decision to resort only to borrowing and to avoid a further drawdown on the reserves reflected King Fahd's assessment that the latter could not be depleted further after having sunk to $40bn. To make matters worse, the reserves were becoming less and less liquid since the government had sold off its more easily realized holdings. Moreover, a significant proportion of the reserves consisted of assets that were unlikely to be collected, such as International Monetary Fund (IMF) reserve positions, aid loans to Arab countries, and assistance to Iraq during the Gulf War.[4] So paramount was this priority that the government preferred to be falling behind on payments to contractors and suppliers. By the fall of 1989, half of 1988's crop subsidy — some $680m. — had not been yet paid. And despite the recovery in oil prices in the second half of 1989, the government was still plagued by payments arrears to both local and foreign firms.

It was not clear why the government was having such cash-flow difficulties, especially since oil revenues were on target and perhaps even higher. The most likely explanation was that an increasing proportion of Saudi oil exports was being earmarked to pay for Saudi imports, especially arms. With arms procurement proceeding in full gear (see below), the government was free to sell less and less oil for cash, hence the recurring budgetary constraints.[5]

The most decisive evidence of King Fahd's determination to stop the drain on the reserves, even at the cost of embarrassment to the kingdom, occurred in December. A leak in a British publication suggested that Riyadh faced a gap in payments for the huge *Tornado* arms deal (see *MECS* 1988, p. 684). Saudi Arabia had already suffered a similar gap in 1987, which it resolved by an overdraft of $1.3bn. This time the gap was much larger — $3.1 bn. — and worse, Riyadh could solve it only by obtaining a formal loan. The gap originated from the fact that more arms and equipment were being delivered than could be covered by the 400,000 barrels per day (b/d) of oil which Saudi Arabia was countertrading. The loan was expected to be raised in London from a consortium put together by British and Saudi banks, the latter being joint venture banks.[6]

One way to alleviate the budgetary constraints was to devalue the riyal. Many Saudi bankers argued for a devaluation because it could boost the domestic spending power of the oil revenues. But King Fahd remained opposed adamantly for fear that living costs in the kingdom might increase substantially. Moreover, in early 1989, the government used strong-arm tactics to end speculation against the riyal. By withholding state payments, it forced the banks to liquidate their own dollar positions to meet riyal withdrawals. The king's unequivocal position also aimed at eliminating any exchange-rate risks, thus making the bond issues more attractive for investors.[7]

Despite the pressing financial challenges, there was an overall sense that the end of the seven-year economic crisis was finally within sight. Such a confident state of mind was reinforced by the 3.2% increase in the GDP in both 1988 and 1989, after five consecutive years of decline. There were also clear signs that the construction industry had recovered from a deep recession.[8] Another positive sign of major importance was the repatriation in 1988 of SR27bn. held by Saudis abroad. True, this was less than 10% of the SR300bn. thought to be held by Saudis overseas, but as the new five-year plan was launched, with its emphasis on the private sector, King Fahd hoped that more Saudis would be motivated to repatriate their capital.[9] Finally, a study by the Riyadh Chamber of Commerce concluded that the kingdom had reached self-sufficiency in many industrial and agricultural products. These included wheat, mineral water, fruit juices, fertilizers, feeds, base petrochemicals, and soap. Virtual self-sufficiency had been obtained in the production of eggs, dairy products, watermelons, sweets, cement, desert coolers, lubrication oils, and paints. There was no doubt that such findings were bound to enhance confidence in the Saudi economy.[10]

ATTEMPTS TO RESTRUCTURE THE ECONOMY

Privatization and Saudization became the catchwords in the efforts to restructure the Saudi economy and prepare it for the 1990s. Indeed, they were the cornerstone of the kingdom's fifth five-year plan, which was to go into effect in 1990. They also dominated the fourth Saudi Businessmen's Conference held in Riyadh in late May (for previous conferences, see *MECS* 1982–83, pp. 748–49; 1984–85, pp. 592–93; 1987, p. 585).

The new five-year plan was predicated on the need to achieve a transition to a private-sector oriented economy. Its main goals were:

(a) Reduction in government expenditure without decreasing public services;

(b) Increase in reliance on private-sector activity, drawing private capital to investments and to development projects;

(c) Encouraging the private sector to employ more Saudi citizens, and replacing non-Saudi manpower with Saudi personnel; and

(d) Achieving balanced development between various regions of the kingdom.[11]

These objectives became the official policy of the Ministry of Planning. In January, a symposium on "the role of the private sector in development" convened in Riyadh. The ministry presented a paper suggesting the creation of a ministerial committee to look into privatization and the transfer of some government bodies to the private sector. Specifically recommended for privatization were parts of the petrochemical industry as well as export-oriented and import-substitution manufacturing sectors. The symposium recommended:

(a) The merger of smaller projects and firms;

(b) The establishment of an export finance bank;

(c) More sales of government stakes in joint-stock companies;

(d) Improvement of government statistical information to help the private-sector decision-making proecess; and

(e) Accelerated recruitment of Saudi personnel.[12]

To show its concern for the development of the private sector, the Commerce Ministry issued renewed notices to foreign contractors stressing the requirement to sublet no less than 30% of their contract work to wholly owned Saudi firms, and to confine services related to transport, catering, land lease, insurance, and banking to Saudi establishments. In addition, reports of progress on government projects frequently emphasized the involvement of Saudi companies. For instance, 400 Saudi contractors were engaged in the construction of King Fahd International Airport in the Eastern Province and materials purchased for the project in the local market totaled SR1.2bn.[13]

The government, however, did not abstain from criticizing the private sector. An assistant under secretary in the Ministry of Planning, Prince Faysal Ibn Sultan, emphasized that in the transfer of projects to the private sector, it was imperative "to introduce adequate rules to restrain its purely profit-making mentality."[14] In the same spirit, Oil Minister and Acting Minister of Planning Hisham Nazir stated that the Saudi private sector "needs to exercise greater self-denial and responsibility for productive investment."[15]

There was an area, however, in which both the government and the private sector could be criticized. A recent study revealed that only 9.5% of the employees in the nongovernment sector were Saudi nationals. If companies belonging to Sabic were excluded from the sample, the proportion of Saudi workers would fall to 4.9%(!).

Arab nationals formed 18% of the work force, with the remaining 72.5%(!) coming from other countries. These alarming figures proved that the private sector did not adhere to its own fine words about Saudization. Moreover, they questioned the government's implementation of the Labor Code's stipulation that the proportion of Saudi workers on a company's payroll should not be less than 75%.

The study leveled specific charges at all parties. Factory owners were blamed for preferring cheaper expatriate labor, for offering short-term employment contracts which provided no job security, and for equipping their plants with sophisticated machinery to which Saudi employees were unaccustomed. The study deemed the training of Saudi personnel highly deficient. Finally, it confirmed the widespread view that the average Saudi only wanted jobs with managerial authority.[16]

The Saudi leadership sought to rectify the situation, using the same old methods of affording preferential treatment to Saudi firms that complied with Saudization programs. Thus, in early 1989 Defense Minister Sultan, in his capacity as chairman of the Manpower Council, issued a set of decrees stipulating that consulting firms would get government contracts only if a minimum 10% of their work force were Saudi nationals. By 1999 this minimum was to rise to 50%. As these regulations contained the same considerations embodied in previous rulings, there was general skepticism as to the effectiveness of the new measures.[17]

It was against this multitude of problems that the fourth Saudi Businessmen's Conference convened in Jidda at the end of May. These problems notwithstanding, the upbeat and constructive conference reflected the perception of the 1,500 delegates that the private sector was clearly in better health than ever since the first conference in 1983. Indeed, while the previous conferences were characterized by complaints and accusations leveled at the government, the emphasis in this conference was on a positive set of recommendations.

Four main topics dominated the three-day sessions: (a) restructuring the private sector; (b) Saudization of the labor force; (c) promoting local investment; and (d) privatization. Specific recommendations on the first issue included calls for more mergers, joint-stock companies, specialized marketing companies, the licensing of national insurance companies, promotion of internal tourism, and provision of project loans. On the second issue, Saudization, few new policies were introduced and the general feeling was rather pessimistic. To encourage more local investment, the conference called for the development of a stock market, more private-sector involvement in the offset program, tax exemptions on schemes to widen share ownership, and consideration of a duty-free zone in the kingdom.

Privatization, however, emerged as the key issue. The goals of any privatization program were described as repatriation of private capital, private-sector involvement in major productive activity, and the creation of a wider and more stable capital market. The conference determined that the first step was to establish a planning body comprising government ministries, businessmen, and consultants. Representing the government in the conference, Commerce Minister Sulayman al-Sulaym gave the entire privatization program unequivocal cabinet support. He indicated the possible privatization of 13 establishments, such as Petromin, Saudia Airlines, the General Railway Organization, and Sabic.

Such a positive atmosphere was tempered by a number of factors. For one thing, there was disappointment that more concrete steps were not laid down. For another, there were doubts whether the private sector had sufficient managerial and organizational skills — not to mention long-term vision and commitment — to develop some of the kingdom's industries. There was also uncertainty as to whether the current dual system of public and private involvement in areas such as health and education should be revised. Nevertheless, a consensus prevailed that the government would be able to dictate its own pace for privatization as long as it opened a few small minority interests in large state companies to the public.[18]

SAUDI OIL POLICIES

Nineteen eighty-nine was most probably the first positive year for Saudi oil since the reversal in the oil market's fortunes in the early 1980s. With a perception that the years of glut were over, 1989 undoubtedly served as a model for Saudi expectations: a sustained period of both oil production and prices rising simultaneously. If this process continued, the Saudi leadership hoped not only to maximize revenues, but also to recover from seven years of consecutive deficits.

Saudi oil policies in 1989 consisted of a combination of continuity and change. In terms of continuity, the overriding Saudi goal was to maintain the kingdom's market share in the Organization of Petroleum Exporting Countries (Opec) and to reject the swing-producer role. Thus, King Fahd repeatedly served notice that any increase in Opec production would have to be shared out by all members proportionately to existing quotas. This was a direct rebuff to Kuwait and the United Arab Emirates (UAE), which sought to get a larger slice of a bigger cake. Repeating the same message on the eve of the Opec meeting in November, Oil Minister Nazir stated that Saudi Arabia would insist on retaining its Opec share [24.6%] in any revised production quota agreement.[19]

Also in terms of continuity, Saudi Arabia was opposed to any unjustified increase in oil prices not commensurate with the market realities of demand and supply. This "moderation" was not aimed at keeping prices down for its own sake. It was designed to prevent the development of alternative sources of energy and the exploration of new oil fields. In other words, the Saudi leadership was determined not to repeat the 1970s pattern when sharp increases in oil prices triggered these adverse consequences. In the words of Hisham Nazir: "We learned that too high a price sets the stage for too low a price."[20]

It was against this background that an unexpected statement by King Fahd created havoc in the oil market. He told an interviewer that he expected oil prices "to reach $26 a barrel at the beginning of 1990, provided production ceilings are strictly adhered to."[21] As a 50% rise in oil prices appeared to be antithetical to Saudi preference for stable prices, the oil minister rushed to explain the discrepancy. The king, Nazir explained, did not want to raise the price to $26 by "reducing production or anything like that." Rather, Fahd wanted to stress that "a commitment by all producers to their quotas will allow the natural balance of supply and demand to work." Consequently, Nazir reasoned, "the natural increase of demand for oil which we witness will eventually raise prices up as the king noted."[22]

It seemed certain that Fahd did not want to see prices climb to $26, nor did he believe they would. His statement, rather, was directed at his fellow Opec members, hence its timing — the eve of Opec's ministerial meeting in Geneva (see chapter on oil developments). Instead of repeating the usual Saudi threats against quota violations,

Fahd decided to opt for a positive approach. The king was trying to coax Opec members by suggesting to them that the best way to maximize revenues was by adhering to, not exceeding, their quota. The emphasis in Fahd's statement was therefore not on the first part, but rather on the latter — "provided production ceilings are strictly adhered to." Such an emphasis made it imperative for the Saudis to deny vehemently that the kingdom itself was producing well in excess of its quota.[23]

Changes in Saudi oil policy were reflected in a number of areas. In June, Nazir called on Opec to abandon its official policy of an $18 target price, and focus its strategy instead on absolute adherence to production ceilings. Such a new approach, Nazir reasoned, would let the market forces set the price and would likely result in prices higher than $18, "which Saudi Arabia no longer considers as its target." Two weeks earlier, Nazir had proposed that instead of the $18 target, Opec adopt a floor price of $15; but he subsequently withdrew the proposal. In the Opec meeting, Saudi Arabia did not succeed in scrapping the $18 reference price. However, this target was given less prominence at the expense of emphasizing the centrality of adhering to production quotas.[24]

Another major shift in Saudi policy centered on the need to raise production capacity substantially. Saudi capacity had been steadily declining since 1982 due to production cutbacks, maintenance delays, the aging of fields, and the mothballing of installations. It was suggested that the kingdom's sustainable capacity might be just a little over 6.5m. b/d, down from 10.5m. b/d in 1981, and plans were already in hand to raise it to 10m. b/d.[25] In addition to increasing revenues, two other reasons underlaid this new policy. First, low crude production was dragging down associated and natural gas output, undermining plans of the petrochemical industry. Second, and in the long run far more important, production capacity affected Saudi Arabia's position in Opec. Two criteria determined Opec's quota distribution system: oil reserves and production capacity. Recently, the latter took precedence over the former as the determinant factor. With Saudi production in decline, a trend in Opec circles tended to downgrade the actual Saudi production capacity. An inevitable outcome was a sharp fall in the Saudi share of overall Opec output: from 30.5% in 1979 and a record 42.3% in 1981 to 20.9% in 1985. The Saudis were determined to reverse this trend and stabilize their 25% share of total Opec production.

For this strategy to succeed, it was imperative also to increase export capacity. The oil minister linked the two, explaining that increasing production capacity to 10m. b/d would be "more in line with increasing export capacity to 14m. b/d." It was with this goal in mind that the government was pressing ahead with upgrading Petroline's capacity from 3.2m. b/d to 4.8m. b/d by 1992. Such a level would enable the Saudis to export almost their entire present output via the Red Sea, relieving them of the anxieties of Persian Gulf turmoil.[26]

Though production and export capacities took precedence over the volume of proven reserves, the latter still remained a major factor in Opec quota distribution. A Saudi move on this front became all the more urgent as in recent years Venezuela, Iran, Iraq, and the UAE had all claimed much higher proven reserves in order to improve their bargaining position in Opec's quota allocation. This had significantly eroded Saudi Arabia's position as Opec's preeminent oil power, being in possession of only 22% of total Opec reserves. Consequently, in the first week of 1989, the kingdom announced a major revision of its proven reserves — from 167bn. barrels to 252bn.

(25% of the world's total). Thus, Riyadh could legitimately demand a far higher production quota, claiming a third of Opec reserves but only a quarter of production.[27]

An element of continuity, though with far greater emphasis, was the Saudi determination to invest heavily in downstream networks. The joint venture with Texaco, signed in November 1988 and named Star Enterprise (see *MECS* 1988, p. 683), provided the Saudis with a secure market for 600,000 b/d. At the signing ceremony, Nazir expressed interest in similar joint ventures also in Europe and Asia, hoping to see the kingdom eventually marketing all its crude through such integrated channels.[28]

Speaking at an oil conference in London in late 1989, Nazir sought to provide a conceptual framework for the idea of downstream ventures, giving it ideological, as well as practical, legitimacy. He said that close cooperation between producing countries and the big oil companies was imperative, because the two were roughly balanced as forces in the international oil industry. It was a question of mutual self-interest: the oil companies depended on the producing countries for access to crude supplies, while the oil producers needed the international marketing networks of the oil companies in order to sell their crude and refined products. Close cooperation, Nazir concluded, would enhance security of markets for producers and security of supply for oil companies and consumers, thereby creating a much more stable oil market.[29] On another occasion, Nazir declared that the kingdom would "welcome approaches from oil companies around the world having downstream refining and distribution facilities but suffering from a declining base of proven reserves."[30]

Nazir's underlying agenda revealed that a whole new strategy of relationships with the global oil markets was in the making in Riyadh. It meant that Saudi Arabia was much more concerned with increasing its market share and securing access to its oil crude and products than with the policies and cohesiveness of Opec. This major reorientation was undoubtedly triggered by the disastrous financial consequences of the oil decline in the 1980s and Saudi determination to avoid the repetition of this syndrome at all costs. Their readiness to commit large sums of money — the Star Enterprise investment reached $812m. — despite spending constraints at home evidenced the long-term importance which the royal family attached to its downstream strategy.[31]

A new major feature in Riyadh's oil policy was the centrality of the US market, which could be illustrated in a number of areas. First, the Saudis gave prominence to the US in their downstream strategy, expressing a desire to enter into joint ventures with American oil companies along the lines of the Star Enterprise. Nazir stated that the kingdom's "moderate oil policies and desire to expand downstream joint ventures made it a particularly attractive partner for the US." Second, there was a considerable reorientation of Saudi oil supplies toward the US market and the better prices obtained there. US imports of Saudi oil increased from 0.75m. b/d in 1987 to 1.06m. b/d in 1988 and to 1.4m. b/d in the first half of 1989. Saudi Arabia became the largest single supplier of foreign oil to the US. To counter arguments that such dependence created a national security risk for Washington, Nazir told an oil conference in Oklahoma that Saudi Arabia was "the most dependable source of oil for the US in the future" and could guarantee "predictable and safe supplies."[32]

Third, the kingdom leased considerable storage capacity in the Caribbean. The

Saudis were holding 3.5m. barrels of crude at any given time in order to supply the Star Enterprise venture and other US customers, and 5m. barrels were held on a discretionary basis. Saudi Arabia was apparently positioning itself to capture a larger market share in the US. This was done partly in response to the aggressive sales campaign which Kuwait, Nigeria, and the UAE had launched earlier in the US. Finally, there were reports that the US and Saudi Arabia were negotiating the lease of Saudi oil to expand the Strategic Petroleum Reserve. A long-term lease would enable the Saudis not only to earn revenue on oil otherwise unsalable due to quota constraints, but also to raise their production capacity as planned (see above).[33]

All in all, 1989 was a very good year for Saudi oil in almost every respect. First, world demand grew considerably; in the industrialized countries it increased in 1988 by a record 5%. Second, most of this increase in demand was supplied by Opec whose production ceiling rose between December 1988 and December 1989 from 18.5m. b/d to 22m. b/d; actual Opec production at the end of 1989 was as high as 23.5 m.b/d. Third, such a sharp rise in supply did not result in price reductions; on the contrary, Opec prices went up from as low as $13 to almost $18 a barrel during 1989. Fourth, Saudi Arabia managed to increase its quota from 4.524 m. b/d in the first half of 1989 to 4.79m. b/d in the third quarter to 5.014m. b/d in the fourth quarter and 5.380m. b/d for the first half of 1990.[34] This 20% increase within one year was achieved without any erosion in the kingdom's claimed 24.5% share of Opec production. The net result was that Saudi oil revenues in 1989 were bound to be considerably higher than the most optimistic budgetary projections. Fifth, the restructuring of the oil industry ended successfully with the establishment of the Saudi Arabian Oil Company (Saudi Aramco), and the Saudi Arabian Refining and Marketing Company, which took over the functions of Petromin.[35] (For an analysis of the restructuring, see *MECS* 1988, pp. 683–84.) Sixth, by upgrading its proven oil reserves to 252bn. barrels, the kingdom reestablished its preeminent role in the international oil market, possessing a quarter of world reserves and a third of Opec's. Finally, and symbolically, in early June, Riyadh announced the discovery of a major oil field 190km. south of the capital. It was the first discovery outside the Eastern Province and the Empty Quarter.[36]

INTERNAL CHALLENGES

Subversion and Hajj

The assassination of a Saudi diplomat in Ankara in October 1988 (see *MECS* 1988, p. 688) was followed by two more assassinations of Saudi diplomats, in Karachi and Bangkok. Whereas the Hizballah's Saudi branch claimed responsibility for the first, a previously unknown group — "the Arab Fury Generation" — claimed the other two. Then, the Saudi imam of the Brussels mosque was murdered, purportedly because of his refusal to condone Khomeyni's death sentence against the writer Salman Rushdie (see chapter on Islamic Affairs).[37]

But most Saudi fears centered on the potential for subversion inherent in the Eastern Province's 400,000-large Shi'i community. What exacerbated the danger was the Shi'is' proximity to Iran and to the oil fields. In early January, ther were reports of disturbances, mass demonstrations, and even the execution of dissidents in the region. Some reports suggested that the Saudis had uncovered an underground group which sought to overthrow the regime. It was in order to demonstrate order and stability and refute such allegations that the cabinet meeting in late January convened in the Eastern Province and not in Riyadh as usual.[38]

Tension again flared in Hasa in June following the death of Ayatollah Khomeyni (see chapter on Iran). Iranian sources claimed that "despite an official ban, some 70,000 people took to the streets, beating on their chests and shouting slogans." Other sources suggested that the Ayatollah's death was greeted with "impassioned outbursts of grief, sometimes officially suppressed." There was consensus, however, that the harsh treatment of Shi'i mourning caused considerable resentment against the authorities.[39]

The biggest security headache was, as usual, the annual pilgrimage. The government sought to enforce the traditional measures: an official identity card to each pilgrim; quotas for Saudi pilgrims; special quotas for Saudi Shi'is; restriction on expatriate Muslim workers; a ban on books, placards, photographs, leaflets, political and ideological literature, and demonstrations; and a ban on carrying any object that might be construed as a weapon.[40]

But the overriding security issue was the possible participation of Iranians. There were some indications that the two countries were heading toward a compromise over the number of Iranian pilgrims, an issue which led Iran to boycott the 1988 Hajj (see *MECS* 1988, pp. 687, 691). Iranian sources leaked that the Saudi Government had abandoned the 45,000 quota and agreed to allow in 150,000 Iranians; the Saudi authorities denied it promptly. Tehran reacted by accusing Riyadh of barring Iranians from performing their religious duties, and Saudi spokesmen reiterated their readiness to accept 45,000 Iranian pilgrims at any time.[41]

It appeared, however, that the issue generated a controversy within the Saudi leadership. With the end of the Iran-Iraq War and the departure of Khomeyni, the Foreign Ministry favored a compromise with Iran. Adding the unused quota from 1988 to Iran's 45,000 allocation was one possible compromise. But the Interior Ministry preferred not to take any security risks by letting the Iranians in. Prince Na'if was anxious lest the Hajj be turned into an excuse for demonstrations in remembrance of Khomeyni or in support of the death sentence on Rushdie. These anxieties were heightened by the revelation that the Iranian regime had sought to recruit hundreds of Muslims in Europe, particularly England, and send them to Mecca to organize political demonstrations during the Hajj. It was the Interior Ministry which prevailed, with the philosophy of "if in doubt, keep them out."[42]

An otherwise peaceful Hajj was marred by two explosions near the Grand Mosque on 10 July, which killed one pilgrim and seriously injured 16. Responsibility for the bombings was claimed by "the Arab Fury Generation" group (see above). Calling the explosions "a warning to the royal family which betrayed Islam and desecrated the holy shrines," it threatened "to liquidate the Al Sa'ud Family if it persists in its policy of treason." The explosions were followed immediately by a wave of recriminations between Riyadh and Tehran. While the Saudis condemned "these criminal acts behind which the Tehran rulers stand," Iranian Parliament Speaker Rafsanjani accused "US agents and the Saudis themselves of perpetrating this crime so they can blame Iran and deprive us from participating in the Hajj."[43]

On 21 September, 16 Kuwaiti Shi'is, most of them of Iranian origin, were beheaded by sword for their role in the bomb attacks. Three other Kuwaitis were sentenced to 15 years' imprisonment and 1,000 lashes, and one Kuwaiti received 20 years and 1,500 lashes. The 20 were convicted of "smuggling explosives and weapons, placing the bombs near the Grand Mosque and planning other acts of terrorism in the kingdom." Nine other defendants were acquitted. The Saudi information authorities moved from complete silence over the investigation to blanket coverage and maximum publicity for the affair: the confessions of the convicted were featured on Saudi television for three hours; the names, ages, nationality, religious affiliation, and ethnic origin of the convicted were repeatedly mentioned; and newspaper editors were told to print the photographs of those executed and their confessions. It was clear that the royal family used the case to deter any future subversive activity.[44]

No less important a goal was to expose Iranian involvement and to signal Saudi determination not to be intimidated. But the implication of Tehran was carried out quite subtly through the medium of the condemned men's confessions rather than by direct Saudi accusations. The Iranian Embassy in Kuwait played a central role, with two diplomats responsible for three aspects: establishment of the terror cell "to undermine security, spread panic among pilgrims, and expose Saudi inability to administer the Hajj; training the group in the use of explosives; supplying the explosives."[45] More information implicating Iran was derived from Egypt. An investigation of 40 members of an underground group produced evidence of Iran sponsoring subversive activities in the ME against Saudi, Kuwaiti, and Iraqi targets.[46]

Reacting to the executions, a Hizballah spokesman vowed to "avenge the blood of these oppressed Muslims who were massacred in an act of terrorism."[47] In mid-October, an employee of the Saudi Embassy in Ankara lost both legs in a bomb explosion. Two weeks later, a Saudi official looking after the kingdom's vacant embassy in Beirut was murdered near his home. In Riyadh, Saudi police defused two bombs planted in the Ministry of Interior. These actions prompted the royal family to tighten security around palaces at home and Saudi embassies and offices abroad, and to instruct members of the family to abstain from unnecessary trips.[48] The bombings in July, the investigation that ensued, and the executions in September accounted, at least partly, for the cancellation of Fahd's planned visits to Washington in July and September (see below).

Military Buildup

Neither the end of the Iran-Iraq War nor the steep fall in oil revenues seemed able to quench Saudi Arabia's thirst for sophisticated weaponry. The year 1989 was characterized by the successful conclusion of some previously negotiated deals, with others running into various complications. But what became almost a constant feature in all arms purchasing programs was the Saudi insistence on bartering for the weapons and on committing the arms seller to offset investments.

On 10 June, Defense Minister Sultan signed a $1.7bn. agreement in Paris for the supply of three missile-armed helicopter-carrying naval frigates and up to 600 *Mistral* man-portable surface-to-air antiaircraft missiles.[49] On the same trip, Sultan signed a contract in Vienna for the supply of 100 155mm. howitzer guns.[50] After protracted negotiations and experiments (see *MECS* 1988, p. 684), the Saudis finally decided to buy both US and Brazilian tanks and to turn down the British *Challenger* and the French AMX-60. The expected order would probably include 315 of the American M1-A1, worth $700m.–$1bn., and 200–300 of the Brazilian *Osorio*. In addition to the tanks, the Saudis were to purchase from the US 200 Bradley infantry fighting vehicles at a cost of $200m., as well as multiple-launch rocket systems, an air-defense radar system, 15 antitank Bell helicopters and 2,000 Mark-84 aerial bombs.[51] But the biggest item in their shopping list was the replacement of the aging F-5 aircraft by up to 110 warplanes — either the F-16 or the F-18A. Another item bound to generate controversy in 1990 was Riyadh's desire to buy 38 F-15E combat jets of the type whose sale was blocked by Congress in 1985.[52]

The lengthy search for submarines was not as yet concluded. French sources, however, claimed that a deal with France was imminent and that it would consist of eight submarines and training and technical support worth $4bn.[53] At the same time, complications arose with regard to the "arms deal of the 20th century" with Great Britain. On the Saudi side, financial constraints led to a payment gap, forcing Riyadh to borrow as much as $3.1bn. (For complications on the British side, see below.) At any rate, there were indications that the supply of *Tornado* and other aircraft slowed down, while the sale of the *Blackhawk* helicopters seemed to be on the verge of being canceled.[54]

There was also a new, and surprising, feature in the 1989 budget: it failed to provide the exact figure allocated for defense. Instead, it stated that a total of SR73.89bn. was earmarked for both "defense and administration," without providing a breakdown. It appeared that this was done to conceal the real dimensions of military outlays, thereby preempting criticisms of the vast defense spending similar to that in 1988 when the kingdom's military expenditures reached an all-time record of 36% of the budget — $13.37bn. (SR50.08bn.). The fact that most deals were paid for through oil supplies and barter made it easier to obscure the real extent of the military budget.

The Saudi state of mind regarding military procurement was best illustrated by Prince Sultan. Interviewed in Paris and asked whether the *Mistral* was an alternative to the canceled US *Stinger* missile deal, he responded: "We do not replace one weapon with another; we always ask for more."[55]

Royal Family Politics
Reports on King Fahd's deteriorating health abounded in 1989. Cited were the old problems of severe overweight, tuberculosis, high blood pressure, and a kidney dysfunction.[56] But it was worsening knee trouble which seriously curtailed his movements. He needed to be supported when standing and had to use an escalator when boarding a plane. Fahd was due to be admitted to a Cleveland hospital for treatment in July, but as the visits to the US were canceled (see below), the plan was aborted. It appeared, however, that all allegations that the king was suffering from "an incurable illness," vehemently denied by Saudi spokesmen, had no foundations.[57]

Such rumors were accompanied by reports that the king's bad health triggered a major power struggle between Crown Prince 'Abdallah and Defense Minister Sultan. The former was reportedly bitter and frustrated at his failure to upgrade, both qualitatively and quantitatively, the weaponry of the National Guard under his command, in a way which would have made it a counterbalance to the armed forces under Sultan's command. Such a power struggle was claimed to have created "uncertainties over the succession and an air of impending turmoil in Riyadh."[58] That these reports circulated in the summer, coinciding with the bombings in Mecca and the investigation, tended to enhance the perception of insecurity and turmoil. It was also against this background that the execution of the 16 Shi'is should be viewed. The Saudi leadership sought to project not only an uncompromising posture *vis-à-vis* Iran, but also to demonstrate the unity and self-confidence of the royal family.

Social Challenges

It appeared that the almost decade-long economic recession exacted a social toll as well. Nearly 65% of all Saudis were under the age of 25. They had spent their formative years in an era when the government provided free tuition and monthly salaries for all university students and well-paying jobs after graduation. With these benefits over, a sense of unrest and malaise began to spread, especially among youth not admitted to universities and among the unemployed. According to a foreign diplomat, criminals executed in October had left notes with their victims saying that "we were forced to do this, because we are university graduates without jobs."[59]

One manifestation of the heightening social crisis was the growing number of executions in 1989, which was three times the 1988 figure. In March and April, for instance, Saudi television announced names of people executed almost every night, in order "to demonstrate the determination of the authorities to maintain order and security." It peaked at the beginning of Ramadan, when 11 people were executed within a week.[60] Charges ranged from murder and highway robbery to drug trafficking. The rising wave of drug-related crimes pointed to the failure of the authorities to combat drug smuggling effectively (see *MECS* 1988, p. 688). According to one source, the problem was so widespread that even royal princes took part in drug smuggling and trafficking.[61]

FOREIGN AFFAIRS

THE INTER-ARAB ARENA

In early 1989, Saudi Arabia resumed its efforts to lay the ground for convening the long-awaited Arab summit, delayed since 1983(!), in Riyadh. Having returned from his trip to Iraq and Egypt, King Fahd stated in April that the kingdom was making "all the necessary steps for the summit." However, by the king's own standards, the necessary prerequisites were not yet in place: Syria was not reconciled with any of its long-time rivals — Iraq, Egypt, and the PLO — and no resolution of the Lebanese crisis was in sight.[62]

Instead, the Saudis were forced to endorse the convening of an extraordinary summit in Casablanca, an initiative launched by King Hasan of Morocco. From Riyadh's perspective, the summit was successful within its limited terms of reference: Egypt was readmitted to the Arab League and the PLO's political agenda was endorsed. Moreover, the weakness and isolation of Syria was amply demonstrated. One of its manifestations was the reference in the final communiqué to the intention to amend the Arab League Charter. King Fahd explained that the articles "requiring unanimity for the implementation of certain resolutions" should be changed so that "a certain majority can be considered sufficient." The allusion to Syria's veto power was clear.[63]

The Saudis wanted to cash in on the Casablanca summit and press ahead with the convening of the regular summit in Riyadh. But by midyear, the king was preoccupied with the Hajj, on the one hand, and his own role in the Arab Tripartite Committee on

Lebanon, on the other. Topping these considerations was the failure to arrive at a "reasonable degree of Arab reconciliation prior to the summit." In King Fahd's words: "An Arab summit is desirable not for its own sake but for the sake of the objectives to be achieved. It must be adequately prepared, politically and diplomatically, so it can achieve its objectives."[64]

The greatest anxiety in the Arab arena was the new Iraqi stature given the end of the Gulf War and Baghdad's ambitions in the region. The anxiety was enhanced by the formation of the ACC (for a detailed analysis, see chapter on inter-Arab relations). Not only were the Saudis left in the dark when the project was launched in February, but they were certain that they were one of the primary targets of the new grouping. The immediate interpretation was that Saddam Husayn strove to intimidate the oil-rich, small Gulf states and move them away from the Saudi-dominated GCC into the Iraqi orbit. The Saudis, it should be noted, denied such interpretations publicly, welcoming "any close cooperation among Arab states."[65]

No wonder then that Saudi Arabia sought to increase its influence again as a broker in inter-Arab affairs. It attributed the resumption of diplomatic relations between Syria and Morocco in early 1989 and between Syria and Egypt at the end of the year to Saudi mediation. It also took credit for breaking the logjam in the Lebanese crisis by hosting the Lebanese Parliament and helping produce the new political program (see chapter on Lebanon).[66]

Relations with Iraq

King Fahd's visit to Iraq from 25–27 March marked the first visit of a Saudi monarch to Baghdad in more than 30 years. Though Fahd stated that he had come "to talk about Palestine, Afghanistan, and Lebanon,"[67] foremost on his agenda was the nature of Saudi-Iraqi relations in the aftermath of the Iran-Iraq War. Saudi crucial support of, indeed the alliance with, Iraq during the war appeared to have obliterated the fact that the two countries were ruled by regimes whose ideologies and *Weltanschauung* were diametrically opposed.

Now that the war and with it the almost total Iraqi dependence on Saudi Arabia were over, the old Saudi suspicions and fear of Iraqi power began to surface. That the Iraqi Army was now much larger and stronger than ever tended to deepen this sense of anxiety. Moreover, the creation of the ACC with Iraq as its linchpin seemed only to be substantiating Saddam Husayn's regional aspirations. That the ACC could be viewed in Riyadh as anti-Saudi was corroborated by the highly provocative inclusion of North Yemen, a country considered to be in the Saudi orbit.[68]

If it was the intention of King Fahd to obtain some Iraqi assurances, and if Saddam Husayn's objective was to allay Saudi anxieties, then Fahd's visit could hardly have been less successful. Only after Fahd's departure, the Iraqis announced that two agreements were signed — one, a form of nonaggression treaty, the other an accord on security cooperation.

In the former, the two countries undertook not to use force, to settle disputes between them by peaceful methods, and to refrain from interference in each other's internal affairs. The reference to "force" was surprising to say the least, given that Saudi Arabia was Iraq's leading ally during the war with Iran. But, as King Fahd commented, everything in the treaty had already appeared in previous agreements; "now it was merely documented in a Saudi-Iraqi accord."[69] An embarrassing discord also surfaced regarding Saudi assistance in rebuilding the Iraqi nuclear reactor (see *MECS* 1980–81, pp. 182–207). The Iraqi News Agency reported Fahd's pledge to finance the plant's reconstruction. But the king strove to disassociate himself from any such offer, claiming that it had been the late King Khalid who had made the promise. Saudi Arabia, he said, would only back the project if reconstruction took place under international supervision and for nonmilitary purposes. Paradoxically, the Iraqi Government itself confirmed that it had been Khalid's promise. An official decree conferring on Fahd the highest Iraqi decoration stated that "when the plant was destroyed in 1981, the Saudi Government pledged to finance its reconstruction."[70]

As Saudi-Iraqi relations appeared to be strained, it seemed that the Saudi leadership could still exercise some leverage over Baghdad, consisting of three elements. First, with an agreement between Iraq and Iran as elusive as ever, the possible resumption of hostilities between the two meant an inevitable renewal of Iraqi dependence on Riyadh. Second, the kingdom remained by far Iraq's biggest creditor, though it did not make public any demand for repayment. Third, the Saudi leaders were in a position to influence Iraq's oil policy not only by virtue of their status in Opec, but principally because they could dictate the Iraqi oil export levels in the IPSA 1 and 2 pipelines going through Saudi territories (see chapter on oil developments).

Relations with Egypt

The enthusiasm and warmth with which King Fahd was welcomed in Cairo, following his trip to Iraq, stood in stark contrast to the air of gloom he had faced in Baghdad. That the Cairo visit in March started precisely on the 10th anniversary of the signing of the Israeli-Egyptian peace treaty and the subsequent severance of relations between Saudi Arabia and Egypt meant that the two countries had come full circle. The first visit of a Saudi monarch in more than a decade signified not only Riyadh's wish to close the chapter on the controversial Egyptian-Israeli peace. It marked Saudi Arabia's return to its "natural" alliance with a regional power that shared Riyadh's pragmatic goals of stability and tranquillity, a decade after the Saudis were forced into siding with their radical rivals — Syria and Iraq — and ostracizing Egypt (see *MECS* 1978–79, pp. 214–17, 219–25).

But Fahd's visit to Cairo carried more than just symbolism; it reinforced the return of Egypt to inter-Arab politics. The Saudi leadership hoped that the Cairo-Riyadh axis would strengthen the pragmatic camp in the Arab world and emphasize further the isolation of Syria. The immediate Saudi goal was to have Egypt readmitted to the Arab League and have President Mubarak participate in Arab summit meetings. To that end, Fahd was even prepared "to support a change in the Arab League's rules" to permit Cairo's readmission by majority vote — a move designed to circumvent Syrian and Libyan objections. Indeed, in the joint communiqué at the end of the visit Fahd stressed that "Egypt's presence within the Arab fold was indispensable support for joint, concrete Arab work in achieving the rights of the Arab nation."[71]

The communiqué stressed unanimity of views on the Lebanese crisis, on the need for a formal end to the Iran-Iraq War, on support for a Mujahidin government in Afghanistan, and on convening an international conference in order to solve the Palestinian problem. On the latter, Saudi support for Egypt was of particular significance given that Mubarak's forthcoming visit to Washington was to focus on that issue. On bilateral matters, a number of agreements were signed aimed at boosting economic cooperation and encouraging Saudi private-sector investments in Egypt; a joint committee was established in order to oversee such cooperation.[72]

So eager were Fahd and Mubarak to project consensus that no reference was made to any controversial issues. Thus, Egypt wished the Saudis to intercede on its behalf in its protracted negotiations with the IMF (see chapter on Egypt) on whose board Saudi Arabia had a seat. Likewise, Mubarak wanted to unfreeze Saudi and other Gulf investments in the Arab Organization of Industry (AOI), established in 1974 and suspended in 1979, to revitalize the AOI and build a defense industry. King Fahd, however, refused to commit himself on either issue.[73]

No sign could be detected of Saudi anger at Egypt over the ACC. This was all the more remarkable given the clear dissatisfaction Riyadh expressed toward the other three members of the ACC — Iraq, Jordan, and North Yemen. It appeared that the Saudi leadership had specific reasons to suspect Iraq (see above), to feel betrayed by Jordan (see below), and to feel outmaneuvered by North Yemen (see chapter on the Yemeni Arab Republic). But Egypt was a different story altogether. Cairo's foreign policy goals allowed the Saudis to view its regional ambitions as devoid of any anti-Saudi component.

The two countries were also coming closer geographically. One of the joint projects agreed upon envisaged the erection of a bridge which would connect the Sinai Peninsula to the Saudi coast across the Straits of Tiran. The Saudi *al-Yawm* described it as "a strategic link which will reduce the distance between the kingdom and Egypt to 10 minutes, give Egypt direct access to the Gulf, and give the Saudis direct access to the African continent."[74] (See also chapter on Egypt.)

Relations with Syria

The end of the Iran-Iraq War and the death of Ayatollah Khomeyni posed the question of whether Presiden Asad's role in Saudi regional policies was still as central as previously. The royal family regarded Syria as a power in decline and its influence with the Iranian leadership as of much less importance than in previous years. But Damascus was still viewed as critically important for the kingdom, serving as a counterbalance to an ever stronger Iraq and possibly also to Egypt.

The rivalries between Syria and a number of Arab states highlighted the kingdom's role as a broker in inter-Arab affairs. Mediating the Egyptian-Syrian dispute was of immediate importance, because the Saudis wanted to have Mubarak participate in the Arab summit in May. The Saudis intensified their efforts in early 1989 and sought to reconvene a reconciliation minisummit in Riyadh with Presidents Asad and Mubarak. There were some news reports that Riyadh offered Asad $800m. for his acceptance of Egypt's return to the Arab League, but Saudi spokesmen vehemently denied such allegations.[75] King Fahd, however, also waved the stick *vis-à-vis* Damascus, warning that the kingdom would support "a change in the Arab League's rules to permit Egypt's readmission by majority vote."[76] It was difficult to assesss the weight of the Saudi efforts among the several factors that had prompted Asad to drop his objection to Egypt's return (see chapters on Syria and inter-Arab relations). That the resumption of Egyptian-Syrian diplomatic relations came only in late 1989 clearly showed that the change in Syria's posture was rooted in changes in its geostrategic status no less than in successful Saudi pressure.

Another effort, undertaken by Crown Prince 'Abdallah, was to mediate differences between Damascus and Baghdad. It assumed all the more importance in view of the escalation of the Syrian-Iraqi rivalry via their proxies in Lebanon, which frustrated the efforts to resolve the Lebanese crisis. A third mediation centered on the Syrian-PLO dispute. Various PLO officials hailed 'Abdallah's attempts to bring about a reconciliation with the Syrian leadership, given the "central Syrian role in Arab and Palestinian politics." According to one source, 'Abdallah promised Asad $65m. if he met with 'Arafat.[77] But no amount of Saudi persuasion and largesse could change Asad's terms for a reconciliation with Saddam Husayn and 'Arafat.

Saudi-Syrian relations in the second half of 1989 were, undoubtedly, shaped by the role King Fahd played in the Arab Tripartite Committee on Lebanon. When the committee first declared on 31 July that it had "reached a dead-end," its statement was overtly critical of Syria "whose direction in this matter is not in agreement with the concept of the committee," i.e., for its refusal to accept a timetable for withdrawal from Lebanon.[78] Syria must have been furious with Fahd as within days the Damascus media distributed news reports about unrest in the kingdom's Eastern Province, serious frictions and tensions within the royal family, and deterioration in Fahd's health.[79]

The Saudi leadership seemed to have been caught off balance, and within a short period forced through a plan which was much more amenable to Syrian interests. It not only omitted the term "Syrian withdrawal" but also assigned to Damascus a significant role in pacifying the country. And as the Ta'if talks reached a deadlock, Foreign Minister Sa'ud al-Faysal flew to Damascus where he stated that "it is impossible to solve the Lebanese crisis without Syria's assistance."[80] The whole episode seemed to have reinforced the notion that Saudi leverage over Syria was inherently limited. (For details on the Saudi role in the Lebanese crisis, see chapter on inter-Arab relations.)

Syrian-Iranian relations continued to be a source of resentment for the royal family. Syria was the only Arab country to declare a week-long mourning for Khomeyni's death. Moreover, Syrian-Iranian cooperation in Lebanon, even after the Ta'if agreement, led Riyadh to suspect whether the Syrians were, indeed, going to abide by any settlement.[81] A source of consolation for the royal family was the Syrian support of the Hajj quota system (see above) in the face of Iranian protestations.

Relations with Jordan

Saudi-Jordanian relations in 1989 were characterized by a short-term rupture that was resolved because of convergence of long-term interests. Saudi anger was rooted in the central role King Husayn played in the establishment of the ACC. That Husayn visited the kingdom on the eve of the creation of the ACC and failed to divulge the new project to Fahd, let alone consult with him, caused a furor in Riyadh. According to one source, the royal family concluded that "Husayn exaggerates his self-importance in a way which does not conform with the substantial financial assistance he gets from the Saudis." The Saudi leadership was reported to have decided to punish Husayn by withholding Saudi financial commitments. It came as no surprise, then, that King Fahd abstained from visiting Jordan during his ME tour in late March.[82]

What changed the Saudi attitude was the riots that broke out in southern Jordan in mid-April, which were perceived as threatening the very stability of the Hashemite Kingdom. A major economic crisis and political turmoil in Jordan had always been deemed as detrimental to Saudi security, let alone when they centered on an area of such close proximity to the Saudi borders and raised the possibility of a spillover. King Husayn, for his part, realized that there was no substitute for Saudi financial assistance. This mutual understanding paved the way for Husayn's visits with King Fahd on 2 May and on 31 July and for mending their differences. Saudi Arabia was reported to have renewed its financial assistance to Amman directly, and indirectly by depositing large amounts of money in Jordanian banks to strengthen the dinar which had lost 75% of its value in one year[83] (see chapter on Jordan).

The reconciliation between Fahd and Husayn reflected their realization that despite all tensions and differences, the two kingdoms shared the most fundamental long-term goals, which forced them to maintain a high level of cooperation and coordination. Thus, at the end of Husayn's latter visit, Fahd hailed the "firmness of our common pillars and principles" and publicly expressed "full confidence in the wise leadership and sound policy of King Husayn."[84]

Relations with the PLO and Attitude Toward the Palestinian Issue

Following the declaration of Palestinian independence in November 1988, Saudi Arabia was among the first to recognize the new "State of Palestine." The Saudi leadership donated one of the most elegant buildings in the diplomatic quarter of Riyadh to serve as "the Palestine Embassy," and the PLO representative, Rafiq al-Natsha, became the first ambassador. Symbolically, the embassy was inaugurated on al-Fath's Day, 1 January 1989.[85]

The financial assistance that the oil-rich Arab states offered the "confrontation states," agreed upon in the Baghdad summit of 1978 (see *MECS* 1978–79, pp. 214–17), expired in late 1988. Under the 10- year pledge, Riyadh paid the PLO a total of $855m. — three annual installments of $28.5m. over 10 years. In early 1989, King Fahd ordered new monthly payments of $6.02m. to help finance the Intifada and to be put at the PLO's disposal. Thus, Saudi annual assistance to the PLO dropped from $85.5m. to $72.24m.[86]

The royal family welcomed the PLO's political program adopted in November 1988 (see *MECS* 1988, p. 696). Saudi leaders emphasized that the only way to solve the Arab-Israeli conflict in general and the Palestinian problem in particular was through an international conference in which the PLO had to participate.[87] It was in this context that Saudi spokesmen and media vehemently assailed Israel's peace plan of May 1989 (see chapter on the ME peace process). They especially rejected the notion of holding elections in the West Bank and Gaza Strip under "conditions of occupation," and interpreted the Israeli proposal as "an attempt to end the Intifada, obliterate the PLO's role, and split the Palestinian people."[88]

PERSIAN GULF AFFAIRS
Relations with Iran

Saudi-Iranian relations in 1989 went through successive ups and downs, fluctuating from *rapprochement* and attempts to restore diplomatic relations to escalation of verbal wars, tensions, and frictions. What further complicated their bilateral relations was the wide range of issues on which they differed and arenas where they collided. These included the Hajj dispute, controversy over Afghanistan, the Rushdie affair, the Islamic conference Organization (ICO), Iranian support of anti-Saudi groups, and Iran's role in attacks against Saudi targets and diplomats. Finally, the power struggle in Tehran, before and after Khomeyni's death (see chapter on Iran), directly affected relations between the two countries.

Indeed, the three attacks on Saudi diplomats in Ankara, Karachi, and Bangkok were reported to have been carried out by three factions — the Hizballah's Saudi branch, "the Arab Fury Generation," and "Soldiers of Justice." A Lebanese weekly, well informed on Iran, argued that the three had been set up by "certain elements within the Iranian Government who wished to undermine the attempt to improve relations with Saudi Arabia."[89] These attacks, the unresolved issue of compensation for the Iranians killed in the 1987 Hajj (see *MECS* 1987, pp. 589–91),[90] and the Saudi recognition of a Mujahidin government in Afghanistan, all made an improvement in relations all the more difficult. Nevertheless, it appeared that meetings in London between Iranian and Saudi officials and the mediation of Oman and Pakistan paved the way for Iranian participation in the ICO's foreign ministers' meeting in Riyadh in mid-March. As Iranian pilgrimage officials expressed hope that "with normalization of relations, Iranian pilgrims will be able to perform the Hajj," the Pakistani foreign minister stated that the resumption of diplomatic relations was just a matter of time.[91]

The mutual desire to improve relations resulted in a compromise at the ICO meeting. While Iran wanted the ICO to endorse Khomeyni's death sentence against Rushdie for blasphemy, the Saudis wished to keep the whole issue off the agenda. The joint communiqué described Rushdie as an apostate, but made no reference to a death sentence. Afghanistan, likewise, did not become a major divisive issue, because there was no vote over recognizing the interim Mujahidin government.[92] (For details, see chapter on Islamic affairs.)

Following the ICO conference, a sense of *rapprochement* prevailed, with both sides making conciliatory statements not heard since Khomeyni's accession to power. Saudi spokesmen and media expressed a desire to see "lasting, cordial ties and full normalization of relations." The Iranians reciprocated by praising the "particular style of influence that Saudi Arabia has always wielded on the politics of the region," and by suggesting that the Saudi king, "by virtue of his regional political weight, is the ideal person to mediate between Iraq and Iran."[93]

Relations, however, started to deteriorate again in April. The assassination of the Saudi imam of the Brussels mosque (see above) was followed by reports that Tehran was pushing the Shi'i Afghan refugees in Iran against the Saudi-sponsored Mujahidin government and toward a deal with the "Communist" regime in Kabul.[94] But what triggered the escalation was the resumption of the controversy over Iranian participation in the Hajj. It appeared that the Iranian leaders had assumed that the *rapprochement* with Riyadh would lead the royal family to abandon the quota (see *MECS* 1988, pp. 690–91). When they realized that Riyadh still adhered to the quota, they began to assail "the Saudi Hajj tactics," arguing that "contrary to earlier positive signs, Saudi Arabia is determined to prevent Iranians from going to Mecca." The Saudi media retorted that "these sickening attacks are evidence that Iran's policies of dissent, sedition, and aggression against all sanctities led to the bankruptcy of the Tehran regime."[95]

But the royal family also made some overtures. King Fahd said that all he asked from Tehran was "mutual respect and good neighborliness," and he expressed hope to see "cooperation between the Arabs and Iran." Defense Minister Sultan stated Saudi readiness "to resume relations and bring an end to the dispute between the two brotherly peoples." For that to happen, he argued, Tehran would have to adopt an approach "devoid of any aggressive behavior toward the kingdom." The Iranian leadership responded that the Saudis could demonstrate their sincerity "by immediately eliminating all obstacles which prevent 150,000 Iranian pilgrims from performing the Hajj."[96]

The death of Khomeyni on 3 June once again heralded signs of *rapprochement*. The Saudi and Iranian foreign ministers, Sa'ud al-Faysal and 'Ali Akbar Velayati, were reported to have discussed the resumption of diplomatic relations. The meeting led to the suspension of the propaganda war, but it failed to produce any progress on the Hajj issue.[97] It came as no surprise, then, that the GCC foreign ministers' meeting in September stressed especially "the need to resolve the difference between Saudi Arabia and Iran." The Iranians also expressed hope to see "cordial relations" with the Saudis. But an Iranian source, who spoke "on condition of anonymity," attributed the Saudi failure to respond to Iranian overtures to the "power struggle over succession which created an atmosphere of uncertainties and turmoil in Riyadh."[98]

The execution of the 16 Shi'is on 21 September (see above) infuriated Tehran. Iranian spokesmen who had vowed "to defend to the death" the convicted Shi'is, renewed their attacks after the executions, promising imminent revenge. Tehran was particularly angered by the Shi'is' confessions which included detailed accounts of Iran's role in the Mecca bombing. Seeking to cash in on this point, King Fahd expressed "extreme amazement at Iran's false accusations, since we have not addressed any accusations to Iran concerning the explosions in Mecca."[99] It became, thus, abundantly clear why the Saudis preferred the convicted Shi'is to implicate Tehran rather than themselves leveling such accusations.

The subsequent attacks on two Saudi diplomats in Ankara and Beirut (see above) did not dissuade Riyadh from trying to mend relations. In October, a Saudi spokesman declared that "the kingdom is ready to respond to any positive initiative of good intent that might heal the rift between the two countries." But the royal family was determined to reach such a *modus vivendi* only on Saudi terms.[100]

In the background of this confusing pattern of overtures and vicious accusations was a Saudi fear that Iran might be deliberately stalling peace talks with Iraq, using the lull in hostilities to rebuild its military machine. If that was the case, then Saudi Arabia had to be prepared to become the target of Iranian ideological and strategic challenges again. However, the evolution of both — the Iranian-Iraqi rivalry and the Iranian attitude toward Riyadh — depended, to a large extent, on the outcome of the power struggle in Tehran, an issue over which the Saudi leadership had no influence.

Relations with Kuwait
Saudi-Kuwaiti relations became strained by the execution of the 16 Kuwaiti Shi'is. Though the Kuwait Government was strikingly reticent with regard to commenting on the Saudi judicial process, it was placed in an extremely uncomfortable position. That the Saudi leadership apparently snubbed all Kuwaiti efforts to intercede on behalf of the 16 made it all the more embarrassing.

Kuwait demonstrated its dissatisfaction with Riyadh by pursuing negotiations with Iran on the resumption of diplomatic relations. The Saudis were reported to have been annoyed at the sight of other GCC states improving their relations with Tehran. Publicly, however, the royal family was at pains to stress "the deep-seated ties with Kuwait which are stronger than all the plots and schemes of those who attempt to spread dissension between the two."[101]

Underlying this controversy were deep-rooted differences of opinion as to how to treat the Iranian threat. A case in point was the contentious issue of the US Navy *Hercules* floating base, central to the US reflagging of Kuwaiti ships since 1987 (see *MECS* 1987, pp. 29–35). The Kuwaitis were anxious to act as though there was no longer a danger of Iranian aggression against Kuwait, now that it had stopped helping Iraq. It therefore removed the US flags and requested the withdrawal of the *Hercules* from near its territorial waters. The Saudis took issue with such an approach, fearing that Kuwait and other GCC members were dropping their guard against Iran too soon. Consequently, Riyadh suggested to Washington that it extend the stationing of the *Hercules* indefinitely under a joint Saudi-American control.[102]

Another major rift evolved over oil issues. The immediate dispute in June was over Opec production quotas, with Kuwait insisting that it could not produce less than 1.5m. b/d because of commitments to customers. The problem was aggravated by both Kuwait and the UAE exceeding their quota by 60%-100%. In October, Kuwait actually produced 1.9m. b/d compared with a 1.149m. b/d quota (UAE's production reached 2.2m. b/d, more than twice its quota of 1.094m. b/d). With the focus of Saudi oil policy shifting to strict adherence to production quotas (see above), the breach with Kuwait was unavoidable. The latter, in turn, accused the Saudis of not consulting with the three other GCC-Opec members — Kuwait, the UAE, and Qatar — confining key discussions only to Saudi, Iranian, and Iraqi officials[103] (see also chapter on oil developments).

THE INTERNATIONAL ARENA
Relations with the United States
Unlike 1988, which had been one of the stormiest years in Saudi-American relations, 1989 was characterized by relaxation of tensions and attempts to sort out differences. The end of the Iran-Iraq War and the beginning of the US-PLO dialogue helped accelerate this process. The US also seemed resigned to the presence in Saudi Arabia of the Chinese-made CSS-2 missiles after having obtained assurances from King Fahd. Finally, the Saudis hoped that the shock of losing the large *Tornado* deal to Britain would galvanize support in Washington for future US arms sales to the kingdom.

The US and Saudi Arabia handled various arms deals throughout 1989 with caution and moderation. The Saudis were reluctant to push officially for arms whose approval by Congress could not be reasonably guaranteed. Instead, they launched large-scale lobbying campaigns both in defense industry circles and among congressmen who, for a variety of domestic and foreign policy considerations, cared more about the defense industry and were in favor of arms sales to the kingdom.[104] The Administration, likewise, embarked on more persuasion campaigns in and consultations with Congress, in order to secure prior congressional approval and avoid major embarrassments.

In January, the outgoing Reagan Administration notified Congress of all possible arms sales in 1989. The list for Saudi Arabia included 315 M1-A1 tanks, 200 Bradley infantry fighting vehicles, multiple-launch rocket systems, battlefield antiair and antiground rockets, an air defense radar system, and 2,000 Mark-84 aerial bombs. Conspicuously missing were aircraft. Instead, the Administration attached a letter indicating that it had not yet decided about selling the kingdom 110 jets — either the F-16 *Falcon* or the F-18A *Hornet* — as replacements for the aging fleet of F-5s. This arrangement reflected, reportedly, a prior understanding with Riyadh. Publicly, the State Department stated that "the Bush Administration is not planning to sell the planes to Saudi Arabia this year." But, privately, Saudi and American diplomats intimated that the sale would most probably occur in early 1990.[105]

Another illustration of Saudi caution was Riyadh's desire to purchase 38 aircraft of the more advanced F-15E type to add to the 62 F-15C jets in its arsenal. The move was bound to challenge congressional restrictions which had placed a limit of 62 on the number that can be in Saudi Arabia at one time. When leaking the information in March, "a senior Saudi official" said that the impact of the *Tornado* deal in US defense circles had been "dramatic" and that "political acceptance of the F-15E request is difficult but not impossible."[106] The leak was intended to test the degree of opposition to the deal. That Riyadh did not submit a formal request until the end of the year reflected the new Saudi line. The Administration's caution was illustrated by the fact that nine months had passed from the January notification of Congress of the 315-tank deal until it was appropriately "packaged" and presented to the Israeli Government in order to avoid attempts to block the deal by pro-Israeli congressmen.[107]

A major problem threatening all arms deals to the kingdom arose from a completely new source. In early April, the *Chicago Tribune* published a series of articles based on US intelligence reports on countries developing chemical weapons. In one article, there was the following reference: "Suspected of being in the next echelon of those who have an interest in a possible access to resources needed to build chemical weapons are Saudi Arabia...." (seven other countries were mentioned). Though the reference was fairly innocuous, made in passing and short, it immediately elicited an official Saudi denial, condemning the allegation as "baseless and fabricated." The lengthy, categorical denial probably served to draw more attention to the kingdom's inclusion in the report than it might otherwise have gained.[108]

It also revealed how sensitive Riyadh had become about US questioning of the deployment of the Chinese CSS-2 missiles. This sensitivity was well founded, because a 1988 amendment to the foreign aid bill explicitly banned future arms sales to Saudi Arabia unless "the US president, in a letter to Congress, certifies that the CSS-2 missiles are not equipped with nuclear, chemical, or biological warheads."[109] The US intelligence report, cited by the *Chicago Tribune,* meant that nothing less than Saudi-American military relations were now at stake. Both governments acted promptly. Following a telephone conversation with King Fahd, President Bush certified to Congress within a week that "Saudi Arabia does not possess biological, chemical, or nuclear warheads for the intermediate-range missiles purchased from China."[110] The way was thus cleared for new arms deals.

In June, the Administration notified Congress of its intention to respond favorably to three Saudi requests: more powerful engines for the F-15 aircraft; maintenance, training, and support services for the F-15 jets; and overhaul of the aging F-5 aircraft.

All three contracts were worth some $850m. In addition, the Saudis concluded a deal with US Bell for the purchase of 15 antitank helicopters at a cost of $84m.[111]

King Fahd was scheduled to arrive in Washington on 27 July for his first meeting with Bush as president. Nine days before his arrival, the two sides announced the postponement of the visit to mid-September, citing the king's role in the Arab Tripartite Committee as the reason. But a number of sources put the emphasis on other factors. First was the king's bad health, particularly his weak knees which prevented him from holding himself up without support. A state visit to Washington would have revealed the extent of his disability. Second was Fahd's anxiety at the explosions in Mecca, which occurred only one week before the postponement was announced. The king wanted to delay his departure long enough to be certain that the bombings were not part of a plan to destabilize the kingdom. Third was the king's attempt to use the postponement as a means of pressuring the Bush Administration to approve a Saudi purchase of F-18 or F-16 aircraft. Another reason was Fahd's reluctance to be in the US at the same time that the Saudi multimillionaire 'Adnan Khashoggi, reputed to have been closely connected to the top echelons of the royal family, was indicted in New York on charges of fraud and obstruction of justice. In fact, the postponement of the visit was announced on the very day Khashoggi was extradited from Switzerland. Considerable embarrassment had already been caused when US government attorneys rejected an official Saudi offer to guarantee Khashoggi's appearance in court, if released on bail, stating that "the guarantee of the Saudi Arabian Government is an empty promise in view of the absence of an extradition treaty between the two countries." The anticipated photographic juxtaposition of Khashoggi in handcuffs and his Saudi monarch at the White House would have only made matters worse.[112]

The visit was scheduled for 14–17 September. But on 4 September the Saudi Government announced a second postponement "until a suitable date," citing again Fahd's role in the Lebanese problem. Little credence was, again, given to this factor. The postponement was caused by the same reasons which had prevailed in July, primarily the seriousness and visibility of Fahd's medical problems. Second, Fahd wanted to stay home at the time of the sentencing and execution of the 16 Shi'is. Third, the king wanted to demonstrate his disappointment at the absence of any ready-to-sign arms deals with the US. Aggravating the situation was a statement by Richard Haas, in charge of the ME at the National Security Council, that Fahd's visit would be confined to purely ceremonial contacts. Fahd himself, however, rejected all these explanations, adhering to the Lebanese crisis as the only reason.[113]

All in all, it appeared that in the aftermath of the Iran-Iraq War and the Soviet withdrawal from Afghanistan, the foreign policy issue increasingly affecting Saudi-American relations was the Arab-Israeli conflict, in particular the Palestinian question. On that, the Saudis had mixed feelings. On the one hand, they were extremely pleased that the US, at long last, had launched a dialogue with the PLO. On the other hand, they were critical of Washington for rejecting an international conference and for endorsing Israel's elections plan for the territories. On the latter, however, Saudi criticism became mute once the PLO itself was engaged in negotiations over the Israeli plan (see chapters on the PLO and the ME peace process). The Saudis were particularly critical of the US failure to condemn the Israeli treatment of the Intifada more categorically. Such an American posture coupled with US defense of Israel at the UN,

Saudi spokesmen argued, harmed Washington's credibility and cast serious doubts on its role as a peace mediator.'[114]

Relations with Western Europe

Following the conclusion of "the arms deal of the 20th century" (see *MECS* 1988, p. 684), London and Riyadh signed an agreement in November 1988 establishing the procedures for British offset investments. The Saudis wanted British industry to invest 25% of the technical component of the *Tornado* deal, an estimated $1.5bn., in Saudi Arabia. Two seminars were held to launch, publicize, and stimulate interest in the offset program, the first in London in January and the second in Jidda in late May. Five joint ventures were proposed by British firms: an aluminum smelter that would export to Britain; a missile engineering facility for maintaining and upgrading weapons; computer training centers; a weapons and ammunition factory; and a plan to produce polyethylene yarn.[115] But complications arose with regard to the entire arms deal. On the British side, a wide range of aspects were investigated: the mechanism of the oil barter agreement; financial risks for Britain; the extent of the offset program; the effect on the British Air Force of new aircraft being sent to Saudi Arabia; the existence of subsidies, discounts, or loans in the sales; the role of Britain as a major world arms supplier; the implications of the loss of trained personnel to become contract workers in the kingdom; and rumors of bribes and commissions paid by and to Saudi and British middlemen.[116]

The latter point was of special sensitivity for the royal family, particularly after a number of publications and news agencies gave prominence to such reports. A Saudi spokesman condemned "this campaign of fabricated defamation and disinformation" and described the "rumors" as "totally untrue — in totality and in details."[117] With such an abundance of issues hampering the deal, the Saudis were determined to demonstrate that business was as usual. Thus, when visiting London in June, Defense Minister Sultan made it a point to emphasize "the success of all effective agreements between the two kingdoms," and the Saudi ambassador described the visit as "one of the most successful ever."[118]

Even more embarrassing for the royal family were the reports on gaps in Saudi payments for the *Tornado*s, which forced Riyadh to borrow as much as $3.1bn. (see above). Some British officials expressed concern that the payment gap had originated not only from financial constraints, but primarily from a new Saudi strategic assessment. They feared that as the Iran-Iraq War was over and especially that Khomeyni had died, Riyadh would seek to change the terms of the arms deal and considerably lower its volume. Indeed, by the end of the year there were indications that the supply of *Tornado* and other aircraft slowed down, while the sale of the *Blackhawk* helicopters was likely to be canceled.[119]

Three years of negotiations with France were crowned with success in June, when Defense Minister Sultan and his French counterpart signed two "cooperation agreements." One stipulated the sale of 600 *Mistral* surface-to-air missiles, very similar to the US *Stinger,* whose sale to Saudi Arabia had been blocked by Congress. The second was a "framework agreement" by which "the kingdom is allowed to purchase from France, and France agrees to supply everything that the kingdom wants to obtain from the French military industries." The purchase of three missile-armed helicopter-carrying naval frigates came under the terms of the latter.[120]

The two agreements reinstated France as a major arms supplier to the kingdom. What could further reinforce such a large-scale military relationship was a Saudi purchase of eight submarines. Though French sources claimed that a \$4bn. agreement was "imminent," one was not signed until the end of 1989.[121]

A new feature in the military relationship was Saudi payment in kind. The June agreements contained a stipulation that in addition to "monetary payments," the deal would be paid for by "manufactured Saudi products such as petrochemicals, agricultural products, or other Saudi exports." Prince Sultan had previously declared that "like agreements with the US and Britain [a reference to 'Peace Shield' and 'Tornado-Yamama' projects]," all military deals with France would include an offset component.[122] Such a feature, however, was missing from the June agreements.

Relations with the Soviet Union

Saudi relations with the Soviet Union remained contingent on a complex set of local, regional, and global developments. But the basic pattern which had evolved throughout the 1980s — Soviet overtures, ambiguous Saudi responses, diplomatic contacts, and a failure to establish diplomatic relations — persisted also in 1989. Such a failure became all the more conspicuous following the completion on 15 February of Soviet withdrawal from Afghanistan which the Saudis had said would pave the way for diplomatic relations.[123]

Expectations for an "imminent" resumption of diplomatic relations reached a peak in late March when King Fahd's visit to Baghdad coincided with the presence there of Vladimir Polyakov, head of the Middle East and Africa division of the Soviet Foreign Ministry. Asked specifically about the correlation between Soviet withdrawal from Afghanistan and diplomatic relations, Foreign Minister Sa'ud replied: "We view the withdrawal as an important and effective step toward improvement in Soviet relations with the whole Islamic world."[124] The spokesman of the Soviet Foreign Ministry also felt obliged to react to the speculations. Repeating "Soviet readiness to exchange ambassadors with the Saudi Kingdom at any time," he stressed that such a move "is awaiting a clear signal from Riyadh" at a time when "our relations are witnessing improvement albeit slow." So eager were the Soviets to establish diplomatic relations that the Saudi recognition of the provisional Mujahidin government in Afghanistan prompted only a lukewarm "regret." Moreover, Moscow sought to generate Saudi interest in mediating Afghan peace talks.[125]

The Soviets were encouraged by King Fahd's statements which praised Gorbachev as "a great leader who carries out historical reforms in his country." It was clear that the royal family viewed the Soviet leader as the antithesis of his dogmatic and doctrinaire predecessors, hardly interested in foreign adventures. The withdrawal from Afghanistan was a case in point. In the following months, Soviet-Saudi diplomatic contacts were reportedly carried out in Washington, London, and Cairo. The Soviet ambassador in Cairo, Gennady Zhuravlev, who reportedly was playing a central role in these contacts, stated in June that the two countries would "exchange ambassadors within a short time."[126] It appeared that despite the *rapprochement,* Saudi Arabia was still reluctant to make the big move for the same old reasons: opposition within certain circles of the royal family and adamant rejection of the idea among the 'Ulama and the religious establishment.

Saudi Relations with China

In the spring of 1989, Saudi Arabia and China moved to implement the agreement they had signed in November 1988 for the opening of trade missions in each other's capital. The Saudis appointed the director of protocol at the Foreign Ministry as head of their Beijing office, and a Chinese delegation of eight diplomats arrived in March to open the Riyadh office. The two offices and their personnel were given diplomatic privileges similar to those granted to embassies. Furthermore, the agreement indicated that the trade offices would be the nucleus of future embassies. This created the impression that the whole arrangement was a prelude to full diplomatic recognition.[127]

But the kingdom could not establish diplomatic ties with China until it decided to abandon its support of Taiwan, and this did not seem likely. The rationale for some form of diplomatic recognition had been a growing volume of trade as well as China's role as arms supplier to the kingdom. In 1987, trade between the two reached $350m., 70% of which was Chinese exports to the kingdom. Saudi Arabia sold petrochemical products and fertilizers, and China exported food products, textiles, and light industrial products. An additional Saudi success was to persuade China to increase the number of Chinese Muslims allowed to make the annual Hajj to Mecca.[128]

NOTES

For the place and frequency of publications cited here, and for the full name of the publication, news agency, radio station, or monitoring service where an abbreviation is used, please see "List of Sources." Only in the case of more than one publication bearing the same name is the place of publication noted here.

1. On the 1990 Saudi budget, see *IHT*, 3 January; R. Riyadh, 3 January — SWB, 4 January; *FT*, 4 January; *CR:* Saudi Arabia, No. 4, 1989, p. 11.
2. *MM*, 9 January; *FT*, 2 August 1989.
3. *FT*, 5 August 1989.
4. R. Riyadh, 3 January — SWB, 4 January; *FT*, 4 January, 2 August 1989.
5. *FT*, 5 August 1989.
6. *MM*, 1 December 1989.
7. *IHT*, 3 January 1989.
8. *FT*, 4 January 1989, 22 January 1990; Sama, *Annual Report 1988*, Riyadh, p. 9; *CR*: Saudi Arabia, No. 4, 1989, p. 12.
9. *Al-Sharq al-Awsat*, 22 July; King Fahd's interview in *al-Siyasa*, Kuwait, 30 October 1989.
10. *CR:* Saudi Arabia, No. 4, 1989, p. 13.
11. Ibid., No. 1, pp. 9–10.
12. Ibid., p. 10.
13. Ibid.
14. *Al-Madina*, 27 January 1989.
15. *Al-Riyad*, 15 January 1989.
16. *CR:* Saudi Arabia, No. 2, 1989, p. 12.
17. Ibid.
18. Ibid., No. 3, pp. 8–9.
19. *'Ukaz*, 26 April; *FT*, 20 October 1989.
20. *FT*, 20 October 1989.
21. *Al-Siyasa*, Kuwait, 3 May 1989.
22. R. Riyadh, 3 May — DR, 4 May; *NYT*, 4 May 1989.
23. *Le Figaro*, 2 May; R. Riyadh, 3 May — DR, 4 May; *Gulf States Newsletter*, 15 May 1989.
24. *IHT*, 31 May 1989.

25. *FT,* 22 January 1990.
26. *Oil Daily,* 4 September; *MM,* 18 September: *CR:* Saudi Arabia, No. 4, 1989, p. 17.
27. *FT,* 11 January 1989.
28. *Gulf States Newsletter,* 1 May 1989.
29. *FT,* 20 October, 1989.
30. *Gulf States Newsletter,* 20 March 1989.
31. *MM,* 3 April 1989.
32. *Gulf States Newsletter,* 20 March; *CR:* Saudi Arabia, No. 3, 1989, p. 13.
33. *IHT,* 12, 13 September, *CR:* Saudi Arabia, No. 3, 1989, p. 13, No. 4, 1989, p. 16.
34. According to the annual report of "Saudi Aramco," average 1988 production was 4.928m.b/d.
35. *MM,* 20 March 1989.
36. *CR:* Saudi Arabia, No. 3, 1989, p. 14.
37. SPA, 6 January — DR, 11 January; *al-Ra'y al-Akhar,* 31 January; *CR:* Saudi Arabia, No. 2, 1989, p. 8.
38. *Al-Ra'y al-Akhar,* 31 January; AFP, 31 March — DR, 31 March 1989.
39. IRNA, 9 June — DR, 9 June; *CR:* Saudi Arabia, No. 3, 1989, p. 5.
40. SPA, 18 June — DR, 19 June 1989.
41. IRNA, 5 April — DR, 6 April; SPA, 7 May, 6 June — DR, 8 May, 7 June; *al-Yawm al-Sabi',* 15 May; R. Tehran, 14 May — DR, 15 May 1989.
42. *Al-Dustur,* London, 10 July; *MM,* 16 October 1989.
43. SPA, 10 July — DR, 11 July; NYT, 11 July; *Ha'aretz, al-Yawm, LAT,* 12 July; *MM,* 24 July 1989.
44. R. Riyadh, 21 September — DR, 21 September; *NYT,* 22 September 1989.
45. Saudi TV, 21 September — DR, 21 September; *al-Dustur,* Amman, 14 August; *MM,* 16 October 1989.
46. *Al-Musawwar,* 3 September 1989.
47. *LAT,* 23 September 1989.
48. *MM,* 13 November; *The Observer,* 5 November; *al-Sha'b,* East Jerusalem, 3 October 1989.
49. AFP, 11 June — DR, 12 June; *The Economist,* 1 July; *MM,* 10, 24 July 1989.
50. *'Ukaz,* 13 June; SPA, 15 June — DR, 19 June; *MM,* 24 July 1989.
51. *FT,* 3 October; *MM,* 16 October; *CR:* Saudi Arabia, No. 4, 1989, pp. 9–10.
52. *The Economist,* 1 July; *CR:* Saudi Arabia, No. 2, 1989, pp. 6,9.
53. *CR:* Saudi Arabia, No. 2, 1989, p. 10.
54. *MM,* 11 December 1989.
55. Sultan's interview in *al-Sharq al-Awsat,* 11 June 1989.
56. *Al-Thawra al-Islamiyya,* August 1989.
57. *WT,* 27 July; R. Tehran, 6 September — DR, 7 September; *Sabah al-Khayr,* Cairo, 16 September 1989.
58. *Al-Kifah al-'Arabi,* 23 October; *TT,* 10 September — DR, 11 September 1989.
59. *LAT,* 14 November 1989.
60. Ibid.; Reuters, 15 April, quoted in *Ha'aretz,* 16 April 1989.
61. *Al-Thawra al-Islamiyya,* May 1989.
62. Fahd's interview to SPA, 5 April — DR, 6 April; Sa'ud al-Faysal's interview in *al-Yamama,* 7 March 1989.
63. Fahd's interviews in *al-Siyasa,* Kuwait, 3 May and *al-Sharq al-Awsat,* 30 May 1989.
64. Ibid.; *al-Ra'y,* 12 July 1989.
65. *FT,* 28 March; *al-Thawra al-Islamiyya,* May; Sa'ud al-Faysal's interview in *al-Musawwar,* 7 April 1989.
66. *Al-Madina,* 10 January; *al-Jazira,* 25 December; *'Ukaz,* 18 November 1989.
67. INA, 25 March — DR, 27 March 1989.
68. *Al-Sair,* 23 January; *CR:* Saudi Arabia, No. 4, 1989, pp. 6–7.
69. *Al-Jumhuriyya,* Baghdad, 28 March; Fahd's interview in *al-Siyasa,* Kuwait, 3 May 1989.
70. INA, 27 March — DR, 29 March; *al-Thawra,* Baghdad, 26 March 1989.
71. *NYT,* 1 April; MENA, 31 March — DR, 1 April 1989.
72. For detailed descriptions of Fahd's visit, see *al-Musawwar* and *al-Hawadith,* 31 March; *al-Mustaqbal,* 1 April; *al-Nadwa,* 2 April 1989.

73. *Al-Mustaqbal*, 1 April; *FT*, 25 March; *CR:* Saudi Arabia, No. 2, 1989, p. 7.
74. *Al-Yawm*, 16 May 1989.
75. *Al-Ittihad*, Abu Dhabi, 3 January, 24 March, 13 April; *Le Point*, 2 January; *CSM*, 11 January; SPA, 9, 12 January — DR, 10, 13 January 1989.
76. *NYT*, 1 April 1989.
77. *Al-Watan*, Kuwait, 6 February; *al-Jazira*, 7 February; *al-Usbu' al-'Arabi*, 27 February 1989.
78. *MM*, 4 September 1989.
79. Quoted in *Ha'aretz*, 28 August; *CR:* Saudi Arabia, No. 3, 1989, p. 6.
80. *CR:* Saudi Arabia, No. 4, 1989, p. 8; *Ha'aretz*, 20 October; R. Damascus, 20 October — DR, 21 October 1989.
81. *Al-Qabas*, 17 January 1990.
82. SPA, 24 January — DR, 25 January; *al-Ra'y*, Beirut, 10 July; *WP*, 23 April 1989.
83. SPA, 2 May, 31 July — DR, 2 May, 1 August; R. Monte Carlo, 1 August — DR, 2 August; *al-Siyasa*, Kuwait, 4 May; *al-Khalij*, 9 August 1989.
84. SPA, 3 August — DR, 4 August 1989.
85. *Al-Riyad*, 1 January 1989.
86. *Al-Madina*, 24 April; *JP*, 16 May; Natsha's statement to SPA, 25 May — DR, 27 May; SPA, 14 August — DR, 15 August 1989.
87. Sa'ud al-Faysal's interview in *al-Yamama*, 9 March; Fahd's interview in *al-Sharq al-Awsat*, 30 May 1989.
88. *Al-Madina,al-Yawm, al-Jazira*, 17 April 1989.
89. *Al-Shira'*, quoted in *NYT*, 8 January; AFP, 5 January 1989.
90. The Saudis denied that they had offered $1.5m. for each Iranian killed; *al-Sharq al-Awsat*, 1 May; SPA, 4 May — DR, 5 May 1989.
91. *'Ukaz, al-Madina*, 10 March; *Kayhan al-'Arabi*, 6 February — DR, 8 February 1989.
92. *IHT*, 14, 15 March 1989.
93. *Al-Madina*, 20 March; *al-Jazira*, 21 March; *TT*, 26 March — DR, 6 April 1989.
94. AFP, 31 March — DR, 31 March; *CR:* Saudi Arabia, No. 2, 1989, p. 8.
95. IRNA, 4 May — DR, 4 May; R. Riyadh, 16 May — DR, 17 May; SPA, 17 May — DR, 18 May; *'Ukaz, al-Yawm*, 18 May 1989.
96. *Al-Siyasa*, Kuwait, 3 May; *al-Majalla*, 24 May; *Kayhan*, London, 27 May 1989.
97. *Al-Masa*, Beirut, 31 July; *al-Mawqif al-'Arabi*, 11 September 1989.
98. GNA, 29 August — DR, 3 September; *al-Masa*, Beirut, 18 September; *TT*, 10 September — DR, 19 September 1989.
99. R. Tehran, 23 September — DR, 25 September; R. Riyadh, 25 September — DR, 26 September 1989.
100. SPA, 16 October — DR, 17 October; *CR:* Saudi Arabia, No. 4, 1989, p. 6.
101. Fahd's interviews with KUNA, 25 September — DR, 26 September, and with *AT*, 30 October; *al-Jazira*, 27 September 1989.
102. *CR:* Saudi Arabia, No. 4, 1989, p. 7.
103. *MM*, 26 June 1989.
104. *Jane's Defence Weekly*, 28 January; *Ha'aretz*, 19 February; *al-Qabas*, 10 July 1989.
105. *Ha'aretz*, 27 January; *Jane's Defence Weekly*, 28 January; *WP*, 2 February; *NYT*, 3 February 1989.
106. *FT*, 17 March 1989.
107. *NYT*, 29 September; *FT*, 30 September 1989.
108. *Chicago Tribune*, 4 April; SPA, 6 April — DR, 7 April 1989.
109. *Ha'aretz*, 16 April, 2 July; *MM*, 17 April 1989.
110. *WP*, 13 April; *al-Jazira*, 15 April; *al-Majalla*, 19 April; *al-Qabas*, 8 May 1989.
111. *Ma'ariv*, 14 June; *Ha'aretz*, 23 June; *CR:* Saudi Arabia, No. 3, 1989, pp. 7–8.
112. SPA, 19 July — DR, 20 July; *MM*, 7 August, 4, 18 September; *al-Bayadir al-Siyasi*, 5 August; *CR:* Saudi Arabia, No. 4, 1989, p. 8.
113. SPA, 4 September — DR, 5 September; *MM*, 4, 18 September; *CR:* Saudi Arabia, No. 4, 1989, p. 8; *al-Siyasa*, Kuwait, 30 October 1989.
114. *Al-Yawm*, 20 January, 11 June; *al-Madina*, 11 June; *al-Bilad*, 14 June 1989.
115. *FT*, 31 January, 1 June; *MM*, 20 February; *CR:* Saudi Arabia, No. 4, 1989, pp. 10–11.

116. *MM,* 15 May; *CR:* Saudi Arabia, No. 2, 1989, p. 10.
117. *The Observer,* 19 March; *FT,* 20 March; SPA, 20 March, 30 April — DR, 22 March, 1 May; AP, AFP, Reuters, 29 April — DR, 30 April; *'Ukaz,* 5 May 1989.
118. Interviews in *al-Sharq al-Awsat,* 31 May, 4 June 1989.
119. *Ha'aretz,* 24 October; *MM,* 11 December 1989.
120. Sultan's interview in *al-Sharq al-Awsat,* 11 June; AFP, 11 June — DR, 13 June; *al-Madina,* 12 June 1989.
121. *CR:* Saudi Arabia, No. 2, 1989, p. 10.
122. SPA, 10 June — DR, 12 June; AFP, 27 March — DR, 29 March 1989.
123. *Al-Sharq al-Jadid,* 14 February 1989.
124. *JP,* 27 March; Sa'ud's interview in *al-Musawwar,* 7 April 1989.
125. *Al-Watan,* 11 April; AFP, SPA, 10 March — DR, 10, 11 March 1989.
126. SPA, 31 March — DR, 1 April; *al-Hayat,* London, 6 May; *al-Watan,* 13 June; *al-Kifah al-'Arabi,* 7 August 1989.
127. *Al-Sharq al-Awsat,* 31 March; *al-Thawra al-Islamiyya,* June 1989.
128. *Al-Sharq al-Awsat,* 24 June; *CR:* Saudi Arabia, No. 1, 1989, p. 5.

Sudan
(Jumhuriyyat al-Sudan)

YEHUDIT RONEN

The military *coup d'état* launched on 30 June 1989 by Brig. Gen. 'Umar Hasan Ahmad al-Bashir put an end to the democratically elected government of al-Sadiq al-Mahdi. The new government became the seventh to govern Sudan since its independence in 1956, when the cycle of alternating civilian and military governments began.

The coup of 30 June was a watershed in Sudan's domestic and foreign affairs. Accordingly, this survey is divided into two equal parts: the first, covering the period of Mahdi's Government (January-June) and the second, of Bashir's Government (June-December).

During the first six months of the year, Mahdi was almost entirely preoccupied with efforts to tighten his grip on the country, whose national, political, and economic disintegration became even more severe. Mahdi's complete failure to cope with Sudan's key problems, or even provide hope of improvement domestically, sealed his fate. Politically, he was caught between strong and contradictory pressures exerted by the Democratic Unionist Party (DUP), the country's second major political force after his own Umma Party (UP), and by the militant National Islamic Front (NIF), the third major actor in Sudanese politics. While the DUP demanded a freeze on the application of Shari'a law as a condition for opening a dialogue with the southern Sudanese People's Liberation Army (SPLA), as agreed between them in late 1988, the NIF opposed this demand vigorously and took moves toward the reapplication of the Shari'a. Given this difference, it was not surprising that Mahdi could not prevent recurrent cabinet crises, which in turn further damaged his already poor record.

His handling of the armed conflict in the south reached its nadir, too. The continuation of the war dealt the Army a serious blow, when it lost large areas to the SPLA.

In foreign affairs Mahdi took no initiative; neither did he score any particular success. In effect, his policies were relatively narrow in scope, being limited to Sudan's immediate neighbors, mainly Libya and Egypt. Libya received his greatest attention, since it was the major, and virtually sole, source of economic and direly needed military assistance. Khartoum's reliance on Tripoli was clearly at the expense of relations with Cairo.

Thus, the public's sharp disappointment and growing sense of *déjà vu* with regard to Mahdi's incompetence and lack of leadership, became greatest toward midyear. The exposure on 18 June of a planned coup surprised no one. In retrospect, the exposure was an effective smokescreen for preparations taking place to change the guard in Khartoum.

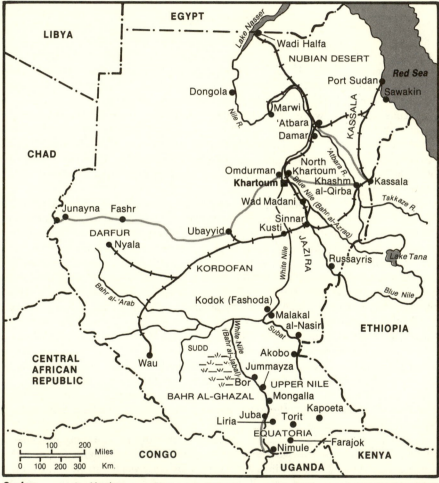

Sudan   –ᵥᵥ– Marshes   ∿ River   +++ Railway   —— Main Road   –·– International boundary

On 30 June, a new group seized power under Bashir's leadership. Neither euphoria nor great expectations seemed to follow the change. The new rulers tried persistently during their first months in power to win the people's support by promising to halt the country's headlong plunge into chaos. But before long it became clear that the new government could not fulfill its promises. It failed completely to offer solutions to the crucial problems facing the country; in fact, it led Sudan more deeply into political crisis, civil war, and economic chaos.

Bashir preferred to deal with relatively simple issues while deliberately evading the twin key problems of the south and the economy, as was plainly evident in his campaign to root out malpractice and corruption. Although he adopted an iron-fist policy, the campaign made no noteworthy improvement in the people's standard of living and certainly did not relieve their grievances. Socioeconomic and political unrest continued; as winter approached the unrest erupted in the form of recurrent demonstrations and strikes.

The resumption of intensive fighting in the south, after a lull of almost six months, did not contribute to the regime's popularity either. It even threatened to erode backing for the Army. This possibility was most perilous, because it was mainly the Army's support and, perhaps, that of the NIF, which had kept the unpopular regime in power during fall-winter 1989.

The government channeled its energies into foreign affairs only as long as they served its immediate interest, i.e., the desperate need for economic and military aid. Therefore, it tried to improve relations with Libya and Egypt and to restore Sudan's neglected ties with Saudi Arabia, Iraq, and the Gulf states. Relations with Libya remained pivotal in Sudan's foreign affairs. The euphoria which dominated Khartoum's links with Cairo in the immediate aftermath of the coup seemed to have faded by late summer, apparently as a result of Egypt's refusal to supply Bashir with arms. Nevertheless, bilateral relations were better than they had been during Mahdi's rule.

All in all, as 1989 neared its end, it became apparent that even the tough military regime had not brought about any change for the better in Sudan.

THE MAHDI ERA

INTERNAL AFFAIRS

The "Swan Song" of the Mahdi Government
Violent Economic Turmoil
Additional shadows were added at the turn of 1988–89 to the already gloomy socioeconomic picture in Sudan. The resolution of the severe economic crisis continued to be put off, the government being almost exclusively preoccupied with its political survival. Having an external debt of c. $14bn.,[1] and the war in the south costing £S2m.–£S10m.[2] daily, Sudan desperately needed additional foreign aid. The International Monetary Fund (IMF) conditioned its further assistance, as it had in the past, on the imposition of a new austerity policy.

On 26 December 1988, apparently unwilling to procrastinate any longer, Mahdi declared new austerity measures, which resulted in steep increases in the price of basic commodities such as bread and sugar; in some cases, the increase was by as much as 500%.[3] The population, which for a number of years had been living at the very edge of its endurance, threw off its self-restraint and poured into the streets of Khartoum and other main towns in stormy protest; some of the demonstrations rapidly turned into bloody riots.[4]

Still fresh was the reaction in late March 1985 to similar IMF-inspired measures which resulted in the rise of the price of basic foodstuffs and helped topple the Numayri regime. Mahdi was, therefore, determined to reduce to a minimum the threat to his government: the imposition of the austerity measures was accompanied by the declaration of a nationwide state of emergency. The violent disturbances were suppressed, but continued to simmer below the surface. Before long, discontent exploded once again, but assumed quite a different character this time.

On 30 December, the leadership of the trade unions which became an important factor in Khartoum politics after the ousting of Numayri, declared a four-day, nationwide general strike (which did not affect the south, immersed as it was in a six-year-old civil war). Most of the vital services were paralyzed, recalling the nationwide strike on the eve of Numayri's downfall in 1985 (see *MECS* 1984–85, pp. 621–24). Then, and again in 1989, the trade unions urged the authorities to do their utmost to solve the country's key problems immediately. The 1989 demand was particularly worrisome to the regime, because of its potential effect on other elements who might be encouraged to challenge Mahdi's leadership.

Tragically, however, not only for Mahdi personally, but much more so for the democratic system and the whole population, the government offered neither relief nor hope. Its incompetence increased the population's hardship and fed its discontent even further. A new wave of strikes soon broke out, disrupting the day-to-day functioning of the economy and administration. In January, Mahdi announced his decision to revoke some of the price rises of basic commodities and to increase salaries of government employees and workers in private industry,[5] but popular grievance did not abate. The last six months of Mahdi's rule were full of uncertainty.

Successive Crises in the Coalition Cabinet; The Threat of the NIF Opposition
In late December 1988, a new tremor shook Mahdi's fragile coalition government, which had been born in great agony only seven months earlier. The DUP, an important coalition partner, left the Cabinet in protest against Mahdi's failure to formally endorse the "peace agreement" signed in November 1988 between the DUP and the SPLA, with the UP's blessing. That document emphasized the eagerness of the two sides to convene the national constitutional conference — an important milestone on the road to settling the devastating civil war. The conference was to convene on 31 December 1988, on condition, above all, as stated in the document, that the two sides consent to freeze the implementation of the controversial law of 1983 concerning Shari'a law until the conference was convened (for other articles of the agreement, see *MECS* 1988, p. 503).

Unfortunately for Sudan, Mahdi could not translate his approval of the agreement into action, since it could have led to political suicide: the militant fundamentalist NIF, which opposed the DUP-SPLA agreement and insisted upon the reapplication of the Shari'a, would probably have tried to remove Mahdi from office if he barred the way to the application of Islamic law. The other horn of his dilemma was that the DUP and the SPLA regarded the freezing of the Shari'a as an elementary, though not sole, condition for enhancing the chances of progress toward peace with the south. The

DUP-SPLA demand to abrogate the military agreement with Libya (signed in 1985) was an additional difficult problem, since Mahdi could not afford, when facing a fiasco in the south and pressure by the Army's high command for immediate reinforcement of its ranks, to endanger the flow of Libyan aid.

Determined above all to maintain his shaky hold on power and aware of the NIF's potential destructive influence, Mahdi appeared resolute not to do anything that could add to the political unrest. Presumably, he hoped that the DUP, a less bellicose and less fanatical element than the NIF, would allow him to continue his political inaction, particularly since the DUP, Mahdi thought, was interested in preserving political order. But as it soon turned out, the DUP upset Mahdi's cards and left the cabinet; coinciding as it did with growing social unrest, it added to the political turbulence. Aware that the DUP's exit from the cabinet would create a political vacuum, which would invite further troubles, Mahdi moved rapidly to establish a new coalition government.

On 1 February, Mahdi announced the formation of his new cabinet, without the DUP. The most conspicuous characteristic of the new cabinet was its strong Islamic coloring. Seven of the portfolios were given to the NIF in comparison to 11 to the UP. Hasan 'Abdallah al-Turabi, the veteran NIF leader, became Mahdi's deputy and foreign minister (see Table 1 below).

Nevertheless, new tensions soon threatened the goverment's survival. On 5 February, Minister of State for Finance al-Tijani al-Tayyib, the architect of the country's short-term economic recovery program, resigned from the cabinet. Al-Tayyib, a well-known Communist leader who had actively opposed the Numayri regime and had joined Sudan's leadership immediately after Numayri's downfall, resigned in protest against the entrenchment of the NIF in the new cabinet, and against the appointment of several ministers to key economic portfolios despite their lack of experience in economic affairs.[6] A day later, a foreign source reported the resignation of Defense Minister 'Abd al-Majid Hamid Khalil,[7] who had assumed office in May 1988; two weeks later the resignation received official confirmation. Mahdi then appointed Salah al-Khalifa as acting defense minister.[8]

Khalil did not state publicly why he had resigned. The government, which had good reasons to play down the affair, did likewise. One can only speculate about Khalil's motives. He might have felt that the combination of the humiliating military fiascos in the south and the likelihood that the Army's performance would not improve plus the political and economic chaos in Khartoum, had become unbearable. He might also have not wanted to be held responsible for further deterioration. Perhaps he also wished to shake up the country's exhausted leadership to get it to mobilize all its resources to deal promptly and efficiently with Sudan's urgent problems, above all the war. One could assume that Khalil himself was exhausted. He was a veteran military figure with a long career in public life. In the late 1970s he had built for himself the image of a "soldier's soldier," thoroughly imbued with a sense of duty and discipline. Until his dismissal by Numayri in early 1982, he had been defense minister, commander in chief of the armed forces, and the first vice president. His dismissal was due to a sharp difference of opinion with Numayri over the role of the military in domestic affairs — a clear similarity to the circumstances in 1989.

On 20 February the armed forces' high command submitted to the Mahdi cabinet a strongly worded memorandum signed by 150 senior officers headed by Commander in Chief Gen. Fathi Ahmad 'Ali,[9] who was known to be a personal friend and confidant of Khalil (see *MECS* 1988, p. 498). Though not containing an explicit threat of a coup, the memorandum was, in effect, an ultimatum. It gave the leadership one week to form a broad-based government and to improve the prospects of ending the civil war. The memorandum also demanded that the armed forces be strengthened and that the economic recession be dealt with more effectively.[10] It was not clear whether the presentation of the memorandum was coordinated with Khalil, but it was undoubtedly affected by his resignation. Mahdi made no public response to the officers' move, but the immediate cancellation of his plan to attend the funeral of Japan's recently deceased emperor and to send Idris al-Banna, the deputy chairman of the State Supreme Council, instead, clearly indicated his anxieties.[11] On the eve of the deadline (26 February), the Army stationed thousands of troops on combat alert in Khartoum.[12] A day later, the trade union leadership submitted a memorandum of its own to Mahdi repeating, in effect, the Army's ultimatum,[13] to add further pressure, without doubt, on the prime minister to respond positively to the officers' demands.

Having no choice, al-Mahdi responded on 27 February to the ultimatum in an address to the Constitutent Assembly which was designed first and foremost to ease tension and to prevent further friction with the Army's top echelon. The exchange of views is "normal between those who hold political responsibilities and those who hold military responsibilities, particularly in circumstances of combat," he stated, adding that "we should not be drawn into a maelstrom of mutual recriminations where the military seeks a political scapegoat and the politicians seek a military scapegoat." Rarely capable of making a decisive move, Mahdi neither announced any dramatic action nor outlined any new policy. Apparently playing for time, he said that he would resign on 5 March if the Army and the trade unions did not assure him of their commitment to "constitutional legitimacy."[14] The army command was not satisfied with Mahdi's reply and kept the troops on full alert.[15]

The last day of February was particularly tense, following rumors about a military coup being thwarted.[16] The daylong closed meeting of the senior-officer corps contributed to the rumor mill and whatever the truth about the attempted coup, no political or military leader referred to it publicly. The political uncertainty continued, reflected, among others, in the reported assassination attempt on Khalil on 3 March.[17] In this case, too, the authorities remained silent.

Aware of the dangers threatening him and knowing that the political unrest was a great peril, Mahdi acted with vigor. On 4 March, he gained a reprieve when he drew all political forces (except for the NIF, and the Army giving its tacit consent) into an agreement on a program setting out policies for a new coalition. The program called for: strengthening the armed forces, convening the constitutional conference on the basis of the DUP-SPLA agreement, finding a solution to the chronic problems of the economy and improving standards of living, and pursuing a balanced foreign policy.[18] The issue of Sudan's foreign relations played a pivotal role in the political crisis, since Mahdi's alignment with Libya had been opposed by the DUP, which demanded closer ties with Egypt (see below).

A day later, however, the wheel turned once again. Addressing a press conference in Khartoum, Mahdi surprised everyone by saying that the NIF would join the new government.[19] His announcement infuriated the political parties and the trade unions, which accused him of reneging on the program to which he had just agreed.[20] Mahdi lost further credibility, and the Army and the trade unions, frustrated by his delaying tactics and skeptical of his ability to comply with their demands, continued to apply pressure on him. On 10 March, they submitted another ultimatum, demanding that he resign within 24 hours.[21] On 12 March, the State Supreme Council formally accepted the resignation of all the ministers and the cabinet was dissolved. The NIF announcement two days later that it would not join the new government[22] paved the way for the formation of a new cabinet, though it was by no means clear that Mahdi could govern without the NIF.

On 25 March, the new government was sworn in (for its composition see Table 1 below). Mahdi, who referred to the enervating process as a positive "exercise in democracy,"[23] felt great relief, but not for long. As expected, the NIF boycotted the new cabinet on the grounds that it was not committed to the reapplication of the Shari'a and because it included trade union elements. At this point, it seemed increasingly likely that the NIF would seek to undermine the cabinet, hoping to see it collapse. During 1986, the NIF as a major opposition force had done just that to the first Mahdi coalition government, virtually paralyzing it (see *MECS* 1986, pp. 581–82).

On 10 April, the Constituent Assembly voted 154 to 53 to ratify the cabinet decision to implement the new draft legal code based on the Shari'a.[24] The decision was called "illogical" by Muhammad Yusuf Muhammad, speaker of the Constituent Assembly and senior NIF member.[25] He resigned as speaker and two days later, Faruq 'Ali al-Barbar, a lawyer, was elected to succeed him. The 10 April vote stirred up stormy demonstrations by NIF supporters in the country's main cities and especially in Khartoum. They continued for several days, with one person being killed and three others injured.[26] The NIF leaders took an active part in the demonstrations; they called on the people to resist as part of "the revolution of the Qur'an,"[27] threatening Mahdi's political position unless he reapplied Shari'a.[28] During May, the NIF was determined to continue "the battle" against the Mahdi government "until its fall or until it changes its decisions to obstruct the Shari'a."[29] Turabi even used the term Jihad (holy war) when referring to the struggle for the reapplication of the Shari'a.[30]

The government was helpless against the NIF subversion, as it was on all other domestic fronts. In late spring 1989, it became clear that Mahdi's regime was sitting on a volcano that was on the verge of erupting.

The Exposure of an Alleged Coup Plan

At this juncture, the desperate domestic circumstances invited an attempt at political change. On 18 June, the government announced that a plot against it had been exposed: army officers and civilians reportedly planned to topple the government and return Numayri to power.[31] Numayri, who had lived in Egypt since his ousting, denied any complicity.[32] (He had reiterated on several occasions his determination to return home; he even stated that he would return to power within four weeks.)[33]

Large-scale arrests of soldiers and civilians followed.[34] The official announcement on the exposure of a coup plan and the authorities' failure to identify its instigators raised doubts about the truth of the matter. Senior officials even called it a fabrication and a "bad play."[35] Whatever the facts, the abortive coup plan was soon eclipsed by a successful military coup that led to Mahdi's downfall.

TABLE 1: MAHDI'S CABINETS, FEBRUARY AND MARCH 1989

Portfolio	1 February	Party Affiliation	25 March	Party Affiliation
Prime Minister	al-Sadiq al-Mahdi	UP	Unchanged	
Defense	'Abd al-Majid Hamid Khalil	UP	Mubarak 'Uthman* Rahman	Independent
Foreign Affairs	Hasan 'Abdallah al-Turabi**	NIF	Sayyid Ahmad al-Husayn*	DUP
Justice and Attorney General	Hafiz al-Shaykh al-Zaki*	NIF	'Uthman 'Umar al-Sharif*	DUP
Agriculture and Natural Resources	Aldo Ago Deng**	Southern Party	Unchanged	
Irrigation and Water Resources	Muhammad Bashir	UP	Unchanged	
Higher Education and Scientific Research	Shaykh Mahjub Ja'far	UP	Unchanged	
Finance and Economic Planning	'Umar Nur al-Da'im	UP	Unchanged	
Local Government	Richard Makobi	Southern Party	Joseph Ukel*	Southern Party
Health	Ma'mun Yusuf Hamid*	NIF	'Abd al-Rahmad Abu al-Kull*	Trade Union
Industry	'Abd al-Wahhab 'Uthman	NIF	Ibrahim Radwan*	DUP
Internal Trade, Cooperation, and Supply	'Ali al-Hajj Muhammad Adam	NIF	Mirghani 'Abd al-Rahman Sulayman*	DUP
Animal Wealth	Isma'il Abakir	UP	Paolino Zizi*	Southern Party
Public Communication	Taj al-Sirr Mustafa 'Abd al-Salam	NIF	Vacant	
Public Works and Housing	Hasan Shaykh Idris*	UP	Isma'il Abakir**	UP
Labor and Social Security	Matthiew Abor	Southern Party	'Ukasha Babikr al-Tayyib*	Trade Union
Culture and Information	Bashir 'Umar*	UP	Husayn Sulayman Abu Salih*	DUP
Social Welfare and Refugees Affairs	Ahmad 'Abd al-Rahman Muhammad	NIF	Awhaj Muhammad Musa*	DUP
Youth and Sports	Joshua Diwal	Southern Party	Robert Bendi*	Southern Party
Public Service and Administrative Reform	Fadlallah 'Ali Fadlallah	UP	Abu Zayd Muhammad Salih*	Communist Party
Tourism and Hotels	Salah al-Din 'Abd al-Salam al-Khalifa	UP	Muhammad Hamad Kuwa*	SNP
Interior	Mubarak 'Abdallah al-Fadil	UP	Unchanged	
Energy and Mining			Bashir 'Umar**	UP

*   New appointment.
**   Reappointed to another portfolio.

Seventh Year of War in the South: Deterioration in Khartoum's Position
and the SPLA Strengthening

Early in 1989, the SPLA and the Army were dragged into renewed cycles of fierce fighting after the Mahdi government's failure to endorse the DUP-SPLA "peace agreement"(see above). Whether because it lost its patience or because it was trying to exert new pressure on the government, or both, the SPLA resumed the armed struggle.

On 26 January, the SPLA won its first victory of the year when it captured al-Nasir, a strategic town in the Upper Nile region.[36] A month later, it also took control of Torit,[37] the former provisional headquarters of Eastern Equatoria and the second major garrison town after Juba, the capital of the south. During March, the SPLA continued its vigorous offensive, taking Liria, Farajok, and Nimule near the Uganda border, and Jummayza and Mongalla, both north of Juba.[38] As a rule, neither the Army nor the Khartoum government initially mentioned the SPLA claims of victories, most of which proved to be true. In some cases, the Army admitted, though not explicitly, the loss of its outposts.

During March and April, encouraged by its impressive victories, the SPLA repeatedly tried to penetrate into southern Kordofan, outside the south's informal border. The SPLA forces arrived at the outskirts of Kadugli, the capital of the region, but the Army repulsed them,[39] in what seemed a concentrated effort to drive off the "rebels" from the area, which reportedly had oil reserves and was a link between the south and the north. The separatist tendencies long endemic to the region, which might lead its population to demand autonomy, as had happened in the south during the 1970s, also troubled Mahdi. (For the Army's foiling of a similar SPLA attempt a year and a half earlier, see *MECS* 1987, p. 624.)

Meanwhile, the SPLA, with its c. 60,000 members and supporters,[40] deployed its forces in the south. The armed clashes continued without interruption and on 11 April the SPLA announced the capture of Akobo, an important garrison town near the Ethiopian border.[41] Six days later, the SPLA claimed to have captured Bor,[42] in the Upper Nile region, the birthplace of the SPLA in 1983. The capture of Bor was important not only symbolically, but much more so because of its strategic location, controlling traffic on the Nile to and from Juba, and the road form Malakal to Juba.

The SPLA followed the capture of Bor with an announcement of the "sealing of its dry season offensive,"[43] and the "clearing [of] the international borders east of the Nile River in southern Sudan,"[44] namely the areas adjacent to the Ethiopian, Kenyan, and Ugandan borders. Given the armed forces' poor performance and thorough demoralization and the SPLA's strengthened military position and high motivation, the course of the war was not surprising. While the high command of the armed forces and the political leadership became ineffective, due largely to the escalating crisis in the capital, the SPLA leadership appeared more united than ever, enabling it to devote itself to winning as much territory as possible, which it could use as bargaining chips when the time for negotiations came. The Army's lack of fuel and ammunition[45] enabled the SPLA to score its victories. During the past two years, the supply of weapons and other equipment by the military's traditional Arab and Western backers fell off dramatically and even stopped, due partly to the country's chronic foreign debt, and partly to a growing recognition among these suppliers that they should help promote peace rather than the armed conflict. Furthermore, Mahdi's reliance on

Libya isolated it from its traditional arms suppliers (see below).[46] The SPLA, in contrast, received a steady supply of arms, mainly from Ethiopia but also from Kenya and Israel.[47] Another source was the Army's deserted or captured posts, the SPLA claimed.[48]

Meanwhile, the political picture changed, culminating in the establishment of a broad-based coalition cabinet in March. In one of its first acts, the government approved in principle though not formally the DUP-SPLA agreement and called for a cease-fire. Early in April, a Sudanese ministerial delegation went to Addis Ababa, where it met with the SPLA to discuss all aspects of a truce.[49]

Expectations of ending the political stalemate were heightened following the reported cooperation of the two warring sides with the UN's relief campaign, known as "Operation Lifeline Sudan," which started on 1 April.[50] Tragically, the relief operation had largely faltered. Not only did it begin late, thus being caught by the rain which complicated distribution because of the impossible roads; it also faced difficulties emanating from the suspicions of each of the conflicting sides that the other would exploit the relief convoys for its own benefit. Each suffered from severe shortages of basic foods and medicines.

The repeated attacks on the relief convoys during April and May[51] threatened to aggravate the human catastrophe in the south even further: in addition to the 250,000 starvation deaths during 1988, 100,000 persons were under the threat of death at the beginning of the second quarter of 1989.[52] The refugee population was estimated at 3m., the majority of them women and children.[53]

On 1 May, SPLA leader Col. John Garang announced an unexpected, immediate unilateral cease-fire. "I here reciprocate the call of Prime Minister al-Mahdi for a temporary cease-fire," he stated, adding that "it [would] expire, unless extended on 31 May....During this period the SPLA units will cease all military operations and remain in their present positions." He conditioned the cease-fire on similar behavior by the Army. Meanwhile, he added, "all will wait from the government to implement the requirements of the [November] peace agreement after which a comprehensive cease-fire will be worked out by a joint technical military committee." Garang, who described his move as "a bold action of statemanship," hinted to the government that this time he was expecting substantial progress, saying that "actions speak louder than words."[54]

Mahdi welcomed, though somewhat belatedly, Garang's initiative and offered to convene a joint military committee on 15 May in Addis Ababa to discuss further aspects of the cease-fire.[55] The SPLA turned down the offer as "premature" and "irrelevant."[56] "Words do not suffice," the SPLA stated.[57] But, once again, and tragically for the whole of Sudan, Mahdi could not translate words into deeds, even if he had so wished. He was caught on the horns of a dilemma: if he suspended the Shari'a law, as the SPLA flatly demanded, then the militant NIF would endanger his grip on power. If he did not, then various political circles, foremost among them the DUP, would most probably plot against him politically, as would the trade unions' leadership. In such a situation, the Army might stage a coup against him, and if so, the SPLA would intensify its war against the government and not only damage Mahdi militarily but also cause him a severe political blow. Another dilemma was connected with the SPLA's insistence upon Sudan's canceling of its military agreements with Libya and Egypt (see above and below). Despite the prime minister's ostensible optimistic statement that "for every step the SPLA makes the government is prepared to make two,"[58] he could not move forward at all.

In late May, it appeared that Garang understood Mahdi's complex situation; fearing that the renewed political momentum might become bogged down once again, he turned to Western political circles and media, hoping that they would put pressure on Khartoum, while simultaneously endowing the SPLA with political respectability. Between late May and the first half of June, Garang was in West Germany, Switzerland, the US, and Britain. While in Bonn and later in London, Garang cunningly gained further prestige by announcing the unilateral extension of the cease-fire, first until mid-June, and then until 1 July. Khartoum denounced Garang's successful public relations campaign,[59] but it did not stop Garang from impressing foreign audiences to whom he explained the situation in Sudan as he saw it, as well as the SPLA program.[60] The SPLA, he said, was not interested in partitioning Sudan; it was fighting for the whole of Sudan, to end the concentration of wealth and political power in the hands of a northern-based minority and to introduce a secular constitution which would promote equal development and popular government.[61]

The SPLA's growing political standing abroad and military position in the south forced Mahdi to meet the SPLA's representatives in Addis Ababa in mid-June. Both sides announced their decision to meet again in Addis Ababa on 4 July to follow up the implementation of the peace agreement and to fix 18 September 1989 as the date for convening the constitutional conference.[62] But Bashir's successful military coup severed the political contacts of the two sides.

FOREIGN AFFAIRS

Libya

During Mahdi's three years in office, in particular the first half of 1989, the Sudanese government became entirely dependent upon Libyan economic and military assistance. Distancing itself politically from the US and the West in general, as well as from Egypt, Saudi Arabia, and the Gulf states, and aligning itself with Qadhdhafi's Libya, Sudan lost its traditional sources of support.

Although the nearly exclusive reliance on Libya had a political price, it did not cause Mahdi any discomfort as he felt morally indebted to Libya for its support and welcome during his years of exile there in the 1970s. Qadhdhafi had then provided Mahdi's followers in Libya, the Ansar, with funds and training, and in mid-1976, Tripoli even collaborated with them in launching an abortive coup attempt against the pro-American and pro-Egyptian regime in Khartoum (see *MECS* 1976–77, pp. 586–87, 597). The strong resentment, perhaps even personal indignation, which Mahdi felt toward Egypt made it easier for him to identify with Tripoli rather than with Cairo.

In February, when the Mahdi government faced a renewed threat to its political survival (see above), Mahdi appealed to Qadhdhafi for emergency aid. The visits of senior Sudanese officials to Tripoli during this period should be seen within this context.

On 4 March, when the political turbulence in Sudan was at its fiercest, Qadhdhafi sent a top-level official to Sudan on a discrete mission.[63] Neither side dwelt on the visit's aims or results. An Egyptian source claimed that Tripoli had threatened to halt aid if the Army overthrew Mahdi and seized power[64] — a not unlikely possibility at that time. Senior Libyan intelligence officials, stationed in Khartoum, were also instructed to keep a close watch on local politics and warn Mahdi in case of real danger.[65]

Somewhat surprisingly against the background of the highly fragile political situation in Sudan, Mahdi arrived in Tripoli for a 24-hour official visit on 7 March. Whatever was the immediate reason for the visit, he made verbal attacks on Egypt before leaving for Libya, another signal that he had no intention of scuttling the special Sudanese-Libyan relationship. The Libyan response was immediate: Libya agreed to give military equipment worth $250m.[66] (a helicopter which landed unexpectedly in the Aswan area in southern Egypt on 26 April was part of this deal).[67] The arrival of a senior Sudanese mission in Tripoli in late March-early April, headed by the new minister of defense, suggested, however, that Libya was far from satisfying Sudan's pressing needs, especially in weaponry. Apparently, the Sudanese visitors hoped to convince Qadhdhafi to increase the quantity and content of the aid. Whether this was also the reason for Mahdi's intention to visit Tripoli in late June,[68] remained unknown as the Army ousted him from office on the eve of his departure. (For Tripoli's view of its relations with Sudan, see chapter on Libya.)

Egypt

The clouds hanging over relations between Sudan and Egypt did not lift during the first half of 1989. On the contrary, Sudan's alignment with Libya dragged relations between the two states down to a new low.

Because of Sudan's most vital importance to Egypt's interests, the latter could not deny itself channels of communication with its neighbor. Cairo, therefore, played an important role in the contacts which had been made in late 1988 between the SPLA and the DUP, Egypt's traditional friend in Sudanese politics. These contacts culminated in the signing of a "peace agreement" between the two Sudanese parties (see above). Mahdi's failure to endorse the agreement, which, in turn, caused the DUP to leave the cabinet, caused additional strain in relations with Egypt.

Another issue that marred bilateral relations was Cairo's ignoring of Mahdi's repeated requests to extradite Numayri, who had lived in exile in Egypt ever since his ouster from power. Mahdi's hostile approach toward Cairo was perhaps also influenced by his animosity to Egyptian President Husni Mubarak, who reportedly had headed the air squadron, which in March 1970 bombed the Aba island, the stronghold of the Ansar and the base of their uprising against Numayri.

It was not surprising, therefore, that Mahdi repeatedly delayed his planned visit to Cairo and eventually announced its cancellation at the beginning of March.[69] Mahdi's arrival, in early March, on an official visit to Libya further heightened tension with Egypt.

In addition to the existing causes of friction, Khartoum became increasingly concerned at the beginning of 1989 at what it viewed as Cairo's leaning toward the SPLA in the war. The arrival of SPLA representatives in Egypt at the beginning of 1989 added to Khartoum's apprehensions.[70] Mahdi's implied criticism was echoed in his statement, released in late February, that "for some reason Egypt takes a neutral stance on our war in the south, on the pretext that it is a domestic problem."[71] Mubarak did not sit idly by either. On 1 March, he strongly criticized Mahdi in public, denying the Sudanese prime minister's allegation of Cairo's having deserted Khartoum and his claim that Sudan had mediated on Egypt's behalf in its dispute with Libya.[72] Since Mahdi was embroiled in a severe political crisis at home, he preferred not to add further fuel to the antagonism; he only expressed his "regret" at Mubarak's remarks.[73]

About a month later, however, when Mahdi felt politically stronger (see above), he pressed ahead with the abrogation of the joint defense agreement which had been signed with Egypt in mid-1976 in response to the subversion launched jointly by Libya and Mahdi's Ansar against the pro-Egyptian Numayri regime. It remained unclear what pushed Mahdi to take this step at this time. Was it in response to immediate Libyan pressure? Was it in response to domestic pressure aimed at paving the way for negotiations with the SPLA, which made the cancellation of the agreement a condition for opening a dialogue? Or was it perhaps in reaction to pressures by senior army officers to placate Qadhdhafi in order to receive additional military aid? Or was Mahdi's decision another expression of his animosity toward Egypt, which he could express once his political position had relatively improved?

Whatever the reasons, the strain in relations between the two countries continued unrelieved. It was plainly reflected in June, when Egypt for the first time allowed Numayri to make public statements after discouraging him from speaking to the press in the past. In all the interviews and statements given to various Arab organs, he assaulted the Mahdi regime virulently and even called for its immediate overthrow.

The visit of a high-ranking SPLA delegation to Egypt in June[74] added to Mahdi's anger, as attested by Khartoum's intention, announced in late June, to grant political asylum to Khalid 'Abd al-Nasser, the son of the late Egyptian president, who had been sentenced to death in Egypt.[75] Whether Mahdi really intended granting asylum or was putting pressure on Mubarak remained unknown and irrelevant, because on 30 June, Mahdi was ousted from office. (On Sudanese-Egyptian relations during this period see also chapter on Egypt.)

THE BASHIR ERA

INTERNAL AFFAIRS

The Coup d'État and Formation of New Government Institutions

At dawn on Friday, 30 June, army forces, most of them paratroopers,[76] carried out a successful coup in Khartoum. The seizure of power was rapid and bloodless, except for two casualties, a civilian and a soldier who were wounded accidentally.[77]

On the very same day, Staff Brig. Gen. 'Umar Hasan Ahmad al-Bashir, who elevated himself to the rank of lieutenant general, was revealed as the leader of the coup. It was argued, however, that the real leader was not Bashir but Zubayr Muhammad Salih,[78] who later became second in command in the new political hierarchy. Zubayr belonged to the group that had tried to topple the Mahdi regime on 18 June (see above). Whatever the actual relations between the two, Bashir was the new regime's leader throughout the rest of 1989, with no political differences or personal rivalries between the two, coming to the surface.

During his first days in office, Bashir clamped down on potential opposition elements by a wave of arrests and purges, especially within the top political and military echelons. The nucleus of the civilian leadership was imprisoned, except for Muhammad 'Uthman al-Mirghani, who was in Rhodes, and Mahdi who had escaped but was caught a week later. A total of 28 senior officers, including the commander in chief and chief of staff, were dismissed;[79] Maj. Gen Ishaq Ibrahim 'Umar became the new chief of staff,[80] and Bashir assumed the post of commander in chief. A nationwide state of emergency was proclaimed, the constitution was suspended, the formal political institutions were dissolved, political parties and trade unions were banned, and all newspapers, except for the army daily, *al-Quwat al-Musallaha,* were closed down. On the day of the coup, Bashir set up a 15-member Revolution Command Council for National Salvation (RCCNS — *majlis qiyadat thawra al-inqadh al-watani*). Its composition was announced as follows:

		Regional Division*
Chairman:	Staff Lt. Gen. 'Umar Hasan Ahmad al-Bashir	Northern Region
Vice Chairman:	Staff Brig. Gen. Zubayr Muhammad Salih	
Other members:	Staff Col. Tijani Adam Tahir	Darfur
	Staff Col. Faysal 'Ali Abu Salih	
	Staff Brig. Gen. 'Uthman Ahmad Hasan	Northern Region
	Staff Brig. Gen. Dominic Kassiano	Equatoria, Southern Region
	Brig. Gen. Ibrahim Nayil Idam	Darfur
	Naval Staff Col. Salah al-Din Muhammad Karrar	
	Staff Col. Sulayman Muhammad Sulayman	Central Region
	Col. Martin Malwal Arap	Bahr al-Ghazal, Southern Region
	Col. Pipo Kuwan	Upper Nile, Southern Region
	Air Staff Col. Faysal Madani	Kordofan
	Staff Lt. Col. Muhammad al-Amin Khalifa	Eastern Region
	Staff Lt. Col. Bakri Hasan Salih	
	Maj. Ibrahim Shams al-Din	

*   No details were available regarding some of the council members.

Members of the RCCNS were drawn from all regions of the country. Three of the members were non-Muslim, representing the three regions of the south. No precise details regarding the political affiliation of the 15 members were available. The new regime, however, appeared anxious to give the RCCNS an image of political independence. "We have come to serve all the people and we do not represent any particular group," its official spokesmen stated repeatedly.[81] Nevertheless, recurrent reports indicated the regime's sympathy and even close links with the NIF; one source even said that eight of the 15 RCCNS members were known to be fundamentalists, including Zubayr Muhammad Salih.[82] These reports motivated Bashir and other top officials to deny them repeatedly,[83] lest they erode support at home and abroad.

While the religious and political affiliation of each of the RCCNS members remained unclear, other biographical details were copious. Bashir himself was born on 1 January 1944 in Shandi, in northern Sudan. His military training had been acquired in Sudan and abroad, reportedly in Malaysia, the USSR, the US, Egypt, and Pakistan. He spent the 1973 war in Egypt, and was appointed military adviser to the United Arab Emirates (UAE) in 1975. After returning home, he became the third ranking paratroop commander and served for two years as a garrison commander in the south. He was later transferred to Khartoum where he headed an armored and parachute brigade.[84] It was unknown whether he was among the 150 officers who signed the February ultimatum (see above).

Important in the new regime's efforts to secure its grip on power was its immediate public statement, justifying the coup:

The fear that Sudan might be lost and we would become a burden and live as refugees in neighboring states prompted us to make the move....We moved to save Sudan...from the destruction and devastation....We want to build a new united Sudanese nation which is free from interparty conflicts, and free of regional and tribal conflicts.[85]

In a large number of statements and interviews, especially in Arab publications, Bashir defined the regime's priorities as ending the civil war and reforming the economy.[86] He also emphasized that "we have not come to rule forever. Once we feel that our people have become capable of electing their own real rulers and making sound decisions without the sectarian and party forms of the past, then we will clear the way, quit, and return to our homes."[87]

In his 10th day in office, Bashir announced the composition of his cabinet:

Portfolio	Incumbent*
Prime Minister and Defense	'Umar Hasan Ahmad al-Bashir
Deputy Prime Minister	Muhammad Salih al-Zubayr
Presidential Affairs	Muhammad Ibrahim al-Tayyib
Foreign Minister	'Ali Sahlul
Interior	Faysal 'Ali Abu Salih
Justice and Attorney General	Hasan Isma'il al-Bili
Culture and Information	'Ali Muhammad Shummu
Finance and National Economy	Sayyid 'Ali Zaki
Agriculture and Natural Resources	Ahmad 'Ali Qunayif
Guidance	'Abdallah Deng Lual
Irrigation and Water Resources	Ya'qub Abu Shura
Energy and Mining	'Abd al-Mun'im Khujali
Industry	Muhammad 'Umar 'Abdallah
Education	Mahjub al-Badawi Muhammad
Housing and Public Works	Muhammad Ma'mun al-Hadi al-Mardi
Trade, Cooperation, and Supply	Faruq al-Bashri
Health and Social Welfare	Shakir al-Sarraj
Relief and Refugees	Peter Orat Adwar
Transport and Communications	'Ali Ahmad Ibrahim
Labor and Social Insurance	George Kinga
Local Government and Religious Coordination	Natali Ambu
Youth and Sports**	Ibrahim Nayil Idam
Defense (Minister of State)	'Uthman Muhammad al-Hasan

* For biographical details about the new cabinet members, see *al-Quwat al-Musallaha, al-Ittihad,* Abu Dhabi, 10 July 1989.

** On 11 November, Bashir issued a decree creating a new portfolio, Ministry of Youth and Sports, which was given to Ibrahim Nayil Idam, an RCCNS member.

Four senior army officers were appointed to key portfolios; a fifth, Ibrahim Nayil Idam was appointed in November. Four southerners, including a Christian cleric, were given fairly minor positions. Not all of the ministers were new faces, and some of them had served in earlier governments, including Numayri's. The only minister of state appointed was Staff Maj. Gen (ret.) 'Uthman Muhammad al-Hasan as minister of state for defense.[88]

Failure to Cope with Internal Challenges
After setting up a new government, which maintained a tight control over domestic affairs, Bashir was expected to translate his verbal commitments into deeds.

But as summer passed and the regime's period of grace came to an end, it became clear that no dramatic change for the better was likely. The new regime, like its predecessors, seemed to lack a program for coping with the twin key problems, the civil war and the economic chaos. Bashir refrained from taking any bold steps in either area, which might endanger his hold on power and probably not win him any immediate political rewards. The regime's inaction should be seen within the context of the complex web of political, religious, and socioeconomic elements. Nevertheless, it appeared that Bashir's incompetence brought the country closer to the brink of an abyss.

Crackdown on Malpractice and Corruption

The new leadership was concerned by the potential threat inherent in the growing hardships of the people and their grievances. Political suppression, which stirred up strong ferment among wide circles, especially in the capital, did not contribute to sympathy for the regime. Therefore, Bashir moved swiftly to tackle a problem, which if solved successfully, could win him immediate popular support. In July, Bashir started a crackdown (which lasted until the year's end) on economic corruption and malpractice. Suspected black marketeers, smugglers, hoarders, and currency traders were arrested, and threatened with execution if found guilty. Simultaneously, he decreased prices of essential items, but sugar, cigarettes, flour, and meat disappeared from the shops.[89] Public transportation almost ground to a halt, because many of the vehicles depended on the black market for gasoline.[90]

As part of the war against corruption, the government established three committees to investigate financial and administrative malpractice, the activities of state institutions, and the country's leadership during Mahdi's era. Special publicity was given to the trial of Idris al-Banna, a former vice president of the Supreme State Council, that began on 12 August before a special military court on charges of "fraudulence and dishonesty."[91] On 2 September, Banna, who was 73, was sentenced to 40 years' imprisonment and confiscation of all his property.[92] Another central figure in the former regime, former minister of housing and attorney general 'Uthman al-Sharif was sentenced to two weeks in prison, later increased to five years, for abusing his authority.[93]

The government used the campaign against corruption and malpractice as an excuse to detain the country's leadership during Mahdi's era. The government also exploited the campaign to neutralize anyone considered a potential political threat.

On 2 December, two men found guilty of illegal currency and drug dealings were sentenced to death. Two weeks later, they were hanged in Khartoum's Kober prison,[94] apparently in the "justice square" which Numayri had created seven years before to hold the large crowds which came to witness the execution of the verdicts given under the Shari'a — the public hanging of leaders of the Republican Brothers, among them Mahmud Taha (see *MECS* 1984–85, pp. 616–17).

Growing Civil Unrest

Though important, the crackdown on corruption was a relatively minor issue and, in any case, it did not ease public unrest to any significant degree. Nor, surprisingly, did it take long for the strong latent discontent to burst into the open again. Even the regime's iron fist policy of eliminating any potential sources of incitement, did not wipe them out. In early August, several leaders of trade unions — it was not clear which — were arrested following publication of a memorandum calling upon the regime to allow the trade unions to resume their activities.[95] Other signs of growing dissatisfaction were the continuing dismissals of officers — allegedly over 400 — and the further purges of senior civil servants.[96] The authorities, sensitive to their image not only in Khartoum but even more so in the Arab world, called these reports "highly exaggerated."[97]

Whatever the true extent of the detentions and dismissals, suspense remained high, and the discovery, also in August, of "large quantities" of weapons in a number of vehicles at the southern entrance into Khartoum added to the political uncertainty.[98]

Tension increased significantly in the second half of September, following the government's imposition of an austerity program which removed subsidies on basic consumer goods, whose price then rose.[99] Bashir urgently needed financial aid from the IMF to which Sudan owed $1bn., which was half the sum due to the IMF from all debtor states.[100] The IMF had conditioned its aid on the government imposing economic austerity measures and the timing of the program was dictated by the IMF World Bank meeting in Washington on 23–27 September.

Popular protest was not long in coming. During the last week of September, two waves of demonstrations swept Khartoum.[101] Whether connected to the demonstrations or being a preemptive act, arrests of members of the dissolved Communist Party followed immediately, accused of "illegal subversive activities."[102] It seemed that the Communists, as had happened during the Numayri dictatorship, not only raised the banner of struggle against the oppressive regime, but also became the regime's scapegoat for any outburst of political discontent.

Aware of the worsening security conditions and wishing to ease political tension, Bashir used the anniversary of the October 1964 revolution — the overthrow of 'Abud's military regime by civilian elements — to release 174 political prisoners.[103] Nevertheless, political turbulence continued and it came out into the open once again a month later.

On 26 November, the officially dissolved physicians' trade union, known for its strong Communist sympathies, declared a strike in Khartoum's hospitals in protest against the political oppression, and the alleged detention of some of its members sometime earlier. The authorities called the strike "an act of treason," and warned that it "would not tolerate a return to strikes and chaos."[104] The strike ended on 2 December, when the government's iron fist came down upon the strikers. Four physicians were arrested and pleaded guilty to causing the strike, to violating the emergency regulations, and to waging war against the state. One doctor was sentenced to death and another to 15-years' imprisonment; the two others were acquitted.[105] An Egyptian source claimed that one of the leading doctors, a central figure in the civil disobedience campaign which had led to Numayri's overthrow, was tortured to death by the security authorities,[106] but they denied this allegation.[107]

In the last week of November, c. 300 university students in Khartoum staged an antiregime protest in the streets, the first such demonstration since the military takeover on 30 June.[108] Two students from Khartoum University were reported to have been shot to death when the police crushed the demonstration. A third death was reported when a Muslim fundamentalist student was killed during a political debate.[109]

On 29 November, Khartoum University students belonging to or sympathetic to the NIF won all 40 seats in elections to their student union.[110] On 3 December, the students were allowed to stage a victory march despite a ban on street demonstrations. Bashir used the occasion of the march to deliver a long speech, highlighting what he called "the masses' support of the 30 June revolution."[111] Khartoum's university students, usually at the forefront of all civilian action, were believed to be solidly behind the NIF and were considered to be staunch supporters of Bashir's government. Despite the government's repeated denials of strong links to the NIF, it became fairly evident at the end of the year that such links did exist.

Further Brewing of the War in the South

On the very day of the coup and in its immediate aftermath, Bashir repeatedly emphasized his determination to end the conflict with the south peacefully. At the same time, however, he announced his objection to the "peace moves" taken by previous regimes, namely the 1986 Koka Dam and the 1988 DUP-SPLA agreements, portraying them as "partisan deceit and lies." Instead, he offered to open a dialogue with Garang and hold a nationwide referendum on the divisive issue of the Shari'a law, if the problem could not be resolved through negotiations between the two sides.[112] In an attempt to add substance to what he considered to be a goodwill gesture toward the SPLA, Bashir announced a monthlong cease-fire on 4 July.[113] It was only symbolic, because not only was the Army paralyzed, but also because the truce which the SPLA had declared two months before, was still in effect. Bashir added to his "olive branch" policy by permitting UN relief efforts in the south to continue, and by declaring a general amnesty for SPLA people.[114] On 25 July, while attending the summit conference of the Organization for African Unity in Addis Ababa, Bashir extended the truce by another month.[115]

It was only in mid-August — six weeks after the 30 June coup — that the SPLA responded officially to the "new junta's" domestic policies in general, and to its attitude toward the war in the south in particular. Delivering a long, venomous speech, Garang attacked the inability of the "junta" in Khartoum to bring the salvation which it claimed as its justification for seizing power. Garang denounced Bashir's cancellation of the 1986 and 1988 "peace agreements," noting that this act damaged Khartoum's credibility. What guarantee was there that the junta would not cancel whatever peace agreement the SPLM-SPLA might reach with it? "Or does Mr. Bashir consider himself the last coup-maker?" he asked cynically. "The junta is behaving as if Sudan came into being on 30 June. It is presumptuous of these officers to throw away all previous peace agreements...and to claim to start from scratch." Garang attacked the "junta's very shallow and distorted perception" of the nature of the civil war, which, he said, was the problem of the whole of Sudan rather than of the south, as Bashir claimed. Garang accused the new regime of lacking "any new radical program" that could improve the chances of peace. Moreover, he termed steps already taken by Bashir as "nonstarters." Garang even denounced Bashir's offer to hold a referendum on the Shari'a issue: "It is blasphemous to say that God's laws should be judged by human beings." Beside this argument, which did not necessarily reflect Garang's real stand and which might have been a tactic to eliminate the referendum idea, a fair plebiscite seemed to be impossible. Not only did the chaotic circumstances in the south (and in the west, though significantly less), prevent it, but with two thirds of the Sudanese being Muslims, the results of a referendum were predictable, to the south's disadvantage.

Nevertheless, despite his criticism, Garang expressed his readiness to talk with the "junta," because it was "the *de facto* leadership." To create a basis for the talks, he presented his view, though in general terms, of the "national paradigm of the new Sudan." He listed four "minimum steps" which the quest for establishing a new Sudan necessitated:

(1) Establishing an interim, broad-based government of national unity, free of any sectarianism;

(2) Establishing a national, nonsectarian, nonregional army made up of the SPLA and the regular Army;

(3) Convening a national constitutional conference to achieve a settlement on the basis of the earlier peace agreements;

(4) Holding free elections.

Garang offered to discuss this program with the "junta," otherwise he would be obliged to mount a "general strike and [stir up] a popular mass uprising to remove it [from office], and have the program implemented by the forces of the uprising and the SPLM-SPLA."[116]

The threat implicit in Garang's speech was amplified against the background of his subsequent visit to Cuba (with which the SPLA maintained cooperating ties).[117] Khartoum became concerned not only about Garang's foreign links, but also about his declared determination to undermine Khartoum's position if it did not meet his demands. This pressure had the immediate effect of bringing the two sides to the negotiating table on 19–20 August in Addis Ababa. Nevertheless, these talks, the first since Bashir's coup, soon broke down, mainly over the issue of the Shari'a. While Khartoum tried to play down the fiasco, and even described the talks as "fruitful" and "successful,"[118] the SPLA, however, said that the collapse of the talks "exposed the real nature of the new rulers, being Muslim fundamentalists."[119]

The failure of the talks did not influence, as had been expected, Khartoum's decision, announced on 21 August, to extend the cease-fire for another month.[120]

On 9 September, while political contacts between the SPLA and Khartoum were in abeyance, Bashir opened a conference in the capital, which he entitled "the national dialogue on the question of peace."[121] The conference, he said, was designed to discuss major national issues, primarily the civil war. Two days before the conference began, Bashir publicly invited Garang to participate,[122] but he refused to attend unless Bashir agreed to a list of preconditions.[123] It seemed that Garang had assumed that Bashir would flatly reject these preconditions, which would provide an elegant excuse to decline the invitation without harming the image as a seeker of peace, which he had acquired abroad, and even in some circles in Khartoum. Later, Garang gave an additional reason for his absence: "no guerrilla leader can be expected to go to the national capital of the government he is fighting."[124] It seemed that his refusal to participate stemmed first and foremost from his view that such a proregime forum, especially with its many fundamentalist members,[125] would in no way positively serve his interests. Furthermore, the participation of southerners with known close ties to earlier governments but without links with the SLPA, substantiated Garang's evaluation of the conference as a "sold game." One could also assume that Garang feared that by attending the conference, he might not only be in personal danger, but he might also contribute to enhancing Bashir's political prestige and to enabling him to gear up for another round of fighting. Not surprising, therefore, was the SPLA's unequivocal condemnation of the conference, as a "gimmick" and a "falsification."[126]

On 20 September, while the conference in Khartoum was still in session, Garang began a three-week tour of southern Africa, covering six countries: Zimbabwe, Zambia, Malawi, Botswana, Mozambique, and Tanzania. On his way home, he paid a short visit to Kenya as well. The tour was aimed at "explaining the prospects of war and peace in Sudan,"[127] or in other words, at buttressing the SPLA's political and moral position. Garang also sought new sources of material support, including arms. As reported later, an arms agreement was signed between the SPLA and the South-West African People's Organization, paid by private sources, which also funded the airlift of the arms from Angola to southern Sudan.[128]

Khartoum was not idle. Senior officials toured the Arab world, seeking financial aid with which to revitalize the economy, but even more important at that juncture, military support. Bashir himself made a comprehensive tour of the Gulf in late 1989, visiting Kuwait, Qatar, Oman,and the UAE. The results soon followed: Iraq, Libya, and China were reported to have supplied the Army with military equipment.[129]

On 30 September, while Garang was still abroad, Bashir extended the ceasefire for yet another month.[130]

On 14 October, the much trumpeted conference in Khartoum ended its six weeks of deliberations. Its major resolution proposed a model of federal rule for Sudan, which it considered "as the best alternative for government in Sudan."[131] The resolution did not go into details, but floating the idea was sufficient to deepen Garang's suspicions of Khartoum's intentions. The whole idea of "divisive federalism," the SPLA stated, was in effect another way for Khartoum to reapply the Shari'a law.[132]

On 21 October, Khartoum extended the cease-fire for still another month, the very day that the SPLA reported the outbreak of "heavy fighting" between the two sides in the Kurmuk area near, but outside, the informal border of the south six days before.[133] According to the SPLA, the Army initiated the renewal of fighting, which Khartoum categorically denied, stating that Garang was the responsible party.[134] The impression, however, was that the initiative came almost entirely from the SPLA. The results of the fighting strengthened that impression: on 28 October, Khartoum announced "a tactical retreat" from Kurmuk town, near the Ethiopian border, following "intensive bombardments by the SPLA from Ethiopian territory."[135] Khartoum repeatedly claimed that the loss of the town, which the SPLA had captured on the same day, was the result of "a foreign aggression" against it. Ethiopia, along with Israel and Cuba, were accused of aiding the SPLA.[136] The latter labeled the accusation "a scandalous lie."[137] Whatever the truth, it did not detract from the serious blow dealt to Khartoum, especially since it served as a reminder of a similar defeat two years earlier (see *MECS* 1987, p. 624). Not only did the loss of Kurmuk associate the incompetence of Bashir's regime with that of Mahdi's and struck at Bashir's efforts to strengthen his government, it also caused Khartoum serious military and strategic damage. The SPLA might use Kurmuk as a point from which to extend its movement northward.Furthermore, Kurmuk's location c. 100 miles from the vital Roseires Dam and hydroelectric power station, which supplied a major part of the capital's water, might pose a serious threat to one of the country's most sensitive nerve centers.

During November, fighting around Kurmuk continued without any letup. The SPLA reported its success in gaining control over at least four garrison towns in that area,[138] but Khartoum recaptured Kurmuk late in the month.[139]

Meanwhile, as hostilities in the south intensified, a new mediation initiative by former US president Jimmy Carter gathered momentum. It was part of his peace initiative in the Horn of Africa which had already involved Ethiopia. As a result, both sides agreed to hold direct peace talks on 1 December in Nairobi. The talks, presided over by Carter, began as scheduled, but collapsed on 5 December principally due to disagreement over the long-standing Shari'a controversy. As in the earlier round of talks in August, a wide gap opened up this time too. While the SPLA blamed the collapse on Khartoum, the latter tried to give the impression that a degree of success had been achieved.[140]

During December, intensive fighting continued and by the end of the month, any hope aroused by Bashir's coup that the war might end seemed to evaporate, or be significantly reduced.

FOREIGN AFFAIRS

Egypt

Egypt's alleged connection with, and even involvement, in Bashir's coup had been repeatedly suggested by various sources both in Sudan and abroad. Cairo's actions in the immediate wake of the coup contributed to the impression that a link existed: the Egyptian official news agency was the first to inform the international community about the coup;[141] Egypt was the first country to recognize the regime;[142] and it quickly sent Sudan a gift of 20,000 tons of oil and medicines, children's food, vehicle spare parts, and ammunition.[143] The immediate exchange of high-level officials between Khartoum and Cairo, and the fact that most of RCCNS officers had been trained at the Nasser Academy in Cairo, and that one of them remained there while the coup took place, was further circumstantial evidence.

It was not surprising, therefore, that Bashir's first foreign trip was to Egypt on 12 July. He expressed his gratitude for Cairo's "direct and quick stand of support."[144] At the same time, he considered it expedient to state publicly that Egypt was not implicated in his seizure of power,[145] apparently not to provoke the antagonism of Qadhdhafi and of Sudanese domestic circles. Egypt's President Husni Mubarak likewise denied his country's involvement in the coup (see chapter on Egypt).

If Egypt was involved, the extent of that involvement remained unknown. In any case, it was not long before the initial enthusiasm began to wane, especially on the Egyptian side. Bilateral relations came under a certain measure of strain over two major issues: the future of southern Sudan (which significantly contributed to the political destabilization of the whole region and which held the key to increasing the flow of the Nile waters, a vital Egyptian concern), and the degree to which the fundamentalist NIF in Sudan might accelerate the fundamentalist pressures already threatening the Egyptian regime. Egypt's refusal to supply the Sudanese Army with heavy weapons or combat aircraft[146] for use against the SPLA, added to the mutual unease. One could also assume that Bashir objected to former president Numayri's vociferous activity in the foreign media, probably with Egypt's consent. Khartoum was also displeased with some Egyptian newspapers that showed considerable disrespect for Bashir.[147]

Nevertheless, both countries had most important interests in maintaining their channels of political contact. Mubarak's mediatory efforts regarding the war in southern Sudan were the major link connecting them during fall-winter 1989.[148]

Garang's "secret" visit to Cairo on 20 November was part of this complex.[149]

In October, fighting resumed between the SPLA and the Sudanese Army. The Army was defeated once again, losing control, among others, of Kurmuk (see above). This grave blow pushed Bashir into speeding up his efforts to mobilize Arab military support to facilitate the recapture of Kurmuk. Egypt was included in these efforts. Khartoum's oft repeated assertions of the validity of their joint defense agreement of 1976 clearly attested to this.[150] (Mahdi's regime had virtually announced the abrogation of the agreement — see above.) Bashir's official visit to Cairo on 23 October further indicated Sudan's need for Egypt's support at a time when fierce battles were raging around Kurmuk. Mubarak reciprocated with a brief visit on 31 December (see also chapter on Egypt).

Libya

The process of reconciliation between Egypt and Libya, which started in May 1989, enabled Sudan to maintain political ties with both of them. Bashir paid a four-day visit to the Jamahiriyya on 2 August, less than two weeks after paying a similar visit to Cairo, without facing any complications.[151] Libya was quick to follow Egypt in rendering assistance immediately after the 30 June coup. Though not referred to publicly by either side, one could assume that Qadhdhafi continued to supply Khartoum with weaponry. In return, Libya was apparently allowed to continue to use the Darfur region in western Sudan where there was no French air cover as a base for Chadian rebels against Ndjamena. Bashir, like his predecessors, did not publicly mention the worrying presence of Libyan forces in western Sudan. Apparently, however, Khartoum's apprehensions increased in the second half of 1989, because problems mounted in the Darfur and Kordofan regions where c. 6m. people were facing serious famine.[152]

On 2 September, Bashir attended the 20th anniversary celebrations in Libya. While there he, as well as the other senior Sudanese officials who arrived in Libya in the winter, discussed primarily the acceleration of Libyan aid to Sudan, particularly military. In late November, Bashir reportedly made an "unannounced visit" to Libya.[153] It followed a stream of senior Sudanese visitors to Tripoli, all of whom were probably occupied with increasing Libyan military aid, which was intended for use in recapturing Kurmuk.

NOTES

For the place and frequency of publications cited here, and for the full name of the publication, news agency, radio station, or monitoring service where an abbreviation is used, please see "List of Sources." Only in the case of more than one publication bearing the same name is the place of publication noted here.

1. *AC*, 12 May; *MEED*, 10 November 1989.
2. Al-Tijani al-Tayyib, the minister of state for finance in an interview with *al-Ittihad*, Abu Dhabi, 11 February, and *al-Quwat al-Musallaha*, 8 July 1989. The official £S/$ rate of exchange in 1988 was 4.5. See *CR: Sudan*, No. 1, 1989.
3. *Africa Report*, January-February 1989.
4. *Al-Dustur*, London, 2 January; *IHT*, 5 January 1989 (reports from Khartoum).
5. *Al-Dustur*, London, 9 January 1989 (a report from Khartoum).

6. *FT,* 6 February 1989 (a report from Khartoum).
7. *Al-Raya,* 6 February 1989.
8. *Alwan,* 25 February 1989.
9. *Al-Ghuraba,* 1 April 1989.
10. For the text of the memorandum, see *al-Raya,* 22 February 1989.
11. *Al-Raya,* 22 September 1989.
12. AFP, 26 February — DR, 27 February 1989, quoting Reuters from Khartoum.
13. R. Omdurman, 27 February — DR, 27 February 1989.
14. R. Khartoum, 27 February — DR, 1 March 1989.
15. *FT,* 1 March 1989, quoting Reuters from Khartoum.
16. *Al-Sharq al-Awsat,* 1 March 1989.
17. MENA, 4 March — DR, 6 March 1989.
18. *Al-Siyasa,* Khartoum, 5 March 1989.
19. *Al-Sharq al-Awsat,* 6 March 1989.
20. *Al-Siyasa,* Khartoum, 6 March 1989.
21. MENA, 10 March — DR, 13 March 1989.
22. *Al-Sudani,* 14 March 1989.
23. Mahdi's interview with *al-Majalla,* 15–21 March 1989.
24. AFP, 10 April — DR, 11 April 1989, from Khartoum.
25. An interview with *al-Sharq al-Awsat,* 4 June 1989.
26. *Al-Sharq al-Awsat,* 18 April; *al-Sudani,* 23 April 1989.
27. *Alwan,* 17 April; for similar expressions, see also Turabi's remarks in *al-Sudani,* 18, 22 April 1989.
28. During the violent protests of the NIF, 'Uthman 'Ali Muhammad Taha, deputy secretary-general of the NIF and leader of the parliamentary opposition, appeared as the party's outstanding leader, eclipsing Turabi somewhat. Taha gave an intensive series of interviews to foreign Arab publications, e.g., *October,* 23 April; *al-Sharq al-Awsat,* 9 May, and *al-Tadamun,* 22–29 May, explaining there his party's perception of the political situation and the war in the south. For other similar opinions of NIF leaders, see e.g., Turabi with *'Ukaz,* 15 March and Yasin 'Umar al-Imam with *al-Sharq al-Awsat,* 25 April 1989.
29. Al-Fatih 'Abdun, former governor of Khartoum and central NIF figure, in a statement to *al-Sharq al-Awsat,* 4 May 1989.
30. Ibid., 9 May 1989.
31. R. Omdurman, 18 June — DR, 19 June 1989.
32. Interviews with the SWB, 19 June — DR, 20 June, and with *al-Anba,* Kuwait, 4 July 1989.
33. SUNA, 19 June — DR, 20 June, quoting an interview with the Kuwaiti *al-Watan.*
34. *Al-Siyasa,* Khartoum, 19 June; *al-Sudani,* 20, 21 June. In July, Bashir released the detainees, who included two of the 15 members of the RCCNS (see below); Bashir's interview with *al-Ahram,* 5 July 1989.
35. 'Abd al-Rahman Farah, the adviser for the security administration, quoted by *al-Sudani,* 22 June, and Muhammad Tawfiq Ahmad, a senior DUP member, as quoted by the SWB, 27 June — DR, 28 June 1989.
36. R. SPLA, 27 January, SUNA, 28 January — DR, 30 January 1989.
37. *Al-Sudani,* 28 February; for a detailed survey on the capture of the town, see *New African,* June 1989.
38. R. SPLA, 4, 6, 7 March — DR, 2, 6, 7, 20 March 1989.
39. *Al-Raya,* 12 March; *al-Sudani,* 9 April 1989.
40. *CR:* Sudan, No. 3, 1989.
41. R. SPLA, 12 April 1989.
42. *Al-Raya,* Khartoum, 18 April 1989, quoting R. SPLA.
43. R. SPLA, 17 April — DR, 19 April 1989.
44. R. SPLA, 12 April — DR, 13 April 1989.
45. *The Economist,* 4 March 1989.
46. Ibid., for a report that the Sudanese defense minister came home empty-handed from an arms-shopping trip to Jordan and Iraq in February.
47. Senior Sudanese officials in statements and interviews with *Alwan,* 1 March; *al-Sudani,* *al-Sharq al-Awsat,* 27 April; *al-'Alam,* London, 29 April, and *'Ukaz,* 17 May 1989.

48. Garang in an interview with MENA, 1 June — DR, 2 June 1989.
49. *Al-Siyasa,* Khartoum, 11 April 1989.
50. For more details on the relief campaign, see, e.g., *IHT,* 27 March; *Africa Report,* May; *CR: Sudan,* No. 2, 1989.
51. For details, see *IHT,* 15 May; AFP, 29 May — DR, 30 May, and *NYT,* 11 July 1989.
52. USIS, 11 April; *al-Majalla,* 12-18 April 1989.
53. *CR: Sudan,* No. 2, 1989. In any case, the situation was better than in previous years.
54. For the full text of Garang's statement, see R. SPLA, 1 May — DR, 3 May 1989.
55. R. Omdurman, 6 May — DR, 8 May 1989.
56. *FT,* 9 May 1989, quoting Nehial Deng, the SPLA spokesman.
57. R. SPLA, 9 May 1989.
58. *FT,* 3 May 1989.
59. E.g., a statement by Sudan's energy minister, Bashir 'Umar, as quoted by MENA, 30 May — DR, 31 May 1989.
60. *CR: Sudan,* No. 3, 1989.
61. *New African,* June 1989.
62. R. SPLA, 12 June — DR, 13 June 1989.
63. *Al-Watan al-'Arabi,* 10 March 1989.
64. MENA, 4 March — DR, 6 March 1989.
65. *Al-Dustur,* London, 5 June 1989.
66. *Al-Jumhuriyya,* Cairo, 8 March 1989.
67. *Al-Majalla,* 10-16 May 1989, quoting the Sudanese defense minister.
68. AFP, 29 June 1989.
69. *Alwan,* 9, 19 January; *al-'Alam,* London, 11 February; Foreign Minister Turabi in a statement to *al-Hawadith,* 27 February 1989.
70. *Al-Majalla,* 25–31 January; *al-Ahali,* 1 February; a top Sudanese politician in *al-Kifah al-'Arabi,* 10 April 1989.
71. R. Khartoum, 27 February — DR, 1 March 1989.
72. As quoted by *Alwan,* 1 March 1989.
73. R. Khartoum, 5 March — DR, 6 March 1989.
74. R. Monte Carlo, 22 June 1989.
75. *Al-Siyasa,* Khartoum, 24 June. Nasser's son denied any intention of residing in Khartoum. *Al-Wafd,* 26 June 1989.
76. *CR: Sudan,* No. 3, 1989; *al-Siyasa,* Kuwait, 19 July 1989 reported that three different army groups were engaged in preparations for launching a coup. When the 30 June coup took place, the two other groups joined Bashir's.
77. For details, see R. Omdurman, 2 July — DR, 2 July; *al-Quwat al-Musallaha,* 5 July 1989.
78. *CR: Sudan,* No. 4, 1989.
79. R. Omdurman, 1, 2 July — DR, 1, 5 July 1989.
80. *Al-Quwat al-Musallaha,* 27 July 1989. In mid-August he was promoted to lieutenant general.
81. E.g., the RCCNS spokesman in an interview with *al-Sharq al-Awsat,* 12 August 1989.
82. *AC,* 28 July. See also *New African,* October 1989. Among the plethora of denials by senior officials, e.g., *al-Sharq al-Awsat,* 12, 13 August 1989.
83. The RCCNS spokesman in a series of interviews, e.g., *al-Sharq al-Awsat,* 12, 13 August; *al-Wafd,* 28 August 1989.
84. For a biographic survey on Bashir and his partners, see *al-Sharq al-Awsat,* 1 July; *al-Ittihad,* Abu Dhabi, 3 July; *al-Musawwar,* 7 July; *al-Jumhuriyya,* Cairo, 10 July; *al-'Alam,* London, 22 July; and *AC,* 28 July 1989.
85. Bashir's interview with the doyen of the Egyptian journalists' syndicate, Markam Muhammad Ahmad, broadcast by R. Omdurman, 2 July — DR, 2 July 1989.
86. Bashir in an interview with R. Cairo, 17 July — DR, 18 July, and with *'Ukaz,* 3 July 1989.
87. Bashir's interview with *al-Ittihad,* Abu Dhabi, 5 July 1989.
88. R. Omdurman, 15 July — DR, 18 July 1989.
89. *The Economist,* 16 September 1989.
90. *AED,* September 1989.
91. SUNA, 13 August — DR, 14 August 1989.

92. R. Omdurman, 2 September — DR, 5 September 1989.
93. SUNA, 16 September — DR, 19 September; for more details, see *al-Dustur*, London, 2 October 1989.
94. USIS, 19 December 1989.
95. DR, 9 August — SWB, 10 August 1989, from "The Focus on Africa" program.
96. *AC*, 11 August 1989. According to the same source, some evaluations placed their number as high as 500.
97. Interviews of Sudanese senior officials, e.g., *al-Sharq al-Awsat*, 12 August, *al-Wafd*, 28 August 1989.
98. *Al-Ittihad*, Abu Dhabi, 10 August 1989.
99. SWB, 25 September — DR, 28 September 1989, from "The Focus on Africa" program.
100. *CR:* Sudan, No. 3, 1989.
101. *Al-Inqadh*, Khartoum, 24 September 1989.
102. MENA, 24 September — DR, 25 September 1989.
103. R. Omdurman, 18 October — DR, 23 October 1989.
104. SUNA, 30 November — DR, 8 December 1989.
105. SUNA, 4 December; R. Omdurman, 10 December — DR, 8, 11 December 1989.
106. *Al-Wafd*, 3 December 1989.
107. Khartoum TV, 4 December 1989.
108. R. SPLA, 28 November — DR, 29 November; *al-Wafd*, 29 November 1989.
109. *MEED*, 29 December 1989.
110. AFP, 16 December — DR, 21 December 1989.
111. R. Omdurman, 3 December — DR, 5 December 1989.
112. For Bashir's first statement, R. Omdurman, 30 June — DR, 3 July; for other similar statements, see e.g., *al-Quwat al-Musallaha*, 2, 4, 9 July; interviews with *'Ukaz*, 3 July; *Akhbar al-Yawm*, 8 July 1989.
113. R. Omdurman, 4 July — DR, 6 July 1989.
114. *Al-Quwat al-Musallaha*, 9 July; R. Omdurman, 4 July — DR, 5 July 1989.
115. R. Omdurman, 25 July — DR, 27 July 1989.
116. For the full text of Garang's two-part speech, R. SPLA, 14, 15 August — DR, 16, 21 August 1989.
117. R. Reloj (Havana), 17 August — DR, 19 August 1989; *AC*, 26 January 1990.
118. Col. Muhammad al-Amin al-Khalifa, a RCCNS member and the head of the delegation, in interviews with *al-Anba*, Kuwait, and *al-Sharq al-Awsat*, 30 August 1989.
119. R. SPLA, 3 September — DR, 7 September 1989.
120. R. Omdurman, 21 August — DR, 23 August 1989.
121. The conference was composed originally of 77 members. Their number steadily increased and eventually reached 106. For more details on its composition, R. Omdurman, 5, 25 September — DR, 12 September, 3 October 1989.
122. R. Omdurman, 7 September — DR, 11 September 1989.
123. For the list of preconditions, R. SPLA, 7 September — DR, 8 September 1989.
124. R. SPLA, 7 October — DR, 10 October 1989.
125. *MEI*, 22 September 1989.
126. R. SPLA, 12 September — DR, 13 September 1989.
127. R. SPLA, 18 October — DR, 23 October 1989.
128. *AC*, 9 February 1989.
129. SWB, 17 October — DR, 20 October, from "The Focus on Africa" program; *MEI*, 3 November, and *CR:* Sudan, No. 4, 1989.
130. R. Omdurman, 2 October — DR, 3 October 1989.
131. For more details, R. Omdurman, 14 October — DR, 17 October 1989.
132. An interview with Mansur al-Khalid, a senior SPLA official, *al-Sharq al-Awsat*, 21 October 1989.
133. Ibid.
134. SUNA, 24 October — DR, 25 October 1989.
135. AFP, 29 October — DR, 30 October 1989, quoting the Army's announcement.
136. R. Omdurman, 2 November — DR, 6 November 1989.
137. R. SPLA, 1 November — DR, 3 November 1989.

138. R. SPLA, 9, 13 November — DR, 13, 14 November 1989.
139. R. Omdurman, 29 November — DR, 30 November 1989.
140. R. SPLA, 8 December, R. Omdurman, 7 December — DR, 8, 12 December 1989.
141. According to *al-Majalla,* 12–18 July 1989.
142. *AED,* 17 July 1989.
143. R. Omdurman, 3 July — DR, 5 July; *ME,* August 1989.
144. MENA, 12 July — DR, 13 July 1989.
145. Bashir's repeated denials, e.g., in interviews with *al-Ittihad,* Abu Dhabi, 5 July; *al-Majalla,* 12–18 July 1989.
146. *AC,* 3 November 1989.
147. *Al-Wafd,*taking the leading role, especially in the last quarter of 1989.
148. For details see, e.g., *al-Anba,* 27 November; *'Uman,* 7 December; *al-Ahram,* 26 December 1989.
149. *Al-Dustur,* London, 20 November 1989.
150. E.g., *Akhir Sa'a,* 15 November; *al-Ahram,* 26 December 1989; SUNA, 30 December 1989 — DR, 4 January 1990.
151. In early summer, tension between Sudan and Chad over the Libyan forces' presence in the Darfur area reached a new crisis. Ndjamena accused Khartoum of serving as a base for Libyan aggression against it. The tension abated after Bashir's coup.
152. *CR:* Sudan, No. 4, 1989.
153. *Al-Sharq al-Awsat,* 22 November 1989.

Syria

(Al-Jumhuriyya al-'Arabiyya al-Suriyya)

GIDEON GERA

During 1989, the emphasis in Syrian politics continued to be on foreign affairs. One could safely carry forward a summing up of internal affairs for 1988:

> Little happened in the domain of domestic politics. Syria's economic crisis has not been resolved, but...has been stabilized. The opposition to Asad's regime is still in disarray....Asad is not a healthy man, yet he refuses to make arrangements for an orderly succession. This...contributes to the barely perceptible but real jockeying for position in which several of his lieutenants are engaged."[1]

The main preoccupations of Syrian foreign policy during 1989 were:

(1) The unceasing civil strife in Lebanon, where despite political achievements (the double election of a president under their cover), the Syrians were unable to eliminate the "rebel" regime of Gen. Michel 'Awn in East Beirut. The well-known arguments against evicting him militarily were still valid (the expected cost in casualties, the likelihood of a sharp Arab and international disapproval, and possibly a harsh Israeli reaction). Thus, the chances of implementing the Ta'if accords on political reforms, which legitimized the Syrian military presence in Lebanon for at least until 1992, were slim.

(2) The continued active hostility (e.g., in Lebanon) of a muscle-flexing Iraq no longer engaged in a war elsewhere.

(3) The possible erosion of the Soviet strategic support, which was the backbone of Syrian policy and strategy for decades. Hafiz al-Asad had to face the new political reality in the Soviet Union and Eastern Europe and its global consequences. While reassuring and supplying him, the Soviets explicitly counseled Asad to scale down his plans for "strategic parity" with Israel and work for a political settlement of regional conflicts.

Under these circumstances Asad continued to perform as an accomplished practitioner of *realpolitik*: he took care to preserve his working alliance with Iran, while giving high priority to reducing Syria's isolation in the Arab world. Under the guise of reinforcing Arab solidarity, he realigned Syria with the changing Arab situation. First, mending fences in the Maghrib and taking care not to alienate Saudi Arabia, he finally reconciled his differences with Egypt, resuming formal relations with it at year's end. Although neither Syria's attitude toward the Arab-Israeli conflict nor its opposition to 'Arafat changed perceptibly, it did not derail the latter's "peace offensive." This, as well as the Lebanese imbroglio, helped Asad keep a channel open to the US.

630

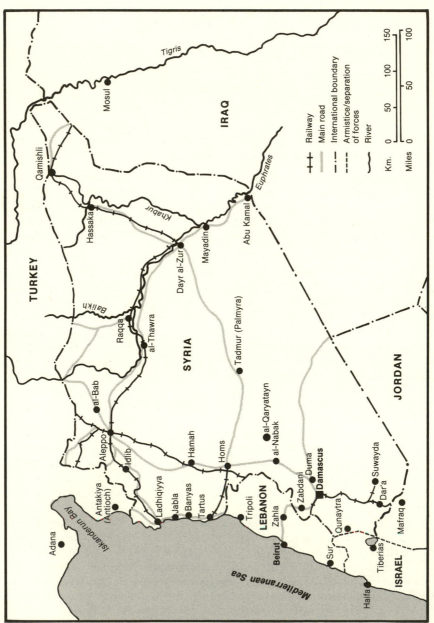

Syria

THE DOMESTIC SCENE

POLITICAL AFFAIRS

The year 1989 was a quiet one domestically for Syria. No personnel changes occurred at the regime's senior levels, nor were there any institutional changes. Indeed, the nonevent of the year was the postponement of the ninth regional congress of the Ba'th Party, from March 1989 to sometime in 1990 (the eighth congress was held in January 1985 — see *MECS* 1984–85, pp. 645–46). The congress was expected to crystallize Syria's political orientation in a world of *perestroika* and clarify the regime's power structure.[2]

Furthermore, the congress was expected to throw light on the curious status of the president's brother, Rif'at, who though nominally still vice president, had been living abroad in political exile since 1985 (see *MECS* 1986, pp. 605–6). Although Rif'at denied periodically serving as his brother's special envoy, he was reportedly following the Syrian political scene rather closely. He was said to have laid the groundwork for a party of his own — Young Syria — to participate in the forthcoming elections to the People's Assembly (see *MECS* 1988, p. 729); his son set up an ostensibly agricultural investments firm at Ladhiqiyya, through which contacts among 'Alawis were financed.[3] Hafiz al-Asad's elder brother, Jamil, was exiled abroad for some time after commercial scandals involving him and his eldest son at Ladhiqiyya became public.[4] Meanwhile, the grooming of the president's favorite son, Basil, for leadership continued and he was entrusted with additional responsibilities in the presidency (see *MECS* 1987, p. 636; 1988, p. 729).[5] There was no confirmation of recurring reports on Asad's ill health. He himself brushed off speculation about the future, saying he was not bothered by what would happen to Syria after him: "Syria...will continue to exist...We have the Ba'th Party...official and popular establishments and constitutional provisions that will meet all possibilities."[6]

No major clashes with the opposition were reported in 1989 (on the incident in Damascus in December 1988, see *MECS* 1988, p. 731), but Iraqi sources reported an increase in armed opposition. In May and November, arrests, presumably of communists, were reported.[7] In April, several Syrian clandestine opposition groups active abroad met in Europe and discussed uniting in a "National Alliance for the Liberation of Syria." It seemed that the meeting was organized by the Iraqis (or at least supported by them), who later reported its success.[8] One may assume that this was an Iraqi reaction to the reorganization of Iraqi opposition groups sheltered by Damascus (see below). A later statement by one of the exiled leaders of the Muslim Brothers, 'Adnan Sa'd al-Din, supporting Gen. 'Awn in Lebanon and calling on all opponents of Asad to unite, cast doubt on a possible consolidation of opposition groups.[9]

In these circumstances, the regime felt confident enough to release more than 500 political prisoners, many of whom were detained since the Hama uprising of February 1982 (see *MECS* 1981–82, pp. 850–53).[10]

In a seasonal ritual of anticorruption drives, which had been recurring periodically since 1985 (see *MECS* 1986, pp. 610–11; 1987, p. 639; 1988, pp. 732–33), the People's Assembly in December discussed misappropriations of public property, neglect of responsibilities, and smuggling. As a result, 49 officials were reportedly dismissed from ministries and public companies.[11] It should be noted, however, that the regime considered corruption in a narrow, highly political sense, as any practice that diminished the regime's power. Patronage and "mediation" were deemed essential to the functioning of the political order, especially by the party apparatus and the armed forces. The need for "mediation" as a device for circumventing legal difficulties or smoothing the inevitable contact with the omnipresent bureaucracy was obvious; the state commanded not only the tools of repression, but also the avenues to careers, economic prosperity, and welfare for most Syrians.[12] This relationship was underlined, for instance, by including the announcement of an impending raise in salaries in the public sector in Asad's anniversary address on 8 March — always a major event. In the same vein, Prime Minister Mahmud al-Zu'bi announced at the beginning of 1990 that the 1989 budget had created 73,400 new jobs.[13]

ECONOMIC AFFAIRS

There was no major change in the basic trends of the Syrian economy in 1989, although some improvement was noticeable (see *MECS* 1988, p. 726). Inflation was high, estimated at 60%, leading the government to decree a 25% increase in salaries as well as increases in pensions and allowances (last increased two years earlier, see *MECS* 1987, p. 640). Controlled prices were not raised, but fuel prices and customs duties were increased by 50%. Thus, the pay awards were clearly insufficient to compensate for inflation.[14]

Although there was a good cotton crop, drought (rainfall was 40% below average) sharply reduced the output of cereals and vegetables. The well-known dependence of Syrian agriculture on the vagaries of rainfall was underscored by the poor wheat harvest (1m.–1.4m. tons, half of the 1988 crop). To avoid the possibility of politically sensitive shortages of bread, the government had to import 1m.–1.5m. tons of wheat and flour at relatively high prices, thus adding to its foreign currency expenditure. Furthermore, as Minister of Economy Muhammad al-'Imadi pointed out, an annual population increase of 500,000 had to be provided for.[15] Among agricultural projects undertaken to secure food supplies, one should note the Upper Yarmuk project. It was to irrigate 75,000 ha. throughout the year and was planned to be completed by 1989, although there was no evidence that this had indeed happened.[16]

The lack of rain also reduced the supply of hydroelectric energy by at least 10%, causing power failures during the summer.[17] These occurred after a year of no cuts in 1988, and after Prime Minister Zu'bi announced that no more power rationing or failures were expected and that power supplies from Jordan were no longer needed.[18] In June, a Syrian newspaper blamed power failures on bad maintenance and poor coordination, arguing that the country could produce sufficient energy.[19] These faults might have contributed to the trouble, but were hardly its main reason, as evidenced by the rationing of water in major cities and in the Damascus district at the same time.[20]

Early optimism about oil production was deflated, when damage was incurred at the 'Umar oil field (near Dayr al-Zor) in spring, after production had been officially inaugurated in mid-February.[21] But at year's end Syria increased its oil output once more, although production was not yet stable. Total output during 1989 was 325,000–360,000 barrels per day (b/d) of which 80,000 b/d were exported. Despite the production of c. 210,000 b/d of light, low-sulphur crude, which was demanded by the market and proximity to the main European refining centers, the selling of Syrian oil was troubled by vagueness in the effective blend buyers could expect.[22] At least during part of the year, Iran continued to supply 20,000 b/d (1m. toms per year) to Syria.[23]

New in the domain of hydrocarbons was the priority the government gave to the development of the country's natural gas resources. The gas was planned both for domestic consumption (including power stations) and for export. The Syrian Petroleum Company focused its development effort on the southern part of the country, following large discoveries of gas in Jordan.[24]

No reliable data on Saudi Arabian financial aid were available. No aid was reported until June, but some promises might have been made after Syria's acquiescence to Egypt's readmission to the Arab League and its cooperation with the tripartite committee in Lebanon (see below).[25]

The 1989 budget included expenditures of £Sy57bn., a nominal increase of c. 10% over 1988. National security (including internal security forces) was allotted c. £Sy18bn. (c. 31.5% of the budget),[26] but actual defense expenditure was estimated to have reached 55% of current expenditures.[27] For obvious reasons, no statistics on the "black" market Syrian economy were available.

Despite all these difficulties, Syria achieved a trade surplus of $930m. in 1989, which indicated a current account surplus of $200m.–$300m. Prime Minister Zu'bi proudly stated that the country's current expenses were covered by local revenues. This could enable Syria to improve its standing with international financial institutions in case of future aid.[28]

SYRIA AND THE ARAB-ISRAELI CONFLICT

MILITARY ASPECTS

In his major annual speech on 8 March, Asad reiterated the well-known Syrian perception of Israel as Syria's principal enemy: "The Arab-Israeli struggle is our major worry and...dominates all of our interests, because it is a struggle of existence and fate." At year's end Asad remarked, rather dryly, that "Israel is Israel" and that Syrian expectations of Israeli steps had not changed nor would they change.[29] Accordingly, the guiding concept of Syrian policy toward Israel — "strategic parity" — remained unchanged (see *MECS* 1988, pp. 733–35). However, such parity had not yet been achieved; such was the message broadcast by Syria's leaders on Army Day (1 August). According to Asad, Syria's only choice in the current circumstances was to persevere in building its military, technological, scientific, economic, and cultural strength. Chief of Staff Gen. Hikmat Shihabi added that despite his satisfaction with Syrian achievements in these domains, there should not be backtracking, reservations, or laxity.[30] Minister of Defense Mustafa Talas underlined the future dimension: quoting Israeli sources describing the Syrian Army as currently the strongest Arab force, he stated that it would be able to wage the conflict on its own in the coming years, but not in the coming days.[31]

Essential to achieving eventual parity was the continued military buildup. During 1989 Syria reportedly completed the installment of a fourth Sam-5 ground-to-air missile battery, near the Jordanian border, thereby adding to its long-range air-defense system.[32] During the year Syria received its first Su-24 advanced light bombers and additional MiG-29 fighter-interceptor aircraft.[33] Unwelcome to Syria was the surprise defection to Israel of a senior MiG-23 pilot with his plane on 11 October.[34]

Syria continued to increase its chemical warfare capability. According to CIA Director William Webster, Syria had begun producing chemical warfare agents in the mid-1980s, having constructed a production facility with the critical assistance of West European firms. Syria possessed a stockpile of a variety of chemical warfare agents, including nerve gas, and the means to deliver them.[35] While attending the Paris international conference on chemical weapons, the Syrian foreign minister as much as admitted his country's possession of such weapons; he argued that the removal of only one category of weapons of mass destruction (allegedly Israel had nuclear weapons) amounted to unilateral disarmament, which Syria rejected.[36] In August, Talas described Israeli reports that Syria was producing chemical weapons as "baseless"; according to him, Syria had decided to forgo chemical and nuclear arms because of the deterrent effect of its treaty with the Soviet Union.[37]

Following a series of Israeli statements during spring concerning a possible Syrian military threat,[38] a senior Syrian official told a Lebanese paper that fighting against Israel from the Golan was out of the question because it meant general war. Syria considered the attrition of Israel by Lebanese "resistance" groups much more effective.[39] This deferment of a military initiative was explicitly set out by Talas: Syria had not yet decided on initiating war, or on the timing and place. In planning a war "we will not brook any mistake, no matter how small....We will not have any party drag us into war...not decided upon by us." His position on opening the Golan border to Palestinian operations against Israel was similar; these would be allowed only if coordinated and decided upon by Syria.[40] At the same time, Syria no longer feared the expected Israeli offensive; it might even welcome it, as it was "bound to make the Soviets take a more hard-line stand toward Israel...and embarrass a good many pro-US Arabs." However, Talas did not suppose that Israel would embark on war.[41] Undoubtedly this line of Syrian thinking was strongly influenced by the Soviet reassessment of its strategic ties with Syria (see below).

TERRORISM

The blowing up over Scotland of a US airliner with heavy loss of life, in December 1988, and the subsequent linking by Western media (relying on US sources) of the attack to the Syrian-based Popular Front for the Liberation of Palestine-General Command (PFLP-GC), evoked — especially in Western Europe — memories of the Hindawi affair (see *MECS* 1986, pp. 613, 618–19).[42] Asad attempted to limit the damage to Syria's international image by stating that he considered PFLP-GC involvement "highly improbable" and that there was no "irrefutable" evidence of it. But he did not exclude the possible involvement of individuals belonging to that group.[43] An annual US report on terrorism did not "detect" Syria's hand in any terrorist incident during 1989 but criticized it for harboring terrorist groups, of which the PFLP-GC was only one.[44]

SYRIA AND THE POLITICAL PROCESS

Syria objected to the various proposals concerning the political process launched during 1989. It regarded these moves as leading to a partial settlement of the conflict, something to which Damascus was opposed as a matter of principle. Thus, it rejected the Israeli plan to hold elections in the West Bank and Gaza and the subsequent Egyptian Ten-Point proposal[45] (for details, see chapter on the Middle East peace process). Syria adhered to the view that "anyone who thinks Israel wants peace is mistaken."[46] The unchanged Syrian position was reiterated by Asad at year's end: Syria, he said, was against any "unilateral deals." Peace had to be based on UN resolutions and be elaborated within the framework of a UN-sponsored conference attended by the parties concerned and the superpowers, or the permanent members of the Security Council.[47]

A different, though unofficial, impression was voiced by Cyrus Vance, the former US secretary of state, after visiting Damascus in early December 1989. He said that Asad's attitude to peace talks with Israel on the Golan had "definitely softened."[48]

SYRIA IN LEBANON

The year 1989 was a critical one in the history of Syria's involvement in Lebanon. Following its failure to bring about the election of a president, Syria faced the prospects of deepening partition in Lebanon, which pitted the cabinet of Salim al-Huss — supported by Syria — against the hostile East Beirut "emergency cabinet" headed by Gen. 'Awn. (See *MECS* 1988, pp. 736, 738.)

In January, the Arab League foreign ministers appointed a committee of six, chaired by the Kuwaiti foreign minister, to advance constitutional reforms and presidential elections in Lebanon, an endeavor that Syria supported.[49] The committee chairman's attempts to mediate between the Syrians and 'Awn came to nothing since the latter rejected the former's well-known positions — political reforms, positively defined relations with Syria, and the replacement of the Lebanese Forces in East Beirut by the Army.[50] Under these circumstances, the Syrians quickly acted to stop renewed clashes between Amal and Hizballah in Beirut and the south, imposing a cease-fire on both rivals at the end of January with the Iranian foreign minister's cooperation.[51]

When 'Awn began to assert his "legitimate" position by prohibiting and blockading "illegal" ports operated by Muslim and Druze militias, thus depriving them of a major source of income and arms, fighting erupted. The alleged shelling by long-range Syrian artillery, which participated in the bombardment of East Beirut on 14 March, led 'Awn to declare a "war of liberation" on Syria and to demand the immediate withdrawal of its troops from Lebanon.[52] This was an unprecedented challenge to the Syrian position in Lebanon, an affront with which Asad had to deal immediately. Denying 'Awn any legitimacy,[53] Syria responded by imposing a land and naval blockade to isolate the enclave and by indiscriminate bombardments, sometimes with siege artillery (240 mm. mortars); this continued intermittently until mid-September.[54] Furthermore, Asad declared that Syria would not allow the defeat of Lebanese nationalist forces and would fulfill their requirements.[55] A half-hearted French attempt to stop the shelling by dispatching some ships to Beirut in April was met with Syrian threats and ridicule (see below).[56]

In July, reports that Iraq was about to supply 'Awn with *Frog*-7 rockets — which (their range being 70 km.) could reach Damascus if suitably positioned — led Asad to warn the Arab countries and the superpowers that such a development would cause a Syrian preventive strike.[57] Syria tightened its naval blockade off Lebanon,[58] and on 13

August the Syrians were reportedly behind an abortive assault by Muslim, Druze, and Palestinian militias on the key stronghold of 'Awn's forces at Suq al-Gharb. A Lebanese newspaper identified the Syrian brigade involved, and reported that the bodies of 37 of its soldiers were counted on the battlefield. Some observers interpreted the attack as a Syrian attempt to escalate the fighting and as a threat to overrun the Christian area if the political solution it proposed was delayed. Damascus, however, denied it had participated in the raid.[59]

The Arab committee of six, ostensibly supported by the Syrians, soon found itself unable to continue its mission. Its attempt to deploy an Arab observer force was thwarted by the continuous shelling.[60] The issue was referred back to the council of Arab foreign ministers and then to a special Arab summit meeting, which was held in Casablanca on 23–26 May 1989 (see chapter on inter-Arab relations).

At the summit, Syria endeavored to repulse attempts to terminate, or even limit, its role in Lebanon, as demanded by 'Awn and his supporters (headed by Iraq). Syria described 'Awn as a criminal, who had foiled all attempts at a cease-fire and lifting the blockade. His call for national liberation was inadmissible. Syria had prevented the internationalization of the Lebanese crisis, which would have linked it to the ME conflict and might have led to partition. The only way out, the Syrians maintained, was an intra-Lebanese political solution through reforms. In the ensuing give-and-take (for concessions on other subjects — see below), Asad succeeded in having the summit appoint a tripartite committee comprising the heads of state of Algeria, Morocco, and Saudi Arabia, which would try to settle the conflict politically. The summit limited the proposed demand for the withdrawal of *all* foreign troops to Israelis in the south, while 'Awn's demand for the departure of the Syrians was not mentioned, although the call for the extension of Lebanese sovereignty over the whole national territory could be considered a substitute.[61]

The tripartite committee's plan was to establish a cease-fire, lift blockades, and secure Beirut by a mixed Lebanese force as preliminary steps to constitutional reform and election of a president. Asad approved and promised his support.[62] Meanwhile, the Syrians consolidated their clients — c. 16 "nationalist groups, Muslim, Druze, and Palestinian" — into a "national front." On 10 July, a meeting of the front with the Syrian and Iranian foreign ministers formalized Syrian-Iranian coordination.[63]

On 31 July the tripartite committee unpleasantly surprised the Syrians by reporting it had reached deadlock on two connected problems: reasserting Lebanese sovereignty over the whole national territory in face of the Syrian military presence, and defining the future relationship between the two countries (both problems obviously echoed 'Awn's demands). In an angry reply, accusing the committee of deviating from the summit's guidelines, Syria's foreign minister clearly set forth his country's position:

(1) Syria's "excessive" interest in implementing the summit resolution encouraged hostile elements inside and outside Lebanon to foil the committee's mission.

(2) The committee failed to describe the position of the 'Awn "military clique" as antithetical to a political solution. It neglected to consult with nationalist and Muslim groups on its political projects. It also neglected to deal with the security of areas not under Syrian control, thus endangering Muslims and nationalists both in East Beirut and the south.

(3) The committee neither stabilized the cease-fire nor lifted blockades. The opposition of Lebanese, Arab, and international forces made the committee renege

on an agreement reached in Damascus to have the ports monitored. Furthermore, the committee was unable to oblige Israel and Iraq to stop sending arms, including advanced systems, to Lebanon. This forced Syria to continue its naval blockade.

(4) On the ground, the goodwill shown by "nationalist and Islamic" forces in Beirut was not reciprocated and shelling resumed.[64]

This Syrian demonstration of force effectively stopped the committee's work. But Asad, who did not wish to face undesirable inter-Arab repercussions (especially in his relations with Saudi Arabia), proceeded to mend his fences. He laid the groundwork for the resumption of the committee's work in talks with the Algerian and Moroccan heads of state in Tripoli on 1 September: the committee would adhere strictly to the Casablanca resolutions, which did not mention Syrian withdrawal; its primary mission would consist of achieving political reforms in Lebanon and setting up a national cabinet based on them. For his part, Asad undertook to withdraw from Lebanon conditionally. When the committee resumed its work at the beginning of September, this understanding was orally worked out in detail:[65] six months after the endorsement of a national reconciliation document with Syria's prior approval, the election of a president, and the formation of a new cabinet, and "provided security circumstances permit" and the Lebanese Cabinet wished it, Syrian forces would begin to withdraw from Beirut. Syrian troops would assist Lebanese forces to extend the authority of the Lebanese state for a period not exceeding two years *after* ratification of national reconciliation, the election of a president, the formation of a reconciliation cabinet, and the constitutional acceptance of political reforms. At the end of this period, the Syrian military would redeploy to the Biq'a and its western approaches (roughly their deployment in May 1982). The future size and duration of the Syrian presence would then be agreed upon. Thus, for the first time Asad had officially agreed to the principle of a Syrian withdrawal from Lebanon, but no explicit statement was issued because formally such a statement, as well as a specific timetable, were matters for the Syrian and the future Lebanese government to discuss. Furthermore, conditioning implementation on the completion of political reforms in Lebanon and limiting it to what was specified in the reconciliation document, legitimized the postponement of the Syrian withdrawal until at least 1992. Reportedly, the US and the Soviet Union approved of this understanding and 'Awn was informed.[66]

After that, the tripartite committee accelerated its work. Having established a cease-fire, it convened Lebanese deputies for a month-long meeting at Ta'if (30 September-24 October). Saudi browbeating made the deputies endorse the reconciliation document, after Asad had agreed to some (mainly cosmetic) changes in the text at Saudi urging (see chapters on Lebanon and inter-Arab relations.)[67]

Syria considered the Ta'if accord a major success. The way for reform and the election of a president now seemed open. After the Syrians acidly rebuffed the criticism of their allies Walid Junblat and Nabih Barri, their only remaining obstacle was 'Awn, who had rejected the accord and castigated Christian deputies who had accepted it.[68]

The next Syrian achievement was the election of René Mu'awwad as president of Lebanon, which took place at Qlay'at air base under their protection on 5 November. Mu'awwad duly reappointed Huss as prime minister. Calling the elections the beginning of a new era, the Syrians described 'Awn as a rebel who now had lost any remaining claim to legitimacy and should leave the presidential palace or be evicted from it by force. Syria depicted 'Awn as a threat to its own security, and said that once it had the prior agreement of the new president it would act militarily; reportedly it began consultations with Arab and other states on the matter.[69]

The assassination of Mu'awwad in Beirut on 22 November, for which the Syrians blamed 'Awn, Iraq, and Israel, spurred Damascus to the speedy election of another president, Ilyas Hirawi.[70] Syria again insisted on the removal of 'Awn without further delay, rejecting international calls for self-restraint as dangerous and interfering. It reminded all concerned that despite Lebanese, Arab, and international responsibilities for implementing the Ta'if accord, it was the only power operationally capable of controlling events. But Syria now adopted a more cautious position: it acceded to Hirawi's request for more time to find a political solution. According to Asad, Syria would assist with its regular forces in a military assault only when asked by Hirawi. His minister of information added that 'Awn would not "drag" the Syrians into storming East Beirut, which they had hitherto avoided doing in order to prevent heavy civilian losses there.[71]

When eventful 1989 drew to an end, Syria had improved its diplomatic and political position in Lebanon. Without abandoning its resolute posture it had consolidated the nationalist camp and managed two sequential presidential elections under adverse conditions; it had reversed some of the Western and Arab hostility, kept both Iranian and Saudi goodwill, and gained US and Soviet approval for its actions, at least while it refrained from military assault on 'Awn. However, Syria had to expend large resources during the year, its hold on the ground did not increase, and 'Awn was still there, posing a major, continuing, and radical challenge to its dominant role in Lebanon.

REGIONAL RELATIONS

Syria's policy toward other Arab states continued to be aimed at reducing its isolation (see *MECS* 1988, pp. 742–44). Its main motivation was the need for Arab support in Lebanon to counteract Iraq's hostile involvement and the perceived erosion of Soviet strategic backing. Syria refrained from associating itself with any of the three regional groupings in the Arab world — the well-established Gulf Cooperation Council (GCC), the Arab Cooperation Council (ACC), and the Arab Maghrib Union (AMU). According to Foreign Minister Shar', Syria's nonparticipation endowed it with a "distinctive status" rather than isolating it. Both the GCC and AMU evinced their interest in strengthened relations with Syria.[72]

RELATIONS WITH IRAQ

The long-standing hostility between the Syrian and Iraqi regimes (see *MECS* 1988, pp. 739–40) revolved in 1989 around two issues: Lebanon and the support by each of movements opposed to the other. As put by the Syrian minister of information, Iraq did not want "natural" relations with Syria and in the past had financed and led sabotage operations against it. Its current support of 'Awn in Lebanon was complementing the role of Israel.[73]

On 7 March, a "joint action charter" to overthrow Saddam Husayn was agreed upon by seven Iraqi opposition groups sheltered by Damascus, including the Kurdish organization led by Mas'ud Barazani (see *MECS* 1988, p. 740), who personally informed the press of it. The groups considered establishing an interim executive committee, but nothing further was publicized in Syria during the year (for Iraqi support of Syrian opposition see above).[74]

Asad typically derided Iraq's involvement in Lebanon as not embodying a strategic concept; it did not seriously serve Iraq. Iraq's relationship with some Lebanese groups was without roots and served only to kill more Lebanese.[75] At the Casablanca summit the two heads of state were at loggerheads; later Syria continued to accuse Iraq of allying itself with Israel and obstructing the work of the tripartite committee.[76] (See also chapter on inter-Arab relations.)

SYRIA AND IRAN

Despite differences in outlook and interests, which occasionally strained their ties (see *MECS* 1988, pp. 739–40), Syria and Iran continued to enjoy a generally good working relationship.[77] The increased Iraqi involvement in Lebanon became a target common to both and made them muzzle the endemic rivalries between Amal and Hizballah. Meanwhile, Arab pressure on Syria to cool its relations with Iran declined with the cease-fire in the Gulf. When Ayatollah Ruhollah Khomeyni died (3 June), Asad pointedly went to the Iranian Embassy to convey his condolences to the ambassador and Prime Minister Zu'bi represented his country at the funeral.[78] The new team in Iran made no change in the relationship.

The Iranian foreign minister paid regular visits to Damascus — in April, July, and August — which were mainly devoted to coordinating policy in Lebanon.[79] In mid-September Syrian Foreign Minister Shar', accompanied by an economic delegation, went to Tehran and signed a memorandum on economic, technical, and scientific cooperation. Iran also backed the Arab tripartite plan for Lebanon. The prospect of a visit by Asad to advance strategic and economic cooperation, first raised in May but presumably postponed on Khomeyni's death, was renewed.[80] Next, Foreign Minister 'Ali Akbar Velayati came to Damascus on 28–29 October to express Iranian opposition to the Ta'if accords, because "Muslims came out losers." But despite Iranian dissatisfaction with the unyielding Syrian position, cooperation between the two countries continued.[81] For the next routine Iranian visit on 24 December, however, the minister sent his first deputy.[82] The Asad visit seemed to have been adjourned.

In these and other contacts with Iranian functionaries, the subject of Western hostages abducted by pro-Iranian groups in Lebanon was frequently raised, but none were released during 1989. This issue became especially topical following the seizure by Israeli troops of the leading Hizballah cleric in South Lebanon, Shaykh 'Abd al-Karim 'Ubayd, at the end of July (see chapter on armed operations).

SYRIA AND EGYPT

The continuing informal dialogue between Syria and Egypt, furthered by Saudi and Jordanian mediation, culminated at year's end with the restoration of diplomatic relations between the two countries.

In January, Syria agreed to Egypt's participation in future Arab summits and to its reinstatement in the Arab League, despite prevailing differences on Lebanon.[83] Accordingly, Syria welcomed Egypt's readmission to the Arab Agricultural Development Organization which met in Damascus in January.[84] In March, Asad defined relations with Egypt as "positive."[85]

The participation of Egypt in the Casablanca summit led to two meetings there between Asad and Egyptian President Husni Mubarak. The former said later he would continue what both had started in Casablanca.[86] Although a cautious note was introduced by Foreign Minister Shar', who argued that strategic and substantive issues could not be solved in a brief meeting,[87] visits by Egyptian trade and professional delegations were proof of the steadily progressing *rapprochement*.[88]

Asad alluded to the impending resumption of relations in terms which reflected his strategic concerns at year's end: he could not allow the estrangement between the two countries to last forever on account of "one document" — a reference to the Camp David Accords — especially as the Egyptian perception of Israeli expansionism did not differ from that of Syria. Only Israel would profit from severed relations. "We must cooperate even if we still have our differences," he stated.[89] Rapid developments followed: on 11 December, direct flights between the two capitals were resumed; then the Egyptian minister of information came to Damascus, followed by a trip by Syrian Vice President 'Abd al-Halim Khaddam to Cairo. On 27 December, Egyptian Prime Minister 'Atif Sidqi came to Damascus and the restoration of diplomatic relations was announced in both capitals.[90] A circle of 12 years of adverseness was thereby declared closed (see also chapter on Egypt).

RELATIONS WITH THE PLO

Syria's antagonism toward PLO policy and leadership continued during 1989, but the wide gap between them appeared less "unbridgeable" (see *MECS* 1988, pp. 740, 742); this was at least partly due to Asad's increased attention to his relations with Arab states, particularly Saudi Arabia and Algeria.[91]

On the practical level, there were continuous contacts between the PLO and Syria to arrange the visit of a high-level Palestinian delegation to Damascus in order to resume talks which began following the funeral of Abu Jihad (see *MECS* 1988, p. 741). The Syrians were urged by both the Algerians (during Asad's March visit there) and the Soviets to renew the direct dialogue with the PLO, and usually responded favorably (especially to a projected visit by "Foreign Minister" Qaddumi). Asad met PLO Chairman Yasir 'Arafat briefly during the summit in Casablanca, and his foreign minister conferred with Qaddumi at the UN General Assembly in October, when the latter's visit to Damascus within "a few weeks" was again announced. This, however, did not occur.[92] According to Foreign Minister Shar', Syria wanted an intra-Palestinian agreement on "Palestinian unity" — probably meaning alignment with the pro-Syrian groups — to precede the resumption of its talks with the PLO.[93] It seemed that Asad did not consider a high-level visit of PLO leaders, not to mention 'Arafat himself, propitious, as they still refused to accept his policies and guidance. Already in February, when 'Arafat refused to meet the Soviet foreign minister in Damascus unless officially invited by Asad, a well-informed Kuwaiti newspaper reported that no Syrian-Palestinian reconciliation meeting would occur in the foreseeable future.[94] Asad took care to point out that his differences with 'Arafat were not "because of the latter being 'Arafat" but for political reasons, and that he would not declare war on account of these differences. According to his biographer, Patrick Seale, Asad regarded 'Arafat as "a small-town politician dazed by the bright lights and unprepared for serious negotiation."[95]

Another practical problem in the relations between the PLO and Damascus was the continued imprisonment of Palestinian activists in Syria. In January, the Syrians released a prominent member of the PFLP and another of the Democratic Front for the Liberation of Palestine, who had been detained for one and two years respectively.[96] In June, the release of 140 alleged Fath members after six years of detention was reported, but Palestinian sources claimed there was only one Palestinian among them, the rest being members of Hizballah and the Ba'th. In July and November, more arrests among Palestinians were reported.[97]

However, the substantial differences between Syria and the PLO were political. An unnamed senior Palestinian leader listed three obstacles to a *rapprochement*:[98]

(1) The Syrians regarded the PLO peace initiative as leading toward a separate Israeli-Palestinian peace agreement containing many concessions to Israel, which would negatively affect the Syrian position in a future peace process. The PLO leadership refused to stop its initiative and to elaborate an alternative plan of action with Syria.

(2) Syria objected to all contacts between senior Palestinians and Israelis or American Jews not within an international conference.

(3) Moreover, Syria did not admit the principle of "independent Palestinian decision making." The Palestinian problem directly concerned Syria and all Arabs and was no "private Palestinain domain."

Later, Vice President Khaddam was even blunter: the Palestine question was a pan-Arab cause. "Palestine, like Syria, is part of *Bilad al-Sham*." Khaddam supported independent Palestinian decisions on matters concerning Palestinians only, but decisions affecting Syria, Lebanon, or Egypt could not be unilaterally made by Palestinians.[99] The PLO rejected this Syrian position.

In practice, the Syrians adopted a watchful attitude toward 'Arafat's peace initiative and stopped short of derailing it. They continually belittled his achievements — which Asad did not think would lead to the happy end expected by some — and derided his alleged concessions to Israel without obtaining anything in return. Thus, they condemned 'Arafat's statement in Paris that the Palestine National Charter was "*caduc*" (null and void) as another unilateral concession to Israel and as an abandonment of inalienable Palestinians right.[100] (See also chapter on the PLO.)

RELATIONS WITH SAUDI ARABIA

Syria took care to preserve its good relations with Saudi Arabia, traditionally a major purveyor of aid. During a visit to Damascus of Crown Prince 'Abdallah at the beginning of January, Syria announced the restoration of diplomatic ties with Morocco, praising Saudi assistance in achieving it.[101] Asad's positive responses to the Saudis before and during the Ta'if negotiations (see above) reinforced cordial relations and possibly generated Saudi financial aid to Syria.[102]

SYRIA AND JORDAN

The relations between Syria and Jordan during 1989 were friendly and practical. The joint ministerial committees established previously continued their work on economic and technical cooperation (see *MECS* 1987, pp. 647–48). Mutual trade was to increase to $200m. A visit by the Jordanian prime minister to Damascus on 9–11 July was reciprocated by a visit of the Syrian foreign minister to Amman on 26–27 August.[103]

Regular three-monthly meetings of the joint committee on the common development of the Yarmuk River basin were held. A meeting in Damascus in October finalized the design of the al-Wahda dam, reviewed progress on its tunnel, and discussed the utilization of water on both sides of the river.[104]

RELATIONS WITH MAGHRIB STATES

The increasing importance of the Maghribi states to Asad's effort to reduce Syria's political isolation in the Arab world was underlined by his three visits to that region during 1989. His first move was to restore diplomatic relations with Morocco on 9 January.[105] In mid-March Asad visited Libya (16–17 March), Algeria (18–19 March), and Tunisia (19 March). Plainly Asad looked for support for his policy in Lebanon, where 'Awn, backed by Iraq, had just declared "war" on him. Reportedly he asked Qadhdhafi to sever ties with 'Awn. Asad also wanted understanding for his attitude toward the PLO. Ties with Egypt were also discussed as well as relations with the AMU.[106] Morocco followed the visit with interest, and in April King Hasan dispatched his foreign minister to Damascus to advance their relations.[107]

On 22 May, on his way to the emergency summit conference in Casablanca, Asad paid a short visit to President Chedli Benjedid. Algeria's part in the Arab efforts in Lebanon was assuming greater importance and Asad probably wanted to ensure its cooperation against his adversaries at the summit.[108] Asad's third visit was to participate in the celebrations of the 20th anniversary of the Libyan Revolution on 1 September.[109] As mentioned above, his understandings there with President Benjedid and King Hasan paved the way for the resumption of work by the tripartite committee on Lebanon.

Syria had a long-standing military relationship with Libya, where some 30 of its pilots served. The commander in chief of the Libyan armed forces, Gen. Abu Bakr Yunis, visited Damascus in February and December 1989.[110]

RELATIONS WITH TURKEY

For some years, two problems troubled Syrian-Turkish relations. The Syrians were worried about the implications of Turkish water development and especially about the filling up to the huge Atatürk Dam reservoir. The Turks wanted to put a stop to the support and shelter the Syrians gave to the Kurdish Workers' Party, which occasionally raided Turkish territory. Both issues were addressed during the July 1987 visit of the Turkish prime minister to Damascus (see *MECS* 1987, pp. 650, 662).

Turkish Foreign Minister Mesut Yılmaz discussed the development of bilateral, especially security and economic, relations in Damascus on 3–5 July. Preceding the visit, it was reported that the Kurdish Workers' Party was cooperating with Barazani's anti-Iraq Kurds supported by Syria (see above).[111] In the fall, the Turkish prime minister made it known that if Kurdish raids organized from the Syrian-controlled Biq'a did not cease, Turkey would reduce the flow of water to Syria.[112] This might have been a hint of future policy, because in December Turkey informed Syria (and Iraq) that the flow of water in the Euphrates would be stopped (or greatly reduced) for a month beginning 13 January 1990, in order to fill up the completed reservoir of the Atatürk dam.[113]

Under these circumstances, the Syrians made every effort to minimize the possible consequences of Syrian fighters having shot down, on 18 October, a Turkish civilian cartograpghic aircraft above the border near Alexandretta, in which all five people aboard perished.[114] (See also chapter on Turkey.)

INTERNATIONAL RELATIONS

SYRIA AND THE SOVIET UNION

Syrian-Soviet relations ostensibly continued in their routine mold during 1989, but the strains put on them by Gorbachev's evolving policies, such as the "de-ideologization of interstate relations" and the need to end regional conflicts, were obvious.[115] In March, Asad expressed satisfaction with Gorbachev's policies and said he perceived no political change in the Soviet Union's relations with Syria, which were based on friendship, cooperation, and mutual benefit. He found no reason to discuss the concept of strategic parity (see above) with the Soviet leader. No correlation existed between an improvement of Soviet relations with Israel and Soviet-Syrian relations: Asad did not expect Moscow to harm Arab interests.[116] However, a Syrian newspaper later defined the relationship in a significantly different way, as "mature, firm, and honest."[117] The Soviets, for their part, endeavored to allay Syrian misgivings and fears by constantly emphasizing the ongoing consultations and coordination between the two, and to guide Syria toward alignment with the new reality. The Soviet effort manifested itself in a visit by two top Soviet officials to Damascus in the spring.

Pointedly, Foreign Minister Eduard Shevardnadze began his tour of ME capitals in Damascus (17-19 February). In what was described as "continuing consultations" at the highest level, he discussed with Asad the political process, regional issues, and the dangers of an arms race. Asad reportedly told Shevardnadze that *perestroika* could be misinterpreted in the West as a sign of weakness; this probably was a signal of his discomfort with some of the Soviet views.[118]

A month later Defense Minister Dmitri Yazov visited Syria (27–30 March), the first Soviet defense chief to do so since 1970. The visit underlined both the continuing military relationship and its limitations. In a press comment, Yazov said that military capabilities in the ME were much greater than the region's economic and demographic weight on the international level. Global disarmament could be hindered by the absence of movement toward a political settlement in the region. Asad possibly referred to this statement when, in his summing-up meeting with Yazov, he mentioned the necessity of confronting maneuvers that kept the region tense.[119] An obviously Syrian-inspired press comment on the visit stated that while differences in political views might emerge, Soviet readiness to improve Syrian military capabilities was a constant feature of the relationship.[120] Indeed, Soviet arms deliveries continued (including the already mentioned Su-24 light bomber aircraft), although reportedly at a reduced level,[121] as well as visits (inspections?) by Soviet military chiefs.[122] Soviet Foreign Economic Relations Minister Konstantin Katushev met with Defense Minister Talas at year's end, possibly to discuss further defense deals.[123]

The Syrians continued to reaffirm their primary reliance on Soviet support for gaining strategic parity and for deterring enemies. To Talas, the Soviet Union represented an "international deterrence." He could not conceive the Soviets content with the role of a spectator if a state friendly to them were attacked.[124]

In an effort at clarification, Soviet Ambassador to Damascus Alexander Zotov frankly outlined the parameters of the relationship, first to Western and then — more soothingly — to Syrian newsmen:

(1) The Soviets had no intent of loosening their ties with Syria, to make it feel insecure, let it feel that it had "lost [its] only friend and pillar of support." But new developments had to be looked at.

(2) Political understanding existed between the two countries and there were no "fundamental" differences on how to solve major regional issues. However, "regional conflicts must be solved peacefully."

(3) The Soviet Union intended to fulfill its commitments to provide military assistance and cooperation capable of guaranteeing Syria's security. The question was: "what is enough?" There were certain limits to countries being saturated with arms, and the strain of military expenditure on Syria was obvious. The Soviets would be guided by their assessment of Syrian "reasonable defense sufficiency," which they defined as the capability to withstand an Israeli strike and then to inflict unacceptable losses on it in a counterattack. A new five-year military cooperation agreement for 1991–95 was being negotiated, with special emphasis on air defense;[125] it would be based on the above assessment, on Soviet limits to provide sophisticated equipment and on Syria's ability to pay.

(4) The figure generally advanced in the West of Syrian debts to the Soviet Union — $15bn. — was greatly exaggerated.

(5) (To the Syrian press, referring to published reports of his interview in the West:) Western media attempted to disturb the good relationship between the two countries by highlighting some points and ignoring other positive ones.[126]

"Reasonable defense sufficiency" — "reasonable" presumably to be defined by the Soviets — was a concept very different from strategic parity. But the centrality of Syria's relationship with the Soviet Union (and its East European clients) for decades caused Damascus to accept, however reluctantly, new Soviet policies, despite evident differences of view and the loss of close personal relations that had existed with past East European leaders. Thus, obvious constraints were put on the Syrian policy toward the Arab-Israeli conflict. Asad attempted to balance this by strongly emphasizing Arab solidarity (see above). The Syrian — indeed, the regime's — need for strategic reinforcement, despite Soviet reassurances, was one of the major reasons for the resumption of its diplomatic links with Egypt.

RELATIONS WITH THE UNITED STATES

During 1989, Asad succeeded not only in keeping a door open to the US, but in perceptibly improving relations with it. The new Administration's ME policies were carefully watched for signs of change. Thus, the Syrian minister of information considered as very positive Secretary of State Baker's statement in May that Israel should give up annexation. In July, the Syrian minister said that high-level contacts between the US and Syria were continuing and that Syria understood the Administration's policy.[127] During the UN General Assembly in the fall, the secretary met with the Syrian foreign minister and among other issues discussed the Golan problem in the framework of the peace process. The Syrians considered the talks positive, but they expressed their unwillingness for any "deals."[128]

Terrorism was again a subject on the agenda between the two countries, particularly after the blowing-up of Pan Am flight 103 over Scotland in December 1988 (see above), which the US linked to the Syrian-based PFLP-GC. Despite group leader

Ahmad Jibril's denial of the organization's involvement, the US urged Asad to make it cease operations. On 3 March, the PFLP-GC apprehended two US military attachés while they were photographing a training camp of the organization near Damascus. While officially accused of "acts not in conformity with their diplomatic mission," the two were not expelled by the Syrians, who had secured their release. Thus, while the Syrians did not act against the PFLP-GC, they took care not to endanger relations with the US.[129] A report by the US ambassador for counterterrorism in April cautiously stated that "Syria has made some efforts to improve its record as a state sponsor of terrorism." On a subject important to the US, it said that Syria had "indicated its willingness to work closely with Western governments to facilitate the release of remaining hostages in Lebanon although its influence is seen as limited."[130] Syria officially expressed its disgust and condemnation of the killing of US hostage Col. William Higgins in July (see chapter on Lebanon).[131] A year later the State Department reported that "Syria's hand" had not been detected in any terrorist incident in 1988 or 1989. But as it sheltered various terrorist groups (especially the PFLP-GC) it bore responsibility for their activities.[132]

When fighting erupted in Lebanon between 'Awn and the Syrians, the US repeatedly urged Syria to stop shelling East Beirut, especially with heavy weapons, and then severely and publicly deplored "unnecessary" bombardments. The US reportedly prevented a Syrian assault on 'Awn when he was rumored to have received missiles from Iraq.[133] On the other hand, the US supported the Arab effort to reach a political solution in Lebanon, which resulted in the Ta'if accords and the two Lebanese presidential elections (see above). This created a common terrain of understanding between Syria and the US.[134]

RELATIONS WITH WESTERN EUROPE

Syria continued its effort to reinforce diplomatic and economic relations with the countries of the European Economic Community during 1989 (see *MECS* 1988, p. 745). A main obstacle was Syria's involvement with terrorism (see above).

Relations with France were clouded because of events in Lebanon. A mid-March visit to Paris by Foreign Minister Shar' served only to underline their differences concerning Lebanon. Syria would not make any concession to France on this issue and rejected French mediation with 'Awn.[135] The dispatch of two French ships to Lebanon after the escalation of fighting was depicted as a "return to the colonial past." However, the Syrians praised President François Mitterrand when he recalled the ships and abandoned "the call to internationalize" the crisis, by disavowing his envoy to Beirut, Jean-François Deniau. When, in August, France again announced the dispatch of ships, this was seen as another attempt to interfere in Lebanon. However, the French reconsidered and twice sent the secretary-general of their Foreign Ministry to Damascus to pacify the Syrians and to express support of the Arab tripartite effort. Obviously this satisfied the Syrians.[136]

Relations with Great Britain were not resumed in 1989 (see *MECS* 1988, p. 745), despite optimism on this score expressed in October by Foreign Minister Shar'.[137]

Terrorism was an important item on Shar''s agenda during a visit to Bonn late in June. An agreement on counterterrorist cooperation was reportedly reached with the Federal Republic of Germany, which was ready to consider the resumption of economic aid and loans, interrupted in 1987 because of Syrian encouragement of terrorism (see *MECS* 1987, pp. 651–52).[138]

RELATIONS WITH CHINA

Since the Soviet Union, in accordance with its arms limitation treaties with the US, refused to supply Syria with SS-23 ground-to-ground missiles, rumors spread that Syria had either asked for or attained the agreement of the People's Republic of China to supply it with M-9 missiles (with a range of 500km.–600km.). The deal was said to have been financed by Saudi Arabia, which denied it.[139] The visit of Chinese Foreign Minister Qian Qichen to Damascus on 23–24 September apparently nourished the rumors.[140] However, after a worried US asked for Chinese reassurances on the matter, the deal was denied by a Beijing Foreign Ministry spokesman. At the beginning of February 1990, Secretary of State Baker said that the Chinese had given "indications of restraint regarding the supply of missiles to the Middle East." Syria was not specifically mentioned.[141]

NOTES

For the place and frequency of publications cited here, and for the full name of the publication, news agency, radio station, or monitoring service where an abbreviation is used, please see "List of Sources." Only in the case of more than one publication bearing the same name is the place of publication noted here.

1. Itamar Rabinovich, "Syria and Lebanon in 1989," *Current History*, 88 (1989), p. 104.
2. *CR*: Syria, No. 4, 1989, p. 4; *al-Nashra*, Nicosia, 20 March 1989.
3. *Al-Nashra*, Nicosia, 20 March; *al-Sharq al-Jadid*, March 1989.
4. *L'Express*, 14 June; *al-Ra'y al-Akhir*, London, 15 August 1989.
5. *CR*: Syria, No. 4, p. 9; *al-Muharrir*, 18 November 1989.
6. Interview by *Time*, R. Damascus, 27 March — DR, 28 March 1989. Interestingly, this answer did not appear in *Time*, 3 April; *CR*: Syria, No. 4, 1989, p. 9.
7. R. Baghdad, 22 August — DR, 23 August; *al-Nashra*, Athens, 8 May; *al-Dustur*, London, 27 November 1989.
8. INA, 21 Paril; *al-Nashra*, Athens, 9 May, 3 July; *al-Dustur*, London, 12 June 1989.
9. *Al-Watan al-'Arabi*, 11 August 1989. The Egyptian monthly *al-I'tisam*, October 1989, reported on a meeting of "a new council" of Syrian Muslim Brothers hostile to the Asad regime.
10. *FT*, 4 July; *al-Nashra*, Nicosia, 24 July 1989.
11. R. Monte Carlo, 3 December; Damascus TV, 13 December — DR, 4, 14 December 1989.
12. Yahya M. Sadowski, "Patronage and the Ba'th: Corruption and Control in Contemporary Syria," *Arab Studies Quarterly*, 9 (1987), pp. 449, 457; Annika Rabo, *"State"and"Identity" in the Middle East*, a paper submitted to the annual conference of the British Society for Middle Eastern Studies, 12 July 1987; *idem*, "Nation-State Building in Syria: Ba'th and Islam — Conflict or Accommodation," in Klaus Ferdinand and M. Mozaffari (eds.), *Islam: State and Society* (London: Curzon Press, 1988), p. 122.
13. R. Damascus, 8 March 1989, 14 February 1990 — DR, 9 March 1989, 15 March 1990.
14. *CR*: Syria, No. 3, p. 10; No. 4, p. 3; R. Damascus, 13, 15 May; *Tishrin*, 16 May; *FT*, 1 June 1989.
15. *CR*: Syria, No. 3, p. 10; No. 4, p. 12; *al-Majalla*, 17 May — DR, 23 May; *FT*, 1 June; *JP*, 22 November 1989.
16. *Al-Ba'th*, 9 January 1989.
17. *FT*, 1 June; *al-Thawara*, Damascus, 23 June; *al-Ba'th*, 29 September 1989.
18. *Tishrin*, 12 January 1989.
19. *Al-Thawra*, Damascus, 7 June 1989.

20. R. Damascus, 10 May; *al-Thawra,* Damascus, 13 May; *FT,* 1 June 1989.
21. R. Damascus, 15 February — DR, 17 February; *MM,* 5 February 1990.
22. *MM,* 5 February 1990; *CR:* Syria, No. 3, pp. 12-13, No. 4, p. 13; *al-Bayan,* Dubai, 15 November — DR, 24 November 1989; for the lower output figure, Arab Banking Corporation, *The Arab Economies — Structure and Outlook* (3rd ed., London: 1989), p. 142.
23. SANA, 4 February 1989.
24. *CR:* Syria, No. 3, 1989, p. 14; *MM,* 5 February 1990.
25. *CR:* Syria, No. 3, p. 4, No. 4, p. 4; *FT,* 1 June 1989.
26. *Al-Jarida al-Rasmiyya,* 29 November 1989.
27. *CR:* Syria, No. 4, pp. 10-11; for a lower estimate — 25% of the budget — *The Economist,* 25 November 1989.
28. *CR:* Syria, No. 4, 1989, p. 4; *al-Hawadith,* 12 January 1990; *Ha'aretz,* 7 February 1990; R. Damascus, 7 February; Damascus TV, 13 February — DR, 9, 15 February 1990.
29. R. Damascus, 8 March; *al-Qabas,* 9 December — DR, 9 March, 11 December 1989.
30. R. Damascus, *al-Ba'th,* 1 August — DR, 2, 18 August 1989.
31. *Al-Anba,* Kuwait, 15 August — DR, 17 August 1989.
32. *FR,* 6 April 1989.
33. *Al-Ra'y al-'Amm,* 26 October — DR, 30 October; *FT,* 20 November; *JP,* 29 December; *CR:* Syria, No. 2, 1989, p. 9. The Su-24 has an estimated range of 1,050 km., US Department of Defense, *Soviet Military Power — 1989* (Washington, DC: 1989).
34. *Ha'aretz,* 12 October 1989.
35. Assessment given to the Senate Foreign Relations Committee on 1 March. USIS Official Text, 4 April 1989.
36. R. Damascus, 7 January. Cf. Talas's comment to a Soviet journal that whenever the US and the West learn that one of the Arab states "had received or produced some defensive weapons," they get agitated. *Aziya i Afrika Segodnya,* January 1989, pp. 19–20.
37. *Al-Anba,* Kuwait, 15 August — DR, 17 August 1989.
38. E.g., Defense Minister Rabin, *Ha'aretz,* 16 February, 12 March; Chief of General Staff Shomron, ibid., 21, 27 February 1989.
39. *Al-Hayat,* Beirut, 19 April; for analysis and rejection of these from a Palestinian and/or Iraqi point of view, *al-Yawm al-Sabi',* 15 May 1989.
40. *Al-Anba,* Kuwait, 15 August — DR, 17 August 1989. Reportedly Syria also took steps to avoid chance naval clashes with Israel off Lebanon, Voice of Free Lebanon, 16 July — DR, 17 July 1989.
41. *Al-Anba,* Kuwait, 15 August, Chief of Staff Shihabi in *al-Ba'th,* 1 August — DR, 17, 18 August 1989.
42. *CR:* Syria, No. 2, p. 10. Reportedly the US presented the evidence in Damascus; *IHT,* 6 November 1989.
43. R. Damascus, 27 March — DR, 28 March 1989.
44. "Patterns of Global Terrorism," USIS Official Text, 1 May 1990.
45. R. Damascus, 12 April, 4 October, *al-Watan,* Kuwait, 1 October — DR, 13 April, 3, 4 October 1989.
46. Foreign Minister Shar', *al-Anba,* Kuwait, 27 July — DR, 31 July 1989; *Ha'aretz,* 5 November 1989.
47. *Al-Qabas,* 9 December — DR, 11 December 1989.
48. *JP,* 14 December 1989.
49. Damascus TV, 12 January; R. Damascus, 18 January, 5 March — DR, 13, 19 January, 6 March. On the composition of the committee see *al-Nahar,* Beirut, 14 January 1989.
50. *Al-Hawadith,* 20 January; *al-Ittihad,* Abu Dhabi, 17 February — DR, 21 February; *al-Ittihad,* 26 February 1989.
51. Voice of Free Lebanon, 3, 4 January; VoL, 4 January — DR, 4, 5 January; *NYT,* 12 January; R. Monte Carlo, *JP,* 16 January; R. Damascus, 23, 25 January; R. Monte Carlo, 23, 24 January; IRNA, 23 January — DR, 24, 25 January; *Le Monde,* 2 February 1989.
52. VoL, 14 March — DR, 15 March 1989.
53. R. Damascus, 15 March; Voice of Free Lebanon, 17 March; R. Damascus, 22 March — DR, 20, 23 March; Foreign Minister Shar', *al-Watan,* Kuwait, 26 April; Asad, R. Damascus, 4 May — DR, 28 April, 5 May 1989.

54. *IHT,* 22–23 April, 10 May; *FT,* 28 April; *The Economist,* 11 November 1989. Testimony of Assistant Secretary of State John Kelly before Europe and ME Subcommittee of the House of Representatives, 19 September — USIS Official Text, 21 September 1989.

55. R. Damascus, 4 May — DR, 5 May; Talas, SANA, 31 July; *al-Anba,* Kuwait, 15 August — DR, 17 August 1989.

56. *Al-Diyar,* 6 April; *Le Monde,* 28 April; R. Damascus, 9 May — DR, 10 May; cf. Shar', *JT,* 28 August — DR, 28 August 1989.

57. Voice of National Resistance, 4 July; R. Monte Carlo, 7 July — DR, 5, 13 July; *The Economist,* 27 May; *al-Sharq al-Awsat,* 20 June; *al-Qabas,* 25 July; denial by 'Awn, *Le Monde,* 12 July 1989.

58. *Al-Qabas,* 10 July, VoL, 11 September — DR, 12 July, 12 September 1989.

59. Voice of the Mountain, 13 August — DR, 14 August; *al-Hayat,* Beirut, 15 August; *CR:* Syria, No. 4, 1989, p. 6.

60. KUNA, 10 May — DR, 10 May 1989.

61. Shar', *al-Watan,* Kuwait, 26 April; R. Damascus, 28 April, Voice of Free Lebanon, 2 June — DR, 28 April, 1 May, 2 June; R. Damascus, 28 May — DR, 30 May; *al-Qabas,* 30 May; *CR:* Syria, No. 3, p. 5; for an Iraqi view of the summit procedings, hostile to Syria, *al-Thawra,* Baghdad, 7 June — DR, 16 June 1989.

62. GNA, 11 June; Damascus TV, 2 July — DR, 12 June, 3 July 1989.

63. *CR:* Syria, No. 4, p. 8; for the composition of the front, R. al-Quds, 16 August — DR, 18 August 1989.

64. R. Damascus, R. Monte Carlo, 7 August — DR, 8 August 1989.

65. KUNA, 9 September; *al-Masira,* 11 September 1989.

66. SANA, 3 October; *al-Qabas,* 6 October — DR, 4, 10 October; *NYT,* 2 October 1989.

67. R. Damascus, 17, 19, 20 September — DR, 18, 20 September; R. Damascus, 3 October; BBC (Arabic Service), 21 October 1989; *CR:* Syria, No. 4, 1989, p. 7.

68. R. Damascus, 23, 31 October; Khaddam in *al-Majalla,* 7 November — DR, 25 October, 1, 3 November 1989.

69. R. Damascus, 7, 30 November — DR, 8, 30 November; *al-Qabas,* 12 November 1989.

70. R. Damascus, 24 November — DR, 27 November 1989.

71. R. Damascus, 1, 4, 7 December; *al-Qabas,* 9 December — DR, 2, 5, 8, 11 December 1989.

72. *Al-Ba'th,* 24 March, Khaddam in *al-Anba,* Kuwait, 30 June — DR, 11 April, 13 July 1989.

73. R. Damascus, 10 September 1989.

74. *Tishrin,* 8 March; SANA, 7 March — DR, 9 March 1989.

75. R. Damascus, 27 March — DR, 28 March 1989.

76. *JP,* 26 May; R. Damascus, 28 May, 12 June — DR, 30 May, 14 June 1989.

77. According to Talas, mutual support between the two countries, despite their ideological differences, was based on common hostility to Israel and the US; *al-Anba,* Kuwait, 15 August — DR, 17 August 1989.

78. R. Damascus, 6 June — DR, 7 June; *al-Dustur,* London, 12 June 1989.

79. R. Monte Carlo, 3 April; IRNA, 8 July; Damascus TV, 14 August; R. Tehran, 15 August — DR, 4 April, 10 July, 15 August 1989.

80. R. Monte Carlo, 15 May; R. Damascus, 18 May, 20 September — DR, 16, 18 May, 21 September; *al-Amal,* Beirut, 22 September 1989.

81. R. Damascus, IRNA, 28 October; R. Monte Carlo, VoL, 29 October — DR, 30 October; *IHT,* 23 November 1989.

82. SANA, 24 December; R. Damascus, 25 December — DR, 26 December 1989.

83. *Al-Usbu' al-'Arabi,* 2 January; *NYT,* 15 January; *al-Wafd,* 18 January; AFP, 19 January — Dr, 23 January; cf. *al-Hayat,* Beirut, 6–7 May 1989.

84. Damascus TV, R. Monte Carlo, 18 January — DR, 19 January 1989.

85. R. Damascus, 27 March — DR, 28 March 1989.

86. R. Damascus, 20 June, Khaddam in *al-Anba,* Kuwait, 30 June — DR, 21 June, 13 July 1989.

87. *Al-Anba,* Kuwait, 27 July — DR, 31 July 1989. The minister of information voiced a more optimistic view, MENA, 21, 22 June; R. Damascus, 22 June — DR, 22 June 1989.

88. E.g., SANA, 28 June; R. Damascus, 31 July — DR, 29 June, 1 August 1989.

89. *Al-Qabas,* 9 December — DR, 11 December 1989.

90. Damascus TV, 11, 27 December; SANA, 17, 23, 27 December; R. Damascus, 12, 23, 27 December — DR, 12, 14, 18, 26, 27, 28 December 1989.
91. *Al-Sharq al-Awsat,* 12 April — DR, 19 April 1989.
92. Ibid.; *al-Siyasa,* Kuwait, 17 April; *al-Ra'y,* 15 September; *al-Qabas,* 3 October; R. Damascus, 4 October — DR, 20 April, 15 September, 5 October; *al-Hayat,* Beirut, 6–7 May 1989.
93. *Al-Majalla,* 12 July; *al-Anba,* Kuwait, 27 July — DR 31 July 1989.
94. *Al-Qabas,* 25–26 February 1989.
95. R. Damascus, 27 March — DR, 28 March; *IHT,* 19 May 1989.
96. AFP, 21 January — DR, 23 January; AFP, 23 January; *al-Usbu' al-'Arabi,* 13 February 1989.
97. *NYT,* 18 June; *al-Nashra,* Nicosia, 24 July; *al-Nashra,* Athens, 13 November; *al-Dustur,* London, 27 November 1989.
98. *Al-Qabas,* 10 March 1989.
99. *Al-Anba,* Kuwait, 30 June — DR, 13 July 1989.
100. *IHT,* 19 January; *al-Hayat,* Beirut, 6-7 May; R. Damascus, 8 May; Khaddam in *La Repubblica,* 20 May — DR, 24 May 1989.
101. R. Damascus, 6, 7 January — DR, 9, 10 January 1989.
102. R. Damascus, R. Riyadh, 1 November — DR, 2 November; *CR*: Syria, No. 4, 1989, p. 7.
103. *Al-Ra'y,* 12, 20 June; R. Damascus, 5, 6, 9, 10, 11 July, 27 August; Damascus TV, 27 August — DR, 11 July, 28 August 1989.
104. JNA, 5 October — DR, 6 October 1989.
105. R. Damascus, R. Rabat, 9 January — DR, 9, 10 January 1989.
106. R. Damascus, 18, 19 March; Algiers TV, 18 March; R. Tunis, 19 March; *al-Sharq al-Awsat,* 22 March — DR, 20, 31 March; *JP,* 17 March; AFP, 20 March; *al-Qabas,* 2 April 1989.
107. *Al-Sharq al-Awsat,* 22 March; R. Damascus, Damascus TV, 2 April — DR, 31 March, 4 April 1989.
108. R. Damascus, 22 May — DR, 23 May 1989.
109. R. Damascus, 2 September — DR, 5 September 1989.
110. R. Damascus, 9 February, 27, 28 December — DR, 10 February, 28, 29 December; *al-Watan al-'Arabi,* 7 July 1989.
111. R. Damascus, 3, 4, 5 July — DR, 12 July; *al-Dustur,* London, 19 June 1989.
112. *Ha'aretz,* 21 October; *al-'Alam,* London, 4 November; *The Economist,* 16 December; cf. Report by ambassador for counterterrorism, Department of State Publication 9705, USIS Official Text, 21 April 1989; "Patterns of Global Terrorism," USIS Official Text, 1 May 1990.
113. *The Economist,* 16 December; *al-Hayat,* Beirut, 16–17 December; *al-Yawm al-Sabi',* 18 December 1989.
114. *Ha'aretz,* 21 October; R. Damascus, 22 October; SANA, 23 October — DR, 23, 24 October 1989.
115. Cynthia Roberts and Elizabeth Wishnik, "Ideology is Dead! Long Live Ideology," *Problems of Communism,* November-December 1989, pp. 58, 64.
116. R. Damascus, 8, 27 March — DR, 9, 28 March; cf. Minister of State for Foreign Affairs Nasir Qaddur in *Magyar Hirlap,* Budapest, 18 May — DR, 7 June 1989.
117. *Tishrin,* 22 July, quoted by R. Damascus, 22 July — DR, 24 July 1989.
118. *NYT,* 22 February; R. Damascus, 19, 23 February — DR 21, 24 February; *al-Watan,* Kuwait, 3 March 1989.
119. R. Damascus, 27, 30 March; Damascus TV, 28 March — DR, 28, 30, 31 March; *FT,* 28 March 1989.
120. *Al-Ittihad,* Abu Dhabi, 28 March — DR, 30 March 1989.
121. Thomas Pickering, US ambassador to the UN, *Ha'aretz,* 6 December 1989; however, Israeli sources estimated overall Soviet aid to Syria in 1989 (weapons, munitions, spares, training) at $1bn., i.e., equal to 1988; ibid., 30 January 1990.
122. Among them: commander of rockets and artillery of Soviet ground forces, Col. Mikhalkin in September; deputy minister of defense for armaments, Army-Gen. Shabanov, in November; commander of Soviet air defense, Army-Gen. Tretyak, in December. SANA, 7

September; R. Damascus, 28 November; Damascus TV, 3 December — DR, 8 September, 29 November, 4 December 1989.

123. R. Damascus, 27 December — DR, 27 December 1989.
124. *Magyar Hirlap*, 18 May; *al-Anba*, Kuwait, 1ƒ August — DR, 7 June, 17 August 1989.
125. See Note 122 above.
126. *FT,* 20 November; *IHT,* 21 November, for the interviews with Western newsmen; R. Damascus, 23 November — DR, 24 November, for the press conference in Damascus. The latter probably was an outcome of the ambassador's "dissatisfaction with news media" conveyed to the Syrian minister of information — Damascus TV, 21 November — DR, 22 November 1989. A further denial of some of Zotov's statements was made by a Soviet official in Cairo; *al-Wafd,* 25 December — DR, 2 January 1990.
127. *FT,* 30 May; *al-Watan al-'Arabi,* 21 July 1989.
128. R. Damascus, 30 September; Damascus TV, 4 October — DR, 2, 6 October; *al-Hayat,* Beirut, 2 October 1989.
129. *IHT,* 11–12 March; AFP, 12, 13 March; Asad's comments on the PFLP-GC: R. Damascus, 27 March — DR, 28 March 1989.
130. Report by ambassador for counterterrorism, Department of State Publication 9705, USIS Official Text, 21 April 1989.
131. R. Damascus, 31 July — DR, 1 August 1989.
132. "Patterns of Global Terrorism," USIS Official Text, 1 May 1990.
133. *IHT,* 18 April; *al-Sharq al-Awsat,* 20 June; *Le Monde,* 16 August; Assistant Secretary of State John Kelly, USIS Official Text, 21 September 1989.
134. Assistant Secretary of State John Kelly, USIS Official Text, 21 September 1989; *al-Nahar,* Beirut, 17 June 1989; Secretary of State Baker, USIS Official Text, 2 February 1990.
135. AFP, 20 March; *al-Qabas,* 23 March; *al-Ittihad,* Abu Dhabi, 24 March 1989.
136. R. Damascus, 9, 12, 14 April — DR, 14 April; *FT,* 11 April; *NYT,* 13 April; R. Damascus, 24 August; R. Monte Carlo, 28 August; *JT,* 28 August — DR, 28, 29 August; *Le Monde,* 16, 30 August 1989.
137. R. Damascus, 4 October — DR, 4 October 1989.
138. AFP, 29 June; *al-Akhbar,* Cairo, 2 July 1989.
139. *Al-Ra'y al-'Amm,* 22 May; *al-Qabas,* 26 July; *al-Ittihad,* Abu Dhabi, 31 July — DR, 28 July, 2 August; *Ha'aretz,* 8 August, 12 December; *JP,* 12 December; *CR*: Syria, No. 4, 1989, p. 9.
140. R. Damascus, 23 September — DR, 25 September 1989.
141. *Ha'aretz,* 8 August; *JP,* 12 December 1989; USIS Official Text, 2 February 1990.

Turkey
(Türkiye Cumhuriyeti)

ANDREW MANGO

The closing year of the decade has also been the most difficult for Turkey since the restoration of parliamentary rule in 1983. Measures of economic austerity introduced in 1988, after the rapid expansion pursued by Turgut Özal during his first term as prime minister (November 1983-November 1987), bit hard in the opening months of 1989. Hardship fed discontent, which was reflected in the defeat of the ruling conservative Motherland Party (MP; *Anavatan Partisi*) in the local-government elections in March. As labor unrest developed and as the opposition clamored for the dissolution of parliament, Özal relaxed his economic policies and allowed salaries and wages to increase more than twofold. However, in spite of economic difficulties compounded by the drought, which decreased agricultural production by an estimated 11%,[1] Özal stood firm in refusing the demand that general elections be held before parliament's election in November of a successor to President Kenan Evren. Undeterred by an opposition boycott, he secured his own election as president by the votes of MP deputies and appointed a political supporter, the speaker of parliament, Yıldırım Akbulut, as the new prime minister.

Difficulties abounded also in the conduct of foreign policy, which was dominated by the flight to Turkey of over 300,000 ethnic Turks from Bulgaria. There were problems in relations with other neighbors — Greece, Syria, and Iran — and while relations with the USSR improved and gained substance through increased trade, the turmoil in the Soviet Caucasus opened up worrying possibilities. There were also disappointments in relations with Turkey's Western partners. Turkey's hopes of admission as a full member of the European Economic Community (EEC) were set back in December, when the European Commission recommended to the council of foreign ministers that there should be no negotiations on the matter until 1993 at the earliest. Relations with the US were soured by a new attempt in Congress to commemorate the deportation of Armenians in the Ottoman Empire in 1915.

Yet there were also signs that Turkey's strength had grown. In spite of the drought and the consequent need to import wheat, there was a surplus in the external current account for the second consecutive year. Direct foreign investment increased, there were no difficulties in refinancing the foreign debt, and the national currency appreciated in real terms. In domestic politics, there was a large consensus that changes had to be sought by constitutional means. And in foreign affairs, adversaries were motivated more by a fear of Turkey than by a perception of Turkish weakness, while partners sought to avoid giving offense even where they did not meet Turkey's wishes.

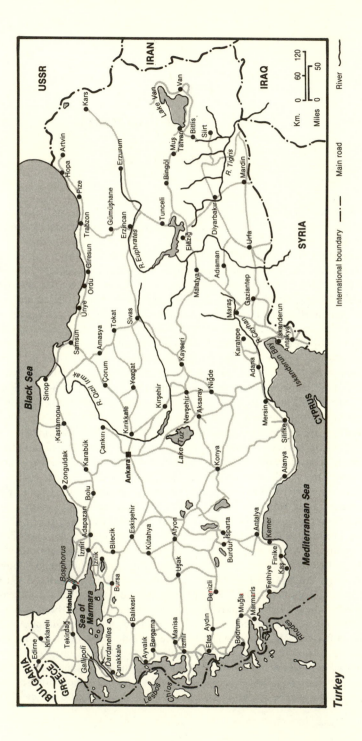

Turkey

DOMESTIC ISSUES

LOCAL-GOVERNMENT ELECTIONS AND MINISTERIAL RESHUFFLE

There were two important dates in the political calendar: 26 March, when local-government elections were held; and 9 November, when the seven-year term of office of President Evren expired. On 26 March, votes were cast for provincial councils (*il genel idare meclisleri,* modeled on the French *conseils généraux*), town mayors and councils (*belediye başkanları ve meclisleri*), and the mayors and councils of metropolitan areas, i.e., the larger conurbations (*büyükşehir belediye başkanları ve meclisleri*). Attention was focused on the distribution of votes in the provincial council elections (since all voters on the national electoral register could take part in these and they were, therefore, a pointer to parliamentary elections), and on the choice of the metropolitan mayors, because of their prominence and of the resources put at their disposal by the fiscal decentralization policies introduced in 1984. (Municipalities at present receive 6% of central government tax revenues, collect property and some indirect taxes, and may borrow abroad.)[2] Nonvoters were not subject to fines, as they had been on several occasions after the reintroduction of parliamentary government in 1983.[3]

As for the presidential elections, the outgoing incumbent, Kenan Evren, had been chief of the general staff before the military intervention of 12 September 1980, when he became president of the Council of National Security and head of state. In accordance with provisional article 1 of the constitution,[4] he was deemed elected president of the republic for a seven-year term on 7 November 1982, when the new constitution was approved by referendum. However, his successors were to be elected by parliament (the Turkish Grand National Assembly — TGNA), as had always been the case. The successful candidate required a two-thirds majority on the first two ballots, or an absolute majority (226 votes in a 450-member parliament) on the third ballot. The constitution provided that parliament would be dissolved if no candidate could obtain an absolute majority. This was a potent consideration in the minds of deputies, most of whom did not want to incur the trouble and considerable expense of a new election, only two years after winning their seats. Another point at issue was whether Turkey was to have a president with a civilian background, for the first time since the military coup on 27 May 1960, and only for the second time since the foundation of the republic on 29 October 1923.

Prime Minister Özal at first attempted to stress the local character of the March elections. But as the opposition based their campaign on criticism of the government's national policy and, in particular, on the hardship caused by the rise in the cost of living, Özal stated that it would be to the advantage of local communities if they were run by people in sympathy with the central government. This was interpreted by the opposition as an attempt to intimidate local electors with a cutoff of central funds to local government bodies controlled by the opposition. Whatever the truth of the accusation, the elections assumed the character of a referendum on government performance. Fearing that discontent with the government might overshadow his local achievements, Bedrettin Dalan, the powerful mayor of the Istanbul metropolitan area (the most populous in the country), placed press advertisements in which he extolled his services to the city, without mentioning his membership of the ruling MP. This did not save him from defeat at the hands of Dr. Nurettin Sözen, the candidate of

Prof. Erdal İnönü's Social Democratic and Populist Party (SDPP; *Sosyaldemokrat ve Halkçı Parti*) who was less known and whose chances had been discounted by local observers. Dalan subsequently resigned from the MP and at the close of the year he was preparing to launch a new democratic center party in opposition to it.

In the Ankara metropolitan area there was less surprise at the election of the SDPP candidate, Murat Karayalçın. In all, the SDPP won control of the six largest metropolitan areas, while ex-prime minister Süleyman Demirel's True Path Party (TPP; *Doğru Yol Partisi,* translated more accurately as Party of the Right Path) and Prof. Necmettin Erbakan's Welfare Party (WP; *Refah Partisi*), of Islamic fundamentalist inspiration, won one each.

The SDPP also won most of the boroughs within the metropolitan areas where they wrested control. Throughout the country, they came first with 650 mayoralties, won on 32.8% of the votes cast.

In the provincial council elections, the SDPP were again first with 28.7% of the total poll, followed by the TPP with 25.1%, and the MP in third place with 21.8%. Of the parties not represented in parliament — because they had failed to cross the threshold of 10% of the total poll in the general elections of November 1987 — the WP received 9.8% of the votes cast for provincial councils, ex-prime minister Bülent Ecevit's Democratic Left Party (DLP; *Demokratik Sol Partisi*) 9.0% and the extreme right-wing Nationalist Labor Party (NLP; *Milliyetçi Çalışma Partisi*), led by Alparslan Türkeş, 4.1%.[5] The first two thus approached the 10% barrier and threatened to introduce further fragmentation in the next legislature.

However, the most significant aspect of the result was that the ruling MP had fallen to third place on a national scale. The fact that its voting strength amounted to barely 22% of the electorate (or even to 15%, according to later public opinion polls)[6] constituted the main argument of the opposition when it claimed that a parliament, shown to be unrepresentative, should not be allowed to elect the new president.

Prime Minister Özal's response was threefold. First, he argued that the parliament's mandate was unaffected by the local polls and that there was no legal reason why it should not serve out its five-year term, scheduled to end in November 1992. Second, he reshuffled the government, as evidence that he had taken to heart the warning which he had received from the electorate. Third, he proceeded to calm down social discontent by concessions to the labor unions.

The main feature of the cabinet reshuffle on 31 March[7] was the departure of the prime minister's brother, Yusuf Bozkurt Özal, and cousin, Hüsnü Doğan, whose presence in the government had been criticized as evidence of "dynastic rule." Another casualty was Minister of Defense Ercan Vuralhan, whose name had been linked with allegations of corruption. A notable promotion was the appointment as deputy prime minister of Prof. Ali Bozer, who retained his portfolio as minister of state in charge of relations with the EEC. Bozer had formerly been a member of the Nationalist Democracy Party, on which the military had pinned their hopes in the 1987 elections, and was known to be close to Evren. Prof. Ekrem Pakdemirli, who as under secretary for the treasury and foreign trade and then as minister of transport, had been closely associated with Özal's economic policies, was promoted to the Ministry of Finance. A notable right-winger, Halil Şıvgın, formerly a supporter of Türkeş, became minister of health. But Mehmet Keçeciler, the leader of the religious faction in the MP, where he was in charge of party organization, was again kept out of the government. On 11

April, the government was endorsed in parliament by 289 votes to 95, the MP voting for it, the SDPP against, while the TPP's 57 deputies boycotted the proceedings.[8]

EASING SOCIAL UNREST

It was generally agreed that the discomfiture of the MP in the local polls was due in the first place to the rapid rise in the cost of living. The consumer price index (CPI) had risen by 75.4% in 1988, and the rise fell only slightly to 70.3% in the first quarter of 1989.[9] The extent of the rise had not been foreseen in collective labor contracts, which usually run for two years and many of which were renegotiated in 1987, when the average level of real wages rose by merely 8%. As a result, real wages fell by an average of 8.7% in 1988. Labor militancy, natural in the circumstances, was reinforced by the desire of the leaders of the main trade-union confederation Türkiş to gain popularity in advance of that body's convention. Legislation introduced by the military after 1980 had circumscribed the right to strike by providing for cooling-off periods, followed by compulsory arbitration; by banning strikes in essential services; by allowing government intervention in the interests of national security; and by denying union membership to numerous categories of public employees. However, in the first half of 1989 labor discontent found many ways to express itself: workers boycotted canteens, demanded medical examinations *en masse,* slowed down production, interrupted traffic, etc. There were also strikes, where legally possible.

Soon after the elections, the government moved to remedy workers' grievances. In May, workers in the public sector received an average raise of 142% for the first year of their renegotiated contracts, with provisions for inflation-linked raises in the second year.[10] On 1 July, civil servants had their salaries doubled in the second annual revision, which brought their raises for the year to 140%–160%.[11] There were consequential increases in pensions. Agreement on these terms was reached fairly easily except in the case of steelworkers, whose strike in the Karabük and Iskenderun mills, originally postponed by the authorities, lasted for 137 days and was not resolved until 17 September.[12]

Another move calculated to enhance the government's popularity was the formation of new provinces. Provincial status extends the range of facilities available to local people. Four new provinces — Aksaray, Bayburt, Karaman, and Kırıkkale — were founded in June, bringing the number of provinces in the country up to 71.[13]

THE PRESIDENTIAL ELECTION

Polemics about the presidential election went on for the seven months between the end of March and the end of October. While the opposition advanced a number of alternatives such as early elections and interparty agreement on a candidate, preferably an independent, Özal insisted on the letter of the constitution and argued that parliament, as constituted, and in effect the MP, which held the absolute majority of parliamentary seats, was entitled to elect the new president.

Opposition hopes that the MP's parliamentary group might not follow its leader, or that it might split, were dispelled when the new session opened in September. Akbulut, the candidate favored by Özal, was elected speaker on the third ballot on 11 September. He received 250 votes against 173 votes cast for a candidate also belonging to the MP.[14] This meant that only some 30 MP deputies were prepared to disregard their leader's wishes.

Özal proceeded, nevertheless, to make assurance doubly sure by sending a questionnaire to the MP parliamentary group, asking deputies whether they were prepared to support him as presidential candidate. They were, and on 18 October Özal announced his decision to stand. He was not deterred by threats voiced by the SDPP that they would resign their seats. Özal called their bluff by saying that resignations would lead not to general elections but to by-elections, and if the SDPP boycotted them, there were plenty of other candidates prepared to stand. Unable to persuade even Ecevit not to field candidates from his own DLP, if by-elections were held, the SDPP contented themselves with joining Demirel's TPP in boycotting the elections in parliament. Nevertheless, Özal was not unopposed, since Fethi Çelikbaş, a veteran politician from the MP, made the quixotic gesture of standing against his leader.

In the first round of voting on 20 October, Özal received 247 votes against 18 for Çelikbaş; in the second, 256 against 17.[15] As no candidate had received the requisite two-thirds majority, a third ballot was held on 31 October and Özal was elected by an absolute majority of 263 votes against 14 votes cast for Çelikbaş.[16] Özal thus became the eighth president of the Turkish republic. His next assignment was to choose his successor both as prime minister and as leader of the MP, a post which he had had to vacate on his election as president of the republic, in accordance with the constitution.

THE NEW GOVERNMENT

As soon as the new president had been elected, the MP decided to hold an extraordinary convention on 17 November to elect its new leader. Normally the leader of the majority party is given the task of forming the government. However, Özal decided to reverse the process and preempt the convention. A former minister of education, Hasan Celal Güzel, whom Özal had excluded from his last government, immediately announced that he would seek both the prime ministership and the party leadership. Özal had other plans. On 9 November, as soon as he took over the presidency from Evren in a ceremony boycotted by the opposition, Özal appointed not only the prime minister, but the entire Cabinet. Speaker of parliament Akbulut was chosen as prime minister. The choice was unexpected, in view of Akbulut's background as a provincial lawyer. (He had a practice in his home town of Erzincan, where he headed the organization of Demirel's Justice Party before the 1980 coup. Akbulut first became deputy in 1983, had little knowledge of the outside world, and spoke no foreign languages.)

With no time for a reshuffle, all departmental ministers in the old cabinet retained their portfolios, but the number of ministers of state was increased to 15 (including deputy prime minister Bozer).[17] Among them were Özal's cousin Doğan and MP strongmen like Keçeciler and the former secretary-general of the party, Mustafa Taşar, both of whom entered the government for the first time. The program of the new government was rushed to parliament, and endorsed on 15 November by 278 votes to 95, the SDPP voting against, while the TPP absented itself. Then on 18 November, after intensive ministerial lobbying, Prime Minister Akbulut was elected to the leadership of the MP, by 739 votes against 382 cast for Güzel.[18]

The last important vacancy was filled on 21 November, when Kaya Erdem was elected speaker of parliament, again on the third ballot, by 270 votes to 94. Erdem had been an old associate of Özal and had served him as deputy prime minister, but the two fell out when Erdem resigned in the belief that Özal had not shielded him from accusations of involvement in a banking scandal. The press had attributed the accusations to Bülent Şem'iler, the young president of the public-sector Emlâk Bank (Real Estate Bank). Şem'iler then had to resign, but was immediately appointed by Özal as his chief banking adviser. Erdem's return to favor and the inclusion of faction leaders as ministers of state in the new government left Güzel as the focus of dissent within the MP. However, as the year ended, dissent had not come out into the open: 279 MP deputies voted solidly for the 1990 budget, which was approved on 27 December.[19] During the preceding months, only six deputies had resigned from the MP, which continued to enjoy a solid majority in parliament.

DISSENSION AMONG SOCIAL DEMOCRATS

After their victory in the local-government elections, the SDPP held a rule-book conference in Ankara on 4 June. The leadership, headed by party president İnönü and secretary-general Deniz Baykal, succeeded by 489 votes to 374 to make changes strengthening the national executive's powers.[20] However, the latter's right to suspend local organizations did not always produce the results intended. Thus, in the unruly Istanbul party organization, the local leftist SDPP leader Ercan Karakaş — who had been elected on 5 June 1988 and reelected on 10 July 1988 (after his first election had been disallowed), then removed from office by the national executive in November 1988 — was again reelected in August 1989, defeating the candidate supported by the party's secretary-general.[21]

However, it was the refusal of the leadership to accommodate Kurdish national sentiment which caused the most trouble. An SDPP deputy, İbrahim Aksoy, who had advocated Kurdish cultural rights in a speech at a meeting of the Turkey-EEC joint parliamentary commission in Strasbourg, was expelled from the party on 6 February.[22] This did not stop another seven SDPP deputies from flouting the wishes of the leadership by attending a conference on Kurdish national identity and human rights, opened by the French president's wife, Danielle Mitterrand, in Paris on 14 October.[23] Mme. Mitterrand had been to southeastern Turkey in April-May in order to visit the camps in which the Turkish authorities had given shelter to Kurdish insurgents from northern Iraq, and although she had been received courteously, her statement that Turkey had to recognize the existence of the Kurds caused controversy.[24] When the seven SDPP deputies returned home from Paris, they were expelled from the party.[25] The expulsions were followed by the resignation of several prominent members of the party's left wing. These included Abdullah Baştürk, who had led the Marxist labor confederation Disk (*Devrimci Isçi Sendikaları Konfederasyonu* — Confederation of Revolutionary Trade Unions), banned by the military in 1980; Prof. Aydın Güven Gürkan, who had led the Populist Party before its merger with the Social Democrats and subsequently became deputy leader of the SDPP; Cüneyt Canver, a vocal militant from Adana, and others. As a result, the SDPP, which had won 99 seats in parliament in the November 1987 elections, was reduced to 81 seats.[26] In the southeast, the party organization was gravely weakened by widespread resignations and suspensions. Plans by former Social Democrats to form a new left-wing party did not materialize by the end of the year. Within the SDPP criticism persisted, with secretary-general Baykal facing accusations of packing party organs with his own supporters, and Chairman İnönü accused of vacillation, particularly during the presidential election campaign. The leadership thereupon decided to call another party convention in January 1990, which resulted in a clear victory by Baykal.

A public-opinion survey toward the end of the year suggested that Demirel's center-right TPP had replaced the SDPP in first place and led voters' preferences. Demirel's unchallenged ascendance over his party prevented serious internal trouble, although there were two resignations from the parliamentary group. Throughout the year Demirel's preferred method of fighting the government was through public meetings, which attracted considerable crowds, but made no impression on government policies.

TERRORISM, KURDISH AND OTHER

The secessionist Kurdish Workers' Party (*Parti-ye Karkaran-e Kurdistan* — PKK) pursued its terror campaign in the southeast of the country, in particular in the mountainous area south of Lake Van. The campaign cost some 250 lives during the year,[27] with the worst incident occurring on 24 November, when a PKK band coming from Iraq murdered 28 people, including 13 children, in the frontier village of İkiyaka.[28] Two gendarmerie commanders in charge of antiterrorist operations, Generals Hulusi Sayın and İsmail Selen, retired in quick succession, as security forces mounted a number of operations, the largest of which took place in July and August in and around Mount Cudi. Some villages were forcibly evacuated and a few suspected terrorist sympathizers were exiled from the region. There were several incidents in which the Army was accused of brutality: in January it was claimed that an army officer had forced Kurds in Yeşilyurt village (Cizre District, Mardin Province, near the Syrian frontier) to eat human excrement;[29] in July there were reports that seven persons killed by the Army in Hakkâri Province were not terrorists, but innocent villagers;[30] in September, a similar claim with regard to seven local people killed by the Army led to the stoning of the district officer's (*kaymakam*) house at Silopi (on the Syrian frontier).[31] There were also arrests of alleged PKK members outside the southeast, with the authorities claiming that they had foiled PKK attempts to move their campaign to the main cities.[32]

Outside the southeast, the worst incident occurred in August in Gümüşhane Province (northern Anatolia) when seven gendarmes and one civilian were killed in an attack attributed to Tikko[33] (*Türkiye Isçi Köylü Kurtuluş Ordusu* — Turkish Worker-Peasant Liberation Army, said to be the military wing of TKP/ML — Turkish Communist Party/Marxist-Leninist),[34] a terrorist organization active among the (Zaza) Kurds in the mountainous province of Tunceli.

THE ISSUE OF RELIGION

The long-standing feud between secularists and Islamists focused on the attempts by the latter to remove the ban on women students wearing headscarves on university premises. A law allowing them to do so was referred to the Constitutional Court by President Evren on 4 January[35] and annulled on 7 March as a violation of the secular character of the state.[36] The grounds for annulment, published on 5 July, stated: "The way of life which is contrary to Atatürk's principles and reforms and which a section of the public, inspired by certain religious beliefs, has been trying to implement for many years, is symbolized in dress, and brings about the creation of separate camps in society." The Constitutional Court concluded unambiguously: "The republic and democracy are the antithesis of the regime of the Shari'a."[37]

The annulment was followed by widespread demonstrations of protest and by tension between Turkey and Iran, which attacked Turkish secularists (both in broadcasts and in debates in the Majlis). Before the annulled law had been passed in November 1988, the Council of Higher Education (*Yüksek Öğretim Kurumu* — Yök) had sought to lift the ban on headscarves by a change in university regulations. Although this was challenged by the highest administrative tribunal (*Danıştay* — Council of State), Yök tried again on 28 December, when it left universities free to interpret the term "civilized attire," which the regulations prescribe for students and staff.[38] According to first reports, seven universities then decided to keep the ban. An attempt to set up a private university in Istanbul, which would have an Islamic character, was blocked by Yök.

Repercussions of the Salman Rushdie affair (see chapter on Islamic affairs) were limited in Turkey. There were small-scale demonstrations outside mosques, but the view of the Turkish official religious establishment, expressed by President of Religious Affairs (*Diyanet İşleri Başkanı*), Prof. Mustafa Said Yazıcıoğlu was that according to Islamic precepts a penalty (*scil*) against Rushdie could only be handed out by competent courts after the defendant had been heard.[39] On another occasion, Yazıcıoğlu said that Rushdie's *Satanic Verses* should not be published in Turkey: its publication could do no harm to Islam, but could provoke the public. The prime minister's younger brother, Yusuf Bozkurt Özal, who was at the time minister of state, was more matter of fact. "Increased tension between the Muslim world and the West will secure foreign-trade advantages to Turkey," he said. "The Salman Rushdie affair is God's gift to us. It broke out just as we were developing our exports. Get ready (to sell)!"[40]

Both the annulment of the law permitting headscarves and the Salman Rushdie affair figured in speeches made by candidates put up by the WP in the local-government elections. Soon afterward, Ibrahim Çelik who was elected mayor of Şanlıurfa (formerly known simply as Urfa) on the WP ticket, was detained for 14 days, following reports that he had declared that he was not a follower of the republic's founder Mustafa Kemal Atatürk. He was released without trial, the prosecutor of the State Security Court announcing that Çelik had accepted Kemalism.[41]

The armed forces continued to stand firm on the principle of secularism. On 8 April, the Chief of General Staff Gen. Necip Torumtay announced that 95 cadets had been expelled for "reactionary activities."[42] On 20 May, it was reported that 28 gendarmerie privates had been detained for deserting their duties after their NCO had refused to excuse them from morning drill during the Ramadan.[43]

HUMAN RIGHTS

The scene was set at the beginning of the year, when Foreign Minister Mesut Yılmaz declared: "I agree that we must make further efforts in this field [of human rights]."[44] However, a few days later his under secretary, Nüzhet Kandemir, told Western ambassadors that the human rights issue had been exploited to ensure Turkey's exclusion from the process of political and economic integration in Europe.[45]

On 18 February, the Turkish Ministry of Foreign Affairs replied to an Amnesty

International (AI) report which claimed that there had been 239 deaths from torture in Turkey. The ministry said that 146 cases had been investigated. Of these, 10 persons listed by AI as dead were still alive, 34 had committed suicide, 42 had died from natural causes, 22 had been shot while trying to escape, one was killed by other prisoners, and three had died in hunger strikes. There were 32 suspected deaths from torture, leading to sentences on 14 officials, and four acquittals for lack of evidence; 12 trials were still in progress, and two cases were under preliminary investigation.[46] On 1 June it was reported that five policemen had each been sentenced to four years and five months in prison for causing the death of a prisoner.[47]

In April, a bill was tabled in parliament for the commutation of 235 death sentences (which included those passed on 121 left-wing and 20 right-wing terrorists and on four Palestinians who had attacked the Egyptian Embassy in Ankara).[48] While the use of the death penalty thus remained suspended, a government bill published in September retained the death penalty but reduced its scope and provided that all death sentences awaiting ratification would be commuted, but that in the future, death sentences not ratified within two years would be executed.[49] However, parliament had not passed the bill by the end of the year.

On 4 August, it was reported that two members of the PKK terrorist organization (one under sentence of death and the other still on trial) had died from the effects of a hunger strike on being transferred from Eskişehir to Aydın prison.[50] On 9 August, there were said to be 877 hunger strikers in 12 prisons. They were protesting against the tightening of prison regulations on 1 August 1988, following the escape of several prisoners. The hunger strike in Aydın ended on 19 August after 51 days, when Minister of Justice Oltan Sungurlu promised a more humane prison regime.[51] The revised regulations (published in the *Official Gazette* only on 6 January 1990) provided for the prisoners' right to confidential access to their lawyers; prohibited cruel, inhuman, and group punishment; and outlined a complaints procedure.[52]

In September, it was announced that Turkey would recognize the jurisdiction of the European Court of Human Rights. The required written declaration, which was deposited with the Council of Europe on 26 December, stated that the jurisdiction of the court would be recognized for three years, that it would be limited to cases examined by the European Commission of Human Rights under the restricted recognition given to it by the Turkish Government in 1987, and that it could not be applied to cases *sub judice* before the declaration was made.[53] This would seem to exclude a reference to Strasbourg of the protracted case against Nabi Yağcı (alias Haydar Kutlu) and Nihat Sargın, the leaders of the still illegal Turkish United Communist Party (*Türkiye Birleşik Komünist Partisi*), who have been in prison since their return to Turkey on 16 November 1988. Nevertheless, the communists held a press conference on 15 December to declare their intention to operate openly, to end their clandestine work, and to accept a pluralist democracy. They then held open meetings in several cities. The authorities reacted patchily, taking no action in some cases, while detaining commmunist organizers in others.[54]

On 12 July, it was reported that the Ministry of Culture had banned a cassette of songs in Kurdish on the basis of Law 2033 in force since 21 October 1983, which bans "the expression, dissemination, and publication of thought in any language which is not the first official language of states recognized by the Turkish state."[55]

STAGFLATION IN THE ECONOMY

The year 1988 had witnessed a succession of measures to reduce overheating in the economy. They included increases in taxation and in the prices of goods and services produced by the public sector, and (in October 1988) the decontrol of bank interest rates, except on official deposits (see *MECS* 1988, pp. 763–64). As a result, banks raised the interest which they paid on one-year deposits by some 20 points to 85% p.a. The measures had the twin effect of raising the CPI and of reducing economic activity much faster than had been expected. By the end of 1988, the CPI had risen by 75.4% (nearly double the figure for the previous year), while the value of real wages fell by 8.7%. The growth of the gross national product (GNP) was revised downward twice, and finally worked out at 3.4% (as against 7.4% in 1987). Public-sector fixed investments fell by 14.1% (and total investments by 1.6%, against a rise of 5.5% in 1987).[56]

However, the government did succeed in improving the external current account. In view of lower domestic demand, imports increased by only 2.6% (27.5% in 1987), while exports rose by 1.4% (36.7% in 1987). Helped also by strong growth in tourist revenue, Turkey had ended 1988 with a current-account surplus of $1,503m. (against a deficit of $982m. in 1987).[57]

The economic slowdown continued into 1989. According to a survey by the Istanbul Chamber of Industry, manufacturing production fell in the first quarter, stagnated in the second, and started to rise in the third. According to the third revised estimate of the State Institute of Statistics (SIS), industry grew by 4.2% overall (against 2.05% in 1988). But this increase was wiped out by a sharp fall of 10.8% in agricultural production, which was badly hit by drought (in 1988 agricultural production had increased by 7.03%). Consequently, according to the SIS's third estimate, the GNP growth rate fell to 1.7%, well below the rate of population increase, which was estimated at 2.5%.[58]

In the meantime, prices continued to rise strongly. True, the rise in the CPI decelerated from 82.7% in the last quarter of 1988 to 70.3% in the first quarter and 64.4% in the second quarter,[59] but then rose again to 73.0% in the third quarter, before falling once again to produce an end-year figure of 69.6%.[60] (The formula for calculating both the CPI and the wholesale price index was changed in January 1990, and the new formula reduced the rise in the CPI between 1 February 1989 and 31 January 1990 to 63.0%.)[61]

Stagflation — stagnation in production and inflation in prices — was partly the result of a deliberate government policy seeking to stabilize the economy before resuming growth and partly of an explosion in wages, forced on the government by labor unrest and by its defeat in the March local-government elections (see above). Because of the multiplicity of allowances and benefits, exact wages were difficult to calculate, but according to a provisional estimate by the Organization for Economic Cooperation and Development (OECD), real wages in the private sector rose by 29.1%, and in the public sector by 21.0%.[62] Moreover, given that the larger wage increases were conceded from May onward, that many were governed by collective contracts running for two years, and that these contracts included elements of indexation for inflation during the second year, the effects of the increases would still be felt strongly in 1990. Nominal wage increases conceded in mid-1989 exceeded 100%

in most cases. There were also large rises in subsidies. Thus, the support price for wheat, the country's main crop, was increased by 95%.[63]

However, subsidies for exports were theoretically reduced, as were duties and taxes on imports. Direct subsidies for exports (disguised as "tax drawbacks") ended with contracts signed by the end of 1988 and ceased to be payable after the last deliveries had been made under these contracts in mid-1989. They were replaced by cheap credits provided by a new foreign trade bank (Türk Eximbank). While some minor subsidies (toward energy costs, those provided by the Price Support and Stabilization Fund, etc.) remained, the degree of protection afforded to exporters and to home manufacturers decreased. The exact amount of the decrease was difficult to determine, because of the proliferation of levies on imports. Even so, the economy succeeded in withstanding such measures as were taken to liberalize foreign trade. Exports increased marginally, to $11.627bn., against $11.662bn. in 1988, and imports rose more strongly from $14.335bn. to $15.763bn. during the 11 months.[64] Thanks to a slight growth in tourist revenue (where a fall had been expected) and a considerable rise in the remittances of Turkish workers abroad, the year ended with a surplus in the external current account for the third time in succession ($966m. as against $1.59bn. in 1988).

The capital account also moved into surplus — of $775m. as against a deficit of $958m. in 1988. Here the main item was direct foreign investment, which reached $442m. for the first 10 months of 1989,[65] a record figure for Turkey, although small in comparison with the foreign investment attracted by Portugal, let alone Spain.

The restriction of domestic demand, which ensured a healthy balance of payments, coupled with signs that the recession was bottoming out, steadied the Turkish lira (TL). During the year, the TL lost only 27.3% against the US dollar,[66] while domestic consumer prices rose by nearly 70%. The fact that the consequent considerable appreciation of the lira in real terms did not do more damage to exports was a tribute to the endeavors of Turkish exporters. However, the cumulative effects of the appreciation, which continued into the new year, remained to be seen. Clearly, a further rise in domestic prices unmatched by devaluation will discourage exports, encourage imports, and discourage both tourism and remittances by emigrant workers.

Money supply doubled during the year, from TL22.4 trillion on 25 November 1988 to TL44.2 trillion on 24 November 1989,[67] thus exceeding the rate of inflation. Money rates fell approximately from 85% to 65% on one-year deposits. The foreign debt was slightly reduced according to the old criteria although a recalculation according to World Bank rules showed an increase to $41.021bn. by the end of the year.[68] Domestic public debt also increased, from $36,444m. in September 1988 to to $36,303m. in September 1989, while domestic public debt increased, from TL18.6 trillion in November 1988 to TL34.4 trillion in November 1989.[69] Share prices on the young Istanbul Stock Exchange (ISE) increased almost sevenfold, the index reaching 2218 at the end of the year (1986: 100).[70] However, the number of securities quoted remained small and the market was dominated by the public sector. It seems that the ISE served more for speculation than for raising equity capital for the private sector.

There were early indications that fixed investments continued at a low level, with a squeeze on public investments, and private investments sluggish in the first half, but picking up in the second half of the year. However, progress continued to be made on the vast Southeast Anatolia Development Project (*Güneydoğu Anadolu Projesi* —

GAP), and in particular on the construction of its two main constituents, the Atatürk dam on the Euphrates and the Urfa tunnel which will draw water from the dam lake to irrigate the Harran plain, between the city of Şanlıurfa and the Syrian frontier. As the year ended, Turkey was preparing to begin impounding water in the dam, which was reported 80% completed.[71] May 1991 remained the target date for the operation of the first of the eight 300MW turbines. The Urfa tunnel was reported to be 80% excavated and 45% concreted, and the target date for completion was also 1991. Progress was made with another major project: the motorway that bypasses Istanbul and feeds traffic into the second Bosphorus bridge (the Fatih Bridge), which was completed in 1988.

FOREIGN AFFAIRS

During the long years of the decline of the Ottoman Empire, Turkish statesmen had been preoccupied with the question "How can our state be saved?" After the successful conclusion of the War of Independence, the question became "How can our republic be defended in the territories which it has won?" Then, as the perception of external threat faded, thanks largely to membership in Nato, a gradual change set in and the question "How can our country develop to West European levels?" assumed primacy. Turgut Özal's answer to this question has been "Through integration with the world free-market system." As a result, ever since his accession to power as prime minister in 1983, Turkish foreign policy has been giving increasing importance to economic objectives. Turkey has sought to give economic substance to friendly political relations and to resolve political differences by promoting trading links.

In relations with OECD countries this has led to efforts to increase trade with and attract investments from the US and Japan, while seeking an organic relationship with Europe through full membership in the EEC. Economic cooperation was also to be the key to improved relations with the USSR, to closer relations with Muslim countries, and to the resolution of political problems with Turkey's smaller neighbors: Greece, Bulgaria, Syria, and Iran. In 1989, this approach to foreign policy produced limited results.

SETBACK ON THE ROAD TO THE EUROPEAN ECONOMIC COMMUNITY

When Özal attended the Nato Council meeting in Brussels at the end of May, he discussed the Turkish application for full membership in the EEC with President François Mitterrand and with Prime Minister Felipe González of Spain, the country which held the community chairmanship at the time. They both refused to commit themselves or to anticipate the report which the EEC Commission was drawing up for submission to the council. As news from Brussels indicated that Turkey's original request for immediate negotiations on full membership would not be met, the Turkish Government reduced its expectations and asked that the community should at least indicate on what date, after the completion of the single market at the end of 1992, it was prepared to initiate discussions on full membership. An even lesser expectation was that the community should commit itself to the principle of negotiating full membership, without specifying a date.

These Turkish hopes were disappointed when the commission presented its report to the council of foreign ministers of the community on 18 December.[72] The commission recommended that there should be no negotiations on the admission of any new members before 1993 at the earliest. In the case of Turkey, it listed both economic and political obstacles to membership: the disparity in levels of development between Turkey and the community's southern members — Greece, Portugal, and Spain — let alone the community as a whole; shortcomings in the practice of democracy, such as the treatment of minorities (which, as Commissioner Abel Matutes, who presented the report, explained, included the Kurds);[73] difficulties in Turkey's relations with a member country (Greece); and the unsolved problem of Cyprus. However, the commission acknowledged that Turkey was eligible for membership and recommended a number of measures to strengthen Turkey's links with the community in the framework of the existing Treaty of Association (the Treaty of Ankara of 1963). Chief among them was the completion in 1995 of the customs union between Turkey and the EEC, as provided in the treaty.

Responding to the report, the Turkish Foreign Ministry and Özal, who had in the meantime become president, regretted the absence of commitment to either a date or even the principle of membership negotiations, and the references to minorities and to problems with Greece and Cyprus. But they welcomed the acknowledgment of Turkey's eligibility and indicated that they would go along with the recommendation that concrete steps be taken to strengthen Turkey's links with Europe.[74] At the same time, Turkey continued its efforts to persuade the council of the community to commit itself to membership negotiations. These efforts failed when the council discussed the report in Brussels on 5 February 1990, endorsed its main recommendations, and asked the commission to work out specific measures for closer relations with Turkey.[75]

In the meantime, integration with Europe suffered a setback in June when the UK imposed visas on Turkish visitors. The immediate cause of the British decision was the arrival of several thousand Turkish citizens, who sought political asylum as Kurdish refugees. Ireland followed the British example. In both cases, Turkey retaliated by demanding from British and Irish visitors entry-point visas (granted on payment of £5).

DIFFICULTIES WITH GREECE
Political instability in Greece, where two general elections were held in the course of the year, precluded any initiative to improve Greek-Turkish relations, while putting a premium on nationalist gestures. In particular, Greek elections brought out the uneasy condition of the Muslim minority in Greek western Thrace. The number of Muslims in Greece (mainly in western Thrace, but with a handful in the Dodecanese Islands) was estimated at 120,000. Most of them were Turkish-speaking and had received some education in Turkish, but the Greek authorities refused to acknowledge them as Turks, insisting on the description of "Muslims of Hellenic nationality," which was used in the treaty of Lausanne (1923). In 1923, the Turks of western Thrace and the Greeks of Istanbul were both excluded from the Greek-Turkish exchange of population. They were given similar minority rights and their numbers were of the same order. However, since then the Greek minority in Istanbul had all but disappeared, while the number of Turks in Greece remained roughly stable, departures being made up by a high birthrate. Greeks, who were, in any case, worried that the natural increase of the Turkish community was exceeding emigration, felt that they would be only reciprocating Turkish attitudes if they squeezed out their Turks. The

emigration of ethnic Greeks from the USSR, which was expected to speed up, created an opportunity to increase the number of Greeks in western Thrace and, in particular, to settle the homecomers on Turkish-owned land. Defensive feelings among Greeks had been growing since the landing of Turkish troops in Cyprus in 1974 in order to protect the island's Turkish minority. This fed Greek fears that a similar intervention in western Thrace might not be inconceivable. At the same time, the vogue for human rights did not fail to inspire the Turkish minority in western Thrace. Where in the past, it had been content to work through the Greek political party system, it now became more self-assertive. This mood was expressed by independent candidates in Greek parliamentary elections, who unambiguously proclaimed themselves to be ethnic Turks and gave vigorous voice to the complaints of their kinsmen.

The human rights campaign among the Turks in western Thrace was led by Dr. Sadık Ahmed. He had been put on trial in 1988 for securing the signatures of 20,000 ethnic Turks to a petition complaining of oppression by the Greek Government. Ahmed was sentenced to 30 months in prison, and a companion to 15 months, subject to appeal.[76] On 1 February, it was reported that Greece had refused to accept a Turkish note protesting the sequestration of Turkish land in western Thrace.[77] Tension in the community increased when 6,000 dönüms (6m. sq. meters) of land were expropriated.[78] However, after meeting his Greek opposite number in Vienna at the beginning of March, Turkish Foreign Minister Mesut Yılmaz announced that he had been assured that pressure on the Turkish minority would cease.[79] A Greek note complaining that the Turkish public-service broadcasting organization TRT had supported independent Turkish candidates and had thus interfered in Greek internal affairs was rejected by the Turkish ambassador in Athens.[80]

Dr. Ahmed was elected as an independent deputy, but when he put his name forward again for the November elections, his candidacy was invalidated on a technicality. Ahmed and another independent candidate (Ibrahim Şerif) then tried to stand for the elections scheduled for April 1990. In January 1990, they were both put on trial, sentenced to imprisonment, and this time kept in prison pending an appeal.[81] Their trial was followed by a riot in the town of Komotini (Gümülcine), during which Turkish property was damaged and Turks injured.[82] The Turkish consul general in Komotini was expelled for referring to the Turkish minority as "kinsmen," and Turkey retaliated by expelling the Greek consul general in Istanbul.

Greek-Turkish friction obstructed the work of the Conference on Security and Cooperation in Europe (CSCE) in Vienna in January 1989, when Greece insisted that the Turkish port of Mersin (lying opposite Cyprus and serving as a supply base for the Turkish troops on the island) should be included in the area where force reduction would apply. A compromise, under which the line delimiting the area was left undefined from a point just north of Mersin to the Mediterranean, saved the conference, but did not prevent the continuation of the argument during the rest of the year.[83]

A technical dispute, which caused great excitement in Greece in January, concerned the publication of a Turkish decree under which Turkey promised to undertake search and rescue operations in the eastern part of the Aegean Sea (Greece claiming that it was responsible for this service in the whole of the Aegean). An assurance by Özal that the decree would be frozen calmed the storm.[84] The disagreement about airspace (Greece claiming 10 miles beyond its shores and Turkey recognizing only six) rumbled on. On 27 February, Turkey refused to accept a note by the Greek ambassador alleging violation of Greek airspace by Turkish military aircraft.[85]

On several occasions, Özal expressed the hope that Greek-Turkish disputes would not be allowed to escalate. Greek and Turkish ministers met regularly on the sidelines of international gatherings, but Özal's visit to Athens in 1988, made in the framework of the Davos process (see *MECS* 1988, pp. 764–66), was not returned either by Greek Prime Minister Papandreou or by his successors. Nor was any progress made in listing disagreements between the two countries, prior to their step-by-step solution, as envisaged in Davos in January 1988.

Cyprus was mentioned whenever Greek and Turkish ministers met, but officially Turkey remained on the sidelines, insisting that the solution of the problem be sought in intercommunal talks. The Turkish-Cypriot leader, Rauf Denktaş, continued to visit Turkey, where he was received as the president of the Turkish Republic of Northern Cyprus and was given assurances of support. Attempts by the Greek-Cypriot president of Cyprus, George Vassiliou, to arrange a meeting with Özal, prompted the latter to suggest that both Cypriot leaders as well as the prime ministers of Greece and Turkey should meet.[86] This suggestion, which put Vassiliou on an equal footing with Denktaş, was not acceptable to the Greeks. The Turkish Foreign Ministry spokesman periodically issued statements supporting the Turkish-Cypriot position: on the course of the talks; on their interruption in July after Greek-Cypriot women had forced their way across the green line; on the purchase of French weapons by Greek-Cypriots, etc.

TURKISH EXODUS FROM BULGARIA

Turkey had been giving vigorous expression to its concern at the oppression of Bulgaria's Turkish minority ever since 1985, when the Zhivkov regime introduced its policy of forcible assimilation (through the change of all Muslim names, a prohibition on the use of Turkish and on Muslim customs and ceremonies, and similar measures). However, Turkey had been spared any concrete burdens, since the Bulgarian authorities did not allow any ethnic Turks to leave the country and Turkish assurances that Turkish refugees would be welcomed in Turkey could not, therefore, be tested. With the exception of a few well-publicized escapes (such as the defection of the weight lifter Naim Süleymanoğlu, who subsequently won an Olympic gold medal for Turkey), the problem remained frozen until May 1989. Encouraged by the spirit of *glasnost,* Bulgarian Turks then held a number of demonstrations on the eve of the CSCE meeting in Paris, on 30 May, and demanded an end to the policy of forcible assimilation.[87] The Bulgarian authorities brutally suppressed the demonstrations with several Turks killed (estimates ranged from eight to 50). At the same time, the Bulgarian Government, in a clear reversal of policy, began expelling the presumed ringleaders of the protest movement. They did not wait for them to obtain Turkish visas and forced them to travel on trains and aircraft going to Belgrade, Budapest, and Vienna. All of them were admitted to Turkey a few days later. Recognizing implicitly the failure of their policy of assimilation, the Bulgarian Communist authorities staged demonstrations outside the Turkish Embassy in Sofia and demanded that Turkey should open its frontier to recalcitrant ethnic Turks. The Turkish Government responded by suspending visa requirements on 30 May.

The scale and speed of the resulting exodus took both governments by surprise. At first Özal declared that Turkey was willing to welcome all those of its kinsmen in

Bulgaria who wished to come. Reception camps were established near the Bulgarian frontier, from which those refugees who had no relatives in Turkey were moved to schools and other public buildings. At the same time, the Turkish Government used every diplomatic opportunity to demand that the Bulgarian Government treat its Turkish minority in accordance with the principles of the Helsinki Final Act, and should negotiate a migration agreement with Turkey to cover those ethnic Turks who wished to seek refuge in Turkey. The help of the Soviet Government was enlisted in order to put pressure on the Zhivkov regime. But neither the shuttle diplomacy of the Soviet ambassador in Ankara, Albert Chernishev, nor Turkish denunciations at international gatherings produced any effect on the Bulgarian attitude. Inside Turkey, angry protest meetings were not matched by any noticeable public willingness to make sacrifices for the refugees. The government had to take action before classes reopened, forcing the refugees out of their temporary encampment in schools and colleges, and before autumn rains made their camps uninhabitable. On 22 August, as the number of refugees exceeded the 310,000 mark and with no evidence of any slowdown in the exodus, the Turkish Government reimposed visas on Bulgarian passport holders. By the end of the year some 15,000 visas were issued, first to members of split families. But by that time the movement back had begun. At first, only a limited number of refugees, who found themselves without home or work, swallowed their pride and returned home. But the movement back gathered momentum, particularly after Zhivkov had been deposed in Bulgaria. By the end of the year, some 100,000 refugees had returned to Bulgaria, in spite of a Bulgarian nationalist backlash after Zhivkov's successors had promised to put an end to the policy of forced assimilation.

In the meantime, Kuwaiti mediation had led to a resumption of contacts between Turkey and Bulgaria. A first meeting between Foreign Minister Yılmaz and Bulgarian Deputy Prime Minister Georgi Yordanov in Kuwait on 30 October produced little beyond an agreement to meet again in December.[88] The fall of Zhivkov led to the postponement of the meeting to 9 January, when Yılmaz met the new Bulgarian foreign minister, Boiko Dimitrov, again in Kuwait. There was no formal agreement, but a similarity of approach was noted.[89] Turkey agreed to wait until relevant resolutions by the Bulgarian parliament and Communist Party congress had taken effect, in the hope that arrangements to regulate migration could be put in place in the spring of 1990.

RELATIONS WITH THE SUPERPOWERS

The Chernishev mission was a pointer to the improvement of Turkish relations with the USSR, which was underpinned by the growth of trade. In the first 10 months of 1989, Turkish exports to the USSR grew by 110% to $442m., while imports increased more slowly, by 20%, to $425m.[90] True, Turkish-Soviet trade still represented only 4% of Turkey's total foreign trade. But rapid growth was forecast in step with the conversion of Ankara and Istanbul to Soviet natural gas, and as a result of an agreement to build a second gas pipeline from the Caucasus. (The first pipeline enters Turkey from the west after crossing Bulgaria.)

There was also growth in the much more considerable trade exchanges with the US, which represented 11.5% of Turkey's foreign trade: exports grew by 38% to $735m., and imports by 43% to $1,753m. American military aid continued and US firms won contracts in the framework of the Turkish armed forces modernization program (notably for armored personnel carriers and for electronics for the F-16s manufactured under license in Turkey). However, political relations were soured by controversy over the resolution introduced by Senator Robert Dole, the Republican minority leader, to commemorate the 50th anniversary of the deportation of Armenians from eastern Turkey. The Turkish Government had hoped to rebut charges that there had been an Armenian genocide by announcing on 2 January that Ottoman archives on the Armenians would be opened to all scholars.[91] In protest at the perceived failure of the Bush Administration to throw its weight against the Dole resolution, the Turkish authorities stopped courtesy visits by US warships, US training flights over the Konya plain, and the modernization of US installations in Turkey.[92]

In Nato meetings, Turkey went along with the majority view that caution was needed in responding to changes in Eastern Europe. As the deadlock with Greece persisted, the two countries continued to veto each other's country chapters (which spell out their respective contributions to the alliance) and Nato infrastructure projects, with Greece still refusing to take part in Nato maneuvers in the Aegean.

West Germany continued to provide modest military aid to Turkey, the only Nato country to do so apart from the US. It also remained Turkey's main trading partner, with a 16% share of Turkey's foreign trade in the first 10 months of 1989 (unchanged from 1988, although in absolute terms there was a 7% growth of imports from West Germany and a 2% increase in Turkey's exports to it).

RELATIONS WITH MUSLIM COUNTRIES
On the trade front, exports to Muslim countries dropped by 19%,[93] largely due to Turkey's unwillingness to extend further credits to Iraq, pending progress in settling the latter's debt to Turkey (for Iraq's foreign debt problem, see chapter on Iraq). Imports from Muslim countries remained virtually unchanged, the slight increase in oil prices being balanced by a slight decrease in Turkey's imports of crude as a result of the economic slowdown. Total imports from Muslim countries at $2,920m., were marginally in excess of Turkish exports at $2,871m. In regional cooperation projects, there was no progress on Turkey's offer to build a water pipeline (the so-called "peaceline") to the Arabian Peninsula. There was agreement in principle to link Turkey's electricity grid with those of Syria and Iraq,[94] a project which, by the end of the year, was still at the feasibility-report stage.

In political relations, there were problems with Syria and Iran. Relations with Iran were strained when the Fatwa condemning Salman Rushdie to death was posted outside Iran's consulate in Istanbul. Worse was to follow in March, when the Iranian Majlis demanded that relations with Turkey be reviewed as a result of the Turkish Constitutional Court's decision to maintain the ban on headscarves for women university students (see above). The Turkish ambassador was recalled from Tehran, and Iranian Ambassador Manuchehr Mottaki (who had been warned repeatedly that his staff had infringed diplomatic privileges by misusing the diplomatic bag, not to mention the attempted abduction of an Iranian dissident in the boot of a car) was ordered out of Turkey.[95] In June, there were attacks on the Turkish Embassy in Tehran and on Turkish journalists attending Khomeyni's funeral, as the Iranian regime condemned Turkish press coverage of the event.[96] However, there was an improvement at the end of the year, symbolized by the decision of the new Iranian ambassador, Muhammad-Reza Bagheri, to pay his respects to the mausoleum of Atatürk, the founder of the secular Turkish republic. This contrasted with the previous refusal of members of the Iranian Islamic regime to set foot in the place.

Relations with Syria deteriorated sharply on 21 October, when Syrian MiGs shot down a Turkish land-survey aircraft over the Turkish province of Hatay (which as the *sanjak* of Alexandretta had been part of French-mandated Syria, and which the Syrians still claim) with the loss of five Turkish lives.[97] At the same time, Turkey made it known that Syria had broken the promises it had made during Özal's visit to Damascus in July 1987 (see *MECS* 1987, pp. 674–75), by allowing, or failing to prevent, the infiltration of Kurdish terrorists into Hatay. Turkey decided to activate the mechanism of consultation agreed upon in 1987 and as a result, Syrian Deputy Foreign Minister Yusuf Shakur arrived in Ankara on 20 November.[98] The Syrian delegation accepted responsibility for the downing of the aircraft, but dragged its feet over compensation.

In November, Turkey gave notice to both Syria and Iraq that it would begin filling the Atatürk dam on the Euphrates and that all the water reaching the dam would be impounded for a month starting on 13 January.[99] At the same time, Turkey disclaimed any intention of using its control of the headwaters of the Euphrates and Tigris as a political weapon, and said that it would keep its promise to release to Syria an annual average flow of Euphrates water amounting to 500 cu. meters per second. This represents roughly half the flow in the river. Meanwhile, the Euphrates was hardly used for irrigation in Turkey, all the water being released after activating turbines in Turkish hydroelectric stations. However, the situation was to change when work was completed on the Urfa tunnel, which would draw water from the Atatürk dam lake to irrigate the Harran plain north of the Syrian border. The completion of the Urfa tunnel should follow the filling of the Atatürk dam. Disagreements between Turkey, on the one hand, and Syria and Iraq, on the other, were thus likely to persist.

NOTES

For the place and frequency of publications cited here, and for the full name of the publication, news agency, radio station, or monitoring service where an abbreviation is used, please see "List of Sources." Only in the case of more than one publication bearing the same name is the place of publication noted here.

1. *Haber Bülteni, Ankara, 30 March 1990.
2. OECD Economic Surveys, *Turkey,* Paris, January 1990, p. 67.
3. *Milliyet,* 21 March 1989.
4. Directorate General of Press and Information [DGPI], Prime Ministry, Republic of Turkey, *The Constitution of the Republic of Turkey,* Ankara, 1982, p. 118.
5. The final results of the local elections were published in *Resmi Gazete,* 28 May 1989.
6. Poll carried out in May by KONDA, results reported in *Milliyet,* 4 June 1989.
7. List of cabinet and biographies of ministers in *Newspot* (published by DGPI in Ankara), 6 April 1989.
8. *Milliyet,* 12 April 1989.
9. OECD, *Turkey,* p.25, Table 7.
10. *Milliyet,* 18 May 1989.
11. Ibid., 8 July 1989.
12. Ibid., 18 September 1989.
13. Ibid., 22 June 1989.

14. Ibid., 12 September 1989.
15. *Newspot,* 26 October 1989.
16. Result and Özal's biography in *Newspot,* 2 November 1989.
17. Cabinet list, biographies, and vote of confidence in *Newspot,* 16 November 1989.
18. Election of party leader and parliamentary speaker in *Newspot,* 23 November 1989.
19. Ibid., 4 January 1990.
20. *Milliyet,* 6 June 1989.
21. Ibid., 21 August 1989.
22. Ibid., 7 February 1989.
23. Ibid., 15 October 1989.
24. Ibid., 1 May 1989.
25. Ibid., 23 November 1989.
26. Turkish Press Review (compiled by DGPI), 20 December 1989.
27. *Turkey Briefing,* January 1990.
28. Turkish Press Review, 26 December 1989.
29. *Milliyet,* 28 January 1989.
30. Ibid., 28 July 1989.
31. Ibid., 19, 20 September 1989.
32. Ibid., 11 July 1989.
33. Ibid., 16 August 1989.
34. Ibid., 12 January 1989.
35. Turkish Press Review, 5 January 1989.
36. *Milliyet,* 8 March 1989.
37. Ibid., 6 July 1989.
38. *Turkey Briefing,* January 1990.
39. *Milliyet,* 10 March 1989.
40. Ibid., 2 March 1989.
41. Ibid., 30 April 1989.
42. Ibid., 9 April 1989.
43. Ibid., 21 May 1989.
44. Ibid., 3 January 1989.
45. Turkish Press Review, 17 January 1989.
46. *Milliyet,* 19 February 1989.
47. Ibid., 1 June 1989.
48. Ibid., 14 April 1989.
49. Turkish Press Review, 15 September 1989.
50. *Milliyet,* 4 August 1989.
51. Ibid., 20 August 1989.
52. *Turkey Briefing,* January 1990.
53. Ibid.
54. Ibid.
55. *Milliyet,* 12 July 1989.
56. OECD, *Turkey,* p.16, Table 3.
57. Ibid., p. 45, Table 14.
58. *Haber Bülteni,* 30 March 1990, p. 1.
59. OECD, *Turkey,* p.25, Table 7.
60. *Haber Bülteni,* 4 January 1990.
61. Ibid., 4 February 1990.
62. OECD, *Turkey,* p. 29, Table 8.
63. Ibid., p. 122.
64. *Haber Bülteni,* 16 March 1990.
65. *ANKA Review,* Ankara, 27 March 1990, p. 9.
66. *Milliyet,* 1 January 1990.
67. *ANKA Review,* 27 March 1990, p. 9.
68. *Turkey Confidential,* No. 8, April 1990, p. 15.
69. Ibid., p. 26, Tables 25 and 26.
70. *Milliyet,* 1 January 1990.

71. G. Tansey, "Impounding at Atatürk Risks Final Bottom Outlet," communication to *World Water,* January 1990.
72. Commission des Communautés Européennes, *Avis de la Commission sur la demande d'adhésion de la Turquie à la Communauté* (Commission document SEC (89) 2290 final), Brussels, 18 December 1989.
73. Unpublished minutes of press conference given by Commissioner Abel Matutes in Brussels on 18 December 1989.
74. *Newspot,* 21 December 1989.
75. Statement by Foreign Ministry spokesman in Ankara, reported in Turkish Press Review, 9 February 1990.
76. Turkish Press Review, 21 December 1988.
77. *Milliyet,* 1 February 1989.
78. Ibid., 3 March 1989.
79. Ibid., 8 March 1989.
80. Ibid., 7 June 1989.
81. Turkish Press Review, 29 January 1990.
82. Ibid., 30 January 1990.
83. *Milliyet,* 15 January 1989.
84. Ibid.
85. Ibid., 3 March 1989.
86. Ibid., 30 May 1989.
87. Details in Andrew Mango, "Turkish Exodus from Bulgaria" in *The World Today,* October 1989.
88. *Newspot,* 2 November 1989.
89. Ibid., 11 January 1990.
90. SIS, *October 1989: Summary of Monthly Foreign Trade,* pp. 4–5, Tables 2–3.
91. *Milliyet,* 3 January 1989.
92. The nature of the sanctions was never officially divulged. Their lifting was, however, announced by the Foreign Ministry; see Turkish Press Review, 2 March 1990.
93. *Haber Bülteni,* 16 March 1990, p. 8.
94. Turkish Press Review, 2 August 1989.
95. *Milliyet,* 3 April 1989.
96. Ibid., 9 June 1989.
97. *Newspot,* 26 October 1989.
98. Ibid., 23 November 1989.
99. Ibid., 21 December 1989.

United Arab Emirates
(Al-Imarat al-'Arabiyya al-Muttahida)

UZI RABI

Regional stability attracted unprecedented Arab and international business interest from which the United Arab Emirates (UAE), Abu Dhabi, and Dubai in particular, stood to benefit. As in the past, the UAE spared no efforts to express its Arab-nationalist policy, seeking to achieve a pan-Arab concensus on the region's most pressing issues. The UAE improved its status in the Arab world still further after having initiated several successful mediation attempts in recent years. It enlarged the scope of its international links by establishing diplomatic ties with East European countries. However, dissension among the emirates over the federal budget and oil production still inhibited the development of a federal outlook. Relations with the Organization of Petroleum Exporting Countries (Opec) reached an impasse when the UAE refused to step into line with other producers and reiterated its demand for what it considered an equitable quota of 1.5m. barrels per day (b/d).

INTERNAL AFFAIRS

POLITICAL CHANGES

Shaykh Hazza' Ibn Zayid Al Nuhayan was named deputy chief of the newly established state security organ.[1] The proximity of the UAE, and particularly Dubai, to Iran, made it a convenient site for anti-Iranian activity. The new post reflected a growing concern of being implicated in such activity. An embarrassment of that kind was felt in June when an Iranian dissident, a former colonel in the late shah's army, was shot dead in his Dubai hotel room, allegedly by Iranian agents.[2] The incident went unreported in the UAE media. In another change, the Federal Ministry of Justice was coupled with the Ministry of Islamic Affairs and Awqaf (religious endowments) to form the Ministry of Justice, Islamic Affairs, and Awqaf under Shaykh Muhammad al-Khazraji. This change, which implied greater religious involvement in legal matters, was a discouraging sign for the financial community, which was striving to extract repayments from debtors who sheltered behind Islamic law.[3]

UAE Minister of State for Supreme Council Affairs, Shaykh 'Abd al-'Aziz Ibn Humayd al-Qasimi resigned after 11 years in the post; it could not be confirmed whether or not he was replaced. UAE Deputy Prime Minister Shaykh Hamdan Ibn Muhammad Al Nuhayan died on 11 October, but the cause of death was not revealed, although he was known to be undergoing medical treatment in the US and West Germany.[4]

THE DEATH OF SHAYKH SHAKHBUT

Shaykh Shakhbut Ibn Sultan al-Nuhayan, the former ruler of Abu Dhabi and elder brother of Zayid, the present ruler, died aged 83 on the evening of 11 February in the town of al-'Ayn. The conservative shaykh had ruled Abu Dhabi for more than four decades, from 1922 to 8 August 1966. When oil revenues began to pour in in the early 1960s, Shaykh Shakhbut was reluctant to spend them fearing the old ways would be destroyed. As a result, he was deposed — with the help of British connivance — and Zayid took over, in one of the Middle East's few bloodless *coups d'état*. Shaykh Shakhbut went into exile for a few years, but later returned to live in al-'Ayn. Federal government departments and institutions throughout the UAE were closed for three days in mourning for the deceased.[5]

OIL AFFAIRS: THE POLICY OF OVERPRODUCTION

The UAE pursued its policy of adhering to Opec's production quotas, while reiterating its demand for what it considered an equitable quota of 1.5m. b/d. The UAE's chief argument for this policy was that it had borne more than its share of the burden by reducing output to underpin oil prices in the early 1980s and that now it wanted to compensate itself.[6] Moreover, Abu Dhabi, which was the federation's chief producer, could not afford to play the role of swing producer — i.e., to safeguard the Opec quota set for the entire UAE by cutting back its own — as long as Dubai continued to place pressure on the UAE quota by producing close to its maximum output capacity of 400,000 b/d.[7] Once again it was shown that the UAE's being composed of seven separate emirates tended to complicate its relations with multilateral organizations, since the two leading emirates — Abu Dhabi and Dubai — did not always adopt an identical stand in foreign policy or oil production.

Having no means to enforce its decisions on its member states, Opec vainly attempted to appease the UAE by raising its quota from 988,000 b/d for the first half of 1989, to 1,041,000 b/d for the third quarter and to 1,095,000 b/d for the fourth. The UAE, however, remained adamant; oil output in the year reviewed fluctuated at c. 2m. b/d, double its certified quota. By the end of the year, the UAE increased its quota demand to 1,900,000 b/d, thereby making it harder for Opec to make ends meet.[8] The UAE was pushed out of the Opec quota system, having alienated some Opec members, such as Saudi Arabia, which firmly rejected the UAE's quota demands. Against this backdrop of discord, the UAE was anxious to prove that its demands were justified. It claimed that its proven recoverable reserves had trebled from 31 bn. to 92 bn. barrels, a rise which seemed to owe more to political wishful thinking than to geology.[9] A similar note lay behind the federation's attempts to get its production capability on line as a recognized criterion for increased quotas. The UAE's more selfish, less pragmatic policy in oil matters was attributable to the change in the Abu Dhabi oil industry's decision-making apparatus, i.e., the establishment of the Supreme Petroleum Council in June 1988 (for details, see *MECS* 1988, pp. 461–63). According to a UAE official, the new body speeded up decision making and removed a considerable number of superfluous bureaucrats.[10] In the short term, however, the change had not achieved the aim of settling the differences between Abu Dhabi and Dubai, the federation's chief oil producers. (See also chapter on oil affairs.)

ECONOMIC AND SOCIAL AFFAIRS

Despite the impression created by its independent and often disruptive oil policies, the UAE's economy was more mixed than that of most of the members of the Gulf Cooperation Council (GCC): it relied on oil to provide 73% of its revenue compared with 90% for the GCC. Regional stability led to renewed business confidence and increasing trading opportunities from which the UAE — Abu Dhabi and Dubai in particular — stood to benefit. By nature, efforts were focused on diversifying the economy away from oil. Dubai, for instance, maximized the opportunity afforded by the Gulf War cease-fire. Close to Iran, Dubai became particularly attractive to foreign companies interested in Iran's impending reconstruction efforts. The Jabal 'Ali Free Zone in particular was well placed to benefit from the upturn in trade due to its stable atmosphere and the access to lucrative GCC markets. At the same time, however, due to political uncertainties in Iran, Dubai began shifting from Iran to extraregional trade partners, chiefly in the Far East; reexports to China increased significantly.[11] Small wonder that Dubai's non-oil trade rose by 22% during the first half of 1989, compared with the same period in the previous year.[12] The aluminum industry — which produced the UAE's most prominent non-oil export — underwent a $100m. expansion program, to increase profitability.[13] The UAE's garment exports to the US was secured following the conclusion of a three-year quota agreement, which allowed for a more flexible export quota than that imposed by the US in June 1988.[14] The clement economic climate also enabled the UAE to strengthen its position in the European downstream market. The Abu Dhabi-based International Petroleum Investment Company increased its holding in the Madrid-based Compañia Española de Petróles' refinery from 10% to 20%.[15]

As a winter holiday resort and a stopover *en route* to the Far East, Abu Dhabi and Dubai took a serious look at tourism. In light of the growing number of visitors, hotels had to be expanded and new holiday resorts erected. The UAE's seventh international airport was being built north of al-'Ayn.[16] The growing interest in the UAE, best reflected in the fact that in 1989 it was the fifth among Arab recipient countries of Arab investments, indicated that conditions were favorable for organizing a domestic capital market.[17] Undoubtedly, the opening of exchanges in Bahrain and Oman in 1989 had an effect; the first sign was the setting up of the UAE's first publicly quoted stocks index. Although dealing was still limited to UAE nationals, the new arrangement was seen as an alternative to the long-term goal of a full-fledged stock exchange.[18] However, the peacetime profits which replaced wartime horrors could not bale the UAE out of all its difficulties, chiefly the federal budget and the excessively high proportion of foreigners in its population.

In principle, the UAE's budget was provided by 50% of each constituent government's revenues. However, in fact only Abu Dhabi and Dubai, the federation's richest emirates, provided funds. Prominent among those who did not was Sharja, which in recent years did not contribute to the federal budget due to its dire financial straits. The severe reduction of revenue as a result of the worldwide oil glut made the problem of an effective federal budget all the more critical; the UAE had to contend with a steadily rising deficit in recent years, although the 1989 budget — agreed upon only in November due to disagreement over each emirate's contribution — foresaw a 1.1% reduction in the overall deficit, estimated at UAEDh1.81bn.[19] Many hopes were pinned on a rise in oil prices and in non-oil revenue, although neither seemed to offer grounds for optimism. The growth in non-oil revenues was too small; if the UAE continued to increase its revenue by constantly exceeding its quota, it risked retaliation from other GCC states, notably Saudi Arabia. In the 1990s, the federal government may have to seek other methods of raising revenue.

The UAE's demographic problem, too, became more acute. According to official figures, the UAE population, which in 1985 was 1.6m., of which 70% were expatriates, would grow to 2.2m., an increase of 36% by 1990.[20] These data showed that the UAE had one of the world's highest rates of population growth and was also one of the world's most foreign-labor dependent economies. These figures were a grave economic and social challenge to the government, the most prominent being growing unemployment. The drive to replace expatriates with nationals was stepped up; a five-year deadline for employing nationals in the federal government was decreed, regardless of the effect on the civil service.[21] The ousted expatriates were to be replaced by UAE nationals completing their education and training abroad or at home. Concerted efforts were made to create vocational schools as part of this effort.

THE ARMED FORCES

Defense spending was a major item in the UAE budget. Disagreements with France over the contract for arms and avionics for the *Mirage* 2000 fighter were finally resolved. The first shipment of the aircraft arrived in the UAE and appeared in the military parade marking the federation's 18th National Day in December;[22] the plane became the backbone of the UAE Air Force. In an effort to provide a mix of quality for a denser air defense network, a deal was concluded with Britain for 12 *Hawk* 100 trainer jets.[23] These developments showed clearly that the Air Force had become the cornerstone of the UAE's defense. Given the UAE's manpower shortage and its very long borders, the maintenance of large ground and naval forces was unrealistic. Speaking of the UAE's armed forces, Heir Apparent and Deputy Supreme Commander of the UAE Shaykh Khalifa Ibn Zayid Al Nuhayan said:

> The UAE always seeks peace and respects neighborhood and friendship. Its need for a capable army is a continuous goal not for a desire to invade or fight other states. The UAE wants to safeguard the national accomplishments of its people and take up its role along with other Arab armies out of its belief in the unity of destiny and goal.[24]

FOREIGN POLICY

REGIONAL AFFAIRS

The relief felt in the UAE following the Gulf War cease-fire was tinged with uncertainty because of the faltering peace negotiations between Iran and Iraq. The UAE repeatedly called on the UN to make every effort to bring about a new round of talks, in order to overcome the obstacles to regional peace.[25] UAE relations with both belligerents were generally close, but cautious. Like other GCC states, the UAE made it clear to Iran that relations had to be based on good intentions "so that this will be reciprocated."[26] The UAE tried to soothe some of Iran's harsh feelings toward some of the states within the GCC. Careful not to antagonize Iran, the UAE kept aloof from regional disputes involving Iran, such as the one with Saudi Arabia (for details, see chapter on Saudi Arabia). Likewise, it appealed to Iran's Islamic sentiments in an apparent attempt to prevent Tehran from feeling isolated; Zayid's offer to establish an Islamic common market should be viewed in this context.[27] Throughout the year, official visits were exchanged and new air routes established, but the UAE was firm in preempting Iranian activity which could prove dangerous to the region, as was evidenced in the interception of a cargo of mustard gas destined for Iran.[28] UAE-Iraqi relations were marked by the establishment of a direct air route between Abu Dhabi and Baghdad.[29] A UAE representative attended the reinauguration festivities of Faw, in October.

Looking at the other side of the peninsula, the UAE was gratified by the PDRY's gradual moderation. In May, the UAE opened its first embassy in Aden.[30] The initial indication of *rapprochement* came in March, when PDRY Foreign Minister Dr. 'Abd al-'Aziz al-Dali visited the UAE and discussed bilateral relations with his counterpart, Rashid 'Abdallah. Also in March, UAE sent relief to the PDRY to help it cope with the considerable flood damage.[31] (For details see chapter on the PDRY.)

THE UAE'S INTER-ARAB POLICIES

Having initiated several successful mediation attempts in recent years, the UAE stood a chance to play a more active role in defining an Arab consensus on the most pressing regional issues. The UAE took part in the six-member Arab committee entrusted with tackling the Lebanese crisis. Shaykh Zayid asserted that the UAE would do everything possible to "achieve a national consensus in Lebanon and preserve the country's integrity."[32] Talks to that effect were also held with Syria, which had a vested interest in Lebanon, during a visit by Syria Foreign Minister Faruq al-Shar' to the UAE in April.

The UAE reiterated its support for the Intifada, urging its escalation since "there is nothing more important to the Arabs and the Palestinians."[33] The UAE also preached solidarity to the Palestinians. "It is unacceptable that some Palestinians," Shaykh Zayid lamented, "make statements which others contradict."[34] For its part, the UAE maintained contacts with figures representative of the various PLO factions, such as George Habash of the Popular Front for the Liberation of Palestine and Na'if Hawatima of the Democratic Front for the Liberation of Palestine; PLO chairman Yasir 'Arafat visited the UAE many times throughout the war. The creation of the two Arab groupings — the Arab Cooperation Council (ACC) and the Arab Maghrib Union (AMU; for details, see chapter on inter-Arab relations) — was seen as offering an opportunity to lessen the polarization in the Arab world. The founding of these groups underlined that the GCC was beneficial not only to its member states, but also "represent[ed] a strength to the larger Arab body."[35] Zayid explained that "...understanding among three opinions [ACC, AMU, GCC] is better than understanding among 22." Accordingly, Arab states such as Syria were urged to join one of the newly established Arab groupings[36] and the UAE offered to unite the three groupings into one economic body, "The Arab Cooperation and Development Council."[37]

Nevertheless, the UAE was associated primarily with the moderates in the Arab world. It hailed Egypt's full-fledged return to the Arab League and was delighted at the return of Taba to Egyptian sovereignty, calling it "a triumph for all Arab states."[38] Both the UAE and Egypt coordinated their stands during Mubarak's two-day visit to the UAE in February. In a reciprocal visit by the UAE heir apparent in May, talks dealt with military cooperation, i.e., promotion of the activities of the Arab Organization for Industry (AOI) in which both countries had a common interest. Shaykh Khalifa also attended an air show featuring Egyptian-made aircraft.[39] The UAE also served as a test site for some of the AOI military products.[40] Ways to enhance bilateral security were discussed during the November visit to the UAE of Egyptian Interior Minister Maj. Gen. Zaki Badr.

The amicable UAE-Jordanian relations were given financial expression when the UAE, together with other GCC states, took part in a $300m. loan to help Jordan overcome its economic crisis.[41] As for the Maghrib, relations with Morocco and Algiers were generally close; Shaykh Zayid visited Morocco in November, when he conferred with King Hasan. UAE-Algerian relations were chiefly on economics; the UAE participated in setting up an aluminum smelter in Algiers.[42] However, UAE ties were not restricted to the moderates. The UAE expressed solidarity with Libya, following the clash in January between US and Libyan jets over the Mediterranean (see chapter on Libya). "We consider US threats against the Jamahiriyya [Libya] to be threats directed against the Arab nation," asserted Zayid in a written message to Qadhdhafi delivered by the UAE's minister of state for foreign affairs.[43] Libyan envoys came to the UAE twice bearing messages to Zayid.

THE INTERNATIONAL ARENA

Relations with Britain and France

Relations with Great Britain — perhaps the UAE's most important extraregional ally — were marked by official visits in both directions. Foreign Secretary Sir Geoffrey Howe came in January, while Minister of State at the Foreign Office William Waldegrave visited the UAE in May. Shaykh Zayid paid his first state visit to Britain, since taking over in 1966. In addition to discussing military cooperation and further arms sales (see above), the issue of peace in the Gulf and in other parts of the region was discussed at most of the meetings. Shaykh Zayid said that more than other European states, "Britain has a special responsibility in helping achieve peace in the region in view of its former links in the area."[44]

France's role as a major arms supplier to the UAE again came to the fore with the completion of the *Mirage* 2000 fighter jet deal (see above). Further discussions on the subject were held with Defense Minister Jean-Pierre Chevênement who visited the UAE in December, when he attended the 18th annual celebrations of the federation's independence.[45] The Lebanese crisis was also dealt with in view of France's special relations with the warring sides in Lebanon. The crisis was also probably among the topics discussed during President François Mitterrand's stopover in February in Dubai, while returning to France from India.

Relations with the People's Republic of China

The cementing of UAE-PRC relations reflected a Chinese eagerness for wider economic links in the wake of the Western economic boycott triggered by the Tiananmen Square protests. Several Chinese officials, such as Deputy Premier Tian Jiyun, negotiated for UAE loans and other forms of economic cooperation. Chinese plans for setting up a large chemical fertilizer plant in Dubai's Jafz were discussed.[46] A direct airlink between Abu Dhabi and Beijing was expected to boost tourism.[47]

Cultural cooperation was enhanced following the visit of Chinese Culture Minister Liu Deyou to the UAE in May.

Relations with Eastern Europe

UAE-USSR relations were hitherto limited chiefly to fact-finding missions and cultural activities, but in 1989 the two countries signed a memorandum of understanding in the fields of economy, trade, and investment — agreed upon in March during a visit to the UAE by a Soviet trade delegation — which was ratified during a visit to the USSR by UAE Minister of Economy and Trade Sayf al-Jarwan at the end of the year.[48] This agreement was the first between the two countries. Further signs of cooperation were seen in tourism, when the first group of Soviet tourists visited the UAE.[49] In March, a TASS correspondent was posted in Abu Dhabi. Nonetheless, the changed Soviet attitude toward the Israeli-Arab conflict in general and the Palestinian issue in particular did not go unnoticed by the UAE media which termed it a "retreat and unusual stand in Soviet relations with the central Arab cause."[50]

Moscow's *perestroika* opened the door to closer bilateral ties with other East European states: diplomatic relations were slated with Romania and Poland, while East Germany held its first industrial fair in the UAE.

NOTES

For the place and frequency of publications cited here, and for the full name of the publication, news agency, radio station, or monitoring service where an abbreviation is used, please see "List of Sources." Only in the case of more than one publication bearing the same name is the place of publication noted here.

1. *Al-Ittihad*, Abu Dhabi, 4, 7 June 1989.
2. *Al-Dustur*, London, 12 June; AFP, 10 June — DR, 16 June 1989.
3. *MEER*, April 1989.
4. GNA, 12 October — DR, 12 October; *The Gulf States*, 30 October 1989.
5. *The Gulf States*, 20 February; *CR:* UAE, No. 2, 1989.
6. See, e.g., Shaykh Khalifa's interview with *al-Ittihad*, Abu Dhabi, 17 January 1989.
7. *CR:* UAE, No. 4, 1989.
8. Ibid.
9. *MM*, 23 January 1989.
10. *The Gulf States*, 20 August 1989.
11. *Memo*, 13 February; *CR:* UAE, No. 4, 1989.
12. *The Gulf States*, 16 October 1989.
13. *CR:* UAE, No. 3, 1989.
14. Ibid., Nos. 1 and 2, 1989.
15. *Memo*, 13 February 1989.
16. Ibid., 2 June 1989.
17. *CR:* UAE, No. 4, 1989.
18. See, e.g., *The Gulf States*, 17 April; *ME*, October 1989.
19. *CR:* UAE, No. 4, 1989.
20. Ibid., *Country Profile*, 1989–90.
21. *ME*, April 1989.
22. Ibid., February 1990.
23. *CR:* UAE, *Country Profile*, 1989–90.
24. GNA, 28 March — DR, 29 March 1989.
25. GNA, 3 October — DR, 3 October 1989.

26. GNA, 17 July — DR, 18 July 1989.
27. *Memo,* 16 March 1989.
28. *JP,* 3 July 1989.
29. *Al-Bayan,* Dubai, 27 March 1989.
30. *The Gulf States,* 29 May; *CR:* PDRY, No. 2, 1989.
31. *Al-Bayan,* Dubai, 4 April 1989.
32. *Al-Dustur,* London, 17 April 1989.
33. Ibid.
34. *Al-Bayan,* Dubai, 5 December 1989.
35. GNA, 17 July — DR, 18 July 1989.
36. *Al-Hawadith,* 27 July; *al-Bayan,* Dubai, 5 December 1989.
37. *Al-Ra'y al-'Amm,* 16 April 1989.
38. GNA, 22 March — DR, 23 March 1989.
39. MENA, 15 May — DR, 15 May 1989.
40. *Al-Jumhuriyya,* Cairo, 11 January 1989.
41. *CR:* UAE, No. 4, 1989.
42. Ibid.
43. JANA, 18 January — DR, 19 January 1989.
44. GNA, 5 January — DR, 6 January 1989.
45. GNA, 1, 4 December — DR, 11 December 1989.
46. GNA, 16, 19 March — DR, 21 March; *Memo,* 21 April 1989.
47. GNA, 14 September — DR, 15 September 1989.
48. *Al-Bayan,* Dubai, 22 February 1989; GNA, 5 January — DR, 5 January 1990.
49. *ME,* March 1990.
50. *Al-Bayan,* Dubai, 3 November 1989.

North Yemen (YAR)
(Al-Jumhuriyya al-'Arabiyya al-Yamaniyya)

JACOB GOLDBERG

President 'Ali 'Abdallah Salih's success in stabilizing the political system in the Yemeni Arab Republic (YAR) was a remarkable achievement. His 12 years in power made him the most capable and long-lasting president in the YAR's history since the revolution of 1962. Salih accomplished this through policies of modernization, development, centralization, and a unique partnership between the military and the technocrats. The incorporation of diverse political and social groups into the political system through the 1988 elections (see *MECS* 1988, pp. 774–75) significantly broadened the basis of support for the regime and for Salih personally. At the same time, *détente* with the People's Democratic Republic of Yemen (PDRY), the relaxation in superpower rivalry, and the Soviet policy of *glasnost,* all created a regional atmosphere conducive to internal stability. All of these developments made 1989 the most peaceful year since Salih's accession to power in 1978.

The economic and financial scene reflected a mixture of positive developments and adverse processes. On the whole, however, the initial optimistic outlook caused by expected oil wealth was fundamentally tempered and replaced by a more realistic assessment of the country's economic future. On the negative side, there were growing budgetary and balance of payment deficits, increased foreign debt, and a decline in foreign aid. The positive developments included a constant, impressive growth in the gross domestic product (GDP), a first rise in remittances after a six-year decline, and higher oil prices which resulted in larger revenues. Underlying the government's approach toward the economy was a realization that oil wealth could not solve all of North Yemen's problems, and that the country would need more foreign aid and investments in order to create a solid infrastructure and achieve rapid development.

In foreign affairs, the YAR continued to proclaim the principle of "nonalignment" as governing its foreign policy. This was successfully translated in the global arena into "diversification of the sources of armaments and economic assistance" to include not only the US and the USSR, but also Western Europe and China. On the regional level, however, "nonalignment" and "Arab solidarity" were tested by the YAR's membership in a new Arab bloc — the Arab Cooperation Council (ACC). YAR leaders sought to dispel the notion of divisiveness inherent in membership in any Arab grouping by emphasizing the pan-Arab character of the ACC, its mainly economic significance, the absence of any military-political aspects, and its being open for other Arab states to join. They also intensified their mediation efforts in inter-Arab rivalries (mainly the Egyptian-Libyan dispute), and voiced public support of widely agreed, mainstream Arab causes, such as the Palestinian Intifada.

Topping the list of foreign affair priorities, however, were the unity talks with the

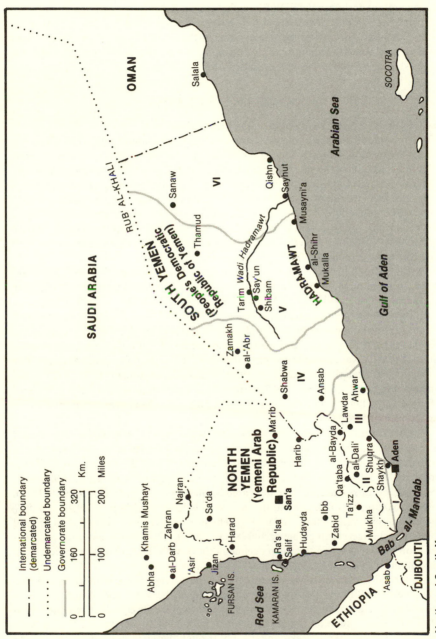

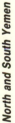

North and South Yemen

PDRY. With the process of democratization in Aden gathering more momentum and a concomitant decline in the PDRY's radicalism, the YAR leadership was increasingly inclined to expedite negotiations and move forward toward a union. Given its numerical superiority (9m. people vs. 2m. in the PDRY), its oil production and revenues (10 times those of the PDRY), and its more stable political basis, the YAR leadership could conceivably hope to be politically dominant in a unified Yemen.

DOMESTIC AFFAIRS

ECONOMIC AND FINANCIAL CHALLENGES

The economic difficulties of the YAR were not uncommon among other oil-producing Third World countries. In fact, the roots of the problems represented a familiar syndrome: a country recently becoming an oil exporter, launching major development programs based on optimistic projections of oil revenues, enjoying very high rates of economic growth, running budgetary and balance of payment deficits, and incurring increased foreign debt. Exacerbating the crisis were oil exports and earnings lower than expected, and fears that existing oil reserves would be nearing exhaustion by the mid-1990s. Mitigating the crisis were higher oil prices throughout 1989 and new oil and gas discoveries in the Ma'rib-Jawf area (see below).

In early March, President Salih announced the YAR's budget for 1989. Revenues were projected at 16.041 bn. Yemeni riyals (YR) = $1.642bn., and expenditures were estimated at YR20.79bn. = $2.128bn. A deficit of YR4.747bn. = $486m. was thus built into the budget. The gravity of the economic problems is amply demonstrated when the 1989 budget is compared with 1988 figures. While revenues were only 16.9% higher, expenditures went up by 33.8% and the projected deficit soared by 160%. Similar anxiety was caused by the rapid deterioration in the balance of payments. The current account deficit of $125m. in 1986 increased dramatically to $452m. in 1987 and reached an all-time record of $694m. in 1988. Of particular concern was the level of imports. As high as they were in 1988 — $1.3bn. — the 1989 projection envisaged a further rise to $1.6bn.[1]

The consecutive deficits in the budget and in the balance of payments, combined with a relaxation of the Central Bank's tight fiscal policy, led to an inevitable rise in borrowing, especially in the international markets. Total debt at the end of 1987 amounted to $2.155bn., and was projected to reach $2.6bn. by the end of 1989. As a result, the country's debt service increased by alarming proportions: from $102m. in 1986 to $145m. in 1987, $189m. in 1988, and as high as $279m. in 1989 — a 50% increase in one year. Thus, the YAR's debt service ratio rose from 9% to 25% of foreign exchange earnings between 1987 and 1989. The critical external payment position was reflected in the steep decline in the YAR's international reserves: from $285m. in late 1988 to $139m. in mid-1989.[2]

Salih tried to minimize the seriousness of the foreign debt, arguing that it was "relatively small in view of the large population of the YAR and the considerable burden of development." He also claimed that most of the foreign debt benefited from favorable terms, such as low interest rates; beginning of repayment having been deferred for a number of years; and most of the debt being long-term. Salih justified the increased foreign debt, stressing that it all emanated from "investments in development of productive projects — in agriculture, dams, canals, the oil industry — and not from purchase of consumer goods."[3]

The economic outlook was further clouded by the dramatic, six-year drop in remittances from Yemenis working in Saudi Arabia and the Gulf states. In 1982, YAR's expatriate workers sent $1.4bn. home through the banks alone; more money was transferred by clandestine means such as smuggling . Remittances declined to $1bn. in 1984, $750m. in 1987, and a record low of $330m. in 1988. Thus, the overall decline exceeded 75% in six years.[4]

Foreign aid fell too. The YAR's new status as an oil producer and exporter was bound to cause multilateral and bilateral aid agencies to scale down their allocations to Yemen. Foreign aid donors included such countries as the US, the USSR, China, and Saudi Arabia, and such international agencies as the UN Funds for Development and Housing, the World Health Organization, the World Food and Agriculture Organization, Unesco, the World Bank, and the International Monetary Fund (IMF). Saudi Arabia, for one, decreased its financial assistance over the last few years because of its own budgetary and monetary constraints. Total foreign aid had fallen from $462m. in 1982 to $111m. in 1988.[5] The new oil revenues could hardly make up for the decline in foreign aid and remittances.

Yet another problem was caused by the growing consumption of *qat,* the narcotic leaf so popular in Yemen. As *qat* had become a very profitable business, many farmers abandoned other crops, to grow *qat* bushes, thereby grossly distorting agriculture. The production of coffee, once the staple cash crop, was down too. As a result, the YAR's grain imports had risen in the 1980s from 100,000 tons to 600,000 tons.[6]

During the year, however, a number of positive developments began to crystallize, which reversed the adverse trends to some extent. In response to the looming payment crisis and the IMF's call for fiscal restraint, the government imposed in early 1989 a $900m. ceiling on imports, a 45% cut from the projected $1.6 bn. The new restrictions were in line with Salih's emphasis on imports directed to investments in development and not to the purchase of consumer goods. The ceiling was not likely to be met, because of inadequate central control over imports and a number of measures which had effectively liberalized the import regime. Nevertheless, there was a good chance that imports could be limited to $1.3bn. Another positive development was the unexpected increase in remittances, caused probably by the higher level of economic activity in Saudi Arabia and the Gulf states. Having hit a low of $330m. in 1988, remittances rose to over $450m. in 1989.[7]

The curb on imports, larger oil revenues caused by higher oil prices, and rising remittances all significantly improved the payment situation. Immediately affected was the 1989 current account deficit, which was down to $350m. from a projected $460m. When the debt service was added, the account deficit approached $630m. — down 10% from its 1988 level, marking the first decline in the deficit ever. Another revealing indicator was the GDP. Following a 4.8% increase in 1987, it registered a rise, massive by any standards, of 19.2% in 1988, and settled on an impressive 6% increase in 1989.[8] Oil production, oil industry-related activities, and sectors stimulated by oil wealth were all expected to generate an overall higher level of economic activity and growth.

Also on the positive side, the government hoped that despite financial constraints and the relatively small markets, foreign businesses would be drawn in by the wide range of investment opportunities. These were especially in the sectors of tourism, health, and primarily agriculture. For food production, North Yemen offered comparative advantages greater than any other country in the Arabian Peninsula and the Red Sea region. In some areas there was a climatic environment and enough rainfall to permit it to provide seasonal fresh fruit and vegetables to markets all around the Middle East.[9]

Future oil earnings were unlikely to make up for the loss of revenue caused by the decline of remittances and foreign assistance. But oil income had a positive angle which was bound to have a great impact on the political-economic structure. Whereas workers' remittances were spread mainly among individuals, oil revenues led to a greater concentration of foreign currency in the hands of the government. The result would be an increase of available funds for government planners targeted for sectors such as agriculture and human services.[10]

OIL DEVELOPMENTS

The year 1988 was the first of the YAR's membership in the "exclusive club" of oil-producing countries. By mid-1989, there were four commercial oil fields in the country, all in the northeastern Ma'rib-Jawf region. The concession was operated by the Yemen Exploration and Production Company (Yepco), which was a joint venture between Yemen Hunt (51%) and Exxon Yemen (49%). The Alif and Azal fields produced the bulk of Yemeni oil, while Raydan and Sayf Ibn Dhi Yazin were minor oil fields. Total production of all four increased from 150,000 barrels per day (b/d) in 1988 to an average of 190,000 b/d in 1989. However, previous optimistic projections that production and export would increase to 250,000 b/d in 1989 and to 400,000 b/d in 1990 did not materialize and were unlikely to do so.[11]

Hampering an increase in the fields' output was the limited capacity of the only pipeline, 440 km. in length, carrying oil from the Ma'rib-Jawf region to Ra's 'Isa on the Red Sea coast. It was possible to double the pipeline's capacity to 400,000 b/d, but the reserves discovered so far in the four fields did not warrant such expansion. In the absence of refineries, the YAR exported the entire oil output and, in turn, purchased refined oil products.[12]

In July, various government officials and the media announced the discovery of new fields in the Red Sea district of al-Madmura. Much more important was Yepco's statement on 7 August that the Asad Kamil field, discovered in December 1987, had been declared commercial. Production was set to start as soon as the field was connected to the export pipeline to the Red Sea. According to preliminary projections, the field was capable of immediately producing 4,000 b/d of oil and 57.5m. cu. ft. of gas. Estimated reserves were as high as 200m. barrels of oil and 2.7 trillion cu. ft. of gas. It was expected that within a short time, the field — some 15 km. north of the Azal field — would boost the YAR's production to 225,000 b/d.[13]

Oil output and revenues continued to be allocated according to the system used since the beginning of oil production in 1987: the government's share was 80,000 b/d, i.e., 40% of the 200,000 b/d produced by the end of 1989. In the beginning of the year, revenue projections were based on an average price of $14 per barrel, which translated into some $400m. for the year. Rising oil prices during 1989, however, revised the average price to $16–$16.5 per barrel, bringing annual earnings to $480m. With an estimated production of 225,000 b/d in 1990, oil income could very likely top the

$500m. mark. By the end of 1989, the YAR had produced within two years 135m. barrels of oil.[14]

Meanwhile, there were new gas discoveries in the oil region of Ma'rib-Jawf. In view of the growing domestic demand for natural and liquid gas, the government began to lay greater emphasis on gas production. Proven gas reserves were put at 7 trillion cu. ft. But there were growing indications that the Ma'rib-Jawf area contained no less than 20 trillion cu. ft. of gas, which was enough to satisfy local demand for the next century. This enhanced expectations that the YAR's future might lie in gas rather than oil. One immediate result was the government studying the possibility of using nonassociated gas to fuel power stations.[15]

In November 1988, the YAR and the PDRY signed an agreement establishing the joint Yemeni Company for Investment in Oil and Mineral Resources (YCIOMR). The company was to manage oil exploration in a 2,200 sq. km. area in the border region between the main oil-producing fields of the two countries. With an authorized capital of $10m., the company had two managers, one from each country, and was headquartered in San'a. In early 1989, Rashid al-Kaf — the PDRY's under secretary of oil — was appointed chairman of the board. On 11 January, the YAR's Consultative Assembly approved the joint oil project.[16]

Once the joint venture was announced, no fewer than 32 multinational companies expressed interest in acquiring exploration permits. The companies' scramble for oil concessions was undoubtedly triggered by geological assessments that there was an excellent chance of commercial discoveries in the border area. The exploration and development contract was eventually awarded in August to a multinational consortium comprising companies from four states: the American Exxon-Hunt partnership held 37.5%; a Kuwaiti company, 25%; a joint venture of two Soviet firms, 18.75%; and the French CFP-Total, 18.75%. Though the YCIOMR and the consortium had some differences over the terms of the concession, it was expected that the actual exploration of the region would begin in early 1990. High hopes were pinned on this joint venture whose revenues were to be equally shared between the two countries.[17]

POLITICAL AND SOCIAL STABILIZATION
Decades of internal struggle and civil war exacerbated by a strong tribal background left the Yemeni society inherently divided and fragmented. Salih recognized this diversity which spanned a wide spectrum of the social, political, and religious scene of the YAR — tribal or rural vs. urban-based, conservative vs. left-wing, Zaydi vs. Shafi'i. Salih realized that there was no way of controlling all the rival factions through governmental coercion. Thus, for the purpose of both internal reconciliation and political stability, he sought to co-opt as many groups as possible into the political system by enabling them to participate in government institutions (see *MECS* 1987, pp. 679–80 and *MECS* 1988, p. 773).

The 1988 elections to the semiparliamentary Consultative Assembly represented a major milestone in the implementation of this concept. Needless to say, the 128 elected members and the 31 appointed by Salih were individuals who did not represent any political parties. In an interview with an Egyptian weekly, Salih explained that "the constitution banned the activities of political parties, because factionalism hurts the national interest; we ought to learn from what happened in Lebanon and Sudan."[18]

But the 159 representatives included leftist, Islamic, and conservative elements whom Salih wanted to function overtly, as part of the system, and under the open eye of his regime. Thus, the assembly provided a wide basis of support for the president and the state. This could also explain why 1989 was such a peaceful year.

Despite the growing political stability, Salih's regime continued to encounter some of Yemen's perennial problems. One of them was the widespread possession of weapons by individuals and tribes. According to one estimate, there were 17m. personal weapons in Yemen, a country of c. 9m. people. Some tribes were said to possess tanks and armored cars left over from the country's civil war in the 1960s. The personal weapons were used by both tribes and individuals at roadblocks which were described as "setting the boundaries between new government and old fiefdom."[19]

Foreign Minister 'Abd al-Karim al-Iryani attributed the government's difficulties to "Yemen's mountainous geography and to a history of clannish people living far from central control." He said that the regime was determined "to break this isolationism." But the government found out that extending roads into remote and isolated areas did not necessarily guarantee acceptance of authority. The attempt to have all cars in the country registered was a case in point. In the summer, government troops fought tribesmen near the town of Ma'rib — center of the oil region — for four days to force them just to register their cars. About 20,000 cars were registered by official count, but a dozen people were killed in the process. The government had to settle the dispute over the dead by paying blood money to the bereaved in the old way.[20]

Other traditional problems persisted as well. About 75% of Yemen's adults were still illiterate. The rate of population growth, 3%, was among the highest in the world. Many children still died in their early years from curable ailments, such as the dehydration that accompanied diarrhea. Government ministers complained that unchecked population growth strained budgets and nullified the financial gains accruing from oil earnings. Foreign Minister al-Iryani admitted that while "the YAR is going fast with development, we are not able to come in with state infrastructure." He concluded that "the state cannot impose its authority everywhere, because it does not have the means."[21]

An acute social problem was the widespread use of *qat*, a daily habit among wider sectors of the society. According to some estimates, farmers who grew the narcotic leaf earned around $1.2bn. a year, i.e., equivalent of about 75% of all government revenues in 1989(!). Truly, such profits kept the farmers on the land, avoiding the overurbanization of many Third World countries. But there were also adverse consequences. The huge profits distorted agriculture, encouraging farmers to abandon traditional crops, such as coffee and various grains, and switch to *qat*. A daily chew of the narcotic — costing some $10 for one man — stripped many household budgets in the cities, while many farmers prospered. Moreover, "if you are spending 70% of your income on *qat*," as one Yemenite said, "how are you going to feed your wife and children?"[22]

In March, Salih called on the armed and security forces to combat widespread smuggling. It was estimated that up to half of the imports were brought in unofficially, sometimes in exchange for expatriates' earnings, which had also been brought in illegally. The problem, by and large, emanated from the unwillingness of the northern tribes in particular to have their activities in this respect controlled by the central government. Successive attempts by the regime to clamp down on the smuggling trade had been largely unsuccessful. It was clear that given the as yet imperfect hold of the government over the periphery and the need for careful maneuvering, the problem was politically sensitive.[23]

FOREIGN AFFAIRS

ATTITUDE TOWARD THE PEOPLE'S DEMOCRATIC REPUBLIC OF YEMEN AND UNITY TALKS

The legacy of mutual suspicion and distrust between the YAR and the PDRY abated significantly in 1989. Consequently, unity talks between the two states registered some major advances, and the YAR's attitude toward unity became much more favorable. (For a detailed account of the unity talks, see chapter on the PDRY.) Though San'a's spokesmen emphasized that much more preparatory work was needed in order to reach an agreement on unity, they sounded much more optimistic about the eventual creation of a unified Yemen.

YAR leaders continued to attach importance to unity talks not only for the sake of the projected union but also as a vehicle for resolving a number of outstanding problems and controversies. It was in this context that they saw the efforts to resolve the following issues: clashes among tribes along the undemarcated border; increased military presence and erection of fortifications on the PDRY's side of the border; the presence in San'a of former PDRY leader 'Ali Nasir Muhammad and 40,000 of his supporters; and oil exploitation in the Ma'rib (YAR) and Shabwa (PDRY) regions along the disputed border, which had increased tension and military activity.

Some of these problems were successfully resolved during the talks, while significant progress was made on others. The controversy over the undemarcated boundary was alleviated by the agreement to allow citizens of both states to cross the border freely. The oil dispute ended in an agreement on a joint exploration of the border region, granting the concession to a multinational consortium, and sharing future revenues (see above). Finally, the visit of the PDRY's chief of staff to San'a in late 1989 ended in the signing of a protocol stipulating the dismantling of the border fortifications.[24]

Salih sought to use these agreements and arrangements to promote the YAR's preference for a step-by-step integration of the two states, the long-term goal being a full-fledged federal union. Salih argued that "the very implementation of these agreements and other unionist projects will deepen the confidence between the two leaderships and peoples and consolidate the efforts toward the restoration of Yemeni unity." Prime Minister 'Abd al-'Aziz 'Abd al-Ghani stated that the joint exploration for and exploitation of oil "is one of the elements which paves the way for the creation of joint institutions and draws us closer toward a union."[25]

One of the major remaining stumbling blocks along the road toward unity was the degree of political pluralism allowed in the unified state. While the PDRY was inclined to institute a multiparty system, the YAR leadership continued to oppose it, insisting that all political forces should function within the framework of the General People's Congress. Salih stated that the Yemeni people had drawn a lesson from "the tragic experience of Lebanon and Sudan" caused by the multiplicity of political parties and would, therefore, not repeat it. In the absence of agreement on the internal political structure, Salih suggested that they start with the unification of the foreign and defense policies of the two states and proceed incrementally until a full merger was achieved.[26]

Though emphasizing the gradual nature of the union, the YAR leadership struck an optimistic, even enthusiastic, note when referring to unity. Minister of Unity Affairs Yahya al-'Arshi declared that "as the people in the YAR and PDRY demand that we expedite our work, and as developments in the Arab and international arena are opportune, unity now is more natural and appropriate than ever before." This was clearly different from Salih's cautioning in 1988 that attaining unity required bridging-over ideologically, politically, and economically different systems.[27] The change in the YAR's attitude reflected a more confident state of mind in San'a, caused by a growing sense that given the *perestroika* in the USSR, and the decline in the revolutionary fervor in the PDRY, San'a had nothing to fear from a unified Yemen. Moreover, in view of the YAR's overwhelming numerical superiority, it would most likely be the dominant force in such a union.

THE YEMENI ARAB REPUBLIC AND THE ARAB COOPERATION COUNCIL
Perception of the Arab Cooperation Council
All official YAR statements regarding the formation of the ACC sought to dispel the notion that the new grouping had been the idea of one leader (King Husayn) or an attempt by another (Saddam Husayn) to achieve regional dominance. (For a detailed account and analysis of the ACC, see chapter on inter-Arab relations.) Salih repeatedly stated that "it was the idea of all four leaders who found that there was large room for cooperation and integration among the four states in the form of a new Arab grouping." He explained that rather than weakening Arab solidarity, "the ACC is a tributary which, along with other Arab regional groupings — the Gulf Cooperation Council [GCC] and the Arab Maghrib Union [AMU] — would bolster the Arab League's role and enhance Arab cooperation."[28]

Salih described the ACC as "a historic, unionist achievement for the whole Arab nation and a qualitative contribution toward realizing comprehensive Arab unity." Ghani suggested that the ACC could play a central role "in enhancing cooperation among the three Arab groupings, because geographically we are in the middle between the GCC and the AMU."[29] Being an instrument of Arab unity, Salih declared, the ACC would be based on "the open-door principle." This meant that the grouping would not be confined to the four founding states, but would rather be open to all Arab countries, without any exception, who wished to join it. Thus, "Syria, Sudan, Lebanon, and any other Arab sister were welcomed." Even the PDRY could join the ACC if this was acceptable to the other three founding members.[30]

YAR spokesmen were at pains to reject any notion of the ACC being a political bloc or a military alliance aimed against other Arab states. Foreign Minister al-Iryani stressed that as far as political cooperation was concerned, there existed "coordination of the general frameworks of the four states' foreign policy," but that did not mean that they all spoke "with one voice."[31]

Asked about the military aspects of the ACC, Ghani responded that "security and military coordination is an important issue, but this kind of cooperation should be among all Arab states and be based on agreements and charters." Moreover, Iryani elaborated that all ACC members were committed by the Joint Arab Defense Pact, and the grouping had no intention of forming its own separate military industry. Speaking at the UN General Assembly, Iryani described the YAR's perception of the ACC as a grouping "seeking to achieve the highest levels of cooperation, coordination, and integration among its states in the economic, cultural, and social fields";[32] references to "political" and/or "military" were conspicuously absent.

Indeed, most official Yemeni statements focused on economic cooperation as being at the center of San'a's strategy in joining the ACC. The most explicit formulation was Salih's himself, declaring that the ACC "is actually a realistic formula for economic integration among its four founders."[33] It was, therefore, assumed that the YAR had hoped to reap substantial economic benefits from the new bloc. But as these were unclear, various analysts growingly viewed the economic advantages of the grouping as having been overstated. Moreover, as the other members of the ACC were suffering serious economic and financial problems, none had much financial help to offer the Yemenis.

That the YAR was unlikely to derive much short-term benefit from its membership in the ACC was indicated by a number of facts. For one, the ACC's statute lacked any details on economic measures beyond vague, general references. For another, the much prepared Alexandria summit in June did not produce any major move toward the stated goal of economic integration. On the contrary, the four states rejected the idea of lifting trade and tariff barriers in the short term and agreed that "further economic ties" would be studied. Consequently, the YAR's expectations had to be confined to technical assistance, and trade and other cooperation arrangements. This was precisely what the San'a summit in September produced: a series of 16 accords stipulating economic, social, and agricultural cooperation; joint struggle in combating drug use and trafficking; and the setting up of a parliamentary committee.[34]

Indeed, it was hard to explain both the YAR's willingness to join the ACC and its inclusion by the other three states on purely economic grounds. It appeared more likely that the impetus might have been primarily political rather than economic. For Iraq, Egypt, and Jordan, the YAR represented a strategic location and a relatively large population; for Iraq, particularly, Yemen's inclusion served as a means of weakening and outflanking Saudi Arabia (for details, see chapters on Saudi Arabia and inter-Arab relations). For Salih, the ACC membership had a political significance, both external and internal. In foreign policy, the ACC provided the YAR with a counterweight to Saudi dominance and with an unprecedented opportunity to demonstrate its independence of Saudi Arabia. In fact, both Baghdad and San'a shared the interest of weakening Riyadh's inter-Arab stature and hegemony in the Arabian Peninsula. From another perspective, in joining the ACC, the YAR retaliated for its exclusion by Saudi Arabia in 1980 from the GCC which it had wanted so much to join. Another version took this interpretation one step further, arguing that Salih's real goal was to join the GCC, and membership in the ACC was designed merely to pressure Riyadh into admitting the YAR into the GCC.[35]

In domestic politics, the political significance of the country's membership in the ACC lay in the prestige it bestowed upon Salih and his regime. Having consolidated his power base and reconciled the diverse groups in the 1988 elections (see *MECS* 1988, pp. 773–75), Salih needed a foreign policy success which would confer on his regime an all-Arab legitimacy as a means of bolstering his position at home. Being in one league with such major Arab countries as Egypt and Iraq was expected to provide just that.

Relations with Arab Cooperation Council Members

The establishment of the ACC followed a previous strengthening of the YAR's bilateral links with Egypt, Jordan, and Iraq. In October 1988, the joint Egyptian-Yemeni Economic Committee held its first meeting, which resulted in seven accords on cooperation in technology, agriculture, health, science, investment, and manpower. Following a visit by King Husayn to San'a in January, the joint Jordanian-Yemeni Higher Committee convened in Amman and reached agreements to boost cooperation in security, trade, housing, planning, agriculture, energy, education, telecommunications, and research. Yemeni-Iraqi relations were also expanded. While Saddam Husayn was visiting San'a in late January, the joint Iraqi-Yemeni Higher Committee convened in Baghdad and concluded agreements in the fields of economics, culture, and oil.[36]

The establishment of the ACC in February provided a multilateral formalization of existing bilateral links between the YAR and its three partners. Future accords were negotiated and concluded within the ACC framework. Still some accords were reached on a bilateral basis. On 4 March, a two-year cooperation protocol was signed between the Iraqi Ba'th Party and the YAR's General People's Congress. In mid-March, the joint Yemeni-Iraqi Permanent Committee for Oil and Gas met in San'a. The two sides agreed on boosting bilateral oil industry cooperation and on Iraqi technical assistance to the YAR's oil sector, as well as on holding regular consultations "to review world oil prices in order to secure stability in world oil markets." The Iraqi oil minister also agreed to send Iraqi oil experts to the YAR and to accept Yemeni students in Iraqi colleges.[37]

Bilateral agreements were likewise concluded with Egypt and Jordan. In May, a memorandum of understanding was signed between the Faculty of Agriculture at the University of San'a and its counterpart in Alexandria. It called for joint scientific research, exchange of experts and students, and scholarship programs. In September, the Jordanian and YAR Ministries of Education signed a cooperation agreement involving exchange programs in higher education, archaeology, and sport.[38]

RELATIONS WITH SAUDI ARABIA

The number of issues and controversies straining relations between Saudi Arabia and the YAR increased in 1989, with San'a's membership in the ACC topping the list. The Saudi leaders were ill-pleased with the emergence of a new bloc centered on powerful and ambitious Iraq. They were even more anxious that the new bloc included the YAR — the Saudi "backyard" — which they had always considered part of their legitimate sphere of interest. The Iraqi-YAR axis was, most probably, seen in Riyadh as evidence of a "pincer movement," and the legacy of continuous border problems between Saudi Arabia and the YAR only further fueled Saudi apprehensions. This development was viewed as all the more detrimental to Saudi interests when seen in the context of the YAR becoming an oil-exporting country, and thus less sensitive to Saudi concerns, and against the background of the YAR-PDRY unity talks which raised the specter of a powerful, united Yemen.

Salih was aware of the unease with which the Saudis viewed the YAR's "defection."

On the one hand, Salih wished to convey the impression that his very joining of the ACC, let alone without consulting Riyadh, demonstrated that "Yemeni decision-making is independent." On the other hand, however, he sought to allay Saudi fears, by dispatching messengers to Riyadh — immediately after the creation of the ACC — assuring the Saudi leadership that the new grouping would not hurt Saudi interests and publicly declaring that "Yemeni-Saudi relations are special."[39]

The perennial territorial dispute emanating from the undemarcated boundary between Saudi Arabia and the YAR persisted in 1989. A common interpretation in the Arab world was that San'a had always refused to demarcate the boundary, because it refused to negotiate from an inferior bargaining position. Salih hoped that the ACC umbrella would significantly enhance his bargaining stand *vis-à-vis* Riyadh.[40]

Publicly Salih strove to minimize the issue, describing it as "similar to all border disputes between neighboring countries, including similar disputes between sisterly Arab states." He stressed that there was "nothing that prevents us from resolving the dispute," that he and King Fahd were dealing with the issue "in a brotherly way through direct contacts," and that "more time is needed to arrive at a final resolution." An important milestone was the agreement in August to establish four checkpoints along the common border. But tribal skirmishes and smuggling from Saudi territory into the YAR exacerbated the dispute. Moreover, Saudi influence on some northern Yemeni tribes and San'a's suspicion that the Saudis were encouraging them to shift their loyalty to Riyadh further strained relations.[41]

At the same time, a sensitive problem involving c. 1m. Yemeni workers in Saudi Arabia was solved to San'a's satisfaction during Salih's visit to Riyadh in July. As the Saudi authorities imposed more restrictions on foreign workers and limited their presence to three to five years, the position of Yemeni expatriate workers was endangered. A royal decree issued in May, regulating the residence of non-Saudis, explicitly exempted YAR citizens who, as a result, enjoyed in many respects similar rights to Saudi citizens. Yemeni leaders praised the Saudi measure, describing it as "a reflection of the brotherly relations between the two peoples linked by a common fate."[42]

On the whole, the two countries strove to project good relations and "business as usual" despite the many controversies. Salih consistently referred to relations with "fraternal" Saudi Arabia as "excellent," "strong," "special," and "distinctive," and described its assistance to the YAR as "manifold." In addition to ongoing aid organized within the Yemeni-Saudi Coordination Council, the Saudi Government announced in late 1989 that "a bilateral economic pact is expected to be finalized within the coming months." In a further sign of the extent of Riyadh's assistance, the Saudis provided $30m. for the expansion of the San'a air base, which Defense Minister Sultan inaugurated in September.[43]

RELATIONS WITH OTHER ARAB STATES

YAR leaders sought to base their inter-Arab policies on the principle of nonalignment. Their oft-proclaimed goal was to promote Arab solidarity and cooperation by helping Arab states overcome their differences. Such an approach made it imperative for the YAR not to be entangled in regional disputes which might have poised it against other Arab countries.

The YAR's membership of the ACC seemed to have called this policy into question, because the San'a-Baghdad axis was bound to alienate Damascus. That Syria was kept in the dark regarding the YAR's joining the ACC further antagonized the Syrian leadership. San'a's emphasis on the economic character of the new bloc was not taken seriously in Damascus. The final communiqué of the ACC's Alexandria summit in June, signed by the YAR, accepted the Iraqi position on Lebanon and called for the withdrawal "of all non-Lebanese forces" — a clear allusion to the Syrian troops.[44] The significance of this statement should be seen against the backdrop of the Arab Casablanca summit, only one month earlier, which had refused to endorse such an anti-Syrian formula.

Salih was aware of Syrian sensitivities and sought to minimize the challenge directed at Damascus. Thus, when explaining the ACC's "open door" policy (see above), he put Syria at the top of the list of countries which could join the bloc. Asked specifically whether contacts had been held with Damascus, he said: "We have consulted Syria and contacts are under way on this subject." The Syrians, likewise, were not interested in harming relations with San'a, and the joint Yemeni-Syrian Higher Committee convened regularly. In February, it reached a number of cooperation agreements on agriculture, industry, trade — including barter deals — culture, and information.[45]

The YAR embarked on a number of mediation efforts in order to demonstrate its inter-Arab stature as well as its nonaligned policy. The most conspicuous attempt was to reconcile Egyptian President Mubarak with Libya's leader Qadhdhafi. Yemeni spokesmen sought to take credit for the reconciliation between Cairo and Tripoli after Mubarak had praised Salih at the Egyptian People's Assembly. Solidarity with Arab causes was also reflected in San'a's denying allegations that the PLO paid the YAR for the facilities put at its disposal in the country.[46]

THE INTERNATIONAL ARENA

Yemeni leaders frequently stressed their desire to pursue a nonaligned, nonpartisan policy in the international arena. Hence, the YAR sought to have good relations with all political blocs and to remain neutral on international disputes. This approach accounted for the YAR's goal of diversification of its sources of weaponry and economic assistance. Salih expressed pride at his success in having both American and Soviet experts working in the YAR, at times "even on the same projects — civilian or military."[47] In reality, however, there was a clear division: while the Soviet Union centered on Yemen's military needs, the US concentrated on the YAR's nonmilitary sectors.

The USSR provided a significant amount of military assistance to San'a; it had not been as successful in the economic aspect of their bilateral relations. A number of agreements were concluded during the year. In late 1988, the "first agreement of friendship and trade" was signed in San'a, and in early April 1989, the Interior Ministries of the two states signed a cooperation protocol. In late October, minutes for economic cooperation were signed in preparation for the fourth session of the joint Yemeni-Soviet committee for economic, technical, and trade cooperation scheduled to convene in early 1990. The minutes contained agreements in principle on cooperation in the fields of oil, agriculture, electricity, ports, cement, textile, roads, and trade exchange. However, to appreciate these agreements in their proper proportions, it is useful to bear in mind that, according to statistics published by the

Organization for Economic Cooperation and Development, gross official development assistance to the YAR from all Eastern Bloc countries did not exceed $3.1m. in 1987.[48]

The US, in contradistinction, allocated over $31m. in economic assistance to the YAR in 1988. In 1989, the US Agency for International Development agreed to provide San'a with $40m. to increase high- quality crop production, and to improve irrigation and agricultural methods. A former American ambassador to the YAR pointed out that the US was involved in health, clean water, education, agriculture, and training, and that there was a substantial presence of Peace Corps volunteers. In addition, the major oil company involved in exploration, production, and construction in the country was the Hunt Company from Texas.[49]

There was also a dramatic rise in the volume of trade between Washington and San'a. The US became the YAR's largest supplier in 1987, with $128m. of exports, and the fourth largest in 1988 with $80m. worth of exports. Yemeni sales to the US soared from $4.5m. in 1987 to $129m. in 1988, the first year of major oil production.[50] Relations, however, were clouded over by political differences, particularly the US position in the Arab-Israeli conflict in general and toward the Palestinians in particular. Thus, top Yemeni leaders described Washington's denying a visa to PLO chairman 'Arafat in November 1988 (see *MECS* 1988, chapter on the PLO) as "a disgraceful act which violates international law." The downing of two Libyan jets by the Sixth Fleet in January 1989 was called "a provocative act" and "a blatant aggression which does not serve the cause of peace." It was expected that Salih's forthcoming visit to Washington, scheduled for early 1990, would clear the air and further expand relations between the two countries.[51]

In its efforts to diversify its foreign relations, the YAR sought to expand beyond the framework of the two superpowers. In May, San'a reached an agreement with the European Economic Community (EEC), by which the latter undertook to finance several industrial projects. Previously, EEC financing was limited to infrastructural projects. In January, the British foreign minister visited San'a and offered $60m. in grants and loans, provided the YAR accepted proposals involving British companies. In December 1988, a contract for the construction of a 127km.-long road, from the Ma'rib oil region to south of San'a, was signed with a Chinese company. The financing came from a Chinese loan under a December 1987 aid protocol. In March, a Chinese Foreign Ministry delegation held talks in San'a on "expanding an agreement on cooperation between the two countries."[52]

NOTES

For the place and frequency of publications cited here, and for the full name of the publication, news agency, radio station, or monitoring service where an abbreviation is used, please see "List of Sources." Only in the case of more than one publication bearing the same name is the place of publication noted here.

1. R. San'a, 8 March — DR, 15 March; *CR:* Saudi Arabia, 1989, No. 2, pp. 10, 32, No. 3, pp. 11, 38.
2. *CR:* Saudi Arabia, No. 1, pp. 11, 33, No. 4, p. 38; *FT,* 22 March 1989.
3. Interviews with *al-Usbu' al-'Arabi*, 6 October; *Ruz al-Yusuf,* 21 August; *al-Siyasa,* Kuwait, 2 October 1989.
4. *CR:* Saudi Arabia, No. 3, p. 38; *NYT,* 24 October 1989.

5. *FT,* 22 March; *al-Yawm al-Sabi',* 12 October 1989.
6. *NYT,* 3 October 1989.
7. *CR:* Saudi Arabia, No. 1, p. 10, No. 3, pp. 11, 38; *al-Muharrir,* 19 February 1989.
8. *CR:* Saudi Arabia, 1989, No. 2, p. 11, No. 3, p. 11, No. 4, pp. 11, 35.
9. *FT,* 22 March 1989.
10. USIA, 9 February 1989.
11. *Al-Dustur,* Amman, 7 October; *al-Siyasa,* Kuwait, 22 July; Salih's TV interview, quoted in *MEES,* 9 May 1988.
12. *PIW,* 20 February 1989.
13. *CR:* Saudi Arabia, No.1, p. 33, No. 3, p. 38, No. 4, pp. 35–36; *al-Siyasa,* Kuwait, 18 July 1989.
14. *CR:* Saudi Arabia, No. 3, p. 11, No. 4, p. 11; Salih's interview with *al-Hayat,* London, 4 October 1989.
15. *Al-Siyasa,* Kuwait, 18 July; *CR:* Saudi Arabia, 1989, No. 2, p. 33.
16. *CR:* Saudi Arabia, 1989, No. 1, p. 33.
17. Ibid., No. 4, pp. 10, 36.
18. Salih's interview with *Ruz al-Yusuf,* 21 August 1989.
19. *NYT,* 24 October 1989.
20. Ibid.
21. Ibid.
22. Ibid.
23. *CR:* Saudi Arabia, 1989, No. 2, p. 31.
24. *Al-Yawm al-Sabi',* 8 January 1990.
25. Interview in *al-Ufuq,* 9 July; *al-Usbu' al-'Arabi,* 23 October 1989.
26. Interviews with *al-Yawm al-Sabi',* 9 October 1989, 8 January 1990.
27. Interviews with *al-Sharq al-Awsat,* 18 November 1989; *al-Ra'y al-'Amm,* 11 October 1988.
28. Interview with *al-Ra'y al-'Amm,* 23 February 1989.
29. R. San'a, 23 February — DR, 24 February; interview with *al-Anba,* Kuwait, 25 June 1989.
30. Interviews with *al-Ra'y al-'Amm,* 23 February; *al-Anba,* Kuwait, 25 June 1989.
31. Interview with *al-Hawadith,* 6 October; MENA, 24 September — DR, 26 September 1989.
32. Interviews with *al-Anba,* Kuwait, 25 June; MENA, 24 September — DR, 26 September; *al-Yawm al-Sabi',* 4 September; R. San'a, 6 October — DR, 11 October 1989.
33. Interview with *al-Hawadith,* 6 October 1989.
34. *CR:* Saudi Arabia, No. 2, p. 31, No. 3, p. 36; MENA, 24 September — DR, 25 September; R. San'a, 25 September — DR, 26 September 1989.
35. *Al-Sharq al-Awsat,* 21 September 1989.
36. *CR:* Saudi Arabia, No. 1, p. 32; *JT,* 23 January; R. San'a, 23 January, 30 November — DR, 23 January, 1 December 1989.
37. *CR:* Saudi Arabia, No. 2, p. 32; INA, 13 March — DR, 17 March; R. San'a, 15 March — DR, 17 March 1989.
38. *Al-Akhbar,* Cairo, 28 May; *al-Dustur,* Amman, 23 September 1989.
39. Interview with *al-Hawadith,* 6 October; R. San'a, 4 March — DR, 9 March 1989.
40. *Al-Safir,* 20 March 1989.
41. Interview with *al-Siyasa,* Kuwait, 20 May; *al-Ra'y al-'Amm,* 23 February; *al-Nahda,* Kuwait, 4 March; *al-Yawm al- Sabi',* 4 September 1989.
42. *CR:* Saudi Arabia, No. 3, p. 37; R. San'a, 10 July — DR, 11 July; interview with *al-Yawm al-Sabi',* 4 September 1989.
43. Interview with *al-Siyasa,* Kuwait, 20 May; *al-Ra'y al-'Amm,* 23 February; *CR:* Saudi Arabia, No. 4, 1989, p. 34.
44. *CR:* Saudi Arabia, No. 3, 1989, p. 37.
45. Interview with *al-Ra'y al-'Amm,* 23 February; R. San'a, 6 February — DR, 7 February; R. Damascus, 7 February — DR, 8 February; *CR:* Saudi Arabia, No. 2, 1989, p. 32.
46. Interviews with *al-Ittihad,* Abu Dhabi, 21 May; *al-Anba,* Kuwait, 25 June; *CR:* Saudi Arabia, No. 3, 1989, p. 37.
47. Interview with *Ruz al-Yusuf,* 7 August 1989.
48. *Al-Ittihad,* Abu Dhabi, 15 December; R. San'a, 4 April, 24 October — DR, 5 April, 26 October; *CR:* Saudi Arabia, No. 2, 1989, p. 34.

49.   *CR:* Saudi Arabia, 1989, No. 2, p. 34, No. 4, p. 38; USIA, 9 February 1989.
50.   *CR:* Saudi Arabia, 1989, No. 1, p. 33, No. 2, p. 34, No. 4, p. 37.
51.   R. San'a, 14 December 1988, 4 January 1989 — DR, 15 December 1988 and 4 January 1989; *WP,* 21 December 1989.
52.   *CR:* Saudi Arabia, 1989, No. 1, p. 34, No. 3, p. 40; R. San'a, 14 March — DR, 17 March 1989.

South Yemen (PDRY)

(Jumhuriyyat al-Yaman al-Sha'biyya al-Dimuqratiyya)

JOSEPH KOSTINER

During 1989, the People's Democratic Republic of Yemen (PDRY) initiated reforms in its main domestic and foreign policies and institutions. These reforms resulted from the PDRY leaders' attempts to overcome an inherent problem of South Yemeni modern history, i.e., how to establish a Marxist regime in unfavorable economic and political conditions. Motivated by the Marxist values they had acquired during their struggle for independence against Britain in the 1960s, PDRY leaders sought to carry out a revolutionary policy in the Arabian Peninsula, to establish a collective, state-run economy and a highly centralized polity run by the ruling Yemeni Socialist Party (YSP). But these ambitions clashed with conditions prevailing in the area: an unskilled population, a lack of economic assets, and uncompromising neighbors. The PDRY suffered from prolonged economic difficulties and chronic political instability, which often erupted into crises and, in January 1986, even into a civil war. There were obvious limitations to the benefits from the aid given by the PDRY's patron, the Soviet Union. This aid concentrated on military and technical support, and forced Aden to seek financial assistance from the anti-Marxist, but oil-rich Gulf states.

Thus, PDRY leaders tried to establish a Marxist regime, but were forced to compromise and change their policies. In 1968, after independence, President Qahtan al-Sha'bi's regime had to stop economic collectivization in favor of stimulating the economy through private, mostly foreign, financial assistance. In the early 1970s, 'Abd al-Fattah Isma'il and Rubay' 'Ali attempted to export the PDRY's revolution to Oman, and the Yemeni Arab Republic (YAR) and establish a party-led polity at home. But in the mid-1970s, it became evident that Marxist structures had developed very slowly, regional subversion had failed, and the economy had not improved. This prompted Rubay' to seek financial assistance from the Gulf states and even the West between 1976 and 1978. Rubay' was defeated by Isma'il and during the latter's presidency (June 1978-April 1980) the efforts to reinforce the Marxist regime and encourage regional insurgency reached their peak. But Isma'il's attempt clashed with the interests of the Gulf states and even of Moscow in regional *détente,* and further weakened the PDRY economy. Isma'il's deposition led to an opposing policy: his successor, 'Ali Nasir Muhammad, improved relations with the PDRY's neighbors, sought financial assistance from the Gulf states, and liberalized the economy somewhat. 'Ali Nasir's attempt in January 1986 to dispose of his opponents developed into a civil war, which resulted in his defeat.[1]

The new government denounced 'Ali Nasir's "deviationist" policies and attempted to reestablish a solid Marxist economy and political structure, but again their ambitions clashed with realities. The economic crisis and political divisions deepened because of the growing interfactional hatred, and the physical destruction during the civil war. 'Ali Nasir formed a faction of exiled former political activists and refugees residing in the YAR, which threatened to topple the PDRY Government. The PDRY foreign policy, which sought good relations with states in the region, failed both to allay most Arab states' fears of Aden's Marxist policy and to obtain foreign financial assistance (see *MECS* 1986, pp. 530–32, 535–37).

These failures led the PDRY leaders to reform their domestic and foreign policies, the Soviet *perestroika* being their model. The possibility of joining an Arab regional organization, such as the newly established Arab Cooperation Council (ACC), or at least of benefiting from relations with its member states, gave the PDRY leaders new hope of obtaining economic assistance. Their unanimous belief in the need for reforms, and particularly for improving relations with 'Ali Nasir's faction and other tribal and religious political groups, encouraged the leaders to take this road.

The PDRY did not develop an elaborate program of reforms or a clear strategy of how to achieve them. The reform process rather reflected the leaders' immediate preferences or results of inconclusive debates on the nature of reforms. As a result of the reforms: (1) The regime became more tolerant of Islamic and tribally organized groups and of 'Ali Nasir's allies. Toward the end of 1989, the regime even declared its readiness to permit a multiparty system, which was an attempt to increase the population's trust in the regime, and thereby to reinforce its socio-political base. (2) There were new initiatives to encourage foreign investment, to privatize the economy to an extent, and to obtain financial assistance. (3) The PDRY increased its efforts to unite with the YAR and improve relations with Arab states in order to encourage Arab technical and financial support for the PDRY.(4) A new atmosphere of renewal and change pervaded the country, as was evident in a liberalization of the press and an openness toward the West. Aden's foreign policy thus became more diversified and less dependent on Moscow, by seeking improved relations with both the Eastern and Western Bloc. The country's relations with the Soviet Union did not particularly develop during 1989, although they remained stable and friendly.

Reform is not new in South Yemen. Concerning his own reform attempt, 'Ali Nasir noted ironically: "We were ahead of the Soviet Union as far as reforms were concerned, but that was considered a form of deviation from the principles of revolution and submission to 'reaction and imperialism'."[2] It remains to be seen whether the new attempt at reforms will endure longer than 'Ali Nasir's.

FROM "PAST MISTAKES" TO REFORM

REASONS FOR REFORM
The drive for reforms was paved by two related motives: a negative one — the determination to overcome past failures and to inhibit their widespread ramifications — and the positive incentive of taking advantage of new strategic and economic realities conducive to reforms. Unwilling openly to bring into question the nature of the 22-year-old Marxist rule in the PDRY, the leaders did not systematically discuss what they referred to as "past mistakes," nor did they elaborate on their extent and

causes. Even so, their testimony revealed a wide range of problems waiting for solution.

The statement in January 1989 of 'Ali Salim al-Bayd, secretary-general of the YSP, that mistakes were made by "left-wing and right-wing opportunist streams,"[3] and the PDRY Council of Ministers' decision in August "to rectify the mistakes which accompanied the construction of the authorities [e.g., the government] and various organizations...over the past two decades,"[4] attested to the dissatisfaction with the PDRY's leadership and governing institutions. Severe socioeconomic problems were indicated by the admission in January of President Haydar al-'Attas that "the PDRY's main difficulty lies in insufficient financing of projects," and that the "productive infrastructure is weak."[5] This was true also of a YSP statement in October that "the real challenge facing the party" was "the economic and living conditions of our masses."[6] In the same vein, in a speech in June, al-Bayd emphasized stimulating "the energies of the people and drawing them into the process of progressive construction and the creation of a broad social base,"[7] thereby demonstrating the necessity of rebuilding the regime's sociopolitical foundation. Foreign Minister 'Abd al-'Aziz al-Dali's statements in October that "Aden had made faulty evaluations of foreign relations" and that it had become necessary to establish "balanced and positive relations"[8] with many states, similarly attested to the problems inherent in the PDRY's continuous anti-Western and revolutionary foreign policy. And the indication by YSP Deputy Secretary-General Salim Salih Muhammad that the PDRY had been wrong to build its state institutions by copying from Arab and Eastern Bloc states, demonstrated the leaders' wish to abandon their old state-building model.[9] These "past mistakes" were the negative phenomena Aden had to overcome and change.

South Yemeni leaders were encouraged to rectify past mistakes by several developments which came to a head in early 1989, and influenced the PDRY's strategic and economic conditions. The foundation of the ACC in February 1989, which included the PDRY's neighbor, the YAR (see chapters on inter-Arab relations, and on the YAR), and the ongoing development of the Gulf Cooperation Council (GCC), which comprised the Gulf states (see chapter on the Gulf States), were perceived in Aden as proof that economic improvement and political stability could be achieved through broad regional cooperation and integration. The PDRY's leaders believed that they could tap these two regional organizations and benefit from their economic enterprises, and possibly even join the ACC (see below). Moreover, their very determination to embark on widespread changes was inspired by the reforms made during 1989 by the PDRY's patron, the Soviet Union and its Eastern Bloc allies. Salim Salih Muhammad clarified in September that "what is now happening in the Soviet Union and other Eastern Bloc states reinforces what is happening to us...we are influenced by the events there."[10] The openness, search for change, and readiness to scuttle established practices, typical of the Soviet *perestroika,* and the implied economic promise of the ACC, convinced the PDRY leaders that by following such new models they would be able to overcome the PDRY's weaknesses.

The Practical Implications of Past Mistakes

What were the implications of these past mistakes? Their wide range indicates that the regime's strategies were ineffective. Three main areas in which the government's policy had been vamped after the 1986 civil war were:

(1) Rebuilding the country's Marxist institutions, which had been eroded by 'Ali Nasir's liberalizing steps and later almost completely destroyed during the civil war. The leaders who rose to power after the civil war sought to reestablish the YSP's dominant role in society and a Marxist economy, free of any "deviationist," liberalizing features.

(2) Subordinating foreign policies to internal rehabilitation. Aden, therefore, sought to establish friendly relations with its neighbors, to seek financial assistance from the Gulf states, and to help build the PDRY.

(3) Continuing to rely on the Soviet Union for long-term defense and economic development (see *MECS* 1986, pp. 532–40).

These strategies, however, proved ineffective in both foreign and internal affairs.

In foreign affairs, Aden obtained Soviet military and technical assistance, and a small amount of financial aid from the Gulf states. This combination could, perhaps, have developed into a valuable strategic asset in the long run, but did not provide an effective solution to current problems. Being struck by economic recession, the Gulf states had been decreasing foreign aid. Furthermore, the new order in Aden, which was an unknown entity to other countries, startled conservative Gulf leaders. The new government's persistence in portraying itself and its party as revolutionary and its refusal to settle differences with 'Ali Nasir, whom Gulf leaders respected as a moderate and popular statesman, made it an object of continuous suspicion by the Gulf leaders. The South Yemeni Government, therefore, failed to tap the Gulf economies effectively. Its reliance on the Soviet Union also proved insufficient: the reformist Soviet regime supplied means of defense and technical advice, but could not provide for South Yemen's economic rehabilitation.

The PDRY's convoluted relationship with the YAR was likewise a source of many problems. During the last three years there had been friction between Aden and San'a over the extraction of oil in their undemarcated border zones. This friction decreased somewhat after the two states finally signed an agreement for the joint operation of the field in May 1988. There was also conflict over the activities of 'Ali Nasir's faction which had close links with the YAR, and which San'a wanted to settle but Aden was unwilling to do so. There were additional difficulties in the efforts of the two Yemens to achieve unity. The Gulf states feared that the PDRY might renew its insurgence in the YAR and the Soviet Union favored growing cooperation between the two Yemens, but under Soviet influence (see below and chapters on the PDRY and the YAR in *MECS* 1987 and 1988).

At home, the civil war resulted in heavy destruction — about 10,000 dead, $500m.-worth of Soviet military hardware destroyed,[11] cadres and political institutions eliminated, and extensive quarters of the main cities ruined — which impeded construction. The c. 65,000 people who fled the PDRY and joined 'Ali Nasir in exile in the YAR became both a center of opposition to Aden, and a catalyst for strife between tribal groups within the remaining YSP leading faction[12] (see *MECS* 1986, pp. 527–32).

The government's failure to solve these political and economic problems impeded the attempt to reconstruct the Marxist regime. In addition, the government's failure to mend its fences with 'Ali Nasir's faction continued to provoke internal conflict in 1989. There were elements within the YSP who either supported 'Ali Nasir, or at least opposed the government's refusal to settle the dispute with him. They called for a *rapprochement* with 'Ali Nasir's supporters, and especially for an amnesty for the sentenced leaders of this faction and permission for their return (see *MECS* 1988, pp. 665–67, 668). Such elements were particularly numerous in the provinces of Abyan and Shabwa, which had traditionally supported the deposed leader. More South Yemeni dissidents continued to join 'Ali Nasir's faction,[13] and according to South Yemeni opposition sources, the disagreement over the faction caused intercommunal strife in Aden, which led to arrests.[14] There were also reports of conservative, tribal, and religiously motivated groups, without Marxist convictions, who had come to the fore during the 1986 civil war and resurfaced in 1989. Opposition sources noted that urban centers in Hadramawt had been affected by the emerging wave of Islamic fundamentalism, which prompted demonstrations of zealous Muslims. They called for the elimination of corruption and disbelief and for the adoption of an orthodox education and life-style, prompting the government to arrest some of them. According to these sources, 22 years of Marxist experience did not obliterate tribal and religious loyalties, which continued to simmer beneath the Marxist superstructure, and came to the surface because of political and economic pressures.[15] Since these groups eroded the regime's power, Aden was determined to stabilize its relations with the opposition groups.

The PDRY's unresourceful, state-run economy failed to utilize optimally the limited financial assistance from the Gulf states. The money was immediately used to complete state-run projects, such as road construction and communication networks. Although these were doubtless essential, the government failed to allot sufficient funds to encourage the exports needed to improve the PDRY's balance of payments. Neither did it do enough to create conditions conducive to investment by Gulf entrepreneurs.

Economic difficulties were first and foremost evident in the limited productivity of major economic facilities and industries. The port of Aden, which before independence in the 1960s had accommodated 6,000 ships a year (surpassed only by Liverpool, London, and New York) received only 2,000 ships in 1988. Since cargo ships had increased their range, and thereby reduced their dependence on refuelling ports such as Aden, the prospects for full reactivation of the port seem discouraging. The oil refinery, built in Aden in 1954, used outdated equipment and refined only small quantities due to the Gulf states' relatively limited economic cooperation with the PDRY. With a capacity of 8.3m. tons of oil a year, Aden had processed less than 3m. tons a year since 1985.[16] Since then, the oil fields at Shabwa had not lived up to the high expectations, i.e., 200,000 barrels per day (b/d). The PDRY's agreement with the YAR for mutual exploitation of oil and the efforts of the Soviet Union to increase production and construct a pipeline to Bir 'Ali on the coast (to be completed in early 1990) had limited results. In May 1989, oil production was 7,000 b/d and could possibly reach an optimum of 70,000 b/d in 1990 through the pipeline. Given both the relatively low price of oil and the low level of production, it was hardly surprising that the PDRY leaders were dissatisfied with their oil industry.[17]

The limited productivity of the major economic facilities and industries resulted in severe financial difficulties. 'Attas admitted that the PDRY's main difficulty was to "finance projects."[18] The lack of foreign currency was intensified by a drop in oil remittances from South Yemeni expatriates (the lifeblood of the PDRY economy) by half in the last five years, to an annual $250m. or less, because of a general recession in the Gulf states.[19] The PDRY's total debt at the end of 1987 was $1,669m.[20]

Consequently, average per capita income fell from SYD115 (c. $335) in 1987 to SYD113 (c. $328) in 1988, at an average negative growth rate of 1.7%.[21] There were reports of food shortages and rationing. Another source of trouble was heavy rainfall at the end of March, which flooded some districts in the provinces of Shabwa, Hadramawt, and Mahra and left c. 30,000 people homeless.[22]

The Road to Reform

The prevailing problems led South Yemeni leaders to reform the system during the first half of 1989. Inspired by Soviet *perestroika* and taking advantage of new possibilities of regional cooperation, these changes indicated a preferable and feasible course of reforms.

Some of the changes concerned regional economic endeavors. Following the PDRY-YAR agreement of May 1988 (see chapter on the YAR in *MECS* 1988, p. 776), the two states jointly established in early January 1989 the Yemeni Company for Investment in Oil and Mineral Resources (YCIOMR), which was capitalized at $10m.[23] The company aimed to explore for and produce oil in 2,200 sq.km. in the Ma'rib-Shabwa region along the border. In turn, the YAR became an ACC founding member in February. The YCIOMR then sought a suitable contractor to carry out oil exploration and production in this region. The best offer came from a consortium which included American companies (Hunt and later also Exxon), French (Total), Soviet (Technoexport, actually representing the Soviet Ministry of Minerals and Petroleum) and a Kuwaiti company (Kuwait Foreign Petroleum Exploration Company).[24] These developments showed Aden that joint economic enterprises, which cut across states and even political blocs, were endorsed by many parties, including the Soviet Union, and that Marxist convictions should not impede such cooperation. Moreover, it was also understood that large-scale regional enterprises combining technical knowledge and solid financial bases may hold the key to profits and successful industrialization.[25]

The ensuing cooperation with the YAR persuaded the leaders in Aden to pursue even more seriously a settlement with the YAR-based 'Ali Nasir faction. Negotiations were conducted in March between envoys of the two sides under the YAR's auspices. 'Ali Nasir demanded that all sentences pronounced against his men be canceled and that they return to their previous positions in the PDRY. He also wanted all the dead in the civil war, including those of his own faction, to be declared "victims for their homeland." He also demanded that direct negotiations start with him. These conditions were unacceptable,[26] but Aden was prepared to release 25 of 'Ali Nasir supporters from PDRY prisons, and grant amnesty to several of his YAR-based senior aides who had been sentenced to various periods of imprisonment. These included a former minister of education, Hasan Salami; a former minister of minerals, 'Abd al-Qadir Ba-Jammal; and a former Politburo member, Anis Yahya.[27] PDRY Minister of the Interior Salih Munassir al-Siyayli reiterated that the government showed no readiness for conciliation with 'Ali Nasir, and that the amnesty had already been granted as part of "finding a solution to the aftermath of the 13 January 1986 incidents."[28] But he did not reject the efforts at reconciliation. Furthermore, during a visit of YAR Minister of State for Union Affairs Yahya al-'Arshi to Aden in March, the possibility was raised of granting PDRY governmental guarantees to the well-being of 40,000 South Yemeni refugees, who would return from the YAR to the PDRY, but to no avail. In return for the PDRY's concessions, 'Ali Nasir had to shut down his radio station in the YAR which broadcast against the Aden regime; he probably also had to cease his faction's operations against the PDRY.[29]

These steps indicated that the PDRY government was ready to grant amnesty and even readmit key figures of the until recently much-detested faction of 'Ali Nasir. This was the price of economic cooperation with the YAR, but also the result of the awareness that an opposition (notably after it had ceased broadcasting anti-PDRY propaganda) could be tolerated and incorporated within the system. This pluralism was also manifested in respect of other groups. In April, the government established a council of clerics who would provide religious services and deal with all matters relating to religious observance in the provinces.[30] This step was an attempt by the government to strengthen its supervision of the growing Islamic and tribal groups, but in a manner that would legitimize their activities. In May, the organization of members of the press held a special conference and issued a call, which must have had the government's backing, for a law guaranteeing the people's right of free expression, and the development of their chosen fields of interest.[31] This indicated that the intelligentsia may want to obtain intellectual freedom. Political pluralism was conceived not just as appeasement of the opposition, but also as a means of motivating "all forces" to unite in reform, and thereby contribute to its effectiveness.[32]

Three main aims could, therefore, be attributed to the PDRY reform:

(1) To reach out to tribal and Islamic groups and to 'Ali Nasir's faction, and show them more tolerance in order to enlist their support for the government and stabilize the regime.

(2) To encourage foreign investment, mainly by tapping the new interstate enterprises, in order to stimulate the economy.

(3) To intensify cooperation with Arab states, particularly with the YAR and with Eastern and Western Bloc states, conducive for reforms.

This attempt to achieve cooperation through pluralism was most evident in 1989. While PDRY leaders differed in the past over the attitude to take toward 'Ali Nasir's group, and suffered from internal tribal divisions (see *MECS* 1987, p. 572), a situation which probably still prevailed in 1989, there was unanimity among the leaders about the need for reform, which took precedence over other deep-seated divisions.[33]

DOMESTIC REFORMS

POLITICAL AND CONSTITUTIONAL CHANGES

By mid-1989, the first signs of reform were evident in the unprecedentedly free media and in public debates, focusing on the meaning of democracy and the political structure appropriate for the PDRY. These debates reflected the PDRY leaders' lack of experience in integrating economic and pluralistic concepts into a political structure. Salim Salih Muhammad expressed this confusion by explaining that the PDRY would not "mechanically copy" the changes in Eastern Europe, but rather "look at reality" and discover in the experience of different states what was suitable for the PDRY.[34] There were those who called for adopting democracy patterned on the Western way of life: introduction of basic individual rights, unrestricted political participation, and cadre recruitment from various social elements.[35] Others, however, stressed the need to preserve a leading role for the YSP — by advancing democratic procedures, social recruitment, and representation via the YSP.[36] In a series of discussions at the end of June in the People's Council, which were televised nationwide, the delegates stressed the need for *glasnost,* that is, openness to Western influences and the recruitment of foreign capital. Some delegates mildly criticized the executive authorities inefficiency in strengthening the economy. Others, such as YSP Central Committee member 'Abd al-Razzaq Musa'id, demanded reforming the ruling party by restoring its original structure and ideology which had prevailed prior to the YSP's foundation in 1978. He implied that the socialist structure and groups later incorporated into the YSP had led the PDRY to disaster.[37] The actual steps of reform reflected this variety of opinions, but lacked a clear-cut program.

Reform was discussed in a programmatic speech by Bayd on 30 July and published in the YSP paper, *al-Thawri.* The plan he outlined fell short of a Western-style democracy, but included promises to reshape the leadership, rotate the presidency, guarantee civil rights, and allow the publication of new newspapers. It undertook to rectify previous "wrong attitudes on Arab and Islamic culture and religion" by adopting a more positive attitude toward "rebuilding mosques" and treatment of "clergy and religious institutions."[38] It also included pledges to recruit foreign finance and change foreign policy. The speech covered many issues, but was not a detailed strategy on how to achieve reform.

The leaders were uncertain about the order of reform and its implementation. The changes were made one at a time, in order to allow each change to be absorbed separately, before moving on to the next one.

In late August the People's Council accepted a new law of elections to the people's councils in the provincial governments, which was described as a "real basis of democratic development."[39] It was a means of reviving recruitment from the regime's grass-root cadres and electorate, without upsetting the top political echelons. Elections were supposed to be held in October,[40] but did not take place until the end of 1989.

A step toward replacement of senior officials and major institutional change was taken in late September, when the YSP Central Committee decided to streamline the party's structure and administration, and abolish duplication of offices in the YSP and the government. The YSP foreign affairs, economics, and security offices would thus close down. A government reshuffle was also contemplated.[41] This move was aimed at a moderate change in the PDRY power structure, but by the end of the period under review, the effectiveness of this decision and the nature of its implementation were yet to be seen.

In early December, the YSP Central Committee decided to permit the establishment of other political parties and instructed the Politburo to devise a policy concerning political parties "that had fought colonialism and remained loyal to the principles of the revolution."[42] The decision may have indicated that the YSP sought to grant political freedom only to leftist and Arab nationalist groups, whose convictions were similar to those of the YSP, rather than to each and every group that aspired to run for government.

Thus, in 1989, political reforms in the PDRY permitted a limited pluralization of the body politic. There was a liberalization of the press and tolerance of religious activities, and in December the Council of Ministers reviewed a law to effect freedom of the press.[43] In Salim Salih's view, an atmosphere of cooperation and teamwork prevailed in the PDRY during the reform period, which reflected an improved relationship between the rulers and the ruled, and among the leaders themselves.[44] This improvement did not, however, eliminate dissension in the YSP and among the PDRY elite. A group of 46 army officers and an unspecified number of top officials (including the governor of the Mudiyya Province and the president's personal translator) fled to the YAR, where they joined 'Ali Nasir. Particularly embarrassing was the desertion to the YAR of some officers from Prime Minister Yasin 'Abduh Nu'man's home province, Sabiha.[45] Nevertheless, 'Ali Nasir was definitely influenced by the discussions, held with the leading faction in Aden, and by YAR pressure, with the result that his attitude toward Aden became more moderate. His speeches and interviews indicated more sympathy toward Aden and a lesser commitment to act against it, which brought the PDRY elite much relief.[46]

ECONOMIC CHANGES

Many observers have stressed the need to recuperate from economic difficulties as the main motive for reform.[47] The acquisition of funds to encourage profitable industries featured prominently on the leaders' agenda. Nu'man's visit to Saudi Arabia in early August to encourage South Yemeni expatriates to invest in the PDRY, notably in foreign currency bonds,[48] was the zenith of efforts to that effect. Foreign and local investors were called upon to develop industries producing electric cables, paper cartons, sacks, and toilet paper, among others.[49] The government approved an amended investment bill on 6 September, with a capital threshold of SYD50,0000 ($146,000) to encourage investment in large-scale projects.[50] The secretary of the YSP Central Committee, Fadil Muhsin 'Abdallah, stressed that the aim was to develop the "private sector" and attract the "petty and national bourgeoisie." Aden port was to become a tax-free zone[51] in order to attract trade. Results were still unknown by the end of the year.

While investment was the focus of economic reforms, the government also enabled private investors to build apartment houses for rent, thereby easing housing problems.[52] Farmers and fishermen were allowed to sell their surplus on the free market.[53] Flood-relief operations accompanied by planned work on irrigation, electricity, and road-building projects were also reported.[54]

The organization of the oil industry improved, but not its profits. The establishment of YCIOMR to produce oil jointly in the Ma'rib-Shabwa region and the negotiations with the multinational consortium attested to the new type of international organization that would operate the oil industry both in the PDRY and the YAR. But late in the year, when the consortium's proposals fell short of the demands of the two Yemens, PDRY Minister of Minerals and Oil Salih Abu Bakr Ibn Husaynun threatened to consider proposals from other bidders. In December, the consortium made new offers and the parties resumed negotiations.[55] Other Western companies were searching for oil in different regions.[56] The Soviet company Technoexport was building a 200km.-long pipeline to carry oil from Shabwa to Bir 'Ali on the coast[57] but, meanwhile, the PDRY had to transfer the oil in lorries, and production was limited to the earlier mentioned 7,000 barrels per day.

These changes attested to Aden's readiness to convert its economy into one more capitalist-structured and market-oriented, as evident in new organizational forms, but the effectiveness of the changes remained to be seen.

FOREIGN POLICY UNDER THE IMPACT OF REFORM

During the last few years, Aden had devised a foreign policy one of whose mainstays was befriending the Gulf states and inducing them to support the PDRY economy (see *MECS* 1988, pp. 669–71). These moves were compatible with reform. But in 1989, the PDRY's foreign policy was completely subjected to the cause of reform and assumed additional dimensions: it was designed to support domestic pluralism, economic openness, and notably the attraction of financial investment.

South Yemen devised two strategies to implement its reform-oriented foreign policy. First, in February 1989, the PDRY found itself surrounded by two powerful political and economic regional organizations, the GCC and the ACC. The rulers apparently decided to make the best of it by seeking to join the ACC, and until this took place, to benefit from these two regional blocs' economic enterprises and financial assistance. Thus, the secretary of the YSP Central Committee, 'Abdallah Muhsin, stressed that the PDRY had "new thoughts about international contacts" and the need to reinforce them.[58] Minister for (Yemeni) Union Affairs Rashid Muhammad Thabit emphasized that the PDRY had to consider participation in "economic forms of unity which evolve in the Arab homeland and the world."[59] This motive, of joining a regional organization or benefiting from its economic enterprises, guided Aden in its attempts to strengthen union with the YAR and, more generally, to seek economic cooperation with a number of Arab states (see below).

Second, given the PDRY's own objectives of reform and the Soviet Union's diminished endeavors to advance revolutionary aims, the PDRY seemed to have abandoned all the radical goals it had earlier sought to realize through foreign policy. In the past few years, these goals included the reconstruction of the "rejectionist bloc" of Arab states, or the formation of a strong revolutionary axis, via cooperation with Ethiopia, Libya, or Syria (see *MECS* 1987, p. 577). In 1989, the desire for economic benefits completely overshadowed any of Aden's remaining revolutionary aspirations. Instead, Aden developed a stand more typical of the YAR (see chapter on the YAR), namely, a neutral foreign policy, nonalignment with any of the Arab camps, and a more diversified policy in global affairs.

The declared aims were "to respect each state's integrity and sovereignty," and seek cooperation among states.[60] Foreign Minister 'Abd al-'Aziz al-Dali stated in August that the PDRY was, in fact, occupying a middle ground among Arab camps and maintained good relations with all of them.[61]

RELATIONS WITH THE YEMENI ARAB REPUBLIC

From the PDRY's vantage point, during the last few years, improved relations with the YAR were the key to solving several of its major political and economic problems. Through improved relations with the YAR, Aden hoped to mend its fences with 'Ali Nasir. Aden wished to alleviate tensions which sometimes emerged along the border between the two states; to facilitate the large-scale search for and production of oil, and to demonstrate to the Gulf states its good neighborliness, which could win Aden their financial assistance. The two states stated that their improved relations were a step toward unity, although in fact they feared prompt unification as long as their political systems and interests were markedly different (see chapters on the YAR and the PDRY in previous volumes of *MECS*). Their relations focused on defusing the above problems or intensifying economic cooperation. Therefore, in 1988, the two Yemens had agreed to ease border tension, to engage in joint oil prospecting and production, and to defuse 'Ali Nasir's threat against Aden. However, they took only marginal steps to unite the two states (see *MECS* 1988, pp. 668–69).

In the first half of 1989, Aden continued this policy, seeking mainly to settle a variety of problems, to encourage economic cooperation and to improve its economic and political conditions. The two states thus established YCIOMR in January with a South Yemeni president, a North Yemeni director-general, and a joint board of directors.[62] The company started to search for contractors who would advance oil exploration and production in the Ma'rib-Shabwa region (see above).

The formation of the ACC, with the YAR as a member, left the PDRY isolated, which could have renewed the friction between the two Yemens. But the pragmatic attitude of the PDRY leaders prevailed. Dali explained that the ACC was not a new "political axis," but rather a product of Arab aspirations for unity, which would encourage Yemeni unity and permit a united Yemen to achieve a regional role within the new bloc. He and other spokesmen were careful to underline that the PDRY would possibly join the ACC, but that for the time being, it was studying its nature and implications.[63] Thus considering that it was uncertain whether the PDRY could join the ACC, the PDRY's leaders did not look upon their exclusion from it as a cause for emotional, vengeful reactions. Meanwhile, they sought to benefit from the promise of broad economic integration and assets inherent in the ACC, or in the words of 'Attas, from the "utilization of Arab resources as a basis for Arab joint action."[64] The PDRY wanted to take advantage of increased Arab investment, technical assistance, and financial aid that might be channeled through the ACC and to attempt gradually to join the new bloc. In March, PDRY leaders used a meeting between the two Yemens' ministers of union affairs in San'a[65] to advance these interests. At the same time, the YAR helped facilitate a *rapprochement* between the PDRY and 'Ali Nasir, although the basic problem of facilitating the return of tens of thousands of South Yemeni refugees from the YAR to the PDRY was not solved.[66]

Little progress was made over unification during this period. The communiqué following a meeting in San'a on 21 March of PDRY Prime Minister Yasin 'Abduh Nu'man and his YAR counterpart, 'Abd al-'Aziz 'Abd al-Ghani, expressed satisfaction with the steps already taken toward unity, but urged the ministerial unity committees to continue working "until they complete their task."[67] This formulation implied that problems still set the two states apart. The attitude of the leaders in Aden was that unity could be deferred. Bayd reiterated that "unity should not be treated emotionally...it requires patience...the suitable conditions of unity require careful planning."[68]

However, leaders of the two Yemens changed their minds. In July they began to formulate a unification program. There were several reasons for this change: (1) With the PDRY's search for economic construction peaking, there was a strong desire to benefit from the ACC's economic power. The only feasible way to achieve this goal was through formal unity with the YAR.[69] (2) As part of their reform program, PDRY leaders adopted a more tolerant attitude toward tribal and religiously organized groups, which were the socioeconomic backbone of the YAR regime. Aden, therefore, reversed its earlier objection to collaborating with these elements and thus became more receptive to unification with San'a. (3) Similarly, the PDRY adopted a policy of nonalignment with regard to inter-Arab affairs, which brought it closer to the YAR leaders' viewpoint and encouraged it to embark on unity with the YAR. For the PDRY leaders, unification became an integral part of and stimulus for reform.

The YAR, in turn, favored the PDRY's reform as expressed in its wish for reconciliation with 'Ali Nasir, in Aden's readiness to accommodate non-Marxist political groups, a free-market economy, and a nonaligned inter-Arab policy. The PDRY shed its image as a rabid backer of insurgents and became a partner for unification. Moreover, the PDRY's need to benefit from the YAR's access to the ACC economy was paralleled by the YAR's need of the PDRY's services in carrying its oil from Ma'rib to the south coast via the pipeline the Soviets were building. The construction of such a pipeline through the mountainous area separating Ma'rib from the Red Sea was technically very difficult and expensive. Export of YAR oil through the South Yemeni pipeline was more feasible.[70] Unification with the YAR would put the seal on economic cooperation between the two states, notably over oil (see also chapter on YAR).

There were reports that the Soviet Union also encouraged unity between the two Yemens in order to reinforce cooperation between the two states which Moscow regarded as its clients, in particular the PDRY.[71]

A unification program was discussed in San'a during visits of YSP Central Committee Secretary Fadil Muhsin 'Abdallah in July, and of PDRY Secretaries of Defense and Union Affairs Salih 'Ubayd Ahmad and Rashid Muhammad Thabit, respectively, in September. Thabit's declaration in July that "it is time to abandon the old political school" concerning unity, namely, to cease giving it low priority, attested to the parties' effort to achieve it.[72] The program finally adopted reflected a combination of two proposals. The YAR suggested step-by-step unification of certain political organs and of policies: unified representation in international organizations and a uniform foreign policy, unification of the defense and military establishments, a unified parliament, and a supreme federal government;[73] in the words of YAR President 'Ali 'Abdallah Salih, through "a gradualist approach...with the two halves assimilating in one melting pot,"[74] that is, by a slow process of evolution to which the two sides could accommodate. The PDRY initially sought a confederal structure that would leave the governments and political organization of the two states intact. The PDRY proposal reflected its wish to preserve its Marxist regime and its old doubts about full-scale unity and, notably, about the YSP's integrity.[75]

During the coming weeks, however, the YAR position gained more leverage. PDRY leaders were becoming more receptive to Salih's proposal as their reform campaign advanced and their willingness to forsake old convictions grew. They were at least ready to accept the federal framework as suitable for a united Yemen. During this period, there were two important meetings, at which a unification program was formulated. Salim Salih Muhammad met with YAR Foreign Minister 'Abd al-Karim al-Iryani in Ta'izz, on 31 October; they decided to establish a Unified Political Organization Committee (Upoc), which would seek to develop cooperation between the YSP and the ruling political organization in the YAR, the General People's Congress, aiming at their ultimate merger.[76] Salih then visited Aden in late November, and presented his program to PDRY leaders in private discussions and in a public speech.[77] During Salih's visit to Aden, he and Bayd decided to take two major steps toward unity: (1) They agreed upon the draft constitution of a united Yemen, which had been prepared by a joint committee some years previously and had been finally drafted on 31 December 1988. They referred the draft to the parliaments of both states for ratification within six months. (2) They decided to set up a joint ministerial committee with the two states' ministers of the interior to supervise this procedure.[78] The agreement over the constitution indicated that they also concurred on the basic structure of unity, but did not publicize this fact. Reports stressed that they had decided to gradually merge the two Ministries of Defense, and Foreign Affairs and Judicial Affairs, and then continue with the merger of other ministries "until [they have achieved] complete unification." They also decided to establish a federal government to supervise these processes.[79] They thus agreed on the major principles of unification, but remained unwilling to compromise the independent existence of their governments and political organizations. At the moment of decision it thus seemed that the two sides, particularly the PDRY, were still hesitant about a complete unification. 'Attas explained that the Upoc would decide in two months whether to unify the two ruling parties, but that the political leaders in both states wished to preserve their independence within the framework of a "broad national front." He hoped that the new atmosphere would eliminate all points of disagreement, but that these "are natural."[80] Thus, 1989 witnessed the emergence of conditions favorable to the unification of the two Yemens and major steps were taken in this direction, but whether the process would be completed still remained uncertain.

RELATIONS WITH OTHER ARAB PARTIES

Once the ACC was formed, the PDRY eagerly examined the possibilities of joining it. However, the ACC founding states proved rather reluctant to add new members, especially the Marxist PDRY. Nevertheless, they were prepared to negotiate this issue with the PDRY leaders. Aden settled for entering the ACC gradually, by improving relations, notably in economic areas, with individual ACC members.[81]

Dali visited Egypt in late April and put forward his country's wish to join the ACC. While Egypt's response to this request was unclear, Dali succeeded in warming up Aden's relations with Cairo in other respects. Egyptian Foreign Minister 'Ismat 'Abd al-Majid agreed to visit Aden at an unspecified date and to establish an Egyptian-Yemeni Council, headed jointly by both foreign ministers.[82] Aden also paid homage to Egypt's growing role in the Arab world when Dali expressed the PDRY's strong support for Egypt's readmission to the Arab League. 'Attas visited Cairo shortly in May and again in August,[83] and in September he declared his state's support for Egyptian President Husni Mubarak's peace plan "to negotiate on equal terms to find a just solution to the Palestinian question"[84] (see chapter on the ME peace process).

In September, 'Attas and Dali visited Jordan and signed three agreements of cooperation: for the exchange of services and agricultural products, development of science and education (notably teacher training in these fields), and liberalization of trade and transport between the two countries. Several protocols were signed to facilitate these agreements.[85] In 'Attas's words, the "foundations for improved relations with Jordan were thus laid."[86] For Aden, which had earlier deemed Jordan a "reactionary state" unworthy of cooperation, the conclusion of these agreements marked a real change of policy.

The PDRY's relations with Iraq, which started developing in 1988 (see *MECS* 1988, pp. 670–71), intensified in 1989. An agreement of cooperation in radio and television development was signed between them in late April,[87] and South Yemen's airline opened a regular line to Baghdad in July. A month later, 'Attas hailed the "prospects for further constructive cooperation" between the PDRY and Iraq.[88]

Aden's interest in maintaining good relations with the Gulf states was motivated primarily by its need of financial assistance. In 1988, Arab commitments to South Yemen totaled over $130m., mostly from the Gulf states. Dali explained that the PDRY's relations with these countries were based on mutual respect for the sovereignty of all states in the region and were, therefore, cordial and cooperative. "The negative effect...that accompanied 13 January [1986, namely the PDRY civil war] had completely disappeared. Matters have not only returned to normal, but have even become better than before."[89]

In early June, Saudi and South Yemeni frontier patrols clashed about 300 km. west of Shabwa at their undemarcated border. The incident reflected Saudi sensitivity over South Yemeni initiatives in this oil-rich region (see also chapter on Saudi Arabia), but both sides acted swiftly to contain the problem and maintain "brotherly relations."[90] In the months that followed, the Saudis indeed demonstrated good neighborliness. To this end, the Saudi Government in July exempted Yemeni nationals from a royal edict restricting the rights and activities of foreign nationals, and in August, during Nu'man's visit to Saudi Arabia, the kingdom eased the regulations on the transfer home of remittances of PDRY expatriates.[91] In November, the Saudi ministers of foreign affairs and finance, Sa'ud al-Faysal and Muhammad Aba al-Khayl, visited Aden, when technical, cultural, and commercial agreements were concluded.[92]

The PDRY also changed its policy toward most of its former revolutionary allies. Replying to a question about the defense alliance Aden had signed with Libya and Ethiopia in August 1981, Dali replied: "I believe it was never born. At any rate, the circumstances that called for that alliance have changed. This issue is not being discussed anymore." He also condemned Ethiopia's allowing Jews to leave in return for Israeli financial and military assistance, leading to the resumption of diplomatic relations between Addis Ababa and Jerusalem.[93] 'Attas visited Libya in August and early September and discussed "bilateral and regional relations,"[94] but there were no reports of further contacts.

Aden developed close relations with Syria. Damascus helped to mediate Aden's dispute with 'Ali Nasir, with the result that the two states which had been left out of the ACC also developed common economic interests. The visit of Syrian Prime Minister Mahmud al-Zu'bi in Aden in June focused on both issues. It was decided to establish a joint committee of both countries' presidents; agreements on cooperation in economic, medical, and agricultural fields were also concluded.[95] Aden's Minister of Information Muhammad Jirghum went to Damascus in August and discussed cooperation in the areas of information and the media.[96] Syria's President Hafiz al-Asad met 'Attas in Tripoli in early September.[97]

The only Arab group with which Aden maintained close relations anchored in its revolutionary past was the Palestinian left wing. A delegation of the Democratic Front for the Liberation of Palestine, led by the secretary-general Na'if Hawatima and his deputy, Naji Talal, visited Aden in March and April.[98] The PDRY's relations with the main leaders of the PLO were more restricted in 1989, Aden's new interests appearing to be the reason. However, there was no evidence of any friction between the parties. 'Arafat visited Aden in August and praised the PDRY's early recognition of the State of Palestine and its granting the PLO representative in Aden the status of ambassador.[99] The PDRY was reportedly trying to persuade Syria to host the second anniversary celebrations of the Palestinian uprising in the Israeli-occupied territories, but to no avail.[100]

RELATIONS WITH THE SUPERPOWERS

The Soviet Union played a rather passive role in PDRY affairs in the year under survey. At the end of 1989, Dali expressed what seemed to be Aden's view of the Soviet Union's policy toward South Yemen during the year. "So far," he said, "they continue to implement their agreements with us," implying that Moscow had not stopped honoring its commitments. Enmeshed in its own reforms, the USSR did not undertake new commitments and might not do so.[101] The USSR continued to assist the PDRY in oil drilling in Shabwa, building the pipeline to the coast, and providing military assistance. Senior Soviet officials visited the oil fields and played host to top PRDY leaders, such as Salim Salih (in October) and Chief of Staff Haytham Qasim Tahir (in November).[102]

The reforms in the Soviet Union were a source of inspiration for the PDRY, and Soviet leaders were reportedly encouraging some of the PDRY's reform measures, as well as increasing the search for oil and the process of unification with the YAR. But, as in the case of its other Eastern Bloc allies, Moscow did not push the PDRY openly or vigorously toward reform nor did it help implement them. The Soviets were also not reported as financing the cost of the reforms or committing themselves to their completion. Soviet spokesmen rather went on record as stressing their lack of objections to these reforms.[103]

Aden's response was twofold. On the one hand, PDRY leaders became more independent of Moscow. Salim Salih explained that the PDRY would not "mechnically copy" Eastern Bloc reforms, thus implying regret at having done so in the past.[104] Ibn Husaynun indicated the PDRY's dissatisfaction with the Soviet progress in the oil fields, which prompted Aden to seek the assistance of Western companies.[105]

On the other hand, the PDRY did not want to leave the Soviet strategic defense orbit, particularly during this time of change, and Moscow presumably shared this view. It was manifested in a new 20-year agreement of friendship and cooperation signed on 25 October, which called for cooperation in the economic, scientific, and technical fields, the exchange of information and the development of cadres in educational and cultural areas, the increase of mutual visits and, notably, coordination of foreign policy. The two states agreed not to enter military pacts aimed at either of them.[106] This agreement was signed despite the existence of a 20-year friendship and cooperation agreement signed in October 1979 during the incumbency of 'Abd al-Fattah Isma'il. It stressed mutual revolutionary interests and military cooperation, notably against "a threat which has arisen or [in order of] restoring peace."[107] The 1979 pact was not abolished in 1989 but bypassed in view of the interest in peaceful relations and *rapprochement* with other nonrevolutionary parties in the region. Hence, the 1989 agreement only stressed mutual nonaggression and co-ordination in foreign policy between Aden and Moscow.[108] The PDRY thus increased its room for maneuver within the Soviet bloc.

The PDRY's traditional criticism of the US "aggression" against Libya continued at the beginning of 1989. But, as the year went on, Aden's spokesmen expressed growing interest in restoring diplomatic relations with Washington, which Aden had terminated in 1969 as a gesture toward its leftist revolutionary style. Aden deemed the restoration of relations with the US essential for seeking Western aid. The Kuwaiti Government mediated between the parties and initiated a dialogue between the South Yemeni and American envoys at the UN,[109] but relations were not renewed during 1989.

South Yemen's search for improved relations with the West went as far as breaking the ice with Great Britain, South Yemen's former colonial master, by hosting a visit of Royal Navy ships in Aden in July,[110] and a visit by the British Deputy Foreign Secretary William Waldegrave in early October.[111]

NOTES

For the place and frequency of publications cited here, and for the full name of the publication, news agency, radio station, or monitoring service where an abbreviation is used, please see "List of Sources." Only in the case of more than one publication bearing the same name is the place of publication noted here.

1. On PDRY political fluctuations, see J. Kostiner, *South Yemen's Revolutionary Strategy, 1970–1985: From Insurgency to Bloc Politics* (Tel Aviv: Jaffee Center for Strategic Studies, 1990).
2. 'Ali Nasir's interview, *MEED,* 10 November 1989.
3. Bayd was quoted by *Pravda Bratislava,* 18 January — DR, 26 January 1989.
4. R. Aden, 8 August — DR, 10 August 1989.
5. 'Attas's interview, *al-Sharq al-Awsat,* 9 January 1989.
6. R. Aden, 2 October — DR, 11 October 1989.
7. R. Aden, 21 June — DR, 28 June 1989.
8. Dali's interview, *al-Majalla,* 12 October 1989.
9. Salim Salih Muhammad's interview, *Fourteenth October,* 21 September 1989.
10. Ibid.
11. *FT,* 11 May 1989.
12. *JP,* 20 June 1989.
13. *Al-'Amal,* Cairo, 26 March, 17 July 1989.
14. Ibid., 26 March, 5 June 1989.
15. Ibid., 5 June 1989.
16. *FT,* 17 May 1989.
17. Ibid., 11 May; *MEED,* 1 September 1989.
18. 'Attas's interview, *al-Sharq al-Awsat,* 9 January 1989.
19. *JP,* 20 June 1989.
20. *CR:* South Yemen, No. 1, 1989, pp. 36–38.
21. *Al-Usbu' al-'Arabi,* 27 February; R. Aden, 19 September — DR, 22 September 1989.
22. *CR:* South Yemen, No. 2, 1989, pp. 36–40.

23. *MEED*, 27 January 1989.
24. Ibid., 28 July 1989.
25. *Al-Hayat*, London, 8 February; 'Attas's interview, *al-Siyasa*, Kuwait, 12 September 1989.
26. *Al-Ittihad*, Abu Dhabi, 5 March 1989.
27. AFP, 4 March; *al-Ittihad*, Abu Dhabi, 5 March 1989.
28. Siyayli's interview, *al-Sharq al-Awsat*, 21 March 1989.
29. *Al-Mustaqbal*, 11 March 1989.
30. *Al-Ittihad*, Abu Dhabi, 15 April 1989.
31. *Al-Thawri*, Aden, 20 May 1989.
32. *Fourteenth October*, 24 January, 26 March 1989.
33. Salim Salih Muhammad's interview, ibid., 21 September 1989.
34. Ibid.
35. Ibid., 11, 12 July 1989.
36. Ibid., 24 May 1989.
37. AFP, 26 June, 20 July 1989.
38. *Al-Thawri*, Aden, 30 July 1989.
39. Ibid., 26 August 1989.
40. *Fourteenth October*, 19 December 1989.
41. *MEED*, 20 October; *CR:* South Yemen, No. 4, 1989, pp. 39–45.
42. AFP, 11 December 1989.
43. *CR:* South Yemen, No. 4, 1989, pp. 39–45; *al-Watan al-'Arabi*, 20 October 1989.
44. Salim Salih's interview, *Fourteenth October*, 21 September 1989.
45. *Al-Shira'*, 19 December 1989.
46. *Al-Hayat*, London, 16 August 1989.
47. *Al-Tadamun*, 27 March 1989.
48. *MEED*, 11 August 1989.
49. *CR:* South Yemen, No. 2, 1989, pp. 36–38.
50. Ibid., No. 4, 1989, pp. 39–45.
51. R. Aden, 21 October — DR, 23 October 1989.
52. *MEED*, 8 September 1989.
53. *JP*, 20 June; *CR:* Yemen, No. 4, 1989, pp. 39–45.
54. *CR:* Yemen, No. 3, 1989, pp. 41–44; *Fourteenth October*, 13 July 1989.
55. *MEED*, 8 September, 23 December 1989.
56. Ibn Husaynun's interview, *al-Sharq al-Awsat*, 12 April 1989.
57. Ibn Husaynun's interview, *al-Hayat*, London, 7 April; R. Aden, 22 January — DR, 23 January 1989.
58. Muhsin's interview, *Nidal al-Sha'b*, 14 April 1989.
59. Dali's interview, *al-Sharq al-Awsat*, 13 January 1989.
60. Dali's interview, *al-Safir*, 10 August 1989.
61. *Al-Hayat*, London, 8 February 1989.
62. Dali's interview, *al-Ra'y*, 27 February 1989.
63. 'Attas's interview, *al-Watan al-'Arabi,*, 20 October 1989.
64. Ibid.
65. R. San'a, 4 March — DR, 13 March 1989.
66. *Al-Ittihad*, Abu Dhabi, 18 March 1989.
67. R. Aden, 24 March — DR, 31 March 1989.
68. Bayd's interview, *al-Yawm al-Sabi'*, 23 January 1989.
69. Thabit's interview, *al-Watan al-'Arabi*, 10 November 1989.
70. *MEED*, 25 August 1989.
71. *Al-Shira'*, 20 March 1989.
72. *Al-Fursan*, 8 July 1989.
73. Salih's interview, *al-Yawm al-Sabi'*, 9 October; 'Arshi's interview, *al-Sharq al-Awsat*, 18 November 1989.
74. Salih's interview, *al-Ra'y al-'Amm*, 21 November 1989.
75. Salim Salih Muhammad's interview, *Fourteenth October*, 21 September 1989.
76. R. Aden, 2 April — DR, 7 April 1989.
77. R. San'a, 29 November — DR, 3 December 1989.

78. R. San'a, 1 December — DR, 1 December 1989.
79. AFP, 22 November 1989.
80. 'Attas's interview, *al-Sharq al-Awsat,* 9 December 1989.
81. *Al-Siyasa,* Kuwait, 27 February; Dali's interview, *al-Safir,* 10 August 1989.
82. MENA, 3 May—DR, 4 May 1989.
83. Ibid.
84. *Sawt al-Sha'b,* 12 September 1989.
85. *Al-Siyasa,* Kuwait, 11 September 1989.
86. Ibid., 12 September 1989.
87. R. Aden, 27 April — DR, 2 May 1989.
88. INA, 30 August — DR, 1 September 1989.
89. Dali's interview, *al-Sharq al-Awsat,* 18 September 1989.
90. *Al-Hadaf,* Damascus, 11 June; R. Aden, 9 June — DR, 12 June 1989.
91. *Al-Hayat,* London, 27 July; *al-Yawm al-Sabi',* 7 August 1989.
92. R. Riyadh, 28 November — DR, 30 November 1989.
93. Dali's interview, *al-Ahali,* 13 December 1989.
94. R. Aden, 29 August — DR, 30 August 1989.
95. R. Aden, 17 June — DR, 19 June; *al-Ittihad,* Abu Dhabi, 30 June, 5 July 1989.
96. *Al-Ba'th,* 30 August 1989.
97. R. Damascus, 2 September — DR, 6 September 1989.
98. R. Aden, 5 March — DR, 14 March, 1 May 1989.
99. R. Aden, 26 August — DR, 27 August 1989.
100. *Al-Ittihad,* Abu Dhabi, 15 October 1989.
101. Dali's interview, *al-Ahali,* 13 December 1989.
102. R. Aden, 20 October, 28 November — DR, 23 October, 30 November 1989.
103. Interview of the Soviet Union's ambassador to the YAR, *al-Ittihad,* Abu Dhabi, 6 July 1989.
104. Salim Salih Muhammad's interview, *Fourteenth October,* 5 December 1989.
105. *Al-'Amal,* Cairo, 7 September 1989.
106. *Al-Thawri,* Aden, 28 October 1989.
107. S. Page, *The Soviet Union and the Yemens* (New York: Praeger, 1985), pp. 94–95.
108. R. Aden, 26 December — DR, 27 December 1989.
109. USIS Report, 27 October; *al-'Amal,* Cairo, 18 October 1989.
110. *Al-Shira',* 24 July 1989.
111. *Al-Sharq al-Awsat,* 25 November 1989.

INDEX

NOTE

Page numbers in **bold** type indicate principal references. Alphabetical order is word-by-word.